TUTORIAL: FAULT-TOLERANT COMPUTING

Victor P. Nelson and Bill D. Carroll

IEEE Computer Society Order Number 677
Library of Congress Number 86-46205
IEEE Catalog Number EH0254-3
ISBN 0-8186-0677-0

THE COMPUTER SOCIETY OF THE IEEE

THE INSTITUTE OF ELECTRICAL AND ELECTRONICS ENGINEERS, INC.

COMPUTER SOCIETY PRESS

Published by IEEE Computer Society Press
1730 Massachusetts Avenue, N.W.
Washington, D.C. 20036-1903

COVER DESIGNED BY JACK I. BALLESTERO

Copyright and Reprint Permissions: Abstracting is permitted with credit to the source. Libraries are permitted to photocopy beyond the limits of U.S. copyright law for private use of patrons those articles in this volume that carry a code at the bottom of the first page, provided the per-copy fee indicated in the code is paid through the Copyright Clearance Center, 29 Congress Street, Salem, MA 01970. Instructors are permitted to photocopy isolated articles for noncommercial classroom use without fee. For other copying, reprint or republication permission, write to Director, Publishing services, IEEE, 345 E. 47 St., New York, NY 10017. All rights reserved. Copyright © 1987 by The Institute of Electrical and Electronics Engineers, Inc.

IEEE Computer Society Order Number 677C (case)
IEEE Computer Society Order Number 677 (paper)
Library of Congress Number 86-46205
IEEE Catalog Number EH0254-3
ISBN 0-8186-0677-0 (paper)
ISBN 0-8186-4677-2 (microfiche)
ISBN 0-8186-8677-4 (case)

```
QA
76.9
.F38
T88
1987
```

Order from: IEEE Computer Society   IEEE Service Center   IEEE Computer Society
            Post Office Box 80452   445 Hoes Lane   Avenue de la Tanche, 2
            Worldway Postal Center   Piscataway, NJ 08854   B-1160 Brussels,
            Los Angeles, CA 90080   Belgium

 THE INSTITUTE OF ELECTRICAL AND ELECTRONICS ENGINEERS, INC.

Preface

Interest in the field of fault-tolerant computing has grown in recent years because of increased demands for safer, more reliable, and more available systems, the declining cost and increasing complexity of hardware, and the maturing of the field. This tutorial is designed to provide an introduction to the field of fault-tolerant computing. A combination of original material developed specifically for this volume and selected reprints of key papers in the field provide the reader with definitions of terms, introductions to theories and concepts, and case studies of experimental and production systems. Hardware and software techniques are covered both conceptually and as actually applied in fault-tolerant systems.

The original material is written at an introductory level, whereas that of the reprints ranges in difficulty from introductory to advanced. An undergraduate level understanding of logic circuits, computer organization, computer architecture, computer programming, operating systems, and probability theory is recommended as prerequisite.

This tutorial is intended for design engineers, computer scientists, technical managers, or students who want an introduction to or update on the field of fault-tolerant computing. New researchers in the field or researchers in other computer fields will also find this book useful. Hence, it is ideally suited for use as a textbook for tutorials, short courses, advanced undergraduate or graduate courses; as a reference book; or for self-study.

Chapter 1 provides a general overview of the field through a historical perspective, definitions of terms, and a discussion of fault-tolerance design issues. Reliability modeling and redundancy techniques are introduced in Chapter 2. A survey of systems designed for high-reliability aerospace applications and for high-availability communication systems is presented in Chapter 3. Chapter 4 is devoted to real-time industrial process control systems and to commercial transaction-processing systems. Chapter 5 covers software fault tolerance. The design of fault-tolerant memory systems is discussed in Chapter 6, while the implementation of redundancy techniques through very large scale integration (VLSI) is considered in Chapter 7.

Table of Contents

Preface iii

Chapter 1: Introduction to Fault-Tolerant Computing 1

Fault-Tolerant Computing—Concepts and Examples 5
    D.A. Rennels (*IEEE Transactions on Computers*, December 1984, pages 1116-1129)
Fault-Tolerant Systems in Commercial Applications 19
    O. Serlin (*Computer*, August 1984, pages 19-30)
Fault-Tolerant Software 31
    H. Hecht (*IEEE Transactions on Reliability*, August 1979, pages 227-232)
Fault Modeling 37
    J.P. Hayes (*IEEE Design & Test*, April 1985, pages 88-95)

Chapter 2: Reliability Modeling and General Redundancy Techniques 45

On Reliability Modeling and Analysis of Ultrareliable Fault-Tolerant Digital Systems 68
    F.P. Mathur (*IEEE Transactions on Computers*, November 1971, pages 1376-1382)
Reliability Modeling Technique for Self-Repairing Computer Systems 75
    W.G. Bouricius, W.C. Carter, and P.R. Schneider (*Proceedings of ACM Annual
    Conference*, 1969, pages 295-309)
A Unified Reliability Model for Fault-Tolerant Computers 90
    Y.W. Ng and A.A. Avižienis (*IEEE Transactions on Computers*, November 1980,
    pages 1002-1011)

Chapter 3: Fault-Tolerance in Aerospace and Communication Systems 101

The STAR (Self-Testing and Repairing) Computer: An Investigation of the Theory and
Practice of Fault-Tolerant Computer Design 107
    A. Avižienis, G.C. Gilley, F.P. Mathur, D.A. Rennels, J.A. Rohr, and D.K. Rubin
    (*IEEE Transactions on Computers*, November 1971, pages 1312-1321)
Redundancy Management Technique for Space
Shuttle Computers 117
    J.R. Sklaroff (*IBM Journal of Research and Development*, January 1976,
    pages 20-28)
FTMP—A Highly Reliable Fault-Tolerant Multiprocessor for Aircraft 126
    A.L. Hopkins, Jr., T.B. Smith III, and J.H. Lala (*Proceedings of the IEEE*,
    October 1978, pages 1221-1239)
SIFT: Design and Analysis of a Fault-Tolerant Computer for Aircraft Control 145
    J.H. Wensley, L. Lamport, J. Goldberg, M.W. Green, K.N. Levitt,
    P.M. Melliar-Smith, R.E. Shostak, and C.B. Weinstock (*Proceedings of the IEEE*,
    October 1978, pages 1240-1255)
Fault-Tolerant Design of Local ESS Processors 161
    W.N. Toy (*Proceedings of the IEEE*, October 1978, pages 1126-1145)
Pluribus—An Operational Fault-Tolerant Multiprocessor 181
    D. Katsuki, E.S. Elsam, W.F. Mann, E.S. Roberts, J.G. Robinson,
    F.S. Skowronski, and E.W. Wolf (*Proceedings of the IEEE*, October 1978,
    pages 1146-1159)

Chapter 4: Commercial Systems for Industrial Control and Transaction Processing 195

Fault-Tolerant Computers Ensure Reliable Industrial Controls 198
    J.H. Wensley (*Electronic Design*, June 25, 1981)

Programmable Control of a Chemical Reactor Using a Fault Tolerant Computer 205
    J.H. Wensley and C.S. Harclerode (*IEEE Transactions on Industrial Electronics*,
    November 1982, pages 258-264)
REBUS, A Fault-Tolerant Distributed System for Industrial Real-Time Control 212
    J.-M. Ayache, J.-P. Courtiat, and M. Diaz (*IEEE Transactions on Computers*,
    July 1982, pages 637-647)
New System Manages Hundreds of Transactions per Second 223
    R. Horst and S. Metz (*Electronics*, April 19, 1984, pages 147-151)
Making Processing Fail-Safe 228
    R. Freiburghouse (*Mini-Micro Systems*, May 1982, pages 255-264)
Multiprocessor Architecture Ensures Fault-Tolerant Transaction Processing.....................234
    A.D. Inselberg (*Mini-Micro Systems*, April 1983, pages 165-172)
Fault-Tolerant Mini Needs Enhanced Operating System 239
    S.D. Glazer (*Computer Design*, August 1984, pages 189-198)

Chapter 5: Software Fault Tolerance..247

Software Reliability Models: Assumptions, Limitations, and Applicability 257
    A.L. Goel (*IEEE Transactions on Software Engineering*, December 1985,
    pages 1411-1423)
A Survey of Analytic Models of Rollback and Recovery Strategies..............................270
    K.M. Chandy (*Computer*, May 1975, pages 40-47)
System Structure for Software Fault Tolerance 277
    B. Randell (*IEEE Transactions on Software Engineering*, June 1975, pages 220-232)
The N-Version Approach to Fault-Tolerant Software 290
    A. Avižienis (*IEEE Transactions on Software Engineering*, December 1985,
    pages 1491-1501)
Redundancy in Data Structures: Improving Software Fault Tolerance 301
    D.J. Taylor, D.E. Morgan, and J.P. Black (*IEEE Transactions on Software
    Engineering*, November 1980, pages 585-594)
DMERT: A Fault Tolerant Environment for Diverse Applications................................311
    D.J. Fitch, A.M. Guercio, K.W. Johnson, and G.T. Surratt (*Proceedings of the
    Fourteenth Annual International Symposium on Fault-Tolerant Computing Systems*,
    June 1984, pages 336-340)

Chapter 6: Fault-Tolerant Memory Systems..317

Error-Correcting Codes for Semiconductor Memory Applications: A State-of-the-Art
Review 326
    C.L. Chen and M.Y. Hsiao (*IBM Journal of Research and Development*,
    March 1984, pages 124-134)
Fault-Tolerant Design Techniques for Semiconductor Memory Applications 337
    F.J. Aichelmann, Jr. (*IBM Journal of Research and Development*, March 1984,
    pages 177-183)
Fast RAM Corrects Errors on Chip...344
    A. Khan (*Electronics*, September 8, 1983, pages 126-130)
Fault-Tolerant 256K Memory Designs 349
    R.M. Tanner (*IEEE Transactions on Computers*, April 1984, pages 314-322)
Error-Correction Technique for Random-Access Memories 358
    F.I. Osman (*IEEE Journal of Solid-State Circuits*, October 1982, pages 877-881)

Chapter 7: VLSI Implementations of Redundancy Techniques.......................................363

A Study of Standard Building Blocks for the Design of Fault-Tolerant Distributed
Computer Systems 366
    D.A. Rennels, A. Avižienis, and M. Ercegovac (*Proceedings of the Eighth
    Annual International Symposium on Fault-Tolerant Computing Systems*, June 1978,
    pages 144-149)

Fault Tolerance of a General Purpose Computer Implemented by Very Large Scale
Integration 372
    R.M. Sedmak and H.L. Liebergot (IEEE Transactions on Computers, June 1980,
    pages 492-500)
The Intel 432: A VLSI Architecture for Fault-Tolerant Computer Systems. .381
    D. Johnson (Computer, August 1984, pages 40-48)
The Design of C.fast: A Single Chip Fault Tolerant Microprocessor 390
    M.M. Tsao, A.W. Wilson, R.C. McGarity, C.-J. Tseng, and D.P. Siewiorek
    (*Proceedings of the Twelfth Annual International Symposium on Fault-Tolerant*
    Computing Systems, June 1982, pages 63-69)
Design Approach for a VLSI Self-Checking MIL-STD-1750A Microprocessor 397
    M.P. Halbert and S.M. Bose (Proceedings of the Fourteenth Annual International
    Symposium on Fault-Tolerant Computing Systems, June 1984, pages 254-259)
Fault Tolerance Techniques for Array Structures Used in Supercomputing. .403
    R. Negrini, M. Sami, and R. Stefanelli (Computer, February 1986, pages 78-87)

Bibliography. 413

Author Biographies. 419

Chapter 1: Introduction to Fault-Tolerant Computing

Historical Background

The electronic computer has evolved into a powerful tool that can be applied to a wide variety of problems. In fact, the computer has become an indispensable element in many aspects of our daily lives. A properly functioning computer is necessary for the completion of telephone calls, the control of modern aircraft and spacecraft, the processing of bank transactions, the monitoring of nuclear power plants, and the monitoring of critically ill patients in a hospital just to mention a few. The list of applications will continue to grow as more powerful, smaller, and less expensive machines become available.

However, a computer like any physical system is subject to failure, with the consequences ranging from inconvenience to catastrophy. For example, the failure of a telephone-switching computer may temporarily prevent the completion of a call, whereas the failure of an aircraft control computer could cause a fatal crash. Therefore, computer reliability, availability, and/or safety must be considered during system design.

The field of fault-tolerant computing has evolved over the past twenty-five years and addresses issues affecting the design of reliable computer systems. Fault-tolerant computing begins with the assumption that digital systems are susceptible to many kinds of failures, and then attempts to meet the reliability goals of a particular application by incorporating various types of redundancy into the design. This redundancy can, in some cases, allow a system to continue operating in spite of the presence of one or more faults. In other cases, the redundancy might attempt to minimize the damage caused by a fault with no attempt to keep the system operational. In still other cases, the redundancy may simply facilitate diagnosis and repair of a system to minimize downtime. The amount of fault tolerance needed depends on the nature of the application and the potential consequences of system failure.

Initially, fault-tolerant design principles were developed for a few specialized applications such as space flight and telephone switching. The costs associated with redundant hardware and/or software could be justified when weighed against the costs of system failure. Many of these fault-tolerant systems were developed for space programs in which millions of dollars were invested in spacecraft and/or in which human lives were entrusted to the correct operation of guidance, navigation, and control computers. The Voyager unmanned spacecraft is an example of an early fault-tolerant system, while both the Apollo and the Space Shuttle are examples of manned spacecraft that employ fault-tolerant computer systems.

The communications industry, primarily led by Bell Laboratories, developed early fault-tolerant telephone-switching system computers. Such systems were motivated by the potential consequences of lost revenues and other problems associated with the failure of electronic switching systems. Bell's No. 1 Electronic Switching System (ESS) and its successors are examples.

More recently, as the cost of computer equipment has declined, fault-tolerant techniques have been extended to industrial process-control systems that control nuclear power plants, hazardous materials processing, and other critical equipment and elements, and to commercial transaction-processing systems used by banks, airline reservation systems, credit card companies, and others who have critical databases to be protected. The Tandem Non-Stop II is an example of a successful, commercially available, fault-tolerant transactions processing system.

Indeed, the point has been reached when a number of fault-tolerant features are regularly incorporated into the design of many medium- to large-scale systems. The reader wanting a more complete overview of the development of fault-tolerant computing is referred to the reprints by Rennels [REN84] and by Serlin [SER84] in this chapter.

Definitions and Concepts

This section contains definitions of terms and brief descriptions of basic concepts that are used throughout the book.

Failure—Any departure of a system or module from its specified correct operation. A failure is a malfunction.

Fault—A condition existing in a hardware or software module that may lead to the failure of the module. Hardware faults are caused by physical factors resulting from wear-out, external disturbances, design mistakes, or manufacturing defects. Software faults, on the other hand, result from design or implementation mistakes.

Error—An incorrect response from a hardware or software module. An error is the manifestation of a fault. In other words, the occurrence of an error indicates that a fault is present in the module, that the module has been given an incorrect input, or that the module has been misused. An error will lead to the failure of a system unless tolerance of the underlying fault has been provided. Conversely, a fault may exist without the occurrence of an error under certain conditions.

Faults may be further characterized by a number of properties which describe their effects on a system. The reader is referred to the reprints in this chapter by Hayes [HAY85] for further discussion of hardware faults, and by Hecht [HEC79] for more on software faults.

Type—The fault can be in software or hardware.

Cause—A fault can be the result of improper design, failure of a hardware component, or external disturbances.

Model—A fault is typically represented by some model, ranging from simple "stuck-at" models of digital logic lines in which lines become fixed at logical 1 or 0 values, to more complex models in which faults take on indeterminate values or result in timing errors or other nonlogical behavior.

Duration—A fault is said to be *permanent* if its cause will not disappear without repair and if its effect is always present. An *intermittent* fault also will not disappear without repair but its effect may not always be present. A *transient* fault will exist for some period of time and then disappears without the need for any repair action.

Level—The level at which a hardware fault occurs may be that of a component, a module, a subsystem, or a system, while software faults can exist in programs or microprograms.

Extent—The extent of a fault refers to the scope of its effect on the system and ranges from localized, in which case only a single component at the level of interest is affected, to global, in which case damage has propagated to other system components.

Latency—The property of a fault which allows it to go undetected by virtue of not causing an error.

The following definitions introduce fundamental design approaches and fundamental measures of fault-tolerant systems. Further discussion of these topics is found in Chapter 2.

Fault-Avoidance—The use of high-quality components and conservative design as a means to prevent the occurrence of faults.

Fault-Tolerance—The use of protective redundancy to permit continued correct operation of a system after the occurrence of specified faults.

Protective Redundancy—The use of extra hardware, software, information, or time to mask faults or to reconfigure a faulty system.

Graceful Degradation—The ability of a system to enter an operational yet degraded state after the occurrence of a sequence of specified multiple faults.

Fail-safe—The ability of a system to fail but not produce a catastrophic result.

Reliability—The probability that a system will not fail within time t given that it was operating correctly at time 0.

Availability—The probability that a system will be operating correctly at time t.

Maintainability—The probability that a system will be restored to operation within time t given that it was in a failed state at time 0.

Mean-Time-to-Failure (MTTF)—The expected value of system failure time.

Mean-Time-to-Repair (MTTR)—The expected value of system repair time.

Mean-Time-Between-Failure (MTBF)—The expected value of the time between successive failures of a system, expressed as $MTBF = MTTF + MTTR$.

Fault Tolerant Design Issues

An important step in the design of a fault-tolerant system is the establishment of reliability requirements. The design of highly reliable, maintainable, or available systems requires the use of a combination of techniques. Both fault-avoidance and fault-tolerance approaches are usually employed. However, the selection of specific redundancy techniques is highly dependent on the application intended and the established requirements. It should be noted that a system can be reliable without being fault tolerant; indeed it can be fault tolerant without being reliable. The use of high-quality components and proper design principles can make a system reliable, although it might be intolerant of a fault should one occur. In contrast, if redundancy is applied to a system built with inherently unreliable components, it is possible for reliability to actually decrease, in spite of the fact that some faults are tolerated. Other system requirements are likely to include limits on weight, space, and power.

Requirements of some typical applications will illustrate the range of possibilities. In the case of an aircraft control computer or of a military weapons system, any erroneous output from the computer can be catastrophic. Consequently, the probability of such errors must be extremely low at all times. This precludes the use of nonredundant designs and requires that all individual components be of the highest quality. In the case of telephone-switching systems, some instantaneous errors are considered acceptable, provided that correct operation can be restored within some preselected minimum amount of time. Given these requirements, the amount of redundancy needed is not as great as the amount needed for military or aerospace systems. In transaction-processing systems, the most critical element is the database, which must be protected even if the system must be shut down. Hence continuous operation is not required, but redundancy techniques are necessary for protecting the database.

Designers must make a number of decisions in developing a strategy to provide fault tolerance in a system. The following issues must be addressed:

Fault Detection—Most strategies will require a means of detecting the presence of a fault so that corrective and/or protective action can be taken. This is most often accomplished through the detection of errors that result from the fault. However, diagnostic testing can also be used in some applications. In other cases, it may be sufficient to simply mask the effects of a fault for some length of time without actually being aware of its presence.

Fault Confinement—In most systems, it is desirable to confine the effects of a fault to as small an area as possible to protect the rest of the system.

Fault Diagnosis—Automatic identification of faulty modules is necessary in systems that have a high availability requirement. Such a feature is also needed in systems that provide for reconfiguration around faulty modules. In most cases it is sufficient to diagnose only to the level of a replaceable module or system.

Repair and/or Reconfiguration—The system must either be repaired to eliminate the faulty component or else be reconfigured so that the faulty component can no longer affect the operation of the system. This might require degrading the operation of the system to some acceptable, but lesser, configuration and possibly undoing the damage resulting from the fault.

Recovery—The system must be placed into an acceptable operating state from which it can continue operation, unless the effects of the fault have been masked from the rest of the system.

In selecting an overall fault-tolerance strategy, one must address the above issues, given the reliability and performance requirements of the intended application. For example, in an aircraft control computer, instantaneous errors could be catastrophic. Consequently, this application must continuously mask errors. Given the duration of a particular mission, detection, and automatic repair might be needed to ensure that the system remains reliable over the entire duration of the mission. If the duration of the mission is relatively short, continuous masking might be sufficient, eliminating the need for automatic repair. In the case of a commercial system, however, extensive fault diagnosis and some degree of fault confinement might be sufficient, with manual procedures utilized to effect repair and recovery.

In all cases, some form of redundancy is required in the system to implement the selected fault-tolerance strategies. The various forms of redundancy all have some inherent costs, including those of hardware, redundant design efforts, effects on system speed and performance, size and power penalties, and so on. Redundancy techniques can usually be classified into the following categories:

Hardware Redundancy—Extra hardware is employed to provide fault detection, fault masking, fault diagnosis, or functional spares. Error detection may be provided by code checkers, watchdog timers, replicated modules, and so on. Multiple copies of hardware elements can be provided, with two copies allowing faults to be detected via disagreements between the copies and three or more copies allowing identification of a faulty unit through majority voting procedures. Repair usually consists of replacing one hardware module with a spare unit.

Information Redundancy—Coding techniques can be applied to data, instructions, and other information within a computer system in which redundant bits are utilized to allow detection and/or correction of errors within that information.

Software Redundancy—Extra software can be utilized to provide fault detection, fault diagnosis, fault masking, or fault tolerance of hardware and/or software faults. Diagnostic software can be used to detect and identify faulty hardware or software. Multiple software modules implementing a given algorithm may be utilized either concurrently or sequentially to allow errors resulting from the execution of any one of those modules to be detected and/or corrected.

Temporal Redundancy—Operations ranging from single bus cycles to program executions can be repeated to allow recovery from transient and intermittent faults.

Each of these approaches is characterized by its effect on system reliability and the penalty incurred through its use. Consequently, no single strategy is optimal for all applications. Therefore, the fault-tolerance approaches and case studies examined in this tutorial will examine a wide variety of applications, and will consider the trade-offs associated with the selection of any of the above redundancy techniques.

Outline of the Tutorial Text

The original material and reprinted papers contained in this book have been written and/or selected to provide an overview of the complete field of fault-tolerant computing. Each chapter begins with introductory material that presents definitions, concepts, and techniques needed for the reader to easily grasp the significance of the reprints that follow. Reprints were selected either for their contribution to the development of fault-tolerance principles or for their coverage of important case studies that illustrate the application of principles. A view of the near future of this dynamic field is also captured in the original material and in the reprints.

The reprints in this chapter, Chapter 1, provide an interesting overview of the development and present state of fault-tolerant computing. They also provide additional definitions of terms and summaries of various fault-tolerant systems.

Chapter 2 begins with a tutorial on basic reliability modeling methods and tools. A discussion of basic redundancy techniques follows. Then a thorough discussion of error-detecting and error-correcting codes is presented. Coding is perhaps the most widely used redundancy technique and is a fundamental component of the design of most of the systems examined throughout this tutorial. The reprints in this chapter go into further depth in discussing techniques for modeling the reliability of fault-tolerant systems and provide an overview of several reliability modeling tools available to designers.

Chapter 3 presents a series of case studies of fault-tolerant computing projects related to the development of aerospace and communications systems. These two areas are highlighted because they represent pioneering efforts in the development of fault-tolerant design principles. The systems examined include long-term spacecraft computers, aircraft control systems, telephone electronic switching systems, and computer network communication systems.

Chapter 4 examines the recently developing area of commercial fault-tolerant systems with emphasis on process-control and transaction-processing systems. The case studies presented examine a number of actual systems which either are or have been commercially available, and they examine the different approaches taken to meet the various reliability goals of these two applications.

Chapter 5 presents an overview of software reliability and software fault-tolerance techniques. Unlike hardware, software does not "fail" in the sense of going from a correct to an incorrect state. If a software fault exists in a system, it is the result of the software design or implementation process. Consequently, the approaches taken to tolerate such faults and to evaluate the reliability of a software system are often different from those techniques applied to hardware design. The papers presented in this chapter examine the various techniques that have been proposed to provide tolerance of software faults and they examine several principles that have been applied to database and operating-system design in actual applications.

Chapter 6 provides an overview of fault-tolerance techniques as applied to the design of memory systems. To date, fault-tolerant memory systems have been incorporated into a number of commercial systems, as well as into other designs, primarily because of the relatively low cost of the redundancy associated with error-coding techniques as compared to other forms of redundancy. In addition to two papers that provide an overview of the various design techniques applicable to fault-tolerant memory design, several case studies are included which illustrate the trend toward the use of fault tolerance in VLSI designs, presenting designs of memory chips that incorporate on-chip fault-tolerance features.

The final chapter, Chapter 7, presents an overview of fault-tolerant design as applied to VLSI devices in general. The increasing density of such devices is making the use of on-chip redundancy for fault tolerance more attractive both to increase the reliability of these components and to improve manufacturing yields and testing procedures. The case studies presented in this chapter include designs of several fault-tolerant chips that have been developed in the past few years, ranging from microprocessors to various other system components. Several of these papers present designs involving low-level fault tolerance, in which faults are effectively masked from, or at least reported to, the world outside the chip. The remaining papers discuss design techniques for VLSI devices that support fault tolerance on a system level, including wafer-scale integration approaches to large array-processors.

The field of fault-tolerant computing is an exciting one, in that the decreasing cost of hardware has allowed the development of unique designs to implement ultra-reliable systems, and it has pushed these designs out of research laboratories onto factory floors and into offices. As the number of these applications increase, the demand for even greater degrees of fault tolerance will continue to promote the development of new design techniques, as will the development of new and unique hardware elements, distributed system designs, and artificial intelligence and other software tools.

Fault-Tolerant Computing—Concepts and Examples

DAVID A. RENNELS

Abstract—This paper presents a brief history of fault-tolerant computing. This is followed by a survey of architectural approaches to fault-tolerant design, emphasizing the basic concepts employed in the design of these systems, and the tradeoffs and alternatives available to the system designer in attempting to meet applications requirements. Classes of fault-tolerance applications are identified, along with design approaches which are applicable, and several problem areas are identified in which new research results are badly needed.

Index Terms—Computer architecture, fault-tolerant computing, fault-tolerant design.

I. Introduction

THE objective of fault-tolerant computing is to develop and certify computing systems which perform in a satisfactory fashion in the presence of faults. In this context, faults are deviations from the intended functionality of the system which can be caused by device anomalies, design errors, or even operator mistakes. A community (or perhaps several overlapping communities) of interest has developed over the years, as evidenced by an IEEE Technical Committee and an IFIP Working Group 10.4 devoted to this subject, as well as special issues of technical journals. Several research groups in industry and academia have made continuing contributions for many years, several fault-tolerant machines have been built for government and utility companies, and more recently a number of companies have been formed to supply fault-tolerant machines in the commercial marketplace.

Many of the design techniques for fault-tolerant machines were used in early relay and vacuum-tube machines. Since they were prone to error, techniques such as error detection codes, instruction retry, and diagnostics were used—usually in an ad hoc fashion, to help these machines compute correctly most of the time. It was not viewed as practical to produce a computer which continued computation in the presence of major errors and faults which are hard to handle, e.g., failures in control, transient faults, etc. There was one notable exception in Prague where a team led by A. Svoboda developed a computer (SAPO) with comprehensive fault detection and recovery capabilities. Due to very poor quality of available components (and, as he often described it, threats from the ruling authorities), he found it necessary to build three processors and vote their results in order to circumvent frequent relay errors to achieve acceptable performance [29].

Manuscript received June 12, 1984; revised August 20, 1984. This work was supported by the National Science Foundation under Grant MCS 83-07026.

The author is with the Department of Computer Science, University of California, Los Angeles, CA 90024.

With the development of transistor machines, component reliability was greatly improved. Automated fault recovery was not viewed as being cost effective since redundant hardware and fault recovery mechanisms would add considerably to the initial cost of the system. Emphasis was placed on minimizing downtime when a fault occurred by including fault detection mechanisms in the design and providing comprehensive diagnostics to allow a repairman to quickly isolate faulty logic and replace it.

Research into circuit testing and fault diagnosis is probably the oldest active area in the fault tolerance field. By the mid 1960's effective algorithms had been implemented for testing combinational circuits (Roth's *D* algorithm being perhaps the best known [38]), and the use of microprogramming allowed diagnostic programs to be written in microcode giving much improved access to internal logic for more effective testing. By the mid 1960's extensive fault-detection logic, retries of single instructions, and microdiagnostics were in use in many (e.g., IBM) mainframes.

In the 1960's several applications arose for which the potential cost of computer failure was very high, and automatic fault recovery was needed so that computations could continue uninterrupted in the presence of faults. Among these applications were computer-controlled spacecraft (which cost several hundred million dollars each), and computer controlled telephone switching systems. These were probably the first requirements for fully fault tolerant systems, and they caused a new advance in the state of the art. In addition to the previously developed functions of fault detection and diagnosis, these systems were required to automate the recovery process.

Two fault-tolerant space computers were built and flown in the OAO satellite and the Apollo guidance system, while fault-tolerant electronic switching systems (ESS) were developed for telephone switching. The OAO computer was one of the last computers built with discrete transistors, and its approach to fault tolerance was unique to that technology. Each transistor was replaced by four in a series parallel circuit and was designed in such a way that if any transistor failed, the others could continue to provide the proper logic function [23]. This approach could not be continued with integrated circuits because independence of failure could no longer be guaranteed. With all four transistors on the same piece of silicon, a fault could damage all of them.

The next machine, the Apollo guidance computer, used design techniques which are still useful with modern technology. There were three processors running the same programs, and their results were voted to mask out an error by any single processor. This technique is designated triple modular redundancy (TMR). Two memories were used and data were written to both of them and encoded in an error detecting code. If one of the memories failed, its data would be incorrectly coded, and the processors would then use data from the other memory [2].

The initial ESS designs used a different approach. Two computers executed the same programs and their outputs were compared. If one failed they would disagree, and diagnostics were executed to find which machine was faulty [43]. Later designs used two processors each of which is specially designed to detect its own internal faults so that the faulty machine can usually identify itself when the computers disagree.

The JPL-STAR computer was developed for long unmaintained life during deep space missions during this period [5]. It used a fourth approach. The computer was subdivided into functional units (memories, an arithmetic processor, a control processor, an I/O processor, and a test and repair processor.) Each unit was designed to detect and signal its own internal faults concurrent with regular program execution. The triplicated Test and Repair Processor was charged with replacing a faulty unit with a spare so that computations could continue. This architecture was finely subdivided into small functional units, and in most cases only one unit of each type was powered at a time. This "standby replacement" system was chosen because of very limited power availability on the spacecraft and the need for very long unattended life.

By the end of the 1960's nearly all of the basic forms of fault-tolerant architecture to be found in later designs had been built and experimented with (e.g., triplication with voting, duplication and comparison, self-checking units, and backup sparing). These concepts were refined and adapted to more modern hardware and software technology in subsequent computers.

In the 1970's, several fault-tolerant machines were developed for commercial aircraft control. Two very advanced research machines were developed to the same specifications by the same NASA sponsor, and were built and tested as prototypes (the fault-tolerant multiprocessor (FTMP) and software implemented fault tolerance (SIFT)). Simplified block diagrams of the two architectures are shown in Fig. 1. Both systems execute three copies of a program in different hardware and vote the results to mask faults but they do it in very different ways. All processors in the FTMP are clock synchronized and voting is done by hardware. Processors in SIFT use independent clocks, and voting and synchronization are carried out by software.

In the FTMP structure, a set of processors and memories are connected to five redundant buses through special redundant bus guardian circuits. Processors and memory modules can be dynamically assigned to be a member of a group of three processors and three memories which will run the same computation (designated a triad). This is done by commanding their associated bus guardians to communicate over specially assigned buses. The guardian circuits in the processors vote the three copies of data arriving from their assigned memories, and conversely the memories' guardians

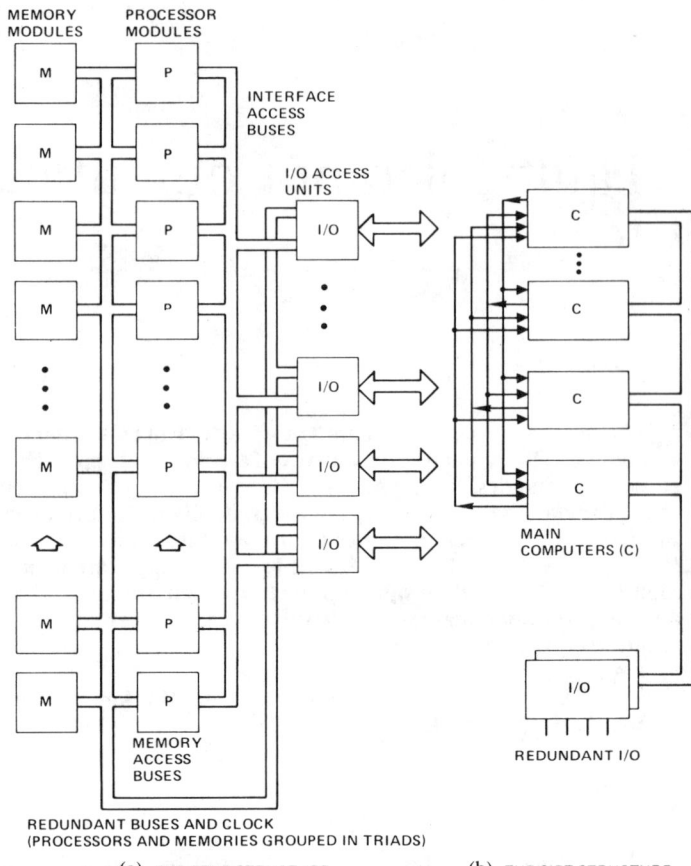

Fig. 1. Simplicated block diagrams of the FTMP and SIFT flight control computers.

vote on information from their assigned processors. If a bus, processor, or memory fails there will still be two valid copies of information at each voter, and the fault will be masked, allowing the triad to continue. When such a failure occurs, a different triad can sense the condition and reconfigure the affected triad by sending commands to bus guardians to assign a new processor, memory, or bus to the affected triad. In this system the common clock had to be specially protected since its failure would disable everything. A special redundant hardware clock design was developed which is immune to single-point failures [19].

The SIFT computers are totally connected. Each computer can broadcast a message over a serial line to dedicated buffers in all the other computers. The computers operate with unsynchronized hardware clocks, and synchronization occurs by a software voting process. Each computer contains a synchronous software executive, and software voting procedures. Periodically, the computers exchange messages containing their views of the time, and develop to a consensus as to its value. As user processes are scheduled in a time-synchronous fashion, they are executed at approximately (but not exactly) the same time and send their results to the other processors where a software voting procedure is invoked to mask faults. If a computer fails and generates disagreeing outputs, the other two ignore it [45].

In practice the FTMP architecture has two major advantages over SIFT in dedicated real-time control applications.

It runs faster than SIFT because its voting is done by hardware. The SIFT computers use a significant percentage of their processing time running the software voting and synchronization programs. More importantly, the fault-tolerance features of FTMP are nearly software transparent. Nearly any software executive can be run on FTMP with fault recovery procedures written to run under it. (Remember the triads will continue to operate under fault conditions until a reconfiguration procedure is invoked.) SIFT, on the other hand, is constrained to using its custom synchronous executive which implements the fault-tolerance features. The U.S. Navy recently selected the FTMP developer (Draper Laboratory) to implement a fault-tolerant version of a Navy-standard minicomputer. One of their most important requirements was the ability to use an executive and applications software already in widespread use.

In this author's opinion, FTMP may have been more practical, but SIFT has probably made the more important research contribution of the two programs. The SIFT program developed pioneering work on proving the correctness of software, the use of formal specifications, has developed new software voting and synchronization concepts, and allowed for the use of selective redundancy. In the SIFT system the processors can schedule different (nonredundant) programs in three machines some of the time while running highly protected triplicated programs at other times. This type of approach has considerable merit in commercial systems where resources can be assigned individually to noncritical tasks, then brought into a redundant configuration for more important uses (such as periodically waking up a fault-tolerant monitoring and system recovery process).

A highly redundant computing system was used on the Space Shuttle [42]. This system has five computers. During critical mission phases four execute identical programs, and the control outputs of the four are voted in the control actuators. The fifth is used as a nonredundant backup and contains totally different programs in the hope that if an uncorrectable design or software error occurs in the four primary machines, the fifth can be switched-in to replace them. Two sets of programs have been written by different contractors (the four are programmed by IBM and the fifth by Rockwell). Incompatabilities between the two sets of programs have caused check-out problems and a delayed launch, but the system now appears to be working satisfactorily.

Also during the 1970's more advanced fault-tolerant computers were developed for communication switching, and the expansion of fault-tolerant computing into process control for critical transportation applications [20].

Recently, two parallel developments have accelerated application of fault-tolerant computing. The first is the increased degree to which the public depends upon computing systems, greatly multiplying the inconvenience and public awareness of an occasional computer fault. A failure of computing for automated bank tellers for a large city one or two times a year, or temporary outages of credit card checks can inconvenience thousands, as can failure of just one computerized ignition system on a freeway at rush hour. The second is the enormous decrease in the cost of computer hardware. The primary cost associated with implementing hardware fault tolerance is associated with redundancy that is added to provide fault detection and recovery. Although the relative hardware cost of a highly fault-tolerant computer may be several times that of a nonfault-tolerant machine, hardware prices have dropped an even greater relative amount making fault tolerance cost-effective for a larger number of applications.

A number of new companies have been formed to enter the commercial marketplace with fault tolerance. The best known is Tandem Computers which has grown to a large size within a very short time by supplying this technology to the transaction industry [7], [22]. Other companies (August Systems, Stratus, Synapse, etc.) have since been formed to enter this expanding marketplace.

A new and exciting area is the development of fault-tolerant local area networks. A large amount of redundancy is naturally available in collections of identical machines, and the individual machines have the built-in intelligence (with properly written programs) to provide sophisticated recovery algorithms at very low cost when other machines fail. It is instructive to briefly discuss two examples, Locus and the Draper Laboratories AIPS systems.

Locus is a network operating system which exploits the hardware redundancy in a local network to provide very high availability. It is running on a 20 VAX network at UCLA and provides a network-transparent UNIX environment. The user can log onto any machine in the system, except when restricted by administrative fiat, and see an identical environment (passwords, files, mail, etc.). Files are duplicated at two different sites, and as his programs execute, data are paged out to those sites. If the user's machine crashes, he or she connects to a different machine and continues using the system [30]. This system is based on the use of commercial hardware with little or no hardware modifications.

AIPS is an extension of the FTMP concept to distributed systems as shown in Fig. 2. A group of processing sites is connected through switching nodes to a redundant intercommunication structure which behaves like a triply redundant bus, but which can be circuit switched over different paths to provide physical damage tolerance. Each processing site may be a fault-tolerant multiprocessor (FTMP), a triplicated (TMR) fault-tolerant processor (FTP), a duplicated pair of processors, or a single nonredundant machine. Each site has a local clock which synchronizes computers at that site, but clocks are not synchronized between sites. Hardware voting is done throughout the system. Within a site containing triplicated (TMR) processors, voting is straightforward because the processors are clock-synchronized and are executing identical programs. Voting of triplicated data sent between processing sites with different local clocks requires a hardware synchronization operation, but the data skew can probably be kept small and hardware voting is still feasible. This design recognizes the need for selective redundancy. In a complex system, not all processes are sufficiently critical to justify triplicating their processors. Thus, duplex and single processors can also be included [1]. This system is a candidate for use on the Space Station.

Future research will have to deal with much more complex distributed systems. Since powerful processors have become just another chip, we can expect large numbers of processors forming multilevel hierarchic systems in which fault toler-

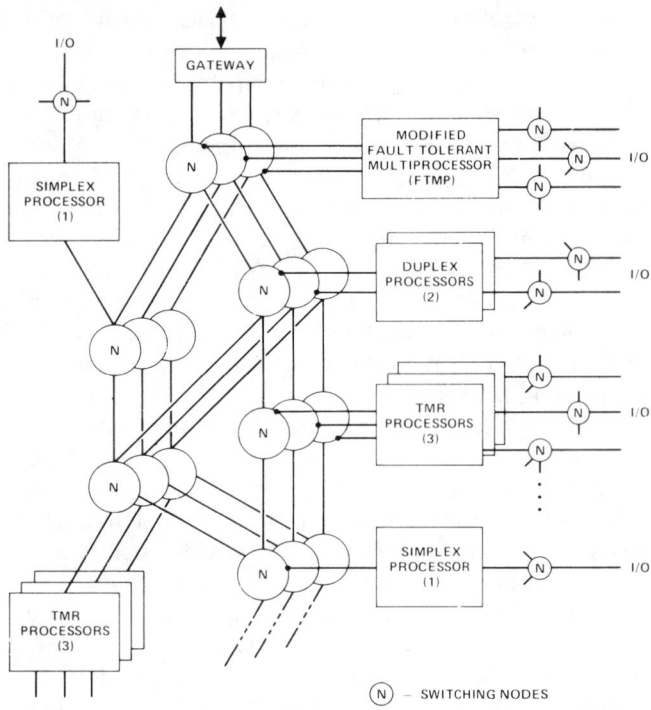

Fig. 2. One configuration of the advanced information processing system (AIPS).

systems with many embedded computers, and fault tolerance must be implemented in this type of distributed environment. System development usually proceeds from a set of user specifications (including fault-tolerance requirements) to an architecture concept. The architecture is then refined and partitioned into subsystems, each with specific functions to provide. The subsystems are then further partitioned and protective redundancy is added in the form of fault detection and recovery mechanisms.

A. Hierarchic System Partitioning

Complex systems are naturally partitioned at several levels based on funtions provided by specific subsystems. A fault-tolerant system displays similar functional partitioning, but in addition it contains redundant components and recovery mechanisms which may be employed in different ways at different levels. It is reasonable to view a fault-tolerant system as a nested set of machines (subsystems) each of which may display varying levels of fault tolerance. For example, at the highest level, a distributed system may recover from a failed computer by shifting its computations to other machines. At the next lower level, a single computer may be capable of replacing a faulty memory module with a spare and switching to alternative communication channels to circumvent a failed port, but not be able to recover when a short occurs on the local memory–processor bus or when its power supply fails. At a lower level, the memory modules may be capable of replacing defective RAM chips with spares or the chips may contain redundancy and be capable of tolerating certain failures but not others.

A descriptive model must capture this hierarchic property of systems and the way in which fault-tolerance features are apportioned within the various levels. To do this we will introduce the terminology of embedded partitions. A redundant partition (RP) is a set of modules which contains sufficient redundancy that if one fails, acceptable performance can be achieved with those remaining. (The RP may contain spare modules to replace those which fail, or they may redistribute functions when one fails and operate in a degraded fashion.) Recovery from a fault within the RP may be effected within the domain itself, or may require action by higher levels within the system. An RP may be made up of heterogeneous modules (e.g., a computer with its communications ports and disks backed up by a similar computer which has different disks and I/O facilities), and a module in one RP will often contain other nested RP's. An example would be a redundant set of computers, where each computer contains redundant memory modules, processors, and I/O circuits. Fig. 3 shows a typical system which is partitioned into several levels.

In Fig. 3, the highest level partition (RP) is the intercommunications bus and its backup spare. Typically, the computers are grouped into several independent partitions by their dedicated interconnections to external devices. Computers 1 and 2 with devices X1 and X2 form a redundant partition and, if no other computers have devices similar to X1 and X2 and therefore cannot back up their services, they are the only computers in the partition. The computers contain two nested redundant partitions: memory modules and I/O ports, and the memory modules contain nested partitions

ance will be employed in different ways at different places within the system. Research has been initiated into autonomous systems in which an embedded fault-tolerant computing facility is used as an automated repairman — to take over decision making currently being done by humans and to initiate repair. An autonomous satellite demonstration has been initiated by the Air Force, which uses an on-board computer to diagnose and repair faults within its host system [4].

In a typical design for this type of system, redundant sets of computers is embedded in various subsystems (e.g., attitude control, command, payload, etc.) which control redundant electromechanical devices. These local computers are responsible for fault recovery in their associated subsystems since they have the most diagnostic information available and are programmed by subsystem contractors most familiar with their intended operation. The subsystem computers may be autonomously fault tolerant by themselves, or they may depend upon assistance from higher level command and control computers within the system to implement and control recovery from their faults. The result is a hierarchy of fault-tolerance mechanisms: 1) local software for recovery from subsystem faults, 2) local software and hardware for recovery from faults in the subsystem computers, 3) software in high-level command and control computers to recover from failed subsystems, and 4) hardware and software for recovery of faults in the command and control computers. New models and design techniques will be needed for this new class of nested fault-tolerant machines.

II. Hardware Fault-Tolerance Concepts

We review next some of the basic concepts and design issues in the implementation of fault-tolerant systems. The availability of low-cost single chip processors is resulting in

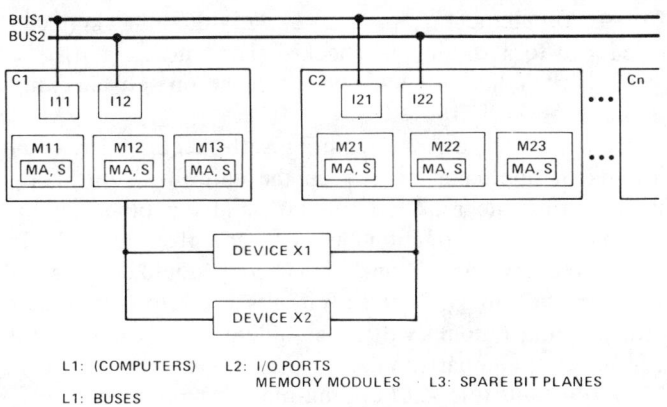

Fig. 3. Nested redundant partitions.

of spare bit planes (ma-memory array, s-spare).

Associated with each module is a fault-tolerance interface which goes along with its functional interface. The fault-tolerance interface communicates with modules in its own partition or higher level partitions with requests to supply recovery services that it cannot provide for itself [3], [35]. For example, if a memory chip fails, its memory interface unit (the next highest level) may switch in a spare bit plane and reconstruct damaged data automatically. If a memory module fails, the whole computer is likely to be disabled requiring services two levels higher. Other computers may be required to diagnose the fault, activate a new memory module, reload and restart the failed computer.

Fig. 4 is an idealization of the fault-tolerance interface needed between modules of a three-level distributed system. This type of hierarchic computer architecture is already beginning to appear in spacecraft, and probably in industrial automation also. The lowest level (but often the most expensive) redundant partitions are at the electromechanical sensors and actuators for which spares are provided. At the next level, redundant computers are dedicated to specific subsystems (e.g., attitude control on a spacecraft), and at the next level, a set of redundant computers provide high-level executive and control functions.

The subsystem-embedded computers provide a degree of fault tolerance for their associated electromechanical subsystems using software which can detect anomalies and effect recovery within the subsystem. The system executive computers provide system-level recovery functions. If a subsystem temporarily ceases to operate while a component is being replaced, systemwide recovery implications can result. For example, a spacecraft may have to reacquire orientation in space, or a command sequence may have to be modified. The system-level computers must also provide fault tolerance for themselves and may be capable of assisting the subsystem computers in local recovery.

Each level can be characterized by its possible response to various internal faults. The two primary categories are faults that the level is designed to handle locally, and faults beyond its range of coverage. If one level recognizes a fault for which it was properly designed, it can notify higher system levels in one of three ways: 1) it can indicate that the fault was recovered locally, 2) request specific help in recovering the fault within its local level, or 3) notify higher levels of a failure which cannot be recovered at its level. Notifying higher

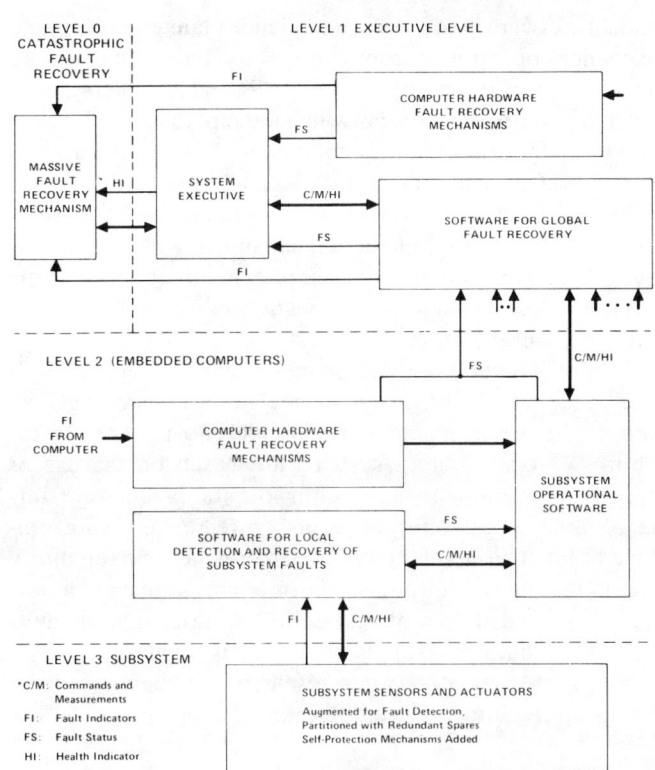

Fig. 4. Fault-tolerance interfaces in a recovery hierarchy.

levels of faults may be implicit or explicit. If the lower level module provides outputs encoded in an error detection code, or if it is one of a set of duplicated or triplicated modules whose outputs can be easily compared by the next higher level, we view this as an implicit error indication.

Much more difficult are faults which were overlooked in the design at the partition at which it occurred. In this case, no explicit notification will be forthcoming when the fault occurs. Here the higher level must employ reasonableness checks and acceptance tests on the functional outputs of the module. This is shown in the figure as "health indicators." Each level should be designed so that its functioning can be checked for reasonableness. For example, data may be specified whose rate of change cannot exceed some specified threshold, calibration data may be included within real measurements, and special procedures may be executed to check data for consistency. Control flow checks (locks and keys on procedure entry) and time-out-counters also fall into this category. This heuristic checking can be used to provide a second line of defense against faults which may not be detected at the level where they occurred.

For many dedicated systems reasonable checks of this type can be quite powerful. For example, the attitude control subsystems of many spacecraft execute complicated differential equations to keep the system pointed to the Sun and a star. If sensors indicate loss of lock or excessive loss of control gas, a fault in this subsystem is nearly certain to have occurred whether or not it was detected locally within the subsystem.

Reasonableness checks, although useful in detecting that a subsystem is no longer functioning, provide little information about the cause of failure. Fault recovery at this level can require expert systems. A recovery algorithm may involve substituting redundant elements (and possibly activating redundant software modules) in a sequence planned to optimize the chances of restoring correct operation based on educated guesses as to what might be wrong. Research is being conducted into on-board systems which attempt to restore correct operation, but go so far as to replan mission operational sequences if only partial operation can be restored.

Several distributed systems using commercial machines have very limited fault detection capability within the computers. Thus, the systems often employ heuristics of this type for fault detection such as heartbeat checks and checking of time counts in the other machines.

Multilevel models of fault tolerance have not yet been well developed, but this is the way that technology is moving. The state of the art in mathematical models to predict the reliability of fault-tolerant systems are based on the use of Markov models whose number of states become unmanageable when multiple levels of redundancy are employed [28]. The development of performance and reliability models for future multilevel fault-tolerant systems is a new and badly needed area of research. The extension of fault-tolerant computing to supply autonomous repair to complex systems is also a relatively new research area which will have increasing importance in the future.

B. Fault Detection

If a module fails, a recovery mechanism must detect it in order to take corrective action. This is the process of fault detection. Modules at all levels (computers, logic modules, or on-chip redundancy) fall between two basic types. At one extreme are circuits which can detect internal faults concurrently with normal operation—these we will call "self checking" (SC)—and at the other extreme are modules which have no internal fault detection capability which will be designated "nonself-checking" (NSC). When used in a redundant partition, SC modules can be operated singly, since faults will be detected, if an external recovery mechanism can substitute a spare module for one which has failed. NSC modules must be duplicated and operated two-at-a-time with outputs compared for fault detection and, three-at-a-time and voted if a faulty module is to be identified quickly (or if transient faults are to be located).

A methodology for designing self-checking logic has been developed, and it has been shown that a self-checking computer can be developed at an approximate 10 percent increase in hardware complexity [12]. The reason for this relatively low cost is that the majority of a computer's logic is memory which due to its regular structure can be designed to detect faults with a few extra bits per word. Irregular logic must often be duplicated, but this makes up a small percentage of many modern machines. An important characteristic of this methodology is the fact that self-checking checkers have been developed which signal faults in the checking circuitry as well as in the operational circuits being continually checked [11]. This largely solves the problem of "who checks the checker?" Checking signals are implemented as complementary "morphic" pairs which alternate between values 1, 0 and 0, 1 when no error exists. Upon detecting an error in the circuits being checked or in the checking circuits, these signals take on values 1, 1 or 0, 0 indicating a fault has occurred. A reduction circuit was developed so that a number of these complementary pairs from individual checkers can be reduced to a single self-checked pair which serves as a master fault indicator. A useful reference on self-checking circuits is Wakerly [44].

One approach to implementing self-checking logic on VLSI is to duplicate circuits on the chip, with one copy implementing the required function and the other implementing the same function but with complementary logic functions (every logical "one" in one copy would be a logical "zero" in the other). If these circuits are error free, their corresponding outputs will be complementary pairs, and a self-checking comparison can be performed [40].

The JPL fault-tolerant building-block computer (FTBBC) architecture was designed to use a small set of VLSI building-block circuits to interconnect existing microprocessor and memory chips to form self-checking computer modules (SCCM). The SCCM's contain redundant communications interfaces to facilitate their use in fault-tolerant distributed systems on spacecraft. Self-checking (morphic) logic is used throughout the SCCM design. Odd parity checks are split into two halves covering portions of words being checked to generate complementary signals, and random logic is duplicated with the outputs of one member of a duplex pair inverted to also generate complementary output signals. These are reduced to provide self-checking check circuits. The SCCM is shown in Fig. 5. The four building-block types are: 1) a memory interface building block which implements Hamming codes and spare chip replacement in memory, 2) an I/O building block, 3) a bus interface building block which allows the SCCM's to be connected with similar SCCM's into a network, and 4) a Core building block which compares the outputs of two duplicated processors, checks information on internal buses for proper coding, and collects fault messages from other building blocks. The Core, on detecting a fault, can initiate a program rollback to correct transient faults, and disable the SCCM if the fault persists—indicating a permanent fault [36]. A breadboard system was constructed, and faults were inserted into both the operational logic and the check circuits by shorting randomly selected wires to ground to experimentally evaluate the effectiveness of its fault-detection mechanisms.

Possibly a more practical approach was taken by INTEL in some of their chips for the 432 system, which are designed to be duplicated and compared. Every chip contains a set of output comparators, and a control line indicating whether the chip is to serve as an active chip generating outputs, or whether it is to serve as a checker. Two chips are tied together with one designated the active unit and the other designated the checker. Both receive the same inputs and compute the same logic functions but the check chip does not output. It blocks its outputs and compares them to what the other chip generated, signaling an error if a disagreement occurred [21]. In a highly competitive commercial environment, few vendors will sacrifice performance of their chips by devoting a large amount of chip area to concurrent error checking. Intel's comparator approach costs little in real estate or performance on the chip, and it gives the user the option to buy two if concurrent fault detection is to be implemented.

In many systems circuit modules may fall somewhere in between SC and NSC and be partially self-checking. Many

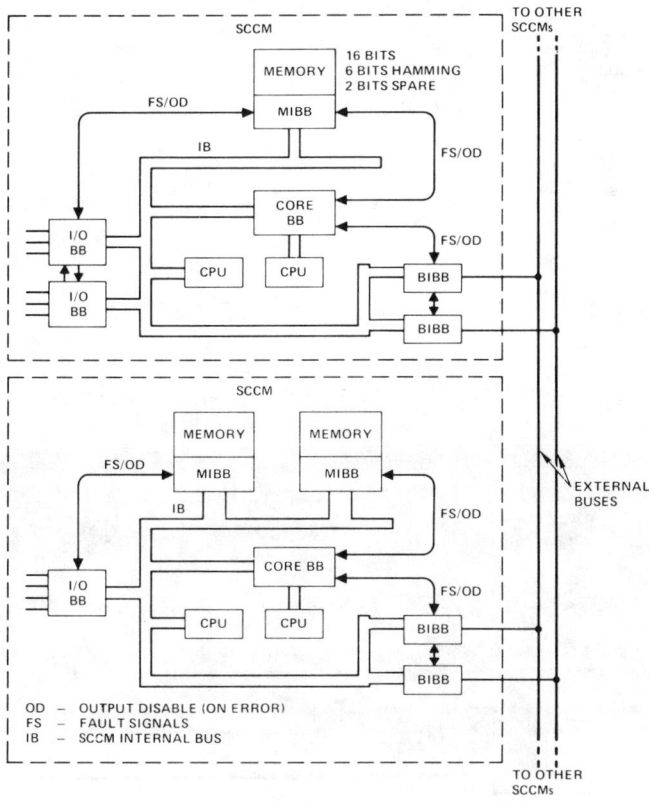

Fig. 5. Self-checking computer modules (SCCM).

commercial computers which are used in (at least partially) fault-tolerant distributed systems have hardware to detect of some (e.g., memory parity) faults while other internal faults cannot be detected.

We will characterize the checking of modules in a recovery partition by two parameters: fault-detection coverage, and detection latency time. The fault-detection coverage for a given detection procedure is the probability given that a fault occurs, that it is detected by applying the procedure. The detection latency is the time between the occurrence of the fault and the time that the fault is detected through observations of erroneous results. We simplify this parameter by giving it three values, *I* (instantaneous), *EC* (error-concurrent), and *NC* (nonconcurrent). Instantaneous fault detection implies that a fault is detected when a fault first occurs, and is impractical to achieve since many faults do not cause signals to take on incorrect values (i.e. errors) until the system reaches particular states. For example, a stuck-at-zero cell in memory causes no error while the stored word has a zero in the faulty bit position. An error only occurs when an attempt is made to store a "one" there. Error-concurrent fault detection (concurrent is the term used by Avižienis and others) implies that a fault is detected before a fault-induced logic error travels beyond its point of origin. In many cases this requires that an error be detected within the same clock cycle that it first appears (although in some designs this can be relaxed to a few cycles), and before damaged data leave the module. An NSC module, having nonconcurrent detection, may run for many cycles before a fault is detected, and massive error propagation can be expected.

Self-checking modules exhibit concurrent but not instantaneous fault detection. An interesting potential area of research is the design of self-checking and self-testing logic which not only detects fault-induced errors, but also flushes out faults within a guaranteed time by exercising, during normal operation, all logic states necessary for faults to cause detectable logic errors. Considerable research has been carried out on test-set generation with hundreds of papers to be found in the literature [10]. Recent research has focused on generating tests and checking responses directly on a VLSI chip, e.g., one approach partitions the chip into small enough logic groups that exhaustive testing can be carried out [9]. (Other approaches have been proposed using probabilistic testing, generating pseudorandom test sequences and signature analysis on chip but the coverage of such tests are very hard to determine.)

This area can integrate the separate specialties of VLSI logic synthesis (e.g., state assignment) design for test and fault-tolerant architecture. If chips are made to detect their own internal faults, and can also be made to perform self-tests during normal operation (by interleaving test cycles with operational cycles, or better yet, exercising circuits that are temporarily idle) it may be practical to build circuits which thoroughly test themselves in a few seconds of normal operation. An interesting question is how to mechanize state saving on-chip with little area penalty to allow interleaving of testing and normal operation.

C. Fault Recovery Using SC and NSC Modules

There are three common ways of providing fault tolerance within a redundant set of modules: triplication and voting; duplication and comparison (with later identification of a faulty module); and standby replacement.

To achieve comprehensive fault tolerance using nonself-checking modules it is necessary to provide fault detection and recovery by massive redundancy techniques. Three NSC modules may be operated concurrently and their outputs voted to detect and mask out a fault in one. This approach is commonly known as triply modular redundancy (TMR). When spare modules can be used to replace the faulty units in a TMR set, the configuration is designated as hybrid redundancy. TMR and hybrid architectures were previously described in the discussions of the SIFT, FTMP, and Apollo systems. Alternatively, two NSC modules be operated together and their outputs compared to detect faults. Upon detecting a fault, both are commanded to run diagnostics and the one which succeeds will be deemed operational. The early ESS processors used duplicated processors. This technique, designated duplex redundancy (DR) sometimes fails for transient faults since both modules are likely to pass the diagnostic and it may be impossible to tell which contains fault-damaged data. When a computer fails in a TMR system, the system may revert to duplex operation, and when a duplex system fails it is often possible to find the good unit of the pair and continue nonfault-tolerant operation with a single machine.

If a module is capable of detecting its internal faults, it is possible to operate only one unit and, upon detecting a failure, turn it off and replace it with a spare or assign its function to some other module. This approach is known as standby redundancy (SR). This form of redundancy was used in the JPL STAR and FTBBC computers because it uses minimal power and is well suited to long unattended life [34].

The three approaches are shown symbolically in Fig. 6 for the simple case where a single module is redundantly protected.

From Fig. 6 it is easy to see that standby redundancy has a major advantage for long life unmaintained systems (if unpowered equipment has a lower failure rate) because more of the total hardware is available as spares. It has a disadvantage of lower fault coverage than the voted configuration, which can detect and recover from any single fault within one module. The self-checking module in an SR configuration must make use of internal error detection techniques which may not be capable of detecting certain obscure multiple error conditions such as those induced by clock and power supply noise.

Standby redundant configurations must make use of program rollback techniques. Since computations may not be recoverable from the point at which a fault was detected, it is necessary to save the system state in the form of rollback points in programs and, after detection and removal of a fault, return to the most recent rollback point to recover computations [37]. Especially difficult is the problem of nonrepeatable events where a computer may generate an output to external systems and then generate it again after rolling back. A similar problem of this type occurs if a file is advanced by a record, a fault is detected, and it is advanced again during the rollback as previous code is repeated. Solutions to these problems have been developed by the software community under the more general category of atomic transactions and stable storage [25]. The approach is to make it possible to back out of I/O operations if an error is detected and a rollback or restart initiated. When a series of external events are requested, none is carried out until it is assured that the computer has safely progressed to the next rollback point. The Unified Data System system, for example, buffered all outputs and executed them all at once when the next rollback segment was reached (as indicated by a real-time interrupt [33]).

Remapping Processes to Redundant Hardware: In distributed systems TMR, Duplex, and Standby redundancy may be used at different sites. AIPS, discussed in Section I allows all three types to be used in different places. TMR/Hybrid redundancy may be used for critical processes, while standby redundancy is used for less critical applications, thus freeing up more processors for increased throughput.

In multiple processor systems the fault recovery process is complicated by the process of remapping the computations of failed processors onto different elements which remain functional (examples are shown in Fig. 7). For small systems, this remapping can be relatively simple. For example, the JPL-STAR computer was divided into a set of functional units, each of which had dedicated backup spares which could be switched-in to replace a faulty unit [Fig. 7(a)]. SIFT and FTMP are homogeneous structures which allow any spare module of a given type to be substituted for any active module of similar type. If spares are available, the "next" spare is substituted for any module of its type which fails.

When a system is designed to operate in a degraded fashion if no spare elements are available, the remapping process becomes more difficult and sometimes involves complex decisions [Fig. 7(b)]. It is necessary to select computational

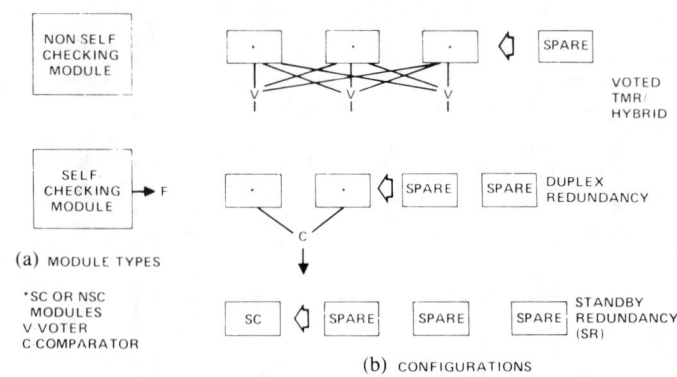

Fig. 6. TMR/hybrid, duplex, and standby redundant configurations.

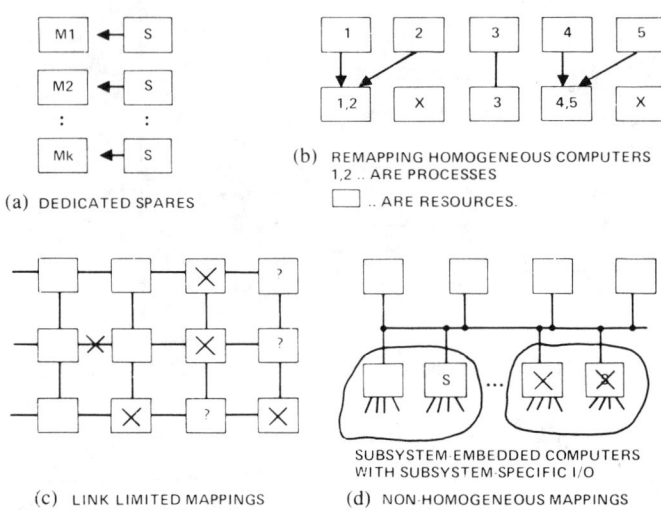

Fig. 7. Mapping processes to redundant hardware.

services which may be delayed (slowed down) or dropped altogether, and for dedicated control systems entirely new operating modes may have to be developed.

This process of remapping becomes most complex when systems contain large numbers of processors. Large networks 1) have limited interconnections between processors, and 2) are often heterogeneous. Fig. 7(c) shows a processing network in which the failure of links can make processors unavailable, and the failures of processors can make links unavailable. It is desirable to limit the number of communications links to an individual processor for economic reasons, but the interconnection structure must be as redundant as possible to minimize losses when a failure occurs. Several researchers have applied graph theory to study the general problem of fault diagnosis and the remapping of processes in large connection-limited networks. Hayes has analyzed the problem by specifying processes to be carried out and physical resources as separate graphs, and has considered the problem of designing networks which can tolerate some number of failures and still be capable of carrying out the required computations. This is equivalent to finding an isomorphism between the process and resource graphs in the presence of failures [18]. A considerable amount of work has also been done on the problem of diagnosing faults in large collections of machines [31], [39]. Kuhl and Reddy have developed techniques by which processors in a large unsynchronized network can diagnose failures using distributed algorithms and come to a mutual agreement on the availability of resources [24].

A number of researchers have studied specific network structures in an attempt to optimize this fault-induced remapping process for performance, various technology constraints, and long-life availability [16], [32].

In systems with a large number of resources, the concept of reliability is no longer a simple question of whether it works or not. Various degraded levels of performance are to be expected and evaluation must be made on the basis of both reliability and performance. A new area of performability modeling has been developed which attempts to evaluate the functionality to be expected from a system, considering the fact that failures will occur at various times during its life [26]. This type of modeling can provide comparative evaluation of design approaches in terms of a user's objectives — extra services gained for a fault-tolerance investment.

Finally, to achieve fault tolerance in very large systems, new distributed operating systems concepts will be needed. Functional languages and high-level data flow concepts will apply.

D. The Need for Independence of Failures

In order for most fault-tolerant designs to work properly, random component faults must occur independently in the modules into which a system has been partitioned. There are a variety of techniques for detecting a fault in one module and effecting recovery (either by suppressing its outputs using voting, or by disconnecting it using switching), but few if any existing designs can deal with the occurrence of a fault which affects more than one module simultaneously. This need to localize a fault to only one module leads to very stringent design requirements which may be from a minimum of placing modules of a redundant partition on different chips to encapsulating each module in shielded boxes with ground and power isolation.

A subtle problem of "lurking faults" is encountered. Two faults may occur independently, and at different times, in different modules that may result in simultaneously occurring errors for a particular common data input. This occurrence of simultaneous errors under these circumstances may appear to be simultaneous faults in two modules. It is possible for a fault to occur in logic which is seldom used, and thus not cause a detectable error until the faulty logic is exercised. If an undetected fault occurs in one module and lurks there until a fault in a different module causes an unusual set of computational states which causes the first fault to generate an error, then errors will appear as if the modules had experienced dependent faults. A new requirement occurs to fully exercise and test each module periodically in order to flush out lurking faults and preserve independence. This area was described before as offering interesting research opportunities because three often disjoint disciplines are involved for optimal solutions: combining architecture, design of fault-detecting logic, and design of circuit testing procedures.

III. THE DESIGN SPACE

Having briefly discussed some of the principals of fault-tolerant design, several systems will now be examined in terms of their particular fault-tolerance objectives and the tradeoffs involved in their designs. Ideally, all computing systems should be fully fault tolerant but most only achieve limited capabilities for economic reasons. All fault-tolerant systems have an objective of improved availability, i.e., to minimize downtime. In addition, three principal characteristics which define a space of requirements for fault-tolerant design as shown in Fig. 8.

A. Computational Integrity

One axis is computational integrity. At the high end, there are systems which make no mistakes and have no delays when a fault occurs and is recovered. Intermediate performance on this axis involves delays during fault recovery and/or loss of some computations between the time of the fault and a previous rollback point at which the system state was saved for recovery.

In order to achieve complete computational integrity (without time delays for fault recovery) it is necessary to carry out at least two self-checked computations or three non-self-checked computations concurrently. If a fault occurs in one machine carrying out the computation, another can continue it without delay. This is hardware-expensive and has in the past been reserved for critical applications such as airframe control. As described before, the SIFT, FTMP, and Space Shuttle computers all run multiple copies of computations in different machines and use fault masking through voting to provide instantaneous correction of errors.

Only recently has the price of hardware dropped to the point where this level of redundancy can be introduced into commercial machines. The Stratus Computer system uses a pair of self-checking processors, running the same software concurrently. At a price of about $100 per chip, this system includes eight 68 000 processors running as four self-checking pairs. Two pairs run executive programs, and two pairs run user programs, with one pair backing up the other.

For many applications, computational integrity requirements can be relaxed. These computing applications do not require instantaneous recovery and can use less expensive standby redundancy. A computation is run in a single machine which is backed up by other computers running different computations. The machine's state is periodically saved as rollback points. If a transient fault occurs, the computer returns to the last rollback point to restart its computations. For a permanent fault, provisions may be added for a different computer to obtain the rollback state and continue the interrupted computations. In either case the computation is delayed.

In the JPL-STAR computer (which as previously described used standby redundancy) the recovery delay could take hundreds of milliseconds. This may not be a problem in some commercial applications, but for real-time systems the worst case recovery time must be accounted for in the design of the surrounding system. For example, a spacecraft might be

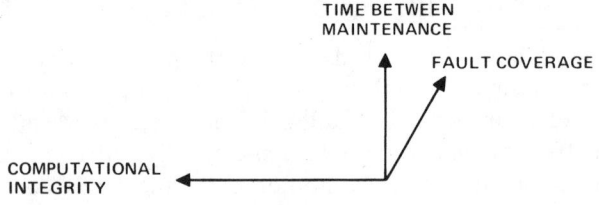

Fig. 8. Fault-tolerance characteristics.

scheduled to start a sequence of periodic commands to a subsystem during the time that a fault recovery was in progress. After the recovery the applications programs would be required to account for the fact that a delay occurred and the command generation program would have to send the command later. This might cause other commands to be modified to related subsystems, etc.

A standby redundant system cannot guarantee computational integrity if inputs are lost or if outputs are forgotten during a program rollback. It is seldom recognized that special hardware must be included to capture any input which occurred between the time that a rollback point was established, and a fault-induced rollback to that point. Clearly, if inputs are ignored the computational results will be modified by the occurrence of a fault. Similarly, outputs can not be repeated when a rollback is attempted.

To summarize, computational integrity can be maintained rather easily when expensive fault masking techniques are employed (TMR/Hybrid or duplex self-checking). Time delays are introduced with the less expensive standby redundancy and, if careful design is not employed, computational integrity cannot be guaranteed. Probably the best solution is the selective use of redundancy. If noncritical programs are run on single machines, while occasional critical programs are triplicated, a cost-effective solution can be obtained. A system is currently being developed at UCLA which will cause critical computations to be run in triplicate on a distributed computing facility, while the majority of (noncritical) programs will be run in a standby redundant fashion [6].

B. Time Between Scheduled Maintenance

The next axis of Fig. 8 is Time Between Scheduled Maintenance. Maintenance in this context is human intervention to replace faulty components. A fault-tolerant machine will recover from a fault by invoking redundant hardware, but the faulty hardware must be replaced to restore the system since the system will ultimately fail when spare hardware is exhausted. There are a number of applications for which maintenance is impossible (in this case, time between scheduled maintenance is the total life of the system), and others for which maintenance is inconvenient or expensive (resulting in months to years during which the system should operate without manual repair). For example, many space computers are unrepairable. Many military systems have severe logistic problems for repair, as do systems at remote places. This requires the design of long-life systems with sufficient redundancy to survive some prescribed time (with a specified level of confidence), between scheduled maintenance. Often these systems are also constrained by limited power availability and a requirement to be fitted into a small volume.

These systems must employ more redundancy than a regularly maintained system, and must use the redundancy that they have in an efficient fashion. This can be in conflict with the need for computational integrity which, as we have seen, requires massive redundancy during operation. For example, a long-life system which requires three operating processors must provide sufficient redundancy to guarantee that three processors will survive until end of life. (If the system degrades to two processors or less, transient error recovery cannot be guaranteed.) Due to power constraints and the fact that many semiconductor technologies (NMOS, Bipolar) have a higher failure rate when powered, many long-life systems are designed to operate with only one copy of a computation being run at one time. Self-checking design is needed so that when the system degrades to only a single working computer, transient faults can still be recovered and reliable computing can still be carried out. Computational integrity is sacrificed to attain longer life with a given amount of redundant hardware.

In order to use redundancy in an efficient fashion, long-life computers are often partitioned more finely than are frequently maintained systems because this allows longer life to be achieved with a given amount of redundant hardware. For example, the FTBBC computer developed for unmanned spacecraft at the Jet Propulsion Laboratory allows faulty computers to be replaced with spares, but each individual computer contains internal redundancy which allows individual memory modules, processors, and even memory chips to be replaced with spares to enhance the life of each processor at a small increase in hardware cost [36].

C. Fault Coverage

Coverage (c) is a measure of how well the fault-tolerance mechanisms work. It is defined as the conditional probability given that a fault occurs, that the system will recover properly. It has been shown to be a very sensitive parameter in achieving fault tolerance over long periods of time [8]. This can be easily seen since if N faults occur, the probability of correct operation will be bounded by $c**N$, no matter how much redundant hardware is employed in the system.

As a system requirement, the level of coverage reflects the criticality of the application to which the computer is applied and what levels of performance people are willing to accept. The SIFT and FTMP computers were designed to a requirement that there be less that one chance in a billion of computer failure during any a ten hour aircraft flight (between ground maintenance). Since there is a reasonable chance of a fault occurring within that time, coverage was required to be a nearly perfect (0.999999···). Other applications, such as spacecraft control, typically require a smaller value of coverage (e.g., >0.98–0.99). The FTBBC would be deemed successful with this coverage level because a computer outage is not as critical. The surrounding system is designed with interlocks which would prevent erroneous commands or loss of computations from destroying the spacecraft, and remote ground intervention would be possible to manually reconfigure the on-board computer to a working configuration should that be necessary on rare occasion. The users of some general purpose systems might be satisfied with reducing the average crash rate from once a month to once a year allowing a coverage of 0.93.

Extremely high levels of coverage against random faults in hardware is very difficult to achieve. To design for coverage of 0.999999 would require knowing with near absolute certainty which faults will occur in practice. This is clearly impossible, so the designers use the only alternative available. Three computers are operated simultaneously and their outputs voted. Here we do not have to know how a computer will fail; it is assumed that no two computers will fail at the same time, and if one fails, the correct result will appear in the output vote.

There are a number of less expensive techniques to effect fault detection and recovery at a lower level of coverage. Most of the logic in computer systems has a very regular structure and can be protected using error detection and correction codes. For example, a 32-bit memory can be provided with single error correction and double error detection at an additional seven bits per word. If the individual bit positions are packaged on separate chips, spare bit planes can be added to replace faulty bits and greatly extend the expected life of the memory system. This occurs at an additional cost of about 25 percent.

It was shown that a conventional computer could be made self-checking at a cost of about an additional 10 percent in hardware. Clearly, two machines of this type running the same computation could provide fault tolerance with high computational integrity and this would be considerably less expensive than running three machines and voting. If rollback and restart are acceptable, even cheaper standby redundancy could be employed. Unfortunately, these approaches have lower coverage than the use of massive voted redundancy. The efficient coding techniques used inside are susceptable to multiple faults, and it is not possible to guarantee against the occurrence of such faults induced in a common clock, power supply, and electromagnetic environment. It may be possible to prove coverage of 98–99 percent in these types of low-cost designs, but proof of extremely high coverage is probably impossible. You get what you pay for.

IV. Applications Classes

A. Critical Applications

For highly critical applications where the loss of human life or expensive machinery can occur, it is likely that massive voting redundancy will always be used. By running three or more machines and comparing their outputs, it is not necessary to know the fault mechanisms which occur within a module. The only assumption required is that they will fail randomly and independently. If only one machine fails at a time, an output vote will deliver a correct result, and very high coverages can be assumed. The guarantee of no computational delays during fault recovery is often very important. Uncertainty as to interruption of computations can complicate design of the system which the computer may be expected to control — sometimes with unpredictable effects.

Thus, machines which use fault masking, such as SIFT and FTMP, are the types best suited to these applications.

B. Long-Life Applications

For systems with long periods of time between scheduled maintenance, standby redundancy is attractive where limited power is available or where the failure rates of unpowered spares can be shown to be lower than the failure rate of powered units [5]. But this conflicts with the fact that coverage is lower than that available in voted systems, and inadequate fault coverage will limit the expected life of the system. With inadequate coverage, it does no good to add additional spares to extend life because a high probability will exist that the fault-recovery mechanisms will fail.

In distributed systems, the selective use of both voting and standby redundancy possibly offers the best solution to this problem. A small hard core portion of a system is configured using hybrid redundancy to run critical processes and fault-management functions. The remainder of the system uses less expensive standby redundancy depending upon the core to supply high-coverage fault recovery to the whole system. The FTBBC architecture assumed that critical processes would be run in two or three self-checking processors while others would use standby redundancy.

These long-life systems should display implementations which are finely partitioned (e.g., the use of spare bits in memory, spare microprocessor chips, and redundant I/O circuits) inside of individual computers in order to squeeze the maximum useful life out of a given amount of redundant hardware. This was done in the SCCM [36].

C. Commercial Applications

For commercial applications, we can expect to see customers become more demanding of fault tolerance. In this environment, we see increasing costs of maintenance calls and interrupted service while the cost of hardware is going down rapidly. The emergence of systems such as Tandem and Stratus have shown that fault tolerance can be achieved at acceptable costs and, as people depend more heavily on these computers for banking and commerce, this market will continue to grow. Until recently, commercial systems compromised fault coverage due to an assumption that customers would not pay for redundant processor units. For example, most current systems are designed to handle easily detectable processor faults, but subtle transients can go by undetected because the processor is essentially nonredundant. The availability of cheap single-chip processors allows duplication or triplication of processors for detection of all transient faults and very high fault coverage (at least for medium performance machines). This has been recognized and implemented in the Stratus system [15].

D. Institutional Computer Networks

Nearly all large computing systems in the future will be distributed processors due to the simple fact that processors have become remarkably inexpensive. Many current systems, use networks of time-shared super minicomputers (e.g., VAX's at universities). Since the hardware is off-the-shelf and relatively expensive, partial fault tolerance is implemented in software. One of the better systems of this type, Locus, provides a distributed UNIX environment with a high degree of transparency. As described previously, a user can log on from any machine and have access to identical services and data. Files are automatically maintained in the secondary storage of two machines so that if one machine fails, the user can log onto a different processor and resume computations [30]. These networks rely upon a unified naming and file management scheme which is both redundant and consistent across the network.

The SIFT results point toward an approach which is can be used to supply "hard" fault tolerance in such a network in a cost-effective fashion. It should be possible to schedule and run selected programs in three different machines, voting their results. This can allow crash-free and error-free results for critical programs while allowing most of the computations in the network to be scheduled on single machines. A capability of this type is currently under development at UCLA [6].

But a second revolution is beginning in systems of this type. While many institutions pride themselves on the number of time-shared super minicomputers tied together into a network, there is a move afoot toward collections of microcomputer workstations which often give greater processing power to the user than the "slice" he would get from a larger machine at considerably lower cost. (For example, it has been estimated that the annual cost of maintenance of the VAX network at UCLA will be higher than the hardware cost of replacing it with workstations of similar performance although the cost of transferring software would probably make such a change unfeasible.) Some shared facilities will still be needed, and they are expected to evolve toward specialized servers which provide services not available in workstations. Large storage systems, high-performance numerical processors, and database machines will be needed as the specialized servers within large networks of workstations. These unique nodes will be depended upon by multiple users and therefore need considerable fault tolerance. Thus, research into fault-tolerant mass memory systems, special purpose number crunchers, and database processors should gain additional impetus.

E. Ultrahigh Performance Processing

There exists a class of dedicated system applications (e.g., signal processing) which needs special purpose processing functions to be carried out at enormous speeds. Often the desired processing rates are in the range of billions of multiplies per second. In most of these applications, the value of individual measurements is very small due to the large number being taken, and an occasional error in an individual measurement is not very important, but system availability should be high. Here the designer is pressed to use nearly all of the available VLSI chip area to increase speed, and the use of silicon real estate for fault tolerance is viewed as highly expensive. This is a controversial area because fault-tolerance specialists feel that the VLSI area costs of concurrent fault detection and other fault-tolerance features is justified. Users often do not.

These systems are very complex and may even require wafer-scale integration to achieve satisfactory performance. Due to that complexity, failures are likely to occur and redundant hardware must be employed to maintain operation in the event of failure. Here the fault-tolerance techniques are likely to be semiconcurrent fault detection (i.e., a fault should be detected and isolated within a second or so of its occurrence and spare hardware should be substituted and a system restart invoked to restore correct operation).

A promising approach is to implement fault detection locally within the high-performance system and to rely upon external control computers (which are slow and highly fault tolerant) to effect diagnosis and recovery within the high-performance frontend processors. Proposed fault detection and isolation mechanisms have included 1) insertion of "dummy" calibration data into the input stream and having an external computer identify this calibration data in the processed output to certify correct operation, 2) using internal duplexing where a spare logical module (checker) periodically duplicates the function of several active modules and compares outputs to verify correct operation, and 3) the use of low-cost error detecting codes in all arithmetic. In any case, it appears that a hierarchic fault-tolerance approach is needed where special purpose very high performance parallel processors are maintained by simpler and much more fault-tolerant external processors. Applicable fault-tolerance techniques will be better understood when VLSI layouts for these systems are completed and a database of applications is better established.

V. Design Faults — The Achilles Heel of Fault Tolerance

A number of fault tolerant systems have been demonstrated which can deal with random faults, but these systems have little or no capabilities to handle design faults. Examples of faults not covered include the following.

1) Semiconductor processing faults such as contamination which might make all chips fail after a period of time;
2) logic design faults in a processor or other hardware — the most subtle ones which cause all redundant copies to make the same mistake when a rarely occurring data or control state is reached are the most difficult to deal with;
3) software faults — in most systems software errors cause faults more often than hardware faults, and as above, the subtle ones are difficult to test for since they may only occur when an unusual set of inputs or rare timing relationships exist.

A. Process Verification

To eliminate processing faults, military and space programs spend millions of dollars in detailed inspection of semiconductor parts. There are rigorous and expensive parts screening procedures defined as military standards which must be carried out before parts are qualified for use in many systems [27]. Both government and privately sponsored research is being conducted into development of test circuits for VLSI wafers and into analysis of circuit failures which have been found. The designer who cannot afford military quality parts is wise to use well-established parts whose bugs have already been found through widespread use. Even then it is advisable to get parts from different processing batches for redundant circuit elements so as to avoid correlated failures.

B. Hardware Testing and Functional Verification

Most current systems make use of extensive tests for hardware to try to uncover any design faults and physical faults that may exist. In the past circuit designers and testers have worked independently. With the enormous complexity of VLSI and the limited number of access pins for testing, it has become necessary to include testability in the initial design. One approach to testability is level sensitive scan design (LSSD) in which internal flip-flops can be tied together to form a serial shift register to scan-in test patterns and scan out results [14]. Another approach uses multiplexing of internal data paths to improve external access to internal logic [46]. Some methodologies go so far as designing test pattern generators and checkers on-chip [41].

Proof of design correctness is a promising area of research. Proving the correctness of algorithms in hardware is considerably simpler than proving correctness of programs because most hardware operations can be broken into a fixed number of functions (e.g., microprogram segments) each of which is usually carried out in a small number of steps (clock cycles). Software programs, on the contrary, are often very long and deal with complex data structures and external timing relationships. Innovative research has been conducted in this area from correctness proofs of microprograms to modeling and proof of fault recovery processes [13], [45]. A recent project has developed a methodology for verifying the correctness of layered communications protocols between sets of fault-tolerant machines [17].

C. Software Error Protection

Various techniques have been used for protection against software errors in computing systems for many years, especially in time-shared systems. Most of these techniques often can be viewed as building firewalls around executing processes so that they cannot damage other users' programs and data. The use of virtual memory systems, privileged instructions, and communication between user programs and the executive via interrupt mechanisms have provided hardware enforcement of the isolation of processes by constraining users to only those resources granted by the operating system.

Although proving correctness of a large and varying set of user programs is seldom if ever done, there has been designs of proveably correct kernels of the operating system. Although this approach cannot prevent single users from failing due to software errors, it allows other users to be protected and prevents user-induced system crashes [30].

VI. Toward Tolerance of Design Faults

Most of the techniques above are directed at eliminating design faults. Assuming that the occurrence of these faults can be greatly reduced by extensive testing and partial correctness proofs, there still remains the possibility that some faults remain. There are at least two approaches which have been taken. The first, recovery blocks, uses modular programs, and acceptance checks are run as the program modules execute to determine if they are working properly. If an acceptance check fails, a redundant (but different) program module is executed in place of the one for which an acceptance check failed. This approach is similar to standby redundancy in hardware [3].

A second approach relies upon design diversity and is intended to deal with design faults both in hardware and software. A computing algorithm is specified, independent sets of programmers write different programs, and they are run on different computers. At specified points, voting takes place between the independent programs to determine if a fault has occurred and also to mask out the fault and reinitialize a faulty processor and its program. As long as any two processors with their programs are free of design errors in any voted program block, computations will proceed correctly, and if the faulty processor/program can be reinitialized upon disagreement the triplicated computations will continue. This allows faults to exist in all three copies, so long as no two are faulty in one voted computational block. This type of approach is quite expensive, but is justified in life-critical applications where fault coverage (for both design and random faults) must be extremely high.

VII. Conclusions

Fault tolerance has gone through a seat-of-the-pants phase in which the artistry of individual designers was employed to create computers which were tolerant of a wide range of random component faults. As several fault-tolerant machines have been developed and evaluated, this art has been systemized, and design methodologies have been widely disseminated (e.g., software voters, redundant hardware clocks, and self-checking logic). Reliability prediction models have been developed which attempt to predict the lifetime and performance levels that can be expected of a fault-tolerant system when it is used many years into the future. Techniques have been developed for proving correctness of portions of the software within these machines.

Future advances of the state of the art are likely to require a multidisciplinary approach. We have many special interest areas relating to fault-tolerant system development: 1) VLSI fault physics, 2) logic testing and design for test, 3) system architecture, 4) software correctness proofs, 5) robust operating systems, 6) reliability and performance modeling, and 7) fault-tolerant software through recovery blocks or design diversity. Future research into fault tolerance will require the integration of all these disciplines if comprehensive and fully optimized designs are to be achieved, yet many practitioners of these areas speak different languages. This remains a challenge to the fault-tolerance community.

One thing is certain. Fault-tolerant computing will provide considerable opportunities both for entrepreneurs and researchers for the forseeable future. The field has reached adolescence. Systems and design techniques have been developed, yet its greatest opportunities remain in the future.

ACKNOWLEDGMENT

Special thanks are due to Reviewer B who contributed many helpful comments.

REFERENCES

[1] *Advanced Information Processing System (AIPS) System Specification*, prepared for Johnson Space Center by C. S. Draper Laboratory, Cambridge, MA, May 15, 1984 (distribution limited).
[2] J. Anderson and F. Macri, "Multiple redundancy applications in a computer," in *Proc. 1967 Annu. Symp. Reliability*, Washington, DC, Jan. 1967, pp. 553–562.
[3] T. Anderson and P. Lee, *Fault Tolerant Principles and Practice*. Englewood Cliffs, NJ: Prentice-Hall, 1981.
[4] W. Arens and D. Rennels, "A fault-tolerant computer for autonomous spacecraft," in *Proc. 13th Int. Symp. Fault-Tolerant Computing*, Milan, Italy, June 1983, pp. 467–470.
[5] A. Avižienis et al., "The STAR (self-testing-and repairing) computer: An investigation into the theory and practice of fault-tolerant computing," *IEEE Trans. Comput.*, vol. C-20, pp. 1312–1321, Nov. 1971.
[6] A. Avižienis and J. Kelly, "Fault tolerance by design diversity: Concepts and experiments," *Computer*, Aug. 1984.
[7] J. Barlett, "A nonstop operating system," in *Computer Structures Principles and Examples*, D. Siewiorek et al., Eds. New York: McGraw-Hill, 1982, pp. 480–485.
[8] W. Bouricius et al., "Reliability modeling techniques for self repairing computer systems," in *Proc. 24th Nat. Conf. ACM*, 1969.
[9] S. Bozorgui-Nesbat and E. McCluskey, "Structured design for testability to eliminate test pattern generation," in *Dig. 10th Int. Symp. Fault-Tolerant Computing*, 1980, pp. 158–163.
[10] M. Breuer and A. Friedman, *Diagnosis and Design of Reliable Digital Systems*. Potomac, MD: Computer Science Press, 1976.
[11] W. Carter et al., "Computer error control by testable morphic Boolean functions—A way of removing hardcore," in *Dig. 2nd Int. Symp. Fault-Tolerant Computing*, Newton, MA, June 1972, pp. 154–159.
[12] W. Carter et al., "Cost effectiveness of self-checking computer design," in *Dig. 7th Int. Symp. Fault-Tolerant Computing*, Los Angeles, CA, June 1977, pp. 117–123.
[13] F. Christian, "A rigorous approach to fault tolerant system development," IBM Res. Rep. RJ 4008 (45056), Sept. 1983.
[14] E. Eichelberger and T. Williams, "A logic design structure for LSI testability," in *Proc. 14th Design Automat. Conf.*, June 1977, pp. 462–468.
[15] R. Freiburghouse, "Making processing fail safe," *Mini-Micro Systems*, May 1982, pp. 255–264.
[16] B. Grey et al., "A fault tolerant architecture for network storage systems," in *Proc. 14th Int. Symp. Fault-Tolerant Computing*, Orlando, FL, June 1984.
[17] P. Gunningberg, "Voting and redundancy management implemented by protocols in distributed systems," in *Dig. Int. Symp. Fault-Tolerant Computing*, Milan, Italy, June 1983, pp. 182–185.
[18] J. Hayes, "A graph model for fault-tolerant computing systems," *IEEE Trans. Comput.*, vol. C-25, pp. 875–884, Sept. 1976.
[19] A. Hopkins, "FTMP—A highly reliable fault-tolerant multiprocessor for aircraft," *Proc. IEEE*, vol. 66, pp. 1221–1239, Oct. 1978.
[20] H. Ihara et al., "Fault-tolerant computer system with three symmetric computers," *Proc. IEEE*, vol. 66, pp. 1160–1177, Oct. 1978.
[21] "The INTEL 432 System Summary," Intel Corp., Aloha, OR, 1981.
[22] J. Katzman, "The Tandem 16: A fault-tolerant computing system," in *Computer Structures Principles and Examples*, D. Siewiorek et al., Eds. New York: McGraw-Hill, 1982, pp. 470–479.
[23] R. J. Kuehn, "Computer redundancy: Design, performance, and future," *IEEE Trans. Rel.*, vol. R-18, no. 1, pp. 3–11, Feb. 1969.
[24] J. Kuhl and S. Reddy, "Distributed fault tolerance for large multiprocessor systems," in *Proc. 7th Annu. Symp. Comput. Arch.*, May 1980, pp. 23–30.

[25] B. Lampson, "Automic transactions," in *Distributed Systems Architecture and Implementation, An Advanced Course*. Berlin: Springer-Verlag, 1981.
[26] J. Meyer, "Closed form solutions of performability," in *Dig. 11th Int. Symp. Fault-Tolerant Computing*, Portland, ME, June 1982, pp. 66–71.
[27] U.S. Military Standard MIL-M-38510, Class S parts.
[28] Y. Ng and A. Avizienis, "A unified reliability model for fault-tolerant computers," *IEEE Trans. Comput.*, vol. C-29, pp. 1002–1011, Nov. 1980.
[29] J. Oblonsky, "A self correcting computer," in *Digital Information Processors*, W. Hoffman, Ed. New York: Interscience, 1962, pp. 533–542.
[30] J. Popek et al., "LOCUS, A network transparent, high reliability distributed system," in *Proc. 8th SOSP*, Monterey, CA, Dec. 15–17, 1981.
[31] F. Preparata, G. Metze, and R. Chien, "On the connection assignment problem of diagnosable systems," *IEEE Trans. Comput.*, vol. EC-16, no. 6, pp. 848–854, Dec. 1967.
[32] C. Ragavendra et al., "Reliability optimization in the design of distributed systems," in *Proc. 3rd Int. Conf. Distrib. Comput. Syst.*, Miami, FL, Oct. 1982.
[33] D. Rennels et al., "The unified data system: A distributed processing network for control and data handling on a spacecraft," in *Proc. NAECON*, Dayton, OH, May 1976, pp. 283–289.
[34] D. Rennels, "Architectures for fault-tolerant spacecraft computers," *Proc. IEEE*, vol. 66, pp. 1255–1268, Oct. 1978.
[35] D. Rennels et al., "Fault tolerant design considerations for future spacecraft systems," Dep. Comput. Sci., Univ. California, Los Angeles, CA, Rep. prepared for Aerospace Corp., Aerospace Lib. A81-04858, Oct. 1981.
[36] D. Rennels, A. Avizienis, and M. Ercegovac, "Fault-tolerant computer study final report," JPL Pub. 80-73, Jet Propulsion Lab., Pasadena, CA, Feb. 1981.
[37] J. Rohr, "STAREX self-repair routines: Software recovery in the JPL-STAR computer," in *Dig. 2nd Int. Symp. Fault-Tolerant Computing*, Palo Alto, CA, June 1973.
[38] J. Roth et al., "Programmed algorithms to compute tests to detect and distinguish between failures in logic circuits," *IEEE Trans. Electron. Comput.*, vol. EC-16, pp. 567–580, Oct. 1967.
[39] J. Russell and C. Kime, "System fault diagnosis: Closure and diagnosability with repair," *IEEE Trans. Comput.*, vol. C-20, pp. 1078–1088, Nov. 1975.
[40] R. Sedmack and H. Liebergot, "Fault tolerance of a general purpose computer implemented by very large scale integration," *IEEE Trans. Comput.*, vol. C-20, pp. 492–500, June 1980.
[41] D. Siewiorek and R. Swarz, *The Theory and Practice of Reliable System Design*. Bedford, MA: Digital, 1982.
[42] J. Sklaroff, "Redundancy management technique for space shuttle computers," *IBM J. Res. Devel.*, vol. 20, pp. 20–28, Jan. 1976.
[43] W. Toy, "Fault-tolerant design of local ESS processors," *Proc. IEEE*, vol. 66, pp. 1126–1145, Oct. 1978.
[44] J. Wakerly, *Error Detecting Codes, Self-Checking Circuits and Applications*. New York: North-Holland, 1978.
[45] J. Wensley, "SIFT: The design and analysis of a fault-tolerant computer for aircraft control," *Proc. IEEE*, vol. 66, pp. 1240–1255, Oct. 1978.
[46] T. Williams and K. Parker, "Testing logic networks and design for testability," *Computer*, vol. 12, pp. 9–22, Oct. 1979.

David A. Rennels was born in Terre Haute, IN, in 1942. He received the B.S.E.E. degree from Rose-Hulman Institute of Technology, Terre Haute, in 1964, the M.S.E.E. degree from the California Institute of Technology, Pasadena, CA, in 1965, and the Ph.D. degree in computer science from the University of California, Los Angeles, in 1973.

Since 1965 he has been associated with the Jet Propulsion Laboratory of the California Institute of Technology, where he has been instrumental in the design of several fault-tolerant computing systems, and is currently an Academic Member of the Technical Staff. In 1978 he joined the Faculty of the University of California, Los Angeles, where he is currently an Associate Professor in the Department of Computer Science.

A wide choice of multiprocessor systems featuring hardware fault tolerance is now available from a growing number of commercial suppliers; fault-tolerant software design remains a problem.

Reprinted from *Computer*, August 1984, pages 19-30. Copyright © 1984 by The Institute of Electrical and Electronics Engineers, Inc.

Fault-Tolerant Systems in Commercial Applications

Omri Serlin, ITOM International Company

Although fault-tolerant techniques were employed in some of the earliest digital computers, the advent of solid-state devices—first the transistor, and later integrated circuits—greatly improved the overall reliability of computer systems. One notable exception to this trend, however, is the popular dynamic MOS RAM: memory systems based on such ICs are actually less reliable than the magnetic cores they replaced. In fact, the reliability of solid-state memory systems has been made to equal that of the older, magnetic-core systems only through the use of error correcting codes; however, parity and ECC schemes are applicable only to subsystems that do not perform any data transformations, but perform only pure data transport (such as computer buses and I/O channels) or offer pure storage (such as main memory and disks).

As a result of the improvement in basic component reliability on the one hand and the development of error-correcting codes on the other, the initial interest that computer scientists had in developing fault-tolerant techniques soon faded. During the 1960's and early 1970's, interest in such techniques remained limited to a number of specific applications areas, including computer-controlled telephone switching systems, military and commercial real-time monitoring and control systems, commercial time-sharing systems, and airline reservations systems.

Early dual-processor systems

Computer-controlled, electronic switching systems began to appear in central offices of the public telephone network in the US and in France around 1965. Because of the nature of the services they render, the computers incorporated in such switching complexes must provide very high availability. A typical requirement is that there be no more than two hours of system outage (downtime) in 40 years.

To achieve the goal of high availability, various techniques have been devised by AT&T Bell Laboratories for use in its family of ESS computers, of which the latest is the 3B20D processor used in the No. 5 ESS and recently released as a commercial product (see Figure 1). Details differ in each ESS implementation, but the general scheme is to duplicate all critical components (such as the control unit and memory system). The running system utilizes one set of subsystems, while a duplicate set is either in a "hot backup" mode or is executing synchronously with the on-line set. The system detects errors either by matching the results produced by both sets (as in the No. 1A ESS) or by constructing each set from self-checking modules, which are themselves duplicates that match one another's results (as in the No. 3A ESS and 3B20D).

In real-time monitoring and control applications, a computer system is integrated into its environment through various sensors that permit it to monitor the state of physical devices and processes. If the computer is also entrusted with the task of controlling some devices or processes with a variety of actuators, it becomes a "closed-loop" system. Applications include industrial process control, both continuous and discrete; power plant monitoring, both conventional (fossil fuel) and nuclear; aerospace telemetry and on-board control systems; air traffic control systems; and military command and control systems.

To address the high-availability issues inherent in these applications, dual-processor configurations similar to the one shown in Figure 2 were (and in many cases, still are) employed. The particular system depicted in the figure closely resembles the SEL 88 system, manufactured between 1970 and 1974 by Systems Engineering Laboratories.

In the SEL 88 system, four-port memory modules allowed access from two pairs of CPUs and direct memory access I/O processors. Modules connected in this way created a shared memory region, which mapped into the high end of each processor's address space. This shared memory was typically used to hold "global common" areas (the main programming language was Fortran), which allowed programs running in the two separate processors to share data. In addition, the operating system copy in each processor, which occupied the low end of the address space, could use the shared, high-address locations to communicate with each other at high speeds.

To coordinate the use of shared memory, the system supported a *test bit and set* instruction, which was used to manage semaphores. This instruction read the word containing the addressed bit, set the bit to "one" and the condition code to reflect the status of the bit prior to setting, then rewrote the word into the shared memory—all in one uninterruptible sequence. In this way, a program running in one processor could both test a flag and, upon finding it clear, set the flag to indicate that it was about to modify a certain region of memory; the other CPU was then expected to refrain from modifying (or even reading) the same region.

A special "peripheral switch" permitted I/O controllers to be accessed by either one (but not both) of the I/O processors. Each controller attached to the switch (up to 14 could be accommodated) was actually controlled by a single-pole, double-throw switch, with the peripheral controller at the center position and the I/O processors at the two "throws." This was simplified, since the I/O processor normally communicated with the controllers over coaxial cables in bit-serial fashion, but parallel interfaces could also be similarly switched. Both manual and computer-controlled switching were supported. Typically, the "process I/O" interfaces (such as analog-digital converters and discrete I/O lines) and one or more disk controllers were attached to the peripheral switch.

In addition to the usual parity checking and various error traps, each CPU in this system was equipped with a "watchdog timer" designed to detect "stalls." This timer (actually a downtime counter) could be loaded with an initial count by the CPU; it then counted down at a fixed, clock-controlled rate. The operating system or the applications programs running in each CPU were expected to reload periodically the initial value into their timers. An interrupt signal was sent *to the other CPU* if the program failed to do so before the watchdog timer counted down to zero.

Assuming that no branch of either the system or user programs took longer to execute than the countdown time, such a situation could only come about either because of a complete CPU failure or because of a program bug or hardware error leading to an "infinite loop." In any event, the receipt of the watchdog timer interrupt at a given processor signaled that the other CPU was probably "stalled."

Dual- or multiple-processor systems, similar to the one just described, whether with or without the shared-memory feature, were available from a number of suppliers, including DEC, Data General, and Perkin Elmer's Interdata Division. The five-computer complex that supported the NASA Manned Space Flight Center was of this type, as were the IBM 9020 systems installed in the en-route air

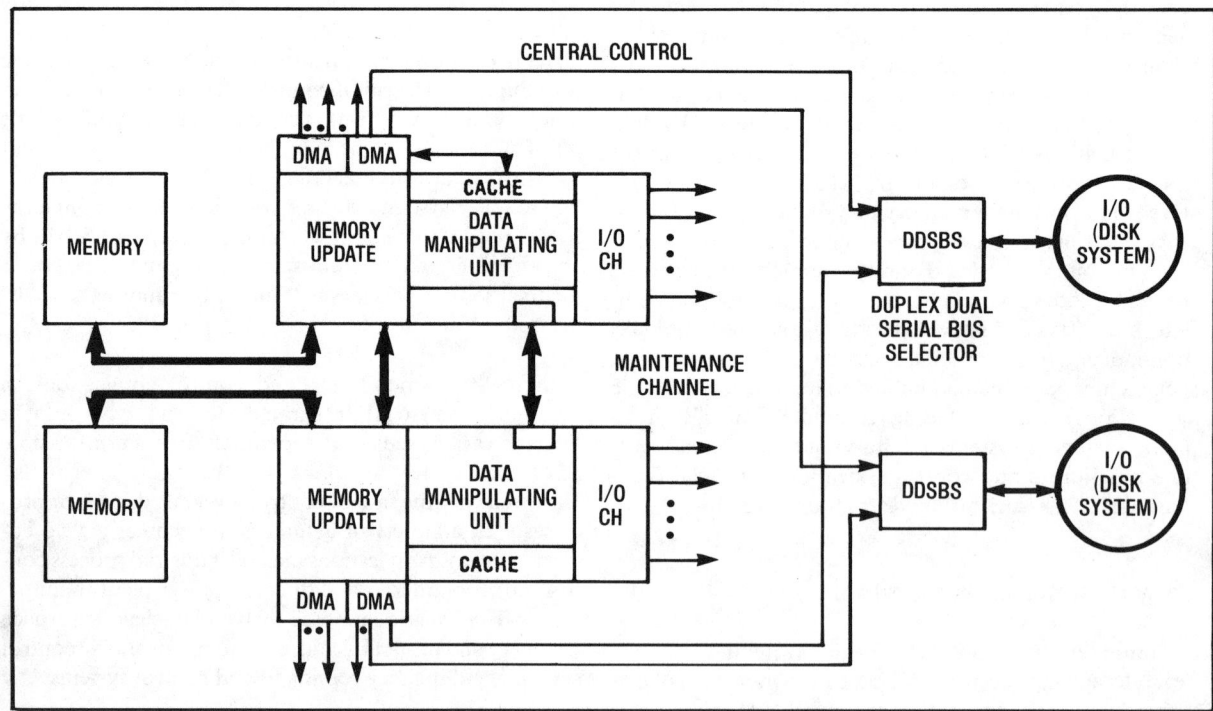

Figure 1. General block diagram of the 3B20D system.

traffic control centers. Variants of this arrangement are still available from several manufacturers, including Hewlett-Packard and, in the UK, Computer Technology, Ltd.

However, these systems provide only the illusion of fault tolerance. For example, they incorporate a number of "critical points," the failure of any of which can bring the entire system down. Examples of such critical points include the shared memory, the peripheral switch, and the shared controllers and devices attached to the switch. Such deficiencies are part of the reason that computer-based "closed-loop" control systems are not permitted in certain critical applications in the US (for example, nuclear power plant control).

Equally serious is the fact that failed components can neither be removed nor be returned to service without powering down one or both processor systems. Furthermore, few of these systems can accept additional processors to accommodate growing workloads.

The most notable limitation of such systems is that they include practically no software support. It is generally left to the end user to supply even the most basic mechanisms for interprocessor communications and control of shared memory and shared peripherals; recovery procedures are entirely within the user's own responsibility.

The main reason for these and other deficiencies is that the elements employed in these multiprocessor systems were never designed for fault-tolerant operation. Indeed, even SEL's four-port memories and bit-serial peripheral controllers were—and still are—highly unusual. By and large, these systems were (and are) "force-fitted" into the fault-tolerant application by incorporating only superficial hardware and software modifications into products that were originally meant to function in a stand-alone, single-processor environment.

Variations of this architecture have been employed in commercial time-sharing systems and in airline reservations systems. Both environments are particularly sensitive to downtime, not only because of the actual monetary losses resulting from such disruptions, but also because of the large number of users affected, both internal employees and outside customers.

On-line transaction processing

Airline reservations systems, initially based on Univac and IBM computers, were quite unlike other real-time systems in several important respects—not least of which was that the hardware manufacturers actually undertook to develop the specialized operating systems, terminal communications protocols, and applications interfaces. This task proved so onerous for Univac, especially at United Airlines, that the company could never recover its original momentum. Only a handful of airlines now use Univac's USAS reservation system.

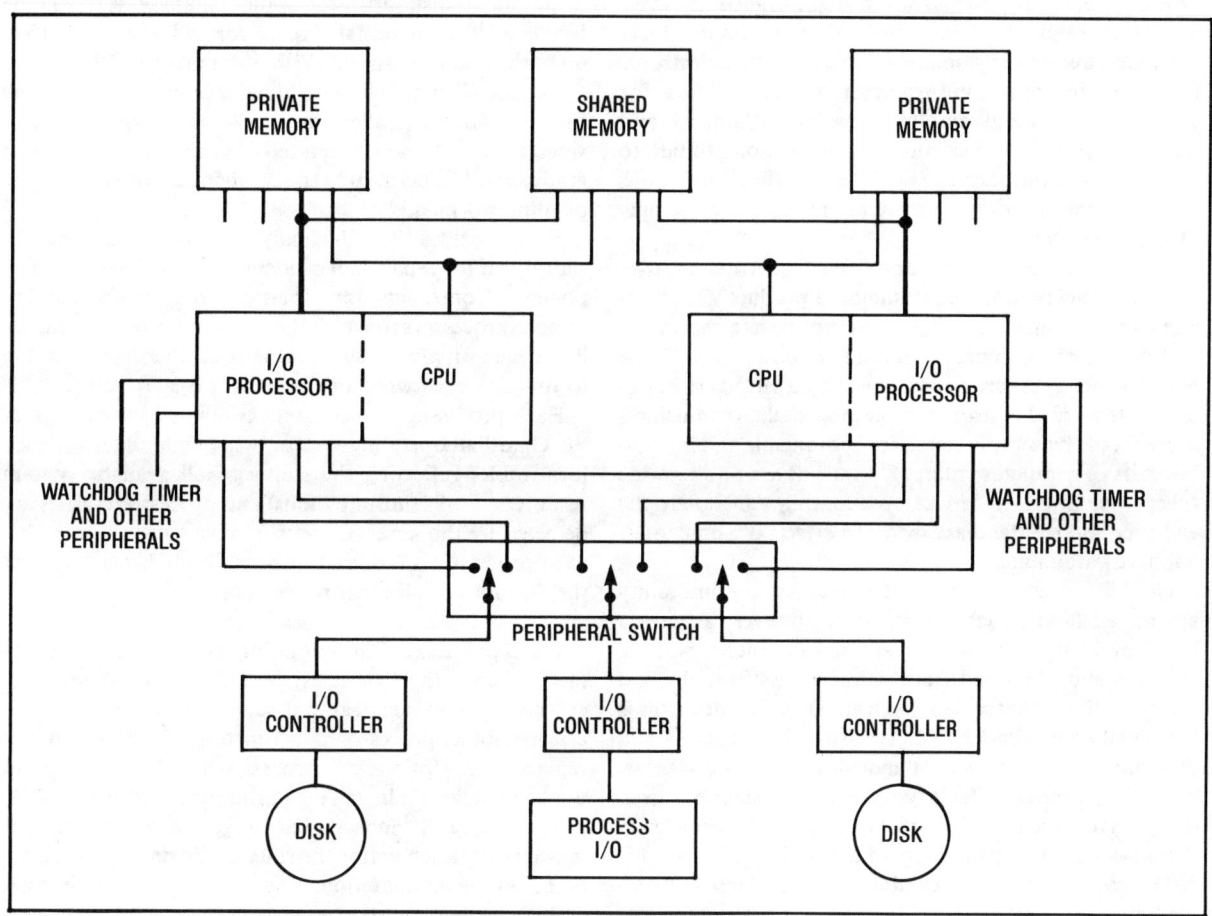

Figure 2. SEL 88-type dual processor (ca.1970).

IBM hardware and the IBM PARS and IPARS software systems became de facto airline industry standards in the US and abroad. The underlying software, the Airline Control Program, is now fully interfaced to SNA, IBM's "grand design" in computer networking. Under SNA's multisystems networking facility, user terminals can access application programs throughout a network of mainframes, even when the application is physically located in a processor to which the terminal has no direct connection. ACP has been so successful that it is now offered by IBM as a more or less standard product for such applications as on-line banking and credit verification.

Unlike real-time monitoring and control systems, which make little use of disk-resident data because disk accesses are too lengthy relative to the required response time, airline reservations systems are created expressly for the manipulation of disk-resident databases. The issues of shared access from a large number of terminals, database consistency and integrity, and system recovery are therefore of prime importance. ACP, for example, includes facilities for periodic dumping of critical data items, called "keypoints" and "globals," to different disk modules. The concepts of checkpointing, audit trails, record locking and disk mirroring or shadowing, also supported by ACP, originated largely from the requirements of on-line transaction processing, or OLTP, of which airline reservations systems were early examples.

The explosive growth in on-line applications is responsible to a large extent for the recent increased interest in FT systems. On-line systems are being installed at ever-increasing rates to handle support of automatic teller machines, automatic gasoline pumps, and other electronic fund-transfer applications; reservations systems for airlines, hotels, and auto-rental agencies; lottery and wagering systems; and videotex or information utilities, to name a few. Even such classical "back office" functions as billing and inventory control are handled increasingly by on-line systems.

The obvious attractions of on-line systems are that they allow a business to increase employee productivity, exercise tighter controls through more up-to-date reporting, and offer new or improved services to customers. These benefits, however, are accompanied by a serious risk: on-line systems at the heart of a business make the business more fragile by sharply increasing the tangible and intangible costs of computer failure. FT systems are finding wide acceptance in OLTP service because they can isolate the end user and the database from the effects of some internal hardware faults.

No FT system can guarantee 100 percent immunity against all faults; such systems can, however, achieve a high level of probability that internal faults will be detected and recovered from before they affect the end users and the database. How well an FT system does this is measured by its *depth,* which is the number of faults of a particular kind that can be handled; and by its *coverage,* which is the range of fault types that the system has been designed to anticipate. FT coverage and depth vary greatly from system to system. Even within a given system, different components may exhibit different depths: ECC-equipped memory systems, for instance, can withstand several successive faults; processors and I/O controllers typically have zero depth in conventional systems and a depth of one or more in FT systems.

The Tandem approach

In 1975, Tandem took a new and more systematic approach to fault tolerance. The Tandem multiprocessor architecture eliminated single points of failure by, among other things, eliminating "master/slave" relations among processors and providing dual paths to all subsystems. Moreover, for the first time in a commercial system, it provided for on-line repair, i.e., the ability to remove defective components (for example, printed circuit boards) and return repaired ones to service without impacting running applications programs. The key architectural features of the Tandem system that underlie these capabilities are processor replication, dual-access I/O controllers, a redundant power system, and a message-based operating system.

A Tandem Nonstop system (Figure 3) includes from two to 16 processors, each with its own memory and I/O channel. These minicomputer-type processors communicate over a high-speed, duplexed, 16-bit parallel bus system called Dynabus. All I/O controllers are dual ported; each is accessible from two I/O channels, typically of two different processors. Disk drives are, in addition, dual-ported; each is attachable to two controllers. Disk data therefore remains accessible even when both a processor and a disk controller have failed.

Should a disk drive fail, the database can still be recovered if the optional disk mirroring has been in effect up to the point of failure. With disk mirroring, the system automatically maintains two identical copies of designated files on two independent drives. A special utility is provided to restore a newly repaired drive to mirror conditions gradually while permitting the surviving drive to satisfy the ongoing workload.

Each processor is individually powered and thus can be shut down for repair independently of other system components. Controllers draw their power from the supplies of both processors to which they are connected; the capacity of each supply is such that the controllers can continue to function even when one processor is shut down.

Each processor in the system contains its own copy of the Guardian operating system, which maintains for each local tables reflecting the status of all available system resources. Stalls (infinite loops) and processor crashes are detected by the absence of "I'm alive" messages, which each processor is required to periodically broadcast over the Dynabus to all other processors.

Checkpointing. Checkpointing is the key recovery mechanism in the Tandem system. For each running process, there is an identical, but semi-inactive, backup process in another processor. The function of the backup is to replace the "primary" process should there be an unrecoverable fault in the primary's processor. The primary process sends its backup periodic "checkpoint messages," which define the state of the process at critical points in the computation. The operating system in each processor "wakes up" the relevant backup process upon discovering that its corresponding primary has failed. The backup can then resume the task from the state defined in the last checkpoint.

Checkpointing is conceptually simple, but its efficient application requires a high degree of programming skill and understanding of system details. Checkpointing is still employed internally by Tandem-supplied system components. One such component is the transaction monitoring facility, or TMF, which maintains database consistency by undoing the effects of aborted or incomplete transactions and supports database recovery. Another checkpointing-based Tandem product, Pathway, is responsible for handling communications with the user terminals. User applications can now be implemented through higher level abstractions called *requesters* and *servers,* which are interjected between the TMF-enhanced DBMS and Pathway. These requesters and servers can be coded as conventional high-level language programs; their loss entails no more than a manual restart of an interrupted transaction.

Message system. Isolation of user processes from configuration details is accomplished by forcing all interprocess communications to be carried out via the *message system*. For example, a user process needing some disk data formulates a "message" addressed to the logical disk controller process. By consulting its resource tables, the local operating system copy determines the actual location of the destination process. The user process therefore does not need to know which two processors are currently connected to the disk in question or which of the two processes is currently the primary.

The isolation of user tasks from configuration details is essential for on-line repair. Furthermore, such isolation facilitates "graceful growth," or the ability to increase the transaction-processing capacity of the system by merely plugging in additional processors. Although this capability is not entirely "seamless," it is, nevertheless, one of the key advantages Tandem has over conventional systems, in which growth involves painful "upgrades." In addition, a

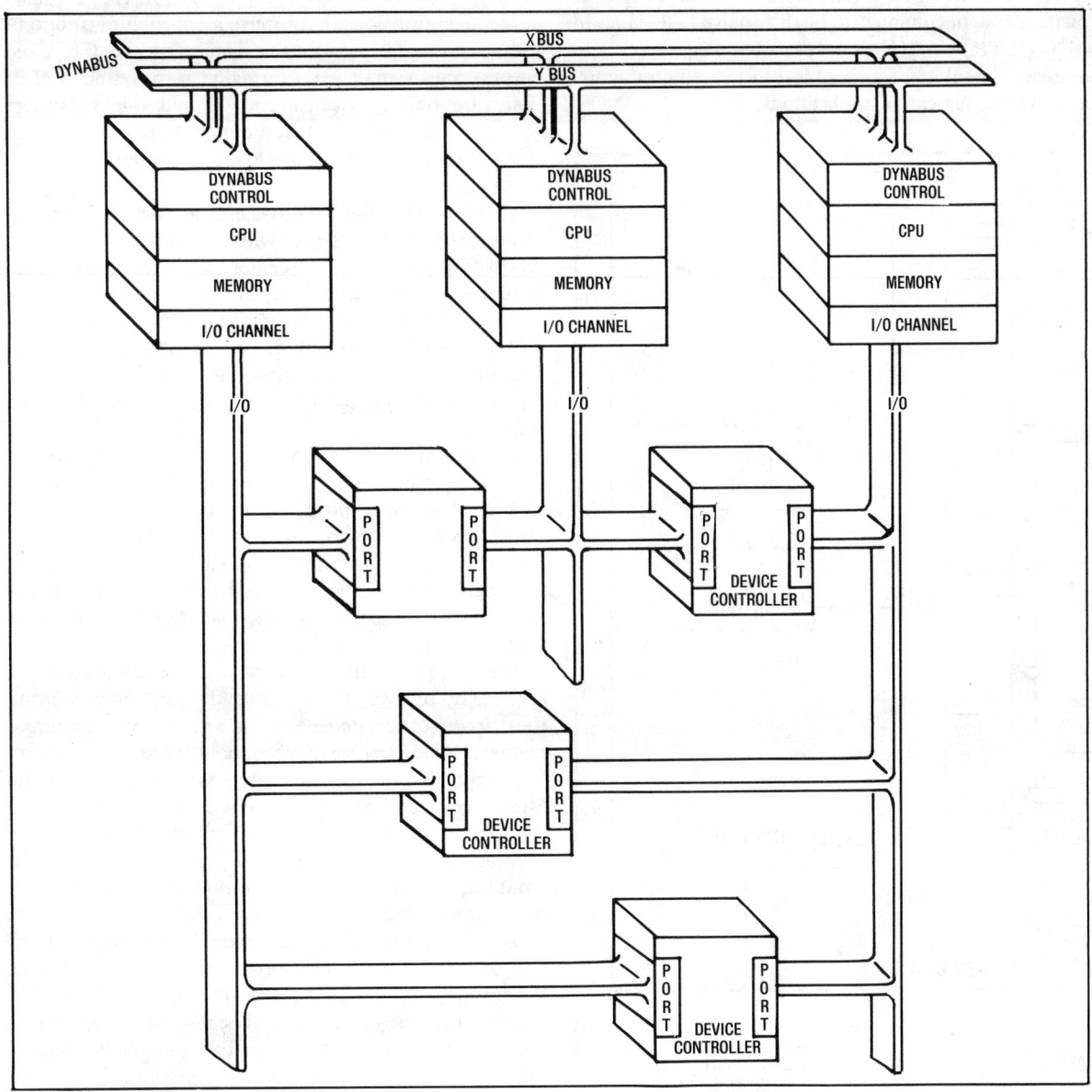

Figure 3. Tandem Nonstop architecture.

network of geographically remote Tandem systems can be created. A relatively minor enhancement to the basic message-based Tandem software is needed to support this important capability.

The Tandem system has undergone a number of notable improvements. Along with enhanced performance, the Nonstop II, introduced in 1981, added "extended addressing" to allow data access beyond the 64K-word limitation of the original product. The Nonstop TXP,[1] introduced in November 1983, achieved a substantially higher performance level through an additional 64K-byte cache and other refinements; the model is expected to receive an enhancement later this year to allow execution of programs larger than 64K-word.

By combining minicomputer technology with architectural innovation, Tandem brought to market an attractive FT system with a substantial price-performance edge over mainframe-based, redundant backup systems. As a result, it enjoyed five years of vigorous growth in revenues and earnings. Despite some recent moderation in its rate of growth, Tandem continues to be the undisputed leader in the FT/OLTP field. It has an especially strong presence in the areas of banking, financial institutions, manufacturing, and communication applications.

Over the last several years, a number of new FT/OLTP suppliers have emerged. They are using powerful, low-cost, 16/32 MPUs to create innovative FT designs that were not economically feasible only a few years ago. Most are targeting the OLTP applications that are being addressed by Tandem.[2-5]

Pair and spare

One particularly interesting strategy, dubbed *self-checking,* is employed by Stratus Computer of Natick, Massachusetts, and, to some extent, by the Intel 432 MPU family (see Johnson article, pp. 40-48) and the AT&T 3B20D processor. Stratus, a 1980 start-up which went public in August 1983, developed an architecture (Figure 4), informally known as "pair and spare," in which major functions are replicated four times. First, each subsystem (a printed circuit board) has an identical counterpart, its "spare." Both are self-checking: each consists of a "pair" of identical functions that receive identical inputs; output comparators generate an error signal whenever the paired outputs are mismatched. Normally, a subsystem and its spare are tightly synchronized; should one subsystem detect an internal mismatch, it merely "pulls out" and its spare continues to carry the load, all without missing a beat.

To assure that faulty subsystems are detected rapidly, Stratus equips its systems with automatic dialers that report faults to a support center. When a repaired subsystem is returned to service, an interrupt informs both CPUs (or the spare CPU, if the repaired system is the other CPU). The CPU then brings the repaired system to full synchronism with its running counterpart; for example, a repaired memory subsystem will copy the contents of the functioning memory.

Self-checking is employed throughout the Stratus system;[6] the pair-and-spare strategy is restricted to the CPU and memory proper only. Disk controllers have duplicate read and write circuitry; the controller will not write to the disk, or the duplex system bus, unless both sections agree. Communications controllers are similarly self-checking: each handles half the load, but either can take over all ports.

The Stratus scheme is attractive for several reasons. It requires no recovery from a fault: the work goes on using the "spare" subsystem. Since no recovery is required, neither are such artifices as checkpointing and "I'm alive" broadcasts. To the user (and most system functions), the Stratus computer appears to be a conventional machine that requires no special FT programming considerations.

Stratus is able to implement a degree of redundancy that would have been out of the question with minicomputer technology, and yet offer a surprisingly low price ($180,000 for a typical, basic system) because of its liberal use of off-the-shelf microprocessors. A basic Stratus system may contain as many as 18 Motorola 68000 and Zilog Z80A microprocessors. Because of the product's convincing FT architecture and low system cost, Stratus has had considerable market success, growing from about $5 million in revenues in 1982, its first year of shipments, to $20 million in 1983. A significant number of indepen-

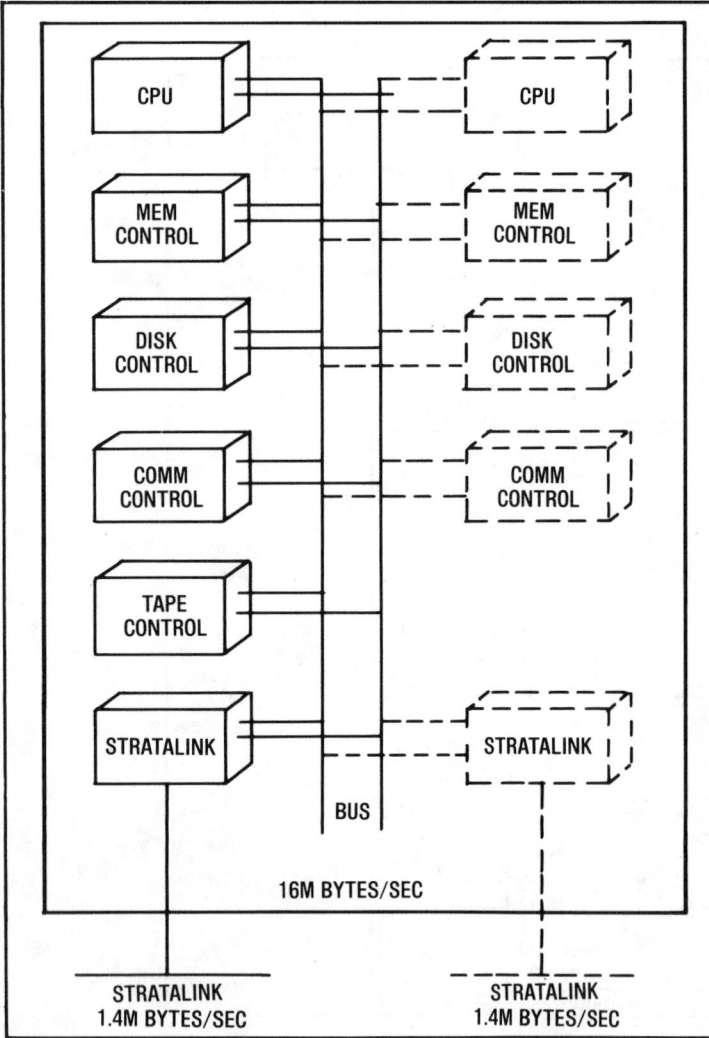

Figure 4. Stratus "pair and spare" architecture.

dent software vendors have adopted vertical market applications, especially in banking and finance, to the Stratus system.

Members of the Intel 432 microprocessor family feature functional redundancy checking, which facilitates the construction of pair-and-spare and/or self-checking systems. The comparators needed to implement self-checking are built into each chip and can be activated with an external signal. Thus, a self-checking module can be created by connecting all corresponding input and output pins of a pair of identical chips. As noted earlier, the AT&T 3B20D processor also employs self-checking and mirror-image memories, although it differs in implementation details from the Stratus approach and cannot be expanded beyond the basic, two-CPU configuration.[7]

Tightly coupled systems

A disadvantage of the pair-and-spare strategy is that when growth becomes necessary, the basic unit must be "cloned" in its entirety. Stratus can accommodate up to 32 processing modules, interconnected over a duplexed, ring-type local area network. However, the PMs are, in effect, stand-alone computers that are not normally able to share resources with other PMs.

Synapse Computer, a well-funded, 1980 start-up in Milpitas, California, has developed an architecture (Figure 5) that avoids this limitation. In this scheme, multiple 68000-based processors are "tightly coupled" through a duplexed, high-speed, 32-bit parallel bus to a common, shared-memory system, which holds the only copy of the operating system. The processors, some of which are specialized for I/O while others concentrate on running the transaction-processing applications, act as a pool from which resources are drawn as required to service the load. The processors are self-dispatching: when idle, they look up work queues in main memory and assign themselves to the next task that needs doing. A somewhat similar architecture is employed in the System 9000 from GEAC Computers International (Markham, Ontario, Canada); variations have been used in the BTI 8000 and the Elxsi systems as well.

Synapse calls its architecture $N+1$: by configuring just one more processor than the N required to service some workload, essentially the same FT depth can be achieved as in a $2N$ scheme, in which each processor or process is backed by a duplicate counterpart.

Applications and I/O processors schedule work for each other by making entries in various dispatching queues in main memory. I/O processors have substantial local buffers, while each application processor is equipped with a 16K-byte, high-speed cache that minimizes memory bus utilization.

The caches are managed under a "non-write-through" policy,[2] which leaves updated data in the cache as long as possible. This technique improves the hit rate but creates a problem when shared data structures or I/O buffers are involved. Synapse evolved an elegant "ownership" scheme to allow the multiple processors to hold shared data in their caches. It handles read-only accesses, such as instructions, simply by giving each requester a copy of the requested item; shared memory continues to "own" such items.

When a processor issues a write request against a shared data item, ownership of the item, along with the item itself, is transferred from main memory to the requesting processor. Should another processor need access to that item, the owner will either furnish a copy (for read-only access) or generate a "busy" response. All caches monitor bus traffic for requests for the data items they hold. IOPs have special privileges that allow them to write data to shared memory without previously reading it; all caches note such writes and invalidate any corresponding entries.

A high degree of graceful growth is possible with this approach. Additional processors can be added to handle independent growth either in applications (transaction) load or in I/O load.

Processor failures are handled through a semi-transparent checkpointing system. Users need not code explicit checkpoint calls; they must instead build their applications from small "program units" by following a set of design rules. The system then undertakes to insert checkpoints automatically between such program units; this activity can be suppressed. A relational database

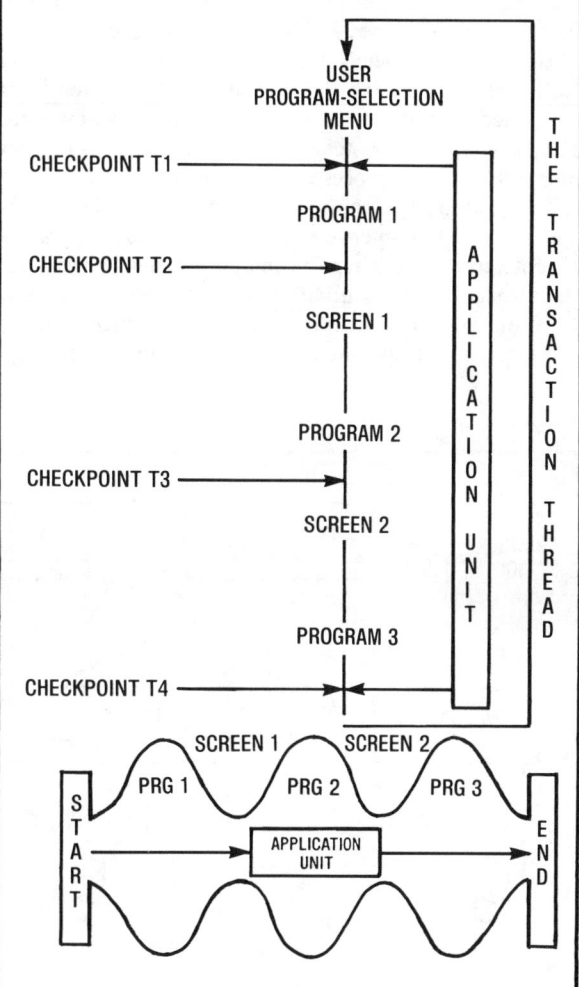

Figure 5. Synapse checkpoint model.

system, integrated with (rather than grafted onto) the operating system facilitates a "Commit" strategy which assures transaction atomicity (that is, the transaction either completes successfully or its effects are removed). A "write-ahead log" technique is used.

The shared-memory system is a single point of failure. A memory failure is the most severe problem that can occur, since it can wipe out work queues, the disk buffers, or parts of the operating system. The memory controller detecting the fault deals with this problem by interrupting all running processors. The mass-storage controller in the highest-priority I/O slot then reloads the operating system, taking care to bypass the failed memory module. Should it fail to do so within a given time period, the next-highest priority I/O controller will try. After a successful reboot, the database recovery process examines the mirrored log file and proceeds to implement all pending committed transactions while undoing the effects of uncommitted (incomplete) transactions. End users should suffer no more than the loss of the screen data they were manipulating at the time of the crash. This recovery process may take up to a few minutes.

Other approaches

Auragen Systems of Fort Lee, New Jersey, also a 1980 start-up, has developed an architecture that is conceptually similar to Tandem's but includes several interesting hardware and software improvements. The system[8] is composed of multiple "clusters" connected to a duplexed, 32-bit, parallel-bus system. Each cluster contains at least three 68010-based processors: two of them execute user tasks and global system processes, while the third manages the system's bus interface and executes most operating system kernel functions. The operating system is based on Unix System III but is modified both internally (to support FT, a message system, and a multiprocessor environment) and externally (to present a more friendly user interface).

For fault recovery, Auragen employs "synchronization" (Figure 6), an interesting variation of the checkpointing idea. After a primary process and its backup have been brought to identical states (synchronized), the backup receives and saves all messages sent to its primary; it also keeps track of the number of messages issued by its primary since the last synchronization. Should the primary fail, the backup would reprocess the saved input messages, suppressing output messages already issued by the primary while it was still functioning.

Synchronization occurs under system control and requires no insertion of checkpoints in the applications code. Moreover, synchronization can occur at a lower frequency than conventional checkpointing and involves less data. The penalty is that more processing steps are involved during recovery, since the backup goes through the motions of some of the actions already completed by the primary. The suggested justification is that the reduction in overhead during normal operation is well worth the longer recovery from rare (one hopes) faults.

Tolerant Systems (San Jose, California), founded in 1982, also employs a synchronization scheme but within the context of a distributed architecture. The basic system building blocks, each based on a pair of National Semiconductor Corporation's NS16000 microprocessors, are interconnected over a duplexed Ethernet local area network.[9]

Computer Consoles, Inc., (Rochester, New York), is developing a multiple processor architecture based on its successful Directory Assistance System. The CCI FT system, dubbed Power 5/55, provides full point-to-point connections among as many as eight 68000-based processors and eight disk controllers. These connections enable the system to implement an interesting generalization of the disk-mirroring scheme: multiple copies of the database are automatically maintained by the system to reduce greatly the response time for inquiry-only transactions, which generally constitute 70 to 90 percent of the transaction load. A local area network connects all pro-

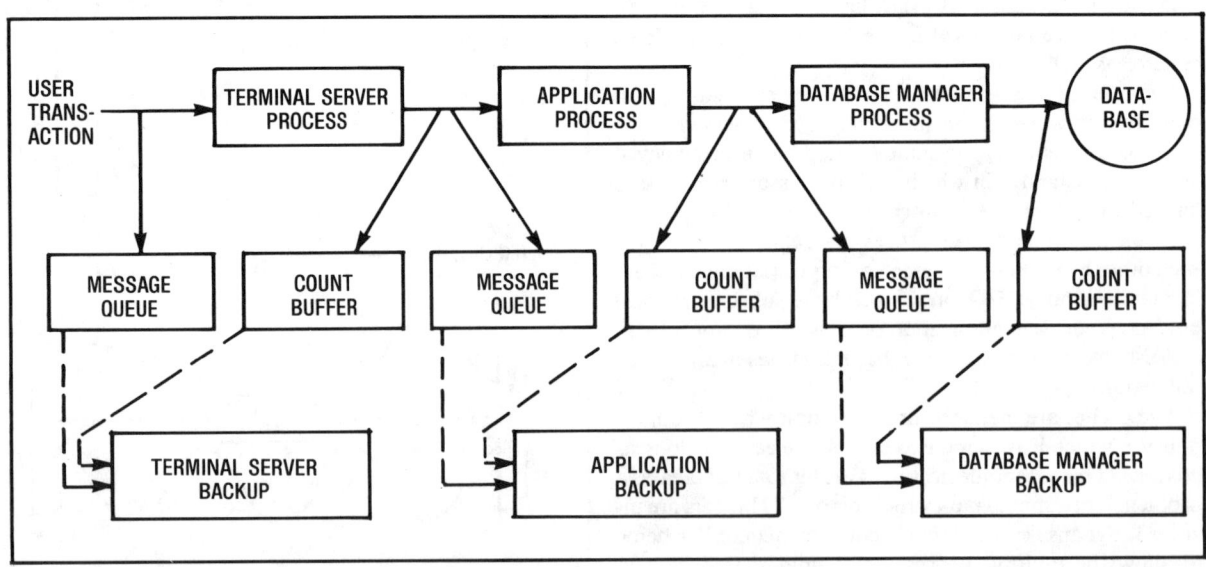

Figure 6. Auragen synchronization scheme (simplified).

cessors to all front-end communications and terminal controllers.

Sequoia Systems (Marlboro, Massachusetts), founded in 1981, is preparing to introduce an FT/OLTP system that combines self-checking processors within a tightly coupled, shared-memory architecture.[10] Encore Computer is also believed to be developing a transaction-processing system along similar lines. Interestingly, Stratus has recently introduced new, "extended architecture" models in which four or six self-checking processors share the duplexed memory system within a Processing Module.

A few firms are addressing FT systems to the special needs of the process control and industrial automation environments. August Systems (Tigard, Oregon) has a system that employs TMR in its front end (analog/digital interfaces) while the triple-processor main engine runs an interesting variation of TMR called SIFT (software-implemented fault tolerance). The three 8086-based processors perform identical computations and periodically "vote" on the results by reading each other's memory (the links are strictly read-only to prevent one processor from corrupting another's memory). The repetitive nature of the computation involved in process applications makes this approach viable. Voting occurs just prior to launching the next iteration of the algorithm.[11]

Autech (Pompano Beach, Florida) has a system in which duplexed basic units, designed and packaged for harsh-environment service, can be interconnected over a duplexed local area network to a supervisory computer. Hewlett-Packard offers a conventional, hot backup, dual-processor system—dubbed Systemsafe 1000—for supervisory control applications.

The comparison table on pp. 28-29 summarizes the salient features and intended applications of several FT systems now being offered commercially by US manufacturers.

Some open issues

Moves by the established suppliers. Most of the established mainframe and minicomputer manufacturers are known to be considering FT systems. The problem they face is that offering convincing FT architectures may well cause them to lose a great part of their large investments in existing software. This loss clearly would be unacceptable to both vendors and users. Consequently, the established manufacturers can be expected to introduce a variety of solutions involving slightly modified existing products. Examples of this approach are the Vax Cluster from DEC, the NCR V8500/V8600 cluster, the IBM Series/1 ring, and the Perkin Elmer Series 3200 Resilient System, to name a few.

The absence of the established manufacturers from the FT/OLTP scene is both a boon and an obstacle for the existing FT suppliers. Lack of competition from the established vendors helps the newcomers sell their solutions. However, the proprietary nature of the new architectures is limiting their appeal to new applications only: the effort involved in converting existing applications may be too large. This has been a problem for Tandem and is likely to continue to be the principal factor limiting the acceptance of the new FT systems.

Long-range prospects. As more functions are compressed onto fewer and fewer chips, the reliability of a system providing constant functionality and performance can be expected to improve. The suggestion has been made that this will eventually lead to a loss of interest in FT techniques.

A much more likely scenario is that very simple machines, equivalent to today's desktop microcomputers, will indeed become so reliable as to obviate the necessity of equipping them with special FT features. Even today it can be argued plausibly that the correct FT strategy for desktop systems is to stock spare machines and simply replace a malfunctioning unit.

However, the spread of such desktop computing resources is likely to create demand for "file servers" at several levels of the corporate hierarchy. Such file servers, or "group computers," will be used mainly as custodians of shared data (database managers) and as electronic mail hubs, rather than as shared computing (time-sharing) resources.

These computers are likely to continue to be fairly complex. Furthermore, as more workers begin to depend on file servers for the performance of their daily duties, the demand for FT features in such systems will intensify.

Reliable power. As fewer electronic parts are required to implement computing systems, the role of factors other than electronics in system availability will become more pronounced. Several firms (Arete, No Halt, Parallel Computers) are beginning to offer built-in battery-backup systems to counteract the effects of power failures, already a major source of system downtime. Due to the reduced power requirements of today's smaller disks and progress in small-battery technology, such systems can often maintain the complete computer configuration for up to several hours.

Transaction throughput. Almost without exception, today's FT architectures are based on multiplicities of relatively low-powered processors. While these architectures are justified by the nature of transaction processing, which is characterized by relatively limited CPU requirements and fairly heavy I/O loads, they are inherently less efficient than ones in which a relatively small number of very powerful processors can take advantage of economies of scale. It is likely that both approaches will eventually find market acceptance. Meanwhile, FT suppliers are answering the need for higher throughput by adding performance-enhancing features within the context of their basic architectures. The Tandem TXP and the Stratus XA models are examples of such moves.

Software fault tolerance. As the hardware becomes more reliable, software faults—already recognized as being more of a problem than hardware faults in many situations—will become even more visible. High hopes raised by a variety of panaceas ("structured programming," "correctness proofs," "reusable software," "recovery blocks," etc.) have proven premature.

COMMERCIAL FAULT-TOLERANT SYSTEMS

COMPANY/SYSTEM	ADDRESS & PHONE	TARGET MARKETS	CPU TECHNOLOGY	OPERATING SYSTEM NAME & TYPE
August Systems, Inc./ Can't Fail 300	18277 SW Boones Ferry Rd. Tigard, OR 97223 (503) 684-5330	Industrial automation and process monitoring/control.	Three Intel Corp. 8086-based processors run identical code when in FT mode.	RTTS (real-time task scheduler), one copy per CPU
Augragen Systems Corp./ System 4000	2 Executive Dr. Ft. Lee, NJ 07024 (201) 461-3400	On-line transaction processing (OLTP); medium to large applications.	Up to 32 clusters of three Motorola 68010 each; clusters interconnect over a high-speed, duplex 32-bit bus.	AT&T Bell Laboratories' Unix with internal modifications; one copy per cluster.
Autech Corp./ DAC-6000	Data Systems Division 1301 W. Copens Rd. Pompano Beach, FL 33064 (305) 979-2700	Industrial automation and process monitoring/control.	Dual 6800-based Displaymaster and Decmaster, Zilog, Inc. Z80A-based process I/O modules.	Aide process control development system plus read-only memory routines in Decmaster's controller and process I/O modules.
Computer Consoles, Inc./ Power 55/5	97 Humboldt St. Rochester, NY 14609 (716) 482-5000	OLTP, medium to large applications.	Up to eight 68000-based CPUs with 68000-based disk and terminal controllers.	Perpos (perpetual processing OS), Unix-based, one copy per CPU plus special control in inter-computer controllers. (ICC).
Hewlett-Packard Co./ Systemsate/1000	Data Systems Division 11000 Wolfe Rd. Cupertino, CA 95014 (408) 257-7000	Industrial automation and process monitoring/control.	Two HP1000 Models 60 or 65 working in "hot backup" mode (16-bit, microprogrammed).	RTE-6/VM, real-time, multitasking, virtual memory, one copy per CPU.
Parallel Computers, Inc./ Parallel 300	3004 Mission St. Santa Cruz, CA 95060 (408) 429-1338	OLTP, very small to small applications.	Two 68010's on a multibus.	Berkeley Unix; kernel in both CPUs; one does I/O.
Sequoia Systems/ No name yet	3 Metropolitan Corp. Center Marlboro, MA 01752 (617) 480-0800	OLTP, medium to large applications.	Up to 64 CPUs and 96 IOPs, all 68010-based and self-checking.	UNIX-based with new kernel, one copy in shared memory.
Stratus Computer, Inc./ FT200, XA400, XA600	17 Strathmore Rd. Natick, MA 01760 (617) 653-1466	OLTP, small to large applications.	Self-checking CPUs based on Motorola 68000s. Each Processing Module can have duplexed CPU, memory and controllers. Maximum 32 Processing Modules on a ring-type local area network.	VOS (Virtual OS), one copy per CPU (FT200) or four CPUs (XA400) or six CPUs (XA600).
Synapse Computer Corp./ Synapse N + 1	801 Buckeye Ct. Milpitas, CA 95035 (408) 946-3191	OLTP, medium to large applications.	Up to 28 68000-based CPUs and IOPs (I/O processors) working with a shared memory via a duplexed, high-speed 32-bit parallel bus.	Synthesis, one copy in shared memory.
Tandem Computers, Inc./ NonStop I, II, TXP	19333 Valico Pkwy. Cupertino, CA 95014 (408) 725-6000	OLTP, medium to large applications.	Up to 16 CPUs on a duplexed, high-speed, 16-bit parallel bus. CPU is 16-bit microprogrammed.	Guardian, one copy per CPU.
Tolerant Transaction Systems/Eternity	81 E. Daggett Dr. San Jose, CA 95134 (408) 946-5567	OLTP, small to medium applications. Also real time.	Two National Semiconductor Corp. 16000's in each system building block.	Transaction executive, transaction operator interface elements may be replicated in same or multiple system building blocks.

© 1984 ITOM International Co.

MEMORY SYSTEM	PERFORMANCE/CPU (MIPS and TPS)	FT STRATEGY	CPU FAULT DETECTION*	RECOVERY SCHEME
32K bytes per CPU on-board; up to 1M byte per CPU on Multibus.	Approximately 0.4 MIPS—up to 256 A/D points. TPS not relevant.	CPUs: SIFT; analog front end; TMR	At start of each iteration, three CPUs check state data and vote out odd processor.	Repaired processor reads programs from read-only link or from disk; synchronized at next voting point.
Up to 8M bytes per cluster (1M byte/board).	0.85 MIPS/cluster (company figure). Nominally 27 MIPS/system at full expansion. 1.5 TPS/CPU (estimate).	Queue and count	Self-detect via idle diagnostics and absence of "I'm alive" messages.	Backup process reprocesses input messages since last sync, discarding outputs already effected.
64K bytes to 256K bytes per CPU, with parity; battery backup on board; CMOS static.	Decmaster supports up to 256 process points. TPS: not relevant.	Hot backup	Timeouts, cross diagnostics.	Auto switchover to backup Decmaster on Stall (timeout).
512K bytes to 4M bytes per CPU, error checking and correction; battery backup. Each of two ICCs has 512K bytes.	Nominally 5.6 MIPS (0.7 per 68000). Two TPS/CPU (ITOM estimate) due to multicopy database.	Checkpointing	ICC timeout transactions; bad ICCs detected by CPU voting scheme.	Next available CPU completes stalled transaction.
256 bytes to 2M bytes per CPU; 1 parity bit/16 bits of data.	1 MIPS (200K floating-point operation/sec. mod 65); TPS not relevant.	Hot backup	Watchdog timer times out.	Peripheral switch flips over; hot backup CPU informed via interrupt.
Maximum 4M bytes/processor.	0.7 MIPS.	Hot backup	Hardware and software synchronization between CPUs.	Manual replace and restart.
2M bytes to 64M bytes with ECC (seven bits per 32-bit word).	Sequoia claims up to 40 MIPS at full expansion.	Automatic reassignment	Self-checking subsystem electrically disconnects.	Next available CPU picks up stalled transaction.
FT200; 8M bytes logical XA400; (16M bytes physical) XA600. 16M bytes logical (32M bytes physical).	0.7, 2.0, 3.0 MIPS; 2, 4, 6 TPS; for FT200, XA400, and XA600, respectively.	Pair and spare	Self-checking subsystem pulls out and generates red-light interrupt to operating system.	Re-education procedures synchronize repaired module with one that's running.
16M bytes/system (1M byte boards), error checking and correction.	0.7 MIPS/CPU; system MIPS depend on how many CPUs configured. 2 TPS/CPU (ITOM estimate) if supported by enough I/O processors.	Checkpointing	Timeout mechanisms.	Next available processor picks up stalled transaction that's been checkpointed into shared memory.
8M bytes/CPU (2M bytes/board), error checking and correction.	0.7, 0.8, 2 MIPS; 1, 1.5, 5 to 6 TPS for Nonstop I, II, and TXP, respectively.	Checkpointing	Absence of "I'm alive" message; each CPU must broadcast over Dynabus each second.	Backup process in another CPU picks up transaction from last good checkpoint sent by primary.
1M byte to 4M bytes per system building block.	1.5 MIPS/system building block (Tolerant estimate).	Checkpointing	Timeouts and "I'm alive" message.	Backup system building block takes over.

*Beyond conventional parity and error traps.

An intriguing idea is that software creation might be brought up to a fault-free level comparable to that of hardware design if software designers had available the equivalent of computer chips—small, well-tested, widely used off-the-shelf packages. With the increasing popularity of rehostable-kernel operating systems, such as Unix, universally applicable packages could become a reality within the foreseeable future. Still, the design of reliable software is very much an intractable problem today. Whoever solves it will gain a well-deserved place of honor in the history of computing. ✻

References

1. R. Horst and S. Metz, "New System Manages Hundreds of Transactions/Second," *Electronics,* Apr. 19, 1984, pp. 147-151.
2. O. Serlin, "New Microprocessor-Based Computer Architectures," *AFIPS Conf. Proc.*, Vol. 54, 1984 NCC, AFIPS Press, Reston, Va.
3. O. Serlin, "Fault Tolerance," *Computerworld Buying Guide,* Aug. 1983.
4. O. Serlin, *Fault-Tolerant Transaction Systems*, Datamation (OEM edition), Jan. 1983.
5. O. Serlin, *Fault-Tolerant Systems,* ITOM International Co., Aug. 1982.
6. R. Freiburghouse, "Making Processing Fail-Safe," *Mini-Micro Systems,* May 1982.
7. W. N. Toy and L. E. Gallaher, "Overview and Architecture of the 3B20D Processor," *Bell System Technical J., *Jan. 1983, part 2.
8. A. Borg, J. Baumbach, and S. Glazer, "A Message System Supporting Fault Tolerance," *Proc. Ninth ACM Symp. Operating Systems Principles,* Oct. 1983.
9. "Computer System Isolates Faults," *Computer Design,* Nov. 1983.
10. "Sequoia Unveils Self-Checking, Shared-Memory FT System," *FT Systems Newsletter,* ITOM International Co., May 1984, pp. 2-7.
11. J. H. Wensley, "Industrial Control System" *Electronics,* Jan. 27, 1983, pp. 98-102.

Omri Serlin heads ITOM International Company, a research and consulting firm in Los Altos, California, which he established in January 1980. For 18 years prior to establishing ITOM, he worked in various technical, management and product planning capacities in the computer industry. He is the author of a popular market research study on fault-tolerant systems and writes a monthly newsletter on the subject. Among his other interests are supermicros and local area networks. He is a member of the IEEE 802 Committee.

Serlin received a BS degree in electrical engineering from Bridgeport University in 1961 and an MS degree in the same field from Rutgers University in 1964.

His address is ITOM International Company, PO Box 1415, Los Altos, CA 94022.

Fault-Tolerant Software

Herbert Hecht, Senior Member IEEE
SoHaR Inc., Los Angeles

Key Words—Software reliability, System reliability, Redundant software

Reader Aids—
Purpose: Widen state-of-the-art
Special math needed: None
Results useful to: Software engineers

Abstract—Limitations in the current capabilities for verifying programs by formal proof or by exhaustive testing have led to the investigation of fault-tolerance techniques for applications where the consequence of failure is particularly severe. Two current approaches, N-version programming and the recovery block, are described. A critical feature in the latter is the acceptance test, and a number of useful techniques for constructing these are presented. A system reliabiliy model for the recovery block is introduced, and conclusions derived from this model that affect the design of fault-tolerant software are discussed.

1. INTRODUCTION

The fault-tolerance features for software described here are primarily aimed at overcoming the effects of errors in software design and coding. In fortuitous circumstances they may also circumvent failures due to hardware design deficiencies or malfunctions in input channels. Fault-tolerance for random computer failures is outside the scope of the present discussion. In practice, the user wants computer system fault-tolerance, i.e. toleration of failures due to all causes, and this can be provided by a combination of established hardware fault-tolerance techniques [1] and the fault-tolerant software described here.

It is generally recognized that even very carefully designed and manufactured computer components may fail, and hardware redundancy is therefore provided in applications where interruptions of service can not be tolerated. That software may fail is also widely recognized; yet this seems to have been perceived as a temporary shortcoming: today's software contains design and coding errors but it is expected that these will be eliminated once improved development and test methodologies or efforts at formal verification become fully effective. Deliberate use of redundant software to tolerate software faults is not an established practice today.

It is expected that the many efforts to improve software quality and reliability will indeed reduce failures but will not completely eliminate them. A number of thoughtful articles have pointed out the limitations of current test methodology [2] and of formal verification [3 - 5]. Sometimes it is believed that maturity can provide freedom from software errors but that is not borne out by the experience on extensively used operating systems [6]. For the foreseeable future even the most carefully developed software will contain some faults, probably of a subtle nature such that they were not apparent during software and system testing. These faults will manifest themselves during some unusual data or machine state and will lead to a system failure unless fault-tolerance provisions are incorporated in the software. In the Bell Laboratories' Electronic Switching Systems (which employ hardware redundancy and thoroughly tested software such) software faults accounted for approximately 20% of all failures [7].

Fault-tolerance always involves some redundancy and therefore increases the resource expenditure for a given function. Software fault-tolerance of the type described here is therefore primarily aimed at applications where the consequences of failure are particularly severe, e.g. advanced aircraft flight control systems [8, 9], air traffic control programs, and nuclear reactor safety systems. Sometimes fault-tolerance applied to a small segment of a large software system can provide a hardened kernel that can then be used to organize the recovery from failures in other segments [10]. Such applications are today under study or in early development. Experience with these techniques in an operational environment has not yet been reported.

A survey of current approaches to software fault-tolerance is presented in the next section. This is followed by a discussion of a particularly critical component, the acceptance test that determines when the primary software routine has failed. In the final section a system reliability model for fault-tolerant software is described.

2. CURRENT APPROACHES

Two different techniques for achieving fault-tolerance in software have been discussed in the recent literature: the recovery block and N-version programming. In the latter a number ($N \geq 2$) of independently coded programs for a given function are run simultaneously (or nearly so) on loosely coupled computers, the results are compared, and in case of disagreement a preferred result is identified by majority vote (for $N > 2$) or a predetermined strategy. This approach had been suggested in a general way by Elmendorf [11] and has more recently been developed into a practical form by Avizienis & Chen [12, 13] who report results on the use of this technique on a classroom problem.

The success of this technique is obviously governed by the degree of independence that can be achieved in the N-versions of the program. Ref. [13] states "Wherever possible, different algorithms and programming languages or translators are used in each effort." One might also want to see different data structures so that the requirements document rather than the specification (which usually defines data structures quite rigorously) becomes the common starting point for the N versions. In addition, the voting algorithm and the housekeeping for 'results' prior to and after voting have been identified as critical items for this technique.

A specific constraint on N-version programming is the requirement for N computers that are hardware independent yet able to communicate very efficiently so that rapid comparisons of results can be achieved. These N computers must all be operating at the same time, and a hardware failure in any one of them will at best force the system into a different operating mode and may, in minimal configurations, cause loss of the fault-tolerance provisions. An example of a system that seems well suited to host N-version programming is SIFT [9]. N-version programming is capable of masking intermittent hardware faults, and this can be an advantage in some applications. It also has the ability to aid in detection of permanent hardware faults, although detail fault-tolerance provisions for these may best be handled by dedicated hardware/software reconfiguration provisions.

The recovery block technique [14, 15] can be applied to a more general spectrum of computer configurations, including a single computer (which may also include hardware fault-tolerance). The simplest structure of the recovery block is:

Ensure T

    By P

    Else by Q

Else Error

where T is the acceptance test condition that is expected to be met by successful execution of either the primary routine P or the alternate routine Q. The internal control structure of the recovery block will transfer to Q when the test conditions are not met by executing P. Techniques have been described for purging data altered during processing by P when Q is called [15].

For real-time applications it is necessary that the execution of a program be both correct and on time. For this reason the acceptance test is augmented by a watchdog timer that monitors that an acceptable result is furnished within a specified period. The timer can be implemented in either hardware or software or a combination. The structure of a recovery block for real time application modules is shown in fig. 1 [16]. In normal operation only the left part of the figure is traversed. When the acceptance test fails, or if the time expires, a transfer to the alternate call is initiated, a flag is set, and process Q is executed. If its result satisfies the acceptance test, the normal return exit in the right part of the figure is taken, and processing continues. If the acceptance test fails again, or if a timeout is encountered in the execution of Q (with the flag now set), an error return results.

A fault-tolerant navigation module using these techniques

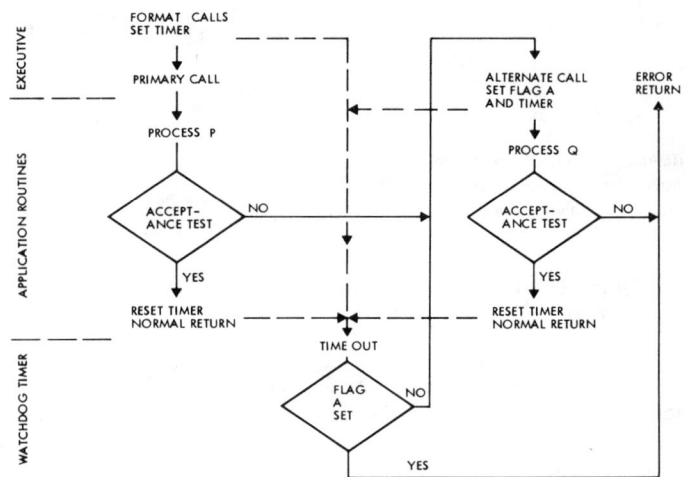

Fig. 1. Recovery Block for Application Modules

is described in [16], and the interaction of fault-tolerant application modules with the executive is also discussed there. Principles of a fault-tolerant scheduler based on the recovery block technique have also been described [17]. The number of alternate routines is not restricted, and where it seems desirable any number of back-ups can be entered successively on failure of the acceptance test. Recovery blocks can also be used in concurrent processes and multi-level structures [18, 19].

As in N-version programming, it is desirable that the redundant routines in a recovery block be as independent of one another as possible. A specific and critical feature of the recovery block is the acceptance test. Alternate routines will be useless if failure of the primary one is not promptly detected. Thus acceptance tests must be thorough. On the other hand, the acceptance test is traversed on every program execution, and the amount of code required for it should therefore be minimized. Few formal guidelines exist for satisfying these partly contradictory requirements. The following section attempts to classify techniques that have been used as a first step towards a systematic study of the design of acceptance tests.

3. ACCEPTANCE TESTS

Acceptance tests can be devised against two criteria: to detect deviations from expected program execution, or to prevent unsafe output. The first is more restrictive, and will result in more frequent transfer to the alternate routine. However, the penalties for unnecessary transfer are usually small, whereas the penalties for failure to switch when necessary can be much greater. For software that has been in use a long time, testing for unsafe output may be preferable because it can be simpler and it avoids unnecessary transfers. However, for programs just emerging from development, testing for expected program execution has 3 benefits:

1) Unexpected behavior of the primary system will be noted even in cases where only a mild degradation is encountered. This aids in program evaluation.

2) Switching to the alternate program is exercised more often under realistic (unplanned) conditions. Providing realistic testing of the fault-tolerance mechanism is a difficult undertaking.

3) As a program matures it is usually easier to relax acceptance conditions than to make them more restrictive.

The four types of acceptance test described below can usually be designed to test either for expected execution or for unsafe output.

1. *Satisfaction of requirements.*

In many cases the problem statement imposes conditions which must be met at the completion of program execution. These conditions can be used to construct the acceptance test.

In the 'Eight Queens' problem it is required that eight queens be located on a chessboard such that no two queens threaten each other. A suitable acceptance test for a computer program solving this problem is that the horizontal, vertical, and the two diagonals identified with the location of a given queen do not contain the location of any other queen. If testing for these conditions is already included in one or more of the routines in a recovery block, then the acceptance test should use a different sequence and a different program structure.

The acceptance test for a sort problem described by Randell is also a test for satisfaction of requirements [15]. The test involves checking at the completion of the execution that the elements are in uniformly descending order, and that the number of elements in the sorted set is equal to the number of elements of the original set. This test is not exhaustive: changes in an element during execution would not be detected. A stronger test, to determine that the elements of the sorted set are a permutation of the original set, was rejected because of excessive programming complexity and execution time.

An important subset in this class is the inversion of mathematical operations, particularly those for which the inverse is simpler than the forward operation. A typical example is the square root which is frequently handled as a subroutine call whereas squaring a number is a one-line statement. The effectiveness of inversion for the construction of acceptance tests is limited by the fact that some logical and algebraic operations do not yield a unique inverse, e.g. OR, AND, absolute value and trigonometric operations.

Testing for satisfaction of requirements is usually most effective when carried out on small segments of a computer program because at this level requirements can be stated simply. On the other hand, for efficiency of the overall fault-tolerant software system, it is desirable to construct acceptance tests that cover large program segments. The classes of acceptance tests described in the following two sections have better capabilities in this regard but are more limited in the types of programs which they can handle. For text editing systems, compilers, and similar programs, tests for satisfaction of requirements constitute at present the most promising approach.

2. *Accounting Checks*

Commercial accounting had to struggle with the problem of maintaining accuracy in systems with many records and arithmetic operations long before the advent of the digital computer. Most of the procedures that had evolved for checking manual operations were taken over when bookkeeping evolved into data processing. These accounting checks can be very useful for acceptance tests in software that serves transaction oriented applications. Airline reservation systems, library records, and the dispensing of dangerous drugs all can be checked by these procedures.

The most rudimentary accounting check is the tally which in computer usage has become the checksum. Whenever a volume of financial records (checks, invoices, etc.) is transmitted among processing stations, it is customary to append a tally slip representing the total amount in the records. On receipt, a new total is computed and compared with the tally. The corresponding use of checksums is widespread in data processing. The digital presentation of information makes it possible to apply the checksum to non-numerical information as well.

When a large volume of records representing individual transactions is aggregated, it is almost impossible to avoid errors due to incorrect transcriptions or due to lost or misrouted documents. In the commercial environment such errors are not always of an innocent nature since an employee may be able to pocket the amount corresponding to an improper entry. The double-entry bookkeeping system evolved as an effective means of detecting such errors. In this procedure the total credits for all accounts must equal the total debits for all accounts for any arbitrary time period, provided only that corresponding transactions have been entered into all accounts. This equality can also be used as a criterion in acceptance tests.

Another worthwhile accounting check is the reconciliation of authorized transactions with changes in physical inventory over a period of time. For example, in storage of nuclear material it is possible to determine the quantity in inventory by means of radiation counters which can feed data directly into a computer. At specified intervals the change in radiation level can be compared to that independently calculated for normal decay of the material and authorized inventory transactions. This furnishes an overall check, including most computer and software errors.

Accounting checks are suitable only for transaction-oriented applications and they cover only elementary mathematical operations. Within this sphere, accounting checks provide a time-tested and demonstrably complete means for assessing the correctness of computer operations. They can test recovery blocks containing large software segments, and portions of the input operations and physical inventory can be checked in the same process.

3. *Reasonableness Tests.*

This heading includes acceptance tests based on precomputed ranges of variables, on expected sequences of program states, or on other relationships that are expected to prevail for the controlled system. The dividing line between reasonableness tests and testing for satisfaction of requirements can become blurred, but in general reasonableness tests are based on physical constraints whereas testing for requirements uses primarily logical or mathematical relationships.

Reasonableness tests for numerical variables can examine the individual values (e.g. to be within range), increments in individual values of the same variable (increments between successive values or deviations from a moving average), or the correlation between values of different variables or of their increments. Examples of these different types are examined for an airspeed calculation. The indicated airspeed (typically an input quantity), and the true airspeed (a computed quantity) must each be within a range that is dictated by the aerodynamic and structural capabilities of the airframe, e.g. 140 to 1100 km/hr. Obviously only gross malfunctions of either the sensor or of the computing process can be diagnosed by such a test. The airspeed range is a function of aircraft configuration (flap position, etc.) and an acceptance test with narrower limits can be constructed if adjustments for configuration are included.

A much more sensitive test for sudden malfunctions (and these are usually the most critical ones) can be devised by examining the increments in each quantity. Changes in speed are equivalent to acceleration, and in the normal flight mode changes in forward speed are well below the 1 g level. Even if the acceptance test is based on the maximum allowable acceleration for structural integrity (which may be 6 g), the corresponding change in speed is limited to 213 km/hr/sec. Individual speed calculations can be carried out ten times per second, yielding an allowable speed increment between successive values of 21.3 km/hr. To suppress noise in the sensor output, the acceptance test may operate on averaged readings so that the effective sampling interval is increased, but even under these circumstances the acceptance test based on increments will for sudden malfunctions be much more sensitive than one based on range.

The correlation between increments of indicated and true airspeed can be used for further refinement, but an even more useful correlation can be obtained by comparing increments in true airspeed with the acceleration measured by an appropriately oriented accelerometer. In this case, limits of the acceptance test will depend on the noise characteristics of the instruments used, elastic deformations of the aircraft, and other secondary characteristics. For filtered observations the acceptance region can probably be reduced by an order of magnitude over that obtained in the test based on increments alone.

The use of correlated measurements for acceptance tests always raises the problem that errors might be introduced by the variable added to provide the refinement (in this case the accelerometer output). The consequences of a spurious failure of the acceptance test must be evaluated to determine whether the refinement is indeed warranted. To be particularly avoided is the use of a variable in the acceptance test that is also used in the back-up routine because this could cause transfer to the back-up at exactly the time when its data source is unreliable. The importance of keeping the back-up program independent of software structures and data used in the acceptance test is discussed further in connection with reliability modeling.

An example of a reasonableness test based on state transition is found in an electronic telephone switching system. Once a call has proceeded to the 'connected' state it is inadmissible for it to subsequently go to 'ringing' or 'busy'. Inappropriate transitions of this type can therefore be used to signal the need for switching to an alternate routine.

Tests for reasonableness of numerical or state variables are a very flexible and effective way of constructing acceptance tests for fault-tolerant software. They permit acceptance criteria to be modified as a program matures. Reasonableness tests can be devised for most real-time programs that control physical variables, and they may monitor overall performance of a computing system, e.g. by reasonableness tests on output variables.

4. *Computer Run Time Checks*

Most current computers provide continuous hardware-implemented testing for anomalous states such as divide by zero, overflow and underflow, attempts to execute undefined operation codes, or writing into write-protected memory areas. If such a condition is detected, a bit in a status register is set, and subsequent action can then be defined by the user. When fault-tolerant software is being executed, encountering one of these conditions can be equated with failure of the acceptance test and transfer to an alternate software routine is then effected. The previously mentioned watchdog timer can be tied into this status reporting scheme.

Run-time checks can also incorporate data structure and procedure oriented tests that are embedded in special support software or in the operating system. Checking that array subscripts are within range is already implemented in many current computer systems. Array value checking (for being within a given range, being in ascending or descending order, etc.) has also been proposed [20]. Under the title "Self-checking Software" and "Error-Resistant Software" a number of interesting run-time monitoring techniques have been described, many of which are akin to acceptance tests mentioned earlier in this section [21, 22]. A particularly appropriate concept for a run-time acceptance test is an Interaction Supervisor [22]. In its simplest form this requires declaration for each module of authorized callers and authorized calls. The Interaction Supervisor will cause failure of the acceptance test if access to, or exit from, a module involves unauthorized locations.

The value of run-time checks is not restricted to prevention of failures due to errors arising directly from the attribute that is being monitored. They cover a much wider area, e.g. attempts to write into write-protected memory may have as their original cause an improper indexing algorithm, a failure to clear a register, or similar more subtle software discrepancies. It is therefore appropriate to use all of these facilities that modern computers, operating systems, and programming languages can contribute to implementing acceptance tests even if the occurrence of the monitored conditions per se could be prevented by other means. Run-time checks are not exhaustive but they require very little development time or other resources. They supplement the previously mentioned types of acceptance tests for critical segments, and they can be used by themselves as

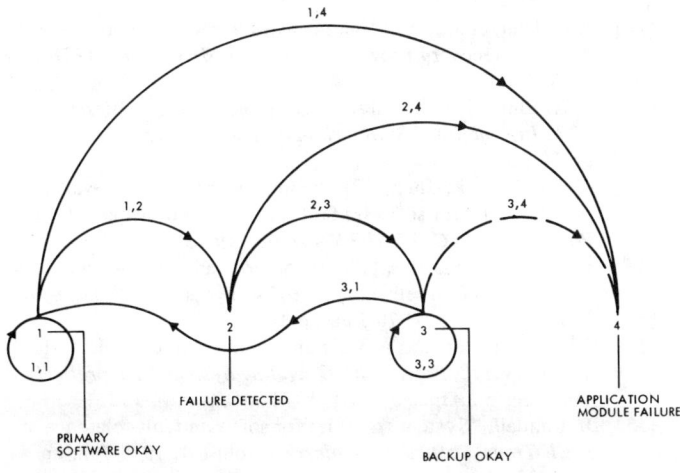

Fig 2. Transition Model

the acceptance test for non-critical segments operating as part of an overall fault-tolerant software system.

Ultimately one would like to see a classification of acceptance tests that characterize them by error detection capability, run-time penalty, and storage requirements, thus permitting a rational selection for each application. This stage, unfortunately, has not yet been reached. But that need not deter advancing with practical applications; there is little methodology for the routine testing of software which is being carried out all the time, and occasionally even with satisfactory results.

4. SYSTEM RELIABILITY MODELING

A potential advantage of the fault-tolerant software approach over other techniques for software reliability improvement is that it permits using (with some modifications) system reliability modeling techniques that have been developed in the hardware field. The qualifying 'potential' in the previous sentence reflects the fact that adequate parameters for the models do not yet exist although a methodology for obtaining them has been defined [23, 24]. Interesting insights can be achieved by modeling even at the present stage.

This will be demonstrated with a transition model shown in fig. 2 for a recovery block consisting of a primary and an alternate routine [16]. Reliability models can also be developed for N-version programming and for recovery blocks having multiple alternates.

Along the bottom of the figure are four possible states for the recovery block (here identified as an application module). Starting at state 1, primary routine operating, the immediate transitions are:

Loop 1, 1 — Primary routine continues to operate
Arc 1, 2 — Failure in primary routine detected
Arc 1, 4 — Undetected failure in the primary routine

Out of state 2, a transient state after detection of failure, two transitions are possible:

Arc 2, 3 — Transition to a satisfactory alternate
Arc 2, 4 — Failure at transition

State 3 is defined as satisfactory operation of the back-up routine through at least one complete program pass, and once this is achieved, the further possible transitions are:

Loop 3, 3 — Back-up continues to operate
Arc 3, 1 — Reversion to primary routine
Arc 3, 4 — Uncorrelated failure of the back-up

The word 'uncorrelated' is inserted because failures in the back-up routine occasioned by the transition from state 2 are represented by the arc 2, 4 as will be further discussed. The uncorrelated failures (arc 3, 4) are extremely unlikely, given thoroughly tested software and the usually limited time period for operation in the back-up mode. This transition is therefore shown in dashed symbols.

The major sources for failure of the recovery block are expected to be undetected failures of the primary routine and correlated failures in the back-up. The former are caused by deficiencies in the acceptance test. The previous discussion of this subject has shown that design of acceptance tests is far from an established discipline, and the possibility of undetected failures must be accounted for. Correlated failure of the back-up routine (arc 2, 4) can be caused by two circumstances: correlated deficiencies in the primary and back-up routine software, and correlation of faults in the acceptance test with those in the back-up routine. Insistence on independent design and coding of the two software routines, and, wherever possible, use of independent data sources, will minimize the first of these. The second cause of these correlated failures is particularly insidious, since the failure occurs even though the primary software may execute correctly! Possible sources of such correlated failures of the acceptance test and the back-up routine must therefore be thoroughly investigated in the design of a recovery block. The use of common data, common algorithms, and common subroutines should be avoided. Where some commonality is unavoidable (cf. the Eight Queens problem in section 3) at least the detailed software design should be varied.

Use of this transition model, even with the very inadequate data available, has led to some interesting insights into the measures necessary to obtain software reliability consistent with critical flight control applications [17]. A substantial advantage of the recovery block approach illustrated by this model is that the requirement for demonstrated reliability of the primary and alternate routines can be held several orders of magnitude (in terms of failure probability) below that required for the recovery block as a whole.

5. DIRECTIONS FOR THE FUTURE

Complete fault-tolerant software systems can for the foreseeable future be considered only for the most demanding and safety-critical applications, e.g. fly-by-wire passenger aircraft or safety systems for nuclear reactors. But fault-tolerant segments in otherwise conventional software may find much wider use. Such segments may be needed only temporarily, e.g. when a new operating system is being introduced, or they may be permanently installed, e.g. for back-up file management in a reservation or inventory control system.

Even more widespread may be the use of fault-tolerant techniques (short of a formal recovery block or *N*-version segment). In many applications it may be sufficient to halt operations (or to flag output) when errors occur. Acceptance tests or the previously referenced techniques for self-checking software will be used here. In other tasks, e.g. in the accounting field, the availability of back-up routines and data caches may be important, while the acceptance test might be relegated to a human observer or to a separately running audit routine.

Research will more and more apply the basic techniques outlined here to multi-tasking and multi-processing environments, and to the multi-layered operating systems of time-shared computers.

All of the present and most of the foreseeable applications are dictated by a need for greater reliability in the computing function without specific economic trade-offs of one technique versus another (the choices are very limited). It is questionable whether at some future time good criteria can be developed on where to apply software fault-tolerance and where to apply intensive validation methods. Where highly reliable illumination is desired we use long-life bulbs, redundant bulbs, and separate emergency lighting systems. Sometime all of these are used together and sometimes they are used separately. Any one of them is better than reliance on a single standard light bulb. Future generations may look in the same way at our efforts to produce more reliable software.

ACKNOWLEDGEMENT

Portions of the work reported here were carried out under subcontracts to C.S. Draper Laboratory and SRI International in connection with efforts by these organizations for the NASA Langley Research Center under contracts NAS1-15336 and NAS1-15428, respectively.

REFERENCES

[1] *Proc. IEEE*, Special Issue on Fault-Tolerant Digital Systems, vol 66, 1978 Oct.

[2] W.E. Howden, "Theoretical and empirical studies of software testing", *IEEE Trans. Software Engineering*, vol SE-4, 1978 Jul, pp 293-297.

[3] S.L. Gerhart, L. Yelowitz, "Observations on the fallibility in applications of modern programming methodologies", *IEEE Trans. Software Engineering*, vol SE-2, 1976 Sep, pp 195-207.

[4] C. Reynolds, R.T. Yeh, "Induction as the basis for program verification", *IEEE Trans. Software Engineering*, vol SE-2, 1976 Dec, pp 244-252.

[5] S.L. Gerhart, "Program verification in the 1980s: Problems, perspectives, and opportunities", ISI/RR-78-71, Information Sciences Institute, Marina del Rey, Calif, 1978 August.

[6] L.A. Belady, M.M. Lehman, "A model of large program development", *IBM Systems Journal*, vol 15, no. 3, 1976, pp 225-252.

[7] W.N. Toy, "Fault tolerant design of local ESS processors", in [1], pp 1126-1145.

[8] A.L. Hopkins, et al., "FTMP — A highly reliable fault-tolerant multiprocessor for aircraft", in [1], pp 1221-1239.

[9] J.H. Wensley, et al., "SIFT: The design and analysis of a fault-tolerant computer for aircraft control", in [1], pp 1240-1254.

[10] K.H. Kim, et al., "Strategies for structured and fault-tolerant design of recovery programs", *Proc. COMPSAC '78*, 1978 Nov, pp 651-656.

[11] W.R. Elmendorf, "Fault-tolerant programming", *Digest of the 1972 International Symposium on Fault-Tolerant Computing*, pp 79-83.

[12] A. Avizienis, L. Chen, "On the implementation of *N*-version programming for software fault-tolerance during execution", *Proc. COMPSAC '77*, 1977 Nov, pp 149-155.

[13] L. Chen, A. Avizienis, "*N*-Version programming: A fault-tolerance approach to reliability of software operation", *Digest of Papers, FTC – 8*, 1978 Jun, pp 3-9.

[14] J.J. Horning, et al., "A program structure for error detection and recovery", *Proc. Conf. Operating Systems: Theoretical and Practical Aspects, IRIA*, 1974 Apr, pp 174-193.

[15] B. Randell, "System structure for software fault-tolerance", *IEEE Trans. Software Engineering*, vol SE-1, 1975 Jun, pp 220-232.

[16] H. Hecht, "Fault-tolerant software for real-time applications", *ACM Computing Surveys*, vol 8, 1976 Dec, pp 391-407.

[17] Advanced Programs Division, The Aerospace Corporation, "Fault-tolerant software study", NASA CR 145298, 1978 Feb.

[18] J.S.M. Verhofstad, "The construction of recoverable multi-level systems", PhD Dissertation, University of Newcastle upon Tyne, 1977 Aug.

[19] K.H. Kim, C.V. Ramamoorthy, "Failure-tolerant parallel programming and its supporting system architectures", *AFIPS – Conf. Proc.*, vol 45 (NCC 1976) pp 413-423.

[20] L.G. Stucki, G.L. Foshee, "New assertion concepts for self-metric software validation", *Proc. 1975 International Conf. Reliable Software*, IEEE Cat. 75CH0940-7CSR, 1975 Apr, pp 59-71.

[21] S.S. Yau, R.C. Cheung, "Design of self-checking software", same source as [20], pp 450-457.

[22] S.S. Yau, R.C. Cheung, D.C. Cochrane, "An approach to error-resistant software design", *Proc. Second International Conf. Software Engineering*, IEEE Cat. 76CH1125-4C, 1976 Oct, pp 429-436.

[23] J.D. Musa, "Measuring software reliability", *ORSA/TIMS Journal*, 1977 May, pp 1-25.

[24] H. Hecht, et al., "Reliability measurement during software development", NASA CR-145205, 1977 Sep.

AUTHOR

Herbert Hecht; SoHaR, Inc.; 1040 S. LaJolla Ave.; Los Angeles, CA 90035 USA.

Dr. Hecht (M'47,SM'54) is president of SoHaR Incorporated, an organization engaged in studies and consulting in computer software and hardware reliability problems. In prior employment he was Director of Computer Technology in the Advanced Programs Division of The Aerospace Corporation and Department Head for Helicopter and Light Aircraft Flight Controls at the Flight Systems Division of the Sperry Rand Corporation. Hecht received a Bachelor of Electrical Engineering degree from City College, New York and a Master's degree in the same subject from Brooklyn Polytechnic Institute. He obtained a PhD in Engineering from UCLA. He has published many papers on computer and control system reliability subjects and has conducted a short course in Software Reliability at UCLA. He is registered as a Professional Engineer (Control Systems) in California. He is Vice Chair'n of the IEEE Computer Society Technical Committee on Software Engineering and has initiated efforts to standardize software terminology and practices.

Manuscript SI79-08 received 1978 December 1; revised 1979 January 18.

FAULT MODELING

D&T Tutorial

The fault models used for design, simulation, and test generation can reduce testing time and cost, as well as provide more accurate analysis.

John P. Hayes, University of Michigan

Computers and other digital systems are subject to any number of faults caused by design errors, inadequate quality control during manufacture, and the wear and tear of normal operation. How many and what kinds of faults depend mainly on the circuit technology used (TTL, CMOS, etc.) and the circuit's operating environment. For example, the faults occurring during IC manufacture with MOS technologies stem from many causes:[1,2] defects in original silicon wafer; holes in gate oxide of transistors; short circuits in metal, diffusion or polysilicon interconnections; open circuits in interconnections; high-resistance contacts between interconnections; transistor threshold voltage shifts due to ionic contamination; excessive leakage currents or charge loss; and missing or extra conductor, semiconductor or oxide regions.

Fault modeling is concerned with the systematic and precise representation of physical faults in a form suitable for simulation and test generation.[3] Such a representation usually involves the definition of abstract or logical faults that produce approximately the same erroneous behavior as the actual physical faults. Different fault models are necessary for each level of abstraction—electrical, logical, functional—at which the circuits of interest are modeled. For example, at the electrical level, faults are characterized by changes in voltage, current, or resistance. Electrical parameters are meaningless at the logic design level, and faults must be defined indirectly in terms of the more abstract 0 and 1 logic values.

Consider the physical fault caused by minute holes in the thin oxide insulation layer separating the gate electrode from the substrate of an NMOS transistor. This fault, a common IC failure, prevents the transistor from being switched on. It is modeled in electrical terms by a short-to-ground fault F_1 of the kind shown for transistor Q_1 in the NOR circuit of Figure 1a. Here, a connection to ground is added to gate terminal g of Q_1, which approximates the failure-induced path through Q_1's gate oxide layer to its substrate. (The substrate is normally

---

Summary

Fault models for physical failures in digital systems attempt to combine computational simplicity with an accurate modeling of real failures. The single-stuck-line, or SSL, model is the most popular model today. It is simple and compatible with methods to test logic circuits. The model has been successfully applied to a wide variety of circuit types under varied operating conditions. The deficiencies of SSL models for some circuit types such as CMOS can be mitigated by the use of workaround circuits that adapt the original circuit to the SSL model. Alternatively, switch-level circuit models that use the more accurate generalized SSL model can be employed.

Functional fault modeling is suitable for systems where logic circuits are either unobtainable or too complex to use. The general functional model covers a wide range of physical faults but can be used only with small combinational circuits and very small sequential ones. Less general heuristic fault models are often most appropriate for larger systems.

held at ground potential.) In actuality the oxide defect creates a high-resistance leakage path to ground. The abstract model F_1, which assumes an ideal zero-resistance path to ground, only roughly approximates this state; however, more accurate fault models that account for resistive or capacitive effects greatly complicate fault analysis. Another approach is to replace F by other, functionally equivalent, electrical fault models, such as the combination of transistor Q_1 stuck off and transistor Q_4 stuck on.

Figure 1b shows the logical model of the circuit (1a) as a two-input NOR gate. For this simplified circuit model, we need equally simple fault models. Note that many of the concepts used in formulating the electrical fault model are inapplicable at the logic-gate level. Because the internal structure of the gate is no longer accessible, we cannot predict the results if we attempt to insert short or open circuits in the input-output lines of the gate model. For example, if 0 and 1 are applied to x_1 and x_2 respectively, what happens if x_1 and x_2 are shorted together? To circumvent these difficulties, we need a different type of fault model. In the model in Figure 1b, input x_1 (which controls transistors Q_1 and Q_4 in the original electrical circuit) is overridden by a constant 0 signal. This fault F_1' is an instance of the widely used "stuck-at-0/1" fault model for logic circuits.

In comparing fault models F_1 and F_1' of Figure 1, we see that more accuracy can be achieved at the lower electrical level, but at the expense of more computation. Thus, at the electrical level we must deal with six components and many interconnections, all subject to failure; whereas, at the logic level, we have a single component with only three interconnections and a more restricted set of failure modes. At the electrical level, signals are continuous or analog; at the logic level they are confined to the digital values 0 and 1. On the other hand, physical failure modes such as excessive current leakage and threshold voltage shifts, which have fairly simple electrical models, are impossible to model directly in logical terms.

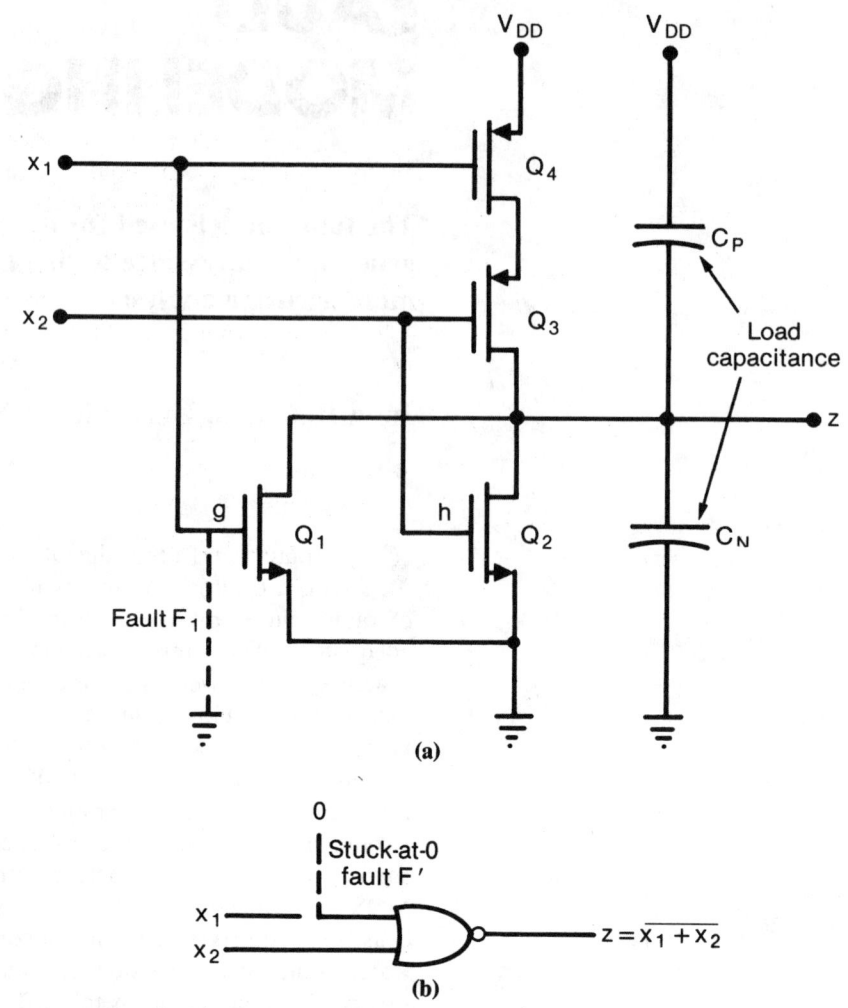

Figure 1. Two types of fault modeling for an IC failure: an electrical model (a), which depicts a CMOS NOR circuit with a short-circuit fault, and a logical model (b), which depicts a NOR logic gate with a stuck-at-0 fault.

Fault model characteristics

What constitutes a good fault model? First, it should match the type of circuit (electrical, logical, functional) in which it is to be used. Second, the complexity of the faults and the number to be considered should not entail excessive amounts of computation. Finally, a fault model should reflect the behavior of the underlying physical faults with sufficient accuracy for the intended applications. In short, good fault models should be straightforward, accurate, and easy to use. Unfortunately, these requirements are frequently at odds with one another.

In many situations, a relatively simple abstract fault model $\mathbf{F}_a$ can be used to adequately represent a large number of physical fault types $\mathbf{F}_p$. In test generation, for example, a basic task is to compute a sequence of test patterns to detect all known or expected $\mathbf{F}_p$-type faults in a circuit N_p. The tests are determined using an appropriate circuit model N_a of N_p, and a test-generation algorithm designed to compute tests $\mathbf{T}$ for all faults of type $\mathbf{F}_a$ in N_a. If experiment or analysis can show that $\mathbf{T}$ will detect all—or, more likely, almost all—$\mathbf{F}_p$ faults, then fault model $\mathbf{F}_a$ is considered sufficiently accurate for test generation. In this situation, F_a is said to *cover* F_p. The percentage of physical faults F_p that can be detected by tests derived from F_a is called the *fault coverage* of F_a. Although normally difficult to measure precisely, fault coverage serves as a useful indication of fault model quality.

A number of general characteristics are used to classify fault models for digital systems. One is fault variability with respect to time; faults can be permanent, transient (nonpermanent and nonrecurring), or intermittent (nonpermanent but recurring). Another classification characteristic is the effect of faults on the functional behavior of a circuit's components and interconnections. Also important are changes in operating speed induced by faults. Finally, faults are distinguished by the number of distinct faults that may be present simultaneously. A convenient approach is to assume that only one type of fault is present at a time, thereby eliminating the possibility of two or more distinct faults possibly interacting in complex ways during testing.

Types of fault models

Table 1 lists some representative fault models that have been proposed for digital circuit testing,[4,5,6] all of which aim to model physical failures whose effects can be defined in logical as well as electrical terms. By far, the most widely used and studied of these is the single-stuck-line model (also called the stuck-at-0/1 or stuck-at model), which has been used for fault analysis and test generation in all types of logic circuits. Only permanent faults are considered in the following discussion, although some nonpermanent faults may be represented by the models discussed earlier, with additional data on their frequency of occurrence. In general, intermittent and transient faults are very difficult to model.[1]

Single-stuck-line model. An SSL fault is inserted into logic line x by conceptually cutting x and applying a constant signal d, which may be 0 or 1, to the output of x. Line x is now said to be stuck-at-d (s-a-d), and is unaffected by the normal logic signal applied to x by the remainder of the circuit. SSL faults are often restricted to the input-output lines of gates and flip-flops. Figure 1b shows the SSL fault x_1 s-a-0, which has been inserted into an input line of the NOR gate. The SSL fault model allows only one line to be faulty at a time. SSL faults are permanent and do not affect either the function or speed of the circuit components with which they are associated.

> **SSL faults are well suited for use with test-generation procedures like the D-Algorithms.**

The SSL fault model meets the general criteria of circuit-level compatibility and low computational complexity noted earlier. In a circuit containing n lines that may be faulty, $2n$ distinct SSL faults are possible. This number is modest compared to the corresponding number of short-circuit faults between pairs of lines [$n(n-1)/2$], or the number of multiple stuck-line faults (3^n-1). The SSL model is obviously compatible with standard logic circuits and does not lead to the complex behavior associated with shorts or opens in logic circuits. For example, a combinational (memoryless) circuit always remains combinational in the presence of SSL faults. Not so obvious is the range of physical faults that can be adequately represented by the SSL model.

SSL faults are particularly well suited for use with test-generation procedures like the D-Algorithm.[3,7] These methods attempt to compute circuit conditions that enable an error signal to propagate from the fault site to an observable primary output line. Consider the logic circuit in Figure 2, whose indicated 0/1 signal values have been derived to test for the SSL fault $F_2 = a$ s-a-1. Under fault-free conditions, the signals appearing along the input-output path *abcde* are 01010. If fault F_2 is present, these signals become 10101. Thus the primary input pattern $T_1 = x_1 x_2 x_3 x_4 x_5 = 10000$ serves as a test for F_2, producing the response $z = 1$ when F is present, and $z = 0$ when no fault is present. The path *abcde* (heavy lines in Figure 2) is said to be *sensitized* to the fault F_2 because an error signal can propagate along this path from a to the primary output z. As the other heavy lines in Figure 2 indicate, a typical test often sensitizes several paths at once. Indeed, maximizing the number of simultaneously sensitized paths is the goal of some test-generation methods.[3] A given test pattern detects an SSL fault associated with every line along the sensitized paths it creates. Thus, T_1 detects all the following faults in Figure 2: a s-a-1, b s-a-0, c s-a-1, d s-a-0, e s-a-1, f s-a-1, and g s-a-1. We can therefore easily generate tests for a larger number of SSL faults simultaneously, reducing the number of test patterns, which in turn decreases the cost of test generation and the testing time.

Because of these advantages, most existing test-generation programs aim at producing tests to detect all SSL faults in gate-level logic circuits. A natural question is what physical fault coverage is achieved by such tests? This problem may be tackled by careful analysis of actual physical faults.[8,9] While exact coverage figures are difficult to obtain, substantial empirical evidence shows that for general combinational or sequential logic circuits implemented with common MOS or bipolar technologies, the SSL model provides very good coverage of permanent physical faults.

One indication of SSL model effectiveness is that tests for SSL faults tend to thoroughly exercise all logic gates of a circuit. For example, an n-input gate G of the AND, OR, NAND, or NOR variety has $2(n+1)$ distinct SSL faults F_G associated with its input-output lines. A unique set of $n+1$ test patterns T_G are sufficient to detect F_G. Table 2 lists the six members of F_G for the two-input NOR gate given in Figure 1b and the test patterns needed to detect them. It follows immediately that $T_G = \{00,01,10\}$. Thus, to detect all

SSL faults in this or any other two-input gate, 75 percent of all possible test patterns must be applied. Also, the remaining test pattern $x_1x_2 = 11$ may be applied to the NOR gate as a side-effect of tests aimed at other gates in the same circuit. For one-input gates (inverting and noninverting buffers), $T_G = \{0,1\}$ represents 100 percent of the possible input patterns. As gate fan-in increases, the ratio of the number of tests in T_G to the number of possible gate input patterns—$(n+1)/2^n$—diminishes rapidly. In many circuits, the average gate fan-in is between two and three, hence SSL-based tests tend to apply almost all possible input patterns to most gates. With this nearly exhaustive exercising of each gate, most physical faults are likely to be revealed through an incorrect logical signal at the gate output, which is then propagated along a sensitized path to a primary output of the circuit.

SSL model extensions. We have concluded that the electrical fault $F_1 = g$ shorted to ground in Figure 1a is functionally equivalent to the SSL fault $F_1' = $ line x_1 s-a-0 in Figure 1b. Now, suppose that F_1 is replaced by fault F_3, an open circuit in g. Like F_1, this fault causes Q_1 to become independent of its gate control signal, but does not affect Q_4. Consider what happens when the input pattern $x_1x_2 = 10$ (the test for F_1 and F_1') is applied to the NOR circuit with F_3 present. Transistors Q_1, Q_2 and Q_3 are switched off; hence, output z is disconnected from both power (V_{DD}) and ground. Because the output load capacitance (C_N and C_P in Figure 1a) is substantial, line z remains in its previous 0 or 1 state for a relatively long period. Consequently, the behavior of the NOR circuit changes from combinational to sequential, behavior that cannot be directly modeled by an SSL fault. Moreover, as discussed by Wadsack,[10] F_2 can escape detection even if an exhaustive set of tests is applied to the gate in question. Suppose, for instance, that all four combinations of x_1x_2 are applied to the NOR gate in the sequence 00,01,10,11. The fault-free response appearing at z is 1,0,0,0. The corresponding response when the open-circuit fault is present is also 1,0,0,0, because when $x_1x_2 = 10$ is applied, z produces the response $z = 0$ to the preceding test $x_1x_2 = 01$; this response is stored in the now isolated load capacitance C_P. If we change the order of the input test patterns to 11,01,00,10, we will get an incorrect response sequence 0,0,1,1 with F_3 present.

Table 1.
Fault models used for digital systems.

Fault Model	Definition	Comments
Single stuck line	One interconnection line may be stuck at 0 or 1	Most widely used; applies to all types of logic circuits
Multiple stuck line	Several lines may be stuck at 0 or 1 simultaneously	Number of possible faults is very large
Generalized single stuck line	SSL model with multiple strength levels for stuck values	Applies to switch-level logic circuits
General functional	Truth or state table may change arbitrarily	Requires very long (exhaustive) tests
Coupling faults	State transitions in one memory cell affect other memory cells	Applies mainly to RAMs

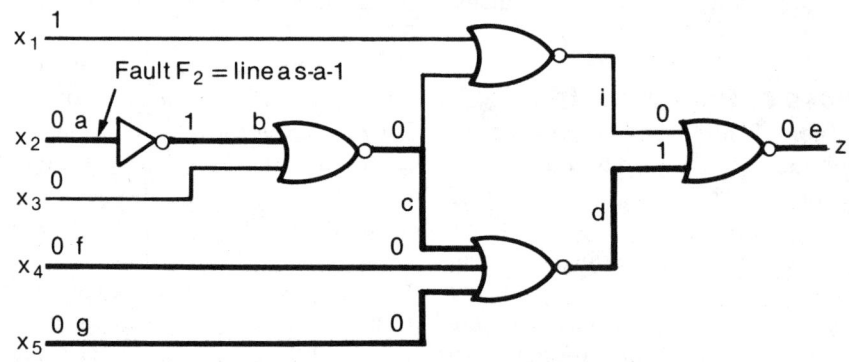

Figure 2. Testing a logic circuit for single-stuck-line faults.

Table 2.
SSL faults and tests for the NOR gate in Figure 1b.

SSL Fault F	Tests for F
x_1 stuck-at-0	$x_1x_2 = 10$
x_1 stuck-at-1	$x_1x_2 = 00$
x_2 stuck-at-0	$x_1x_2 = 01$
x_2 stuck-at-1	$x_1x_2 = 00$
z stuck-at-0	$x_1x_2 = 00$
z stuck-at-1	$x_1x_2 = 01$ or 10 or 11

A physical fault like F_3 can be represented by an equivalent SSL fault in a more complicated logical model of the original circuit. Figure 3 shows a logic circuit that can reproduce the NOR gate behavior with F_3 present. A D-latch and five gates have been added to the basic two-input NOR gate G_0. The gates in Figure 3 are assumed to have zero propagation delay, while the D-latch has the same propagation delay τ as the physical NOR gate being modeled. Under fault-free conditions, clock signal CK is 1, and the circuit generates the output

$$z(t) = \overline{x_1(t-\tau) + x_2(t-\tau)}.$$

The six SSL faults listed in Table 2 can be inserted directly into the corresponding lines of G_0 in Figure 3.

Suppose that SSL fault $F_3' = g'$ s-a-1 is introduced into the augmented circuit model. When $x_1 x_2$ becomes 10, F_3' changes CK to 0 causing the D-latch to hold z at its previous state indefinitely. Thus, F_3' simulates the behavior of the open-circuit fault $F_3 =$ line g stuck open shown in Figure 1a. The NOR circuit of Figure 3 has also been designed to allow the companion fault, line h stuck open, in Figure 1a to be modeled by the SSL fault h' s-a-1. This circuit can be further extended to allow almost any type of permanent physical fault to be modeled by SSL faults.[4,10] However, because modified circuits are so complex, fault modeling in this manner must be restricted to a small number of frequently occurring failure types. Moreover, most of the SSL faults that can be inserted into the added circuitry are either meaningless (do not represent the behavior of any physical fault in the original circuit) or undetectable.

The SSL fault model can also be generalized by removing the single-fault restriction, thereby allowing more than one line to be stuck at 0 or 1. The resulting *multiple-stuck-line* model causes a massive increase in the number of possible faults from $2n$ to $3^n - 1$ for an n-line circuit. This large number makes using the MSL model impractical for all but the most trivial circuits. On the other hand, for test generation, a test set **T** for all SSL faults will usually cover all MSL faults. This assumption is based on the fact that **T** contains tests to detect each of the m SSL faults that compose every m-line MSL fault. The detection of one of these component SSL faults, however, could be blocked by some other SSL fault. For example, if fault $F_4 = i$ s-a-1 and target fault $F_2 = a$ s-a-1 occur simultaneously in the circuit of Figure 2, the latter is no longer detected. However, other test patterns are easily found in **T** that will detect the

> **Switch-level circuits allow direct modeling of major failure modes without elaborate workarounds.**

double fault $\{F_2, F_4\}$. For an MSL fault to escape detection by a complete set of SSL tests, its component faults must mask one another. Since the conditions necessary for this mutual masking are complex and rarely encountered in real circuits,[3] we can safely assume that, for practical test generation, the SSL model will cover MSL faults.

A new circuit representation called the switch-level, or transistor, model has recently been developed for VLSI design and simulation.[4,11,12] Falling midway between the classical gate and electric circuit levels, switch-level circuits employ a small set **L** of signal values of the form (v,i), where v denotes voltage-like values including 0,1 and the high-impedance state Z, while i denotes current-like values termed logical strength. The strength parameter can be interpreted as the current-driving capability of the signal. As these values suggest, switch-level circuits capture some of the attributes of analog electrical circuits. The logic elements used include switches representing MOS switching transistors and digital elements that can model resistive and capacitive effects. Figure 4 shows a switch-level model[11] for the CMOS NOR gate in Figure 1. The model employs ideal on-off switches $S_1:S_4$ to represent transistors $Q_1:Q_4$ and digital charge-storage elements W_N and W_P termed wells to represent load capacitors C_N and C_P.

Switch-level circuits allow direct and accurate modeling of the major failure modes in MOS circuits, without the need for elaborate workaround circuits, such as those in Figure 3. The SSL model may be extended to a *generalized single-stuck-line* model[3] which allows any line in a switch-level circuit to be stuck-at-d, where d is any value (v, i_j) in the available signal set **L**. For example, the open-circuit fault g s-a-1 (Figure 1a) can be represented by the GSSL fault g s-a-$(Z,0)$ in the switch-level circuit of Figure 4, where $(Z,0)$ denotes the normal high-impedance state.

Suppose we have an input combination of the form $x_1 x_2 = (0, i_j)(1, i_j)$, corresponding to $x_1 x_2 = 01$ in the gate-level representation. The GSSL fault then isolates z from the rest of the circuit, causing z to assume a logic value (v_k, i_k) defined by the charge packets stored in W_N and W_P. For instance, if the last value of z was $(1, i_j)$, then W_N is charged, and z remains at the logical 1 level, generating an output signal $(1, i_k)$ derived from W_N.

While SSL faults can represent only "strong" faults, in which the faulted line is effectively connected to power or ground, GSSL can represent "weak" faults such as a partial short to ground. Thus, if $(0, I_0)$ denotes the ground signal in Figure 4, the GSSL fault $F_4 =$ line a s-a-$(0, I_j)$ where $I_j 5 I_0$, has the effect of decreasing the current-carrying ability of line a; that is, it increases the line's resistance. This fault therefore represents a condition midway between a short and an open. Similarly, other GSSL faults can be used to modify the capacitance of a line. By altering digital resistance and capacitance parameters, GSSL-type faults can directly mimic the behavior of many important physical failures in digital circuits.

General functional model. The gate- and switch-level fault models discussed so far have been successfully applied to circuits containing tens of thousands of transistors. With much larger circuits, the number of possible faults becomes prohibitive, even when high-speed, computer-aided fault analysis techniques are used. A further problem is that the detailed logic and transistor circuit diagrams needed to employ SSL-type fault models may be unavailable. For instance, when faced with the task of designing tests for off-the-shelf VLSI circuits, the user often has access only to high-level (register-transfer) circuit diagrams; input-output interface specifications; and, in the case of programmable devices, instruction-set listings. High-level fault models and testing procedures must therefore be devised on the basis of meager design information of this sort. Such fault models are termed *functional,* since their primary purpose is to exercise and check the basic functions performed by the circuit under test. They are also *implementation independent* in that they do not require detailed knowledge of the circuit's internal structure or of the specific IC technology being used. Unlike the precise fault models discussed so far, functional fault models are usually inexact and heuristic in nature.

Perhaps the most powerful model in this context, which is referred to here as the *general functional* model, is one that allows arbitrary changes to a circuit's truth table (combinational case) or state table (sequential case). The maximum number of states, which can be taken to be one in the combinational case, is assumed to remain constant when faults are present. (The number of states was increased by the stuck-open faults considered earlier for the CMOS NOR gate.) Detection of GF faults requires essentially exhaustive testing procedures. For an n-input combinational circuit, all 2^n distinct input patterns must be used as test set **T**. GF detection is thus feasible for moderate numbers of input lines, say $n \leq 20$. **T** can be generated very simply by means of a free-running counter that produces all possible n-bit binary numbers in sequence. A hardware-implemented counter can generate **T** at the maximum clock rate of the unit under test. At a 1-MHz clock rate,

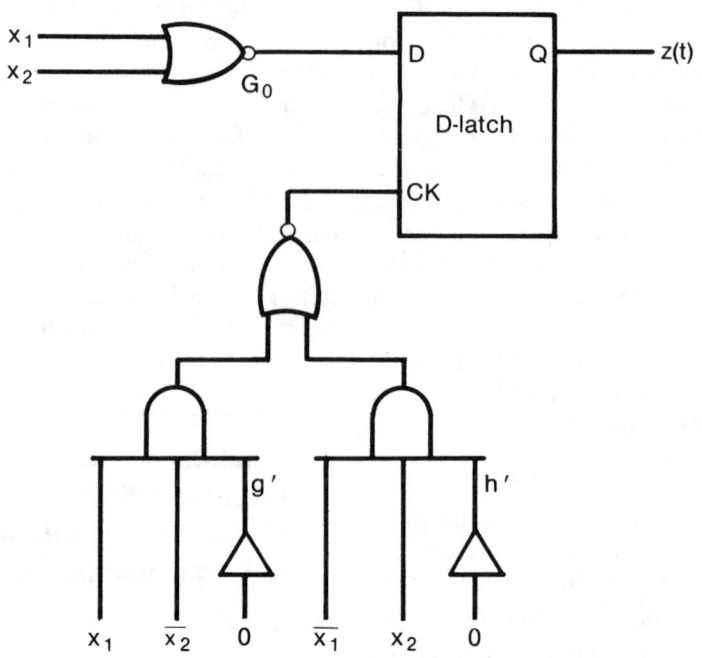

Figure 3. Modified NOR circuit to allow representation of open-circuit faults by the single-stuck-line model.

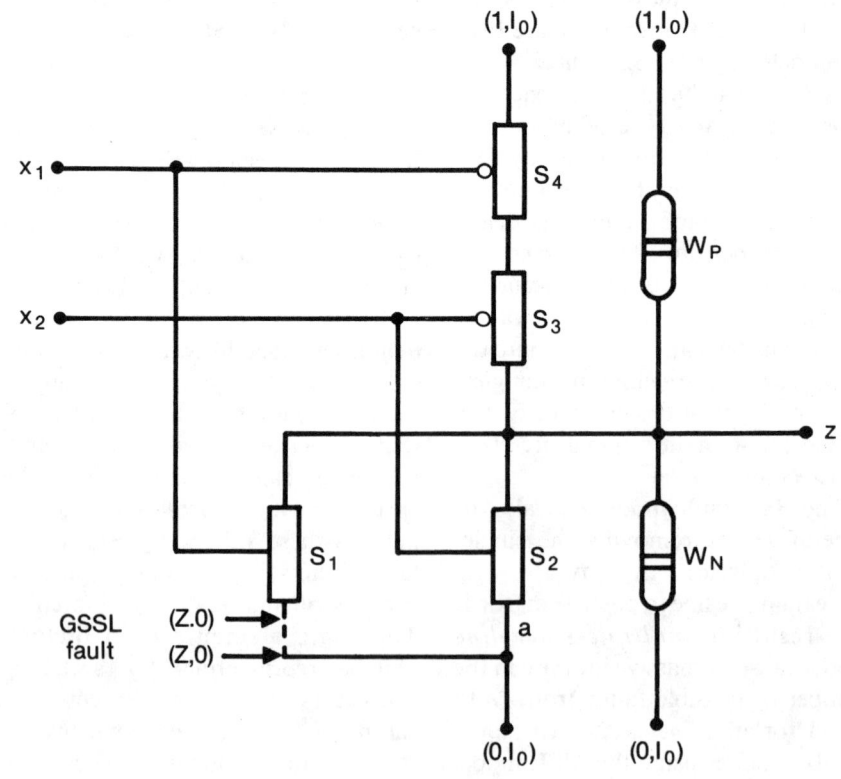

Figure 4. Switch-level model of the CMOS NOR circuit.

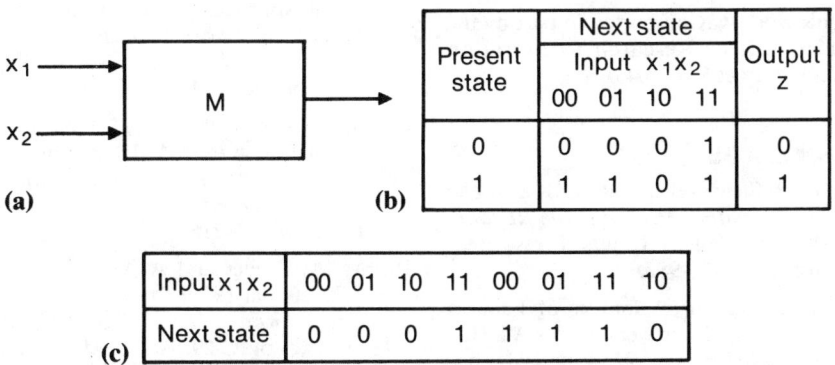

Figure 5. Checking sequence: (a) memory element *M*; (b) its state table; (c) on input sequence for *M*.

10^6, or 2^{20}, tests can be produced in one second. At the same rate, we would need 30 hours to obtain all 2^{40} 40-bit test patterns, so this approach is not feasible for combinational circuits with very large numbers of inputs. If a circuit is composed of small combinational modules, however, each module could be tested exhaustively for GF faults.

A test for GF faults in a sequential circuit is termed a *checking sequence*, the derivation of which is a classical switching theory problem.[13] The concept is illustrated in Figure 5a, which shows a one-bit memory element M resembling a D flip-flop. The behavior of M is described by the Moore-type state table in Figure 5b. The input sequence given in Figure 5c detects all GF faults in M, assuming that the initial state is 0. This checking sequence is relatively short because the internal state of M is directly observable at its output z. Therefore the checking sequence need exercise every state transition only once.

In circuits where the internal state is not directly observable, each state transition must be traversed repeatedly to check it. Consequently checking sequences for general sequential circuits tend to be extremely long and difficult to compute, and the GF model is practical only for circuits containing a few memory elements. It has, however, been applied successfully to the representation of certain types of pattern-sensitive faults in RAMs,[5] and to testing simple bit-sliced microprocessors.[14]

Other functional models. When we are dealing with circuit models in which ALUs, RAMs and the like are treated as primitive components, we cannot practically describe functional behavior by means of truth tables or state tables. Instead, we need more concise descriptive tools such as register-transfer languages to define both normal and faulty behavior. Such languages also allow us to construct simple fault models to describe very complex physical failure modes. No standard or widely used languages for functional fault modeling exist but a few languages have been devised for use with specific simulation and test generation systems.[15,16]

Consider once more the NOR gate in Figure 1. Suppose that a physical fault f exists that changes the output function from NOR to NAND and increases the input-output propagation delay from four to eight time units. If we describe this fault using stuck-type fault models of the sort examined earlier, we must use complicated workaround circuits. The following description of f is in the Function Definition Language developed at AT&T Bell Laboratories, which has been incorporated into the Lamp fault simulator.[15]

INPUTS: x_1, x_2;
OUPUTS: z;
INTERNAL_FAULTS: f;
DEF:
IF f THEN AT 0,
    $z = \neg(x_1(-8) \& x_2(-8))$
ELSE AT 0,
    $z = \neg x_1(-4) \& \neg x_2(-4)$
FI
FED

FDL is easily read by anyone familiar with a high-level programming language such as Fortran or Pascal. The present output z of the circuit (at time $t=0$) is the NAND function of the input values of x_1 and x_2 at $t = -8$, that is, eight time units earlier, when f is present; z is the NOR function of x_1 and x_2 at $t = -4$ when no fault is present. Note that this FDL model is independent of the internal structure of the NOR circuit. Devising a stuck-line fault model like that in Figure 3 to reproduce the same faulty behavior is by no means easy.

Functional fault models have been developed for a few specific circuit families, notably RAMs[6] and microprocessors.[17] An example of a fault model designed for RAMs is the coupling model, which allows a state transition occurring in one memory element M_i to change the state of some other element M_j. This model can represent a variety of physical faults affecting the RAM's addressing logic. Coupling faults are detected by applying read and write operations to M_i and M_j in turn and checking the responses to the reads. Coupling fault modes implicitly underlie such widely used memory testing procedures as the column bars and the galloping 0's and 1's tests.[3]

Functional fault models are much harder to construct for microprocessors. One attempt in this direction is the S-graph model,[17] which represents functional behavior by means of a directed graph. The nodes of this graph denote registers and IO ports. A directed edge (arrow) labeled I_{jk} is drawn from node R_i to node R_j if the kth subcycle or phase of instruction I_j causes data to flow from R_i to R_j. The functional faults that can be defined in terms of S-graphs include instruction opcode and address decoding faults and incorrect storage or transfer of data. The model does not account for data-processing faults involving the ALU, interrupt control, or the like. Tests are obtained directly from the

S-graphs in the form of instruction sequences for execution by the microprocessor to be tested. In practice, microprocessors and other programmable systems are more often tested by ad hoc test programs that systematically but incompletely exercise all functional units.[18] The main difficulty in using these approaches, and, indeed, in most functional testing, is how to estimate the fault coverage achieved.

All the fault models proposed for digital circuits attempt to combine computational simplicity with an accurate modeling of real failures. The simplification or abstraction inherent in fault modeling means that some physical failures at which a particular fault model is aimed will not be covered. Also, models that provide adequate fault coverage for bipolar TTL, for example, may be inadequate for CMOS. Determining actual fault coverage is difficult. The quality of a fault model is often gauged informally by field experience, and test procedures are generally based on such experience.

The SSL model has achieved widespread use in design verification, test generation, and design for testability. Design-for-testability techniques such as LSSD may allow the SSL model to be used with very large sequential logic circuits.[19] Although not yet widely used, the GSSL model allows higher accuracy to be achieved, with a corresponding increase in computational effort.

Another type of model is the functional fault model, which is suitable for large systems in which logic circuits are either unobtainable or too complex to use. The general functional model covers a wide range of physical faults but can be used only with small combinational circuits and very small sequential ones. More practical fault models in this category limit themselves to testing a small representative sampling of a circuit's possible functions. Little theory is yet available to help in the construction of functional fault models or testing techniques. The designer's experience remains the best guide. □

Acknowledgments

This work was supported in part by the Semiconductor Research Corporation under Contract 84-01-045.

References

1. D. P. Siewiorek and R. S. Swarz, *The Theory and Practice of Reliable System Design,* Digital Press, Bedford, Mass., 1982.
2. T. E. Mangir, "Sources of Failures and Yield Improvement for VLSI," *Proc. IEEE,* Vol. 72, June 1984, pp. 690-708.
3. M. A. Breuer and A.D. Friedman, *Diagnosis and Reliable Design of Digital Systems,* Computer Science Press, Woodland Hills, Calif., 1976.
4. J. P. Hayes, "Modeling Faults in Digital Logic Circuits," in *Rational Fault Analysis,* R. Saeks and S. R. Liberty eds., Marcel Dekker, New York, 1977, pp. 78-95.
5. J. P. Hayes, "Fault Modeling for Digital MOS Integrated Circuits," *IEEE Trans. Computer-Aided Design,* Vol. CAD-3, No. 3, July 1984, pp. 200-207.
6. M. S. Abadir and H.S. Reghbati, "Functional Testing Of Semiconductor Random Access Memories," *Computing Surveys,* Vol. 15, Sept. 1983, pp. 175-198.
7. J. P. Roth, *Computer Logic, Testing and Verification,* Computer Science Press, Potomac, Md., 1980.
8. G. R. Case, "Analysis of Actual Fault Mechanisms in CMOS Logic Gates," *Proc. 13th Design Automation Conf.,* June 1976, pp. 265-270.
9. C. C. Beh et al. "Do Stuck Fault Models Reflect Manufacturing Defects?", *Digest 1982 Int'l Test Conf.,* Oct. 1982, pp. 35-42.
10. R. L. Wadsack, "Fault Modeling and Logic Simulation of CMOS and MOS Integrated Circuits," *Bell System Tech. J.,* Vol. 57, May-July 1978, pp. 1449-1474.
11. J. P. Hayes, "A Unified Switching Theory with Applications to VLSI Design," *Proc. IEEE,* Vol. 70, Oct. 1982, pp. 1140-1151.
12. R. E. Bryant, "A Switch-Level Model and Simulator for MOS Digital Systems," *IEEE Trans. Computers,* Vol. C-33, Feb. 1984, No. 2, pp. 160-177.
13. A. D. Friedman and P. R. Menon, *Fault Detection in Digital Circuits,* Prentice-Hall, Englewood Cliffs, N.J., 1971.
14. T. Sridhar and J. P. Hayes, "A Functional Approach to Testing Bit-Sliced Microprocessors," *IEEE Trans. Computers,* Vol. C-30, No. 8, Aug 1981, pp. 563-571.
15. S. G. Chappell et al., "Functional Simulation in the LAMP System," *J. Design Automation and Fault-Tolerant Computing,* Vol. 1, May 1977, pp. 203-215.
16. M. A. Breuer and A. D. Friedman, "Functional Level Primitives in Test Generation," *IEEE Trans. Computers,* Vol. C-29, No. 3, Mar. 1980, pp. 223-235.
17. S. M. Thatte and J. A. Abraham, "Test Generation for Microprocessors," *IEEE Trans. Computers,* Vol. C-29, No. 6, June 1980, pp. 429-441.
18. A. C. L. Chiang and R. McCaskill, "Two New Approaches Simplify Testing of Microprocessors," *Electronics,* Vol. 49, No. 2, Jan. 1976, pp. 100-105.
19. R. G. Bennetts, *Design of Testable Logic Circuits,* Addison-Wesley, London, 1984.

John P. Hayes is a professor in the Department of Electrical Engineering and Computer Science at the University of Michigan, Ann Arbor, where he teaches and conducts research in VLSI design, computer architecture, digital system testing, and switching theory. From 1972 to 1982 he served on the faculty of the University of Southern California. He is the author of *Computer Architecture and Organization* and *Digital System Design and Microprocessors* (McGraw-Hill, publisher).

Hayes received a BE from the National University of Ireland, Dublin, and an MS and a PhD in electrical engineering from the University of Illinois. He is a fellow of the IEEE and a member of ACM and Sigma Xi.

Hayes's address is Dept. of Electrical Engineering and Computer Science, University of Michigan, Ann Arbor, MI 48109.

Chapter 2: Reliability Modeling and General Redundancy Techniques

Overview

This chapter introduces the redundancy techniques and reliability modeling methods needed for a study of fault-tolerant systems. Redundancy schemes will be discussed in terms of hardware implementations. However, many of the techniques can be implemented in software or be applied to software fault tolerance as discussed in Chapter 5. Reliability modeling is also presented from a hardware-level or system-level point of view. Software reliability modeling is fundamentally different from hardware reliability modeling and is introduced in Chapter 5.

This presentation begins with the basic principles of failure models and reliability computations including the military standard reliability models. Redundancy techniques including N-modular redundancy (NMR), sparing, a hybrid system, and coding are then described. Reliability models of several redundancy techniques are presented and compared.

The chapter concludes with three reprints which each describe the development of reliability models for fault-tolerant systems. A brief summary of each paper is given below. However, the beginning reader should defer reading the papers until after reading the introductory material on reliability modeling and on redundancy techniques.

Mathur [MAT71] presents combinatorial reliability models that cover NMR, sparing, and hybrid systems. Quantitative evaluations of system reliability as a function of various parameters are given for selected cases. Also, a notation is introduced that unifies the description of various system configurations. The notation is used later in this chapter as well. The CARE (Computer-Aided Reliability Estimation) program employs these models and was used to produce the quantitative results given in the paper.

Bouricius, Carter, and Schneider [BOU69] introduced the concept of coverage in reliability modeling. A combinatorial model for sparing that incorporates coverage is developed and used to examine thoroughly the effect of coverage on system reliability. An interesting design case study is also included.

Ng and Avizienis [NG80] present Markov reliability models that can be used with simplex, sparing, or hybrid systems. One model is for systems without repair while another model includes repair. Both models incorporate coverage and allow the modeling of systems that provide graceful degradation. The ARIES (Automated Reliability Interactive Estimation System) program is based on these models.

Reliability Modeling

This section begins with definitions of the most common measures employed in the evaluation of system reliability and fault tolerance. Combinatorial modeling methods are then introduced for systems that satisfy an independent component failure assumption and that do not provide for repair. Finally, Markov modeling methods are presented for systems that are repairable and have constant hazard functions.

The *reliability*, $R(t)$, of a system is defined as the probability that the system will not fail within time t, given that it was not failed at time 0. The *probability of failure*, $F(t)$ (often called the "unreliability"), of a system is the probability that the system will fail within time t, given that it was not failed at time 0, and is given by

$$F(t) = 1 - R(t). \quad (2\text{-}1)$$

The *failure density function*, $f(t)$, is defined as

$$f(t) = dF(t)/dt. \quad (2\text{-}2)$$

The *hazard function*, $z(t)$, is defined as

$$z(t) = \frac{f(t)}{1 - F(t)} \quad (2\text{-}3)$$

Figure 2.1 shows the hazard function that has been empirically observed for electronic parts and systems that do not employ redundancy. This curve is often referred to as the "bathtub" curve because of its shape.

The hazard function has units of failures per unit time and is sometimes called the failure rate-function. Three phases can be observed in the life of systems that are characterized by Figure 2.1. The first phase is often called the *burn-in period* or *infant mortality period* and is characterized by failures due to marginal components or faulty construction. Phase two is referred to as the *operational period* or *useful life period* and is characterized by random failures of the components. The third phase is called the *wearout period* and is characterized by failures caused by components reaching the end of their useful life.

The hazard function during the operational period is usually approximated as a constant, λ. A constant failure rate implies

$$f(t) = \lambda e^{-\lambda t}, \quad (2\text{-}4)$$

$$F(t) = 1 - e^{-\lambda t}, \quad (2\text{-}5)$$

and

$$R(t) = e^{-\lambda t}. \quad (2\text{-}6)$$

Coverage is a measure of the capability of a system to tolerate the occurrence of a fault and is defined as the conditional probability that the system will recover given that a fault has occurred. The term coverage is also used in an informal sense to describe the classes of faults that a system can tolerate. Hence, coverage is a measure of the capability of a system to detect a fault, tolerate the fault, and recover from the fault.

The *mean-time-to-failure* (MTTF) of a system is defined as the expected value of the time to failure of the system and is given by

$$\text{MTTF} = \int_0^\infty R(t)\, dt. \quad (2\text{-}7)$$

For $R(t) = e^{-\lambda t}$, MTTF $= 1/\lambda$.

The *maintainability*, $M(t)$, of a failed system is defined as the probability that the system will be restored to operation within time t, given that it was in a failed state at time 0. Maintainability is difficult to model and is usually approximated as $1 - e^{-\mu t}$ where μ is the repair rate. *Mean-time-to-repair* (MTTR) is the expected value of system repair time, and equals $1/\mu$ for the exponential model.

Mean-time-between-failures (MTBF) is the expected value of the time between failures for a system with repair. Hence, MTBF is dependent on both failure rate and repair rate and is given by MTBF = MTTF + MTTR for systems with constant rates.

Availability, $A(t)$, is defined to be the probability that a system is operational at time t. $A(t) = R(t)$ for systems without repair. For systems with repair, failures may have occurred and repair accomplished prior to time t. In general, for large t, $A(t)$ will reach a steady-state value, A, which is given below for systems with constant λ and μ. This result will be derived later when Markov modeling is introduced.

$$A = \frac{\mu}{\lambda + \mu} = \frac{\text{MTTF}}{\text{MTTF} + \text{MTTR}} \quad (2\text{-}8)$$

Military Standard 217B AND 217C

The United States Department of Defense publishes reliability model standards MIL-HDBK-217B and 217C. These standards define parameters for computing the failure rate λ for electronic parts. MIL-HDBK-217B specifies the following model for λ.

$$\lambda = \pi_l \pi_q (c_1 \pi_t + c_2 \pi_e) \pi_p \quad (2\text{-}9)$$

where π_l is the learning factor, π_q the quality factor, π_t the temperature acceleration factor, π_e the environmental factor, π_p is the pin multiplier factor, and c_1 and c_2 are complexity factors. Parameters are published for specific devices after qualification testing. Table 2.1 shows examples of λ derived from the above model for several classes of memory devices.

Combinatorial Modeling Techniques

Systems are often classified for reliability modeling purposes as series, parallel, or *m*-out-of-*n*. A *series* configuration implies that proper system function requires all system components to function properly. Figure 2.2 shows the functional decomposition of such a system. The reliability,

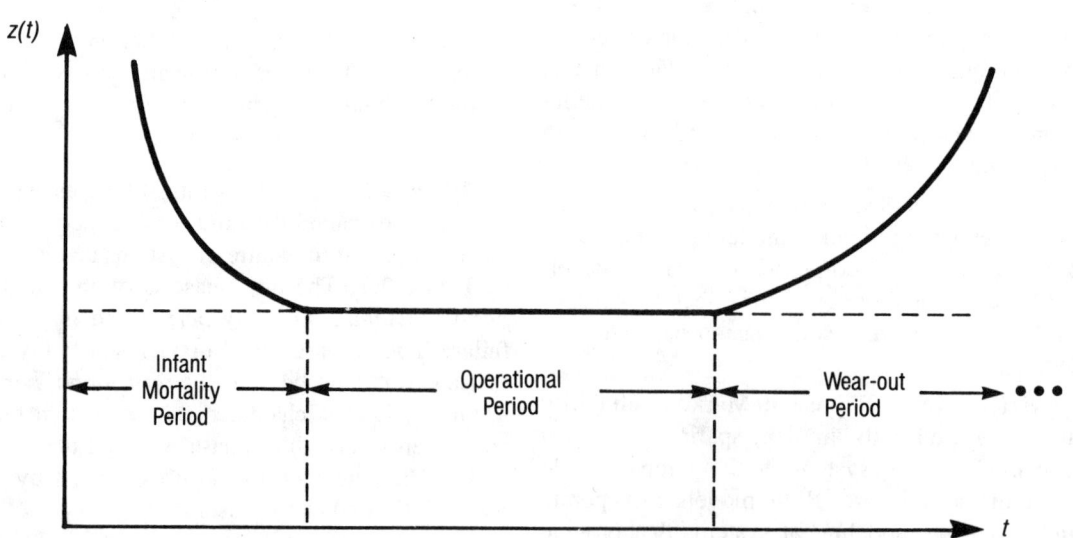

Figure 2.1 Hazard function of typical electronic components, showing the three phases of a component's lifetime.

Table 2.1 Typical values of λ^* ($\pi_q = 16$, $\pi_l = 1$, $\pi_e = 1$, $T_j = 50°C$)

Bits/Chip	Bipolar ROM	Bipolar RAM	MOS ROM	MOS RAM
1K	0.8647	1.5006	1.4331	2.4928
64K	11.7009	20.2001	18.679	32.382

*Failures per million hours

R_s, of a series system is given by the product of the reliabilities of the individual components. Hence,

$$R_s = \prod_i R_i \text{ for } i = 1, \ldots, n \qquad (2\text{-}10)$$

where R_i is the reliability of component i and where failures are independent. If $R = R_i$, then $R_s = R^n$. Systems without redundancy are modeled as series configurations. The model clearly indicates that the reliability of such systems is dominated by the least reliable component.

A *parallel* system configuration implies that proper operation will occur if at least one system component functions properly. Figure 2.3 shows a diagram of such a configuration. The reliability of a parallel system can best be modeled by first finding the probability of failure, F_p, and then using $R_p = 1 - F_p$. Hence,

$$F_p = \prod_i (1 - R_i) \text{ and} \qquad (2\text{-}11)$$

$$R_p = 1 - \prod_i (1 - R_i) \text{ for } i = 1, \ldots, n. \qquad (2\text{-}12)$$

$$R_p = 1 - (1 - R)^n \text{ if } R_i = R. \qquad (2\text{-}13)$$

Systems that employ sparing may be classified as parallel if system failure occurs only after all components have failed and if component failures are independent.

A system can be modeled as an *m*-out-of-*n* configuration when proper operation is achieved if at least m components operate properly. The reliability model of such a system is given by

$$R_{m/n} = \sum_k \binom{n}{k} R^{n-k}(1 - R)^k \qquad (2\text{-}14)$$

for $k = 0, \ldots, m - 1$ and where R is the reliability of each component. This model is useful for systems employing NMR.

Some systems cannot be modeled as simple series, parallel, or *m*-out-of-*n* structures. Combinations of the basic structures can sometimes be used as models. However, other systems require modeling techniques that are beyond the scope of this book.

Markov Modeling Techniques

The application of Markov processes to reliability modeling will now be introduced. A more complete treatment of the subject can be found in [SHO68] and in [TRI82]. The discussion will be limited to discrete-event, continuous-time models with constant hazard functions. Such models can be used for systems with or without repair, with dependent component failures, and with sparing.

A Markov model consists of a set of states and a set of transition probabilities. States are mutually exclusive, and each state represents a distinct combination of good and failed components of a system. Transition probabilities give the probability of moving from one specific state to another. State probabilities can be derived as illustrated in the following examples.

Figure 2.4 shows two Markov models for a simple single-component system. State S_0 corresponds to a working system, while state S_1 corresponds to a failed system. Hence, the probability of being in S_0 at time t is the reliability, R, of the system. The probability of failure, F, of the system is given by the probability of being in S_1.

Figure 2.4(a) corresponds to a system without repair with a constant hazard function λ. This implies that a system remains in the failed state once a failure occurs. The corresponding transition probabilities are given in the following matrix:

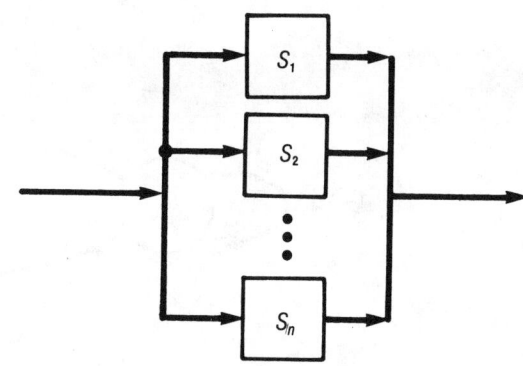

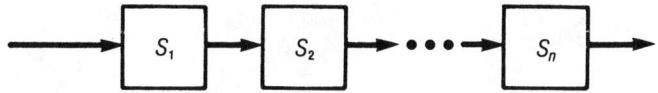

Figure 2.2 A series system of modules $S_1 \ldots S_n$. All must be operable for the system to be operable.

Figure 2.3 A parallel system of modules $S_1 \ldots S_n$. Only one module is needed for system operation.

$$P = \begin{bmatrix} 1 - \lambda \Delta t & \lambda \Delta t \\ 0 & 1 \end{bmatrix} \quad (2\text{-}15)$$

Let P_0 and P_1 be the probabilities of being in states S_0 and S_1, respectively. State probabilities at time $t + \Delta t$ can be given in terms of state probabilities at time t and state transition probabilities by the following matrix equation:

$$[P_0(t+\Delta t), P_1(t+\Delta t)] = [P_0(t), P_1(t)] \times P. \quad (2\text{-}16)$$

The above can be rewritten as follows:

$$P_0(t+\Delta t) = (1 - \lambda \Delta t) P_0(t) \quad (2\text{-}17a)$$

and

$$P_1(t+\Delta t) = \lambda \Delta t P_0(t) + P_1(t) \quad (2\text{-}17b)$$

Algebraic manipulation yields

$$[P_0(t+\Delta t) - P_0(t)]/\Delta t = -\lambda P_0(t) \quad (2\text{-}18a)$$

and

$$[P_1(t+\Delta t) - P_1(t)]/\Delta t = \lambda P_0(t) \quad (2\text{-}18b)$$

A set of simultaneous differential equations follows by taking the limit as Δt approaches 0.

$$dP_0(t)/dt = -\lambda P_0(t) \quad (2\text{-}19a)$$

and

$$dP_1(t)/dt = \lambda P_0(t) \quad (2\text{-}19b)$$

Solving the differential equations results in

$$R(t) = P_0(t) = e^{-\lambda t} \quad (2\text{-}20a)$$

and

$$F(t) = P_1(t) = 1 - e^{-\lambda t} \quad (2\text{-}20b)$$

which are the expected results.

The power of Markov modeling is more clearly demonstrated by the example given in Figure 2.4(b) which models a single component system with repair. Here, the probability, $P_0(t)$, of being in state S_0 is equivalent to system availability, $A(t)$. The corresponding P matrix is given below.

$$P = \begin{bmatrix} 1 - \lambda \Delta t & \lambda \Delta t \\ \mu \Delta t & 1 - \mu \Delta t \end{bmatrix} \quad (2\text{-}21)$$

A derivation similar to the previous one yields the following set of differential equations:

$$dP_0(t)/dt = -\lambda P_0(t) + \mu P_1(t) \quad (2\text{-}22a)$$

and

$$dP_1(t)/dt = \lambda P_0(t) - \mu P_1(t) \quad (2\text{-}22b)$$

Solving the equations produces

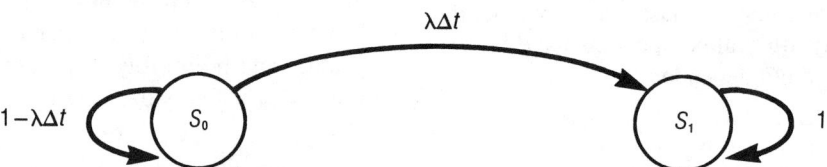

(a) Without repair—state S_1 is never left once entered.

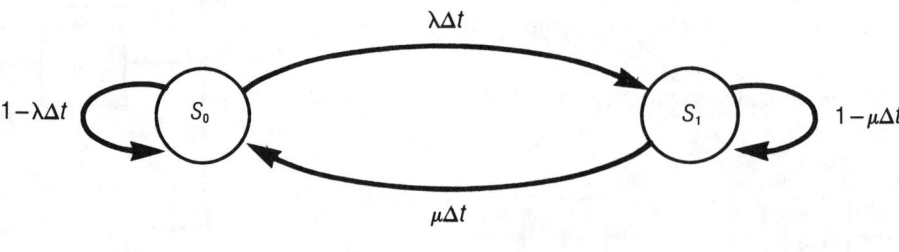

(b) With repair.

Figure 2.4 Markov models for a single-component system. S_0 is the operational state, and S_1 is the failed state of the component.

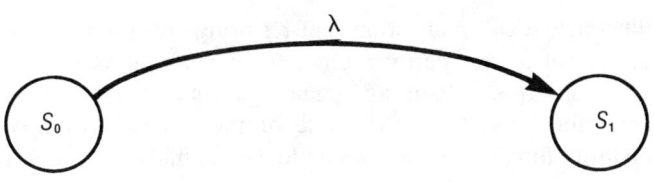

(a) Without repair.

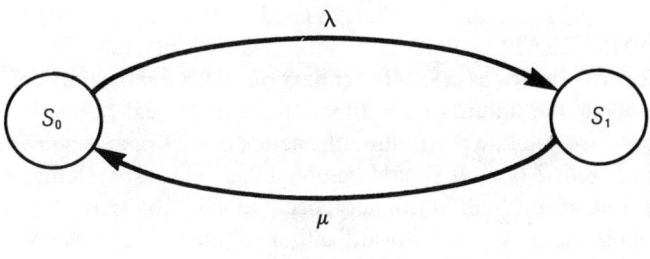

(b) With repair.

Figure 2.5 Simplified forms of the Markov model state diagrams of Figure 2.4.

$$P_0(t) = \frac{\mu}{\lambda + \mu} - \frac{\lambda}{\lambda + \mu} e^{-(\lambda+\mu)t} = A(t) \quad (2\text{-}23a)$$

and

$$P_1(t) = \frac{\lambda}{\lambda + \mu} + \frac{\lambda}{\lambda + \mu} e^{-(\lambda+\mu)t} \quad (2\text{-}23b)$$

The first term of $A(t)$ gives the steady-state availability as discussed earlier in the chapter.

Direct derivation of the differential equations can be obtained from a modified form of the Markov model state diagram. Figure 2.5 shows modified state diagrams corresponding to those given in Figure 2.4. The state transitions given in a state diagram can also be described in matrix form. Transition matrices for the diagrams in Figure 2.5 are the following:

$$T_a = \begin{bmatrix} -\lambda & \lambda \\ 0 & 0 \end{bmatrix} \quad (2\text{-}24)$$

and

$$T_b = \begin{bmatrix} -\lambda & \lambda \\ \mu & -\mu \end{bmatrix} \quad (2\text{-}25)$$

The set of differential equations corresponding to a Markov model with transition matrix T can be written in matrix form as follows:

$$[P_0'(t), P_1'(t)] = [P_0(t), P_1(t)] \times T. \quad (2\text{-}26)$$

Redundancy Techniques

System reliability can be improved by the use of protective redundancy at one or more levels of application in the system. Redundancy techniques can be classified as spatial, informational, or temporal. Spatial techniques involve replication of system hardware and include N-modular techniques, sparing techniques, or hybrid techniques. Informational techniques involve the introduction of redundant data and include numerous coding schemes. Some spatial techniques and some coding techniques are equivalent at low levels of application. Temporal techniques involve repetition of processes in time and include rollback and timeouts. While the above describe primarily hardware approaches, similar redundancy techniques can be applied in software as well. Software approaches will be discussed in Chapter 5.

Redundancy methods may be classified in other ways as well. Static or masking techniques include N-modular redundancy and coding. Dynamic techniques involve the use of sparing or other methods of reconfiguration. Both static and dynamic techniques are employed in hybrid methods. Redundancy may be employed for fault detection only, for fault tolerance only, or for both. Table 2.2 summarizes the classifications of redundancy methods. Each method will now be discussed in more detail.

Table 2.2 Summary of redundancy techniques

Configuration \ Domain	Spatial	Informational	Temporal
Static	NMR Quadding N-Version Programming	Coding Duplication	Timeouts Rollback
Dynamic	Sparing Backup Hybrid	Checkpointing	Restart Recovery Blocks

Replication Methods

N-Modular Redundancy

N-modular redundancy or NMR is sometimes referred to as massive redundancy because of the large amount of extra hardware needed for implementation. Though expensive, NMR has the capability of masking the occurrence of a fault without the need for reconfiguration. Hence fault tolerance is achieved without a time penalty for detection, reconfiguration, and recovery. However, the extra hardware reduces the long-term reliability of the system as will be shown later in this chapter. Furthermore, the masking effect may result in latent faults that cause catastrophic failure should a second fault occur.

An NMR realization of a unit, U, consists of N identical copies of U feeding a restoring organ, V. Figure 2.6(a) illustrates such a realization. The restoring organ is usually a voter, but it may perform other functions such as median selection. If the restoring organ is a voter, the output is determined by a majority vote of the inputs. A simple majority function is usually employed but higher thresholds are sometimes used.

Let T be the threshold of a voter. Then an NMR realization can tolerate the failure of $N - T$ functional units. Note however that the failure of a single voter cannot be tolerated.

Triple modular redundancy (TMR) is the simplest form of NMR. The TMR voter is a 2-out-of-3 majority gate. Figure 2.6(b) illustrates a TMR realization. This realization can tolerate the failure of one functional unit. A realization that can also tolerate the failure of one restoring organ is shown in Figure 2.6(c). It should be noted that, in most systems, a single result will ultimately need to be produced at the interface to the "real world," although much study has gone into the development of redundant sensors and actuators for spacecraft, process controls, and similar applications.

A simple reliability model for a TMR system with ideal voter can be obtained from Equation (2-14) by setting $m = 2$, and $n = 3$, and simplifying. The following is the result:

$$R(3,0) = 3R^2 - 2R^3 \qquad (2\text{-}27a)$$

where R is the reliability of a unit U and where $R(i,j)$ denotes the reliability of a system with i on-line units and j spares.

A TMR system using a single voter with reliability R_v has a reliability model of

$$R^*(3,0) = R_v [3R^2 - 2R^3] . \qquad (2\text{-}27b)$$

The above model can be easily generalized for the NMR case as

$$R(N,0) = R_v \left[\sum_k \binom{N}{k} R^{N-k} (1 - R)^k \right] \qquad (2\text{-}28)$$

where $k = 0, \ldots, T-1$.

The above models are considered pessimistic because there are some cases of failure of two or more units that do not cause system failure. Less pessimistic models of TMR reliability are given in [MAT71].

Redundancy may be applied at the subsystem level. Figure 2.7 shows two simple cascades of TMR subsystems. Each case can be modeled as a series system. Hence, the reliability model for Figure 2.7(a) is given by the product of the individual subsystem reliabilities as follows.

$$\prod_i R_{vi} [3R_{mi}^2 - 2R_{mi}^3], \text{ for } i = 1, \ldots, l \qquad (2\text{-}29)$$

where R_{vi} is the reliability of voter i and R_{mi} is the reliability of a single functional unit in module i.

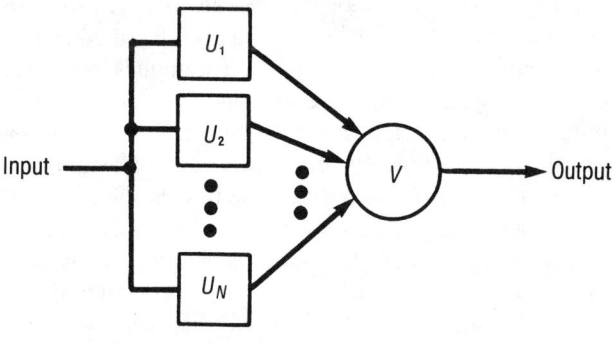

(a) General configuration.

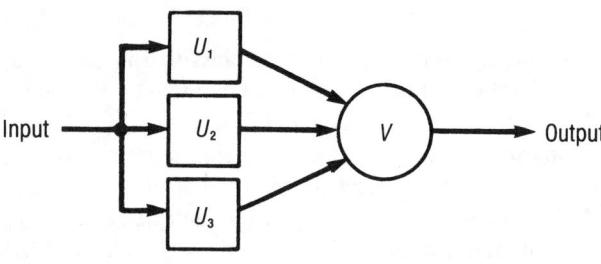

(b) TMR with single voter.

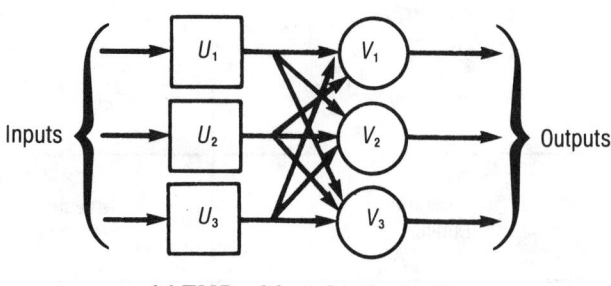

(c) TMR with redundant voter.

Figure 2.6 Simple N-modular redundant configurations.

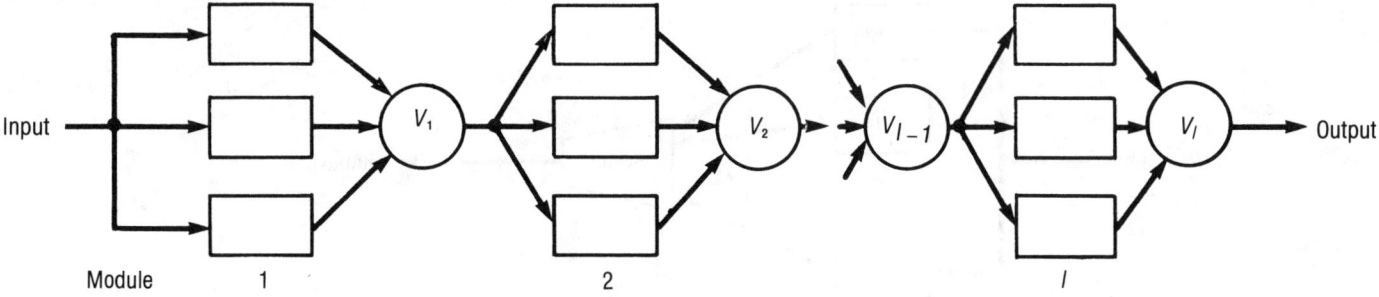

(a) Simplex voters.

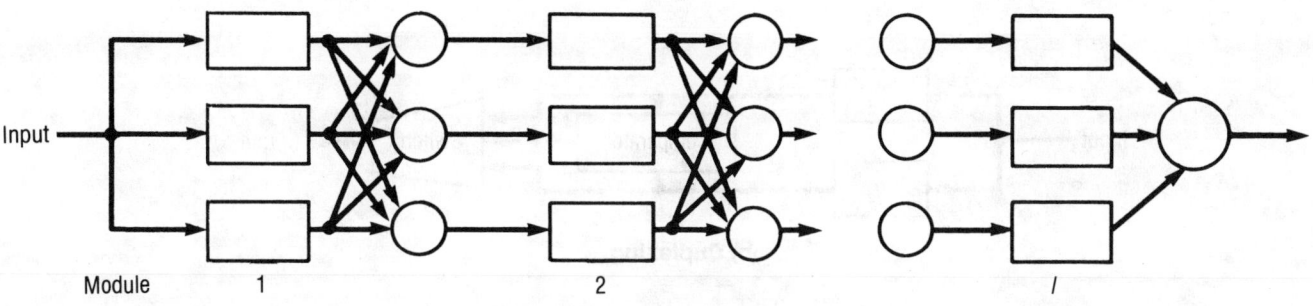

(b) Redundant voters.

Figure 2.7 TMR cascades.

The reliability model of Figure 2.7(b) is obtained by treating each voter/module pair as a series unit within the larger series system. The resulting equation is given below

$$R_{cas} = [3R_{m1}^2 - 2R_{m1}^3] \prod_i \{3(R_{mi}R_{vi-1})^2 - 2(R_{mi}R_{vi-1})^3\}R_{vl}, \quad (2\text{-}30)$$

for $i = 1, \ldots, l$.

Systems with structures more complex than cascades present difficult modeling problems whose solutions will not be discussed here. The reader wanting to pursue this topic is referred to [ABR74] and [SIE82].

The MTTF of a TMR system with ideal voter where $R = e^{-\lambda t}$ is $5/6\lambda$ whereas the MTTF of the corresponding simplex system is $1/\lambda$. Hence, $\text{MTTF}_{\text{TMR}} < \text{MTTF}_{\text{simplex}}$. This results because, as the systems deteriorate, the TMR realization is more likely to experience a failure because of its added complexity than is the less complex simplex system.

Sparing

Sparing is often referred to as stand-by redundancy since the redundant or spare units usually are not operating online. Figure 2.8(a) shows the general organization of a system that employs sparing. The restoring organ for sparing is a switch. However, an error detector is also required to determine when the on-line unit has failed. Spares may be active (powered) or dormant (unpowered). When active spares are employed, fault detection may be accomplished by comparing the output of the on-line unit with the output of one of the spares.

Duplexing is a form of sparing that uses an on-line unit plus an on-line active spare as shown in Figure 2.8(b). Error detection is accomplished by comparison of the two outputs. A pair and a spare system as shown in Figure 2.8(c) is obtained by including an off-line spare with a duplexed system.

A reliability model for a system with one on-line unit and $N-1$ spares can be obtained from Equation (2-13) and is given below (this expression assumes perfect coverage, i.e. ideal operation of error detection and switching circuitry):

$$R(1, N-1) = [1 - (1 - R)^N] R_s \quad (2\text{-}31)$$

where R is the reliability of each unit U and R_s is the reliability of the switch and comparator combined.

Equation (2-31) for a duplex system ($N = 2$) and $R_s = 1$, again for perfect coverage, becomes

$$R(1,1) = 1 - (1 - R)^2 \quad (2\text{-}32a)$$

$$= 2R - R^2. \quad (2\text{-}32b)$$

If $R = e^{-\lambda t}$, MTTF is $3/2\lambda$.

Other reliability models for sparing have been proposed and some of these will now be discussed for the case of duplexing. It should be noted that there are two modes of operation for duplex systems, one with the spare unit active and continuously comparing its output to that of the primary unit, and the other with the spare unit inactive. The two approaches differ in the computation of the "coverage"

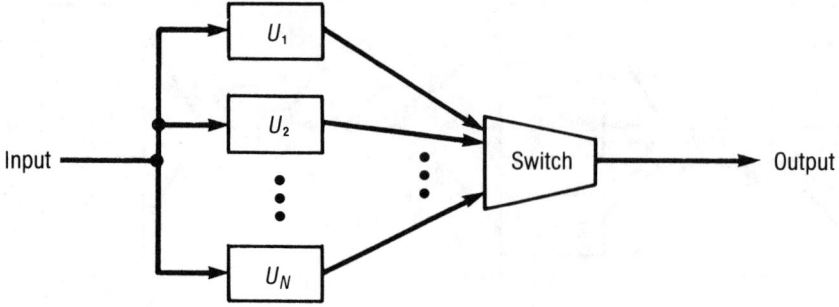

(a) General configuration.

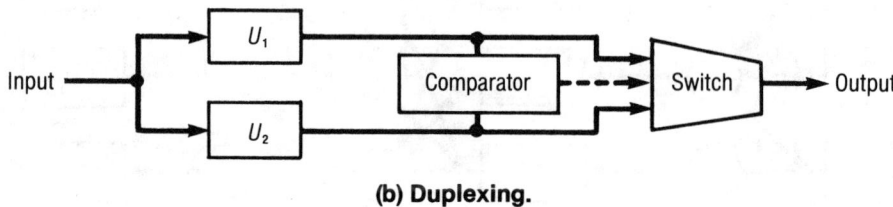

(b) Duplexing.

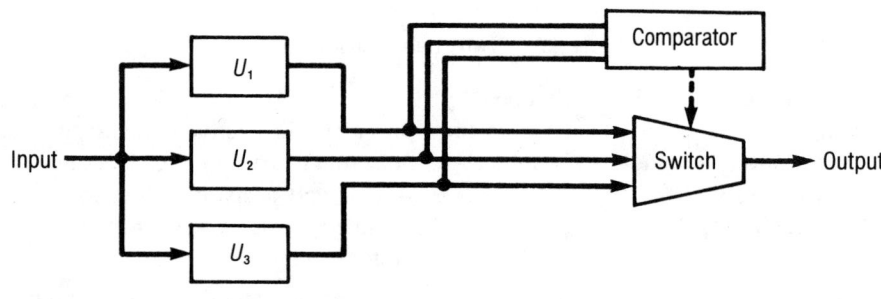

(c) A pair and a spare.

Figure 2.8 Stand-by redundancy configuration.

terms, since they utilize different error-detection mechanisms, but they are otherwise identical for modeling purposes.

Assuming perfect coverage, $R(1,1)$ can be derived by adding the probability of two units not failing to the probability of one unit failing and one unit not failing. The result is given below.

$$R(1,1) = R^2 + 2R(1-R) \qquad (2\text{-}33)$$

Coverage (C) can be introduced into Equation (2-33) to produce the following model.

$$R^c(1,1) = R^2 + 2R(1-R)C \qquad (2\text{-}34)$$

where C is the probability that the error-detection and switching mechanisms operate correctly, given the failure of one of the modules. A generalization of Equation (2-34) can be found in [BOU69].

The stand-by model can also be used to obtain a reliability model for sparing. Let R and F be the reliability and probability of failure, respectively, of the units in a duplex system. The stand-by reliability model, $R_{sb}(t)$, of the system is given by

$$R_{sb}(t) = R(t) + F(t_1) R(t - t_1) . \qquad (2\text{-}35)$$

If $R(t) = e^{-\lambda t}$, then

$$F(t_1) = \int_0^t \lambda e^{-\lambda t_1} \, dt_1$$

and

$$R(t - t_1) = e^{-\lambda(t - t_1)} .$$

Performing the calculus produces

$$R_{sb}(t) = e^{-\lambda t} + (\lambda t)e^{-\lambda t} \qquad (2\text{-}36)$$

and
$$\text{MTTF}_{sb} = 2/\lambda \,. \tag{2-37}$$

Design issues in the application of sparing include the number of spares needed, the switching mechanism, the use of active or inactive spares, the error detection mechanism, and the synchronization of units.

Hybrid Systems

Hybrid redundancy combines features of NMR and sparing by providing an on-line NMR core with a pool of spares. A spare may replace any failed unit in the core. A hybrid configuration with a TMR core and two spares is shown in Figure 2.9.

A combinatorial reliability model for a hybrid system with an NMR core and S spares is given by

$$R(N,S) = R_{vsd} \left[\sum_i \binom{N+S}{i} R^{N+S-i} (1-R)^i \right] \tag{2-38}$$

where R is the reliability of a functional unit, R_{vsd} is the reliability of the voter/switch/detector combination, and $P = \lfloor N/2 \rfloor + S$. If $P_{vsd} = 1$ and $R = e^{-\lambda t}$, then the MTTF of a hybrid with TMR core and two spares is $77/60\lambda$.

Reliability Comparisons

Comparison of reliability models of the various redundancy techniques presented above is useful when evaluating the relative merits of the techniques. Figure 2.10 gives plots of system reliability versus module reliability, R, for several types of redundancy. The plots show that TMR provides the least potential for reliability improvement. Sparing has the best potential for reliability gain followed by hybrid redundancy. Clearly, the gains that sparing and hybrid redundancy produce are highly dependent on the number of spares.

However, the models plotted in Figure 2.10 assume that the restoring organs (voters, switches, comparators, etc.) are ideal. Voters are simpler devices to implement than are switches. Hence, voters are inherently more reliable and less expensive than switches. TMR is a more viable alternative when this is considered. TMR also masks the effect of a fault without the need for detection or reconfiguration. Therefore, no time penalty for reconfiguration is imposed. Hybrid redundancy also masks faults.

Figure 2.11 shows plots of reliability versus time for a simplex system and a TMR system. Reliability of the simplex system is assumed to be $R = e^{-\lambda t}$. It can be seen that for $t > 0.693/\lambda$, $R(3,0) < R$. Hence, TMR is indicated for short-term missions where fault masking is necessary. Sparing redundancy is useful for long-term missions where time to reconfigure is available. Hybrid redundancy is useful when both masking and reconfiguration are desired.

The parallel and standby reliability models for a duplex system are compared in Figure 2.12.

All of the reliability comparisons in Figures 2.10 and 2.11 assumed ideal coverage, i.e. error-free operation of voting, switching, and disagreement detection (VSD) circuitry. However, it should be realized that as the complexity of the modules being duplicated increases, a similar increase in complexity of the VSD circuitry can be expected. In [SIE82], the effects of VSD unreliability on the reliability of an HMR system were examined. The system reliability can be expressed as:

$$R_{HMR} = R^{n\alpha} \{1 - nR(1-R)^{n-1} - (1-R)^n\}$$

where R is the reliability of the nonredundant module, n is the total number of modules, and α is a factor relating the complexity of one "slice" of the VSD circuitry (there are n slices) to that of the nonredundant module. Figure 2.13 shows the effect of the $R^{n\alpha}$ term on the overall reliability of the system for a complexity factor of 0.1 for various simplex

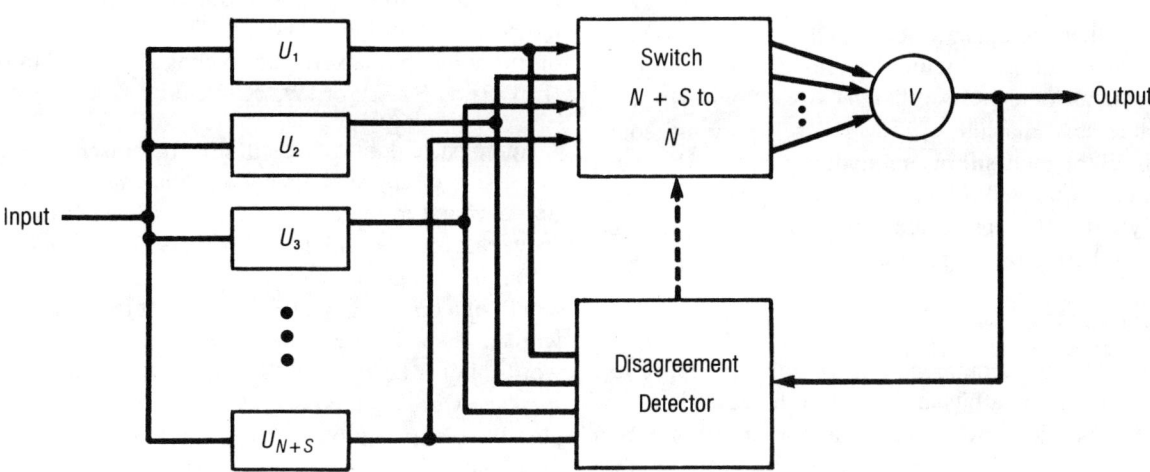

Figure 2.9 Hybrid modular redundancy configuration.

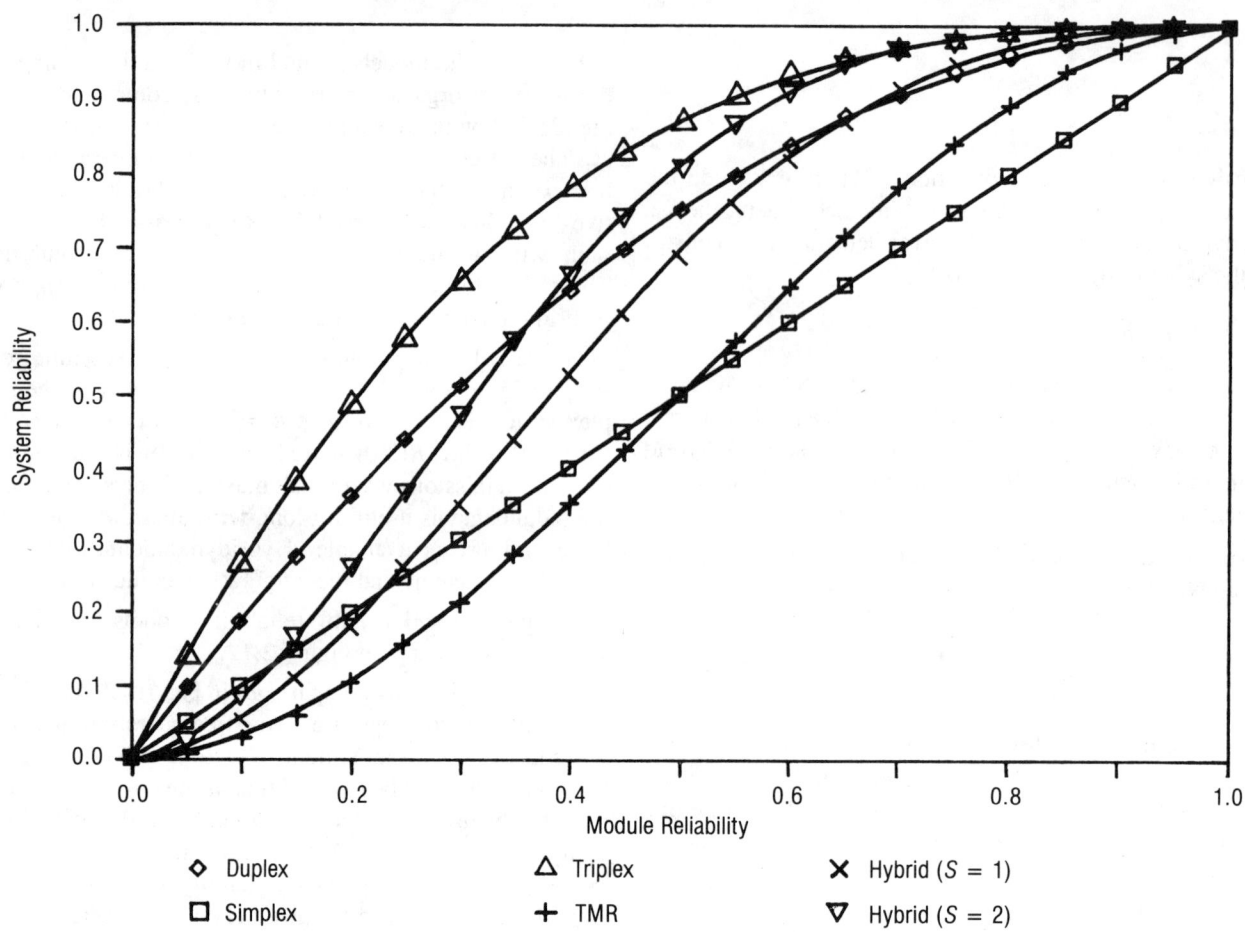

Figure 2.10 (a) Reliability comparisons. (Full range, ideal coverage)

module reliabilities. Note that the overall reliability *decreases* when the degree of redundancy is increased above a certain amount. Consequently, while the assumption of ideal coverage simplifies the development of first-order approximations to reliability models, the actual coverage effects must be considered in high-reliability applications.

Other Redundancy Schemes

Several other redundancy schemes have been proposed over the years. These include quadded logic [TRY62, JEN63], radial logic [KLA69], interwoven logic [PIE65], coded finite state machines [ARM61], self-purging redundancy [LOS76], and sift-out redundancy [DES78]. These methods have received little acceptance in practice. Therefore, they will not be presented here. The reader interested in pursuing these topics is referred to [SIE82].

Coding Methods

Perhaps the most common form of redundancy in use today is coding. Extra bits are added to the basic information code to provide error detection and/or error correction capabilities. In a broader sense, coding can be used for other purposes such as encryption, compaction, or information transfer. However, the discussions here will be limited to error-detection and error-correction codes.

Coding is widely used because of its effectiveness in providing error detection and/or correction, its efficiency in terms of redundant bits per "code word," and its relative ease of implementation. A number of coding techniques have been developed in theory, and many have been applied in practice. Some of the more commonly used coding methods will be defined below. The reader wanting broader or more in-depth coverage of coding is referred to [LIN70], [LIN83], [PET72], or [WAK78].

Some basic definitions will now be presented prior to the discussion of any specific codes. A *message* is the information encoded in the code. A code is *binary* if messages are sequences of 0's and 1's. *Block* codes have messages divided into fixed-length segments called blocks. Let k be the length of a binary message word and M be the set of all such words. Then there can be as many as 2^k unique message words. Let n be the length of a binary n-tuple into which message words can be encoded, and let U be the set of all possible binary n-tuples. There are 2^n elements in U. However, only 2^k of the elements in U correspond to message words. Let C be the set of such elements of U. C is called

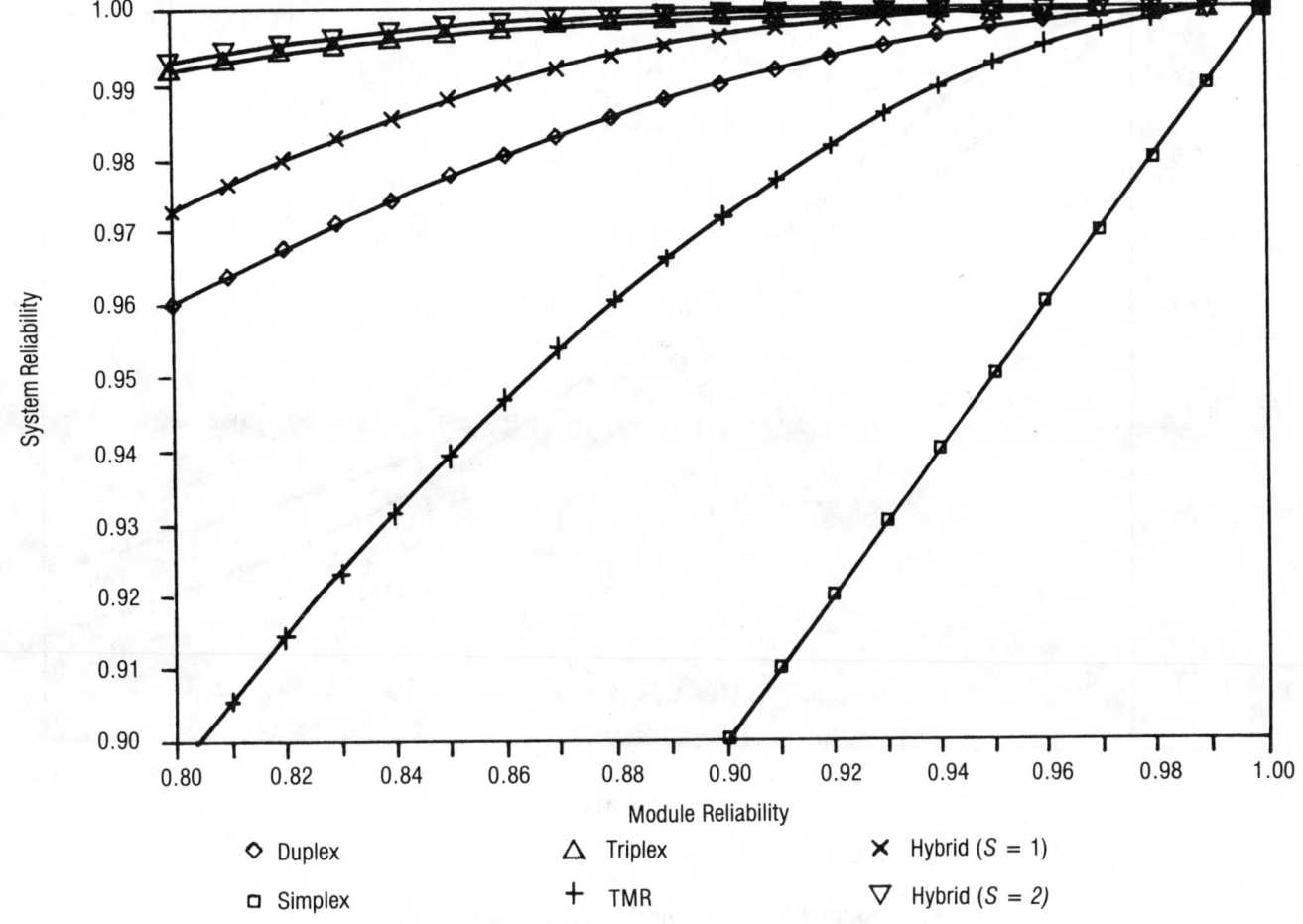

Figure 2.10 (b) Reliability comparisons. (Limited range, ideal coverage)

the *codespace*, and the elements of C are called *code words*. Elements of $U-C$ are non-code words. Let X be a code word, and let Y be an erroneous representation of X caused by a fault. The error can be detected if Y is a non-code word but is undetectable if Y is itself a code word. These definitions and concepts are illustrated in Figure 2.14. The error-detection and error-correction properties of codes will be discussed in general and for specific cases in the following paragraphs.

Let X and Y be binary *n*-tuples. The *Hamming weight* of X, $w(X)$, is defined as the number of non-zero components of X. For example, if $X = 1010$, then $w(1010) = 2$. The *Hamming distance* between X and Y, $d(X,Y)$ is defined as the number of components in which X and Y differ. In general, $d(X,Y) = w(X-Y)$, where $(X-Y)$ is computed by performing modulo-2 subtraction in each bit position of X and Y. For example, if $X = 1010$ and $Y = 1101$, then $d(1010,1101) = w(0111) = 3$. The *minimum distance*, d_{min}, of a code C is defined as the minimum of the Hamming distances between all possible pairs of code words.

A code is called a *separable* code if the original (i.e. unencoded) data can be directly extracted from a code word without performing a transformation. Separable codes are needed when information must be extracted quickly. A code is called *systematic* if the encoding and decoding processes are implemented by applying simple arithmetic transformations to the words being manipulated.

The next section covers several error detection codes including parity, *m*-out-of-*n*, Berger, checksum, and arithmetic. A later section provides an introduction to linear block, i.e., parity-check, error-detection and error-correction codes.

Error-Detection Codes

The error-detection capability of a code is related to the code's minimum distance. A code C with minimum distance d_{min} can detect up to p errors if and only if $p + 1 <= d_{min}$. For single error detection ($p = 1$), code words must be at least distance two apart, otherwise an error in a single bit in one code word could produce another code word as illustrated in Figure 2.15.

Simple Parity Codes

Simple parity codes have been in common use in computer systems for many years. Applications include encoding of data in memory, on buses, and on communications channels. The general format of a simple parity code is shown in Figure 2.16. Odd or even codes can be defined.

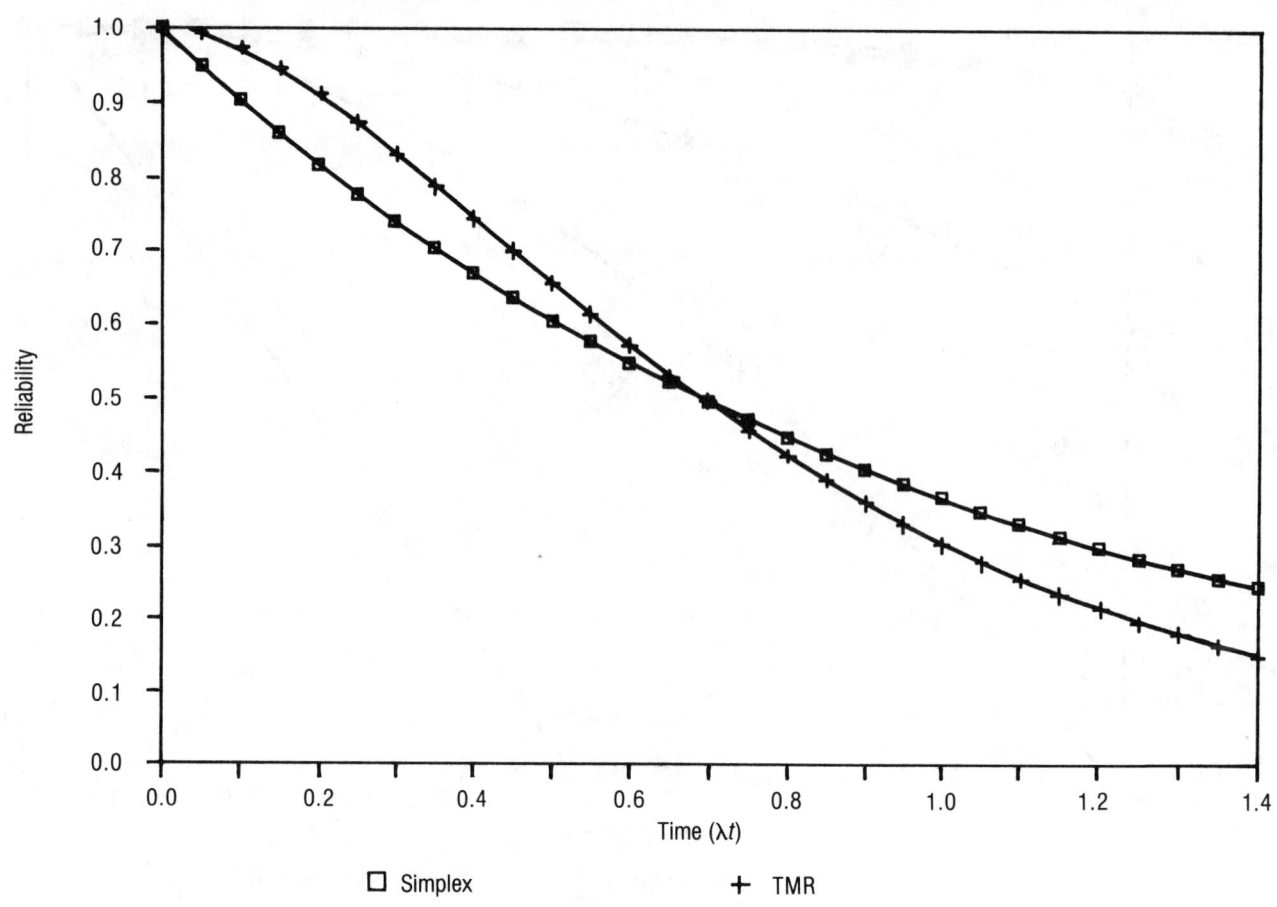

Figure 2.11 Reliability vs. time. (Ideal voter)

Table 2.3

Message Vector	Odd-Parity Code	Even-Parity Code	Berger Code
0 0 0 0	0 0 0 0 1	0 0 0 0 0	0 0 0 0 1 1 1
0 0 0 1	0 0 0 1 0	0 0 0 1 1	0 0 0 1 1 1 0
0 0 1 0	0 0 1 0 0	0 0 1 0 1	0 0 1 0 1 1 0
0 0 1 1	0 0 1 1 1	0 0 1 1 0	0 0 1 1 1 0 1
0 1 0 0	0 1 0 0 0	0 1 0 0 1	0 1 0 0 1 1 0
0 1 0 1	0 1 0 1 1	0 1 0 1 0	0 1 0 1 1 0 1
0 1 1 0	0 1 1 0 1	0 1 1 0 0	0 1 1 0 1 0 1
0 1 1 1	0 1 1 1 0	0 1 1 1 1	0 1 1 1 1 0 0
1 0 0 0	1 0 0 0 0	1 0 0 0 1	1 0 0 0 1 1 0
1 0 0 1	1 0 0 1 1	1 0 0 1 0	1 0 0 1 1 0 1
1 0 1 0	1 0 1 0 1	1 0 1 0 0	1 0 1 0 1 0 1
1 0 1 1	1 0 1 1 0	1 0 1 1 1	1 0 1 1 1 0 0
1 1 0 0	1 1 0 0 1	1 1 0 0 0	1 1 0 0 1 0 1
1 1 0 1	1 1 0 1 0	1 1 0 1 1	1 1 0 1 1 0 0
1 1 1 0	1 1 1 0 0	1 1 1 0 1	1 1 1 0 1 0 0
1 1 1 1	1 1 1 1 1	1 1 1 1 0	1 1 1 1 0 1 1

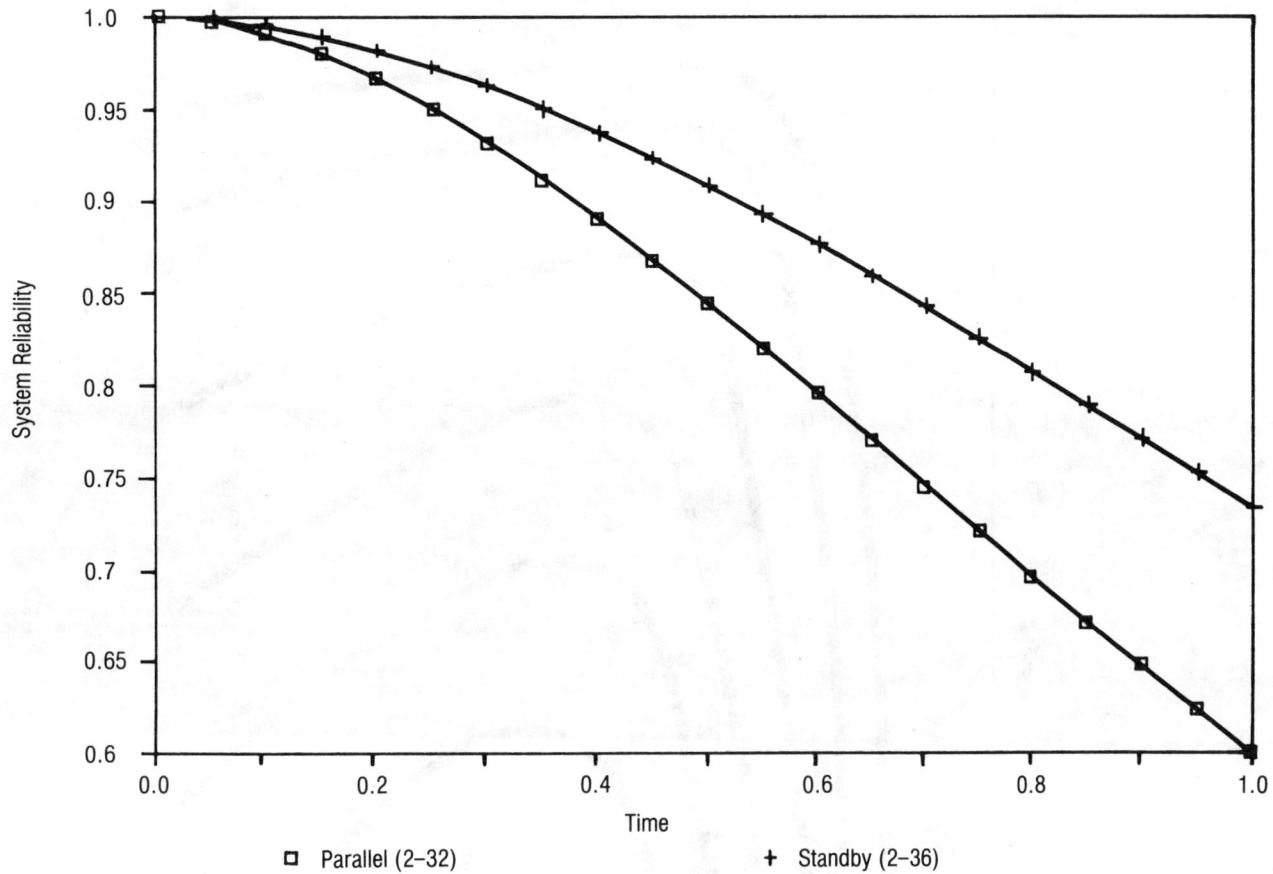

Figure 2.12 Parallel vs. standby models. (Perfect coverage)

Encoding of a simple parity code involves the selection of the appropriate parity bit value for a given set of data bits. The parity bit is selected so that the total number of 1's in the codeword is odd (even) for an odd-parity (even-parity) code. Parity codes are illustrated in Table 2.3.

Decoding of simple parity codes involve checking for the appropriate parity of a received word. Simple parity codes have $d_{min} = 2$. Hence, they are single-error detection codes. Moreover, all errors involving an odd number of bits can be detected because such errors will produce an incorrect parity. Note, however, that errors involving an even number of bits usually cannot be detected. An all-0's error cannot be detected using even parity but it can be detected using odd parity. Also, an all-1's error can be detected using odd parity if the word length is even but cannot be detected using even parity. Hence, odd parity is often preferred over even parity for these reasons.

Circuits for encoding or error detection can easily be implemented using trees of EXCLUSIVE-OR gates, called *parity trees*. Figure 2.17 shows such circuits for the odd-parity code from Table 2.3.

Error-detection coverage of parity codes can be increased by using multiple parity bits defined over distinct subsets of the data bits, each of which is referred to as a parity group. Moreover, multiple parity bits improve the *diagnostic reso-lution* of the error detection. That is the location of the error can be more precisely identified by taking the intersection of the different parity groups detecting the error. Byte-parity, interlaced parity, bit-slice parity, and chip parity are examples of such implementations and are illustrated in Figure 2.18.

A comparison of the fault coverage of each of the implementations of Figure 2.18 shows that the different organizations are capable of detecting different types of multiple faults. For example, the byte-parity scheme of Figure 2.18(a) can detect a single fault within either or both of the two separate data bytes. The interlaced scheme of Figure 2.18(b), in addition to being able to detect simultaneous single faults within each of the three parity groups, can detect any combination of three adjacent errors, since each bit would be in a separate group. The bit-slice parity scheme of Figure 2.18(c) detects an entire 4-bit slice as faulty, since each bit of a given slice is within a separate parity group. Finally, the chip parity scheme of Figure 2.18(d) detects simultaneous single faults within each of the 4-bit-wide chips, as well as identifying the faulty chip, since each chip forms its own parity group.

Consequently, the selection of a particular parity scheme depends on the desired degree of diagnostic resolution, as well as the desired multiple fault coverage.

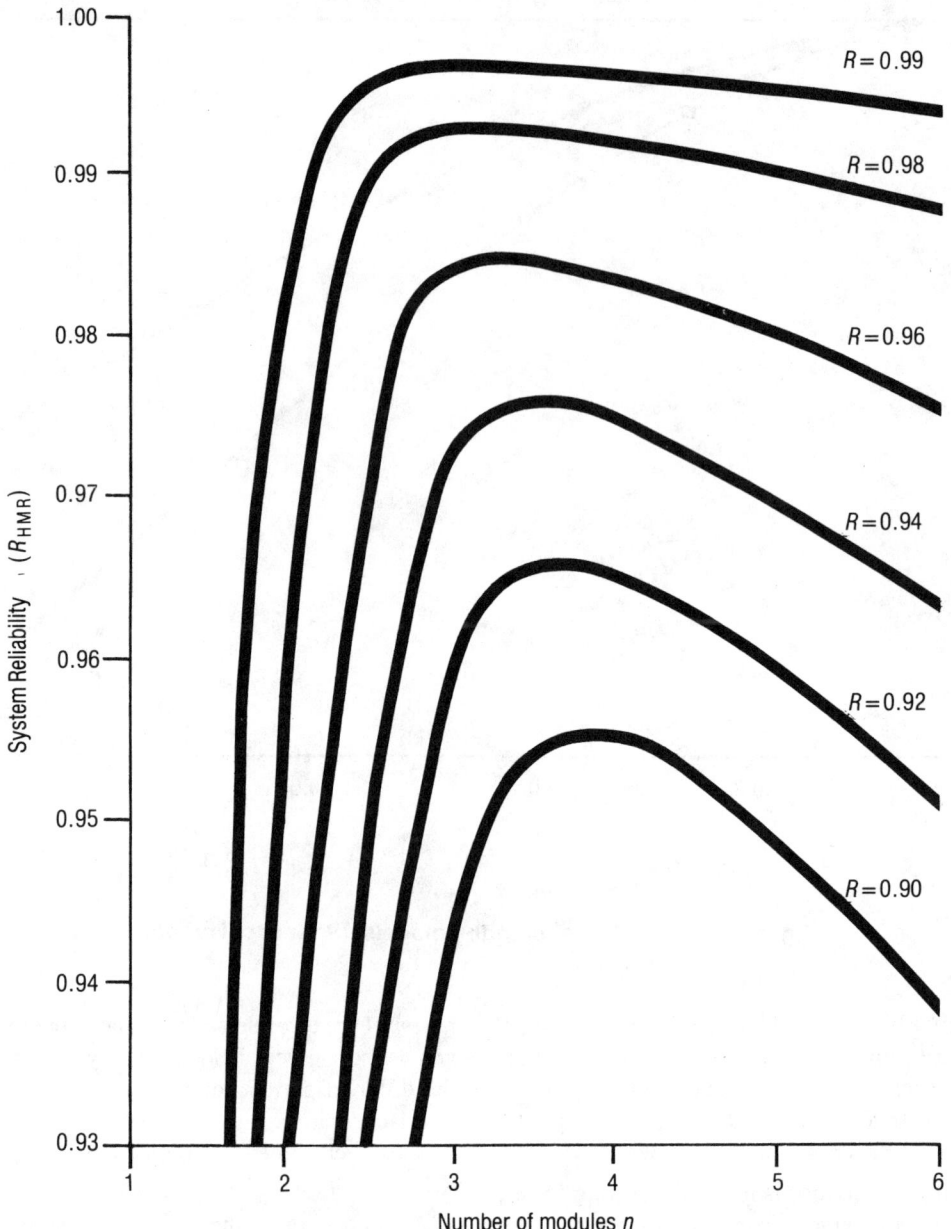

Figure 2.13 Effect of imperfect coverage in voting, switching, and disagreement detection circuits for an HMR system of *n* modules, each of reliability *R*. Complexity factor $\alpha = 0.1$.

M-Out-Of-N Codes

An *m*-out-of-*n* (*m/n*) code has block length *n* with each code word containing exactly *m* 1's. Hence, there are $\binom{n}{m}$ code words for given values of *m* and *n*. The maximum number of code words for a given *n* is obtained when $m = \lfloor n/2 \rfloor$. Table 2.4 illustrates several *m*-out-of-*n* codes.

An *m*-out-of-*n* code can be used for detection of any multiple unidirectional error. Serial error detection can be simply accomplished with a counter. However, parallel error detection requires a complex combinational circuit. Clearly, *m*-out-of-*n* codes are nonsystematic which makes the encoding and decoding processes for numeric data complex. Hence, *m*-out-of-*n* codes are more often used to encode non-numeric data such as control signals and control fields of microprogram instructions. Also, they are useful in the design of self-checking circuits.

Berger Codes

Berger codes are separable codes that can be used to detect multiple unidirectional errors, as might be expected within parallel buses where bus drivers or other common circuits fail, causing all lines to take on either a high or low value. Codewords contain *k* data bits and $\lceil \log_2 (k+1) \rceil$ check bits. The check bits are the bit-wise complement of the

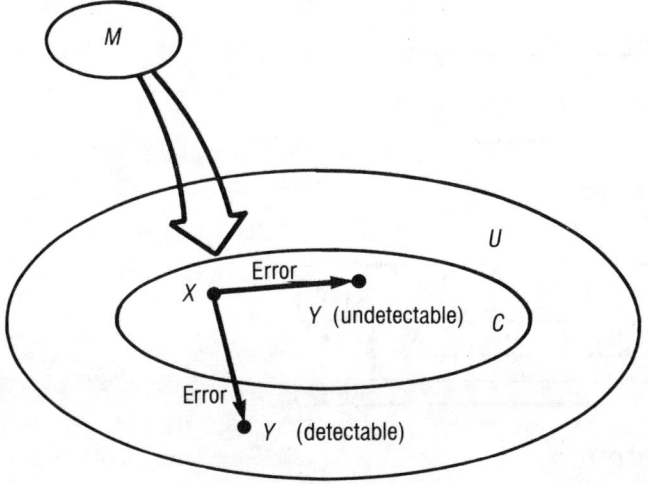

Figure 2.14 Codespace.

binary representation of the number of 1's in the data bits. An example of a Berger code is given in Table 2.3. Berger codes offer efficient redundancy and easy encoding, decoding, and error detection.

Checksums

Checksum coding is accomplished by concatenating an extra string of bits, the checksum, to a block of data words. The checksum is the arithmetic sum, mod x, of the s words in the data block. The checksum computation is illustrated in Figure 2.19. Checksumming is simple and inexpensive to implement. However, it is best suited for block data, has a long error latency, and has low diagnostic resolution. Hence, the technique is most often used in applications such as sequential storage devices, block-transfer peripherals, read-only memory, microstore, data structures, and program code.

Let n be the data word length in bits, and let s be the data-block length in words. A single precision checksum has length n and is computed with mod 2^n addition. Error-detection coverage is a function of the block size and the columns in error. Coverage is highest for the least significant bit.

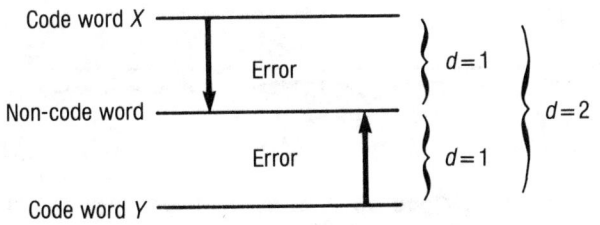

Figure 2.15 Single Error Detection.

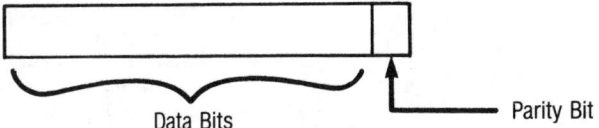

Figure 2.16 Simple parity code format.

An extended checksum can be used to provide the same coverage for all bit positions that the single-precision checksum provides for the least significant bit. This is accomplished by increasing the length of the checksum by A, $s < 2^A$, bits and by using mod 2^{n+A} arithmetic. The reader wishing to learn more about checksumming is referred to [SIE82] and [JAC75].

Arithmetic Codes

The codes discussed above are useful for error detection in data storage and data transmission applications, but the codes are not preserved by arithmetic operations. On the other hand, arithmetic codes are preserved by arithmetic operations. That is $A(x*y) = A(x)*A(y)$ where $*$ is any arithmetic operation and $A(x)$ is the code of x. Error-detection and/or error-correction arithmetic codes are available.

For example, an *AN* code is a nonseparable arithmetic code. A datum X is encoded by multiplication by a *check base A* to form the codeword. An *AN* code has error detection capability if and only if A is not a power of two. A *residue code* is an example of a separable arithmetic code. A

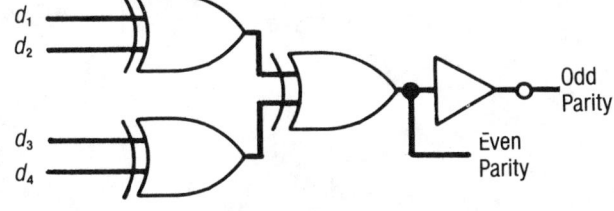

(a) Parity bit generator.

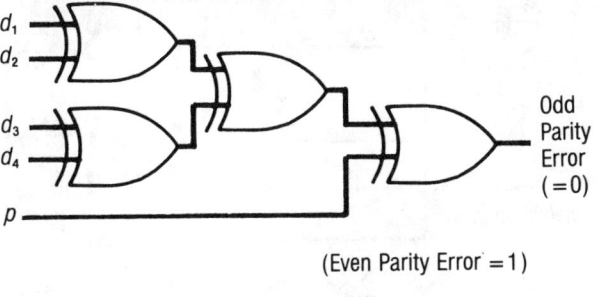

(b) Parity checker.

Figure 2.17 Parity trees for odd-parity code.

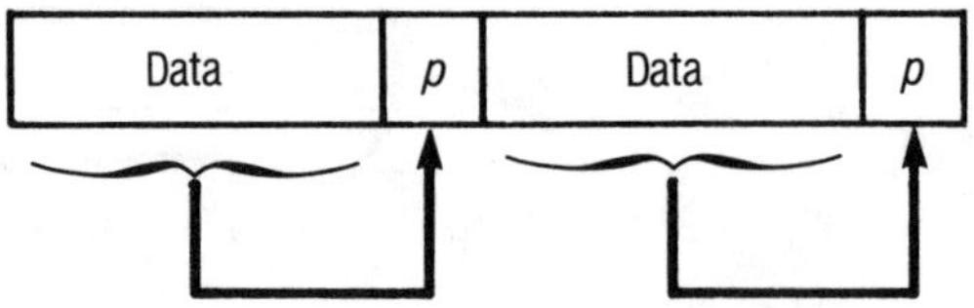

(a) Byte parity.

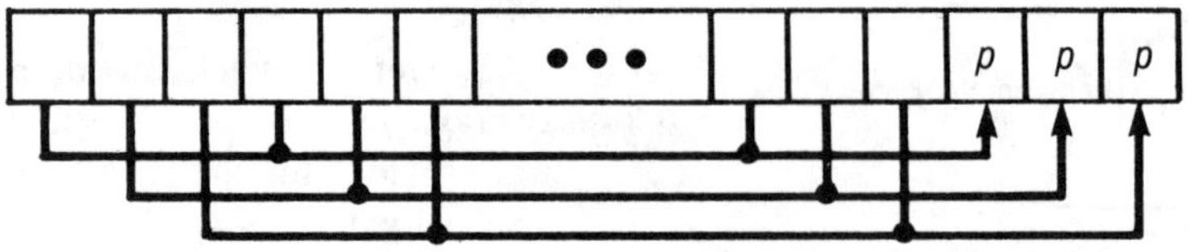

(b) Interlaced parity.

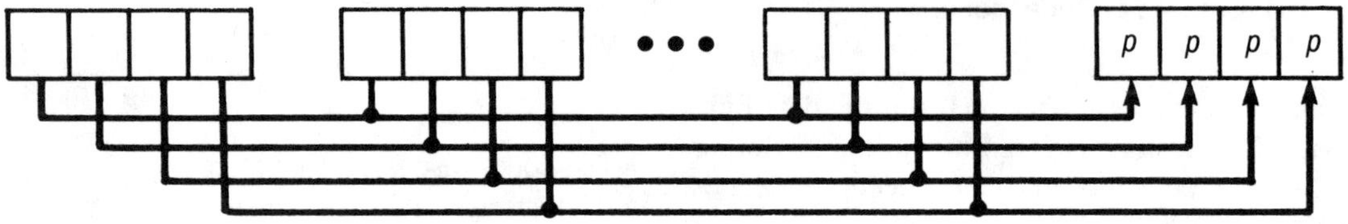

(c) Bit-slice parity.

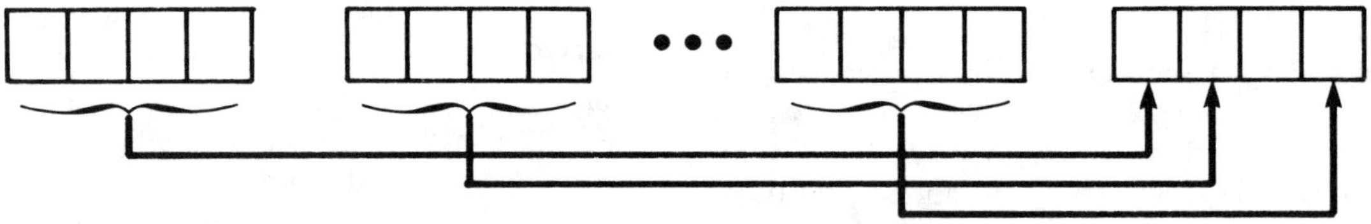

(d) Chip parity.

Figure 2.18 Multiple parity schemes.

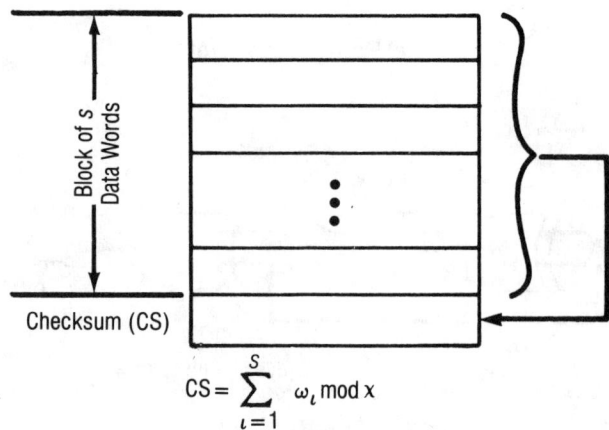

$$CS = \sum_{\iota=1}^{S} \omega_\iota \bmod x$$

Figure 2.19 Checksum coding.

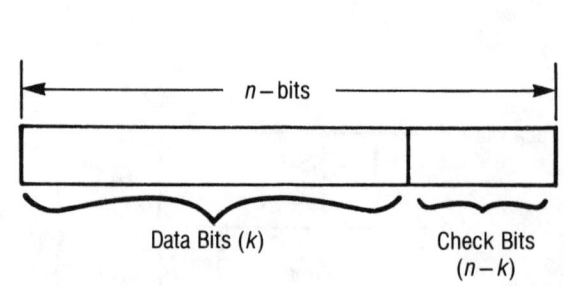

Figure 2.20 Code word format of a systematic (n,k) parity-check code.

codeword for *X* is found by concatenating *X* with (X mod A) where A again is not a power of two.

The reader wanting more information on arithmetic codes is referred to [WAK78] and [RAO74].

Parity-Check Codes

A *parity-check or linear block code* is a subspace of the vector space of binary *n*-tuples. Parity-check codes are often referred to as (n,k) codes where *n* is the block length of the code and *k* is the number of bits in a message word. A parity-check code is *systematic* if a code word has the form shown in Figure 2.20.

A systematic (n,k) parity-check code can be described by a $k \times n$ *generator matrix*, G, of the following form.

$$G = \begin{bmatrix} 1 & 0 & 0 & 0 & \ldots & 0 & p_{11} & p_{12} & \cdots & p_{1,n-k} \\ 0 & 1 & 0 & 0 & \ldots & 0 & p_{21} & p_{22} & \cdots & p_{2,n-k} \\ 0 & 0 & 1 & 0 & \ldots & 0 & p_{31} & p_{32} & \cdots & p_{3,n-k} \\ \vdots & & & & & & & & & \vdots \\ 0 & 0 & 0 & 0 & \ldots & 1 & p_{k1} & p_{k2} & \cdots & p_{k,n-k} \end{bmatrix} \quad (2\text{-}39a)$$

where $p_{ij} = 0$ or 1.

The following is a generator matrix for a (7,4) code:

$$G = \begin{bmatrix} 1 & 0 & 0 & 0 & 1 & 1 & 0 \\ 0 & 1 & 0 & 0 & 0 & 1 & 1 \\ 0 & 0 & 1 & 0 & 1 & 1 & 1 \\ 0 & 0 & 0 & 1 & 1 & 0 & 1 \end{bmatrix}. \quad (2\text{-}39b)$$

The code word *c* corresponding to a message block *m* can be obtained from G as follows.

$$c = mG \quad (2\text{-}40)$$

Table 2.5 shows the code words generated by the code defined by (2-39b).

A parity check code with generator matrix given by (2-39) has the following *parity-check matrix*, H.

$$H = \begin{bmatrix} p_{11} & p_{21} & \cdots & p_{k1} & 1 & 0 & 0 & \ldots & 0 \\ p_{12} & p_{22} & \cdots & p_{k2} & 0 & 1 & 0 & \ldots & 0 \\ p_{13} & p_{23} & \cdots & p_{k3} & 0 & 0 & 1 & \ldots & 0 \\ \vdots & \vdots & & \vdots & & & & & \vdots \\ p_{1,n-k} & p_{2,n-k} & \cdots & p_{k,n-k} & 0 & 0 & 0 & \ldots & 1 \end{bmatrix} \quad (2\text{-}41a)$$

The H matrix that follows from (2-39b) is the following:

$$H = \begin{bmatrix} 0 & 1 & 1 & 1 & 1 & 0 & 0 \\ 1 & 1 & 1 & 0 & 0 & 1 & 0 \\ 1 & 0 & 1 & 1 & 0 & 0 & 1 \end{bmatrix}. \quad (2\text{-}41b)$$

An *n*-tuple *c* is a code word generated by G if and only if

$$Hc^T = 0 \quad (2\text{-}42)$$

Let *r* be a received word corresponding to a code word *c* corrupted by an error pattern *e*. Then,

$$r = c + e \quad (2\text{-}43)$$

The *syndrome s* corresponding to *r* is given by

$$\begin{aligned} s &= Hr^T \\ &= H(c + e)^T \\ &= Hc^T + He^T \\ &= 0 + He^T \end{aligned} \quad (2\text{-}44a)$$

and

$$= He^T \quad (2\text{-}44b)$$

Syndromes corresponding to Equation (2-41b) are given in Table 2.6.

The minimum distance, $d_{\min}$, of a parity-check code is equal to the minimum weight of its nonzero code words. Let H be the parity-check matrix of a parity-check code. The code has minimum weight *d* if no $d-1$ or fewer columns of H add to 0. Moreover, the minimum weight of the code is equal to the smallest number of columns of H that sum to 0.

A parity-check code can correct an error pattern of up to *t* errors and detect an additional *p* errors if and only if

$$2t + p + 1 <= d_{\min} \quad (2\text{-}45)$$

Columns 1, 6, and 7 of (2-41b) add to 0. Hence, the corresponding code has $d_{\min} = 3$ which implies single-error correction.

Decoding of a parity-check code can be accomplished for a received word, *r*, as follows:

1. Compute the syndrome of *r* by Equation (2-44a).
2. Decode the syndrome to identify the error pattern *e*.
3. If *e* is a correctable error, compute $c = r + e$.

Parity trees can be used to encode a message word and to compute the syndrome from a received word. Circuits corresponding to Equations (2-39b) and (2-41b) are given in Figures 2.21(a) and (b), respectively. The corresponding syndrome decoder and error-correction circuit is shown in Figure 2.21(c) and (d), respectively.

Hamming Codes

Hamming [HAM50] introduced the first parity-check codes for error correction in 1950. Hamming codes and their variations are widely used data storage and data communications systems.

Table 2.4 m-Out-of-n code examples

2-out-of-4	3-out-of-5	3-out-of-6	4-out-of-6
0 0 1 1	0 0 1 1 1	0 0 0 1 1 1	0 0 1 1 1 1
0 1 1 0	0 1 0 1 1	0 0 1 0 1 1	0 1 0 1 1 1
1 0 1 0	1 0 0 1 1	0 1 0 0 1 1	1 0 0 1 1 1
0 1 0 1	0 1 1 1 0	1 0 0 0 1 1	0 1 1 0 1 1
1 0 0 1	1 0 1 1 0	0 0 1 1 1 0	1 0 1 0 1 1
1 1 0 0	1 1 0 1 0	0 1 0 1 1 0	1 1 0 0 1 1
	0 1 1 0 1	1 0 0 1 1 0	0 1 1 1 1 0
	1 0 1 0 1	0 1 1 0 1 0	1 0 1 1 1 0
	1 1 0 0 1	1 0 1 0 1 0	1 1 0 1 1 0
	1 1 1 0 0	1 1 0 0 1 0	1 1 1 0 1 0
		0 0 1 1 0 1	0 1 1 1 0 1
		0 1 0 1 0 1	1 0 1 1 0 1
		1 0 0 1 0 1	1 1 0 1 0 1
		0 1 1 0 0 1	1 1 1 0 0 1
		1 0 1 0 0 1	1 1 1 1 0 0
		1 1 0 0 0 1	
		0 1 1 1 0 0	
		1 0 1 1 0 0	
		1 1 0 1 0 0	
		1 1 1 0 0 0	

Table 2.5 (7,4) Parity-check code

Message Vector	Code Words
0 0 0 0	0 0 0 0 0 0 0
0 0 0 1	0 0 0 1 1 0 1
0 0 1 0	0 0 1 0 1 1 1
0 0 1 1	0 0 1 1 0 1 0
0 1 0 0	0 1 0 0 0 1 1
0 1 0 1	0 1 0 1 1 1 0
0 1 1 0	0 1 1 0 1 0 0
0 1 1 1	0 1 1 1 0 0 1
1 0 0 0	1 0 0 0 1 1 0
1 0 0 1	1 0 0 1 0 1 1
1 0 1 0	1 0 1 0 0 0 1
1 0 1 1	1 0 1 1 1 0 0
1 1 0 0	1 1 0 0 1 0 1
1 1 0 1	1 1 0 1 0 0 0
1 1 1 0	1 1 1 0 0 1 0
1 1 1 1	1 1 1 1 1 1 1

A Hamming code with the following properties exists for any positive integer $m >= 3$.

Code length: $n = 2^m - 1$
Number of data bits: $k = 2^m - m - 1$
Number of check bits: $n - k = m$
Error-correction capability: $d_{\min} = 3$ ($t = 1$)

The parity-check matrix **H** of such a code consists of all nonzero m-tuples as its columns. **H** can be arranged in the following systematic form.

$$\mathbf{H} = \mathbf{P}|\mathbf{I}_m \qquad (2\text{-}46)$$

where $\mathbf{I}_m$ is an $m \times m$ identity matrix and **P** consists of $2^m - m - 1$ columns of the m-tuples with weights $>= 2$. The generator matrix corresponding to (2-46) is the following.

$$\mathbf{G} = \mathbf{I}_{2^m - m - 1}|\mathbf{P}^T \qquad (2\text{-}47)$$

Note that the code defined by Equations (2-39b) and (2-41b) is a Hamming code. Another Hamming code is illustrated in Figure 2.22(a). The code in Figure 2.22(b) is a modified Hamming code obtained from Equation (2-41b) by adding a fourth check bit and an all 1's row. The modified code has $d_{\min} = 4$, and therefore is a Single Error Correction

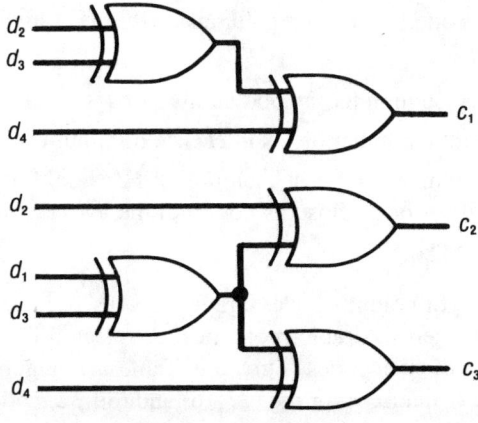

(a) Check-bit generator.

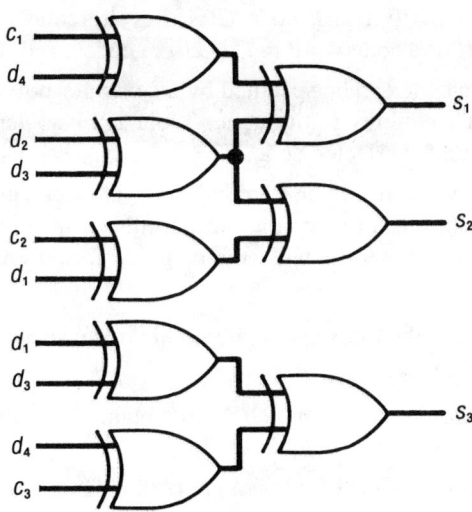

(b) Syndrome generator.

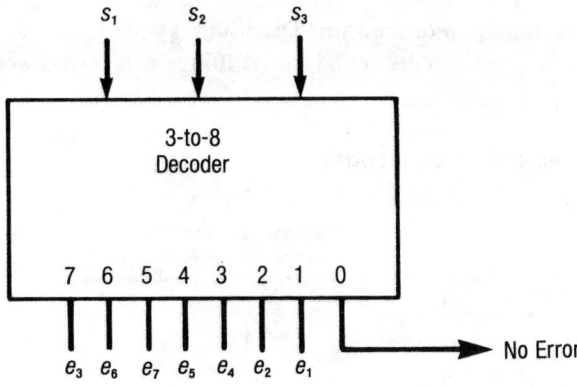

(c) Syndrome decoder.

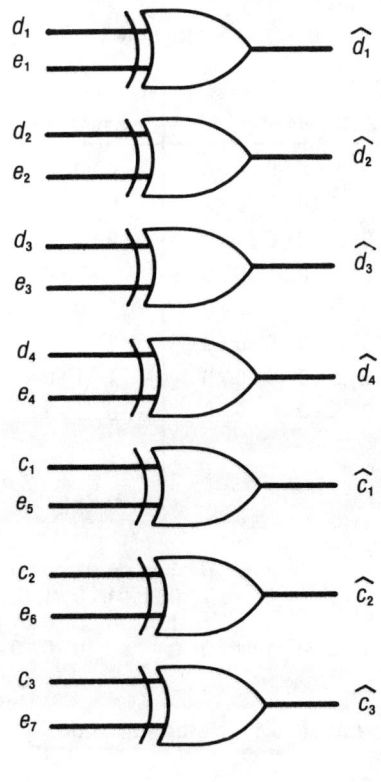

(d) Error corrector.

Figure 2.21 Parity-check code circuits.

($t = 1$) and Double Error Detection ($p = 1$) or SEC/DED code.

Shortened Hamming codes can be produced by deleting columns from the parity-check matrix of a Hamming code. The resulting codes have $d_{min} >= 3$. The code in Figure 2.22(c) is a shortened Hamming code obtained from Figure 2.22(a) by deleting all columns with an even number of 1's. Note that no three columns of the reduced code add to 0. Hence the code has $d_{min} = 4$, and therefore is a SEC/DED code. This is an example of a class of Hamming codes to be discussed below known as Odd-Weight-Column codes.

Odd-Weight-Column Codes

These codes were discovered by Hsiao [HSI70] and are a subset of the class of shortened Hamming codes. They provide SEC/DED capability as well as other desirable properties. For example, the codes specified in Figure 2.22(b) and (c) are both SEC/DED codes. However, the second code is preferred since it permits simpler and faster encoding and decoding circuitry because of the smaller number of 1's in the **H** matrix.

The parity-check matrix, **H'**, of an odd-weight-column code is obtained from the parity-check matrix, **H**, of a

Table 2.6   Syndrome table

Error Pattern	Syndrome
0 0 0 0 0 0 0	0 0 0
0 0 0 0 0 0 1	0 0 1
0 0 0 0 0 1 0	0 1 0
0 0 0 0 1 0 0	1 0 0
0 0 0 1 0 0 0	1 0 1
0 0 1 0 0 0 0	1 1 1
0 1 0 0 0 0 0	1 1 0
1 0 0 0 0 0 0	0 1 1

```
1 0 1 1 1 0 0 0 1 1 1 1 0 0 0
1 1 0 1 1 0 1 1 0 0 1 0 1 0 0
1 1 1 0 1 1 0 1 1 0 0 0 0 1 0
1 1 1 1 0 1 1 0 0 1 0 0 0 0 1
```

(a) A (15,11) Hamming code.

```
0 1 1 1 1 0 0 0
1 1 1 0 0 1 0 0
1 0 1 1 0 0 1 0
1 1 1 1 1 1 1 1
```

(b) An (8,4) modified Hamming code.

```
0 1 1 1 1 0 0 0
1 0 1 1 0 1 0 0
1 1 0 1 0 0 1 0
1 1 1 0 0 0 0 1
```

(c) An (8,4) shortened Hamming code.

Figure 2.22 Parity matrices of selected error-correction codes.

Hamming code by deleting columns so that $\mathbf{H}'$ satisfies the following:

1. Every column has an odd number of 1's.
2. The total number of 1's in $\mathbf{H}'$ is a minimum.
3. The number of 1's in each row of $\mathbf{H}'$ should be made equal to (or as close as possible) the average number of 1's per row of $\mathbf{H}'$.

Odd-weight-column codes are widely used in practice because of their desirable properties. A selected list of the parameters of such codes is given in Table 2.7. Figure 2.23 shows the $\mathbf{H}$ matrices for the (22,16) and (39,32) codes.

Cyclic Redundancy Check (CRC) Codes

Cyclic codes form a subclass of parity-check codes that are often used for encoding data for transmission over communication channels or for storage in secondary storage devices. A parity-check code C is a cyclic code if every cyclic shift of a code word in C is also a code word in C.

A cyclic code can be specified by a generator polynomial $G(X)$, using modulo-2 arithmetic. Table 2.8 lists generator polynomials for selected codes.

A message word can be encoded in a cyclic code using an algebraic approach or using a linear feedback shift register. An algebraic procedure will now be given for a systematic code.

1. Express the message in polynomial form, $m(X)$.
2. Multiply $m(X)$ by X^{n-k}.
3. Divide $X^{n-k}m(X)$ by $G(X)$ to obtain the remainder $b(X)$.
4. Compute $b(X) + X^{n-k}m(X)$ to obtain the code word.
5. Translate the code word polynomial to binary form.

A linear feedback shift register can also be used to encode and to decode a cyclic code. Figure 2.24 shows a linear feedback shift register for the code named example in Table 2.8. Encoding can be accomplished by clearing the shift register and then shifting the message word through the shift register. The check bits can be found in the shift register upon completion of the shift. Decoding is accomplished by clearing the shift register and then shifting the received word

Table 2.7   Parameters of selected odd-weight-column codes

Code	Total Number of 1's in H	Average Number of 1's per row
(8,4)	16	4
(14,9)	32	6.4
(22,16)	54	9
(39,32)	103	14.7
(72,64)	216	27

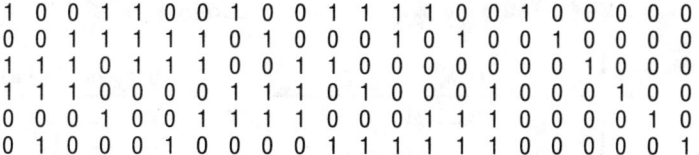

(a) A (22,16) code.

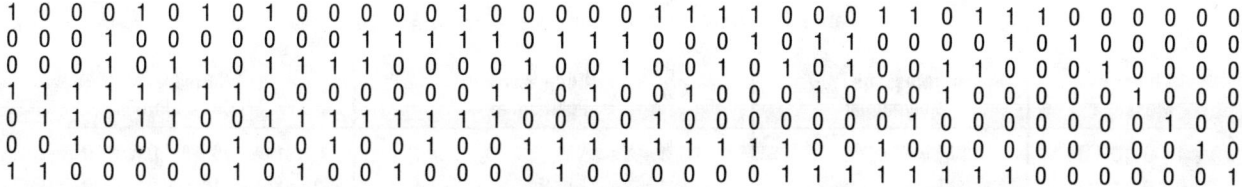

(b) A (39,32) code.

Figure 2.23 Parity-check matrices for selected odd-weight-column codes.

through the shift register. The final contents of the shift register will be zero if and only if the received word is a code word. Table 2.9 shows the encoding for selected messages for the example code.

Self-Checking Circuits

Error detection codes are effective for detecting faults that produce non-code words at the output of a functional circuit. However, some faults may actually cause an incorrect code word to be produced. In the latter case, the fault would not

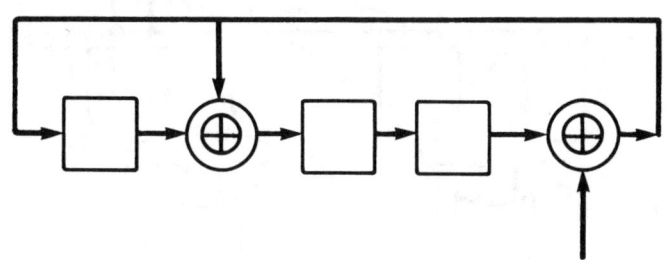

Figure 2.24 Linear feedback shift register for $G(X) = X^3 + X + 1$.

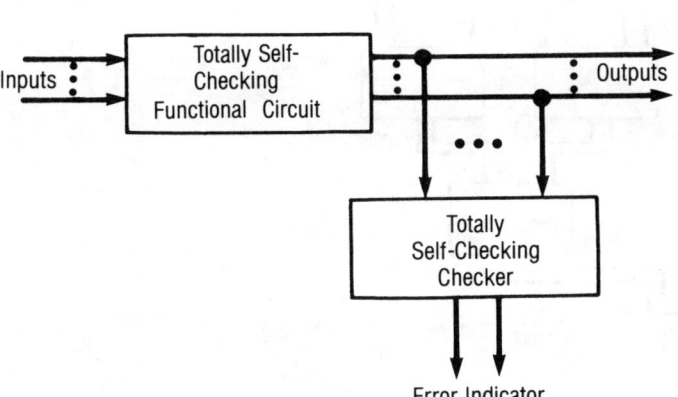

Figure 2.25 General diagram of a totally self-checking circuit.

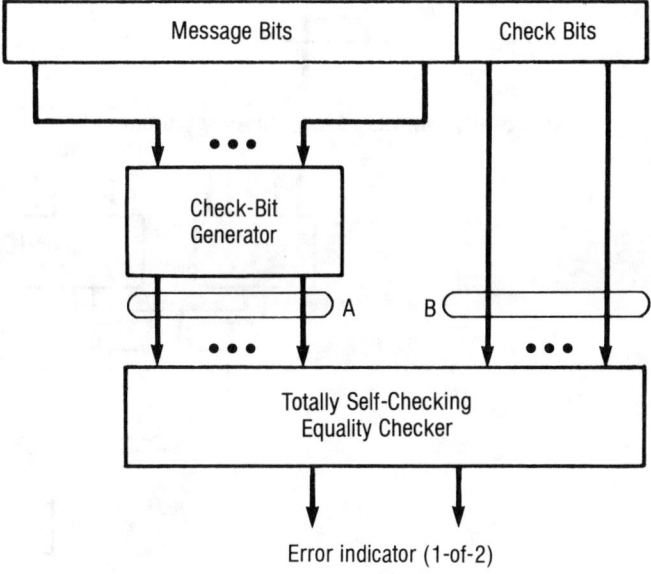

Figure 2.26 Totally self-checking checker for systematic codes.

Table 2.8 Selected cyclic codes

Name	(n,k)	Generator Polynomial
Example	(3+k,k)	X^3+X+1
CRC-12	(12+k,k)	$X^{12}+X^{11}+X^3+X^2+X+1$
CRC-16	(16+k,k)	$X^{16}+X^{13}+X^2+1$
CRC-CCITT	(16+k,k)	$X^{16}+X^{12}+X^5+1$

Table 2.9 Selected message encodings

Binary Message	Message Polynomial	Code Word Polynomial	Binary Code Word
1 0 0 0	$X^0=1$	$1+X+X^3$	1 1 0 1 0 0 0
0 0 1 0	X^2	$1+X+X^2+X^5$	1 1 1 0 0 1 0
1 0 1 0	$1+X^2$	$X^2+X^3+X^5$	0 0 1 1 0 1 0
0 1 0 1	$X+X^3$	$1+X+X^4+X^6$	1 1 0 0 1 0 1
1 0 1 1	$1+X^2+X^3$	$1+X^3+X^5+X^6$	1 0 0 1 0 1 1
1 1 1 1	$1+X+X^2+X^3$	$1+X+X^2+X^3+X^4+X^5+X^6$	1 1 1 1 1 1 1

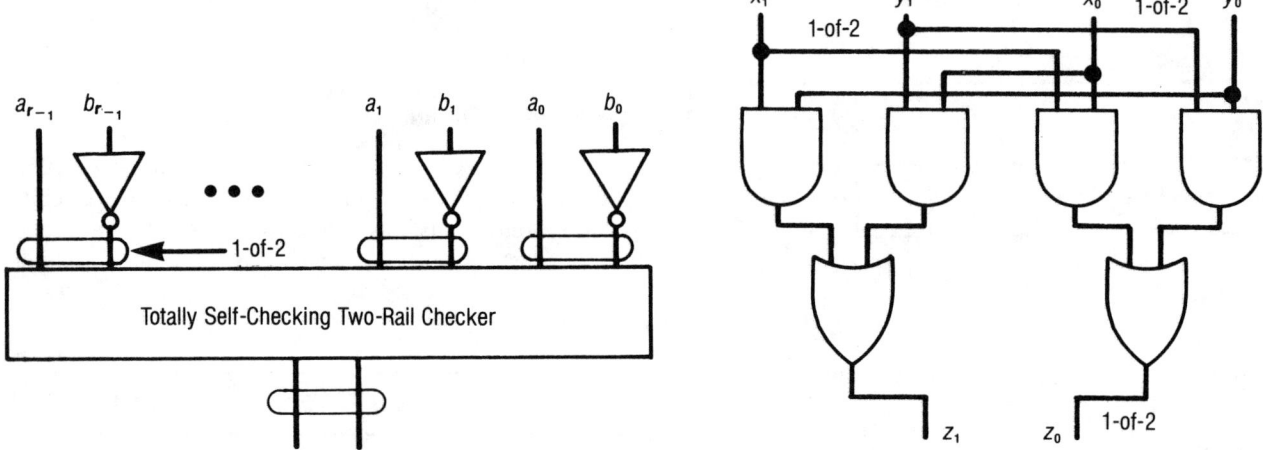

(a) Totally self-checking equality checker.

(b) Totally self-checking two-rail checker ($k=2$).

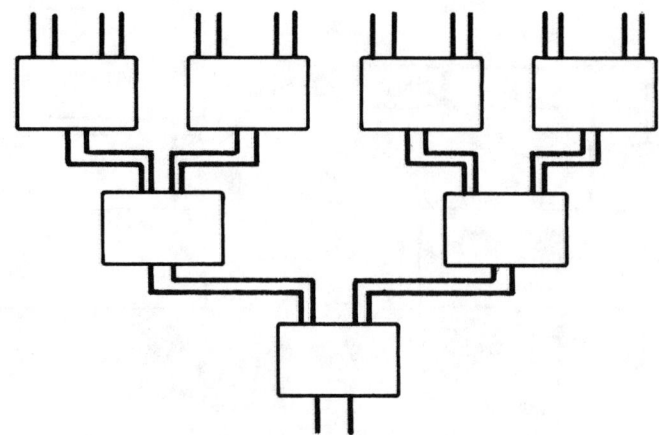

(c) Totally self-checking two-rail checker ($k=8$).

Figure 2.27 Realization of a totally self-checking equality checker.

be detectable using error-detection codes. Self-checking circuits have properties that guarantee faults from a specified set to be detectable. Self-checking circuits are employed in several systems, including the Bell Laboratories Electronic Switching Systems and an experimental fault-tolerant MIL-STD-1750A processor. Each of these systems is discussed in more detail in Chapters 3 and 7, respectively.

Some introductory remarks on self-checking and totally self-checking circuits will be presented. The interested reader is referred to [WAK78] for a more in-depth treatment of the subject.

Let X and Z represent the input code space and the output code space, respectively, of a circuit, and let F represent a set of faults. A circuit is *fault-secure* for F if, for any fault in F, the circuit never produces an incorrect output code word for any input code word. That is, for any $x \in X$ and any $f \in F$, $z(x) = z_f(x)$ or $z_f(x) \notin Z$. A circuit is *self-testing* for F if, for any fault in F, a non-code word is produced for at least one code word input. That is, for any $f \in F$ there exists $x \in X$ such that $z_f(x) \notin Z$. A circuit is *totally self-checking* for F if and only if it is both fault-secure and self-testing.

Figure 2.25 shows a general block diagram of a totally self-checking circuit. Specific designs depend upon the type of code used for the functional circuit output. A totally self-checking circuit for separable codes has the form shown in Figure 2.26.

A circuit is *code-disjoint* if and only if for all $x \notin X$ then $z(x) \notin Z$. A circuit is a *totally self-checking checker* if and only if it is both totally self-checking and code-disjoint.

A totally self-checking equality checker can be realized using two-rail logic. Two-rail logic uses two complementary variables, x_i, y_i, to represent a binary signal i. Hence, under normal conditions, a signal is represented by 01 or 10. An abnormal condition is thus indicated by 00 or 11.

Figure 2.27(a) shows a realization of a totally self-checking equality checker that employs inverters for two-rail encoding and a totally self-checking two-rail checker. An r-variable two-rail checker can be realized by using a tree interconnection of two-variable two-rail checkers. A two-variable two-rail checker is illustrated in Figure 2.27(b). The tree structure for an eight-variable checker is shown in Figure 2.27(c).

On Reliability Modeling and Analysis of Ultrareliable Fault-Tolerant Digital Systems

FRANCIS P. MATHUR, MEMBER, IEEE

Abstract—The processes of protective redundancy, namely, standby replacement (SR) redundancy and hybrid redundancy (a combination of SR and multiple-line voting redundancy), find application in the architecture of fault-tolerant digital computers and enable them to be ultrareliable and self-repairing. The claims to ultrareliability lead to the challenge of quantitatively evaluating and assigning a value to the probability of survival as a function of the mission durations intended. This note presents various mathematical models, and derives and displays quantitative evaluations of system reliability as a function of various mission parameters of interest to the system designer.

Index Terms—Fault-tolerant digital systems, hybrid redundancy, hybrid/simplex redundancy, measures of reliability, protective redundancy, reliability modeling, self-repair, ultrareliability.

INTRODUCTION

The use of protective redundancy to enhance reliability [1], [2]—once every step has been taken, under the limitations of the prevailing state of technology, to select, screen, and package highly reliable components—has, as a result of the research conducted and the applications made in this field over the last decade [3], [4], found wide acceptance as a fundamental procedure and is a process which nature in her apparent working sanctions [5]. These processes of protective redundancy, namely, standby replacement (SR) redundancy [6], multiple-line voting redundancy [5], [7], [17] and hybrid redundancy [9]–[13] (a combination of SR and multiple-line voting redundancy), find application in the architecture of fault-tolerant digital computers and enable them to be ultrareliable and self-repairing.

The claim to ultrareliability leads to the challenge of quantitatively evaluating and assigning a value to the probability of survival as a function of the mission durations intended. This note presents some mathematical models and derives and displays quantitative evaluations of system reliability as a function of various mission parameters of interest to the system designer.

The significant reliability parameters besides reliability (i.e., the probability of surviving for the length of the mission) are the mean life of the system, the reliability at the mean life, the maximum mission duration for a system at a given reliability, and the reliability gain which may be with respect to either the nonredundant design or competitive designs. These reliability parameters are evaluated under the assumption that the underlying failure law of nonredundant units is exponential. The exponential failure law, apart from its mathematical tractability, is justifiable on the basis of equipment complexity and the utilization of a high degree of replication or replacements [14]. The exponential distribution indicates that the failure rates are constant; different failure rates apply depending on whether the units are active, dormant, or inert. These designations indicate whether the standby unit is undergoing relatively greater, lesser, or equal failure stress as compared to the powered unit. These interrelationships between the failure rates λ, μ, and the dormancy factor K are summarized in Table I.

The lack of accurate statistical data on the parameters (such as failure rates) limits estimates of absolute reliability, but does not affect the relative reliability comparison of competitive redundancy configurations which use identical technologies.

UNIFYING NOTATION

A unifying notation, developed to describe the various system configurations using selective, massive, or hybrid redundancy, is illustrated in Fig. 1.

TABLE I
BASIC PARAMETERS AND SPARE MODES RELATIONSHIPS

SPARE MODE	FAILURE RATE, μ OF THE SPARE	DORMANCY FACTOR, $K = \lambda/\mu$	RELIABILITY, R_s OF THE SPARE	ASSUMPTION
ACTIVE	$\mu = \lambda$	$K = 1$	$R_s = R$	CONSERVATIVE
INERT	$\mu = 0$	$K = \infty$	$R_s = 1$	OPTIMISTIC
DORMANT	$0 < \mu \leq \lambda$	$1 < K < \infty$	$R_s \geq R$	REALISTIC

In Fig. 1 N refers to the number of replicas that are made massively redundant (NMR); S is the number of spare units; W refers to the number of cascaded units, i.e., the degree of partitioning; $R(\ )$ refers to the reliability of the system as characterized in the parentheses; TMR stands for triple modular redundant system ($N=3$); the NMR stands for N-tuple modular redundancy.

A hybrid redundant system $H(N, S, W)$ is said to have a reliability $R(N, S, W)$. If the number of spares is $S=0$, then the hybrid system reduces to a cascaded NMR system whose reliability expression is denoted by $R(N, 0, W)$; in the case where there are no cascades, it reduces to $R(N, 0, 1)$, or more simply to $R(\text{NMR})$. Thus the term W may be elided if $W=1$. The sparing system $R(1, S)$ consists of one basic unit with S spares.

Furthermore, the convention is used that R^* indicates that the unreliability $(1-R_v)$ due to the overhead required for restoration, detection, or switching has been taken into account e.g., $R^*(\text{NMR}) = R_v \cdot R(\text{NMR})$; if the asterisk is elided then it is assumed that the overhead has a negligible

---

Manuscript received June 3, 1971. This paper represents research that has been carried out at the Jet Propulsion Laboratory, California Institute of Technology, Pasadena, Calif., under NASA Contract NAS7-100. With the exception of the work on hybrid/simplex modeling, the material presented here formed part of the author's doctoral dissertation in the Department of Computer Science, University of California, Los Angeles, Calif.

The author is with the Astrionics Division, Jet Propulsion Laboratory, California Institute of Technology, Pasadena, Calif.

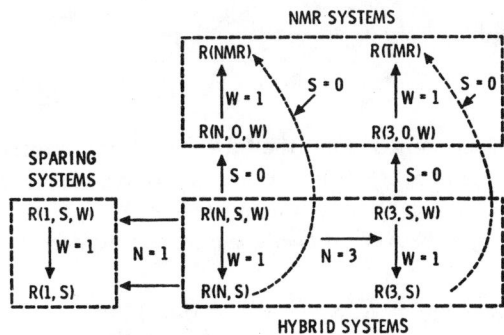

Fig. 1. Unifying notation.

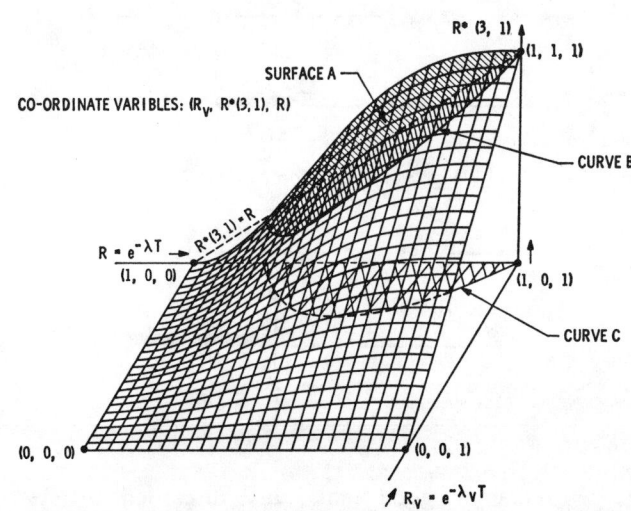

Fig. 2. Reliability surface of $H(3, 1)$ system versus R and R_v.

probability of failure. This proposed notation is extendable and can incorporate a number of functional parameters in addition to those shown here by enlarging the vector or lists of parameters within the parentheses, e.g., $R(N, S, W, \cdots, X, Y, Z)$.

Hybrid Redundancy

Standby replacement systems using selective or dynamic redundancy in combination with the general TMR systems (NMR) result in the class of protectively redundant systems designated as being hybrid redundant [9]–[13]. The hybrid scheme was first described by Goldberg [15] from an architectural standpoint. In a private communication to the author it was stated that his inspiration was received while considering the self-repair model of Kruus [8]. The first reliability equation describing this system appears in [11] (rewritten in the notation of this paper) as:

$$R(3, S) = 1 - (1 - R)^{S+2}[1 + (S + 2)R] \qquad (1)$$

and is simply the probability of any two out of the total $S+3$ identical units surviving the mission duration.

The detailed analysis of the reliability model of the $H(3, S)$ system, where the spares are considered to be dormant, is presented in [12] and the model is extended to the general $H(N, S)$ system in [13].

Briefly, the hybrid (N, S) system consists of an NMR core with an associated bank of S spare units such that when one of the N active units fails, the spare unit replaces it and restores the NMR core to the all-perfect state. The $H(N, S)$ system reduces to a NMR system when all the spares have been exhausted. Notationally, hybrid (3, 0) system is equivalent to a TMR system and thus from the standpoint of mathematical modeling the classical NMR systems form a proper subset of the hybrid redundant systems.

The implementation of such a system is realized by means of disagreement detectors, restoring organs, and a switching network [10], [13]. The tradeoffs involved between the system reliability R^*, the reliability of the detection-restoration-switching net R_v, and the reliability R of the nonredundant system is illustrated in Fig. 2. The surface A is the region above the intersection bounded by the curve B. The curve C is the projection of the intersection on the R, R_v plane. The intersection is obtained by moving the line of unit slope, $R^*(3, 1) = R$, along the R_v axis. The area above the intersection indicates the conditions under which $R^*(3, 1) > R$; thus curve B is the locus of points such that $R^*(3, 1)/R = 1$.

Two major observations of practical value to the designer of such systems may be made from this graph: 1) if $R < 0.233$ then $R^*(3, 1) < R$, irrespective of the value of R_v; and 2) if $R_v < 0.73$ then $R^*(3, 1) < R$, irrespective of the value of R. These constraints establish a tight bound on the inherent reliabilities of systems to which hybrid redundancy may be gainfully applied. Similar graphical representation of the behavior of conventional TMR systems is given in [18] where it is shown that the above two conditions for an $R^*(3, 0)$ system are $R < 0.5$ and $R_v < 0.89$, respectively. Thus the applicability constraints of a TMR system is much more restricted than that of a hybrid system.

Hybrid/Simplex Redundancy

The hybrid redundant system $H(3, S)$ uses the conventional TMR system along with a bank of standby spares. A variant of the TMR scheme, called the TMR/simplex system [16], [17], yields increased reliability by adopting the following strategy. In a triplicated majority voted system, upon the first failure of a unit, that unit is discarded; however, one of

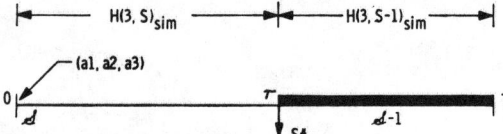

Fig. 3. Illustration of Case 2.

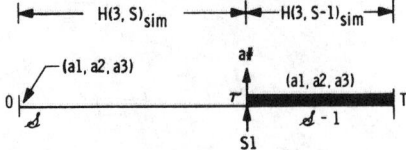

Fig. 4. Illustration of Case 3.

the two remaining good units is also discarded, the system from then on being operated in a simplex mode.

The reliability equation for such a system may be expressed as follows:

$$R(3, 0)_{sim}[T] = R^3[T]$$
$$+ 3 \int_0^T \lambda e^{-\lambda \tau} \cdot e^{-2\lambda \tau} \cdot R[T - \tau] \cdot d\tau. \quad (2)$$

This equation is the summation of the probabilities of those events leading to mission success.

Equation (2) when solved reduces to: $R(3, 0)_{sim}[T] = 1 \cdot 5R - 0 \cdot 5R^3$ and its mean life, MTF$(3, 0)_{sim}$ is $4/3\lambda$.

Now if a hybrid redundant scheme is devised which combines standby replacement units with the above variant of a TMR system, a new scheme called hybrid/simplex redundancy results. The derivation of the reliability equation of such a system will now be indicated.

Three cases may be distinguished that yield the success of the system for any mission time T. These three cases are shown in Figs. 3 and 4. The notation of these figures is explained in [13], and has been adapted from a similar notation commonly used to describe the dynamic behavior of queues in the sister branch of queuing theory.

Case 1: All units survive mission time T. This event has the probability $R^3 R_s^S$, where $R = \exp(-\lambda \tau)$ and $R_s = \exp(-\mu \tau)$.

Case 2: A spare unit is the first unit to fail (Fig. 3). At some time τ $(0 < \tau < T)$ a spare unit $S\#$ of the set of spares $S = \{S1, S2, \cdots, SS\}$ fails, reducing the $H(3, S)_{sim}$ system to an $H(3, S-1)_{sim}$ system for the unelapsed time $(T-\tau)$. The probablity of this event is

$$S \int_0^T e^{-3\lambda \tau} \cdot \mu e^{-\mu \tau} \cdot e^{-(S-1)\mu \tau} \cdot R(3, S-1)_{sim}[T-\tau] \cdot d\tau.$$

Case 3: An active unit is the first unit to fail (Fig. 4). At some time τ one of three multiplexed units $a\#$ fails and is replaced by the spare $S1$, thus leaving the system in the reduced $H(3, S-1)_{sim}$ mode for the unelapsed time $(T-\tau)$. The probablity of this event is

$$3 \int_0^T \lambda e^{-\lambda \tau} \cdot e^{-2\lambda \tau} \cdot e^{-S\mu \tau} \cdot R(3, S-1)_{sim}[T-\tau] \cdot d\tau.$$

Summing up these three cases yields:

$$R(3, S)_{sim}[T] = R^3 R_s^S + (3\lambda + S\mu) \int_0^T e^{-(3\lambda + S\mu)\tau}$$
$$\cdot R(3, S-1)_{sim}[T-\tau] \cdot d\tau. \quad (3)$$

It should be noted that the above integral equation is recursive, i.e., the equation for the case of S spares is defined in terms of the case of a system having $(S-1)$ spares. This equation by substitution $t = T - \tau$ may be rewritten as:

$$R(3, S)_{sim}[T] = R^3 R_s^S \left\{ 1 + (3\lambda + S\mu) \int_0^T e^{(3\lambda + S\mu)t} \right.$$
$$\left. \cdot R(3, S-1)_{sim}[t] \cdot dt \right\}. \quad (4)$$

It may be shown that this recursive integral equation has the solution:

$$R(3, S)_{sim}[T]$$
$$= R^3 R_s^S \left\{ 1 + 1.5 \left(\frac{1}{R^2 R_s^S} - 1 \right) \prod_{i=1}^{S} \left(\frac{3K + i}{2K + i} \right) \right.$$
$$- \prod_{j=1}^{S} \frac{(3K+j)}{j} \sum_{i=0}^{S-1} \binom{S}{i} (-1)^i \left(\frac{1}{R_s^{S-i}} - 1 \right)$$
$$\left. \cdot \frac{3K^2}{(2K+i)(3K+i)} \right\}$$

for $S > 0$ and $\mu > 0$ (5)

and

$$= (1 \cdot 5)^{S+1} R - R^3 [(1 \cdot 5)^{S+1} - 1]$$
$$- R^3 \sum_{i=1}^{S} \frac{(3\lambda T)^{S+1-i}}{(S-i)!} [(1 \cdot 5)^i - 1]$$

for $S > 0$ and $\mu = 0$. (6)

For the case $S=1$, $K=1$ (5) reduces to $R(3, 1)_{sim} = R^4 - 2R^3 + 2R$ for a hybrid/simplex system as compared to $R(3, 1) = 3R^4 - 8R^3 + 6R^2$ for a hybrid system.

The behavior of (5) for the H/S system is shown in Fig. 5 along with reliability curves of standby sparing, hybrid, and TMR systems for dormancy factor K of 1 and infinity.

The mean life is the area under the reliability curve and may be obtained by integrating the reliability function from zero to infinity with respect to time. The equations for the mean life of the H/S system are the following:

$$\text{MTF}(3, S)_{sim}$$
$$= \frac{1}{3\lambda + S\mu} \left\{ 1 + \frac{(1 \cdot 5)(2K + S)}{K} \prod_{i=1}^{S} \frac{3K + i}{2K + i} \right.$$
$$\left. - 3K^2 \prod_{j=1}^{S} \frac{3K+j}{j} \sum_{i=0}^{S-1} \binom{S}{i} \frac{(-1)^i (S-i)}{(2K+i)(3K+i)^2} \right\}$$

for $S > 0$ and $\mu > 0$ (7)

and

$$= \frac{1}{\lambda} \left\{ (1 \cdot 5)^{S+1} - \sum_{i=1}^{S+1} [(1 \cdot 5)^i - 1] \frac{(S+1-i)}{3} \right\}$$

for $S > 0$ and $\mu = 0$. (8)

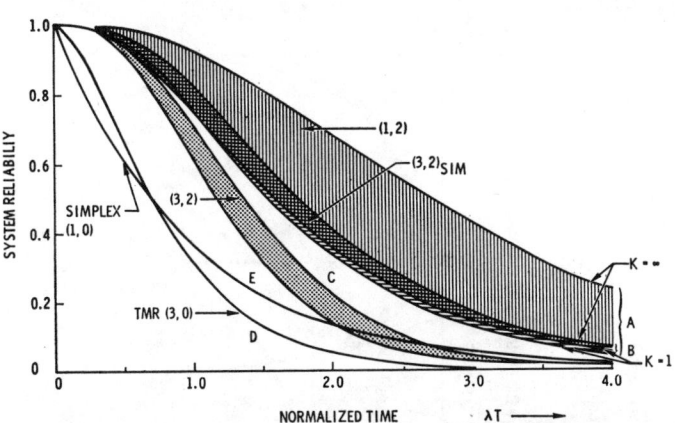

Fig. 5. System reliabilities of protectively redundant systems. (*Notation:* A = Standby replacement 2 spares (1, 2), B = hybrid/simplex redundant (3, 2)$_{sim}$, C = hybrid redundant (3, 2), D = triple modularly redundant (3, 0), and E = simplex (1, 0).)

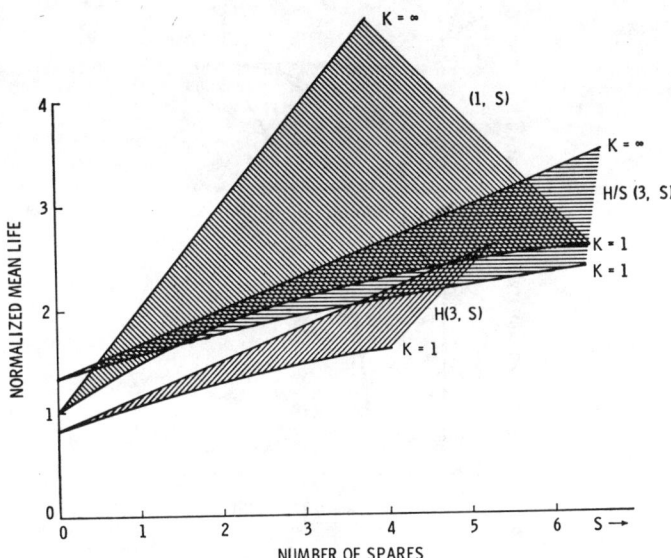

Fig. 6. Normalized mean life versus S of systems (1, S), $H(3, S)$, and H/S (3, S) for $K=1$ and $K=\infty$.

The mean lives of standby sparing, hybrid, and hybrid/simplex systems as a function of the number of spares is shown in Fig. 6. For $S=1$ and $K=1$ (7) has the value MTF $(3, 1)_{sim} = 19/12\lambda$.

MEASURES OF RELIABILITY

In order to make effective evaluation of contrasting properties, measures of reliability are required. The probability of survival function is the most general reliability function and completely describes the reliability properties of the system; however, specific comparative measures are often needed. Herein a number of measures varying from the obviously simple to the more sophisticated are presented and their values shown by illustrative examples. These measures fall into two major categories where the measures pertain to: 1) relative difference, gain, or improvement as a result of direct comparisons of the survival probabilities; and 2) the time domain of the systems, e.g., the mean life of the system, the maximum length of time for which the system has a reliability greater than a specific value, or the maximum length of time it takes for system reliability to drop from some initial value to an acceptable terminal value. Within each category, whether the survival probability or the time domain, comparisons may be made relative to either a nonredundant system (simplex) or a competitive system.

An organization of reliability measures, though by no means exhaustive, is shown in Table II. In particular, the class of measures obtained by taking logarithms of the basic reliability parameters and combinations thereof have not been included here.

TABLE II
CLASSIFICATION OF MEASURES OF RELIABILITY

	TIME DOMAIN			SURVIVAL PROBABILITY DOMAIN	
ABSOLUTE	RELATIVE TO SIMPLEX SYSTEM	RELATIVE TO COMPETITIVE SYSTEM	ABSOLUTE	RELATIVE TO SIMPLEX SYSTEM	RELATIVE TO COMPETITIVE SYSTEM
MTF	MTF(Normalized)	RATIF	R	SIMREL	DIFF
TMAX	SIMTMAX		R [MTF]	SIMDIFF	RIF
	SIMTIF			SIMGAIN	GAIN
				SIMRIF	

ABSOLUTE MEASURES OF RELIABILITY

The absolute measures of reliability, shown in Table II, are the probability of survival R, the reliability at the mean life, the mean life (MTF), and the maximum mission time for some desired minimum mission reliability (TMAX). The latter two are in the time domain.

The first three measures are well known. Since reliability is a function of time and dependent on mission length, the measure MTF is often used to characterize systems. However, MTF is an average and can often be misleading, e.g., the mean life of a simplex system is greater than the mean life of a TMR system even though the reliability of a TMR system is greater than that of the simplex system for all normalized mission times less than 0.694. Because of this undesirable feature of MTF, the measure "reliability at the mean life" was proposed since it was considered that this would yield a representative reliability of the system. A detailed discussion of MTF and R[MTF] was presented in [18] with reference to cascaded NMR systems. It was shown that the reliability at the mean life cannot be a satisfactory measure of reliability due to its asymptotic properties.

The measure TMAX is the maximum mission time at a specified minimum mission reliability, i.e., the time it takes for the system reliability to drop from some reference reliability $R2$ (usually taken to be 1.0) to some terminal reliability $R1$. TMAX may be plotted as a function of $R1$ for some fixed $R2$ [18].

COMPARATIVE MEASURES OF RELIABILITY

The reliability of a nonredundant (simplex) system will be referred to as SIMREL, an abbreviation for simplex reliability. Some comparative measures relative to the nonredundant design are the following.

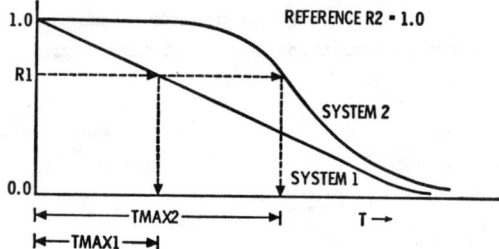

Fig. 7. Illustration of TMAX and RATIF.

1) The normalized mean life, MTF (normalized) is the the system mean life divided by the mean life of the simplex system. Since the mean life of a nonredundant system is $1/\lambda$, this enables the computation of the normalized mean life for a system without having to know the failure rate of the nonredundant system.

2) The simplex maximum mission time, SIMTMAX is the maximum mission time at a specified minimum mission reliability (for a simplex system), i.e., the time it takes for the simplex reliability to drop from some reference reliability $R2$ (usually taken to be 1.0) to some terminal reliability $R1$.

3) The simplex time improvement factor, SIMTIF is defined to be TMAX $(R1)$/SIMTMAX $(R1)$.

4) The simplex difference, SIMDIFF is the difference in reliability relative to a simplex system defined to be $R(\text{System})[t] - R(\text{Simplex})[t]$.

5) The simplex gain, SIMGAIN is the gain in reliability relative to a simplex system, defined to be $R(\text{System})[t]/R(\text{Simplex})[t]$.

6) The simplex reliability improvement factor, SIMRIF is defined to be $[1 - R(\text{Simplex})[t]/[1 - R(\text{System})[t]]]$.

The above measures reflect the improvement of a system with respect to the nonredundant design. SIMRIF is particularly useful when the two reliability numbers being compared are very close to 1.0 and differ only in the lower decimal positions. For example, if $R2 = 0.9995$ and $R1 = 0.995$, then SIMRIF $= 10.0$, whereas SIMDIFF $= 0.0045$.

Some comparative measures relative to competitive systems are the following.

1) The difference in reliability, DIFF is defined to be $R2(t) - R1(t)$.

2) The gain in reliability, GAIN is defined to be $R2(t)/R1(t)$.

3) The reliability improvement factor, RIF is defined to be $[1 - R1(t)]/[1 - R2(t)]$.

4) The relative time improvement factor, RATIF is defined to be TMAX2$(R1)$/TMAX1$(R1)$ where TMAX2$(R1)$ and TMAX1$(R1)$ are shown in Fig. 7.

Thus for a specified terminal reliability $R1$, RATIF states how much further System 2 will last as compared to System 1. The behavior of RATIF as $R1$ is varied may be shown by plotting RATIF versus $R1$ [18]. The CARE (computer-aided reliability estimation) program [19], an interactive computer program written in Fortran V and consisting of some 4000 cards, incorporates the preceding definitions and

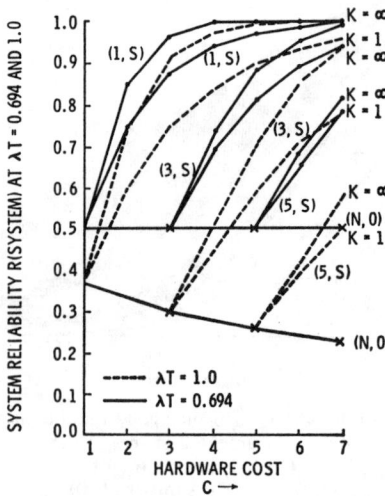

Fig. 8. System reliability versus cost ($\lambda T = 0.694$ and 1.0).

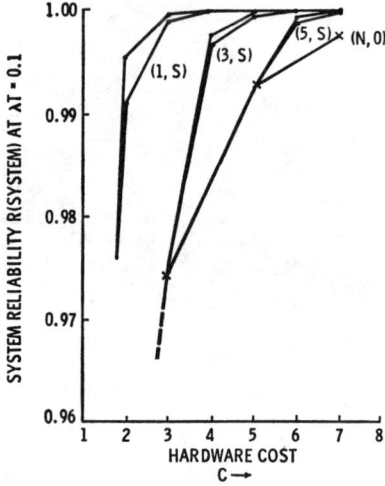

Fig. 9. System reliability versus cost ($\lambda T = 0.1$).

was used to generate the reliability data and graphs presented here.

Comparative Reliability Versus Cost Tradeoffs

One of the major parameters in any systems evaluation is cost. In systems using redundancy, cost is almost directly proportional to the order of replication of the nonredundant system. In order to compare the relative costs of protectively redundant systems, the total number of replicated units in the system may be taken as a relative index of cost.

It is of interest to evaluate the cost-performance or the cost-reliability tradeoffs between the simplex, NMR, hybrid and standby replacement systems. One method of making such a comparison is to compare the system reliabilities as a function of the degree of replication at a particular time slice. In order to make the comparison fair a number of time slices need to be judiciously selected. In Figs. 8 and 9 such a comparison is graphically shown with time slices for the normalized mission time λT taken to be 0.1, 0.694, and 1.0.

TABLE III
COMPUTED VALUES OF RELIABILITY MEASURES ($\lambda T = 0.1$ AND 1.0)

	SIMPLEX (1,0)	NMR (7,0)	HYBRID (3,4)		HYBRID (5,2)		SR (1,6)	
	K = 1	K = 1	K = 1	K = ∞	K = 1	K = ∞	K = 1	K = ∞
TOTAL # OF UNITS:	1	7	7	7	7	7	7	7
COST:	1	7+	7+	7+	7+	7+	7+	7+
R_{sys} @ $\lambda T = 0.1$	0.905	0.998	0.999995	0.9999995	0.99986	0.99996	0.9999999	0.9999999
R_{sys} @ $\lambda T = 1.0$	0.368	0.23	0.79	0.94	0.51	0.58	0.96	0.99992
SIMDIFF @ $\lambda T = 0.1$	0	0.0929	0.0951	0.0952	0.0950	0.0951	0.0952	0.0952
SIMDIFF @ $\lambda T = 1.0$	0	0.137	0.43	0.57	0.14	0.21	0.59	0.63
SIMGAIN @ $\lambda T = 0.1$	1	1.1027	1.1052	1.1052	1.1050	1.1051	1.1052	1.1052
SIMGAIN @ $\lambda T = 1.0$	1	0.63	2.16	2.54	1.38	1.57	2.61	2.72
SIMRIF @ $\lambda T = 0.1$	1	42.0	20×10^3	177×10^3	685	1.1×10^3	1.3×10^6	6.4×10^6
SIMRIF @ $\lambda T = 1.0$	1	0.82	3.1	9.8	1.3	1.5	15.7	7.6×10^3
MTF (NORMALIZED)	1	0.76	1.6	2.2	1.1	1.2	2.6	7.0
R [MTF]	0.368	0.430	0.432	0.44	0.434	0.437	0.42	0.45
LAMTMAX ($R_1 = 0.9$)	0.105	0.33	0.79	1.13	0.52	0.57	1.27	3.89
SIMTIF ($R_1 = 0.9$)	1	3.1	7.5	10.7	4.9	5.4	12.1	37.0

These three values of time were taken with reference to $\lambda T = 0.694$ since at this value the NMR systems remain static as a function of the degree of replication.

An allocation of seven units can be used to produce the (7, 0) (3, 4), (5, 2), and (1, 6) systems. The results of the reliability comparison of these cost-equivalent systems are shown in Table III for a "short" normalized mission time of 0.1 and a "long" mission time of 1.0. For each system the computed values of all the reliability measures described earlier are tabulated.

Under the constraints of this analysis, the tables clearly demonstrate that, from a quantitative reliability standpoint, standby replacement systems are superior to hybrid systems which in turn are superior to NMR systems.

CONCLUSION

This note spans the general area of reliability analysis. A proposed unifying notation for characterizing some important classes of protective redundancy, the analysis of hybrid and hybrid/simplex redundant system, and some measures of reliability and their classification along with a reliability cost-performance evaluation are presented. A large number of quantitative results gathered in the course of this research are made available to the reader in the form of tables and two- and three-dimensional plots.

ACKNOWLEDGMENT

The guidance and encouragement given by Prof. A. Avižienis that has enabled this effort to be brought to fruition is gratefully acknowledged. The author also wishes to thank his colleagues in the Spacecraft Computers Section, G. Milligan, D. Rennels, J. Rohr, D. Rubin, and A. Weeks, whose extensive discussions also helped to this end. To the management of the Astrionics Division of the Jet Propulsion Laboratory, J. Scull, W. Scott, and J. Wedel, a special acknowledgment with thanks for providing the atmosphere conducive to this research. The author also wishes to thank secretaries, Mrs. E. Griggs and Miss J. Rekers for the typing efforts involved.

REFERENCES

[1] E. F. Moore and C. E. Shannon, "Reliable circuits using less reliable relays," *J. Franklin Inst.*, vol. 262, pt. I, pp. 191–208, and pt. II, 281–297, 1956.
[2] A. Avižienis, "Design of fault-tolerant computers," in *1967 Fall Joint Comput. Conf., AFIPS Conf. Proc.*, vol. 31. Washington, D. C.: Thompson, 1967, pp. 733–743.
[3] A. Avižienis, F. P. Mathur, D. Rennels, and J. Rohr, "Automatic maintenance of aerospace computers and spacecraft information and control systems," in *Proc. AIAA Aerospace Comput. Sys. Conf.*, Los Angeles, Calif., Sept. 8–10, 1969, Paper 69-966.
[4] J. E. Anderson and F. J. Macri, "Multiple redundancy applications in a computer," in *1967 Proc. Annu. Symp. Reliability*, 1967, pp. 553–562.
[5] J. von Neumann, "Probabilistic logics and the synthesis of reliable organisms from unreliable components," in *Automata Studies*, C. E. Shannon and J. McCarthy, Eds. Princeton, N. J.: Princeton Univ. Press, 1956, pp. 43–98.
[6] B. J. Flehinger, "Reliability improvement through redundancy at various system levels," *IBM J. Res. Develop.*, vol. 2, pp. 148–158, Apr. 1958.
[7] J. K. Knox-seith, "Improving the reliability of digital systems by redundancy and restoring organs," Ph.D. dissertation, Dep. Elec. Eng., Stanford Univ., Stanford, Calif., Aug. 1964.
[8] J. Kruus, "Upper bounds for the mean life of self-repairing systems," Coord. Sci. Lab., Univ. Illinois, Urbana, Rep. R-172, July 1963.
[9] J. Goldberg, M. W. Green, K. N. Levitt, and H. S. Stone, "Techniques for the realization of ultra-reliable spaceborne computers,"

Stanford Res. Inst., Menlo Park, Calif., Interim Sci. Rep. 2, Project 5580, Oct. 1967.
[10] W. G. Bouricius, W. C. Carter, J. P. Roth, and P. R. Schneider, "Investigations in the design of an automatically repaired computer," in *1st Annu. IEEE Comput. Conf. Digest*, Sept. 1967, pp. 64—67.
[11] J. P. Roth, W. G. Bouricius, W. C. Carter, and P. R. Schneider, "Phase II of an architectural study for a self-repairing computer," SAMSO TR-67-106, Nov. 1967.
[12] F. P. Mathur, "Reliability modeling and analysis of a dynamic TMR system utilizing standby spares," in *Proc. 7th Annu. Allerton Conf. Circuit and System Theory*, Oct. 8–10, 1969, pp. 243–252.
[13] F. P. Mathur and A. Aviẑienis, "Reliability analysis and architecture of a hybrid redundant digital system: Generalized triple modular redundancy with self-repair," in *1970 Spring Joint Comput. Conf.*, *AFIPS Conf. Proc.*, vol. 36. Montvale, N. J.: AFIPS Press, 1970, pp. 375–383.
[14] R. F. Drenick, "The failure laws of complex equipment," *J. Soc. Ind. Appl. Math.*, vol. 8, pp. 680–690, Dec. 1960.
[15] J. Goldberg, "Network schemes for combined fault-masking and replacement," presented at the Workshop on Reliability, Pacific Palisades, Calif., Feb. 1966 (unpublished).
[16] M. Ball and F. Hardie, "Majority voter design considerations for—TMR computer," *Comput. Design*, pp. 100–104, Apr. 1969.
[17] ——, "Architecture for an extended mission aerospace computer," IBM Rep. 66-825-1753, May 1969.
[18] F. P. Mathur, "Reliability modeling and architecture of ultrareliable fault-tolerant digital computers," Ph.D. dissertation, Dep. Comput. Sci., Univ. California, Los Angeles, Microfilm reorder no. 71-662, June 1970.
[19] F. P. Mathur, "Reliability estimation procedures and CARE: The computer-aided reliability estimation program," *Jet Propul. Lab. Quart. Tech. Rev.*, vol. 1, Oct. 1971.

RELIABILITY MODELING TECHNIQUES FOR SELF-REPAIRING
COMPUTER SYSTEMS

W. G. Bouricius, W. C. Carter and P. R. Schneider
IBM Watson Research Center
Yorktown Heights, New York

Abstract

This paper develops techniques for generating and using mathematical models applicable to architectural evaluation of the tradeoffs involved in designing self-repairing highly reliable computers for long missions.

These systems must use standby sparing and their reliability is shown to be extremely sensitive to small variations in a new design parameter, the coverage, c, defined as the probability of system recovery given the existence of a failure. Interactive terminal calculations show c to be the single most important parameter in high-reliability system design. Changing the coverage from 1 to .98 can result in orders of magnitude change in system mission time with a specified reliability.

Most techniques for increasing system reliability (e.g. adding more spares) are shown to be futile in the face of an inadequate .99 coverage. Adding checking, diagnostics, etc. to improve failure coverage is shown to be the most advantageous technique by examples of system tradeoff evaluation. This mandates extensive application of modeling techniques throughout all computer system design phases.

1. Modeling Highly Reliable Computers

1.1 Introduction

In the design of highly reliable, highly available computers, introducing various forms of redundancy is a necessity. In such systems extreme sensitivity of the overall reliability to small variations in certain system design parameters mandates extensive application of modeling techniques throughout all phases of design [1,2]. The purpose of this paper is to develop techniques for generating and using computer reliability models applicable to the architectural evaluation of trade-offs involved in designing highly-reliable computers.

A scientific model is a symbolic, mathematical or physical representation of some subject undergoing scrutiny and is used for the purposes of prediction, evaluation and control [3]. A model is never more than a partial representation of the subject being studied and is usually judged by how accurately it can predict (despite its inherent incompleteness) the effect of changes in some parameters or aspects of the subject. Two more criteria for judgement are the convenience with which the model can be used and the ability to derive useful results from the model. This leads to the major reason for employing models: explanation of a subject's response under a variation in certain of its parameters or aspects is usually more conveniently obtained from a model than from the real subject.

The models discussed in this paper are primarily mathematical and are concerned with investigating the gross trade-offs between reliability and many of the various parameters or aspects of a computer system. The models are extremely useful in making architectural decisions concerning the design of highly reliable computer systems. It is to be emphasized that it is not the specific models being developed that are considered to be of prime importance but rather the basic techniques for generating such models and the design criteria obtained from them. This is a necessary consequence of the fact that it is impractical to generate _precise_ models for all the distinct situations arising in the design of computer systems. Thus the burden of model accuracy falls directly on the user who is forced to live with the "Garbage In-Garbage Out" axiom. However, to assist the user in employing these models the restrictive assumptions employed in obtaining each model are specified.

1.2 Basic Model Assumptions

High reliability for long missions can be obtained by standby redundancy using spares with an appropriate mechanism for automatic system reconfiguration [1,4]. Figure 1.1(a) shows a typical interface for a system using standby sparing with two possible sending modules (SM_1, SM_2), three possible receiving modules (RM_1, RM_2, RM_3) and a status register (SR) containing a specification of the current state of the interface. Figure 1.1(b) shows a typical selection switch for one of the receiving modules. The method of operation is as follows.

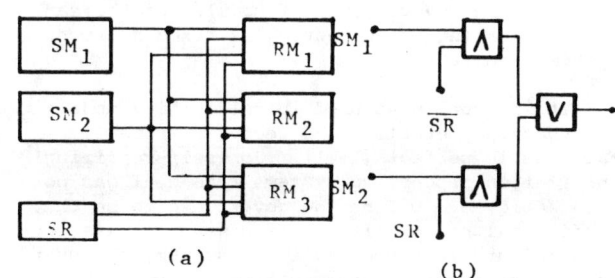

Figure 1.1 Basic Standby Configuration

Initially SR = 0 to denote the fact that SM_1 is the active sending module from which data is to be taken. In each receiving module the selection switch has its upper AND gate activated to transmit the data received from SM_1. When it is determined, by diagnosis or checking, that SM_1 has failed, its spare SM_2 is selected by setting SR = 1. This activates the lower AND gate in each receiving module and blocks the upper one. The selection process on the modules RM_1, RM_2 and RM_3 is performed by another status register at their outputs. It is obvious that extension to the case where each sending module has N output data lines merely involves using N independent selection trees, one for each data line, in each of the receiving modules.

The previous discussion shows that automatic reconfiguration using standby spares can be made feasible and that through appropriate design of the selection switches their failures can be made indistinguishable from failures in the receiving modules [5]. Thus the failure rates of the selection switches are lumped with those of the receiving modules.

Failures in the status register usually prevent the interface from achieving all its possible states. While not exactly catastrophic, in the sense of independently bringing the system down, the status register does deserve some protection. For this reason redundancy is added to it in the form of error correction coding; e.g., TMR [6], quadding [7], etc. One goal is to make the small amount of circuitry in the status register orders of magnitude more reliable than the modules being switched so that its contribution to the system unreliability becomes negligible. This permits the designer to ignore the extremely complex interaction between failures in the modules and failures in the status register, and to concentrate solely on the module reliability. The assumption of extremely reliable status registers (through redundancy when necessary) will be used throughout this paper.

1.3 Notation

The number of spares initially available, s, clearly affects system reliability and has been discussed in general [11] and for computers [1,2,4]. Reliability is not the only computer requirement; throughput and capacity are two others. The quantity, q, of modules of the same type, operating concurrently, is fixed by such system requirements.

It is usually assumed in reliability modeling that the detection and recovery from all failures is perfect [2,11]. For self-repairing information processing systems this goal has not been achieved. Define the coverage c to be the conditional probability that, given the existence of a failure in the operational system, the system is able to recover, and continue information processing with no permanent loss of essential information, i.e.,

$c = \Pr[\text{system recovers} \mid \text{system fails}]$.

Exactly what constitutes recovery is a matter for the individual system designer to settle; at this point it is just a system parameter. In some situations recovery may only mean detection, location and automatic repair of the hardware failure, while in others it may also include very complex restoration of an operating data base. In the latter case the coverage c would be lower than in the former. In a sense, c can be interpreted as a probability of surviving a failure without irreparable damage.

Now consider the case of a module designed to tolerate up to f single failures before it becomes inoperative. The ability to recover from one of these failures and continue operation is governed by a coverage c as before. For simplicity, the same value of c will be used for the first 1 to f failures, where the same module is used, and for the $(f+1)^{st}$ failure where recovery is to a new module.

The parameters which have a major effect on the form of the system reliability equations are s, q, c, and f. In order to display the status of these parameters, each reliability formula will be written in tensor notation as ${}^f_c R^q_s$. When any of the parameters q, c, f, or s are elided, convention establishes the values q = 1, c = 1, f = 0, or s = 0.

The simplex module reliability depends upon its failure rate, usually denoted by λ, and the time, t, for which the module operates [11]. The module failure rate, in turn, depends upon both the amount and type of physical circuitry in the module.

A variation in the automatic reconfiguration mechanism involves using the status register to turn power off on the unused sending module and a simple buffering of the signals at the receiving module. Such a scheme will not be discussed in detail here since it adds little to the reliability modeling study. However, if it is assumed that computer hardware has a lower failure rate with power off than with power on, the system reliability can be increased by keeping the spare modules in the power off state until they are required to replace failed modules [8]. The power-off failure rate will be denoted by μ to distinguish it from the power-on failure rate λ. The parameters λ and μ are both dependent on physical quantities and are assumed to be independent of the other parameters (e.g. s, q, etc.) and constant during the system comparisons made in this paper.

The general reliability function is written as ${}^f_c R^q_s(t,\lambda,\mu)$, showing the specific dependence upon all 4 system parameters affecting form and the 3 module variables. Frequently it is assumed that $\mu = \lambda$; in this case the function is written as ${}^f_c R^q_s(t,\lambda)$. For convenience, if only t is important, the function ${}^f_c R^q_s(t)$ is used with $\mu=\lambda$ and λ understood. Finally the short form ${}^f_c R^q_s$ with $\mu = \lambda$ and λ, t understood is used to shorten formulae. This terminology together with short definitions of terms are listed in the appendix.

The parameters s (number of spares), c (coverage) and f (failure tolerance) are the parameters whose increase produce improvements in reliability. Increasing s simply means adding more modules: the effect of this is analyzed directly using equations derived from the formulae of Section 2. To analyze the impact of coverage, the following two questions concerning the lack of perfect coverage must be answered:

"How much does non-perfect coverage degrade the mission time?"

and

"How much extra equipment can be added to the module to achieve perfect coverage without making the module itself so unreliable as to defeat the effect of obtaining perfect coverage?"

Similar questions can be posed concerning the impact of failure tolerance. The formulae and examples in Sections 2 and 3 provide answers to these questions.

1.4 Figures of Merit for System Reliability

The usual figure of merit for system reliability is MTBF (Mean Time Between Failures). Applying the usual definition of mean, the following well known result is obtained [11].

$$MTBF = \int_0^\infty {}_c^f R_s^q(t, \lambda, \mu) dt$$

A simplex system with a single module described by a Poisson distribution with failure rate λ has

$$MTBF = 1/\lambda$$

This is convenient for hand calculation.

It is now shown that MTBF's are very misleading when it comes to comparing the performance of various highly reliable computer system configurations [4,6]. The basic reason for this is that the MTBF computation evaluates the reliability function for $0 \leq t \leq \infty$, when in actual self-repairing computer operation the only region of concern is $0 \leq t \leq T$, where T is some specified mission time. The crucial point is that to meet operational specifications the reliability is always quite high (say > .9) and what happens to it for $t > T$ is not particularly relevant to the mission. For two systems with reliability $R_A(t)$ and $R_B(t)$ as shown in Figure 1.4:1 the MTBF for $R_B(t)$ may be higher, but for the indicated mission time $R_A(T) >> R_B(T)$. (The graph of $R_A(t)$ shows a typical high redundancy system characteristic: when the system "rounds the knee" of its curve it <u>really</u> goes bad.)

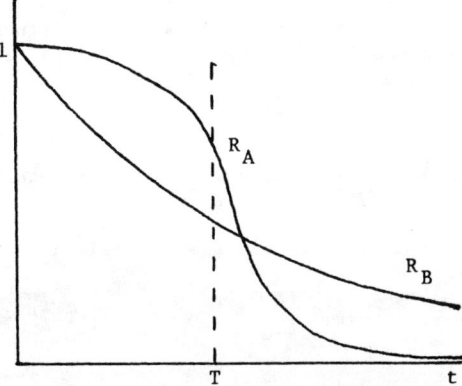

Figure 1.4:1 System MTBF and mission comparison.

The values of the reliability for $0 \leq t \leq T$ are a possible second figure of merit. In the above example, $R_A(t) >> R_B(t)$ during the mission, so the comparison is easy. However, for highly reliable computer systems the numbers being compared may be .990 and .995. Since these appear almost equal, the probability of failure $P_A = 1 - R_A$, is frequently used. For the previous illustrations, these numbers become .01 and .005, indicating a difference of a factor of 2. If the mission time T is fixed, then $P_A = 1 - R_A$ is a satisfactory figure of merit.

In most cases a certain computer system reliability level must be maintained and, although a minimum mission time is imperative, the longer this reliability is maintained the better. A third figure of merit is the length of time T during which a specified reliability is exceeded, i.e., T where $R_A(t) \geq R_{Spec}$ for $0 \leq t \leq T$ with $R_A(T) = R_{Spec}$. Thus a meaningful method of system comparison is to compute the ratio of mission times during which a specified reliability level is achieved [4]. Let two systems A, B have reliability given by $R_A(t)$ and $R_B(t)$, and let $R_A(t) \geq R_{Spec}$ for $0 \leq t \leq T_A$ and $R_B(t) \geq R_{Spec}$ for $0 \leq t \leq T_B$. Now let

$$I = T_B/T_A$$

give the mission time improvement of system B relative to system A for the specified reliability level. The worth of this figure of merit is illustrated later.

Since $R_A(T_A) = R_B(T_B) = R_B(IT_A)$, the functions for R_A and R_B may be substituted and the resulting equations solved for I. In some cases the resulting equations are too complicated for easy hand computation, however they are well suited for use with an interactive terminal computing system, e.g., APL [9].

2. Basic Reliability Formulae

A Poisson distribution of hardware failures [11] is assumed so that the simplex module reliability becomes

$$R = e^{-\lambda t} \quad (2{:}1)$$

using the assumptions about eliding parameters described in the previous section.

The following formulae are derived in the appendix.

$$_{c}R^{q}_{s}(t,\lambda,\mu) = (R)^{q} \sum_{k=0}^{s} \binom{k-1+q\lambda/\mu}{k} c^{k}(1-e^{-\mu t})^{k} \quad (2{:}2)$$

If λ/μ is an integer, then

$$_{c}R^{q}_{s}(t,\lambda,\mu) = \left[\frac{e^{-\mu t}}{1-c(1-e^{-\mu t})}\right]^{q\lambda/\mu} \times$$

$$[1-[c(1-e^{-\mu t})]^{s+1} \sum_{i=0}^{q\lambda/\mu-1} \binom{s+i}{i}[1-c(1-e^{-\mu t})]^{i}] \quad (2{:}3)$$

while a similar but more complicated formula holds if λ/μ is non-integral. If $c = 1$,

$$R^{q}_{s}(t,\lambda,\mu) = 1-(1-e^{-\mu t})^{s+1} \sum_{i=0}^{q\lambda/\mu-1} \binom{s+i}{i} e^{-i\mu t} \quad (2{:}4)$$

It is shown in the appendix that

$$_{c}R^{q}_{s}(t,\lambda,\mu) \leq \left[\frac{e^{-\mu t}}{1-c(1-e^{-\mu t})}\right]^{q\lambda/\mu} \quad (2{:}5)$$

with $_{c}R^{q}_{s}$ approaching the bound slowly but monotonically as $s \to \infty$.

In addition it is proved that

$$\text{MTBF}(_{c}R^{q}_{s}(t,\lambda,\mu)) = \sum_{i=0}^{s} \frac{c^{i}}{q\lambda+i\mu} \leq \frac{s+1}{s+q\lambda/\mu} \cdot \frac{-\ln(1-c)}{c\mu} \quad (2{:}6)$$

The equations for the ratio of mission times during which a specified reliability level is achieved will be derived in the text, since this figure of merit is less well known.

If the parameter s is changed by adding more modules, then its effect follows from analyzing (2:2) and (2:3) or by solving

$$_{c}R^{q}_{s+j}(IT,\lambda,\mu) = _{c}R^{q}_{s}(T,\lambda,\mu)$$

for I. Alternatively the bound (2:5) may be used.

The parameter c may be modified by adding extra equipment to the module so the coverage, c, becomes 1. The basic module failure rate is now $a\lambda$, where $a>1$ is a multiplicative factor showing how much circuitry has been added. Now one system has perfect coverage (c=1), failure rates $a\lambda$ and $a\mu$ and mission time IT, while the other has coverage $c < 1$, failure rates λ and μ and mission time T. Then I can be obtained by solving

$$_{c}R^{q}_{s}(IT, a\lambda, a\mu) \geq _{c}R^{q}_{s}(T,\lambda,\mu) \quad (2{:}7)$$

If $q=1$ and $\lambda=\mu$, substituting in Equations (2:4) and (2:2) using (2:1) yields

$$aI \leq \frac{-1}{\lambda T} \ln[1- \{1-e^{-\lambda T} \sum_{i=0}^{s} [c(1-e^{-\lambda T})]^{i}\}^{1/s+1}]. \quad (2{:}8)$$

This equation gives a bound on the augmentation/mission time improvement trade-off which is obtainable at a fixed reliability level. As always, if the full potential of aI is not used it can be traded for an increase in the original reliability level.

If q is not equal to 1, it is not possible to obtain a closed form solution for aI. However, using an interactive terminal system [9], the basic design questions can be answered.

3. Reliability Analyses Using the Previously Defined Figures of Merit

3.1 Analyses Using the Mission Time Ratio, I.

3.1.1 Maximum Improvement Possible by Adding Spares. The inequality (2:5) can be used to establish the maximum mission time improvement obtainable through sparing. Assume that a single module has reliability $R(T) = e^{-\lambda T}$ for mission time T, $\lambda=\mu$, $q=1$, and $c < 1$. Then the maximum mission time improvement achievable <u>at this reliability</u> through adding spares is found by substitution in (2:5).

$$e^{-\lambda T} = \frac{(e^{-\lambda T})^{I_{max}}}{1-c[1-(e^{-\lambda T})^{I_{max}}]}$$

$$I_{max} = \frac{-1}{\lambda T} \ln \frac{(1-c)e^{-\lambda T}}{1-ce^{-\lambda T}}$$

$$(3.1{:}1)$$

The table below computes I_{max}. This data is also plotted in Figure 3.1:1.

I_{max}	c				
	.99	.95	.9	.8	.7
R .99	69.5	18.3	9.6	4.9	3.3
.95	35.8	14.0	8.2	4.6	3.2
.9	23.7	11.1	7.1	4.2	3.0
.8	14.6	8.0	5.6	3.6	2.7

Table 3.1:1

It is clear that unless the coverage is made much greater than .9 most of the potential mission time improvement can never be achieved (if c = 1, $I_{max} = \infty$, for any R).

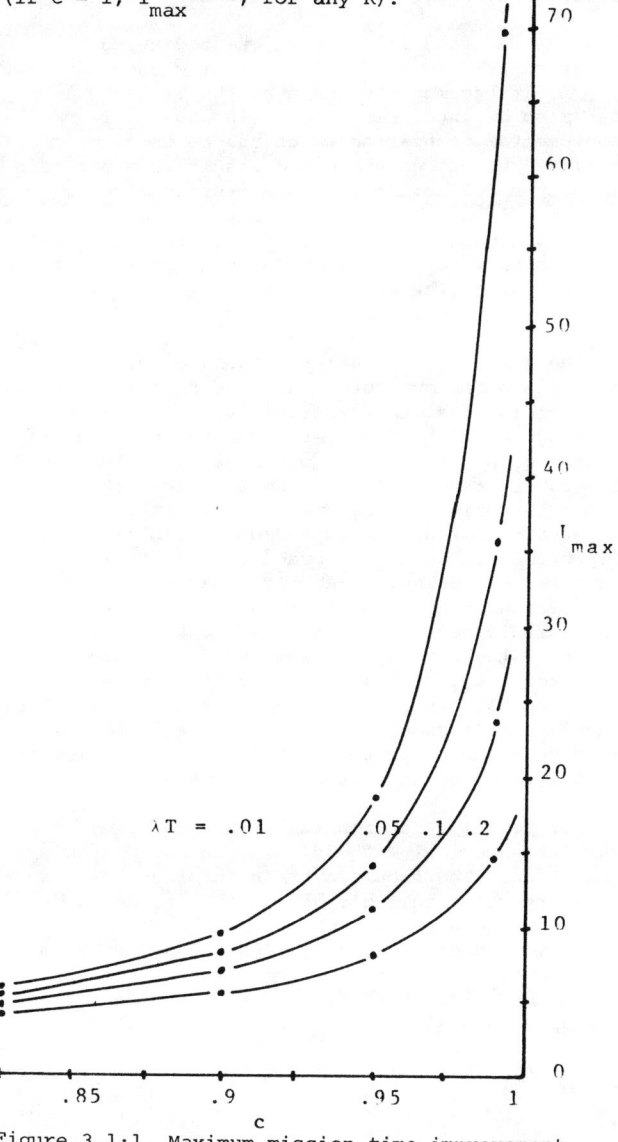

Figure 3.1:1 Maximum mission time improvement (through using an infinite number of spares) vs given coverage.

The following example shows the advantage of improving c rather than adding more spares.

Consider a storage unit which has $\lambda = \mu = 10^{-3}$ and T = 105 for R_1 = .99. If the failure coverage is only .8 the correct mission time with $_8R_1$ = .99, is T = 44 hours. Using Equation (2:8) it is clear that as long as a < 2.4 extra equipment can be added to this imperfectly covered storage unit to bring c to 1 a mission time improvement over the existing 44 hours will occur. On the other hand, using the inequality (2:5) with $_8R_s(t)$ = .99 shows that just adding more spare storage units of the same imperfectly covered variety will never give a mission time better than 50 hours.

3.1.2 Improvement by Increasing c. The first question concerning the lack of perfect coverage is:

"How much does non-perfect coverage degrade the mission time?"

To answer this, tabulate solutions to Equation (2:8) with a = 1 (no increase in circuitry).

Table 3.1:2 shows the potential mission time improvement, I, which could be obtained if the module's coverage were increased from the given value to that corresponding to perfect coverage, i.e. to c = 1. As a specific example, when λT = .01, s = 2 and the imperfect coverage is c = .9 there is the possibility of increasing the mission time by over an order of magnitude (I = 10.55) if the coverage can be made perfect.

I	s 1	2	3	I	s 1	2	3
.99	1.05	1.32	2.03	.99	1.42	4.78	10.55
.95	1.23	2.00	3.14	.95	2.46	8.29	16.22
.9	1.43	2.52	3.85	.9	3.35	10.55	19.6
.8	1.77	3.23	4.76	.8	4.66	13.5	23.78
	λT = .1				λT = .01		

Table 3.1:2

Figure 3.1:2(a) is a plot of this potential I vs the existing imperfect coverage for the case λT = .01. It is clear that when imperfect coverage exists, a great potential mission time improvement is available if the coverage can be made perfect.

An alternate way to view these results is to plot the mission time degradation D, the reciprocal of I, obtained by not having perfect coverage: this is done in Figure 3.1:2(b) for λT = .01. Reading off this curve one sees that for a system with λT = .01, s = 2 and c = .9 the mission time is only 1/10 that which could be obtained if the coverage were perfect.

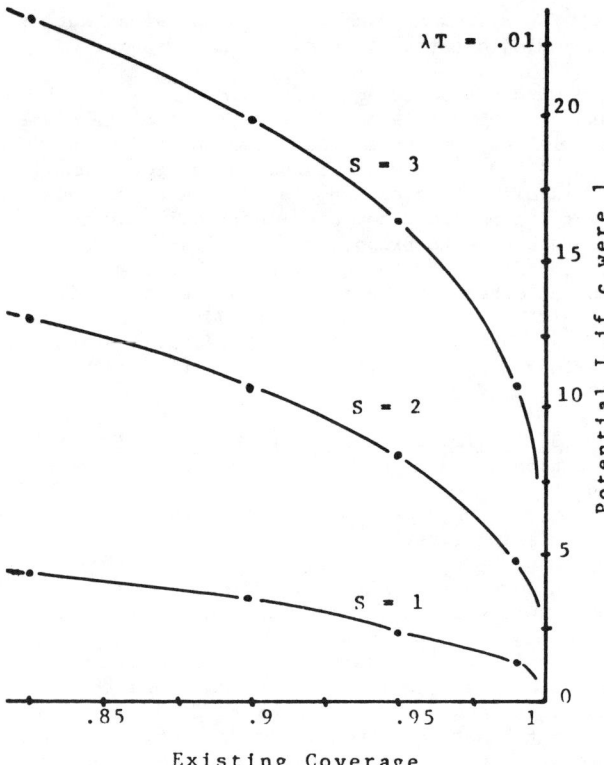

Figure 3.1:2(a) Potential Mission Time Improvement if existing c made perfect.

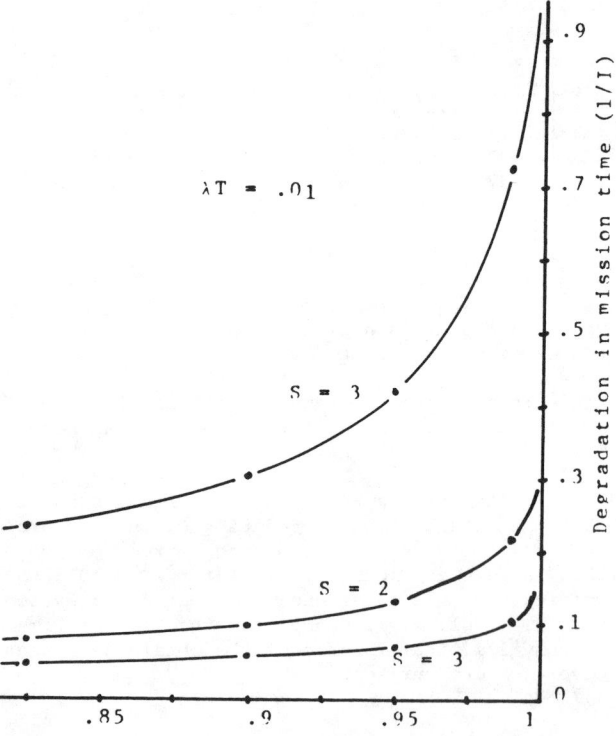

Figure 3.1:2(b) Degradation in mission time due to existing imperfect coverage.

Since gains in mission time at a fixed reliability can be traded for gains in reliability at a fixed mission time, the previous example also shows the tremendous potential gain in reliability that can be achieved.

Perhaps the biggest danger pointed out in this analysis is that assuming perfect coverage when the coverage is only "near" perfect produces grossly inaccurate results. Viewing the rapid drop in the curves of Figure 3.1:2(b) it is clear that c = .99 is not anywhere near perfect!

The second question, "How much extra equipment can be added to the module to achieve perfect coverage without making the module itself so unreliable as to defeat the effect of obtaining perfect coverage?" will now be answered.

The Tables 3.1:2 were calculated using Equation (2:8) with a = 1. If in the same equation I = 1, it becomes obvious that the Tables 3.1:2 can also be interpreted as giving the <u>maximum</u> equipment augmentation which can be used to achieve perfect coverage <u>and</u> result in a net gain in system reliability. Since mission time improvement and system reliability can be traded this also can be interpreted as giving a net gain in mission time. Consider the case in which there are 2 spares, the coverage is .9 and R_0 = .99.

Now, s = 2, c = .9 and λT = .01. Referring to the Tables 3.1:2, as previously considered, there is a maximum potential mission time improvement of 10.55 at this reliability level if the coverage could be made perfect without adding any extra equipment. On the other hand, if the coverage can be made perfect using less than 10.55 times the original equipment, it is still possible to obtain a mission time and/or reliability improvement. In actual practice, constraints such as powering, delay, size, etc., may prevent the use of equipment augmentations of the magnitude of those indicated. However, the clear rule is that whenever the coverage is low, adding reasonable amounts of extra equipment to improve the coverage is both permissible and highly advisable. The fact that each individual module is becoming more unreliable due to the added equipment is more than off-set by increasing the coverage.

If q > 1, Equation (2:7) can be solved using various numerical methods, e.g., using Newton's iteration. The tabulated results of such an exercise are shown in Table 3.1:3 for $\lambda=\mu$ and a range of s, λT, q and c. Each entry is a sequence of three values of aI corresponding to q = 1, 2, 3 (the entries for q = 1 can be compared with those in Table 3.1:2). The effect of q > 1 is to decrease the aI values slightly.

	s				s		
aI	1	3		aI	1	3	
	1.049	2.025	1		1.415	10.55	1
.99	1.033	1.672	2	.99	1.292	8.444	2
c	1.025	1.470	3 q	c	1.226	7.137	3 q
	1.426	3.854	1		3.348	19.60	1
.9	1.301	3.153	2	.9	2.800	15.78	2
	1.233	2.717	3		2.480	13.41	3

$\lambda T = .1$ $\qquad\qquad\qquad$ $\lambda T = .01$

Exact aI values for q = 1, 2, 3

Table 3.1:3

The improvement in mission time achieved at a fixed reliability level by keeping the spares in the power off state so $\lambda \ne \mu$ is given below for the special case q = 1 over a range of parameters commonly encountered in practice. Again, the results were obtained by numerical solution of

$$_c R^q_s (IT, \lambda, \mu) \ge\ _c R^q_s (T, \lambda)$$

λ/μ $\qquad\qquad\qquad$ λ/μ

I for c = 1

		2	10		2	10
	1	1.154	1.348		1.152	1.344
s	2	1.260	1.656		1.256	1.649
	3	1.337	1.933		1.333	1.923

R = .99 $\qquad\qquad\qquad$ R = .9

I for c = .99

		2	10		2	10
	1	1.097	1.203		1.144	1.323
s	2	1.007	1.012		1.176	1.395
	3	1.003	1.005		1.074	1.127

R = .99 $\qquad\qquad\qquad$ R = .9

I for c = .9

		2	10		2	10
	1	1.020	1.037		1.092	1.194
s	2	1.003	1.005		1.050	1.091
	3	1.002	1.004		1.027	1.049

R = .99 $\qquad\qquad\qquad$ R = .9

Table 2.3:4

The tables clearly show the strong dependence of I on c. However, even under the best conditions (c, λ/μ, R and s all large) the mission time improvement is not very great.

3.2 Analyses Using the MTBF

By (2:6)

$$MTBF(_c R^q_s (t, \lambda, \mu)) = \sum_{i=0}^{s} \frac{c^i}{q\lambda + i\mu} \le \frac{s+1}{s + q\lambda/\mu} \frac{-\ln(1-c)}{c\mu}$$

Since $q\lambda/\mu \ge 1$, this means that no matter how many spares are added, the MTBF cannot exceed

$$\frac{-\ln(1-c)}{c\mu} \qquad \text{or} \qquad \frac{-\ln(1-c)}{c}$$

times the power off MTBF of a single module in this system. Further, this bound is approached very slowly as s is increased.

For the two cases c = .9 and c = .99 this bound together with the exact MTBF values for s = 2, 5, 10 are given below. The entries are in terms of the power-off MTBF of a single module, i.e. $1/\mu$.

c	$MTBF(_c R_2)$	$MTBF(_c R_5)$	$MTBF(_c R_{10})$	$\frac{-\ln(1-c)}{c}$
.9	$1.72/\mu$	$2.13/\mu$	$2.39/\mu$	$2.56/\mu$
.99	$1.82/\mu$	$2.41/\mu$	$2.94/\mu$	$5.1 /\mu$

Table 3.2:1

Notice that the multiplicative factor $\frac{-\ln(1-c)}{c}$ for the MTBF is very small compared with 100 to say nothing of the ∞ theoretically possible with c = 1.

The changes in the MTBF tabulated above are difficult to interpret clearly. All these figures show is a strong dependence on c - with a potential very sharp increase for a c greater than .99. This shows that for practical as well as theoretical reasons the MTBF is a poor figure of merit for highly reliable computers.

3.3 Analyses Using the Reliability, $_c^f R^q_s(t, \lambda, \mu)$.

Equation (2:2) shows that adding an extra spare to an $_c R^q_s(t, \lambda, \mu)$ system increases the reliability by an increment

$$e^{-q\lambda T} \binom{s + q\lambda/\mu}{s+1} [c(1 - e^{-\mu T})]^{s+1}$$

for a mission of length T.

The first term in the Taylor expansion of this increment involves $(\mu T)^{s+1}$. Since the Taylor expansion of Equation (2:2) contains terms involving $(\mu T)^i$ and $(\lambda T)^i$ for all $i < s + 1$, with coefficients that vanish as $c \to 1$ (c.f. Equation (2:4)), it is clear that the net reliability gain due to addition of another spare is not very great unless $c \approx 1$, i.e. for $c \ne 1$ the lower terms dominate.

As a specific example, with $\lambda=\mu$,

$$_cR_1 = 1-(1-c)\lambda T + (1-3c)\frac{(\lambda T)^2}{2} - (1-7c)\frac{(\lambda T)^3}{6} + \ldots$$

$$_cR_2 = 1-(1-c)\lambda T + (1-3c+2c^2)\frac{(\lambda T)^2}{2}$$
$$- (1-7c+12c^2)\frac{(\lambda T)^3}{6} + \ldots$$

$$_cR_3 = 1-(1-c)\lambda T + (1-3c+2c^2)\frac{(\lambda T)^2}{2}$$
$$- (1-7c+12c^2-6c^3)\frac{(\lambda T)^3}{6} + \ldots$$

and for reliable systems (small λT) unless c is close to 1, the reliability gain is small by going from one spare to two or three, and the incremental gain by adding more spares is less.

Since the bound in (2:5) is 1 for c = 1, it is clear that perfect coverage provides for unlimited reliability potential if enough spares are used. With less than perfect coverage, not only is the reliability potential bounded no matter how many spares are used, but since the partial derivative of the bound with respect to c is

$$q\lambda/\mu \; [\frac{e^{-\mu t}}{1-c(1-e^{-\mu t})}]^{q\lambda/\mu} \; \frac{(1-e^{-\mu t})}{1-c(1-e^{-\mu t})} \geq 0$$

as the coverage decreases, $(c \to 0)$, the reliability bound monotonically decreases toward $e^{-q\lambda t}$.

The following table gives reliability bounds over common ranges of c and $e^{-\mu t}$ for $\mu=\lambda$, q=1.

Bound $_cR_\infty$	c				
	.99	.95	.9	.8	.7
$e^{-\mu t}$ .99	.999899	.999495	.998990	.997983	.996978
.95	.999473	.997375	.994764	.989583	.984455
.9	.998890	.994475	.989010	.978260	.967741
.8	.997506	.987654	.975609	.952380	.930232

Table 3.3:1

The rapid rate of approach of $_cR_s$ to this bound as spares are added is illustrated below for c = .9 and R = .9. As contrast, the values of R_s for c = 1 and R = .9 are also given.

	s				
	0	1	2	3	5
$_{.9}R_s =$	.9	.981	.98829	.988946	.989010
$_1R_s =$	.9	.99	.999	.9999	.999999

Table 3.3:2

The equation

$$_cR^f = R \sum_{k=0}^{f} \frac{(c\lambda T)^k}{k!}$$

is the probability that a module operates reliably with f or less recovered failures with q = 1 and $\lambda=\mu$. Using a simple enumeration procedure, the system reliability can be shown to be

$$_cR_s^f = _cR^f \sum_{i=0}^{s} [c^{f+1}(1-{}^fR)]^i$$

This series can be expressed in closed form as

$$_cR_s^f = _cR^f \; \frac{1-c^{(f+1)(s+1)}(1-{}^fR)^{s+1}}{1-c^{f+1}(1-{}^fR)}$$

As must be expected, when f=0 these latter two equations do reduce to the forms previously given. In this system the reliability increment when the number of spares is increased from s to s+1 is

$$_cR^f \; c^{(f+1)(s+1)} (1-{}^fR)^{s+1}$$

which means the smallest term in $c\lambda T$ added to the power series expansion is

$$\frac{(c\lambda T)^{(f+1)(s+1)}}{[(f+1)!]^{s+1}}$$

When c is not near 1 this term is negligible compared to the first (f+1)(s+1) - 1 terms already in the series.

4. A System Design Study

For the purpose of illustrating how the models in the previous chapter can be used by the system architect, a typical reliability design study is carried out on a hypothetical computing system. The goal of such a study is to analyze the particular mix of redundancy techniques used throughout the system in order to locate both weak links in the system (comparatively low reliability) and excessively strong links in the system (comparatively high reliability). Available methods for alleviating these difficulties include adding hardware to improve the coverage, relaxing the coverage requirements, adding spare modules, removing spare modules, etc. Selected system modifications can then be evaluated to ascertain the "best" method for balancing[1] the subsystem's reliability.

---

[1] From a reliability standpoint, balancing means redesign to eliminate the obvious under- and over- design of any subsystems' reliability.

Figure 4:1 is the block diagram for the system to be studied. Table 4:1 contains a list of each subsystem, its mnemonic as used on the block diagram, and the applicable reliability model. The system requirements call for 2 Channels, 6 Main Stores, 3 Control and Local Stores,[2] 4 Arithmetic Logic Units, 1 Special Operation Unit (e.g. a trigonometric function), 1 Storage Control Unit, 1 Instruction Control Unit and 3 Power Supplies to be operational. Standby sparing is to be used on all these subsystems.

The main clocking oscillator is TMR'd [6]. The System Status and Interconnection Control[1,2] is designed to employ error correction encoding so that it can tolerate f failures before malfunctioning. Two of the busses, the Data Input Buss and the Storage Buffer Buss, are 36 bits wide with s spare lines provided [1]. The remaining busses are error correction encoded or provided with interconnection control switching [2] to provide failure intolerance.

---

[2] The control store and local store are assumed to be of the same physical structure and technology.

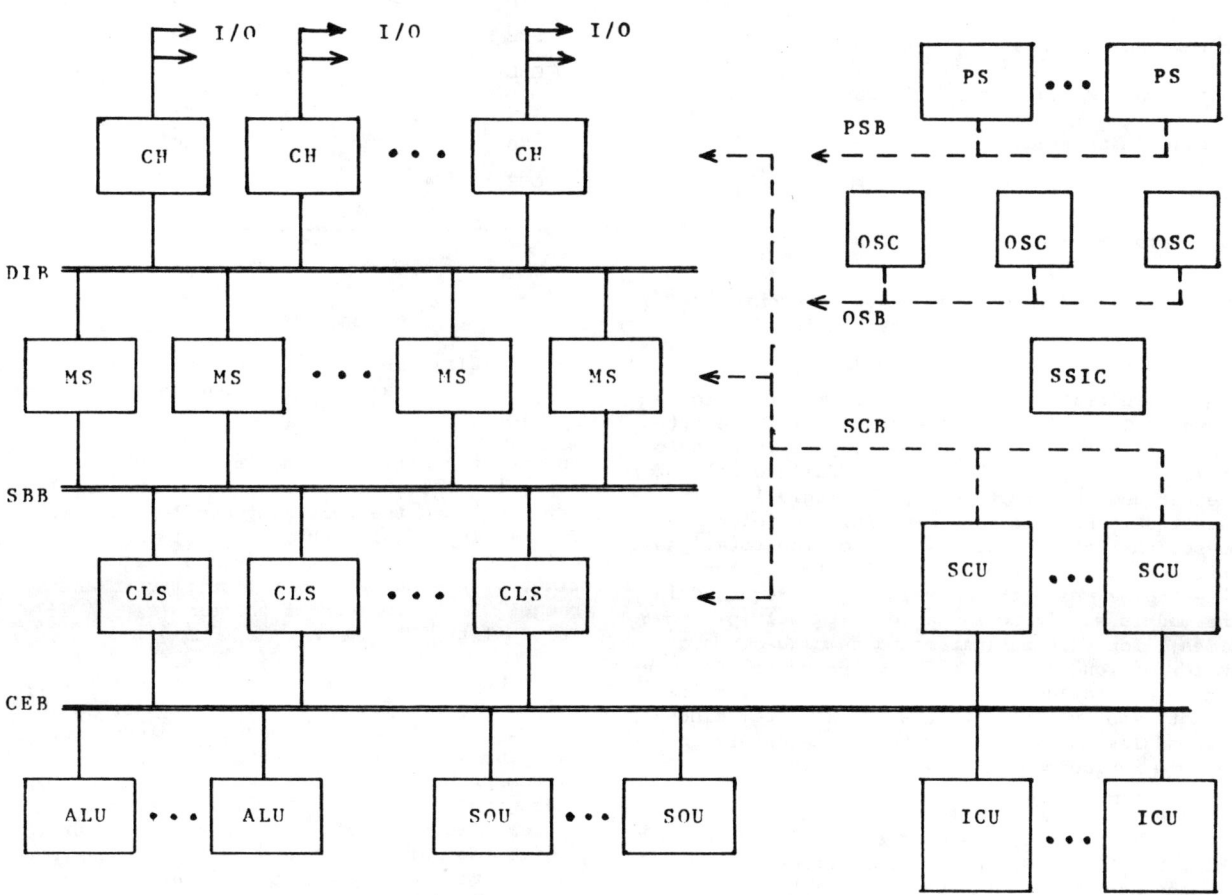

Figure 4:1 Hypothetical System Structure.

System Component	Mnemonic	Model
Channel	CH	$R_c^2 R_s$
Main Storage	MS	$R_c^6 R_s$
Control and Local Storage	CLS	$R_c^3 R_s$
Arithmetic Logic Unit	ALU	$R_c^4 R_s$
Special Operation Unit	SOU	$R_c R_s$
Storage Control Unit	SCU	$R_c R_s$
Instruction Control Unit	ICU	$R_c R_s$
Power Supply	PS	$R_c^3 R_s$
Oscillator	OSC	R_{TMR}
System Status & Inter-Connection Control	SSIC	$_f R_c$
Data Input Buss	DIB	$R_c^{36} R_s$
Storage Buffer Buss	SBB	$R_c^{36} R_s$
Control and Execute Buss	CEB	$_f R_c$
Storage Control Buss	SCB	$_f R_c$
Power Supply Buss	PSB	$_f R_c$
Oscillator Buss	OSB	$_f R_c$

Table 4:1 System Components, Mnemonics and Reliability Models.

The initial hypothetical system structure is shown in Table 4:2(a). The assumed failure rates assigned to each subsystem module are in units of failures per million hours. The failure rates for the DIB and SBB are those for a single line in the set of 36. For the remaining failure tolerant busses the failure rate is that of the total buss. This particular method of quoting the failure rates coincides with the values of λ required in the models specified in Table 4:1. Multiplying q times λ for each subsystem and summing gives an approximation to the total simplex system failure rate: 527 failures/10^6 hours. This failure rate is not exactly that of the simplex system since the modules contain the switching necessary to perform replacement in standby sparing.

The balancing of this system will take place for a mission time of 4 months: it is assumed this will be the tentative time between scheduled maintenance. The total system reliability is computed as

$$R_{sys} = \prod_{\text{all subsystems}} R_{subsystem}$$

	λ	S	C	%P
CH	15	2	.97	9.9
MS	45	5	.99	30.7
CLS	30	3	.97	29.1
ALU	10	2	.99	5.4
SOU	5	1	.99	1.3
SCU	10	1	.97	5.6
ICU	10	1	.97	5.6
PS	10	2	.99	3.8
OSC	2	-	1.00	.4
SSIC	5	f=1	.97	1.9
DIB	.25	1	.99	2.1
SBB	.25	1	.99	2.1
CEB	5	f=1	.97	1.9
SCB	5	f=1	.97	1.9
PSB	5	f=1	.99	.9
OSB	2	f=1	.99	.3

$R_{sys} = .969750$

$P_{sys} = .030250$

Table 4:2(a) Initial System Configurations with Failure Contribution at T=4 Months.

on an interactive terminal system [9] where the subsystem reliability models are obtained from Table 4:1 and the pertinent model parameters from Table 4:2(a). The goal is to obtain a balanced system, for the given 4 month mission time, with total system reliability in the range .97-.99 instead of the simplex reliability .21.

Table 4:2(a) shows an initial system reliability of .96975, or a probability of failure of .03025. The column headed %P gives, for each subsystem, the percent of the total system probability of failure contributed by that given subsystem. Thus, in the initial system structure, 30.7% of the failures are due to the Main Stores and 29.1% are due to the Control and Local Stores. This parameter, %P, is the one to be balanced across the set of subsystems.

Since 60% of the failures are due to the MS and CLS the balancing process should start with the improvement of these subsystems. As a first possible solution an extra spare will be added to both the MS and CLS. The two rightmost columns in Table 4:3 show that increasing the number of spares has little effect on the balance and total system reliability. Examination of the left column also shows that decreasing the number of spares has little effect! To the knowledgeable designer it is apparent that <u>the trouble lies with the low coverage not with the number of spares</u> (c.f. Section 3).

		INITIAL			FINAL
λ	CH	15	15	15	16.5
	MS	45	49.5	49.5	49.5
	CLS	30	33	39.93	39.93
c	CH	.97	.97	.97	.98
	MS	.99	.999	.999	.999
	CLS	.97	.98	.999	.999
%P	CH	9.9	13.7	17.4	14.3
	MS	30.7	11.2	14.2	14.8
	CLS	29.1	31.8	12.9	13.4
R_{sys}		.96975	.97829	.98291	.98352
P_{sys}		.03025	.02171	.01709	.01648

Table 4:4 Variation as Coverage is Improved.

	No. of Spares in MS and CLS		
%P	1 Less	Initial	1 More
CH	4.2	5.3	6.4
MS	33.2	30.7	29.5
CLS	34.7	29.1	28.5
R_{sys}	.96270	.96975	.97092
R_{sys}	.03730	.03025	.02908

Table 4:3 Variation in MS and CLS with Spares.

The leftmost column in Table 4:4 gives λ, c and %P for the initial CH, MS and CLS structure. Suppose the system designer determines that by redesigning the CH and CLS the coverage can be raised to .999 and .98, respectively, at an extra cost of 10% more hardware per module. Entering this change in the terminal, the result is shown in the second column of Table 4:4. At this point the CLS is the weak link in the system; contributing 31.8% of the total system failures. Another CLS redesign shows that an additional 20% increase in hardware brings the coverage to .999 and results in the system shown in the third column. In general this system looks fairly good. However, while the MS and CLS were being improved it was natural that the percent failure contributions of the other subsystems should rise slightly. In particular the third column in Table 4:4 shows that the channel now contributes 17.4% of the system failures. The final system structure in the last column is obtained by assuming that the system designer invests 10% more hardware in the channel to raise its coverage to .98.

A complete enumeration of all subsystem parameters for this final system structure is shown in Table 4:2(b). Although the Oscillator and Oscillator Buss make very low contributions to the probability of failure their level of redundancy cannot be reduced without drastic impact on the system.

The final system is balanced at an assumed mission time of 4 months. Table 4:5 shows how the relative subsystem balance is affected as the mission time varies from 1 month to 12 months in one month increments. Since the subsystems have widely varying reliability models for which $\delta R/\delta T$ differs greatly, one would expect to see the system become unbalanced for T different from 4 months. The unbalancing with changing T appears to be most prevalent when subsystems with wide variations in λ are present (e.g., the MS and SOU in this system have a λ ratio of 10). This unbalancing illustrates the danger in using such a system in a mission environment other than the one for which it was designed.

The change in system reliability with mission time for the final system is shown in Figure 4:2. As guides there are reliability plots for the cases where all coverages are perfect (c = 1) and where all coverages equal to .95. It is seen that the high coverages in the dominant subsystems (i.e. MS, CLS, etc.) are reflected by the nearness of the final system plot to that for c = 1. The tremendous penalty for poor coverage is also clearly indicated by the spread between the c = 1 and c = .95 curves.

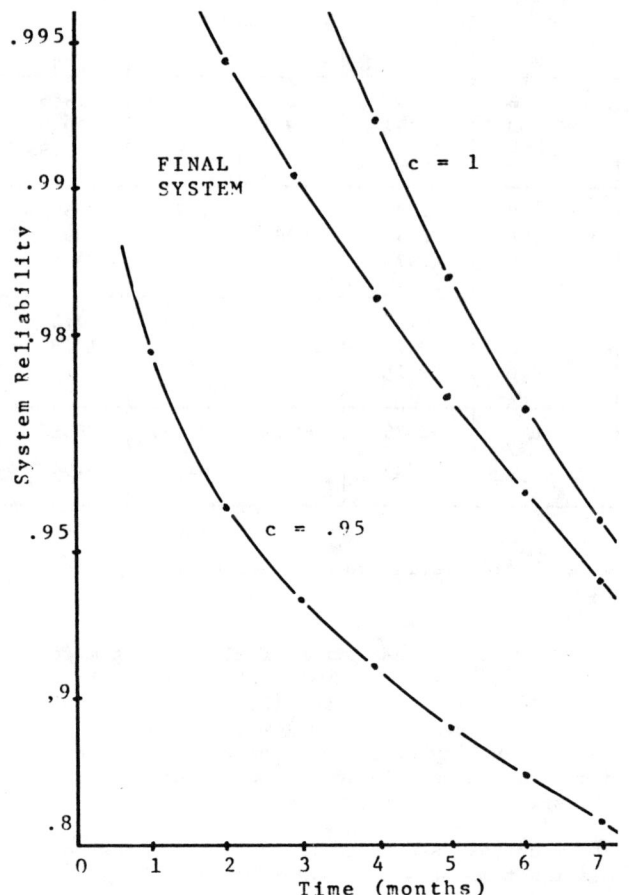

Figure 4:2 System Reliability vs Mission Time

	λ	S	C	%P
CH	16.5	2	.98	14.0
MS	49.5	5	.999	14.4
CLS	39.93	3	.999	13.1
ALU	10	2	.99	9.7
SOU	5	1	.99	2.1
SCU	10	1	.97	10.0
ICU	10	1	.97	10.0
PS	10	2	.99	6.6
OSC	2	–	1.00	.7
SSIC	5	f=1	.97	3.3
DIB	.25	1	.99	3.7
SBB	.25	1	.99	3.7
CEB	5	f=1	.97	3.3
SCB	5	f=1	.97	3.3
PSB	5	f=1	.99	1.6
OSB	2	f=1	.99	.6

$R_{sys} = .983515$

$\overline{R}_{sys} = .016485$

Table 4:2(b) Final System Configurations with Failure Contribution at T = 4 Months.

%P	FINAL SYSTEM Mission Time (Months)											
	1	2	3	4	5	6	7	8	9	10	11	12
CH	19.5	17.9	16.2	14	11.9	10	8.5	7.3	6.4	5.7	5.3	4.9
MS	8.8	8.6	10.2	14.4	20.8	27.6	34	39.5	43.8	47.1	49.8	51.8
CLS	3.9	5.7	9	13.1	16.7	19.3	20.9	21.8	22.2	22.5	22.6	22.8
ALU	11.9	11.3	10.6	9.7	8.6	7.6	6.7	6	5.4	5	4.7	4.5
SOU	2.1	2.3	2.4	2.1	1.9	1.7	1.4	1.2	1.1	1	0.9	0.8
SCU	10.7	11.2	10.9	10	8.6	7.4	6.2	5.2	4.5	4	3.6	3.2
ICU	10.7	11.2	10.9	10	8.6	7.4	6.2	5.2	4.5	4	3.6	3.2
PS	8.8	8.3	7.6	6.6	5.7	4.9	4.3	3.7	3.4	3.1	2.8	2.7
OSC	0.3	0.5	0.6	0.7	0.6	0.6	0.6	0.5	0.5	0.4	0.4	0.4
SSIC	4.6	4.3	3.8	3.3	2.7	2.1	1.7	1.4	1.2	1	0.9	0.8
DIB	3.5	3.8	3.9	3.7	3.3	2.8	2.4	2.1	1.8	1.7	1.5	1.3
SBB	3.5	3.8	3.9	3.7	3.3	2.8	2.4	2.1	1.8	1.7	1.5	1.3
CEB	4.6	4.3	3.8	3.3	2.7	2.1	1.7	1.4	1.2	1	0.9	0.8
SCB	4.6	4.3	3.8	3.3	2.7	2.1	1.7	1.4	1.2	1	0.9	0.8
PSB	1.8	1.8	1.8	1.6	1.4	1.2	1	0.9	0.8	0.6	0.5	0.5
OSB	0.7	0.7	0.6	0.6	0.5	0.4	0.3	0.3	0.3	0.3	0.2	0.2
System Prob. of Failure	.002507	.005658	.010004	.016485	.026353	.040972	.061568	.089009	.123669	.165376	.213445	.266777

Table 4:5 Subsystems Percentage Contribution to Probability of System Failure for Various Mission Time.

5. Conclusions

Modeling

The extreme sensitivity of high reliability computer system designs to certain system parameters (c.f. system parameters below) dictates a careful, well thought out modeling process prior to design. The particular reliability models developed here are considered extremely useful in indicating those changes in key system parameters which result in the maximum rate of increase in system reliability. It is to be emphasized that absolute numbers are not considered of prime importance here; relative results are. This is dictated in part by a general uncertainty in many parameters relating to computer system design. In those cases where an adequate data base is not available it may be necessary to resort to more extensive hardware models for data acquisition.

System Parameters

For systems which must operate at high reliability levels for <u>long</u> mission times, standby sparing has, by far, the greatest potential. However, interactive terminal calculations have shown that the coverage, defined to be the probability of system recovery given the existence of a failure, is the single most important parameter in high-reliability system design. Changing the coverage from 1 to about .98 can result in orders of magnitude degredation in system mission time. Most techniques for increasing system reliability (e.g. adding more spares, etc.) are futile in the face of inadequate coverage: here inadequate means c as large as .99.

Adding checking, diagnostics, etc. to improve failure coverage is shown to be the most advantageous technique by examples of system tradeoff evaluation. Accurate estimation of the coverage, c, is difficult and requires accurate measurement of the effect of component errors, but may be done by using known techniques [12,13]. This mandates extensive application of modeling techniques throughout all computer system design phases.

Reliability Performance Measures

Since MTBF places undue emphasis on the tail of the distribution, it is not a meaningful measure for comparing complex high-reliability systems. The ratio of mission times to achieve a given reliability level was repeatedly shown to be a superior method for comparing such systems.

Warning

It is important to remember that in performing computer system reliability modeling or tradeoff studies the burden of model <u>accuracy</u> must fall directly on the system designer. The model builder can only assure the <u>precision</u> of the model. Only the designer can determine whether his particular system fits the particular model he is using. Thus the designer must always be prepared to live with the "Garbage In-Garbage Out" axiom.

Appendix – Notation Summary and Proof Of Formulae Used

Notation Summary

System Parameters.

- s – number of spares initially available.
- q – number of modules required to be operating at all times (power on).
- c – the conditional probability that after a failure in the operational system the system is able to recover and continue information processing with no permanent loss of essential information.
- f – number of single failures tolerated by a module before correct module operation ceases.
- T – mission time, time interval of reliability study.
- I – mission time improvement ration (T_B/T_A).
- MTBF – Mean Time Between Failures.

Module Parameters.

- t – time
- λ – failure rate during power on.
- μ – failure rate during power off.
- a – multiplicative factor for varying amount of circuitry in a module.

Reliability Formulae.

$_c^f R_s^q (t,\lambda,\mu)$ nothing elided

$_c^f R_s^q (t,\lambda)$ $\mu = \lambda$

$_c^f R_s^q (t)$ $\mu = \lambda$, λ understood

$_c^f R_s^q$ $\mu = \lambda; \lambda$, t understood

In addition, whenever f, q, c, or s is elided its value is assumed to be 0, 1, 1, or 0 respectively.

Proofs

A Poisson distribution of hardware failures [11] will be assumed so that the basic module reliability becomes

$$R = e^{-\lambda T} \qquad (A:1)$$

The formulation of $_c^{}R_s^q$ with the spare modules kept in a power off state until they are required to replace failed modules is recursive.

$$_cR^q_0(T,\lambda,\mu) = e^{-q\lambda T}$$

$$_cR^q_s(T,\lambda,\mu) = {_cR^q_{s-1}}(T,\lambda,\mu) \quad (A:2)$$
$$+ \int_0^T c^s \frac{d}{dt}[1-R^q_{s-1}(t,\lambda,\mu)]e^{-\mu t} e^{-q\lambda(T-t)} dt$$

This formulation says the reliability with s spares is due to reliable operation with s-1 spares augmented by the reliability increment due to having the sth spare. This latter term is expressed as the integral over [0,T] of the product of:

1) $\frac{d}{dt}[1-R^q_{s-1}(t,\lambda,\mu)]$; the probability density of having the system with s-1 spares fail at some time t, $0 \le t \le T$;

2) $e^{-\mu t}$; the probability that the sth spare has survived in the power-off state until time t when it is needed;

3) $e^{-q\lambda(T-t)}$; the probability that after replacing the failed module with the sth spare the refurbished system survives the remaining time until T;

4) c^s; the probability that s successful recoveries have occurred.

The solution to this recursive equation is

$$_cR^q_s(T,\lambda,\mu) = e^{-q\lambda T} \sum_{i=0}^{s} \binom{k-1+q\lambda/\mu}{k} c^k (1-e^{-\mu T})^k$$
(A:3)

where $\binom{k-1+q\lambda/\mu}{k}$ are generalized binomial coefficients since λ/μ may not be integral. The derivation of this result is inductive with the inductive step for s > 2 using

$$\frac{d}{dt} R^q_{s-1}(t,\lambda,\mu) = -q\lambda e^{-q\lambda t}\binom{s-1+q\lambda/\mu}{s-1}(1-e^{-\mu t})^{s-1}$$
(A:4)

in Equation (A:2) to obtain (A:3) followed by a demonstration that differentiating (A:3) with respect to t, with c = 1, does give the form of Equation (A:4). This proves formula (2:2).

The following lemma, easily proved by induction, leads to another useful form for $_cR^q_s$.

<u>Lemma A:1</u> For n integral, $y \le 1$ and $z \ge 0$

$$\sum_{i=0}^{n} \binom{z+n+1}{i} y^i (1-y)^{n-i} = \sum_{i=0}^{n} \binom{z+i}{i} y^i$$

By the lemma,

$$_cR^q_s(T) = e^{-q\lambda T}[1-c(1-e^{-\mu T})]^s$$
$$\times \sum_{i=0}^{s} \binom{s+q\lambda/\mu}{i} [c(1-e^{-\mu T})]^i [1-c(1-e^{-\mu T})]^{-i}$$

By the generalized binomial theorem [10],

$$\left[\frac{1}{1-c(1-e^{-\mu t})}\right]^{s+q\lambda/\mu} = \sum_{i=0}^{s} \binom{s+q\lambda/\mu}{i} \left[\frac{c(1-e^{-\mu T})}{1-c(1-e^{-\mu T})}\right]^i$$
$$+ \sum_{i=s+1}^{\infty} \binom{s+q\lambda/\mu}{i} \left[\frac{c(1-e^{-\mu T})}{1-c(1-e^{-\mu T})}\right]^i$$

So,

$$_cR^q_s(T,\lambda,\mu) = e^{-q\lambda T}\left\{\frac{1}{[1-c(1-e^{-\mu T})]^{q\lambda/\mu}}\right.$$
$$\left. - \frac{[c(1-e^{-\mu T})]^{s+1}}{1-c(1-e^{-\mu T})} \times \sum_{i=s+1}^{\infty} \binom{s+q\lambda/\mu}{i}\left[\frac{c(1-e^{-\mu T})}{1-c(1-e^{-\mu T})}\right]^{i-s-1}\right\}$$

and this may be rewritten as

$$_cR^q_s(T,\lambda,\mu) = \left[\frac{e^{-\mu T}}{1-c(1-e^{-\mu T})}\right]^{q\lambda/\mu}\{1-[c(1-e^{-\mu T})]^{s+1}$$
$$\times [1-c(1-e^{-\mu T})]^{q\lambda/\mu - 1} \quad (A:5)$$
$$\times \sum_{i=s+1}^{\infty} \binom{s+q\lambda/\mu}{i}\left[\frac{c(1-e^{-\mu T})}{1-c(1-e^{-\mu T})}\right]^{i-s-1}\}$$

The terms in the infinite series in (A:5) will alternate in sign after a certain point. If all pairs of terms are grouped after alternation of sign begins and $c(1-e^{-\mu T}) < 1/2$ then the resulting series has positive terms and $_c R^q_s(t,\lambda,\mu)$ is bounded by $\left[\dfrac{e^{-\mu T}}{1-c(1-e^{-\mu T})}\right]^{q\lambda/\mu}$ as stated in formula (2:5). By comparing expansions for s and s+1 it can be proved that if

$$c(1-e^{-\mu T})^{\frac{1}{\alpha}} < \frac{s+2}{s+1+q\lambda/\mu}, \quad \alpha > 1,$$

then the bound is approached monotonically as stated in Section 2.

If λ/μ is an integer, the binomial expansion is finite and repeated applications of Lemma A:1, together with a change in order of summation, give

$$_c R^q_s(T,\lambda,\mu) = \left[\frac{e^{-\mu T}}{1-c(1-e^{-\mu T})}\right]^{q\lambda/\mu} \times \{1-[c(1-e^{-\mu T})]^{s+1}$$

$$\times \sum_{i=0}^{q\lambda/\mu - 1} \binom{s+i}{i}[1-c(1-e^{-\mu T})]^i\}$$

(A:6)

which is formula (2:3).

The MTBF is, as usual, easy to calculate.

$$\text{MTBF}(_c R^q_s) = \sum_{k=0}^{s} c^k \binom{k-1+q\lambda/\mu}{k} \int_0^\infty e^{-q\lambda t}(1-e^{-\mu t})^k dt$$

(A:7)

Define

$$I(q+j\mu/\lambda, k-j) = \int_0^\infty e^{-(q+j\mu/\lambda)\lambda x}(1-e^{-\mu x})^{k-j}dx$$

Then integration by parts proves

$$I(q+j\mu/\lambda, k-j) = \frac{k-j}{j+q\lambda/\mu} I(q+(j+1)\mu/\lambda, k-j-1)$$

so, by iteration,

$$I(q,k) = \frac{1}{\lambda q} \frac{1}{\binom{k+q\lambda/\mu}{k}}$$

(A:8)

Now, since $q\lambda/\mu \geq 1$,

$$\text{MTBF}(_c R^q_s(t,\lambda,\mu)) = \frac{1}{\mu}\left[\frac{1}{q\lambda/\mu} + \frac{c}{1+q\lambda/\mu} + \ldots + \frac{c^s}{s+q\lambda/\mu}\right]$$

$$\leq \frac{s+1}{s+q\lambda/\mu} \frac{1}{c\mu}\left[c + \frac{c^2}{2} + \ldots + \frac{c^{s+1}}{s+1}\right]$$

$$\leq \frac{s+1}{s+q\lambda/\mu} \frac{-\ln(1-c)}{c\mu}$$

(A:9)

BIBLIOGRAPHY

1. J. P. Roth, W. G. Bouricius, W. C. Carter and P. R. Schneider, Phase II of an Architectural Study for a Self-Repairing Computer, SAMSO TR-67-106, Nov. 1967.

2. A. Avizienis, "Design of Fault-Tolerant Computers", FJCC, Vol. 31, pp. 733-743, 1967.

3. C. W. Churchman, R. L. Ackoff and E. L. Arnoff, Introduction to Operations Research, Chapter 1, Wiley, New York, 1957.

4. J. K. Knox-Seith, A Redundancy Technique for Improving the Reliability of Digital Systems, Stanford Electronics Laboratory, TR No. 4816-1, Dec. 1963.

5. W. G. Bouricius, W. C. Carter, J. P. Roth and P. R. Schneider, Investigations in the Design of an Automatically Repaired Computer, First Annual IEEE Computer Conference, Sept, 1967.

6. J. von Neumann, "Probabilistic Logics and the Synthesis of Reliable Organisms from Unreliable Components", Automata Studies, Annals of Mathematics, No.34, pp.43-98, Princeton, 1956.

7. J. G. Tryon, Quadded Logic, Redundancy Techniques for Computing Systems, Spartan Books, 1962.

8. P. O. Nerber, "Power Off Time Impact on Reliability Estimates", IEEE Int. Convention Rec., Part 10, pp. 1-5, March 22-26, New York.

9. A. D. Falkoff and K. E. Iverson, The APL Terminal System, Instructions for Operation, IBM Watson Research Center, Yorktown Heights, N. Y., March 1966.

10. R. Courant, Differential and Integral Calculus, Vol. 1, P. 330, Nordemann Publishing Co., 1937.

11. W. S. Feller, An Introduction to Probability Theory and Its Application, Volume I, Wiley, New York, 1957,

12. W. C. Carter and P. R. Schneider, Design of Dynamically Checked Computers, IFIPS '68, Edinburgh, Scotland.

13. W. G. Bouricius, W. C. Carter, K. A. Duke, J. P. Roth and P. R. Schneider, Interactive Design of Self-Testing Circuitry, Purdue Centennial Symp. on Information Processing, May 1969.

A Unified Reliability Model for Fault-Tolerant Computers

YING W. NG, MEMBER, IEEE, AND ALGIRDAS A. AVIZIENIS, FELLOW, IEEE

Abstract—The diversified nature of fault-tolerant computers led to the development of a multiplicity of reliability models which are seemingly unrelated to each other. As a result, it becomes difficult to develop automated tools for reliability analysis which are both general and efficient. Thus, the potential of reliability modeling as a practical and useful tool in the design process of fault-tolerant computers has not been fully realized. This paper summarizes the results of an extended effort to develop a unified approach to reliability modeling of fault-tolerant computers which strikes a good compromise between generality and practicality. The unified model developed encompasses repairable and nonrepairable systems and models, transient as well as permanent faults, and their recovery. Based on the unified model, a powerful and efficient reliability estimation program ARIES has been developed.

Index Terms—Computer reliability, fault tolerance, graceful degradation, reliability estimation, reliability modeling, transient fault analysis.

I. INTRODUCTION

BECAUSE of the flexibility and low cost with which reliability estimates can be made, reliability modeling has been an important and popular tool in the design and evaluation of fault-tolerant computer systems. For this purpose, many important reliability models have been developed in the past for a variety of fault-tolerant computer structures. Up to now, most of these models have been developed in an "ad hoc" fashion, leading to scattered and sometimes unnecessarily complex results that are difficult to apply. Consequently, it also becomes difficult to develop automated tools for reliability analysis that are both powerful and efficient. Thus, the potential of reliability modeling as a practical and useful tool in the design process of fault-tolerant computers has not been fully realized.

A recent effort [1] has led to a unified approach to the reliability modeling of fault-tolerant computer systems. By applying Markov modeling techniques in a systematic manner, a unified reliability model was developed which strikes a good compromise between generality and practicality. The model not only allows the reliability estimation of a wide spectrum of repairable and nonrepairable systems with permanent and transient fault recovery capabilities, but does so in a computationally efficient manner. Because of the availability of such a model, it becomes possible to develop a reliability estimation program with capability and efficiency far superior to existing programs of its kind.

Previous publications [2]–[5] have presented various aspects of this modeling approach. The present paper endeavors to summarize and present, in a unified framework, the results of this research effort. We will begin by summarizing the parameters of this unified model. After that, we will solve the modeling problem for closed systems, i.e., the subclass of fault-tolerant systems which do not allow manual repair. We will next extend this solution to repairable systems with an attempt to maintain efficiency and compatibility of the solution without overly sacrificing generality. We will next demonstrate the technique used in incorporating transient fault recovery modeling into the general model. Finally, a description of ARIES, which is an interactive program developed for flexible and efficient reliability estimation based on the modeling results described previously, will be presented.

II. PARAMETERS OF THE UNIFIED RELIABILITY MODEL

A fault-tolerant computer system is treated as a set of homogeneous subsystems, such as memories, processors, busses, etc. Each homogeneous subsystem consists of a set of identical modules that are either in *active* or in *spare* status. "Active" here means "participating in the computing process," i.e., a powered spare is *not* active, although its failure rate is normally the same as that of an active module. It is assumed that every subsystem must survive in order for the system to survive. With this assumption, the system reliability is the product of the individual reliability of each subsystem. The parameters described in this section represent one homogeneous subsystem, i.e., set of identical modules.

The parameters that characterize one homogeneous set of modules can be divided into two classes.

1) Parameters describing the static properties of the set. These include the *physical* properties, *structural* properties, and the off-line *repair* properties.

2) Parameters describing the dynamic properties of the set, that is, the quality of *fault-detection* and *fault-recovery* techniques.

The goal of this section is to define and briefly explain all the parameters and basic assumptions of the model. Further

---

Manuscript received August 22, 1977; revised April 10, 1980. This work was supported by the National Science Foundation under Grant MCS72-03633 A04.

Y. W. Ng was with the Department of Computer Science, University of California, Los Angeles, CA 90024. He is now with Bell Laboratories, Naperville, IL 60540.

A. A. Avizienis is with the Department of Computer Science, University of California, Los Angeles, CA 90024.

discussion of the rationale behind the choice of these parameters are given in subsequent sections.

A. Physical Parameters

The *physical* parameters characterize the physical reliability properties of the modules. For *permanent* faults they are

λ = failure rate of one active module ($\lambda > 0$)

μ = failure rate of one spare module ($\mu > 0$).

All spares are assumed to have the same failure rate. This implies that they are either all powered (then $\lambda = \mu$) or all unpowered (then $\mu \leq \lambda$). Constant failure rates are assumed in accordance with current experience.

For *transient* fault characterization we use two transient environment parameters:

τ = transient fault arrival rate of one active module

$\overline{D}$ = mean duration of a transient fault.

The currently preferred assumptions are: a Poisson process with a constant arrival rate for transient arrival and an exponential distribution for transient duration [3]. It is assumed that spare modules are not affected by transient faults.

B. Structural Parameters

The structural parameters are chosen by the designer to satisfy the computing performance requirements and to meet the reliability goals. They are:

N = initial number of modules in the active configuration

D = number of degradations allowed in the active configuration

S = number of spare modules

Y = sequence of allowed degradations of the active configuration.

The choice of N is determined by the computing requirements of the system, while the choice of S determines the extent of "self-repair" capability. Parameters D and Y characterize the "graceful degradation" capability of the system. Y is actually a vector $(Y[1], \cdots, Y[D])$ of integers where $Y[i]$ specifies the number of active modules remaining after the ith degradation.

C. Repair Parameters

When a fault-tolerant homogeneous set of modules is supported by off-line repair [4], two new parameters are introduced:

M = number of repair facilities ("repairmen")

ψ = repair rate of one repair facility.

By assumption, repair rate is a constant and multiple repair facilities, when they exist, are independent. Repair policy is discussed in Section IV.

D. Detection and Recovery Parameters: Permanent Faults

The *coverage* parameter ($0 \leq C \leq 1$) is defined as the conditional probability of recovery, given that a fault has occurred. It was first introduced by Bouricius et al. [9]. Coverage quantitatively characterizes the adequacy of fault-detection and recovery methods. The present model uses the following set of coverage parameters with respect to *permanent* faults:

Ca = coverage for recovery from a permanent fault in an active module

Cd = coverage for recovery from a permanent fault in a spare module (when that module is tested or switched into the active configuration)

CY = coverage vector for degraded active configurations.

The coverage vector CY has the form $CY = (CY[1], \cdots, CY[D])$, in which $CY[i]$ is the coverage associated with the transition to the degraded configuration described by $Y[i]$.

The estimation of coverage is, in practice, a difficult problem because it is a complex parameter dependent on both fault mechanisms and recovery capability of the system. The best attempt to date to analyze and estimate coverage can be found in [10].

For transient faults, a coverage parameter also exists. However, this parameter is derived from more basic parameters characterizing transient fault environment and recovery, as will be discussed in Section V.

E. Detection and Recovery Parameters: Transient Faults

Additional parameters are needed when transient fault-recovery processes are added to the reliability model. Transient fault recovery is modeled as a multiphase process described by the following parameters [3]:

n = number of recovery phases

r = recoverability

ρ = interference rate

T = recovery duration vector

E = recovery effectiveness vector.

The recovery duration and effectiveness vectors have the following forms:

$$T = (T[1], \cdots, T[n]) \quad E = (E[1], \cdots, E[n])$$

where $T[i]$ is the duration of the ith phase of recovery and $E[i]$ is its effectiveness, defined as the conditional probability that the ith recovery phase is successful, given that it was initiated against a noncatastrophic transient fault.

The *number* n of recovery phases depends on the designer's decision. For example, the first phase can be an intentional delay of duration $T[1] > 0$ and effectiveness $E[1] = 0$. It is then followed by one or more active recovery processes, such as instruction retry, program rollback, etc.

The *recoverability* r ($0 \leq r \leq 1$) is defined as the conditional probability that the fault is noncatastrophic, given that a fault occurs. A catastrophic fault leads to an immediate failure during phase 1.

The *interference rate* is the failure rate of all the hardware engaged in the execution of the transient recovery processes. We made the conservative assumption that interference (a second independent fault, transient or permanent), which occurs in this hardware while it is executing a recovery process, always leads to system failure.

Together with the (previously defined) parameters τ and $\overline{D}$, the above parameters provide the quantitative basis for the modeling of transient faults.

III. Modeling Closed Systems

By closed systems [6], we mean systems which, once put into operation, must maintain operation on its own without external intervention. When the first system failure occurs, the useful life of the system is considered terminated. Many fault-tolerant computer systems, in particular those in aerospace applications, are closed systems.

Since closed systems do not allow manual repair, fault tolerance must be achieved through redundancy techniques. These have been very well developed in the past. They fall into three main categories: static or masking redundancy, dynamic redundancy or self-repair, and hybrid redundancy [7]. Because these techniques are so diverse both in their basic philosophies and their implementations, reliability models for the resulting fault-tolerant system designs tend to be developed in an independent and unrelated manner. In the following, we will demonstrate that the modeling of a diverse set of closed systems can be brought under one roof and described by one single Markov reliability model. In addition, this single model yields a computational procedure for reliability estimation which is highly efficient.

A. A Unified Reliability Model for Closed Systems

Following accepted practice in modeling, a computer system is modeled as a cascade of stochastically independent subsystems. The reliability function of a system is the product of the reliability functions of its homogeneous subsystems. Each subsystem of a closed system consists of a homogeneous set of modules, i.e., a set of identical disk drives, or a set of memory modules, etc. Its reliability, with respect to permanent faults, is completely characterized by the following subset of the parameters discussed in Section II:

N = initial number of modules in the active configuration
D = number of degradations allowed in the active configuration
S = number of spare modules
Ca = coverage for recovery from active module failures
Cd = coverage for recovery from spare module failures
λ = failure rate of one active module
μ = failure rate of one spare module ($\mu = \lambda$ if spare is powered)
Y = sequence of allowed degradations of the active configuration
CY = coverage vector for transitions into degraded configurations.

We will represent the set of parameters by the notation $(N, D, S, Ca, Cd, \lambda, \mu, Y, CY)$. The unified Markov model for closed systems characterized by this set of parameters is shown in Fig. 1. In its special cases, it reduces to well-known reliability models given in Table I [1].

The parameters $(N, S, Ca, Cd, \lambda, \mu)$ define the self-repairing capability of the system being modeled. In a self-repairing system, an active configuration of N modules (with failure rate λ per module) is supported by a bank of S spare modules (with failure rate μ each), which may be powered down to conserve power or to take advantage of possibly lower failure rates. On an active module failure, the system will attempt to recover from the failure and switch in a spare (in a predetermined sequence) to replace the failed active module. Since the fault detection, location, and recovery mechanisms are probably different for failures in an active and in a spare module, a separate coverage parameter is provided for each. In Fig. 1, recoverable failures, whether in an active or spare module, cause transitions on the upper row of states, from an initial state $(N, S, 0)$ to (eventually) the state $(N, 0, 0)$, which represents a system that has exhausted all its spares, but still operates at full capacity. Further failure would cause it to go into a degraded configuration (if degradation is allowed). An unrecoverable failure in an active module leads to system failure immediately. This is represented by the transition to the failed state (F). However, an unrecoverable failure (e.g., undetectable) in a spare does not cause immediate system failure, only when the system attempts to switch it into service. Effectively, the failure blocks the use of spares that follow it in the selection sequence. Furthermore, it destroys the ability of the system to degrade (if it can), because the system would have failed before it can use up all its spares. This effect is incorporated in the model by transitions to the states with an overbar ($\overline{(N, S-1, 0)}$, $\overline{(N, 0, 0)}$, etc., which are states of a corresponding system that cannot degrade the active configuration. This means that the system in states $(N, i, 0)$ and $\overline{(N, i, 0)}$ have the same active configuration and the same number of *usable* spares, but the system at state $\overline{(N, i, 0)}$ has lost its ability to degrade because of the presence of a "lurking" unrecoverable failure in one of its spare modules.

When all the spares are exhausted in a dynamically redundant system, and one more failure of an active module in that system occurs, the system usually is considered to have failed. However, in some applications, as long as the failed modules can be successfully isolated or their effect masked so that they will not interfere with useful processing, the system can still be considered operational, although it is "degraded," i.e., it has a reduced set of active modules (and hence, a possible degradation in performance). This continues until the degraded active configuration falls below a specified minimal configuration, at which time the system fails. This "graceful degradation" capability is described by a vector $Y = (Y[1], Y[2], \cdots, Y[D])$ where $Y[i]$ is the number of modules in the active configuration after the ith degradation. Since systems in a degraded mode of operation might not have the same resources devoted to fault detection and recovery, the model allows the customizing of the coverage factor to each degraded configuration. This is provided by a vector $CY = (CY[1], \cdots, CY[D])$, where by convention, $CY[i]$ is the coverage associated with the transition to the state with configuration $Y[i]$ (with this convention, $CY[1] = Ca$).

Statically redundant active configurations (such as TMR)

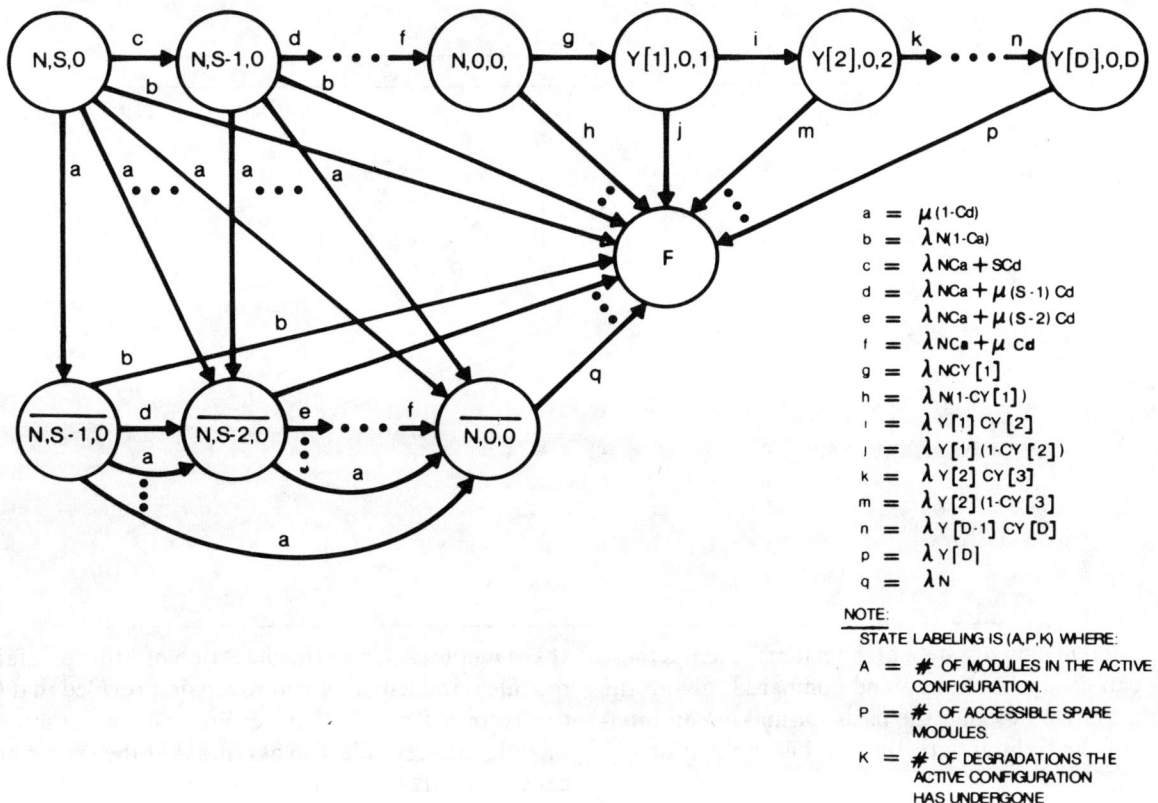

Fig. 1. Markov reliability model for closed systems.

and hybrid redundant configurations with a static core [15] also have an active configuration which degrades to some extent before system failure occurs. Hence, they can be described in the same manner as the "degradable" active set. The manner of degradation, of course, depends on the redundant design. For example, a TMR configuration degrades from three to two modules upon the first module failure, while a TMR/Simplex configuration [9] degrades from three to one.

The model as described above is very general. In its special cases (e.g., $S = 0$ or $D = 0$) it models systems which are self-repairing [9], static redundant, or hybrid redundant [15]. In fact, it covers not only all the systems listed in Table I, but many more other (not previously analyzed) systems. What is more important, the reliability can be estimated using a very efficient procedure, as discussed in the following.

B. Reliability Estimation for Closed Systems

As shown in [1], the reliability function $R(t)$[1] of all closed systems has a certain regular form, as follows.

Theorem: A closed fault-tolerant computer system has a reliability function of the form

$$R(t) = \sum_i A_i e^{-\sigma_i t} \quad (1)$$

where i indexes through all the good (i.e., nonfailed) states i of the Markov reliability model of the system and where σ_i is the failure rate of the system configuration in state i.

[1] Reliability $R(t)$ at time t is defined as the probability that the system has remained operational throughout the period of time $(0, t)$.

Corollary: Mean time to first occurrence of system failure is

$$\text{MTFF} = \sum_i \frac{A_i}{\sigma_i}. \quad (2)$$

While the σ_i in (1) are always simple arithmetic functions of the modeling parameters, the coefficients A_i, when expressed as a function of the parameters, can be quite complicated (e.g., the TMR/S model in [16]). However, for the unified model for closed systems in Fig. 1, $R(t)$ has a more specific form

$$R(t) = X(t) \cdot A \cdot W(t)$$

where

$$X(t) = (e^{-Y[0]\lambda t}, \cdots, e^{-Y[D]\lambda t}), \quad \text{with } Y[0] = N$$

$$W(t) = (1, e^{-\mu t}, \cdots, e^{-S\mu t})$$

$$A = \begin{bmatrix} A_{S,0}^0 & \cdots & A_{S,0}^D \\ \cdot & & \cdot \\ \cdot & & \cdot \\ \cdot & & \cdot \\ A_{S,S}^0 & \cdots & A_{S,S}^D \end{bmatrix}. \quad (3)$$

The coefficients $A_{i,j}^k$ in matrix A are functions of the parameters and can be computed by the very efficient algorithm of Table II. This algorithm is the key to efficient reliability estimation for closed systems and forms a backbone for the implementation of ARIES, which will be discussed in Section VI. Note that although the form of the solution differs from those of previous models ([9], [15], etc.), it yields the same numerical results.

With the power and capability of ARIES, the reliability

TABLE I

System	N	D	S	Ca	Cd	λ	μ	Y	CY	References
Simplex	n	0	0	1	1	λ	λ			
Static Redundancy										
TMR	3	1	0	1	1	λ	λ	2	1	(9)
TMR/Simplex	3	1	0	1	1	λ	λ	1	1	(9)
NMR	2n+1	n	0	1	1	λ	λ	2n,...,n+1	1,...,1	(8)
NMR/Simplex	2n+1	n	0	1	1	λ	λ	2n-1,...,3,1	1,...,1,1	(8)
k-out-of-n	n	n-k	0	1	1	λ	λ	n-1,...,k	1,...,1	
Dynamic Redundancy										
$_cR^q{}_s$	q	0	S	C	C	λ	μ			(9)
$R^*(N,S,A_C^a,A_C^d)$	N	0	S	A_C^a	A_C^d	λ	μ			(11)
K-out-of-N	N	N-K	0	C	C	λ	λ	N-1,...,K	C,...,C	(12)
R(2,S)	2	1	S	1	1	λ	μ	1	1	(13)
Hybrid Redundancy										
H(N,S,D)	N	D	S	1	1	λ	μ	N-1,...,N-Q	1,...,1	(14)
R(N,S)	2n+1	n	S	1	1	λ	μ	2n,...,n+1	1,...,1	(15)
R^* TMR/S	3	2	S	1	1	λ	μ	2,1	1,1	(16)

behavior of different closed system architectures (such as those in Table I) can easily be studied and compared, giving the fault-tolerant system designer the basis for making an intelligent choice of the right architecture for his application.

IV. MODELING REPAIRABLE SYSTEMS

Many papers exist on the modeling of repairable systems, although few of them are specific to fault-tolerant computing and usually do not include important parameters, such as coverage. On the other hand, the few known modeling efforts for repairable fault-tolerant computers [18]–[20], [10] deal with specific architectures. Thus, there is a need for a more general approach to the modeling of repairable fault-tolerant computer systems. Our approach is to extend the previous result for closed systems to cover the same (nonrepairable) fault-tolerant architectures as covered by the closed system model, but, in addition, incorporate repair in these architectures.

It is evident that there are many ways of extending the closed system model to cover repairable systems, depending on different ways of modeling the repair process. In the following, we outline the assumptions we make on repair time distribution, repair policy, etc. As in the case of closed systems, attention is restricted to the modeling of a homogeneous subsystem.

A. Basic Repair Assumptions

We assume that repair is a memoryless process, i.e., repair time is exponentially distributed. While, in general, this may not be a fully accurate characterization of real-life repairs, it makes usable approximation and allows us to use the same Markov modeling techniques as used for closed systems. Under this assumption, repair is characterized by a (constant) repair rate ψ. In the model to be developed, we allow for multiple independent repair facilities, each with the same repair rate.

The repair policy that we assume is "first-come–first-serve." The architectures we are modeling can have both active and spare modules. Upon the detection of failure, a failed active module is immediately sent to repair, provided that the system can recover from the failure. We assume the same for spare module failures. We also assume that the spares are periodically checked for failure. Consequently, as in the case of active modules, the time between occurrence of failure and start of repair is assumed to be negligibly small in comparison with the time scale of reliability prediction.

After a failed module is repaired, it is assumed to be in a new condition. It is then returned immediately to an active state if the subsystem is operating in degraded mode; otherwise it is returned to the head of the spare pool, i.e., where the next spare will be fetched for the replacement of a failed active module. As in a closed system, a spare which fails unrecoverably does not cause the system to fail immediately. It will remain in the spare pool until it is called into service, at which time the system crashes. The flow of spares through the system is depicted in Fig. 2. Of course, an unrecoverable failure in an active module causes system failure immediately.

B. Unified Reliability Modeling for Repairable Systems

With these assumptions, a repairable fault-tolerant subsystem is now characterized by the same set of modeling parameters as in closed systems, plus two additional parameters:

M = number of repairmen (or repair facilities)
ψ = repair rate of one repairman.

The full set of parameters for a repairable system then is given by $(N, D, S, Ca, Cd, \lambda, \mu, Y, CY, M, \psi)$. Corresponding to this set of modeling parameters, a Markov model based on general Markov theory and tailored to our specific systems has been developed. Details of the modeling can be found in [1]. As an illustration, a repairable system with two spares, two repairmen, and capability to "gracefully degrade" twice ($D = 2$) after spares are exhausted would have the simplified Markov state diagram of Fig. 3. It should be emphasized that the general model for repairable systems is a fully compatible extension of the general model for closed systems described

TABLE II
ALGORITHM FOR EVALUATING $A_{SK,T}$ OF (3)

STEP 1

Start with $A_0^0 = 1$. Go to Step (2) if $D = 0$.
For $I = 1$ to D, iterate the following computations:

$$A_J^I = \frac{CY[D-I+1] \; Y[D-I] \; A_J^{I-1}}{Y[D-I] \; Y[D-J]} \quad \text{for } J = 0, \ldots, I-1$$

$$A_I^I = 1 - \sum_{J=0}^{I-1} A_J^I$$

STEP 2

Set $A_{0,0} = 1$.
Using results of Step (1), set $A_{0,0}^K = A_{D-K}^D$ for $K = 0, \ldots, D$.

For $M = 1$ to S, iterate the following computations:

STEP 2(a)

$$A_{M,J} = \frac{(NCa\lambda + MCd\mu) A_{M-1,J} + (1-Cd)\sum_{I=J}^{M-1} A_{I,J}}{(M-J)\mu}$$

for $0 \leq J < M$

$$A_{M,M} = 1 - \sum_{J=0}^{M-1} A_{M,J}$$

STEP 2(b)

$0 < K \leq D$:

$$A_{M,J}^K = \frac{(NCa\lambda + MCd\mu) A_{M-1,J}^K}{(N-Y[K])\lambda + (M-J)\mu} \quad \text{for } 0 \leq J < M$$

$$A_{M,M}^K = 0$$

STEP 2(c)

$K = 0$:

$$A_{M,J}^0 = \frac{(NCa\lambda + MCd\mu) A_{M-1,J}^0 + (1-Cd) \sum_{I=J}^{M-1} A_{I,J}}{(M-J)\mu}$$

for $0 \leq J < M$

$$A_{M,M}^0 = 1 - \sum_{(K,J) \neq (0,M)} A_{M,J}^K$$

---

previously, i.e., in the special case when $M = 0$ (or $\psi = 0$), it reduces to the model of Fig. 1.

Reliability computations follow a similar procedure as in the case for closed systems. It was shown in [1] that the reliability equation of a repairable system has the same standard form as in closed systems

$$R(t) = \sum_i A_i e^{-\sigma_i t} \quad (4)$$

but here the values σ_i cannot be expressed as simple functions of failure rates. Instead, the σ_i's have to be computed as eigenvalues of the transition probability matrix of the Markov model. The coefficients A_i are still computable as a relatively simple function of the eigenvalues and the modeling parameters.

Thus, reliability estimation for repairable systems has much in common with that for closed systems, the basic difference being the procedure for computing σ_i and A. For this reason it was possible to develop ARIES in an integral and nonredundant manner to provide flexible and efficient capabilities for the reliability analysis of both closed and repairable systems. The application of ARIES to the study of repairable systems is extensively documented in [1].

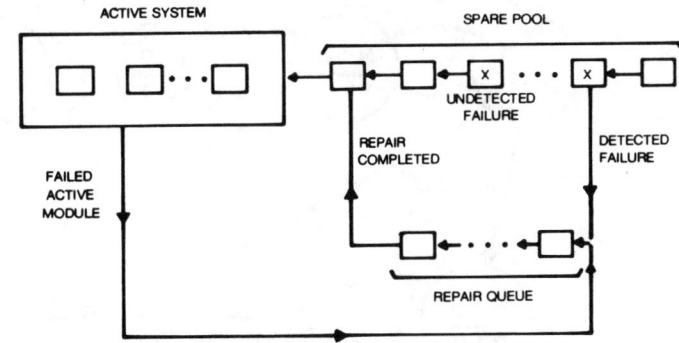

Fig. 2. Placement of spare modules.

V. MODELING TRANSIENT FAULT RECOVERY

Because the capability of transient fault recovery is so important in fault-tolerant systems, there is a need to model it in order to have a means of evaluating its effectiveness in a given system and to identify methods of optimizing this effectiveness. In order to create a realistic model, it is necessary to make generally acceptable assumptions about the causes and nature of transients and about the methods of recovery.

A. Nature of Transient Faults and Recovery Methods

Transient faults are physical events, whose logical symptoms manifest themselves intermittently in an unpredictable manner, but do not generally lead to permanent damage of the hardware. Transient faults can be due to environmental disturbances, such as heat and noise, marginal hardware components which fail intermittently, or residual design and construction flaws. In our modeling effort, we adopt the viewpoint that the transient fault environment can be characterized by two fundamental parameters—transient arrival rate and transient duration [7], [22]. These are modeled by τ and $\overline{D}$, as given in Section II-A. In the absence of accurate data on the stochastic nature of transient fault environment and in the interest of applying a unified Markov technique to model transient faults as well, we assume that both the transient arrival and transient duration are governed by a Poisson process.

Transient fault recovery methods are many and varied. Since no permanent hardware damage results, recovery usually involves "repairing" or "reconfiguring" the information structure of the system so that it can continue to function acceptably. At a functional recovery level, this includes techniques such as instruction retry, I/O operation retry, program rollback, etc. At a system recovery level, this would include system reboot, system reconfiguration, etc., with possible loss of jobs and/or performance. There are also supporting techniques such as "environmental records" [21] and transient recovery delay [22].

It is important to realize that no single recovery technique is totally effective against all transient faults. Thus, for effective transient fault tolerance, a recovery strategy comprising of several stages of recovery and which encompasses an effective combination of recovery techniques, is needed. The modeling of this type of recovery is discussed below. But first, let us look at how transient fault recovery can fail.

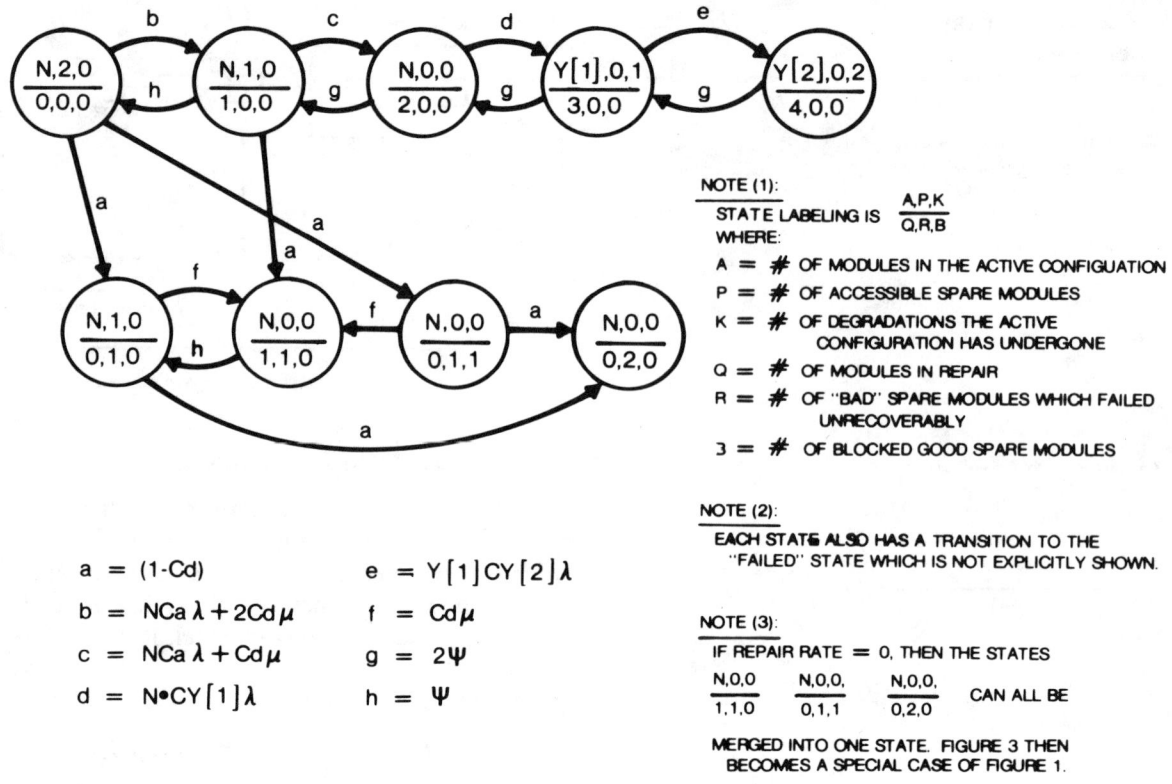

Fig. 3. State diagram for a simplified repairable system ($S = 2$, $D = 2$, $M = 2$).

Each stage of the recovery process can fail in many ways. These are modeled by parameters defined in Section II-E., which are summarized below.

1) Persistent Transients: If a transient fault persists through the entire recovery stage, the recovery will fail, and the next recovery stage will be entered (if the fault persists through all recovery stages, it will be treated as a permanent fault). The probability of that is governed by τ and $\overline{D}$ as well as the recovery duration modeled by $T[i]$.

2) Catastrophic Fault: A fault is "catastrophic" if it causes so much damage that recovery becomes impossible. The probability of this is modeled by the recoverability parameter r. A catastrophic fault leads to system crash even before the first phase of transient recovery is executed.

3) Ineffective Recovery: Although a transient fault is noncatastrophic, a particular recovery technique might not be effective against it. This is modeled by an effectiveness parameter $E[i]$ for the ith recovery stage.

4) Interference: Transient recovery commands certain resources in the system. We take the conservative view that, if a fault occurs in the resources performing recovery, the system will fail. This is modeled by the interference rate ρ, which is the failure rate of the recovery system hardware. This hardware includes both dedicated recovery hardware and those elements used to store, deliver, and execute recovery software.

B. A Model for Transient Fault Recovery

Transient fault recovery is modeled as a multiphase process as depicted in Fig. 4. There are three possible outcomes of the transient fault recovery process. Either the system crashes due to a catastrophic fault or interference during recovery; or the transient fault is treated as permanent due to persistent fault or ineffective recovery; or transient recovery succeeds and system resumes normal processing. If we define

C_T = transient coverage
= Prob(transient recovery succeeds | fault occurs)
L_T = transient leakage
= Prob(fault is treated as permanent | fault occurs)
F_T = Prob(system crashes | fault occurs),

then these three measures characterize the transient fault recovery capability of the system and determines the reliability of the system in the presence of transient faults. In [1], we show how these three measures can be estimated from the basic modeling parameters. An evaluation of this model reveals some interesting insights on effectiveness of transient fault recovery [3]. For example, the usefulness of recovery delay [22] as a technique for optimizing recovery effectiveness (i.e., maximizing transient coverage) is highly dependent on the transient fault rate and transient fault duration as shown in Fig. 5.

The transient fault recovery model as described above can be integrated into the unified reliability model as discussed in Sections III and IV. Fig. 6(a) shows, on a "localized" basis, the incorporation of the transient fault recovery model into the unified reliability model. Two additional states are introduced between each pair of successive "operational" states of the subsystem to represent the existence of the transient and permanent fault recovery processes. In addition to the original set of parameters, transitions between states are also governed by the three transient fault recovery parameters: C_T, L_T, and F_T.

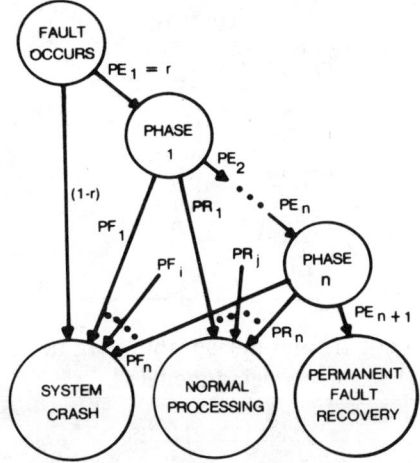

Fig. 4. Transient fault recovery process.

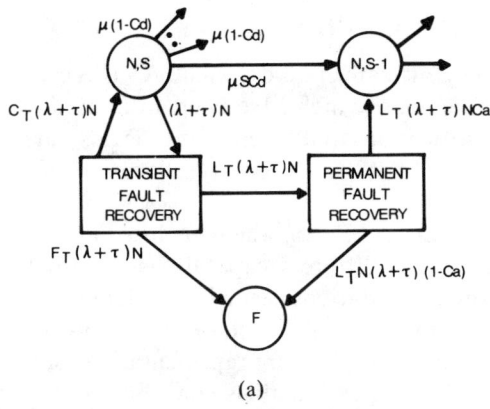

(a)

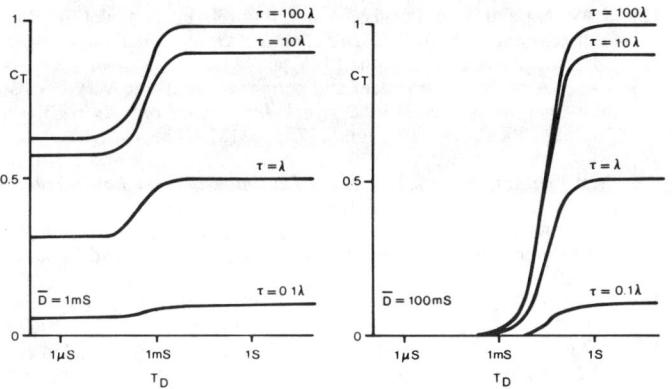

Fig. 5. Effect of transient recovery delay on transient coverage.

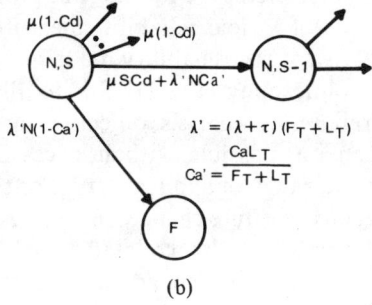

(b)

Fig. 6. (a) Transient recovery in the Markov model. (b) Equivalent form of the Markov model.

We have made the assumption that transients have no effect on the operational status of spare modules. Hence, transitions between states caused by spare module failures remain the same. Although the system spends a finite amount of time in these two recovery states, for all practical purposes one can assume that the recovery process is instantaneous because, even in the worst case, recovery time is several orders of magnitude smaller than the average time between failures of the hardware. With this assumption, the two recovery states are "merged" into the operational states and Fig. 6(a) becomes Fig. 6(b).

Thus, the general model is preserved even when the transient fault recovery model is incorporated. The main effect of this incorporation is to change the effective failure rate of each module from λ to λ' and the effective coverage factor from Ca to Ca', as shown in Fig. 6(b).

VI. ARIES—AN INTERACTIVE RELIABILITY ESTIMATION PROGRAM

The previous sections summarize the main facets of a unified approach to reliability modeling and analysis for fault-tolerant computer systems. The unified model encompasses a wide range of systems, some of which have been previously modeled, and provides a unified method for reliability estimation. But, despite the analytical unity it achieves, the unified model is of little practical utility by itself unless it is automated as a general, flexible, and efficient reliability evaluation tool for the fault-tolerant computer designer. When implemented as an interactive program, it allows a designer to enter parameters at a terminal and immediately returns reliability estimates. This allows him to explore many design alternatives in a convenient and productive manner.

The REL interactive program [9] has been the pioneering effort in this field. Following REL, a few other software packages based on reliability models of redundant structures were developed to perform automated reliability analysis, among them CARE [23], RELCOMP [24], and RMS [11]. Experience gained in the use of these programs has revealed several shortcomings. The programs either deal with only one class of redundant configurations, or they tend to become very complex and time-consuming when a variety of configuration is provided, such as in CARE. The reason for the complexity is that these programs include several diverse reliability models which were developed with "ad hoc" methods, and therefore, they contain much redundant analysis and representations. Simplicity has been maintained only by limiting the scope of application to a few of the existing models.

Based on the unified reliability modeling as developed above, an interactive computer program ARIES (automated reliability interactive estimation system) has been implemented in APL, which overcomes in large part the shortcomings found in earlier programs of its kind. It is general and efficient, as it is based on general models having wide coverage and on unified and efficient procedures for reliability computations. It is also designed with flexibility and ease of use in mind.

A. Description of ARIES

At the present state of development, ARIES consists of over 20 APL functions, which have been structured to facilitate future modifications and extentions. ARIES currently runs quite well in an APL workspace allocation of around 48 kbytes.

The functions in ARIES, which are listed in Table III, form two groupings of different capabilities. Group 1 functions perform the computations needed to evaluate σ_i and A_i as in (1) and (4). In addition, it includes functions to create and manipulate objects which are representations of the systems being modeled. These functions contribute to the efficiency and flexibility of ARIES. Group 2 consists of functions for explicit reliability computations. These functions operate on the modeling objects created by the first group to yield numerical estimates of various reliability measures, which is the ultimate objective of the reliability modeling effort.

The design philosophy of ARIES is to allow the user to achieve his reliability analysis objective in as simple and flexible a manner as possible, without excessive compromise on efficiency and range of applicability. For this reason, and with the possibility of future changes in mind, ARIES has been implemented as a loosely interrelated set of APL functions. Although there is obvious dependence of Group 2 functions on Group 1 functions, most of the main functions within each grouping are independent of each other. In fact, the choice of even a small subset of functions from ARIES (e.g., DEFINE, GENERATE, CHECK, RELIABILITY, COMPUTE, TAKE) would give the user substantial reliability analysis capability (for closed systems), while fitting into a much smaller workspace. Likewise, additions to ARIES can be made to enhance its usefulness with little or no restructuring of the present system. A detailed description of the functions and examples of their use can be found in [25].

VII. Conclusion

In this paper, we presented the results of an extended effort to develop a unified approach to reliability modeling of fault-tolerant computer systems. We have shown that it is not only possible to develop a unified model which covers a wide spectrum of repairable and nonrepairable systems and which models both permanent and transient fault recovery, but also to do it in such a manner as to allow efficient reliability estimation of these systems as well. Based on the modeling results, we have developed a general, flexible, and efficient reliability estimation tool which could be of practical value to designers of fault-tolerant computer systems.

Much work remains to be done in the modeling field. The most difficult task is to create models which accurately reflect the real-life complexity of computing system organization, programming, and operation, and yet are sufficiently concise for efficient computing of the various reliability measures. Progress in the field of reliability modeling will only be assured if researchers will pay equal attention to the use of the most sophisticated mathematical tools at their disposal and to the selection of realistic and measurable parameters for the description of the systems being modeled.

TABLE III

GROUP 1	GROUP 2
DEFINE	RELIABILITY
CONFIGURE	COMPUTE
RECONFIGURE	MTFF
CHECK	MISSIONTIME
UPDATE	RATIO
TAKE	BALANCE
MATREP	RIF
REDUCE	PLOT
EIGEN	ΔFMT
GENERATE	
GENERATE	
CAL	
LIST	
TRANSLATE	

References

[1] Y. W. Ng, "Reliability modeling and analysis for fault-tolerant computers,". Dep. Comput. Sci. Univ. California, Los Angeles, Tech. Rep. UCLA-ENG-7698. Sept. 1976.

[2] Y. W. Ng and A. Avizienis, "A unifying reliability model for closed fault-tolerant systems," in *Dig. 5th Int. Symp. on Fault-Tolerant Comput.*, Paris, France, June 1975, pp. 224.

[3] ——, "A model for transient and permanent fault recovery in closed fault-tolerant systems," in *Dig. 6th Int. Symp. on Fault-Tolerant Comput.*, Pittsburgh, PA, June 1976, pp. 182–188.

[4] ——, "A reliability model for gracefully degrading and repairable fault-tolerant systems," in *Proc. 7th Int. Conf. on Fault-Tolerant Comput.*, Los Angeles, CA, June 1977, pp. 22–28.

[5] ——, "ARIES—An automated reliability estimation system," in *Proc. 1977 Annu. Reliability and Maintainability Symp.*, Philadelphia, PA, Jan. 1977, pp. 108–113.

[6] E. J. Kletsky, "Upper bound on mean life of self-repairing systems," *IRE Trans. Rel. Qual. Contr.*, vol. RQC-11, pp. 43–48, Oct. 1962.

[7] A. Avizienis, "The methodology of fault-tolerant computing," in *Proc. 1st USA-Japan Comput. Conf.*, Tokyo, Japan, Oct. 1972, pp. 405–413.

[8] F. P. Mathur and P. T. de Sousa, "Reliability models of NMR systems," *IEEE Trans. Rel.*, vol. R-24, pp. 108–112, June 1975.

[9] W. G. Bouricius et al., "Reliability modeling for fault-tolerant computers," *IEEE Trans. Comput.*, vol. C-20, pp. 1306–1311, Nov. 1971.

[10] B. R. Borgerson and R. F. Freitas, "A reliability model for gracefully degrading and standby-sparing systems," *IEEE Trans. Comput.*, vol. C-24, pp. 517–524, May 1975.

[11] D. A. Rennels and A. Avizienis, "RMS: A reliability modeling system for self-repairing computers," in *Dig. IEEE 3rd Int. Symp. on Fault-Tolerant Comput.*, Palo Alto, CA, June 1973, pp. 131–135.

[12] H. Wyle and G. Burnett, "Some relationship between failure detection probability and computer system reliability," *Proc. Fall Joint Comput. Conf., AFIPS Conf. Proc.*, vol. 31. Washington, DC: Spartan, 1967, pp. 745–756.

[13] D. A. Rennels, "Fault detection and recovery in redundant computers using standby spares," Dept. Comput. Sci., Univ. California, Los Angeles, Tech. Rep. UCLA-ENG-7355, July 1973.

[14] J. L. Bricker, "A unified method for analyzing mission reliability for fault tolerant computers," *IEEE Trans. Rel.*, vol. R-22, pp. 72–77, June 1973.

[15] F. P. Mathur and A. Avizienis, "Reliability analysis and architecture of a hybrid-redundant digital system: Generalized TMR with self-repair," in *Proc. Spring Joint Comput. Conf., AFIPS Conf. Proc.*, vol. 36. Washington, DC: Spartan, 1970, pp. 376–384.

[16] D. S. Taylor, "A reliability and comparative analysis of two standby system configuration," *IEEE Trans. Rel.*, vol. R-22, pp. 13–19, Apr. 1973.

[17] R. E. Barlow and F. Proschan, *Mathematical Theory of Reliability*. New York: Wiley, 1965.

[18] T. F. Arnold, "The concept of coverage and its effect on the reliability model of a repairable system," *IEEE Trans. Rel.*, vol. R-22, pp. 251–254, Mar. 1973.

[19] D. Chow, "Reliability of redundant systems," *IEEE Trans. Rel.* vol. R-22, pp. 223–228, Oct. 1973.

[20] R. Teoste, "Design of a repairable redundant computer," *IRE Trans. Electron. Comput.*, vol. EC-11, pp. 643–649, Oct. 1962.
[21] D. L. Droulette, "Recovery through programming system/360-system/370," in *Proc. Spring Joint Comput. Conf., AFIPS Conf. Proc.*, vol. 38. Washington, DC: Spartan, 1971, pp. 467–476.
[22] P. M. Merryman and A. Avizienis, "Modeling transient faults in TMR computer systems," in *Proc. 1975 Annu. Rel. Maintainability Symp.*, Washington, DC, Jan. 1975, pp. 333–339.
[23] F. P. Mathur, "Automation of reliability evaluation procedures through CARE—The computer-aided reliability estimation program," in *Proc. Fall Joint Comput. Conf., AFIPS Conf. Proc.*, vol. 41. Washington, DC. Spartan, 1972, pp. 65–82.
[24] J. L. Fleming, "RELCOMP: A computer program for calculating system reliability and MTBF," *IEEE Trans. Rel.*, vol. R-20, pp. 102–107, Aug. 1971.
[25] Y. W. Ng and A. A. Avizienis, "ARIES 76 user's guide," Dep. Comput. Sci., Univ. California, Los Angeles, CA, Tech. Rep. UCLA-ENG-7894, Dec. 1978.

Ying W. Ng (S'73–M'76) received the B.A. degree in mathematics from the University of California, Berkeley, and the M.S. and Ph.D. degrees in computer science from the University of California, Los Angeles, in 1973 and 1976, respectively.

From 1973 to 1976 he was a Post-Graduate Research Engineer in the Department of Computer Science, University of California, Los Angeles. In 1976, he joined Bell Laboratories, Holmdel, NJ, as a member of the Technical Staff. Since 1977, he has been associated with Bell Laboratories, Naperville, IL. His research interests are in the area of computer architecture and fault tolerance.

Dr. Ng is a member of the Association for Computing Machinery.

Algirdas Avizienis (S'55–M'56–F'73) was born in Kaunas, Lithuania, in 1932. He received the B.S., M.S., and Ph.D. degrees, all in electrical engineering, from the University of Illinois, Urbana-Champaign, in 1954, 1955, and 1960, respectively.

In 1960 he joined the Spacecraft Computers Section, Jet Propulsion Laboratory (JPL), California Institute of Technology, and initiated research on reliability of computing and fault tolerance. He organized and directed the JPL-STAR Experimental Computer Research Project from 1964 to 1972. He joined the Faculty of the University of California, Los Angeles (UCLA) in 1962. Currently, he is a Professor in the Department of Computer Science, UCLA, where since 1972 he has been the Principal Investigator of the "Reliable Computing and Fault-Tolerance" Research Project. He teaches courses in computer system architecture, computer arithmetic, and fault tolerance, and is the author or coauthor of over 100 publications in these fields of study. He has served as a Consultant in studies of computer systems design and fault tolerance sponsored by the U.S. Air Force, U.S. Navy, NASA, and the National Bureau of Standards. He has also served on a number of study groups and panels, including the Hardware Systems Committee of the NSF COSERS Study, and a three-year term as a member of the Advisory Panel on Computer Science and Engineering for the National Science Foundation, Office of Computing Activities.

Dr. Avizienis has received numerous awards, among others the AIAA Information Systems Award, the Honor Roll of the IEEE Computer Society, the NASA Apollo Achievement Award, and Best Paper selection from the 1971 IEEE TRANSACTIONS ON COMPUTERS. In the IEEE Computer Society, he founded and was the first Chairman of the Technical Committee on Fault-Tolerant Computing (1969–1973), and was the organizer and General Chairman of the First International Symposium on Fault-Tolerant Computing in 1971. He also served for four years (1971–1974) as a member of the Governing Board of the IEEE Computer Society. In international activities, he is a member of the Working Group 10.3 of the IFIP TC-10 on "Digital System Design." He has lectured and conducted joint research at the National Polytechnic Institute of Mexico, the University of Sao Paulo, Brazil, and the Laboratoire d'Automatique et d'Analyse Systemes in Toulouse, France. In 1974 he spent a five-month research visit, sponsored by the U.S. National Academy of Science, at the Institute of Mathematics and Cybernetics, Lithuanian Academy of Sciences, Vilinius, Lithuania.

Chapter 3: Fault Tolerance in Aerospace and Communication Systems

Introduction

The aerospace and communication industries have been the primary sponsors of fault tolerant digital system research and design since the 1960s, motivated by high reliability requirements which are the result of anticipated consequences of failures in their systems. The nature of these requirements differ very greatly among the different classes of systems.

In the case of manned aerospace systems, life-threatening situations can develop if system failures affect guidance, navigation, or control functions. In the case of unmanned, longer range missions, billions of dollars are spent on deep space probes that must be protected from system failures to ensure success of these missions. In contrast, temporary failures of communication systems used in telephone switching and computer network applications are considered more of a nuisance than a critical problem, so long as such failures can be kept to very limited durations and provided that a system can gracefully recover from such failures. This chapter will examine the reliability requirements in these two different application areas and the various approaches that have been used to meet them.

Reliability Requirements

Different application areas view reliability in different ways, resulting in a wide variety of reliability parameters. A manned aircraft controller, for example, must exhibit a high instantaneous reliability for the duration of its mission, i.e., the probability of any error being generated at any time during the mission must be negligible, to ensure the continuous real-time operation needed to avoid danger to personnel and equipment. A deep space probe, on the other hand, is not subject to the same real-time constraints as an aircraft control system. Consequently, some temporary loss of a system might be tolerable if the system can be automatically repaired within a given time, and the damage resulting from the fault corrected in some acceptable manner. Communication systems have completely different reliability goals. In such systems, temporary outages are viewed as tolerable, as long as the system is available to potential users some reasonable percentage of the time. The different reliability requirements of these three types of applications have led to the use of a wide variety of approaches to fault-tolerant system design.

On-Board Computers for Manned Missions

In the overall set of requirements for guidance, navigation, and control systems, instantaneous reliability is of utmost importance, i.e., the probability that a system component failure will result in the introduction of errors into the system functions at any time during the operation of the system must be below some acceptable threshold since such failures can lead to serious consequences. For early aircraft and space vehicle control systems, typical reliability requirements included 99% reliability over a 250-hour mission for the Saturn V launch vehicle computer [DIC64], 97% reliability over 240 days and no longer than 1 second repair time for the Skylab system [COO76], and 95% reliability over 5 years plus 100% coverage of all faults with a non-negligible probability of occurrence for the Fault-Tolerant Spaceborne Computer (FTSC) [STI76,BUR76]. The Space Shuttle computer complex requirements include allowing no single failure to affect operation and no double failure to endanger the crew [SKL76]. A goal of no greater than 10^{-9} failure probability over 10 hours for the flight control computer complex was set by NASA when it defined the requirements that were to be met by two more recent competing projects, SIFT [WEN72,WEN78] and FTMP [HOP71,HOP75,HOP78]. In the earlier systems, very few critical functions were entrusted to the on-board computers. However, as more of the critical guidance, navigation, and control functions were implemented, the corresponding reliability requirements have increased. These requirements can be met only through the use of massive redundancy to mask errors as they occur and then to repair the system before further errors occur.

Even in the earliest manned missions, fault-tolerant design techniques were used to minimize the probability that an error would jeopardize a mission. It should be realized that the probability of correct operation for a system is given by

$$P(\text{success}) = P(\text{no fails}) + P(\text{success/fails})*P(\text{fails})$$

where $P(\text{no fails})$ is related to the inherent reliability of the components of the system and $P(\text{success/fails})$ represents the effect of the fault-tolerance scheme utilized. In most aerospace applications, the requirement for $P(\text{success})$ is sufficiently high that the value of $P(\text{no fails})$ for the system cannot meet that requirement by itself, and hence fault tolerance must be applied to the system design.

Triple modular redundancy (TMR) at the subsystem level with a special duplex memory was used in the Saturn V launch vehicle [DIC64] to tolerate all single faults to meet its modest reliability goal, raising the predicted reliability from .943 for the simplex (non-redundant) unit to .9972 for the fault tolerant unit. Some form of TMR was proposed for use in the critical phases of a number of other on-board aircraft and spacecraft systems to meet even higher goals. As these systems have developed, the TMR has moved from the subsystem level to the system level, as in the Space Shuttle computer complex [SKL76], which uses four redundant processors during critical phases. Both the FTMP and SIFT systems use TMR, but in a hybrid rather than a static configuration, as will be discussed below.

The Space Shuttle computer system and some longer term spaceborne systems differ from the systems described above in that their reliability requirements vary according to the criticality and computing requirements of each phase of the mission. During those phases in which guidance, navigation, and control functions are critical (takeoff and reentry), instantaneous reliability is important, requiring TMR to guarantee that reliability. Reliability requirements are relaxed during the non-critical phases, allowing the system configuration to be altered by breaking up the TMR triad, and using only one of the processors with the others powered down.

One interesting point that should be noted in the Space Shuttle fault-tolerance requirements is the attention to multiple faults. Most fault-tolerance schemes tend to begin with the basic assumption that at most one fault will exist at any one time, so that the various fault-tolerance mechanisms used will need only to deal with a single fault. For longer term missions, and missions in which environmental conditions are sub-optimal (eg. in the presence of radiation, electromagnetic interference, etc.), the single-fault assumption may not be valid. Consequently, highly reliable systems intended for such applications must provide mechanisms that can deal with multiple faults.

Unmanned Missions

In systems that are unmanned, some instantaneous errors might be tolerable, provided that proper operating conditions can be restored quickly enough to allow the mission to continue without serious loss of control. The Self-Testing-and-Repairing (STAR) [AVI71] computer, developed at the Jet Propulsion Laboratory (JPL), utilized the concept of power switching of spare units to replace faulty ones. Here the system was simply rolled back and restarted from various points in response to detected faults, with processing halted during the repair period. Sufficient spares are provided to achieve the desired mission lifetime. Since this operation requires the availability of a special Test and Repair Processor (TARP) to perform these operations, the TARP used a hybrid TMR configuration. A system based on the STAR architecture was used in the Thermoelectric Outer Planet Spacecraft (TOPS) for deep space probes [MAR70].

Telephone and Network Communication Systems

Next to the aerospace programs, communication systems have received the most attention with regard to requirements for fault tolerance. However, these reliability requirements are considerably different from aerospace application requirements. First, most errors in communication systems are not "life threatening," and thus a mishandled phone call or network communication is seen as more of a nuisance than a severe problem. As a secondary consideration, communications systems are products of companies whose business is to make money, and hence system cost is a larger consideration than it is for most aerospace systems. Consequently, reliability must be high enough to ensure the satisfaction of the system users, but it need not be as high as that for aerospace applications in terms of preventing the instantaneous occurrence of all errors.

Consequently, system availability for communication systems is a more critical requirement than instantaneous reliability is. Some instantaneous errors are acceptable, provided that repair is automatic and quick. Availability is expressed as

$$A = \mu / (\mu + \lambda)$$

where μ is the system repair rate (inverse of repair time) and λ is the system failure rate. To achieve a high availability, one must make $\lambda \ll \mu$. This can be done by increasing μ, decreasing λ, or both. One can minimize λ either by using high quality components with low failure rates or by using fault-masking techniques, such as TMR and error-correcting codes, to mask the effects of some minimum number of failures. Either approach is quite expensive if the λ requirement is high. The alternative is to increase availability by increasing the repair rate, μ. This typically requires some form of automatic system-repair capability, driven by good fault-detection facilities.

Realistically, the most cost-effective approach is to use sufficient redundancy to provide good error-detection capabilities and standby spare units to replace failed ones, coupled with an automatic repair facility. This is the approach that has been used in the development of two successful fault-tolerant communication computer systems: the Electronic Switching System (ESS) processors of Bell Labs [DOW64,BOW778,TOY78], and the Pluribus system developed for ARPANET network communications applications [ORN76,KAT78]. The ESS project has recently been extended to commercial computing applications in the 3B20 computer from AT&T [HAN83,FIT84].

All three of these systems were developed to achieve high availability at reasonable cost, without attempting to mask instantaneous failures. In the case of the ESS systems and the 3B20, the availability goal is reported as 2 minutes per year of down time. Recognizing the different potential sources of error, this two minutes is broken down into four parts: 0.4 min/yr because of hardware failures, 0.3 min/yr because of software deficiencies, 0.7 min/yr because of recovery deficiencies, and 0.4 min/yr because of operator or procedural errors. In the ESS systems, an additional reliability goal requires no more than 0.01% of all calls to be processed incorrectly. In the case of Pluribus, maximum availability of the system within the ARPANET is the primary goal, with graceful system recovery following faults receiving the most attention. No attempt is made to mask errors in either system, but the attempt rather is to detect errors quickly and to repair the system quickly and gracefully.

Fault-Tolerant Design Features

Aerospace Systems

Given the requirements for extremely high instantaneous reliability, fault masking through massive redundancy has been the primary approach in most aerospace system designs. Systems designed for the Saturn V launch vehicle [DIC64], the Space Shuttle [SKL76], FTMP [HOP78], and SIFT [WEN78] have all used modular redundancy with voting to mask some minimum number of element failures. In the JPL STAR computer [AVI71], a similar approach was used for TARP, which is the critical portion of the system, with this subsystem then made responsible for the monitoring and repair of the rest of the system. In all of these systems, a single failure anywhere in the system will not introduce errors into the operation of the system. While TMR allows single failures to be tolerated, additional failures within a voting group of elements can result in complete system failure. In the case of the Saturn V launch vehicle computer, the probability of a second error was considered negligible, given that system's reliability goals and the relatively short mission time of the system. In a TMR configuration, the probability of having no more than a single error is given by

$$R_{TMR}(t) = R(t)^3 + 3R(t)^2(1 - R(t)).$$

Assuming the reliability of a single module to be

$$R(t) = e^{-\lambda t}$$

then the overall reliability of the TMR configuration is given by

$$R_{TMR} = 3e^{-2\lambda t} - 2e^{-3\lambda t}.$$

Since failure of a TMR system requires two of three modules within a voting group to fail, if mission time t is relatively small, resulting in a small value of λt, then the corresponding system failure probability will likewise be small.

In the case of the JPL STAR system, the mission time is expected to be on the order of 8-10 years. Hence the probability of double errors in its TMR core is non-negligible. In this case, a failed unit within the triad is replaced with a spare unit as soon as possible after detection to bring the system back to a full triad, i.e., hybrid modular redundancy (HMR) is utilized. In the SIFT and FTMP systems, the overall mission times are relatively short, but the reliability requirements are so high that the instantaneous probability of occurrence of a double fault cannot be minimized sufficiently with available components. In both systems a failed element of a triad is replaced by a spare unit to restore the triad to its full configuration.

For hybrid modular redundant systems, a simple combinatorial reliability model is no longer sufficient to compute the system failure probability. In these systems, system failure is the result of a second failure occurring within a triad before the triad has been restored to full capacity by the replacement of the first failed unit. A simplified version of the reliability models for these systems is presented in Figure 3.1. In this figure, state 3 represents the state in which all three elements in a triad are good, state 2 the state in which one is faulty and two are good, and state 1 the state in which at least two units are faulty. The parameters λ and μ represent the failure and repair rates, respectively. Consequently, the overall failure rate is the probability that state 1 is entered.

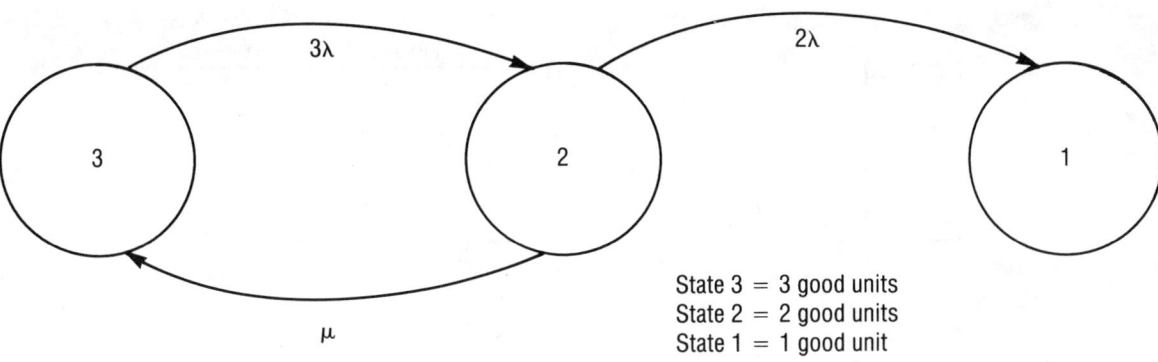

State 3 = 3 good units
State 2 = 2 good units
State 1 = 1 good unit

Figure 3.1. Markov model of a repairable TMR system having failure rate λ and repair rate μ.

Perhaps an indication of the importance of automatic repair can be seen by examining the mean time to repair (MTTR) of the above system, which can be derived as

$$\text{MTTR} = (5\lambda + \mu) / (6\lambda^2).$$

Assuming values of $\lambda = 0.001$ hr^{-1}, and $\mu = 0.1$ hr^{-1}, we get an MTTR for the TMR case of 833 hours, and an MTTR for the HMR case of 17,500 hours! Note that an acceptable system reliability is assured by ensuring that the repair rate is large relative to the failure rate, so that repair will take place before the occurrence of a second system failure.

The actual implementation of the TMR configurations differs widely between systems. In the earlier systems, such as the Saturn V, TMR was applied to subsystems within a single computer. Since reconfiguration was not required, the voters were fixed in their positions within the individual triads. A different approach was required as levels of integration increased and dynamic reconfiguration became necessary. Entire processors were treated as "throw-away" modules to be replaced as a result of any detected processor error. In the STAR TARP, this replacement was performed by simple power switching of static spares. In contrast, both the FTMP and SIFT systems are multiprocessors in which processors are dynamically allocated to triads, with multiple triads operating concurrently, depending on the number of available healthy processors. As failures occur, processors are reassigned to restore full TMR operation, with the system performance degrading gracefully (i.e. fewer triads) as processors are used up. In the FTMP system, all voting is done by hardware at the input to each processor, while in the SIFT system, all voting is done in software. Hence in both systems, any processor can be a member of any triad, providing a flexible system organization.

As the use of VLSI components increases and as system computing requirements increase, multiprocessor configurations are being utilized as system solutions. Given the availability of a large number of processors, memories, and other components within a system, the potential exists for fault tolerance by exploiting the inherent redundancy in such systems. Considering the example shown in Figure 3.2, if a failure occurs in a uniprocessor-based system, then the system must stop its operation completely while system repair and reconfiguration take place. On the other hand, if the resources are properly managed, only a small dip in performance might be noted upon losing a processor or other resource in a multiprocessor. The key to this phenomenon is the proper management of these resources, which requires new fault detection capabilities, system reconfiguration algorithms, and so on in the presence of the large number of resources.

While both the SIFT and FTMP approaches display the potential for such multiprocessor configurations, architectures such as those proposed by Rennels [REN78a,REN78b] show considerable promise as building blocks for large systems. This approach uses a number of self-checking computer modules with which to construct large systems. Each processor, memory, and I/O module is responsible for detecting its own internal errors, allowing it to be isolated without totally disrupting the processing activities of the rest of the system. In addition, the self-checking modules described in [REN78b] allow the use of a variety of microprocessors, memories, and other components rather than requiring the development of a special purpose processor, as was done for all of the other systems described previously.

Communication System Implementations

In contrast to the aerospace systems described above, the ESS and Pluribus architectures do not incorporate any fault-masking techniques, other than the occasional use of error-correcting codes in memory arrays and retries of faulty operations. Instead, both use relatively simple error detection mechanisms, such as parity checks, bus timing checks, and software diagnostics, and then incorporate extensive system recovery mechanisms to restore correct operational states following the detection of various faults. Consequently, neither system attempts to prevent errors from

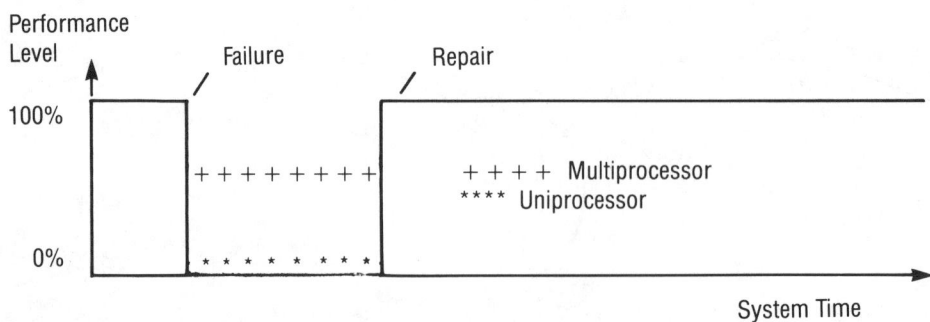

Figure 3.2. Comparison of performance degradation of uniprocessor configurations vs. multiprocessor configurations due to a processor failure.

occurring, but rather each concentrates on detecting errors as soon as possible after their occurrence and then gracefully restores the state of the system as quickly as possible so to minimize the effect on the users of the system. Thus, there will be some mishandled phone calls in ESS, which will have to be redialed by the callers, and some erroneous communications in Pluribus, which will usually be dealt with within the ARPANET layered network protocol.

The two systems differ considerably in their mechanisms used for error detection. The earliest ESS systems, the Number 1 and 1A processors, use a duplex architecture for their control computers (CC's) with parity coding in the various memories and buses and various time-out checks on I/O and bus operations. The duplex CC's were designed to operate in lock-step, with a number of internal points within the CC's being compared during each cycle of the machine. Any mismatches detected during these comparisons initiate recovery routines that determine which of the two units are faulty and then allow the healthy unit to continue until the faulty one is replaced manually. Similar actions occur following error detection by any of the other mechanisms. In the Number 3A processor, the duplex operation was maintained, but rather than comparing internal points within the CC's, each CC was designed around self-checking circuits that continuously detect errors within the CC, including the check circuits themselves. This approach eliminates the need to determine which unit in the duplex configuration is faulty, as well as relaxing the requirements for synchronizing the operation of the duplex units. The 3B20 system architecture is similar to that of the 3A processor.

In contrast, the Pluribus system relies heavily on software diagnosis of errors, with the only hardware error checking features being simple parity checks on the buses, and some time-out checks on the buses and I/O channels. The primary error checking mechanisms are embedded in the STAGE operating system, which periodically examines various data structures, including redundant information, system configuration tables, and so forth. In addition, the application programs perform similar checks of their own data structures and other information. In contrast to the ESS systems, which are logically uniprocessors, the Pluribus system is a tightly coupled system consisting of three types of modules: processor, shared memory, and I/O. This allows the power of the system to be tailored to each particular set of requirements. One spare module of each type is included for replacement purposes, with all modules interconnected to facilitate reconfiguration. This allows reconfiguration to a fully operational state after a single failure, with the potential for graceful degradation following additional failures that might occur before repair can take place.

After error detection, both the ESS and Pluribus systems initiate extensive diagnosis and recovery software mechanisms that quickly (1) locate the source of the fault, (2) evaluate the extent of the damage to the system to determine the amount of system recovery needed, (3) reconfigure the system resources to bypass the failed component(s), and (4) re-establish a correct operating state. In both cases some loss of data may occur, but this typically affects only a small number of users (typically one), and is thus considered acceptable so long as the system achieves a correct operational state quickly and gracefully.

An additional requirement for both the ESS and Pluribus systems is to facilitate manual repair. Consequently, both systems make extensive use of software diagnostic routines to detect and isolate failures and to maintain error histories that can be used by service personnel to perform repairs. In the ESS systems, the goal of the diagnostic software is to isolate the fault to one or two replaceable boards. This allows a service person to perform simple spare replacements quickly and to restore the system to its full configuration before the second unit can fail. A second fault would, of course, result in complete system failure. Extensive signature analysis and diagnosis algorithms for ESS are described in [BOW77].

Summary

The development of fault-tolerant computing systems for both aerospace and communication applications has led the way in the development of fault-tolerant computing principles and practices that have recently begun to appear in other application areas. The high reliability requirements of these systems, coupled with fewer budget restraints than one might find in most commercial applications, have been largely responsible for this emphasis on fault tolerance. With the availability of VLSI components, this trend can be expected to continue.

The papers reprinted in this chapter of the tutorial represent some of the landmark, and most comprehensive, work done in fault-tolerant computing, covering both manned and unmanned aerospace control systems, along with two representative communication-oriented systems. Avizienis and his coworkers [AVI71] present both the design and reliability analysis of the STAR computer, designed for long-term, deep space unmanned applications. To address the requirements for manned spacecraft, Sklaroff [SKL76] presents a description of the fault-tolerance requirements and the design of the redundancy management hardware for the Space Shuttle computer complex. Hopkins and his coworkers and Wensley and his [HOP78,WEN78] present the designs and reliability analyses of the FTMP and SIFT projects, respectively. These two projects have been the most comprehensive to date, and were driven by extremely high reliability requirements to be used for aircraft control. Consequently, both SIFT and FTMP utilize massive redundancy, and both projects make extensive use of both combinatorial and Markov reliability modeling techniques to analyze the overall system reliability.

The final two papers in this chapter examine communication systems. The paper by Toy [TOY78] examines the evolution of the Bell System ESS processors, presenting the designs of the Number 1A and the Number 3A ESS processors. The former utilized duplication with matching at the register level as its basic error detection mechanism, while the latter makes extensive use of self-checking logic and error detection codes. The final paper by Katsuki and his coworkers [KAT78] presents a description of the Pluribus multiprocessor, which was designed as an interface message processor (IMP) for the ARPANET. As was the case with the ESS processors, the emphasis of the Pluribus design is on rapid recovery after a fault, with automatic reconfiguration provided to minimize, but not to eliminate, downtime.

The STAR (Self-Testing And Repairing) Computer: An Investigation of the Theory and Practice of Fault-Tolerant Computer Design

ALGIRDAS AVIŽIENIS, MEMBER, IEEE, GEORGE C. GILLEY, MEMBER, IEEE, FRANCIS P. MATHUR, MEMBER, IEEE, DAVID A. RENNELS, JOHN A. ROHR, MEMBER, IEEE, AND DAVID K. RUBIN, MEMBER, IEEE

Abstract—This paper presents the results obtained in a continuing investigation of fault-tolerant computing which is being conducted at the Jet Propulsion Laboratory. Initial studies led to the decision to design and construct an experimental computer with dynamic (standby) redundancy, including replaceable subsystems and a program rollback provision to eliminate transient errors. This system, called the STAR computer, began operation in 1969. The following aspects of the STAR system are described: architecture, reliability analysis, software, automatic maintenance of peripheral systems, and adaptation to serve as the central computer of an outerplanet exploration spacecraft.

Index Terms—Fault-tolerant computers, replacement systems, self-repairing computers.

I. INTRODUCTION: CHRONOLOGY AND RATIONALE

THIS paper presents a summary of the theoretical results and design experience obtained in an investigation of fault-tolerant computing which is being conducted at the Jet Propulsion Laboratory (JPL). Initial studies (1961–1965) led to the conclusion that dynamic (also called standby) redundancy offered the greatest promise in the design of fault-tolerant digital computer systems [1]. The *dynamic* redundancy [2] approach requires a two-step procedure for the elimination of a fault: first, the presence of a fault is determined; second, a corrective action is taken (e.g., replacement of failed unit, repetition of program, reconfiguration of systems, etc.). The alternative to the dynamic approach is *static* (masking) redundancy [2], which was already being utilized in existing component-redundant [3], [4] and triple-modular-redundant (TMR) [4]–[6] computers. Early analytic studies of dynamic redundancy with idealized series-parallel system models indicated that mean life gains of an order of magnitude and more over a nonredundant system could be expected from dynamically redundant systems with standby spares replacing failed units [7]–[10]. This gain compared favorably with the mean life gain of less than two in the typical TMR systems.

Manuscript received March 15, 1971; revised June 1, 1971. This research has been carried out at the Jet Propulsion Laboratory, California Institute of Technology, Pasadena, Calif., under National Aeronautics and Space Administration Contract NAS 7-100.
A. Avižienis and G. C. Gilley are with the Jet Propulsion Laboratory, California Institute of Technology, Pasadena, Calif. 91103, and the Department of Computer Science, University of California, Los Angeles, Calif. 90024.
F. P. Mathur, D. A. Rennels, J. A. Rohr, and D. K. Rubin are with the Jet Propulsion Laboratory, California Institute of Technology, Pasadena, Calif. 91103.

Other qualitative advantages of the dynamic over the static redundancy were: 1) greater isolation of catastrophic (nonindependent) faults which is especially important for densely packed microelectronic circuitry; 2) survival of system until all spares of one type are exhausted; 3) ability to eliminate errors which are caused by transient faults by the use of program rollback; 4) ready adjustability of the number and type of spare units; 5) utilization of the potentially lower failure rate of unpowered components in spare units; 6) avoidance of the circuit-related problems of static redundancy: increases in fan-out, fan-in, power requirements, and the need for isolation and synchronization of separate channels; and 7) facilitation of the checkout of spare units by means of standard diagnostic programs.

The attainment of the apparent advantages of a dynamically redundant system had been shown to depend very strongly on the successful execution of the detection and replacement operations [9], [10]; these observations have since been formalized as the concept of "coverage" [12].

The second phase of the investigation (1965–1970) was focused on the identification and solution of the problems involved in the design of a general-purpose digital computer possessing the properties attributed to the abstract model of a dynamically redundant computing system. Three major areas of investigation were: 1) an investigation of fault-detection methods; 2) a study of computer architecture with emphasis on partitioning into subsystems with minimal interconnection requirements; and 3) a study of the "hard-core" problem, i.e., the alternate technologies and logic organizations for implementing the detection and switching functions. The choices among feasible alternatives in all three areas are strongly affected by assumptions on the available component technology and on the computing tasks to be required of the computer. In order to retain contact with the practice of computer design, it was decided to design and construct an experimental general-purpose digital computer which would incorporate dynamic redundancy (i.e., fault detection and replacement of failed subsystems) as integral parts of its structure. The design objectives have been carried out and the system, called the STAR (self-testing and repairing) computer, began operation in 1969. The modular nature of the STAR computer has allowed systematic expansion and modifications that are still being continued.

The first objective of the design is to study the class of

Fig. 1. The STAR computer.

problems which are encountered in transforming the theoretical model of a self-repairing system into a working computer. State-of-the-art integrated circuit and memory technology was employed in the design. The STAR computer characteristics were chosen to satisfy all predictable requirements of a spacecraft guidance, control, and data acquisition computer which would be used in the very long (ten years and more) unmanned missions exploring the outer planets of the solar system [13]. The second objective was to provide a tool for laboratory studies of fault-tolerant computing, including the injection of transient as well as permanent faults of catastrophic nature. Very extensive displays of registers, manually controlled clocking, and provisions for convenient modification of subsystems were incorporated into the experimental STAR computer breadboard (Fig. 1).

The STAR computer employs a balanced mixture of coding, monitoring, standby redundancy, replication with voting, component redundancy, and repetition in order to attain hardware-controlled self-repair and protection against transient faults. The principal goal of the design is to attain fault tolerance for a variety of faults: transient, permanent, random, and catastrophic. The actual construction (rather than simulation) of the STAR breadboard has two significant advantages. First, the design process has uncovered interesting new hardware-related problems and led to numerous improvements. Second, the computer serves as a vehicle for further experimentation and refinement of the recovery techniques.

During the studies of fault-tolerant architecture and the design of the STAR computer, concurrent investigations were being conducted in other closely related areas of fault-tolerant computing, including studies of software, reliability prediction, and extension of dynamic redundancy to peripheral devices [14]. A complete redesign of the STAR computer is being performed to match the exact requirements of a control computer for the thermoelectric outer planet spacecraft (TOPS) [15]. This effort led to the evaluation of additional fault-recovery techniques. The results of the efforts described above are summarized in the following sections of this paper.

II. Architecture of the STAR Computer

A. Methods of Fault Tolerance

The STAR computer is a replacement system that provides one standard configuration of functional subsystems with the required computing capacity. The standard computer is supplemented with one or more spares of each subsystem. The spares are unpowered and are used to replace operating units when permanent faults are discovered. The principal methods of error detection and recovery are the following.

1) All machine words (data and instructions) are encoded in error-detecting codes and fault detection occurs concurrently with the execution of the programs.

2) The computer is divided into a set of replaceable functional units containing their own instruction decoders and sequence generators. This decentralization allows simple fault location procedures and simplifies system interfaces.

3) Fault detection, recovery, and replacement are carried out by special-purpose hardware. In the case of memory damage, software augments the recovery hardware.

4) Transient faults are identified and their effects are corrected by the repetition of a segment of the current program; permanent faults are eliminated by the replacement of faulty functional units.

5) The replacement is implemented by power switching: units are removed by turning power off and connected by turning power on. The information lines of all units are permanently connected to the buses through isolating circuits; unpowered units produce only logic "zero" outputs.

6) The error-detecting codes are supplemented by monitoring circuits which serve to verify the proper synchronization and internal operation of the functional units.

7) The "hard core" test and repair processor (TARP) is protected by triplication and replacement of failed members of the triplet.

B. Hardware System Organization

The block diagram of the STAR computer is shown in Fig. 2. Communication between the units is carried out on two four-wire buses: the memory-out (M-O) bus, and the memory-in (M-I) bus. The abbreviations designate the following units.

COP Control processor, contains the location counter and index registers and performs modification of instruction addresses before execution.

LOP Logic processor, performs logical operations on data words (two copies are powered).

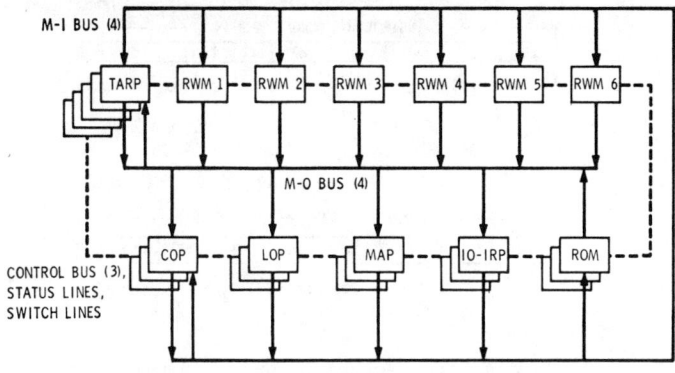

Fig. 2. STAR computer organization.

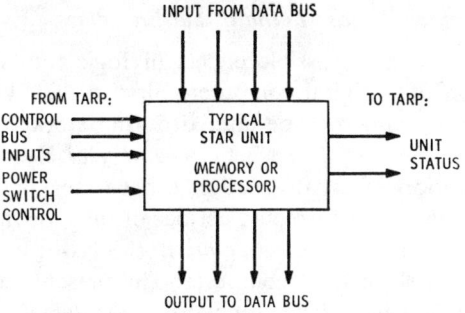

Fig. 3. Functional unit of STAR computer.

MAP   Main arithmetic processor, performs arithmetic operations on data words.
ROM   READ-ONLY memory, 16 384 permanently stored words.
RWM   READ-WRITE memory unit with 4096 words of storage (at least two copies powered; 12 units are directly addressable).
IOP   Input/output processor, contains I/O buffer registers.
IRP   Interrupt processor, handles interrupt requests.
TARP   Test and repair processor, monitors the operation of the computer and implements recovery (three copies are powered).

The functional units (processors and memories) of the STAR computer communicate by means of the M-I and M-O (four-wire) information buses. The 32-bit words are transmitted on these two buses as eight bytes of four bits each. Three control signals are sent from the TARP on the three-wire control bus to synchronize the operations of the functional units and to initiate recovery. Otherwise the functional units operate autonomously. Unless otherwise noted, one copy of each unit is powered at a given time. The decentralized organization allows a standard interface between each unit and the remainder of the computer. Each STAR unit interfaces with the computer by the means of 14 signal lines. Eleven lines, both in active and spare units, are permanently connected to the computer system buses, and three are connected to the TARP array. An unpowered unit cannot produce logic one outputs. The external connections of a STAR unit are shown in Fig. 3.

The four input and four output lines are connected to the data M-I and M-O buses. They receive and send coded machine words in four-bit bytes. The power switch control input causes power to be applied to the unit. The three control bus input signals are: CLOCK, a basic timing input; SYNC, a periodic synchronization signal; and RESET, a signal that forces the unit into a standard initial state. Two unit status lines send information on the internal operation of the unit to the TARP. These lines carry multiplexed information which will be discussed in a following section. Each functional unit is autonomous and contains its own sequence generator as well as storage for the current operation code, operands, and results. The internal design of a unit may be altered without affecting other units as long as the interface specifications are observed.

It is to be noted that the IOP and IRP units are shown combined in Fig. 2.

C. Standard Operation

The STAR computer has two modes of operation: the standard mode and the recovery mode (under TARP control). During the *standard mode* the stored programs are carried out. The TARP processor issues the principal CLOCK signal and SYNC signal which occurs when a new step is initiated in the execution of an instruction. Ten CLOCK periods form the basic time unit (cycle) of the computer. During the first period, a four-bit "step code" (in 2-out-of-4 encoding) is issued by the TARP to the M-O bus. The next eight periods are employed to transmit or manipulate one eight-byte machine word. During the tenth period a four-bit "condition-code" byte may be broadcast by one of the functional units. The ten-period cycle is needed because of the series-parallel organization of the computer.

One instruction is executed in two or three steps. In the first step, the address of the instruction is sent from the location counter in the COP to the memory (ROM and RWM) units. In the second step, the addressed memory unit broadcasts on the M-O bus the operation code and address of the instruction to all functional units. The address is indexed in the COP which transmits it to the M-I bus if necessary. The appropriate units recognize the operation code, store the address, and initiate execution. In the third step the instruction is executed: an operand is placed on the appropriate bus and accepted by the destination unit. The first two steps require one cycle each; the duration of the third step depends on the instruction and requires 0, 1, or more cycles. Program interrupts begin without the first step. During the second step an instruction is broadcast by the interrupting unit (IO-IRP or TARP).

The instruction set consists of 180 single-address instructions, about one-third of which are indexable. It includes fixed-point arithmetic, maskable logic, and shift operations. Loop-facilitating and subroutine link register instructions are provided. There are 28 interrupts which can be masked out and tested under program control. A special class of instructions aids in fault tolerance. They include diagnostic instructions which exercise unit status messages and the fault-location logic in the TARP. Others perform updating of the "rollback" register in TARP units, name assignment and cancellation of RWM units, power control of spare units, duplexing of ROMs and processors, and absolute read or write operations in RWM units.

D. Computer Words: Formats and Encoding

There are two possible effects of logic faults upon the operation of a digital computer. First, a data word or an instruction word may be altered during storage, transmission, or processing. The effect is a *word error*. Second, during the execution of an instruction a processor or a memory module may act incorrectly, act out of turn, or fail to act at all. The effect is a *control error*. Both classes of errors are detected in the STAR computer. The present section considers coding techniques for word error detection; control errors are considered later.

Complete duplication offers the simplest word-error detection at the highest cost. Low-cost arithmetic error-detecting codes [16] are attractive because they are preserved during arithmetic processing and mandatory duplication of an arithmetic processor is avoided. An intensive study of error codes led to the choice of modulo 15 arithmetic checking which is especially effective for a byte-organized computer with four-bit bytes [17].

All words in the STAR computer are encoded as shown in Fig. 4. The 32-bit numeric operand word [Fig. 4(b)] consists of the 28-bit binary number b, and a 4-bit check byte $c(b)$. The check byte is a binary number which has the value

$$c(b) = 15 - |b|_{15}$$

where $|b|_{15}$ means "the modulo 15 residue of b." This check byte causes the 32-bit word to be a multiple of 15. The checking algorithm casts out 15s, that is, it computes the modulo 15 residue of the entire coded word. A zero residue, represented by 1111, indicates a correct word; all other values of the residue indicate a fault. The casting out 15s is implemented with a four-bit "end-around carry" adder and takes place concurrently with the transmission of a word on the bus.

The 32-bit instruction word [Fig. 4(a)] consists of a 12-bit operation code and a 20-bit residue-coded address part. The 16-bit address is encoded in the same residue code as the operands, and the same checking algorithm is used. The operation code is divided into three bytes, and each byte is encoded in a 2-out-of-4 code. This code permits each byte to be checked individually. There are six valid forms of each byte, giving a total of 216 valid op-code variants. The structure of a bus checker circuit which performs word checking is shown in Fig. 5. The single step-code and condition-code bytes also use the 2-out-of-4 code and are checked by the bus checker.

The initial choice of error codes in the STAR computer emphasized variety for the purpose of comparison and evaluation, and the arithmetic product (or AN) code was used for operands [16]. Two reasons for the change to the present encoding of operands were: 1) the residue code is separable and allows the use of the more efficient two's complement algorithms for binary arithmetic, and 2) multiple precision and floating-point arithmetic is much more readily implemented with residue encoding. Residue encoding is also suitable for operation codes in STAR instructions. Its advantage is that an identical checking algorithm is applied to instructions and operands; an explicit identification is not required for checking, and loading of

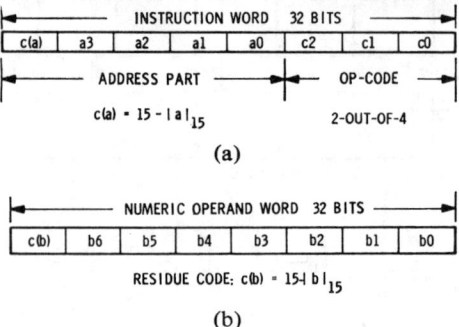

Fig. 4. (a) STAR instruction word format. (b) STAR operand word format.

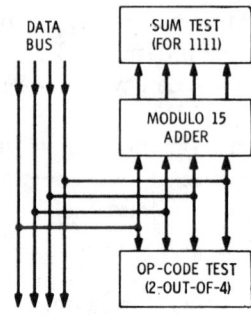

Fig. 5. The bus checker circuit.

programs is facilitated. The drawback is that the bytes of the op-code cannot be checked individually as in the 2-out-of-4 encoding.

E. Control Error Detection

It has been observed that a large number of faults which cause control errors also cause word errors and are detectable by the use of error codes. Some critical control errors, however, do not fall into this category and require other methods of detection.

The principal method of control fault detection in the STAR computer is the validation that every unit is active at the proper time and that the proper algorithm is carried out within the unit. The initial design [11] used a four-wire status line for every replaceable unit to transmit one of six possible "2-out-of-4" coded status messages. Experience has shown that the diagnostic logic in the TARP is significantly simplified when status messages are conveyed to the TARP at predetermined clock times within each ten-unit cycle of operation. In the revised design, each status message is conveyed on two wires (in 1-out-of-2 encoding) and each message covers the time interval between two messages of the same type. The status-message originating circuits are duplicated in each unit to allow the detection of a fault in the status message.

The "output active" message indicates that the unit has produced a nonzero output to the bus in the preceding time interval. It serves to identify improperly active units which otherwise would destroy the information being transmitted on a bus, and make it impossible to locate the source of error. The absence of an expected active message is also a fault condition, since the all-zero word is not a validly coded operand or instruction. The checking of output activity is the most critical of all status monitoring functions.

The other status messages are multiplexed and sent over the same pair of wires as the output active messages because the activity information is not required continuously in the byte-serial machine structure. The status messages which are listed below aid in increasing the probability of immediate detection of incorrect operation.

The "disagree with bus" message is needed for duplex operation (discussed in the next section). Two identical units produce outputs to a bus which acts as an OR gate. Each unit compares the bus word to its internally held output word and records a disagree message if a mismatch occurs. The message is conveyed to the TARP at a specified time. The bus checker result together with disagree message permits a rapid identification of a faulty unit. In simplex operation this message helps to identify improper activity of another unit.

The "complete" message is essential for functional units which have variable-duration algorithms. Memory units issue "write complete" and "read complete" messages which are essential for immediate detection of incorrect storage events.

The "internal fault" message is produced by internal monitoring circuits within each unit. Its function is to indicate incorrect internal algorithms detected by duplication of critical signals, special test circuits, and "inverse microprogramming" in which an operation is deduced from active gating signals.

In addition to the above listed four types of messages, time is provided for a "special" status message which varies for different units. For example, the IO/IRP uses it to report to the TARP the arrival of an external interrupt request.

F. Properties of Functional Units

The main arithmetic processor (MAP) input consists of an operation code followed by a coded operand, and the output is a coded result followed by a condition-code byte, indicating either one of three singularities (sum overflow, quotient overflow, zero divisor) or the type of a good result (positive, zero, negative). The control processor (COP) stores the condition code and uses it to implement conditional branches instructions. The COP also contains the location counter LC, two index registers, and a four-bit adder to implement indexing of residue-coded addresses and incrementing the LC. The logic processor (LOP) performs the bit-by-bit logic operations and code conversions on input words. The arithmetic coding is removed from the operand before the operation, since error codes are not preserved during logic operations, and the final result is again encoded. The LOP operation is checked by operating two copies which issue disagree status messages when their outputs differ. The IO/interrupt processor (IO/IRP) receives external interrupt requests, initiates allowable interrupts, and carries out input/output buffering functions.

The READ-ONLY memory (ROM) contains the permanent programs and the associated constants. The present machine uses a "braid" assembly of transformers and wires for the permanent storage of 16 384 words. Complete replicas of the ROM are used as replacements. Each 4096 word READ-WRITE memory (RWM) unit has two modes of operation. In the *absolute* mode a RWM unit recognizes its own wired-in absolute name. In the *relocated* mode a RWM unit responds to an assigned name. All relocated units with the same assigned name store and read out the same locations simultaneously. In case of a disagreement with the word on the M-O bus, the RWM unit sends a disagree status message to the TARP. The relocated mode provides duplicate or triplicate storage for critical programs and data. When a RWM unit fails, its replacement unit can be assigned the same name, avoiding a discontinuity in addresses. Assignment and cancellation of assigned names is performed under program control; this provision allows selective redundancy of storage. A record of RWM name assignments is retained (in nonvolatile storage) in all active TARP units. The accessing of storage locations within a RWM unit is checked by permanently storing the 4-bit check byte of its 12-bit internal address in every location. This byte is read out and checked against the contents of the address register during every read and write operation.

In the STAR computer only the logic processor and the RWM memory unit containing critical system programs are duplexed for normal operation. For experimentation, complete provisions have been made for optional duplex operation of all memory and processor units under program control. The combination of duplication and coding offers detection of all errors as well as a fast identification of one faulty unit. In order to permit duplex operation of processor and ROM units, active TARP units hold a record of units which are operating in duplex.

G. The Test and Repair Processor (TARP) and Recovery Mode

The "hard core" monitor of the STAR system is designated as TARP (test and repair processor) in Fig. 2. The TARP monitors the operation of the STAR computer by two methods: 1) testing every word sent over the two data buses for validity of its code; and 2) checking the status messages from the functional units for predicted responses. An incorrect word or a deviation from predicted response causes an interruption of normal computing and an entry into the recovery mode of operation. The block diagram of one TARP is shown in Fig. 6. It is functionally divided into two sections. One section provides standard mode machine control and fault location, and the other controls the recovery mode operation and effects the switching of replaceable units.

1) The Control and Test (CAT): This section contains the standard mode control logic consisting of an op-code decoder, a clock, and a counter which generates the step-code signals for standard mode operation. The machine-state prediction logic uses the current instruction and step-code to predict which status messages should be received from each powered functional unit. It also predicts the information source and the type of encoding expected on each bus. The fault location logic compares the status and bus checker (Fig. 5) results to the prediction. In most cases, it can localize an error to a particular functional unit. Upon detecting an

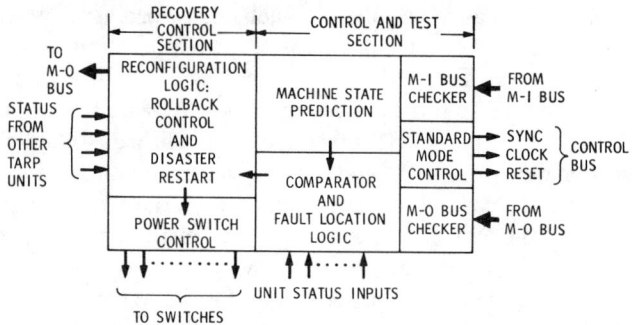

Fig. 6. Test and repair processor (TARP) organization.

error, the CAT section stops the machine and transfers its error information to the recovery control section.

2) Recovery Control (REC): This section of the TARP contains a "rollback point" address register which specifies the location of the instruction at which normal operation is to be resumed after a recovery. This register is updated under program control. Before every updating, the contents of all processor registers needed for recovery is stored in duplexed memory units. Upon receipt of an error message from the CAT section, the REC section issues the "reset" signal which causes all powered units to be set to an initial state, and then broadcasts an unconditional jump instruction, which causes the program to be resumed at the "rollback" address. A repeated fault indication in the same unit leads to its replacement. The number of repetitions before replacement can be specified in the experimental TARP. To replace, power is turned off in the unit, a spare is turned on, and another reset (and jump) is issued. For cases of temporary power loss and other fault conditions which cannot be resolved by the fault location logic, the REC section contains a wired-in "disaster restart" procedure.

The TARP is the hard core of the system. Three fully powered copies of the TARP are operated at all times together with n standby spares ($n=2$ in the present design). The outputs of the TARPs are decided by a 2-out-of-$(n+3)$ threshold vote. When one powered TARP disagrees with the other two, the recovery mode is entered and an attempt is made to set the internal state of the disagreeing unit to match the other two units. If this TARP rollback attempt fails, the disagreeing unit is returned to the standby condition and one of the standby units receives power, goes through the TARP rollback, and joins the powered triplet. The computer is now restarted, a rollback performed, and standard operation continues. Because of the three unit requirement, design effort has been concentrated on reducing the TARP to the least possible complexity. Experience with the present model has led to several refinements of the design.

The replacement of faulty functional units is commanded by the TARP vote and is implemented by power switching. It offers several advantages over the switching of information lines which connect the units to the bus. The number of switches are reduced to one per unit, power is conserved, and strong isolation is provided for catastrophic failures. Magnetic power switches have been developed which are part of each unit's power supply and are designed to open for most internal failures. The threshold function is inherent in the control windings of the switch. The information lines of each unit are permanently connected to the buses through component-redundant isolation circuits. The signal on a bus is the logic OR of all inputs from the units, and unpowered units produce only logic zero outputs. The power switch and the buses utilize component redundancy for protection against fatal "shorting" failures.

III. COMPARATIVE RELIABILITY ANALYSIS

This section considers the reliability (with respect to permanent failures) which can be expected for the STAR computer. The approach is to estimate the relative reliability with respect to an existing reference system. An absolute reliability prediction is not made because the failure rates for components which are being developed for a flight model are not yet adequately established.

The reference computer for reliability estimation is the nonredundant Mariner Mars 1969 (MM'69) computer, which was the on-board computer for the successful Mariner 6 and 7 missions to Mars. It was chosen because a detailed description and extensive failure rate data are readily available. With respect to computing performance it must be noted that the MM'69 computer is a bit-serial machine with a bit rate of 2.4 kHz and an instruction set of 16 op-codes, whereas the STAR is a byte-serial machine with a 0.5 MHz clock and an instruction set of 130 op-codes. This gain in performance is not used as a factor in reliability estimation.

Reliability models 1) the MM'69 computer, 2) a simplex computer equivalent in performance to the STAR, and 3) the STAR computer are shown in Fig. 7. The MM'69 computer [Fig. 7(a)] is assigned a complexity of unity. It is assumed that the simplex computer [Fig. 7(b)] consisting of eight functional units is $8 \times CF$ times as complex as the MM'69 computer. The relative complexity factor CF is defined as the ratio of complexity (component count) of a single STAR unit to the complexity of the entire MM'69 computer. The value $CF = 1/3$ was established by detailed comparison and is used in the subsequent analysis. The comparison is made with respect to MM'69 technology, i.e., it is assumed that the simplex and the STAR computers employ the same components and packaging techniques as the MM'69 computer.

The STAR model [Fig. 7(c)] consists of eight functional units plus the test and repair processor (TARP) array in series reliability. All units are considered to be of similar complexity and are allocated an equal number of spares. Results for $S=2$ and $S=3$ are presented. The reliability model applied to all units except the TARP is the standby-replacement redundancy model with dormant spares [12], [19]. The TARP was modeled as a hybrid-redundant $H(3, S)$ system [18]. Details of the reliability models and measures are presented in [19]. The logic processor LOP is assumed to have an internal duplication of the circuits which are not protected by the error-detecting codes. Two sets of three RWM units each are shown; this is a pessimistic assumption, since the computer can function with only one of the six RWM units surviving.

The fault coverage factor [12] in the STAR model is

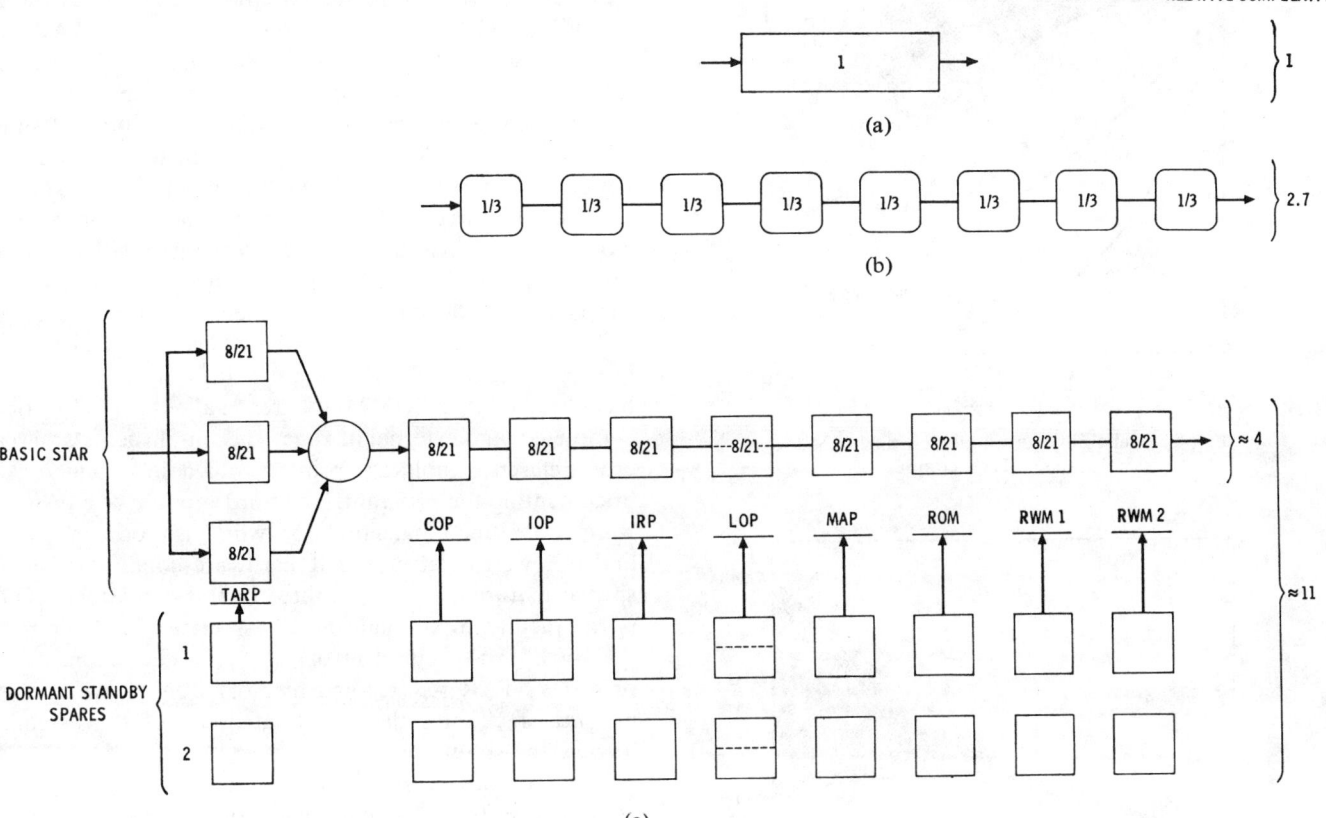

Fig. 7. Reliability models. (a) Mariner Mars 1969 computer. (b) Simplex computer. (c) STAR computer.

taken into account in two ways: 1) by including the fault detector and recovery initiator as a separate processor (the TARP), and 2) by applying a self-testing factor (STF) to the relative complexities of the units. Note that the simplex computer [Fig. 7(b)] does not contain a processor corresponding to the TARP in the STAR computer since the simplex computer is a computationally equivalent nonredundant machine without "test and repair" capabilities. Since 4 bits of the 32-bit STAR word serve for error detection, a STF equal to 8/7 was chosen. The STF expresses the overhead due to the self-testing and repairing features within each STAR unit, that is, a STAR unit has 8/7 of the complexity of the same unit in the "simplex" computer. Applying CF=1/3 and STF=8/7 a STAR unit has the relative complexity of 8/21 with respect to the entire MM'69 computer.

Examples of reliability predictions based on the MM'69 data are shown in Tables I and II and Figs. 8 and 9. The *lower bound* ($K=1$) assumes equal failure rates of powered and spare units (K is the failure rate ratio). The *upper bound* ($K=\infty$) assumes a zero failure rate of spare units. Two-spare ($S=2$) and three-spare ($S=3$) STAR systems are considered. Table I and Fig. 8 show the predicted reliability as a function of time. Table II shows the time (in years) for which the reliability remains above a specified value. Fig. 9 presents the predicted reliability gain, defined as the ratio STAR reliability/MM'69 reliability.

The computing operations for the foregoing analysis, the generation of tables, and the plotting of graphs was done with the aid of the computer-aided reliability estimation (CARE) program [21], which was developed as a design tool during the reliability study. CARE is a software package developed on the Univac 1108 computer system at JPL. CARE may be interactively accessed by a designer from a

TABLE I
RELIABILITY VERSUS TIME FOR VARIOUS CONFIGURATIONS (CF = 1/3)

Mission Time (h)	MM'69 Computer	Simplex Computer	STAR Computer with S Spares Upper Bound ($K=\infty$)		Lower Bound ($K=1$)	
			$S=3$	$S=2$	$S=3$	$S=2$
4368 ($\approx$ 6 months)	0.928	0.82	0.9999998	0.99997	0.999995	0.99982
43 680 ($\approx$ 5 years)	0.475	0.14	0.997	0.97	0.966	0.87
87 360 ($\approx$ 10 years)	0.225	0.019	0.96	0.79	0.71	0.45

TABLE II
MISSION DURATION FOR SPECIFIED RELIABILITY (CF = 1/3)

	Mission Duration in Years					
Desired Mission Reliability	MM'69 Computer	Simplex Computer	STAR Computer with S Spares Upper Bound		Lower Bound	
			$S=3$	$S=2$	$S=3$	$S=2$
0.9	0.7	0.3	12.5	7.5	6.7	4.5
0.8	1.5	0.6	16.0	9.7	8.5	6.0
0.7	2.4	0.9	18.5	11.7	10.0	7.0
0.6	3.5	1.3	20.5	13.5	11.3	8.3

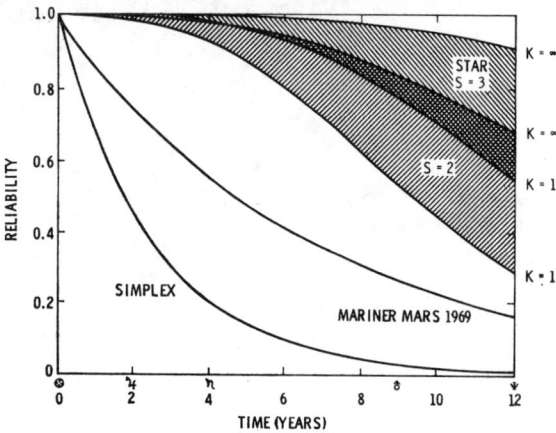

Fig. 8. Reliability versus mission time MM'69, simplex, and STAR computers.

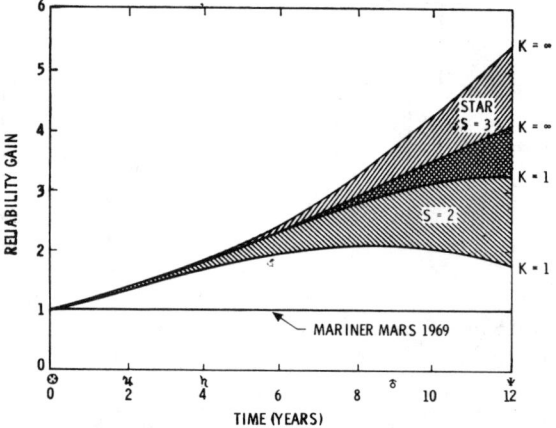

Fig. 9. Reliability gain of STAR computer with respect to the MM'69 computer.

teletype console to calculate his reliability estimates. The input is in the form of a system configuration description followed by queries on the various reliability parameters of interest and their behavior with respect to mission time, fault coverage, failure rates, dormancy factors, allocated spares, and partitioning. The CARE program is extensible, and it may be updated to incorporate new reliability models as they become available.

IV. STAR Computer Software System

Early in the design of the STAR computer it became evident that the fault-tolerant architecture would impose unconventional constraints on its software. The development of the software system for the STAR computer was initiated in 1968 and closely followed the hardware development. It is partitioned into two subsystems. The programming subsystem consists of three modules: an assembler, a loader, and a functional simulator. An executive program facilitates coordinated use of these modules. The operating subsystem consists of two modules: the resident executive module and the applications programs module. The programming subsystem has been implemented on the Univac 1108 computer of the Scientific Computing Facility at JPL. The first version of a resident executive for the STAR computer is nearing completion.

SCAP (the star computer assembly program) is the first module of STAR software. Programs for the STAR computer are written in the assembly language SCAL. SCAP is a traditional two-pass assembler incorporating machine instructions, pseudo-operations, and macrofacilities. A unique feature of SCAP is the encoding of instruction and data words as required by the STAR computer. SCAP calculates the code required and generates the encoded value of the word. Another feature of SCAP is the COMPILE pseudo-operation which implements automatic compilation of simple arithmetic statements by the assembler.

The second module LOAD (the loader) reads the program into the simulated STAR computer memory. After all decks have been read, a COMMON area is allocated, relocation is completed, and external linkage is accomplished. A map and cross-reference table are printed to aid in debugging and documenting the program. The third module of STAR software is the functional simulator, which is modular in nature and follows the latest STAR hardware configuration. Two special features are incorporated in the simulator. The first is the facility to simulate hardware errors in order to test the software aspects of error recovery. The second feature provides STAR register and memory dumps. An executive program facilitates the coordinated use of the assembler, loader, and simulator.

The modules of the operating subsystem of the STAR computer software system consist of the resident executive module and the applications programs module. The STAR resident executive augments the self-testing and repairing features of the hardware in addition to its normal functions. The standard features include interrupt control, input/output processing, and job scheduling. Novel features incorporated due to the fault-tolerant architecture of the STAR computer include a "cold start" capability, reconfiguration processing, rollback assistance, and diagnosis of faulty units. The cold start capability resets the hardware and software after a disaster restart as well as prior to an initial load. Reconfiguration processing is required for memory replacement, since software assistance is required to load a newly activated memory unit. All programs running on the STAR computer require rollback (recovery) points. The resident executive provides rollback status storage and controls events which are nonrepeatable i.e., they may not occur more than once even if a rollback takes place. Finally, it implements diagnosis for faulty units to determine the cause and extent of failures for possible partial reuse. The present application programs module includes floating-point arithmetic subroutines, and test and demonstration programs. The applications programs which will be required for space missions are a part of the TOPS control computer subsystem project discussed later in this paper.

V. Extension of STAR Techniques to Peripheral Systems

The STAR techniques of fault tolerance can be systematically extended beyond the boundaries of the computer to effect automatic maintenance of various peripheral systems that communicate with the computer. The case which was investigated in connection with the STAR computer development is the implementation of automatic maintenance for a simplified model of the JPL thermoelectric outer planet spacecraft (TOPS) which is being proposed for the exploration of the outer planets [15]. The potentially lower failure rates of unpowered spare units and the constant power demand of a replacement system are exceptionally important in missions requiring a ten year survival of the spacecraft under very strict power constraints.

The methodology of extending the STAR techniques consists of several steps: 1) identification of the replaceable peripheral units; 2) selection of internal error detection functions which are economically feasible within the units themselves; 3) identification of possible functional redundancy, in which either another type of peripheral unit, or the computer itself can take over the function of a failed unit; 4) algorithmic description of the monitoring and recovery procedures to be performed for each unit by the computer; 5) development of fault-tolerant communication between the peripheral units and the I/O and interrupt processors of the computer; 6) translation of the monitoring and recovery procedures which have been assigned to the computer into computational requirements: speed, instruction set, storage size, input/output and interrupt system complexity; and 7) estimation of reliability and mean life attainable for each peripheral unit. Several iterations of the design process lead to a system for which a balanced gain in reliability has been attained by means of computer-controlled automatic maintenance. A detailed case study of the application of these techniques is presented in [20].

The investigation has identified and quantized the computing capability required from the STAR computer in order to effect the automatic maintenance of the TOPS spacecraft. Furthermore, the results have shown that: 1) the fully automatic maintenance of a complex long-life spacecraft is feasible through a systematic extension of STAR techniques, and 2) the automatic maintenance requirements of the spacecraft systems can be algorithmically described to the detail required to produce computer programs for their implementation. The results of the investigation have systematically extended dynamic redundancy to various peripheral subsystems of an information processing system. Beyond the specific example of a spacecraft, the methodology is applicable to computer-controlled automatic maintenance of other complex data processing, communication, and control systems.

VI. Design of the TOPS Control Computer

The most recent step in the development of the STAR computer concept has been the design of a control computer subsystem (CCS) for the thermoelectric outer planet spacecraft (TOPS) [15]. After the TOPS requirements were quantified as described in the preceding section, the CCS design had still to meet four major externally-imposed constraints: 1) the weight of the subsystem was not to exceed 40 lb; 2) power consumption was not to be greater than 40 W; 3) probability of successfully completing a 100 000 h mission was to be equal to or greater than 0.95 (using TOPS approved part failure rates, and 4) it could not, as a consequence of any single internal fault, result in a failure mode catastrophic to the mission.

Because of these constraints, it was not possible merely to "shrink" the STAR computer into a flight package. The STAR design was simplified by retaining only the capabilities needed to meet the TOPS functional requirements. The entire self-test and repair ability of the larger machine has been retained; in fact, the TOPS CCS has expanded failure detection and recovery capability. A variety of advances arising from the years of work on the STAR computer that preceded the TOPS effort have been incorporated into its design.

The CCS operates at a clock frequency of 500 kHz. The CCS word is the same length as the STAR word, 32 bits. The word-processing cycle, ten byte-times long in the STAR computer, has been reduced to nine in the CCS: eight for processing or transferring information and one (two in STAR) for the messages and decision making between words. The execution (including fetch) of an instruction requires one to three cycles. The STAR instruction set with over 200 variants has been reduced to less than 100. To detect word errors, the CCS uses the same residue code as the STAR computer. Unlike the STAR, however, the CCS employs the residue encoding also for operation codes of instructions. In addition to these failure detection measures, the CCS incorporates dual control logic and clocking, memory address checking simultaneous with all memory accesses, and a nondestructive read-after-write option on all store instructions.

The CCS consists of the seven STAR computer functional units designated the COP, LOP, IOP, IRP, ROM, RWM, and TARP (Fig. 2). The IO/IRP has been split into independent IOP and IRP units in order to improve failure detection and isolation in a completely unattended environment. The MAP is deleted because software multiplication and division are sufficient, while addition and subtraction are done in the LOP. Simplifications in the instruction set have resulted in reduced hardware in the COP, LOP, IOP, and IRP. Conversely, there is increased hardware in the RWM and TARP for added failure detection. A 4096-word ROM and two 4096-word RWM units constitute the program storage capability of the CCS. In addition, another 4096-word RWM (designated SHM) is shared (by use of two independent ports) by the CCS and measurement processor subsystem (MPS). All the CCS RWM units are identical; any one of them can be assigned either as a CCS internal memory or as the SHM. The SHM contains the MPS operating program and the most recent samples of spacecraft variables gathered by the MPS. Because the SHM is available to the CCS as part of its own memory, these samples are conveniently available to it for fault diagnosis and monitoring of spacecraft activity [20].

VII. Current Research

The research and development program which led to the STAR computer is continuing in several directions. The design of several improved second generation STAR functional units is under way, including a new arithmetic processor, a control processor for medium-scale integrated-circuit implementation, and the shared READ-WRITE memory unit for the storage of automatic maintenance information from the spacecraft telemetry system. Analysis of automatic maintenance algorithms and design of a command/data bus for their implementation are under intensive study. Other current investigations are concerned with the following areas: 1) hardware–software interaction in a fault-tolerant system with recovery, especially the interaction of the TARP and the operating system; 2) studies of advanced recovery techniques, i.e., post-catastrophic restart, TARP replacement schemes, recovery from massive interference, partial utilization of failed units; 3) advanced component technology, especially methods to attain bus and power switch (i.e., hard core) immunity to faults; 4) heuristic studies of fault tolerance by interpretation of extensive experiments with the STAR breadboard as the instrument; 5) design of a second-generation STAR-type computer with universal processor and storage modules, and their implementation by large-scale integration; 6) Computational utilization of the spare units for supplemental tasks in a multiprocessing mode.

At the present time it is evident that the STAR computer design and construction effort has led to valuable new insights into the problem of fault-tolerant computing; further results in this field are expected from the research program in the future.

Acknowledgment

The research and development of the STAR computer has been performed in the Spacecraft Computers Section of the JPL Astrionics Division, and recognition is due to most of the Section's members for support in their respective specialties. The STAR concept of computer architecture is due to A. Aviẑienis, who has directed the overall research effort. The hardware design is directed by D. A. Rennels, the software effort by J. A. Rohr, reliability analysis by F. P. Mathur, and the implementation of peripheral automatic maintenance by G. C. Gilley. Technical contributions to the design have been made by P. H. Sobel and A. D. Weeks, and consultation has been contributed by R. K. Caplette, E. Greenberg, G. R. Hansen, E. H. Imlay, G. R. Kunstmann, J. Nievergelt, J. J. Wedel, and L. J. Zottarelli. The STAR effort has been administered by J. R. Scull, W. F. Scott, and J. J. Wedel. The power switch has been developed by the Stanford Research Institute, Menlo Park, Calif., and a fault-tolerant READ-ONLY memory has been designed by the M.I.T. Instrumentation Laboratory, Cambridge, Mass., under subcontracts from JPL. Construction of the computer was performed by J. Buchok, J. L. Cline, N. B. Funsten, J. C. Schooler, and B. Stall. The design of the TOPS Control Computer is due to D. K. Rubin, with technical contributions by N. Deo, G. Milligan, and M. Vineberg. A special acknowledgment is due to R. V. Powell of the JPL Research and Advanced Development Program Office, and F. J. Sullivan, Director, Electronics and Control, J. L. East, J. I. Kanter, T. S. Michaels, and G. A. Vacca of the NASA Office of Advanced Research and Technology, Washington, D. C., for their continued support and encouragement of the STAR computer effort.

References

[1] A. Aviẑienis, "Design of fault-tolerant computers," in *1967 Fall Joint Comput. Conf., AFIPS Conf. Proc.*, vol. 31. Washington, D. C.: Thompson, 1967, pp. 733–743.

[2] R. A. Short, "The attainment of reliable digital systems through the use of redundancy—A survey," *IEEE Comput. Group News*, vol. 2, pp. 2–17, Mar. 1968.

[3] T. B. Lewis, "Primary processor and data storage equipment for orbiting astronomical observatory," *IEEE Trans. Electron. Comput.*, vol. EC-12, pp. 677–686, Dec. 1963.

[4] R. E. Kuehn, "Computer redundancy: Design, performance, and future," *IEEE Trans. Rel.*, vol. R-18, pp. 3–11, Feb. 1969.

[5] J. E. Anderson and F. J. Macri, "Multiple redundancy applications in a computer," in *Proc. 1967 Annu. Symp. Rel.*, Washington, D. C., pp. 553–562, 1967.

[6] R. E. Lyons and W. Vanderkulk, "The use of triple-modular redundancy to improve computer reliability," *IBM J. Res. Develop.*, vol. 6, pp. 200–209, Apr. 1962.

[7] I. S. Reed and D. E. Brimley, "On increasing the operating life of unattended machines," RAND Corp., Memo. RM-3338-PR, Nov. 1962.

[8] J. Kruus, "Upper bounds for the mean life of self-repairing systems," Coordinated Sci. Lab., Univ. Illinois, Urbana, Rep. R-172, AD-418 174, July 1963.

[9] B. J. Flehinger, "Reliability improvement through redundancy at various systems levels," *IBM J. Res. Devel.*, vol. 2, pp. 148–158, Apr. 1958.

[10] J. E. Griesmer, R. E. Miller, and J. P. Roth, "The design of digital circuits to eliminate catastrophic failures," in *Redundancy Techniques for Computing Systems*. Washington, D. C.: Spartan, 1962, pp. 328–348.

[11] A. Aviẑienis, "An experimental self-repairing computer," in *Information Processing '68, Proc. IFIP Cong.*, vol. 2, pp. 872–877, 1968.

[12] W. G. Bouricius, W. G. Carter, and P. R. Schneider, "Reliability modeling techniques for self-repairing computer systems," in *Proc. 24th Nat. Conf. Ass. Comput. Mach.*, pp. 295–309, 1969.

[13] J. E. Long, "To the outer planets," *Astronaut. Aeronaut.*, vol. 7, pp. 32–47, June 1969.

[14] A. A. Aviẑienis, F. P. Mathur, D. Rennels, and J. Rohr, "Automatic maintenance of aerospace computers and spacecraft information and control systems," in *Proc. AIAA Aerosp. Comput. Syst. Conf.*, Paper 69-966, pp. 1–11, Sept. 8–10, 1969.

[15] "TOPS outer planet spacecraft," *Astronaut. Aeronaut.* (Special Issue), vol. 8, Sept. 1970.

[16] A. Aviẑienis, "Concurrent diagnosis of arithmetic processors," in *Dig. 1st Annu. IEEE Comput. Conf.*, pp. 34–97, 1967.

[17] ——, "Arithmetic error codes: Cost and effectiveness studies for application in digital system design," this issue, pp. 1322–1331.

[18] F. P. Mathur and A. Aviẑienis, "Reliability analysis and architecture of a hybrid-redundant digital system: Generalized triple modular redundancy with self-repair," in *Proc. Spring Joint Comput. Conf., AFIPS Conf. Proc.*, vol. 36. Montvale, N. J.: AFIPS Press, 1970, pp. 375–383.

[19] F. P. Mathur, "On reliability modeling and analysis of ultrareliable fault-tolerant digital systems," this issue, pp. 1376–1382.

[20] G. C. Gilley, "Automatic maintenance of spacecraft systems for long-life, deep-space missions," Ph.D. dissertation, Dep. Comput. Sci., Univ. California, Los Angeles, Sept. 1970.

[21] F. P. Mathur, "Reliability estimation procedures and CARE: The computer aided reliability estimation program," *Jet Propul. Lab. Quart. Tech. Rev.*, vol. 1, Oct. 1971.

J. R. Sklaroff

Redundancy Management Technique for Space Shuttle Computers

Abstract: This paper describes how a set of off-the-shelf general purpose digital computers is being managed in a redundant avionic configuration while performing flight-critical functions for the Space Shuttle. The description covers the architecture of the redundant computer set, associated redundancy design requirements, and the technique used to detect a failed computer and to identify this failure on-board to the crew. Significant redundancy management requirements consist of imposing a total failure coverage on all flight-critical functions, when more than two redundant computers are operating in flight, and a maximum failure coverage for limited storage and processing time, when only two are operating. The basic design technique consists of using dedicated redundancy management hardware and software to allow each computer to judge the "health" of the others by comparing computer outputs and to "vote" on the judgments. In formulating the design, hardware simplicity, operational flexibility, and minimum computer resource utilization were used as criteria.

Introduction

The Space Shuttle avionics system contains five identical general purpose digital computers, each capable of communicating with the avionic subsystems to perform flight-critical and non-critical functions. During time-critical mission phases (i.e., recovery time less than one second), such as boost, reentry, and landing, four of these computers operate as a redundant set, receiving the same input data, performing the same flight-critical computations, and transmitting the same output commands. (The fifth computer performs non-critical computations.) In this mode of operation, comparison of output commands and "voting" on the results in the redundant set provide the basis for efficient detection and identification of two flight-critical computer failures. After two failures, the remaining two computers in the set use comparison and self-test techniques to provide tolerance of a third fault. This paper describes the computer set configuration, its operation in collecting and transmitting data, the redundancy management requirements, design considerations in meeting the requirements, and the actual design implementation.

The Space Shuttle represents the first planned operational use of multiple, internally simplex computers to provide continuous correct system operation in the presence of computer hardware failures. The concept was flight-proven in the Tactical Aircraft Guidance (TAGS) research and development program [1], which demonstrated a helicopter flight control system using three simplex digital computers to provide single-fault tolerance. The F-8 aircraft research and development program [2], currently under way, also uses three digital computers in a triply redundant flight control system. By comparison, previous space programs used either specially designed, internally redundant computers or multiple computers in a prime-backup configuration to provide fault-tolerant operation. The Saturn IB and Saturn V launch vehicle digital computer was a triply redundant design providing redundancy at a modular level within the computer [3]. The Orbiting Astronomical Observatory processor was four-fold redundant at the circuit level. The Skylab program used dual computers in an active/standby mode (in-orbit), relying on self-test techniques to detect failures in the active computer, and redundant hardware to switch to the standby computer (up to 2.75 s switchover time) [4].

Internally redundant computers use considerable extra circuitry to provide the required fault tolerance for continuous system operation [5]. This circuitry also provides the means to detect failures by making logical comparisons at selected points in the data flow within the computer. The concept of redundancy, when employed at the computer unit level, uses comparisons of data generated at the normal computer interface and thus does not incur the cost of special computer or circuit development. The Space Shuttle avionics design, constrained to the use of standard, off-the-shelf comput-

Copyright 1976 by International Business Machines Corporation; reprinted with permission.

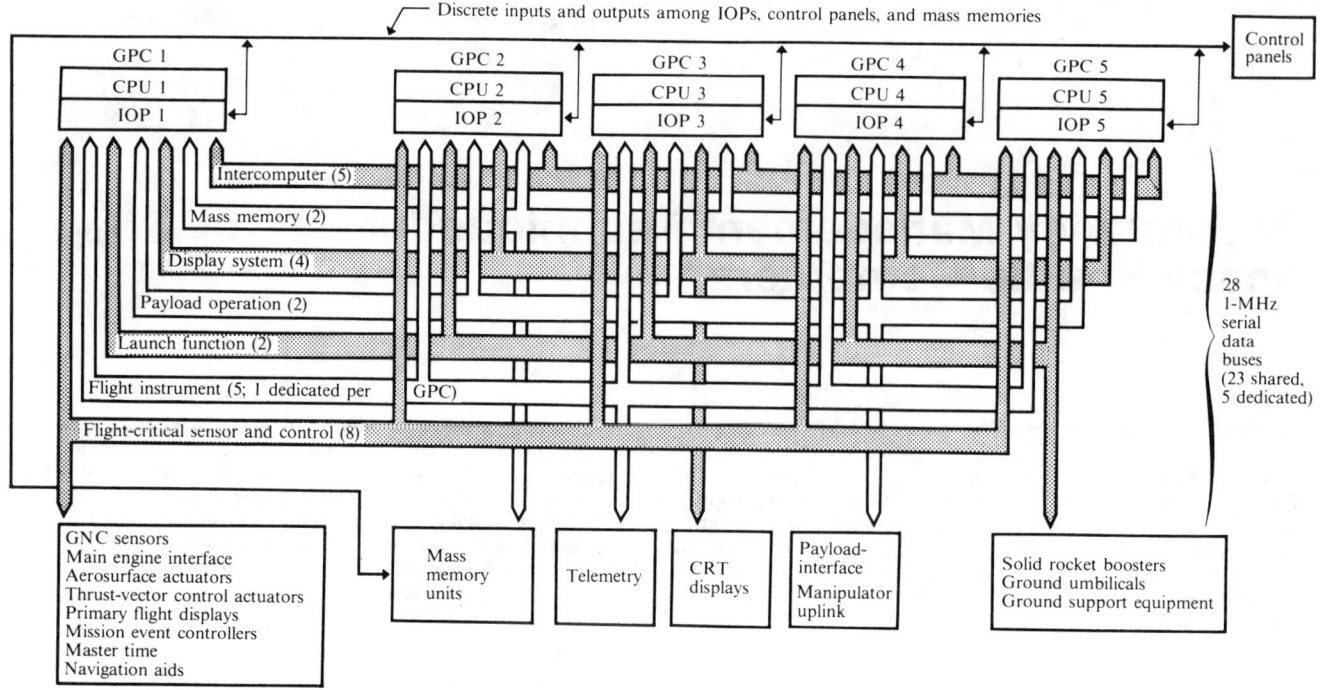

Figure 1 Space Shuttle avionics system block diagram.

ers, presented a unique engineering opportunity to properly utilize redundance at the unit level to provide the necessary failure coverage and fault tolerance.

System configuration

The digital processing subsystem defined for the Space Shuttle [6, 7] contains five general purpose computers (GPCs) communicating with the avionic subsystems over serial data buses (Fig. 1). Four of the five GPCs are identically programmed to perform flight-critical functions, such as guidance, navigation, and control. The fifth computer is programmed to perform non-flight-critical avionic functions.

A GPC consists of an IBM AP-101 central processor unit (CPU) and an input/output processor (IOP). Each IOP is transformer-coupled to the buses, and can transmit or receive 1-MHz serial digital data over each of 24 bus channels. The data buses, in turn, are transformer-coupled to multiplexer/demultiplexer units (MDMs) and digital subsystems. The MDMs (containing analog-to-digital and digital-to-analog converters) interface with analog subsystems, such as flight control sensors and effectors.

Subsystems performing similar functions are assigned to the same data-bus group. (There are seven such groups in total.) Subsystems have varying levels of redundancy at the unit level, depending on their criticality; e.g., there are three inertial measurement units, two radar altimeters, and four air data transducer assemblies. Each unit is addressable by a command word over the bus. To prevent the loss of more than one redundant unit when one data bus fails, no two redundant units interface with the same bus.

Some subsystems are internally redundant, such as the hand controllers and keyboard units. Also, all safety-of-flight critical effector subsystems, such as the actuators for the main engine and for the aerosurfaces, the main engine interface units, and mission event controllers are internally redundant at different levels. Such subsystems receive redundant commands on separate input channels and, using internal algorithms, generate one output. The algorithms detect incorrect commands and eliminate such commands from consideration in the output.

An example of a four-input "voting" effector is the aerosurface actuator, which uses four independent servo channels driving a four-element force-summed actuator. Failure of any three of the four channels can be tolerated without loss of operational capability. Hydraulic fault detection is provided by sensing the pressure differential at each element of the secondary actuator. With more than two channels operating, the actuator element is automatically bypassed when the threshold pressure differential is exceeded for a given time. With two channels operating, no actuator element is bypassed when the pressure differential is exceeded, thereby producing a "standoff" until one of the channels is manually reset.

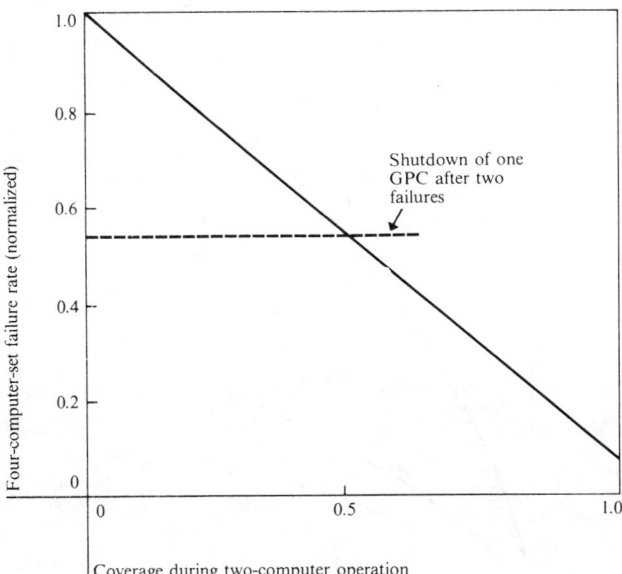

Figure 2 Effect of coverage during two-computer operation on the failure rate of a four-computer redundant set; coverage of the first two failures is one. Normalization is to the zero-coverage failure rate. The GPC failure rate is 8×10^{-2} per hour.

The use of voting effectors provides, in effect, downstream protection against failures in the redundant computer set. It allows a computer to transmit incorrect commands to critical subsystems for an indefinite number of cycles without actually having adverse effects on system operation. Thus, it is not necessary to detect computer failures immediately and stop the transmission of the incorrect output. This feature significantly relaxes the failure detection time constraint, which is one of the requirements that control the selection of the redundancy management technique.

Another feature of the system that facilitates the selection of a redundancy management technique is the interconnection of buses to computers. This feature allows each computer to have access to all flight-critical data received or transmitted by the other computers and makes possible the comparison of identical computations among computers.

System operation

Each bus within a data-bus group is assigned, under software control, to operate in either a command or a listen mode. In the command mode, data requests and commands are issued to the subsystems over the bus and data are received over this same bus. In the listen mode, data are only received on the bus.

In the flight-critical sensor and control-data-bus group (two subgroups of four buses), one bus in each subgroup is assigned to operate in the command mode (in each redundant-set computer) and the remaining three are assigned to operate in the listen mode. In the inter-computer channel (ICC) data-bus group (five buses), one bus (in each computer) is in the command mode and the remaining four are in the listen mode.

For data collection, since each of the redundant subsystems is connected to a different bus, a different computer requests data from each of the subsystems and the returned data are available to all other computers in the set. The listening computers are alerted that the subsystem data are available by receiving a listen command, which is issued by the command computer just prior to issuing the data request command to the subsystem. When operated in this manner, identical input data are available to each computer in the redundant set.

For data output, since each channel of the effector subsystem is connected to a different bus of the group, a different computer transmits command data to each of the voter-effector channels. Thus, a voter-effector subsystem requiring four inputs receives inputs from four different computers. Also, since the buses are interconnected to all computers, the capability exists for each computer to listen to the command data sent out by each of the other computers.

For inter-computer information transfer, each computer communicates with all other computers, passing data to the others, requesting data from the others, and performing any other tasks required to operate the computer set. No subsystem is connected to the ICC buses.

As a consequence of the distributed control of redundant sensors among computers, an unacceptable time-skew may exist between redundant inputs unless the computers are synchronized prior to initiating the inputs. Similarly, unacceptable data-skew may exist at the voting effectors unless synchronization occurs prior to initiating outputs. Moreover, unacceptable command differences may exist at the voting effectors unless synchronization occurs at appropriate points during program execution. Synchronization is accomplished in the Space Shuttle computer set by using inter-computer discrete signals and synchronization software.

Program synchronization is required because computers that do not use exactly the same data for computing flight-control outputs experience command divergence [8]. The time required to synchronize program execution depends on the design of the flight software operating system. A fixed time-slice system (i.e., one in which all processes are run within a given cycle time) requires one synchronization point in each computational cycle. An interrupt-driven system must synchronize at all points at which data are calculated in one process and used in another, and at all points needed to preserve identical process sequences in all computers of the set.

Redundancy management design

• *Requirements*

Five redundancy management (RM) design requirements established for the GPCs are presented and discussed below.

1. A failed computer must be identified to the crew, prior to assignment to the redundant set, using self-test techniques that provide at least 96 percent coverage. (Coverage is defined as the probability of detecting a failure, given that a failure has occurred.)

The purpose of this requirement is to enable the crew to identify a failed computer (a) before lift-off (to abort the mission) or (b) before a critical in-orbit phase (to reallocate the data bus assignments or to attempt to restore a GPC using an initial program load (IPL) from mass memory). A goal of 96 percent coverage of computer failures in an autonomous environment (i.e., no external test equipment or cooperative use of other GPCs) was established. A computer fail-discrete interface with the crew panel suffices for GPC failure identification.

2. Of four GPCs in the redundant set, the first two to fail and cause incorrect flight-critical output must be automatically identified to the crew as failed; the third should also be identified as failed, but only by achieving as much coverage as is possible within a limited processing and storage overhead.

The purpose of this requirement is to enable the crew to take appropriate action during flight based on complete knowledge of the failure status, such as aborting the mission, de-energizing the computers, or reallocating bus assignments. Moreover, in the case in which a critical failure occurs when only two GPCs are operating, if the crew can reconfigure accordingly, the voting effectors will continue to operate without simply arriving at a standoff.

The relation between failure coverage during a two-computer operation and the probability of an N-unit system loss is presented in the Appendix. The result shows that for a system which achieves total coverage on the first $N - 2$ failures, system loss is a linear function of coverage during the two-unit operation and is the same as in the one-unit operation when the coverage is 0.5. Thus, for any coverage of more than 50 percent, the probability that the redundant set will fail when two computers are operating is less than the failure probability when only one is operating.

The result in the Appendix has been applied to a typical Shuttle mission. The graph shown in Fig. 2 illustrates the importance of providing adequate coverage in the two-computer operation. If two computers are allowed

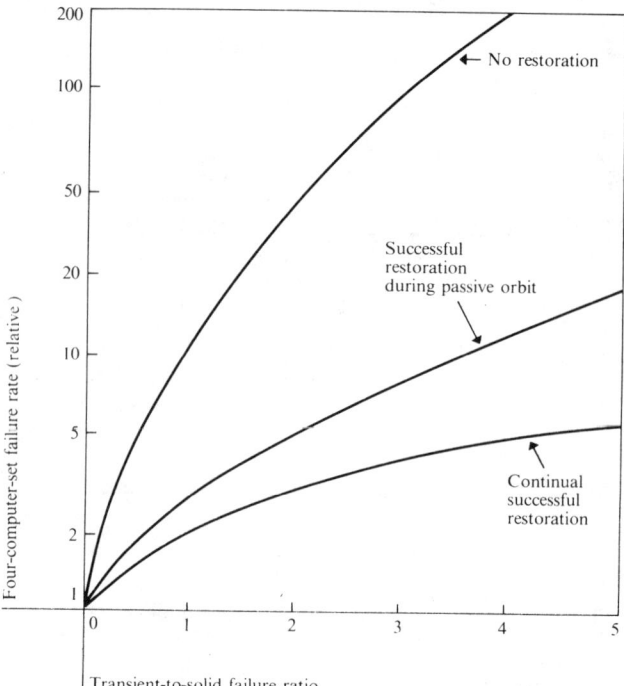

Figure 3 Effect of GPC transient failures on the computer-set failure rate as a function of restoration policy, in relation to the zero-transient failure rate. The operational-hour equivalents are 6.6, ascent; 128, passive orbit; 43, active orbit; and 4.4, reentry/landing.

to operate until one critically fails and is removed 100 percent of the time (coverage = 1), the probability that the computer set will fail is 5.5 times lower than if one fails and is removed only 50 percent of the time (coverage = 0.5). Also, if two computers are allowed to operate without ever removing one that fails, the computer-set failure rate is 5.5 times greater than if one computer is arbitrarily shut down.

3. A GPC indicated as failed should be capable of automatically inhibiting all transmission, but this capability must be enabled by the crew.

The purpose of this requirement is to provide the crew with the option of automatic reconfiguration of the redundant set.

4. A GPC failure should not cause another GPC to either identify itself as failed or generate an incorrect output.

The purpose of this requirement is to minimize the occurrence of (a) a non-failed computer being identified as failed because of the redundancy management design implementation and (b) a failed computer causing another computer to execute an incorrect program.

5. Restoration of a GPC in which a permanently incorrect critical output exists because of a transient failure should be accomplished wherever practical.

The purpose of this requirement is to minimize the impact of transient GPC failures on system operation. Figure 3 illustrates the effect that such transients have on the number of computer-set losses, depending on the restoration policy used. If restoration is never attempted, computer-set losses increase by a factor of 16 over those of a continual restoration policy at a 2:1 "transient-to-solid" (i.e., intermittent-to-permanent type) failure ratio, and by 60× at a 4:1 ratio. However, if computer restoration takes place only during passive orbit (non-time-critical phase), computer-set losses increase only 1.6× over a continual restoration policy at a 2:1 transient-to-solid failure ratio, and 2.8× at a 4:1 ratio. For a continual restoration policy, an undue amount of computer resource and operational complication is involved in restoring and adding a computer to the redundant set during time-critical mission phases. Consequently, the redundancy management implementation need not automatically attempt restoration on detecting a computer failure. Instead, restoration can be attempted under crew control during passive orbit, when no maneuver takes place.

• *Considerations*
Several factors must be considered in developing computer redundancy management techniques to satisfy the requirements listed in the previous section. One of the more significant considerations is whether faults (hardware defects) or manifestations of faults to the output interfaces should be detected. Detection of faults is helpful from a hardware maintenance standpoint, but is of little practical operational value. A computer fault is of interest when the effect of the fault shows up in an operational output. Therefore, redundancy management design for the Space Shuttle should be oriented to the detection of failures that affect commands on the flight-critical buses.

Another important consideration is the amount of resource needed to attain the total coverage required for the one- or two-failure case. Such coverage cannot be attained in single off-the-shelf computers, as specified for the Space Shuttle. Therefore, cooperative testing techniques must be established among the computers. Comparison of identical computations is one method of attaining high coverage and is practical in the Shuttle computer set, without a significant amount of additional hardware, as a consequence of the normal system operation of command and listen modes, synchronization, and grouping of buses.

Other design decisions and rationales in developing the redundancy management technique are as follows.

1. Minimize the need to depend on the computer to detect and identify its own failure by using special hardware logic dedicated to the RM process.

Even though the comparison-of-output technique can detect a very high percentage of failures, identification is not certain if the failed GPC is simply notified that it has failed. Therefore, non-failed computers in the set must have the capability of forcing the failed computer to indicate itself as having failed. This requires hardware dedicated to the redundancy management identification process.

2. Use computer software to judge the "health" of other computers.

If a computer cannot correctly monitor and test other computers, then it probably cannot compute correct output itself and will be judged bad by the others. Thus, the output-compare process need not be a part of the RM hard logic, but may be done by software.

3. Use sum-checking of critical outputs as the comparison basis.

A large range of output-compare data exists. Each separate word transmitted on the flight-critical buses could be compared, but this would result in considerable computer and bus overhead. A more effective method of reducing overhead, without losing the required coverage, is to sum the outputs to be transmitted over the flight-critical buses during one computational cycle and then compare the sum-check.

4. Transmit the compare word over the ICC buses.

Eight flight-critical buses and the ICC buses are available for transmitting the selected compare word to the other computers. Input/output processor transmission and reception on the flight-critical buses are checked when transmitting commands to the sensors and receiving data from the sensors using special communication tests, e.g., IOP BITE (built-in test equipment) and bus channel timeout. The ICC buses are available for use without interfering with the critical bus traffic.

5. Detect faults in dedicated RM hardware by programmed testing of the logic.

Faults in any redundancy management logic added to the individual computers do not propagate to the flight-critical channels and show up as critical failures. However, faults in this logic are critical, and it is important that they be detected in order to satisfy design requirement 4. Hence, faults in this logic should be detected by a test program executed in each CPU.

Design implementation

The hardware and software elements developed for the Space Shuttle and used to meet the redundancy management requirements are listed in Table 1. The elements and their operational use support failure detection, identification, and reconfiguration. These functions are performed according to which of the following conditions prevails during flight: (a) four or three GPCs operating in the redundant set (quad or triplex configuration); or (b) two GPCs operating in the redundant set (duplex configuration).

• *Quad/Triplex operation*

When more than two GPCs are operating in the redundant set, the level of achievable coverage can be significantly improved over that provided by self-testing by using cooperative techniques. Moreover, the resource utilized in obtaining this coverage with cooperative techniques is significantly less than that required for self-testing.

Two cooperative tests are performed in the Shuttle to detect a failed GPC when more than two GPCs are in the redundant set. These are the compare word test and the bus channel timeout test.

The *compare word test* consists of

a. Computing a compare word by summing critical GPC command outputs (to the effectors);
b. Transmitting the compare word on the ICC bus to the other computers in the RM set;
c. Receiving compare words from other computers and storing them in designated locations in main memory;
d. After a time has elapsed which ensures receipt of all compare words, comparing the received words with the computed word on a bit-by-bit basis; and
e. Identifying another GPC as failed if two successive non-compares are assigned to it.

The compare word test, performed after the critical GPC commands have been computed in each computation cycle, is implemented using both CPU and IOP software. The test uses less than 0.2 percent of the CPU processing capability and achieves nearly total coverage.

The *bus channel timeout test* consists of waiting a given time after synchronization for another computer to perform an input transaction on its dedicated bus. This test, plus the compare word test, provides total coverage in the computer set of all flight-critical functions.

The compare word test uses the dedicated redundancy management hardware, shown in Fig. 4, for cooperative identification as follows:

Failure-vote register (FVR) Each IOP contains a four-bit register, which is used to judge another GPC as failed as the result of a cooperative test. When a failure is detected, a bit is set in this register. Each position of the FVR is associated with another GPC within the computer set. The FVR is set and reset under control of the software and is automatically reset for any reset of the IOP.

Failure-vote discrete driver/receiver Each output of the FVR is logically connected to an independent, discrete driver. Each failure-vote discrete driver has two dedicated outputs, one to indicators on the crew panel and the other to a discrete receiver in the IOP of one of the GPCs (the one corresponding to the dedicated FVR position). Thus, each GPC contains four failure-vote discrete drivers for transmission of the results of the compare word test to other GPCs (and to the crew panel) and four failure-vote discrete receivers for acceptance of the votes.

Voter logic and fail-latch The voter logic accepts the outputs of the fail-vote discrete receivers and generates an output to set a voter fail-latch whenever two or more failure-vote discretes are received from other GPCs. The voter fail-latch is reset by an IOP power-on reset or a halt-discrete input from a crew panel switch and is set by the voter logic. The output of the latch is transmitted to the computer-fail driver, failure-vote inhibitor, and transmission termination control logic.

Computer-fail driver (fail-discrete) During flight the computer-fail driver is used to transmit a GPC critical failure indication to the controls and display console as a result of both cooperative and self-test GPC failure identification. When the voter fail-latch is set, the computer-fail driver transmits an output discrete to the crew panel. No fail indication is present when a GPC is on and operating normally, is off, or has received a halt-discrete input.

Table 1 Summary of the elements of redundancy management.

Function	Element
Fault detection	Compare word test Bus channel timeout test Built-in test equipment Self-test programs Watchdog timer
Fault identification	Failure-vote-discrete out GPC-fail-discrete out
Reconfiguration	Failure-vote inhibit, voter- and timeout-IOP reset (RM-initiated) IOP-master reset (software-initiated) IOP-fail reset (BITE-initiated) Power off and halt-discrete in (crew-initiated)

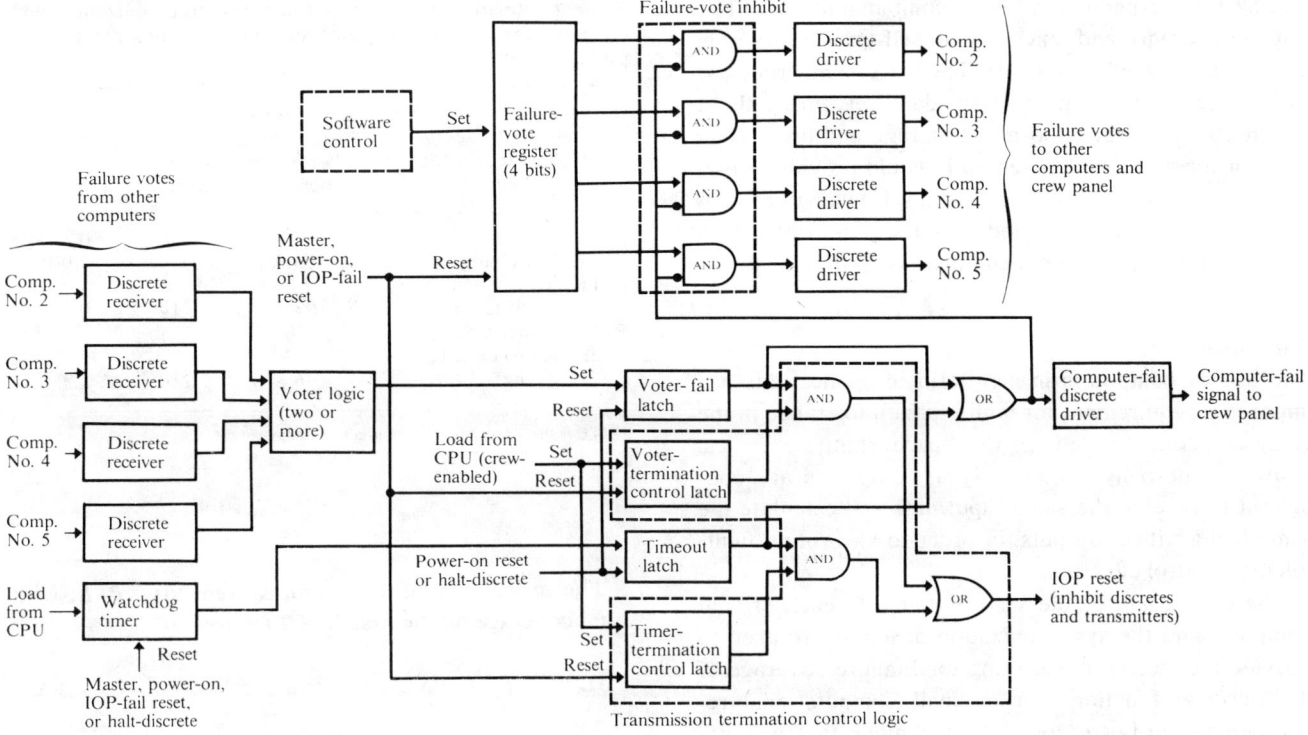

Figure 4 Dedicated redundancy management logic, shown for computer 1.

The hardware shown in Fig. 4 is also used for reconfiguration, which involves termination of the role of a GPC as a functioning member of the redundant GPC set. One manifestation of reconfiguration is an IOP reset, which can occur automatically when the GPC has been identified as failed; another is automatic inhibition of the transmission of failure votes to other GPCs, which means that the logic operates to prevent a failed GPC from further participation in cooperative failure detection.

- *Duplex operation*

When only two GPCs are operating in the redundant set, identification as a result of cooperative testing is not possible, although detection of a disagreement is possible through the compare word test. Therefore, self-testing must be used to distinguish which of two GPCs has failed. The cooperative tests are still useful, however, in providing a program cue to scheduling any planned self-test program execution. As such, cooperative tests should be run continuously in the duplex mode. Thus, whenever a failure vote is set by either of the two computers, that computer can also run self-test.

The sources of self-test coverage that can be used in the duplex mode fall into three categories:

BITE (*built-in test equipment*) BITE consists of any hardware logic or microcode which causes an interrupt to the CPU, during its normal program operation, when a GPC failure is detected.

Self-test programs These programs detect GPC failures, but must be specifically executed under program control. They can consist of either main-memory-resident (macrocode) or control-storage-resident (microcode) routines.

Watchdog timer A watchdog timer (shown in Fig. 4), located in the IOP and periodically loaded by the CPU, is used to detect failures that affect cyclic program execution by the CPU and is a means of indicating that the GPC has failed after fault detection by the CPU. Whenever the time loaded into the timer elapses, a timeout latch is set to identify the failure to that GPC.

The level of coverage of critical hardware that can be achieved by self-test techniques during duplex operation is limited by the resource utilization constraints imposed by flight-program budgets. An example of the relation between coverage and resource utilization is shown in Table 2 for the central processor (the example does not include memory or power supply). The level of CPU coverage achievable for the amount of storage and processing time expended, when a combination of BITE, watchdog timer, and microcoded self-test program is used, is considered acceptable. The use of a macrocoded self-testing program in the redundant set during flight operation would take too much storage and processing time for the additional coverage it would provide. However, the execution of a macrocoded self-testing program prior to assignment to the redundant set, to meet the 96 percent coverage requirement discussed previously, is necessary.

Summary

The use of computers in flight-critical applications has imposed a requirement for multiple-fault tolerance in the computer configuration. In the Space Shuttle avionics, multiple, internally simplex digital computers are configured to receive the same input data and calculate the same flight-critical outputs, in order to use voting fault-tolerant control effectors.

The calculation of the same outputs by each critical computer and the synchronization of inputs are used to provide the means of achieving total failure coverage of flight-critical functions for a small computational resource and hardware cost. The technique that was implemented uses each computer to judge the "health" of the others through a bit-by-bit comparison of critical data and an I/O transaction timeout test. The judgement process was implemented in software for greater flexibility, and the vote on the judgements and the generation of the failure indication were implemented in dedicated hardware for greater failure identification reliability.

When more than two computers are operating, the level of failure detection and identification achievable using data comparison between computers and voting techniques is significantly higher than that obtainable using self-testing. When only two are operating, an acceptable level of failure detection and identification can be obtained, within limited storage and processing time, by using built-in test equipment and a watchdog timer on a continual basis and scheduling special test microcode to follow the occurrence of a non-compare.

Acknowledgments

The author appreciates the useful comments received from F. G. Kilmer, H. A. Padinha, R. E. Poupard, and A. R. Stevens. This paper covers work performed under Space Shuttle contract M4J3XMS-483027 between Rockwell International Corporation, Space Division, and International Business Machines Corporation, Federal Systems Division.

Appendix

Here we develop the relation between coverage during two-unit operation and the probability of multiple-unit system loss.

Table 2 Relation between self-test resource utilization and coverage for the central processor (not including memory or power supply).

Central processor self-test coverage source	Coverage of critical hardware (percent)	Storage (half-words)	Processing time (ms)
BITE*	36.9	0	0
BITE/Watchdog timer	68.5	4	0.005
BITE/Timer/Microcoded self-testing	88.7	14	0.15
BITE/Timer/Micro- and macro-coded self-testing	96.8	110	1.3

*BITE is the abbreviation for built-in test equipment.

The probability of an N-unit system loss, PSL, with total coverage on the first $N-2$ failures, is

$$PSL = \int_0^T P_2(t) \, PSL^*(T-t) \, dt, \quad (A1)$$

where T = mission length; $P_2(t)$ = probability of failing to a two-unit system at time t; and $PSL^*(T-t)$ = probability of system loss during two-unit operation. In turn, PSL^* has been derived [9] as

$$PSL^* = (1 - e^{-u}) - [(2c-1)/(2k+1)]$$
$$\times e^{-u}[1 - e^{-(2k+1)u}], \quad (A2)$$

where $u = \lambda_c(T-t)$; λ_c = unit failure rate; c = failure coverage during two-unit operation; $k = \lambda_b/\lambda_c$; and λ_b = failure rate of components that do not affect the unit's function, i.e., the false alarm rate.

Equation (A2) shows that, for this particular system, system loss is a linear function of coverage c. Moreover, this loss, during two-unit operation, is the same as in one-unit operation when $c = 0.5$.

References

1. F. G. Kilmer and J. R. Sklaroff, "Redundant System Design and Flight Test Evaluation for the TAGS Digital Control System," *Proceedings of the 29th Annual National Forum of the American Helicopter Society*, Washington, D.C., May 1973.
2. C. Jarvis, "A Digital Fly-by-Wire Technology Development Program Using an F-8C Test Aircraft," presented at the AIAA 12th Aerospace Sciences Meeting, Washington, D.C., January 1974.
3. F. B. Moore and J. B. White, "Application of Redundancy in the Saturn V Guidance and Control System," AIAA Paper 67-553, *Proceedings of the AIAA Guidance Control and Flight Dynamics Conference*, Huntsville, Alabama, August 1970.
4. "Apollo Telescope Mount Digital Computer Program," Contract NAS 8-20899 Information Document, Part 1, *TR 72-WO-0039*, IBM Federal Systems Division, Huntsville, Alabama 35805, December 1971.

5. H. Hecht, "A Comparison of Fault Tolerant and Externally Redundant Computers," *SAMSO TR 74-66*, Aerospace Corporation, El Segundo, California, January 1974; available as document *AD777166/0* from the U.S. National Technical Information Service, Springfield, Virginia 22151.
6. S. Z. Rubenstein and L. O. Shroyer, "Digital Processing Subsystem for the Space Shuttle," presented at the National Aviation Electronics Conference (NAECON), May 1974.
7. E. A. O'Hern, "Space Shuttle Avionics Redundancy Management," presented at the AIAA Digital Avionics Systems Conference, Boston, April 1975.
8. H. A. Padinha, "Divergence in Redundant Guidance, Navigation and Control Systems," *Proceedings of the ION National Aerospace Meeting*, Washington, D.C., March 1973.
9. D. R. Thomas and F. G. Kilmer, "Redundancy Management Policies for a Dual Redundant Computer Configuration," *TR 75-C65-0013*, IBM Federal Systems Division, Owego, New York 13827, February 1975.

Received February 24, 1975; revised August 15, 1975

The author is located at the IBM Federal Systems Division, Owego, New York 13827.

FTMP—A Highly Reliable Fault-Tolerant Multiprocessor for Aircraft

ALBERT L. HOPKINS, JR., SENIOR MEMBER, IEEE, T. BASIL SMITH, III, MEMBER, IEEE, AND JAYNARAYAN H. LALA, MEMBER, IEEE

Reprinted from *Proceedings of the IEEE*, Volume 66, Number 10, October 1978, pages 1221-1239. Copyright © 1978 by The Institute of Electrical and Electronics Engineers, Inc.

Abstract — FTMP is a digital computer architecture which has evolved over a ten-year period in connection with several life-critical aerospace applications. Most recently it has been proposed as a fault-tolerant central computer for civil transport aircraft applications. A working emulation has been operating for some time, and the first engineering prototype is scheduled to be completed in late 1979.

FTMP is designed to have a failure rate due to random causes of the order of 10^{-10} failures per hour, on ten-hour flights where no airborne maintenance is available. The preferred maintenance interval is of the order of hundreds of flight hours, and the probability that maintenance will be required earlier than the preferred interval is desired to be at most a few percent.

The design is based on independent processor-cache memory modules and common memory modules which communicate via redundant serial buses. All information processing and transmission is conducted in triplicate so that local voters in each module can correct errors. Modules can be retired and/or reassigned in any configuration. Reconfiguration is carried out routinely from second to second to search for latent faults in the voting and reconfiguration elements. Job assignments are all made on a floating basis, so that any processor triad is eligible to execute any job step. The core software in the FTMP will handle all fault detection, diagnosis, and recovery in such a way that applications programs do not need to be involved.

Failure-rate models and numerical results are described for both permanent and intermittent faults. A dispatch probability model is also presented. Experience with an experimental emulation is described.

I. INTRODUCTION

THE FTMP (Fault-Tolerant Multiprocessor) is a computer architecture that has been studied, simulated, modeled, and emulated extensively over the past several years. It is scheduled to be implemented in an engineering prototype form within two years of this writing. The principal goal of FTMP is to be extraordinarily survivable without being difficult to program, operate, or maintain. It is presently predicted that the overall FTMP failure rate will be less than 10^{-9} failures per hour, provided that maintenance is available within no more than ten hours of dispatch. In most cases, however, it will not be necessary to maintain the FTMP at intervals of less than 200–300 hours.

The FTMP structure can be described as an arbitrary number of processor modules with local, or *cache*, memories, and an arbitrary number of memory modules, interconnected by redundant serial buses. Modules are associated into groups of three to perform triply redundant functions. All data is distributed synchronously and in triplicate, and every module contains a voting element to mask bus disagreements. All modules contain special circuits to create logical and physical boundaries to halt the propagation of faults from one module to another.

The FTMP is intended for use as one of at least two central computers in a redundant distributed digital system designed to serve as a highly survivable avionics system [1].

A. Background and Context

The development history of the FTMP dates to 1965, with a serial-bus multiprocessor concept for spaceborne control applications [2], [3]. Increasingly redundant versions were conceived, including one in 1969 intended to serve as a preliminary design baseline for a manned spacecraft, i.e., the space shuttle [4]. At that time, a concept was stated for the systematic design of a redundant, fault-tolerant vehicle, employing fault-tolerant "regional" computers, each of which was to be the master of an I/O bus connected to a number of dedicated (micro-) computers, local to each of a number of sensor and effector components or subsystems [5]. In the early 1970's, some of the basic concepts were tested by simulation in a laboratory multiprocessor arrangement called Cerberus. The National Science Foundation sponsored most of this testing effort.

There were two particularly significant outcomes of this work. One was a network I/O data communication structure to replace the topologically leaner, and therefore more vulnerable, I/O bus [6]. The second was a significant improvement in the redundancy management capability of the architecture [7], [8]. As a result of these developments, the Draper Laboratory undertook the construction of breadboard emulations of the new multiprocessor and the network as independent Research and Development projects. Evaluations of various aspects of these emulations were sponsored by the National Science Foundation, the Office of Naval Research, the NASA Langley Research Center, and Draper itself.

The Draper study concerned itself with the design of a robust integrated avionics systems concept suitable for control-configured aircraft, and numerous other life-critical applications. This concept was to use a fault-tolerant central computer with a second remote identical computer available to take over in case of damage to the first. The concept also used the I/O network as a fault-tolerant and damage-tolerant medium for maintaining access to all surviving system elements. The third prong of the concept was a redundant sensor and effector architecture, with algorithms executed centrally to determine which, if any, of the sensors and effectors were malfunctioning [9]. The entire system concept came to be called OSIRIS, (onboard, survivable, integrated, redundant information system, [10]).

Manuscript received March 1, 1978; revised May 12, 1978. This work was supported by the NASA Langley Research Center under Contract NAS1-13782, and the National Science Foundation under Grant DCR74-24116.

The authors are with the Charles Stark Draper Laboratory, Inc., Cambridge, MA 02139.

Meanwhile, NASA Langley sponsorship further developed the fault-tolerant multiprocessor architecture in the direction of civil transport aircraft application, along with a competing architecture developed at SRI International, called SIFT [11]. In 1977, a design specification was drawn up for an engineering prototype of the multiprocessor, to be built by a major avionics manufacturer. At this point, the name FTMP was adopted to signify this particular architecture and its derivatives.

The FTMP represents a major architectural advance beyond the contemporary practices of computer redundancy in aircraft systems. All too often, computers have been interconnected in the simplest possible way, leaving as a programming task the detection and isolation of each fault and the subsequent recovery. This approach has serious problems, including the means of granting authority to a valid module without granting it to an invalid one. It is also virtually impossible in such approaches to separate the redundancy management software from the applications programs, with the result that both are greatly complicated. Validation is a difficult problem in these systems.

The FTMP is quite different from some other fault-tolerant computers for different applications. A fault-tolerant spacecraft computer, for example, has a similar task, but a dissimilar survival requirement. Other fault-tolerant architectures are meant to serve general data processing tasks in a benign environment with maintenance available. The next subsection attempts to show how the architecture of the FTMP corresponds to the class of applications it is designed to serve.

B. Rationale of the FTMP Approach

The intended use of the FTMP is to support critical control functions in vehicles, process plants, life-support, or any similar application in which maintenance is available periodically or after a delay, and where loss of control leads with significant probability to high cost in terms of life or property. The failure rate at the system level must be remote. In civil transport aircraft this generally means the order of 10^{-9} failures per hour in flights of up to ten hours.

One can immediately rule out some of the classical approaches to redundant systems on the grounds that they do not permit the detection and location of faults concurrent with critical operation. Other approaches can be dismissed because of insufficient redundancy and fault coverage. Still others are unusable because they depend excessively on the applications software.

The approach must have the ability to mask, i.e., correct, errors without requiring program rollback. All resources, including those used only in case of malfunction, must be capable of being individually verified during system operation. The approach must further be capable of surviving a multiplicity of faults, although not necessarily all at the same time.

Apparently, the most efficient way to furnish the multiple fault tolerance and concurrent testing is in a multiprocessing or multicomputing structure. Moreover, in order to provide error masking, all critical transactions must be at least triplicated. This is the course that has been followed in both the FTMP and the SIFT architectures. The result is a variant of classical redundancy of the TMR-Hybrid type [12], in which spare elements are placed in a pool so that they can substitute for any element in any of several parallel TMR triads. We find it convenient to refer to this redundancy form as "parallel-hybrid" redundancy. Both FTMP and SIFT employ three times the resources nominally required by the application, plus an arbitrary level of spares, plus the hardware and software overhead necessary to manage the redundancy, i.e., fault detection and isolation, reconfiguration, and recovery. These two architectures employ graceful degradation as an important means of trading system cost against criticality. In projected aircraft, the flight critical functions account for a minority of the resource utilization. These functions are therefore supported with highest priority as resource pools diminish due to aggregated failures.

Beyond this point, FTMP and SIFT have gone separate ways. The FTMP has adopted a fully synchronous approach, which allows hardware-implemented bit-by-bit voting of all transactions. This in turn allows system management to be effected by majority rule, and means that the modules can be reassigned under executive control to different triads, or to spare status. Modules can be reconfigured in order to diagnose the location of a fault, to test the reconfiguration mechanisms, to activate spares for purposes of test and recovery, and to retire modules diagnosed as failed.

The next section discusses the theory of the FTMP architecture, and enlarges on several of the points that have been introduced here.

II. Theory of the FTMP

A. Nominal Organization

Loosely defined, a multiprocessor is a computer with several processors and a single (possibly multiport) memory accessible to all processors. In the extreme, all instructions and data reside in a common memory available to any processor, so that processors are "anonymous." Given a suitable state vector, any processor can execute any procedure from any starting point. Motivations for multiprocessors are typically to increase productivity and availability at the same time, although these two purposes are competitive. At any rate, parallelism is intrinsic to the multiprocessor, as each processor is able to execute a different concurrent procedure subject to limitations imposed by resource sharing and sequential constraints on the procedures.

1) Memory Access: A "canonical form" of a multiprocessor is illustrated in Fig. 1, which introduces the notion of memory private to each processor in addition to the common memory. The rationale for this private, or cache, memory stems from the limitations imposed on parallel operation by memory access constraints. In a multiprocessor with highly parallel memory access, memory conflicts would occur only when individual units of data are simultaneously requested, or are locked for sequential conflict resolution. This would be the optimum structure for parallelism, and the cache memory's role is reduced to a possible enhancement of processor execution speed.

In the FTMP, on the other hand, the memory access is highly serial, for reasons dictated by reliability and economy. This essentially means that the memory has a single port, and that the throughput of the multiprocessor is governed by the bandwidth of this memory port. In this case, the cache memory has a significant role in enhancing parallelism. The combination of processor and cache is a true computer, capable of performing elaborate operations on input data in response to terse commands. This means that the common memory can contain programs written in a language level

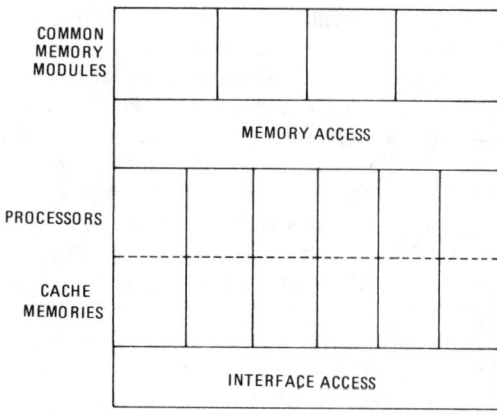

Fig. 1. Multiprocessor functional form.

higher than the processor's machine-language level, and that the processor-cache unit can interpret the higher level statements during the time that other processor-cache units are accessing the common memory. In this mode of system operation, which is really a form of "virtual machine," a memory port of moderate bandwidth can support an instruction execution "bandwidth" that is, at least in principle, almost arbitrarily large.

The degree to which the instruction execution bandwidth can exceed the common memory port bandwidth depends on the parameters of the cache memory, the terseness of the higher level language, and the relative amount of input and output data for each independent procedure. Clearly, the enlargement of the cache memories tends toward a multicomputer organization. Indeed, at some point the total cache capacity becomes adequate to contain everything in common memory, and the usefulness of common memory is reduced to the buffering of interprocess data. Processor anonymity is significant to this application because of the frequent reconfigurations that need to take place in this computer for latent fault exposure. Anonymity also provides an intrinsic mechanism for dynamic load distribution among available processing resources. The cache memory, however, acts to reduce the anonymity of the processor. To put it another way, the degree of anonymity is determined by the ease of reloading the cache memory. With zero cache memory, anonymity is greatest. As cache memory is increased to support instruction bandwidth enhancement, the anonymity of the processor-cache units depends on the amount of cache memory whose contents are unique to one processor. Note that the incorporation of identical procedural and other constant data, or indeed identical variable data, in every cache memory has no adverse impact on anonymity.

The use of a cache memory in a sampled-data control application, such as the aircraft application considered here, is generally productive. The typical job step uses rather few data samples as input, and produces one data sample as output. The procedures used tend to lend themselves well to expression as macrooperations, i.e., higher level operations, such as floating point arithmetic, linear combination, elementary functions, vector and matrix operations, and so forth. The incorporation of procedures of this level as cache subroutines is reasonable and profitable in today's technology. The current high annual rate of memory density increase prompts one to observe that a fairly extensive set of procedures, and indeed a hierarchy of procedures, is increasingly appropriate for inclusion in cache memories.

The cache memory structure of the FTMP includes memories for data and procedures, partly read-write, partly read-only, designed to enhance instruction bandwidth with rather little loss of processor anonymity. The common memory, although highly modular, acts as a single-port paged memory, accessible to one processor at a time via a serial bus with a built-in contention mechanism.

2) Functional Resource Allocation: The programmer sees this multiprocessor as a machine for executing job steps, largely corresponding to periodic sampled-data updates. The magnitudes of these job steps will vary considerably from one control function to another, but will require something of the order of a few milliseconds, on the average, of processor time per job step. The procedure for each job step is written in a suitable language, and resides in common memory. Typically, each job step is scheduled to occur at a given time or following a given event. The relevant dispatch data for each scheduled job step is kept in a queue, where it is frequently examined to see if the job step is eligible to be run, or *invoked*. The frequent examinations are conducted by processors that have completed their earlier assignments, and are available to undertake new ones. When an available processor finds one or more eligible job steps, it selects one of them to invoke. In this way, job allocation is dynamic, and adjusts itself to the momentary load distribution and to module failures.

Input-output management in a multiprocessor can be more complex than it is in a single multiprogrammed computer, because as a single-port resource, it impinges on program parallelism. Depending on the statistics of external data traffic and of internal job steps, different access strategies may be appropriate. The most straightforward of these is to treat interface access as a single resource that is allocated to a single process for its exclusive use for the short period of time that a process requires access. Access may be granted on a priority basis or a first come first served basis. That is, when a processor needs interface access, it ascertains by means of flags in memory whether the interface is free. If not, the processor waits (with appropriate safeguards against lock-up) until it becomes free.

B. Redundant Organization

The physical organization of the FTMP is substantially more complex than the nominal organization outlined in the preceding section. A simplified module diagram of the computer is shown in Fig. 2. Superficially, this diagram appears much the same as the nominal multiprocessor. The principal differences are that the buses for memory and interface access are redundant, and that the actual number of modules is three times the number of nominal modules plus some number of spares.

All activity is conducted by triads of modules and triads of buses. A module triad is formed by associating any three like modules with one another. This means that any module can serve as a spare for any triad. Such flexibility permits the best possible utilization of surviving modules. A single triad of bus lines is active at any one time for each of the

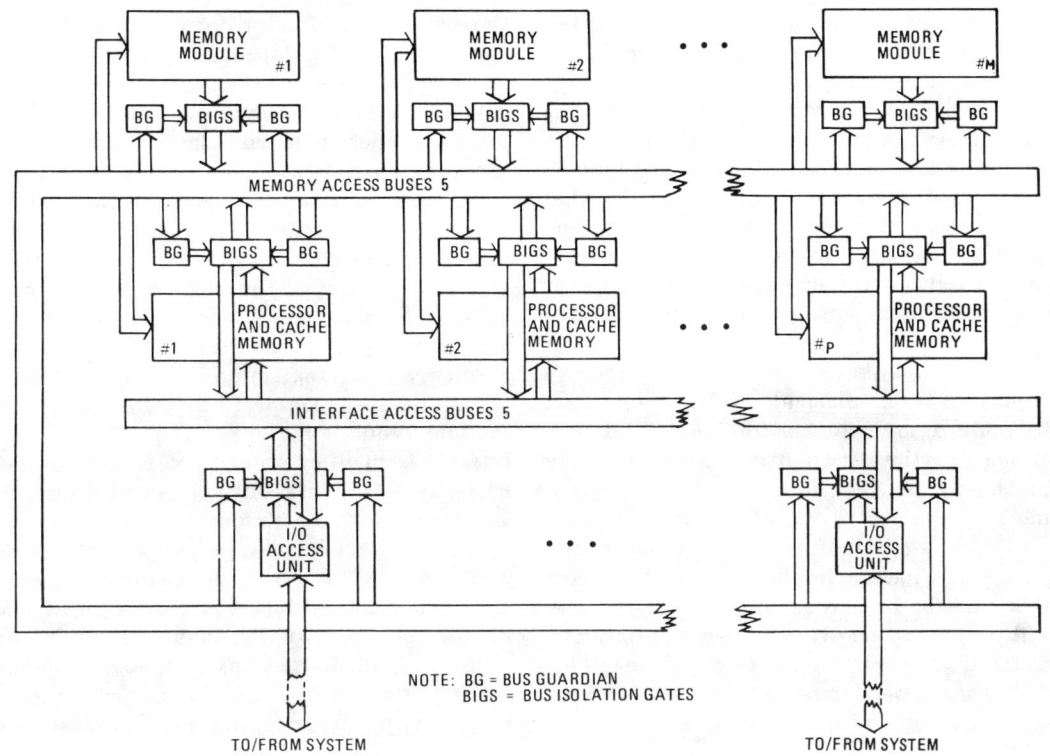

Fig. 2. Simplified physical diagram of the FTMP.

memory and interface accesses. In other words, a three-member subset of N bus lines is chosen on a quasistatic basis to serve as a bus triad.

Every module of every kind is able to receive data from all incident bus lines, and contains a decision element to formulate a corrected version of bus data. It is necessary for each module to know which three bus lines are the active ones. These three lines are connected to a voter in each module, thus constituting a TMR element. The three active bus lines carry three independently generated versions of the data, each version coming from a different member of the triad that is transmitting the data. To accomplish this, it is necessary to assign each module to transmit on one specific bus line. Now if totally flexible module configuration is to be possible, it follows that the assignment of a module's transmission to a single bus line must be quasi-static and reconfigurable.

1) Bus Guardians: In addition to the redundancy described in the preceding few paragraphs, the redundant organization differs from the nominal one by virtue of the inclusion of independent submodules called bus guardian units in each processor, memory, and input–output access unit. Guardians are charged with governing the status of their associated modules. This includes power-on status, memory bus triad and transmission selection, and certain self-test configuration selections.

Each of the functions of the guardian has the characteristic that its failure modes have safe directions as well as unsafe ones. By biasing the failure modes toward the safe directions, it is possible to increase the probability of system survival. In general, the safe failure modes of a module are power-off, and bus transmission disconnected. To bias in this direction, one can employ redundant guardians in each module, and require agreement among them to establish power-on and bus transmission enable.

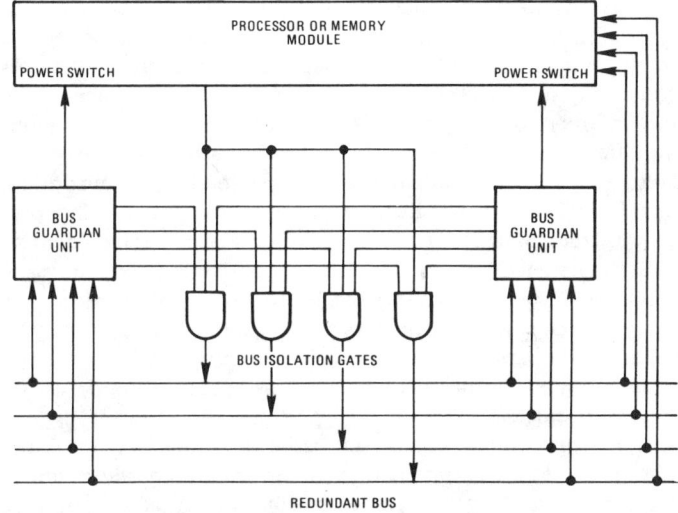

Fig. 3. Bus guardian connections.

The connection of bus guardians is illustrated in Fig. 3. It should first be noted that the guardian principle depends heavily on fault independence. Therefore, each guardian derives its power, its bus inputs, and its timing reference independently of all other guardians. It is moreover physically isolated from all other guardians and all modules. A particularly critical area from the isolation viewpoint is the control of the module's transmission interface onto the various bus lines. The bus isolation gates must be highly independent of one another, as must the guardian's enable signals to these gates. This is one of the crucial electrical and mechanical design aspects of the entire computer.

Bus guardians are addressable as part of the common memory address space, and are capable of receiving messages from any processor triad via the active memory bus triad. A message to a guardian contains commands which are staticized by the guardian and applied to its outputs until superseded by a new command message. In this way, the probability is remote that a failed module can assert more than one erroneous data stream. As a result, correct data can be determined by the bus voters, and the malfunctioning module can be switched to a silent state. It is noted in passing that certain failures of a bus isolation gate can render a bus line useless, in which case the active bus triad must be reconfigured. However, most guardian failures are biased to appear as passive failures of the unit to which the particular guardian unit pertains.

Guardians are used as agents to convey the computer's configuration authority to all elements of the computer. They are highly secure against the random or willful malfunction of any single active transmitting module. They make possible the highly flexible reconfiguration on which the FTMP depends.

2) Processor and Memory Modules: All modules and buses are organized into triads. In the case of processors and memories, there can be numerous triads in existence at the same time, but only one memory bus triad and only one interface bus triad. Each processor triad acts as one functional processor, of which several can work in parallel. Each memory triad acts as a page of memory, of which several can exist at one time, but only one can communicate at a time with a processor triad.

When a processor fails, its triad will attempt to complete its current job step, which it will be able to do unless a second failure prevents it. The period of vulnerability to a second failure will be a fraction of a second. When the job step is complete, one of the other processor triads is assigned the task of reconfiguring the injured triad. When the erroneous module is identified, it is removed by commands to its guardians. If a spare is available, it is connected to the appropriate bus by its guardians, likewise upon command by the processor triad assigned to the reconfiguration. Triad identity will be assigned to the spare processor by a direct message. If no spares are available, the injured triad is retired. The resources of the multiprocessor are diminished by one processing unit, and the two unfailed members of the former triad are now available to be used as spares, should further failures occur.

The situation is much the same for memory modules. The principal difference is that memories are not anonymous. In fact, a read-only memory module is totally dedicated to its assigned function, and cannot be used as a spare. When a read-only memory triad is injured by the loss of a memory module, a read-write memory module can be used as a spare. It must be loaded to agree with the surviving triad members before a second failure occurs. If no spare is available, the triad is reduced to a dyad, which is vulnerable to the next failure, at which time one memory page is lost. This is a significant departure from the flexibility offered by the anonymous processor triads. The eventuality of read-only memory failure must clearly be covered by the inclusion of adequate spares, either read-write memories for flexible pooled use, or extra dedicated copies of read-only memory.

3) Input-Output Access: Fig. 2 indicates the existence of input-output access modules connected to the internal interface bus and also the external environment.

The external interfaces of the computer can alternatively support dedicated, bussed, or networked link structures to the sensor and effector components. The redundancy structure at this point depends on the redundancy desired in the external interface.

The simplest conceptual structure is a triple-redundant interface, such as a redundant external bus, where the triple modular redundancy structure is extended through to the component interfaces. Each external bus line can be dedicated to a different input-output access module, which in turn is assigned by its guardian units to transmit on one of the active interface bus lines. More complex variants are possible, in which each access module performs error correction by voting on incoming data from the external bus.

When an external interface is nonredundant, the strategy would be to assign it to a single access module, where the module would transmit on all three active interface bus lines. A malfunctioning access module could pollute the entire interface bus, but with suitable encoding and protocol there would be no serious consequences to the state of the system. The offending access module could be discovered and disconnected by bus guardian commands conducted over the memory bus, the major penalty being a time loss on the remainder of the input-output interface of the computer. For dedicated links, the loss of the link is noncritical by hypothesis. For a network, whose survival is assumed critical [6], the computer must interface with the network in several places via several distinct access modules. Each such interface would be simplex, but the system would survive the failure of all but one of them.

C. Synchronization

The employment of independent redundancy requires some form of synchronization among the independent data sources. Soft, or loose synchronization involves such operations as buffering, comparing or voting, signalling consensus, and marking completed intervals. These can be done by program, given suitable intermodule data links. Hard, or tight synchronization involves hardware comparison or voting, and a common time reference, whereas loose synchronization can employ separate time references.

Tight synchronization is employed in the FTMP. It provides the basis for solving some problems, and it presents some problems of its own. A common time reference, or clock, that supports hardware voting, allows instantaneous validation of internal data, configuration control, and, in some cases, interface data. In this way, it helps to make the redundant multiprocessor resemble the nominal one, which is advantageous to programmers at all levels.

The problems of common clocking stem primarily from the fact that it is critical to computer operation in the dynamic sense. The timing reference must be continuous and must remain within tolerances. A second consideration is that common clocking results in time-correlated data transfer, which is subject to correlated malfunction if subjected to external radiation of electromagnetic energy beyond the levels tolerated by shielding. The second problem is intrinsic to all synchronization, but is more severe for tight synchronization. The problem also exists in principle for any degree of shielding. When the statistics of such interference are known, the problem can be addressed in the time domain by encoding for error detection, rerun for recovery, or repetition for time independence.

The problem of maintaining a continuous timing reference is solved by a fault-tolerant redundant clocking arrangement,

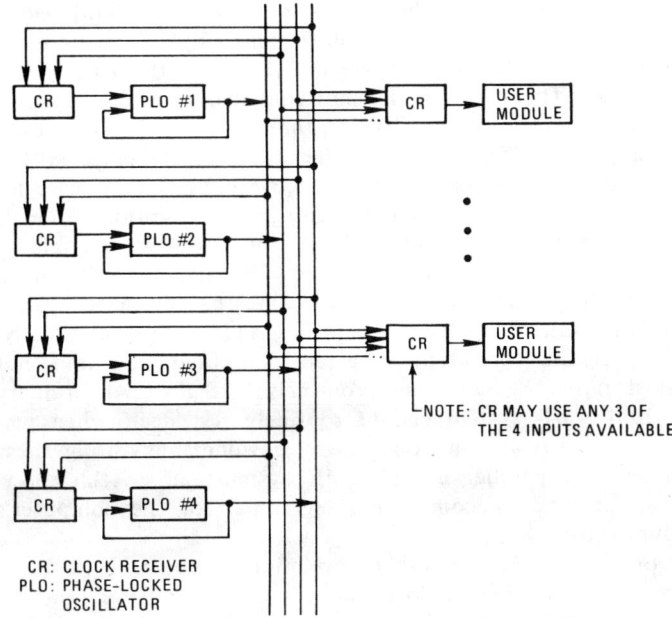

Fig. 4. Fault-tolerant clock system.

based on a majority logic algorithm described in reference [13]. A more recent embodiment, using voltage-controlled crystal oscillators, will be described in future reports. The basic principle of the system is shown in Fig. 4, which shows a set of independent phase-locked oscillators arranged so that the failure of one of the oscillators does not destroy the phase lock of the survivors. The clock signal from each oscillator is distributed to every module and guardian, so that each can make an independent determination of clocking edges. These independent determinations are made by circuits called clock receivers, whose operational principles are closely similar to the clock receivers described in [13]. In normal, nonfailed operation, the outputs of all the clock receivers are in phase lock with each other and with all the oscillators. The same phase lock holds when an oscillator fails. The failure of a clock distribution line appears as an oscillator failure, and the failure of a clock receiver appears as a failure of the module or guardian that contains it. The approach is discussed further in Section III-D6.

D. Malfunction Management

The unusually high level of dependability required in the FTMP makes it mandatory to consider all possible sources and effects of probable malfunctions. The probabilities associated with exposure to hazards are important here, as they are in any reliability analysis. The fact that reconfiguration and recovery are needed to meet reliability goals raises other issues of importance, having to do with the probabilities associated with the detection and identification of malfunctions, reconfiguration and recovery of the system, and the system status following a malfunction event. All those considerations relate both to the design and the evaluation of the system.

1) Malfunction Sources: A malfunction is a general term for anomalous behavior. Numerous kinds of malfunctions are distinguished, ranging from microscopic disorders in an integrated circuit to total aircraft impairment. Within the information processing segment of the total system, we are concerned about avoiding malfunctions that preclude the availability of viable contingencies. We can think of potential malfunctions as being infinitely rich in number and variety, and tractable solely because they can be treated as classes and subclasses.

The first class of malfunctions to be examined is that resulting from externally induced phenomena, such as physical penetration, radiation (atomic, electromagnetic), temperature extremes, or excursion of prime power. The common thread in these diverse physical environments is that their effects can not be confined or localized to one or a few subportions of the information system. The entire system is vulnerable at one time, and for an arbitrarily high exposure it can not be made otherwise. That is, the shielding, structure, environmental control, and prime power generation must all be designed to withstand stated levels of exposure to known hazards. Exposures in excess of these levels are potentially catastrophic.

The second malfunction class is that of random malfunctions whose sources are internal to the system. Typically, these result from circuit failures. When idealized, such malfunctions are permanent, isolated, unambiguous, visible, and recoverable. Actual faults are apt to be marginal, intermittent, correlated, hidden, uncovered, and/or not perceived uniformly by multiple observers. This is the category of malfunctions that redundancy addresses, although the nonideal attributes of actual faults tend to undermine the effectiveness of all redundant systems.

The third class of malfunction sources will simply be denoted as "other sources." The first two classes are broadly enough defined to be stretched to cover everything, but it is useful to emphasize certain sources separately. Thus we include in this third category the deficiencies resulting from lapses in system specification, that is, where the domain of operation and the domain of design are not matched. Software in this sense is a specification. It specifies the sequential rules of hardware utilization. Logic design is also a specification in this sense, as are design factors related to the human interfaces and the sensor and effector interfaces. The architectural implications of this category are that the system must be tractable and understandable enough to reduce the probability of occurrence of such malfunctions to a negligible level.

2) Malfunction Consequences: It has been useful to characterize the various possible malfunctions according to the levels at which they affect the system [14]. There are *physical malfunctions* that occur within hardware elements, such as a short circuit in a transistor. These have been referred to by various writers as faults and failures, and in this paper the word "failure" refers to this category. A physical malfunction may or may not result in a *logic malfunction*, in which a logic variable is at some time or another complementary to its correct value. Where authors use the word "fault" for physical malfunction, they use "failure" for logic malfunction, and vice versa. A logic malfunction can occur in the absence of a physical malfunction, notably from induced sources.

A logic malfunction may or may not produce a *data malfunction*, often called an error. A data malfunction can occur in the absence of a logic malfunction, notably from specification lapses. A data malfunction, in turn, may or may not produce a *subsystem malfunction*, which in turn may or may not produce *system malfunction*.

We have portrayed a propagation chain from physical malfunctions to system malfunction, with some external entry points. Whether propagation takes place from one level to another depends on whether a causal link exists in the first place, and whether the phenomenon is masked by a redundancy. Thus a logic malfunction produces a data malfunction only if it impacts the outcome of an operation. Even then, it may not, as for example when the data results from the voting of three inputs, only one of which suffers a data malfunction.

A key point, often overlooked in simplistic treatments of redundancy, is that redundancy always has a limited capacity to mask malfunctions, and this capacity can degrade to zero without affecting the apparent behavior of the system. Therefore, a system designed to have tolerance may in fact have none at the inception of a critical mission. Alternatively it may have some tolerance, but less than the design level, and less than what is assumed. Masking is a two-edged sword. On one hand it is a mechanism for holding malfunctions at a low system level, while on the other hand it may obscure the fact that the malfunction has occurred and thereby has reduced the system's tolerance to future malfunctions [15].

3) Tolerance Renewal Principles: The primary advantage of hybrid redundancy over TMR is that injured triads are reconfigured back to a state where they can once again mask malfunctions. This is a process of tolerance renewal. In principle, the system failure rate is restored to its design value by the reconfiguration process. If reconfiguration were to fail, the system failure rate would increase, possibly by many orders of magnitude.

In practice, there are several ways in which an injured triad can fail to be reconfigured. These include exhaustion of spare modules, malfunction of the reconfiguration mechanism, failure to detect the need to reconfigure, and perhaps the use of a defective spare module. We can characterize the process of tolerance renewal as the detection and location of any physical malfunction, the removal of vulnerability from the triad containing the malfunction, the replacement, by spares, of functions thus removed, and the initialization of the reconstituted triad. All mechanisms involved in this process are subject to malfunction, of course, and such malfunctions constitute injury to their triads, and require that tolerance renewal be carried out on the appropriate modules.

The tolerance renewal mechanism in the FTMP is largely contained in the voters and the bus guardian units. Both the voters and the guardian units possess bus line interfaces, and therefore are both capable of degrading elements (i.e., bus lines) outside of their own modules (e.g., processor, memory, interface access). This by itself is not qualitatively different from a single malfunction. The important concern is that all guardians in a single module may fail in such a way as to enable that module to transmit on more than one bus line. Design steps are taken to minimize the probability of this eventuality, but the probability is finite that it will happen. A subsequent failure of the module in a malevolent state could cause an entire central computer to malfunction.

4) Fault Detection, Identification, and Recovery: The FTMP is designed to have a highly improbable loss of capability, with a total failure rate of less than 10^{-9} failures per hour in a flight of up to ten hours. This virtually rules out the use of ordinary triple modular redundancy, as the MTBF's achievable in large scale production have been consistently too low for such reliability without replacement of failed modules. Therefore some form of hybrid redundancy is needed. In a simplistic view, hybrid redundancy works by substituting a spare the first time the TMR voters disagree. This view has the shortcoming of not taking latency of faults into account. That is, the first fault may not result in any voter disagreements, whereas when combined with a second fault, it may frustrate recovery. A prerequisite for achieving highly improbable failure in a hybrid system is therefore to expose latent faults by systematic exercising, or "flexing" of all logic elements. The flexing period must be of the order of seconds for a reasonably sized system with module MTBF's in the ten-thousand hour range. Clearly, then, flexing cannot be relegated to preflight checkout, but must rather be conducted routinely in flight. An ordinary hybrid TMR system cannot routinely test itself when performing critical functions, as it is vulnerable during these times. A parallel hybrid TMR system can do this, however, and this becomes an integral part of the computer's architecture.

In the FTMP, an error correction mechanism exists in every module in the form of a voter. Each voter must be tested routinely to ensure that its error correcting capability is undiminished. Bus voters under normal conditions will correct single bus errors and will set error latches to indicate which of the buses was in disagreement. At this time the processor can record the identity of the nominal user of the bus for diagnostic purposes. A processor triad can flex its own voters during a test job step by having each triad member purposely utter independent bus data that causes all possible kinds of bus errors. To pass the test, all triad members must receive the same data, form the same corrected result, and indicate the same disagreement patterns in their error latches. This is a relatively simple test procedure, which can be conducted by a processor triad under test while other triads carry on normal functions. In a sense it qualifies the triad to conduct further testing, in which the triad's voters are the decision elements.

The remainder of the system testing function is carried out under the assumption that the processor voters and error latches are operational. The test process involves the conversion of every fault into an error, by making calculations whose results are sensitive to each logic variable. Each bus and module, including voters, guardians, isolation gates, clock receivers, oscillators, and data and power interfaces must be exercised in depth.

We might summarize the fault detection process as the arrival of disagreement errors at the voters of a processor triad, stimulated by normal or test activity. The detection of a fault initiates the process of fault identification, which is the discovery of the module, bus, or other isolated element in which the failure resides. During the testing process for latent faults, there is relatively little ambiguity in the determination of faulty modules. In normal operation, however, an error on the bus can come from a number of sources. The identification of the faulty module generally requires the "rounding up of suspects," that is, the listing of elements that transmit on the disagreeing bus. If a module fault is permanent, the module can be found by moving it to another bus. If the bus is faulty, reconfiguration will not move the error to another bus.

Intermittent faults are less easy to identify. When the source of an error eludes detection by disappearing, all of the suspect elements are assigned one demerit, and a reconfiguration is then made to distribute the suspects evenly on different buses. Subsequent error occurrences and reconfigurations will cause a preponderance of demerits to accumulate in the name of the faulty module or bus.

The recovery process is one of assignment and initialization for modules, and voter and transmitter selection for buses. These are all accomplished by the bus guardian units upon receipt of commands from active triads executing system software. Recovery can take place even if single errors are present on the buses. In principle, therefore, an injured processor triad can reconfigure itself.

The use of program restart, or rollback, as a recovery mechanism is secondary, because it is neither sufficiently effective nor easy to implement. The first level of system defense is the masking of errors by the TMR method. The additional system failure rate reduction achievable by rollback can not be measured, *a priori*, without an understanding of the applications software. It should be anticipated, however, that any event that defeats the TMR masking is apt to destroy the vehicle's state vector, which may or may not be catastrophic. In any event, some degree of program rerun should be included to support power-up initialization and to deal to some extent with the eventuality of uncovered errors. This will affect both system software and application software.

III. Description of an Engineering Prototype of the FTMP

During the 1978 and 1979 time frame the Charles Stark Draper Laboratory is planning the construction, for NASA, of an engineering prototype of the FTMP. The hardware is to be built by a major avionics manufacturer using specifications provided by CSDL. CSDL will retain program responsibility, provide all system software, and will conduct the integration, test, and evaluation of the system. The project is being sponsored by the NASA Langley Research Center as a part of the Energy Efficient Aircraft Program. The implementation of the prototype is discussed in this Section.

The proposed system is to be constructed of ten identical line replaceable units (LRU's) connected as indicated in Fig. 5. Each LRU contains one processor/cache module, one memory module, one I/O port, one clock generator, and related peripheral support and control circuitry. Fig. 6 shows how an LRU is divided into fault-containment regions. The principal region is detailed in Fig. 7.

Up to three processor triads can be in operation simultaneously, utilizing nine of ten available processor/cache modules. The tenth module serves as a spare. With three triads operating simultaneously, the system is functioning as a three-processor multiprocessor.

Up to three memory triads can be formed from nine of the mass memory modules. The tenth module is a spare. Each memory triad is assigned to service a single 16k work region of the shared mass memory address space. With three memory triads operating simultaneously, 48k words of contiguous shared mass memory address space can be serviced.

The I/O ports use MIL-STD-1553 data formats and signalling protocols. MIL-STD-1553 is a United States Air Force standard for a bit serial, time multiplexed avionics data bus. A single I/O port accepts the bit serial data from a processor triad, votes to mask any errors in that triad, and generates a single version of the I/O transmission. This version is electrically transformed to conform with MIL-STD-1553 specifications, and is transmitted to the outside world

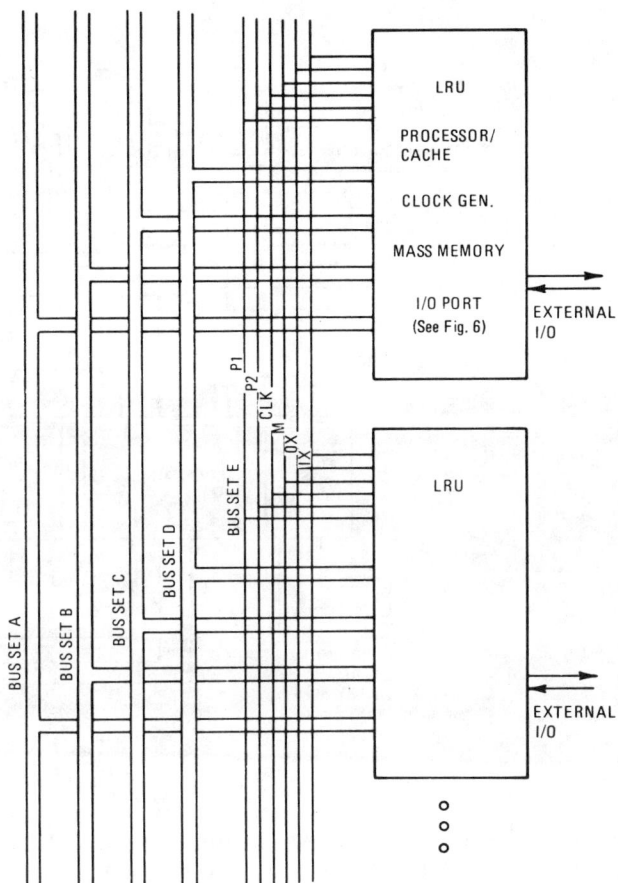

Fig. 5. LRU and Bus interconnections.

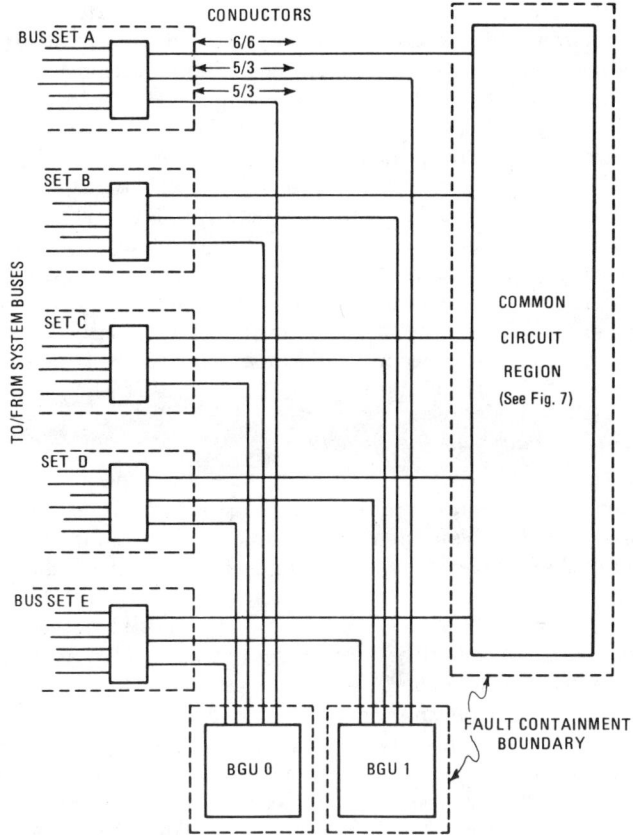

Fig. 6. LRU fault containment boundaries.

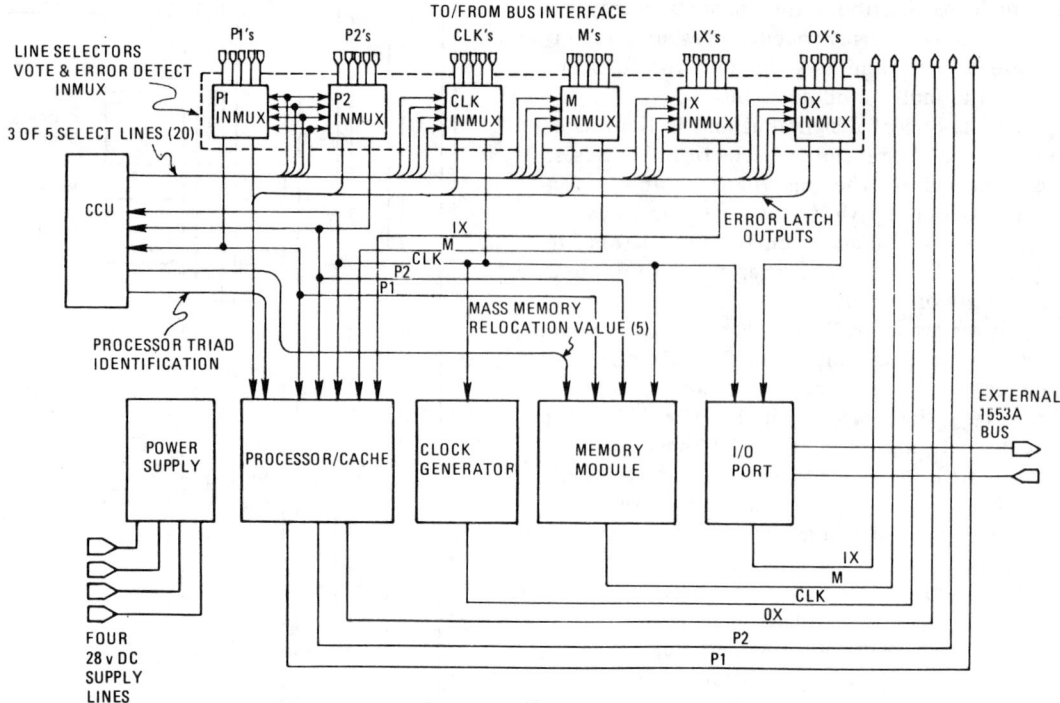

Fig. 7. Common circuitry region.

on one member of a full-duplex transmission pair. Received data from this MIL-STD-1553 transmission pair is accepted by the I/O port, converted to an internal signal level, and distributed to all processors. At least one port and its associated external transmission pair must remain functional for the system to remain operational. Error detection and correction outside the multiprocessor relies upon data encoding and time redundancy in communications to and from remote terminals.

This engineering prototype differs from the basic FTMP design in that it groups a processor, a memory unit, and an I/O port together in a single LRU with common power supply, bus guardians, isolation gates, and other common-failure elements. The reason for doing this arises from the physical form factors involved. Meanwhile, this design preserves the necessary features to allow processors, memory units, and I/O ports to be assigned independently of each other, and for the system to diagnose and recover from simultaneous failures of all three.

A. The Redundant Bus Structure

The bus system shown in Fig. 5 is quintuple-redundant. Each bus has lines dedicated to processor transmission, (the two P bus lines); memory module transmissions, (the M line); clock generator transmission, (the CLK line); and I/O transmissions, (the IX and OX lines). Subsets of three of the five buses are assigned to carry processor and memory triad data. A subset of four of the five is used to carry clock generator transmissions. A single bus of the five is used to carry I/O port transmissions.

The processor uses two bus lines, $P1$ and $P2$, to transmit data and commands to common memory and status register devices. The processor triads also contend for control of the bus system via a cooperative, competitive allocation technique which uses these bus lines.

A triad of memory modules uses the memory bus lines to transmit data requested by a processor triad. Since memory triads only speak on command, there is no mechanism, such as the competitive poll used by the processors, to grant permission to transmit. The processor in control of the P bus implicitly grants transmission permission by issuing a read request.

B. LRU Interfacing to the Bus System

Each LRU of the system must be interfaced to the bus system in a fashion that protects the fault-tolerant architectural features of the logical design. Several design constraints must be met in order to meet this requirement. Fig. 6 illustrates a suitable interface.

Each of the five buses is connected to the LRU through a dedicated bus interface. Each of these bus interfaces represents an independent fault containment region. Design requirements for a fault containment region limit the physical impact of a fault to that region. Signal lines into and out of the region are buffered at the region's edge so that a fault on any of these lines external to the region will not affect the correct operation of the circuitry within the region, excepting possibly these output of input buffers. The principal concept of a fault containment region is the containment of physical damage to one region by the surrounding regions. The logical containment of the effects of a fault are provided by other means. For example, a fault such as a short circuit to power on all lines into and out of a bus interface has two partitionable effects. First, data transmitted through that bus interface is likely to be received incorrectly. This is the logical impact of the fault. The logical failure is not contained by the fault containment region. The second effect is physical. The fault will electrically stress the receiving and transmitting buffers of attached regions. This stress may induce physical faults within these buffers, but the design of these regions is such that these internal faults do not propagate beyond these buffer circuits.

The remaining portion of an attached region's circuitry continues to function correctly, although it may be operating on incorrect data. Since there are no fault propagation paths between regions, a fault within a single bus interface cannot affect the correct operation of another bus interface. A single bus interface failure, therefore, can at most cause the apparent loss of a single bus.

The remaining portions of the LRU are divided into three additional fault-containment regions. Each Bus Guardian Unit is a fault-containment region. The third region, or *principal region*, consists of common voters, processor/cache, mass memory, I/O port, clock generator, and power supply. The bus interface provides separately buffered copies of the *P*1, *P*2 and *CLK* lines to both bus guardians and the principal region. Since a fault within one of these attached regions cannot affect the separately buffered *P*1, *P*2 and *CLK* lines used by the other two regions, they each appear to have independent access to the bus system. In order for a bus interface to allow principal region transmissions onto a system bus line, it must have enabling signals from both bus guardians. Thus either guardian can block access to a particular bus line. Each of the guardians has what is effectively independent access to all incoming bus data. It can independently mask single bus errors via voting, and it processes incoming processor triad transmissions, responding only to write commands to its particular address location. The contents of these write commands alter the static enabling signals from the guardians. Each guardian provides an enable line to each bus interface for the *P* lines, *M* line, *CLK* line, and *OX* line.

The LRU interfacing is designed to protect the integrity of the bus system despite multiple sequential faults. A worst case bus interface failure can at most disable all of the lines of only one of the quintuple bus sets. The system can then be reconfigured to use the remaining lines of other buses. One element of a triad or the clock quad, if it fails, can impact at most one of the active bus sets. Again, reconfiguration commands can isolate that faulty unit from the bus and assign a spare to replace it, thereby restoring system health. To cause a system failure, four of the five bus sets must fail, or two bus guardians within the same LRU must fail, enabling the principal region to access all bus lines, and in addition, the principal region must fail.

C. System Control Units

The bus guardian unit is a particular case of a generalized unit called a *system control unit*. Each LRU has four system control units. They are designated bus guardian unit 0 (BGU 0); bus guardian unit 1 (BGU 1); configuration control unit, (CCU); and the interprocessor triad communication unit, (IPC unit). The CCU and IPC units are part of the principal fault containment region. As previously stated, BGU 0 and BGU 1 are each a fault containment region.

All of these system control unit types are similar and can be constructed from the same circuit. Fig. 8 illustrates the functional requirements for such a common circuit. Essentially the circuit must take the serial processor command data, *P*1, *P*2, and *CLK*, pass it through error-correlation circuitry, if this data is in redundant form, and convert it to a parallel form. A system control unit only responds to a memory write command to its own particular memory address.

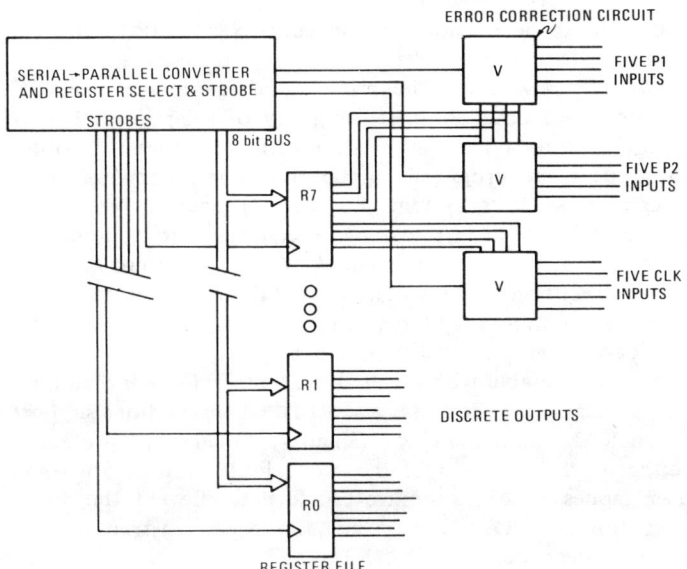

Fig. 8. System control unit.

Register contents may be supplied as static enabling or data signals to circuitry external to the system control unit, or they may be used internally to control the error correction circuitry (if present).

A power monitoring circuit switches the register store to battery power when primary power to the unit is not within specification. When battery powered, the register contents are protected, and the enabling lines from the guardians are in the disable state. Total loss of all power to a guardian clears the register contents to the disable state.

D. The Principal Fault-Containment Region

All of the circuitry of an LRU is within the bounds of the principal fault-containment region excepting the two bus guardians and the bus interfaces.

The principal region can be viewed as being made up of seven subregions. These are: 1) input processing; 2) configuration control; 3) processor/cache; 4) memory, 5) I/O ports; 6) clock generator; and 7) power supply, as shown in Fig. 7.

1) Input Processing: All input to the principal region is from the bus interfaces, and is first processed by shared signal selectors, voters, and error detection circuits. The input circuitry generates a single version of the *P*1, *P*2, *CLK*, *M*, *IX*, and *OX* lines to be used by all modules within the region. This single version of each line is the appropriate majority function of the selected group of 3 out of 5 lines. Additionally, the voting circuitry detects and latches any error condition on the bus lines, and provides this information as input discretes to the processor. The selection of one of the ten possible groups of 3 out of 5 buses to be used by the majority circuitry or the selection of which IX line to be used, is made by selector discretes provided by the Configuration Control Unit.

2) Configuration Control Unit (CCU): The Configuration Control Unit (CCU) is a system control unit. The CCU is used to control the INMUX circuitry, is used to assign the processor/cache unit to a processor triad and to start and stop the processor, and is used to assign the mass memory module to a memory triad.

3) Processor/Cache Module: The processor/cache memory module is the most complex of the principal region. It can be partitioned into a number of submodules. These are: a) processor, b) cache memory, c) bus controller, d) IPC unit, and e) MIL-STD-1553 controller.

a) The processor: The principal design requirements of the processor could be met using any of a large number of general purpose 16-bit minicomputer architectures. In order to support the projected computational requirements of an integrated avionics system, the basic processor has a raw instruction execution rate roughly equivalent to 500 000 16-bit fixed-point adds per second. A 16 bit fixed-point multiply has an execution time six times that of the fixed point add.

The instruction set of the processor is suitable for avionics applications and, in addition, provides for the following: 1) code is relocatable without modification; 2) Code is read-only and reentrant; 3) the CALL and RETURN instructions support dynamic program loading efficiently; 4) memory protect is supported for a region of the cache RAM; and 5) privileged user modes of operation are provided to prevent the direct execution of I/O and mass memory access instructions by applications code.

The processor is adapted to use the output of the *CLK* generator as its time base and incorporates a microcode interlock with the bus controller which allows three processors to be synchronized by using particular bus events, such as bus grant.

b) Cache memory: The cache memory is a 4k × 16 semiconductor RAM and 4k × 16 semiconductor PROM array. It interfaces to the processor over the processor's internal parallel bus. Access time for this memory is 400 ns. There is no requirement for nonvolatility in the RAM portion of this memory.

c) Bus controller: The bus controller is responsible for the bit-by-bit control of the processor side of bus activity. On command of the processor, the bus controller conducts a competitive polling sequence to acquire control of the main memory bus. The controller then holds the bus until instructed to release it. It makes use of the triad identification provided by the CCU and a priority field provided by the processor during the polling sequence. While holding the bus, it performs memory reads and writes as requested by the processor. Data and memory address transfers between the processor and controller are handled in parallel. The controller performs the necessary timing, serial to parallel and parallel to serial conversions for the processor. The processor handles block transfers performing the necessary housekeeping, streaming parallel memory addresses, and accepting whole word data streams from the controller and storing them in cache memory, or streaming parallel addresses and data to the controller for storage in the common memory.

d) Interprocessor triad communication unit: The Interprocessor Triad Communication Unit (IPC) is used by the executive for direct processor-triad to processor-triad communications. The IPC registers are available as discretes to the processor.

e) MIL-STD-1553 controller: A MIL-STD-1553 controller interfaces to the processor over the processor's internal parallel bus. It conforms to the standard format, except that the outgoing and incoming data paths have been split so as to provide full-duplex transmission paths.

4) Memory Module: The memory module contains a 16K × 16 CMOS memory array with the appropriate control circuitry to respond to processor triad memory read and write commands.

Input to the memory control circuitry is the bit-serial quantity represented by the outputs of the *P*-INMUX outputs and *CLK*-INMUX. The most significant bits of the incoming address are compared to the relocation register provided by the CCU. If they match, a read or write operation is performed. If they do not match, the incoming command is ignored. Read responses are made using the *M* bus. Responses are clocked using the output of the *CLK*-INMUX.

5) I/O Port: The I/O port is principally a signal level shifter and data synchronizer. A single corrected version of I/O output data, *OX*, is accepted by the I/O port from the common input module, and is buffered to conform to MIL-STD-1553 specifications. The transmitting processor triad is responsible for formatting the *OX* lines signal to conform to the MIL-STD-1553 format.

The I/O port receives I/O input data, synchronizes it so that transitions do not occur near system clock edges, converts the signal levels to an internal standard, and transmits the signal on an *IX* line to all processors.

6) Clock Generator: As discussed in Section II-C, the entire fault-tolerant multiprocessor rests on an assumption of synchronized operation based on a common timing reference. Each LRU includes a clock generator which can be synchronized to the common reference, and which, if gated by the BGU's onto a *CLK* bus, could serve as a contributing element to the common reference in the manner shown in Fig. 4. The clock generation circuit of an LRU interacts with the *CLK* bus lines, the *CLK*-INMUX, and the other clock generators. To understand the function of the clocking system, it is necessary to discuss all of these components as they interrelate with one another.

The clock bus is a component part of the quintuple redundant busing system. Each of the five bus sets includes one clock bus line, *CLK*. Normally, four of the five *CLK* lines are active and one is inactive. Four clock generators are chosen as the clock sources, each being assigned to a different clock bus. Each transmits a clock signal which is phase-locked to the other three active clock generators. Thus the system has available at all points a quad-redundant time base. Each clock receiver listens to three of the four active clock buses and generates a derived clock which remains correct even if one of the three input signals fails. It is therefore possible to tolerate a single failure of one of the elements of the clock quad without affecting the correctness of the derived clocks generated throughout the system.

Each bus guardian and each *CLK*-INMUX uses a clock receiver to generate its own corrected version of the system clock, despite single faults in the clock quad.

Each clock generator, whether active or in standby mode, phase locks its output to its *CLK*-INMUX output. Thus the clock generator outputs a clock which is in phase with the majority of three *CLK* buses. When active, the output of the clock generator is gated onto one of the four CLK buses, and its associated *CLK*-INMUX is adjusted to listen to the other three *CLK* buses. In this configuration the correctly functioning clock generators will produce multiple phase-locked clocks which will remain phase-locked despite any failure of a single clock element of the quad.

When a failure is detected, the system reconfigures, replacing the failed *CLK* bus or clock generator. Standby clock generators are already phase-locked to the corrected system clock, so that they can be switched in to replace a failed clock generator with minimal transients in clock frequency and with negligible risks. This restores the fault-tolerant character of the clocking system, positioning it to tolerate the next clocking component failure.

7) Power Supply: The power supply provides regulated power to the LRU. The power supply can draw power from any of the four primary 28-V dc power buses. A circuit breaker or fuse protects each of these buses from a short circuit within the LRU. The power supply must have adequate energy storage so that its output remains within regulation for the time it takes these protective devices to act and the bus voltages to return to normal after a short circuit within another LRU. The output of the power supply is overvoltage protected, possibly with serial redundant protection.

The bus interface devices will be designed to operate safely for all power supply voltages beneath the overvoltage protection limit; that is, the bus interface will present a high impedance load on the bus for all voltage levels if the corresponding enables from the BGU's are unasserted.

The BGU's will monitor power supply voltages. If out-of-regulation voltages are detected, the contents of the BGU registers will be frozen, and all enabling outputs will revert to the unasserted state.

A battery backup is used to provide power to the CMOS memory array, and to the BGU and CCU register files, when primary power is lost. If this battery power fails when primary power is down, the register files of the BGU's and CCU will be cleared.

E. Primary Power

Power is distributed to all LRU's of the system by means of four 28-V dc power buses. Four 400-Hz 110-V dc to 28-V dc power converters provide power to these buses. These power supplies are overvoltage and overcurrent protected. If an overcurrent condition arises, the 28-V dc output will current-limit but return to normal when the protective devices within the shorting LRU open. Energy storage with the power supply must be adequate to tolerate momentary power interruptions such as are typically caused by power switching in aircraft power distribution systems.

IV. Survival and Dispatch Probability Models for the FTMP

The FTMP has several different failure modes, each of which is amenable to a different mathematical tool. Specifically, the probability of failure due to exhaustion of spares can be adequately modeled using combinatorial methods, whereas Markov processes are better suited to modeling coverage-related problems. Fortunately, each of these failure modes predominates in a different time segment, and therefore can be modeled and analyzed independently.

A. Survival Probability Models

The computation of survival probability of the FTMP for random hard failures is divided into the following three phases:

1) probability of failure due to the lack of perfect coverage using a Markov process model;
2) probability of failure due to exhaustion of spares using a combinatorial model;
3) probability of failure due to BGU failures in enable mode using a combinatorial model.

In the FTMP some time is required to detect, isolate, and recover from any failure. During this time a second failure may arrive in such a place as to be catastrophic. Therefore, the coverage [16] is imperfect. This phenomenon is most conveniently modeled using Markov processes, as each distinct failure or recovery moves the system into a state that is dependent only on the present state of the system. However, to limit the number of states to a reasonable level, it is necessary to make some approximations. The most effective of these approximations is to assume that recovery from a failure returns the system to a perfect state, which is the initial state of the system, rather than to a computationally degraded state. In effect, this implies an unlimited supply of spare units of each kind. The probability of failure due solely to exhaustion of equipment can be computed independently using combinatorial methods. The basic premise which allows one to decouple and model these two modes of failures separately is the predominance of each mode during a different time span. As will be shown in the following sections, in the short run (0-50 hr) it is the threat of near simultaneous failures which most affects system survivability, whereas in the long run (>100 hr) the system is likely to fail due to a lack of equipment. In addition to these, there is a third failure mode peculiar to the FTMP architecture that has to be accounted for. This relates to two bus guardian units in an LRU failing so as to enable a failed unit (processor, memory, etc.) to transmit simultaneously on a number of buses. It will be shown that this mode does not affect the reliability since its probability is insignificant at all times.

The following three subsections describe the models and the results.

1) Lack of Coverage: Markov Model: Since all the information as well as all the computations in the FTMP computer are triply redundant, any single failure in the system is completely masked by the majority voters. Therefore, if the system starts out in a totally fault-free state, it takes at least two successive failures without recovery to produce a catastrophic system failure. However, not all double failures are catastrophic. In fact, most double failures can be tolerated by the FTMP without any problem. The following is a list of all the catastrophic double failure combinations:

1) two processors in a triad fail;
2) two memory modules in a triad fail;
3) two active buses fail;
4) one active bus fails and a processor or memory enabled on another active bus fails;
5) two active oscillators fail;
6) one active bus fails and an oscillator enabled on another bus fails;
7) one LRU fails in common mode and an associated processor, memory, or bus fails;
8) two associated LRU's fail in common mode.

The common mode LRU failure refers to a failure of any of the LRU components that are shared by the processor, memory, and I/O port in that LRU. These include the local power supply, the oscillator, the two BGU's, and the selectors and voters. A local power supply failure in an LRU, for example, will result in the simultaneous loss of the processor, memory, and I/O port in that LRU. The BGU failures include only the disable mode, since the enable mode is taken care of separately. Finally, the bus failure includes a failure of any of

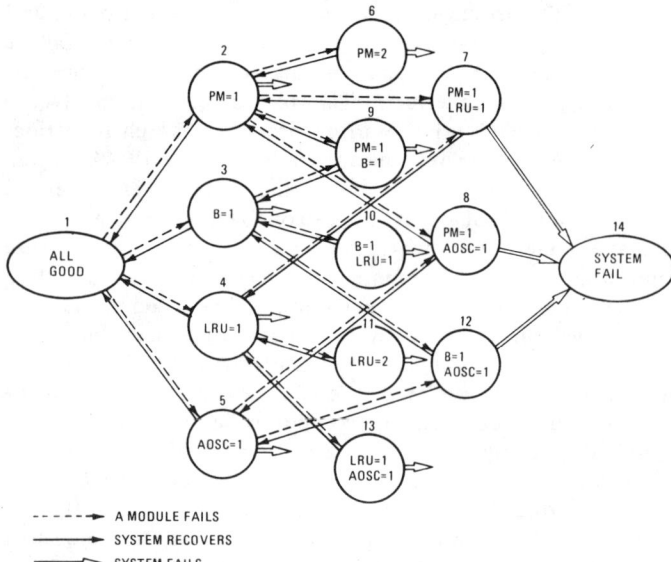

Fig. 9. Reliability model for lack of coverage.

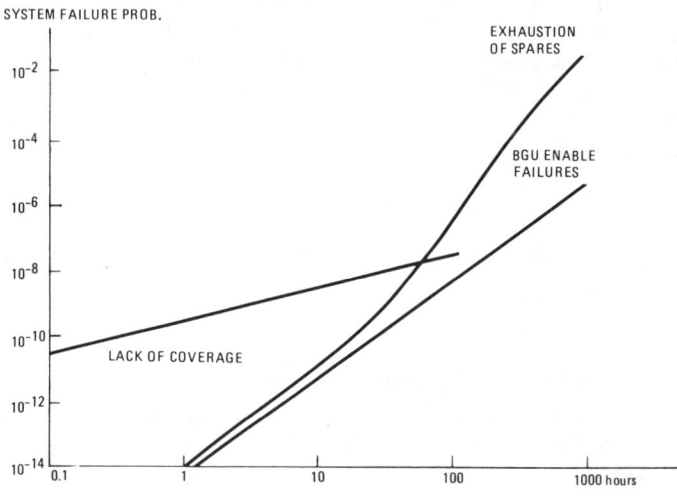

Fig. 10. System failure probability.

TABLE I
Baseline Parameter Values

SYSTEM CONF.		CMC	FAILURE RATE (PER HOUR)	MTBF (HRS)	RECOVERY TIME (SEC)
# PROCESSORS	10	5	2×10^{-4}	5,000	0.25
# MEMORY UNITS	10	2	2×10^{-4}	5,000	0.25
# IO UNITS	10	1	5×10^{-5}	20,000	
# BUSES	5	3	10^{-5}	100,000	0.25
# MAIN POWER SUPPLY UNITS	4	1	10^{-4}	10,000	
# BGUs	20		EN = 10^{-6} DIS = 10^{-5}	1,000 100,000	
# LRUs	10		CMF = 1.46×10^{-4}	7,000	0.25
# OSCILLATORS	10	3	10^{-5}	100,000	1.0

the five lines constituting a bus or a failure of any of the ten bus interface gates connected to that bus.

A Markov model of the FTMP computer reliability based on the above discussion is shown in Fig. 9. The system is initially in a completely fault-free state or "ALL GOOD" state. It will be shown shortly that at time $t = 0$, such as a take-off time, the probability of having a latent failure in the system should be about 10^{-6} to achieve a system failure rate of 10^{-9} failures per hour. That is, one must be certain with a probability of about 0.999999 that the system is initially fault-free. In the following discussion, it is assumed that the system is initially fault-free. Some of the other assumptions used in developing the model are outlined below.

As explained earlier, it is assumed that reconfiguration around a failed unit returns the system to the perfect state. It is also assumed that all the failed buses are active and that all triple undetected faults cause system failure. These simplifying assumptions reduce the number of states in the model considerably without significantly altering the system failure probability. For example, contribution of triple faults to the system failure probability is found to be less than two per cent.

A baseline set of failure and recovery rates, as shown in Table I, was used to obtain a numerical solution of the Markov model. The values shown in Table I are the mean values. The model uses random values that are exponentially distributed around these means. One may argue about the fidelity of exponential distributions, although it is our contention that they represent the actual reconfiguration time distributions sufficiently well for this purpose [17].

The results of the Markov model are shown in Fig. 10 by the curve labelled "lack of coverage." It shows the system failure probability as a function of time on a log-log scale for the baseline hazard and recovery rates. The failure probability is seen to be a linear function of time (linear and unity slope on the log-log graph) which can be explained as follows. After an initial transient, which may take several hundred seconds to settle down, the state probabilities for all states except the system fail state become nearly constant. During this equilibrium there is a constant leakage of probability into the trapping state since all the transition rates are time invariant.

Since the total leakage rate is only about 10^{-9} per hour, the state probabilities diminish extremely slowly, and a state of equilibrium would hold for hundreds of hours. For the baseline case, the system failure rate due to lack of coverage is found to be about 3×10^{-10} per hour.

The reason for having an initial latent-failure probability of 10^{-6} now becomes clear. This is the probability of the system being in states 2 through 5, that is, the single-undetected-failure states (see Fig. 9). The transition rate from those four states into the system fail state or the probability of arrival of a second catastrophic failure is of the order of magnitude of 10^{-3} per hour. To prove that the system is initially fault-free with absolute certainty is not possible. The triple redundancy prevalent in the system immediately points to any obvious disagreements and component failures, and a systematic exercise of all parts of the system using diagnostic routines can uncover most undetected faults. But this still leaves some types of faults, such as pattern sensitive memory locations, which can not be uncovered without exhaustive testing. The probability of such latent failures, has to be reduced to an insignificant level.

2) Exhaustion of Spares Combinatorial Model: In order to compute the probability of not having sufficient equipment, it is necessary to define the minimum equipment necessary to operate successfully. This is mission dependent as well as architecture dependent. The minimum equipment required to fly an aircraft shall be denoted as the Critical Minimum

Complement (CMC). The architecture-dependent parameters of the CMC include the power supply units and buses. One main power supply unit is deemed sufficient to run the whole computer. Similarly, two buses are adequate at the minimum to support communication between processors and memories, as well as the distribution of the clock. However, for one pathological clock failure mode it would be necessary to have three buses. The minimum number of processors and memories required is mission dependent. The throughput of the FTMP computer in a fully operational state is estimated to be 500 000 operations per second and the minimum throughput necessary to support all flight-critical functions is estimated to be about 200 000 operations per second. Similarly, the total storage capacity of the computer is 48 000 words while the critical programs are estimated to be less than 16 000 words. Thus two processor triads and one memory triad have to be operational to support the critical functions. There are a number of ways of achieving this, one of which uses 5 processors and 2 memories. It is, of course, possible to lose another processor in the fully populated triad and still be operational, although the probability of such an event is only 3/5. The number of I/O ports necessary to interface with the I/O network is one. Table I lists the critical minimum complement based on the above discussion. This table lists the minimum number of oscillators as 3, which is what is needed to generate a clock. However, this is dominated by a larger requirement of 5 or more oscillators necessary to operate 5 processors, 2 memories, and an I/O port, all of which may be in different LRU's.

Fig. 10 shows the overall failure probability due to lack of equipment for a period of up to 1000 hr. In the short run, the number of buses is critical, while in the long run it is the number of LRU's. The number of power supplies is adequate at all times.

3) Bus Guardian Unit Failures—Combinatorial Model: This section discusses the system failure probability due to BGU failures in the enable mode. Although this mode can be made about an order of magnitude less likely than the normal disable failure mode, it is nonetheless present and must be accounted for. As explained earlier, one single BGU may disable a unit from transmitting on a bus, while both BGU's in an LRU must agree before a unit is enabled on a bus. Under the normal circumstances, an active unit (processor, memory, etc.) will be enabled on a single bus. With two BGU's failed in the enable mode, a unit would be enabled on more than one bus. This by itself presents little, if any, problem since three members of a triad transmit in tight synchronism on three buses. However, if the unit enabled on multiple buses fails and does not transmit in synchronism, a number of buses immediately become useless, and this may result in a catastrophic system failure. Thus it takes at least three related failures in a single LRU for the system to fail. The BGU enable mode failures are nonrecoverable. That is, the system can not be reconfigured around a failed BGU. The results for the baseline parameter values are shown in Fig. 10. It is seen that the system failure probability due to this peculiarity of the architecture is at all times insignificant.

4) Unified Survival Probability Results: The following conclusions can be drawn from Figure 10.

1) During a typical commercial flight of one to ten hours the most likely threat of the FTMP computer failure is due to an arrival of two failures so close that system reconfiguration is not possible. The probability of this event, however, is acceptably low (about 3×10^{-10} per hour) because of high component MTBF's and fast reconfiguration times.

2) There is very little chance that the FTMP computer will run out of spares during a ten-hour flight, assuming that the system initially has all ten LRU's fully operational. In longer flights, however, failure would be quite possible as evidenced by the sharply rising failure probability curve after 50 hours. Lack of equipment is a critical item as far as the dispatch reliability of the computer is concerned, and is discussed in detail in Section IV-C.

3) Finally, the system failure rate due to BGU enable mode failures is substantially lower than other system failure modes. Therefore it does not contribute significantly to the overall system failure probability.

The overall system failure probability due to all causes, up to about 50 hours, is dominated by the probability of failure due to near simultaneous failures. During this time the probability of exhaustion of spares is several orders of magnitude lower. Beyond 100 hours the opposite is true. Strictly speaking, the overall failure probability is a complex function of all the contributing failure probabilities. However, under certain circumstances, it can be approximated very closely by just the predominant failure probability.

B. Impact of Intermittent Faults

An intermittent fault in a digital computing system may be defined as a fault that persists only part of the time. Physically, this may correspond to a loose connection between components, a loose bond within a semiconductor device, a temperature sensitive device, etc. Since an intermittent fault manifests itself only a fraction of the time, it injects an additional level of latency to the problem of fault detection. This would lead to longer fault detection and isolation times, thereby reducing the system reliability. The actual extent to which the system reliability would be degraded due to intermittent faults would depend on the degree of latency of the fault. That is, the higher the percentage of time a fault stays in the good state, the higher the chance of it being undetected. With the presence of such a lurking fault in a triad, for example, a second fault in another member of the triad leads to a situation where two out of three members of the triad are at one time or another malfunctioning. If this situation is not redressed promptly by reconfiguration of faulty elements it can result in a catastrophic system failure. On the other hand, the presence of two intermittent faults in two members of a triad can be tolerated as long as one or both of them stay in the lurking mode. This apparently should result in an increased level of fault-tolerance. The following study was undertaken to analyze these contradictory impacts of intermittent faults on the FTMP reliability.

To incorporate intermittent faults in the FTMP survivability models, it is necessary first to define various states and their transition rates corresponding to intermittent faults. In the simplest form, an element with an intermittent fault may be represented by two states: a failed state and a pseudofailed state [18]. In the first state the fault is actually present, that is, use of the element will produce an incorrect output. In the second state, the fault is in a benign mode, and use of the element will not corrupt the output. An intermittent fault will oscillate between these two states with a frequency that is dependent upon the characteristics of the fault. In general, the transition rate from the failed to the pseudofailed state may not be the same as the rate in the other direction (see

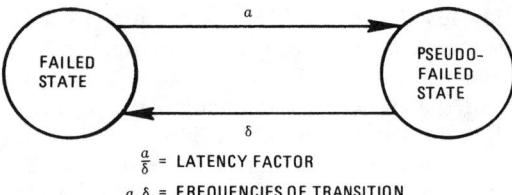

Fig. 11. Intermittent failure model.

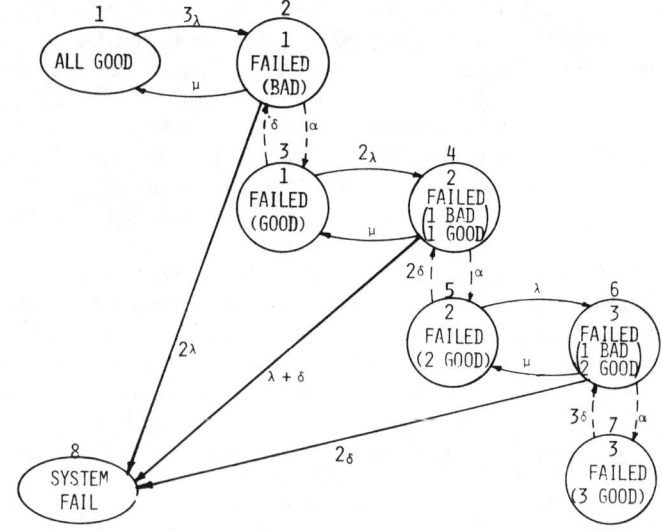

Fig. 12. Intermittent failure model of a TMR-hybrid system.

Fig. 11). The ratio of transition rates, α/δ, is a measure of the additional latency due to the intermittent nature of the fault. The higher the ratio α/δ, the higher is the percent of time a fault stays in the pseudofailed state and is invisible a longer time. For $\alpha/\delta = 0$, the intermittent fault really becomes a hard fault since all the time is spent in the failed state.

Certain assumptions have been made regarding the use of this basic model to keep the overall models and the number of parameters tractable. For example, α and δ are assumed to be constant with respect to time. In addition, all faults are assumed to be intermittent with the same transition frequencies and duty cycles. In practice there will be faults with various frequencies which will most likely vary with time as the intermittent faults transition into hard faults. However, the present purpose is to get an insight into how an intermittent fault affects the system survivability. This is best done by simulating a situation where all the failures are intermittent and stay intermittent during the course of investigation.

A Markov process coverage model of a triple modular redundant (TMR) system incorporating the intermittent failure model was developed, as shown in Fig. 12. The reasons for modeling a TMR before going to a full-fledged multiprocessor model are twofold. It involves fewer parameters, making it easier to establish a cause and effect relationship between reliability and various parameters. It also involves fewer states and can be analyzed for a wider range of parameter values. Since the FTMP multiprocessor under investigation is a combination of a number of triads, the TMR results can generally lead to a good understanding of the FTMP reliability behavior.

Fig. 12 shows three different ways in which a catastrophic system failure can result. The first is the occurrence of two simultaneous failures, that is, the failure of a second element before the first failure has been diagnosed and recovered from (transition 2-8). This is the only mode of failure in a TMR system if all the failures were hard failures. However, due to the intermittent nature of our assumed failures, the system can survive even in the presence of two failures as long as at least one of the faulty elements is in the pseudofailed state (states 4, 5, 6, 7). In such a case, the arrival of another failure in the third element (transition 4-8), or the transition of an element from a pseudofailed to a failed state (transition 6-8), leads to a catastrophic system failure. The model was solved numerically for a number of different values of α, δ, λ, and μ. Some of the important results are shown graphically in Fig. 13. It is found that the failure probability is not a monotonic function of α or δ. However, if the ratio α/δ is held constant, the failure probability increases with δ as shown in Fig. 13. Similarly, for a constant δ, the failure probability generally increases with α/δ. In the steady state, the ratio of state probabilities P_3 to P_2 is given by α/δ. That is

$$P_3/P_2 = \alpha/\delta.$$

This is assuming there is no leakage from state 2 to the system fail state 8. Physically, the ratio α/δ represents the relative time a fault stays in the lurking mode. That is, the higher the variable α/δ, the higher is the latency factor of the intermittent fault. For a fixed ratio α/δ, increasing δ implies a higher leakage rate from state 4, resulting in a higher failure probability. In other words, since the ratio α/δ is fixed, the duty cycle between failed and pseudofailed states is a constant, and, therefore, increasing the frequency of transition between these two states only increases the chance of a lurking fault suddenly crashing the system. It is evident from these results that the worst situation arises where the latency of intermittent faults is high (a high α/δ) and the frequency of transition from pseudofailed to failed state is high (a high δ).

The worst case system failure probability with intermittent faults, for the range of parameters investigated, is about fifty times higher than that due to hard failures (see Fig. 13). The critical frequencies, that is, the worst case α and δ, depend upon the recovery time. The faster the recovery time, the higher these frequencies are. For example, for a recovery time of 36 s, the critical δ is 10^4 per hour or about 3 Hz, while for a recovery time of a one-quarter second, it is about 30 Hz. Increasing the transition frequencies beyond the critical levels does not further deteriorate the reliability appreciably.

To extend these results to the FTMP computer, a 49-state Markov model was developed. This is basically an expanded version of the 14-state hard failure model described in Section 4.1. All the assumptions of that model carry forward here. This model was solved for the base-line parameter values shown in Table I. The FTMP reliability behavior with respect to α and δ was found to be in close agreement with that of the TMR-hybrid system qualitatively as well as quantitatively. As shown in Fig. 13, the FTMP curve is remarkably close to the TMR curve with typical FTMP failure and recovery rates.

Finally, it should be noted that some of the high-frequency intermittent faults, which could do the most damage, may actually look like hard faults. A fault in a processor module, for example, may cause that module to go out of synchronism with the other two triad members, thereby making its presence felt after it disappears. Therefore, the overall impact of the intermittent faults may not be as severe as suggested here.

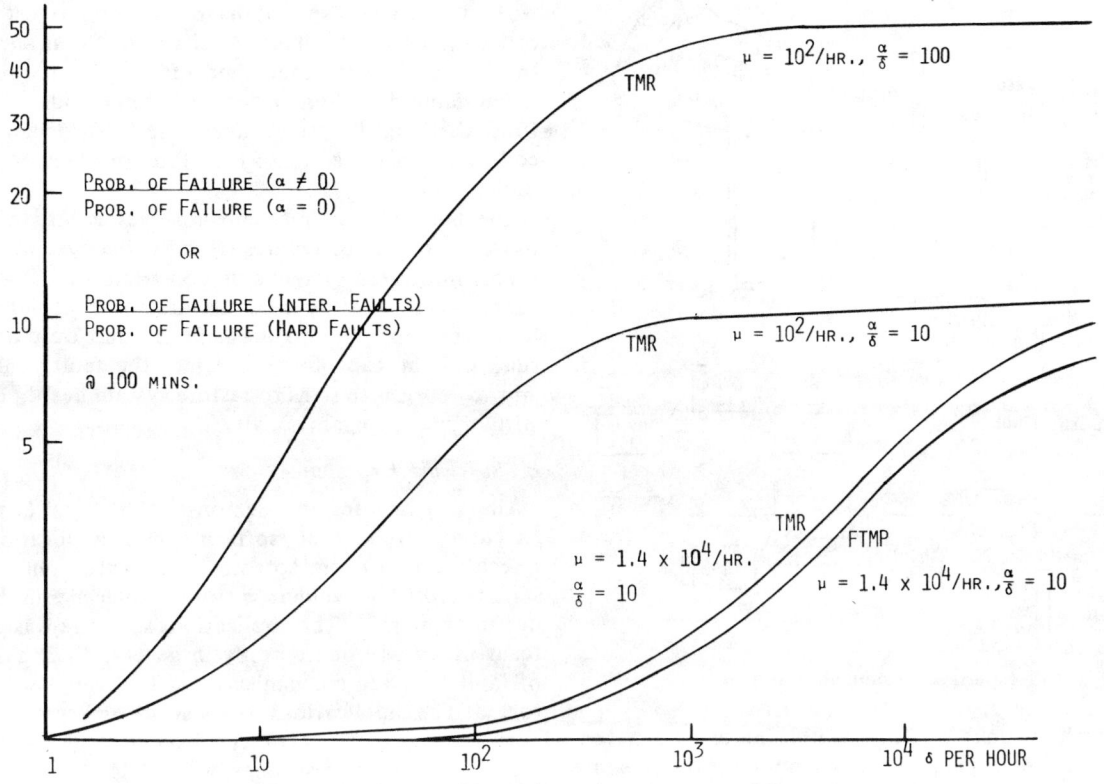

Fig. 13. Influence of intermittency on the system failure rate.

C. Dispatch Reliability of the FTMP Computer

Availability of equipment, in general, is an important concern in the commercial air transport industry. Availability of avionics equipment, in particular, is economically more important since it tends to be at the heart of "Go/NoGo" decisions. A central computer with digital "fly-by-wire" authority certainly falls into this category. It is imperative, therefore, that the dispatch reliability of the FTMP computer be commensurate with its high survival probability. A preliminary estimate of the dispatch reliability is carried out in this section.

Let the "dispatch minimum complement" (DMC) denote the amount of equipment (processors, memories, etc.) necessary to be operational before take-off for the computer to survive through the flight with a given probability. Using a trial-and-error approach with the combinatorial models of Section IV-A(2), the DMC for the baseline case was found to be as follows:

Dispatch Minimum Complement:
   Processors   = 8
   Memories   = 6
   Buses   = 4
   Power Supplies = 3

The question to be answered at this point is, how long would it take an initially fully operational FTMP to degrade below the DMC and thereby fail the dispatch criteria? The probability of this event at time t, assuming no maintenance, is shown as a function of time in Fig. 14. It is seen from this figure that there is a seven per cent chance that the computer will be below the dispatch minimums if the maintenance is scheduled every 300 hours. The probability of requiring unscheduled maintenance can be reduced to just over two per cent by carrying an extra LRU or by shortening the mainte-

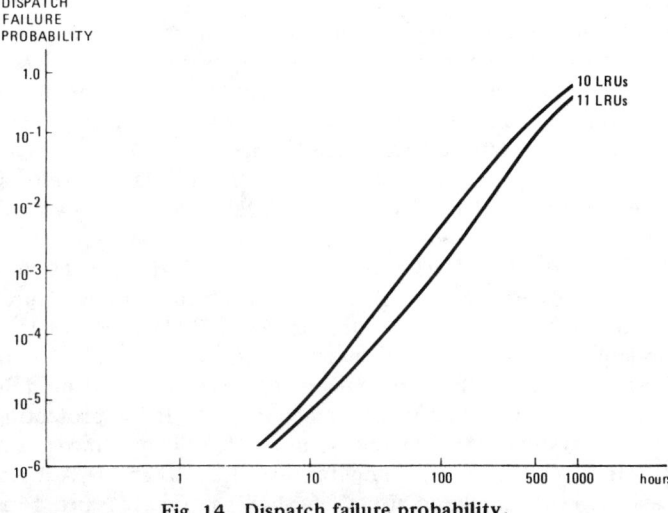

Fig. 14. Dispatch failure probability.

nance interval to 200 hours. This would seem to satisfy the needs of most airlines as far as the computer dispatch reliability is concerned. Beyond this, however, the dispatch reliability is bounded by the reliability of main power supply units. That is, the dispatch reliability can be improved only by modifying the architecture to include five or more main power supply units.

V. Experimental Results

In order to demonstrate and validate as many of the design concepts as possible, a breadboard multiprocessor was used to emulate many of the design features of the proposed system. This demonstration was of an integrated nature in that the experimental setup duplicated much of the information en-

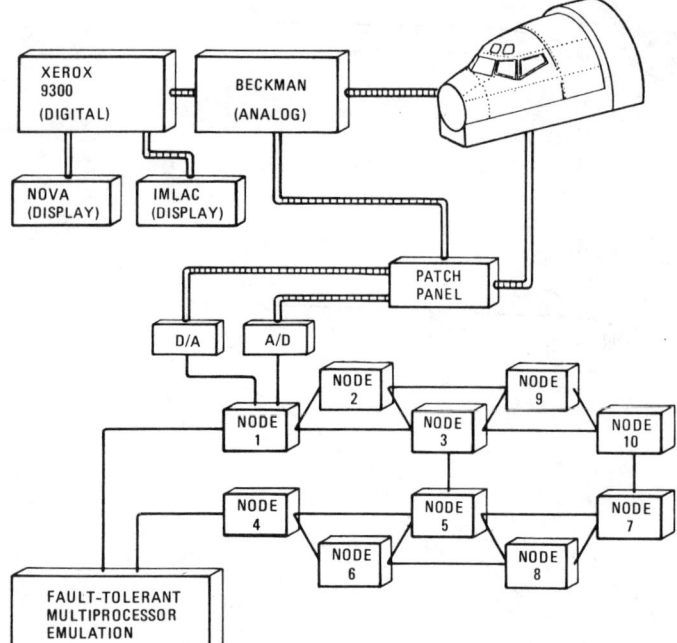

Fig. 15. Experimental simulation system.

vironment which a final product of this nature might encounter, and was therefore able to verify not only the separate design pieces forming the whole, but was also able to confirm predicted interactions between disjoint pieces, and in some cases unearth unexpected interactions.

The basic experimental apparatus consisted of a fault-tolerant multiprocessor, modeled along the lines of the FTMP. The multiprocessor served as the control computer for a Boeing 707 aircraft simulation on a hybrid computer. The experimental fault-tolerant multiprocessor consists of 14 National Semiconductor IMP-16-based processor modules, seven common memory modules of $2k \times 16$ words, two I/O ports, and ten I/O nodes. The processor modules include 1k RAM/1k ROM cache memory storage. With the 14 processor modules it is possible to operate up to 4 triads of processors simultaneously. With the seven RAM modules it is possible to operate two memory triads. The redundant data busing system is triply redundant, and each attached module has two Bus Guardian Units associated with it for protecting the bus system. An I/O node remote from the multiprocessor and local to the hybrid computer provides A/D and D/A interfacing to the simulated aircraft as shown in Fig. 15. Fig. 16 is a photograph of the multiprocessor emulation hardware.

A. Fault Diagnostic Capabilities

Each processor module of the experimental system includes special circuitry for noting and recording disagreements among the three copies of each bus line. All other modules or receiving elements have only error masking circuits. The error detection circuitry functions as expected. Most faults manifest themselves as bus errors, and are therefore easily detected. Certain classes of latent faults are detected by diagnostic programs which basically force bus errors if a latent fault exists. Records kept by diagnostic programs and fault isolation procedures enable the location of both transient and hard failures.

Most faults are detectable as one of a large class of faults. For example, all processor failures are detected at the bus without the aid of special diagnostic code to test the processor or knowledge of the fault mechanism. Some special attention to specific failure modes and effects was required to devise latent fault detection programs. While code was not written for unearthing all possible latent faults, sufficient latent testing code was written so as to establish considerable confidence in the method.

The bus isolation mechanism serves as intended and is able to isolate processor failures from the bus system.

This integrated system's demonstration illustrates all significant aspects of the FTMP architecture. It demonstrates the hardware capability to mask faulty unit outputs in the short run, and the capability to detect the fault, isolate the unit, and to reorganize so as to restore system health, all concurrent with normal program activity.

B. Software Experience

The software for the demonstration consists principally of executive or system software and applications software. Executive or system software was written and debugged by staff thoroughly familiar with the experimental hardware and design objectives. The applications software was provided by a team which was briefed only in general terms as to the nature of fault recovery mechanisms and the overall system architecture. The applications software team was provided with detailed explanations of the executive-to-applications interfaces and executive services, as well as a reasonably short list of programming constraints.

1) Multiprocessor Executive: The multiprocessor executive provides a simple task dispatch mechanism. Tasks awaiting their time of execution are organized in a queue sorted by scheduled start time. As processor triads become free (having finished a previous task) they consult this list and take the next scheduled job. Jobs may be inserted into any relative position of the time queue as long as it remains properly sorted. Executive functions provide for the routine iterative scheduling of the same job step, as might be required for an autopilot iteration, for example. Alternatively, any job, by a call to the executive, can insert a job into the time queue. The executive also handles the removal of a job from the queue when it is taken up for execution.

In addition to the time queue, the executive handles an event queue. Jobs in the event queue have their execution blocked waiting for a particular event to occur. When the event does occur, the affected job is moved from the event queue to the top of the time queue. Jobs can be inserted into the event queue by any job, through a call to the executive. Events can be signaled by the executive or by another job through a call to the executive.

The executive also provides interfaces for all I/O traffic, common memory to/from cache data transfers, real time clock, and for other relatively simple functions commonly thought of as executive-related.

Critical to the success of the demonstration are the executive functions which provide for automatic error logging and recovery. Executive functions perform all common memory to/from cache transfers, and all I/O. During these functions any errors that might occur will become visible. The executive handles the proper logging of the error, schedules recovery action, and, via voting, masks the error for the applications task which was using the executive function. Thus, to the applications task, error handling is completely invisible. Additionally, since hardware monitoring is used, error checking,

Fig. 16. Multiprocessor emulation hardware.

error masking and majority voting do not impact the applications execution speed.

The executive schedules error diagnostics, latent test routines, and error recovery routines, using basically the same mechanisms used to schedule applications tasks. These executive tasks, running concurrently with the applications tasks, but in different processor triads, maintain the system, repairing faults, searching out latent failures, configuring processor triads and memory triads, and starting and stopping triads as required. Thus in the background, behind the system application, continuous activity is in progress to maintain the integrity of the system, assuring faultless and error-free execution of applications software.

An executive providing these functions was written for the experimental test hardware. Although it is not complete, in that only representative latent faults were tested, the executive does provide the basic facilities for providing error free execution of both executive and applications code. The software framework for latent test procedures is fully developed, although it is only sparsely populated. Error detection and recovery from all classes of faults is demonstrated in the simulated environment without interfering with the applications tasks.

2) Cache Memory Management: The experimental hardware and the proposed future system both have a common memory shared by all processor triads and private cache memories which are part of the processor modules. Programs are executed exclusively out of a processor's cache memory. Clearly, the burden of program loading from common memory, program overlaying, and other functions associated with bringing sections of code from common memory to the cache for execution could not be placed on the applications coding.

In the experimental computer, a software cache-memory management system was provided as part of the executive. At the subroutine call interface, conventions were adopted that provided for the automatic loading of called routines. A last used, first out algorithm clears space in the cache if unused space is not available. If a calling routine is dropped from the cache to make room for loading of the called routine, it is reloaded by the subroutine return interface.

The efficiency of this process of loading instructions into the cache before execution depends a great deal on the number of times an instruction is executed each time it is brought from common memory. Each word brought from common memory will take about 5 μs in the FTMP. Thus one triad executing 190k instructions per second could completely fill the bus capacity. In the experimental system, it is found that the applications programs execute between 10 and 40 instructions for every instruction brought from common memory. If an overall average of 20 can be maintained in the proposed system, a processor triad now projected to have a raw computing power of 200k instructions per second would load the bus with 10k instruction fetches per second. With reasonable allowances made for data transfers and queuing overheads, this suggests a maximum capacity of 4 or 5 processor triads before saturating the memory bus.

VI. Conclusion

A. Critical Areas of the FTMP Design

The following are areas where the FTMP has required, or will require, special care in conception, analysis, and/or design.

1) The phase-locked redundant clock has presented problems in latent fault exposure and in theoretical validation. Both of these are believed to be solved.

2) Mechanical and electrical design of bus guardians, bus isolation gates, and the buses themselves, must be done with care in order to prevent undesired fault propagation. The engineering prototype design to achieve this is partially complete at this writing.

3) Cold start capability requires the default formation of a triad or the equivalent. This has not yet been designed.

4) Self-test programs must be virtually complete, including perhaps attempts at finding pattern-sensitive failures over a period of time that is large compared to the basic test cycle. These programs will operate by producing bus errors as results of logic malfunctions. They do not need to diagnose the nature of the fault.

5) Mechanisms must be provided in hardware and software to screen or inhibit interferences caused by a lower priority procedure from impinging on a higher priority procedure. The opposite may or may not be possible.

6) Finally, validation must be made effective to a higher degree than ever before. Although some approaches are available, it remains to show how effective they will be.

B. Summary

The FTMP is a complex multiprocessor computer that employs a form of redundancy related to TMR-Hybrid redundancy, denoted here as Parallel-Hybrid redundancy, in which each major module can substitute for any other module of the same type. Despite the conceptual simplicity of the redundancy form, the implementation has many intricacies owing partly to the low target failure rate, and partly to the difficulty of eliminating single-fault vulnerability.

An extensive analysis of the computer through the use of such modeling techniques as Markov processes and combinatorial mathematics shows that for random hard faults the computer can meet its requirements. It was also shown that the maintenance scheduled at intervals of 200 hr or more can be adequate most of the time. The probability of requiring unscheduled maintenance during this time interval can be reduced to about two per cent by carrying one or two spare LRU's.

A study of intermittent faults revealed that the longer a fault stays in a pseudofailed state the worse is the system failure probability. Furthermore, high frequency faults also tend to affect the system failure probability adversely. This places an obvious burden upon the computer design and production activities to limit the intermittent failure arrivals and/or their duty cycles and frequencies to values such that the overall failure criterion can be met.

Acknowledgment

The authors would like to thank Dr. Jean-Claude Laprie of L.A.A.S., Toulouse, France, for his verification of the numerical results for intermittent faults. Dr. John M. Myers and Dr. Anatol Holt were responsible for an analytical validation of the phase-locked fault-tolerant clock.

References

[1] J. J. Deyst, Jr., and A. L. Hopkins, Jr., "Highly survivable integrated avionics," *Astronautics and Aeronautics*, to be published.

[2] R. L. Alonso, A. L. Hopkins, and H. A. Thaler, "Design criteria for a spacecraft computer," in *Proc. Seminar on Spaceborne Multiprocessors*, sponsored by NASA Electronic Research Center, Boston, MA, Oct. 1966.

[3] R. L. Alonso, A. L. Hopkins, Jr., and H. A. Thaler, "A multiprocessing structure," in *Dig. IEEE Computer Conf.*, Chicago, IL, Sept. 1967, IEEE Cat. No. 16C51.

[4] A. L. Hopkins, Jr., "A fault-tolerant information processing concept for space vehicles," *IEEE Trans. Comput.*, vol. C-20, no. 11., pp. 1394–1403, Nov. 1971.

[5] —, "A new standard for information processing systems for manned space flight," IFAC 3rd Symp. Control Systems in Space, Toulouse, France, Mar. 1970.

[6] T. B. Smith, III, "A damage-and fault-tolerant input/output network," *IEEE Trans. Comput.*, vol. C-24, no. 5, pp. 505–512, May 1975.

[7] A. L. Hopkins, Jr., and T. B. Smith, III, "The architectural elements of a symmetric fault-tolerant multiprocessor," *IEEE Trans. Comput.*, vol. C-24, no. 5, pp. 498–505, May 1975.

[8] —, United States Patent No. 4 015 246, Synchronous Fault-Tolerant Multiprocessor System, March 29, 1977.

[9] J. C. Deckert, M. N. Desai, J. J. Deyst, and A. J. Willsky, "F8-DFBW sensor failure identification using analytic redundancy," *IEEE Trans. Automat. Contr.*, vol. AC-22, no. 5, pp. 794–803, Oct. 1977.

[10] A. L. Hopkins, Jr., and T. B. Smith, III, "OSIRIS–A distributed fault-tolerant control system," in *Digest 14th IEEE Computer Society Int. Conf.*, San Francisco, CA, Mar. 1977.

[11] N. D. Murray, A. L. Hopkins, Jr., and J. H. Wensley, "Highly reliable multiprocessors," in AGARDograph #224, *Integrity in Electronc Flight Control Systems*, P. Kurzhals, Ed., AGARD-NATO Neuilly-Sur-Seine, France, Apr. 1977.

[12] F. P. Mathur, "On reliability modeling and analysis of ultrareliable fault-tolerant digital systems," *IEEE Trans. Comput.*, vol. C-20, no. 11, pp. 1376–1382, Nov. 1971.

[13] W. M. Daly, A. L. Hopkins, Jr., and J. F. McKenna, Jr., "A fault-tolerant clocking system," in *Dig. 1973 Int. Symp. Fault-Tolerant Computing*, Palo Alto, CA, June 1973, IEEE Computer Society, IEEE Cat. No. 73CH0772-4C.

[14] A. A. Avizienis, "Architecture of fault-tolerant computing systems," in *Dig. 1975 Int. Symp. Fault-Tolerant Computing*, Paris, France, June 1975, IEEE Cat. No. 75CH0974-6C.

[15] A. L. Hopkins, Jr., "Design foundations for survivable integrated on-board computation and control," in *Proc. Joint Automatic Control Conf.*, San Francisco, CA, pp. 232–237, June 1977.

[16] W. G. Bouricius, W. C. Carter, D. C. Jessep, P. R. Schneider, and A. B. Wadia, "Reliability modeling for fault-tolerant computers," *IEEE Trans. Comput.*, vol. C-20, no. 11, pp. 1306–1311, Nov. 1971.

[17] J-C Laprie, "Reliability and availability of repairable structures," in *Dig. 1975 Int. Symp. Fault-Tolerant Computing*, Paris, France, June 1975, IEEE Cat. No. 75CH0974-6C.

[18] M. A. Breuer, "Testing for intermittent faults in digital circuits," *IEEE Trans. Comput.*, vol. C-22, no. 3, pp. 241–246, Mar. 1973.

[19] J. H. Lala and A. L. Hopkins, Jr., "Survival and dispatch probability models for the FTMP computer," in *Dig. 1978 Int. Symp. Fault-Tolerant Computing*, Toulouse, France, June 1978, IEEE Computer Society.

SIFT: Design and Analysis of a Fault-Tolerant Computer for Aircraft Control

JOHN H. WENSLEY, LESLIE LAMPORT, JACK GOLDBERG, SENIOR MEMBER, IEEE,
MILTON W. GREEN, KARL N. LEVITT, P. M. MELLIAR-SMITH, ROBERT E. SHOSTAK,
AND CHARLES B. WEINSTOCK

Abstract—SIFT (Software Implemented Fault Tolerance) is an ultrareliable computer for critical aircraft control applications that achieves fault tolerance by the replication of tasks among processing units. The main processing units are off-the-shelf minicomputers, with standard microcomputers serving as the interface to the I/O system. Fault isolation is achieved by using a specially designed redundant bus system to interconnect the processing units. Error detection and analysis and system reconfiguration are performed by software. Iterative tasks are redundantly executed, and the results of each iteration are voted upon before being used. Thus, any single failure in a processing unit or bus can be tolerated with triplication of tasks, and subsequent failures can be tolerated after reconfiguration. Independent execution by separate processors means that the processors need only be loosely synchronized, and a novel fault-tolerant synchronization method is described. The SIFT software is highly structured and is formally specified using the SRI-developed SPECIAL language. The correctness of SIFT is to be proved using a hierarchy of formal models. A Markov model is used both to analyze the reliability of the system and to serve as the formal requirement for the SIFT design. Axioms are given to characterize the high-level behavior of the system, from which a correctness statement has been proved. An engineering test version of SIFT is currently being built.

I. INTRODUCTION

THIS paper describes ongoing research whose goal is to build an ultrareliable fault-tolerant computer system named SIFT (Software Implemented Fault Tolerance). In this introduction, we describe the motivation for SIFT and provide some background for our work. The remainder of the paper describes the actual design of the SIFT system. Section II gives an overview of the system and describes the approach to fault tolerance used in SIFT. Sections III and IV describe the SIFT hardware and software, respectively. Section V discusses the proof of the correctness of SIFT.

A. Motivation

Modern commercial jet transports use computers to carry out many functions, such as navigation, stability augmentation, flight control, and system monitoring. Although these computers provide great benefits in the operation of the aircraft, they are not critical. If a computer fails, it is always possible for the aircrew to assume its function, or for the function to be abandoned. (This may require significant changes, such as diversion to an alternative destination.) NASA, in its Aircraft Energy Efficiency (ACEE) Program, is currently studying the design of new types of aircraft to reduce fuel consumption. Such aircraft will operate with greatly reduced stability margins, which means that the safety of the flight will depend upon active controls derived from computer outputs. Computers for this application must have a reliability that is comparable with other parts of the aircraft. The frequently quoted reliability requirement is that the probability of failure should be less than 10^{-9} per hour in a flight of ten hours duration. A good review of the reliability requirements associated with flight control computers appears in Murray *et al.* [1]. This reliability requirement is similar to that demanded for manned space-flight systems.

A highly reliable computer system can have applications in other areas as well. In the past, control systems in critical industrial applications have not relied solely on computers, but have used a combination of human and computer control. With the need for faster control loops, and with the increased complexity of modern industrial processes, computer reliability has become extremely important. A highly reliable computer system developed for aircraft control can be used in such applications as well. Our objective in designing SIFT is to achieve the reliability required by these applications in an economic manner. Moreover, we want the resulting system to be as flexible as possible, so it can be easily adapted to changes in the problem specification.

When failure rates are extremely small, it is impossible to determine their values by testing. Therefore, testing cannot be used to demonstrate that SIFT meets its reliability requirements. It is necessary to *prove* the reliability of SIFT by mathematical methods. The need for such a proof of reliability has been a major influence on the design of SIFT.

B. Background

Our work on SIFT began with a study of the requirements for computing in an advanced commercial transport aircraft [2], [3]. We identified the computational and memory requirements for such an application and the reliability required for the safety of the aircraft. The basic concept of the SIFT system emerged from a study of computer architectures for meeting these requirements.

The second phase in the development of the SIFT system, which has just been completed, was the complete design of the hardware and software systems [4], [5]. This design has been expressed formally by rigorous specifications that describe the functional intent of each part of the system. A major influence during this phase was the Hierarchical Design Methodology developed at SRI [10]. A further influence has been the need to use formal program proving techniques to ensure the correctness of the software design.

The current phase of the development calls for the building of an engineering model and the carrying out of tests to

---

Manuscript received May 20, 1978. This work was supported by NASA-Langley Research Center under Contract NAS1-13792.
The authors are with SRI International, Menlo Park, CA 94025.

demonstrate its fault-tolerant behavior. The engineering model is intended to be capable of carrying out the calculations required for the control of an advanced commercial transport aircraft. SRI is responsible for the overall design, the software, and the testing, while the detailed design and construction of the hardware is being done by Bendix Corporation. The engineering model is scheduled to be built by the middle of 1979, with testing to be completed by the end of that year. Work is also continuing at SRI on proving the correctness of the system.

The study of fault-tolerant computing has in the past concentrated on failure modes of components, most of which are no longer relevant. The prior work on permanent "stuck-at-one" or "stuck-at-zero" faults on single lines is not appropriate for considering the possible failure modes of modern LSI circuit components, which can be very complex and affect the performance of units in very subtle ways. Our design approach makes no assumptions about failure modes. We distinguish only between failed and nonfailed units. Since our primary method for detecting errors is the corruption of data, the particular manner in which the data are corrupted is of no importance. This has important consequences for failure-modes-and-effects analysis (FMEA), which is only required at the interface between units. The rigorous, formal specification of interfaces enables us to deduce the effects on one unit of improper signals from a faulty unit.

Early work on fault-tolerant computer systems used fault detection and reconfiguration at the level of simple devices such as flip-flops and adders. Later work considered units such as registers or blocks of memory. With today's LSI units, it is no longer appropriate to be concerned with such small subunits. The unit of fault detection and of reconfiguration in SIFT is a processor/memory module or a bus.

Several low-level techniques for fault tolerance, such as error detection and correction codes in memory, are not included in the design of SIFT. Such techniques could be incorporated in SIFT, but would provide only a slight improvement in reliability.

II. SIFT Concept of Fault Tolerance

A. System Overview

As the name "Software Implemented Fault Tolerance" implies, the central concept of SIFT is that fault tolerance is accomplished as much as possible by programs rather than hardware. This includes error detection and correction, diagnosis, reconfiguration, and the prevention of a faulty unit from having an adverse effect on the system as a whole.

The structure of the SIFT hardware is shown in Fig. 1. Computing is carried out by the main processors. Each processor's results are stored in a main memory that is uniquely associated with the processor. A processor and its memory are connected by a conventional high bandwidth connection. The I/O processors and memories are structurally similar to the main processors and memories, but are of much smaller computational and memory capacity. They connect to the input and output units of the system which, for this application, are the sensors and actuators of the aircraft.

Each processor and its associated memory form a *processing module*, and each of the modules is connected to a multiple bus system. A faulty module or bus is prevented from causing faulty behavior in a nonfaulty module by the fault isolation methods described in Section II-B.

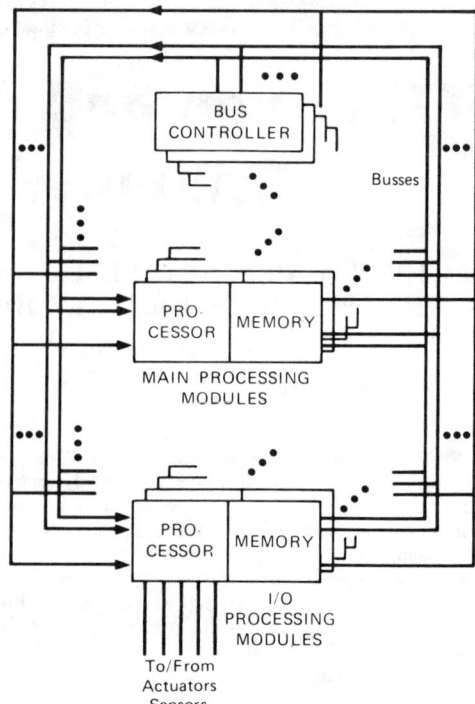

Fig. 1. Structure of the SIFT system.

The SIFT system executes a set of *tasks*, each of which consists of a sequence of *iterations*. The input data to each iteration of a task is the output data produced by the previous iteration of some collection of tasks (which may include the task itself). The input and output of the entire system is accomplished by tasks executed in the I/O processors. Reliability is achieved by having each iteration of a task independently executed by a number of modules. After executing the iteration, a processor places the iteration's output in the memory associated with the processor. A processor that uses the output of this iteration determines its value by examining the output generated by each processor which executed the iteration. Typically, the value is chosen by a "two out of three" vote. If all copies of the output are not identical, then an error has occurred. Such errors are recorded in the processor's memory, and these records are used by the executive system to determine which units are faulty.

SIFT uses the iterative nature of the tasks to economize on the amount of voting, by voting on the state data of the aircraft (or the computer system) only at the beginning of each iteration. This produces less data flow along the busses than with schemes that vote on the results of all calculations performed by the program. It also has important implications for the problem of synchronizing the different processors. We must ensure only that the different processors allocated to a task are executing the same iteration. This means that the processors need be only loosely synchronized (e.g., to within 50 μs), so we do not need tight synchronization to the instruction or clock interval.

An important benefit of this loose synchronization is that an iteration of a task can be scheduled for execution at slightly different times by different processors. Simultaneous transient failures of several processors will, therefore, be less likely to produce correlated failures in the replicated versions of a task.

The number of processors executing a task can vary with the task, and can be different for the same task at different times—e.g., if a task that is not critical at one time becomes critical at another time. The allocation of tasks to modules is in general different for each module. It is determined dynamically by a task called the global executive, which diagnoses errors to determine which modules and buses are faulty. When the global executive decides that a module has become faulty, it "reconfigures" the system by appropriately changing the allocation of tasks to modules. The global executive and its interaction with the individual processors is described in Section IV.

B. Fault Isolation

An important property required in all fault-tolerant computers is that of fault isolation: preventing a faulty unit from causing incorrect behavior in a nonfaulty unit. Fault isolation is a more general concept than damage isolation. Damage isolation means preventing physical damage from spreading beyond carefully prescribed boundaries. Techniques for damage isolation include physical barriers to prevent propagation of mechanical and thermal effects and electrical barriers—e.g., high-impedance electrical connections and optical couplers. In SIFT, such damage isolation is provided at the boundaries between processing modules and buses.

Fault isolation in SIFT requires not only damage isolation, but also preventing a faulty unit from causing incorrect behavior either by corrupting the data of the nonfaulty unit, or by providing invalid control signals. The control signals include those that request service, grant service, effect timing synchronization between units, etc.

Protection against the corruption of data is provided by the way in which units can communicate. A processing module can read data from any processing module's memory, but it can write only into its own memory. Thus a faulty processor can corrupt the data only in its own memory, and not in that of any other processing modules. All faults within a module are treated as if they have the same effect: namely that they produce bad data in that module's memory. The system does not attempt to distinguish the nature of a module fault. In particular, it does not distinguish between a faulty memory and a processor that puts bad data into an otherwise nonfaulty memory.

Note that a nonfaulty processor can obtain bad data if that data is read from a faulty processing module or over a faulty bus. Preventing these bad data from causing the generation of incorrect results is discussed below in the section on fault masking.

Fault isolation also requires that invalid control signals not produce incorrect behavior in a nonfaulty unit. In general, a faulty set of control signals can cause two types of faulty behavior in another unit.

1) The unit carries out the wrong action (possibly by doing nothing).
2) The unit does not provide service to other units.

In SIFT these two types of fault propagation are prevented by making each unit autonomous, with its own control. Improper control signals are ignored, and time-outs are used to prevent the unit from "hanging up" waiting for a signal that never arrives. The details of how this is done are discussed in Section III.

C. Fault Masking

Although a faulty unit cannot cause a nonfaulty processor to behave incorrectly, it can provide the processor with bad data. In order to completely mask the effects of the faulty unit, we must ensure that these bad data does not cause the processor to generate incorrect results. As we indicated above, this is accomplished by having the processor receive multiple copies of the data. Each copy is obtained from a different memory over a different bus, and the processor uses majority voting to obtain a correct version of the data. The most common case will be the one in which a processor obtains three copies of the data, providing protection from a single faulty unit.

After identifying the faulty unit, the system will be reconfigured to prevent that unit from having any further effect. If the faulty unit is a processing module, then the tasks that were assigned to it will be reassigned to other modules. If it is a bus, then processors will request their data over other buses. After reconfiguration, the system will be able to withstand a new failure—assuming that there are enough nonfaulty units remaining.

Because the number of processors executing a task can vary with the task and can be changed dynamically, SIFT has a flexibility not present in most fault tolerant systems. The particular application field—aircraft control—is one in which different computations are critical to different degrees, and the design takes advantage of this.

D. Scheduling

The aircraft control function places two types of timing requirements on the SIFT system.

1) Output to the actuators must be generated with specified frequency.
2) Transport delay—the delay between the reading of sensors and the generation of output to the actuators based upon those readings—must be kept below specified limits.

To fulfill these requirements, an iteration rate is specified for each task. The scheduling strategy must guarantee that the processing of each iteration of the task will be completed within the "time frame" of that iteration. It does not matter when the processing is performed, provided that it is completed by the end of the frame. Moreover, the time needed to execute an iteration of a task is highly predictable. The iteration rates required by different tasks differ, but they can be adjusted somewhat to simplify the scheduling.

Four scheduling strategies were considered for SIFT:

1) fixed preplanned (nonpreemptive) scheduling;
2) priority scheduling;
3) deadline scheduling;
4) simply periodic scheduling.

Of these, fixed preplanned scheduling in which each iteration is run to completion, traditional in-flight control applications, was rejected because it does not allow sufficient flexibility.

The priority-scheduling strategy, commonly used in general-purpose systems, can meet the real-time requirements if the tasks with the fastest iteration rates are given the highest priorities. Under this condition, it is shown in [6] that all tasks will be processed within their frames, for any pattern of iteration rates and processing times—provided the processing load does not exceed $\ln(2)$ of the capacity of the processor (up to about 70 percent loading is always safe).

The deadline-scheduling strategy always runs the task whose deadline is closest. It is shown in [6] that all the tasks will be processed within their frames provided the workload does

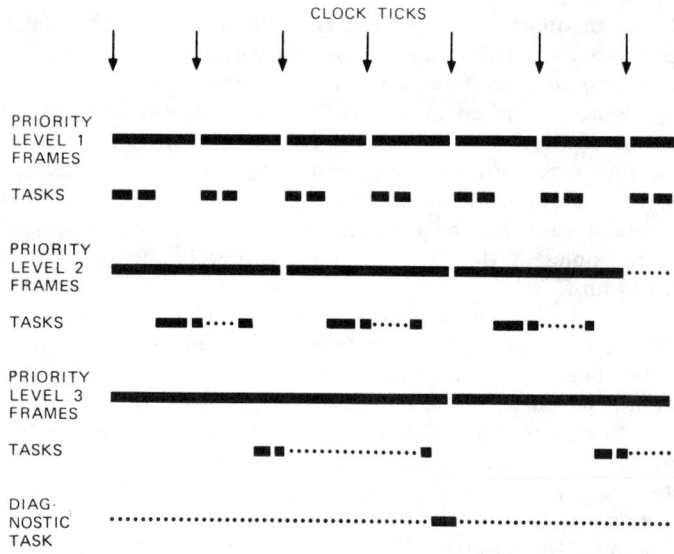

Fig. 2. A typical schedule.

not exceed the capacity of the processor (100 percent loading is permissible). Unfortunately, for the brief tasks characteristic of flight-control applications, the scheduling overhead eliminates the advantages of this strategy.

The simply periodic strategy is similar to the priority strategy, but the iteration rates of the tasks are constrained so that each iteration rate is an integral multiple of the next smaller rate (and thus of all smaller rates). To comply with this requirement, it may be necessary to run some tasks more frequently than their optimum rate, but this is permissible in a flight control system. It is shown in [6] that if the workload does not exceed the capacity of the processor (100 percent loading is possible), then simply periodic scheduling guarantees that all tasks will complete within their frames.

The scheduling strategy chosen for the SIFT system is a slight variant of the simply periodic method, illustrated by Fig. 2. Each task is assigned to one of several priority levels. Each priority level corresponds to an iteration rate, and each iteration rate is an integral multiple of the next lower one. In order to provide very small transport delays for certain functions, and to allow rapid detection of any fault which causes a task not to terminate, the scheme illustrated in Fig. 2 is modified as follows. The time frame corresponding to highest priority level (typically 20 ms) is divided into a number of subframes (typically 2 ms). The highest priority tasks are run in specific subframes, so that their results can be available to other tasks run in the next subframe, and they are required to complete within one subframe.

E. Processor Synchronization

The SIFT intertask and interprocessor communication mechanism allows a degree of asynchronism between processors and avoids the lockstep traditional in ultrareliable systems. Up to 50 μs of skew between processors can readily be accommodated, but even this margin cannot be assured over a ten-hour period with free-running clocks unless unreasonable requirements are imposed on the clocks. Thus, the processors must periodically resynchronize their clocks to ensure that no clock drifts too far from any other.

For reliability, the resynchronization procedure must be immune to the failure of any one clock or processor, and to a succession of failures over a period of time. In order to guarantee the high reliability required of SIFT, we cannot allow a system failure to be caused by any condition whose probability cannot be quantified, regardless of how implausible that condition may seem. This means that our synchronization procedure must be reliable in the face of the worst possible behavior of the failing component, even though that behavior may seem unrealistically malicious. We can only exclude behavior which we can *prove* to be sufficiently improbable.

The traditional clock resynchronization algorithm for reliable systems is the median clock algorithm, requiring at least three clocks. In this algorithm, each clock observes every other clock and sets itself to the median of the values that it sees. The justification for this algorithm is that, in the presence of only a single fault, the median value must either be the value of one of the valid clocks or else it must lie between a pair of valid clock values. In either case, the median is an acceptable value for resynchronization. The weakness of this argument is that the worst possible failure modes of the clock may cause other clocks to observe different values for the failing clock. Even if the clock is read by sensing the time of a pulse waveform, the effects of a highly degraded output pulse and the inevitable slight differences between detectors can result in detection of the pulse at different times.

In the presence of a fault that results in other clocks seeing different values for the failing clock, the median resynchronization algorithm can lead to a system failure. Consider a system of three clocks A, B, and C, of which C is faulty. Clock A runs slightly faster than clock B. The failure mode of clock C is such that clock A sees a value for clock C that is slightly earlier than its own value, while clock B sees a value for clock C that is slightly later than its own value. Clocks A and B both correctly observe that the value of clock A is earlier than the value of clock B. In this situation, clocks A and B will both see their own value as the median value, and therefore not change it. Both the good clocks A and B are therefore resynchronizing onto themselves, and they will slowly drift apart until the system fails.

It might be hoped that some relatively minor modification to the median algorithm could eliminate the possibility of such system failure modes. However, such hope is groundless. The type of behavior exhibited by clock C above will doom to failure any attempt to devise a reliable clock resynchronization algorithm for only three clocks. It can be proved that, if the failure-mode behavior is permitted to be arbitrary, then there cannot exist any reliable clock resynchronization algorithm for three clocks. The impossibility of obtaining exact synchronization with three clocks is proved in [9]. The impossibility of obtaining even the approximate synchronization needed by SIFT has also been proved, but the proof is too complex to present here and will appear in a future paper. The result is quite general and applies not only to clocks, but to any type of integrator which is subject to minor perturbations as, for example, inertial navigation systems.

Although no algorithm exists for three clocks, we have devised an algorithm for four or more clocks which makes the system immune to the failure of a single clock. The algorithm has been generalized to allow the simultaneous failure of M out of N clocks when $N > 3M$. Here, we only describe the single-failure algorithm, without proving it correct. (Algorithms of this type often contain very subtle errors, and extremely rigorous proofs are needed to ensure their correctness.) The general algorithm, and the proof of its correctness, can be found in [9].

The algorithm is carried out in two parts. In the first part, each clock[1] computes a vector of clock values, called the *interactive consistency vector*, having an entry for every clock. In the second part, each clock uses the interactive consistency vector to compute its new value.

A clock p computes its interactive consistency vector as follows. The entry of the vector corresponding to p itself is set equal to p's own clock value. The value for the entry corresponding to another processor q is obtained by p as follows.

1) Read q's value from q.
2) Obtain from each other clock r the value of q that r read from q.
3) If a majority of these values agree, then the majority value is used. Otherwise, the default value NIL (indicating that q is faulty) is used.

One can show that if at most one of the clocks is faulty, then: 1) each nonfaulty clock computes exactly the same interactive consistency vector; and 2) the component of this vector corresponding to any nonfaulty clock q is q's actual value.

Having computed the interactive consistency vector, each clock computes its new value as follows. Let δ be the maximum amount by which the values of nonfaulty processors may disagree. (The value of δ is known in advance, and depends upon the synchronization interval and the rate of clock drift.) Any component that is not within δ of at least two other components is ignored, and any NIL component is ignored. The clock then takes the median value of the remaining components as its new value.

Since each nonfaulty clock computes exactly the same interactive consistency vector, each will compute exactly the same median value. Moreover, this value must be within δ of the original value of each nonfaulty clock.

This is the basic algorithm that the SIFT processors will use to synchronize their clocks. Each SIFT processor reads the value of its own clock directly, and reads the value of another processor's clock over a bus. It obtains the value that processor r read for processor q's clock by reading from processor r's memory over a bus.

F. Reliability Prediction

A sufficiently catastrophic sequence of component failures will cause any system to fail. The SIFT system is designed to be immune to certain likely sequences of failures. To guarantee that SIFT meets its reliability goals, we must show that the probability of a more catastrophic sequence of failures is sufficiently small.

The reliability goal of the SIFT system is to achieve a high probability of survival for a short period of time—e.g., a ten-hour flight—rather than a large mean time before failure (MTBF). For a flight of duration T, survival will occur unless certain combinations of failure events occur within the interval T or have already occurred prior to the interval T and were undetected by the initial checkout of the system. Operationally, failures of the latter type are indistinguishable from faults that occur during the interval T.

To estimate the probability of system failure we use a finite-state Markov-like *reliability model* in which the state transitions are caused by the events of fault occurrence, fault detection, and fault "handling". The combined probability of all event sequences that lead to a failed state is the system failure probability. A design goal for SIFT is to achieve a failure rate of 10^{-9} per hour for a ten hour period.

For the reliability model, we assume that hardware fault events and electrical transient fault events are uncorrelated and exponentially distributed in time (constant failure rates). These assumptions are believed to be accurate for hardware faults because the physical design of the system prevents fault propagation between functional units (processors and buses) and because a multiple fault within one functional unit is no more serious than a single fault. The model assumes that all failures are permanent (for the duration of the flight), so it does not consider transient errors. The effects of uncorrelated transient errors are masked by the executive system, which requires a unit to make multiple errors before it considers the unit to be faulty. It is believed that careful electrical design can prevent correlation of transient errors between functional units. The execution of critical tasks in "loose" synchronism also helps protect against correlation of fast transient errors. Failure rates for hardware have been estimated on the basis of active component counts, using typical reliability figures for similar hardware. For the main processors, we obtain the rate 10^{-4} per hour; for I/O processors and buses, we obtain 10^{-5} per hour.

For a SIFT system with about the same number of main processing modules, I/O processing modules, and buses, it can be shown that the large difference in failure rates between a main processing module and an I/O processing modules or bus implies that we need only consider main processing module failures in our calculations. We can therefore let the state of the system be represented in the reliability model as a triple of integers (h, d, f) with $h \leq d \leq f$, where such a state represents a situation in which f failures of individual processors have occurred, d of those failures have been detected, and h of these detected failures have been "handled" by reconfiguration. There are three types of possible state transition.

1) $(h, d, f) \rightarrow (h, d, f+1)$, representing the failure of a processor.
2) $(h, d, f) \rightarrow (h, d+1, f), d < f$, representing the detection of a failure.
3) $(h, d, f) \rightarrow (h+1, d, f), h < d$, representing the handling of a detected failure.

This is illustrated in Fig. 3.

The first two types of transition—processor failure and failure detection, represented in Fig. 3 by straight arrows—are assumed to have constant probabilities per unit time. However, the third type of transition—failure handling, represented in Fig. 3 by wavey arrows—represents the completion of a reallocation procedure. We assume that this transition must occur within some fixed length of time τ.

A state (h, d, f) with $h < d$ represents a situation in which the system is reconfiguring. To make the system immune to an additional failure while in this state is a difficult problem, since it means that the procedure to reconfigure around a failure must work despite an additional, undetected failure Rather than assuming that this problem could be solved, we took the approach of trying to insure that the time τ that the system remains in such a state is small enough to make it highly unlikely for an additional failure to occur before reconfiguration is completed. We therefore made the pessimistic assumption that a processor failure which occurs

---

[1] In the following discussion, a clock is assumed to be capable of logical operations. In SIFT, such a clock is actually a processor and its internal clock.

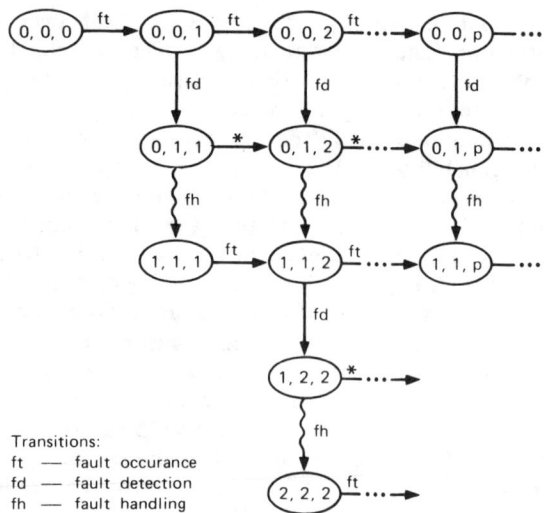

Transitions:
ft — fault occurance
fd — fault detection
fh — fault handling
* — double fault

Fig. 3. The reliability model.

TABLE I

(T = 10 hours)

FAILURE CAUSE	FAILURE PROBABILITY
Exhaustion of spares	5×10^{-12}
Double Fault (τ = 100 ms.)	7×10^{-11}
Double Fault (τ = 1 sec.)	7×10^{-10}

while the system is reconfiguring will cause a system failure. Such failures are represented by the "double-fault" transitions indicated by asterisks in Fig. 3. In our calculations, we assume that each of these transitions results in a system failure.

We have calculated the probability of system failure through a double fault transition, and also through reaching a state with fewer than two nonfaulty processors, for which we say that the system has failed because it has "run out of spares."[2] A brief summary of these failure probabilities for a five processor system is shown in Table I.

III. THE SIFT HARDWARE

The SIFT system attempts to use standard units whenever possible. Special design is needed only in the bus system and in the interfaces between the buses and the processing modules.

The major parameters of the SIFT system are shown in Table II. The column heading "Engineering Model" indicates the system intended for initial construction, integration, and testing. The column heading "Maximum" indicates the limits to which the engineering model can be expanded with only the procurement of additional equipment.

As described in Section II, the fault-tolerant properties of SIFT are based on the interconnection system between units and upon the software system. The particular design of the processors and memories is irrelevant to our discussion of fault tolerance. We merely mention that the main processors and memories are based on the BD*micro*X computer—a modern, LSI-based 16-bit computer designed and manu-

---

[2] The probability of system failure because of multiple *undetected* faults has not been computed precisely, but is expected to be comparable to the double fault values.

TABLE II

Major Parameters of the SIFT System, Engineering Model

System Parameters	Engineering Model	Maximum
Main Processors	5*	8
Main Memories	5	8
I/O Processors	5	8
I/O Memories	5	8
Busses	5	8
External Interfaces	5	8
Main Processors		
Word Length	16 bits	Same
Addressing Capability	32K words	64K
Speed	500K IPS	Same
Arithmetic Modes	Fixed point Double length Floating point	Same
Type	Bendix BDμX	Same
Main Memories		
Word Length	16 bits	Same
Capacity	32K words	64K
Type	Semiconductor+ RAM	Same
I/O Processors		
Word Length	8 bits	Same
Type	Intels 8080	Same
I/O Memories		
Word Length	8 bits	Same
Capacity	4K bytes	Same
Busses		
Speed	< 10 microsec. per word Bit serial	Same
I/O Interfaces		
Type	1553A MILSTD	Same

* In addition, a spare unit of each type is to be built.
+ Program memory would be read only memory (ROM) for actual flight use.

factured by Bendix Corporation specifically for avionics or similar applications. The I/O processors are based upon the well-known 8080 microprocessor architecture.

To help the reader understand the operation of the units and their interaction with one another, we describe the operation of the interconnection system in abstract terms. Fig. 4 shows the connections among processors, buses, and memories. The varying replications of these connections are shown for each type of unit. Within each unit are shown a number of abstract registers that contain data or control information. Arrows that terminate at a register indicate the flow of data to the register. Arrows that terminate at the boundary of a unit indicate control signals for that unit.

We explain the operation of the interconnection system by describing how a processor p reads a word of data from location w of memory m via bus b. We assume normal operation, in which no errors or time-outs occur. Processor p initiates the READ operation by putting m and w into the register PREQUEST(p, b). Note that every processor has a separate PREQUEST register for each bus to which it is connected. When this register is loaded, a BUSREQUEST line is set to request attention from the appropriate bus. The processor must now wait until the requested bus and memory units have completed their part of the operation.

Each bus unit contains a counter-driven scanner that continuously scans the PREQUEST and BUSREQUEST lines from processors. When the scanner finds a processor that requires its attention (BUSREQUEST high), it stops and the bus is said to have been *siezed* by that processor. The bus' counter then contains the identifying number of the processor that has seized it. When seized, the bus transfers the value w from the processor to a register connected to memory m. When this transfer has been completed, the MEMREQUEST line is raised calling for attention from that memory. The bus then waits for the memory to complete its actions.

Memory units contain counter-driven scanners that operate in the same manner as those in the bus units—i.e., they con-

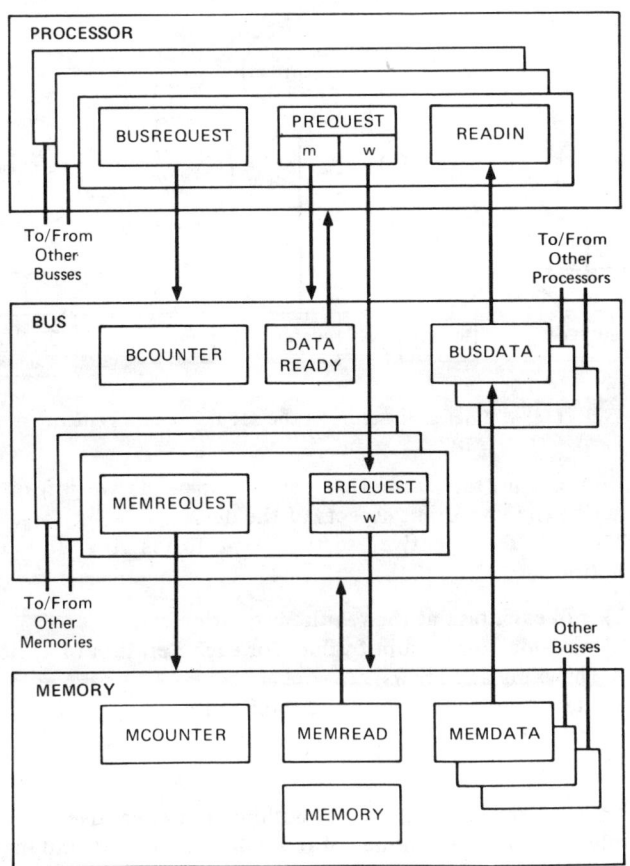

Fig. 4. An abstract view of data transfers.

tinuously scan all busses to determine which of them (if any) is requesting service. When a request is detected, the memory is said to be seized, and it reads the value w from the bus. The memory then reads the contents of its location w into MEMDATA register, and raises the MEMREAD line to inform the bus that the data are available. The memory leaves the state of MEMDATA and MEMREAD unchanged until it detects that the MEMREQUEST line from the bus has dropped, indicating that the bus has received the data from the MEMDATA register. The memory then drops the MEMREAD line and resumes scanning the buses for further requests.

When the bus detects that the MEMREAD line from the memory is up, it transfers the data in the MEMDATA register to the BUSDATA register, drops the MEMREQUEST line, and raises the DATAREADY line—indicating to the processor that the data is available. The bus leaves the state of the BUSDATA and DATAREADY lines unchanged until it detects that the BUSREQUEST line from the processor has dropped, indicating that the processor has received the data word. The bus then drops the DATAREADY line and resumes scanning the processors for further requests.

Meanwhile, the processor that made the original request has been waiting for the DATAREADY line to be raised by the bus, at which time it reads the data from the BUSDATA register. After completing this read, it drops the BUSREQUEST line and continues with other operations.

These actions have left the units in their original states. They are therefore ready to take part in other data transfer operations.

TABLE IIII

```
Data:
    READIN(p,b)
    A set of registers, one for each bus b, that receive
    data read from another processor.

    PREQUEST(p,b)
    A set of registers, one for each bus b, that hold the
    parameters of a request to read one word from another
    module's memory over that bus.

    BUSREQUEST(p,b)
    A set of booleans that indicate a request from bus b.

    ___
    A constant that is the maximum time a processor will
    wait for a bus action.

    BUS FAIL(p,b)
    A boolean indicating that processor p timed-out before
    receiving data from bus b.

External Data (generated by other units):
    DATAREADY, BUSDATA from BUS module

Abstract Program:
    REQUEST(p,b) := m,w
    D := REALTIME
    WAIT ON (DATAREADY(b) OR REALTIME >(D + ___))
    IF DATA READY (b)
        THEN BEGIN READIN(p,b) := BUSDATA(b)
                   BUSREQUEST(p,b) := FALSE
                   WAIT ON ((DATA READY = FALSE)
                           OR (REALTIME > (D + ___))
              END
        ELSE BEGIN BUS REQUEST := FALSE
                   BUSFAIL(p,b) := TRUE
              END
```

The precise behavior of the units can be described by abstract programs. Table III is an abstract program for the processor to bus interface unit.[3] It shows the unit's autonomous control, and the manner in which the unit requests service. Note how time-outs are used to prevent any kind of bus or memory failure from "hanging up" the unit. Abstract programs for the other units are similar.

The interconnection system units designed especially for the SIFT system are:

1) the processor-to-bus interfaces;
2) the busses;
3) the bus-to-memory interfaces.

These units all operate autonomously and contain their own control, which is implemented as a simple microprogrammed controller. For example, the bus control scanner that detects the processors' requests for service is controlled by a microprogram in a programmable read-only memory (PROM). The contents of this PROM are used for two purposes: first, part of the data is fed back to the PROM's address register to determine which word of the PROM is to be read next; second, part of the data is used as logic signals that control the operation of the unit in which the PROM resides. For example, this second part could contain data to open gates to allow the flow of information from one unit to another. Input signals to the controller are applied to some of the bits of the PROM's address register, thereby affecting which PROM words are read.

The interface units (items 1 and 3 above) consist mainly of a few registers, the controller, and the gates necessary to effect the data flow. The bus with its controller (item 2) contains a larger set of such gates, since each bus can allow data flow from every memory to every processor. We estimate that the complexity of a bus unit, consisting of a bus together

---

[3] This program is only meant to illustrate the unit's main features; it does not accurately describe the true behavior of the unit.

with all its interfaces, is about 10 percent of that of a main processing module. The logical structure is such that an LSI version of an entire bus unit will be practical for future versions of SIFT. However, the engineering model will be a mixture of LSI and MSI (medium scale integration) technology.

The design of the interfaces permits simultaneous operation of all units. For example, a processor can simultaneously read data from its memory and from another memory, while at the same time another processor is reading from the first processor's memory. Such simultaneous operation is limited only by contention at a memory unit. This contention is handled by conventional cycle-stealing techniques and causes little delay, since the memory cycle time is small (250 ns) compared to the time needed to transfer a full word through the bus (10 μs).

Since several processors may attempt to seize the same bus, or several busses may attempt to seize the same memory, a processor can have to wait for the completion of one or more other operations before receiving service. Such waiting should be insignificant because of the small amount of data that is transmitted over the busses.

IV. The Software System

The software of SIFT consists of the application software and the executive software. The application software performs the actual flight control computations. The executive software is responsible for the reliable execution of the application tasks, and implements the error detection and reconfiguration mechanisms discussed in Section II. Additional support software to be run on a large support computer is also provided.

From the point of view of the software, a processing module —with its processor, memory, and associated registers—is a single logical unit. We will therefore simply use the term "processor" to refer to a processing module for the rest of the paper.

A. The Application Software

The application software is structured as a set of iterative tasks. As described in Section II-D, each task is run with a fixed iteration rate which depends upon its priority. The iteration rate of a higher priority task is an integral multiple of the iteration rate of any lower priority task. Every task's iteration rate is a simple fraction of the main clock frequency.

The fact that a task is executed by several processors is invisible to the application software. In each iteration, an application task obtains its inputs by executing calls to the executive software. After computing its outputs, it makes them available as inputs to the next iteration of tasks by executing calls to the executive software. The input and output of a task iteration will consist of at most a few words of data.

B. The SIFT Executive Software

Formal specifications of the executive software have been written in a rigorous form using the SPECIAL language [7] developed at SRI. These formal specifications are needed for the proof of the correctness of the system discussed in Section V. Moreover, they are also intended to force the designer to produce a well-structured system. Good structuring is essential to the success of SIFT. A sample of these SPECIAL specifications is given in the Appendix. The complete formal specifi-

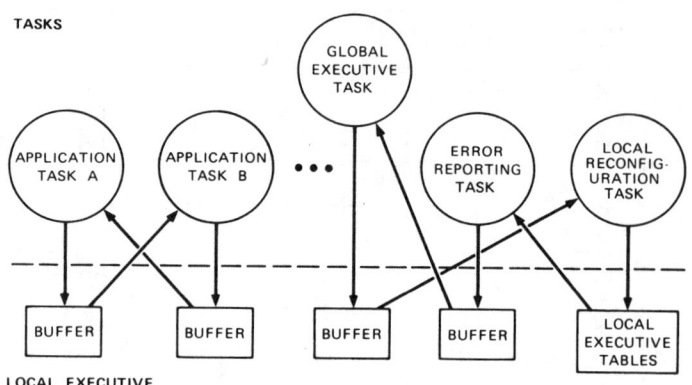

Fig. 5. Logical structure of the SIFT software system.

cation is omitted from this paper. Instead, we informally describe the important aspects of the design.

The SIFT executive software performs the following functions:

1) run each task at the required iteration rate;
2) provide correct input values for each iteration of a critical task (masking any errors);
3) detect errors and diagnose their cause;
4) reconfigure the system to avoid the use of failed components.

To perform the last three functions, the executive software implements the techniques of redundant execution and majority voting described in Section II. The executive software is structured into three parts:

1) the global executive task;
2) the local executive;
3) the local–global communicating tasks.

One global executive task is provided for the whole system. It is run just like a highly critical application task—being executed by several processors and using majority voting to obtain the output of each iteration. It diagnoses errors to decide which units have failed, and determines the appropriate allocation of tasks to processors.

Each processing module has its own local executive and local-global communicating tasks. The local–global communicating tasks are the error reporting task and the local reconfiguration task. Each of these tasks is regarded as a separate task executed on a single processor rather than as a replication of some more global task, so there are as many separate error reporting tasks and local reconfiguration tasks as there are processors.

Fig. 5 shows the logical structure of the SIFT software system. The replication of tasks and their allocation to processors is not visible. Tasks communicate with one another through buffers maintained by the local executives. Note that the single global executive task is aware of (and communicates with) each of the local executives, but that the local executives communicate only with the single (replicated) global executive task and not with each other. In this logical picture, application tasks communicate with each other and with the global executive, but not with the local executives.

Fig. 6 and Fig. 7 show where the logical components of Fig. 5 actually reside within SIFT. Note how critical tasks are

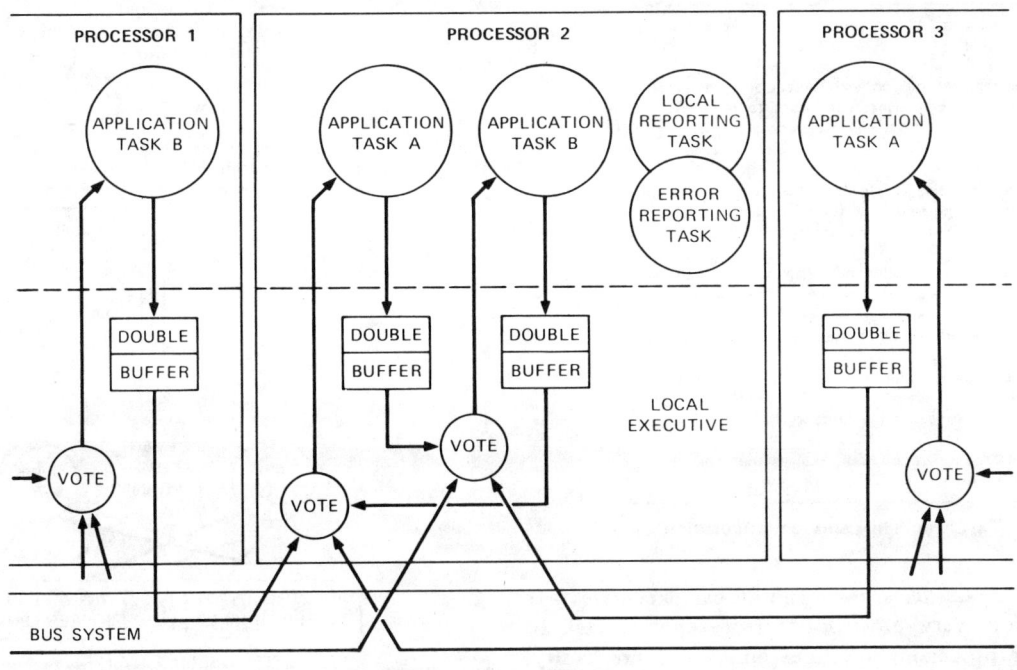

Fig. 6. Arrangement of application tasks within SIFT configuration.

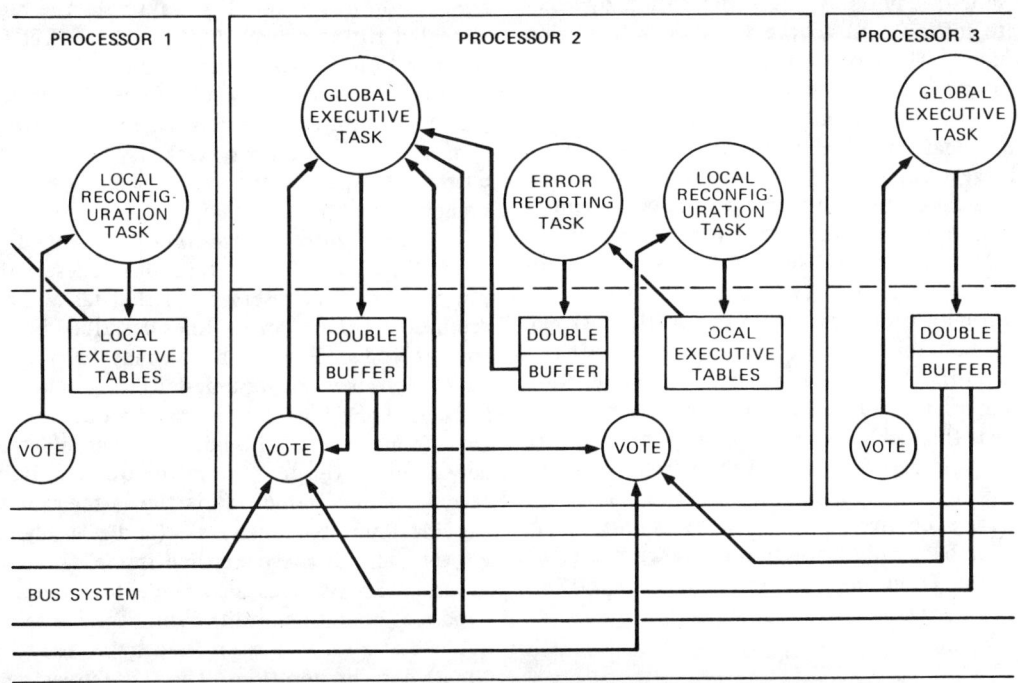

Fig. 7. Arrangement of executive within SIFT configuration.

replicated on several processors. For the sake of clarity, many of the paths by which tasks read buffers have been eliminated from Fig. 6 and Fig. 7.

1) The Local-Global Communicating Tasks: Each processor runs its local reconfiguration task and error reporting task at a specified frequency, just like any other task. These two tasks communicate with the global executive via buffers.

The local executive detects an error when it obtains different output values for the same task iteration from different processors.[4] It reports all such errors to the error reporting task. The error reporting task performs a preliminary analysis of these errors, and communicates its results to the global executive task. These results are also used by the local executive to detect possibly faulty units before the global executive has diagnosed the errors. For example, after several error reports involving a particular bus, the local executive will attempt to use other busses in preference to that one until the global executive has diagnosed the cause of the errors.

The local reconfiguration task maintains the tables used by the local executive to schedule the execution of tasks. It does this using information provided to it by the global executive.

The interaction of the global executive and the local-global communicating tasks is shown in Fig. 8.

---

[4] It can also detect that a time-out occurred while reading from the memory of another processing module.

1. Error handler in each processor puts reports in error table.

2. Error reporter task in each processor reads error table and decides what conditions to report to the global executive. This report is put in a buffer.

3. Global executive (triplicated) reads each processor's buffer over three busses (to guard against bus errors) and votes for a plurality.

4. Global executive, using the diagnosis provided by the error reporter, determines what reconfiguration, if any, is necessary. If a reconfiguration is necessary, a report is put in a buffer.

5. Local reconfiguration task in each processor reads report from each of the global executive buffers and votes to determine plurality.

6. Local reconfiguration task changes the scheduling table to reflect the global executive's wishes.

Fig. 8. Error reporting and reconfiguration.

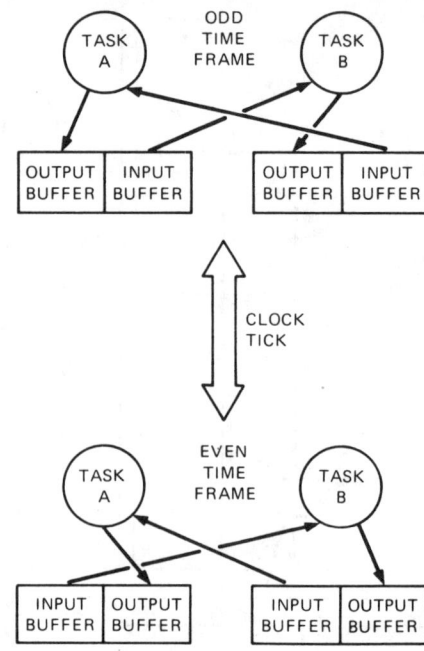

Fig. 9. The double buffering mechanism.

2) The Global Executive Task: The global executive task uses the results of every processor's error reporter task to determine which processing modules and buses are faulty. The problem of determining which units are faulty is discussed in Section IV-C below. When the global executive decides that a component has failed, it initiates a reconfiguration by sending the appropriate information to the local reconfiguration task of each processor. The global executive may also reconfigure the system as a result of directives from the application tasks. For example, an application task may report a change of flight phase which changes the criticality of various tasks.

To permit rapid reconfiguration, we require that the program for executing a task must reside in a processor's memory before the task can be allocated to that processor. In the initial version of SIFT, there will be a static assignment of programs to memories. The program for a critical task will usually reside in all main processor memories, so the task can be executed by any main processor.

3) The Local Executive: The local executive is a collection of routines to perform the following functions: 1) run each task allocated to it at the task's specified iteration rate; 2) provide input values to, and receive output values from each task iteration, and 3) report errors to the local executive task.

A processor's local executive routine can be invoked from within that processor by a call from a running task, by a clock interrupt, or by a call from another local executive routine. There are four types of routines:

1) error handler;
2) scheduler;
3) buffer interface routines;
4) voter.

The *error handler routine* is invoked by the voter when an error condition is detected. It records the error in a *processor/bus error table*, which is used by the error reporting task described above.

The *scheduler routine* is responsible for scheduling the execution of tasks. Every task is run at a prespecified iteration rate that defines a sequence of time frames within which the task must be run. (For simplicity, we ignore the scheduling of the highest priority tasks in subframes that was mentioned in Section II-D.) A single iteration of the task is executed within each of its frames, but it may be executed at any time during that frame.

The scheduler is invoked by a clock interrupt or by the completion of a task. It always runs the highest priority task allocated to the processor that has not yet finished executing the iteration for its current time frame. Execution of a task may be interrupted by the clock, in which case its state is preserved until execution is resumed—possibly after the execution of a higher priority task. A task that has completed its current iteration is not executed again until after the start of its next time frame.

The *buffer interface routines* are invoked by a task when it generates output for an iteration. These routines put the output into a buffer reserved for that task. These output values are used by the voter routines described below to obtain input for the tasks. Because a task may be run at any time during its time frame, the double-buffering scheme shown in Fig. 9 is used. Each buffer consists of a double buffer. In any one time frame, one of the buffers is available for new data being generated by the task while the other contains the data generated last time frame. It is the latter values that are used to provide input to other tasks (and possibly to the same task). At the start of the next time frame, the buffers are switched around. Provision is also made for communication between processes operating at different frequencies.

The *voter routine* is invoked by a task to obtain the inputs for its current iteration. The task requests a particular output from the previous iteration of second task—which may be the same task. The voter uses tables provided by the local reconfiguration task to determine what processors contain copies of that output, and in which of their buffers. It reads the data from each of these buffers and performs a majority vote to obtain a single value. If all the values do not agree, then an error has occurred, and the error reporter is called.

C. Fault Detection

Fault detection is the analysis of errors to determine which components are faulty. In SIFT, fault detection is based upon the processor/bus error table, an m by n matrix, where m is the number of processors and n the number of busses in the system. Each processor has its own processor/bus error table that is maintained by its local executive's error handler. An entry $Xp[i, j]$ in processor p's table represents the number of errors detected by processor p's local executive that involve processor i and bus j. Suppose that processor p is reading from processor q using bus r. There are five distinct kinds of errors that cause a matrix value to change:

1) the connection from bus r to processor q is faulty;
2) the connection from processor p to bus r is faulty;
3) bus r is faulty;
4) processor q is faulty;
5) processor p is faulty;

Processor p's error reporting task analyzes the processor/bus error table as follows to determine if any of these cases hold. Let $e > 0$ be a threshold of errors that will be tolerated for any processor/bus combination. It can deduce that case 1 holds if the following conditions all hold: (i) $Xp[q, r] > e$, (ii) there exists a bus j such that $Xp[q, j] \leq e$, and (iii) there exists a processor i such that $Xp[i, r] \leq e$. Either case 2 or 3 may hold if $Xp[i, r] > e$ for all active processors i. These two cases can only be distinguished by the global executive task, which has access to information from all the processors. (Case 3 holds if all active processors report bus r faulty, otherwise case 2 holds.) The error handler can deduce that case 4 holds if $Xp[q, j] > e$ for all active buses j. The error handler cannot be depended upon to diagnose case 5, since the failure of the processor executing it could cause the error handler to decide that any (or none) of the other four cases hold.

Once the error handler has performed this analysis, the appropriate action must be taken. In case 1, processor p will stop using bus r to talk to processor q. In cases 2 and 3, processor p will stop using bus r, and will report to the global executive that bus r is faulty. In case 4, processor p will report to the global executive task that processor q is faulty.

The global executive task makes the final decision about which unit is faulty. To do this, it reads the faulty processor reports provided by the error reporting task. If two or more processors report that another processor is faulty, then the global executive decides that this other processor has indeed failed. If two or more processors report that a bus is faulty, then the global executive decides that the bus has failed.

The global executive may know that some unit produced errors, but be unable to determine which is the faulty unit. In that case, it must await further information. It can obtain such information by allocating the appropriate diagnostic tasks. If there is a faulty unit (and the error reports were not due to transient faults), then it should obtain the necessary information in a short time.

It can be shown that in the presence of a single fault, the above procedure cannot cause the global executive to declare a nonfaulty unit to be faulty. With the appropriately "malicious" behavior, a faulty unit may generate error reports without giving the global executive enough information to determine that it is faulty. For example, if processor p fails in such a way that it gives incorrect results only to processor q, then the global executive cannot decide whether it is p or q that is faulty. However, the majority voting technique will mask these errors and prevent a system failure.

D. The Simulator

An initial version of the SIFT system has been coded in Pascal. Since the avionics computer is not available at this time, the executive is being debugged on an available general-purpose computer (a DEC PDP-10). To facilitate this, a simulator has been constructed. The simulator uses five asynchronous processes, each running a SIFT executive and a "toy" set of application tasks. The controlling process simulates the actions of the SIFT bus system and facilitates interprocess communications. Faults are injected, either at the processor or the bus levels, and a visual display of the system's behavior is provided. This gives us a means of testing software in the absence of the actual SIFT hardware.

V. The Proof of Correctness

A. Concepts

Estimates of the reliability of SIFT are based upon the assumption that the software operates correctly. Since we know of no satisfactory way to estimate the probability that a piece of software is incorrect, we are forced to try to guarantee that the software is indeed correct. For an asynchronous multiprocess system such as SIFT, the only way to do this is to give a rigorous mathematical proof of its correctness.

A rigorous proof of correctness for a system requires a precise statement of what it means for the system to be correct. The correctness of SIFT must be expressed as a precise mathematical statement about its behavior. Since the SIFT system is composed of several processors and memories, such a statement must describe the behavior of many thousands of bits of information. We are thus faced with the problem that the statement of what it means for the SIFT software to be correct is too complicated to be humanly comprehensible.

The solution to this problem is to construct a higher level "view" of the SIFT system that is simpler than the actual system. Such a view is called a *model*. When stated in terms of the simple model, the requisite system properties can be made comprehensible. The proof of correctness is then performed in two steps: 1) we first prove that the model possesses the necessary correctness properties; and 2) we then prove that the model accurately describes the SIFT system [12].

Actually, different aspects of correctness are best expressed in terms of different models. We use a hierarchy of models. The system itself may be viewed as the lowest level model. In order to prove that the models accurately describe the SIFT system, we prove that each model accurately describes the next lower-level one.

B. Models

We now make the concept of a model more precise. We define a model to consist of a set S of possible states, a subset S_0 of S consisting of the set of possible initial states, and a *transition relation* $\rightarrow$ on S. The relation $s \rightarrow s'$ means that a transition is possible from state s to state s'. It is possible for the relations $s \rightarrow s'$ and $s \rightarrow s''$ both to hold for two different states s' and s'', so we allow nondeterministic behavior. A *possible behavior* of the system consists of a sequence of states $s_0, s_1, \cdots$ such that s_0 is in S_0 and $s_i \rightarrow s_{i+1}$ for each i. Correctness properties are mathematical statements about the possible behaviors of the system.

Note that the behavior of a model consists of a linear sequence of transitions, even though concurrent operations occur in the SIFT system. Concurrently activity can be represented by transitions that change disjoint components of the state, so that the order in which they occur is irrelevant.

Each state of the model represents a collection of states in the real system. For example, in the reliability model discussed in Section II-F, the state is a triple of integers (h, d, f)

which contains only the information that f processors have failed, d of those failures have been detected, and h of the detected failures have been handled. A single model state corresponds to all possible states the system could reach through any combination of f failures, d failure detections, and h reconfigurations.

We now consider what it means for one model to accurately describe a lower level one. Let S, S_0, and $\rightarrow$ be the set of states, set of initial states, and transition relation for the higher level model; and let S', S'_0, and $\rightarrow'$ be the corresponding quantities for the lower level model. Each state of the lower level model must represent some state of the higher level one, but different lower level states can represent the same higher level one. Thus there must be a mapping REP: $S' \rightarrow S$, where REP(s') denotes the higher-level state represented by s'.

Having defined a correspondence between the states of the two models, we can require that the two models exhibit corresponding behavior. Since the lower level model represents a more detailed description of the system, it may contain more transitions than the higher level one. Each transition in the lower level model should either correspond to a transition in the higher level one, or else should describe a change in the system that is invisible in the higher level model. This requirement is embodied in the following two conditions.

1) REP(S'_0) is a subset of S_0.
2) For all s', t' in S': if $s' \rightarrow' t'$ then either:
   (a) REP(s') = REP(t'); or
   (b) REP(s') $\rightarrow$ REP(t').

If these conditions are satisfied, then we say that REP defines the lower level model to be a *refinement* of the higher level one.

If a model is a refinement of a higher level one, then any theorem about the possible behaviors of the higher level model yields a corresponding theorem about the possible behaviors of the lower level one. This is used to infer correctness of the lower level model (and ultimately, of the system itself) from the correctness of the higher level one.

A transition in the higher level model may represent a system action that is represented by a sequence of transitions in the lower level one. For example, the action of detecting a failure may be represented by a single transition in the higher level model. However, in a lower level model (such as the system itself), detecting a failure may involve a complex sequence of transitions. The second requirement means that in order to define REP, we must define some arbitrary point at which the lower level model is considered to have detected the failure. This problem of defining exactly when the higher level transition takes place in the lower level model turns out to be the major difficulty in constructing the mapping REP.

C. The Reliability Model

In the reliability model, the state consists of a triple (h, d, f) of integers with $h \leq d \leq f \leq p$, where p is the number of processors. The transition relation $\rightarrow$ is described in Section II-F, as is the meaning of the quantities h, d, and f.

Associated with each value of h is an integer sf(h) called its *safety factor*, which has the following interpretation. If the system has reached a configuration in which h failures have been handled, then it can successfully cope with up to sf(h) additional (unhandled) failures. That is, the system should function correctly so long as $f - h$, the number of unhandled failures, is less than or equal to sf(h). The state (h, d, f) is called *safe* if $f - h \leq$ sf(h).

To demonstrate that SIFT meets its reliability requirements, we must show two things.

1) If the system remains in a safe state (one represented by a safe state in the reliability model), then it will behave correctly.
2) The probability of the system reaching an unsafe state is sufficiently small.

Property 2) was discussed in Section II-F. The remainder of Section V describes our approach to proving 1).

The reliability model is introduced specifically to allow us to discuss property 2). The model does not reflect the fact that SIFT is performing any computations, so it cannot be used to state any correctness properties of the system. For that, a lower level model is needed.

D. The Allocation Model

1) An Overview: SIFT performs a number of iterative tasks. In the *allocation model*, a single transition represents the execution of one complete iteration of all the tasks. As described in Section II-D, most tasks are not actually executed every iteration cycle. For the allocation model, an unexecuted task is considered to perform a null calculation, producing the same result it produced during the previous iteration.

The input used by a task in its tth iteration is the output of the $(t-1)$st iterations of some (possibly empty) set of tasks. Input to SIFT is modeled by a task executed on an I/O processor which produces output without requiring input from other tasks. The output which an I/O processor produces is simply the output of some task which it executes.

In the allocation model, we make no distinction between main processors and I/O processors. Bus errors are not represented in the model. SIFT's handling of them is invisible in the allocation model, and can be represented by a lower level model.

The fundamental correctness property of SIFT—property 1) of Section V-C above—is stated in terms of the allocation model as follows: if the system remains in a safe state, then each nonfaulty processor produces correct output for every critical task it executes. This implies the correctness of any critical output of SIFT generated by a nonfaulty I/O processor. (The possibility of faulty I/O processors must be handled by redundancy in the external environment.)

The allocation of processors to tasks is effected by the interaction of the global executive task, the local–global communicating tasks, and local executives, as described in Section IV. The output of the tth iteration of a local-global communicating task uses as input the output of the $(t-1)$st iteration of the global executive. During the tth iteration cycle, the local executive determines what the processor should be doing during the $(t+1)$st cycle—i.e., what tasks it should execute, and what processor memories contain the input values for each of these tasks. The processor executes a task by fetching each input from several processor memories, using a majority vote to determine the correct value, and then computing the task's output.[5] We assume that a nonfaulty processor will compute the correct output value for a task if majority voting obtains the correct value for each of the task's inputs.

The only part of the executive software that is explicitly represented in the allocation are the local–global communicating tasks. Although each processor's local–global communicating task is treated in SIFT as a separate task, it is more convenient to represent it in the allocation model as the execu-

---

[5] The fault diagnosis performed by the global executive is not represented in the allocation model.

tion on that processor of a single replicated task whose output determines the complete allocation of tasks to processors.

2) The States of the Allocation Model: We now describe the set of states of the allocation model. They are defined in terms of the primitive quantities listed below, which are themselves undefined. (To show that a lower level model is a refinement of the allocation model, we must define these primitive quantities in terms of the primitive quantities of that lower level model.) The descriptions of these quantities are given to help the reader understand the model; they have no formal significance.

- P A set of processors. It represents the set of all processors in the system.
- K A set of tasks. It represents the set of all (critical) tasks in the system.
- LE An element of K. It is the single task that represents all the local–global communicating tasks, as described above.
- e A mapping from the cross product of K and the set of nonnegative integers into some unspecified set of values. The value of $e(k, t)$ represents the correct output of the tth iteration cycle of task k. Thus, e describes what the SIFT tasks should compute. It is a primitive (i.e., undefined) quantity in the allocation model because we are not specifying the actual values the tasks should produce. (These values will, of course, depend upon the particular application tasks SIFT executes, and the inputs from the external environment.)
- sf The safety factor function introduced in the reliability model. It remains a primitive quantity in the allocation model. It can be thought of as a goal the system is trying to achieve.

We define the allocation model state to consist of the following components.[6] (Again, the descriptions are to assist the reader and are irrelevant to the proof.)

- t A nonnegative integer. It represents the number of iteration cycles that have been executed.
- F A subset of P. It represents the set of all failed processors.
- D A subset of F. It represents the set of all failed processors whose failure has been detected.
- c A mapping from $P \times K$ into some unspecified set of values. The value $c(p, k)$ denotes the output of task k as computed by processor p. This value is presumably meaningless if p did not execute the tth iteration of task k.

3. The Axioms of the Model: We do not completely describe the set of initial states S_0 and the transition relation $\rightarrow$ for the allocation model. Instead, we give the following list of axioms about S_0 and $\rightarrow$. Rather than giving their formal statement, we simply give here an informal description of the axioms. (Uninteresting axioms dealing with such matters as initialization are omitted.)

1) The value of $c(p, LE)$ during iteration cycle t, which represents the output of the tth iteration of processor p's local–global communicating task, specifies the tasks that p should execute during cycle $t + 1$ and the processors whose memories contain input values for each such task.

2) If a nonfaulty processor p executes a task k during

---
[6] To simplify the discussion, one component of our actual model has been omitted.

iteration cycle t, and a majority of the copies of each input value to k received by p are correct, then the value $c(p, k)$ it computes will equal the correct value $e(k, t)$.

3) Certain natural assumptions are made about the allocation of tasks to processors specified by $e(LE, t)$. In particular, we assume that a) no critical tasks are assigned to a processor in D (the set of processors known to be faulty), and b) when reconfiguring, the reallocation of tasks to processors is done in such a way that the global executive never knowingly makes the system less tolerant of failure than it currently is.

To prove that a lower level model is a refinement of the allocation model, it will suffice to verify that these axioms are satisfied.

4) The Correspondence with the Reliability Model: In order to show that the allocation model is a refinement of the reliability model, we must define the quantities h, d, and f of the reliability model in terms of the state components of the allocation model—thereby defining the function REP.

The definitions of d and f are obvious; they are just the number of elements in the sets D and F, respectively. To define h, we must specify the precise point during the "execution" of the allocation model at which a detected failure is considered to be "handled." Basically, the value of h is increased to $h + 1$ when the reconfiguration has progressed to the point where it can handle $sf(h + 1)$ *additional* errors. (The function sf appears in the definition.) We omit the details.

5. The Correctness Proof: Within the allocation model, we can define a predicate $CF(t)$ that expresses the condition that the system functions correctly during the tth iteration cycle. Intuitively, it is the statement that every nonfaulty processor produces the correct output for every task it executes. The predicate $CF(t)$ can be stated more precisely as follows.

If $e(LE, t-1)$ indicates that p should execute a task k in K during the tth iteration cycle, and p is in $P - F$, then the value of $c(p, k)$ after the tth iteration equals $e(k, t)$.

[A precise statement of how $e(LE, t-1)$ indicates that p should execute task k requires some additional notation, and is omitted.]

We can define the predicate SAFE(t) to mean that the system is in a safe state at time t. More precisely, SAFE(t) means that after the tth iteration cycle, $sf(h) \geq f - h$, where f and h are defined above as functions of the allocation model state. The basic correctness condition for SIFT can be stated as follows.

If SAFE(t') is true for all t' with $0 \leq t' \leq t$, then $CF(t)$ is true.

A rigorous proof of this theorem has been developed, based upon the axioms for the allocation model. The proof is too long and detailed to include here. It will appear in the final report to NASA at the conclusion of the current phase of the project.

E. Future Work

The basic correctness property of SIFT has been stated and proved for the allocation model. What remains to be done is to show that the actual system is a refinement of the allocation model. Current plans call for this to be done in terms of two lower level models. The first of these is the *operating-system model*. The allocation model represents all the computations in a given iteration cycle performed by all the processes as a single transition. The operating-system model will represent the asynchrony of the actual computations. It will essentially be a high-level representation of the system that embodies the mechanisms used to synchronize the processors. The proof that the operating-system model is a refinement of the allocation model will be a proof of correctness of these synchronizing mechanisms.

The next lower level model will be the *program model*. It will essentially represent the PASCAL version of the software. We expect that proving the program model to be a refinement of the operating-system model will be done by the ordinary methods of program verification [11].

Finally, we must verify that the system itself is a correct refinement of the program model. This requires verifying first that the Pascal programs are compiled correctly, and second that the hardware correctly executes programs. (In particular, this involves verifying the fault-isolation properties of the hardware.) We have not yet decided how to address these tasks. Although most of this verification is theoretically straightforward, it presents a difficult problem in practice.

VI. Conclusions

The SIFT computer development is an attempt to use modern methods of computer design and verification to achieve fault-tolerant behavior for real-time, critical control systems. We believe that the use of standard, mass-produced components helps to attain high reliability. Our basic approach, therefore, involves the replication of standard components, relying upon the software to detect and analyze errors and to dynamically reconfigure the system to bypass faulty units. Special hardware is needed only to isolate the units from one another, so a faulty unit does not cause the failure of a nonfaulty one.

We have chosen processor/memory modules and bus modules as the basic units of fault detection and reconfiguration. These units are at a high enough level to make system reconfiguration easy, and are small and inexpensive enough to allow sufficient replication to achieve the desired reliability. Moreover, new advances in Large Scale Integration will further reduce their size and cost.

By using software to achieve fault-tolerance, SIFT allows considerable flexibility in the choice of error handling policies and mechanisms. For example, algorithms for fault masking and reconfiguration can be easily modified on the basis of operational experience. Novel approaches to the tolerance of programming errors, such as redundant programming and recovery blocks [8] can be incorporated. Moreover, it is fairly easy to enhance the performance of the system by adding more hardware.

While designing SIFT, we have been concerned with proving that it meets its stringent reliability requirements. We have constructed formal models with which to analyze the probability of system failure, and we intend to prove that these models accurately describe the behavior of the SIFT system. Our effort has included the use of formal specifications for functional modules. We hope to achieve a degree of system verification that has been unavailable in previous fault-tolerant architectures.

Although the design described in this paper has been oriented toward the needs of commercial air transports, the basic architectural approach has a wide applicability to critical real-time systems. Future work may extend this approach to the design of fault-tolerant software and more general fault-tolerant control systems.

Appendix A:
Sample special Specification

This appendix contains an example of a formal specification extracted from the specifications of the SIFT executive software. The specification is written in a language called SPECIAL, a formally defined specification language. SPECIAL has been designed explicitly to permit the description of the results required from a computer program without constraining the programmer's decisions as to how to write the most efficient program.

The function that is specified here is the local executive's voter routine, described informally in Section IV-A. This function is called to obtain a value from one of the buffers used to communicate between tasks. The value required is requested over the bus system from every replication of this buffer, and a consensus value that masks any errors is formed and returned to the calling program. Errors are reported and provision is made for buses that do not obtain a value (due to a nonresponding bus or memory) and for the possibility that there is no consensus.

Notes following the specification are keyed to statements in the specification.

```
OVFUN read_buffer (buffer_name i; address k; value safe)
        [processor a; task t]
            → result r;                                              [1]

EXCEPTIONS                                                           [2]
        CARDINALITY(activated_buffers(a,i)) = 0;
        0 > k OR k >= buffer_size(i);

EFFECTS                                                              [3]
    EXISTS SET_OF response
            w = responses(a, activated_buffers(a,i), k):
        EXISTS SET_OF response
            z = {response b | b INSET w AND b.flag }:

        IF(EXISTS value v;                                           [4]
            SET_OF response x |
            x = {response c | c INSET (w DIFF z)
                    AND c.val = v }:
```

```
            FORALL value u;                                              [5]
                SET_OF response y |
                    y = {response d | d INSET (w DIFF x DIFF z)
                        AND d.val = u }:
                CARDINALITY (x) > CARDINALITY(y))

        THEN(EXISTS value v;                                             [6]
            SET_OF response x |
                x = {response c | c INSET (w DIFF z)
                    AND c.val = v } :

            FORALL value u;                                              [6]
                SET_OF response y |
                    y = {response d | d INSET (w DIFF x DIFF z)
                        AND d.val = u }:
                CARDINALITY(x) > CARDINALITY(y);
            EFFECTS_OF errors(a, w DIFF x);                              [7]
            r = v)
        ELSE(EFFECTS_OF errors(a, w);                                    [8]
            r = safe);
```

Notes

1) The function 'read_buffer' takes three arguments and returns a result. The buffer_name 'i' is the name of a logical buffer which may be replicated in several processors, while the address 'k' is the offset of the required word in the buffer and 'safe' is the value to be returned if no consensus can be obtained. The parameters 'a' and 't' need not be explicitly cited by the caller of this function but are deduced from the context.

2) Exception returns will be made if there are no active instances of the named buffer or if the offset is not within the buffer.

3) A response is obtained by interrogating a buffer in another processor. Each response is a record (also known as a "structure", containing a value field ("val") and flag field ("flag"), the latter set if no response was obtained from the bus or store. The set 'w' of responses is the set obtained from all of the activated buffers known to processor 'a'. The set 'z' is the subset of no-response responses.

4) First we must check that a plurality opinion exists. This section hypothesises that there exists a consensus value 'v' together with the subset of responses 'x' that returned that value.

5) Here we consider all other values and establish for each of them that fewer responses contained this other value than contained the proposed consensus value.

6) Having established that a consensus value exists, we may now validly construct it, repeating the criteria of stages [4] and [5]. It is important to note that these are not programs but logical criteria. The actual implementations would not repeat the program.

7) This section requires that any responses not in the set 'x' (the set 'x' is the set reporting the consensus value) should be reported as errors, and the result is the consensus value 'v'. The expression

EFFECTS_OF errors(a, w DIFF X)

indicates a state change in the module that contains the 0-function "errors". The specification indicates that an error report is loaded into a table associated with processor "a."

8) If there is no consensus value, as determined by stages [4] and [5], then all the responses must be reported as errors, and the safe value returned as the result.

Acknowledgment

The authors wish to acknowledge the help of other members of the Computer Science Laboratory who contributed to the development of SIFT. In particular, Dr. William H. Kautz helped in the formulation of the reliability model and with the diagnosis problem. Marshall Pease developed a proof showing that synchronization could not be achieved with three clocks. Lawrence Robinson indirectly aided the project by his creation of the hierarchical development methodology. We are indebted to numerous individuals of NASA-Langley Research Center: Nicholas D. Murray, the Project Monitor has provided early and continuing guidance and encouragement, Billy Dove has provided inspiration and support within the context of a long-range NASA program of technology development for reliable aircraft control, Earl Migneault first alerted us to problems with the "obvious" solutions to the clock synchronization problem, Sal Bavuso has continually reviewed our work on reliability modeling, and Brian Lupton and Larry Spencer have provided considerable valuable comments during the course of the work.

References

[1] N. D. Murray, A. L. Hopkins, and J. H. Wensley, "Highly reliable multiprocessors," AGARDograph No. 224, *Integrity in Electronic Flight Control Systems*, P. R. Kurzhals, Ed., Advisory Group for Aerospace Research and Development, Neuilly Sur Seine, France, pp. 17.1-17.16, Apr. 1977.

[2] J. H. Wensley, et al., "Architecture," vol. I of *Design of a Fault Tolerant Airborne Digital Computer*," SRI International Technical Report for NASA, CR-132252, SRI International, Menlo Park, CA. Oct. 1973.

[3] R. S. Ratner, et al., "Computational requirements and technology," vol. II of *Design of a Fault Tolerant Airborne Digital Computer*, SRI Technical Report for NASA, CR-132253, SRI International, Menlo Park, CA, Oct. 1973.

[4] J. H. Wensley, "SIFT software implemented fault tolerance," in *Proc. Fall Joint Computer Conf.*, AFIPS Press, Montvale, NJ. 1972, vol. 41, pp. 243-253.

[5] J. H. Wensley, M. W. Green, K. N. Levitt, and R. E. Shostak, "The design, analysis, and verification of the SIFT fault tolerant system," *Proc. 2nd Int. Conf. Software Engineering*, IEEE Catalog No. 76, ch 1125-4 C, IEEE Computer Society, Long Beach, CA, pp. 458-469, 1976.

[6] P. M. Melliar-Smith, "Permissible processor loadings for various

scheduling algorithms," Memorandum, SRI International, Menlo Park, CA. 1977.
[7] L. Robinson and O. Roubine, "SPECIAL—A specification and assertion language," Technical Report CSL-46, SRI International, Menlo Park, CA, Jan. 1977.
[8] B. Randell. "System structure for software fault tolerance," *IEEE Trans. Software Eng.*, vol. SE-1(2), pp. 220–232, June 1975.
[9] M. Pease, R. Shostak, and L. Lamport, "Reaching agreement in the presence of faults," manuscript in preparation.
[10] L. Robinson, K. N. Levitt, P. G. Neumann, and A. K. Saxena, "A formal methodology for the design of operating system software," in *Current Trends in Processing Methodology*, vol. 1, R. T. Yeh, Ed. Englewood Cliffs, New Jersey: Prentice-Hall. 1976.
[11] R. W. Floyd, "Assigning meanings to programs," *Mathematical Aspects of Computer Science*, vol. 19, J. T. Schwartz, Ed. Providence, RI: Amer. Mathematical Society, 1967, pp. 19–32.
[12] R. E. Shostak *et al.*, "Proving the reliability of a fault-tolerant computer system," *Proc. 14th IEEE Comput. Soc. Int. Conf.*, San Francisco, CA, 1977.

Fault-Tolerant Design of Local ESS Processors

W. N. TOY, SENIOR MEMBER, IEEE

Abstract—The stored program control of Bell System Electronic Switching Systems (ESS) has been under development since 1953. During this period, the No. 1 ESS, the No. 2 ESS, and the No. 3 ESS have been developed and used extensively by Bell System operating companies to provide commercial telephone service. These systems serve all types of telephone offices: The large-capacity No. 1 ESS serves metropolitan offices, the medium-capacity No. 2 ESS was designed for suburban offices, and the No. 3 ESS can be found in many small rural offices. The fault tolerant design of ESS processors provides the same highly dependable telephone service established by the previous electromechanical systems. Pertinent processor architecture features used to achieve ESS reliability objectives are discussed. A detailed discussion of the maintenance design of the 3A Processor is also included.

I. INTRODUCTION

NEXT TO COMPUTER systems used in space-borne vehicles and U.S. defense installations, no other application has a higher availability requirement than a Bell System Electronic Switching System (ESS). These systems have been designed to be out of service no more than few minutes per year. Furthermore, design objectives permit no more than 0.01 percent of the telephone calls to be processed incorrectly [1]. For example, when a fault occurs in a system, few calls in progress may be handled incorrectly during the recovery process.

At the core of every ESS is a single high-speed central processor [2]–[4]. To establish an ultrareliable switching environment, redundancy of system components and duplication of the processor itself has been the approach taken to compensate for potential machine faults. Without this redundancy, a single component failure in the processor might cause a complete failure of the entire system. With duplication, a standby processor takes over control and provides continuous telephone service.

When the system fails, the fault must be quickly detected and isolated. Meanwhile, a rapid recovery of the call processing functions (by the redundant component(s) and/or processor) is necessary to maintain the system's high availability. Next, the fault must be diagnosed and the defective unit repaired or replaced. The failure rate and repair time must be such that the probability is very small for a failure to occur in the duplicated unit before the first one is repaired.

II. ALLOCATION AND CAUSES OF SYSTEM DOWNTIME

The outage of a telephone (switching) office can be caused by facilities other than the processor. While a hardware fault in one of the peripheral units generally results in only a partial loss of service, it *is* possible for a fault in this area to bring the system down. By design, the processor has been allocated

Manuscript received March 20, 1978. This article will be included in the book *Microprogrammed and Reliable Design of Small Computers*, to be published by Prentice-Hall, in 1979.
The author is with the Processor Design Group, Bell Laboratories, Naperville, IL 60540.

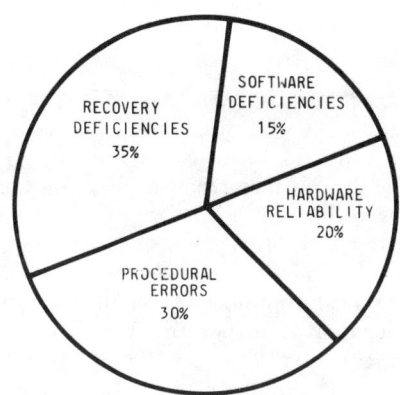

Fig. 1. System outage allocation.

two-thirds of the system downtime. The other one-third is allocated to the remaining equipment in the system.

Field experience indicates that system outages due to the processor may be assigned to one of four categories shown in Fig. 1 [5]. The percentages in this figure represent the fraction of total downtime attributable to each cause. The four categories are as follows.

A. Hardware Reliability

Before the accumulation of large amounts of field data, total system downtime was usually assigned to hardware. We now know that the situation is more complex. Processor hardware actually accounts for only 20 percent of the downtime. With growing use of stored program control, it has become increasingly important to make such systems more reliable. Redundancy is designed into all subsystems so that the system can go down *only* when hardware failures occur simultaneously in duplicated units. However, the data now show that good diagnostic and trouble location programs are very critical parts of the total system reliability performance.

B. Software Deficiencies

Software deficiencies include all software errors that cause memory mutilation, and program loops that can only be cleared by major reinitialization. Software faults are the result of improper translation or implementation of the original algorithm. In some cases, the original algorithm may have been incorrectly specified. Program changes and feature additions are continuously incorporated into working offices. Software accounts for 15 percent of the downtime.

C. Recovery Deficiencies

Recovery is the system's most complex and difficult function. Deficiencies may include the shortcomings of either hardware or software design to detect faults when they occur. When faults go undetected, the system remains extensively impaired until the trouble is recognized. Another kind of recovery problem can occur if the system is unable to properly isolate a faulty subsystem and configure a working system around it.

The many possible system states which may arise under trouble conditions make recovery a complicated process. Besides those already mentioned, unforeseen difficulties may be encountered in the field, and lead to inadequate recovery. Because of the large number of variables involved and because the recovery function is so strongly related to all other components of maintenance, recovery deficiencies account for 35 percent of the downtime.

D. Procedural Errors

Human error on the part of maintenance personnel or office administrators can also cause the system to go down. For example, someone in maintenance may mistakenly pull a circuit pack from the on-line processor while repairing a defective standby processor. Inadequate and incorrect documentation (e.g., users' manuals) may also be classified as human error. Obviously, the number of manual operations must be reduced if procedural errors are to be minimized. Procedural errors account for about 30 percent of the downtime.

The shortcomings and deficiencies of current systems are being continually corrected to improve system reliability.

III. Duplex Architecture

When a fault occurs in a nonredundant single processor, the system will remain down until the processor is repaired. In order to meet the ESS reliability requirement, *redundancy* is included in the system design; continuous and correct operation is maintained by duplicating all functional units within the processor. If one of the units fails, the duplicated unit is switched in, maintaining continuous operation. Meanwhile, the defective unit is repaired. Should a fault occur in the duplicated unit during the repair interval, the system will, of course, go down. If the repair interval is relatively short, the probability of simultaneous faults occurring in two identical units is quite small. This technique of redundancy has been used throughout each ESS.

The first-generation ESS processor structure consists of two store communities: Program store (PS) and call store (CS). The program store is a read-only memory (ROM) containing the call processing, maintenance, and administration programs; it also contains long-term translation and system parameters. The call store contains the transient data related to telephone calls in progress. The memory is electrically alterable to allow its data to be changed frequently. In one particular arrangement, shown in Fig. 2, the complete processor is treated as a single functional block and is duplicated. This type of single-unit duplex system has two possible configurations: Either Processor 0 or Processor 1 can be assigned as the on-line working system, while the other unit serves as standby backup. The mean-time-to-failure (MTTF), a measure of reliability, is given by the following expression [6]:

$$MTFF = \mu/2\lambda^2$$

where μ is the repair rate (reciprocal of the repair time), and λ is the failure rate.

The failure rate (λ) of one unit is the summation of failure rates of all components within the unit. For medium and small ESS processors, Fig. 2 shows a system structure contain-

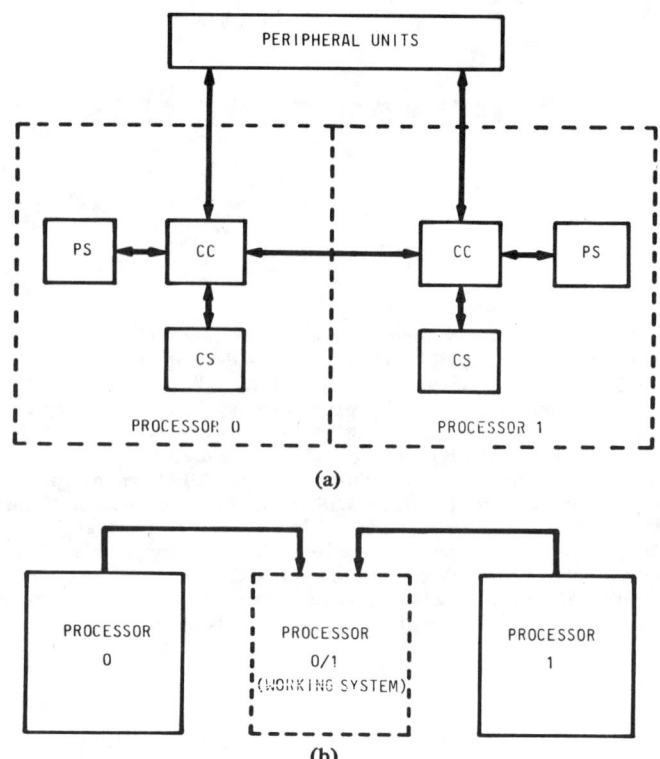

Fig. 2. Single-Unit duplex configuration. (a) Processor structure. (b) Two possible configurations.

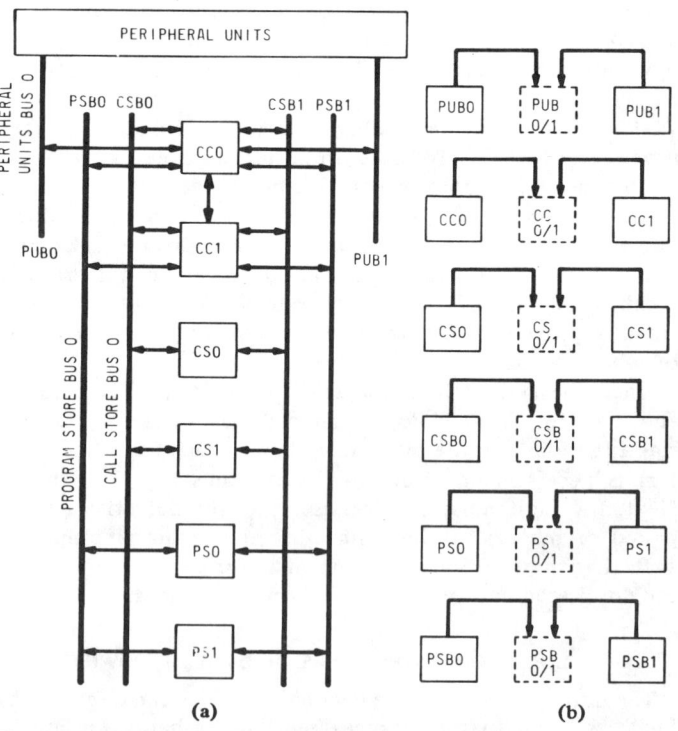

Fig. 3. Multiunit duplex configuration. (a) Processor structure. (b) 64 possible configurations.

ing several functional units which are treated as a single entity, with λ still sufficiently small to meet the reliability requirement. The single-unit duplex configuration has the merit of being very simple in terms of the number of switching blocks in the system. This configuration simplifies not only the recovery program but also the hardware interconnection. It does this by eliminating the additional access required to make each duplicated block capable of switching independently into the on-line system configuration.

In the large No. 1 ESS, which contains many components, the MTTF becomes too low to meet the reliability requirement. In order to increase the value of the MTTF, either the number of components (failure rate) or the repair time must be reduced. Alternatively, the single-unit duplex configuration can be partitioned into a multiunit duplex configuration as shown in Fig. 3. In this arrangement, each subunit contains a smaller number of components and is able to be switched into a working system. The system will fail only if a fault occurs in the redundant subunit while the original is being repaired. Since each subunit contains fewer components, the probability of two simultaneous faults occurring in a duplicated pair of subunits is reduced. The MTTF of the multiunit duplex configuration can be computed by taking into consideration the conditional probability of a subunit failing during the repair time of the original subunit.

An example of a multiunit duplex configuration is shown in Fig. 3. A working system is configured with a fault-free CCx-CSx-CSBx-PSx-PSBx-PUBx arrangement, where x is either Subunit 0 or Subunit 1. This means there are 2^6, or 64, possible combinations of system configurations. The MTTF is given by the following expression:

$$\text{MTTF} = \frac{r\mu}{2\lambda^2} \quad (1)$$

where

$$r = \frac{1}{(\lambda_{CC}/\lambda)^2 + (\lambda_{CS}/\lambda)^2 + (\lambda_{CSB}/\lambda)^2 + (\lambda_{PS}/\lambda)^2 + (\lambda_{PSB}/\lambda)^2 + (\lambda_{PUB}/\lambda)^2}. \quad (2)$$

The factor r is at a maximum when the failure rate (λ_i) for each subunit is the same. In this case

$$\lambda_{CC} = \lambda_{CS} = \lambda_{CSB} = \lambda_{PS} = \lambda_{PSB} = \lambda_{PUB} = \lambda_i \quad (3)$$

or

$$\lambda_i = \frac{\lambda}{s} \quad (4)$$

where

s = number of subunits in (2), $s = 6$, and $r = s$.

At best, the MTTF is improved by a factor corresponding to the number of partitioned subunits. This improvement is not fully realized since equipment must be added to provide additional access and to select subunits. The partitioning of the subsystem into subunits as shown in Fig. 3 results in subunits of different sizes. Again, the failure rate for each individual subunit will not be the same; hence, the r-factor will be smaller than 6. Because of the relatively large number of components used in implementing the No. 1 ESS, the system is arranged in the multiunit duplex configuration in order to meet the reliability requirement.

Reliability calculation is a process of predicting, from available failure rate data, the achieveable reliability of a system and the probability of meeting the reliability objectives for ESS applications. These calculations are most useful and beneficial during the early stages of design in order to assess various types of redundancy and determine the system's organization. In the small and medium ESS's, the calculations have supported the use of single-unit duplex structures. For large ESS's, it was necessary to partition the system into a multiunit duplex configuration.

IV. Fault Simulation Techniques

One of the more difficult tasks of maintenance design is fault diagnosis. Its effectiveness in diagnostic resolution can be determined by simulation of the system's behavior in the presence of a specific fault. By means of simulation, design deficiencies can be identified and corrected prior to any system being deployed in the field. It is necessary to evaluate the system's ability to detect faults, to recover automatically back into a working system, and to provide diagnostic information where the fault is within a few replaceable circuit packs. Fault simulation, therefore, is an important aspect of maintenance design.

There are essentially two techniques used for simulating faults of digital systems: physical simulation or digital simulation. Physical simulation is a process of inserting faults into a physical working model. This method produces more realistic behavior under fault conditions. A wider class of faults can be applied to the system, such as a blown fuse or shorted backplane interconnection. However, fault simulation cannot begin until the design has been completed and the equipment is fully operational. Also, it is not possible to insert faults interior to an integrated circuit.

Digital fault simulation is a means of predicting the behavior under failure of a processor modeled in a computer program. The computer used to execute the program (the host) is generally different from the processor being simulated (the object). Digital fault simulation gives a high degree of automation and excellent access to interior points of logic to monitor the signal flow. It allows diagnostic test development and evaluation to proceed well in advance of unit fabrication. The cost of computer simulation can be quite high for a large, complex system.

The physical fault simulation method was first employed to generate diagnostic data for the Morris Electronic Switching System [7]. Over 50 000 known faults were purposely introduced into the central control to be diagnosed by its diagnostic program. Test results associated with each fault were recorded. They were then sorted and printed in dictionary format to formulate a trouble locating manual (TLM). Under trouble conditions, by consulting the TLM, it was possible to determine a set of several suspected circuit packs which might contain the defective component. Using the dictionary technique at the Morris system, the average repair time was kept low and maintenance was made much easier.

The experience gained in the physical fault simulation was applied and extended in the No. 1 ESS development [1]. Each plug-in circuit pack was replaced by a fault simulator which introduced every possible type of single fault on the replaced package one at a time and then recorded the system reaction on magnetic tape. This was done for all circuit packs in the system. In addition to diagnostic data for dictionaries, additional data were collected to determine the adequacy of

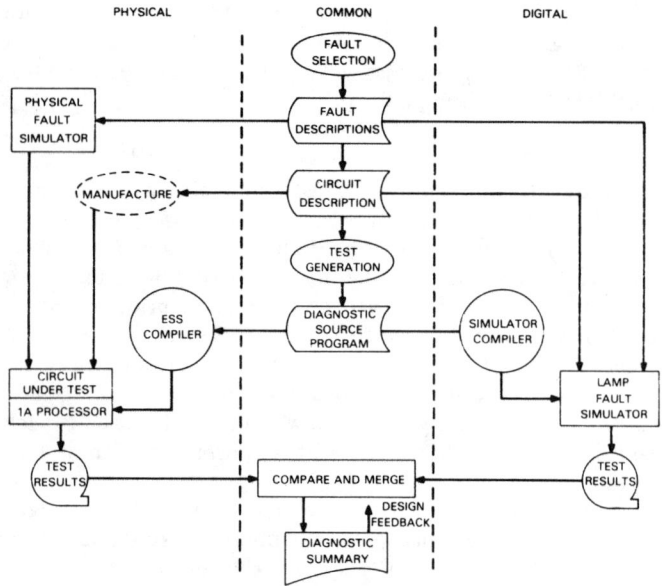

Fig. 4. Complementary fault-simulation system.

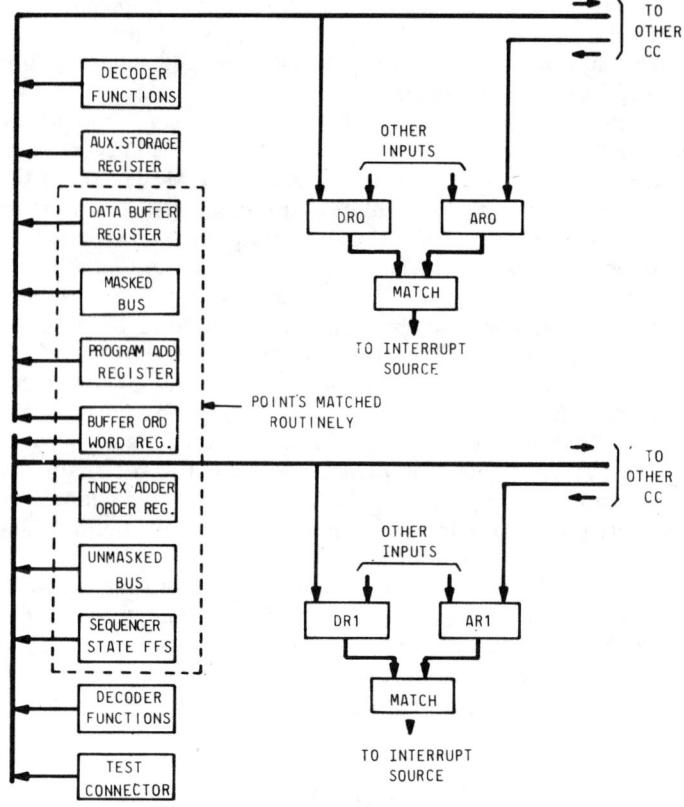

Fig. 5. No. 1 CC match access.

hardware and software in fault detection and system recovery. Deficiencies were corrected to improve the overall maintenance of the system.

A digital logic simulator called LAMP [9] was developed for the No. 1A ESS development. It played an important role in the hardware and diagnostic development of the No. 1A Processor. The simulator is capable of simulating subsystem with as many as 65 000 logic gates. All classical faults for standard logic gates are simulatable with logic nodes stuck at "0" or stuck at "1." Before physical units are available, digital simulation can be very effective in verifying the design, evaluating diagnostic access, and developing diagnostic tests. Physical fault simulation has been demonstrated in the No. 1 ESS to give a very realistic behavior under fault conditions. The integration of both techniques was employed in the development of the No. 1A Processor to take advantages of both processes. The use of complementary simulation allows faults to be simulated physically (in the system laboratory) and logically (on a computer). Most of the deficiencies of one simulation process are compensated for by the other. The complementary method provided both a convenient method for validating the results and more extensive fault simulation data than would have been normally if either process were used individually. Fig. 4 shows the complementary process of fault simulation used in the No. 1A Processor development [10], [11]. Maximum diagnostic performance was achieved from an integrated use of both simulation methods.

V. FIRST GENERATION ESS PROCESSORS

The world's first ESS provided commercial telephone service at Morris, IL, in 1959 for about a year on a field trial basis [8]. The system demonstrated the use of stored program control and the basic maintenance philosophy of providing continuous and reliable telephone service. The trial established valuable guides for designing a successor, the No. 1 ESS.

A. No. 1 ESS Processor

The No. 1 ESS was designed to serve large metropolitan telephone offices, ranging from several thousand to 65 000 lines [12]. As in most large switching systems, the processor represents only a small percentage of the total system cost. Therefore, performance and reliability were of primary importance in the design of the No. 1 Processor; cost was secondary. In order to meet the reliability standards established by electromechanical systems, all units essential to proper operation of the office are duplicated (see Fig. 3). The multiunit duplex configuration was necessary to increase the MTTF of the processor because of the large number of components in each of the functional blocks.

Even with duplication, troubles must be found and corrected quickly to minimize exposure to system failure due to multiple troubles. All units are monitored continually so that troubles in the standby units are found just as quickly as those in the on-line units. This is accomplished by running the on-line and standby units in the synchronous and match mode of operation [1]. Synchronization requires that clock timing signals be in close tolerance so that every operation in both halves is performed in step, and key outputs are compared for error detection. The synchronization of duplicated units is accomplished by having the on-line oscillator output drive both clock circuits. There are two match circuits in each central control (CC). Each matcher compares 24 bits within one machine cycle of 5.5 μs. Fig. 5 shows that each matcher has access to six sets of internal nodes (24 bits per node). In the routine match mode, the points matched in each cycle are dependent upon the instruction being executed. The selected match points are those most pertinent to the data processing steps occurring during a given machine cycle. The two matchers in each CC compare the same sets of selected test points. The capability of each CC to compare a number of internal nodes provides a highly effective means of detecting hardware errors.

If a mismatch occurs, an interrupt is generated, which causes the fault-recognition program to run. The basic function of this program is to determine which half of the system is faulty. The suspected unit is removed from service and the appropriate diagnostic program is run to pinpoint the defective circuit pack.

The No. 1 ESS was designed during the discrete component era (early 1960's) using individual components to implement logic gates [13]. The CC contains approximately 12 000 logic gates. Although this number appears small when compared to large-scale integration (LSI) technology, the No. 1 Processor was a physically large machine for its time.

The match circuits capable of comparing internal nodes are the primary tools incorporated into the CC for diagnosing as well as detecting troubles. Specified information can be sampled by the matchers and retained in the match registers for examination. This mode of operation obtains critical data during the execution of diagnostic programs.

The early program store used permanent magnet twister (PMT) modules as basic storage elements [14]. They are a form of ROM in which system failures cannot alter the information content. Experience gained from the Morris field test system, which used the less reliable flying spot store, indicated that Hamming correction code was highly effective in providing continuous operation. At the time of development, it was felt that PMT modules might not be reliable enough. Consequently, the program store word included additional check bits for single-bit error correction (Hamming code). In addition, an overall parity check bit which covers both the data and their address is included in the word. The word size consists of 37 bits of information and seven check bits. When an error is corrected during normal operation, it is logged in an error counter. The maintenance program has access to this counter. Also, detection of a single error in the address or a double error in the word will cause an automatic retry.

The call store is the temporary read and write memory for storing transient data associated with call processing. Ferrite sheet memory modules are the basic storage elements used in implementing the call store in the No. 1 ESS [15]. The call store used in most No. 1 offices is smaller than the program store. (At the time of design, the cost per bit of call store was considerably higher than that of program store.) Also, ferrite sheet memory modules were considered to be very reliable devices. Consequently, single-bit error detection rather than Hamming correction code was provided in the call store.

There are two parity check bits: one over both the address and data, and the other over the address only. Again, as in the program store, automatic retry is performed whenever an error is detected, and the event is logged in an error counter for diagnostic use.

Troubles are normally detected by fault-detection circuits, and error-free system operation is recovered by fault recognition programs [1]. This requires the on-line processor to be capable of making a proper decision. If this is not possible, an emergency action timer will "time out" and activate special circuits to establish various combinations of subsystems into a system configuration. A special program which is used to determine whether or not the assembled processor is sane takes the processor through a series of tests arranged in a maze. Only one correct path through the maze exists. If the processor passes through successfully, the timer will be reset, and recovery is successful. If recovery is unsuccessful, the timer will time out again, and the rearrangement of subsystems will be tried one at a time (e.g., combinations of CC, program store, and program store bus systems). For each selected combination, the special sanity program is started and the sanity timer is activated. This procedure is repeated until a working configuration is found. The sanity program and sanity timer determine if the on-line CC is functioning properly. The active CC includes the program store and the program store bus.

B. Operational Results of No. 1 ESS

The No. 1 ESS has been in commercial operation since 1965. Over 1000 systems are providing telephone service to more than 15 million subscribers. The performance of the No. 1 ESS has continually improved over a decade of continued effort to improve all phases of software and hardware.

Fig. 6 shows the result of field data accumulated over many machine operating hours. This curve was derived from data in a paper [16] presented at the 1974 International Switching Symposium in Munich, Germany, and data supplied by W. C. Jones of Bell Laboratories.

When the No. 1 ESS were first cut into commercial service, many outages occurred because of software and hardware inadequacies that could only be weeded out with field experience. The inexperience of maintenance personnel also contributed heavily towards system outages. Most hardware and software bugs were corrected during the early years of operation. However, deficiencies still exist, and designs are continually upgraded in working systems. Continual improvements include better diagnostic access, more complete fault recognition and isolation programs, and more effective system recovery.

Improved diagnostic capability reduces repair time and human errors by decreasing the amount of human interaction required by the machine. Better maintenance procedures and more experienced craftpersonnel also contribute to improved system performance. The curve in Fig. 6 shows that the outage rate improved as machine design and operating personnel matured.

C. No. 2 ESS Processor

The No. 2 ESS was developed during the mid-1960's [17]. This system was designed for medium-size offices ranging from 1 000 to 10 000 lines. The processor's design was derived from experience with the common stored program control of a private branch exchange (PBX), the No. 101 ESS [18]. Since the capacity requirement of the No. 2 ESS was to be less than that of the No. 1 ESS, cost became one of the more important design considerations. (Reliability is equally important in all systems.) The No. 2 ESS contains much less hardware than the No. 1 ESS. Understandably, its component failure rate is also substantially less. Its CC contains approximately 5000 gates (discrete components). To reduce cost and increase reliability, resistor-transistor logic (RTL) gates were chosen for the No. 2's processor since resistors are less expensive and more reliable than diodes [the No. 1 Processor used diode-transistor logic (DTL)].

Because the No 2's CC, program store, and call store are smaller, they are grouped together as a single switchable block in the single-unit duplex configuration shown in Fig. 2. Calculations indicate that its MTTF is approximately the same

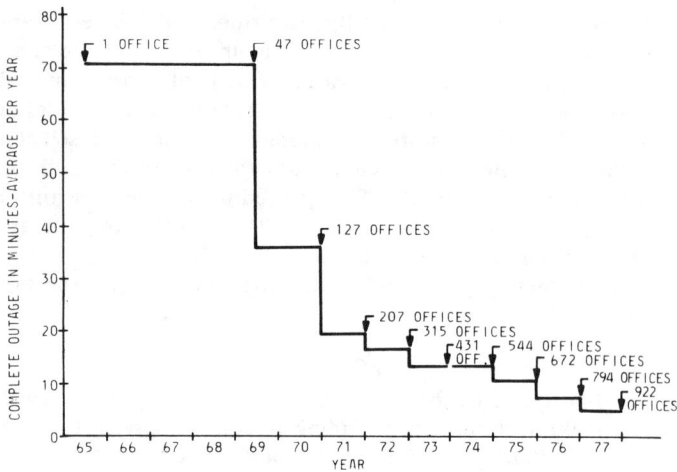

Fig. 6. No. 1 ESS Service performance.

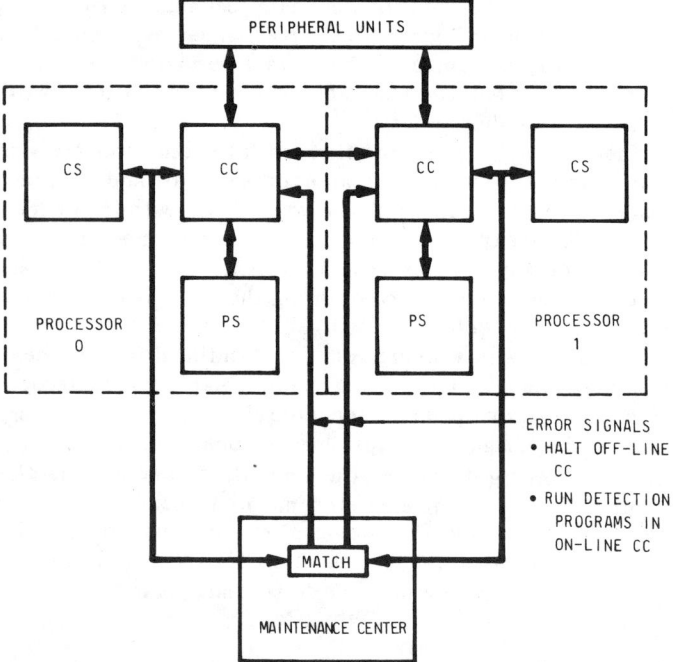

Fig. 7. No. 2 CC match access.

as the No. 1 multiunit duplex structure, with each of the functional blocks and associated store buses grouped together as a switchable block. The use of only two system configurations reduces considerably the amount of hardware needed to provide gating paths and control for each functional unit. Moreover, the recovery program is simplified, and the reliability of the system is improved.

The No. 2 Processor runs in the synchronous and match mode of operation [19]. The on-line oscillator output drives both clock circuits in order to keep the timing synchronized. The match operation is not as extensive as it is in the No. 1 ESS. For simplicity, there is only one matcher in the No. 2 ESS; it is located in the nonduplicated maintenance center (see Fig. 7). The matcher always compares the call store input registers in the two CC's when call store operations are performed synchronously. A fault in almost any part of either CC quickly results in a call store input register mismatch. This occurs because almost all data manipulation performed in both the program control and the input–output (I/O) control in-

volves processed data returning to the call store. The call store input is the central point whereby data eventually funnel through to the call store. By matching the call store inputs, an effective check of the system equipment is provided. Compared to the more complex matching of the No. 1 Processor, error detection in the No. 2 Processor may not be as instantaneous since only one crucial node in the processor is matched. Certain faults in the No. 2 Processor will go undetected until the errors propagate into the call store. This interval is probably no more than tens or hundreds of microseconds. During such a short interval, the fault would affect only a single call.

The No. 2 ESS matcher is not used as a diagnostic tool as is the matcher in the No. 1 Processor. Therefore, additional detection hardware is designed into the No. 2 Processor to help diagnose as well as detect faults.

When a mismatch occurs, the detection program is run in the on-line CC to determine if it contains the fault. This is done while the standby processor is disabled. If a solid fault in the on-line processor is detected by the mismatch detection program, the control is automatically passed to the standby processor, causing it to become the on-line processor. The faulty processor is disabled and diagnostic tests are called in to pinpoint the defective circuit pack.

The program store also uses PMT modules as basic storage elements, with a word size of 22 bits, half the width of the No. 1's word size. Experience gained in the design and operation of the No. 101 ESS (PBX) showed that PMT stores were very reliable. The additional protection provided in the No. 1 Processor against memory faults by error correction was not considered to be as essential in the No. 2 Processor. This and the need to keep the cost down led to the choice of error detection *only* instead of the more sophisticated Hamming correction code.

Error detection works as follows: one of the 22 bits in a word is allocated as a parity check bit. The program store contains both program and translation data. Additional protection is provided by using odd parity for program words and even parity for translation data. This detects the possibility of accessing the translation data area of memory as instruction words. For example, a software error may cause the program to branch into the data section of the memory and execute the data words as instruction words. The parity check would detect this problem immediately. The program store includes checking circuits to detect multiple-word access. Under program control, the sense amplifier threshold voltage can be varied in two discrete amounts from its nominal value to obtain a measure of the operating margin. The use of parity check was the proper choice for the No. 2 ESS in view of the high reliability of these memory devices.

The No. 2 Processor call store uses the same ferrite sheet memory modules as the No. 1 Processor. However, the No. 2's data word is 16 bits wide instead of 24. Fault detection depends heavily upon the matching of the call store inputs when the duplex processors run in the synchronous mode. Within the call store circuit, the access circuitry is checked to see that access currents flow in the right direction at the correct time and that only two access switches are selected in any store operation. This ensures that only one word is accessed in the memory operation. Similarly, threshold voltages of the sense amplifiers may be varied under program control to evaluate the operating margins of the store. No parity check bit is provided in the call store.

Each processor contains a program timer which is designed to back up other detection methods. Normally, the on-line processor clears the timer in both processors at prescribed intervals if the basic call processing program cycles correctly. If, however, a hardware or software trouble condition exists (e.g., a program may go astray or a long program loop may prevent the timer from being cleared), the timer will time out and automatically produce a switch. The new on-line processor is automatically forced to run an initialization restart program which attempts to establish a working system. System recovery is simplified by using two possible system configurations rather than the multiunit duplex system.

VI. Second Generation of ESS Processors

The advent of silicon integrated circuits (IC's) in the mid-1960's provided the technological climate for dramatic miniaturization, improved performance, and cost-reduced hardware. "1A technology" refers to the standard set of (IC) devices, apparatus, and design tools that were used to design the No. 1A Processor and the No. 3A Processor [20]. The choice of technology and the scale of integration level was dictated by the technological advances made between 1968 and 1970. Small-scale integration (SSI), made possible by bipolar technology, was capable of high yield production. Because of the processor cycle time, high-speed logic gates with propagation delays from 5 to 10 ns were designed and developed concurrent with the No. 1A Processor.

A. No. 1A Processor

The No. 1A Processor, successor to the No. 1 Processor, was designed primarily for the control of large local and toll ESS with high processing capabilities (the No. 1A ESS and No. 4 ESS, respectively) [21]. An important objective in developing the No. 1A ESS was to maintain commonality with the No. 1 ESS. High capacity was achieved by implementing the new No. 1A integrated technology and a newly designed system structure. These changes made possible an instruction execution rate that is four to eight times faster than the No. 1 Processor. Compatibility with the No. 1 ESS also allows the No. 1A Processor to be retrofitted into an in-service No. 1 ESS, replacing the No. 1 Processor when additional capacity is needed. The first 1A Processor was put into service in January 1976, as control for a No. 4 ESS in Chicago. Less than one year later, the first No. 1A ESS was put into commercial operation. By 1980, several hundred will be in service [22].

The No. 1A Processor architecture is similar to its predecessor in that all of its subsystems have redundant units and are connected to the basic CC via redundant bus systems [10]. One of the No. 1A Processor's major architectural differences is its program store [23]. It has a writable random-access memory (RAM) instead of PMT ROM. By combining disk memory and RAM, the system has the same amount of memory as a system with PMT, but at a lower cost. Backup copy of program and translation data is kept on disk. Other programs (e.g., diagnostics) are brought to RAM as needed; the same RAM spare is shared among different programs. More important is the system's ability to change the content of the store quickly and automatically. This simplifies considerably the administration and updating of program and translation information in working offices.

The additional disk (file store) subsystem adds flexibility to the No. 1A Processor [23], but it also increases the complex-

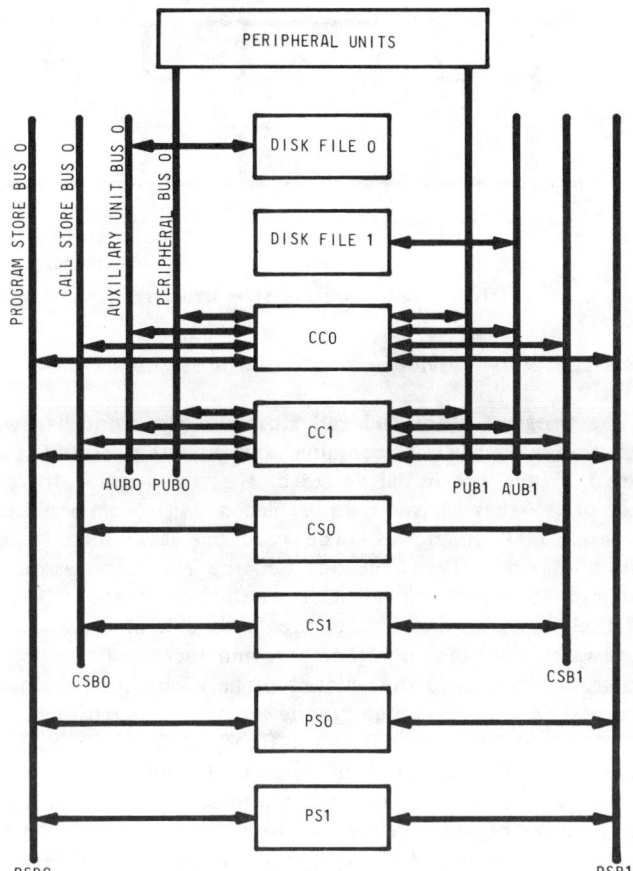

Fig. 8. No. 1A Processor configuration.

ity of system recovery. Fig. 8 shows the multi-unit duplex 1A Processor. This configuration is similar to the No. 1 Processor arrangement (see Fig. 3) with a duplicated file store included. The file store communicates with the program store or call store via the CC and the auxiliary unit bus. This allows direct memory access between the file store and the program store or the call store. The disk file and the auxiliary unit bus are grouped together as a switchable entity.

Error detection is achieved by the duplicated and matched synchronous mode of operation, as in the No. 1 Processor. Both CC's operate in step and perform identical operations. The matching is done more extensively in the 1A to obtain as complete a check as possible. There are two match circuits in each processor. Each matcher has the ability to compare 24 internal bits to 24 bits in its mate once every machine cycle. (A machine cycle is 700 ns.) Any one of 16 different 24-bit internal nodes can be selected for comparison. The choice is determined by the type of instruction being executed. Rather than compare the same nodes in both CC's, the on-line and the standby CC's are arranged to match different sets of data. Four distinct internal groups are matched in the same machine cycle. This ensures the correct execution of any instruction.

The No. 1A Processor design is an improvement of the No. 1 Processor design. The No. 1A Processor incorporates much more checking hardware throughout various functional units in addition to matching hardware. Checking hardware speeds up fault detection and also aids the fault recovery process by providing indications that help isolate the faulty unit. The matching is used in various modes for maintenance purposes.

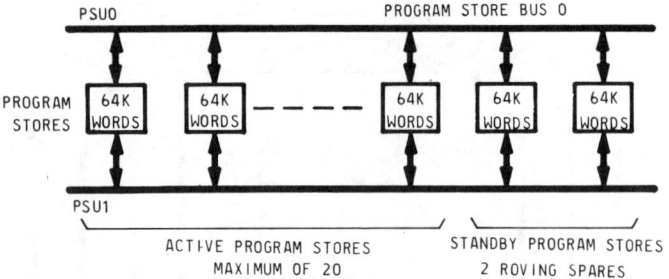

Fig. 9. No. 1A program store structure.

This capability provides powerful diagnostic tools in isolating faults.

The program store and call store use the same hardware technology. The CC contains approximately 50 000 logic gates. While the initial design of the stores called for core memories, they have been replaced with semiconductor dynamic MOS memories. The word size is 26 bits: 24 data bits and two parity check bits. In the No. 1 Processor, the program store and the call store are fully duplicated. Because of their size, duplication requires a considerable amount of hardware, resulting in higher cost and increased component failures. To reduce the amount of hardware in the No. 1A Processor's store community, the memory is partitioned into blocks of 64K words, as shown in Fig. 9. Two additional store blocks are provided as roving spares. If one of the program stores fails, a roving program store spare is substituted and a copy of the program in the file store is transferred to the program store replacement. This type of redundancy has been made possible by the ability to regenerate data stored in a failing unit. Since a program store can be reloaded from the file store in less than a second, a roving spare redundancy plan is sufficient to meet the reliability requirement. As a result, Hamming correction code was not adopted in the No. 1A program store. However, it is essential that an error be detected quickly. Two parity check bits are generated over a partially overlapped, interleaved set of data bits and address. This overlapping is arranged to cope with particular memory circuit failures which may affect more than one bit of a word.

The 1A call stores contain both translation data backed up on the file stores and call-related transient data which are difficult to regenerate. The roving spare concept is expanded for the call stores to include sufficient spares to provide full duplication of transient data. If a fault occurs in a store that contains translation data, one of the duplicated stores containing transient call data is preempted and loaded with the necessary translation data from the duplicated copy in the file store. A parity check is done in the same manner as in the program store, using two check bits.

The combination of writable program store and file store provides a very effective and flexible system architecture for administrating and implementing a wide variety of features which are difficult to obtain in the No. 1 ESS. However, this architecture also complicates the process of fault recognition and recovery. Reconfiguration into a working system under trouble conditions is an extensive task, depending on the severity of the fault. (For example, it is possible for the processor to lose its sanity or ability to make proper decisions.) An autonomous hardware processor configuration (PC) circuit is provided in each CC to assist in assembling a working system. The PC circuit consists of various timers which ensure that the operational, fault recovery, and configuration programs are successfully executed. If these programs *are not* executed, the PC circuit controls the CC-to-program memory configuration, reloading program memory from file store when required, and isolating various subsystems from the CC until a working system is obtained.

B. No. 3A Processor

The No. 3A Processor was designed to control the small No. 3 ESS [24], which can handle from 500 to 5000 lines. One of the major concerns in the design of this ESS was the cost of its processor. The low cost and high speed of integrated logic circuitry made it possible to design a cost-effective processor that performed better than its discrete component predecessor, the No. 2 Processor. The No. 3A project was started in early 1971. The first system cut into commercial service in late 1975.

Because the number of components in the No. 3A Processor is considerably less than in the No. 1A Processor, all subsystems are fully duplicated, including the main store. The CC, the store bus, and the store are treated as a single switchable entity rather than individual switchable units as in the No. 1A Processor. The system structure is similar to the No. 2 ESS. Experience gained in the design and operation of the No. 2 provided valuable input for the No. 3 Processor design.

The 3A's design makes one major departure from previous ESS processor designs: it operates in the nonmatched mode of duplex operation. The primary purpose of matching is to detect errors. A mismatch, however, does not indicate *where* (which one of the processors) the fault has occured. A diagnostic fault-location program must be run to localize the trouble so that the defective unit can be taken off-line. For this reason, the No. 3A Processor was designed to be self-checking, with detection circuitry incorporated as an integral part of the processor. Faults occurring during normal operation are discovered quickly by detecting hardware. This eliminates the need to run the standby system in the synchronous and match mode of operation, or the need to run the fault recognition program to identify the defective unit when a mismatch occurs.

The synchronous and match mode arrangment of the No. 1 Processor and the No. 2 ESS provides excellent detection and coverage of faults. However, there are many instances (e.g., periodic diagnostics, administration changes, recent change updates, etc.) when the system is not run in the normal match mode. Consequently, during these periods, the system is vulnerable to faults which may go undetected. The rapid advances in integrated circuit technology make possible the implementation of self-checking circuits in a cost-effective manner. This eliminates the need for the synchronous and match mode of operation. Self-checking design is covered in more detail in the next section.

Another new feature in ESS processor design is the application of microprogram technique in the No. 3A [25]. This technique provides a regular procedure of implementing the control logic. Standard error detection is made part of the hardware to achieve a high degree of checkability. Sequential logic, which is difficult to check, is easily implemented as a sequence of microprogram steps. Microprogramming offers many attractive features: it is simple, flexible, easy to maintain, and easy to expand.

The No. 3A Processor paralleled the design of the No. 1A Processor in its use of an electrically alterable (writable) memory. However, great strides in semiconductor memory technology after the No. 1A became operational permitted the use of semiconductor memory in the 3A rather than core memory.

The 3A's call store and program store are consolidated into a single store system. This reduces cost by eliminating buses, drivers, registers, and controls. A single store system no longer allows concurrent access of call store and program store. However, this disadvantage is more than compensated for by the much faster semiconductor memory. Its access time is 1 μs (the earlier PMT stores had an access time of 6 μs).

Normal operation requires the on-line processor to run and process calls while the standby processor is in the halt state, with its memory updated for each write operation. For the read operation, only the on-line memory is read, *except* when a parity error occurs during a memory read. This results in a microprogram interrupt, which reads the word from the standby store in an attempt to bypass the error.

As discussed previously, the No. 2 Processor (first generation) is used in the No. 2 ESS for medium-size offices. It covers approximately 4000 to 12 000 lines, with a call handling capability of 19 000 busy-hour calls. (The number of calls is related to the calling rate of lines during the busy hour.) The microprogram technique used in the No. 3A Processor design allows the No. 2 Processor's instruction set to be emulated. This enables programs written in the No. 2 assembly language to be directly portable to the No. 3A Processor. The ability to preserve the call processing programs permits the No. 2 ESS to be updated with the No. 3A Processor without having to undergo a complete, new program development.

The combination of the No. 3A Processor and the peripheral equipment of the No. 2 ESS is designated as the No. 2B ESS. It is capable of handling 38 000 busy-hour calls, twice the capability of the No. 2 ESS [26]. The No. 2B ESS can be expanded to cover about 20 000 lines. Furthermore, when an existing No. 2 ESS system in the field exceeds its real-time capacity, the No. 2 Processor can be taken out and replaced with the No. 3A Processor. The retrofit operation has been carried out successfully in working offices without disturbing telephone service.

VII. Maintenance Design of no. 3A Processor

The 3A Processor is the most recent Bell System ESS processor. Self-checking hardware has been integrated into the design to detect faults during normal system operation. This simplified fault recognition technique is required to identify a subsystem unit when it becomes defective. Reconfiguration into a working system is immediate, without extensive diagnostic programs to determine which subsystem unit contains the fault. The problem of synchronization, in a much shorter machine cycle (150 ns), is eliminated by not having to run both processors in step. The No. 3A Processor uses low-cost IC's to realize its highly reliable and flexible design.

A. General System Description

The general system block diagram of the No. 3A Processor is shown in Fig. 10. The CC, the main store, and the cartridge tape unit are duplicated for reliability. These units are grouped as a single switchable entity rather than individual switchable units. The quantity of equipment within the switchable block is small enough to meet the reliability requirement; therefore, the expense and complexity of providing

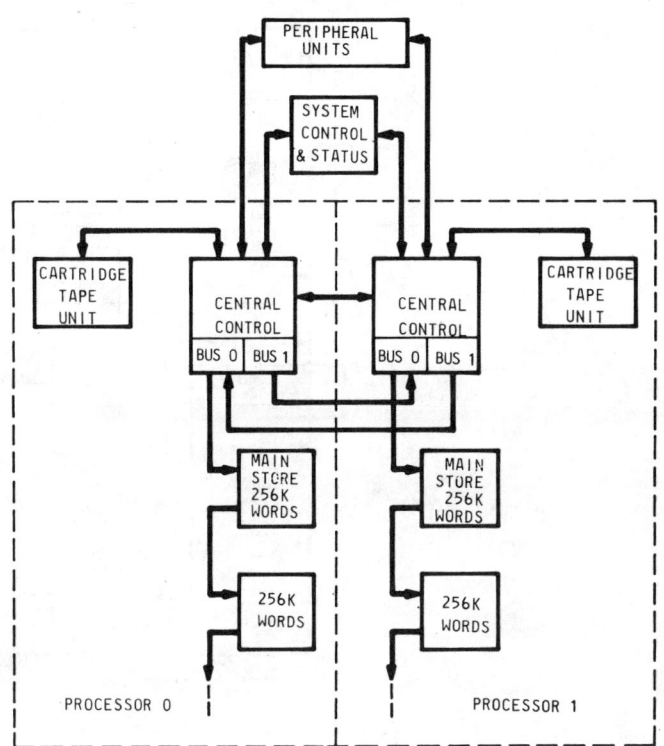

Fig. 10. No. 3A Processor organization.

communication paths and control for switchable units within the system are avoided. Each functional unit was designed to be as autonomous as possible, with a minimum number of output signal leads. This provides the flexibility necessary to expand the system and make changes easily.

As shown in Fig. 10, the standard program store and call store are combined as a single storage unit to reduce cost. Although the processors are not run in the synchronous and match mode of operation, both stores (on-line and standby) are kept up to date. This is achieved by having the on-line processor write into both stores simultaneously when call store data are written or changed. Because of the volatile nature of a writable memory, low-cost bulk storage backup (cartridge tape) is required to reload the program and translation data when the latter are lost due to a store failure. The pump-up mechanism or store loader uses the microprogram control in conjunction with an (I/O) serial channel to transfer data between the cartridge tape unit and the main store. Other deferrable, infrequently used programs (i.e., diagnostics or growth programs) are stored on tape and paged in as needed.

The system control and status panel, a nonduplicated block, provide a common point for the display of overall system status and alarms. Included in this unit is the emergency action circuitry which allows the maintenance personnel to initialize the system or force and lock the system into a fixed configuration. Communication with the processor takes place via the I/O serial channel.

B. General Processor Description

Fig. 11 shows a detailed block diagram of the CC. It is organized to process input data and handle call processing functions efficiently. The processor's design is based on the register type of architecture. Fast-access storage in the form of flip-flop registers provides short-term storage for information

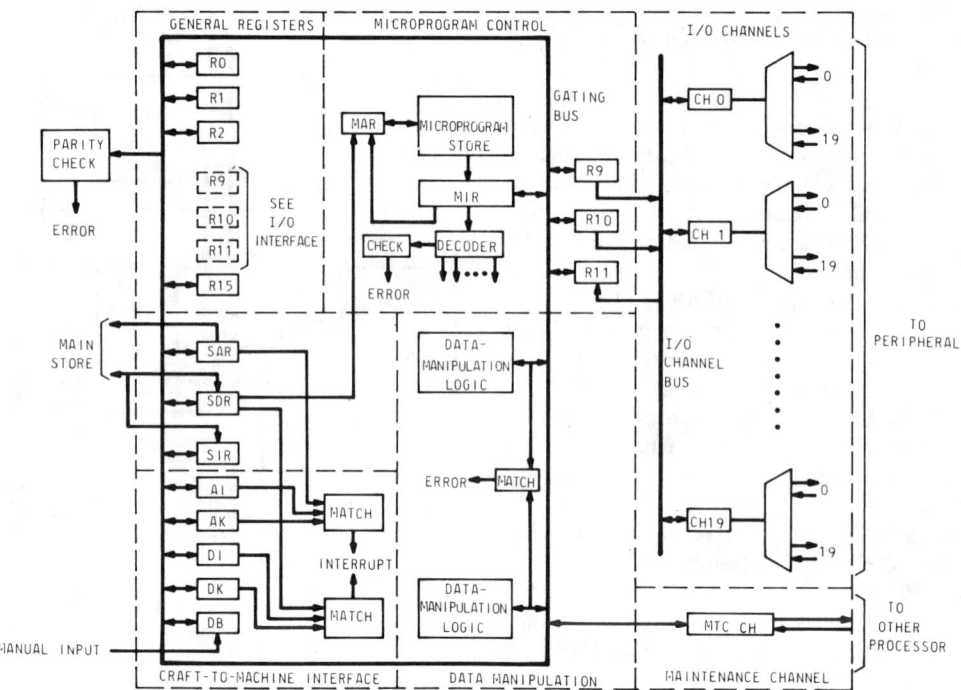

Fig. 11. No. 3A central control.

being used in current data processing operations. Sixteen general-purpose registers (GPR's) are provided as integral parts of the structure.

Microprogram control is the heart of the No. 3A Processor. It provides nearly all of the complex control and sequencing operations required for implementing the instruction set. Other complicated sequencing functions are also stored in the microprogram memory. Examples:

1) the bootstrap operation of reloading the program from the backup tape unit;
2) the initializing sequence to restart the system under trouble conditions;
3) the interrupt priority control and saving of essential registers;
4) the emergency action timer and processor switching operation;
5) the craft-to-machine functions.

The regular structure of the microprogram memory makes error detection easier. The microprogram method of implementation also offers flexibility in changing control functions.

The data manipulation instructions are designed specifically for implementing the call processing programs. These instructions are concerned with logical and bit manipulation rather than with arithmetical operations. However, a binary ADD is included in the instruction repertoire for adding two binary numbers and for indexing. This allows other arithmetical operations to be implemented conveniently by the software combination of addition and logical operations, or by a microprogram sequence if higher speed is essential. The data manipulation logic contains rotation, Boolean function of two variables, first zero detection, and fast binary ADD.

The remaining functional blocks in Fig. 11 deal with external interfaces. The 20 main I/O channels, each with 20 subchannels, allow the processor to control and access up to 400 peripheral units by means of 21-bit (16 data, 2 parity, and 3 start code bits) serial 6.67-MHz messages. The system is expandable in modules of one main channel (20 subchannels). The I/O structure allows up to 20 subchannels (one from each main channel) to be active simultaneously. In addition, the craft-to-machine interface, with displays and manual inputs, is integrated into the processor. This interface contains many of the manual functions which will assist in hardware and software debugging. The control logic associated with this part of the processor is incorporated as part of the microprogram control. Lastly, the maintenance channel enables the on-line processor to control and diagnose the standby processor. The use of a serial channel reduces the number of leads interconnecting the two processors and causes them to be "loosely coupled." This facilitates the split mode or stand-alone configuration for factory test or system test.

C. Detection Techniques

1) Control Circuitry: The major feature of the No. 3A Processor's control logic is that it is microprogrammed. Microprogramming provides a more regular approach than the conventional technique to the design of control logic. It also permits checking techniques to be applied more readily. The simplified microprogrammed structure of the system is shown in Fig. 12. Each microprogram store word contains the address of the next instruction and a FROM and TO control field which specifies the source and destination for a data transfer operation. The store word may also specify some other types of operation. The microprogram address register (MAR) receives its contents from either the OPCODE of the main machine instruction to be executed (this forms the initial address of the microprogram which performs the instruction) or the last microprogram store word. One instruction from the main store results in the execution of a sequence of microinstructions. System operation consists of continually reading instructions from the main store and executing the specified sequences of microinstructions.

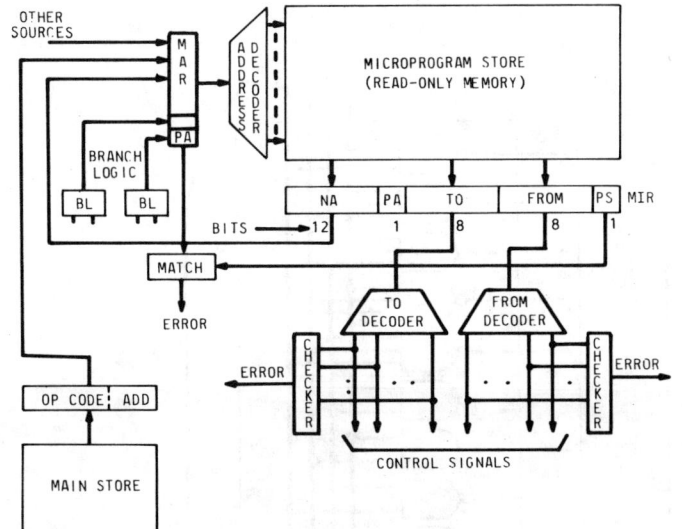

Fig. 12. Microprogram control.

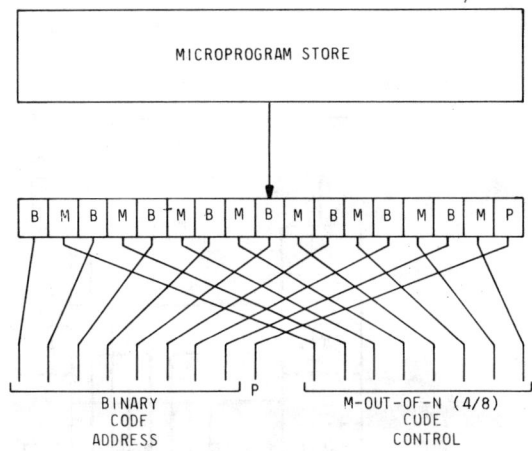

Fig. 13. Microprogram store coding techniques.

In designing the hardware check for the microprogram control, it is essential to recognize the types of failures which are most probable. Matching the checking techniques with the type of faults that actually occur yields the best results with the least amount of hardware. The microprogram control is constructed from integrated circuits: LSI for the memory and SSI for the associated control logic. Because of the method of isolating components and because of the physical proximity of devices on an integrated circuit chip, multiple faults within a chip have been analyzed and found to be of the type which would tend to affect the bits in the unidirectional manner: it affects adjacent bits, rather than nonadjacent bits in the word [27]. Unidirectional error refers to a fault which causes a data bit(s) to assume a wrong value of one type: 0 or 1, but not both simultaneously. (For example: 01100 to 01111, not to 01010.)

The checking technique used in the implementation of the microprogram control takes advantage of the error characteristics mentioned above. The microprogram store contains two types of data: control and address information. The control fields are immediately decoded and checked to provide control signals. A more efficient nonsystematic check code, such as the m-out-of-$2m$ code, would give the maximum detectability at the least possible cost in hardware. This code can detect all multiple-unidirectional errors. However, for the address field, it is desirable to maintain the data in binary form for addressing and to provide immediate binary data to several sources. Consequently, the choice of a systematic check code for the address field is essential to give this flexibility. By recognizing that the multiple-bit faults tend to affect adjacent bits rather than randomly disperse them throughout the word, the binary field is interleaved with the m-out-of-$2m$ code as shown in Fig. 13. Any multiple-adjacent-bit fault would then affect both the binary and the m-out-of-$2m$ code. Consequently, a single parity check bit is adequate to detect single-bit faults in the binary field, and multiple adjacent bit faults would be detected by the m-out-of-$2m$ check.

In checking the binary address field, parity is maintained on the address in the MAR and checked by 1) storing the correct parity (see Fig. 12) in the word addressed in memory, and 2) comparing the two after the word is read out. The next address field in the microprogram store output register (MIR) also has a parity bit which becomes the parity bit of the MAR when it is gated into the MAR. The condition branch logic is checked by duplication. A match is not necessary to check the duplicated logic since its output must change both the low-order bit and the parity bit of the MAR. One of the branch logic circuits feeds the low-order bit, and the other feeds the parity bit (P_A) (see Fig. 12) so that branch logic failure is detected because of the resultant bad parity of the MAR.

The checking techniques (such as m-out-of-$2m$, interleaves parity, and duplication) are integrated into the No. 3A's design to detect the failures that may occur in the microprogram control. These types of checks are provided to detect the multiple-unidirectional type of faults that are possible with the integrated technology.

2) 4-out-of-8 Decoder and Check: The TO and FROM control fields are each eight bits wide and encoded as a 4-out-of-8 code. There are 70 valid combinations in an 8-bit field; each combination has four 1's and four 0's. The fields, which are decoded to drive the control points of the processor, are checked by a self-checking checker which detects faults in the decoder and the input codes [28].

Because of the large number of output leads in a fully decoded 4-out-of-8 code to 70 outputs, the decoder circuitry is divided into two groups. A control function is represented by two outputs, one from each group. Fig. 14 shows the decoding arrangement whereby each group is sorted into five logic subgroups with 4, 3, 2, 1, and 0 inputs and designated as 4(1), 3(1), 2(1), 1(1), and 0(1), respectively. The numbers of gates belonging to the respective subgroups are 1, 4, 6, 4, and 1, as shown in the figure. Similarly, the second four bits in the 4-out-of-8 code are decoded and divided into the same subgrouping. The A subgroups are paired with the B subgroups to obtain the 70 possible 4-out-of-8 code combinations. The $4_a(1)$ group pairs with the $0_b(1)$ group to give one combination; the $3_a(1)$ group pairs with the $1_b(1)$ group to give 16 combinations; and so on, as indicated in Fig. 14. The 0(1) subgroup is redundant, and, therefore, it is not used.

The total number of decoder outputs from each group is 15 instead of 16. Within a decoder group, more than one output may be active simultaneously. For example, the 1111 input code can cause all gates to be active. This is entirely satisfactory since only the gate in the corresponding subgroup of the second decoder [in this case the 0(1) subgroup] would be active; gates in the other subgroups would *not* be active. Hence, one and only one pair of decoder outputs is active.

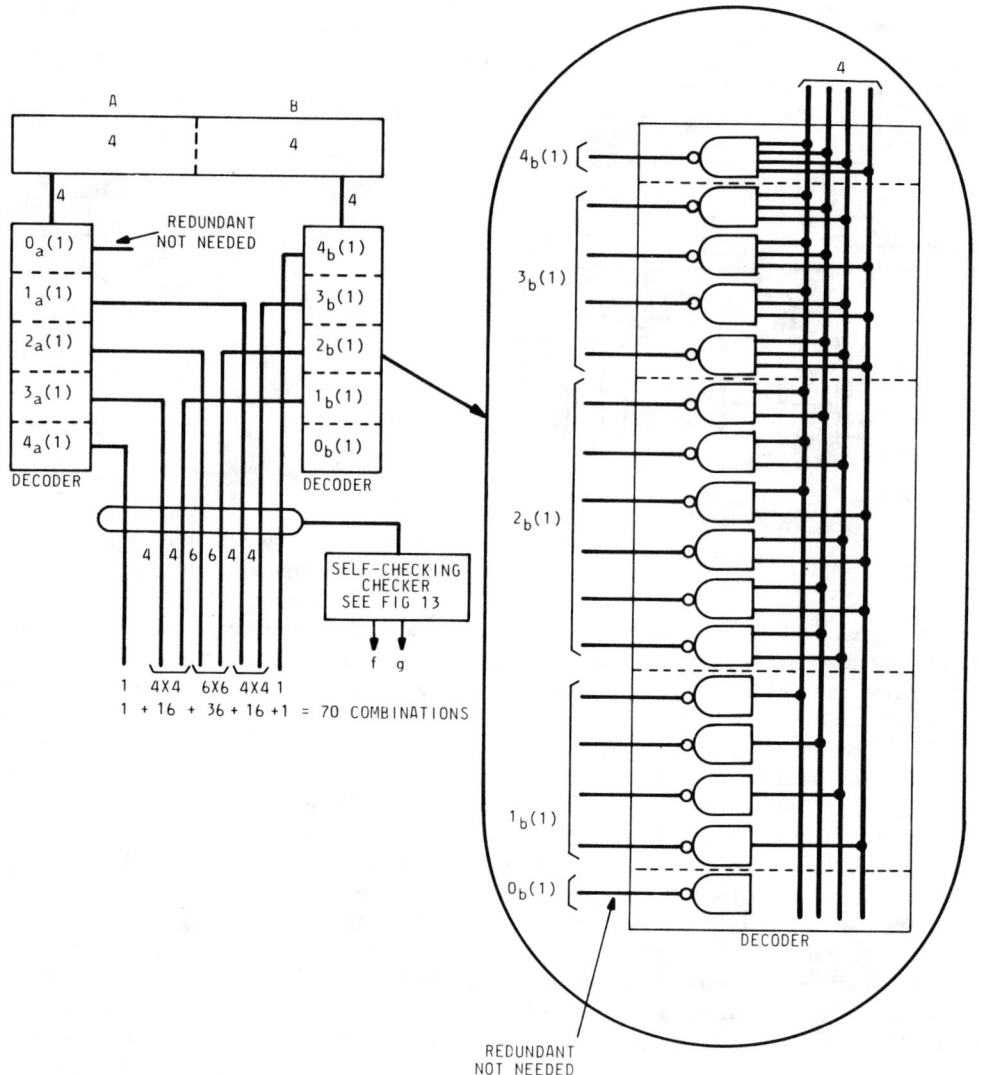

Fig. 14. 4-out-of-8 decoding arrangement.

This condition uniquely defines one of the possible 70 combinations in the 4-out-of-8 codes.

The decoder design provides the proper outputs which facilitate the implementation of the self-checking 4-out-of-8 checker. The self-checking circuit is realized by subdividing the checker into two separate independent subcircuits. Each subcircuit generates a single output whose values are arranged to be complementary for normal 4-out-of-8 input codes. For any errors in the input code, decoder, or check logic, the two outputs are alike (00 or 11).

A totally self-checking checker has the advantage of not requiring periodic tests in order to ensure that any faults occurring in the functional circuits will be detected immediately. The check scheme involves pairing the subgroups, corresponding to exactly four 1's, as follows: $0_a(1)-4_b(1)$, $1_a(1)-3_b(1)$, $2_a(1)-2_b(1)$, $3_a(1)-1_b(1)$, $4_a(1)-0_b(1)$. An output is generated for each pairing. The alternating pairs are divided into separate groups, f and g, as indicated in Fig. 15. Since only one pair will be active for a correct 4-out-of-8 input, the response from f and g will be 10 or 01 for the normal operating condition. If the input is other than a 4-out-of-8 code, the f and g outputs will be 11 or 00. For example, if the input is 11100011, the $3_a(1)$, $2_a(1)$, $1_a(1)$, and $0_a(1)$ from the A group and the $2_b(1)$, $1_b(1)$, and $0_b(1)$ from the B group will be active. This means two pairs of subgroups will be active: $3_a(1)-1_b(1)$ in the f group and $2_a(1)-2_b(1)$ in the g group. The alternating pairs are chosen to be in separate groups

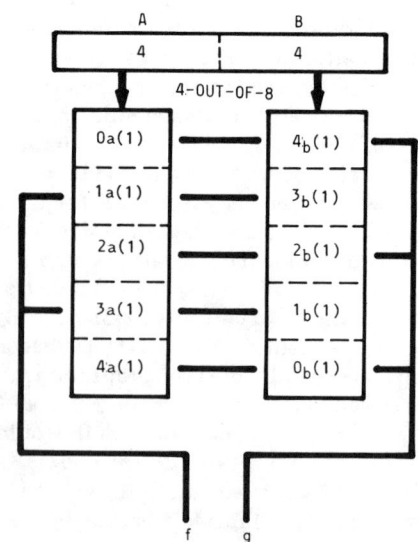

Fig. 15. General diagram of 4-out-of-8 checker.

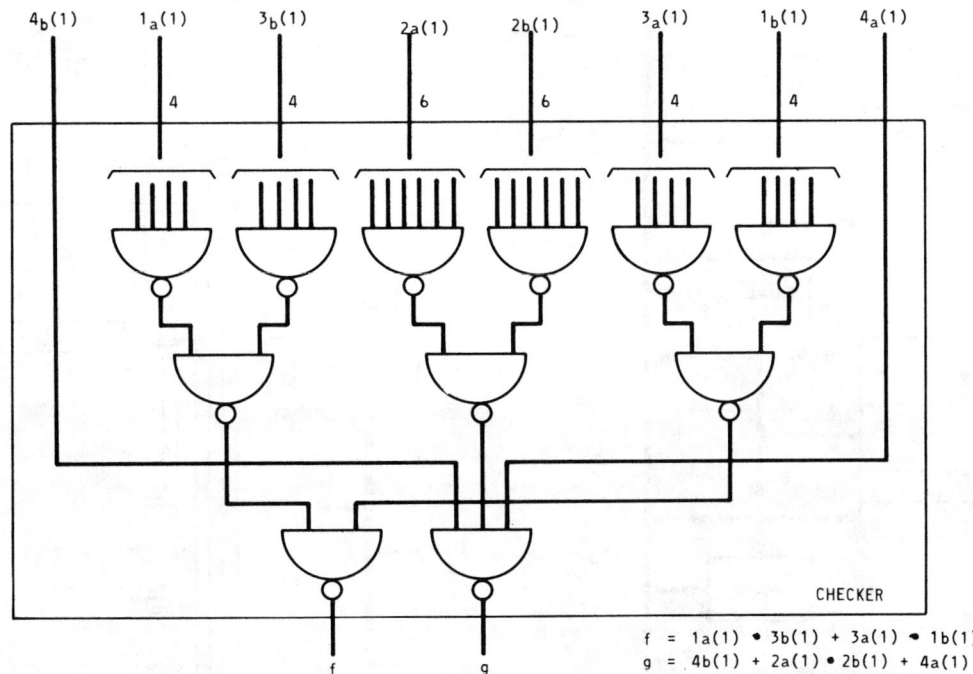

Fig. 16. 4-out-of-8 checker.

$f = 1a(1) \cdot 3b(1) + 3a(1) \cdot 1b(1)$
$g = 4b(1) + 2a(1) \cdot 2b(1) + 4a(1)$

to ensure that when there is more than one pair active, the resultant fg output is 11, representing an input with more than four 1's. If the input contains less than four 1's, none of the four pairs will be active. For example, if the input is 01110000, the $3_a(1)$, $2_a(1)$, $1_a(1)$, and $0_a(1)$ of the A group and the $0_b(1)$ of the B group will be active. These are outputs from each group, but none of them belong to a pair, hence, the fg output is 00, corresponding to an input combination with less than four 1's. The logic implementation of the 4-out-of-8 checker is shown in Fig. 16.

The $0(1)$ subgroup represents the condition of 1 or any number of 1's in the 4-bit input. This means the $0(1)$ gate is always active and redundant. The pairing of $4_a(1)$–$0_b(1)$ does not need to include the $0_b(1)$ subgroup at all. Its gate and output is ignored in the implementation.

The FROM and TO decoder outputs fan out to various functional units for controlling logical operations or data transfers within the CC. Those that go to the data transfer logic control the gating of data from one register to another via the data bus. The circuitry of this functional block is paritioned on a 2-bit slice; all logic gates associated with the two bits are contained on a single circuit board. Since the decoder outputs fan out to 2 bits, any malfunction of the control within a circuit board would affect only those 2 bits of data. When the word is used at a later time, the error will be detected by the parity check on the data. Consequently, it is sufficient to check the control signals prior to entering the data transfer block. This is also true for the data manipulation block since the circuitry is duplicated.

A number of microoperations consist of setting or clearing individual flip-flops or enabling dedicated paths where the use of a single TO or FROM field crosspoint would be inefficient. A miscellaneous decoder is provided; it takes inputs from both the TO and FROM fields. In this way, a 10×10 matrix (100 crosspoints) is generated by assigning only 10 of the 70 combinations from each of the TO and FROM fields. Most of these types of crosspoints control duplicated circuitry;

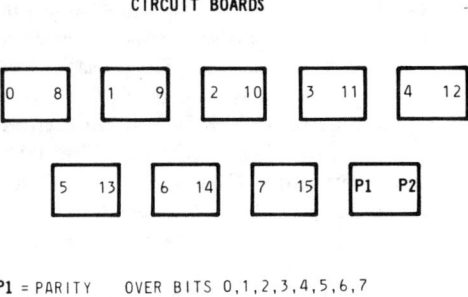

P1 = PARITY   OVER BITS 0,1,2,3,4,5,6,7
P2 = PARITY   OVER BITS 8,9,10,11,12,13,14,15

Fig. 17. Layout of general registers.

hence, the decoding gate itself is duplicated. A fault in this area will result in an error in the data path and will be detected by a parity check.

3) Data Registers: There are two types of internal data registers: general purpose and special purpose. The latter type is dedicated to specific functions. Examples are the interrupt status register (IS) and the error register (ER). The general-purpose registers are involved with the handling of data associated directly with the instructions. The checking of the data transfer logic is done by partitioning two bits of the register on a single circuit board and then carrying two parity bits. This partitioning and the definition of the parity bits is illustrated in Fig. 17, with the first circuit board containing two bits of every general-purpose register. Partitioning the registers in this way ensures that any fault on a circuit board will not affect more than two bits of any register. This also ensures that the fault will be detected by the two parity bits. If all of one register's bits were grouped on a single board, a catastrophic failure of that board could affect all of the bits, and the failure would not necessarily be detectable by the two parity bits. The main memory is also organized as a 2-bit slice per circuit pack plus two parity check bits. A consistent parity check is done throughout the entire system; I/O is included.

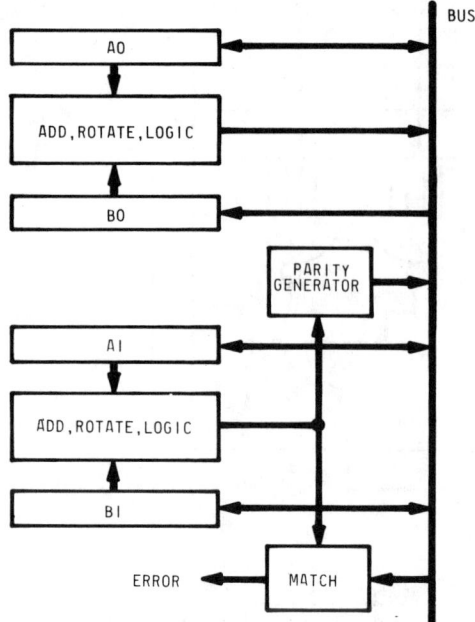

Fig. 18. Duplicated data manipulation logic.

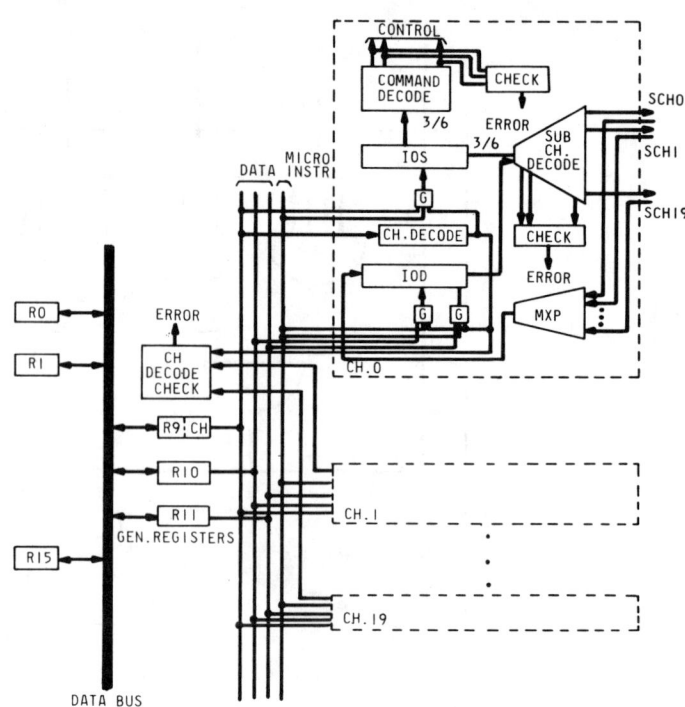

Fig. 19. I/O channel structure.

For any data transfer, the information from the source register is checked by the parity checker at a common point: the data bus. In a register-to-register transfer, the data in the destination register are not checked. This is satisfactory since it will be checked when the data are used either to address the store or to be operated on by the data manipulation logic.

4) Data Manipulation Logic (DML): The DML contains rotation, Boolean function of two variables, first zero detection, and fast binary ADD. The DML is duplicated and matched to allow full checking in this area. Other coding techniques, such as parity prediction and residue coding, are available for arithmetical functions. However, for all logical functions of two variables, duplication is the simplest method of checking. Duplication eliminates the need for checking if the data arrived at the modification logic correctly.

As shown in Fig. 18, a match circuit detects faults, and a parity generation circuit supplies parity on the DML output to interface with the rest of the system.

5) I/O Channels: The 20 I/O channels are 6.67-MHz serial channels. Each channel has 20 subchannels. Fig. 19 shows the data flow from the processor to the I/O buffers. Three of the general-purpose registers, R9 through R11, are used: R9 loads the control buffer (IOS), R10 loads the data buffer (IOD), and R11 receives data from the I/O channel. All command and selection signals are encoded in 3-out-of-6 codes and decoded to 1-out-of-20 codes. The channel address stored in R9 is used to direct the data and microinstructions to one of the 20 specified main channels. The decoding of the enable address is done individually in each main channel, with the output returning to a common point for checking. This is done to ensure that only the right channel is enabled. The command decoding and subchannel selector within each channel are similarly checked for proper decoding of 3-out-of-6 codes. The data message containing two parity check bits from R10 is transmitted by the channel and checked by the peripheral unit. In addition, prior to transmission of the message, the data are brought back by the microprogram sequence to the data manipulation logic and compared with the content of R10 to ensure that the data have been loaded properly. Messages received from the peripheral unit also have two parity bits, which are checked when they are placed on the bus.

6) Maintenance Channel (MCH): The MCH is used for interprocessor communication, as well as for the diagnosis of one processor by the other processor. The MCH's structure is similar to the I/O channel and, therefore, the checking technique is the same. The data field uses the standard 2-bit parity in order to remain consistent with the rest of the processor. The command field is encoded in 3-out-of-6 codes.

7) Method of Checking Error Detection Circuits: Any circuitry used for checking purposes is incorporated as part of the system. Such circuitry should be as fail-safe as possible so that a failure in the system will cause a failure alarm. It has been shown that such a check circuit can be realized if the output is in the form of a 1-out-of-2 code, with 01 or 10 for the normal operation and 00 or 11 for the error condition [29]. Ultimately, these two outputs must be monitored to generate a single error output.

The final gate is not completely fail-safe. A failure in this gate will prevent the circuitry from giving any error indication, and faults normally detected will be ignored. A good design allows only a small portion of the detection hardware to be non-fail-safe. The checking of the non-fail-safe portion of the check logic is essential to guarantee reliable operation of these circuits. This is accomplished by a combination of hardware and software. This approach has been proved to be very effective in checking the check circuits, with both hardware and software costs kept to a minimum. The hardware provides the means of simulating test conditions or circuit faults which are extremely difficult or awkward to set up normally in the system. A flip-flop register, called the maintenance state (MS) register, is used for this purpose. Each bit represents an error or test condition. By appropriately setting up the MS register and applying a well designed test sequence, the detection circuitry can be checked on a periodic basis to ensure its proper application.

8) Method of Detecting Hard-Core Circuit Faults: Although the system is designed to be nearly self-checking, it contains a small hard-core portion which must be operating properly prior to running a program sequence. The circuitry usually includes the sequencing logic of the microprogram control and the addressing and fetching of instructions from the main store. For example, if the control to advance the program counter (PC) cannot be activated, the PC remains in one particular state. The same address is used at each reading, resulting in the same outputs from the store. The program, therefore, is stuck at one location, executing the same instruction repetitively, with no means of advancing through the program sequence to produce any useful work. The amount of hard-core circuitry is strongly dependent upon the system design and is difficult to eliminate. In a duplicated and matched system, when both processors are running in a synchronous mode with important outputs being matched continuously, any error in the hard-core circuitry will be detected instantaneously.

In the nearly self-checking design, the system does not run in a synchronous and match mode. This is done to reduce the complexity of software, thereby increasing reliability. A hardware timer is used to detect faults in the hard-core circuitry and also as backup to protect the system from control by an insane CC due to either hardware or software troubles. The use of a timer depends upon the program meeting an obstacle or a series of tests arranged in a maze. If the program is successfully completed through the maze, the timer is reset by the maintenance control program. On the other hand, if the program strays off course, the timer will time out and the emergency action circuit will select a new configuration. The sanity test is repeated to verify a fault-free system.

The telephone processing program is cyclic in nature. It returns to the starting point at each scan upon completion of a series of tasks required by the call processing [30]. Although the scan time may vary from scan to scan, depending on the amount of work required of the program, the maximum time can be easily determined.

The use of a hardware timer is closely tied with the system program. It is arranged so that a reset is generated for the timer only if the program proceeds through the scan correctly within the prescribed period. If the program deviates from the normal course, no reset will occur. In this case, the timer automatically times out, stops processing, and switches to the standby system.

There are two timers, one located in each processor; both are active at all times. Duplication is necessary in order to guarantee that the system be capable of recovery. It is possible that a single fault can disable one processor and its timer, thus necessitating the standby to perform the function. The timers are periodically reset by the on-line program. If they are not reset, the on-line timers will time out first. If the on-line timer does not work, the off-line timer will perform the task at a later time.

D. Recovery Techniques

Fault detection is the first and most important step in realizing a highly reliable system. Two other functions of equal importance are: 1) rapid recovery of the system to process calls, and 2) the protection of calls in progress in face of either hardware or software difficulties. This means the mechanism for switching controls must be highly reliable. Proper steps have been taken to give a smooth transition in the transfer of controls. In the design of the system, the combination of hardware and software is so intertwined as to provide the utmost protection against an insane CC from taking control of the system. A rapid and successful recovery is achieved by a combination of hardware and software so that continuity is maintained [31].

1) Automatic Recovery: When an error is recognized in the on-line processor, several things may happen depending on the type of error. Error signals are buffered in the error register (ER) for diagnostic purposes. In addition, the error signals are sorted out and divided into three groups, with each group causing a different set of system actions. The least severe of the three are the errors associated with the I/O or MCH. These errors will cause an interrupt in which the processor has complete control in determining the exact cause of the trouble. If the error is a transient fault, it will be recorded and compiled for later analysis. If the error is determined to be a hardware fault within the switchable block of the processor, the interrupt program will initiate a reconfiguration to the standby machine by means of the MCH. This would be an orderly switch to the other processor; there would be no detrimental effect on the system.

The second type of error involves faults occurring in the standby portion of the system. These faults directly influence the on-line operation. For example, the system is organized to operate both stores asynchronously. Whenever data are written into the on-line store, they are written into the off-line store simultaneously. The processor waits for a store completion signal from both stores before proceeding with the next operation. If a response signal originates only from the on-line store, there is a 32-μs pause, and then a special timer times out and generates an error signal, indicating trouble in the off-line store. Under this condition, the processor is interrupted at the microinstruction level and appropriate action is taken to continue call processing with the standby store isolated.

The third type of error involves hardware faults within the on-line processor. An extension of the previous discussion will serve as a good example: If the store completion signal is received from the standby store and *not* from the on-line store, this error signal causes the system to switch to the standby configuration. In this situation, the system momentarily "hangs up." A restart in the standby machine would then initialize the processor and continue with call processing, affecting, perhaps, only one call in the transient state.

Numerous check circuits are designed and integrated into the system. As soon as an error is detected, immediate action takes place to reconfigure the system into an error-free working system. In addition, duplicated hardware timers are provided to back up undetected hardware faults or software bugs which cause the program to go astray. The recovery process involves two steps:

Step 1: Reconfiguration.
Step 2: Restart or initialization—to enable the new processor configuration a smooth transition into full control of the system.

When a switch to the standby processor occurs, it must be initialized to a known state in order to start smoothly. This operation is divided into three stages, or levels. The first stage involves the elementary control of the microprogram store, ensuring that it can start and execute a sequence of microinstruction properly at a predetermined store location. This is done by hardware before the first microcycle. The operation consists of:

1) setting the MAR to a predetermined address;
2) setting clock circuitry to a well-defined state;
3) setting the block hardware check (BHC) flip-flop to inhibit detection hardware from possibly generating an error signal, thus initiating a switch operation;
4) resetting various control flip-flops (e.g., STOP, FREEZE) which would directly affect the running of the microprogram control.

The second stage of initialization is done by microprogram. The primary function of the microprogram initialization is to set the various control bits or registers which have direct influence on running the main program sequence. For example:

1) set the block interrupt (BIN) flip-flop to inhibit the external interrupt from interfering with the initializing program;
2) reset the update (UPD) flip-flop to inhibit the standby store from being updated;
3) set the isolate (ISO) flip-flop to prevent the off-line store operation from interfering with the on-line operation.
4) reset the hardware timer to prevent it from timing out.

In addition, the microprogram decides whether or not the main store contains valid program data. If it does not, the alternative would be to switch the processor and try the other configuration since the program data are duplicated, with a copy in each store. The objective is to try to use each of the two copies before resorting to the use of a tape unit as a final backup. The sanity of the machine depends very heavily on the memory content. As a result, an arrangement (shown in Fig. 20) has been implemented to allow a systematic way of recovering from system errors. The scheme uses two initialization sanity check bits (ISC1 and ISC2) as markers. They are part of the system status (SS) register. Normally, these two bits are in the 00 state. During the first time through the microprogram level of initialization (ISC1 = 0), this ISC1 bit is set to the 1 condition as a marker for subsequent initialization. The system then proceeds to the main program initialization. If the store contains correct program data, and if the system is fully recovered from the initialization, this marker bit will be reset. However, if the program data have been badly mutilated, the main program may wander aimlessly, executing bad programs.

When a second initialization occurs within the same CC and the first marker bit is set to the 1 state, the initialization at the microprogram level will set the second marker bit to 1. It then directs the control to be passed on to the other processor with the expectation that its main memory and the rest of the hardware are in good working condition. Otherwise, it will switch back to the original processor and try to initialize for the third time. Now, with both marker bits set to 11, the microprogram initialization sequence will recognize this condition and take the drastic step of reloading the main memory from the backup tape unit. These operational steps are depicted in Fig. 20.

The third and final stage of initialization is done by the main program. This stage covers both the internal status of the processor and the main store data pertaining to the peripheral equipment status, transient data, and various data associated with maintenance of the system. The internal state of the processor is saved in the main memory for subsequent analysis

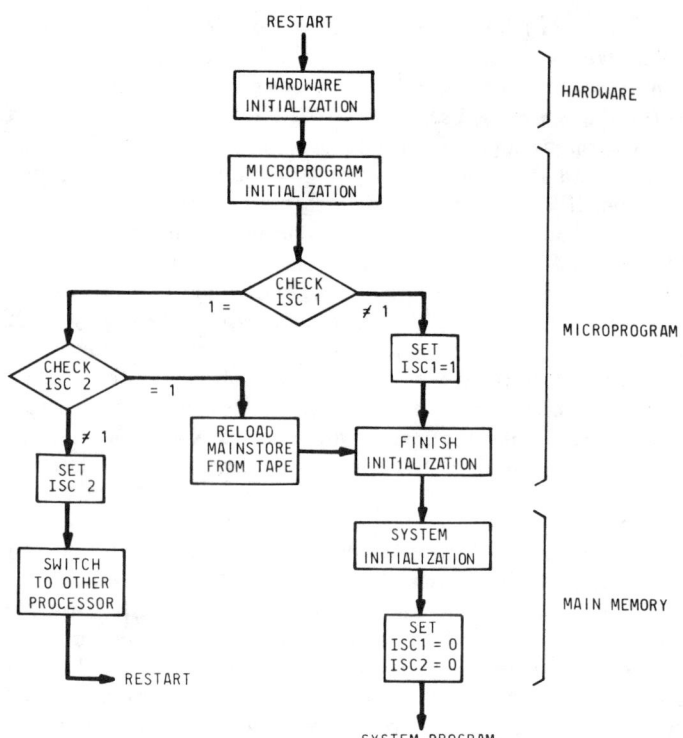

Fig. 20. Initialization sequence.

by the diagnostic program. Next, the various registers are set to a prescribed initial state. All control flip-flops, which were set up by the first two levels of initialization to inhibit various functions (such as block hardware check, block interrupt, and inhibit store update, etc.), are now restored to normal operation. This handling of the memory data, which have direct effect on the operation of the system, depends on the ability of the main program to run successfully and the frequency of initialization. Audit programs are called in to validate and check for consistent data in the memory and peripheral equipment status. The initialization and recovery programs clear selective portions of memory data and take increasingly severe actions on the memory, depending on the rate of system reconfiguration. A high rate indicates the system's inability to maintain its sanity.

2) Manual Recovery: Although the system is designed to recover automatically under trouble conditions, it is conceivable for the system to be unable to reconfigure into a working mode. This can be caused by software bugs, hardware faults, or a combination of both. The processor may be switching continuously, spending all of its available time repeating initialization work. In other words, the control unit has gone insane and is incapable of making any rational decisions. In this case, the ultimate control of the system must be left to the judgment of qualified maintenance personnel. Hardware has been provided to give maintenance personnel the capability of forcing the system into a fixed configuration and the locking it into the mode. Under this condition, the switching operation would be made inoperative and any system initialization would be directed to the locked processor. If both processors are defective, but to different degrees, manual control makes it possible to lock out the most defective one and hope that the system will limp along.

In addition to the manual force and lock functions of the emergency action panel, provision has been made to manually generate initialization and cause different categories of data in the nonwrite protect area of the store be cleaned. These categories include: 1) transient data which are associated with calls in a stable talking state, and 2) recent change data which are associated with changing of customer telephone lines. The automatic recovery program is only allowed to clear the transient data which affects telephone calls in the nontalking state. If an incomplete call is interrupted, the caller must try again. On the other hand, if the stable data are cleared, calls in the talking state are interrupted and the talking state is taken down. Hence, maintenance personnel are given the final control over recovery by taking the additional action of clearing the more important stable and recent change data portions of the store.

Due to the importance of these controls, safeguards have been designed into the manual switches and circuitry to protect against an accidental switch operation. This is necessary to prevent any inadvertent actions which may have severe effects on the system. Emergency controls are grouped together with system alarms and status indicators at the common system control panel, which is readily available to maintenance personnel. Additional redundancy has been designed into the system so that if both processors are down a positive indication must be given to maintenance personnel before the appropriate action can be taken. This is done by another hardware timer in the common system control panel. While the on-line program is progressing through the programs correctly, it must periodically reset this timer. If the on-line processor does not reset the timer, it will time out and set the alarm circuit, immediately bringing the situation to the attention of the craftperson.

E. Diagnostic Hardware

Fault detection determines whether or not a circuit is operating correctly, whereas fault diagnosis localizes the failure to a few replaceable circuit packs. Hardware has been integrated into the design of this system to allow a systematic approach for identifying failures via software. The most commonly used procedure in fault diagnosis [32], [33] is based upon the bootstrap technique. The hard-core portion of the machine can apply test sequences to itself. With a duplicated processor, the fault-free machine is used to check or diagnose the hard-core portion of the defective machine. Once the hard-core portion has been checked and found to be fault-free, it is used to start the diagnostic test of another portion of the processor. Therefore, subunits are tested before being used to check other subunits. This procedure continues until the fault is pinpointed.

In order to facilitate this diagnostic procedure, several important designs have been incorporated into the system. One is the MCH and its associated circuitry. Its primary function is the diagnosis of one processor by the other. The MCH is an autonomous portion of the processor which, under control of the other processor, can provide information about the state of the machine and exercise the machine at its most basic level by direct access to the microprogram control. Another hardware feature is the maintenance instruction, which provides complete access to the system at the most elementary level of hardware.

1) Maintenance Channel Facilities: The MCH interconnects and provides the main source of communication between the two processors. As shown in Fig. 21, the MCH is a high-speed (6.67 MHz), serial, full duplex channel. This method of communication reduces the number of leads at the expense of

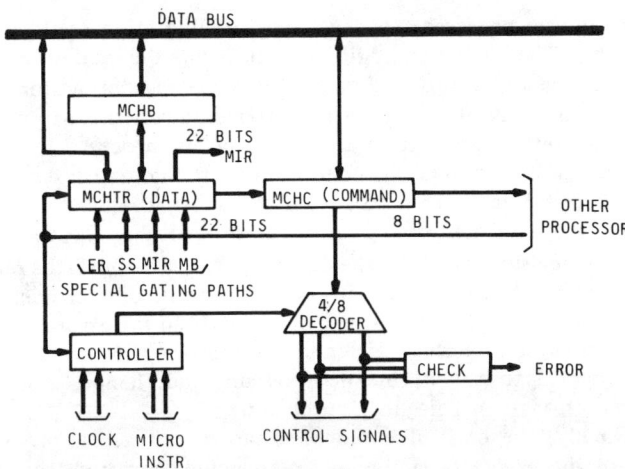

Fig. 21. Maintenance channel.

additional hardware, making the interface easier to maintain. Since there are so few leads, the processors can be said to be "loosely interconnected;" they are isolated from each other in terms of hardware faults. That is, a fault in one processor will not affect the operation of the other processor.

The basic structure of the MCH shown in Fig. 21 consists of a transmit-receive register (MCHTR), a command register (MCHC), and a buffer register (MCHB). The format of a MCH message is 20 bits of data, 2 parity check bits, and 8 bits of command. Although the processor is essentially a 16-bit machine, there are several 20-bit registers for store addressing. Consequently, the MCH message is dictated by the widest data word. For 16-bit data fields, the high four bits are not used. The commands are coded in 4-out-of-8 codes for ease in decoding and checking. The decoded outputs are used to control the primitive functions of the processor so that elementary operations can be observed by the on-line machine. For example, under MCH control, the clock can be stopped and stepped along one clock phase at a time. In between steps, the state of each phase is transmitted back to the other processor for analysis. In this way, the very hard-core is exercised to permit a systematic check of the clock circuitry.

Another basic operation involves transmitting microinstructions over the main channel and executing them one at a time. This is done by gating the received data in the MCHTR directly into the MIR: The command part of the message provides control for gating and executing the microinstruction. This operation allows the on-line processor to step the off-line machine along one microinstruction at a time, thereby gaining access to the entire machine at the most elementary level for fault diagnosis.

The MCHB is used to temporarily store the data transmitted over the MCH. This data source can be used for a variety of operations. For example, in a READ-STORE operation, assume a 20-bit address has been received and buffered in the MCHB at the receiving end. When executed, the maintenance messages which follow (containing microinstructions) will gate the content of MCHB to the store address register (SAR) and read store at that address. In order to bring the store output back into the on-line processor, two more maintenance messages must be sent. The first message gates the store output to the MCHB, and the second message gates the content of the MCHB to the MCHTR and is then transmitted back to the on-line processor. Similarly, the data stored in the MCHB can also be used to write into the store. These operations allow the on-line processor to check the off-line store control circuitry. The MCHB, in addition to buffering the incoming data which are to be directed to any internal register within the processor, may also be used to buffer data which are to be returned to the transmitting processor (on-line processor).

The MCH registers are connected to the common data bus to permit data transfer to any of the internal registers. Also, there are dedicated gating paths, as shown in Fig. 21, to allow special registers (such as the error register, system status register, etc.) to be fetched directly without the aid of microinstructions. Some of these registers, particularly in the error register and the system status register, contain information which may be helpful to the diagnostic program, and, hence, must be saved prior to any diagnostic procedure.

Finally, the controller block, as shown in Fig. 21, provides all of the necessary timing and sequencing operations that the MCH needs to transmit and receive messages. The off-line processor must be able to derive timing signals directly from the incoming serial data stream since the processor's clock may be stopped. Therefore, the MCH circuitry, which is closely integrated into the processor, is really an extension of the other processor since the two are connected by means of an "umbilical" cord.

2) Microdiagnostic Techniques: After the circuits associated with the microprogram control and the main store operation have been checked and verified to be operational, the off-line processor can execute instructions and initiate diagnostic procedures by itself. The microinstruction, being the most elementary operation, provides the best possible access to pinpoint faults within the machine. Therefore, if the diagnosis is performed at the microprogram level, isolating faults to a few replaceable circuit packs becomes a more efficient and effective process. The ideal situation would be to store the diagnostic routines on low-cost tape units and then page them into a writeable microprogram store as needed [34]. However, in this system, the microprogram store is entirely ROM. This is necessary for reasons of cost and reliability. Therefore, it is not practical to store the diagnostic in the ROM because of the increase in the size and cost of the microprogram store.

In order to achieve equivalent microdiagnostic capability, a special microinterrupt (MI) instruction has been incorporated into the design to allow the machine to be exercised at the microprogram level. This is done by allowing the microsequences to be stored in the main memory. The MI instruction simply puts the processor in the interpret mode. While in this mode, the processor stops using the outputs from the microprogram memory and fetches microinstructions from successive main memory words. Any number of microinstructions may now be executed from main memory until the microinstruction, which turns off the interpret mode, is given.

There are several advantages to the microinterpret technique. First, it will allow maintenance routines to be stored in low-cost tape units and paged into main memory as needed at a considerable cost reduction. Since the microprogram memory is a ROM, the microprograms stored in main memory can be changed much more easily than if they were stored in microprogram memory. Secondly, the interpret mode will allow microprogram sequences to be checked out before they are encoded in ROM. Lastly, and most importantly, the maintenance programmer has complete access to every control signal that exists within the machine.

Microprogram sequences in the interpret mode do run slower than the native mode since the main memory is slower than

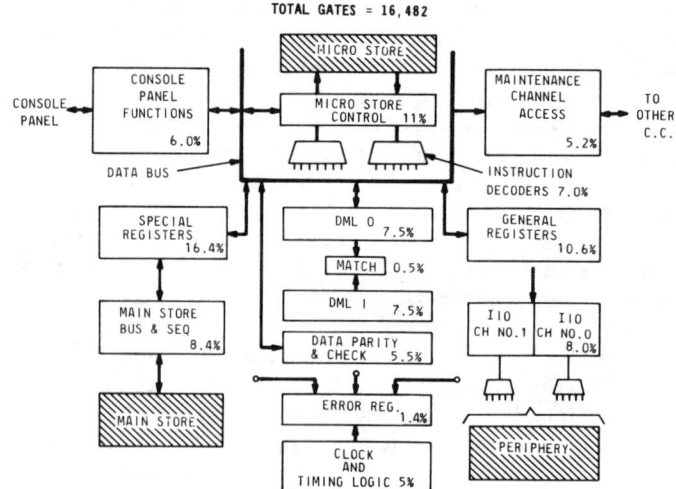

Fig. 22. No. 3A CC gate count.

the microprogram memory. This is not an important disadvantage since diagnostic programs are normally run in the standby machine. However, the microinstructions are executed at the same speed.

F. Repair

When the fault has been diagnosed and located to within a few circuit packs, maintenance personnel must replace the packs one at a time until the defective one has been found. In pack replacement, the power must be turned off to avoid the harmful effects of breaking current on the connector. Since there are a number of leads from the processor to various functional units, power must be turned off "gracefully" so as not to cause any disturbance to the working system. Consequently, the operation is arranged in a sequence to ensure that no harmful transient signals are generated in the process. Similarly, the same protection is given in turning power on.

During the repair process, the working system is manually locked into a selected configuration. This is done to avoid any error conditions which may cause the system to switch control to the machine under repair. Since it is under repair, the machine is without power. Therefore, if an error occurs in the working system, it would be better to restart and attempt to run again with the same configuration. The hardware required to prevent any interaction from the machine under repair is minimal, but is must be integrated into the design at the beginning.

G. Hardware Implementation

Maintenance has been made an integral part of the 3A CC design. It uses the standard No. 1A ESS logic family with its associated packaging technology [20]. Up to 52 silicon integrated circuit chips (SIC's), each containing from four to ten logic gates, can be packed on a 3.25 by 4.00-in 1A ceramic substrate. The substrate is mounted on a 3.67 by 7-in circuit board with an 82-pin connector for backplane interconnections. In the 3A CC, the 53 1A logic circuit packs average about 44 SIC's, resulting in an average of 308 gates per circuit pack, or a total of 16 482 gates. Fig. 22 shows a detailed functional diagram of the 3A CC and the percentage of logic gates used in each functional unit.

Another insight into how the gates are used in the 3A is shown in Fig. 23. The figure shows the relationship between

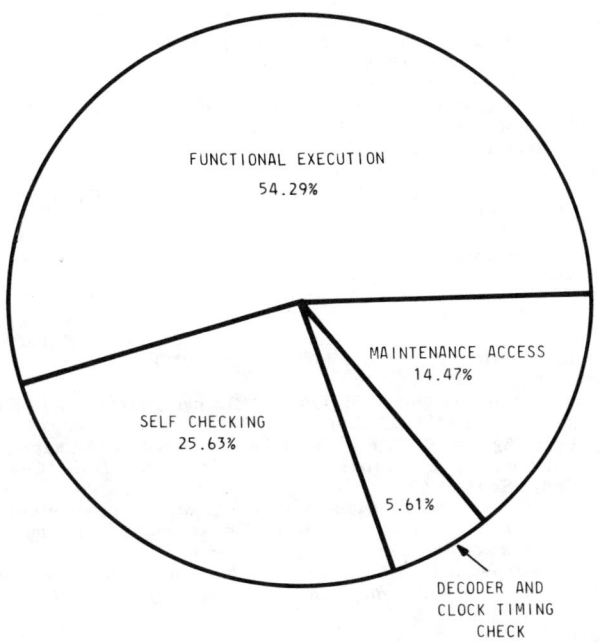

Fig. 23. Logic gates in No. 3A CC. Total gates = 16 482.

working gates, maintenance access gates, and self-checking logic. The working gates are the portion which contribute to the data processing functions, while the maintenance access gates provide the necessary access to make the CC maintainable (i.e., maintenance channel and control panel). The self-checking gates are required to implement the parity bits, the check circuits, and the duplicate circuits that make the CC self-checking. As indicated, about 30 percent of the logic is used for checking. The design covers a high degree of component failures. It is estimated about 90 to 95 percent of the faults would be detected by hardware error detection logic. Certain portions of the checkers, timers, and interrupt logic are not checked. These circuits are periodically exercised under program control to ensure that they are fault-free.

VIII. SUMMARY

In order to achieve the reliability requirements, all ESS subsystem units are duplicated. When a hardware failure occurs in any of the subunits, the processor is reconfigured into a working system around the defective unit. The partitioning of subsystem units into switching blocks varies with the size of the ESS processors. For the medium- or small-size processors such as the No. 2 or the No. 3, the central control, the main memory, the bulk memory, and the store bus are grouped as a single switchable entity. A failure in one of the subunits is considered a failure in the switchable block. Since the number of components within a switchable block is sufficiently small, this type of single-unit duplex configuration meets the reliability requirement. For larger processors such as the No. 1 or the No. 1A, the central control, the program store, the call store, the store buses, and the bulk file store are treated individually as switchable blocks. This multi-unit duplex configuration allows a considerable number of combinations in which a working system can be assembled. The system is down only when two simultaneous failures occur, one in the subunit and the other in the duplicated subunit. A greater fault tolerance is possible with this configuration. This type of configuration is necessary for the large processor because each subunit contains a larger number of components.

The first generation of ESS processors, which includes the No. 1 and the No. 2, have provided commercial service since 1965 and 1969, respectively. The No. 1 ESS serves large telephone offices (metropolitan); the No. 2 is used in medium-size offices (suburban). Their reliability requirements are the same. Both processors depend on integrated maintenance software, with the hardware that must 1) quickly detect a system failure condition, 2) isolate and configure a working system around the faulty subunit, 3) diagnose the faulty unit, and 4) assist the maintenance personnel in repairing the unit. The primary detection technique is the synchronous and match mode of operation of both central controls. Matching is done more extensively in the No. 1 than in the No. 2 since cost is one of major considerations in the design of the No. 2 Processor. In addition to matching, coding techniques, diagnostic access, and other check logic have been incorporated into the basic design of these processors to realize the reliability objectives.

The widespread acceptance of the No. 1 ESS and the No. 2 ESS has created the need for a second generation of ESS processors: the No. 1A and the No. 3A. They offer greater capability and are also more cost-effective. Both processors use the same integrated technology. The 1A Processor extends its performance range by a factor of four to eight times over the No. 1 Processor by using faster logic and faster memory. The 1A design takes advantage of the experience gained in the design and operation of the No. 1 ESS. The No. 1A Processor provides considerably more hardware for error detection and more extensive matching of a large number of internal nodes within the central control. The design of the No. 3A Processor had benefited by the experience gained from the No. 2 ESS. A major departure in the design of the 3A Processor from the design of other ESS processors is the nonsynchronous and the nonmatch mode of operation. The No. 3A Processor uses self-checking as primary means of error detection. Another departure is in the design of the No. 3A Processor's control section; it is microprogrammed. The No. 3A Processor's flexibility permits emulation of the No. 2 Processor quite easily.

ACKNOWLEDGMENT

The author would like to acknowledge the kind assistance of Pat Loprete, Jr.

REFERENCES

[1] R. W. Downing, J. S. Nowak, and L. S. Tuomenoksa, "No. 1 ESS Maintenance Plan," *Bell Syst. Tech. J.*, Sept. 1964.
[2] J. A. Harr, F. F. Taylor, and W. Ulrich, "Organization of the No. 1 ESS central processor," *Bell Syst. Tech. J.*, Sept. 1969.
[3] T. E. Browne, T. M. Quinn, W. N. Toy, and J. E. Yates, "No. 2 ESS control unit system," *Bell Syst. Tech. J.*, Oct. 1969.
[4] R. E. Staehler, "1A processor—organizations and objectives," *Bell Syst. Tech. J.*, Feb. 1977.
[5] R. E. Staehler and R. J. Watters, "1A processor—an ultradependable common control," in *Int. Switching Symp. Rec.* (Japan), 1976.
[6] D. J. Smith, *Reliability Engineering*. New York: Barnes and Noble, 1972.
[7] S. H. Tsiang and W. Ulrich, "Automatic trouble diagnosis of complex logic circuits," *Bell Syst. Tech. J.*, July 1962.
[8] W. Keister, R. W. Ketchledge, and C. A. Lovell, *Proc. Inst. Elec. Eng.*, vol. 107, part B, suppl., no. 20, 1960.
[9] H. Y. Chang, G. W. Smith, and R. B. Walford, "LAMP: System description," *Bell Syst. Tech. J.*, Oct. 1974.
[10] P. W. Bowman et al., "1A processor—maintenance software," *Bell. Syst. Tech. J.*, Feb. 1977.
[11] F. M. Goetz, "Complementary fault simulation," in *Proc. 3rd Annu. Texas Conf. Computing Systems* (Univ. Texas, Austin), Nov. 1974.
[12] W. Keister, R. W. Ketchledge, and H. E. Vaughan, "No. 1 ESS: System organization and objectives," *Bell Syst. Tech. J.*, Sept. 1964.

[13] W. B. Cagle, R. S. Menne, R. S. Skinner, R. E. Staehler, and M. D. Underwood, "No. 1 ESS logic circuits and their application to the design of the central control," *Bell Syst. Tech. J.*, Sept. 1964.

[14] C. F. Ault, L. E. Gallaher, T. S. Greenwood, and D. C. Koehler, "No. 1 ESS program store," *Bell Syst. Tech. J.*, Sept. 1964.

[15] R. M. Genke, P. A. Harding, and R. E. Staehler, "No. 1 ESS call store - A-A0, 2—Megabit ferrite sheet memory," *Bell Syst. Tech. J.*, Sept. 1964.

[16] W. O. Fleckenstein, "Bell System ESS family - Present and future," in *ISS 1974 Rec.* (Munich, Germany), Sept. 1974.

[17] A. E. Spencer and F. S. Vigilante, "No. 2 ESS—System organization and objectives," *Bell Syst. Tech. J.*, Oct. 1969.

[18] E. L. Seley and F. S. Vigilante, "Common control—For an electronic private branch exchange," *IEEE Trans. Commun. Electron*, July 1964.

[19] H. J. Beuscher, G. E. Fessler, D. W. Huffman, P. J. Kennedy, and E. Nussbaum, "Administration and maintenance plan," *Bell Syst. Tech. J.*, Oct. 1969.

[20] J. O. Becker et al., "1A Processor - Technology and Physical Design," *Bell Syst. Tech. J.*, Feb. 1977.

[21] A. H. Budlong, et al., "1A processor—Control system," *Bell Syst. Tech. J.*, 1977.

[22] J. S. Nowak, "No. 1A ESS - A New High Capacity Switching System," in *Int. Switching Symp. Rec.* (Japan), 1976.

[23] C. F. Ault et al., "1A processor—Memory systems," *Bell Syst. Tech. J.*, Feb. 1977.

[24] E. A. Irland and U. K. Stagg, "New developments in suburban and rural ESS (No. 2 and No. 3 ESS)," in *ISS 1974 Rec.* (Munich, Germany), Sept. 1974.

[25] T. F. Storey, "Design of a microprogram control for a processor in an electronic switching system," *Bell Syst. Tech. J.* Feb. 1976.

[26] P. D. Mandigo, "No. 2B ESS: New features for a more efficient processor," *Bell Labs. Rec.*, Dec. 1976.

[27] R. W. Cook, W. H. Sisson, T. F. Storey, and W. N. Toy, "Design of a self-checking microprogram control," *IEEE Trans. Computers*, Mar. 1973.

[28] D. A. Anderson, "Design of self-checking digital networks using code techniques," CSL Rep. R527, Univ. Illinois, Urbana, Ph.D. dissertation, Oct. 1971.

[29] W. C. Carter, K. A. Duke, and D. C. Jessep, "A simple self-testing decoder checking circuit," *IEEE Trans. Computers*, Nov. 1971.

[30] R. J. Andrews, J. J. Driscoll, J. A. Herndon, P. C. Richards, and L. R. Roberts, "Service features and call processing plan," *Bell Syst. Tech. J.*, Oct. 1969.

[31] P. J. Kennedy and T. M. Quinn, "Recovery strategies in the No. 2 ESS," in *Dig. 1972 Fault-Tolerant Computing*, June, 1972.

[32] P. W. Agnew, R. E. Forbes, and C. B. Stieglitz, "An approach to self-repairing computers," in *Dig. 1st Annu. IEEE Computer Conf.*, Sept. 1967.

[33] T. R. Bashkow, J. Friets, and A. Karson, "A programming system for detection and diagnosis of machine malfunctions," *IEEE Trans. Electronic Computers*, Feb. 1963.

[34] N. Bartow and R. McGuire, "System/360 model 85 microdiagnostics," in *1970 Spring Joint Computer Conf.*, AFIPS Conference Proc., 1970.

Pluribus—An Operational Fault-Tolerant Multiprocessor

DAVID KATSUKI, ERIC S. ELSAM, MEMBER, IEEE, WILLIAM F. MANN, ERIC S. ROBERTS, JOHN G. ROBINSON, F. STANLEY SKOWRONSKI, AND ERIC W. WOLF, SENIOR MEMBER, IEEE

Abstract—The authors describe the Pluribus multiprocessor system, outline several techniques used to achieve fault-tolerance, describe their field experience to date, and mention some potential applications. The Pluribus system places the major responsibility for recovery from failures on the software. Failing hardware modules are removed from the system, spare modules are substituted where available, and appropriate initialization is performed. In applications where the goal is maximum availability rather than totally fault-free operation, this approach represents a considerable savings in complexity and cost over traditional implementations. The software-based reliability approach has been extended to provide error-handling and recovery mechanisms for the system software structures as well. A number of Pluribus systems have been built and are currently in operation. Experience with these systems has given us confidence in their performance and maintainability, and leads us to suggest other applications that might benefit from this approach.

I. INTRODUCTION

THE MULTIPROCESSOR discussed in this paper had its beginnings in 1972 when the need for a second-generation interface message processor (IMP) [1] for the ARPA network (ARPANET) [2]-[4] became apparent. At that time, the IMP's Bolt Beranek and Newman (BBN) had already installed at more than thirty-five ARPANET sites were Honeywell 316 and 516 minicomputers. The network was growing rapidly in several dimensions: number of nodes, hosts, and terminals; volume of traffic; and geographic coverage (including plans, now realized, for satellite extensions to Europe and Hawaii). A goal was established to design a modular machine which, at its lower end, would be smaller and less expensive than the 316's and 516's while being expandable in capacity to provide ten times the bandwidth of, and capable of servicing five times as many input-output (I/O) devices as, the 516 [5]. Related goals included greater memory addressing capability and increased reliability.

We decided on a multiprocessor approach because of its promising potential for modularity, for cost per performance advantages, for reliability, and because the IMP algorithm was clearly suitable for parallel processing by independent processors.

The IMP's communicate with host computers and with asynchronous terminals (IMP's with terminals attached are called TIP's [6]). Hosts use the network of IMP's and lines to communicate data messages of up to about 8000 bits; the IMP's divide these messages into packets up to about 1000 bits long. The functions performed by the IMP are those of a communications processor; they include storing and forwarding packets, generating headers, routing, retransmission, error checking, packet and message acknowledgment, message assembly and sequencing, flow control, line error detection, host and line status monitoring, and related housekeeping functions. The IMP's also send status and performance data to a network control center (NCC) which monitors and controls network operations [7], [8]. The ARPANET IMP's operate 24 hours a day, often in unattended locations.

In applications of this sort, reliability requirements differ from those commonly found in other real-time systems. The IMP network forms only a part of a larger system; even a perfectly operating network is not sufficient to guarantee perfect overall system performance. Failures in the host, or in the interface between the host and IMP, may still introduce errors. What this means is that some sort of host-process to host-process error control is required for critical applications; the best that the IMP network can provide is a good environment for host-level error recovery processes. These processes need a network which rarely makes errors and which, when such errors do occur, can effectively process host-to-host retransmissions. In other words, occasional dropped messages and brief outages are acceptable; outages of more than a few minutes are undesirable even if scheduled in advance.

Once we realized that what was needed was not so much reliability as the ability to recover gracefully from failures, we began to see ways to provide a much more robust network by coding this type of fault-tolerance into our operating system and application algorithms, and by including special mechanisms for bypassing and localizing faults in our already-modular hardware designs. The machine that emerged [5], [8]-[11] we call the Pluribus (Fig. 1 shows a typical Pluribus installation). It provides simple checking procedures such as parity, amputation features which allow failing equipment to be isolated and, optionally, redundant components. The software uses these features to detect, report, and isolate hardware failures. Since the symptoms of many subtle software failures are similar to those of intermittent hardware errors, fault-tolerant procedures which adequately recover from one can also recover from the other.

There is a spectrum of fault-tolerant approaches which are appropriate in various applications [12], [13]; our approach opts for a relatively inexpensive system which can quickly reinitialize itself, omitting troublesome components. This approach is especially suitable for applications in which brief outages can be tolerated and where overall correctness can be ensured by other techniques.

II. PLURIBUS SYSTEM ARCHITECTURE

The Pluribus may be characterized as a symmetric, tightly coupled multiprocessor, designed to be flexible and highly modular. Modules are physically isolated to protect against

Manuscript received April 7, 1978.
The authors are with Bolt Beranek and Newman Inc., Cambridge, MA 02138.

Fig. 1. The Pluribus front-end processor at Bolt Beranek and Newman's Research Computer Center.

common failures, and a form of distributed switch is employed for intermodule communications. In this section, we discuss these characteristics and describe the hardware architecture of the Pluribus.

A. Major Design Decisions

In order to make the basic operation of the Pluribus clearer, it is useful to examine some of the major design decisions that have directed its development, and to consider those decisions in the context of other options for multiprocessor system design. We have identified three areas which we believe are key aspects of the Pluribus approach to multiprocessing, each of which is considered in greater detail below.

Processor Symmetry: One dimension of multiprocessing involves the degree of inter-processor symmetry within the system [15, p. 83]. In this dimension, one extreme might be a typical general purpose computer system, including a central processor, a front-end processor, and perhaps one or more channel processors. Such an asymmetric system is relatively inflexible in power since increasing its central processing capacity requires the introduction of a more powerful central processor. Building redundancy into an asymmetric system can be expensive, since replication of all critical resources involves duplicating virtually the whole machine.

At the other extreme are systems like the Pluribus in which all processors are identical. In such systems, the advantages of redundancy and flexibility are much easier to achieve since they include only one type of processing unit. Even without explicit redundancy, a symmetric system can provide graceful degradation of throughput when a processing element fails. Pluribus systems which are sized for fully redundant operation include just one extra processing module; thus the degradation which results from failure of any processing module consists only of a loss of excess throughput capacity.

Processor Coupling: Another multiprocessing dimension is the level at which processors cooperate to accomplish overall system requirements. At one extreme the processors might run totally separate programs under the direction of a supervisor program, communicating only at arm's length. Such processors may be described as "loosely coupled" [15, p. 15]. At the other extreme, which is characterized by array processors such as ILLIAC IV [16], the processors run in lockstep, with a single program operating simultaneously on a number of data streams. The Pluribus lies between these extremes. Its processors are tightly coupled in the sense that all processors can access all system resources and perform all parts of the operational program; they operate independently except for necessary software interlocks on specific I/O devices and data structures.

Flexibility: Although one of the goals in the creation of the Pluribus was to develop a machine with high throughput, this goal was complemented by the need for a smaller, cheaper machine with relatively low throughput. Similarly, although the Pluribus was conceived as having at least two of every resource to permit recovery after failures, it was also clear that not all applications required or could afford a fully redundant system. Thus it was desirable for the architecture to be flexible in at least two ways: The size-flexibility goal was to smooth large incremental steps in the cost-performance curve by utilizing a highly modular design, which could provide processing capacity well beyond our anticipated needs. Flexibility in the area of fault-tolerance and fault-recovery was a related goal, since the need for fault-tolerance involves primarily economic considerations and we wanted to allow our customers to select fault-tolerance features independent of their throughput requirements. Also implied in each of these goals was the requirement for easy expansion to meet changing requirements.

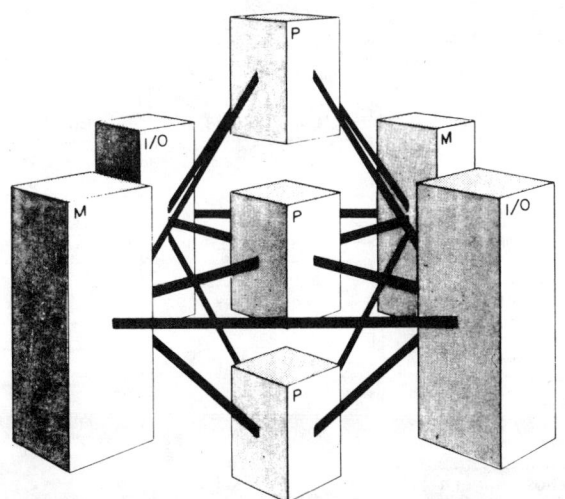

Fig. 2. A simplified view of the functional modules in a typical Pluribus system showing their interconnectivity. No physical relationships are implied.

B. System Overview

A central requirement in any multiprocessor is that processing elements be able to communicate both among themselves and with shared resources such as memories and I/O equipment. Ease of communication is always desirable and is vital in tightly coupled systems, since any delays or unwieldiness would immediately impact system operation and reduce programmability. These considerations, together with a natural desire for symmetry and simplicity, led us to adopt a unified addressing structure in which all common memory and I/O devices share the same address space. The Pluribus development was strongly influenced by previous unified-bus architectures in which processing, memory, and I/O units share not only a common address structure but also a single, time-multiplexed bus (the DEC PDP-11 is perhaps the most familiar example of this). Although multiprocessors based on the unified bus are both easily extensible and conceptually simple structures, they are vulnerable to single failures anywhere along the bus. In addition, the maximum throughput of such multiprocessors is limited both by the design bandwidth of the bus as well as by contention for common resources. To avoid these problems we used a unified bus to create the functional modules which make up the system, but not to form the main connection structure. We defined three basic functional modules which share a common address space but have separate intermodule communications paths: processor *buses*, memory *buses*, and I/O *buses*. A simplified system diagram is shown in Fig. 2.

(In the following sections we will often use the term *bus* to mean a logical and physical module, as in "processor *bus*," rather than just an interconnection system. All such usages will be italicized for clarity.)

The system for interconnecting these modules had several major requirements. It had to be easily extensible to support as many as eight memory or I/O *buses* (common *buses*) and eight or more processor *buses*. It had to permit the operating software to remove malfunctioning modules from the system and incorporate newly acquired or repaired modules. In addition, it had to impose minimal cost penalties for smaller systems, while scaling up smoothly to produce large systems. Finally, it had to have no common point of failure which could lead to total system failure.

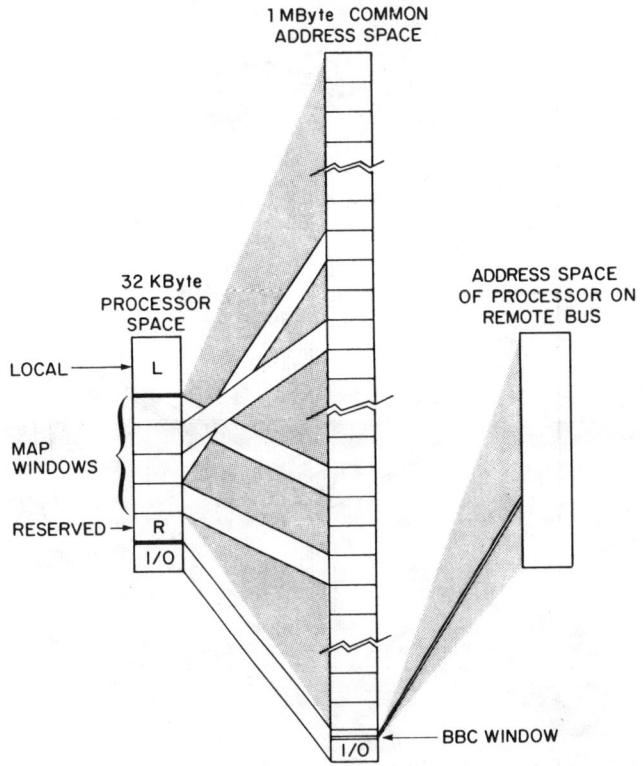

Fig. 3. Pluribus system address space, showing the mapping of processor "local" address space into the system space. "Backwards bus-coupling" path from one processor *bus* through an I/O *bus* to another processor *bus* is shown on the right.

The approach we finally adopted is similar in function to a central crossbar switch although it differs greatly in implementation. The crossbar switch approach allows an extremely high-bandwidth interconnection scheme and has been used to advantage in several multiprocessors [17]. However, the usual implementation techniques are vulnerable to single-point failures. To avoid these problems, we distributed the components of the switch among the various system modules in such a way that no single failure points remain. Switch elements are called bus couplers and consist of two circuit boards connected by a cable.

The bus couplers function by recognizing a range of addresses on processor or I/O *buses*, and initiating an access request on the appropriate common *bus* as a result. Since memory and I/O *buses* share a 20-bit address space, bus couplers must map 16-bit processor addresses into 20-bit system addresses under program control (see Fig. 3). In addition to handling inter-*bus* communications, bus couplers perform several other functions which will be described later.

Modularity: Since the basic Pluribus was modular at several levels, an unusual degree of flexibility was available when we set out to define standard structures within the system. The three basic system modules described above have clear logical functions within the system, but their actual implementation depended on various tradeoffs between cost, throughput, and available physical components.

It was decided early that the goals of flexibility and symmetry could be achieved by segmenting the operational tasks into strips of code (task distribution routines, task-oriented application routines, timers, etc.) which could be run by any available processor. The concept was that the code should be

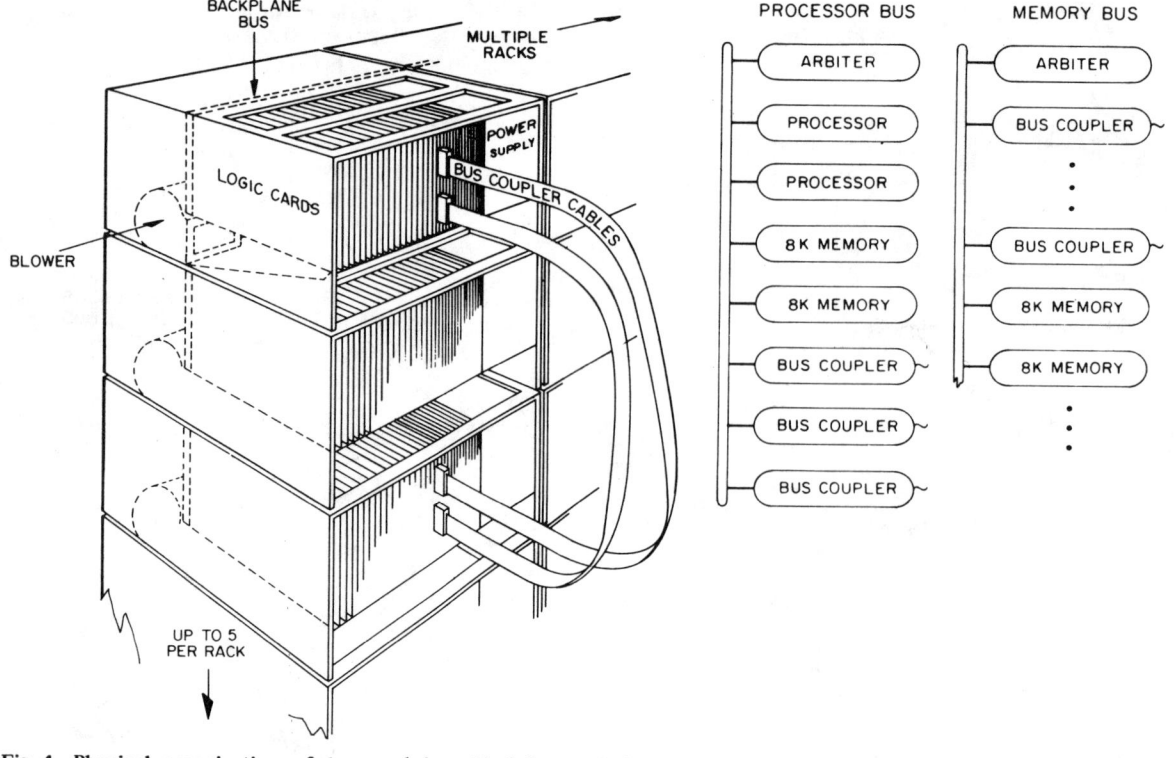

Fig. 4. Physical organization of *bus* modules. Modules are independently supplied with power and cooling.

Fig. 5. Local bussing structure and contents of the three kinds of *bus* modules.

both reentrant and accessible to all processors at all times. The primary function of the common memory modules is to provide space for data buffers, program work areas, and interprocessor communications areas. Code storage is divided into two parts: lightly used code is stored on common memory *buses* and is shared between processors; heavily used code is replicated in local memory on each processor *bus*. This strategy minimizes contention for access to common memory while holding down costs, especially since, in most applications, only a small part of the code is heavily used. The I/O modules were intended to support both polled low-speed I/O devices and high-speed interfaces capable of direct memory transfers. Couplers provide direct paths both from processor *buses* to I/O *buses* for control and polling, and from I/O *buses* to memory *buses* for direct memory transfers.

All normal processor-to-processor communication occurs through locations in common memory. However, to initialize the system, it must be possible for one processor to access the local memory and control registers of a processor on a different *bus*. To allow this, the bus couplers provide a limited reverse path through any common I/O *bus*.

In the following sections, we describe the physical implementation of these system modules and detail several support functions required by the architecture.

C. Physical System Structure

As mentioned in previous papers [5], [8], we chose the Lockheed SUE minicomputer as the point of departure for our system. It is a 16-bit machine, generally similar to the DEC PDP-11, which incorporates a unified address structure and an asynchronous, time-multiplexed bus. It also permits the attachment of a flexible combination of processors, memory, and I/O units. In contrast to the PDP-11, the SUE has its bus arbitration logic physically separated from the processor. This feature permits a bus to have one or several processors, or none at all. The Pluribus uses the bus, arbitration logic, processors, memories, and several minor I/O units of the SUE.

The basic Pluribus building block is the *bus* module. This module contains a modified SUE bus and card cage for up to twenty-four cards, together with completely self-contained cooling fans and power supply. Two *bus* modules can be connected to form an extended *bus*. A Pluribus system rack contains up to five *bus* modules, and each rack is typically supplied with a separate source of ac power. Systems sized to be fully redundant allow any *bus* module or any rack to be powered down for maintenance without affecting system availability (see Fig. 4).

Bus Structure (See Fig. 5): A processor *bus* contains one or two processors and their associated local memory, a bus arbiter, and one bus coupler per logical path. Our current applications require 8 to 12K words of local memory for each processor. The flexibility of the processor *bus* allows us to easily vary this parameter as memory prices or the requirements of the application change.

The common memory *bus* contains an arbiter, bus coupler cards for all the connected paths, and enough memory modules to support the application. Up to 512K words of common memory can be supported in a system, although that amount of memory would probably not be concentrated on one memory *bus*. Typical Pluribus systems have from 32K to 80K words of memory on each *bus*, depending on the application.

In addition to the bus arbiter and bus coupler cards, an I/O *bus* also contains cards for each of the various types of I/O interfaces that are required, including interfaces for modems, terminals, host computers, etc., as well as interfaces for

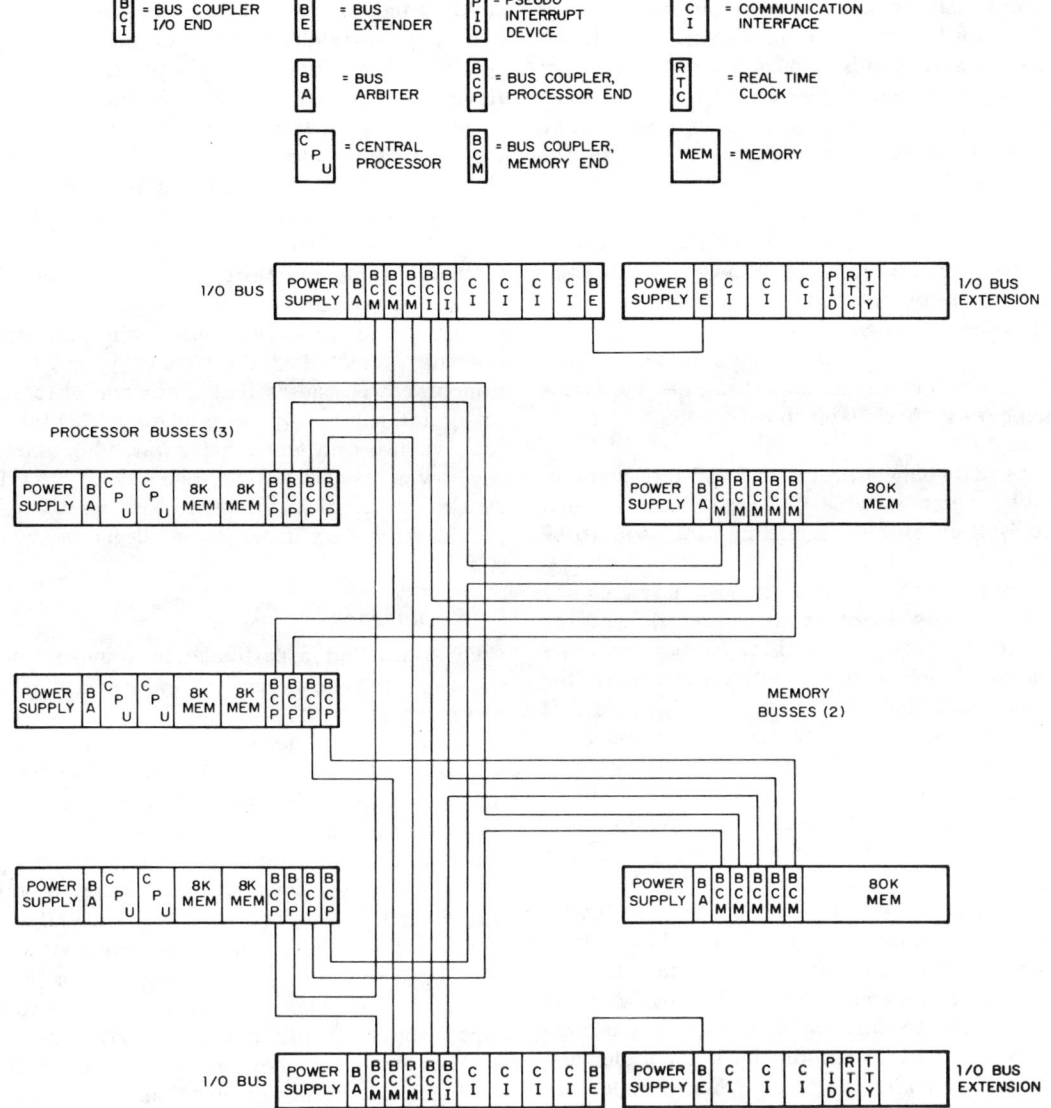

Fig. 6. Logical organization of a typical Pluribus system, showing interconnections of the distributed switch (bus coupler) structure.

standard peripherals. The I/O *bus* also houses a number of special units including 1) a real-time clock (RTC) which is used by the system for timing processes and communications links 2) a special hardware task disbursing unit known as the pseudo-interrupt device (PID) discussed further below and 3) a reload card which monitors up to eight communication lines, watching for (and processing) specially formatted reload messages from the outside world.

Inter-Bus Connection System: Since all processors in our system must be able to perform any system task, *buses* are connected so that all processors can access all shared memory and control the operation and sense the status of any I/O unit (see Figs. 2 and 6).

To connect processors and common memory, one card of a bus coupler is installed on a common memory *bus*, and the other on a processor *bus*. Similar connections are made from every processor *bus* to every common I/O *bus*. Coupler cards are connected by cables which may be up to 30 ft long, although most systems require a maximum of 10 ft.

The memory or I/O end of a bus coupler contains address-recognition circuitry and may be strapped to recognize and pass on to the memories or I/O devices any desired address range. When a processor makes a reference to common memory or I/O *buses*, the bus coupler cards on the processor *bus* all map the 16-bit address on the processor *bus* into a 20-bit system address and pass it to bus couplers at the other ends of the connecting cables. If the address is within the recognition range of a memory or I/O end bus coupler, it will request a service cycle on its *bus*. Data from the selected memory cell or device register are then passed back along the coupler path to the processor. This feature differentiates the system address space so that requests for memory or I/O *bus* access only cause service cycles on appropriate *buses*, thereby avoiding unnecessary contention.

Given a bus coupler connecting each processor *bus* to each common memory *bus*, all processors can access all common memory; I/O devices which do direct memory transfers must also access the common memories. These I/O devices are attached to as many I/O *buses* as are required to physically accommodate the number of devices and allow redundancy if necessary. Couplers connect each I/O *bus* to each memory *bus*. This coupler path is much like the processor-to-memory coupler path except that no address mapping needs to be done. I/O devices must respond to processor requests for action or information and in this respect the I/O devices act like memories. Bus couplers are also used to connect each processor *bus* to each I/O *bus*. Here also, a mapping must be done between the 16-bit processor address space and the 20-bit system space (see Fig. 3).

Processor *buses* need to access each other in order to start and stop each other and reload local memories. We provide this low bandwidth interconnection by allowing a processor to access another processor *bus* via its processor-to-I/O bus coupler. The coupler provides a small (4-word) mapping window from I/O space to each processor's space. A processor accesses another processor on a different *bus* by setting up and referencing this "backwards bus-coupling" window in system I/O space.

The coupler paths that connect processor *buses* into memory and I/O *buses* have program-settable enabling switches at their far (memory and I/O) ends, thus permitting processors to be cut into and out of ("amputated" from) the system. The reverse paths in the processor-to-I/O couplers also have enabling switches; normally the forward paths are turned on and the backwards paths are shut off. Since these paths represent a hazard whereby a "sick" processor or device could damage the system, we have arranged that only by storing a password at the proper address can a switch be changed. A processor can neither enable or disable its own access paths but one processor, deciding that another is sick and should be eliminated from the system, can amputate the *bus* of the offending processor. Reinstatement of an amputated *bus* happens in a similar manner.

Parity: To aid in detecting faulty bus couplers or defective memory, we compute and check parity across all bus coupler paths using a parity computation based on both data and address [18]. The scheme detects both "all zeros" and "all ones" failures. For writes to common memory, parity is computed at the processor or I/O end of the bus coupler and stored in the memory cell with the data. When the memory cell is read, the stored parity is checked at the processor or I/O end of the bus coupler. For accesses from processors to units on the I/O *buses* we use "feedback" parity; for writes to I/O the parity is computed by a special card on the I/O *bus*. The parity is then sent back up the coupler to the processor *bus* where it is compared with parity computed on that *bus*. For reads from I/O the special I/O parity card computes parity and compares it with recomputed parity on the processor *bus*.

Pseudo-Interrupt Device: Real-time systems or, more generally, systems requiring fast response, employ priority interrupt mechanisms to direct the attention of the processor to the most urgent tasks. Reliability and load sharing requirements make it desirable that any processor be able to service any I/O device, but also raise such questions as which processor to interrupt for servicing. We have opted for a simple yet flexible method: each "interrupt event" (DMA completion, RTC tick, software events, etc.) instead of actually interrupting a processor, writes a value associated with its priority to a hardware queuing device called the PID. The software is designed to allow each processor to put aside the context of its present computation periodically and check the PID. The PID, upon being read, will produce the highest value that has been stored in it and simultaneously delete that value from its internal queue. The processor can then use that value as an index to a table of tasks to be performed. The software uses the PID in a similar manner: each time a "strip" of code completes, it writes the number of the next strip in that task to the PID. When that becomes the highest number in the PID, the next available processor will execute the associated strip.

Our system does have two traditional interrupts, however. One is a 60-Hz clock interrupt. Each bus has its own 60-Hz clock, but conceptually this is an interrupt going to all processors; its main function is to time out locked data structures. The other classical interrupt is the power-fail/power-restore interrupt; each processor handles a power-fail interrupt from its own *bus* in the traditional way. Furthermore, bus couplers connected to processor *buses* will pass on any power-fail interrupt detected at their memory or I/O ends. A restoration of power causes first a *bus* master-reset and then a processor interrupt. We have adapted this interrupt mechanism to serve also as a *bus* activity watchdog timer. If any *bus* fails to show access activity for one second, a hardware timer fires, causing an artificial power-restore reset and interrupt. This provides recovery from some illegal hardware and software states.

D. Redundancy

To assure that a particular machine has enough redundant resources to allow survival in the face of component failures, we include at least one extra *bus* of each type so that a failure of any one resource, or the *bus* holding that resource, will not result in system failure. This approach also permits the system to survive many combinations of multiple failures. Thus if a system requires four processors to function at minimum acceptable throughput, six processors would be provided for reliability since the failure of any processor *bus* would disable two processors. Similarly, if a machine required at least 60K of memory to function, we would provide two *buses* each containing 60K of memory, or three *buses* each containing 30K of memory. It is important to note that redundant resources configured into a given machine are not idly standing by since they are used by the running machine to produce performance greater than the acceptable minimum.

I/O ports pose a special problem, since the devices and lines to which they are connected are frequently not doubled. For reliability, I/O interfaces can be doubled on separate I/O *buses*, but both interfaces must usually drive a single cable leaving the machine. We allow this by constructing all of our I/O port drivers with circuits that present a high impedance while unpowered. In addition, each I/O interface has a watchdog timer which, if not held off by repeated processor accesses, will disconnect the driver circuits within a second. Thus the likelihood that malfunctioning or unpowered I/O interfaces will interfere with the signals put on the external cable by the backup I/O interface is kept to a minimum.

III. THE PLURIBUS OPERATING SYSTEM[1]

Unlike most conventional systems, the principal responsibility for maintaining reliability in the Pluribus is placed on the system software rather than in the hardware structure. The Pluribus hardware was designed to provide an appropriate vehicle for software reliability mechanisms. Besides normal error checking and reporting in the hardware itself, programmed

---

[1] Portions of Sections IV, V, and VII of this paper have appeared in "Software Fault-Tolerance in the Pluribus," J. G. Robinson and E. S. Roberts, *AFIPS Conference Proceedings*, vol. 47, copyright AFIPS Press, Montvale, NJ. Reproduced with permission.

tests using known data patterns are run at intervals. When hardware errors are detected, system software exploits the redundancy of the hardware by forming a new logical system configuration which excludes the failing resource, using redundant counterparts in its place.

Pluribus systems also check the validity of their software structures. Redundant information is intentionally introduced into the data structures at various points and checked by processes operating upon those structures. An example of this technique applied to buffer structures is described in Section IV In addition, periodic background processes are used to recompute certain variables which are maintained by the operational system. If the recomputation uncovers a discrepancy, the variables are fixed directly or a more drastic recovery procedure is initiated.

In many cases, a failure is not detected at the exact time of occurrence but later when the software encounters some failure-induced discrepancy. By this time, the effects of the failure may be more widespread and the actual cause of the failure may be difficult to determine. In such cases, the system is not able to perform instantaneous recovery and seeks instead to restore normal operation as quickly as possible.

The remainder of this section discusses the organization of the Pluribus operating system and some of the techniques used for achieving coordination of multiple processors. These techniques are further explored below where two examples of Pluribus fault-tolerant software strategies are presented. One of these examines the Pluribus IMP buffer system in detail, and the other covers strategies for understanding failures when they occur and effecting necessary repairs.

A. General Responsibility of the Operating System

The software reliability mechanisms for a Pluribus system are coordinated by a small operating system (called STAGE) which performs the management of the system configuration and the recovery functions. The overall goal of the operating system is to maintain a reliable, current map of the available hardware and software resources. The map must include accurate information not only about the hardware structure of the machine, but also about variables and data structures associated with the processes that use that hardware. Moreover, the operating system must function correctly even after parts of the system hardware have ceased to be operational. New resources, as they are discovered (e.g., because hardware has been added or repaired), should be incorporated as part of the ongoing operation of the application system.

Since any component of the system may fail at any time, the operating system must monitor its own behavior as well as that of the application system. It may not assume that any element of hardware or software is working properly—each must be tested before it is used and retested periodically to ensure that it continues to function correctly. The operating system must be skeptical of its current picture of the system configuration and continually check to see if the environment has changed.

Based on these considerations, the Pluribus operating system builds the map of its environment step by step. Each step tests and certifies the proper operation of some aspect of the environment, relying on those resources certified by previous steps as primitives. Early steps examine the operation of the local processor and its associated private resources. Subsequent steps look outward and begin to discover and test more global resources of the system, giving the checking process a layered appearance. In the Pluribus operating system, each processor begins by checking its own operation and by finding a clock for use as a time base. Once these resources have been verified, the processor can begin to coordinate with the other active processors to develop an accurate picture of the system.

At the same time, the system must balance the need for reliable primitives with the need to accomplish normal operation efficiently. When all the environment has been certified, the system should spend most of its processing power on advancing the operational algorithms and return only occasionally to the task of reverifying its primitives. When failures of the environment have been detected, however, the power of the system must be brought to bear on the task of reconfiguring to isolate the failure.

B. Hierarchical Structure of the STAGE System

The Pluribus operating system is organized as a sequence of stages which are polled by a central dispatcher. A processor starts with only the first stage enabled. As each stage succeeds in establishing a proper map of its segment of the system state, it enables the next stage to run. Each stage may use information guaranteed by earlier stages and thus may run only if the previous stage has successfully completed its checks. Once enabled, a stage will be polled periodically to verify that the conditions for successful completion of that stage continue to apply. The system applies most of its processing power to the last stage that is enabled but returns periodically to poll each earlier stage. The application system is the final stage in the sequence and may run only after the earlier stages have verified all the configuration information of the application and the validity of the data structures.

Table I lists each stage of the Pluribus operating system, together with the aspects of the environment it guarantees. Many of the functions listed will not be discussed further but are provided to illustrate the layering of stages.

Since processors continue to perform each of the stages periodically, changes in the environment will eventually be noted. Any stage detecting a discrepancy in the configuration map will disable all later stages until the discrepancy is repaired. Then, all the later stages, which might depend on data verified by the disabling stage, will be forced to run all their checks, guaranteeing that they will make any further modifications to the configuration map necessitated by the first change. A serious failure, such as a nonexistent-memory interrupt, disables all but the first stage. In these cases, some reconfiguration might be needed, and all stages should perform all their checks before the application system is resumed.

C. Establishing Communication

So far, we have described the progress of one processor through the staged checking procedures of the operating system. All processors in the Pluribus perform the same checks, since it is important that they agree about the state of the system resources. Coordination of multiple processors with potentially different views of the hardware configuration requires two mechanisms: the processors must agree on an area of common memory in which to record the machine configuration map, and they must cooperate in their decisions to modify the map.

The first step in coordinating the multiple processors of a Pluribus is to agree on a page of memory through which to communicate. The procedure for initially establishing the

TABLE 1
Pluribus Operating System Stages

stage	function
0	Checksum local memory code (for stages 0,1,2). Initialize local interrupt vectors, and enable interrupts. Discover Processor bus I/O. Find some real-time clock for system timing.
1	Discover all usable common memory pages. Establish page for communication between processors.
2	Find and checksum common memory code (for stages 3,4,5). Checksum whole page ("reliability page").
3	Discover all common busses, PIDs, and real-time clocks.
4	Discover all processor bus couplers and processors.
5	Verify checksum (from stage 2) of reliability page code (for rest of stages plus perhaps some application routines). External reloading of missing code pages is possible once this stage is running.
6	Checksum all of local code.
7	Checksum common memory code. Maintain page allocation map.
8	Discover common I/O interfaces.
9	Poll application-dependent reliability and initialization routines. Periodically trigger restarts of halted processors.
10	Application system.

page for communication is clearly delicate. Prior to establishing the page, the processors have no way to communicate about where it will be. The procedure must operate correctly in the face of failures which might leave some of the processors seeing a different set of common memory pages from the rest. Processors which are unable to see the communication area will attempt to use another memory page and must be prevented from interfering with the unaffected processors.

Any processor that is first starting up (or restarting after some massive failure) can assume nothing about the location of the communication page. Any page may be used, and therefore a small area for communication control variables is reserved on each page of common memory. Part of this area is used for a brief memory test, which must succeed before the page may be used at all. Every processor attempts to establish the lowest numbered (lowest address in memory space) page that it sees as the page through which to communicate. To be valid, any page must have a pointer to the current communication page, and the communication page must point to itself.

Each processor looks at the pointer on the lowest numbered page it can see. There are three possible states for the pointer. First, if it points to the page itself, the processor has found the communication page and may now proceed to interact with other processors about the common environment. If it points to a higher numbered page, the processor may just fix the pointer, as the requirement that the communication page be lowest makes this case inconsistent. If it points to a lower numbered page, the processor must attempt to check if the indicated communication page is active. It must assume that the data might simply be old or invalid and must time it out using a dedicated entry in a special array of timers which is allocated on each page. The processor increments the timer and, if it ever reaches a certain threshold, unilaterally fixes the communication pointer and starts to use this page for communication. The processor is prevented from doing this by any other processor which is successfully using the lower numbered communication page; all such processors periodically zero all the timers on all memory pages in the system.

Consider what happens during various possible hardware failures. If the memory *bus* containing the communication page is lost, all processors will attempt to establish a new communication page on the other *bus*. Using their timers on the new lowest page (which initially points to the old one after the failure), they await the threshold. No one is holding the timers to zero, so the new page becomes the communication page when some processor's timer first runs out.

A processor blinded to the communication page by a *bus* or coupler failure will try to establish a higher numbered page for communication. From the point of view of the failing processor, this case is indistinguishable from the previous case, where the common *bus* failed. Since the rest of the processors are satisfied with the communication pointer, they will hold all timers to zero, and the failed processor will never be able to change the communication page pointer. If the processor sees a set of pages disjoint from the rest of the system, it behaves as if no other processors are running, but there is no memory where it may interfere and now we have two systems operating independently. In this case it is likely that the two systems will interfere over other resources; since multiple failures are required for this situation to occur in a Pluribus, we choose not to attempt recovery here.

D. The Consensus Mechanism

When configuration data must be updated, it is crucial to coordinate the Pluribus processors before making the modification. The mechanism to accomplish this goal we call consensus. Each stage has a consensus which is maintained as part of its environment. The first step in forming a consensus is to determine the set of processors that is executing the corresponding stage. This set has certified the primitives necessary to maintain successfully this stage's portion of the configuration map. In order for the system to respond to failures, the consensus must be kept current—new processors must be able to join it rapidly and processors that may have halted or ceased to run the stage must be erased from the set.

Each processor, based on its hardware address in the Pluribus, is assigned a bit in three consensus arrays, called "next," "smoothed," and "fix-it." As part of running the corresponding stage, every processor periodically sets its bit in the next consensus array to show that it wishes to participate in the consensus. After enough time has elapsed for each properly running processor to set its bit, this array is copied into the smoothed consensus and cleared. The set of processors in the smoothed array will then be used as a basis for decisions to reconfigure some portion of the resource map.

Any processor which wishes to modify some configuration information sets its bit in the appropriate fix-it array. Processors that agree with the configuration map clear their bits, and bits corresponding to processors not in the smoothed array are also cleared.

In effect, the bits in the fix-it array represent the votes of the individual processors in favor of a potential modification. In most cases, it is desirable that all processors agree before making the change. All processors wait until the fix-it array matches the smoothed array before implementing the fix. Other modifications might require only majority or two-thirds agreement. The choice of policy often depends on some tradeoff between resources (e.g., should we use more memory or more processors?). The Pluribus approach allows us to make this choice independently at each stage.

Since each processor in the Pluribus performs each stage of the checking code, the consensus mechanism provides the coordination needed to change the configuration map gracefully. When a stage detects a failure, the processor sets the appropriate fix-it bit and disables the following stages. When enough processors detect the failure they implement the fix to the configuration map. Now these processors can complete the later stages, devoting their attention to any further changes required by the failure. A processor which sees a different picture of the resources and cannot reach agreement with the rest of the system hangs forever at the point of detecting the discrepancy. This technique effectively prevents the processor from damaging the system.

E. Application-Dependent Checking

In general, it is desirable for the application system to perform its own checks before initiating or resuming normal operation. The last stage provides a mechanism which polls application-oriented processes to perform consensus-driven checks and repairs of their own data structures. This stage uses the results of the hardware (application-independent) discovery stages to certify its own data structures. For example, it could allocate or deallocate device parameter blocks as the I/O devices are discovered or disappear and initialize spare memory pages for use as data buffers as they become available. User-written reliability checks can be performed on any of the application data structures, and the appropriate reinitialization invoked to remedy failures.

Occasionally, it is possible for a processor checking application data structures to implement minor repairs to the data structures unilaterally. For major reconfigurations of the data structures, such as complete application system reinitialization, the checking routines must signal to the stage dispatcher that consensus is needed. The last concurring processor is then permitted to perform the reinitialization routine. Just as the early stages guarantee the hardware map, the application-dependent routines have the consensus mechanism at their disposal to validate the system data structures before entering the system. In addition, the application system data structures are rechecked periodically during normal system operation.

IV. AN EXAMPLE OF APPLICATION RELIABILITY

We use two general techniques to ensure the validity of data structures in the Pluribus. First, redundant information, where it exists, is checked for discrepancies, and appropriate action taken if they exist. Second, since detailed examination of all data for inconsistency is deemed impossible for any system of nontrivial complexity, we use watchdog timers to ensure the correct operation of the application system at various levels. As an example, we will discuss the buffer management strategy for the Pluribus IMP system.

Buffers in the Pluribus IMP circulate through the system from queue to queue; in some cases, they may be shared between two or more processes. Since a compromised queue structure may, in general, rapidly degrade the performance of the system, elaborate checking methods are built into the IMP program at various levels. In particular, we must be able to detect queues that are crossed or looped and buffers that have been lost (are on no queue at all).

Associated with each buffer in the system is a set of use bits corresponding to various processes that consume buffers. Any process that enqueues a buffer for some other process first sets the use bit for that process. When a process dequeues a buffer, the appropriate use bit must be on or the buffer will not be processed. As a special case, buffers on the system free list must have all their bits turned off. The buffer-freeing routine only returns a buffer to the free list if the last remaining use bit is that of the freeing process.

This technique intentionally generates redundant information and continually validates it as a buffer circulates through the system. In other words, the existence of a buffer on a queue informs the system that some processing is desired for that buffer. In principle, the use bit signals the same thing. Each buffer-processing routine could scan all the buffers in the system for those with its use bit set, but such a strategy would clearly be inefficient. The redundancy check gives preference to neither the queue nor the use bit as an indication of need for service, but rather requires agreement between the two indicators. When they disagree, the system assumes that a failure has indeed occurred and attempts to correct it by forcing the queue to be empty, so that the effects of the failure can be contained as much as possible.

The use bits allow the prompt detection of looped and crossed queues. In addition, an improper buffer pointer will often lead to a failure of the use bit check.

We must also consider the case of a buffer which has been lost from all queues. This condition could arise due to a program bug or as a result of a queue being emptied after a use bit failure. We could employ a classical garbage-collection scheme for this purpose; unfortunately, the demand for buffers is often great in a high-speed communication system, and the requisite locking of the buffer resources during such a garbage collection would likely result in lost inputs.

The recovery scheme we have chosen is a watchdog timer mechanism. Each buffer has associated with it a flag set by normal activity of the buffer which, in this case, is defined to be the periodic appearance of that buffer on the free list. Whenever a buffer is freed, its flag is set. In addition, flags for all the buffers on the free list are set periodically. In the high-speed communications environment, where data passes through a network node very rapidly, each buffer must appear on the free list at least once every two minutes. Therefore, each buffer flag is checked every two minutes to be sure it is set, and then cleared. A zero flag indicates that the buffer has dropped out of normal activity, and the buffer is unilaterally freed and its use bits cleared. In this way, any lost buffer is detected within at most four minutes and returned to normal usage.

V. ADVANTAGES OF THE PLURIBUS APPROACH TO FAULT-TOLERANCE

Two factors help to make our approach a cost-effective one. First, fault-tolerance is implemented primarily in software. This not only allows us to use unspecialized off-the-shelf hardware for much of our system, but also gives us considerable flexibility by allowing us to try new ideas as the product develops. When the time comes to upgrade machines in the field, a new software release is infinitely preferable to hardware modification. Implementing most fault detection in software also allows more complete error reporting than is characteristic of static-redundancy approaches.

The second factor is the modular nature of the Pluribus. Initially, the modular approach was chosen to permit easy expansion of the capabilities of a system to fit an application without being hampered by system-size boundaries. Our system expands by adding the same hardware modules as those which are duplicated to create a dynamic fault-tolerant system. Thus any system with more than the minimum number of processors for a given application both performs well and is fault-tolerant. A processor failure in such a system merely causes it to run a little slower. Since individual processors are relatively inexpensive, the percentage increase in system cost for processor redundancy is usually small, especially in large systems.

Sometimes the system requirements justify only limited fault-tolerance. An example is the large front-end processor which services the BBN Research Computer Center [22]. Here the bulk of the machine is fully redundant, but several of the host interfaces are used only occasionally for experimental systems, and their users can tolerate an occasional outage. Therefore, these interfaces are not duplicated, with a resultant savings in cost.

An additional factor contributing to cost-effectiveness is the relatively low percentage of processing power spent in explicit error detection (about 1 percent for current systems). We depend to a large extent on checks embedded in the operating program (such as code checksums) to detect errors, since the program is able to recover from failures whose effects are detected well after the fact. It is common practice for large software systems to include checks for some "impossible" software states and bad data structures. We have expanded these checks to be comprehensive, including checks which catch many types of hardware errors as well as lingering software problems.

One interesting effect of our approach is to make even a minimal, nonredundant machine significantly more resilient to transient failures caused by either hardware or software. All of the fault-tolerant mechanisms which run in the large systems run also in the small ones, and there are many transient failures which cause only momentary confusion which is usually solved by some level of reset or reinitialization. Obviously, a solid failure of some critical component or destruction of the program cannot be resolved without redundant resources, but these are by no means the only possible failures.

One result of our modular approach is that in contrast to the usual state of affairs, we expect larger systems to be more reliable than smaller ones, since more resources are available to be redistributed in case of trouble.

VI. Recent Field Experience

During the past year, we have had the opportunity to observe eight Pluribus IMP systems both under general operational conditions and in controlled field tests; the availability of these machines has been above 99.7 percent (by availability we mean uptime divided by scheduled uptime, excluding power and air-conditioning failures). Almost all the downtime was caused by program bugs which have been corrected since. Most recently, availability has been above 99.9 percent and we expect it to improve further as the machines reach maturity.

In evaluating this experience in terms of fault-tolerant performance, we feel that it is important to go beyond overall availability numbers and discuss the kinds of faults that the Pluribus system can report, the kinds we observed in the field, and the effects these faults had on system behavior.

The concepts of availability and fault-tolerance are complex when applied to a Pluribus since failure of a component generally results in a reduction in, rather than a complete loss of, performance. In many applications this is an advantage since extra capacity is useful during periods of peak load and reduced service is tolerable while repairing faults. For example, if an I/O interface or an entire I/O *bus* fails, the machine automatically substitutes a spare element with only a momentary (often unnoticeable) interruption of service and with no loss in performance. In the case of processors and memory, however, all resources are normally in use (none are in a standby mode) and the loss of any one (or several) of them forces a reduction in performance, but does not keep the system from running.

When used as an IMP, the principal measure of Pluribus performance is throughput. In the tests described below, the presence of program bugs (since corrected) resulted in somewhat lower availability than we had expected, but the three machines easily exceeded their contractual requirements and were able to deliver better than 92 percent of their rated throughput capacity 99.76 percent of the time and better than 50 percent of capacity 99.83 percent of the time.

Under normal operating conditions, it is possible to observe an IMP only by means of its reports to the NCC or by the reports of its neighbors in the network. Since IMP's often operate unattended, emphasis has been placed on the ability of each Pluribus to evaluate and report its internal hardware and software health. Three varieties of trouble-report messages are sent to the NCC.

Since the Pluribus continually evaluates the state of its hardware (see the discussion of the STAGE system), one type reports trouble in the hardware area. Examples of this are I/O errors, memory parity errors, power failures, and changes in configuration. The second type reflects the results of numerous interlocks and consistency checks which are made regarding tables, queues, variables, and other software entities. The third category concerns the Pluribus' role as part of the network. These reports monitor normal throughput statistics and temporary discontinuities in IMP-IMP message handling protocols, and are normally not directly pertinent to the fault-tolerance of the Pluribus itself. In a few cases the reports are received some time after a fault has been detected and dealt with by the Pluribus, but most fault messages appear within a few seconds.

In the normal course of building and operating Pluribus systems during the past year, we observed a number of unexpected hardware and software faults, but to verify our ideas and procedures we also wanted to observe a number of failure modes which would be expected to occur infrequently under normal operating conditions. To this end, we conducted an extensive series of tests over a three-month period using three four-processor Pluribus IMP's with redundant I/O interfaces, interconnected by high-speed terrestrial and satellite links. These tests demonstrated how the Pluribus handles many of the possible faults that might be encountered during the life of the equipment. We believe that the combination of the unexpected and planned faults we experienced constitutes a valid sample of the wide variety of intermittent failures in either hardware or software which such systems are likely to encounter. Examples of the types of fault recovery which were provoked or observed during these tests are discussed in the following.

1) Failures on the Processor Bus: We powered off various combinations of processor *busses* to demonstrate that the system would continue with traffic processing. We also tried placing bad instructions in various processors' local memories.

In power failure situations, the remaining processors continued to operate without reinitialization. Data handled by the failed processor(s) was recovered by network protocols and a number of trouble-reports indicated this fact. Data structures which were "locked" by the failed processors were "unlocked" by a software watchdog timer. When power was restored, the processors were smoothly readmitted to the system. Processors with bad local memory either halted or looped, and were quickly reloaded by other processors and brought back into operation automatically.

2) Errors in or Loss of Common Memory: We created situations whereby the system suddenly saw common memory disappear. In some cases we powered off the memory *bus*; in others we "removed" memory from usability tables. We also observed some spontaneous parity errors. Since common memory pages are assigned specific roles at initialization time, loss of one or more pages caused a variety of reactions, depending on the role of the lost memory and the amount remaining. At one extreme, loss of all common memory prevented the system from continuing. At the other, loss of one of several pages of message buffers caused only a brief adjustment of memory assignments by the Stage program. Most Pluribus systems are organized for fully redundant operation and have spare code and variables pages. Loss of a primary code or variables area caused a short transient in operations while the spare was initialized. As an example, loss of one-half of physical common memory (several pages of code, variables, and buffers) caused a reconfiguration lasting 15 s or less. During this period, all processors agreed on the reallocation of the remaining memory and reevaluated its usability. As a further test, we destroyed the integrity of various pages of common memory by storing random data in checksummed areas. The system reacted by restoring the contents of the affected page from the backup copy. This process required about 10–12 s. We also created test conditions in which the system found that all copies of critical programs in common memory were unusable (their checksum was bad). At this time the system automatically requested that it be reloaded (from another of the Pluribus IMP's or the NCC). It should also be emphasized that the integrity of message buffers is also protected by software checksums; data harmed in any way is reported to the NCC, and the originator is notified so that retransmission can take place.

3) Loss of I/O Device: We both created and observed several situations wherein I/O devices were either removed or experienced errors. In these cases, the I/O device was eliminated from usability tables by all processors and a backup device substituted. The system continued to operate, although in some cases, depending on the configuration being used, reinitialization was required. Loss of an entire I/O *bus* was handled in much the same way.

4) Loss of Critical Hardware: We observed that redundantly configured Pluribus systems would survive the loss of the RTC and the PID by swapping to the backup. Very little time was lost before the system continued. Errors in PID and RTC operation also are checked for and reported.

5) Internal Software Errors: As previously mentioned, the STAGE system and the IMP code are designed to check on the internal consistency of various software structures. In addition, the system ensures that none of the asynchronous processes is allowed to remain in a waiting state or in a loop. On a very infrequent basis, we observed that a Pluribus will report that such a condition was detected and corrected. We also forced many of these situations to occur by destroying key data structures or by causing queues to be looped or crossed. The system detected these, reported the problem, and continued normally, reinitializing if necessary.

6) Artificial Pathological Conditions: We did not attempt to cause pathological behavior of Pluribus hardware components which would, for example, write zeros to portions of memory or amputate *buses* at random, although we simulated these conditions with the software. Our observations of pathological behavior in the field, although infrequent, convince us that many of these cases can be withstood by the fault-tolerant software. For example, during field tests we observed that some extraneous data appear occasionally in certain critical tables causing the Pluribus to reinitialize quickly or to suspend activity on a communications link briefly. The problem was traced to a special reloading device which was being improperly activated. This situation was eliminated by a minor program change.

We have now gained enough experience with the Pluribus fault-tolerant mechanisms to have confidence in their ability to detect and cope with failures. In the field, spontaneous failures have been of a relatively minor nature and have been successfully dealt with. Under test conditions, all the major and minor failures which occurred or which we created were well tolerated and the systems continued to function within their rated capacities.

VII. Pluribus System Maintainability

Most fault-tolerant systems are designed to be repaired, sooner or later, by humans. Maintainability thus becomes a significant factor in long-term system performance. Since many systems are designed to recover from any single failure, but not from all multiple failures, the mean time to repair (MTTR) directly influences on-line spares requirements and hence the system cost for any given performance goal. To minimize MTTR, the system must provide accurate and unambiguous information about the nature of the detected fault and the automatic recovery process initiated. The environment in which the system operates is also important since the maintaining authority must be notified and must initiate the repair process as soon as possible.

The actual repair process may be carried out at several levels depending on the accuracy of the diagnostics and the obscurity of the failure symptoms. At the lowest level, the repair is accurately defined by the diagnostic and involves only the replacement of a faulty component. At the highest level, the failure may be caused by a design bug in either hardware or software. For the latter, the system must provide sufficient tools to permit overriding the operational recovery procedures. They must permit the repair personnel to reconfigure the system and run any required diagnostic procedures. The more powerful repair tools must be guarded to avoid operator-induced errors. Ideally this "fool-tolerance" [14, p. 32] should extend into all phases of repair. In practice we use only a two-level protection scheme that relies on experienced personnel not to make catastrophic errors.

Although we tend to think of hardware malfunctions as separate from software malfunctions, the symptoms of failure and the recovery procedures are frequently similar. In the Pluribus, the first detection of a fault is usually through failure of an embedded check in the main program, and frequently this is all that is required to initiate a correct recovery procedure. When the diagnostic value of an embedded check is insufficient to define a recovery procedure, various modular diagnostics may be run on the system. Thus in the case of a memory whose checksum is discovered to be wrong, the recovery action is to run a brief memory diagnostic and, if the memory appears usable, to restore the code from a spare copy.

Including a spare copy of some resource helps system recovery only if that spare resource works. Although it is traditional to run modular diagnostics on spare resources, our strategy has been to force the system to rotate use of resources from time to time. In some cases we use manual procedures, but the tendency has been to include automatic rotation procedures in the operational system software. This technique is clearly more appropriate to our application than it would be to a more traditional fault-tolerant requirement, since rotating faulty hardware into the operational system could cause a transient malfunction. On the other hand, it provides a better test of the hardware than modular diagnostics would provide.

One advantage of our reliance on embedded checks for failure detection is that we can detect that class of failure which is rarely caught by diagnostics. It is axiomatic that the operational program is the best program for certifying the hardware, but our operational program has also become the most comprehensive diagnostic for the hardware. In our experience, some of the most subtle hardware failures occur during operation of the application system, even though hardware diagnostic programs detect no errors. By augmenting the operational system with diagnostic capabilities, we have often been able to isolate even obscure or intermittent failures without interrupting normal operation.

A. Reporting Facilities

In the Pluribus IMP, the mechanism for reporting errors, recovery operations, and change-of-status information is the system trap (i.e., a supervisor call). Traps are reported locally on the system terminal and are also sent via trouble-reports to the network log at the NCC, where they serve a variety of diagnostic purposes. Understanding the nature of a failure in the running system requires fairly accurate knowledge of the state of the machine at the instant of the failure. The initial implementation of the trap mechanism recorded only the code number of the trap, which set of processors had encountered it, and a total occurrence count. This proved inadequate for accurate diagnosis and we have augmented the original trap mechanism to allow for saving a large snapshot of the instantaneous state of the processor, including such information as the contents of general registers, the global system time, map register settings, the last value read from the PID, and other important local data. These snapshots allow us to examine diagnostic information about the failure after the recovery code has taken effect and normal operation of the system has resumed. In an operational IMP, the snapshot information is sent to a data collection program at the NCC, where it is both stored for future reference and printed out on a log terminal. The snapshot facility is usually only enabled for that set of traps which indicate system malfunctions of some kind, since there are many normal traps which indicate such things as network topology changes. The same data collection program also keeps track of the current configuration of each machine and reports any changes on the log terminal. Thus the reconfiguration resulting from some module failure is immediately apparent. Correlating a reconfiguration with preceding snapshot error messages is usually sufficient to isolate solid failures.

B. Remote Diagnosis and Repair

Where the failure is intermittent, or error indications are ambiguous, we can make further diagnosis from the NCC using the remote connection capabilities of the network. This allows personnel at the NCC to interact with a system at a remote site exactly as if they were using the system control terminal at the site. We have provided a command structure in the system which allows us to make either "soft" or "firm" overrides of the configuration control structure, loop communications links, and run a variety of special diagnostics, monitors, and traffic generators. This enables us to diagnose many problems from the NCC even before dispatching repair personnel to the site (this can be especially appropriate for diagnosing program bugs). The current software is best at diagnosing the solid failures typical of mature hardware and treats most long-term intermittents as unrelated transients. Although we plan to implement heuristics which can deal with this type of problem, the diagnosis of long-term intermittents currently requires human intervention. Fully redundant Pluribus systems may be thought of as networks of paths and *buses*, so by causing the system not to use a particular path or *bus* and watching the trap log, we are usually able to localize the source of a hardware intermittent. Partitioning the *bus* and using some subset of the modules on the *bus* further localizes an intermittent traced to a particular *bus*, and repairs can then proceed. The same tools for reconfiguration are, of course, also available to maintenance personnel on site through the system control terminal, and trap reports sent to the NCC are duplicated also.

C. Partitioning

In extreme cases, when all normal diagnostic approaches have been exhausted, it is also possible to partition a fully redundant machine into two separate machines and run the operational system in one half while running stand-alone diagnostics or another copy of the system in the other half. We originally expected to use this approach quite frequently, but experience has shown the technique to be less useful than we expected. Splitting a system is a combination of many "firm" overrides of the configuration control which are not currently protected against operator error (i.e., deleting the last copy of a resource from the use tables, or overlapping system resources across the partition). There is also the problem of identifying fault-free components to include in the operational system half. In general, being able to identify a faulty module which is to be excluded from the operational system implies that we can fix the fault by replacing the module, which usually obviates the need for partitioning into two machines. And finally, once a machine has been split, any new failures are likely to cause fatal problems that the machine might have been able to cope with had it not been split. Our current feeling is that the risks of splitting an operational system usually outweigh the advantages.

D. Reloading and Down-line Loading

An important facility provided by the Pluribus hardware allows us to load and start the machine with no onsite personnel. This is accomplished by special-format messages which trigger a simple reload device when received over the network. This device is used to load a software package capable of dumping or reloading the operating system and application code. The source of reload code may be either some other Pluribus IMP on the network, or a disk file at the network control center. These reloading facilities are also used for distributing software updates to the machines in the field. A Pluribus IMP which discovers all copies of some application code page to be compromised will attempt to get a down-line reload from a neighbor IMP. This request is reported to the NCC where an operator then sets up the reload source for the transfer. Its use enables an IMP without duplicated resources to recover quickly from transient failures caused by hardware or software.

E. Maintenance Experience

The prototype Pluribus systems performed their error recovery functions well in many cases. Minor problems were often bypassed so effectively that the users and maintenance personnel were never aware of the problem. Even following drastic failures, such as the loss of a common memory bus, normal system operation was restored within seconds. From our experience with these early systems, however, certain deficiencies in our original strategies have become clear.

In some failure cases, one repair would lead to another, until eventually a fairly major reinitialization would be performed, with obvious effects on the users of the system. Unfortunately, the massive recovery often destroyed evidence of the original failure, or masked evidence necessary for effective diagnosis. While the goal of restoring the system to normal operation was achieved, we were left without any idea of why the reinitialization was required. This was particularly frustrating when the frequency of occurrence was on the order of hours or days.

In other cases, normal operation seemed to continue while some hardware failure occurred undetected. Either the failure was covered by effective recovery at a fairly low level in the system or it occurred in a redundant portion of the hardware which was not being exercised. A second failure in conjunction with the first would remove the last copy of some critical resource, causing the system to fail.

These initial experiences led through several intermediate steps to the current set of maintenance tools and diagnostics. In the prototype systems, we were forced to remove the system software and run stand-alone diagnostics when trouble arose. Development of the original recovery algorithms into early versions of the current STAGE system allowed diagnosis and repair while running the operational system; however, system programmers were required to interpret the traps and wrestle the system into different configurations during repair. The usual repair team during this period included a system programmer (usually at the NCC) watching and interpreting the traps, with a maintenance technician on site replacing components.

At present, the tools and diagnostics are well enough defined and documented so that usually only maintenance personnel are required for a repair. Hardware and software staff at the NCC may offer suggestions when maintenance personnel are dispatched to a site and may still direct occasional repair efforts if a difficult problem or inexperienced personnel require it, but this is the exception rather than the rule.

VIII. Other Applications and Extensions

Since the Pluribus has evolved from a communications application where overall system availability rather than total fault-coverage is the goal, our approach is most obviously suitable for similar applications. We have opted for an approach which depends heavily upon reconfiguration and reinitialization when faults are detected, and which requires very little special hardware beyond that needed to implement our multiprocessor architecture. Our approach would not be suitable for applications where absolutely no downtime can be tolerated, where total computational context must be preserved over failures, or where overall correctness must be ensured. In these cases, traditional approaches involving some form of static redundancy or execution redundancy are indicated [12], [13]. Techniques somewhat similar to ours, but for a redundant uniprocessor, are in use in the Bell System's latest Electronic Switching System [19]. Although we have not closely investigated applications outside the communications area, we believe our approach is suitable for many other tasks, and we discuss several of these briefly below.

A. Message Systems

We have made an extensive study of the possibility of using the Pluribus computer as the basis for a message system. By message system we mean not only traditional message-switching such as is done in the Telex system, but also a system of mailboxes and files by which users can exchange and file messages without recourse to the U.S. Postal System, secretaries, or filing cabinets, and which will permit complicated searches and sorts of message files. Such a system must have high availability but could easily tolerate brief outages after a failure.

B. Real-Time Signal Processing

We have already built one system which is the front-end and control processor for a seismic data collection network, and which performs some preprocessing of seismic data [20]. We believe this application can be extended to other areas of real-time signal processing with requirements for high overall system availability. Since many signal processing tasks can be broken into parallel components, the multiprocessor architecture would be especially appropriate.

C. General-Purpose Timesharing Systems

It seems to us that explicit use of fault-tolerant techniques could benefit general purpose timesharing systems and large operating systems. These systems operate continuously and are subject to minor hardware errors and subtle software bugs, but do not require totally uninterrupted operation. Although most large systems include some self-checking in the software, software fault-tolerance, to be truly effective, must be well integrated into the overall system design, and into the special hardware features which are usually required.

One of the primary purposes of most large operating systems is to provide disk and tape handling features. In this context, reinitialization in response to faults is a much more serious problem than, for example, in the IMP. Various checkpointing procedures may be required to restore the overall system state to a point where restart is possible [21, pp. 340–353]. Large operating systems often support a variety of checkpointing services since the best techniques to use under these circumstances depend in part on the applications being serviced; in cases involving on-line database updates, the application programs themselves must be designed around their fault-tolerance requirements.

C. Reservations Systems

Airline, hotel, and car rental reservation systems provide good examples of on-line database systems which could benefit from well-designed software fault-tolerance systems. Once a reservation has been accepted, it must not be lost. Backup techniques such as dual updating of two copies of the database, perhaps located in different cities with independent central processors and telecommunications systems, may be worthwhile. On the other hand, minor problems (hardware or software) may be tolerated, especially if the problems can be resolved by reentering on-line transactions which were affected by the fault. Even with dual machines in remote locations, using a machine like the Pluribus would increase the reliability of each site separately, and provide substantial computing power in an expandable package. Further research will be required to understand fully the implications to the Pluribus of database integrity requirements for reservation systems.

D. Process Control

Our approach is clearly more appropriate to some areas of process control than to others. We envision a typical application in the area of overall supervisory systems coordinating a number of subsidiary systems or controllers, and incorporating tasks such as inventory control and job scheduling. Processes that could afford to stop momentarily would be controlled directly. End-to-end error correction and fault-masking hardware would be used in the machine interface for applications needing overall fault-tolerance. As with the previous applications, some form of checkpointing would be built in to preserve context over restarts.

ACKNOWLEDGMENT

Much of the initial development of the Pluribus computer was supported by the Information Processing Techniques Office of the U.S. Defense Advanced Research Projects Agency, under Contract Numbers DAHC15-69-C-0179, F08606-73-C-0027, and F08606-75-C-0032, and by the Defense Communications Agency under Contract DCA200-C-616. Additionally, a number of the applications systems were developed under contracts from various branches of the U.S. Government.

Many people have contributed to the Pluribus project; Frank Heart has led the effort since its inception.

REFERENCES

[1] F. E. Heart, R. E. Kahn, S. M. Ornstein, W. R. Crowther, and D. C. Walden, "The interface message processor for the ARPA computer network," in *AFIPS Conf. Proc.*, vol. 36, pp. 551-567, June 1970. Also in W. W. Chu, Ed., *Advances in Computer Communications*. Dedham, MA: Artech House, 1974, pp. 300-316. Also in P. E. Green and R. W. Lucky, Eds., *Computer Communications*. New York: IEEE Press, 1975, pp. 375-391. Also in R. P. Blanc and I. W. Cotton, Eds., *Computer Networking*. New York: IEEE Press, pp. 60-76, 1976.

[2] L. G. Roberts and B. D. Wessler, "Computer network development to achieve resource sharing," in *AFIPS Conf. Proc.*, vol. 36, pp. 543-549, June 1970.

[3] F. E. Heart, "The ARPA network," in *Computer Communication Networks*, R. L. Grimsdale and F. F. Kuo, Eds. (Proceedings of the NATO Advanced Study Institute of Sept. 1973, Sussex, England), Leyden, The Netherlands; Noordhoff Int. Publ., 1975, pp. 19-33.

[4] E. W. Wolf, "An advanced computer communication network," in *AIAA Computer Network Systems Conf. Rec.*, Apr. 1973.

[5] F. E. Heart, S. M. Ornstein, W. R. Crowther, and W. B. Barker, "A new minicomputer/multiprocessor for the ARPA network," in *AFIPS Conf. Proc.*, vol. 42, pp. 529-537, June 1973.

[6] S. M. Ornstein, F. E. Heart, W. R. Crowther, S. B. Russell, H. K. Rising, and A. Michel, "The terminal IMP for the ARPA computer network," in *AFIPS Conf. Proc.*, vol. 40, pp. 243-254, June 1972. Also in W. W. Chu, Ed., *Advances in Computer Communications*, Dedham, MA: Artech House, 1974, pp. 317-328. Also in P. E. Green and R. W. Lucky, Eds., *Computer Communications*. New York: IEEE Press, 1975, pp. 354-365.

[7] A. A. McKenzie, B. P. Cosell, J. M. McQuillan, and M. J. Thrope, "The network control center for the ARPA network," in *Proc. 1st Int. Conf. Computer Communication* (Washington, DC), pp. 185-191, Oct. 1972. Also in R. P. Blanc and I. W. Cotton, Eds., *Computer Networking*. New York: IEEE Press, 1976, pp. 319-325.

[8] S. M. Ornstein and D. C. Walden, "The evolution of a high performance modular packet-switch," in *Conf. 1975 Int. Conf. Communications*, vol. I, pp. 6-17 to 6-21, June 1975.

[9] R. D. Bressler, M. F. Kraley, and A. Michel, "Pluribus: A multiprocessor for communications networks," in *14th Annu. ACM/NBS Technical Symp.—Computing in the mid-70's: an Assessment*, pp. 13-19, June 1975.

[10] S. M. Ornstein, W. R. Crowther, M. F. Kraley, R. D. Bressler, A. Michel, and F. E. Heart, "Pluribus—A reliable multiprocessor," in *AFIPS Conf. Proc.*, vol. 44, pp. 551-559, May 1975.

[11] F. E. Heart, S. M. Ornstein, W. R. Crowther, W. B. Barker, M. F. Kraley, R. D. Bressler, and A. Michel, "The Pluribus multiprocessor system," in *Multiprocessor Systems*: Infotech State of the Art Report, Infotech International Ltd., Maidenhead, Berkshire, England, 1976, pp. 307-330.

[12] A. Avizienis, "Approaches to computer reliability—Then and now," in *AFIPS Conf. Proc.*, vol. 45, pp. 401-411, June 1976.

[13] —, "Architecture of fault-tolerant computing systems," in *1975 Int. Symp. Fault-Tolerant Computing*, Jan. 1975.

[14] J. Goldberg, "New problems in fault-tolerant computing," in *1975 Int. Symp. Fault-Tolerant Computing*, pp. 29-34, Jan. 1975.

[15] P. H. Enslow, Jr., Ed., *Multiprocessors and Parallel Processing*. New York: Wiley, 1974.

[16] G. H. Barnes *et al.*, "The Illiac IV computer," *IEEE Trans. Comput.*, vol. C-17, pp. 746-757, Aug. 1968.

[17] W. A. Wulf and C. G. Bell, "C.mmp—A multi-mini-processor," in *AFIPS Conf. Proc.*, vol. 41, pp. 765-777.

[18] U.S. Patent 4 035 766, July 1977.

[19] M. N. Myers *et al.*, "Maintenance software," *Bell Syst. Tech. J.*, vol. 56, no. 7, pp. 1139-1167, Sept. 1977.

[20] R. T. Gudz, "Application of the Pluribus multiprocessor in a distributed data collection and processing network," in *Conf. Rec. OCEANS 77*, Oct. 1977.

[21] E. Yourdon, *Design of On-Line Computer Systems*. Englewood Cliffs, NJ: Prentice Hall, 1972.

[22] W. F. Mann, S. M. Ornstein, and M. F. Kraley, "A network-oriented multiprocessor front-end handling many hosts and hundreds of terminals," in *AFIPS Conf. Proc.*, vol. 45, pp. 533-540, June 1976.

Chapter 4: Commercial Systems for Industrial Control and Transaction Processing

Introduction

Traditionally, the development of fault-tolerant computer systems has been confined to aerospace and communications applications for which major research organizations have developed systems for high-reliability applications. Recently, however, a number of computer systems have been developed for commercial applications that have similar reliability requirements but could not previously afford the redundant hardware and/or software characteristic of fault-tolerant systems.

The two most prominent applications in which fault-tolerant systems have appeared are industrial control and transaction processing. Industrial control applications are characterized by the need for continuous correct operation over varying durations of time, depending on the nature of the process. Transaction-processing systems, however, require processing of small, individual transactions on databases, with the database being the critical element. Consequently, both types of systems have unique reliability and performance requirements that make the use of fault-tolerant systems attractive, provided that they can be made cost effective. This chapter will discuss further the reliability requirements of these applications and will then outline the approaches being taken by a number of commercially available systems to meet these requirements in a cost-effective manner.

Reliability Requirements

Process Control Applications

Industrial process control systems for such applications as control of hazardous processes, exothermic reactions, and nuclear plants; toxic substance handling; and similar critical operations require extremely reliable control systems [MCG84,WIL84]. Of special importance are several considerations, including potential damage to the environment, equipment, and personnel, loss of revenue due to stoppage in processing, and loss of material due to erroneous irreversible processes. These control systems range in complexity from single-process loop controllers to large hierarchical configurations in which a number of individual low-level process loops are coordinated by one or more higher level controllers. Depending on the nature of the process, it may be acceptable in some cases to suffer the loss of one control loop provided that control is maintained over the rest of the control loops in a plant. In other cases, the consequences of failure may require that absolutely no errors be introduced into a given process loop. Occasionally, one might wish to trade off reliability for performance, with resources combined for fault-tolerance purposes during critical phases of a process, and then separated and used concurrently to gain performance during less critical phases. Each of the systems examined in this tutorial addresses one or more of these performance requirements.

Transaction Processing Systems

In a transaction-processing system, the consequences of a failure are strictly financial, not life-threatening. In applications such as airline reservation systems, on-line banking, and credit card verification, there exist both reliability and availability requirements. First, the availability of the system must be reasonably high, i.e. one must be assured that the system is "up" a sufficient percentage of time so that customers are not discouraged nor are revenues lost. Second, the hearts of these systems are their databases, which must be protected at all costs. Hence it is acceptable to repeat a transaction whenever an operation is suspect, rather than to take the chance of an error being introduced into the database. Response time requirements are typically not as severe as those for process control and other real-time systems. Consequently, unlike process control operations, it is not necessary to completely mask errors, so long as sufficient redundant information is maintained to be able to reconstruct a database following an erroneous action. This is done by either throwing away the results of a transaction or keeping an audit trail from which actions can be reversed. The time lost in performing such recovery is typically not critical, nor is the inconvenience of occasionally requiring an operator or customer to repeat a transaction.

Fault-Tolerant System Design Approaches

Process Control System Design

Fault-tolerant systems developed for process control applications fall into two catetgories: ultrareliable systems designed to prevent any errors from being introduced into a process and large hierarchical systems designed to minimize loss of process control by confining damage to one process loop while ensuring proper overall control of the plant.

The August Systems CS-300 [WEN81,WEN82] (a derivation of the SIFT concept [WEN78]), the Triplex 32 [MCG84], and the experimental c.vmp at Carnegie Mellon

[SIE77] were all designed to prevent instantaneous error introduction into their controlled processes, while maintaining continuous operation in the presence of faulty components. All three systems take a common approach, i.e. utilizing triple modular redundancy (TMR) with voting to allow any single failed component to be masked out by the remaining two modules. The system is susceptible to failure if a second module fails before the first one is repaired, but all three systems alert the operator to the problem so that a "hot repair" can be performed while the system continues to operate, minimizing the time during which the system is vulnerable to a second failure.

In the cases of the two commercial systems, off-the-shelf microprocessors are utilized, allowing the use of standard software development tools and other available software. In both cases the fault tolerance is essentially transparent to the programmers, although the voting processes differ between the two. In the Triplex 32 system, hardware voting circuits are used in each processor module and in the input/output (I/O) modules. In the August CS-300 system, all voting by the processors is handled in software, with all three processors receiving all data and performing all calculations. In both systems, various hardware mechanisms have been developed for implementing voting switches, device actuators, and other fault-tolerant and fail-safe process interfaces that further improve overall system reliability.

In the c.vmp system, an extra feature is the ability of the system to dynamically reconfigure according to the needs of the application process. When a critical process is identified, the three processors go into a lock-step mode with a hardware voter used to mask single faulty processors. During other times, the special voter circuit allows the three processors to operate independently to improve throughput. An interrupt mechanism is responsible for toggling the system between these two states.

In contrast to the above system, the REBUS system [AYA82] has been designed as a large, hierarchical system that manages a large number of process control loops. In this application, the loss of a single loop at any one time is considered acceptable, and hence error-masking techniques are not used in the low-level controllers. However, loss of overall control of the plant is not acceptable, so REBUS employs a fault-tolerant communication protocol that is designed to detect various bus transmission errors. In addition, a robust protocol for passing control among the various system processors is a part of the design to ensure continuous plant operation.

Transaction-Processing System Design

Most commercially available fault-tolerant systems reported over the past ten years have been oriented toward transaction processing applications [KIM84,SER84, ZOR85]. Most of these systems are multiprocessors, allowing the number of processors in the system to be tailored to the volume of transactions required by each individual customer. These multiprocessors include both tightly coupled systems such as the Stratus/32 [FRE82,HEN83], the Synapse N+1 [INS83, COH83, FRA84, NES85], and the Sequoia system [MAR85] as well as loosely coupled systems such as the Tandem NonStop [HOR84,KAT77,KAT82], the Auragen System 4000 [GLA84], and the Tolerant Eternity System [ELE86]. Most of these systems can also be used in geographically-dispersed network configurations as well.

All of these systems are designed for transaction processing, in which small atomic actions are performed on a database in response to user requests. Consequently, most of the database protection features are designed to ensure that each transaction is correctly completed before another is begun, with recovery actions occurring as close as possible to the source of any errors. The individual approaches of the above systems to providing this operation range from all-software- to all-hardware-oriented designs.

The Tandem systems are the oldest and the most successful of the group, utilizing a checkpointing strategy for reliability. To ensure continuous non-stop operation, each transaction process creates a backup process when it is initiated, and periodically sends checkpoint information to the backup, which remains inactive. When an error is detected in the primary process, the backup uses this checkpoint information to reconstruct the state of the process so that processing can continue with minimum delay. Similar approaches are used by the Auragen and Tolerant systems, in that a backup process exists for each active primary process in the system. In the Auragen system, a "queue-and-count" approach is used in which each message sent by a primary process is received by three processes: its own backup process and both copies of the destination process. The Tolerant system likewise sends periodic checkpoint information to backup processes. In all three systems, the backups do not actively process the transaction; they simply take over the processing of a transaction when the primary fails, using a state constructed from the checkpoint data.

The Synapse and Sequoia tightly coupled systems both perform most of their operations in non-write-through caches, with updates posted to shared memory upon completion of each transaction. The Synapse system maintains a write-ahead log, so that disk updates can be reconstructed following a failure, while the Sequoia system uses a "double flush" technique in which two copies of cache data are copied to main memory independently, allowing one good copy of data to exist at all times in spite of the occurrence of faults.

The Stratus/32 differs from all of the previously mentioned systems in that it performs no checkpointing at all. Instead, a hardware approach to fault tolerance is used in which four microprocessors simultaneously execute all programs in the system. These processors are organized as two synchronized pairs, with the processors in each pair continuously comparing their outputs. If a mismatch occurs, the pair isolates itself from the system bus while the other pair continues operations. Similar approaches are used in the peripheral controllers, while error-correcting codes are used in the two copies of the memory. Consequently, the system can continue processing without stopping, despite the presence of any single failure within each class of elements.

Error-detection features differ widely among systems. The Sequoia system uses an approach similar to that of the Stratus/32 in that each processor is duplexed, with continuous matching of results, so that immediate detection of all faults is assured. Another processor pair continues operation when a faulty pair of processors is detected. In both the Sequoia and Synapse systems, a list of transactions is maintained in shared memory so that available processors will continue to select and execute transactions in spite of one or more failed units. Processes from failed processors are simply requeued and then reexecuted by the next available processor. Most transaction-processing systems, other than Stratus/32 and Sequoia, rely on relatively primitive fault detection such as periodic "I'm alive" messages sent to backup processes, time-outs on buses and I/O channels, parity errors in memory or buses, and error-correcting codes in memory. Consequently, errors are often detected farther in time from their sources, and thus these systems restrict all processing to very short atomic actions, and provide more extensive recovery procedures than systems that continuously match the outputs of identical elements.

All of the above systems are similar in their organization of peripheral devices. In particular, they all provide some capability for maintaining "mirrored" disks. Most peripheral controllers allow access by more than one processor, and they maintain two copies of all critical data on duplicate disk drives. Again, the most critical part of a transaction-processing system is the database. Consequently, the maintenance of duplicate data is one of the critical features of these systems. In most cases, a performance bonus is provided by allowing the copy of a duplicated record closest to the read heads of the mirrored disks to be read without waiting for the duplicate copy to arrive, shortening the average read time in the system.

Summary

Whereas the use of redundant processors and other components for commercial applications would not have been cost effective ten years ago, the availability of inexpensive VLSI microprocessors and other components has enabled fault tolerance to be incorporated into various systems designed for transaction processing and industrial control. Consequently, potential users who either have avoided the use of digital systems for reliability considerations or have avoided the use of fault-tolerant systems for cost considerations may now take advantage of the various fault-tolerant technologies that have been developed for the space program, the communications industry, and more recently the business community. In addition, the trend has been toward the use of standard microprocessors, such as the Motorola 68000 family, and variations of standard operating systems, such as UNIX, allowing familiar software and development tools to be utilized.

The papers presented in this section of the tutorial discuss the architectures and other hardware and software features of a number of representative commercial fault-tolerant systems. It can be expected that the growth of such systems will escalate over the next few years as the cost of reliability continues to decrease with improved technology and decreasing component costs.

Sophisticated fault-tolerant computer systems, employing redundant hardware and software, are now within the reach of industrial users, thanks to inexpensive μCs.

Fault-tolerant computers ensure reliable industrial controls

In many industrial process-control applications, a computer failure can result in financially crippling downtime, spoiled production, a loss of quality control, or damage to the environment. In extreme cases, human lives could be jeopardized.

Now, for the first time, a cost-effective control computer can bring to industrial systems a degree of reliability that was formerly available only in vital aerospace equipment, such as manned-spaceflight systems. The Series 300 offers such a dramatic advance in reliability that it has been dubbed the Can't-Fail Computer. Its reliability stems from triple redundancy in the hardware and from a design strategy known as Software Implemented Fault Tolerance (SIFT), originally developed for NASA. The cost effectiveness of the Series 300 stems from its use of standard Intel 8086 microprocessors, patented support circuits with built-in redundancy, and flexible software that restricts redundant operation to critical phases of the application—thus maximizing throughput at other times.

The actual reliability of a Series 300 system is difficult to quantify because it depends heavily on how the system is configured, programmed, and maintained in a specific application (see "How Reliable is the Computer System?"). The Can't-Fail tag is justifiable because the Series 300 is truly fault tolerant. A single hardware failure cannot interrupt continuous and accurate operation. Only if two failures occur simultaneously, or almost simultaneously, can the complete system fail. Since a single failure will not interrupt operation, overall reliability, therefore, depends on the speed with which repairs can be made—before another hardware failure occurs. Because rapid repair is so important, the Series 300 is designed so that circuit boards can be changed and automatically resynchronized without interrupting system operation.

What's in a system?

In the SIFT approach to fault-tolerant computing, redundancy, voting, and isolation are essential:

- Replicated hardware and software ensure that the redundant modules continue to operate correctly if a failure occurs in one module.
- Outputs are compared from modules performing critical functions simultaneously. If the answers disagree, the majority modules will outvote the faulty one to maintain the validity of the output data.
- Although communication between the replicated modules is necessary, they must be isolated so that a malfunctioning unit will not affect the performance of the other units.

For working modules to be able to outvote a faulty module, a minimum of three modules must perform the same function. Reliability could be enhanced by say, quintuple redundancy instead of triple redun-

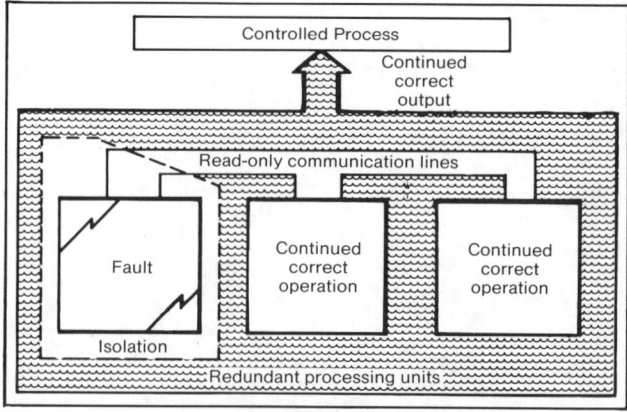

1. The architecture of the fault-tolerant computer is based on triple redundancy. Each of the processor units connects to the others over read-only communication lines. This arrangement, in effect, isolates a faulty unit so that it cannot influence the operation of the other units.

John H. Wensley, Chairman
August Systems, Inc.
2757 19 St., S.E., Salem, OR 97302

Reprinted with permission from *Electronic Design*, Volume 29, Number 13; copyright Hayden Publishing Co., Inc., 1981.

dancy. Then, any two faulty modules would be outvoted by three good ones. In fact, NASA has used quintuple redundancy in some of its systems. However, to minimize cost, triple redundancy is a good compromise. Fortunately, rapid repairs are easier at a typical industrial site than in an aerospace system, and triple redundancy guarantees uninterrupted and valid operation as long as only a single hardware failure is involved.

The triple-redundancy strategy of the Series 300 is illustrated in Fig. 1. Because the individual processing units are connected via read-only communication lines, one faulty unit cannot upset the operation of the two other units. Therefore, the faulty unit is effectively isolated and the output remains uninterrupted and correct. The isolation also contributes to the system's "hot-replacement" and "warm-start" capabilities, by which a faulty module can be removed and replaced without affecting system performance. The new module is brought up to speed during normal system operation by masking the new processor from the initial iteration of any vote, so that it has no effect. When the new unit has been fully "educated" and is in synchrony with the others, the warm-start flag is removed—thereby entering the module as a voting member of the full configuration.

Every system contains three basic types of modules: control-computer modules (CCMs), process interfaces (PIs), and termination modules (TMs). For under $50,000, a basic system could be built from three CCMs, one PI, a CRT terminal, a floppy-disk drive, and a real-time task scheduler (RTTS)—a software module complete with drivers and utilities (Fig. 2).

The system would also include the housing and isolated power supplies for each module.

Each CCM is a complete Intel 8086-based 16-bit microcomputer system with dedicated memory, power supply, peripheral interfaces, and controllers. A CCM has 8 kbytes of EPROM, 32 kbytes of RAM, a serial interface (RS-232C), and a parallel interface for connection to PI modules. The CCMs are available in three chassis sizes to accommodate 3, 9 or 15 Multibus-compatible expansion boards. Maximum addressable memory is 1 Mbyte per CCM.

Three Interfaces are used

A CCM has three main interfaces to other system components: A standard Multibus interface connects memory (RAM and/or ROM), I/O devices, data communications, and various other utility boards; a parallel interface connects the CCMs to the PI modules; and a point-to-point, read-only communications link connects all the other CCMs in the system.

The PI modules provide a convenient way to interface digital and analog devices to multiple CCMs. Because the PI module itself is designed for fault tolerance, it extends fault tolerance beyond the control computer to the fully interfaced system. The module includes hardware "voters" that provide a single output based upon a vote of the outputs received from the multiple computer modules. Input interface boards effectively fan out the input signals to each of the computer modules. The PI module contains independent interface circuitry for each CCM, three independent buses, redundant power supplies, and built-in self-test and alarm capabilities.

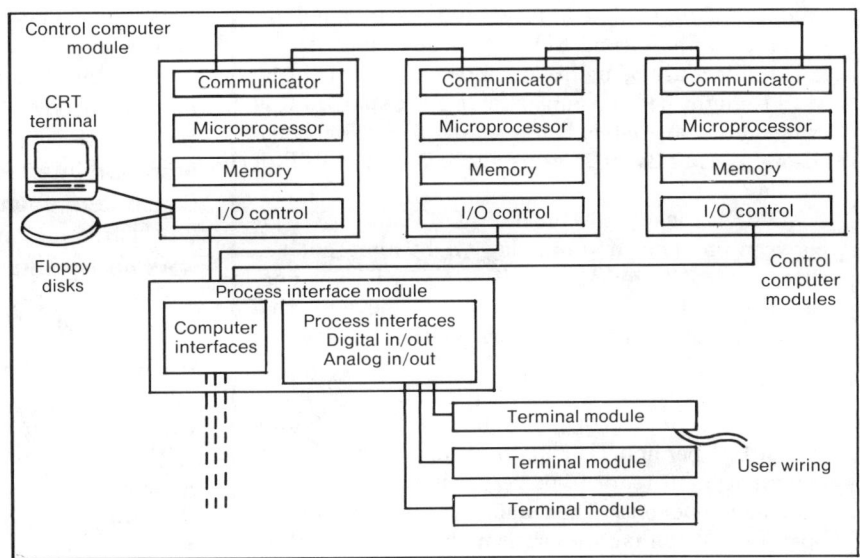

2. The process-interface (PI) module contains the voting hardware and interfaces for all three control-computer modules (CCM). For interfacing processes, additional termination modules (TM) may be required in specialized applications, such as those involving high voltages or currents.

Each bus is independently powered and has a dedicated interface to a CCM. Likewise, all I/O boards (digital/analog, input/output) have three bus interfaces so that any of the CCMs can access any board. Each PI module can accommodate 15 I/O boards in any mix, and up to 15 PIs can be connected via the standard parallel CCM interface.

Like the CCM units, I/O boards are designed so that they can be added or removed without disturbing other system components or data transfer. Also, the fault-tolerant circuitry in the output voters continues to function correctly with a single component failure (see "A Fault-Tolerant Hardware Voter"). Such a failure is detectable, and the user can make repairs to avoid system error or downtime caused by a subsequent component failure. Repair is accomplished by placing the new board in a PI slot that has been specified by the user to be a spare. Once the board is in the spare slot, a maintenance interrupt is generated on the new board, and it is updated by all the computer modules. Once the new board is fully updated, the faulty board can be removed.

Because the CCM modules are compatible with the Intel Multibus, the user has many I/O options. In some situations, Multibus I/O subsystems may be a more practical addition than PI modules. With Multibus I/O, the user can still vote on data—both input and output—via the software vote supported by the RTTS operating system. Standard peripheral controllers can be interfaced to the Series 300 system via the expansion slots in the Multibus motherboard.

The TM termination modules can provide signal conditioning and optical isolation to control high-voltage and high-current devices. Likewise, TMs can convert high-voltage and high-current input signals to levels that can be handled by the PI module. Power, cooling, and alarm functions of the TMs are organized for fault tolerance via redundancy—in the same way as other system modules.

Fault tolerance through the software

Software is the key to cost-effective fault tolerance under the SIFT technique. Software control brings several advantages to the design:

- Several levels of reliability can be maintained. For example, low priority background tasks that do not require extremely high reliability can run on single processors.
- The system can easily adapt to application requirements. Tasks can be added or deleted and priorities can be easily altered.
- In many cases, standard off-the-shelf hardware can be used. This approach lowers the cost; and because the system contains hardware with industry-standard interfaces, a wide variety of plug-compatible controllers, memories, etc., becomes available.
- Efficiency can be improved because the processors need validate only the critical data.

The basic premise behind computational fault tolerance is that a nonfaulty computing module will compute correct output values if it is provided with correct and complete input values. Thus, the first hurdle is to provide each of the computing modules with good inputs. However, this task is not as simple as it might appear. Not only must inputs be correct and complete, but they must be so at the right time. Hence, redundancy without synchronization is not sufficient. A 200-μs time-out limit is maintained by RTTS. If two processors cannot synchronize within the time-out period, an error is recorded. Retries or other actions may be initiated if the error count

---

How reliable is the computer system?

When an engineer designs a high-reliability system, he would like to be able to quantify the reliability by specifying the mean time between failures (MTBF). With software-implemented fault tolerance, however, the reliability is difficult to quantify because it depends on other variables—which are governed by the way the system is used in a specific application. In the August Systems' Series 300, MTBF depends largely on the mean time to repair (MTTR).

In a system in which the processing is triplicated (as in the Series 300), the primary failure mode is that a fault develops in one unit, and then another fault develops in another unit before the first unit is repaired. Therefore, the probability of system failure—defined as an incorrect output signal—depends on the MTTR.

When an additional (fourth) processing unit is included in the system so that it can be switched-in immediately by the system itself, then the MTTR can be very short (a few seconds at most). This approach produces a very high MTBF (more than 2-million years for a one-second MTTR). If replacement of a failed unit must be by human intervention, then the MTTR might be less than an hour if the spare unit is immediately available. However, the Series 300 has a theoretical MTBF of 24 years even with an MTTR of one day.

MTBF is considered a function of MTTR. An MTTR between one hour and one day might represent the time required to replace a unit or repair it. The one-second MTTR indicates what can be achieved with a four-processor system that has software-controlled reconfiguration.

For the purpose of preparing MTBF estimates, each active component is assumed to have a failure rate of 10^{-6} per hour. This figure agrees with industry experience, but tends to be very conservative for the simpler components. The reliability estimates assume operation in the fault-tolerant mode with redundant processors. Because the user can program the system for multiprocessor or single-processor execution of tasks, the onus is on the user to correctly identify the critical phases of the application.

exceeds threshold limits. Once the modules are synchronized, the input values are validated via a voting process supported by the RTTS operating system.

Only program inputs that are necessary to ensure correct processing need be validated. These inputs are referred to as "state variable." Specifically, the state variables of a process are the complete set of good inputs that a program, or piece of a program, needs to calculate its output. Therefore, by ensuring that the state variables are correct, the fault-tolerant system offers a significant improvement in reliability over conventional systems.

Synchronization and voting are accomplished through operating-system services. The user (programmer or system designer) identifies the state variables for each task, and the operating system votes them as part of the dispatching service.

A hard failure in one unit will cause it to be consistently outvoted. The remaining components will note the failure and continue to operate. The failed unit can be repaired or replaced.

A specially designed operating system

The RTTS operating system controls the execution of tasks in a real-time environment (Fig. 3). User tasks can be written in any language capable of producing Intel 8086 executable code that can be linked by standard Intel and August Systems conventions. The user can specify the priority, method for invocation, and scheduled time for execution of each task. The processor code can specify that the particular task will run on any processor, or in replicated mode, or on a particular processor. The latter capability is very important, because the computing modules do not have to be identically configured. Single-mode tasks may require resources that are available only to certain computer modules.

The user interface to RTTS is provided by system startup and system-operation procedures. System-startup procedures allow the user to specify the system-control parameters (Fig. 4). They determine system clock-interval values, place an upper limit on the number of tasks, and define and describe tasks. These procedures create the system tables and controls and relinquish control to the RTTS scheduler. Executive routines are system utilities that let the user interface with the scheduler, to check its status, and change task invocation method, times or intervals.

System-operation tasks can be scheduled to run either periodically (every n time units) or on the occurrence of particular events. Tasks could be scheduled to run in response to hardware interrupts, to incoming characters from a control table, to a request from other tasks, to software interrupts, to specific dates and times, and to the lapse of a certain time from an event.

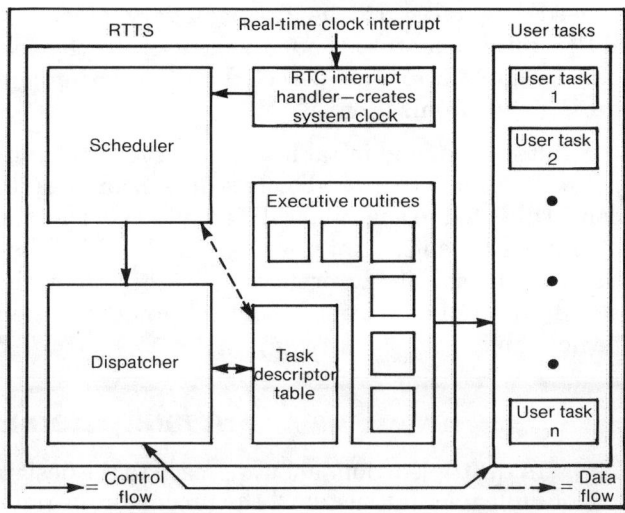

3. The real-time task scheduler (RTTS) is an operating system written specifically to support the unusual tasks required for software-implemented fault tolerance (SIFT). For example, RTTS services handle synchronization and voting procedures.

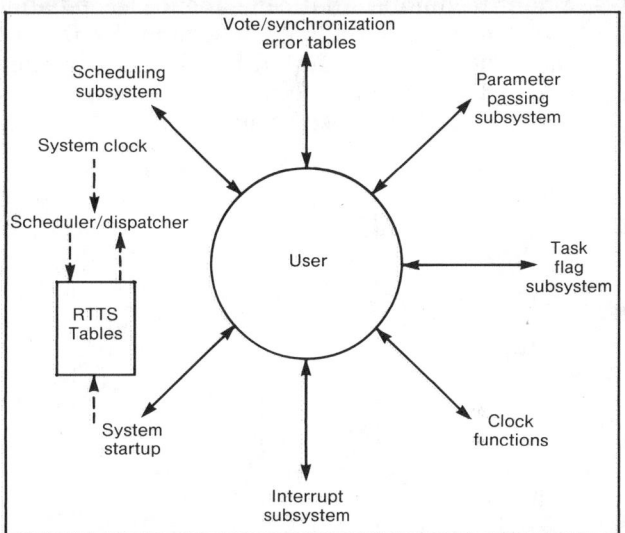

4. User interfaces to the RTTS operating system occur during system startup and during normal operation. After startup, control is relinquished to the scheduler, but the user can still check status and reschedule tasks via executive routines.

Since the RTTS system supports multiple-task priorities (typical in industrial process control), it becomes important to control task execution. The dispatcher determines when the scheduled tasks will actually run. The task to be run at any moment is selected from those that have been marked for execution by the scheduler.

The operating system also contains extensive facilities for error detection. Errors fall into two main categories: those caused by improper operation of the system and those presumed to have been caused by faults. In the first category of errors, RTTS returns a status code to the user. In the second category, errors are detected during voting and during synchronization.

Faults are logged in tables reserved for that purpose. The tables are periodically scanned, and results can be directed to a user-specified device, such as the operator's console, printer, or log file. RTTS allows the user to specify error handlers other than the standard supplied routines should alternative action be desirable.

Some typical applications

In a wide range of industrial applications, cost-effective fault-tolerant computing can rapidly recoup the capital investment it entails. In control systems, fault tolerance avoids problems of damage, danger, and spoiled production. In monitoring systems, high reliability maintains user confidence in the measurements and their subsequent analysis. In alarm systems, fault tolerance prevents false alarms, thus avoiding unnecessary plant shutdowns.

An automatic fault-tolerant system avoids the

A fault-tolerant hardware voter

In the triple-redundancy approach to the design of fault-tolerant systems, the processor outputs are compared in a voting circuit so that a faulty processor cannot influence the actual output determined by the majority. However, this approach doesn't make much sense unless the voting circuit also has built-in fault tolerance.

Fortunately, there are some relatively simple circuit techniques that can enhance the reliability of hardware voters. For example, consider the circuit in Fig. A. Inputs to this voting circuit are received from processors A, B, and C as indicated. Then, if any pair of processors produce identical inputs (for example, if A and B are both high), an output will be produced.

Now consider what happens if the circuit has a latent fault. In Fig. B, one of the switches is shorted; in Fig. C, one of the switches is permanently open. In each of these cases of a single component failure, the voting circuit will continue to function normally. Though one of the A switches is shorted in Fig. B, a discrepancy in the output of processor A will still affect the first leg of the circuit. The same reasoning applies to the fault condition shown in Fig C. Note, however, that a second component failure could produce incorrect results. As with the fault-tolerant computer itself, two faults can cause system failure. Therefore, it is essential to have some means of detecting latent faults so that they can be repaired before a second component failure occurs.

One strength of fault-tolerant I/O is that inputs can be used to monitor outputs—in other words, by feeding back the output of the voter to the processors, each computer module can monitor the operation of the voter. The inputs are voted via software in the computer modules. Once feedback loops have been established in the hardware, voter tests can be accomplished under software control. Suitable test patterns can then be generated on command to verify correct operation of the hardware and its components.

Comprehensive self-test capability is essential for cost-effective, fault-tolerant computing. But fortunately, the addition of self-test features doesn't greatly increase the cost of the system. In the software-implemented approach to fault tolerance, the diagnostic capabilities are added to the operating-system software; hardware costs stay fixed.

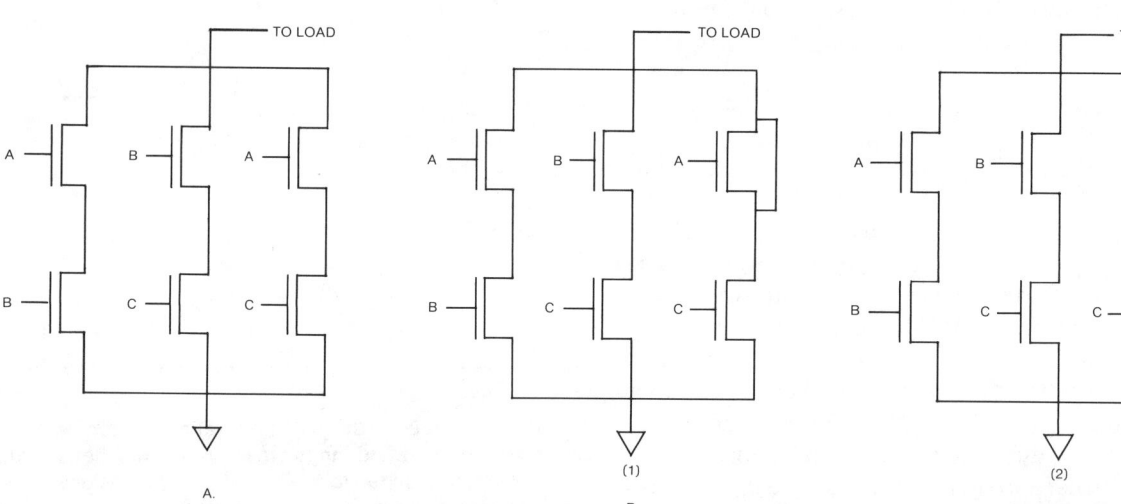

A.   B.(1)   C.(2)

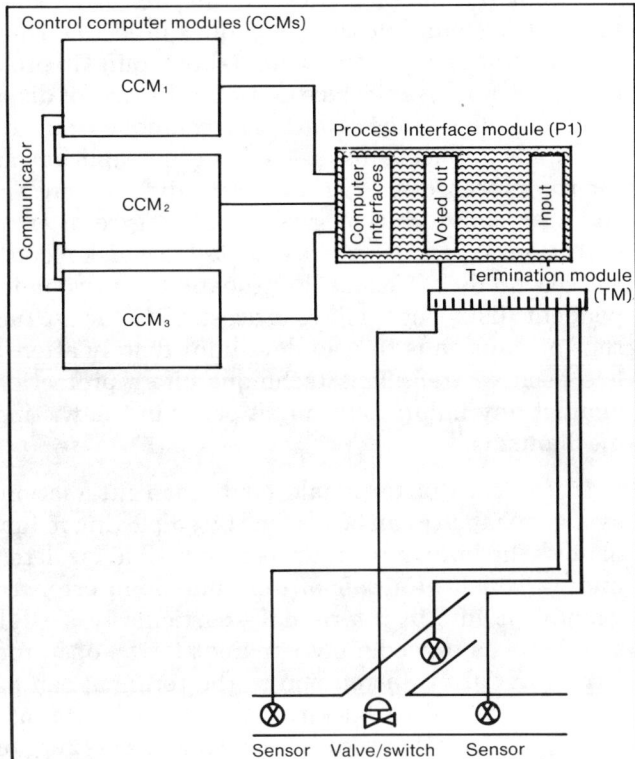

5. In this simple process-control system, each input from a sensor can be read by any or all of the control-computer modules. Analog-to-digital conversion is performed in the process-interface module. A voted output from the fault-tolerant computer is routed by the PI to the actuator. The termination module provides optical isolation and can buffer high voltages and currents.

costs of manually switched backup systems. Backup systems are often less efficient than the primary system, and the speed of the process may make human control impractical. Another advantage of fault-tolerance computing is that maintenance can be scheduled to avoid interrupting production and to optimize the use of the labor force.

Fault-tolerant computing can be advantageous in wind-tunnel control, atomic-particle accelerators, nuclear-power-plant instrumentation, and oil refineries. In all these applications, the cost of a mistake in the control system can be very high. However, the economic benefits of fault tolerance can still be demonstrated for more ordinary tasks, such as elevator control, energy control for buildings, and fluid-level monitoring for storage tanks. As already mentioned, Series 300 is a modular system, and the hardware and software can be tailored to provide maximum reliability when and where it is essential.

In a typical process-control application, a basic system contains three control-computer modules, one process-interface module, and one termination module (Fig. 5). The control system is connected to sensors and actuators via the PI and TM. The PI module routes a voted output to the actuator. The TM, besides providing optical isolation, could interface the PI to high-voltage or high-current devices (up to 280 V ac or 200 V dc and 3 A).

In the example, each of the three sensors is routed via the TM to an input card in the PI module. Each input can then be read by any or all of the CCMs, thus maintaining the advantage of redundant CCMs. The sensors have been placed before and after the actuator—with one in each branch of the pipe. Since the Series 300 provides a reliable way to validate inputs (by synchronizing and voting on those that are critical), this arrangement ensures correct operation of the process-control system.

Expanding the realm of fault tolerance

For situations requiring extreme reliability, redundant sensors and actuators could be added to the system. Three sensors would be provided at each location, instead of a single sensor, and the system would vote on the outputs. Similarly, actuators, such as valves, can be connected in various series and parallel combinations so that if a single actuator fails, the system will continue to work.

Although the use of multiple sensors can theoretically extend fault tolerance beyond the computers to the entire system, some problems can arise unless the system is carefully designed. With analog transducers, it is not unusual to run into what has been termed "the problem of interactive consistency." Simple hardware or software voting systems in a fault-tolerant computer expect to see identical digital words from all three redundant components. However, analog devices such as temperature sensors may give slightly different outputs from correctly functioning units because of inherent inaccuracies. Therefore, the voting procedure must not work on a bit-by-bit basis.

A preferable scheme would be to select the middle value of three as the correct value. The failure of one input would yield a very low or a very high value, which would be ignored in favor of an input closer to the middle value.

However, instead of sticking at a high or low value, the output from the faulty transducer might fluctuate wildly—sending different values to the three computational modules. Again, verification of correct operation by bit-by-bit comparison of the replicated data is impossible. One module may see the sensor output as low and another as high. The faulty input will then confuse a simple voting system.

The solution to this problem is to bring all of the sensor outputs into all of the computational modules (a total of nine readings). Then each CCM determines, by taking the middle value, what the output of the sensor should be. But the values determined by the CCMs may still differ. The difference is resolved

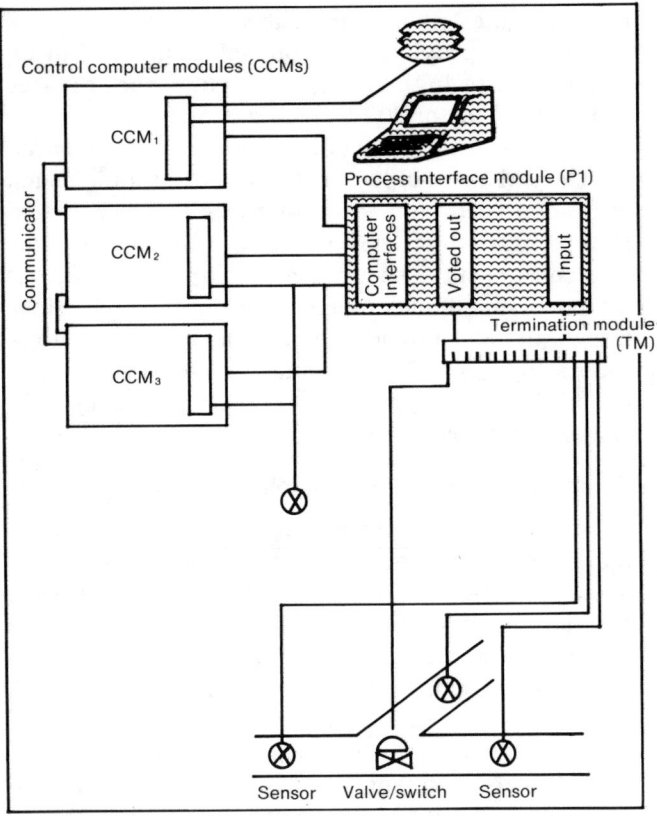

6. Because of its Multibus compatibility, the Series-300 can access a wide range of subsystems to provide special I/O or peripheral-control capabilities. In this example, one transducer is interfaced to CCM_2 and CCM_3 via Multibus subsystems, instead of through the process interface. Also, CCM_1 interfaces to a disk drive and CRT terminal.

by the modules, which again vote on their results and selecting a new middle value. At this point, all channels will agree on a common value for subsequent computation. Thus, the failure of an input sensor in a malicious mode will not invalidate the system.

Taking care of peripherals

The Multibus compatibility of the System 300 increases its versatility by accommodating subsystems offered by other manufacturers. Figure 6 shows a configuration in which Multibus I/O is used along with Series 300 process I/O. In this example, CCM 2 and CCM 3 are connected to a sensor via a Multibus I/O interface board (many types are available). The system includes a CRT terminal and a disk drive connected to CCM 1 via Multibus interfaces or controller boards. When just one disk and CRT as are in the system, tasks requiring these resources should be run on CCM 1.

Peripheral equipment can form part of a fault-tolerant system, but the techniques used to ensure fault tolerance are different from those found in processing or process-interface units. In the case of disks used for bulk storage of data, the technique would be to employ duplicate disks—rather than triplicate, as for the processors. With duplicate disks, there are coding techniques that give a high degree of error detection. When an error is detected in a disk record, the second disk is read. The probability of two independent disks both failing is acceptably low. A further precaution is to read data immediately after it has been written. This technique offers protection against any failure that might occur in the writing mechanisms.

In the case of terminals for human interaction, system reliability can be boosted by employing redundancy. The human operator is responsible for determining which of a pair of terminals is in error. In general, failure in a terminal—particularly a CRT terminal—is immediately apparent to the operator. Errors in data transmission to the terminal can be detected by feeding back the transmitted data into the input of another terminal controller. This type of data check protects against transient faults in the transmission lines.

When the system acts as a node in a network employing communication links, fault tolerance should be implemented at the system level. Messages transmitted throughout the network should be coded to provide for error detection. Protocols should be established for acknowledging the correct receipt of a message, with retransmission if a received message is corrupted.

The Series 300 is designed to allow configurations with shared or redundant peripherals. Up to 15 Multibus boards can be added to each CCM and each CCM can support up to 15 PI modules. Combinations of I/O are supported via drivers and utilities in the RTTS operating system.

Real-time systems must usually be synchronized to the outside world. In some cases, an accurate time reference is essential. In other cases, the system must be synchronized with the process that is being controlled or monitored. The time reference has to be reliable. The Series 300 incorporates a fault-tolerant, crystal-controlled clock in each CCM. Outputs from the clocks are voted prior to use, in the usual best-two-out-of-three fashion so the system will continue to function correctly even with one malfunctioning clock. □

Programmable Control of a Chemical Reactor Using a Fault Tolerant Computer

JOHN H. WENSLEY, MEMBER, IEEE, AND C. SCOTT HARCLERODE, MEMBER, IEEE

Abstract—This paper discusses the operation of a chemical reactor and particularly the need for highly reliable instrumentation and control for critical processes. It describes the use of fault tolerance for the computer control to provide a level of reliability previously unachievable with standard computer control systems. The provision of highly reliable interface equipment to the reactor itself is described and approaches are presented for solving the problem of faults in the sensors and actuators. The paper discusses a specific example chemical reactor and the benefits that are achieveable using a fault tolerant control computer system.

I. INTRODUCTION

AS COMPUTERS are used in more and more critical control applications, it is necessary to ensure reliability of such equipments. The approach described in this paper employs the use of triple modular redundant computers. Such a structure can provide adequately high reliability for the computing function. Beyond the computer function itself, high reliability must also be achieved in the input/output structure of the computer, particularly that part that interfaces to the process itself. A further objective is to provide the facilities whereby faults in the process equipment itself (e.g., sensors or actuators) can be tolerated.

In addition to the need for appropriate hardware redundancy, it is necessary that this redundancy be managed in a manner that is convenient to the user. This management of the fault tolerance is carried out by software. Two objectives were established for this software. Firstly, that the user of the software, typically a control engineer, should not need to concern himself with the details of how fault tolerance is achieved, and secondly, that the user's method of specifying his application should be a form with which he is familiar. This second objective is achieved by a software package that emulates a relay ladder network, a familiar concept to control engineers.

A specific application is discussed, namely the control, monitoring, and safety shutdown of a very high energy chemical reactor. While the complete control system is not described, certain detailed elements are used to illustrate the use of the system.

II. CHEMICAL REACTOR CONTROL

Many chemical reactors, particularly those carrying out mass chemical conversions, are very large, complex, expensive, and involve very high utilization of energy. A reactor vessel can be as long as 100 ft, or have a girth of 40 ft and walls of metal alloys more than 12-in thick. The enormous dimensions of some chemical reactors make the uniform distribution and mixing of feed stocks (reaction components) difficult. This can cause "hot spots" or "cold spots" in various areas within the reactor. This is due to the reaction proceeding at different rates in different areas. These local effects can stress or metalurgically weaken the vessel walls permanently. Some reactions are highly unstable. In particular, some reactions are exothermic and cause the vessel temperature to rise, which in turn causes the rare of reaction to increase—releasing more heat. This thermal runaway is avoided by providing adequate cooling to the reactor vessel. In addition to monitoring the temperature, or perhaps many temperatures in a reactor, other parameters that determine the state of the reaction must be monitored. The state includes pressures and mass flow rates of the feed and product streams. In the event that the reaction fails to stay within the design limits of the process, a shutdown of the reactor may be required for protection of the vessel or safety of the unit personnel.

In addition to the above conditions for shutdown, malfunctions of the process equipment and, in particular, early detection of potential malfunctions must be carried out and shutdown of the plant initiated. Such malfunctions could include increase of temperature or vibration in a compressor bearing suggesting the likelihood of bearing failure, or loss of one of the feed stream flows.

Simple shutdown of the process is seldom possible. The process itself may be self-sustaining, or may produce undesirable reaction by-products which could contaminate or damage expensive catalysts, or require extensive cleaning of the vessel. In certain cases, dumping or ventilating the contents of the reactor during shutdown may be possible, but in other cases, the raw materials or the by-products of the reaction may be either noxious or dangerous, or both. Therefore, appropriate capture of the raw material may be required. In addition, the process of shutting down a reaction may itself be a complex sequence of operations with very rigorous requirements on the order and timing of these operations. For example, during the shutdown of a compressor, valves at both the low- and high-pressure ends of the compressor must be closed. When multistage compressors are used, then certain bypass valves must be either opened or closed. Where a high volume of raw material is flowing through compressors and pumps, then controlled shutdown is required to prevent surging problems in the supply lines.

It can be seen from the above that safety shutdown of such reactor vessels is not a simple trip system involving shutting off power, but must be carefully controlled to produce orderly

---

Manuscript received June 25, 1982.
J. H. Wensley is with August Systems, Inc., Salem, OR 97302.
C. S. Harclerode is at 14903 Hollydale, Houston, TX 77062.

shutdown. Because of the very high cost and danger inherent in the process, this shutdown must be carried out with extremely high realiability. It has, in certain cases, been the practice to duplicate this safety shutdown sequencing. Such duplication greatly reduces the risk of failing to shut down the reactor when conditions warrant such a shutdown. Unfortunately, simple duplication also increases the number of false shutdowns, or "trips" as they are often called. Such false shutdowns can represent a very large economic loss. For example, the cost in lost production of a false trip may be as high as $25 000 per hour for a single reactor. There is also a price paid in accelerated wear on the associated process equipment during the shutdown-startup cycle. It is therefore necessary to utilize control techniques that will guarantee safety shutdown when warranted and also provide reliability in preventing false trips.

Because of the sophisticated logic required for sequencing the shutdown, the use of a computer control is indicated; however, standard control computers do not possess adequate reliability. That is, the catastrophic failure possibility introduced by a single system handling several reactors cannot, in general, be tolerated. Often there are from 4 to 9 reactors in a chemical processing unit, so that if the entire unit is shut down due to control-system failure, the losses could be enormous. In addition, other units in the plant may have to be shut down due to loss of process steam or feed stock. The approach taken is to use a fault tolerant control computer system, i.e., a system that continues correct operation even in the presence of a fault.

III. FAULT TOLERANT COMPUTER CONTROL

The August Systems Series 300 has been designed to provide computerized control systems of very high integrity. By very high integrity, we mean

The right result, at
The right place, at
The right time.

High integrity goes beyond fail-safe or high-availability systems. Further, the Series 300 addresses the issue of high integrity not only in the central processing functions of a control system, but throughout all the interfacing equipment to the process being controlled.

The Series 300 is illustrated in Fig. 1. At the center of the system is the processing function. To provide high integrity, this function is triplicated, i.e., three independent processors each with it's own memory are used to form the control computer module (CCM). This unit carries out the logic and arithmetic calculations, conversion to engineering units, calibration of instruments, and control of the other elements in the system. The triplication of the processing function can be used to ensure that a fault in a processor does not produce any corruption of control signals.

While triplication of the processing function results in high integrity, it is necessary for the CCM to interface to the signals from the process or to the process. Signals from the process (e.g., from sensors) must be distributed to all three of the processing elements of the CCM. Signals from the CCM to the

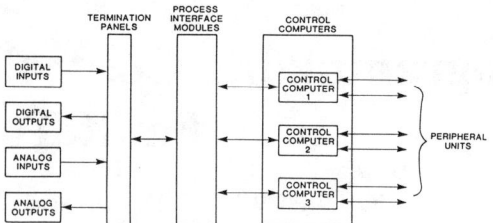

Fig. 1. The CS 330 Fault Tolerant Control System.

process (i.e., to actuators) must be transmitted in such a way that faulty data from one processing element in the CCM is properly masked by the remaining two processing elements so that a fault produces no incorrect control action. In addition, the process signals are frequently very numerous so a capability must be provided to connect to a large number of process points, far larger than can ordinarily be achieved from a processing unit. These functions are carried out in the process interface module (PIM) which also carries out conversions between analog and digital data.

While the CCM's and PIM's operate with voltage and current levels that are appropriate for modern electronics, it is necessary to convert such power levels to those appropriate for the process itself. Frequently, high-voltage and high-power signals to the process need to be switched or controlled. This function is carried out by the use of solid-state relays housed in one or more termination modules (TM's). These TM's provide a convenient means for the large number of wires from the process to be terminated at the Series 300. Another feature of the TM's is that the solid-state relays are optically isolated, thus protecting the control computer from the effect of high-power erroneous signals from the process plant.

A. Control Computer Modules

The control computer modules are based upon the design concept of the SIFT computer [1]-[4]. The SIFT computer was designed for aircraft control and, in particular, for an advanced aircraft type that required a correctly functioning computer system for safe flight. The reliability requirements for that system were exceedingly stringent. Typically, the requirement is that the probability of failure per hour of flight should not exceed 10^{-10}. This translates approximately into a mean time before failure (MTBF) in excess of one million years. To achieve such a high reliability, a large number of processors were included to provide the necessary replication of computers, plus redundant units to be utilized when failures occurred. In its first embodiment, seven independent processors were used.

For control applications, the reliability requirements, though severe, are not as stringent as those found in aircraft control. In general, they can be achieved by a structure containing three independent computing channels. Such a system is referred to as a triple modular redundant (TMR). While the processors of the August Systems Series 300 have been designed so that more than three can be used in one installation, the realiability requirements seldom demand replication beyond three. The use of more than three processors, if it should be warranted, would represent a software design effort, because such an increased number of processors would require different error detection, error correction, voting, diagnosis, and reconfiguration strategies than are used with three processors.

Each individual processor is based upon the Intel 8086 microprocessor. This choice of processing element is based upon design decisions concerned with processing power, memory address-ability, and the availability of a large number of ancilliary components that can be used to construct a complete computer module. The 8086 is a 16-bit microprocessor operating with a clock of 5 MHz and includes modern features for the construction of software. Of particular note are the 20-bit memory addressing capability, a vectored interrupt capability, and the use of stacks for program control.

Fault tolerance is achieved by each of the three processors being able to examine computational results from each of the other two channels. Thus, each channel receives three versions of the results of each critical calculation, one from its own calculation and one each from the other two processors. Following determination of these three results, software in each processor selects the majority value. If no faults have occurred, it can be expected that all three channels will produce the same result. In the event of a fault in one channel, then this will be recognized by the voting software and an error will be reported, but will have no further effect upon the computation. This error report is used to trigger maintenance action on this faulty channel. The reading of critical data from the other two processors is accomplished by a READ ONLY connection. This connection enables each processor to determine values computed by the other two, but because it is READ ONLY, there is no possibility that a faulty channel can corrupt data in the other correctly functioning channels.

Input of the data is accomplished independently by each processor, thus each channel receives an independent view concerning all inputs. Where it is necessary to protect against failure of an input device, then that device itself should be replicated and values from each of the replicated devices should be fed to all computational channels. Thus, each channel can independently carry out a vote of the individual sensors and determine both the correct value to be used and, if there is a fault, to identify the faulty sensor.

When each channel has determined the output to be transmitted to the process, each of them sends its value to circuitry that carries out a hardware vote to remove any data from a faulty computational channel. The method by which this is achieved is described in more detail in the next subsection.

The mode of operation of the computational channels is that for critical calculations, they all carry out identically the same calculation and in the absence of faults, will achieve identically the same results. These calculations are not carried out in a tightly synchronized manner, but the processors are loosely synchronized by software.

B. The Process Interface

It is necessary in a control computer system to interface the inputs and outputs of the computer to specific devices in the process equipment. This interfacing requires many functions to be accomplished such as multiplexing a large number of inputs and outputs, distributing inputs to all the computing channels, carrying out voting of outputs to actuators, and conversion to and from signal levels used in the process equipment.

The multiplexing is required to enable a computer with a relatively small number of input/output channels to connect to many hundreds, or thousands, of process devices. This multiplexing is carried out in the process interface module (PIM). Each PIM contains three interface units, each connected to a computational channel. These interface units implement an independent bus (three in total) in each PIM. Each of these buses communicates with up to 15 input/output cards. The principal input/output cards that are provided are: a 32-bit digital input, a 32-bit digital output, a 32-channel analog input, and a 4-channel analog output.

Up to 15 PIM's can be included in a complete system; thus the maximum number of process points that can be monitored or controlled can be as high at 7200—15 PIM's, each containing 15 cards, each interfacing to up to 32 points. Thus, the relatively small number of input/output lines from the computer modules (24 in the case of the August Systems Series 300) can be multiplexed to a far larger number of processing points.

It is the responsibility of the PIM to take each input variable (either digital or analog) and feed that data independently to each of the computational channels via the three interface units in each PIM. This distribution of input data is carried out by routing this data to three independent circuits in the input card.

For output, it is necessary that the PIM remove all effects of a faulty computational channel. This is accomplished by a voter that carries out the logical "majority function," illustrated in Fig. 2. Such a majority circuit must, however, be protected against faulty components within itself. Such a circuit for discrete outputs is illustrated in Fig. 3. It can be shown that each individual component of that circuit can experience failure without corrupting the output of that circuit, assuming that all data received from the three computational channels are correct. Thus, the combination of three computational channels and the output voter can survive an error in any computational channel, or a faulty component within the voter itself. A double fault, such that a computational unit fails and also the component voter fails, is not always tolerated. Analog voting of output data is far more complex. In the scheme used, the data from each computational channel is first converted to analog form. Because of the inherent slight inaccuracy of digital to analog convertors, the selection of two identical values may not be possible. However, satisfactory operation is achieved by a circuit that selects the middle of the three analog values. Thus, if any computational channel is at fault, so that it generates a totally incorrect value, then that value will be ignored because it will not be the middle value

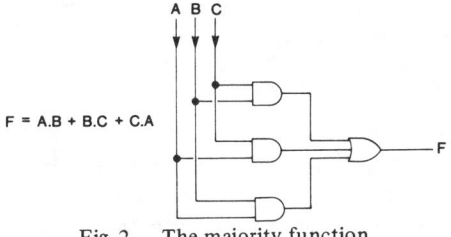

Fig. 2. The majority function.

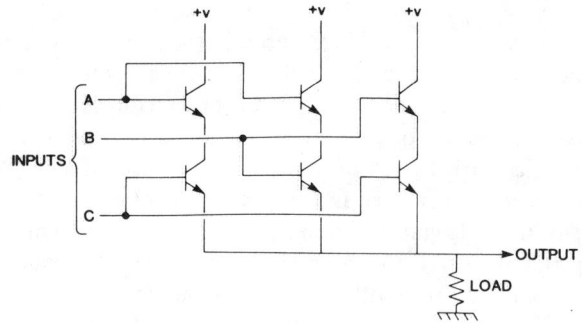

Fig. 3. A fault-tolerant majority (voter) circuit.

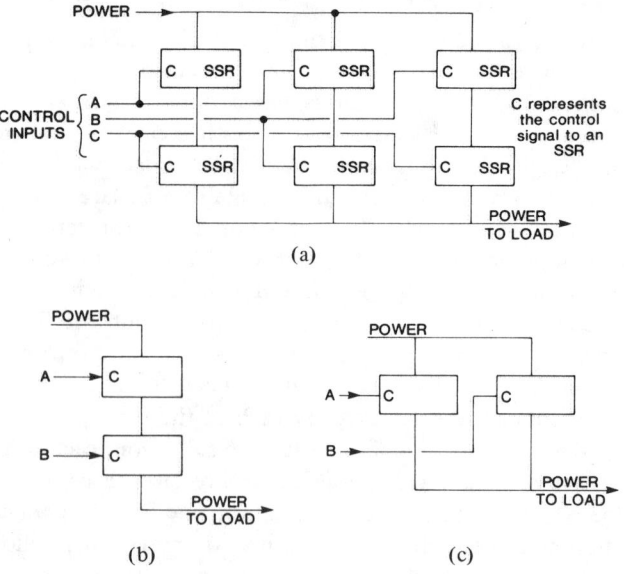

Fig. 4. Circuit schemes to protect against failures in solid-state relays (SSR's). (a) A voter circuit. (b) Reliable turn-off connector. (c) Reliable turn-on connector.

of the three. The design of a circuit to accomplish this voter is complicated by the need to incorporate the following two features:

1) The circuit itself must be fault tolerant so that individual faults in the components cannot corrput the output.
2) Accuracy and linearity of analog data must be maintained.

Such a circuit represents a difficult design challenge and the complexity of that circuit is one of the reasons why the analog output cards of the Series 300 only implement four output channels. Such a limitation on analog output does not represent a significant problem in control systems where in general the number of analog output points is very small compared with analog inputs and discrete inputs and outputs.

Process equipment frequently operates at voltage and power levels that are different from those used in computers. In addition, ac signals are used, as are current loop signals. The conversion of these different signal types to those appropriate for computing equipment (typically 5 V and 0 V) is accomplished by using solid-state relays that also incorporate optical isolation. This isolation protects the circuitry of the control system from any induced high-power transients on input or output lines. The solid-state relays are incorporated in termination modules that also provide a convenient means for attaching user wiring to the system via appropriate terminals. The solid-state relays have very good reliability characteristics and it is seldom necessary to provide fault tolerance for them. However, if it is desired to protect against failure of a solid-state relay, it can be accomplished by connecting them as shown in Fig. 4. In that figure, the first connection scheme provides a voter function that will tolerate any of the solid-state relays failing in an open circuit or closed circuit manner. In Fig. 4(b), a simpler circuit is shown, utilizing only two solid-state relays. This connection scheme is used for a system in which it is necessary to reliably turn off a process unit. Either of the solid-state relays can accomplish this. Thus, if one unit fails to turn off, the other unit properly accomplishes this function. Fig. 4(c) illustrates the case where a process unit must be reliably turned on, even if one solid-state relay fails in the open circuit mode. As mentioned above, such interconnections of multiple solid-state relays are seldom necessary.

IV. SOFTWARE

There are two major software systems with which the user need be concerned. The first is the real time task scheduler (RTTS), and the second is the relay ladder logic simulator (RLLS). These two systems together provide the tools necessary for the user to specify his application and to provide the fault tolerance functions.

The design challenge in these two systems is to provide them in such a way that the user can accomplish his design goals without concern for the details of either the operating system or fault tolerance. The objective is that the user need not be intimately aware of the substructure of these systems, nor must he be skilled in computer technology. The user is viewed as a control engineer with expertise in the process being controlled and the technology of control.

A. Real Time Task Scheduler (RTTS)

The purpose of an operating system is to provide high-level functions that augment the raw hardware capabilities of a computer system in order to make it more convenient to use. Many of the functions provided in RTTS are those found in virtually all operating systems. These include such functions as scheduling, dispatching, interrupt handling, and the like. The detailed actions required to be performed to carry out these functions in general require a detailed understanding of the hardware of the system, such as the particular addressing of registers, timing relationships, and the instruction set of the computer. These functions collectively provide a system with high-level capabilities. One such capability is referred to as multitasking, in which the user can separately define a number of tasks that, in total, define his application and can control the running of those tasks. Tasks may be run on a regular periodic basis by specifying only the period between each running of the tasks. Alternatively, tasks can be specified to run under the occurrence of a particular event. Such events can be hardware interrupts caused by some external signal, or software events, such as a request by one task for a different task to be run. The use of multiple tasks to accomplish a complete application has important advantages in the design of large, complex systems, because it enables the user to focus attention individually on particular components of his total system, with only limited attention being required to consider the interaction between tasks.

In addition to the more conventional facilities mentioned above, RTTS provides facilities that are found only in more advanced operating systems. An example of such a function is the mailbox and message facility. This facility provides a convenient and well-controlled mechanism for tasks to communicate with each other by sending messages to mailboxes that are owned by another task. This message flow is accomplished without the user having to be concerned with such machine dependent factors as storage allocation, buffer allocation, timing relationships between tasks, etc. Another feature provided is a semaphore mechanism. Each semaphore is implemented by a single integer. The capabilities provided in RTTS allow a task to increment this integer, to decrement this integer, and to test whether this integer exceeds a particular value. The purpose of the semaphore subsystem is to provide means whereby multiple tasks can utilize a common resource. As a simple example of the use of semaphores, consider a system with a single terminal. It is assumed that at the beginning of operation the terminal is free to be used by any task. This is indicated in the semaphore for that terminal by setting the value initially to "1". Any task that requests use of the terminal first tests to see if the semaphore has the value "1" or "0". If it is "0", this indicates that the terminal is already in use by another task, and the requesting task must therefore either wait, or proceed with alternate actions. If the semaphore has the value "1", this indicates that the terminal is available for use. The task then immediately decrements the semaphore to the value "0", thus preventing other tasks from utilizing the terminal. The task then proceeds to send or receive a message from the terminal, and upon completion of this action, increments the semaphore from "0" to "1". At this point, another task requesting the terminal may now utilize it. In the event that more than one terminal was available, the initilized value of the semaphore would then be set to the number of available terminals so that more than one task could communicate with the operator simultaneously. This semaphore mechanism provides a convenient means of allocating on a time-by-time basis the use of a shared resource. Other examples include sharing a number of buffers, or sharing common memory. In general, the control engineer need not be concerned with semaphores when using the relay ladder logic system described below. However, for those users who need to specify more complex tasks than can be handled by RLLS, these semaphores represent a user-convenient and machine-efficient mechanism. The functions described above are found in conventional computer operating systems. In the Series 300, the fault tolerance capabilities are also embedded in RTTS. The most obvious such facility is the voting capability whereby critical data in one computer of the triple is compared with the same data computed in the other two channels. In the event of a discrepancy, the erroneous value is ignored and an error report is issued, thus triggering maintenance actions to correct the faulty channel. This voting capability utilizes a lower level function to accomplish the communication of data between the three computing modules. The user need only be concerned with the voting within RTTS without concern for the detailed communication capability implied in this function.

Another capability that is essential in providing fault tolerance is the ability to synchronize the operation of the three computing channels. Because the Series 300 contains three independent processing modules that contain independent clocking circuits, they will tend to operate at slightly different speeds. If the computing channels were not synchronized from time to time, then they would slowly drift apart in time and would be at different stages in their calculations and, thus, it could not be expected that successful voting would take place, even if their were no faults. Thus, before voting on critical data, each of the computing channels enters a synchronization routine at the exit of which all of the computational channels are in close to the same state of execution. In the Series 300, no attempt is made to achieve tight synchronization as used, for example, in computers that operate in "lock step". Rather, the computing channels are synchronized so that they are within 100 μs of each other in their execution. Another function provided by the synchronization routines is to separate the voting of critical data from modification of that data. The problem that is attacked here is that it is possible with no synchronization that one computing channel will be ahead of the other two and will modify a piece of data before the others have voted on it. Thus, it would appear that the faster channel is faulty. This is prevented from occurring by resynchronizing the computing channels between the voting operation and whatever operation modifies the data. This synchronization ensures that all computing channels have completed their voting before any of them modifies the data. The design of synchronization routines has been addressed in the fault tolerant literature [5]-[7].

In fault tolerant computing systems, the intent is that the system as a whole will continue correct operation, even in the presence of a fault. In certain installations, the occurrence of a fault will trigger a maintenance or replacement action by the user, wherein the faulty unit is either repaired or replaced by a properly functioning unit. The replacement ideally should be carried out with the system still continuing to operate. It is necessary for this newly inserted unit to carry out a warm start operation. This operation attempts to set the newly inserted unit into the same state as the units that have been continuing to operate. This msut be accomplished while the process continues to be controlled. The technical problem is that the newly inserted unit must capture all the data that defines the state of the system, while the other units are continuing to change that data. Simple copying of the state data from the good units to the newly inserted unit leaves the possibility of inconsistency between data items because some were changed after this copying process, while others were not. A primitive mechanism for achieving warm start is to temporarily halt the two good units while the new unit copies the state data. This simple mechanism may, in certain cases, be satisfactory, but for some systems, this temporary shutting down of the control system even for a few milliseconds may be unsatisfactory. It is therefore necessary to provide a more sophisticated system whereby the state data is copied from the good processors to the new one in small parts. After each part is

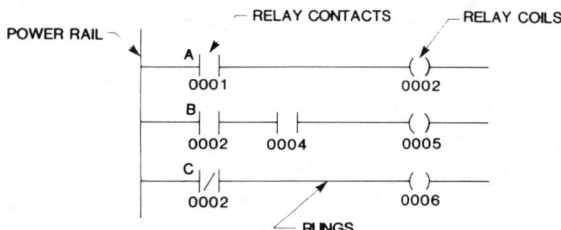

Fig. 5. A simple part of a relay ladder network.

copied, a test is then made to see if any modification to that part was carried out by the processors that were continuing execution. If no modification had occurred, then this part has been consistently copied. If modification had occurred during copying, then the copy is declared invalid and the copying action must be reinitiated. The breaking of the state data into parts is done on the basis that there is independence between the parts, so that consistency need only concern the data in one part, without concern for the state data in another part. In general, the parts are individually associated with a task. The effect is that over a short period of time, the state data of each task is copied into the newly inserted processor which can then carry out the control algorithms associated with that task, thus maintaining the consistency of the data for that task. This warm start capability represents a significant design challenge and its provision in the system provides the user with the capability of replacing faulty units while the system continues operation.

B. Relay Ladder Logic

The purpose of the relay ladder logic system (RLLS), is to provide a means whereby a user can specify the control actions to be performed by the computers without detailed knowledge of the system, or without expertise in the use of computers. The system consists of two parts. The first part referred to as a programming unit, enables the user to specify the control actions required. The second part is the control system that will perform the control actions.

The programmer unit consists of a terminal through which the user interacts with the system, and computer and storage file devices. In the Series 300, this programmer unit is implemented with a single computer because fault tolerance is not required during initial specification of the control tasks. RLLS enables the user to specify the control actions as if they were implemented by a series of relays connected in a network. The primary elements of that network consist of a ground rail, a power rail, relay coils, and relay contacts. A simple example of a part of a network is shown in Fig. 5. In this description, letters (A, B, etc.) are sometimes used to define particular contacts to avoid ambiguity in the description that could be caused by more than one contact associated with a particular relay. In Fig. 5, contact A is presumed to be an external contact, i.e., a switch closure in the process equipment itself. The closing of this switch causes relay coil 0002 to be energized. This in turn closed contact B. This contact closing causes no action because the "rung" on which this contact resides also contains contact 0004, which is still open. Future closing of contact 0004 would energize relay coil 0005, causing some

TABLE I
PRINCIPAL ELEMENTS OF THE RELAY LADDER LOGIC SYSTEM

Element	Symbol
Open Contact	---| |---
Closed Contact	---|/ |---
Coil	---( )---
Horizontal Shunt	----------
Vertical Shunt	|
Stepper Switch	---|STEP|--- |RXXX|
Up Counter	---|PXXX|--- |CTU| ---|RXXX|---
Down Counter	---|PXXX|--- |CTD| ---|RXXX|---
Timer	---|PXXX|--- |T.| ---|RXXX|---
+	---|PXX + PYYY = PZZZ|---
-	---|PXXX - PYYY = PZZZ|---
*	---|PXXX * PYYY = RZZZ|---
/	---|PXXX / PYYY = RZZZ|---
< >	---|PXXX PYYY < PZZZ|---

control action. In addition, contact C that was normally closed, is opened by the energizing of relay coil 0002; thus, relay coil 0006 is de-energized once again providing some control action. It can be seen from this simple example that complex logic can be accomplished using this system in a manner that is convenient and easy to use for the control engineer.

Simple contact closures, contact openings, and relay coils are not sufficient to provide all the capabilities required for building a control system; therefore, other elements are incorporated in RLLS. Principal among these are timers, and means for dealing with analog data.

A timer is a simulated element that can be reset, i.e., turned off, or can be triggered. The triggering action causes the timer to be armed and, after a specified time, the output of the timer is energized. Timers can be used to provide the timing relationships frequently required in a sequential sequence of operations.

The manipulation of analog data in RLLS includes provision of the following function:

1) simple arithmetic operations, e.g., addition, subtraction, multiplication, division;
2) testing of analog data against present values;

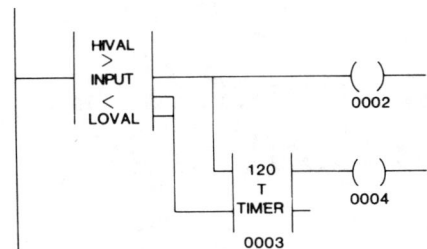
Fig. 6. Detection of flow above upper limit.

3) storing of analog data in a register (this is a simulated register and should not be confused with the arithmetic registers of the control computers).

Some of the principal elements in RLLS are summarized in Table I. Their use is illustrated in Fig. 6. In Fig. 6, a part of the network is set up so that analog data representing fluid flow is compared with a limit. Input and output of process data is accomplished by separately defining those registers that receiver data and/or transmit data to the process. In the event that the flow is above this limit, two actions occur. The first action is to arm an alarm via relay coil 0002. The second action is to trigger the timer. This timer causes the system to wait 120 s and, if this low flow condition persists, then relay coil 0004 will energize, thus causing the sequenced shut down of the system. If the low flow condition is later corrected, then the timer is reset and normal operation continues.

The above discussion illustrates the use of RLLS to specify the control functions to be implemented. In the Series 300, such actions are carried out in a fault tolerant manner.

V. INTEGRATION OF FAULT TOLERANCE INTO THE CONTROL PROCEDURE

The above sections have described mechanisms for fault tolerance and a set of procedures (RTTS and RLLS) for specifying a control system. The Series 300 integrates these functions. The integration of them can best be described in terms of the RLLS system. The basic operation consists of a repetitive process. Each iteration of the process proceeds according to the following steps:

Step 1) all processing channels are synchronized;
Step 2) all data from the process are input into the control modules and voting actions are carried out to remove the effect, if any, of faults;
Step 3) the simulated relay ladder network is scanned and all changes required are carried out, either by energizing relays, de-energizing relays, setting or resetting timers, and the like;
Step 4) computational channels are again synchronized so that timing discrepancies between them are removed;
Step 5) all data to be sent to the process are voted;
Step 6) output data are transmitted to the process.

This repetitive procedure provides a simple means for the incorporation of fault tolerance into a control system without the user needing to be aware of any of the mechanisms used to accomplish it. Thus, the user does not perceive the above steps, and even more importantly, does not need to concern himself with the voting and synchronization operations in the system. Even more importantly, the very detailed operations, such as scheduling, and dispatching, that are incorporated in RTTS are handled automatically with the user being absolved from any design considerations inherent in such processes.

VI. CONCLUSIONS

It has been shown that computer control can be used in situations that demand exceptionally high reliability by using a computer system that employs fault tolerance. The economic return in using such systems is easily demonstrated by the reduction in plant outages, feed-stock loss for other units, as well as cleanup, catalyst replacement, and startup stock. These benefits are a direct result of a reduced number of false or nuisance trips while maintaining adequate protection of the processing plant. It has been further shown that by the use of a software approach specifically designed for process control that the implementation of the software can be carried out economically.

REFERENCES

[1] J. H. Wensley, "SIFT—Software implemented fault tolerance," *Proc. IEEE*, pp. 243–253, 1972.
[2] J. H. Wensley *et al.*, "The design, analysis, and verification of the SIFT fault tolerant system," presented at the 2nd International Conf. on Software Engineering (San Francisco, CA), Oct. 13–15, 1976.
[3] J. H. Wensley *et al.*, "Highly reliable microprocessors," AGARDOGRAPH on "Integrity in flight control systems," #224, Apr. 1977.
[4] J. H. Wensley *et al.*, "SIFT: Design and analysis of a fault-tolerant computer for aircraft control," *Proc. IEEE*, vol. 66, no. 10, Oct. 1978.
[5] S. G. Frison and J. H. Wensley, "Interactive consistency and its impact on the design of TMR systems," presented at the IEEE Fault Tolerant Computer Conf. (Santa Monica, CA), June 1982.
[6] D. Davies and J. F. Wakerly, "Synchronization and matching in redundant systems," *IEEE Trans. Comput.*, vol. C-27, pp. 531–539, June 1978.
[7] S. R. McConnell and D. P. Siewiorek, "Synchronization and voting," *IEEE Trans. Comput.*, vol. C-30, pp. 161–164, Feb. 1981.

REBUS, A Fault-Tolerant Distributed System for Industrial Real-Time Control

JEAN-MICHEL AYACHE, JEAN-PIERRE COURTIAT, AND MICHEL DIAZ, MEMBER, IEEE

Abstract—This paper presents a fault-tolerant distributed system designed for real-time control applications (REBUS), which is one of the research basis of the industrial real-time system MODUMAT 800. It is made up of functional units, i.e., programmable multiloop regulators and operator displays, linked together by a communication structure. The communication hardware consists of a set of serial bus interface boards, one per functional unit, loosely coupled together by a double serial bus and linked to their functional units by a private parallel bus.

The communication software, implemented on each interface board, provides a distributed executive based on a reliable link protocol and a robust bus allocation mechanism. Different fault-tolerant mechanisms are implemented in order to achieve the dependability requirements of industrial control systems.

Index Terms—Distributed systems, fault tolerance, Petri nets, proof, protocols, real-time control, recovery.

I. INTRODUCTION

ADVANCES in technology and data communication have made possible to build real-time distributed processing systems. As a consequence, real-time control may account for the actual distributed organization of people, equipments, and functions. Furthermore, the geographical constraints that usually exist in such systems lead to design their structure as a set of processing units linked by a local network. A simple way to build such a system is to use microcomputers, distributed over the plant, which communicate together through a local network in order to coordinate their activities.

This paper presents such a distributed system intended for real-time control: REBUS, which is one of the research structures of the general purpose industrial real-time control system MODUMAT 800, currently built and sold by Sereg-Schlumberger [1], [2].

In such a general purpose control system there exists
- specific functional processors, for instance, regulators, data loggers, programmable controllers, minicomputers, ...,
- a control or management room with human operators who use appropriate display and management processors.

It may be underlined that the units located in the control room do not directly participate to the plant control; they generate appropriate information to the operators, who, when necessary, modify values, parameters, even set points in the remote specific processors. The actual control is performed by specific processors; the regulators, up to a given number of elementary coordinated control loops—a loop is a pair sensor-actuator related to a physical variable—are handled by these regulators.

Distributed control imposes various functional requirements on the architecture of the distributed system. Among them, the three requirements that have been considered of the utmost importance in the design of REBUS are
- modularity,
- expandability,
- dependability.

In such control systems, dependability is a very important issue [1], [4]. In the specification of REBUS, high dependability requirements have been stated to fulfill the two following propositions:

*P*1) the loss of more than one elementary control loop must be avoided,

*P*2) the global supervision loss of the plant must be most unlikely.

Proposition *P*1 comes from the fact that sensors and actuators are not considered to be redundant because the average number of them is about 500 for a nontrivial industrial plant, and also because they are rather expensive; the cost would be too high if redundancy is provided. The possible loss of one loop, due to the failure of a sensor or an actuator, has therefore to be accounted for in the design of the control algorithms.

Proposition *P*2 is a general requirement, quite obvious; it avoids the situation where in case of supervision loss the distributed control processors continue to work, whereas the human operators cannot observe any more the behavior of the plant.

Having chosen these dependability requirements, the problem was to select some fault hypothesis under which these requirements have to hold.

Taking into account the distributed nature of the system, the following fault hypothesis has been selected: at any moment, only one of the processors (*involved in a distributed cooperating activity*) may be faulty.

This hypothesis is the extension to distributed and cooperating systems of the classical single fault hypothesis: the fault concerns *at most* one processor and *at least* one of the cooperating activities; in fact all the processes which are involved in activities and are located in *the* (*unique*) *faulty processor* should be considered as faulty.

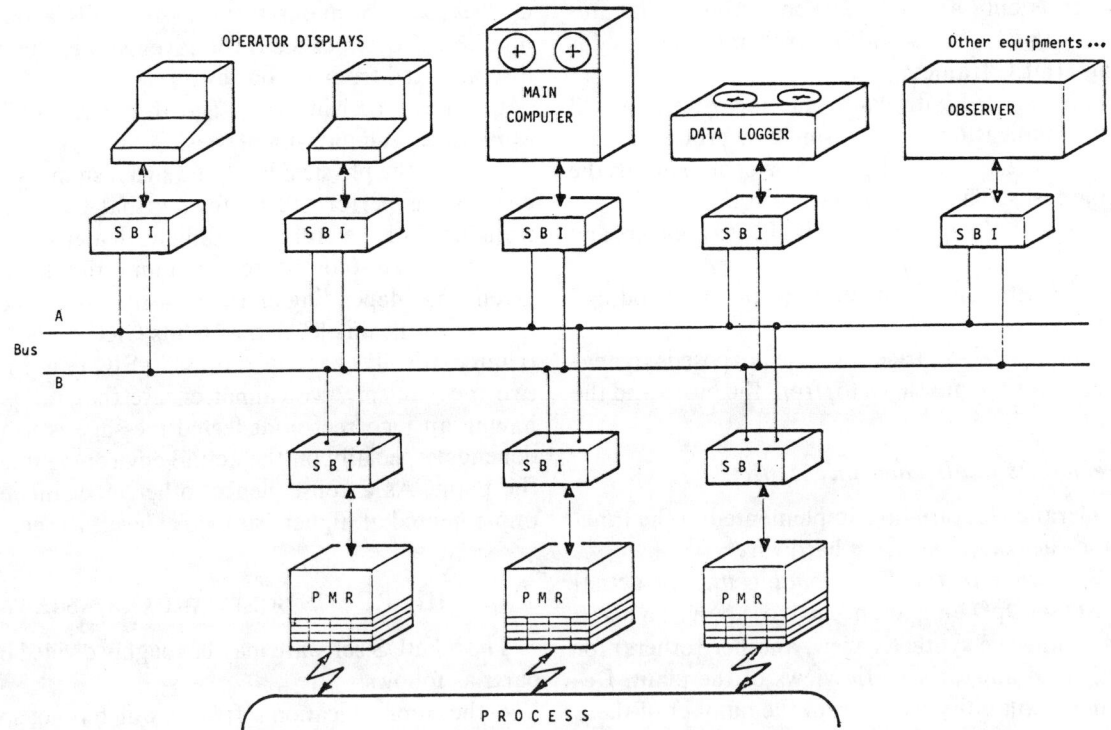

Fig. 1. System hardware architecture.

Another dependability requirement is related to the integrity of information transfer because an incorrect parameter setting or the loss of an alarm message could lead to a critical situation for the plant.

The error rate currently considered in industrial applications needs to be less than 1 message in error per 1000 years operation (for a frame length of less than 100 bits), which corresponds to a residual error rate of 3×10^{-15} at a signaling rate of 1 Mbit/s [4].

In order to achieve the previous dependability requirements, various fault-tolerant and robust mechanisms have been introduced in the architecture of REBUS. They will be developed in the next sections.

II. MODUMAT System Hardware Architecture

The MODUMAT system architecture, the hardware support of REBUS, consists of a set of functional units, stations running some application tasks, linked by a communication hardware (Fig. 1).

A. Basic Functional Units

There are two main types of functional units in the system.

1) Programmable Multiloop Regulators (PMR): Each PMR consists of eight Process Interface Modules (PIM's) and one Multiloop Processing Unit (MPU) which supervises the PIM's.

There is one PIM per control loop, built around a one chip microcomputer which handles the sensor–actuator pair (data filtering and A-D/D-A conversion). It receives orders from the MPU and sends back to it values and status. The MPU runs the regulation algorithms concerning currently up to eight loops and their possible interactions; 18 standard regulation algorithms can be selected in the MPU. The MPU behaves also as an interface for the communication hardware.

2) Operator Displays (OpD): They support the man–machine interface by means of a microcomputer (INTEL SBC 80/20), a color graphic display, and two mini floppy disks. Through them the operator inputs or modifies set points, parameters, or requests for specific data which are then transmitted via the communication structure to the relevant (distant) functional unit. For instance, they are allowed to select various views of the plant: a synthetic view (related to the global control), a local view (related to one MPU), a specific view (related to one PIM, i.e., to a specific control loop). Thus, this unit interprets operator requests by initiating coherent actions in distant units, following a pre-established, possibly complex protocol and it receives reply or alarm messages which are sent to the operator.

The functional units need to communicate with one another (depending on the running application) in order to cooperate and coordinate their activities. This will be implemented through protocols supported by a dedicated communication hardware.

B. The Communication Hardware

On a typical industrial site, the distances between the components of a distributed control system (up to 1.5 km) are, considering wiring costs, large enough to justify the use of serial transmission lines.

It may also be pointed out that a high communication rate, such as achieved for instance through a parallel bus, is not required to exchange informations between the functional units. It follows from these considerations that the communication hardware is only a serial bus connecting Serial Bus Interface boards (SBI). The serial bus transmission speed is 512 kBd using HDLC frames.

One SBI is associated with each functional unit. It will handle the communication mechanisms and protocols, and therefore relieves the functional processor of managing the communication tasks. The SBI boards are composed of
• an interface with the functional unit (FIFO registers and control),
• an interface with the serial buses (biphase encoding-decoding),
• a computing unit, Z-80 based, whose purpose is to analyze/adapt/transmit the messages to/from the buses and the functional unit.

C. Hardware and Its Fault Tolerance Aspects

The fault tolerance features are implemented in the functional units and the communication hardware.

1) Fault Tolerance in the Functional Units: In actual systems, at least two OpD units are needed to supervise a plant: one for maintaining the synthetic view, another (others) for the display of local and/or specific views of the plant. Dependability and availability result from the number of these units.

The problem is more complex for PMR units because only one loop may be faulty (see the aforementioned propositions $P1$ and $P2$). If one PIM is faulty, the requirements are fulfilled because only the control of one loop, the one connected to the faulty PIM, is lost. If the MPU is faulty, then the PMR must perform a recovery. For this purpose each processor in the PIM's checks the correct behavior of the MPU processor in the following way: the PIM's must be polled every 500 ms; if the MPU processor fails and becomes out of service, then the PIM's are not polled and they will set one signal; if all the PIM signals are set, the MPU processor is automatically disconnected and each PIM processor will run a degraded algorithm for regulating its loop (for instance, a proportional integral control algorithm). The corresponding disconnection hardware (a few gates) constitutes the hardcore.

2) The Fault-Tolerant Communication Hardware: The serial bus, because of the poor reliability in transmit/receive hardware and connections for optical fibers, is a shielded twisted electrical pair. It is duplicated for fault tolerance purposes.

There are four main fault-tolerant hardware mechanisms in the board.

a) Each SBI can be directly connected to the PIM's when the MPU processor is disconnected after a recovery. This makes possible the direct access to data inside the PIM's via the bus without using the MPU processor. The same signal is used to disconnect the MPU processor and to connect the interface processor directly to the PIM's.

b) A general board watchdog exists: if not periodically retriggered by software when receiving a message from the bus, it resets the board. This will provide crude reinitialization in case of an unexpected crash.

c) During emission, a watchdog counter checks if the number of transmitted bytes is greater than a given value; this is because continuous transmission kills a bus. When the number of bytes exceeds the given value, the board is then disconnected from the bus by a relay.

d) When receiving a message, there is a twofold verification at physical and data-link levels.
• At the physical level, the signal shape is checked. This checking is performed by testing that 0 and 1 consecutive transitions of the biphase coding lie in a given window (there must be a 1-to-0 or a 0-to-1 commutation for every bit at a given time, depending on the transmission speed).
• At the link level, the 16 bits CRC of the HDLC frame is automatically checked by the Z80-SIO unit. In spite of these two mechanisms, we cannot ensure that the probability of having an incorrect undedected message is negligible. This depends especially on the actual environment constraints in the plant. As a consequence, other mechanisms have been implemented at higher (software) levels as seen later.

III. REBUS SOFTWARE ORGANIZATION

The REBUS software may be roughly divided into two main parts as follows:
• the communication software, which is not specific to any particular application and which is hierarchized following the standard established by ISO [5],
• the application software which is implemented mainly in the functional units and devoted to the control of a specific industrial plant.

Within the frame of REBUS, the communication software represents the main issue. The aim of this study has been indeed the design of a general purpose system which can account for the distributed nature of any industrial process control without being specific to a particular application.

The purpose of the communication software is to support, in a secure way, the cooperation between the user processes. The complexity of the software design comes from the true parallelism, the needed cooperation between the processors and the fault tolerance capabilities which are required.

In order to design a reliable software, a formal specification technique has been used based on the use of Petri nets [6]; as seen later on, a protocol is represented in the following way:
• first, for each of the cooperating processors, the corresponding part of the protocol is modeled by a labeled Petri net [14];
• second, the resulting models are translated into (unlabeled) Petri nets;
• third, those Petri nets are connected together [20] to produce the specification of the global protocol.

This approach has pointed out useful aspects of specification, validation, implementation of the protocols, and of runtime checking.

A. Communication Software Organization

The communication software is fully distributed. Part of it is located on each SBI unit; this part is called the Local Communication Software (LCS).

1) LCS Structure: The structure of a LCS follows the recommendations submitted by the open system architecture

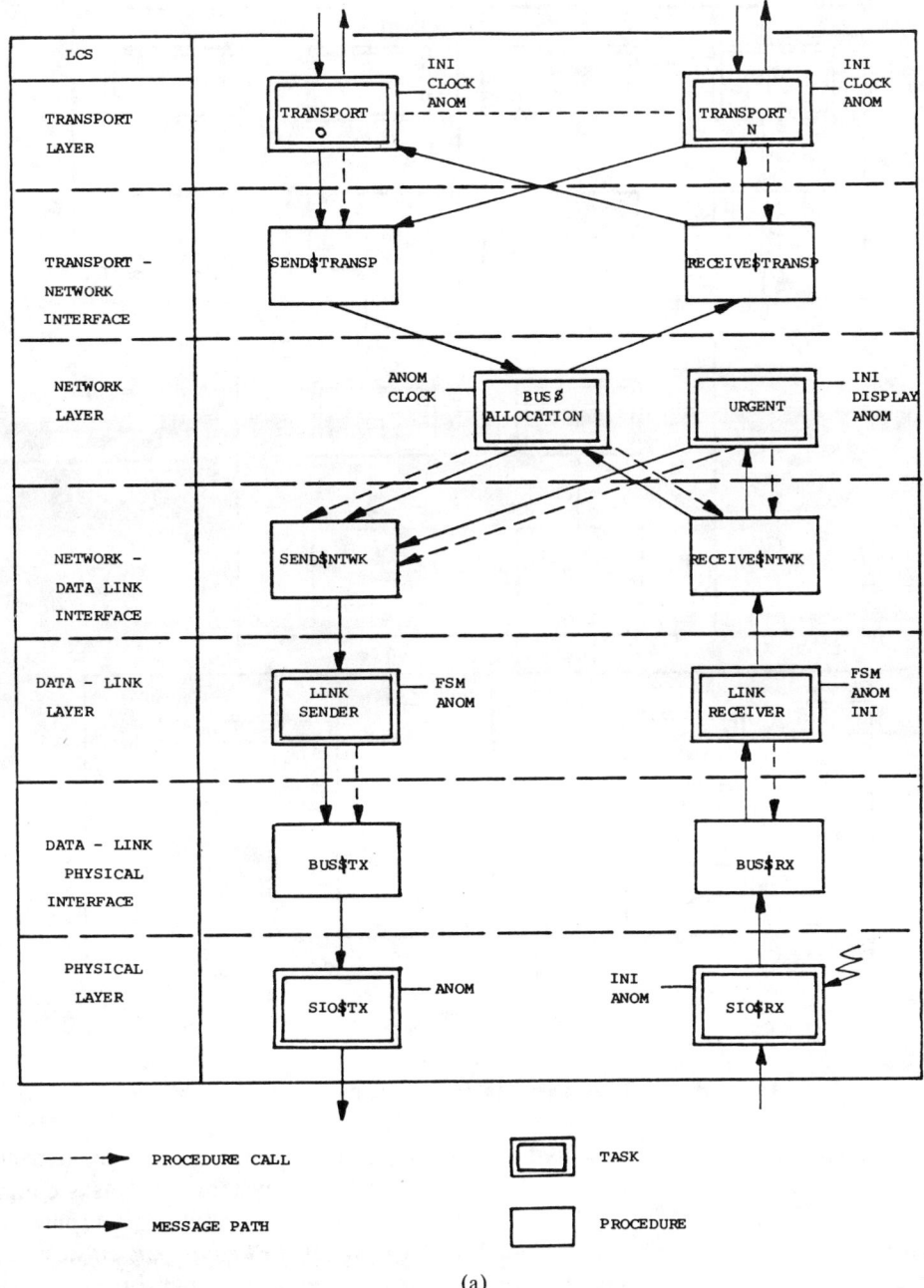

Fig. 2. (a) Local communication software structure.

committee of ISO. Fig. 2(a) shows its hierarchical organization. Each LCS is viewed as logically composed of a hierarchy of entities. The basic concept [5] of this layering is that each layer adds value to services provided by the set of lower layers in such a way that the highest layer is offered the set of services needed to run distributed applications. Cooperation between the entities is specified by the protocols which precisely define how the entities work together by using the services offered by the next lower layer.

In REBUS, four protocol layers have been implemented. Three of them have been designed according to the classical standards: Manchester biphase coding at the physical layer, HDLC at the data link layer, and ECMA drafts at the transport layer (under development).

The fourth one, the network layer, had to be designed in a specific manner. Note that this layer has to hide the bus multipoint structure; it therefore implements

• how the double bus structure is handled; each bus is used alternatively as the system bus for a given period of time; after three unsuccessful attempts to transmit a message, the other bus is selected and an error is reported;

• how to allocate the bus between the processors in order to determine which device (SBI unit) is allowed to transmit data: different classical techniques are available to solve this problem [9]. They range from asynchronous techniques, such as contention [10], [22] to synchronous techniques, such as the "time slots" [9] approach. Although contention is widely used, an original approach which does not need any specific

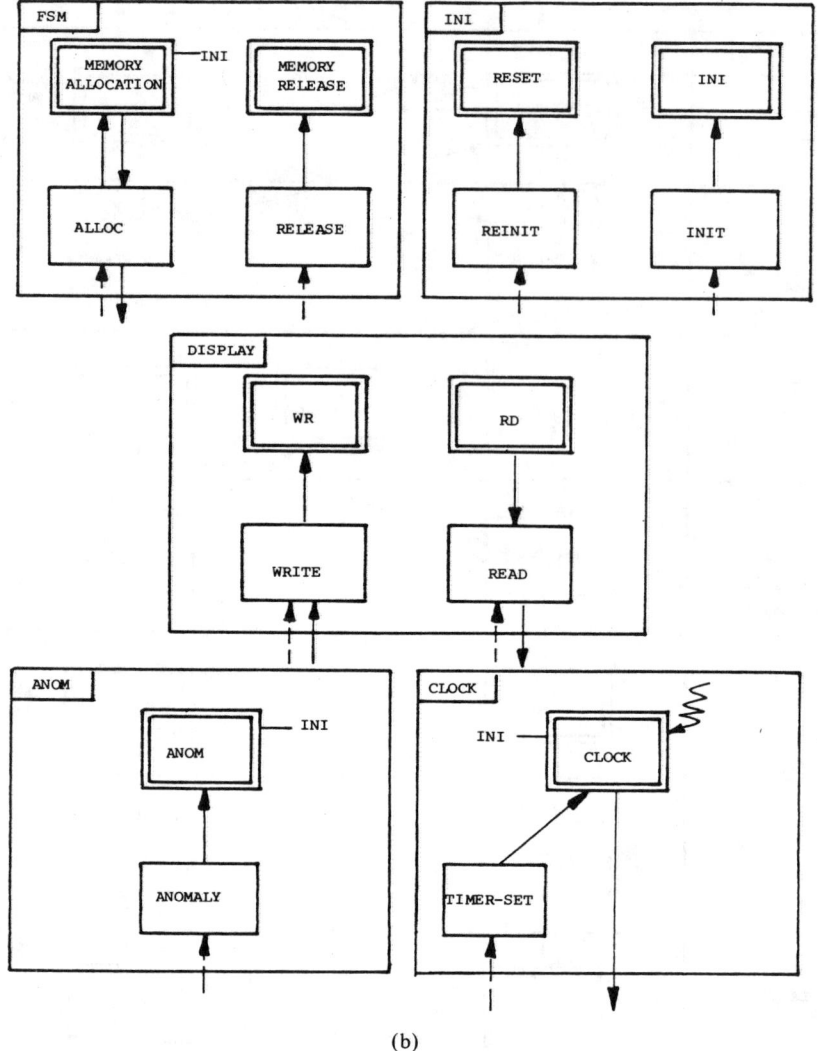

Fig. 2. (*Continued.*) (b) General purpose tasks.

hardware device has been developed and will be presented in Section III-B.

2) LCS Implementation:

a) Structure Translation: At any layer the entities are implemented by a set of tasks. The services provided by the next lower layer are used by calling dedicated procedures. For example, the LCS network layer consists of one entity implemented by task BUS$ALLOCATION [Fig. 2(a)] which can communicate with a remote entity at the same layer through the interface procedures SEND$NTWK and RECEIV-E$NTWK.

b) LCS Kernel: Depending on the considered layer, the tasks are implemented on the SBI unit (physical, data link, network, and transport layers) or in the functional unit (other application layers).

It follows from this organization that a multitasking capability is required to schedule these tasks. Thus, a monitor similar to the multitasking operating system RMX/80 of INTEL [19] has been built in order to direct and coordinate system operation. It initializes system control structures, determines which task should be executed next, supplies timing functions, and provides means for controlling and exchanging data within the system. The tasks communicate with each other in a message-passing synchronization scheme [21].

c) General Purpose Tasks: Beside the tasks which implement the entities, general purpose tasks [Fig. 2(b)] have been implemented to perform some basic functions, such as

- timing (CLOCK), used for time-outs,
- free-space management (FSM), to allocate memory to messages when they are received and to release the memory when the messages have been consumed,
- initialization and reset (INI), to initialize and reset (fully or partially) the LCS system,
- error handling (ANOM), to store some given errors (type, location) and, if necessary, to activate the reset of the system,
- input/output handling (DISPLAY), to debug and to transmit warning messages to a display console.

These tasks (or set of tasks) may be accessed by a simple procedure call.

d) LCS Debugging: The LCS system provides means to transfer data in a secure way between SBI units. In order to increase effectiveness, test and debug capabilities have to be

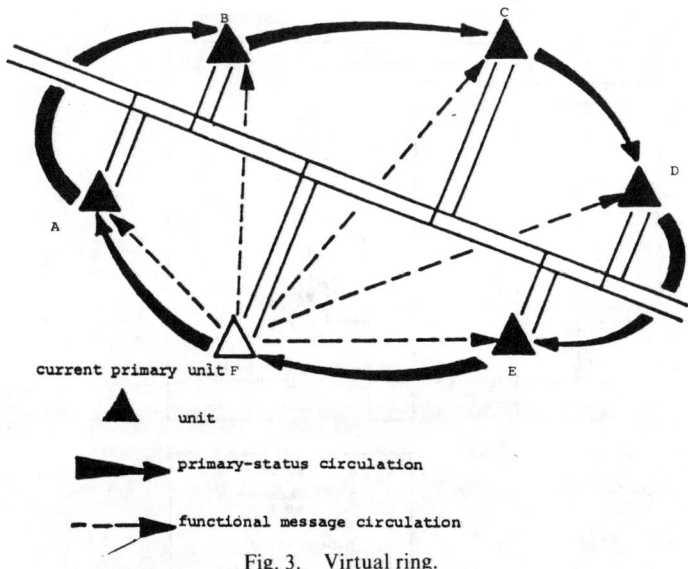

Fig. 3. Virtual ring.

implemented. In particular, the URGENT task [Fig. 2(a)] supplies to the remote SBI units the following capabilities:
- to write (read) in (from) a memory location,
- to reset fully or partially the LCS.

The request to these functions is equivalent to a remote call.

3) Implementation Characteristics: The programs, which implement the various procedures and tasks considered in the previous section, have been written either in assembly language (Z80) for the physical layer and partially for the data link layer or in a PL1-like-language, PLM/80, for the multitasking executive and for the data link and network layers. The size of this operational code is about
- 1.5 kbytes in assembly language,
- 15 kbytes in PLM/80.

The data-link layer implements
- serial input/output handler, i.e., HDLC-like frame, management using a bounded buffer, frame check sequence, over-run (CPU not ready to receive) testing, and verification of the number of transmitted bytes,
- transmit procedures, i.e., time-out triggering (waiting for acknowledgment), retry and stamps management,
- receive procedures, i.e., memory allocation, frame copying.

The service offered by this layer ensures that the frames are not duplicated and provides the transmit status (error indication).

The network layer implements the bus allocation protocol and provides the access to the bus for the upper layers. This protocol concerns a critical point of the system which implies reliability requirements. Hence, the next section is entirely devoted to the specification and validation of this specific protocol.

B. A Fault-Tolerant Bus Allocation Protocol

In the proposed approach, the bus management is performed by a distributed algorithm called the bus allocation protocol. This algorithm is based on a (programmable) "privilege" circulating on a virtual ring [11] and allows one unit at a time to become primary, i.e., to get the access to the bus, whereas the other units are secondary and can only answer to the primary unit. At the end of its privileged state, the primary unit sends the privilege to its successor. The virtual ring (Fig. 3) is a logical organization of the interface units (SBI) ordered in a circular fashion. This ordering is virtual in that only the privilege, called the primary status, must follow the circular path; functional messages sent by the primary unit may be transmitted from it to any other unit and no particular physical organization of the communication medium is implied.

A primary unit, say I, keeps the privilege for a limited amount of time; thus, when its primary-state time is over or when it has no more functional message to send on the bus, it will relinquish the primary status by sending a particular message to its successor [unit $S(I)$] on the virtual ring; the primary status will therefore travel from one unit to another by following the virtual ring.

Three properties will be required for the bus allocation protocol to be reliable and robust

*P*1—at any time, at most one unit is allowed to be primary (exclusion),

*P*2—the loss of primary status may only occur temporarily (robustness),

*P*3—any well-behaving unit must receive the primary status (fairness).

1) Protocol Specification: First, we are concerned with a local specification of the protocol: this specification model [12], [13] describes the behavior of any unit. It specifies the different states of the unit and the messages which may be received and sent in these states. It is deduced from the informal specifications of the protocol and it is close to its implementation.

Nevertheless, a global specification model is required to study the reliability of the protocol (to take into account the interactions between units and possible faults, i.e., loss of messages, hardware failures, etc.).

a) Local Specification: The local specification model is described by means of a labeled Petri net [14] (Fig. 4). The labeling consists in associating with any transition a predicate and a set of actions (procedures or sets of instructions). Thus, if a particular transition is enabled and its associated predicate is evaluated to true, then the transition is fired and the actions are executed. Note that a particular predicate ($X\,?\,m$) represents the reception of a message m from a unit X, a particular action ($Y\,!\,m$) represents the emission of a message m to a unit Y, and ($!!m$) represents the emission of a broadcast message m to all units.

Let I be the current primary unit which broadcasts the message *primary-status* ($S(I)$) by which it loses its privilege and becomes secondary after setting the timer TPS and updating its variable New Primary: NP = $(S(I))$ ($T4$). By receiving this broadcast message, each unit on the virtual ring retriggers its watchdog TPS for TO units of time, updates the new primary NP, and resets the Boolean condition OK-RECOVERY ($T1$). The unit successor of I, the one noted $S(I)$, becomes primary ($T2$) and all the others remain in the secondary state ($T3$).

The condition OK-RECOVERY is set if the watchdog TPS times out ($T8$), i.e., if the message *primary-status* (J) has not

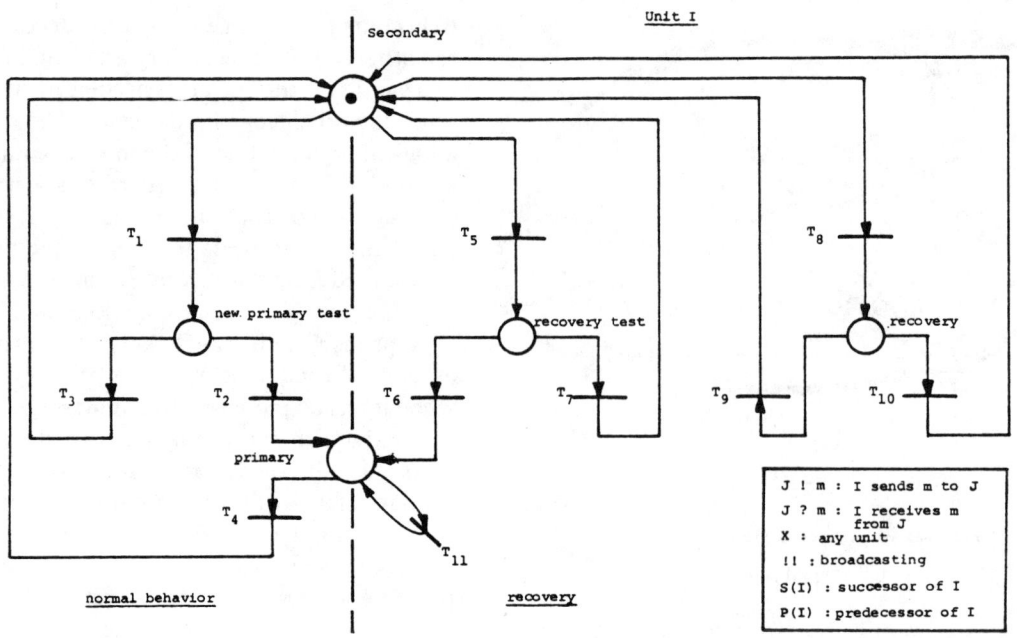

transition		predicate	action
normal behavior	T_1	X ? primary-status (J)	timer-set (TPS,T0) ; N P = J ; OK.RECOVERY = false
	T_2	J = I	
	T_3	J ≠ I	
	T_4		X !! primary-status(S(I));timer-set(TPS,T0);NP=S(I);
recovery	T_5	X ? become-primary	
	T_6	OK.RECOVERY = true	OK.RECOVERY = false ;
	T_7	OK.RECOVERY = false	
	T_8	clock ? time-out (TPS)	NP=S(NP) ; OK.RECOVERY=true ; timer-set(TPS,T0) ;
	T_9	I = S(NP)	delay(t);NP ! become-primary ; OK.RECOVERY=false ;
	T_{10}	I ≠ S(NP)	
	T_{11}	X ? become-primary	

Fig. 4. Local specification model of the virtual ring protocol.

been received after the specified time limit (loss of primary status). In this case the NP variable is updated and indicates, therefore, the successor of the last known primary.

In case of recovery, if unit I is the successor of the successor of the last known primary unit, it indicates the new primary unit by sending the private message *become-primary* to its predecessor ($T9$).

If not, unit I is not concerned with this recovery ($T10$). Unit I may also receive the message *become-primary* ($T5$); if its condition OK-RECOVERY is true ($T6$), it becomes primary, otherwise it remains secondary ($T7$). Reception of *become-primary* ($T11$) does not change the state of an already primary unit.

It may therefore be seen that a unit accepts a recovery only if the two following conditions hold:

1) its own TPS timed out,
2) the unit which receives the message *become-primary*, agrees with that recovery, i.e., if it timed out too (condition OK-RECOVERY = true).

Let us consider an example for which, in Fig. 3, unit A is dead. Let F be the current primary unit known by all units; F leaves the primary state by sending !! *primary-status* (A). This message, not seen by A, will be received by all others units: they perform NP = A and set their timer. After the time $T0$ has elapsed, the units B to F perform NP = $S(A)$ = B and then C (i.e., $S(B)$) will send *become-primary* to B: recovery will occur. The others faulty behaviors are considered in the next paragraph.

It must finally be pointed out that the choice of the time-out value (TO) is of the utmost importance; this value has to be

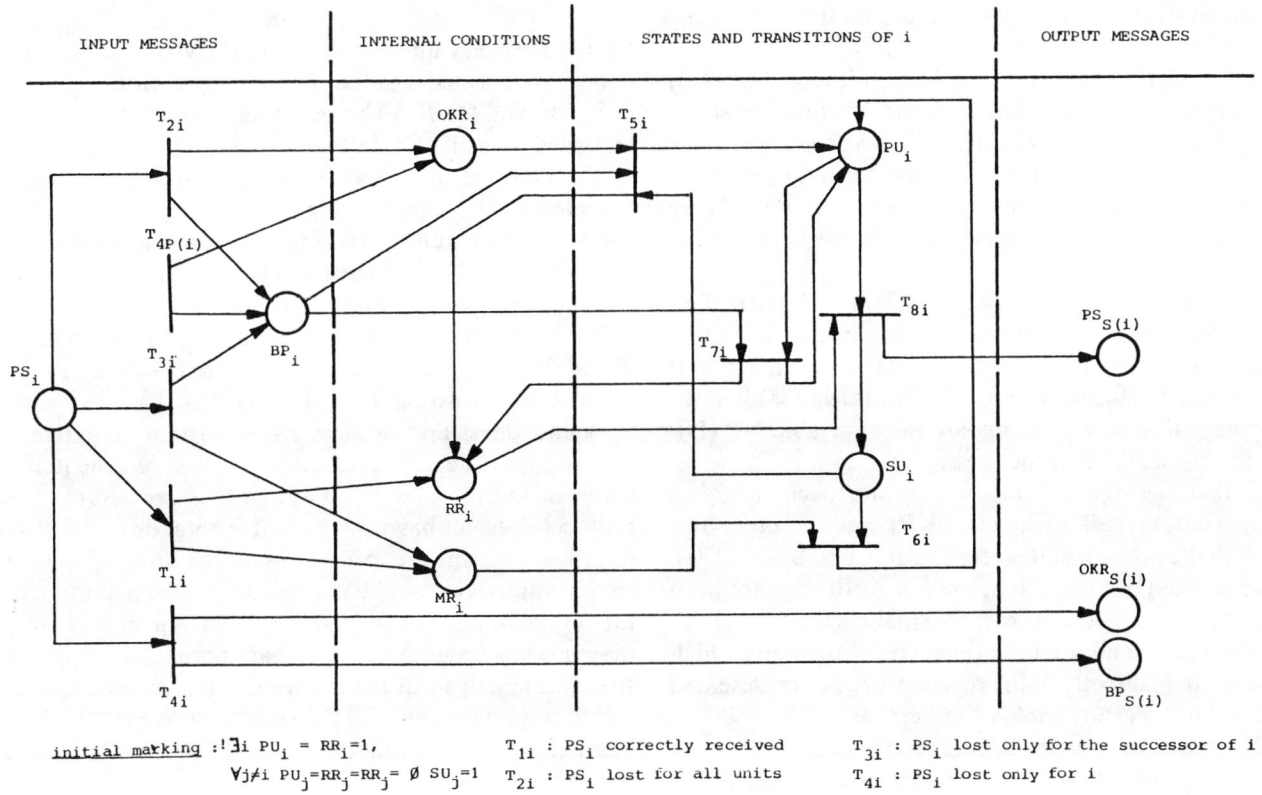

Fig. 5. Global specification model of the virtual ring protocol.

greater than the maximal primary-state time. The retriggerings of TPS are synchronized by the broadcast message, but it is known that it is impossible to ensure that they will time out exactly at the same time [15]. To avoid this problem the unit which is in charge of the recovery enters a delay loop before sending the message *become-primary* ($T9$), in order to allow the other units to time out and to set OK-RECOVERY to true if they have not received the broadcast message *primary-status* (J).

b) Global Specification: The purpose here will be to determine a Petri net model specifying the global protocol behavior. It has to account for the protocol specifications given previously, the interactions existing between the units and different faults that may occur in the communication medium. This model is based on unlabeled Petri nets in order to carry out an automatic validation of the protocol specifications by using the CAD tool OGIVE [18].

i) Fault Assumptions: Different fault cases have been considered in the design of the bus allocation protocol. The protocol will be therefore robust with respect to these (single) faults.

The considered faults are related to faults in the processors or to errors in message transmission on the bus. Different cases have been considered.

1) Transient Faults

• A message may be affected by noise (especially in an industrial environment). This fault can be detected by a 16 bit CRC (Cyclic Redundant Code) checking performed by the receiving unit; if the CRC is incorrect the receiving unit discards the message: the message is lost. The consequence is that in such a case *a broadcast message will be lost for all units*. This fault is referred to as a CRC-error.

• a unit may not be ready to receive a message (e.g., if its buffers are full, if it performs a protected action such that the message interruption is not accounted for . . .). The consequence is that *a broadcast message is lost for this unit*, whereas the other units can receive it correctly.

2) Permanent Faults

• A unit may be "deaf" so that it loses any message which is sent to it.

• A unit may be "dumb" so that any message it tries to send is lost.

Finally, two restrictions on the faults which might occur in the system must be pointed out. First, the watchdogs are supposed to behave correctly, which implies that if a message is lost, each associated watchdog is supposed to time out and it may time out only if the message is lost. Second, the CRC-checking is supposed to be perfect, which means that if the CRC checking is correct, the information contained in the message is supposed to be correct.

ii) The Model: The global specification model is obtained by replicating the Petri net of Fig. 5 as many times as there are units on the virtual ring and by interconnecting them through places representing messages in transit on the bus (PS: *primary-status*, BP: *become-primary*) and places representing the time-outs (OKR: OK-RECOVERY).

Each unit i can be in one of two states PU_i (primary unit) or SU_i (secondary) and has three internal conditions OKR_i, RR_i, and MR_i. The faults, as pointed out before, have been taken into account with respect to the reception of the message

PS$_i$ [*primary-status (I)*] considering the four following cases.

1) PS$_i$ Correctly received (T1$_i$): MR$_i$ (message received) and RR$_i$ (ready to relinquish the primary status) are set to true; unit i becomes primary ($T6_i$) and then secondary through $T8_i$, by sending PS$_{S(i)}$ to $S(i)$: this is the normal behavior.

2) Error Cases During the Transmission of PS$_i$: Three different cases have to be considered, each one being represented by a specific transition.

• *PS$_i$ Lost For All Units (T2$_i$):* This case appears if either unit $P(i)$ is dumb or the message has been affected by noise during the transmission. The last known primary unit is noted $P(i)$; as the broadcast message PS$_i$ is lost for all units, all the units will time out and update their variable NP (NP $= i$); unit $S(i)$ sends then the message BP to unit i; the reception of that message is represented by one token in BP$_i$; as unit i timed out, there is a token in OKR$_i$, and therefore unit i agrees with the primary status recovery initiated by unit $S(i)$. It may be pointed out that, first, the loss of BP has not been accounted for in the model in order to remain in the single fault hypothesis, and second, that the time outs of the units which do not participate directly to the recovery are not represented in the model in order to simplify the Petri net.

• *PS$_i$ Lost Only for the Successor of i (T3$_i$):* This case appears if either unit $S(i)$ is deaf or unit $S(i)$ is not ready to receive the message. Unit i becomes primary ($T6_i$) (PS$_i$ received by i: MR$_i$ set to true); whereas i is primary, there is a recovery initiated by $S(i)$; because it does not agree with the recovery, unit i discards the message BP and remains primary ($T7_i$).

• *PS$_i$ Lost Only for i (T4$_i$):* This case appears if either unit i is deaf or unit i is not ready to receive the message. As unit $S(i)$ did receive the message, there is no recovery initiated by $S(i)$, the recovery is initiated by the unit successor of $S(i)$ to allow unit $S(i)$ to become primary through $T5_{S(i)}$ (BP$_{S(i)}$, OKR$_{S(i)}$ set to true); the mechanism requires that the units timed out twice before the recovery is completed.

2) Protocol Validation: The protocol validation is carried out by the analysis of the properties of the global Petri net model specified in the previous section using a CAD tool, called OGIVE, which has been developed at the LAAS. An industrial version of OGIVE, called OVIDE, is being developed and sold by the French Company ECA-AUTOMATION. Through OGIVE (Outil Graphique Interactif de VErification) it is possible: first, to draw, modify, store Petri nets; second, to analyze their boundedness and liveness properties by classical enumeration of the reachable markings, by reduction rules that simplify the nets keeping their liveness and boundedness properties; third, to obtain net invariants, in fact place and transition invariants: it gives coverings of invariants, basis of invariants, elementary invariants, invariants that contains some given places (respectively, transitions) and that do not contain any given places (respectively, transitions).

It is assumed that at the beginning one unit, say i, is the primary unit which implies that there is one token in place PU$_i$ (shortly, PU$_i = 1$) and also one token in place RR$_i$ (i.e., RR$_i = 1$) in order to enable the transition $T8_i$. The other units are therefore secondary which implies that the places SU$_j$ ($j \neq i$) are marked (SU$_j = 1, j \neq i$).

a) Boundedness and Liveness: The net of Fig. 5 is replicated for every unit belonging to the virtual ring. All these nets are connected together by merging their interface places (PS, BP, and OKR). The resulting global Petri net has been analyzed by using OGIVE.

The Petri net specifying the bus allocation protocol is found bounded for the considered initial marking which implies that whatever the reached marking, the number of tokens of any place is finite. In fact, the bound is one: there is at most one token in any place and the Petri net is therefore safe.

The Petri net is also live which implies that for any transition T and from any reachable marking there is a firing sequence which fires transition T.

Boundedness and liveness are important analytical properties of Petri nets. Boundedness implies that the number of states of the protocol is finite and liveness ensures that the protocol does not have any partial or total deadlock. In order to prove some specific properties on the protocol behavior, a simple approach would be to enumerate the possible states of the protocol. But in concurrent systems the number of states may be very large. A more global approach is supplied by a structural analysis of the net which involves place invariants and transition invariants. These invariants constitute assertions satisfied for any marking of the net, i.e., for any state of the protocol.

b) Net Invariants [16], [17]

i) Place Invariants: A place invariant PI is a vector of size equal to the number of places of the net which satisfies the following (place-invariant) relation for any reachable marking M

$$M \cdot \text{PI} = \text{constant}.$$

This relation holds in particular for the initial marking M_0 of the net, so that it is possible to determine the constant

$$M \cdot \text{PI} = \text{constant} = M_0 \cdot \text{PI}.$$

The following place-invariant relations have been given by OGIVE and are quite interesting in the considered Petri net:

$$R1: \sum_{i=1}^{N} (\text{PU}_i + \text{PS}_i + \text{MR}_i + \text{OKR}_i) = 1.$$

This relation implies in particular that $\sum_{i=1}^{N} \text{PU}_i \leq 1$, which implies that there is at most one unit in the primary state at any time. The property $P1$ of no primary status duplication is therefore proved for the considered protocol.

$$R2: \sum_{i=1}^{N} (\text{PS}_i + \text{BP}_i + \text{RR}_i) = 1.$$

This relation implies in particular that $\sum_{i=1}^{N} \text{BP}_i \leq 1$, which implies that there is at most one unit which may initiate a recovery procedure.

ii) Transition Invariants: By definition transition invariants are dual elements of place invariants. Thus, these are the place invariants of the transposed net, where any place has been changed into a transition and conversely, and where the direction of any arc has been inversed. These transition invariants characterize cyclic firing sequences of the net.

One of the properties (property $P2$, robustness) required by the protocol designer is that no permanent loss of primary status may be possible. This property may be proved in the following way. To prove that no permanent loss of primary status is possible is equivalent to proving that any cyclic firing sequence of the net contains at least one transition $T8_i$ ($i = 1$ to N). The firing of any transition $T8_i$ will indeed indicate that some place PU_i has been marked in order to enable transition $T8_i$ so that a primary unit will exist. By using OGIVE, it has been shown that such a cyclic firing sequence does exist and that there is no cyclic firing sequence which does not contain any transition $T8_i$. This implies the proof of the property and the recovery will ever occur.

The third property (fairness) required by the protocol designer is that any well-behaving unit must receive the primary status, even if one other unit is faulty (single fault hypothesis). This property may be proved in the same way by using transition invariants. When dealing with the fault case, first, one has to choose a well-behaving unit, say i, and to select the transition associated with its good behavior. Second, one has to select the transition associated with the considered fault which appears in a given unit, say j, and to select the transitions associated with the normal behavior of the other units, in order to remain in the single fault hypothesis. Third, one has to show that there is one and only one cyclic firing sequence which contains the prescribed transitions and which does not contain any of the prohibited transitions, and that this cyclic firing sequence does contain the transition $T8_i$ indicating that unit i has been primary (PU_i marked).

Let us consider an example. Unit $P(i)$ (predecessor of i in the virtual ring) is supposed to be dumb, and one wants to prove that unit i will receive the primary status. The dumbness of unit $P(i)$ is represented by the prescription of $T2_i$. The normal behavior of the other units corresponds to the prescription of the transitions $T1_j$ ($j = 1$ to $N, j \neq i$) and the prohibition of $T2_j, T3_j, T4_j$ ($j = 1$ to $N, j \neq i$). By using OGIVE it has been shown that there is only one cyclic firing sequence which contains all the specified transitions and does not contain the prohibited ones. This cyclic firing sequence is

$$\{T8_{P(i)}, T2_i, T5_i, T8_i, T1_{S(i)}, T6_{S(i)}, T8_{S(i)},$$
$$T1_{S(S(i))}, \cdots, T1_{P(i)}, T6_{P(i)}, T8_{P(i)}, \cdots\}.$$

In order to prove completely the property required by the protocol designer, one has only to consider the behavior of unit i for all possible fault cases. The resulting proof has been conducted.

C. Application Software

Various application protocols which use the service provided by the communication software, are available (developed by Schlumberger-Europe). They support
- the man–machine dialogue,
- the synthesis of the plant views,
- the transmission of the operator's orders (set point selection, PID tuning, alarm threshold selection, ...),
- the data display and data modification by remote calls.

These applications that are related to the actual control have been designed following classical techniques and are not given here.

D. General Detection Software

As a basis for debugging, on-line verification and measurements, appropriate mechanisms have been developed.

It appeared when implementing the system that the programming of the processors is rather prone to errors and that these errors are quite difficult to locate and correct. In order to have a self-checking capability for the software, the observer concept [7] was developed. It will be used as follows. An observer is built on a processor by using a Petri net representation of the selected (observed) protocol. This processor, by means of its SBI, is such that it listens to the bus and reads either all the messages or a given subset of the messages related to the selected protocol.

The observer has to check whether the message on the bus is the correct one with respect to the protocol, i.e., allowed by the Petri net representation of the protocol and corresponding to a firable transition. If this is the case then the net is updated; if not, an error is detected and the state, the parameters, the immediate history..., can be obtained.

The corresponding software is implemented on a iSBC 80/30 and its size is about 16K bytes. It is in use at the LAAS and under industrial development at Schlumberger-Europe.

IV. Conclusion

The study has shown the complexity involved in the design of distributed real-time control systems in an industrial environment. In this case, this complexity is due to the fact that REBUS was designed to be really distributed, i.e., without any common memory and common functional processor: we always looked for solutions as general as possible in our context. Two main general conclusions have been found of high interest. On one hand, it appears that it is quite difficult in such systems to reach a satisfactory practical solution without many attempts and without including strong provisions for fault tolerance. On the other hand, some selections of different fault hypotheses pointed out a quite important problem: a little increase in the generality of the selected fault hypothesis leads to a quite unexpected and very high increase in the difficulty and the complexity of a robust solution. The latter point seems to be of fundamental importance when designing reliable distributed systems.

Acknowledgment

The research and implementation described has been done in collaboration with several others, chiefly: J. L. Massieu, J. M. Pons (MITRI-LAAS), Ph. Courthieu, M. Devy, J. Michelena, J. Noubel, M. Shapiro (LC-LAAS), B. Carrichon, A. De Ferry, Ph. Sarquiz, B. Potin (Schlumberger-Europe). They are sincerely acknowledged.

References

[1] J. M. Ayache, B. Carrichon, M. Devy, M. Diaz, B. Potin, and M. Shapiro, "A distributed control system for industrial plants," in *Proc. EUROMICRO*, London, England, Sept. 1980.

[2] J. M. Ayache, B. Carrichon, J. P. Courtiat, M. Diaz, B. Potin, and M. Shapiro, "Fault-tolerance in REBUS, A distributed system for industrial real-time control," in *Proc. Fault-Tolerant Comput. Symp.*, Portland, ME, June 1981.

[3] S. Miranda, "A fault-tolerant decentralized locking protocol for distributed database," in *Proc. Fault-Tolerant Comput. Symp.*, Kyoto, Japan, Oct. 1980.

[4] S. M. Prince and M. S. Sloman, "Communication requirements of a distributed computer control system," *Proc. Inst. Elec. Eng.*, vol. 128, Jan. 1981.

[5] H. Zimmermann, "OSI reference model—The ISO model of architecture for open interconnection," *IEEE Trans. Commun.*, vol. COM-29, Apr. 1980.

[6] J. L. Peterson, "Petri nets," *ACM Comput. Surveys*, Sept. 1977.

[7] J. M. Ayache, P. Azema, and M. Diaz, "Observer: A concept for on-line detection of control errors in concurrent systems," in *Proc. Fault-Tolerant Comput. Symp.*, Madison, WI, June 1979.

[8] D. Katsudi et al., "Pluribus: An operational fault-tolerant multiprocessor," *Proc. IEEE*, vol. 66, Oct. 1978.

[9] K. J. Thurber, "Hardware interconnection technology," in *Distributed Systems, Architecture and Implementation Lecture Notes in Computer Science*, no. 105. New York: Springer-Verlag.

[10] R. M. Metcalfe and D. R. Boggs, "Ethernet: Distributed packed switching for local computer networks," *Commun. Ass. Comput. Mach.*, July 1976.

[11] G. Le Lann, "Distributed computing—Towards a formal approach," in *Proc. IFIP*, Toronto, Ont., Canada, 1977.

[12] G. V. Bochmann and C. A. Sunshine, "Formal methods in communication protocol design," *IEEE Trans. Commun.*, vol. COM-29, Apr. 1980.

[13] P. M. Merlin, "Specification and validation of protocols," *IEEE Trans. Comput.*, vol. C-28, Nov. 1979.

[14] R. M. Keller, "Formal verification of parallel programs," *Commun. Ass. Comput. Mach.*, July 1976.

[15] L. Lamport, "Time, clocks and the ordering of events in a distributed system," *Commun. Ass. Comput. Mach.*, July 1978.

[16] K. Lautenbach and H. A. Schmid, "Use of Petri nets for proving correctness of concurrent process systems," in *Proc. IFIP*, Stockholm, Sweden, 1974.

[17] P. Azema, B. Berthomieu, and P. Decitre, "The design and validation by Petri nets of a mechanism for the invocation of remote servers," in *Proc. IFIP*, Melbourne, Australia, Oct. 1980.

[18] B. Pradin, B. Berthomieu, S. Bachmann, and M. Diaz, "Computer aided design and proof of parallel systems. Application to synchronization software," Int. Rep., LAAS TI.I.41, July 1979.

[19] *RMX/80 User's Guide*, Intel Corp., 1977.

[20] M. Devy and M. Diaz, "Multilevel specification and validation of the control in communications systems," in *Proc. 1st Int. Conf. on Distributed Comput. Syst.*, Huntsville, AL, Oct. 1979.

[21] P. Brinch-Hansen, "The nucleus of a multiprogramming system," *Commun. Ass. Comput. Mach.*, Apr. 1970.

[22] D. Powell, "Performance evaluation and comparison of dependable channel access techniques for locally distributed computing systems," in *Proc. 2nd Int. Conf. on Distributed Comput. Syst.*, Paris, France, Apr. 1981.

Jean-Michel Ayache was born March 3, 1951. He received the Doctorat-Ing. degree in computer science from the University of Grenoble, Grenoble, France, in 1978.

Currently, he is with the French National Institute I.N.R.I.A. and works at the Laboratoire d'Automatique et d'Analyses des Systèmes (L.A.A.S.) Toulouse, France. He has published several papers in fault-tolerant computing and his research interests include the design of distributed systems and self-checking software.

Jean-Pierre Courtiat was born in Konstanz on February 7, 1951. He received the Docteur-Ing. degree in computer science in 1976 from the University of Toulouse, Toulouse, France.

He is now with the Laboratoire d'Automatique et d'Analyse des Systèmes (L.A.A.S.) of the French National Council for Scientific Research, where he works in the Software and Communication team. His research interests include design of fault-tolerant distributed systems, protocol specification, and validation.

Michel Diaz (M'78) received the Doctorat de 3eme Cycle in 1969 and the Doctorat d'Etat in 1974 in electrical engineering and computer science from the University of Toulouse, Toulouse, France.

Presently, he is with the Centre National de la Recherche Scientifique (C.N.R.S.), the French National Council for Scientific Research, and works at the Laboratoire d'Automatique et d'Analyse des Systèmes, Toulouse, France. He has published several papers in fault-tolerant computing and distributed system design. His research interests include the specification, implementation, and validation of fault-tolerant and robust distributed systems. He is the Head of the Research Team Software and Communication at the L.A.A.S.

New system manages hundreds of transactions per second

Parallel data paths, pipelining, large cache memory, and
32-bit hardware combine to increase transaction system performance

by Robert Horst and Sandra Metz, *Tandem Computers Inc., Cupertino, Calif.*

☐ Computer systems for on-line transaction processing have a unique set of requirements that pose an enormous challenge to designers. These systems have to be fault-tolerant, expandable through the addition of modules, and able to process multiple transactions at a reasonable cost, while maintaining data integrity. The coming generation of transaction-processing systems must also address a fast-growing need for very high-volume applications that require the processing of more and more transactions per second.

Designed to handle very high-volume transaction processing, the 32-bit NonStop TXP system reaches two to three times the speed of the NonStop II system it supercedes, while retaining complete software compatibility. Without reprogramming, a TXP system can grow from a single system containing from 2 to 16 processors, to a local cluster of up to 224 processors linked with fiber-optic cables, to a worldwide network of up to 4,080 processors.

Many of the problems in designing the TXP processor had already been solved in the NonStop II processor and system design. The NonStop II extended the instruction set of the NonStop 1+ system to handle 32-bit addressing but did not efficiently support that addressing in hardware. The existing 5-megabyte input/output bus and 26-megabyte Dynabus, Tandem's proprietary bus structure, had more than enough bandwidth to handle a processor with two to three times the performance. The existing packaging had an extra central-processing-unit card slot for future enhancements, and the existing power supplies could be reconfigured to handle a higher-power CPU.

The main problems involved designing a new microarchitecture that would efficiently support the 32-bit instructions at much higher speeds, with only 33% more printed-circuit-board real estate and an existing backplane. This involved eliminating some features that were not critical to performance and finding creative ways to save area on the pc board, including clever uses of programmable array logic and an unusual multilevel control-store scheme.

Since the new TXP processor was to be object-code-compatible with the Nonstop II system yet have a significant price-performance advantage, it was expected that soon after announcement much of the company's produc-

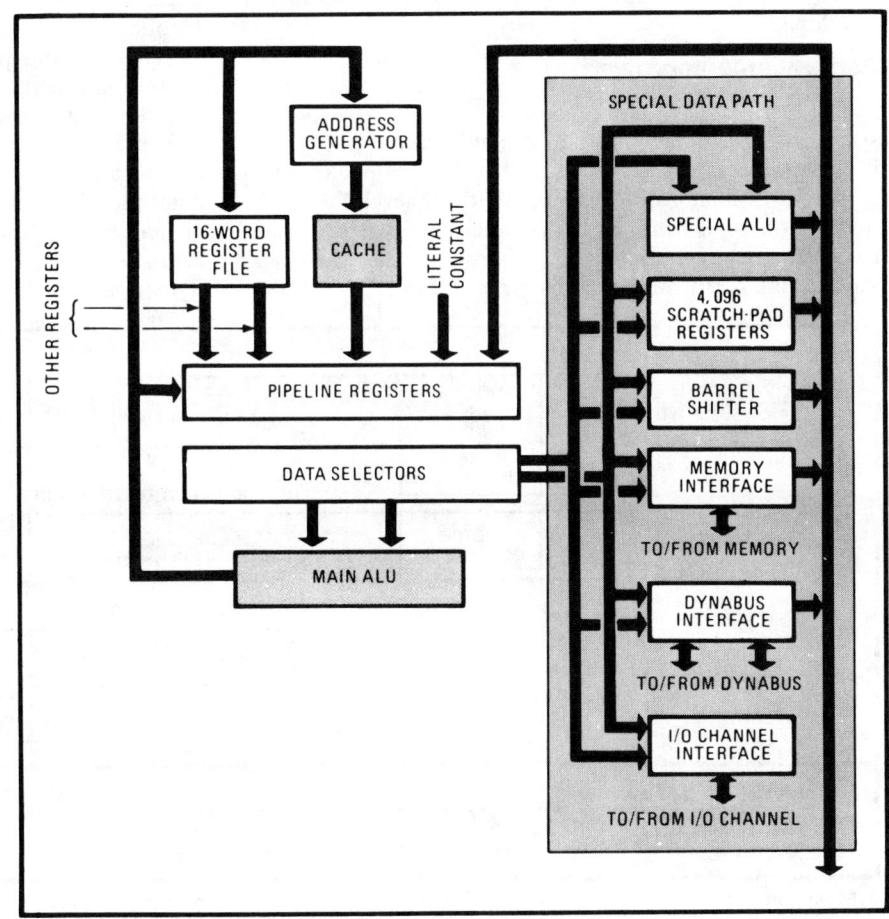

1. Parallel data paths. The NonStop TXP's architecture lets the main arithmetic and logic unit operate in parallel with either a special ALU, one of 4,096 scratch-pad registers, a barrel shifter, the memory interface, the Dynabus interface, or the input/output channel.

TABLE 1: COMPARE-BYTE INSTRUCTIONS (INNER LOOP)

Clock cycle	NonStop TXP		Traditional architecture
	Main ALU	Special ALU	
1	extract byte 1	extract byte 2	extract byte 1
2	compare bytes	—	extract byte 2
3	(repeat)	(repeat)	compare bytes
4	—	—	(repeat)

TABLE 2: DYNABUS-RECEIVE MICROCODE INSTRUCTIONS (INNER LOOP)

Clock cycle	NonStop TXP		Traditional architecture
	Main ALU	Special data path	
1	compute checksum on previous word	read next word from bus queue	compute checksum on previous word
2	address next memory location	write data to cache and memory	read next word from bus queue, increment address
3	(repeat)	(repeat)	write data to cache and memory
4	—	—	(repeat)

tion would have to shift quickly from the NonStop II system to the TXP system. This required that efficient board-testing procedures be in place by the time the product was announced and precluded the use of traditional functional board testers, which need months of programming after the design is finished. Instead, scan logic was designed into the processor and a scan-based board-test system using pseudorandom test vectors was developed.

Performance improvements

The performance improvements in the NonStop TXP system were attained through a combination of advances in architecture and technology. The NonStop TXP architecture uses dual 16-bit data paths, three levels of macroinstruction pipelining, 64-bit parallel access from memory, and a large cache (64 kilobytes per processor). Additional performance gains were obtained by increasing the hardware support for 32-bit memory addressing.

The machine's technology includes 25-nanosecond programmable array logic, 45-ns 16-K static random-access-memory chips, and Fairchild Advanced Schottky Technology (FAST) logic. With these high-speed components plus a reduction in the number of logic levels in each path, a 12-megahertz (83.3 ns per microinstruction) clock rate could be used.

The system's dual-data-path arrangement increases performance through added parallelism (Fig. 1). A main-arithmetic-and-logic-unit operation can be performed in parallel with another operation done by one of several special modules. Among them are a second ALU that performs both multiplications and divisions, a barrel shifter, an array of 4,096 scratchpad registers, an interval timer, and an interrupt controller. Other modules provide interfaces among the CPU and the interprocessor bus system, I/O channel, main memory, and a diagnostic processor.

The selection of operands for the main ALU and the special modules is done in two stages. In the first, data is accessed from the dual-ported register file or external registers and placed into two of the six registers. During the same cycle, the other four pipeline registers are loaded with cache data, a literal constant, the results of the previous ALU operation, and the result of the previous special-module operation.

In the next stage, one of the six pipeline registers is selected for each of the main ALU inputs and one for each special-module operand. Executing the register selection in two stages, so that the registers can be two- rather than four-ported, greatly reduces the cost of multiplexers and control storage, while the flexibility in choosing the required operands is unimpaired.

Some examples of the way microcode uses the parallel data paths are shown in Tables 1 and 2. The first example shows the inner loop of the compare-bytes instruction. Each of the dual ALUs in the TXP system extracts one byte; then the extracted bytes are compared. This operation takes two clock cycles on the TXP system

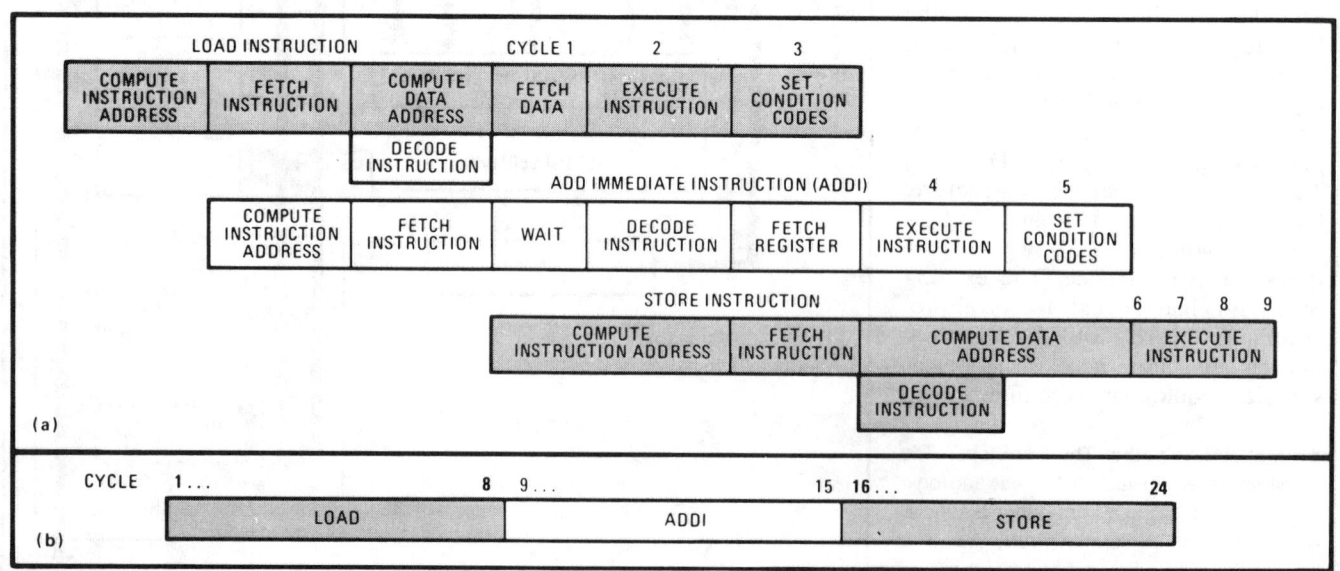

2. Pipelined. The instruction pipeline of the NonStop TXP system allows parts of several instructions to be processed simultaneously (a)—nine cycles are required to execute three typical instructions. Without pipelining (b), 24 clock cycles would be required.

Hardware-performance monitor helps optimize design

While new architectural concepts were being developed for the TXP system, a hardware-performance monitor was built to record measurements of the software-compatible NonStop II processor. Xplor consists of two large Wire-Wrap boards plus a small board to interface to the processor under test. It has approximately 800 Schottky TTL components and took more than two years to develop.

This general-purpose tool is capable of capturing 64 bits of data every 100 nanoseconds and reducing that data to usable form. The 256 kilobits of internal memory can be configured in many different word lengths to record, for instance, a 64-bit count of 4,096 different events, a 32-bit count of 8,192 different events, or a single flag for 256-K events. In addition, Xplor has programmable state machines with which data can be captured based on complex sequences of events; it includes hardware for the emulation of various cache organizations.

Two different Xplor configurations were developed to gather data for the TXP processor. The first was an instruction histogram measurement that records the frequency with which each instruction occurs, the percentage of time spent in each instruction, and the average number of code and data reads and writes performed by each instruction. The data is recorded in 64-bit counters, so in effect an unlimited amount of real-time data can be taken before the counters overflow.

The second Xplor configuration monitors memory addresses and emulates the tag store of a cache. Hit ratios for many different cache organizations can be determined by varying the effective cache size, associativity (one-, two-, or four-way), block size, and replacement algorithm. Because the data is taken in real-time and reduced on-line, the hit-ratio measurements are much more accurate than the traditional technique, in which short address traces are recorded on tape for later analysis. This is especially important in transaction processing, since a large amount of process switching takes place; some individual transactions can last several seconds, during which millions of memory references take place.

Once the measurement methods were working, Xplor was attached to an eight-processor NonStop II system. A typical transaction-processing benchmark was brought up on the system, and transactions then were generated by another system, running software that simulated users at a number of terminals. At that point, histogram and cache measurements were taken for several of the central processing units.

The results of the histogram measurements helped determine some of the data-path widths and organizations for the TXP processor. Once the most frequently executed instructions were known, the design was modified to provide more hardware support for them. Since the measurements distinguished different paths through some instructions, tradeoffs could be made in the microcode to make the frequent cases faster.

The results of the cache measurements brought about some major changes in the original cache organization. In one measurement, the hit ratio went from 97% for the original cache to 99% for the final one, for an overall CPU performance gain of over 15%.

---

but would require three if the extract operations could not be done simultaneously.

The dual 16-bit data paths tend to require fewer cycles than a single 32-bit path when manipulating byte and 16-bit quantities and slightly more cycles when manipulating 32-bit quantities. A 32-bit add takes two cycles rather than one, but the other data path is free to use the two cycles to perform either another 32-bit operation or two 16-bit operations.

Time disadvantage

The time disadvantage in performing a single 32-bit operation is partially offset by the cycle-time advantage for 16- versus 32-bit arithmetic (32-bit arithmetic requires more time for carry propagation). Measurements of transaction-processing applications have shown that the frequencies of 32-bit arithmetic are insignificant relative to data-movement and byte-manipulation instructions, which are handled more efficiently by the dual data paths than by a single 32-bit data path. Most instructions have enough parallelism to let the microcode make effective use of both data paths.

To control the large amount of parallelism in the NonStop TXP system processor, a wide control-store word is required. The effective width of the control store is over 100 bits. To reduce the number of RAMs required, the control store is divided between a vertical control store of 8-K 40-bit words and a horizontal control store of 4-K 84-bit words. The vertical control store controls the first stage of the microinstruction pipeline and includes a field that addresses the horizontal control store, whose fields control the pipeline's second stage. Lines of microcode that require the same or similar horizontal controls can share horizontal-control-store entries.

Unlike microprocessor-based systems that have microcode fixed in read-only memory, the NonStop TXP system microcode is implemented in RAM, so it can be changed along with normal software updates and new performance-enhancing instructions can be added.

The NonStop TXP processor uses three-stage pipelining for both macro- and microinstructions. Figure 2 illustrates the operation of the macroinstruction pipeline for a sequence of three instructions. The first is a load instruction that loads a word into the hardware stack. The second is an add immediate instruction that adds a constant to a register on the hardware stack, and the third is a final store, which stores the result in memory.

With no pipelining, this sequence would require 24 (8+7+9) clock cycles to execute, but because the prefetch and part of the execution of each instruction can be overlapped with previous instructions, the actual execution time is just 9 (3+2+4) clock cycles. Because instructions are pipelined, the TXP processor can execute its fastest instructions in just two clock cycles (167 ns),

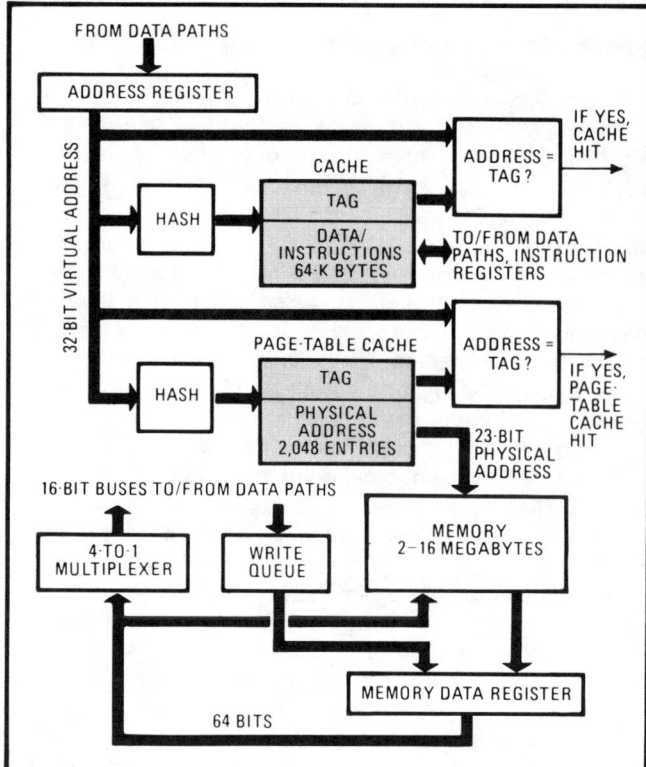

3. Memory access. The simple but extensive organization of the TXP cache provides an average hit ratio of over 96%. With a cache hit, the data is read out of the cache in 83 nanoseconds. When the data requested is not in cache, a cache miss results and the 64-bit-wide access to memory speeds the cache refill.

and it can execute load and branch instructions, which are frequently used, in only three clock cycles (250 ns).

Each NonStop TXP processor has a 64-K-byte cache that holds both data and code. A 16-processor NonStop TXP system has a full megabyte of cache memory. To determine the organization of the cache, a number of measurements were performed on a NonStop II system using a specially designed hardware monitor (see "Hardware-performance monitor helps optimize design," p. 149). The measurements showed that higher cache hit ratios resulted with a large, simple cache (directly mapped) than with a smaller, more complex cache (organized as two- or four-way associative). Typical hit ratios for transaction processing on the NonStop TXP system are in the range of 96% to 99%.

Cache miss

Cache misses are handled in a firmware subroutine rather than by the usual method of adding a special state machine and dedicated data paths for handling a miss. Because of the large savings in cache hardware, the cache can reside on the same board as the primary data paths; keeping these functions proximal reduces wiring delays and contributes to the fast 83.3-ns cycle time.

The cache is addressed by the 32-bit virtual address rather than by the physical address, thus eliminating the extra virtual-to-physical translation step that would otherwise be required for every memory reference. The virtual-to-physical translation, which is needed for refilling the cache on misses and for storing through to memory, is handled by a separate page table cache that holds mapping information for as many as 2,048 pages of 2-K bytes each (Fig. 3).

A cache memory by itself does not necessarily boost a processor's performance significantly. It is of little use for the cache to provide instructions and data at a higher rate than the rest of the CPU can process. In the TXP processor, the cache's performance was tuned to provide instructions and data at a rate consistent with the enhancements to instruction processing provided by increased pipelining and parallelism.

32 bits and more

The two concerns related to a system's word length are capability and performance. The NonStop TXP system has 32-bit virtual addressing built into the hardware, so is capable of addressing a gigabyte of virtual memory. In addition, the TXP processor can manipulate 32 bits of data at a time through its dual 16-bit data paths. Thus the 32-bit NonStop TXP system has the additional advantage of being able to run software that was originally written for the 16-bit NonStop II system; both systems have been provided with instructions that can operate on 8-, 16-, 32-, and 64-bit data types.

In transaction processing, measurements of instruction frequencies show that data-movement instructions (loads, stores, and moves) occur much more frequently than 32-bit arithmetic instructions. For this reason, the NonStop TXP system is optimized to handle data movement by providing 64-bit access to main memory and 32-bit buses and address registers to make memory addressing as efficient as possible.

The NonStop TXP processor was implemented on four large pc boards using high-speed FAST logic, PALs, and high-speed static RAMs. The CPU's logical and physical partitioning was carefully controlled to ensure that the machine's basic cycle time would not be slowed by long propagation delays. The four CPU boards are:
- SQ: containing the control store and sequencing logic.
- CC: containing the I/O channel and various special modules.
- IP: holding the main data paths and cache.
- MC: providing the memory interface, barrel shifter, and interprocessor bus interface.

Each CPU module also has from one to four memory boards. On the initial release, each memory board contains 2 megabytes of error-correcting memory implemented with 64-K dynamic RAMs. A 16-processor NonStop TXP system can therefore contain up to 128 megabytes of physical memory.

The NonStop TXP system was designed to be easy to manufacture and efficient to test. Data and control registers were implemented with shift registers configured into several serial-scan strings. The scan strings are of value in isolating failures in field-replaceable units. This serial access to registers also makes board testing much faster and more efficient because the tester can directly observe and control many control points. A single custom tester was designed for all four CPU boards and for the memory-array board as well.

The NonStop TXP system is the first product to be

MIPS and transactions per second

Determining relative performance among computer systems has never been an easy task. The often-quoted millions-of-instructions-per-second rate is intended as a way to compare basic central-processing-unit-hardware performance. Comparisons are also made on the basis of benchmarks. CPU-intensive benchmarks measure the performance of the CPU hardware and compiler; more extensive benchmarks measure the entire system performance—including the hardware, compiler, operating system, and data-base-management system. In general, the more extensive benchmarks give a more accurate prediction of actual system performance.

Each of the various measurement techniques has pitfalls. The MIPS rate is perhaps the least accurate way to compare systems. One reason is that there is no easy way to relate the power of one instruction set to another. In addition, vendors vary in the way they measure MIPS: some use it for the speed of the fastest instructions, others measure the speed of the most frequently executed instructions, and still others measure the speed of a "typical" mix of instructions. According to these definitions, each NonStop TXP processor is 6, 4, or 2 MIPS, respectively.

---

developed using Tandem's proprietary computer-aided-design system. The CAD system's capabilities for logic entry, logic simulation, and automated pc-board routing were instrumental in reducing the design time. While most high-performance CPUs require four to five years to develop, the NonStop TXP processor took just 2½ years—six months to complete a written specification, one year to construct a working prototype, and another year to reach volume production.

Performance measurement

Some simple benchmark programs have recently become popular in measuring performance (see "MIPS and transactions per second," p. above). One is the Puzzle benchmark, which is a CPU-intensive program to solve a three-dimensional puzzle. Execution times for Puzzle can vary widely for the same machine, depending on whether the program accesses arrays through subscripts or pointers and whether frequently used variables are assigned to registers. Versions of the Puzzle benchmark with pointers and registers were used to compare relative performance for a TXP processor.

Puzzle was written in TAL (transaction application language, the company's system-programming language); the execution time, using a single TXP processor, was measured at 1.67 s. This compares with 4 s on a VAX-11/780 for Puzzle written in C.[1] Because Puzzle does not measure such system features as support for virtual memory, I/O bandwith, and the ability to do fast context switching, a standard benchmark for comparing transaction-processing systems is still needed.

One transaction-processing benchmark has been developed by a third party, however. The U.S. Public Health Service ran an extensive benchmark in 1981 to determine which system to select for a large on-line medical-information system.[2] In that study, a 15-processor Tandem NonStop system running a 1981 version of Tandem's Encompass DBM system performed the benchmark at a rate of 4.5 transactions/s. An International Business Machines Corp. System 370/168-3 running version 3 of the Adabas DBM system performed the same benchmark at 2 transactions/s.

This benchmark gives a data point for comparisons between Tandem and IBM systems. A 15-processor NonStop system performs the Public Health Service benchmark 2.25 times as fast as an IBM 370/168-3. Though it would be desirable to compare the TXP system directly to one of IBM's newest systems, such as the IBM 4381-2, no competitive benchmarks have been published. However, comparisons of the MIPS rate of different processors within a single family are fairly accurate and can be used to extrapolate to newer systems.

According to market research performed by the Gartner Group,[3] the IBM 4381-2 is rated at 2.7 MIPS, compared with the older IBM 370/168-3's 2.4 MIPS rating—a ratio of 1.125 : 1. Company tests have shown the NonStop TXP to have a MIPS rate approximately three times that of the NonStop processor. The extrapolation of the Public Health Service benchmark performance to the two newer systems is shown in Table 3.

Unlike many shared-memory multiprocessor systems, Tandem systems provide linear growth in transaction-processing power as the system expands. A single system can include up to 16 processors, and clusters with as many as 224 NonStop TXP processors may be configured with Tandem's fiber-optic link. Clusters with up to 60 processors are currently in operation, and their users have verified the linear-performance growth within a cluster of this size.

The largest IBM mainframe today is the IBM 3084, which is rated at approximately 23 MIPS. Extrapolation from the benchmark data suggests that the performance of a cluster of 224 TXP processors is on the order of 10 times as powerful as IBM's top-of-the-line 3084 processor. □

TABLE 3: TANDEM VERSUS IBM PERFORMANCE COMPARISONS		
	U.S. Public Health Service benchmark: results (transactions per second)	USPHS benchmark: extrapolated results* (transactions per second)
IBM 370/168-3	2	—
Tandem NonStop 15-processor system	4.5	—
IBM 4381-2	—	2.25
Tandem NonStop TXP 3-processor system	—	2.7
*Not actual measurements		

References
[1] Malcolm A. Gleser, Judith Bayard, and David D. Lang, "Benchmarking for the Best," Datamation, May 1981.
[2] Computer Architecture News, 10 : 1, March 1982, p. 29.
[3] Gartner Group Inc., Stamford, Conn., market research surveys.

NEW SYSTEMS

Making processing fail-safe

ROBERT FREIBURGHOUSE, Stratus Computer, Inc.

Any number of modules, each configurable to be fully redundant, achieves 'continuous processing' for the Stratus/32

Buyers who must have a computer system that continues to function despite failures have not had much of a selection, but their choice has been broadened by the introduction of the Stratus/32 system from Stratus Computer, Inc., Natick, Mass. With 4M bytes of memory, dual 143M-byte disks, a 600-lpm printer and magnetic tape, a typical Stratus/32 sells for $172,000, including COBOL and VOS software licenses. Based on COBOL benchmarks, the system's performance equals or surpasses that of several popular superminis.

The Stratus/32 multiprocessor, fault-tolerant system for commercial applications supports on-line transaction processing, batch processing, word processing and interactive program development. It uses a combination of hardware and software that provides continuous processing of user programs during computer failure without checkpoint/restart programming at the user or system level. Central to the system's fail-safe operation are processing modules, each of which has redundant logic and communication paths, logic and CPU boards and main and disk memory. Twin components operate in parallel with each other; when one fails, its partner carries on.

Architectural overview

The Stratus/32 processing modules are connected via

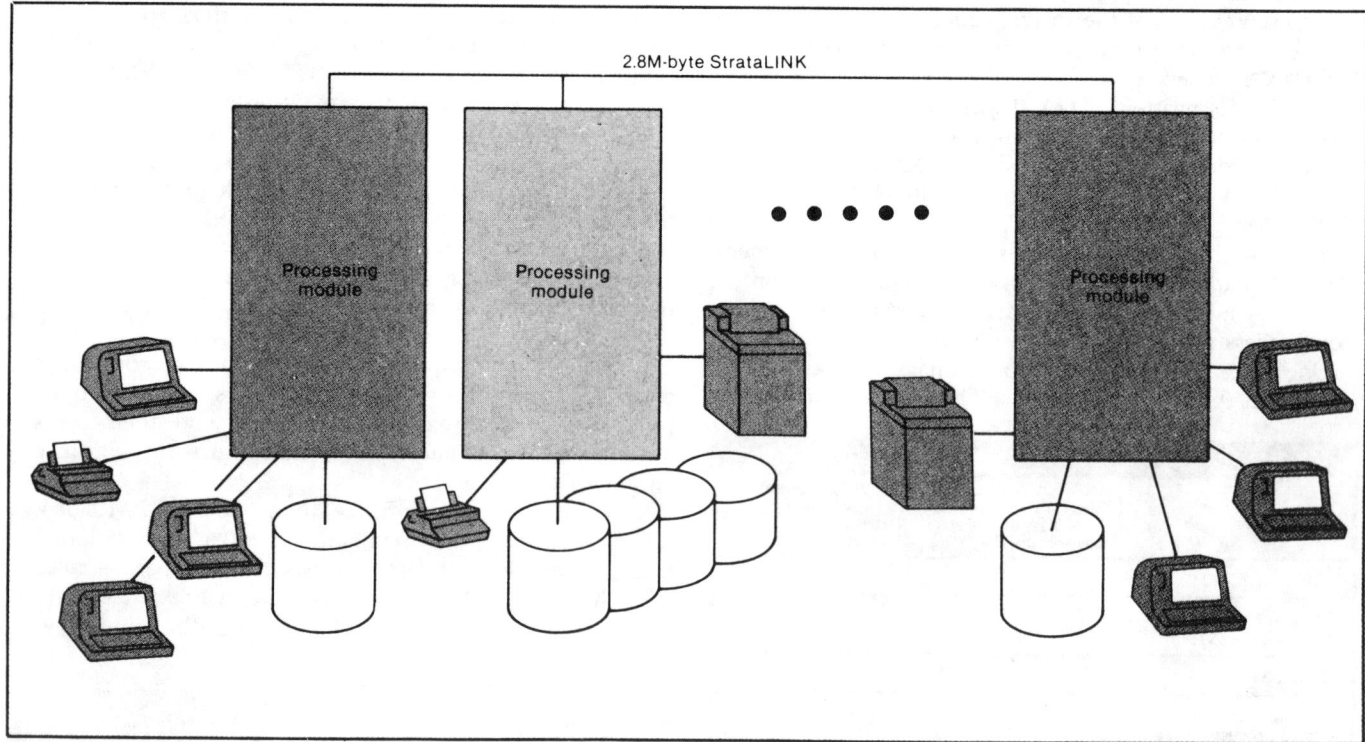

Fig. 1. A Stratus/32 system consists of as many as 32 processing modules *connected by a high-speed coaxial link. The modules can be located anywhere within an office building or can be adjacent to each other.*

> Each processing module can be configured as fully redundant, partially redundant or non-redundant.

the StrataLINK high-speed coaxial link. Each processing module consists of memory, two Motorola Corp. 68000 CPUs, at least one disk and various peripheral controllers and devices (Fig. 1). Both 68000 CPUs are visible to the operating system, and each executes its own instruction stream using a shared memory.

Each processing module can be configured as fully redundant, partially redundant or non-redundant. The degree of a module's redundancy determines the module's resistance to hardware failure. A fully redundant module can withstand failure of essentially any component in the module without performance or data loss and without user program interruption. Multiple modules are used only to achieve greater system capacity; they never serve as backup for other modules.

Stratus's distributed virtual operating system (VOS) runs in each of the processing modules. All modules are equal and can operate independently, but through the use of transparent local networking software, VOS makes the entire set of processing modules appear as a single computer system to programs, programmers and application users.

Although each peripheral device is attached to a processing module, VOS makes all devices available to programs running in any module. Similarly, a program running in a module creates processes to run in the same module or in others. An interactive terminal user can create processes to execute commands or to run programs in any module. The users need not be aware of the module they are using. Likewise, batch jobs can run anywhere in the system.

All VOS service requests have a uniform interface that is independent of the processing module on which the work will be performed. For example, a request to open a file has the same form and arguments regardless of where the file resides. VOS examines the file name, looks in a device table to determine the module that owns the device and performs the requested operation or makes a network request over the StrataLINK to the VOS running the owning module. The requesting program does not see the network request. Consequently, user programs are unaware of the location of files or devices and see the multiple-module network as a single virtual-computer system (Fig. 2).

Examining the hardware

A processing module includes one or more cabinets that contain a complete computer with a logic-board chassis, dual power supplies, peripheral devices and and terminal port. A single cabinet holds a fully redundant module consisting of two 143M-byte disk drives, a magnetic tape, 16M bytes of memory, redundant CPU boards and a set of redundant peripheral controllers (Fig. 3).

A high-speed bus with a 125-nsec. cycle time is central to processing-module organization The bus—virtually two buses operating in parallel—has two sets of data and control-logic paths. The data path on each bus is 32 bits wide, and data can be put on the bus every bus cycle. This results in a potential bus rate of 32M bytes per sec., although processor/memory boards now run at 16M bytes per sec. By comparison a VAX/11-780 bus runs at 13M bytes per sec.

Each logic board that can be attached to the bus can

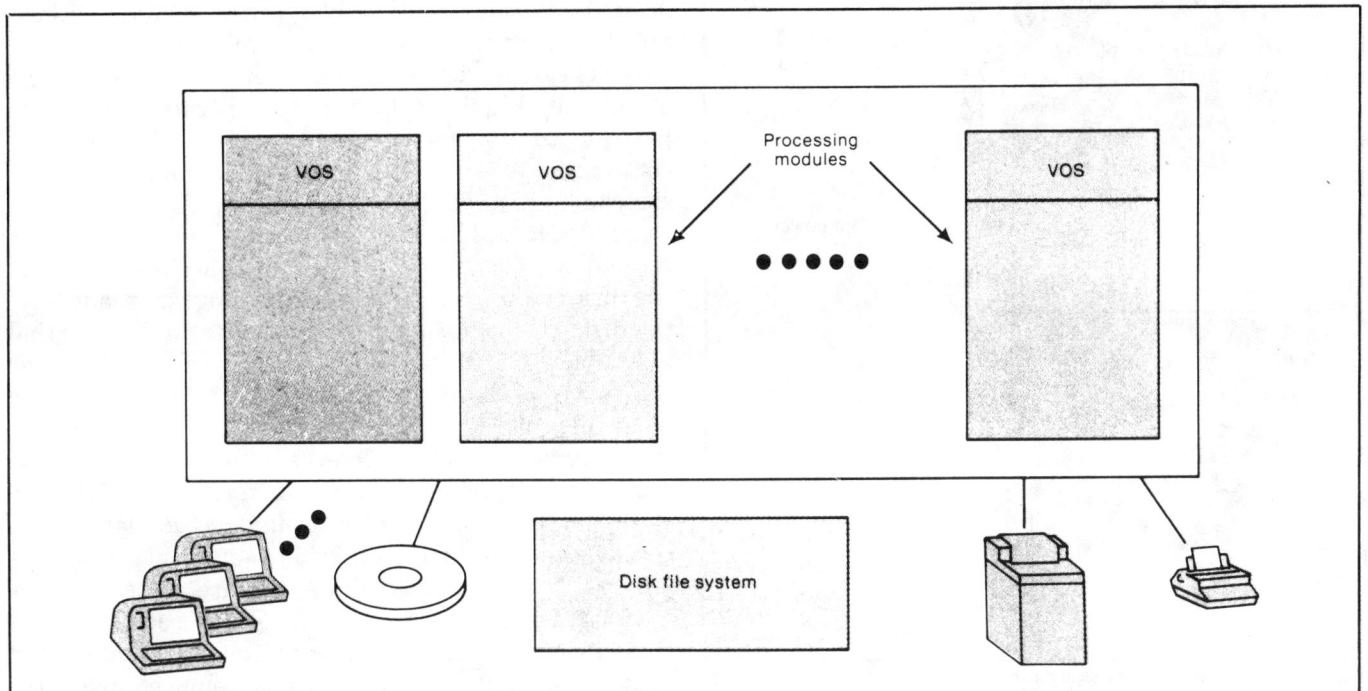

Fig. 2. The Stratus/32 virtual operating system (VOS) *makes all processing modules appear as part of a single virtual system in which all devices, files and system resources are accessible as if it were a single computer.*

> *The bus—virtually two buses operating in parallel—has two sets of data and control-logic paths.*

detect its own failure and shut itself down. It can also run with a redundant board that continues to operate in the event of its partner's failure. Neither logic board is primary, and neither is aware of the other. The pair of boards appears collectively to other system components as a fail-safe entity.

The self-checking technique used by each type of board differs slightly, but generally involves the use of two sets of logic on a board. Each set performs every operation in parallel with the other. When data are to be sent to the bus or to a device, the results produced by the two sets of logic are compared. If identical, the result is sent onto the bus or to the device. Dissimilar results indicate a board failure, and no data are sent. In this case, a red LED on the board is lit, and an interrupt signal is sent on the bus. Until the board is tested and logically reconnected by maintenance software, it remains off-line. The board's redundant partner continues to operate, and no other component of the system is aware of the failure (Fig. 4).

The CPU board contains two complete sets of logic and is self-checking. Four Motorola 68000 processors provide each board with two processors visible to the operating system (Fig. 5). A redundant partner CPU board ensures continuous processing in the event of a failure of a CPU board. At a component price of approximately $100 for each 68000, this is a cost-effective solution to continuous processing that was not practical until the availability of VLSI technology.

Redundancy is achieved by using a pair of logic boards for each logical entity in the system. Each board is attached to both halves of the bus, and both boards operate in parallel, performing identical operations. The output of both boards is placed on the bus at the same instant and is guaranteed to be identical.

Memory is duplicated in a redundant system so that N megabytes of program-visible memory is implemented using 2NM bytes of physical memory with N megabytes attached to each of two memory controllers. When data are written to a given memory location, both memory controllers respond and write the data into their memory. When data are read from memory, both controllers respond and read from their memory.

The controllers and the memory are synchronized and appear to the rest of the system as a single logical entity. Memory subsystems are not paired with CPUs, bus halves or other system components. Memory is implemented from 64K RAMs and is packaged on 1M- or 2M-byte boards. It has a 375-nsec. read-cycle time and is four-way interleaved. A typical processing module has 4M or 8M bytes of memory. In packaged configurations, Stratus sells memory for $5000 per megabyte. A 2M-byte array board lists for $20,000.

The memory system can be dynamically reconfigured to be redundant or non-redundant. This allows a module to use all available memory when full redundancy is not needed. Reconfiguration can occur on-line without affecting running programs.

Disks cannot run completely synchronized with each other; they require help from the operating system to provide continuous processing. Each disk can be configured to have a duplicate. The mirror disk is attached to a separate controller to protect from controller failure. When a program writes a record to a redundant disk, the operating system writes records to the disk and to its mirror. When a program reads from the disk, the operating system reads from the disk that is not busy or whose heads are best positioned to read the record. If a read error occurs, the record is read from the other disk.

An error-correction code stored with each disk record detects media failures during a read. A read error from a redundant disk results in reading the same record from its partner. Non-redundant disks are vulnerable to total disk failure, but are protected from media failures by VOS, which verifies each write. A record that cannot be verified is rewritten to another disk block, and the bad block is removed from the available disk space.

StrataLINKs, like disks, cannot run synchronized.

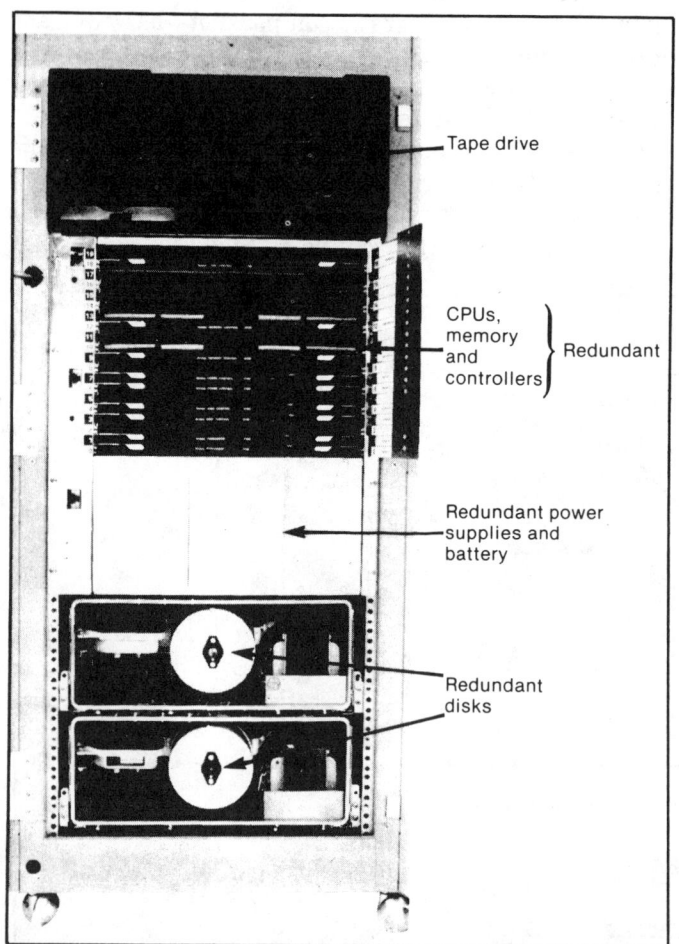

Fig. 3. A Stratus/32 processing module *can contain 16M bytes of memory, a full set of redundant controllers, two 143M-byte disks, a tape drive and two software-visible CPUs. (Additional disks and tapes are held in adjacent cabinets.)*

The CPU board contains two complete sets of logic and is self-checking.

However, the operating system has sufficient software error detection to run dual StrataLINKs as separate parallel links until one fails. Failure of a link is detected, and data are retransmitted over the other link without affecting users of the link. A link failure could cause some performance loss because a dual link has a 2.8M-byte-per-sec. transmission rate, while a single link has a 1.4M-byte-per-sec. rate. But because most links do not operate even close to their maximum rates, it is unlikely that an application would notice the performance difference.

A failure scenario

When a logic board or an attached peripheral device fails, it puts itself off-line, lights a red light on the board and transmits an interrupt to the operating system. Maintenance software in the system then tests the failed board to determine if the failure was transient or hard. In either case, the failure is noted in a hardware-failure log file, and selected terminals are notified of the failure. If the board passes the maintenance-software check, it is resynchronized with its redundant partner and put back on-line, and its red light is turned off. If the board fails the software check, it remains off-line, and a red light on the system control panel is lit.

A failed board can be replaced in a running system by a nontechnical person without special tools and without affecting any user's program. VOS dynamically reconfigures itself when a board is added or removed from the system.

Operating-system software

Each processing module contains two software-visible 68000 processors and a software-visible Z80 µp on each peripheral controller. The VOS off-loads detailed I/O processing to the Z80s and uses one of the 68000s to respond to interrupts and to execute the word processor. The other 68000 executes user code and non-interrupt-driven system code. For example, a user program that calls VOS to perform disk I/O has the user 68000 enter VOS and set up the disk-I/O command chain. The user 68000 is then rescheduled to execute another user's program. The disk-I/O operations are executed by the Z80 on the disk controller, and when the disk operation completes, the "executive" 68000 responds to the interrupt and posts a notification to the scheduler that this I/O event is complete. Depending on the setting of the scheduler's parameters, the user 68000 can be rescheduled to execute the user's program then or at the next scheduling interval.

A "process" is a virtual CPU and a 16M-byte address space in which a sequence of user programs can be executed. A process is created when a user logs onto the system, and is terminated when a user logs off. A process can create additional processes that operate independently of the creating process. VOS uses system processes to monitor terminals for log-in requests, to run the spooler and to perform requests made by other processing modules.

Each process has an address space consisting of 4M bytes for VOS and 12M bytes for a user program (Fig. 6). A program consists of any number of separately compiled subroutines, which can be written in different source languages.

The 16M-byte virtual address space is divided into 4096-byte pages that are mapped into physical memory pages by an address-translation map on the CPU board. The translation occurs within the 125-nsec. clock cycle and does not slow the CPU. The user's program and most of the programs in VOS see only the virtual address space and are unaware of the translation.

The hardware address-translation map informs the scheduling and paging algorithms of which physical pages were recently used and which virtual pages of each process were recently used by that process. Thus, it is possible to determine quickly the real working set

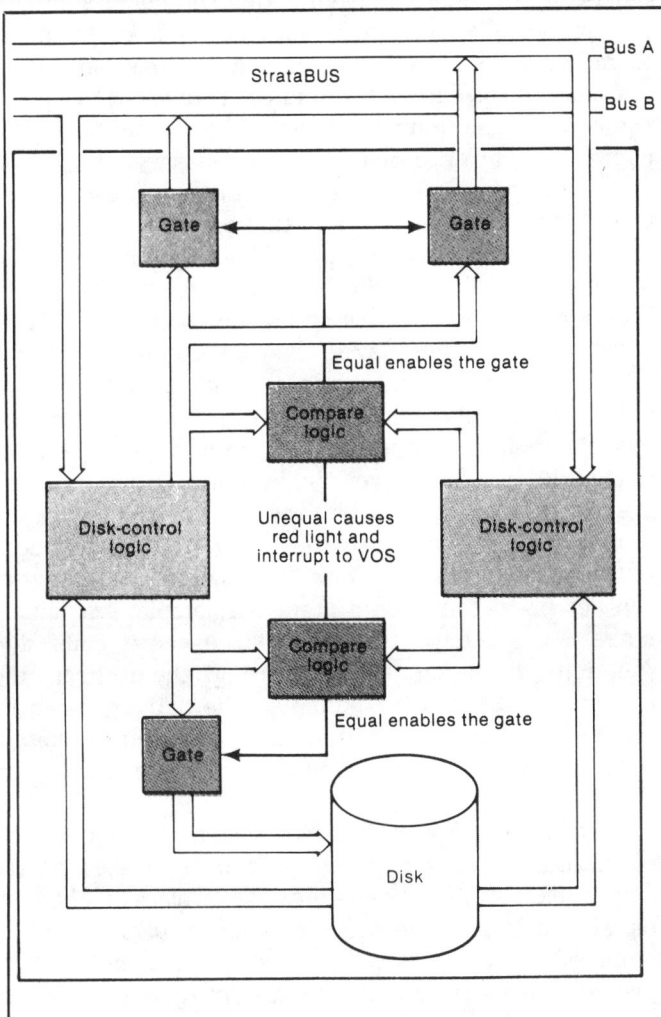

Fig. 4. Self-checking disk controller. *Two sets of logic operate in parallel with each other. If their results differ, a warning light goes on, and no data are sent until the situation is corrected.*

When data are written to a given memory location, both memory controllers respond and write the data into their memory.

of each process and which physical page of memory to replace when a new page is required.

Sharing and protection.

Each page of a process's address space has an associated access code that allows execution, read/write or read-only. The processor has supervisor and user execution states, and, for each state, it has potentially separate access codes for each page of the address space. These access codes are stored in the address-translation map used to translate virtual to physical addresses, and are enforced for every memory reference in both user and supervisor states.

All users share the physical pages of VOS and appear in the address space of each process. Likewise, user programs are shared if executed by more than one process. Sharing user programs and system commands and utilities requires no action on the part of a user and occurs with no visible effect to the user. All code produced by Stratus compilers is pure and reentrant.

A user's program is protected from destruction because each page of program instructions is given an execute-only access code. A user's data are protected from other users because they exist only in the address space of the user. The data are also protected from execution to aid debugging of users' programs.

Inter-process communication facilities of VOS allow a multi-process application to be developed on a single-module configuration and run later without modification on a distributed configuration consisting of multiple processing modules, or even on multiple Stratus systems connected by StrataNET. Consequently, the mechanisms used to start, stop or synchronize processes do not use shared memory; they use the file system as a high-level shared memory.

Every file in the file system has an associated lock and an associated event. In addition, each record in a file has an associated lock. Locks synchronize file access between two or more processes and can be set or reset to indicate reading or updating of the file or records.

Simple notification and waiting for events between processes are performed using event counts. An event count is a large integer that is incremented each time that it is notified by a process.

Most inter-process communication is related to files and consists of notifying processes that data are available to be processed or of waiting for data to arrive for processing. The use of events and locks associated with files is consequently natural and efficient.

User-visible software

The Stratus/32 was introduced with a host of native-mode software, including:

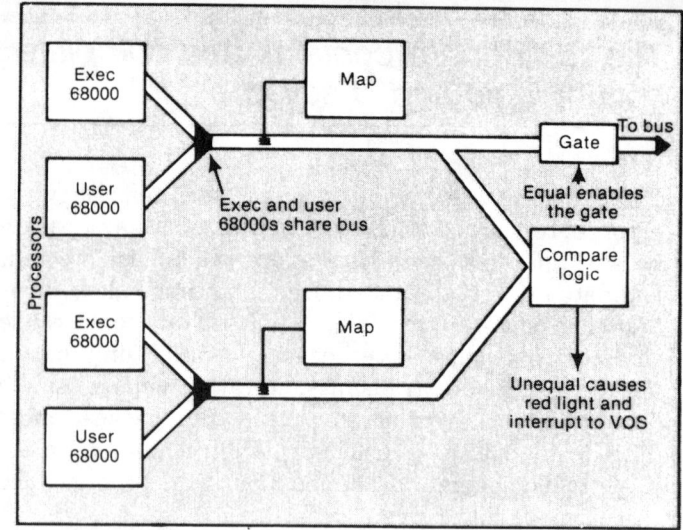

Fig. 5. A single Stratus/32 CPU board contains four Motorola 68000 processors *that provide two software-visible processors. The board is fully self-checking and contains redundant virtual/physical address-translation maps.*

- **CRT menu-oriented commands.** The VOS command interpreter accepts all commands in two forms: a conventional line-oriented form suitable for use on hard-copy terminals or from within command language programs called command macros, and a CRT menu form that displays all command options and their default values. The CRT menu form is invoked by typing the name of the command followed by a function key. A command reference manual is unnecessary.
- **Five industry-standard languages.** These include COBOL 74, FORTRAN 78, PL/I-G, Pascal and BASIC. All languages are supported by optimizing compilers that share an optimizer and a code generator that produces highly optimized relocatable binary code. Subroutines written in all languages can be combined into a program, and all languages can call all VOS service subroutines. All compiled code is pure and reentrant.
- **Program debugging.** Program development in any high-level language can be done entirely within that language without the programmer's knowing the instruction set, data formats or register arrangement of the 68000 processor. For all languages, the debugger can set breakpoints on statements, display variables, make assignments to variables, execute calls and functions, execute gotos, step through the program and execute conditional breakpoints. The debugger can be entered to start execution of a program, when a program fails or to examine a snapshot of a program that has failed.
- **Data security.** Each file has an access-control list consisting of pairs of user IDs and associated access rights (execute, read or read/write). Access rights can be specified by a user or groups of users and are enforced by the VOS I/O system. Access-control lists provide file security without embedding passwords into programs. The lists operate on the basis of people or groups who access the file; consequently, they are easy to administer and use. Security is provided regardless

All languages are supported by optimizing compilers that share an optimizer and a code generator that produces highly optimized relocatable binary code.

of what programs or system commands are used to access files.

• **Networking.** StrataNET permits two or more Stratus systems to run as if they were one system. Just as users of individual processing modules of a system have access to their entire system, users of a networked system have access to the entire network without any network-oriented requests or commands. Normal file operations and inter-process communication operate transparently to the user's program.

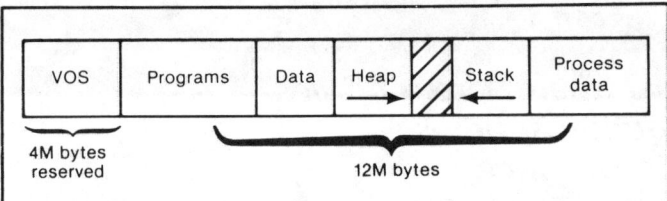

Fig. 6. Stratus/32 virtual address space provides as much as 12M bytes of program and data space per user program. *The stack is the interrupt directory; the heap is handy for temporary data that must be stored randomly. Both expand and contract as needed. User programs and system code are shared without user involvement, and no segment limits are imposed on programs or data.*

• **Transaction processing.** VOS supports the development of transaction-oriented applications by providing CRT forms-design utility and forms I/O statements in all high-level programming languages, multi-terminal transaction control in all high-level programming languages, individual record and file locking, multi-key indexed file access, queued file access and file-system operations to ensure the integrity of transactions.

Data representing a transaction can be processed directly by a user-written transaction-control program, or data can be written into a queued file to be processed by other programs, called transaction servers, which operate asynchronously with respect to the transaction-control program. Transaction servers can run in any processing module, not just modules running the transaction-control program. Likewise, transaction-control programs can run in several modules. The number and distribution of transaction servers can be dynamically altered in response to changes in the transaction rate. ∎

Robert Freiburghouse is co-founder and vice president of software engineering, at Stratus Computer, Inc., Natick, Mass.

SYSTEMS

Multiprocessor architecture ensures fault-tolerant transaction processing

ARMOND D. INSELBERG, Synapse Computer Corp.

Synapse N+1 uses redundant hardware modules and software-protection spheres to achieve fault tolerance

Hardware and software failures in transaction-oriented applications can cause severe losses of time and money. A recent entry in the expanding market for "continuous-processing" systems is a fail-safe computer comprised of tightly coupled general-purpose processors and specialized input/output processors. The processors in Synapse Computer Corp.'s N+1 on-line transaction-processing system use a proprietary non-write-through cache memory and can access reconfigurable, shared main memory over dual 32M-byte-per-sec. buses. Access protection is achieved by integrating the relational database-management system, the transaction-processing manager and the Synthesis operating system into a set of protection spheres. Synchronization of the database and transaction-processing systems provides automatic application checkpointing and recoverability.

The Synapse expansion architecture

The basic Synapse expansion architecture (Fig. 1) consists of as many as 28 tightly coupled multiprocessors centered around the Synapse expansion bus. The processors can be either general-purpose or input/output processors, each of which incorporates a Motorola 68000 microprocessor. The Synapse expansion bus consists of two independent buses that provide a combined data-transfer rate of 64M bytes per sec.

The GPPs execute user programs and Synthesis operating-system software that reside in shared main memory. The IOPs use direct-memory access to access

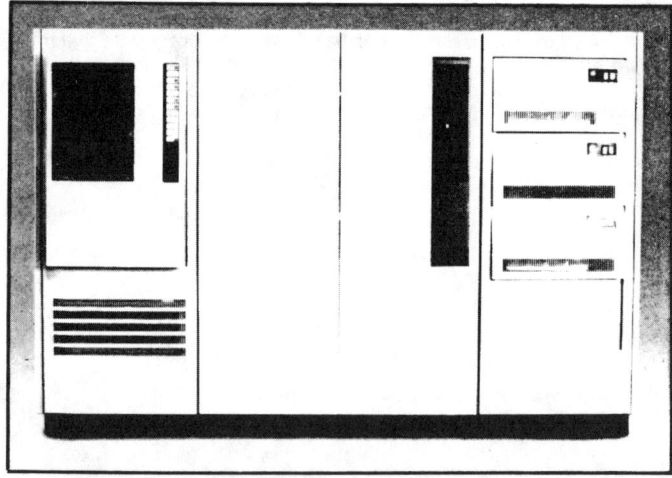

The Synapse N+1 on-line transaction-processing system *is software- and hardware-designed for fault-tolerant operation. A minimum configuration is priced at $340,000 and consists of two general-purpose processors, three input/output processors, 6M bytes of main memory on two main-memory controllers, two 151M-byte disks, a magnetic-tape subsystem and system software.*

shared main memory for data transfers. Each IOP accesses its operating system software from its own 128K bytes of local memory. Each IOP supports as many as 16 I/O adapters that can be either:
• disk controllers, which interface to 151M- and 413M-byte disks,
• advanced communications subsystems, which handle terminal and communication lines or
• multipurpose controllers, which interface to mag-

SYSTEMS

netic tape, line printers, power systems and system clocks.

There are two paths to each I/O adapter via separate IOPs. The path to be used under normal circumstances is software selected, and the secondary path is automatically used in the event of a failure.

The N+1 system requires no more than one additional hardware component of each type beyond the number that is necessary for a specific level of performance. This scheme ensures fault tolerance and provides the additional performance contribution of the extra resource in a fully operational system. No single hardware failure renders the system inoperative.

Tightly coupled multiprocessors

The GPP (Fig. 2) is a single-board processor based on the 16-/32-bit, 10-MHz Motorola 68000. The GPPs serve as execution units for the system software and application programs. Interconnection with the Synapse system is made through the expansion bus. The GPP contains 16K bytes of memory cache. There are 32K bytes of EPROM for a bootstrap loader, diagnostics and a maintenance debugger. The 68000 operates at full speed with no wait states.

The IOP provides an intelligent connection between the expansion bus and the I/O devices (Fig. 3). The main data flow is between the expansion bus interfaces and the I/O bus interface through the DMA controller. The expansion bus interfaces connect the IOP to the expansion bus and the remainder of the Synapse system. The IOP is the master of the I/O bus, initiating all transfers with the adapters. The IOP manages as many as 16 I/O adapters including device controllers and communication subsystems. The adapters can report events to the IOP by generating an interrupt and waiting to be serviced by the IOP. Data are transferred between memory on the I/O adapter cards, IOP local memory and main shared memory. All adapters can transfer concurrently and asynchronously.

The IOP performs the scheduling and dispatching of processes at the completion of a process I/O activity. By

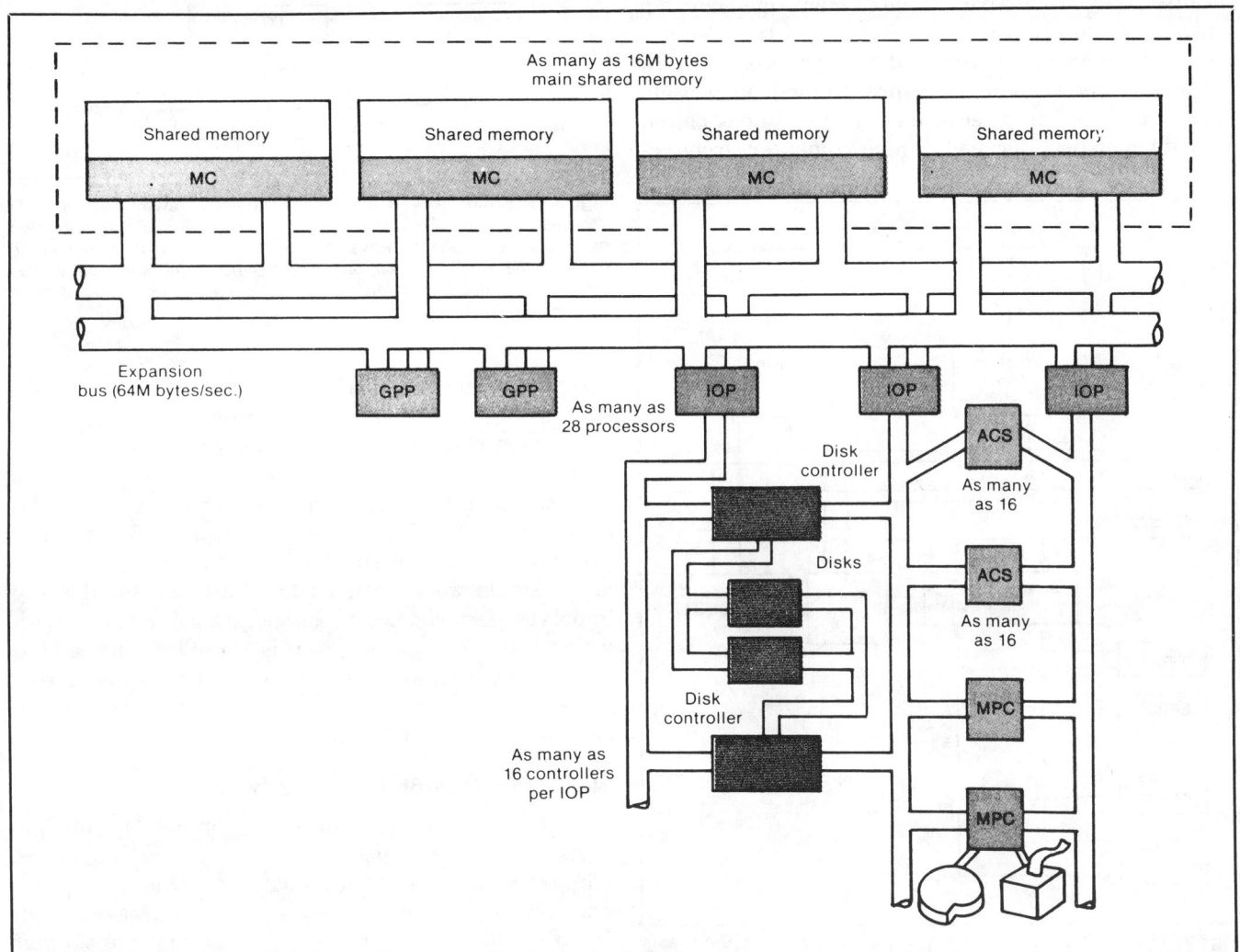

Fig. 1. The Synapse expansion architecture consists of general-purpose processors (GPPs), input/output processors (IOPs), shared main-memory modules and memory controllers (MCs), disk controllers and advanced communications controllers (ACPs). The processors access the main memory via dual 32M-byte-per-sec. buses.

SYSTEMS

taking this responsibility for preparing a process to run, the IOP need not interrupt a GPP at normal I/O completions. The IOP includes 128K bytes of local dynamic RAM for storing IOP operating software and data. The memory has single-bit error correction and double-bit error detection on each 16-bit half-word.

The modularity of GPPs and IOPs allows Synapse systems to be expanded according to the number and types of processors needed. As transaction-processing demands increase on the system, additional GPPs or IOPs can be added on-line to an executing system. A minimum configuration consists of three IOPs and two GPPs.

The work queue containing the list of all processes awaiting a processor is a single queue serving all the tightly coupled processors. Processes are scheduled on a first-in-first-out basis within the context of a priority system. The processors are considered tightly coupled because they collectively share main memory, in contrast to loosely coupled architectures that require each process to be preassigned to a processor's work queue. Processes must be preassigned in loosely coupled architectures because each processor is paired with its memory, forming a multicomputer architec-

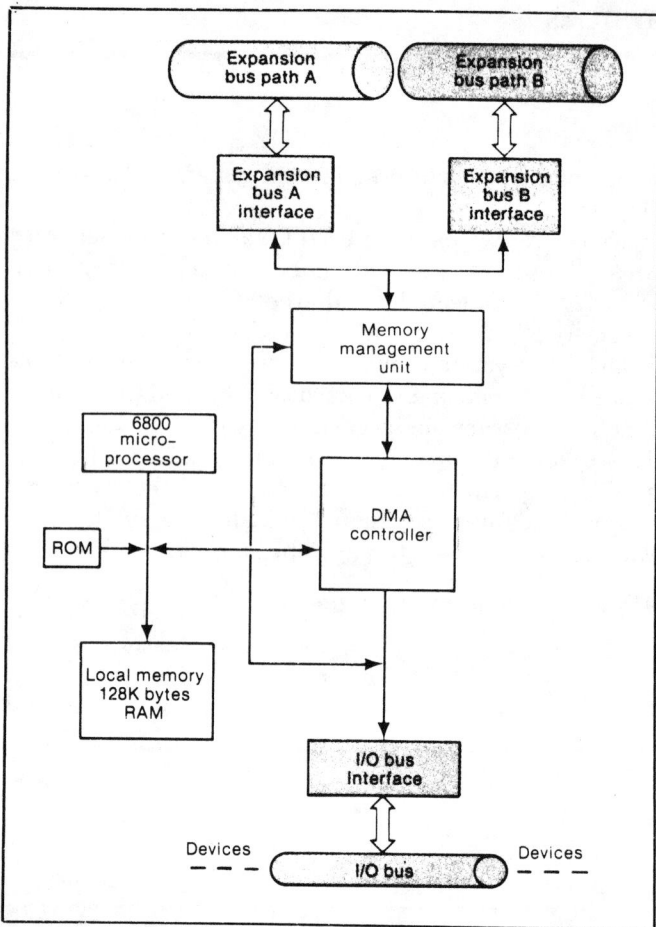

Fig. 3. **The IOP serves as the intelligent gateway** between I/O devices and the Synapse expansion bus. The DMA controller manages the data flow between the expansion bus interface (via the memory-management unit) and the I/O bus interface. The IOP is driven by a 68000 microprocessor and has 128K bytes of local dynamic RAM.

ture. By automatic load balancing, the Synapse approach provides higher throughput and facilitates concurrent software development (Fig. 4).

When I/O is required in a process, the I/O request is dispatched to the appropriate I/O processor, and the executing GPP goes to the work queue for another process. Because of the use of symmetric processors and a single work queue, adding a processor directly improves performance by accelerating the speed with which the single work queue is served. Using shared main memory allows all of the processors to have direct shared access to the entire Synapse relational database, eliminating cross talk and complex configuring.

Non-write-through cache memory

In the past, contention among processors and bus resources has plagued multiprocessor architectures. The recognition that not all data are required by all of the processors and their executing programs led Synapse to improve the typical cache write-through technique. In a write-through operation, any write to a local cache results in the updating of main memory at the time of the write. Synapse uses a proprietary

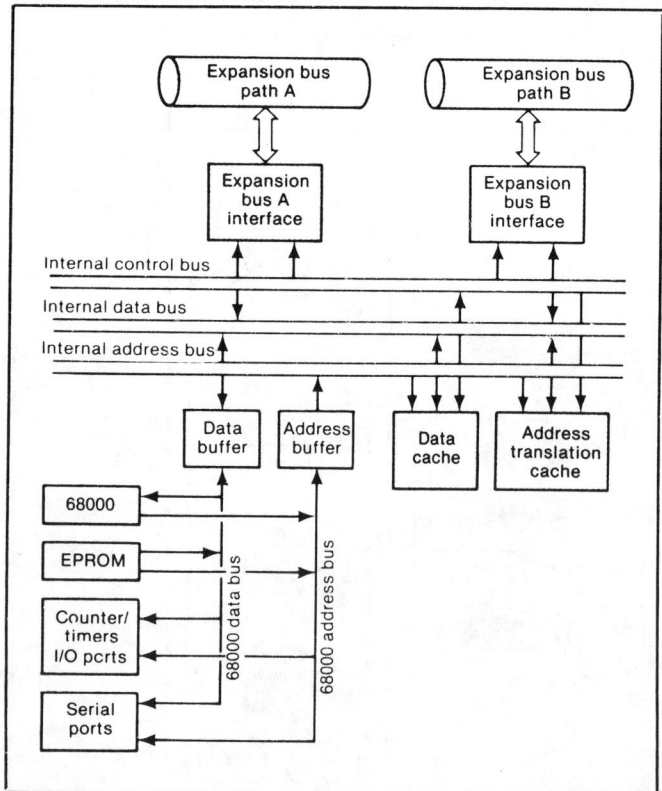

Fig. 2. **The GPP executes user programs and most Synthesis operating software.** The expansion bus connects the GPP to the Synapse system. Each GPP includes a 16-/32-bit 68000 microprocessor, 16K bytes of memory cache, counter/timers, I/O ports and 32K bytes of EPROM.

SYSTEMS

method to reduce the write-through traffic by assigning a usage mode to words contained in cache and in main memory. If the mode dictates no need to perform write-through because of the local usage nature of the data, the main memory copy is not updated. This results in a significant decrease in main-memory system usage.

The tracking of the usage mode of data is distributed throughout all the processors and the memory system itself. Logic is contained in all of the processors and the memory system to acquire and release the responsibility for the latest and only valid copy of a data element. If such data might be used by more than one processor, guarantees and checks ensure that there is only one copy of the latest valid data.

The 16K-byte cache memory in each GPP provides the 68000 with high-speed access to referenced addresses, page table entries, instructions and data. The cache significantly improves Synapse system performance in two ways. First, the average read/write cycle time as seen by the 68000 is decreased because of a high percentage of the accessed data's being present in the cache. The performance of the 68000 and GPP increases approximately in proportion to cycle time decrease. Second, the number of GPP requests to shared memory is significantly decreased, allowing additional GPPs to use the expansion bus and to share memory with minimal contention. Performance is further enhanced by the GPP cache memory using the non-write-through strategy that reduces bus contention and memory usage.

Shared main memory

The shared main memory provides as much as 16M bytes of common storage among all processors connected to the expansion bus. All user processes are contained in the main memory. As many as four shared main-memory controllers can operate in non-interleaved, two-way-interleaved or four-way-interleaved mode. Interleaving is software determined by the Synthesis operating system and can be mixed to allow for reconfiguration of a failed memory component.

The memory subsystem consists of reconfigurable multiple components with the same N+1 fault tolerance found throughout the system. Address ranges are loaded into registers on the memory boards at initial program load or at the time of a reconfiguration. A memory board can be configured to cover any part of the physical address space of the machine. Shared-memory controllers are likewise soft configurable relative to address ranges and interleaving. In the event of a failure on a memory board or controller board, Synthesis readdresses and reinterleaves the remaining resources to create a new, optimal configuration.

It is important to recognize that recoverability is a separate issue from memory failures and reconfigurability. In recovering from memory failures, Synthesis automatically routes around the defective component and then recovers the database and restarts all users. Recovery is always based on mirrored disks, never on memory contents.

Software-protection spheres

Traditional systems have user and supervisor execution modes. In user mode, each program has access only to its own code and data, whereas the supervisor mode has no protection provisions. Synapse provides a

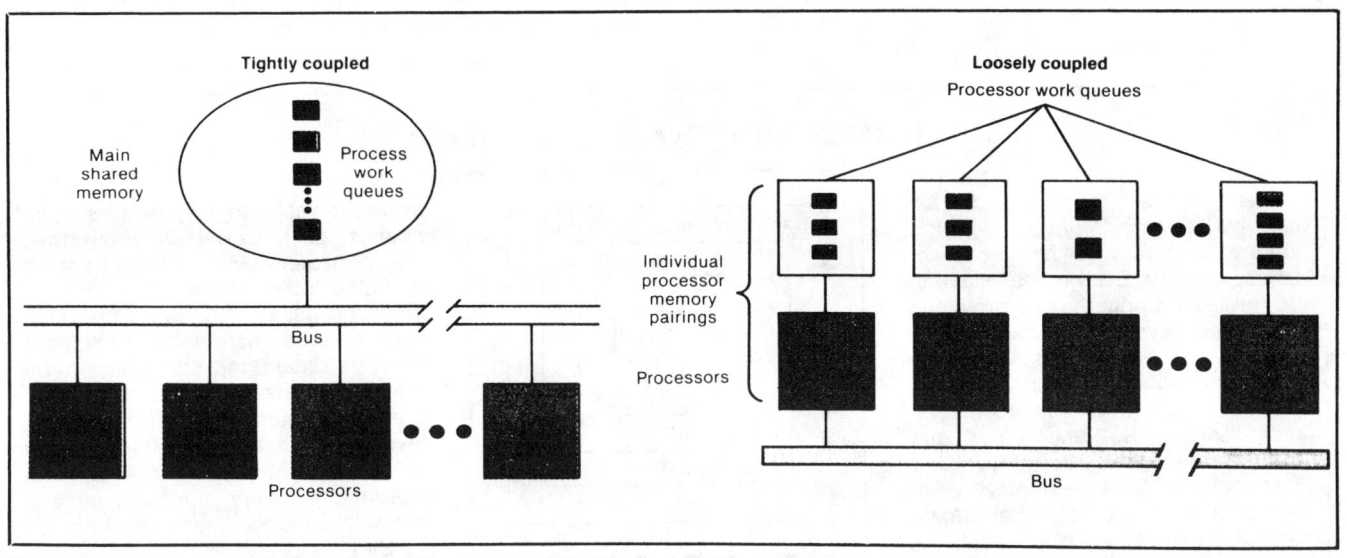

Fig. 4. Two types of processor configurations and work-queue arrangements *can be used in a transaction-processing system. Tightly coupled processors serving a single work queue, as employed in the Synapse N+1 system (left), share a common main memory and operate on a first-in-first-out basis. This arrangement allows any GPP to serve process needs, increasing thoughput by quickly emptying the work queue. Loosely coupled processors serving multiple work queues (right) have dedicated pairings of processors and memory. This arrangement requires portions of the database to be committed to a particular processor/memory pair. When a processor needs data not resident in its memory, inter-processor communications must take place.*

SYSTEMS

more general and well-protected approach in which there are five protection spheres or system levels (see "Synthesis software organization," below).

An execution mode exists for each level of the system, providing a protected execution context. Each system layer manages its own data, making it inaccessible to "higher" layers except through predefined "cross-sphere" calls. A lower level may not "call out" to a higher level. Each process has a 16M-byte address space separated into 1M-byte code and data segments assigned to the various system levels. The access rights to each segment at any time are determined by the level that is currently executing. When a level is entered through a cross-sphere call, the process is given access to all appropriate segments at that level. When the level is exited, the accessibility is removed.

The access protection on a per-process basis is implemented in memory-management hardware in each GPP. Page tables of mapping information are maintained, tracking the location of each logical 2K-byte page in shared main memory. A segment mask register provides access protection for each segment, whereby each register bit indicates whether application access is permitted to the referenced segment. A segment-protection fault is initiated when an access is attempted to a protected segment. Also associated with each page table entry are protection flags, which describe the accessibility of each page as a function of read/write/execute and instruction/data. These are the flags used to permit the proper functioning of the non-write-through cache.

Synchronizing database, transaction processing

The relational DBMS enables transactions to access data associatively from data stored logically in tubular form. The transaction is the unit of both recovery and concurrency. Transaction recovery requires that all updates associated with a transaction be applied or removed as a group. Transaction concurrency requires that other transactions do not see data from an uncompleted transaction.

Shared or exclusive locks can be placed on the data at record, block or table level of granularity to allow a high degree of concurrency. To ensure database integrity, any executing programs are restartable by providing database recovery and concurrency. To provide restartability of a program, points of database consistency must be achieved. This involves not only bringing the database to a known point, but also reestablishing the program and screen states so that the users can continue their work. This collection of information is known as a checkpoint.

The Synapse N+1 has automated the facility for checkpointing and the restartability of user applications. Automatic checkpointing occurs at the point in a process when a program invokes another program to continue processing of a transaction. These "commit points" considerably reduce the amount of checkpoint data needed for a restart. The recovery implementation is based on all changes to the database being recorded in a log file. The log files are mirrored to protect against disk failures. When a transaction is committed, a commit record reflecting all of the recorded changes is added to the log file. This synchronization of the relational database and transaction-processing manager activities enables uncommitted transactions to be removed from the system and committed transactions to be applied when recovery must be performed. □

Armond Inselberg is product manager at Synapse Computer Corp., Milpitas, Calif. He was previously manager of strategic planning at Boole and Babbage and has a Ph.D. in computer science from Washingtion University.

SYNTHESIS SOFTWARE ORGANIZATION

The Synthesis software is divided into five hierarchical layers, with the innermost layers being those of highest priority. Each of these layers, or "protection spheres," is protected from other layers by hardware. The innermost software layer, the kernel operating system, is responsible for process and memory management, processor queue and I/O queue management and reconfiguration management. The next most privileged layer is the relational DBMS, whose capabilities include relational database access, database integrity and deadlock protection, data validation and on-line backup/restore. The extended operating system maintains a hierarchical directory of all system objects, such as tables and forms, and provides device-independent I/O and other user services. The transaction-processing manager performs screen-forms management, screen-input validation and application management/recovery. The user's programs execute at the application level, manipulating the database as a set of related data elements, with integrity, recovery, concurrency and input validation automatically handled by Synthesis.

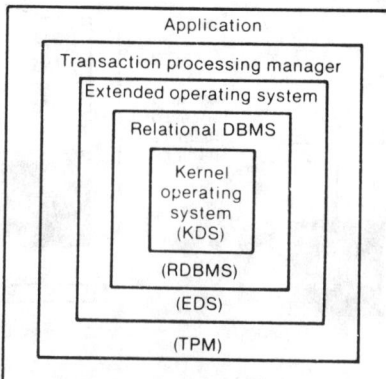

The protection spheres of the Synthesis operating software consist of several functional levels, protected from each other by protection mechanisms residing in hardware. Any sphere not within a process calling sequence remains protected from even the most privileged inner levels.

SPECIAL REPORT ON MINICOMPUTER OPERATING SYSTEMS

FAULT-TOLERANT MINI NEEDS ENHANCED OPERATING SYSTEM

Unix System III application programs run in a user-transparent, expandable minicomputer environment.

Reprinted with permission from the August 1984 issue of *Computer Design*, Copyright 1984, Pennwell Publishing Company.

by Samuel D. Glazer

Minicomputer system designers often require a fault-tolerant architecture to make their systems suitable for transaction processing or other environments where downtime is unacceptable. One approach calls for multimicroprocessor-based, distributed hardware to run an enhanced version of the Unix System III operating system. With a properly designed operating system of this type, a variety of application software can run transparently without the need for special user-created, fault-tolerant code.

One operating system using software that is designed to work well with a fault-tolerant hardware architecture is called Auros. Derived from Unix, this operating system is part of the Auragen System 4000 fault-tolerant minicomputer. To handle fault tolerance, the Auros kernel is set up to control the message-passing communications that allow an active hardware cluster to take over for a failed one.

The Auragen System 4000 minicomputer comprises 2 to 32 tightly coupled, bus-connected multipro-

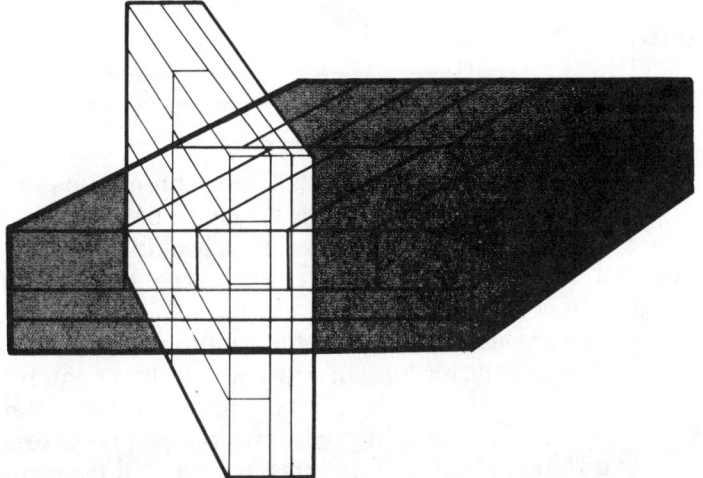

cessor units (clusters). A bus-connected distributed architecture provides modular hardware growth as well as fault tolerance. The multiplicity of dedicated microprocessors ensures that each computing microprocessor is off-loaded from overhead chores.

Each Motorola 68000 family-based cluster contains an executive processor module (to run the Auros operating system for interprocess and intercluster communications), a work processor module (to execute application programs), and a 2-Mbyte memory module (see Fig 1). Clusters expand to contain four disk/tape processor modules (controlled by a bit-slice microprocessor for high speed handling

---

Samuel D. Glazer is director of software development at Auragen Systems Corp, Two Executive Dr, Fort Lee, NJ 07024. He holds a BS in mathematics from Columbia University.

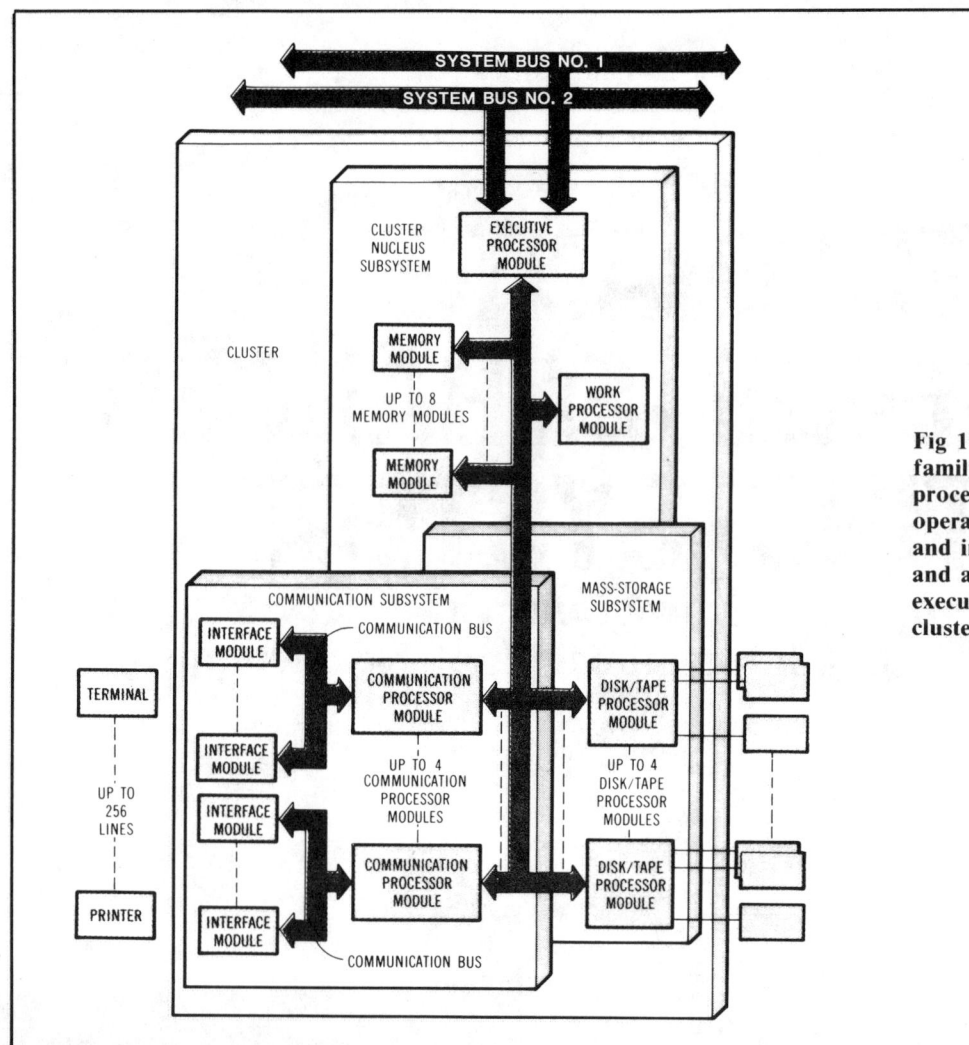

Fig 1 In each Motorola 68000 family-based cluster, an executive processor module runs the Auros operating system for interprocess and intercluster communication, and a work processor module executes application programs. The cluster also has a 2-Mbyte memory.

of disk and tape commands), four communication processor modules (each able to handle 64 lines), and 8 Mbytes of memory (with error checking and correction). Processors connect to external devices via interface modules.

Processors within a cluster communicate over a 20-Mbyte/cluster bus. In contrast, clusters communicate via two 16-Mbyte/s system buses. Disk and tape drives are dual-ported to disk/tape processors in different clusters. Terminals, printers, and various other I/O devices connect to communication processors in different clusters via 4-Mbyte/s communication buses.

A fault-tolerant computer needs more than just the hardware fault tolerance of distributed clusters, however. Its software must enable the clusters to handle the fundamental job of a fault-tolerant computer. In this job, backup software executing in a backup cluster takes over for the failed software process (executing in a cluster whose hardware fails). Backup hardware and its software must replace failed hardware without losing data or program steps, and without effecting an application programmer or end user. The user should be unaware of when failures occur, which cluster executes the application, or when files may be active in another cluster dedicated, for example, to file service (for efficiency).

All fault-tolerant computer systems require hardware and software resource duplication. They differ, however, in the degree to which they allow the backup resources to perform useful work when there is no fault; in the performance loss of the primary computer in maintaining the backup; in recovery time after a fault; and in the ease of programming fault-tolerant applications. They are similar in that they all require that the backup for the primary process (whether or not it executes while the primary process is going on) be able to continue without data loss after a failure (see Panel, "Compare and contrast"). For Auragen's System 4000, Auros is the keystone for addressing these considerations.

Kernel control

The kernel-based message system handles all Auros interprocess communication for normal hardware system operation and fault tolerance. For example, the kernel handles message passing between primary processes executing in a distributed environment and also ensures that the secondary process has all the information it needs to bring itself fully up-to-date if failure occurs.

Unix System III does not have a kernel-based message-passing system. Since it was not designed for a distributed, multimicroprocessor architecture, it does not have the separate system servers necessary for an efficient distributed processing environment. In addition, its file system is not reliable enough for transaction processing applications since it can lose files and become inconsistent, and it does not efficiently manage the processes needed (eg, for transaction processing).

Auros handles these deficiencies in a manner fully compatible with Unix System III software. Each of the System 4000 clusters runs its own cluster-resident copy of the Auros kernel, which contains a so-called "queue-and-count" message system. The message system provides interprocess communication between primary processes and supports fault tolerance by ensuring that every cluster-resident executing program or primary process has a fully informed backup copy on a different cluster. To do its job, Auros supports as many as 256 concurrent tasks in each cluster. In addition to message passing, it features new system calls for transaction processing environments, faster process creation and process switching, and demand-paged virtual memory.

Choice of two

There are two types of Auros software processes. User processes communicate all I/O information by message passing. They have no direct access to any computer peripheral equipment. Actual device I/O (in systems with peripherals) is handled by requests sent to the peripheral server processes. Peripheral server processes take care of specific devices that they access via system calls.

Fault tolerance for user processes is based on the concept that if two processes start out in an identical state and receive identical inputs, they must perform identically and produce identical outputs. As previously stated, each primary software process has an inactive backup resident in a different cluster. A backup process is kept nearly up-to-date, and is provided with the information needed to bring itself fully up-to-date with the primary state and to continue execution as the new primary should a failure occur. Thus, a primary and its backup are initially identical, all the input messages to the primary are available to the secondary, and the backup can recompute to catch up to where a primary failed (by using the same messages the primary used).

Complete recomputation by the backup is not necessary since the primary and backup processes are periodically resynchronized. Between synchronizations, when the backup and the primary are different, all messages to the primary are made available to the backup. Upon synchronization, all messages previously read by the primary process are discarded by the secondary one. If the primary fails, the backup executes—rolls forward—from the last synchronization point (using the saved input).

The message system supporting the relationships between the primary and the secondary fault-tolerant equipment is embedded in the kernel. This message system provides and controls interprocess communication, initiates the creation and deletion of backup processes, and controls the periodic synchronization

---

Compare and contrast

There are two approaches to backing up primary processes that are related but slightly different. One approach requires that the primary process and its backup execute simultaneously on two independent CPUs. If one CPU fails, the other continues without interruption. The duplicate hardware provides no computational advantage, there are no special fault tolerance programming considerations, recovery time is instantaneous, and the performance of the primary is not taxed by the secondary's presence.

An alternative is to maintain an inactive or nonexecuting backup process that executes on a secondary processor upon failure of one processor. The secondary can do useful work while it backs up the primary. There are differences in how the backup is maintained, with consequent differences in primary and backup resource use and recovery time. For example, the state of the backup, as represented by its data space, must either be identical to that of the primary or be capable of being made so (the Auragen approach).

The data space may be kept identical by means of "checkpoint" software which copies the primary's data space to the secondary whenever the dataspace changes. In contrast, Auragen has opted to provide the means for updating the data space by its "queue-and-count" interprocess message system software. When there is a cluster failure, the backup process automatically recreates a data space identical to the primary's at the time of the crash, so a backup process can continue processing as if no failure occurred.

Queue-and-count makes available to the backups the same messages it delivers to the primary. This queue of messages is used during recovery by the backup to recreate the primary data space of the process. In contrast, checkpoints are large messages sent from the primary to the backup each time a normal interprocess message is sent or received. Since user programs must supply checkpoints, checkpoint instructions must be embedded in user programs. Application-program transparent queue-and-count software requires no special programming.

of primary and backup. It further guarantees that the backup can take over in case of failure if it has all the information it needs, and that the backup will interact correctly with the system.

The message system ensures that during normal process execution, all messages sent to the primary (which were unread or arrived after the last synchronization) are available to the backup. It also insists that the primary's state as of the last synchronization time is accessible to the kernel (which controls the backup's processing cluster), and that during a recovery, the backup process reads the available messages in exactly the same order as did the primary. Finally, the message system must see that during recovery the backup will not send any messages already sent by the primary.

Each message sent from one primary process to another is actually sent to three destinations. These are the requested primary destination process, its backup, and the sending process backup (Fig 2). If a message is sent to more than one location, either all locations or none must receive it. The software must guarantee that when a message arrives at each of its three destinations, it is never interleaved with that of any other message. This rule means that a primary and its backup always receive messages in the same order. In addition, if two messages are sent, the first message must reach all of its destinations before the second message arrives at any of its destinations.

> *A primary process and its backup will always receive messages in the same order.*

Each of the three destinations has software that makes use of each received message in a different way. For example, at the primary destination the message is queued for reading by the primary destination process. In contrast, at the backup destination the message is queued and saved for the destination process backup. It is to be read only upon roll forward after a failure. At the sender's backup, a count of the messages sent since the last synchronization is incremented and the message is discarded. Thus, every backup process has a queue of the messages sent to its primary and a count of the messages sent by its primary. The primary keeps a count of the number of messages it has read since the last synchronization.

Stand up and be counted

How software control is transferred from one program to its backup when a fault occurs is important because the method determines how much useful work the backup can do when there are no faults to handle. The control transfer technique also

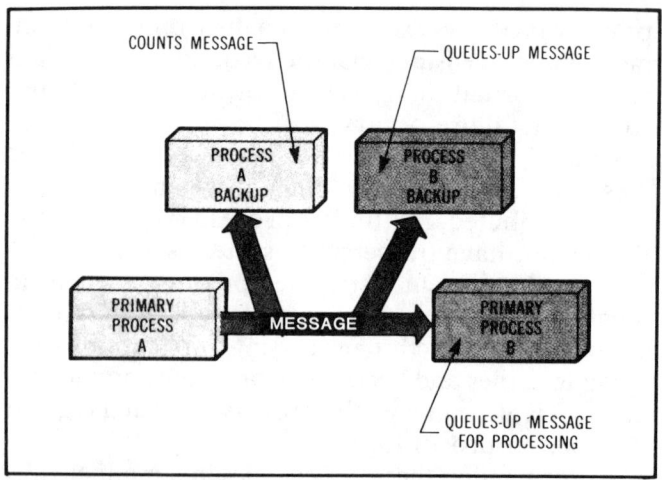

Fig 2 When a message is sent by a primary process to its next process, the primary's backup receives a copy, as does the backup for the next process. If one message fails to arrive, the system bus ensures that none arrive, so the queue-and-count software does not fail.

determines how fast the fault-tolerant computer recovers from a crash.

Auragen was not satisfied with checkpointing for transferring software control (as explained in the Panel, "Compare and contrast"), and developed the queue-and-count design to manage System 4000 interprocess communications. As a manager, queue-and-count performs two chores: ensuring that the 4000's distributed processor clusters appear to the system user to be a single system; and ensuring that secondary (backup) programs always have the correct, latest information so they can take over should a hardware failure that takes out a cluster occur. In the queue-and-count design, whenever a primary process receives a message from Auros, a corresponding backup process also receives the message and saves it in its "queue"—hence the first part of the queue-and-count name. It remains in the queue until the secondary must take over from the primary, at which time the message is processed. Since the secondary must also know what the primary has accomplished up to the time when a failure occurs, it also keeps a count of the primary's outgoing messages (sent to the next primary process). With this "count" part of the queue-and-count scheme, the secondary can avoid sending duplicate messages.

A fault-tolerant system with three primary and three secondary processes illustrates the queue-and-count concept. This example illustrates how a terminal server process handling I/O, an application program, and a file server that handles reads and writes, normally performs and recovers from failure (see Panel, "How queue-and-count software handles recovery"). Remember that the key to recovery is to reproduce the state of a primary at the moment it failed and then continue with normal operations. Except for a several second pause during recovery, the user does not know the fault-tolerant system has

How queue-and-count software handles recovery

Suppose a primary terminal server sends a message (M1) to a primary application program which, in turn, sends a message (M2) to a primary file server to write a record for a disk (see Table, step 1). In the queue-and-count procedure, the message system sets the terminal-server backup count indicator to 1 (indicating that the primary terminal server has sent one message). The message system stores message M1 in the backup application program's queue and sets its count to 1 since the primary application program has sent a message to the primary file server. For the file-server backup, the message system queues M2 but sets no count indicator because the primary file server sent no messages. The primary terminal server then sends message M3 to the primary application program and operations occur as shown in step 2 of the Table.

The primary terminal server (step 3) sends an M5 message which is received by the primary application program. But, assume that the primary application program fails to send M6 to the primary file server. The terminal-server backup has a count of 3 (meaning that the primary terminal server has successfully sent three messages). However, the count on the secondary application program is 2 (since the third message was not sent). The application program backup has M5 queued along with M3 and M1. The secondary file server is unchanged since no step 3 message has been received.

Recovery starts when the previously inactive application program backup becomes active and executes like any other process after checking its queue. Messages in the backup are read in the same order as they were received in the primary application program. This reading order and the count availability ensure that redundant messages are not sent and that the next message to the backup file server is M6.

To initiate recovery, the application program backup (with a count of 2) reads message M1 in its queue, executes it, and generates the appropriate message to be sent to the file-server backup. This new M2 message is not sent to the file-server backup because it is a duplicate of a message the file-server backup already has and is recognized as such because the application program backup's count is 2. Queue-and-count requires a count of 0 before a new message is transmitted since 0 guarantees no previous message transmission.

Since M2 is a duplicate, queue-and-count discards it. The counter on the application program backup is decreased by one and message M3 (the second message received by the primary application program) is read by the secondary application program. M3 is read, executed, and used to generate M4, but M4 is not sent since the count is 1.

The backup application program count is then decreased to 0, the program reads the next message (M5) in its queue, executes it, and generates message M6. Because the application program secondary's count of messages sent by the application program primary to the file server primary is 0, the queue-and-count system knows that the primary file server never got M6. So, the message system sends M6 to the primary file server, which writes its record to a disk, and fault recovery is complete.

Queue-and-Count Example

Queue-and-Count Step	Terminal Server	Application Program	File Server	Terminal Server Backup	Application Program Backup	File Server Backup
1	Sends M1	Receives M1 Sends M2	Writes to File	C = 1	C = 1 Queues M1	Queues M2
2	Sends M3	Receives M3 Sends M4	Writes to File	C = 2 C = 2	C = 2 Queues M1, M3	Queues M2, M4
3	Sends M5	Receives M5 Does not send M6	—	C = 3	C = 2 Queues M1, M3, M5	Queues M2, M4
4	—	—	—	—	C = 2 Read M1 Generate M2' Delete M2' C = 1 Read M3 Generate M4' Delete M4' C = 0 Read M5 Generate M6 Send M6	Queues M2, M4 Receives M6

Legend: M = Message
C = Count

Note: Start at queue-and-count step 1.
Read Horizontally left to right.
Go to next step. Repeat until end.

failed. Of course, the flawed hardware signals its disability to system maintainers.

When a primary process fails, the secondary process uses messages to retrack the primary one's actions until it is in the same state as the primary process before it failed. The secondary process then continues with the calculations. If a failure occurs after many messages have been transferred, it might seem that device restoration to its original state is inefficient. It might also appear that an unbounded message queue wastes memory resources. This is not true, however, because both primaries and the secondaries are periodically synchronized. After each resynchronization the queue restarts, as does the count.

Save that state

A primary and its backup are automatically synchronized whenever the primary has read more than a system-defined number of messages. Synchronization is also implemented if the primary has executed for more than a system-defined amount of time since the last synchronization. Any changes in the address space of the primary (since the last synchronization) are stored so that they are available to the backup. This process is made possible by cooperation between the message system and the computer system's paging mechanism.

Processor synchronization must deal with both real and virtual processor memory. The processor's normal page-fault mechanism ensures that pages changed in real memory since the last synchronization are updated in the virtual memory. The primary also synchronizes its virtual memory with that of the backup when the message queue reaches a system-predetermined value. For efficiency, only the virtual memory that has changed since the last synchronization (that has not been updated in the last real memory page file), is sent to the secondary.

Once the memory space changes are stored, a synchronization message containing certain state information is sent directly to the backup processing unit's kernel. This state information includes a count of the number of reads done by the primary since the last synchronization. The count's availability allows any messages saved for the backup, but already read by the primary, to be discarded. After synchronization the backup will have the correct set of messages available. The arrival of a synchronization message also causes the backup's count of the messages sent since the last synchronization by the primary to be zeroed.

Another concern is that the backup not send (to the next process) any messages that were generated by the primary between the last synchronization and a failure. Remember that the third message destination is the sender's backup, where the message is counted and discarded. So every time the backup (which has become the new primary) begins to execute code and send a message, it checks the value of this count. If the count is positive (meaning this message was already sent by the primary), the count is decreased and the message is not sent. In contrast, if the count is zero, the message is sent.

Synchronization has certain advantages over the checkpointing procedure for backup updates. For one, it is automatically initiated by the operating system, making user program instructions unnecessary. For another, synchronization is needed less frequently than checkpointing. Also, primary processes are not slowed by synchronization, as they are by checkpointing, because they need not wait for synchronization to complete. After synchronization, the contents of message queues and counters are set to zero and any failure recovery proceeds from the new synchronization point.

The operating system differs from Unix in several other respects, all of which are designed to enhance fault tolerance. To allow the 4000's distributed hardware to gain the efficiency benefits of distributed client/server software, the operating system is designed with function separation. Unlike the Unix kernel, the kernel only controls local functions such as memory management, resource control, process scheduling, peripheral, and message handling. Backup servers (peripheral and system) handle global resource management for such services as terminal I/O and file and page management (Fig 3). Communication between servers and any user processes also uses the message system. Peripheral servers which are associated with either logical or physical devices, receive messages in the normal way but must be able to execute certain system calls to control their associated devices.

The operating system automatically initiates synchronization, thus making user program instructions unnecessary.

The result of this separation of global and local resources is, for example, the distribution of front-end (terminal I/O) and backend (file I/O) services across multiple microprocessors and clusters. These servers require somewhat different backup and synchronization schemes than user processes.

Peripheral- and system-server backup processes are created when the primary process executes. In contrast, with user processes, backups are created only when necessary to ensure fault tolerance. Peripheral-server synchronization is different from user-server synchronization since peripheral servers must be core-resident rather than paged, and they communicate with devices directly rather than by message.

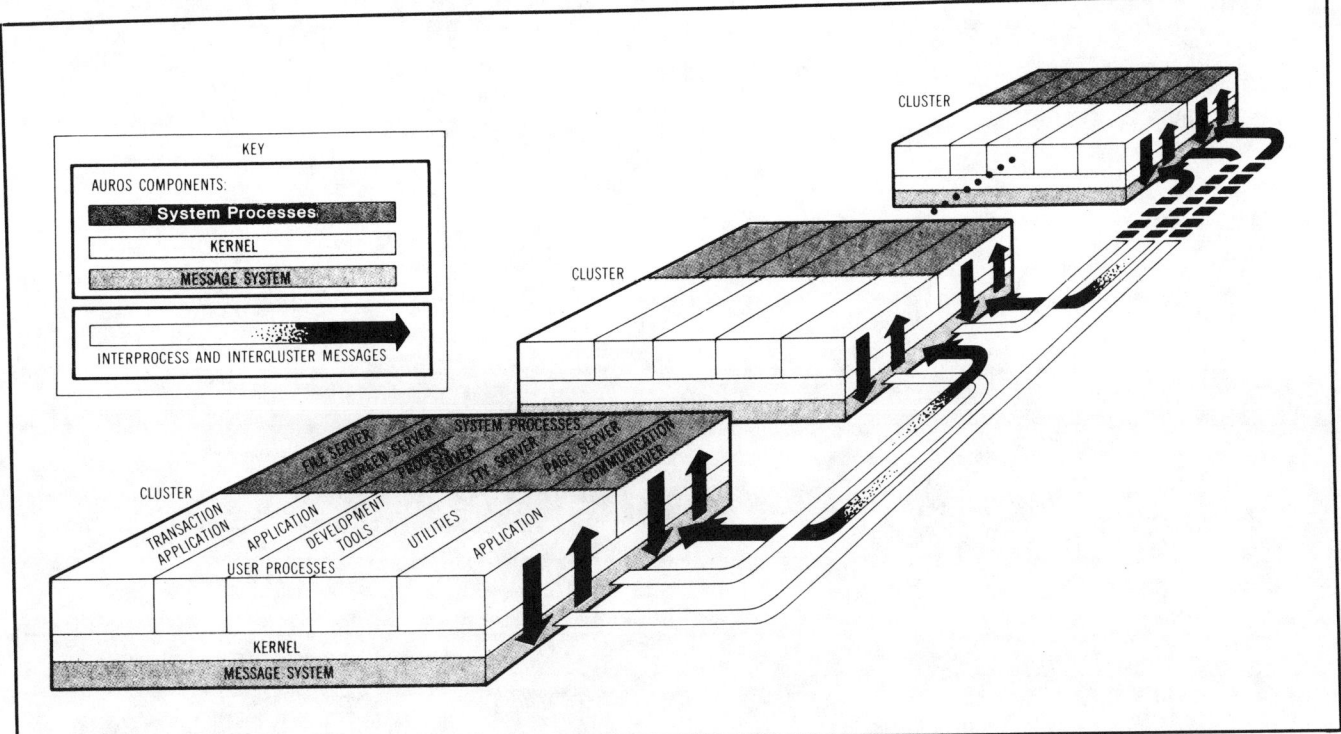

Fig 3 All processes and clusters send and receive messages via the kernel-based message system. Division of the cluster processes into user and system processes allows the kernel to handle local operations while the servers handle global ones.

System-server processes keep track of global system resources via tables in their address space. They are backed up, communicate via message, and execute in the same way as user processes. They differ in that they can be initiated only by the operating system.

All messages transmitted back and forth between processes (whether user or peripheral) are sent by means of a software mechanism known as a channel. Each end of a channel is defined by means of an entry in a cluster's local table known as a routing table. A cluster's routing table resides in kernel space in cluster main memory and is maintained by message system code.

A special process server responsible for system load balancing ensures optimal minicomputer hardware performance. With its proprietary algorithm, the process server determines the cluster on which an application should run. The process server takes into account cluster CPU and memory availability. It also checks to see if the program is already resident in a cluster so that the new process can share resources. The process server, by keeping track of where all processes (primary and secondary) reside, plays a critical part in locating and bringing up secondary processes should a failure occur.

The computer system designer or system integrator opting for a distributed minicomputer is concerned not only with fault tolerance; the easy generation of the application software that must run on the hardware is also a concern. So, among other Unix utilities, Auros supports Programmer's Workbench, file and string manipulation programs, text editors, and document-formatting packages.

In addition to these standard tools, there is a screen manager that allows display creation, a menu system, and a database manager known as Auralate that supports data integrity and concurrency control. This relational database system is based on the high level, English-language-like query language SQL. A transaction processing management system (TPMS) to speed the development of transaction processing-intensive applications is also included.

Software development languages provided include C (the Auros language), Cobol (ANSI 74 with an interpreter), Fortran (ANSI 77), Pascal (conforming to the proposed International Standards Organization version and UCSD extensions), and interpreted Basic. All languages include compilers, source debuggers, and runtime libraries, as appropriate.

Chapter 5: Software Fault Tolerance

Introduction

The reliability of a digital system depends on the individual reliabilities of its components—both hardware and software. Too often the assumption is made that the software is error-free so that the system designers can concentrate on hardware reliability, which is more readily defined and easier to understand and deal with. The primary difference is that software does not "fail" through aging, stress, or similar factors as does hardware. The only source of software faults is through improper design and/or implementation, resulting in the inability of the software to meet its requirements or specifications. Since the probability of such faults or errors is non-zero, in a highly reliable system the designers must ensure an acceptable software reliability as much as possible before the system becomes operational as well as provide the system with means to tolerate any remaining residual errors once it is deployed. Thus the field of software reliability can be subdivided into two categories: fault avoidance through reliable design, testing, and verification, and software fault tolerance. This paper will discuss briefly the various aspects of the former category, and will then examine the current techniques available for tolerating residual errors due to software faults.

It should be noted that the term "software fault tolerance" brings about two connotations: software techniques to deal with hardware faults and the tolerance of software faults. This paper will address the latter definition, although many of the techniques employed for the purpose of tolerating software faults will also serve to deal with various other types of system faults as well.

Software Faults

To properly understand the term "software fault," one must consider the various stages of a software development project. Included in the earliest stage is the specification and definition of requirements for software. Design errors can be introduced at this stage in several forms [LIP77].

1. Incomplete, missing, or inadequate requirements;
2. Requirements not fitting physical models;
3. Inconsistent or incomplete requirements; and
4. Unclear or nonsensical requirements.

From the set of system requirements, the design specification for the software is derived. Then several stages of software development occur. The first is the formulation of the problem solution, or the "design" phase. The second is the "coding" phase, in which the problem solution is translated into the desired programming language on the target machine. Software faults introduced during these two phases have been shown to be divided with about 60% to 65% in the design phase and the rest in the coding phase [TUR76,NEL75,BOE76,BOE75]. Of these, it has been determined that the correction cost is about ten times greater for design errors than it is for coding errors [NEL75,TUR76]. The actual number of errors has been found to be correlated with two factors. The number of errors is roughly proportional to the size of the code [WAG73,NEL75] and it is even more closely proportional to the number of paths through the program [WAG73] for a given application. These proportionalities are used as the basis for various software reliability models [SCH78,KEI83,SCO84].

In a reliable system, faults from each of the above sources must be either eliminated or tolerated in some way. The largest portion of the literature deals with techniques, which fall into several categories, for fault avoidance.

1. Automated design aids, including formal specification languages and other metalanguages [KEL83].
2. Structured programming techniques, including the use of high-level languages, top-down design, and similar techniques which require discipline of the programmer.
3. Formal proof of correctness techniques. This was done extensively in the SIFT project at SRI [SHO77] and in various other projects [LON71].
4. Program testing, both formal and informal, identifies many of the residual errors in a program. However, it is generally recognized that testing does not usually prove that the software is fault-free; it only shows that those states of the software examined are error-free for the specific set of test sequences utilized. Software reliability models based on number of errors detected during testing are described in [SCH78,KEI83,SCO84].

In summary, good design techniques and the use of formal software design tools can minimize the probability of having residual design errors in a system, but they cannot be guaranteed to eliminate them. Hence for an ultrareliable system, one must provide ways to detect and tolerate those design errors that have not previously been identified in the operation and testing of the software.

Software Fault-Tolerance Strategies

As is the case with hardware failures, software faults may be tolerated in different ways, depending on what is deemed acceptable for the given application. In some applications, such as telephone switching, some error propagation is acceptable provided that such events are rare and that the system can recover in a reasonable time. In more critical applications, such as aircraft control, military systems, or life-support systems, error propagation might be completely unacceptable since errors might trigger irreversible actions or else be such that recovery cannot occur within an acceptable time. In commercial systems for transaction processing, the primary concern is protection of the database, with "down time" for system diagnosis and repair typically acceptable. These various applications require different mechanisms to provide the different degrees of fault tolerance required.

As is the case with hardware faults, a software fault-tolerance strategy includes four basic steps.

1. Detection of a software fault.
2. Diagnosis to isolate the source of the fault to a repairable or replaceable module.
3. Repair or reconfiguration to eliminate the source of the fault and its effects.
4. Recovery of the system to either a healthy state or an acceptable degraded state. For time-critical applications and for those applications for which error propagation is unacceptable, the first three steps should be performed concurrently with normal processing, minimizing the need for a time-consuming recovery. This implies that all errors must be either detected or corrected as they occur to confine them to the originating software module without affecting the rest of the system. In this case, the recovery process would not have to correct other system components during the recovery.

If time is not critical, or if a given amount of error propagation is acceptable, then the above fault-tolerance stages can be performed serially with the application software. Although a time penalty is incurred, the number of system resources to support serial (as opposed to concurrent) error detection and diagnosis is typically smaller. In addition, serial techniques tend to be more complete in implementing such features as error diagnosis and analysis.

In all cases, some form of redundancy must be added to the software to support the fault-tolerance features. The various forms of redundancy typically fall into one or more of three categories.

1. Temporal redundancy: execution of a different version of a software module following the detection of an error.
2. Spatial redundancy: concurrent execution of different versions of the software with some form of voting or other comparison of results.
3. Operational redundancy: the inclusion of operations that are not essential to the application algorithms, but do exist solely for fault detection and diagnosis.

Each category specified has various tradeoffs in terms of execution time and required resources. Temporal redundancy has a fixed amount of software overhead associated with its error detection functions, plus the time penalty incurred when repeating operations with different versions of the software. The greatest impact on system performance is the error-detection overhead, since it is incurred whether or not faults exist. Software reexecutions, however, occur only in response to detected errors, which typically are rare, and hence the overall effect on system performance is negligible, unless the application requires real-time response.

Similarly, if operational redundancy is utilized, the software overhead associated with the redundant operations is incurred whether or not faults exist. In the case of software diagnostic routines, "convenient" places in the application are often utilized for these operations, to minimize the overall impact of the overhead.

The use of spatial redundancy eliminates most of the degraded performance associated with temporal or operationally redundant schemes. However, the overhead penalty is substantial in the form of redundant hardware and other resources needed for concurrent execution of multiple versions of the software. Given sufficient redundancy, recovery stages can be completely eliminated because redundancy can potentially mask errors as they occur.

In the following sections, some specific techniques and case studies will be presented to illustrate the various approaches to software fault tolerance. Most of these techniques either have been implemented or have been proposed for a number of commercial and experimental systems.

Recovery Blocks and Other Rollback and Recovery Schemes

Rollback and recovery is a technique by which a system is halted by the detection of an error, rolled back or restored to a known correct state (or checkpoint), and made to repeat the suspect operations in an attempt to eliminate the error. Such schemes have been implemented in one form or another in numerous systems [ROH73,DEA76,MER76,DOW64], ranging from single-instruction retry to the repetition of entire blocks of code. Support for instruction retry is presently being incorporated into a number of commercial machines [BOO80]. Most of these systems employ error-detection codes, duplex operations, or some other form of hardware redundancy to provide the error detection that triggers the rollback events. Almost all of these techniques are effective against both permanent and transient hardware

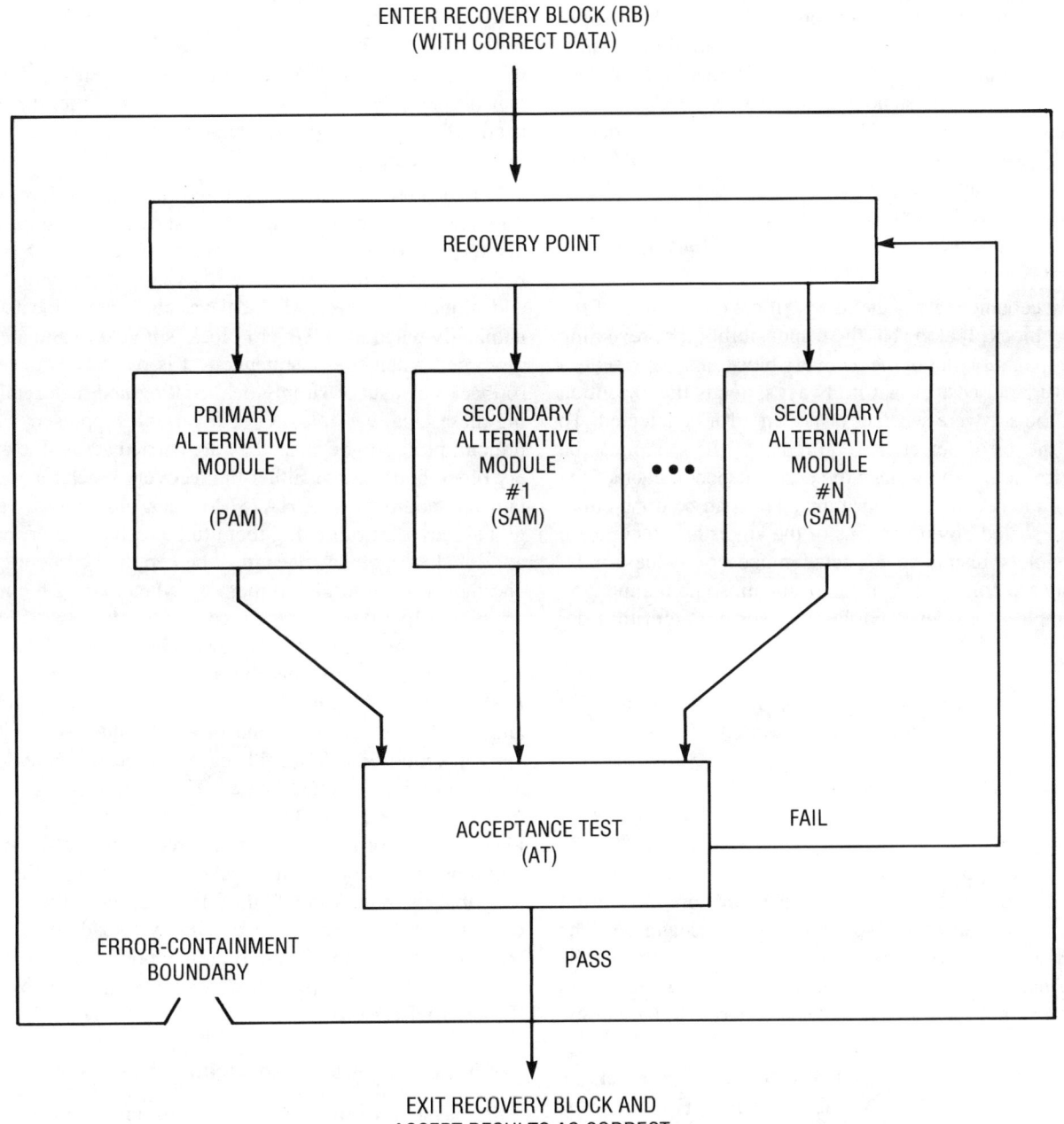

Figure 5.1. Basic Structure of a Recovery Block

faults. In each case, periodic recovery points are established during program execution via special hardware, firmware, and/or software that preserve the state of the program at error-free checkpoints. When an error is detected, the latest error-free state is restored and the program repeated from that point. Thus errors due to transient hardware faults can be eliminated.

The recovery-blocks technique, proposed by Randell [RAN75] and described further in [AND76], utilizes temporal redundancy and a software standby sparing approach both to provide error detection and error correction of software-induced errors in a system as well as to provide similar protection against transient hardware faults. In this approach, all software (application and system) is partitioned into a number of self-contained modules called "recovery blocks" (RB's). Each RB is responsible for validating its own operation within its boundaries, and thus either returns correct information to the system or notifies the system of its failure. In this manner, all software and hardware errors generated during the execution of the RB are either corrected via alternate software procedures, or are at least confined to the boundary of the RB to prevent error propagation to the rest of the system.

As illustrated in Figure 5.1, an RB for a given task consists of three basic components: a "Primary Alternative Module" (PAM), which is the main or preferred algorithms for the task; one or more "Secondary Alternative Modules" (SAM), which act as standby spares for the PAM and are independently designed and/or coded; and an "Acceptance Test" (AT), which is applied to the results of each PAM and SAM to determine their validity. In addition, the RB will contain software to both establish recovery points (RP's) and roll the software back to these RP's following error detection.

The acceptance test is the most critical component of the recovery block. It alone has the responsibility for preventing error propagation out of the recovery block, and represents a fixed overhead cost in that it always extends the execution time of the software whether or not an error is detected. To satisfy the error-detection requirement, the AT must be complete enough to evaluate the performance of each of the primary and secondary algorithms. This can be done either by using scaled-down versions of the algorithm to compare the module's results to expected ranges of values or by checking the consistency of the results in some manner. As an example, consider the following sorting algorithm described in [RAN75].

$$\text{ensure sorted } (S) \wedge (\text{sum}(S) = \text{sum}(\text{prior } S))$$
$$\text{by} \quad \text{quickersort}(S)$$
$$\text{else by quicksort}(S)$$
$$\text{else by bubblesort}(S)$$
$$\text{else error}$$

Here the acceptance test consists of verifying that S is indeed sorted, and that none of the elements of S have been changed (the sum of the components is unchanged). The primary algorithm is a preferred efficient algorithm, while the alternatives are less desirable algorithms. If all three fail the accceptance test, then an error is reported to the calling module.

The overhead costs associated with a recovery block are illustrated in Figure 5.2. As discussed in [CHA75], overhead costs can be divided into fixed costs (incurred for each execution of the recovery block) and variable costs (incurred only when errors are detected). In this figure the fixed costs are represented by t_0 (time to set up the recovery point), t_2 (acceptance test time), and t_3 (time to "accept" or make permanent the results). The total fixed execution time of the recovery block is then:

$$T_{\text{exec}} = t_0 + t_{11} + t_2 + t_3 \quad (1)$$

where t_{11} is the execution time of the PAM. If N successive errors are detected, then:

$$T_{\text{exec}} = t_0 + \sum_j (t_{1j}) + (N+1)t_2 + Nt_4 + t_3 \quad (2)$$

which includes N rollback times (t_4) and N SAM executions ($t_{12}, t_{13}, \ldots, t_{N+1}$). The only term in the above equations that is not an overhead cost is the PAM execution time t_{11}. Consequently, from Equations (1) and (2), it can be seen that the acceptance test should be short to minimize overhead, while being thorough enough to achieve the desired fault coverage.

A major problem in rollback and recovery systems is the implementation of the rollback or state-restoration mechanism. Essentially, one can think of a recovery block as being similar to a PASCAL or ADA procedure having local and global variables. All local variables are allocated dynamically when the recovery block is invoked, and are then discarded when the acceptance test is passed. In this case, rollback consists of simply deallocating and then reallocating these local variables. Global variables represent a more difficult problem, because they are carried across the recovery block boundaries. Either the recovery block must maintain an "audit trail" [CHA75] to track any changes to the global variables, allowing them to be restored later, or else all global variable changes must be kept in a cache memory and then written to global memory when exiting the recovery block. In either case the recovery block keeps all global variable changes in a "recovery cache" [AND76,LEE79], which can be implemented by hardware, software, or both. In the audit-trail approach, the recovery cache would trap and record the addresses and original values of all global variables modified. In a rollback, these global variables are restored to their original values. This approach is described in [LEE79] for a PDP-11 system. The alternate approach is to copy pages of global data to the recovery cache, perform all global operations on the cache, and then copy the cache to global memory when exiting the recovery block. In this case, rollback is performed by simply reloading the cache from global memory, ignoring the previous data in the cache. Other approaches are described in [ROH73,DEA76,MER76].

Rollback and Recovery in Multiprocess Systems

In a system of multiple cooperating processes, an added dimension to the recovery problem exists. A process will most likely communicate with other processes during its execution, the exchanged messages being similar to the global memory updates described above. In rolling a faulty process back to a recovery point, all messages issued by that process must be treated as suspect and must be recalled. This message recall, as described in [RAN75,KIM78], can lead to a "domino effect" by forcing other processes to roll back to recovery points preceding the reception of these recalled messages. This in turn may cause even more messages to be recalled and more rollbacks until the system finally reaches a stable state. Consider the example given in [KIM78], illustrated in Figure 5.3. Assume Process A fails its acceptance test for RB-A2, forcing it to roll back to the beginning of RB-A2 and to recall message $M3$. The recall of

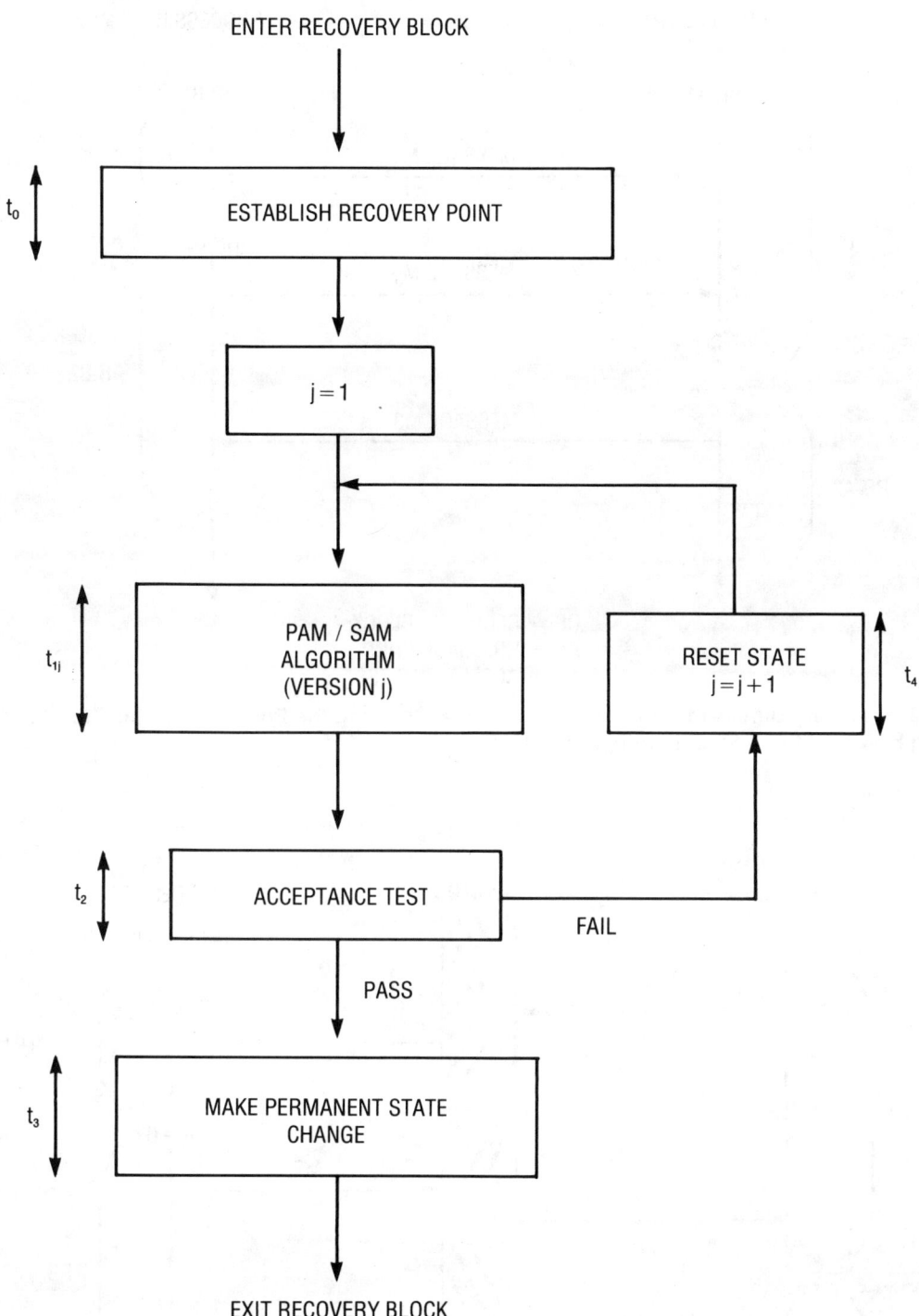

Figure 5.2. Determining Software Overhead Costs Within a Recovery Block

$M3$ will require Process B to roll back to the beginning of RB-B2, recalling $M2$, which in turn forces a rollback of Process A to the beginning of RB-A1 and a subsequent rollback of Process B to the beginning of RB-B1.

Solutions to this problem have been the subject of a number of recent studies [KIM78,KIM82,KIM85,OBR76,-CHA72], the object being to minimize the degree of system rollback in response to any given error. The approach proposed by Kim [KIM78] utilizes two additions to the system of Figure 5.3. First, all messages are passed between processes via a "monitor," which records all messages as changes to its own state and subsequently rolls itself back when any of these messages are recalled. Second, "branch" recovery points are added to the recovery blocks in addition to their "normal" or "base" recovery points to limit the

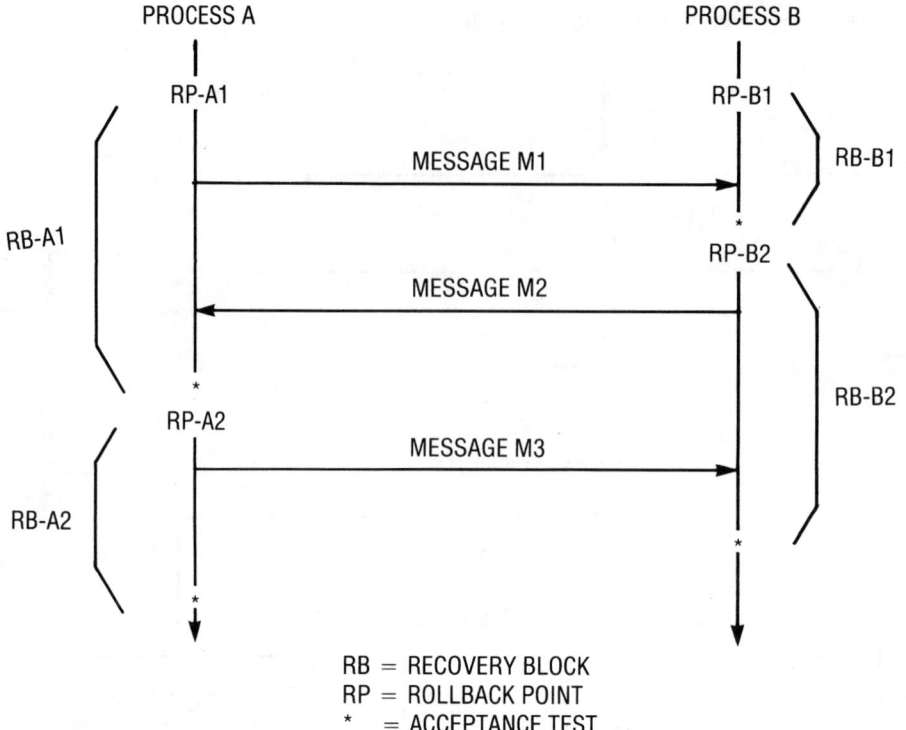

RB = RECOVERY BLOCK
RP = ROLLBACK POINT
* = ACCEPTANCE TEST

Figure 5.3. Recovery Blocks in Concurrent Processes, Showing the Potential for the "Domino Effect" Following Failure of the Acceptance Test in RB-A2.

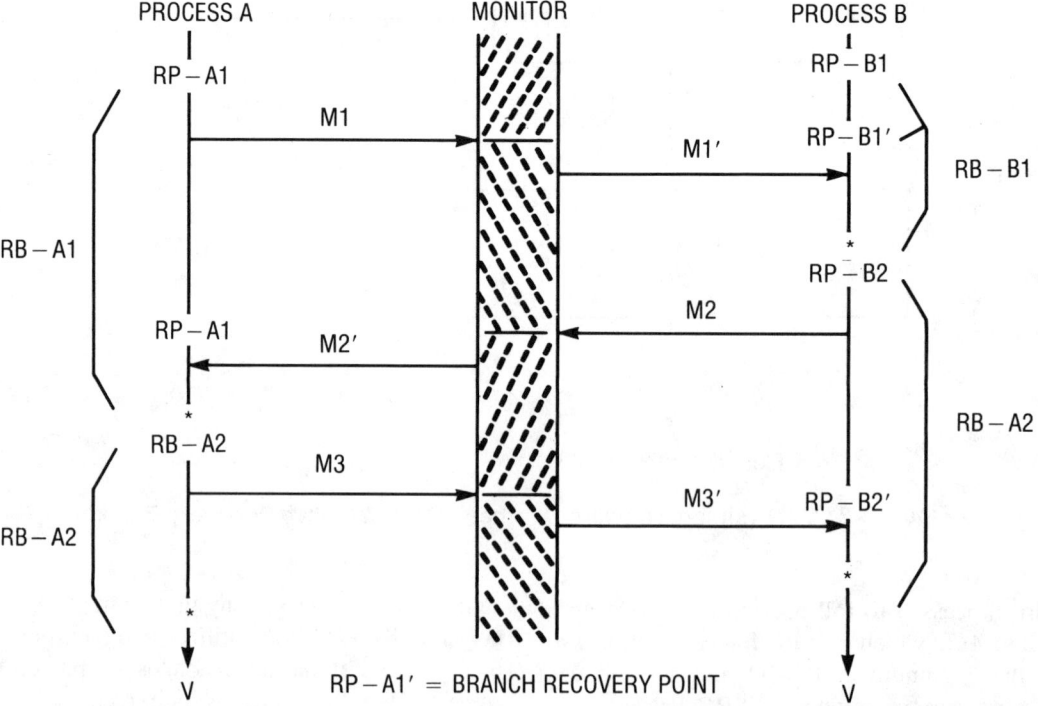

RP−A1' = BRANCH RECOVERY POINT

Figure 5.4. Concurrent Processes With a Communication Monitor and Branch Recovery Points to Minimize Rollback Distance

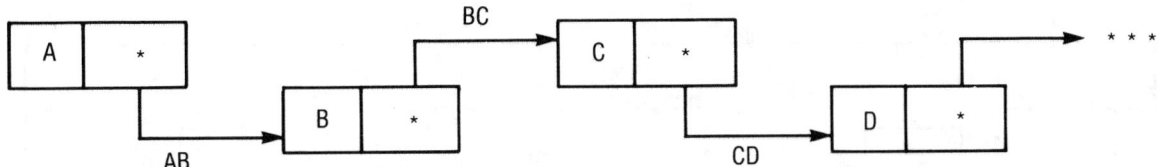

Figure 5.5. Linear Linked List Data Structure with No Fault Tolerance.

rollback distance of a recovery block. These branch recovery points are inserted prior to each monitor reference (message receipt by the monitor) as shown in Figure 5.4, where RP-B1, RP-A1, and RP-B2 are inserted prior to the monitor references $M1'$, $M2'$, and $M3'$, respectively. In this case, if we repeat the above example, the failure of the acceptance test of RB-A2 will force the recall of monitor update $M3$, which in turn will force the monitor to roll back to this point, revoking $M3'$ and thus rolling Process B back to RP-B2$'$. However, the rollback ends at this point, unlike the first example which rolled both processes completely back to their origins.

Of course, the addition of extra recovery points to a system increases the fixed overhead costs of the processes. Methods for optimizing test-point insertion are discussed in [OBR76,KIM80].

Modular Redundancy in Software

The rollback and recovery approaches discussed in the preceding section may be unsuitable in many real-time applications in which minimum response times must be maintained, even if errors have been detected. Failure to respond to an event within an allotted time in such an application represents an error in itself, and must therefore be avoided just as much as other faults. To eliminate time-consuming program rollbacks, on-line detection, and correction of errors is required, using some form of spatial redundancy in the software system. Currently, the most discussed approach utilizes software versions of N-Modular Redundancy, in which multiple copies of each program are executed concurrently, with a majority vote of the redundant results used to determine the final output of the system. The primary overhead costs of this approach include the costly effort to develop multiple versions of the software, redundant hardware to perform the concurrent program executions, and software to implement the voting mechanism. However, if at least three versions of the software are used [AVI77,CHE78], then correct results will continuously be available, which will allow system recovery actions to be postponed until "convenient" times, as is done in FTMP [HOP78] when it reconfigures following a hardware fault.

Software modular redundancy has been used in the SIFT project [WEN78,WEN72] and its commercial version, the August Systems CS-300 [WEN81], as well as in the Space Shuttle [SKL76]. In all three systems, multiple identical copies of each critical software module are executed concurrently, with majority votes taken on all data passed between modules. Unfortunately, the use of identical software modules precludes the detection of software faults, since identical errors would be generated by all copies of the software.

To detect software errors through modular redundancy techniques, the redundant copies cannot be identical. The N-Version Programming approach [AVI77,CHE78,KEL83,AVI85] utilizes independently designed and/or coded versions of each algorithm to implement the redundant system. Theoretically, errors introduced into one version would be detected through comparison with the results of the other versions, with the probability of correlated errors being small. However, this assumption of uncorrelated errors between different versions of software is a much debated issue. Experiments described in [KEL83,AVI85] examine this correlation in actual applications. The N-Version approach has some similarities with the recovery-blocks technique in that multiple versions of the software must be used to obtain correct results. The primary differ-

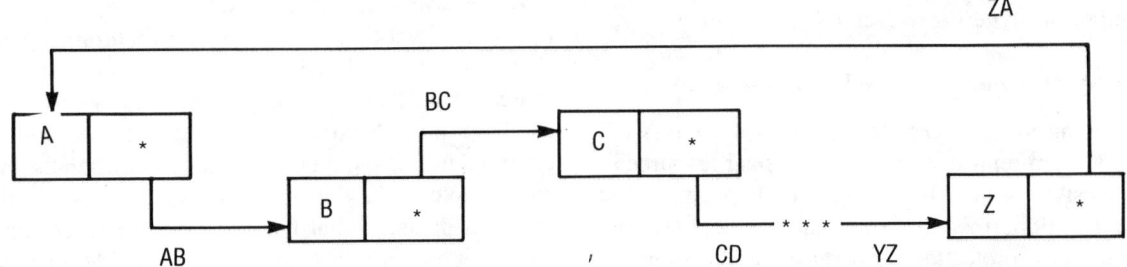

Figure 5.6. Linear Linked List Data Structure With Redundant Tail-to-Head Pointer for Error Detection.

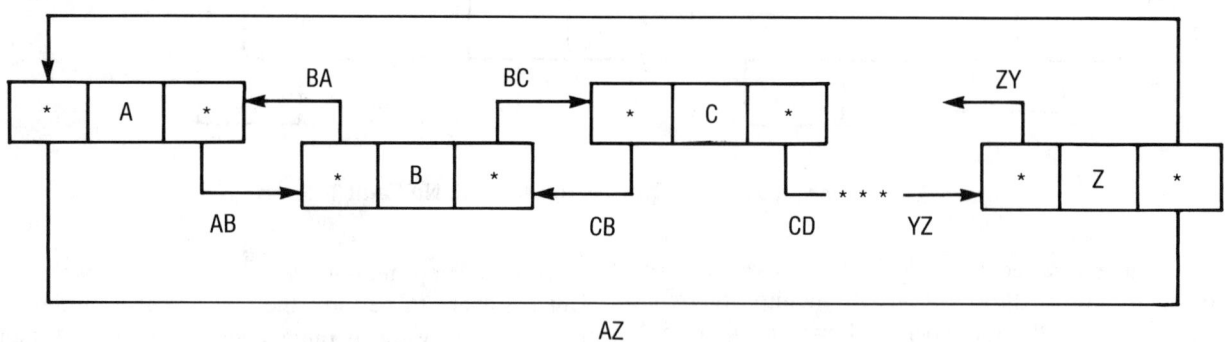

Figure 5.7. Doubly-Linked List Data Structure With Redundant Pointers for Error Correction Capability

ence, however, is that in a recovery block the block is self-checking, with alternates executed serially until the test is passed. In N-Version programming, the versions check each other by exchanging results at various checkpoints in the form of "comparison vectors" [CHE78]. These vectors contain significant program-state information and data which, if found in agreement, verify the correctness of the program versions at the checkpoint. In addition, the exchange process serves both to synchronize the different versions and to detect versions that are unable to respond within acceptable time limits.

In terms of cost, the hardware requirements of N-Version programming are similar to those of SIFT, in that enough processors and other resources must exist to allow parallel execution of the algorithms. Temporal overhead penalties involve only the checkpoint comparison process, which is similar to the software voting of SIFT, although since the program versions are different, the comparison must often be more general than a simple majority vote since minor, but otherwise acceptable, variations may exist. In terms of development costs, the largest factor both in N-Version programming and recovery blocks is the redundant development of independent software modules. This cost consideration has so far made the use of these approaches impractical, especially in commercial applications. Hence, when comparing the two techniques, the trade off is primarily between hardware redundancy for improved error coverage and the time saved in rollback and recovery-time periods. In addition, the constant availability of correct results can minimize the probability of triggering irreversible actions in a system.

Operating System and Database Fault Tolerance

The operating system (O/S) and various databases of a computing system represent extremely critical resources in that they must be shared by the various application processes. In addition, these two system components must provide a layer of protection between the application processes, i.e. a fault in one process should not be allowed to affect another, either directly (through the O/S) or indirectly (through the database). Thus it becomes the responsibility of the O/S and database-management software (DBMS) to provide consistency and validity checks on all operations attempted by the individual application processes, as well as to provide recovery mechanisms where appropriate.

In the design of fault-tolerant O/S's [DEN76, GRZ83, HAN83, FIT84, WUL75], the primary goal is error confinement, i.e. the containment of errors within the boundaries of their originating modules (hardware or software). Secondary goals include the diagnosis of detected errors to identify and isolate their sources and system reconfiguration to eliminate faulty components. These goals can only be met if all process operations agree to invoke the O/S to perform or else coordinate all interprocess operations, with the O/S carefully monitoring these operations.

The "capabilities" approach described by Denning [DEN76] associates with each process in a system a number of parameters which determine, among other things, which resources the process is allowed to access, what operations can be performed, which processes can be communicated with, and which areas of memory can be accessed. Any deviation from a process' allowed activities or privileges will cause it to be flagged as faulty by the O/S, with the rest of the system thus protected. In addition, the O/S can track all system resources and reassign them as needed to prevent one or more from being tied up indefinitely by a faulty process.

In the case of concurrent processes, the O/S has the added responsibility of coordinating or synchronizing access to shared resources [KOH81] to ensure consistency in the shared data. This is done primarily by requiring a shared database to be "locked" prior to using it, excluding all other potential users, and then to be unlocked when the operations are complete. In this manner, no process is allowed to access a database that has been only partially updated by another process, since this would provide an inconsistent view of the database to the second process. The locking mechanism must provide some means for enforcement to protect a database against malicious actions on the part of faulty processes. Thus, all database requests must be "cleared" by the O/S prior to access, to ensure a consistent exclusive access policy. In addition, the O/S must be allowed to forcibly unlock any database or other resource associated with a failed process. In this situation, the O/S should also be given the ability to restore a database to a consistent state following the failure of a process during an update.

The protection of databases is a critical issue in high-reliability systems, especially in commercial systems that rely on their databases more than any other system component. Two things must be considered when providing fault-tolerance schemes for database operations: protection of the data itself and protection of the structure of the database. Of these, the latter is the more critical because a collapse of the structure of a database can result in the loss of all data "downstream" from the fault. Thus, redundancy must be incorporated within the data structures to provide the capability for reconstruction following a fault. If the data themselves cannot be restored, then at least the structure should be.

A number of redundancy techniques for data structures are discussed in [TAY80a,TAY82] that provide resilience to structural faults in a database. These include doubly linked versus singly linked lists, binary trees with redundant pointers not directly related to the tree structure, and combinations of these two structures (chained and threaded binary trees).

Consider the case of the linear linked list of Figure 5.5. An error in link AB resulting from a fault will make all elements beyond A inaccessible. Moreover, we have no direct way to detect this loss of structure. By adding a redundant pointer from the tail of the list, Z, to the head, A, as in Figure 5.6, there is now a way to detect faults by tracing through the list and verifying that it ends back at the beginning. In this structure, however, faults cannot be corrected. The doubly-linked list of Figure 5.7 provides error-correction capabilities by allowing the list structure to be traced either forward or backward through the list. For example, if link BC were to be destroyed, one could trace from A-D-C-B and restore pointer BC as the inverse of pointer CB. Similar usage of redundant pointers for other robust data structures are presented in [TAY80a,TAY80b].

Software Diagnostics and System Evaluation

Almost all commercially available computer systems employ diagnostic software to detect and diagnose errors and permanent faults in both hardware and software. Such diagnostics are typically executed off-line when the processor is not busy with normal activities and exercise the various system components in some way to detect latent (previously undetected) errors in the system. These diagnostic routines may perform various test operations on CPU circuitry, as well as examine memory areas for proper coding. More recently, a number of commercial systems have become available which perform on-line fault diagnosis, i.e. moni-

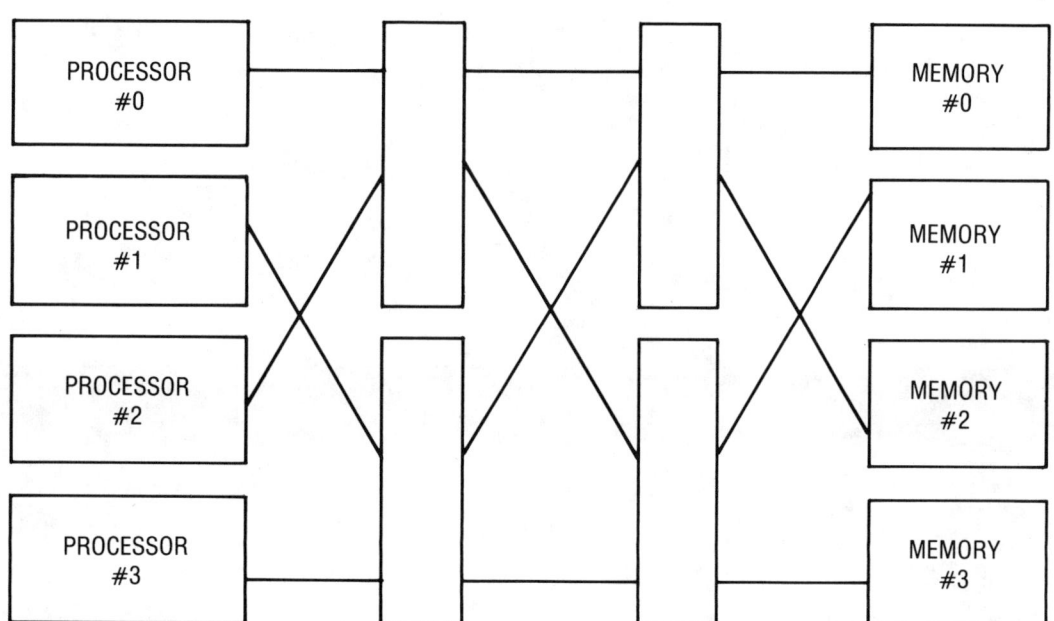

Figure 5.8. The Fault Tolerant/Distributed Computing Lab (FTDCL) Multiprocessor System.

tor various aspects of system operation concurrently with normal activities. This is usually done either by dedicated circuitry [BOO80] or an embedded special purpose processor, as in the Data General MV8000 family [COY80] and in a number of other recent systems [LIU84]. Error statistics are gathered by these maintenance processors from the system for later evaluation by either the system software or maintenance personnel. Extensive diagnostic programs of this type have been in use in the Bell System switches for a number of years [DOW64], as well as in many large mainframe machines. The results of these diagnoses can be used to trigger automatic or manual fault-repair and recovery actions.

As an example, consider the Auburn University Fault Tolerance/Distributed Computing Laboratory (FTDCL) multiprocessor, shown in Figure 5.8 [NEL85]. In this system, the executive software and application software share each of the four processors in the system. The executive, which is identical and independent in each processor, executes a number of diagnostics during the time intervals in which it is preparing to schedule new processes, including integrity checks of the database and connection network hardware, as well as monitoring the real-time clocks maintained by the executives of the other processors. Any irregularities result in recovery procedures being invoked.

Summary

The tolerance of software faults is in most cases more difficult than dealing with hardware faults since most software-fault mechanisms are not well understood and do not lend themselves readily to "nice" techniques such as error coding. Hence, the two most prominent schemes proposed for the tolerance of software faults are based on some form of massive redundancy with an error-checking mechanism. In the case of recovery blocks, the error checker is the acceptance test, which often does not provide complete fault coverage, but is easy to implement on a uniprocessor system with little or no additional hardware. In contrast, N-Version programming uses majority voting, which is more likely to detect and correct all errors with the exception of those few cases in which correlated errors have occurred. However, N-Version programming requires sufficient hardware to execute the multiple versions of the software in parallel. In addition, improved software engineering tools are needed to minimize the degree of correlation between the errors in the multiple program versions. To reduce temporal overhead, more recent schemes have been developed which use a hybrid approach [KIM85], in which primary and secondary algorithms execute in parallel, with acceptance testing then performed on the results.

In the case of operating systems, more attention is being paid to fault detection and protection features, with extensive error-recovery support features [HAN83]. This is especially true in the case of multiprocessors, where errors have the potential to affect multiple processes in the system unrelated to the process which initiated the error.

Software Reliability Models: Assumptions, Limitations, and Applicability

AMRIT L. GOEL, MEMBER, IEEE

Abstract—A number of analytical models have been proposed during the past 15 years for assessing the reliability of a software system. In this paper we present an overview of the key modeling approaches, provide a critical analysis of the underlying assumptions, and assess the limitations and applicability of these models during the software development cycle. We also propose a step-by-step procedure for fitting a model and illustrate it via an analysis of failure data from a medium-sized real-time command and control software system.

Index Terms—Estimation, failure count models, fault seeding, input domain models, model fitting, NHPP, software reliability, times between failures.

Introduction and Background

AN important quality attribute of a computer system is the degree to which it can be relied upon to perform its intended function. Evaluation, prediction, and improvement of this attribute have been of concern to designers and users of computers from the early days of their evolution. Until the late 1960's, attention was almost solely on the hardware related performance of the system. In the early 1970's, software also became a matter of concern, primarily due to a continuing increase in the cost of software relative to hardware, in both the development and the operational phases of the system.

Software is essentially an instrument for transforming a discrete set of inputs into a discrete set of outputs. It comprises of a set of coded statements whose function may be to evaluate an expression and store the result in a temporary or permanent location, decide which statement to execute next, or to perform input/output operations.

Since, to a large extent, software is produced by humans, the finished product is often imperfect. It is imperfect in the sense that a discrepancy exists between what the software can do versus what the user or the computing environment wants it to do. The computing environment refers to the physical machine, operating system, compiler and translator, utilities, etc. These discrepancies are what we call software faults. Basically, software faults can be attributed to an ignorance of the user requirements, ignorance of the rules of the computing environment, and to poor communication of software requirements between the user and the programmer or poor documentation of the software by the programmer. Even if we know that software contains faults, we generally do not know their exact identity.

Currently, there are two approaches available for indicating the existence of software faults, viz. program proving, and program testing. Program proving is formal and mathematical while program testing is more practical and heuristic. The approach taken in program proving is to construct a finite sequence of logical statements ending in the statement, usually the output specification statement, to be proved. Each of the logical statements is an axiom or is a statement derived from earlier statements by the application of an inference rule. Program proving by using inference rules is known as the inductive assertion method. This method was mainly advocated by Floyd, Hoare, Dijkstra, and recently Reynolds [39]. Other work on program proving is on the symbolic execution method. This method is the basis of some automatic program verifiers. Despite the formalism and mathematical exactness of program proving, it is still an imperfect tool for verifying program correctness. Gerhart and Yelowitz [10] showed several programs which were proved to be correct but still contained faults. However, the faults were due to failures in defining what exactly to prove and were not failures of the machanics of the proof itself.

Program testing is the symbolic or physical execution of a set of test cases with the intent of exposing embedded faults in the program. Like program proving, program testing remains an imperfect tool for assuring program correctness. A given testing strategy may be good for exposing certain kinds of faults but not for all possible kinds of faults in a program. An advantage of testing is that it can provide useful information about a program's actual behavior in its intended computing environment, while proving is limited to conclusions about the program's behavior in a postulated environment.

In practice neither proving nor testing can guarantee complete confidence in the correctness of a program. Each has its advantages and limitations and should not be viewed as competing tools. They are, in fact, complementary methods for decreasing the likelihood of program failure.

Due to the imperfectness of these approaches in assuring a correct program, a metric is needed which reflects the degree of program correctness and which can be used

---

Manuscript received February 4, 1985; revised July 31, 1985 and September 30, 1985. This work was supported in part by Rome Air Development Center, GAFB, and by the Computer Applications and Software Engineering (CASE) Center at Syracuse University.

The author is with the Department of Electrical and Computer Engineering and the School of Computer and Information Science, Syracuse University, Syracuse, NY 13244.

in planning and controlling additional resources needed for enhancing software quality. One such quantifiable metric of quality that is commonly used in software engineering practice is software reliability. This measure has attracted considerable attention during the last 15 years and continues to be employed as a useful metric. A commonly used approach for measuring software reliability is via an analytical model whose parameters are generally estimated from available data on software failures. Reliability and other relevant measures are then computed from the fitted model.

Even though such models have been in use for some time, the realism of many of the underlying assumptions and the applicability of these models for assessing software reliability continue to be questioned. It is the purpose of this paper to evaluate the current state-of-the-art related to this issue. Specifically, the key modeling approaches are briefly discussed and a critical analysis of their underlying assumptions, limitations, and applicability during the software development cycle is presented.

It should be pointed out that the emphasis of this paper is on software reliability modeling approaches and several related but important issues are only briefly mentioned. Examples of such issues are the practical and theoretical difficulties of parametric estimation, statistical properties of estimators, unification of models via generalized formulations or via, say, a Bayesian interpretation, validation and comparison of models, and determination of optimum release time. For a discussion of these issues, the reader is referred to Goel [19].

The term software reliability is discussed in Section II along with a classification of the various modeling approaches. The key models are briefly described in Sections III, IV, and V. An assessment of the main assumptions underlying the models is presented in Section VI and the applicability of these models during the software development cycle is discussed in Section VII. A step-by-step procedure for fitting a model is given in Section VIII and is illustrated via an analysis of software failure data from a medium-sized command and control system. A summary of some related work and concluding remarks are presented in Section IX.

II. Meaning and Measurement of Software Reliability

There are a number of views as to what software reliability is and how it should be quantified. Some people believe that this measure should be binary in nature so that an imperfect program would have zero reliability while a perfect one would have a reliability value of one. This view parallels that of program proving whereby the program is either correct or incorrect. Others, however, feel that software reliability should be defined as the relative frequency of the times that the program works as intended by the user. This view is similar to that taken in testing where a percentage of the successful cases is used as a measure of program quality.

According to the latter viewpoint, software reliability is a probabilistic measure and can be defined as the probability that software faults do not cause a failure during a specified exposure period in a specified use environment. The probabilistic nature of this measure is due to the uncertainty in the usage of the various software functions and the specified exposure period here may mean a single run, a number of runs, or time expressed in calendar or execution time units. To illustrate this view of software reliability, suppose that a user executes a software product several times according to its usage profile and finds that the results are acceptable 95 percent of the time. Then the software is said to be 95 percent reliable for that user.

A more precise definition of software reliability which captures the points mentioned above is as follows [30]. Let F be a class of faults, defined arbitrarily, and T be a measure of relevant time, the units of which are dictated by the application at hand. Then the reliability of the software package with respect to the class of faults F and with respect to the metric T, is the probability that no fault of the class occurs during the execution of the program for a prespecified period of relevant time.

Assuming that software reliability can somehow be measured, a logical question is what purpose does it serve. Software reliability is a useful measure in planning and controlling resources during the development process so that high quality software can be developed. It is also a useful measure for giving the user confidence about software correctness. Planning and controlling the testing resources via the software reliability measure can be done by balancing the additional cost of testing and the corresponding improvement in software reliability. As more and more faults are exposed by the testing and verification process, the additional cost of exposing the remaining faults generally rises very quickly. Thus, there is a point beyond which continuation of testing to further improve the quality of software can be justified only if such improvement is cost effective. An objective measure like software reliability can be used to study such a tradeoff.

Current approaches for measuring software reliability basically parallel those used for hardware reliability assessment with appropriate modifications to account for the inherent differences between software and hardware. For example, hardware exhibits mixtures of decreasing and increasing failure rates. The decreasing failure rate is seen due to the fact that, as test or use time on the hardware system accumulates, failures, most likely due to design errors, are encountered and their causes are fixed. The increasing failure rate is primarily due to hardware component wearout or aging. There is no such thing as wearout in software. It is true that software may become obsolete because of changes in the user and computing environment, but once we modify the software to reflect these changes, we no longer talk of the same software but of an enhanced or a modified version. Like hardware, software exhibits a decreasing failure rate (improvement in quality) as the usage time on the system accumulates and faults, say, due to design and coding, are fixed. It should also be noted that an assessed value of the software reliability measure is always relative to a given use environment. Two users exercising two different sets of paths in the same software are likely to have different values of software reliability.

A number of analytical models have been proposed to address the problem of software reliability measurement. These approaches are based mainly on the failure history of software and can be classified according to the nature of the failure process studied as indicated below.

Times Between Failures Models: In this class of models the process under study is the time between failures. The most common approach is to assume that the time between, say, the $(i - 1)$st and the ith failures, follows a distribution whose parameters depend on the number of faults remaining in the program during this interval. Estimates of the prarameters are obtained from the observed values of times between failures and estimates of software reliability, mean time to next failure, etc., are then obtained from the fitted model. Another approach is to treat the failure times as realizations of a stochastic process and use an appropriate time-series model to describe the underlying failure process.

Failure Count Models: The interest of this class of models is in the number of faults or failures in specified time intervals rather than in times between failures. The failure counts are assumed to follow a known stochastic process with a time dependent discrete or continuous failure rate. Parameters of the failure rate can be estimated from the observed values of failure counts or from failure times. Estimates of software reliability, mean tme to next failure, etc., can again be obtained from the relevant equations.

Fault Seeding Models: The basic approach in this class of models is to "seed" a known number of faults in a program which is assumed to have an unknown number of indigenous faults. The program is tested and the observed number of seeded and indigenous faults are counted. From these, an estimate of the fault content of the program prior to seeding is obtained and used to assess software reliability and other relevant measures.

Input Domain Based Models: The basic approach taken here is to generate a set of test cases from an input distribution which is assumed to be representative of the operational usage of the program. Because of the difficulty in obtaining this distribution, the input domain is partitioned into a set of equivalence classes, each of which is usually associated with a program path. An estimate of program reliability is obtained from the failures observed during physical or symbolic execution of the test cases sampled from the input domain.

III. Times Between Failures Models

This is one of the earliest classes of models proposed for software reliability assessment. When interest is in modeling times between failures, it is expected that the successive failure times will get longer as faults are removed from the software system. For a given set of observed values, this may not be exactly so due to the fact

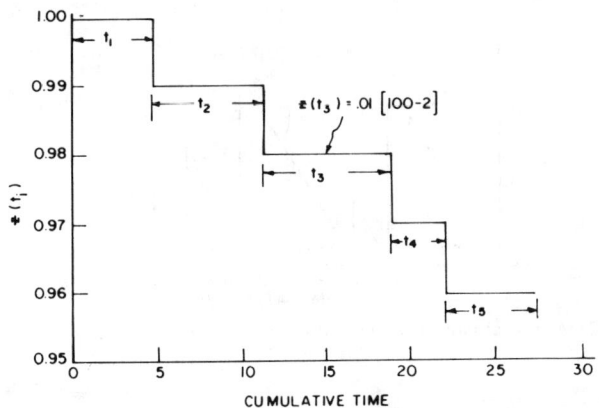

Fig. 1. A typical plot of $Z(t_i)$ for the JM model ($N = 100$, $\phi = 0.01$).

that failure times are random variables and observed values are subject to statistical fluctuations.

A number of models have been proposed to describe such failures. Let a random variable T_i denote the time between the $(i - 1)$st and the ith failures. Basically, the models assume that T_i follows a known distribution whose parameters depend on the number of faults remaining in the system after the $(i - 1)$st failure. The assumed distribution is supposed to reflect the improvement in software quality as faults are detected and removed from the system. The key models in this class are described below.

Jelinski and Moranda (JM) De-Eutrophication Model

This is one of the earliest and probably the most commonly used model for assessing software reliability [20]. It assumes that there are N software faults at the start of testing, each is independent of others and is equally likely to cause a failure during testing. A detected fault is removed with certainty in a negligible time and no new faults are introduced during the debugging process. The software failure rate, or the hazard function, at any time is assumed to be proportional to the current fault content of the program. In other words, the hazard function during t_i, the time between the $(i - 1)$st and ith failures, is given by

$$Z(t_i) = \phi[N - (i - 1)],$$

where ϕ is a proportionality constant. Note that this hazard function is constant between failures but decreases in steps of size ϕ following the removal of each fault. A typical plot of the hazard function for $N = 100$ and $\phi = 0.01$ is shown in Fig. 1.

A variation of the above model was proposed by Moranda [29] to describe testing situations where faults are not removed until the occurrence of a fatal one at which time the accumulated group of faults is removed. In such a situation, the hazard function after a restart can be assumed to be a fraction of the rate which attained when the system crashed. For this model, called the geometric de-eutrophication model, the hazard function during the ith testing interval is given by

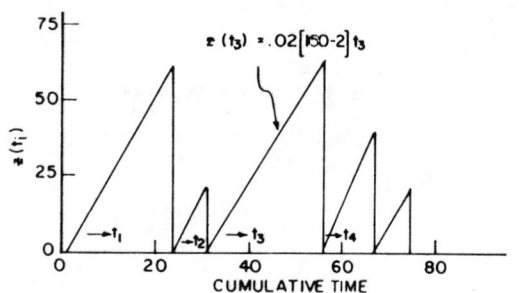

Fig. 2. A typical plot of the hazard function for the SW model ($N = 150$, $\phi = 0.02$).

$$Z(t_i) = Dk^{i-1},$$

where D is the fault detection rate during the first interval and k is a constant ($0 < k < 1$).

Schick and Wolverton (SW) Model

This model is based on the same assumptions as the JM model except that the hazard function is assumed to be proportional to the current fault content of the program as well as to the time elapsed since the last failure [40] is given by

$$Z(t_i) = \phi\{(N - (i - 1))\} t_i$$

where the various quantities are as defined above. Note that in some papers t_i has been taken to be the cumulative time from the beginning of testing. That interpretation of t_i seems to be inconsistent with the interpretation in the original paper, see, e.g., Goel [15].

We note that the above hazard rate is linear with time within each failure interval, returns to zero at the occurrence of a failure and increases linearly again but at a reduced slope, the decrease in slope being proportional to ϕ. A typical behavior of $Z(t_i)$ for $N = 150$ and $\phi = 0.02$ is shown in Fig. 2.

A modification of the above model was proposed in [41] whereby the hazard function is assumed to be parabolic in test time and is given by

$$Z(t_i) = \phi[N - (i - 1)](-at_i^2 + bt_i + c)$$

where a, b, c are constants and the other quantities are as defined above. This function consists of two components. The first is basically the hazard function of the JM model and the superimposition of the second term indicates that the likelihood of a failure occurring increases rapidly as the test time accumulates within a testing interval. At failure times ($t_i = 0$), the hazard function is proportional to that of the JM model.

Goel and Okumoto Imperfect Debugging Model

The above models assume that the faults are removed with certainty when detected. However, in practice [47] that is not always the case. To overcome this limitation, Goel and Okumoto [11], [13] proposed an imperfect debugging model which is basically an extension of the JM model. In this model, the number of faults in the system at time t, $X(t)$, is treated as a Markov process whose transition probabilities are governed by the probability of imperfect debugging. Times between the transitions of $X(t)$ are taken to be exponentially distributed with rates dependent on the current fault content of the system. The hazard function during the interval between the $(i - 1)$st and the ith failures is given by

$$Z(t_i) = [N - p(i - i)]\lambda.$$

where N is the initial fault content of the system, p is the probability of imperfect debugging, and λ is the failure rate per fault.

Littlewood–Verrall Bayesian Model

Littlewood and Verall [25], [26] took a different approach to the development of a model for times between failures. They argued that software reliability should not be specified in terms of the number of errors in the program. Specifically, in their model, the times between failures are assumed to follow an exponential distribution but the parameter of this distribution is treated as a random variable with a gamma distribution, viz.

$$f(t_i|\lambda_i) = \lambda_i e^{-\lambda_i t_i}$$

and

$$f(\lambda_i|\alpha, \psi(i)) = \frac{[\psi(i)]^\alpha \lambda_i^{\alpha-1} e^{-\psi(i)\lambda_i}}{\Gamma\alpha}$$

In the above, $\psi(i)$ describes the quality of the programmer and the difficulty of the programming task. It is claimed that the failure phenomena in different environments can be explained by this model by taking different forms for the parameter $\psi(i)$.

IV. Fault Count Models

This class of models is concerned with modeling the number of failures seen or faults detected in given testing intervals. As faults are removed from the system, it is expected that the observed number of failures per unit time will decrease. If this is so, then the cumulative number of failures versus time curve will eventually level off. Note that time here can be calander time, CPU time, number of test cases run or some other relevant metric. In this setup, the time intervals may be fixed *a priori* and the observed number of failures in each interval is treated as a random variable.

Several models have been suggested to describe such failure phenomena. The basic idea behind most of these models is that of a Poisson distribution whose parameter takes different forms for different models. It should be noted that Poisson distribution has been found to be an excellent model in many fields of application where interest is in the number of occurrences.

One of the earliest models in this category was proposed by Shooman [43]. Taking a somewhat similar approach, Musa [31] later proposed another failure count model based on execution time. Schneidewind [42] took a differ-

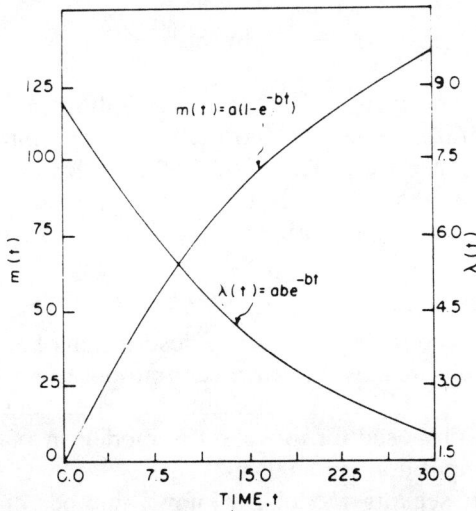

Fig. 3. A typical plot of the $m(t)$ and $\lambda(t)$ functions for the Goel–Okumoto NHPP model ($a = 175$, $b = 0.05$).

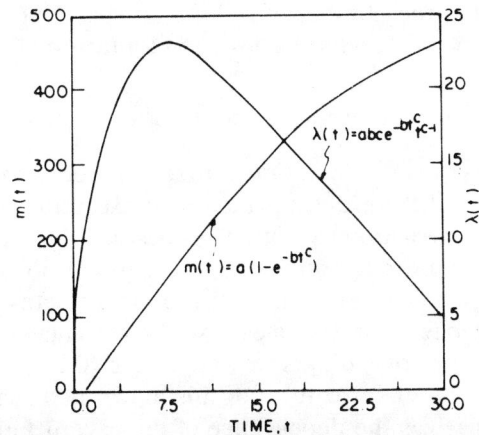

Fig. 4. A typical plot of the $m(t)$ and $\lambda(t)$ functions for the Goel generalized NHPP model ($a = 500$, $b = 0.015$, $c = 1.5$).

ent approach and studied the fault counts over a series of time intervals. Goel and Okumoto [11] introduced a time dependent failure rate of the underlying Poisson process and developed the necessary analytical details of the models. A generalization of this model was proposed by Goel [16]. These and some other models in this class are described below.

Goel–Okumoto Nonhomogeneous Poisson Process Model

In this model Goel and Okumoto [12] assumed that a software system is subject to failures at random times caused by faults present in the system. Letting $N(t)$ be the cumulative number of failures observed by time t, they proposed that $N(t)$ can be modeled as a nonhomogeneous Poisson process, i.e., as a Poisson process with a time dependent failure rate. Based on their study of actual failure data from many systems, they proposed the following form of the model

$$P\{N(t) = y\} = \frac{(m(t))^y}{y!} e^{-m(t)}, \quad y = 0, 1, 2, \cdots$$

where

$$m(t) = a(1 - e^{-bt}),$$

and

$$\lambda(t) \equiv m'(t) = abe^{-bt}.$$

Here $m(t)$ is the expected number of failures observed by time t and $\lambda(t)$ is the failure rate. Typical plots of the $m(t)$ and $\lambda(t)$ functions are shown in Fig. 3.

In this model a is the expected number of failures to be observed eventually and b is the fault detection rate per fault. It should be noted that here the number of faults to be detected is treated as a random variable whose observed value depends on the test and other environmental factors. This is a fundamental departure from the other models which treat the number of faults to be a fixed unknown constant.

In some environments a different form of the $m(t)$ function might be more suitable than the one given above, see, e.g., Ohba [36] and Yamada *et al.* [48].

Using a somewhat different approach than described above, Schneidewind [42] had earlier studied the number of faults detected during a time interval and failure counts over a series of time intervals. He assumed that the failure process is a nonhomogeneous Poisson process with an exponentially decaying intensity function given by

$$d(i) = \alpha e^{-\beta i}, \quad \alpha, \beta > 0, \quad i = 1, 2, \cdots$$

where α and β are the parameters of the model.

Goel Generalized Nonhomogeneous Poisson Process Model

Most of the times between failures and failure count models assume that a software system exhibits a decreasing failure rate pattern during testing. In other words, they assume that software quality continues to improve as testing progresses. In practice, it has been observed that in many testing situations, the failure rate first increases and then decreases. In order to model this increasing/decreasing failure rate process, Goel [16], [17] proposed the following generalization of the Goel–Okumoto NHPP model.

$$P\{N(t) = y\} = \frac{(m(t))^y}{y!} e^{-m(t)}, \quad y = 0, 1, 2, \cdots,$$

$$m(t) = a(1 - e^{-bt^c}),$$

where a is expected number of faults to be eventually detected, and b and c are constants that reflect the quality of testing. The failure rate for the model is given by

$$\lambda(t) \equiv m'(t) = abc\, e^{-bt^c} t^{c-1}.$$

Typical plots of the $m(t)$ and $\lambda(t)$ functions are shown in Fig. 4.

Musa Execution Time Model

In this model Musa [31] makes assumptions that are similar to those of the JM model except that the process modelled is the number of failures in specified execution time intervals. The hazard function for this model is given by

$$z(\tau) = \phi f(N - n_c)$$

where τ is the execution time utilized in executing the program up to the present, f is the linear execution frequency (average instruction execution rate divided by the number of instructions in the program), ϕ is a proportionality constant, which is a fault exposure ratio that relates fault exposure frequency to the linear execution frequency, and n_c is the number of faults corrected during $(0, \tau)$.

One of the main features of this model is that it explicitly emphasizes the dependence of the hazard function on execution time. Musa also provides a systematic approach for converting the model so that it can be applicable for calendar time as well.

Shooman Exponential Model

This model is essentially similar to the JM model. For this model the hazard function [43], [44] is of the following form

$$z(t) = k\left[\frac{N}{I} - n_c(\tau)\right]$$

where t is the operating time of the system measured from its initial activation, I is the total number of instructions in the program, τ is the debugging time since the start of system integration, $n_c(\tau)$ is the total number of faults corrected during τ, normalized with respect to I, and k is a proportionality constant.

Generalized Poisson Model

This is a variation of the NHPP model of Goel and Okumoto and assumes a mean value function [1] of the following form.

$$m(t_i) = \phi(N - M_{i-1}) t_i^\alpha$$

where M_{i-1} is the total number of faults removed up to the end of the $(i - 1)$st debugging interval, ϕ is a constant of proportionality, and α is a constant used to rescale time t_i.

IBM Binomial and Poisson Models

In these models Brooks and Motley [6] consider the fault detection process during software testing to be a discrete process, following a binomial or a Poisson distribution. The software system is assumed to be developed and tested incrementally. They claim that both models can be applied at the module or the system level.

Musa-Okumoto Logarithmic Poisson Execution Time Model

In this model [33] the observed number of failures by some time τ is assumed to be a NHPP, similar to the Goel-Okumoto model, but with a mean value function which is a function of τ, viz.

$$\mu(\tau) = \frac{1}{\theta} \cdot \ln(\lambda_0 \theta \tau + 1),$$

where λ_0 and θ represent the initial failure intensity and the rate of reduction in the normalized failure intensity per failure, respectively. This model is also closely related to Moranda's geometric de-eutrophication model [29] and can be viewed as a continuous version of this model.

V. Fault Seeding and Input Domain Based Models

In this section we give a brief description of a few time-independent models that have been proposed for assessing software reliability. As mentioned earlier, the two approaches proposed for this class of models are fault seeding and input domain analysis.

In fault seeding models, a known number of faults is seeded (planted) in the program. After testing, the numbers of exposed seeded and indigenous faults are counted. Using combinatorics and maximum likelihood estimation, the number of indigenous faults in the program and the reliability of the software can be estimated.

The basic approach in the input domain based models is to generate a set of test cases from an input (operational) distribution. Because of the difficulty in estimating the input distribution, the various models in this group partition the input domain into a set of equivalence classes. An equivalence class is usually associated with a program path. The reliability measure is calculated from the number of failures observed during symbolic or physical execution of the sampled test cases.

Mills Seeding Model

The most popular and most basic fault seeding model is Mills' Hypergeometric model [27]. This model requires that a number of known faults be randomly seeded in the program to be tested. The program is then tested for some amount of time. The number of original indigenous faults can be estimated from the numbers of indigenous and seeded faults uncovered during the test by using the hypergeometric distribution. The procedure adopted in this model is similar to the one used for estimating population of fish in a pond or for estimating wildlife. These models are also referred to as tagging models since a given fault is tagged as seeded or indigenous.

Lipow [23] modified this problem by taking into consideration the probability of finding a fault, of either kind, in any test of the software. Then, for statistically independent tests, the probability of finding given numbers of indigenous and seeded faults can be calculated. In another modification, Basin [2] suggested a two stage procedure with the use of two programmers which can be used to estimate the number of indigenous faults in the program.

Nelson Model

In this input domain based model [35], the reliability of the software is measured by running the software for a sample of n inputs. The n inputs are randomly chosen from the input domain set $E = (E_i : i = 1, \cdots, N)$ where each E_i is the set of data values needed to make a run. The random sampling of n inputs is done according to a probability distribution P_i; the set $(P_i : i = 1, \cdots N)$ is the operational profile or simply the user input distribution. If n_e is the number of inputs that resulted in execution failures, then an unbiased estimate of software reliability $\hat{R}_1$ is $\{1 - (n_e/n)\}$. However, it may be the case that the test set used during the verification phase may not be representative of the expected operational usage. Brown and Lipow [7] suggested an alternative formula for $\hat{R}$ which is

$$\hat{R}_2 = 1 - \sum_{j=1}^{N} \left(\frac{f_j}{n_j}\right) p(E_j)$$

where n_j is the number of runs sampled from input subdomain E_j and f_j is the number of failures observed out of n_j runs.

The main difference between Nelson's $\hat{R}_1$ and Brown and Lipow's $\hat{R}_2$ is that the former explicitly incorporates the usage distribution or the test case distribution while the latter implicitly assumes that the accomplished testing is representative of the expected usage distribution. Both models assume prior knowledge of the operational usage distribution.

Ramamoorthy and Bastani Model

In this input domain based model, the authors are concerned with the reliability of critical, real-time, process control programs. In such systems no failures should be detected during the reliability estimation phase, so that the reliability estimate is one. Hence, the important metric of concern is the confidence in the reliability estimate. This model provides an estimate of the conditional probability that the program is correct for all possible inputs given that it is correct for a specified set of inputs. The basic assumption is that the outcome of each test case provides at least some stochastic information about the behavior of the program for other points which are close to the test point. The specific model is discussed in [3], [38]. A main result of this model is

P {program is correct for all points in $[a, a + V]|$
it is correct for test cases having successive
distances $x_j, j = 1, \cdots, n - 1$}

$$= e^{-\lambda V} \prod_{j=1}^{n-1} \left[\frac{2}{1 + e^{-\lambda x_j}}\right],$$

where λ is a parameter which is deduced from some measure of the complexity of the source code.

Unlike other sampling models, this approach allows any test case selection strategy to be used. Hence, the testing effort can be minimized by choosing test cases which exercise error-prone constructs. However, the model concerning the parameter λ needs to be validated experimentally.

A related model based on fuzzy set theory is discussed in [4].

VI. Model Assumptions and Limitations

In this section we evaluate the implications of the various assumptions underlying the models described above. The main purpose of the following discussion is to focus attention on the framework within which the existing models have been developed. The applicability of such models during the software development cycle will be discussed in the next section.

Before proceeding further, it is helpful to note that a precise, unambiguous statement of the underlying assumptions is necessary to develop a mathematical model. The physical process being modeled, the software failure phenomenon in our case, can hardly be expected to be so precise. It is, therefore, necessary to have a clear understanding of the statement as well as the intent of an assumption.

In the following discussion, the assumptions are evaluated one at a time. Not all of the assumptions discussed here are relevant to any given model but, as a totality, they provide an insight into the kind of limitations imposed by them on the use of the software reliability models. It should be pointed out that the arguments presented here are not likely to be universally applicable because the software development process is very environment dependent. What holds true in one environment may not be true in another. Because of this, even assumptions that seem reasonable, e.g., during the testing of one function or system, may not hold true in subsequent testing of the same function or system. The ultimate decision about the appropriateness of the underlying assumptions and the applicability of the models will have to be made by the user of a model. What is presented here should be helpful in determining whether the assumptions associated with a given model are representative of the user's development environment and in deciding which model, if any, to use.

Times Between Failures Are Independent

This assumption is used in all times between failure models and requires that successive failure times be independent of each other. In general, this would be the case if successive test cases were chosen randomly. However, testing, especially functional testing, is not based on independent test cases, so that the test process is not likely to be random. The time, or the additional number of test cases, to the next failure may very well depend on the nature or time of the previous fault. If a critical fault is uncovered, the tester may decide to intensify the testing process and look for more potential critical faults. This in turn may mean shorter time to the next failure. Although strict adherence to this assumption is unlikely, care should be taken in ensuring some degree of independence in data points.

A Detected Fault Is Immediately Corrected

The models that require this assumption assume that the software system goes through a purification process as testing uncovers faults. An argument can be made that this assumption is at least implicitly satisfied in many testing situations. Sometimes, when a fault is encountered, testing can proceed without removing it. In that case, the future fault detection process can be assumed to behave as if the fault had been physically removed. If, however, the fault is in the path that must be tested further, this assumption would be satisfied only if the fault is removed prior to proceeding with the remainder of the test bucket or if new test cases were generated to get around it.

No New Faults Are Introduced During the Fault Removal Process

The purpose of this assumption is to ensure that the modeled failure process does have a monotonic pattern. That is, the subsequent faults are exposed from a system that has less faults than before. In general, this may not be true if faults are debugged after each occurrence because other paths may be affected during debugging, leading to additional faults in the system. It is generally considered to be a restrictive assumption in reliability models. The only way to strictly satisfy this is to ensure that the correction process does not introduce new faults. If, however, the additional faults introduced constitute a very small fraction of the fault population, the practical effect on model results would be minimal.

Failure Rate Decreases with Test Time

This assumption implies that the software gets better with testing in a statistical sense. This seems to be a reasonable assumption in most cases and can be justified as follows. As testing proceeds, faults are detected. They are either removed before testing continues or they are not removed and testing is shifted to other parts of the program. In the former case, the subsequent failure rate decreases explicitly. In the latter case, the failure rate (based upon the entire program) decreases implicitly since a smaller portion of the code is subjected to subsequent testing.

Failure Rate Is Proportional to the Number of Remaining Faults

This assumption implies that each remaining fault has the same chance of being detected in a given testing interval between failures. It is a reasonable assumption if the test cases are chosen to ensure equal probability of executing all portions of the code. However, if one set of paths is executed more thoroughly than another, more faults in the former are likely to be detected than in the latter. Faults residing in the unreachable or never tested portion of the code will obviously have a low, or zero, probability of being detected.

Reliability Is a Function of the Number of Remaining Faults

This assumption implies that all remaining faults are equally likely to appear during the operation of a system and is used when reliability estimates are based on the number of remaining faults. If the usage is uniform, then this is clearly a reasonable assumption. If, however, some portions are more likely to be executed than others, this assumption will not hold. However, the reliability of the system can be recomputed by incorporating information about differences in usage. In other words, a reliability measure conditioned on usage rather than based on the number of remaining faults, would be more suitable. If, however, such information is not available, the assumption of uniform usage is the only reasonable one to make. In that case, the estimated reliability value should be interpreted with caution.

Time Is Used as a Basis for Failure Rate

Most models use time as a basis for determining changes in failure rate. This usage assumes that testing effort is proportional to either calendar time or execution time. Also, time is generally easy to measure and most testing records are kept in terms of time. Another argument in favor of this measure is that time tends to smooth out differences in test effort.

If, however, testing is not proportional to time, the models are equally valid for any other relevant measure. Some examples of such measures are lines of code tested, number of functions tested, and number of test cases executed.

Failure Rate Increases Between Failures

This assumption implies that the likelihood of finding a fault increases as the testing time increases within a given failure interval. This would be a justifiable assumption if software were assumed to be subject to wearout within the interval. But, generally, this is not the case with software systems. Another situation where such an assumption might be justifiable is where testing intensity increases within the interval in the same fashion as does the failure rate.

Testing Is Representative of the Operational Usage

This assumption is necessary when a reliability estimate based on testing is projected into the operational phase. It is used primarily in input domain based models. The times between failures and fault count models would also need this assumption if they are used to assess operational reliability.

Test cases are generally chosen to ensure that the functional requirements of the system are correctly met. A given user of the system, however, may not use the functions in the same proportion as done during testing. In that case, testing will not reflect the operational usage. If information about usage pattern is available, testing effort can be modified to be representative of the use profile.

VII. Applicability of Software Reliability Models

In this section we suggest the classes of models that might be applicable in various phases of the software development process. Some of the general comments made in the beginning of Section VI about the importance and

TABLE I
LIST OF KEY ASSUMPTIONS BY MODEL CATEGORY

Times Between Failures (TBF) Models
- Independent times between failures.
- Equal probability of the exposure of each fault.
- Embedded faults are independent of each other.
- Faults are removed after each occurrence.
- No new faults introduced during correction, i.e., perfect fault removal.

Fault Count (FC) Models
- Testing intervals are independent of each other.
- Testing during intervals is reasonably homogeneous.
- Numbers of faults detected during nonoverlapping intervals are independent of each other.

Fault Seeding (FS) Models
- Seeded faults are randomly distributed in the program.
- Indigenous and seeded faults have equal probabilities of being detected.

Input Domain Based (IDB) Models
- Input profile distribution is known.
- Random testing is used.
- Input domain can be partitioned into equivalent classes.

interpretation of assumptions are also applicable to the discussion here. In particular, note that a precise statement of assumptions is necessary for modeling even though the development process being modeled is extremely unlikely to be that precise. A partial explanation for this apparent inconsistency lies in the fact that a model is, simply, an attempt to summarize the complexity of the real process in order to understand it and possibly control it. In order to be useful, a software reliability model, thus, has to be simple and cannot capture in detail every facet of the modeled failure process. A realization of such constraints imposed on a mathematical model would be helpful in choosing one which can adequately represent the environment within a given development phase.

In the following discussion, we consider the four classes of software reliability models (see Table I) and assess their applicability during the design, unit testing, integration testing, and operational phases.

Design Phase

During the design phase, faults may be detected visually or by other formal or informal procedures. Existing software reliability models are not applicable during this phase because the test cases needed to expose faults as required by fault seeding and input domain based models do not exist, and the failure history required by time dependent models is not available.

Unit Testing

The typical environment during module coding and unit testing phase is such that the test cases generated from the module input domain do not form a representative sample of the operational usage distribution. Further, times between exposures of module faults are not random since the test strategy employed may not be random testing. In fact, test cases are usually executed in a deterministic fashion.

Given these conditions, it seems that the fault seeding models are applicable provided it can be assumed that the indigenous and seeded fault have equal probabilities of being detected. However, a difficulty could arise if the programmer is also the tester in this phase. The input domain based models seem to be applicable, except that matching the test profile to operational usage distribution could be difficult. Due to these difficulties, such models, although applicable, may not be usable.

The time dependent models, especially the time between failures models, do not seem to be applicable in this environment since the independent times between failures assumption is seriously violated.

Integration Testing

A typical environment during integration testing is that the modules are integrated into partial or whole systems and test cases are generated to verify the correctness of the integrated system. Test cases for this purpose may be generated randomly from an input distribution or may be generated deterministically using a reliable test strategy, the latter being probably more effective. The exposed faults are corrected and there is a strong possibility that the removal of exposed faults may introduce new faults.

Under such testing conditions, fault seeding models are theoretically applicable since we still have the luxury of seeding faults into the system. Input domain based models based on an explicit test profile distribution are also applicable. The difficulty in applying them at this point is the very large number of logic paths generated by the whole system.

If deterministic testing (e.g., boundary value analysis, path testing) is used, times between failures models may not be appropriate because of the violation of the independence of interfailure times assumption. Fault count models may be applicable if sets of test cases are independent of each other, even if the tests within a set are chosen deterministically. This is so because in such models the system failure rate is assumed to decrease as a result of executing a set of test cases and not at every failure.

If random testing is performed according to an assumed input profile distribution, then most of the existing software reliability models are applicable. Input domain based models, if used, should utilize a test profile distribution which is statistically equivalent to the operational profile distribution. Fault seeding models are applicable likewise, since faults can be seeded and the equal probability of fault detection assumption may not be seriously violated. This is due to the random nature of the test generation process.

Times between failures and failure count models are most applicable with random testing. The next question could be about choosing a specific model from a given class. Some people prefer to try a couple of these models on the same failure history and then choose one. However, because of different underlying assumptions of these models, there are subtle distinctions among them. Therefore, as far as possible, the choice of a specific model should be based on the development environment considerations.

Acceptance Testing

During acceptance testing, inputs based on operational usage are generated to verify software acceptability. In this phase, seeding of faults is not practical and the exposed faults are not usually immediately corrected. The fault seeding and times between failures models are thus not applicable. Many other considerations here are similar to those of intergration testing so that the fault count and input domain based models are generally applicable.

Operational Phase

When the reliability of the software as perceived by the developer or the "friendly users" is already acceptable, the software is released for operational use. During the operational phase, the user inputs may not be random. This is because the user may use the same software function or path on a routine basis. Inputs may also be correlated (e.g., in real-time systems), thus losing their randomness. Furthermore, faults are not always immediately corrected. In this environment, fault-count models are likely to be most applicable and could be used for monitoring software failure rate or for determining the optimum time for installing a new release.

VIII. Development and Use of a Model

A step-by-step procedure for fitting a model to software failure data is presented in this section. The procedure is illustrated via analyses of data from a medium size, real-time command and control system. The use of the fitted model for computing reliability and other performance measures, as well as for decision-making, is also explained.

Modeling Procedure

The various steps of the model fitting and decision making process are shown in Fig. 5 and are described below.

Step 1—Study Software Failure Data: The models discussed in this paper require that failure data be available. For most of the models, such data should be in the form of either times between failures or as failure counts. The first step in developing a model is to carefully study such data in order to gain an insight into the nature of the process being modeled.

It is highly desirable to plot the data as a function of, say, calendar time, execution time, or number of test cases executed. The objective of such plots is to try to determine the appropriate variables to use in the model. For example, based on the data and information about the development environment, a model of failures versus unique test cases run may be more important and relevant than a model of failures versus, say, calendar time. Sometimes it is desirable to model several such combinations and then use the fitted models for answering a variety of questions about the failure process. Occasionally, it may be neces-

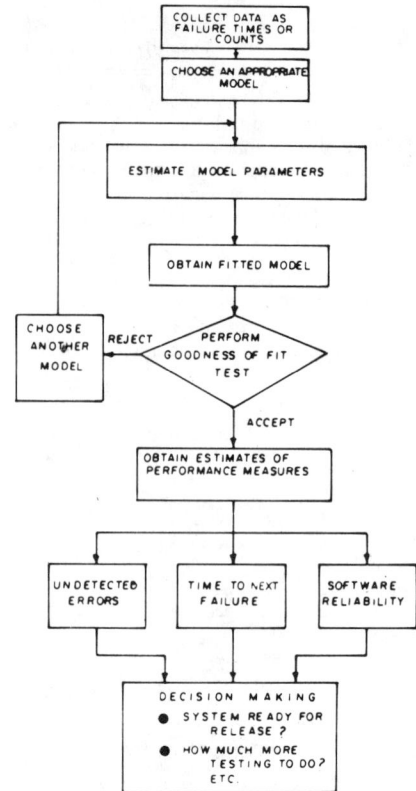

Fig. 5. Flowchart for software reliability modeling and decision making.

sary to normalize the data to, for example, account for changes in system size during testing.

Step 2—Choose a Reliability Model: The next step is to choose an appropriate model based upon an understanding of the testing process and of the assumptions underlying the models discussed earlier. The data and plots from Step 1 are likely to be very helpful in this process. A check about the "goodness" of the chosen model for the data at hand will be made in Step 5.

Step 3—Obtain Estimates of Model Parameters: Different methods are generally required depending upon the nature of available data. The most commonly used one is the method of maximum likelihood because it has very good statistical properties. However, sometimes, the method of least squares or some other method may be preferred.

Step 4—Obtain the Fitted Model: The fitted model is obtained by substituting the estimated values of the parameters in the chosen model. At this stage, we have a fitted model based on the available failure data and the chosen model form.

Step 5—Perform Goodness-of-Fit Test: Before proceeding further, it is advisable to conduct the Kolmogorov-Smirnov, or some other suitable goodness-of-fit test to check the model fit. If the model fits, i.e., if it is a satisfactory descriptor of the observed failure process, we can move ahead. However, if the model does not fit, we have to collect additional data or seek a better, more appropriate model. There is no easy answer to either how much data to collect or how to look for a better model. Decisions on these issues are very much problem dependent and require a clear understanding of the models and the software development environment.

Step 6—Obtain Estimates of Performance Measures: At this stage, we can compute various quantitative measures to assess the performance of the software system. Some useful measures are shown in Fig. 5. Confidence bounds can also be obtained for these measures to evaluate the degree of uncertainty in the computed values of the performance measures.

Step 7—Decision Making: The ultimate objective of developing a model is to use it for making some decisions about the software system, e.g., whether to release the system or continue testing. Such decisions are made at this stage of the modeling process based on the information developed in the previous steps.

An Example of Software Reliability Modeling

We now employ the above procedure to illustrate the development of a software reliability model based on failure data from a real-time, command and control system. The delivered number of object instructions for this system was 21 700 and it was developed by Bell Laboratories. The data were reported by Musa [32] and represent the failures observed during system testing for 25 hours of CPU time.

For purposes of this illustration, we employ the NHPP model of Goel and Okumoto [12]. We do so because of its simplicity and applicability over a wide range of testing situations as also noted by Misra [28], who successfully used this model to predict the number of remaining faults in a space shuttle software subsystem.

Step 1: The original data were reported as times between failures. To overcome the possible lack of independence among these values, we summarized the data into numbers of failures per hour of execution time. The summarized data are given in Table II. A plot of the hourly data is shown in Fig. 6 and a plot of $N(t)$, the cumulative number of failures by t, is shown in Fig. 7. Some other plots shown in Fig. 7 will be discussed later.

Step 2: A study of the data in Table II and of the plot in Fig. 6 indicates that the failure rate (number of failures per hour) seems to be decreasing with test time. This means that an NHPP with a mean value function $m(t) = a(1 - e^{-bt})$ should be a reasonable model to describe the failure process.

Step 3: For the above model, two parameters, a and b, are to be estimated from the failure data. We chose to use the method of maximum likelihood for this purpose [14], [16]. The estimated values for the two parameters are $\hat{a} = 142.32$ and $\hat{b} = 0.1246$. Recal that $\hat{a}$ is an estimate of the expected total number of faults likely to be detected and $\hat{b}$ represents the number of faults detected per fault per hour.

Step 4: The fitted model based on the data of Table II and the parameters estimated in Step 3 is

$$\hat{m}(t) = 142.32(1 - e^{-0.1246t})$$

TABLE II
FAILURES IN 1 HOUR (EXECUTION TIME) INTERVALS AND CUMULATIVE FAILURES

Hour	Number of Failures	Cumulative Failures
1	27	27
2	16	43
3	11	54
4	10	64
5	11	75
6	7	82
7	2	84
8	5	89
9	3	92
10	1	93
11	4	97
12	7	104
13	2	106
14	5	111
15	5	116
16	6	122
17	0	122
18	5	127
19	1	128
20	1	129
21	2	131
22	1	132
23	2	134
24	1	135
25	1	136

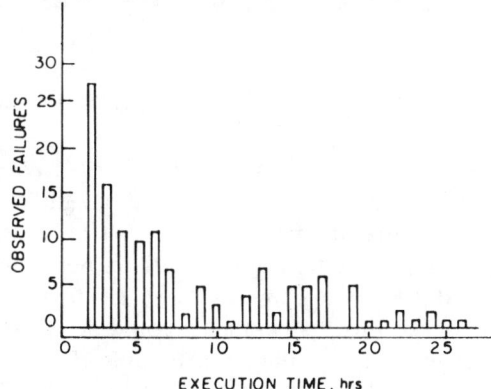

Fig. 6. Plot of the number of failures per hour.

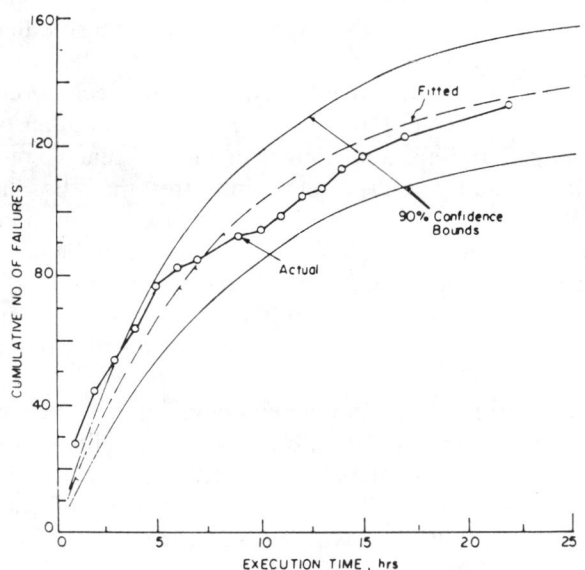

Fig. 7. Cumulative number of failures as a function of execution time and confidence bounds.

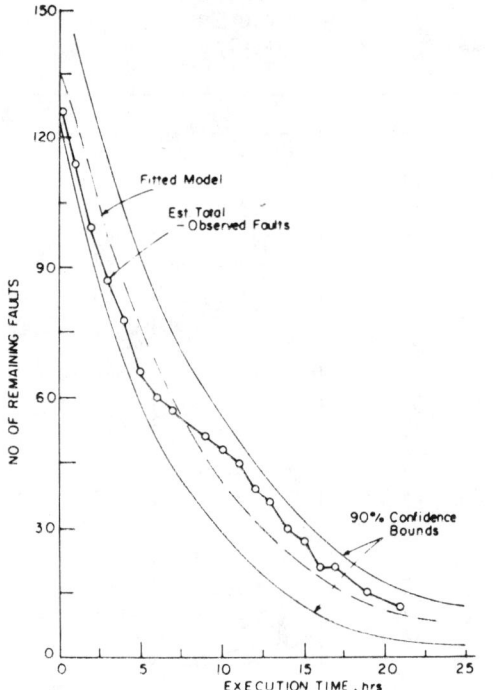

Fig. 8. Estimated remaining number of faults and confidence bounds.

and

$$\hat{\lambda}(t) = 17.73 \cdot e^{-0.1246t}.$$

Step 5: In this case, we used the Kolmogorov–Smirnov goodness-of-fit test for checking the adequacy of the model. For details of this test, see Goel [17]. Basically, the test provides a statistical comparison between the actual data and the model chosen in Step 2. The fitted model in Step 4 passed this test so that it could be considered to be a good descriptor of the data in Table II. The plots in Fig. 7 also provide a visual check of the goodness-of-fit of the model.

Step 6: For illustration purposes, we computed only one performance measure, the expected number of remaining faults, at various testing times. A plot of these values is shown in Fig. 8.

Plots of the confidence bounds for the expected cumulative number of failures, and the expected number of remaining faults are also shown in Figs. 7 and 8, respectively. A study of these plots indicates that the chosen NHPP model provides an excellent fit to the data and can be used for purposes of describing the failure behavior as well as for prediction of the future failure process. The information available from this can be used for planning, scheduling, and other management decisions as indicated below.

Step 7: The model developed above can be used for answering a variety of questions about the failure process and for determining the additional test effort required until the system is ready for release. This type of information can be sought at various points of time and one does not have to wait until the end of testing. For illustrative purposes suppose that failure data through only 16 hours of testing are available, and a total of 122 failures (see Table II) have been observed. Based on these data, the fitted model is

$$\hat{m}(t) = 138.37\,(1 - e^{-0.133t}).$$

An estimate of the remaining number of faults is 16.37 with a 90 percent confidence interval of (4.64–28.11). Also, the estimated one hour ahead reliability is 0.165 and the corresponding 90 percent confidence interval is (0.019–0.310).

Now, suppose that a decision to release software for operational use is to be based on the number of remaining faults. Specifically, suppose that we would release the system if the expected number of remaining faults is less than or equal to 10. In the above analysis we saw that the best estimate of this quantity at present is 16.37, which means that we should continue testing in the hope that additional faults can be detected and removed. If we were to carry on a similar analysis after each additional hour of testing, the expected number of remaining faults after 20 hours would be 9.85 so that the above release criterion would be met.

The above simple example was meant to illustrate the kind of information that can be obtained from a software reliability model. In practice, determination of release time, additional testing effort, etc. are based on much more elaborate considerations than remaining faults. The results from models such as the ones developed here can be used as inputs into the decision-making process.

IX. Concluding Remarks

In this paper, we have provided a review and an evaluation of software reliability models. Four classes of analytical models, along with their underlying assumptions and limitations, were described. The use and applicability of such models during software development and operational phases was also discussed. A methodology for developing a model from failure data was proposed and illustrated via an example. The objective was to provide a model user an insight into the usefulness and limitations of such models that would be helpful in determining which model, if any, to use in a given software development environment.

The material presented here primarily dealt with the development and use of a software reliability model. Several related, but important aspects [19] that were not addressed are model unification issues [22], optimum release time determination [9], parametric estimation problems, comparisons of models [1], [15], [41], [46], and alternate approaches to such models [8], [21].

It should be noted that the above analytical models are primarily useful in estimating and monitoring software reliability, viewed as a measure of software quality. Since they treat the software product and the development process as a blackbox, they cannot be explicitly used for assessing the role of various tools and techniques in determining software quality. For this purpose, more detailed models will be needed that explicitly incorporate information about the software system and the development process.

ACKNOWLEDGMENT

P. Valdes and A. Deb provided valuable help on an earlier version of this paper. Constructive comments by P. Moranda and F. Bastani were very helpful in improving the quality of the paper. The author is grateful to all of them.

REFERENCES

[1] J. E. Angus, R. E. Schafer, and A. Sukert, "Software reliability model validation," in *Proc. Annu. Reliability and Maintainability Symp.*, San Francisco, CA, Jan. 1980, pp. 191-193.

[2] S. L. Basin, "Estimation of software error rate via capture–recapture sampling," Science Applications, Inc., Palo Alto, CA, 1974.

[3] F. B. Bastani, "An input domain based theory of software reliability and its application," Ph.D. dissertation, Univ. California, Berkeley, 1980.

[4] —, "On the uncertainty in the correctness of computer programs," *IEEE Trans. Software Eng.*, vol. SE-11, pp. 857-864, Sept. 1985.

[5] B. W. Boehm, J. R. Brown, M. Lipow, "Quantitative evaluation of software quality," in *Proc. 2nd Int. Conf. Software Eng.*, San Francisco, CA, Oct. 1976, pp. 592-605.

[6] W. D. Brooks and R. W. Motley, "Analysis of discrete software reliability models," Rep. RADC-TR-80-84, Apr. 1980.

[7] J. R. Brown and M. Lipow, "Testing for software reliability," in *Proc. Int. Conf. Reliable Software*, Los Angeles, CA, Apr. 1975, pp. 518-527.

[8] L. H. Crow and N. D. Singpurwalla, "An empirically developed Fourier series model for describing software failures," *IEEE Trans. Rel.*, vol. R-33, pp. 175-183, June 1984.

[9] E. H. Forman and N. D. Singpurwalla, "An empirical stopping rule for debugging and testing computer software," *J. Amer. Statist. Ass.*, vol. 72, no. 360, pp. 750-757, 1977.

[10] S. Gerhart and L. Yelowitz, "Observations of fallibility in applications of modern programming methodologies," *IEEE Trans. Software Eng.*, vol. SE-2, pp. 195-207, May 1976.

[11] A. L. Goel and K. Okumoto, "An analysis of recurrent software failures in a real-time control system," in *Proc. ACM Annu. Tech. Conf.*, ACM, Washington, DC, 1978, pp. 496-500.

[12] —, "A time dependent error detection rate model for software reliability and other performance measures," *IEEE Trans. Rel.*, vol. R-28, pp. 206-211, 1979.

[13] —, "A Markovian model for reliability and other performance measures of software systems," in *Proc. Nat. Comput. Conf.*, New York, vol. 48, 1979, pp. 769-774.

[14] A. L. Goel, "A software error detection model with applications," *J. Syst. Software*, vol. 1, pp. 243-249, 1980.

[15] —, "A summary of the discussion on an analysis of competing software reliability models," *IEEE Trans. Software Eng.*, vol. SE-6, pp. 501-502, 1980.

[16] —, "A guidebook for software reliability assessment," Rep. RADC-TR-83-176, Aug. 1983.

[17] —, "Software reliability modelling and estimation techniques," Rep. RADC-TR-82-263, Oct. 1982.

[18] A. L. Goel, V. R. Basili, and P. M. Valdes, "When and how to use a software reliability model," in *Proc. 7th Software Eng. Workshop*, NASA/GSFC, Greenbelt, MD, Nov. 1983.

[19] A. L. Goel, "Software reliability modeling and related topics: A survey," Dep. of Elec. and Comput. Eng., Syracuse Univ., Syracuse, NY, Tech. Rep., Oct. 1985.

[20] Z. Jelinski and P. Moranda, "Software reliability research," In *Statistical Computer Performance Evaluation*, W. Freiberger, Ed. New York: Academic, 1972, pp. 465-484.

[21] W. Kremer, "Birth–death and bug counting," *IEEE Trans. Rel.*, vol. R-32, pp. 27-47, Apr. 1983.

[22] N. Langberg and N. D. Singpurwalla, "Unification of some software reliability models via the Bayesian approach," *SIAM J. Sci. Statist. Comput.*, vol. 6, pp. 781-790, July 1985.

[23] M. Lipow, "Estimation of software package residual errors," TRW, Redondo Beach, CA, Software Series Rep. TRW-SS-72-09, 1972.

[24] —, "Maximum likelihood estimation of parameters of a software time-to-failure distribution," TRW, Redondo Beach, CA, Systems Group Rep. 2260.1.9.-73B-15, 1972.

[25] B. Littlewood and J. L. Verrall, "A Bayesian reliability growth model for computer software," *Appl. Statist.*, vol. 22, pp. 332-346, 1973.

[26] B. Littlewood, "Theories of software reliability: How good are they and how can they be improved?" *IEEE Trans. Software Eng.*, vol. SE-6, pp. 489-500, 1980.

[27] H. D. Mills, "On the statistical validation of computer programs," IBM Federal Syst. Div., Gaithersburg, MD, Rep. 72-6015, 1972.

[28] P. N. Misra, "Software reliability analysis," *IBM Syst. J.*, vol. 22, no. 3, pp. 262-270, 1983.

[29] P. B. Moranda, "Prediction of software reliability during debugging," in *Proc. Annu. Reliability and Maintainability Symp.*, Washington, DC, Jan. 1975, pp. 327-332.

[30] —, private communication, 1982.

[31] J. D. Musa, "A theory of software reliability and its application," *IEEE Trans. Software Eng.*, vol. SE-1, pp. 312-327, 1971.

[32] —, "Software Reliability Data," DACS, RADC, New York, 1980.

[33] J. D. Musa and K. Okumoto, "A logarithmic Poisson execution time model for software reliability measurement," in *Proc. 7th Int. Conf. Software Eng.*, Orlando, FL, Mar. 1983, pp. 230-237.

[34] G. J. Myers, *Software Reliability, Principles and Practices.* New York: Wiley, 1976.

[35] E. Nelson, "Estimating software reliability from test data," *Microelectron. Rel.*, vol. 17, pp. 67-74, 1978.

[36] M. Ohba, "Software reliability analysis models," *IBM J. Res. Develop.*, vol. 28, pp. 428-443, July 1984.

[37] K. Okumoto and A. L. Goel, "Availability and other performance measures of software systems under imperfect maintenance," in *Proc. COMPSAC*, Chicago IL, Nov. 1978, pp. 66-71.

[38] C. V. Ramamoorthy and F. B. Bastani, "Software reliability: Status and perspectives," *IEEE Trans. Software Eng.*, vol. SE-8, pp. 359-371, July 1982.

[39] J. Reynolds, *The Craft of Programming.* Englewood Cliffs, NJ: Prentice-Hall, 1981.

[40] G. J. Schick and R. W. Wolverton, "Assessment of software reliability," presented at the 11th Annu. Meeting German Oper. Res. Soc., DGOR, Hamburg, Germany; also in *Proc. Oper. Res.*, Physica-Verlag, Wirzberg-Wien, 1973, pp. 395-422.

[41] G. J. Schick and R. W. Wolverton, "An analysis of computing software reliability models," *IEEE Trans. Software Eng.*, vol. SE-4, pp. 104-120, 1978.

[42] N. F. Schneidewind, "Analysis of error processes in computer software," in *Proc. Int. Conf. Reliable Software*, Los Angeles, CA, Apr. 1975, pp. 337-346.

[43] M. L. Shooman, "Probabilistic models for software reliability prediction," in *Statistical Computer Performance Evaluation*, W. Freiberger, Ed. New York: Academic, 1972, pp. 485-502.

[44] —, "Software reliability measurement and models," in *Proc. Annu. Reliability and Maintainability Symp.*, Washington, DC, Jan. 1975, pp. 485-491.

[45] —, "Structural models for software reliability and prediction," in *Proc. 2nd Int. Conf. Software Eng.*, San Francisco, CA, Oct. 1976, pp. 268-273.

[46] A. N. Sukert, "An investigation of software reliability models," in *Proc. Annu. Reliability and Maintainability Symp.*, Philadelphia, PA, Jan. 1977, pp. 478-484.

[47] T. A. Thayer, M. Lipow, and E. C. Nelson, "Software reliability study," Rep. RADC-TR-76-238, Aug. 1976.

[48] S. Yamada, M. Ohba, and S. Osaki, "S-shaped reliability growth modeling for software error detection," *IEEE Trans. Rel.*, vol. R-32, pp. 475-478, Dec. 1983.

Amrit L. Goel (M'75), for a photograph and biography, see this issue, p. 1410.

There are several ways to increase system reliability. Choosing the most cost-effective one is not easy, but models such as those outlined in this paper can help.

Following a brief discussion of the cost-effectiveness of redundancy schemes, attention is then restricted to the analysis of rollback and recovery strategies. The different objectives and constraints of rollback and recovery strategies are discussed, using a data-based system and a process-control system as examples. Approaches to modeling the rollback-recovery process are presented, and the analysis of three specific models is reviewed.

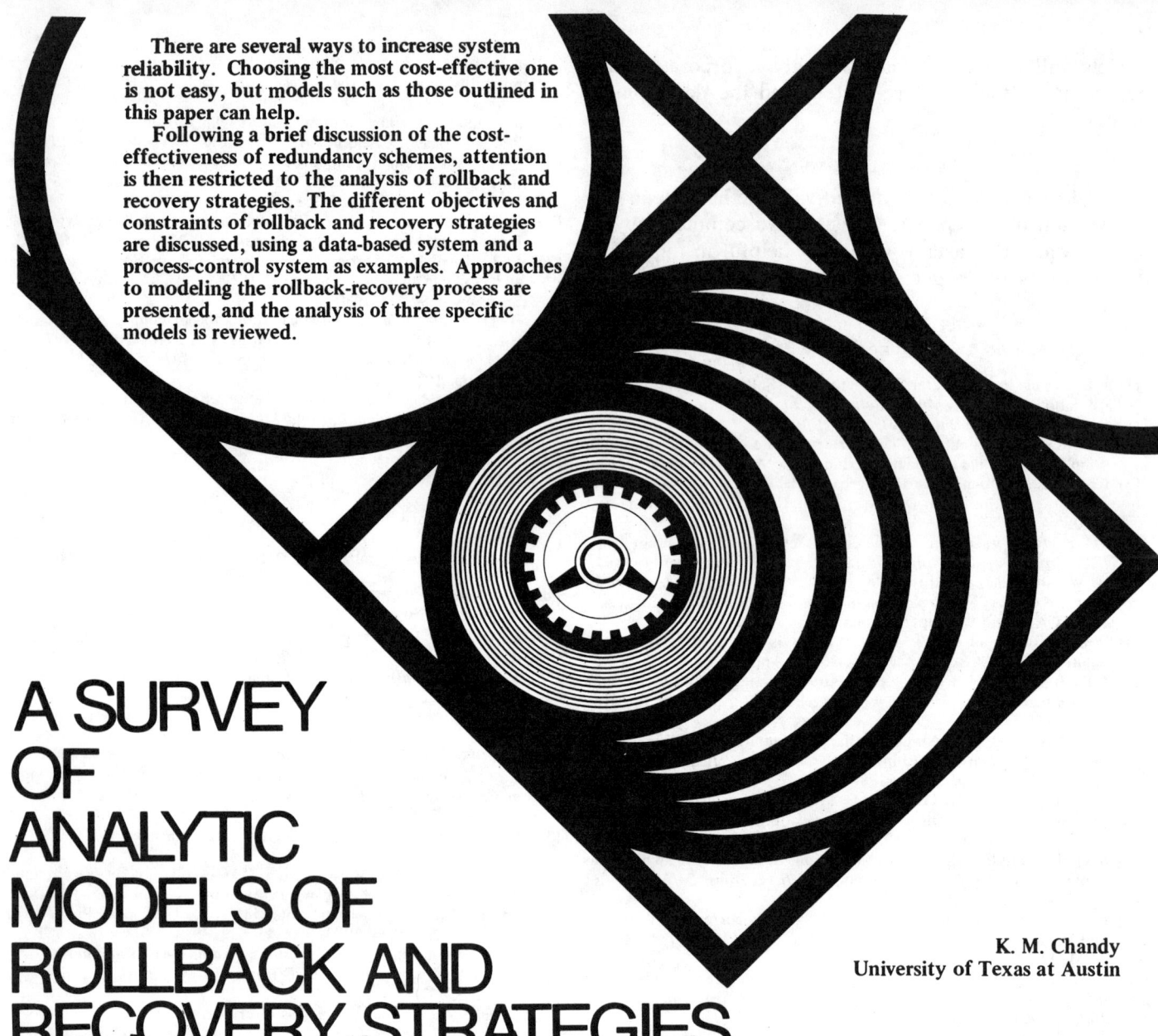

A SURVEY OF ANALYTIC MODELS OF ROLLBACK AND RECOVERY STRATEGIES

K. M. Chandy
University of Texas at Austin

Reprinted from *Computer*, Volume 8, Number 5, May 1975, pages 40-47.
Copyright © 1975 by The Institute of Electrical and Electronics Engineers, Inc.

Introduction

Systems of intrinsically unreliable components can be made more reliable by introducing redundancy into the system. This redundancy may be in hardware, or it may be in "time" (software)—or both.

For example, *triple modulo redundancy* (TMR) is one kind of hardware redundancy. In this scheme, a vote-taker determines the majority output of three identical independent systems. The majority output will be correct provided the vote-taker does not fail and at least two of the three independent systems have the correct output. The TMR system is more reliable than a nonredundant system, but the additional reliability is obtained at the expense of a great deal of additional hardware.

Instruction retry is a method of enhancing reliability by means of both time and hardware redundancy. If an error is detected soon after an instruction is executed, the instruction may be reexecuted. The second execution of the instruction may yield error-free results. Thus, the addition of the instruction-retry facility will allow the system to recover from some transient errors. However, the instruction retry facility requires additional hardware, and the instruction retry itself takes additional time.

Evaluating different redundancy schemes requires comparison of different kinds of "costs": hardware and time. The particular function being performed by the system is important in selecting a redundancy scheme. Hardware techniques are preferred in systems in which delays in performing functions result in large costs. For instance, a missile control system cannot use most time-redundancy schemes, since delays have catastrophic consequences.

The development of a framework for evaluating different redundancy strategies was attempted in Reference 1. In essence, that method compared the costs of (the consequences of) delays introduced by time-redundancy techniques with the costs of hardware in hardware-redundancy schemes. However, the problem of selecting the optimal mix of redundancy strategies for a system is very difficult. Even for a specific strategy, there are often several cost parameters which can be adjusted. This article considers the cost-effectiveness of a specific time-redundancy strategy—the rollback and recovery strategy. Some systems should not use rollback and recovery strategies, either because the overhead cost of checkpointing is not warranted or because the cost of delay incurred due to rollback and recovery strategies is too high.

Error Detection, Error Lifetime, and Error Propagation

Error detection may proceed continuously or intermittently. Parity checking is an example of continuous error detection since parity checking can be carried out all the time a system is available. Some systems have multiple copies of key files, all of which are updated continuously, but which are compared against each other only at specified intervals. This is an example of intermittent detection since an error may be detected only when the copies are compared against one another. An error which is not detected as soon as it occurs might propagate. For instance, if an erroneous data value is used to update an item, the updated item may also be in error. When an error is detected, it is not possible to predict precisely when the error occurred or the amount of error propagation. The lifetime of an error is the length of time between the occurrence of an error and its detection. Clearly, the error lifetime distribution depends upon the error detection schemes used. For instance, if multiple copies of key tables are compared at intervals of fixed duration T, then lifetimes for errors in these tables are less likely to exceed T. Since T is an adjustable parameter, it follows that error lifetimes are sometimes partially controllable. Error lifetime distributions are very hard to measure.

Error propagation is related to error lifetimes. If an error has a short lifetime, it is less likely to be used in updating other data items and is therefore less likely to propagate. Continuous error detection schemes, such as check-sum, operate on every item of data that is queried or used in updating. These schemes tend to limit error propagation. It is sometimes possible to partition a system into subsystems so that errors cannot propagate across subsystem boundaries. The ability to localize the extent of error has a beneficial impact on the rollback and recovery process. Data on error propagation and error lifetimes is not available in the literature, yet these factors have significant impact on the efficacy of most time-redundancy strategies. Assumptions regarding error propagation and lifetimes should be clearly noted.

Correctness, Security, and Reliability

All redundancy techniques for enhancing reliability assume that system programs are written correctly. Replicating incorrect programs will not improve reliability. Security is concerned with protecting a system from an *active* (presumably intelligent) external agent who seeks to defeat system objectives. Reliability means the ability of a system to overcome or recover from *random* errors. Clearly security and reliability are related, although this article restricts attention to reliability.

Rollback and Recovery Models

Rollback and recovery is a method of enhancing the reliability of systems. The objective function and constraints for rollback and recovery strategies may vary substantially from system to system. Two examples will be considered.

1. A data base system with a large number of users which processes a large number of transactions. The execution time for a transaction is small compared to the mean time between failures.
2. A process control system which repeatedly runs a single job or a small set of jobs. The execution time of a job may not be negligibly small compared to the mean time between failures.

The objective in data base systems is generally to maximize system availability, or the fraction of time that the system is up over a long period of time. An alternate objective may be to minimize average response time where response time includes possible wait for a system to recover from errors. There is no severe penalty associated with a single unusually long recovery: the focus is on average *long-term* behavior.

Process control systems are assumed to have high availability. However, if an error does occur, the system must recover very rapidly since a delay in performing vital system functions may have catastrophic results. *Every* recovery should be rapid. There may be an explicit constraint that a recovery should not exceed some given quantity, M time units, in durations. M will depend on the system, may vary from job to job in a given system, and may also depend upon the stage of processing in a given job. The objective is to minimize overhead associated with rollback and recovery. The process control system will be designed to have sufficient capacity to carry out all its tasks and also for overhead associated with rollback and recovery. Thus, the objectives and constraints of rollback and recovery may be different for data base and process control systems.

The checkpointing process may be static or dynamic. Static checkpointing requires carrying out checkpoints at the same time in every shift, day, week, etc., regardless of load. The times at which checkpoints are made will vary from one run of a job to the next, or from day to day, in a dynamic checkpointing environment. This variation will depend on load. It is easy to show that dynamic checkpoints yield better system availability than static checkpoints. However, in data base systems, users prefer predictable checkpoint times since they can learn to avoid using the system at those predetermined times. Thus, static checkpointing is appropriate for data base systems while dynamic checkpointing is more appropriate for process control systems.

In a single-job process control environment it is possible (and necessary) to analyze the job so as to determine the optimal location of checkpoints within the job. In a transaction-oriented data base system, it is not possible to analyze each transaction and determine optimal location of checkpoints within each transaction. Furthermore, it is not necessary to do so since transactions are of short duration.

There are many objectives, constraints, and control parameters even for a specific redundancy scheme. The most appropriate model for a specific system must be carefully selected. There are many systems which do not fall into the data base or process control categories, and they require models other than those described here. There is no single model which is applicable to all systems. Three models (A,B,C) on data base systems are considered next: Young[2] described model A and models B and C are described in Reference 3. Process control models are briefly reviewed later. It must be emphasized that this paper outlines only the modeling approach; the reader is directed to more detailed sources for more information.

Rollback and Recovery in Data Base Systems

In a transaction-oriented data base, a transaction might merely query the data base (without modifying it) or a transaction might change a value or data structure. The total processing time required per transaction is assumed to be small with respect to the mean time between failures.

In many systems a permanent record, generally required for auditing, is made of all transactions which modify the system. A chronological record of all transactions (or transactions which modify the data base), referred to as an *audit trail*, is required to support automated recovery and restart.

At certain points in time called *checkpoints*, a copy of the entire data base is made and stored on magnetic tape (or other archival storage). Special checks may be carried out to ensure that the copy is error-free. This process (checkpointing) may take a long time, possibly hours, if a large volume of data is involved. Note that checkpointing is carried out primarily for rollback and recovery, whereas the audit trail may be required for other reasons. Transactions are not allowed to access the data base during checkpointing; they are stored and processed later when checkpointing is complete.

When an error is detected, the following steps are taken:
1. Transactions are not allowed to query the data base. All incoming transactions are stored for future use.
2. The system fault causing the error is repaired if necessary.
3. The copy of the data base made at the most recent checkpoint is loaded onto the physical devices on which the data base is stored. This process of *loading* the data base may also require a substantial amount of time. After the loading is complete, the entire data or file system is exactly as it was immediately after the last checkpoint.
4. All transactions on the audit trail are reprocessed in chronological order; the system will have recovered when this reprocessing is complete. All transactions on the audit trail are notified of corrections in the data base, if necessary.
5. Incoming transactions which were stored during recovery are processed.

The recovery process will function only if the data base was error-free at the most recent checkpoint.

Costs of Rollback and Recovery

A significant amount of time is required for the checkpointing and recovery processes and for maintaining the audit trail. There are also hardware costs for storage of copies of the data base at different checkpoints, as well as unquantifiable costs deriving from the use of invalid data and from the efforts expended by the individual user processes in protecting their files against error and manually recreating them after detection of errors. Some level of automated reliability management is normally provided in all files and data base systems. The level of automated- or system-level support is usually determined informally on the basis of user complaints.

Hardware costs will be ignored, since once a decision to use rollback and recovery has been made, those costs are largely independent of key parameters in rollback and recovery. In analogy with inventory control theory, time costs are classified as *fixed* and *variable* costs. Fixed costs are independent of the number of errors detected. Variable costs are incurred only if an error is detected. The fixed cost is the time required to make a copy of the entire data base at each checkpoint. The variable cost is the time associated with recovery (i.e., with repair), loading the data base made at a checkpoint, and reprocessing the audit trail. The problem is to choose times for checkpointing which maximize system availability or which minimize costs associated with rollback and recovery.

The recovery time increases with the number of transactions to be reprocessed on the audit trail. Hence, the recovery time increases with the time between the most recent checkpoint and the detection of an error. The greater the intercheckpoint time, the larger will be the average time between a checkpoint and detection of an error. Thus, average recovery time increases with intercheckpoint time. If the intercheckpoint time is too small, too much time is spent in checkpointing, and if the intercheckpoint time is too large, too much time is spent in recovery. (See Figure 1.)

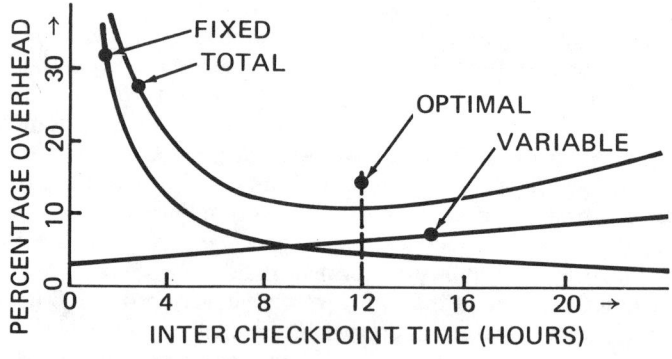

Figure 1. Overhead versus Intercheckpoint Time

Seven assumptions are made for Model A.
1. Fault detections occur at random times; thus, they occur in a (possibly time-varying) Poisson manner. This is a serious assumption. (See the subsection on error detection.)
2. The time required to reprocess the audit trail from a checkpoint is assumed to be directly proportional to the number of transactions recorded on the audit trail since that checkpoint. This is a reasonable assumption.
3. Transactions which arrive when the system is either checkpointing or recovering from an error are stored

until the checkpointing or recovery is complete. The time required to process stored transactions is assumed to be small compared to the mean time between failures.
4. System availability given optimal checkpointing strategies is assumed to be high.
5. No errors occur during recovery, i.e., during the loading of the data base at a checkpoint and during reprocessing of transactions on the audit trail. This assumption is reasonable if recovery time and checkpointing time are small compared to the mean time between failures. This assumption is not necessary for Model B.
6. The transaction arrival rate is constant at all times. This assumption is not necessary for Model C.
7. The checkpoint itself is always assumed to be correct.

These models make no assumptions regarding error propagation. However, this is tantamount to assuming the worst since the entire data base is corrected for a single error.

Definitions

Let F be the expected time required to perform a checkpoint—i.e., the expected time required to save a copy of the system. *Reestablishing* the checkpointed data base after an error is detected consists of repairing any system malfunctions and then loading a copy of the system saved at the most recent checkpoint. Let R be the expected time required to reestablish the checkpointed data base. *Recovering* from an error consists of first reestablishing the most recently checkpointed data base and then processing the audit trail from the checkpoint to the point of error detection. Let $h(t)$ be the expected recovery time, given that an error was detected t time units after the last checkpoint. Clearly, $h(t)$ will be a monotone non-decreasing function of t. Let T be the time between checkpoints. Let $V(T)$ be the total expected time spent in recovery between two successive checkpoints, given that the time between checkpoints is T. Clearly, $V(T)$ is monotone increasing with T. Let $O(T)$ be the total overhead time associated with checkpointing and recovery given the intercheckpoint time T.

$$O(T) = F + V(T)$$

Let $r(T)$ be the expected unit overhead given an intercheckpoint time T. Thus

$$r(T) = \frac{O(T)}{T}$$

It will be shown that $r(T)$ is a convex function for Model A. The availability of the system given intercheckpoint time T is

$$a(T) = 1 - r(T).$$

Let λ be the failure rate: λ is the reciprocal of the mean time between failures. Let t be the time since the initiation of the last checkpoint. Thus, the last checkpoint is initiated at $t = 0$ and the next checkpoint is at $t = T$. The time taken to reprocess the audit trail, given that an error is detected at time t, is proportional to t; let the constant of proportionality be k. We refer to k as the *compression factor*. Let the transaction arrival rate be μ transactions per unit time. Let the average transaction processing rate when the audit trail is being reprocessed be 'b' transactions per unit time. The expected number of transactions which arrive in t time units is μt, and hence the time required to reprocess these transactions is $\mu t/b$. Hence

$$k = \frac{\mu}{b}.$$

Let μ' be the arrival rate of transactions which modify the system. Assume that only transactions which modify the system are stored on the audit trail, and let b' be the corresponding reprocessing rate; in this case $k = \mu'/b'$. The fraction of all transactions which modify the data base is small. Furthermore, μ is generally much smaller than b. Hence, values of k of order 1/10 or less are to be expected. For Model A we have

$$h(t) = R + kt.$$

Figure 2 shows the expected load on the system as a function of time, where the load is the number of transactions processed per unit time. There is a surge of requests immediately after a checkpoint or recovery due to the backlog of transactions. This surge is assumed to be of short duration. Furthermore, checkpoints and recoveries are assumed to take a short time compared to the intercheckpoint time. Model A approximates the load on the system as in Figure 3 where checkpoints and recoveries are assumed to take instantaneous time, but with a cost F

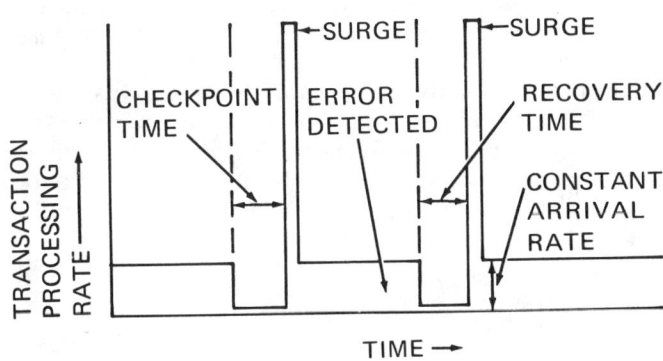

Figure 2. Load on the System

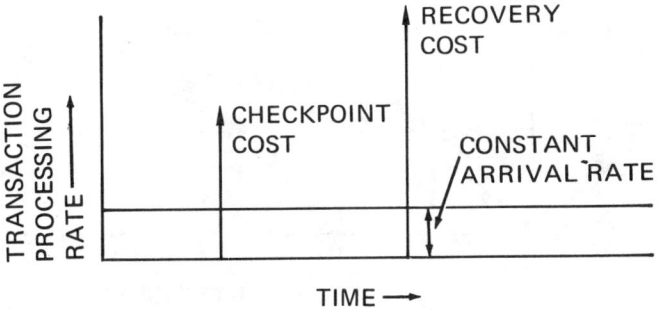

Figure 3. Approximate Load on the System

associated with each checkpoint and a cost h(t) associated with a recovery from an error detected t time units after a checkpoint. Clearly, this approximation is reasonable only if availability is very high.

Analysis of Model A

The expected number of errors detected in time T is λT. Given that an error is detected, the average time between the point of error detection and the most recent checkpoint is $T/2$. If an error is detected t time units after the most recent checkpoint the recovery time is $R + kt$. Hence, the average recovery time is $R + (kT/2)$ and the average total time spent in recovery between checkpoints is $\lambda T(R + kT/2)$. Hence, the total time spent in overhead (i.e., checkpointing and recovery) between two successive checkpoints is

$$O(T) = F + \lambda T(R + kT/2).$$

The overhead per unit time is

$$\rho(T) = \frac{O(T)}{T} = \frac{F}{T} + \lambda R + \frac{\lambda kT}{2}$$

$\rho(T)$ (see Figure 1) is a strictly convex function of T with a minimum at

$$T_{opt} = \sqrt{(2F)/(\lambda k)}.$$

Figure 1 shows curves of $\rho(T)$ as a function of T. The curve of unit overhead $\rho(T)$ as a function of intercheckpoint time T is relatively flat in the region of optimality. This suggests that small errors made in estimating system parameters, such as mean time between failures, compression factors, and checkpoint times, will not result in substantially increased overhead. This fact is important since it is generally very difficult to estimate system parameters precisely. For more on the sensitivity of system overhead to system parameters see Reference 3. See Figure 4 for the variation of T_{opt} with F. The possibility of errors during recovery is considered in Model B in Reference 3; however, Model B is not discussed here.

Model C

In this model it is assumed that the load on the system varies in a cyclic fashion. The load is measured in terms of number of transactions per unit time. The duration of a cycle is typically a day or a week. For instance, the load on a typical system may be light before 7 AM, rise to a peak at midmorning, then decrease with a lull during the lunch hour, rise again to a new peak in midafternoon, and then decrease to an insignificant load after 7 PM. Systems with time-invariant loads are the exception. Furthermore, loads generally vary in a cyclic fashion. The mean time between failures is generally not negligible compared to the cycle's duration. Therefore, models of rollback and recovery which do not consider variations in load are likely to result in poor strategies. Failure rates may increase with load. Neglecting significant variations in failure rates also results in poor strategies.

A checkpoint or recovery during peak load conditions will degrade service for a relatively large number of transactions. Checkpoints during light loads degrade service for much fewer transactions. The objective should be to minimize the number of transactions which receive degraded service rather than to maximize the long-term fraction of time that the system is capable of servicing transactions. If some transactions have high priority, then the objective might be to minimize a weighted-sum of different priority loads which encounter degraded service.

Assume that a cycle is of duration τ. Assume that the cycle is large enough so that there is at least one checkpoint during a cycle. Let $t=0$ denote the start of the cycle and $t=\tau$ the end. The cycle will be broken into M discrete intervals. Let there be M+1 times t_i, $i=0,\ldots,M$ so that $t_0=0$, and $t_M=\tau$, and $t_i < t_{i+1}$, all i. The load function (number of transactions which arrive per unit time) and the failure rate are assumed to be constant within each interval (t_i, t_{i+1}) (see Figure 5). Let $C(t_i, t_j)$ be the total cost incurred in the interval (t_i, t_j), given that there is a checkpoint at t_i and the next one is at t_j; the cost may be one of several possible metrics including number of transactions which encounter a

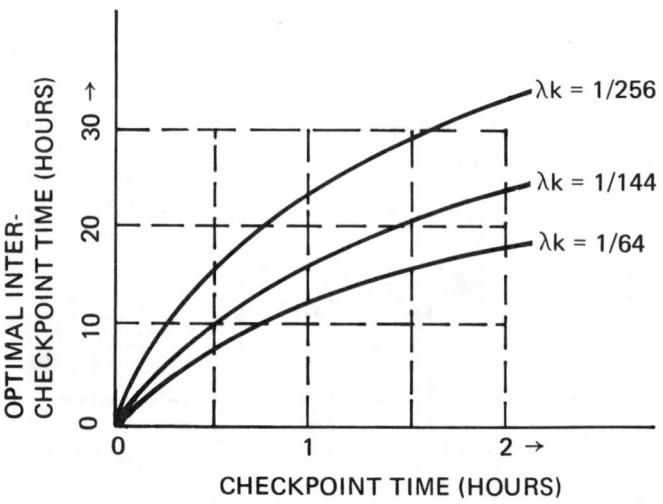

Figure 4. Optimal Intercheckpoint Time as a Function of Checkpoint Time

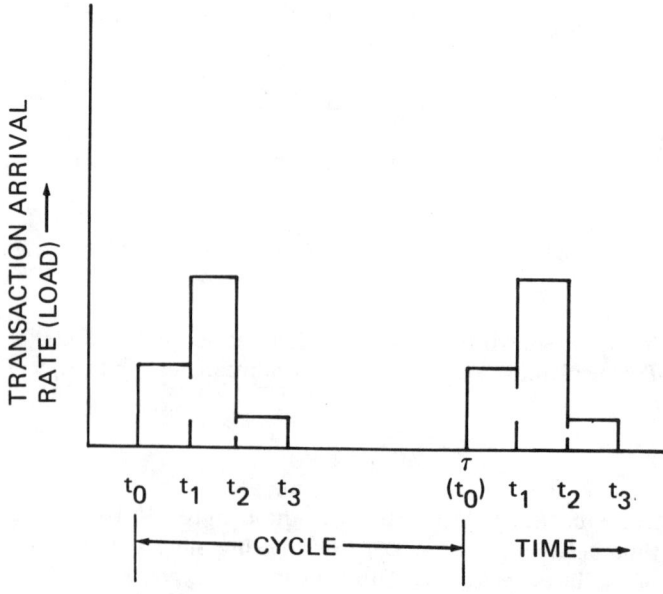

Figure 5. Cyclic Load

down system, or the average delay due to the rollback recovery process. (Formulae for computing costs are found in Reference 3.) If $t_j > t_i$ then (t_i, t_j) is the interval starting at t_i and ending at t_j and is of duration $t_j - t_i$. If $t_i \geqslant t_j$ then the interval (t_i, t_j) starts at t_i and completes at t_j on the *next* cycle; this interval is of duration $\tau - (t_i - t_j)$.

This problem will be solved by using the shortest route model. Consider a graph with vertices t_i, $i=1, \ldots, M-1$ (see Figure 6). Associated with each edge (t_i, t_j) is a cost $C(t_i, t_j)$, and a time $t_j - t_i$ if $t_j > t_i$ and $\tau - (t_i - t_j)$ if $t_j \leqslant t_i$. The problem is clearly to determine an endless path through this graph which minimizes the average cost per unit time. Since the number of vertices are finite, this endless path will consist of repetitions of a circuit: $t_i, t_j, t_k, \ldots, t_i, t_j, t_k, \ldots, t_i, t_j, t_k, \ldots$ It is obvious that to minimize the average cost per unit time, optimal checkpoints should occur at times $t_i, t_j, t_k, \ldots$ etc. The problem of determining endless paths through a graph to minimize average costs falls within the category of unbounded horizon problems (this is described lucidly in Reference 4).

A case study of a data base system is found in Reference 3. Model C is appropriate for many data base systems. However, it suffers from not having a simple closed form solution.

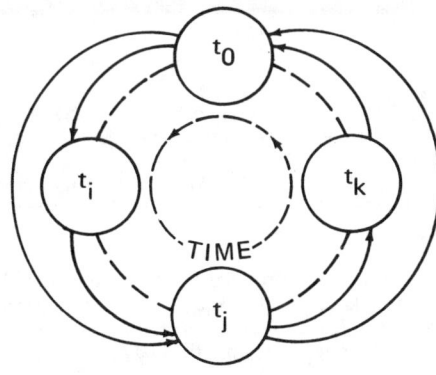

Figure 6. Graph for Time-Varying Load

Process Control Systems

The analysis of process control systems presented in Reference 5 will now be outlined. Each program (job) run by the system is partitioned into several tasks by a programmer. The programmer must construct a task graph which represents the program. Each vertex in the task graph represents a task in the program. All loops in the program are assumed to be "unraveled"; thus if a task is repeated, then each execution of the task is represented by a distinct vertex. Associated with each vertex i is the *maximum* execution time t_i for the corresponding task. The task graph contains edge (i,j) if and only if task i is followed by task j with non-zero probability. Associated with each edge (i,j) of the task graph are two real numbers F_{ij} and R_{ij} which are the checkpoint and reestablishment times soon after task i is processed, given that task j is to be processed next. At each edge (i,j) one may choose to insert, or not insert, a checkpoint. A checkpoint on edge (i,j) implies that after task i is processed, the system will be checkpointed if task j is to be processed next. Checkpoints must be inserted on edges of the task graph so that at every point in the program the maximum recovery time does not exceed M. Checkpoints are not permitted with partially completed tasks. The objective is to minimize the maximum or worst-case time that may be spent in checkpointing.

Note that the process of obtaining model parameters is very time consuming. The programmer must analyze a job, partition it into tasks, unravel loops, and estimate task execution times, checkpoint times, and reestablishment times. The programmer must first consider whether the formal optimal analysis is worthwhile.

Implementation

The recovery time (r) is interrogated after each task completion and used as a basis for making the decision on placing rollback points. r can be determined readily. Let D be the clock time at the end of the last checkpoint, L the time required to load the system at the last checkpoint, E=D−L, and "clock" the current clock time. Then r=clock−E.

Suppose that at some point in the program the task just completed and the task to be processed next are i and j, respectively. Let r be the recovery time at this point. The optimal decision is to insert a rollback point if $r > B_{ij}$ and not to insert a rollback point if $r \leqslant B_{ij}$ where B_{ij} is a constant. *The set of B_{ij} are computed before the program is run.* When task i is completed and if task j is to be processed next, r is compared with B_{ij} and a rollback point is inserted if $r > B_{ij}$. If a rollback point is inserted, then E is updated. Task j is then processed. (A block diagram is presented in Figure 7.) In general r will vary from one run of the program to the next since the time required to execute a task will depend on the input parameters. Hence, the insertion of rollback points will also vary from run to run of the program, since the decision to insert rollback points is based on the value of r.

Analysis

The analysis is outlined here; details are found in Reference 5. Let $g_{ij}(r)$ be a function of recovery time r, $0 \leqslant r \leqslant M$, where $g_{ij}(r)$ is the minimum time spent in checkpointing after task i has been processed and before the completion of the program, given that the next task to be processed after i is j and that the recovery time soon after task i is complete is r. Let $f_j(r)$ also be a function of recovery time r, $0 \leqslant r \leqslant M$, where $f_j(r)$ is the minimum time spent in checkpointing after task j is completed and before the completion of the program, given that the recovery time soon after task j is completed is r. The only difference between the g_{ij} and f_i functions is that the next task to be processed is given in the g function, whereas the next task is not specified in f. The breakpoints B_{ij} will be determined by relating the f and g functions.

Assume that $f_j(r)$ for all $0 \leqslant r \leqslant M$ have been computed. Let r_i be the recovery time after task i is completed. If a checkpoint is not inserted on edge (i,j), the recovery time after task j is completed may be $r_i + t_j$. In this case:

$$g_{ij}(r_i) = f_j(r_i + t_j)$$

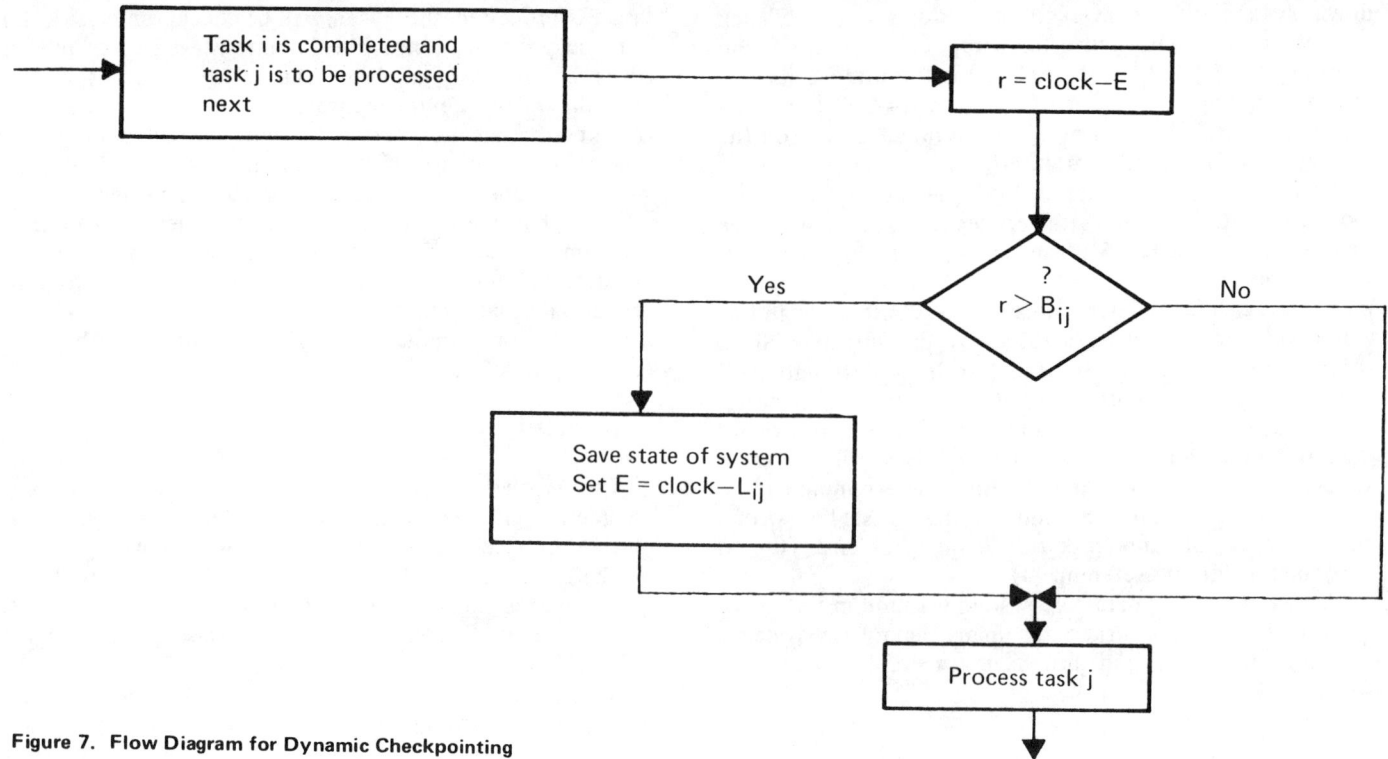

Figure 7. Flow Diagram for Dynamic Checkpointing

If a checkpoint is inserted on edge (i,j), the recovery time after task j is completed may be $R_{ij}+t_j$. Hence

$$g_{ij}(r_i) = f_j(R_{ij} + t_j)$$

If $r_i+t_j > M$, a checkpoint must be inserted on edge (i,j), since if it is not, the recovery time after task j completes may exceed M. Hence

$$g_{ij}(r) = F_{ij} + f_j(R_{ij} + r) \text{ if } r + t_j > M$$
$$= \min\left\{f_j(r + t_j), F_{ij} + f_j(R_{ij} + r)\right\} \text{ otherwise.}$$

It is obvious that B_{ij} is that value of r below which $g_{ij}(r) = f_j(r+t_j)$. It is also obvious that in the worst case

$$f_i(r) = \text{maximum over all edges (i,j) of } g_{ij}(r).$$

These two simple relations are used repeatedly to obtain all breakpoints B_{ij}. ∎

Acknowledgement

Supported in part by contract #F33600-74-C-0134 from the Air Force Logistics Command.

References

1. K. M. Chandy, C. V. Ramamoorthy, and A. E. Cowan, "A Framework for Hardware-Software Tradeoffs in the Design of Fault-Tolerant Computers," *Proc. FJCC,* AFIPS Press, New Jersey, 1972, Vol. 41, Part I, pp. 55-64.

2. J. W. Young, "A First Order Approximation to the Optimum Checkpoint Interval," *CACM,* Vol. 17, No. 9, September 1974, pp. 530-531.

3. K. M. Chandy, J. C. Browne, C. W. Dissly, and W. R. Uhrig, "Analytic Models for Rollback and Recovery Strategies in Data Base Systems," *IEEE Transactions on Software Engineering,* Vol. 1, No. 1, March 1975, pp. 100-110.

4. H. M. Wagner, *Principles of Operations Research,* Prentice-Hall, Englewood Cliffs, New Jersey, 1969.

5. K. M. Chandy and C. V. Ramamoorthy, "Rollback and Recovery Strategies," *IEEE-TC,* Vol. C-21, No. 2, February 1972, pp. 137-146.

K. Mani Chandy is an associate professor of computer sciences and electrical engineering at The University of Texas at Austin. His current research interests include modeling of computer systems, networks, and reliability. He was a consultant to the Computer Sciences Department at the IBM T. J. Watson Research Center. Formerly, he worked as a staff member at the IBM Cambridge Scientific Research Center, 1969-1970, and as an associate engineer at Honeywell EDP, 1966-1967. He received a B.Tech. in 1965 from the Indian Institute of Technology, Madras, and an MS in 1966 from the Polytechnic Institute of Brooklyn, both in electrical engineering. In 1969 he received a PhD in operations research from MIT. He is a member of ACM and IEEE.

System Structure for Software Fault Tolerance

BRIAN RANDELL

Abstract—This paper presents and discusses the rationale behind a method for structuring complex computing systems by the use of what we term "recovery blocks," "conversations," and "fault-tolerant interfaces." The aim is to facilitate the provision of dependable error detection and recovery facilities which can cope with errors caused by residual design inadequacies, particularly in the system software, rather than merely the occasional malfunctioning of hardware components.

Index Terms—Acceptance test, alternate block, checkpoint, conversation, error detection, error recovery, recovery block, recursive cache.

I. INTRODUCTION

THE CONCEPT of "fault-tolerant computing" has existed for a long time. The first book on the subject [10] was published no less than ten years ago, but the notion of fault tolerance has remained almost exclusively the preserve of the hardware designer. Hardware structures have been developed which can "tolerate" faults, i.e., continue to provide the required facilities despite occasional failures, either transient or permanent, of internal components and modules. However, hardware component failures are only one source of unreliability in computing systems, decreasing in significance as component reliability improves, while software faults have become increasingly prevalent with the steadily increasing size and complexity of software systems.

In general, fault-tolerant hardware designs are expected to be correct, i.e., the tolerance applies to component failures rather than design inadequacies, although the dividing line between the two may on occasion be difficult to define. But all software faults result from design errors. The relative frequency of such errors reflects the much greater logical complexity of the typical software design compared to that of a typical hardware design. The difference in complexity arises from the fact that the "machines" that hardware designers produce have a relatively small number of distinctive internal states, whereas the designer of even a small software system has, by comparison, an enormous number of different states to consider—thus one can usually afford to treat hardware designs as being "correct," but often cannot do the same with software even after extensive validation efforts. (The difference in scale is evidenced by the fact that a software simulator of a computer, written at the level of detail required by the hardware designers to analyze and validate

Manuscript received February 1, 1975.
The author is with the Computing Laboratory, University of Newcastle upon Tyne, Newcastle upon Tyne, England.

their logical design, is usually one or more orders of magnitude smaller than the operating system supplied with that computer.)

If all design inadequacies could be avoided or removed this would suffice to achieve software reliability. (We here use the term "design" to include "implementation," which is actually merely low-level design, concerning itself with detailed design decisions whose correctness nevertheless can be as vital to the correct functioning of the software as that of any high-level design decision.) Indeed many writers equate the terms "software reliability" and "program correctness." However, until *reliable* correctness proofs (relative to some correct and adequately detailed specification), which cover even implementation details, can be given for systems of a realistic size, the only alternative means of increasing software reliability is to incorporate provisions for software fault tolerance.

In fact there exist sophisticated computing systems, designed for environments requiring near-continuous service, which contain ad hoc checks and checkpointing facilities that provide a measure of tolerance against some software errors as well as hardware failures [11]. They incidentally demonstrate the fact that fault tolerance does not necessarily require diagnosing the cause of the fault, or even deciding whether it arises from the hardware or the software. However there has been comparatively little specific research into techniques for achieving software fault tolerance, and the constraints they impose on computing system design.

It was considerations such as these that led to the establishment at the University of Newcastle upon Tyne of a project on the design of highly reliable computing systems, under the sponsorship of the Science Research Council of the United Kingdom. The aims of the project were and are "to develop, and give a realistic demonstration of the utility of, computer architecture and programming techniques which will enable a system to have a very high probability of continuing to give a trustworthy service in the presence of hardware faults and/or software errors, and during their repair. A major aim will be to develop techniques which are of general utility, rather than limited to specialised environments, and to explore possible tradeoffs between reliability and performance."

A modest number of reports and papers have emanated from the project to date, including a general overview [12], papers concerned with addressing and protection [6], [7], and a preliminary account of our work on error detection and recovery [5]. The present paper endeavors to provide a rather more extensive discussion of our work on system error recovery techniques, and concentrates on techniques for system structuring which facilitate software fault tolerance. A companion paper [1] presents a proof-guided methodology for designing the error detection routines that our method requires.

II. FAULT TOLERANCE IN SOFTWARE

All fault tolerance must be based on the provision of useful redundancy, both for error detection and error recovery. In software the redundancy required is not simple replication of programs but redundancy of design.

The scheme for facilitating software fault tolerance that we have developed can be regarded as analogous to what hardware designers term "stand-by sparing." As the system operates, checks are made on the acceptability of the results generated by each component. Should one of these checks fail, a spare component is switched in to take the place of the erroneous component. The spare component is, of course, not merely a copy of the main component. Rather it is of independent design, so that there can be hope that it can cope with the circumstances that caused the main component to fail. (These circumstances will comprise the data the component is provided with and, in the case of errors due to faulty process synchronization, the timing and form of its interactions with other processes.)

In contrast to the normal hardware stand-by sparing scheme, the spare software component is invoked to cope with merely the particular set of circumstances that resulted in the failure of the main component. We assume the failure of this component to be due to *residual* design inadequacies, and hence that such failures occur only in exceptional circumstances. The number of different sets of circumstances that can arise even with a software component of comparatively modest size is immense. Therefore the system can revert to the use of the main component for subsequent operations—in hardware this would not normally be done until the main component had been repaired.

The variety of undetected errors which could have been made in the design of a nontrivial software component is essentially infinite. Due to the complexity of the component, the relationship between any such error and its effect at run time may be very obscure. For these reasons we believe that diagnosis of the original cause of software errors should be left to humans to do, and should be done in comparative leisure. Therefore our scheme for software fault tolerance in no way depends on automated diagnosis of the cause of the error—this would surely result only in greatly increasing the complexity and therefore the error proneness of the system.

The recovery block scheme for achieving software fault tolerance by means of stand-by sparing has two important characteristics.

1) It incorporates a general solution to the problem of switching to the use of the spare component, i.e., of repairing any damage done by the erroneous main component, and of transferring control to the appropriate spare component.

2) It provides a method of explicitly structuring the software system which has the effect of ensuring that the extra software involved in error detection and in the spare components does not add to the complexity of the system, and so reduce rather than increase overall system reliability.

III. RECOVERY BLOCKS

Although the basic recovery block scheme has already been described elsewhere [5], it is convenient to include a brief account of it here. We will then describe several extensions to the scheme directed at more complicated situations than the basic scheme was intended for. Thus we start by considering the problems of fault tolerance, i.e., of error detection and recovery, within a single-sequential process in which assignments to stored variables provide the only means of making recognizable progress. Considerations of the problems of communication with other processes, either within the computing system (e.g., by a system of passing messages, or the use of shared storage) or beyond the computing system (e.g., by explicit input–output statements) is deferred until a later section.

The progress of a program is by its execution of sequences of the basic operations of the computer. Clearly, error checking for each basic operation is out of the question. Apart from questions of expense, absence of an awareness of the wider scene would make it difficult to formulate the checks. We must aim at achieving a tolerable quantity of checking and exploit our knowledge of the functional structure of the system to distribute these checks to best advantage. It is standard practice to structure the text of a program of any significant complexity into a set of blocks (by which term we include module, procedure, subroutine, paragraph, etc.) in order to simplify the task of understanding and documenting the program. Such a structure allows one to provide a functional description of the purpose of the program text constituting a block. (This text may of course include calls on subsidiary blocks.) The functional description can then be used elsewhere in place of the detailed design of the block. Indeed, the structuring of the program into blocks, and the specification of the purpose of each block, is likely to precede the detailed design of each block, particularly if the programming is being performed by more than one person.

When executed on a computer, a program which is structured into blocks evokes a process which can be regarded as being structured into operations. Operations are seen to consist of sequences of smaller operations, the smallest operations being those provided by the computer itself. Our scheme of system structuring is based on the selection of a set of these operations to act as units of error detection and recovery, by providing extra information with their corresponding blocks, and so turning the blocks into *recovery blocks*.

The scheme is not dependent on the particular form of block structuring that is used, or the rules governing the scopes of variables, methods of parameter passing, etc. All that is required is that when the program is executed the acts of entering and leaving each operation are explicit, and that operations are properly nested in time. (In addition, although it is not required, considerable advantage can be taken of information which is provided indicating whether any given variable is local to a particular operation.) However, for convenience of presentation, we will assume that the program text is itself represented by a nested structure of Algol or PL/I-style blocks.

A recovery block consists of a conventional block which is provided with a means of error detection (an acceptance test) and zero or more stand-by spares (the additional alternates). A possible syntax for recovery blocks is as follows:

⟨recovery block⟩ ::= **ensure** ⟨acceptance test⟩ **by**

⟨primary alternate⟩

⟨other alternates⟩ **else error**

⟨primary alternate⟩ ::= ⟨alternate⟩

⟨other alternates⟩ ::= ⟨empty⟩ | ⟨other alternates⟩

else by ⟨alternate⟩

⟨alternate⟩ ::= ⟨statement list⟩

⟨acceptance test⟩ ::= ⟨logical expression⟩

The *primary alternate* corresponds exactly to the block of the equivalent conventional program, and is entered to perform the desired operation. The *acceptance test*, which is a logical expression without side effects, is evaluated on exit from any alternate to determine whether the alternate has performed acceptably. A further *alternate*, if one exists, is entered if the preceding alternate fails to complete (e.g., because it attempts to divide by zero, or exceeds a time limit), or fails the acceptance test. However *before an alternate is so entered, the state of the process is restored* to that current just before entry to the primary alternate. If the acceptance test is passed, any further alternates are ignored, and the statement following the recovery block is the next to be executed. However, if the last alternate fails to pass the acceptance test, then the entire recovery block is regarded as having failed, so that the block in which it is embedded fails to complete and recovery is then attempted at that level.

In the illustration of a recovery block structure in Fig. 1, double vertical lines define the extents of recovery blocks, while single vertical lines define the extents of alternate blocks, primary or otherwise. Fig. 2 shows that

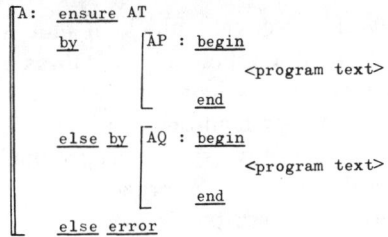

Fig. 1. Simple recovery block.

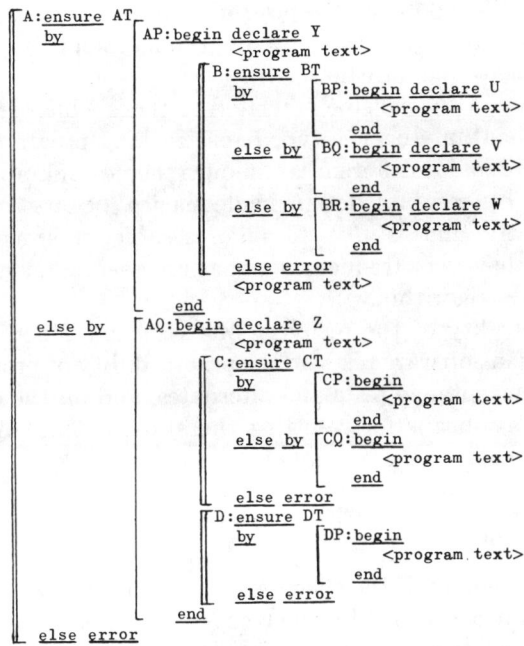

Fig. 2. More complex recovery block.

the alternate blocks can contain, nested within themselves, further recovery blocks.

Consider the recovery block structure shown in Fig. 2. The acceptance test BT will be invoked on completion of primary alternate BP. If the test succeeds, the recovery block B is left and the program text immediately following is reached. Otherwise the state of the system is reset and alternate BQ is entered. If BQ and then BR do not succeed in passing the acceptance test the recovery block B as a whole, and therefore primary alternate AP, are regarded as having failed. Therefore the state of the system is reset even further, to that current just before entry to AP, and alternate AQ is attempted.

Deferring for the moment questions as to how the state of the system is reset when necessary, the recovery block structure can be seen as providing a very general framework for the use of stand-by sparing which is in full accordance with the characteristics discussed earlier, in Section II. There is no need for, indeed no possibility of, attempts at automated error diagnosis because of the fact that the system state is reset after an error, deleting all effects of the faulty alternate. Once the system state is reset, switching to the use of an alternate is merely a matter of a simple transfer of control.

The concept of a recovery block in fact has much in common with that of a sphere of control, as described by Davies [2]. However, we have limited ourselves to preplanned error recovery facilities, and base all error recovery on automatic reversal to a previously reached recovery point. Thus, once a process has "committed" itself by accepting the results of a recovery block, the only form of recovery we envisage involves a more global process reversal, to the beginning of a recovery block whose results have not yet been accepted. In contrast, Davies is prepared to allow for the possibility of recovery following commitment, by means of programmer-supplied "error compensation algorithms."

Although the scheme is related to those which are used in artificial intelligence-type back-tracking programs [4], there are major differences—in our scheme back up, being caused by residual design inadequacies, occurs very infrequently and is due to unforeseeable circumstances, rather than very frequently and as an essential element of the basic algorithm.

The utility of the recovery block scheme for stand-by sparing in software rests on the practicability of producing useful acceptance tests and alternates, and on the cost of providing means for resetting the system state. We will discuss each of these points in turn.

```
ensure sorted (S) ∧ (sum(S) = sum(prior S))
  by quickersort (S)
  else by quicksort (S)
  else by buddlesort (S)
  else error
```

Fig. 3. Fault-tolerant sort program.

A. Acceptance Tests

The function of the acceptance test is to ensure that the operation performed by the recovery block is to the satisfaction of the program which invoked the block. The acceptance test is therefore performed by reference to the variables accessible to that program, rather than variables local to the recovery block, since these can have no effect or significance after exit from the block. Indeed the different alternates will probably have different sets of local variables. There is no question of there being separate acceptance tests for the different alternates. The surrounding program may be capable of continuing with any of a number of possible results of the operation, and the acceptance test must establish that the results are within this range of acceptability, without regard for which alternate can generate them.

There is no requirement that the test be, in any formal sense, a check on the absolute "correctness" of the operation performed by the recovery block. Rather it is for the designer to decide upon the appropriate level of rigor of the test. Ideally the test will ensure that the recovery block has met all aspects of its specification that are depended on by the program text that calls it—in practice, if only for reasons of cost and/or complexity, something less than this might have to suffice. (A methodological approach to the design of appropriate acceptance tests is described by Anderson [1].)

Although when an acceptance test is failed all the evidence is hidden from the alternate which is then called, a detailed log is kept of such incidents, for off-line analysis. Some failures to pass the acceptance test may be spurious because a design inadequacy in the acceptance test itself has caused an unnecessary rejection of the operation of an alternate. In fact the execution of the program of the acceptance test itself might suffer an error and fail to complete. Such occurrences, which hopefully will be rare since the aim is to have acceptance tests which are much simpler than the alternates they check, are treated as failures in the enclosing block. Like all other failures they are also recorded in the error log. Thus the log provides a means of finding these two forms of inadequacy in the design of the acceptance test—the remaining form of inadequacy, that which causes the acceptance of an incorrect set of results, is of course more difficult to locate.

When an acceptance test is being evaluated, any non-local variables that have been modified must be available in their original as well as their modified form because of the possible need to reset the system state. For convenience and increased rigor, the acceptance test is enabled to access such variables either for their modified value or for their original (prior) value. One further facility available inside an acceptance test will be a means of checking whether any of the variables that have been modified have not yet been accessed within the acceptance test—this is intended to assist in detecting sins of commission, as well as omission, on the part of the alternate.

Fig. 3 shows a recovery block whose intent is to sort the elements of the vector S. The acceptance test incorporates a check that the set of items in S after operation of an alternate are indeed in order. However, rather than incur the cost of checking that these elements are a permutation of the original items, it merely requires the sum of the elements to remain the same.

B. Alternates

The primary alternate is the one which is intended to be used normally to perform the desired operation. Other alternates might attempt to perform the desired operation in some different manner, presumably less economically, and preferably more simply. Thus as long as one of these alternates succeeds the desired operation will have been completed, and only the error log will reveal any troubles that occurred.

However in many cases one might have an alternate which performs a less desirable operation, but one which is still acceptable to the enclosing block in that it will allow the block to continue properly. (One plentiful source of both these kinds of alternates might be earlier releases of the primary alternate!)

Fig. 4 shows a recovery block consisting of a variety of alternates. (This figure is taken from Anderson [1].) The aim of the recovery block is to extend the sequence S of items by a further item i, but the enclosing program will

```
ensure consistent sequence (S)
by      extend S with (i)
else by concatenate to S (construct sequence (i))
else by warning ("lost item")
else by S:= construct sequence (i); warning
              (correction, lost sequence")
else by S:= empty sequence; warning ("lost
              sequence and item")
else error
```

Fig. 4. Recovery block with alternates which achieve different, but still acceptable though less desirable, results.

be able to continue even if afterwards S is merely "consistent." The first two alternates actually try, by different methods, to join the item i onto the sequence S. The other alternates make increasingly desperate attempts to produce at least some sort of consistent sequence, providing appropriate warnings as they do so.

C. Restoring the System State

By making the resetting of the system state completely automatic, the programmers responsible for designing acceptance tests and alternates are shielded from the problems of this aspect of error recovery. No special restrictions are placed on the operations which are performed within the alternates, on the calling of procedures or the modification of global variables, and no special programming conventions have to be adhered to. In particular the error-prone task of explicit preservation of restart information is avoided. It is thus that the recovery block structure provides a framework which enables extra program text to be added to a conventional program, for purposes of specifying error detection and recovery actions, with good reason to believe that despite the increase in the total size of the program its overall reliability will be increased.

All this depends on being able to find a method of automating the resetting of the system state whose overheads are tolerable. Clearly, taking a copy of the entire system state on entry to each recovery block, though in theory satisfactory, would in normal practice be far too inefficient. Any method involving the saving of sufficient information during program execution for the program to be executable in reverse, instruction by instruction, would be similarly impractical.

Whenever a process has to be backed up, it is to the state it had reached just before entry to the primary alternate—therefore the only values that have to be reset are those of nonlocal variables that have been modified. Since no explicit restart information is given, it is not known beforehand which nonlocal variables should be saved. Therefore we have designed various versions of a mechanism which arranges that nonlocal variables are saved in what we term a "recursive cache" as and when it is found that this is necessary, i.e., just before they are modified. The mechanisms do this by detecting, at run time, assignments to nonlocal variables, and in particular by recognizing when an assignment to a nonlocal variable is the first to have been made to that variable within the current alternate. Thus precisely sufficient information can be preserved.

The recursive cache is divided into regions, one for each nested recovery level, i.e., for each recovery block that has been entered and not yet left. The entries in the current cache region will contain the prior values of any variables that have been modified within the current recovery block, and thus in case of failure it can be used to back up the process to its most recent recovery point. The region will be discarded in its entirety after it has been used for backing up a process. However if the recovery block is completed successfully, some cache entries will be discarded, but those that relate to variables which are nonlocal to the enclosing environment will be consolidated with those in the underlying region of the cache.

A full description of one version of the mechanism has already been published [5], so we will not repeat this description here. We envisage that the mechanism would be at least partly built in hardware, at any rate if, as we have assumed here, recovery blocks are to be provided within ordinary programs working on small data items such as scalar variables. If however one were programming solely in terms of operations on large blocks of data, such as entire arrays or files, the overheads caused by a mechanism built completely from software would probably be supportable. Indeed the recursive cache scheme, which is essentially a means for secretly preventing what is sometimes termed "update in place," can be viewed as a generalization of the facility in CAP's "middleware" scheme [11] for preventing individual application programs from destructively updating files.

The various recursive cache mechanisms can all work in terms of the basic unit of assignment of the computer, e.g., a 32-bit word. Thus they ensure that just those scalar variables and array elements which are actually modified are saved. It would of course be possible to structure a program so that all its variables are declared in the outermost block, and within each recovery block each variable is modified, and so require that a maximum amount of information be saved. In practice we believe that even a moderately well-structured program will require comparatively little space for saved variables. Measurements of space requirements will be made on the prototype system now being implemented, but already we have some evidence for this from some simple experiments carried out by interpretively executing a number of Algol W programs. Even regarding each Algol block as a recovery block it was found that the amount of extra space that would be needed for saved scalar variables and array elements was in every case considerably smaller at all times than that needed for the ordinary data of the program.

The performance overheads of the different recursive cache mechanisms are in the process of being evaluated. Within a recovery block only the speed of store instructions is affected, and once a particular nonlocal variable has been saved subsequent stores to that variable take place essentially at full speed. The overheads involved in entering and leaving recovery blocks differ somewhat between the various mechanisms, but two mechanisms incur overheads which depend just linearly on the number of different nonlocal variables which are modified. It is our assessment that these overheads will also be quite modest. Certainly it would appear that the space and time overheads incurred by our mechanisms will be far smaller than would be incurred by any explicitly programmed scheme for saving and restoring the process state.

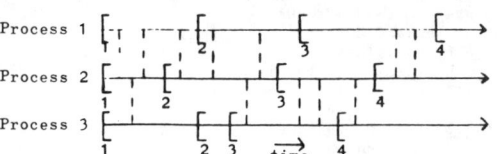

Fig. 5. Domino effect.

IV. ERROR RECOVERY AMONGST INTERACTING PROCESSES

In the mechanism described so far, the only notion of forward progress is that of assignment to a variable. In order to reset the state of a process after the failure of an acceptance test, it was necessary only to undo assignments to nonlocal variables. In practice, however, there are many other ways of making forward progress during computations, e.g., positioning a disk arm or magnetic tape, reading a card, printing a line, receiving a message, or obtaining real-time data from external sensors. These actions are difficult or even impossible to undo. However, their effects must be undone in order not to compromise the inherent "recoverability" of state provided by the recursive cache mechanisms.

Our attempt to cope with this kind of problem is based on the observation that all such forms of progress involve interaction among processes. In some cases, one or more of these processes may be mechanical, human, or otherwise external, e.g., the process representing the motion of the card-reading machinery. In other cases, the progress can be encapsulated in separate but interacting computational processes, each of which is structured by recovery blocks. In this section, we will explore the effect of this latter type of interaction on the backtracking scheme, still restricting each process to simple assignment as the only method of progress. Then in Section V we will explore the more general problem.

Consider first the case of two or more interacting processes which have the requirement that if one attempts to recover from an error, then the others must also take recovery action, "to keep in step."

For example, if one process fails after having received, and destroyed, information from another process, it will require the other process to resupply this information. Similarly, a process may have received and acted upon information subsequently discovered to have been sent to it in error and so must abandon its present activity.

Maintaining, naturally, our insistence on the dangers of attempted programmed error diagnosis, we must continue to rely on automatic backing up of processes to the special recovery points provided by recovery block entries. Each process while executing will at any moment have a sequence of recovery points available to it, the number of recovery points being given by the level of dynamic nesting of recovery blocks.

An isolated process could "use up" recovery points just one at a time by suffering a whole series of ever more serious errors. However given an arbitrary set of interacting processes, each with its own private recovery structure, a single error on the part of just one process could cause *all* the processes to use up many or even all of their recovery points, through a sort of uncontrolled domino effect.

The problem is illustrated in Fig. 5, which shows three processes, each of which has entered four recovery blocks that it has not yet left. The dotted lines indicate interactions between processes (i.e., an information flow resulting in an assignment in at least one process). Should Process 1 now fail, it will be backed up to its latest, i.e., its fourth recovery point, but the other processes will not be affected. If Process 2 fails, it will be backed up to its fourth recovery point past an interaction with Process 1, which must therefore also be backed up to the recovery point immediately prior to this interaction, i.e., its third recovery point. However if Process 3 fails, all the processes will have to be backed up right to their starting points!

The domino effect can occur when two particular circumstances exist in combination.

1) The recovery block structures of the various processes are uncoordinated, and take no account of process interdependencies caused by their interactions.

2) The processes are symmetrical with respect to failure propagation—either member of any pair of interacting processes can cause the other to back up.

By removing either of these circumstances, one can avoid the danger of the domino effect. Our technique of structuring process interactions into "conversations," which we describe next, is a means of dealing with point 1) above; the concept of multilevel processes, described in Section V of this paper, will be seen to be based on avoiding symmetry of failure propagation.

A. Process Conversations

If we are to provide guaranteed recoverability of a set of processes which by interacting have become mutually dependent on each other's progress, we must arrange that the processes cooperate in the provision of recovery points, as well as in the interchange of ordinary information. To extend the basic recovery block scheme to a set of interacting processes, we have to provide a means for coordinating the recovery block structures of the various processes, in effect to provide a recovery structure which is common to the set of processes. This structure we term a *conversation*.

Conversations, like recovery blocks, can be thought of as providing firewalls (in both time and space) which serve to limit the damage caused to a system by errors.

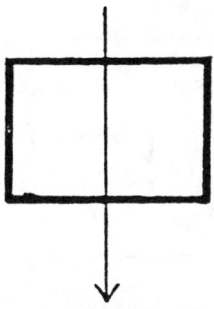

Fig. 6. Recovery block in a single-sequential process.

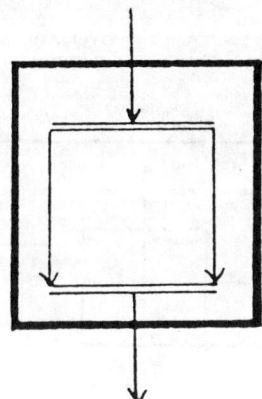

Fig. 7. Parallel processes within a recovery block.

Fig. 6 represents this view of a recovery block as providing a firewall for a single process. The downward pointing arrow represents the overall progress of the process. The top edge of the recovery block represents the environment of the process on entry, which is preserved automatically and can be restored for the use of an alternate block. The bottom edge represents the acceptable state of the process on exit from the recovery block, as checked by the acceptance test, and beyond which it is assumed that errors internal to the recovery block should not propagate. (Of course the strength of this firewall is only as good as the rigour of the acceptance test.) The sides show that the process is isolated from other activities, i.e., that the process is not subject to external influences which cannot be recreated automatically for an alternate, and that it does not generate any results which cannot be suppressed should the acceptance test be failed. (These side firewalls are provided by some perhaps quite conventional protection mechanism, to complement the top and bottom firewalls provided by the recursive cache mechanism and acceptance test.)

The manner in which the processing is performed within the recovery block is of no concern outside it, provided that the acceptance test is satisfied. For instance, as shown in Fig. 7, the process may divide into several parallel processes within the recovery block. The recursive cache mechanisms that we have developed permit this, and place no constraints on the manner in which this parallel-

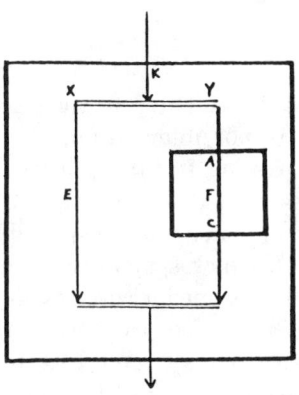

Fig. 8. Parallel processes within a recovery block, with a further recovery block for one of the processes. Interaction between the processes at points E and F must now be prohibited.

ism is expressed, or on the means of communication between these parallel processes.

Any of the parallel processes could of course enter a further recovery block, as shown in Fig. 8. However, by doing so it must lose the ability to communicate with other processes for the duration of its recovery block. To see this, consider the consequences of an interaction between the processes at points E and F. Should process Y now fail its acceptance test it would resume at point A with an alternate block. But there is no way of causing process X to repeat the interaction at E without backing

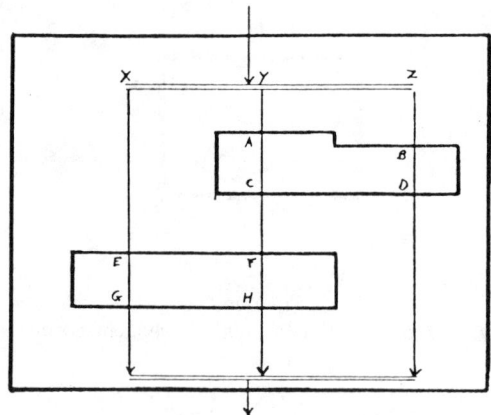

Fig. 9. Parallel processes with conversations which provide recovery blocks for local communication.

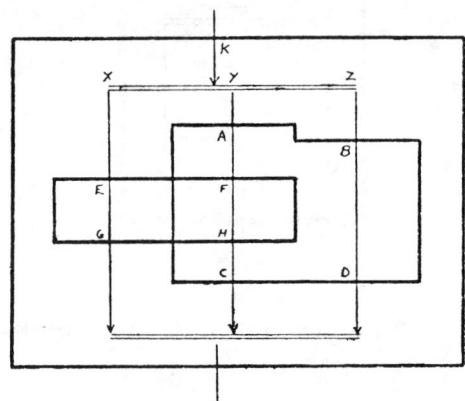

Fig. 10. Example of invalid conversations which are not strictly nested.

up both processes to the entry to their common recovery block at *K*. Thus communication, whether it involve explicit message passing facilities, or merely reference to common variables, would destroy the value of the inner recovery block, and hence must be prohibited.

A recovery block which spans two or more processes as is shown in Fig. 9 is termed a conversation. Two or more processes which already possess the means of communicating with each other may agree to enter into a conversation. Within the conversation these processes may communicate freely between themselves, but may not communicate with any other processes. At the end of the conversation *all the processes must satisfy their respective acceptance tests and none may proceed until all have done so.* Should any process fail, all the processes must automatically be backed up to the start of the conversation to attempt their alternates.

As is shown in Fig. 9, it is possible that the processes enter a conversation at differing times. However all processes must leave the conversation together, since no process dare discard its recovery point until all processes have satisfied their respective acceptance tests. In entering a conversation a process does not gain the ability to communicate with any process with which it was previously unable to communicate—rather, entry to a conversation serves only to restrict communication, in the interests of error recovery.

As with recovery blocks, conversations can of course occur within other conversations, so as to provide additional possibilities for error detection and recovery. However conversations which intersect and are not strictly nested cannot be allowed. Thus structures such as that shown in Fig. 10 must be prohibited, as can be demonstrated by an argument similar to that given in relation to Fig. 8.

V. MULTILEVEL SYSTEMS

We turn now to a method of structuring systems which uses assymetrical failure propagation in order to avoid the uncontrolled domino effect described in Section IV. In so doing we extend the scope of our discussions to cover more complex means of making recognizable progress than simple assignments. Moreover, we also face for the first time the possibility of reliability problems arising from facilities used to provide the means of constructing and executing processes and of using recovery blocks and conversations. The method of structuring which permits these extensions of our facilities for fault tolerance involves the use of what we (and others) term multilevel systems.

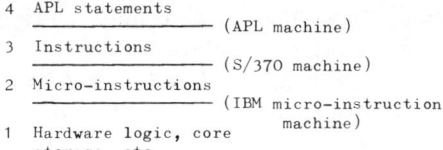

Fig. 11. Fully interpretive multilevel system.

```
8  User Program
7  Access Methods
6  Logical File System
5  Basic File System
4  File Organisation
   Strategy Modules
3  Device Strategy Modules
2  Input/Output Control
   System
1  Central Processor,
   Peripheral Devices, etc.
```

Fig. 12. Multilevel file system interpretive only at level 1 (see Madnick and Alsop [8]).

A multilevel system is characterized by the existence of a sequence of defined "abstract" or "virtual" machines which denote the internal interfaces between the various levels. A given virtual machine provides a set of apparently atomic facilities (operations, objects, resources, etc.). These can be used to construct the set of facilities that constitute a further (higher) virtual machine interface, possibly of a very different appearance. Each virtual machine is therefore an abstraction of the virtual machine below it. Since we are concerning ourselves with computer systems, we in general expect each virtual machine to have the characteristics of a programmable computer. Thus it is capable of executing a program that specifies which operations are to be applied to which operands, and their sequencing.

Our use of the term virtual machine is quite general. In particular our concept of multilevel systems includes systems whose levels are entirely different from each other (as in Fig. 11) as well as systems whose levels have much in common with each other (as in Fig. 12), for example being constructed by applying a protection scheme on a single computer. However, in each case the operations that a given virtual machine provides can be regarded as atomic at the level above it and as implemented by the activity of the level immediately below the virtual machine interface. Thus from the viewpoint of level i of the system in Fig. 12, the whole of the file accessing operation is performed by level 7. Indeed even the operation of addition, and the whole process of instruction fetching and decoding, can be regarded as being provided by level 7. This is the case no matter which actual level below level 7 is in fact responsible for the construction of these facilities out of more basic ones.

Some virtual machine interfaces allow the facilities they provide to be used without much, or even any, knowledge of the underlying structures used to construct these facilities. Virtual machine interfaces which have this characteristic can be termed *opaque* interfaces. Such virtual machine interfaces are total (in the sense that a mathematical function which is defined for all possible arguments is total) and have associated documentation which completely defines the interface. Being total and completely documented are necessary rather than sufficient conditions for a virtual machine interface to be usefully opaque, a characteristic which only well-chosen ones possess in any great measure, but this is a subject which we will not pursue further here.

Opaque virtual machine interfaces facilitate the understanding of existing complex systems, and the design of new ones. They do this by enabling the complexity of the system to be divided and conquered, so that no single person or group of persons has to master all the details of the design. They can therefore in themselves contribute to the overall reliability of a system, by simplifying the tasks of its designers. However, if design errors are made, or operational failures of physical components occur, it will be found that existing methods of constructing opaque virtual machine interfaces are somewhat inadequate. The sought-after opacity of the interface will in many cases be lost, since error recovery (either manual or predesigned) will need an understanding of two or more levels of the system. Hence our interest in providing facilities for tolerating faults, including those due to design errors, which can be used by designers whose detailed understanding of the system is limited to that of a single level and the two virtual machine interfaces that bound it. (A very different approach to these problems, based on the use of programmer-supplied error diagnosis and recovery code, has been described by Parnas [9].)

All this presupposes that the virtual machine interfaces have some physical realization in the operational system. Conceptual levels, though of value during system design and in providing documentation of the behavior of a reliable system, typically play no part in failure situations—for example the levels in the THE system [3] have no relevance to the problem of coping with, say, an actual memory parity error. The actual physical realization in existing multilevel systems can vary widely—from, for example, the provision of physically separate storage and highways for microprograms and programs, to the use of a single control bit to distinguish between supervisor and user modes of instruction execution. What we now describe are additional general characteristics and facilities that we believe any such physical realization of a virtual machine interface should possess in order to support our techniques for system fault tolerance.

A. Errors Above a Virtual Machine Interface

Everything that appears to happen in a given level is in fact the result of activity for which the level below is (directly or indirectly) responsible. This applies not only to the ordinary operations performed at a level but also to any recovery actions which might be required. Consider for example a level *i* which uses our recovery block scheme to provide itself with some measure of fault tolerance, and which makes recognizable progress by means of simple assignment statements. Then it is level *i-1* which is responsible not only for the actual assignments, but also for any saving of prior values of variables and reinstatement of them when required.

Similarly, if the virtual machine which supports level *i* includes any more exotic operations which change the system state as seen by level *i*, e.g., magnetic tape rewind, then level *i-1* will have the responsibility of undoing their effects, e.g., repositioning the tape (whether level *i-1* undertakes this responsibility itself, or instead delegates it to level *i-2* is irrelevant).

Provided that level *i-1* fulfills its responsibilities level *i* can thus assume that error detection will automatically be followed by a return to the most recent recovery point. This will occur whether the detection of a level *i* error occurs at level *i* itself (e.g., by means of an acceptance test) or below level *i* because of incorrect use by level *i* of one of the operations provided to it by level *i-1* (e.g., division by zero).

It should be noted that both progress and fall back, as recognizable in the level above a virtual machine interface, are provided by progress on the level below, i.e., the level *i-1* keeps going forwards, or at least tries to, even if it is doing so in order to enable level *i* to (appear to) go backwards.

For example, level *i* might read cards from an "abstract card reader" while level *i-1* actually implements this abstract card reader by means of spooling. When level *i* encounters an error and tries to go backwards, it must appear to "unread" the cards read during the current recovery block. But level *i-1* implements this "unreading" by merely resetting a pointer in its spool buffer—a positive or forward action on its part.

All this assumes level *i-1* is trouble free—what we must now discuss are the complications caused by level *i-1* being unable, for various reasons, to maintain its own progress, and in particular that progress on which level *i* is relying.

B. Errors Below a Virtual Machine Interface

Needless to say, the programs which provide a virtual machine interface can themselves, if appropriate, incorporate recovery blocks for the purpose of local error detection and recovery. Thus when level *i-1* makes a mistake, which is detected, while performing some operation for level *i*, if an alternate block manages to succeed where the primary alternate had failed the operation can nevertheless be completed. In such circumstances the program at level *i* need never know that any error occurred. (For example, a user process may be unaware that the operating system had to make several attempts before it succeeded in reading a magnetic tape on behalf of the user process.) But if all the alternates of the outermost recovery block of the level *i-1* program performing an operation for level *i* fail, so that the recovery capability at level *i-1* is exhausted, then the operation must be rejected and recovery action undertaken at level *i*.

This case of an error detected at level *i-1* forcing level *i* back to a recovery point in order to undertake some alternative action is very similar to the one mentioned earlier in Section V-A—namely that of an error detected at level *i-1*, but stemming from the incorrect use of an operation by level *i*. The error log which is produced for later offline analysis will indicate the difference between the two cases, but this information (leave alone further information which might be needed for diagnostic purposes) will not be available at level *i*.

The situation is much more serious if level *i-1* errs, and exhausts any recovery capability it might have, whilst performing an inverse operation on behalf of level *i*, i.e., fails to complete the act of undoing the effects of one or more operations that level *i* has used to modify its state. This possibility might seem rather small when the inverse operation is merely that of resetting the prior value of a scalar variable. However when an inverse operation is quite complex (e.g., one that involves undoing the changes a process has caused to be made to complicated data structures in a large filing system) one might have to cope with residual design inadequacies, as well as the ever-present possibility of hardware failure.

When an inverse operation cannot be completed, the level *i* cannot be backed up, so it has to be abandoned. This is perhaps the most subtle cause for level *i-1* to abandon further attempts to execute a level *i* process—more familiar ones include the sudden inability of level *i-1* to continue fetching and decoding level *i* instructions, locating level *i* operands, etc., either because of level *i-1*'s own inadequacy, or that of the level *i-2* machine on which it depends. (For example, level 3 of Fig. 11, the APL interpreter, might find that the file in which it keeps the APL program belonging to a particular user was unreadable, a fault which perhaps was first detected at level 2, by the microprogram.)

There is one other important class of errors detected below a virtual machine interface which can be dealt with without necessarily abandoning level *i*, the level above the interface. After level *i* has passed an acceptance test, but before all the information constituting its recovery point has been discarded, there is the chance for level *i-1* to perform any checking that is needed on the overall acceptability, in level *i-1* terms, of the sequence of operations that have been carried out for level *i*.

For example, level *i* may have been performing operations which were, as far as it was concerned, disk storage operations. Level *i-1* could in fact have buffered the information so stored. Before the present level of fall back capability of level *i* is discarded, level *i-1* may wish to ensure that the information has been written to disk and checked. If level *i-1* finds that it cannot ensure this, but instead encounters some problem from which it itself is unable to recover, then it can in essence cause level *i* to fail, and to fall back and attempt an alternate. This will be in the hope that whatever problem it was that level *i-1* got into (on behalf of level *i*) this time, next time the sequence of operations that level *i* requests will manage to get dealt with to the satisfaction of level *i-1* as well as of level *i*.

In fact an interesting example of this case of level *i-1* inducing a failure in level *i* occurs in the mechanization of conversations. Consider a level *i* process which is involved in a conversation with some other level *i* process and which after completing its primary alternate satisfies its acceptance test. At this moment level *i-1* must determine whether the other process has also completed its primary alternate and passed its acceptance test. If necessary the process must be suspended until the other process has been completed, as discussed in Section IV-A. If the other process should fail, then the first process must also be forced to back up just as if it had failed its own acceptance test even though it had in fact passed it.

C. Fault-Tolerant Virtual Machine Interfaces

We have so far discussed the problems of failures above and below a virtual machine interface quite separately. In fact, except for the highest level and the one that we choose to regard as the lowest level, every level is of course simultaneously below one virtual machine interface and above another such interface. Therefore each interface has the responsibility for organizing the interaction between two potentially unreliable levels in a multilevel system. The aim is to embody *within the interface* all the rules about interaction across levels that we have been describing, and so simplify the tasks of designing the levels on either side of the interface.

If this can be done then it will be possible to design levels which are separated by opaque virtual machine interfaces independently of each other, even in the case where the possibility of failures is admitted. By enabling the design of error recovery facilities to be considered separately for different levels of the system, in the knowedge that the fault-tolerant interface will arrange their proper interaction, their design should be greatly simplified—a very important consideration if error recovery facilities in complex systems are to be really relied upon.

Various different kinds of virtual machine interfaces are provided in current multilevel systems. These range from an interface which involves complete interpretation (e.g., the APL machine interface in Fig. 11 and the lowest interface in Fig. 12), to one where many of the basic facilities provided above the interface are in fact the same as those made available to the level immediately below the interface by some yet lower virtual machine interface (e.g., the other interfaces in Fig. 12). These latter kinds of interface, because of their performance characteristics, can be expected to predominate in systems which have many levels—in theory the multilevel file system (Fig. 12) could be built using a hierarchy of complete interpreters, but this is of course wildly impractical.

It is not appropriate within the confines of this already lengthy paper to give a fully detailed description of even a single kind, leave alone the various different kinds, of fault-tolerant virtual machine interface. However we have attempted, with Fig. 13, to show the main features of a fault-tolerant interface of the complete interpreter kind. For purposes of comparison, Fig. 14 shows the equivalent interface in a conventional complete interpreter.

The basic difference between a fault-tolerant interpreter and a conventional interpreter is that, for each different type of instruction to be interpreted, the fault tolerant interpreter, in general, provides a set of three related procedures rather than just a single procedure. The three procedures are as follows.

1) An Interpretation Procedure: This is basically the same as the single procedure provided in a conventional interpreter, and provides the normal interpretation of the particular type of instruction. But within the procedure, the interface ensures that before any changes are made to the state of the interpreted process or the values of any of its variables, a test is made to determine whether any information should first be saved in order that fall back will be possible.

2) An Inverse Procedure: this will be called when a process is being backed up, and will make use of information saved during any uses of the interpretation procedure.

3) An Acceptance Procedure: This will be called when an alternate block has passed its acceptance test, and allows for any necessary tidying up and checking related to the previous use of the normal interpretation procedure.

When the instruction is one that does not change the system state, inverse and acceptance procedures are not needed. If the instruction is, for example, merely a simple assignment to a scalar, the interpretation procedure saves the value and the address of the scalar before making the first assignment to the scalar within a new recovery block. The inverse procedure uses this information to reset the scalar, and there is a trivial acceptance procedure. A nontrivial acceptance procedure would be needed if, for example, the interpreter had to close a file and perhaps do some checking on the filed information in order to complete the work stemming from the use of the interpretation procedure.

A generalization of the recursive cache, as described in Section III-C, is used to control the invocation of inverse and acceptance procedures. The cache records the descriptors for the inverse and acceptance procedures corresponding to interpretation procedures that have been executed and caused system state information to be saved. Indeed each cache region can be thought of as containing a linear "program," rather than just a set of saved prior values. The "program" held in the current cache region indicates the sequence of inverse procedures calls that are to be "executed" in order to back up the process to its most recent recovery point. (If the process passes its acceptance test the procedure calls in the "program" act as calls on acceptance procedures.) The program of inverse/acceptance calls is initially null, but grows as the process performs actions which add to the task of backing it up. As with the basic recursive cache mechanism, the cache

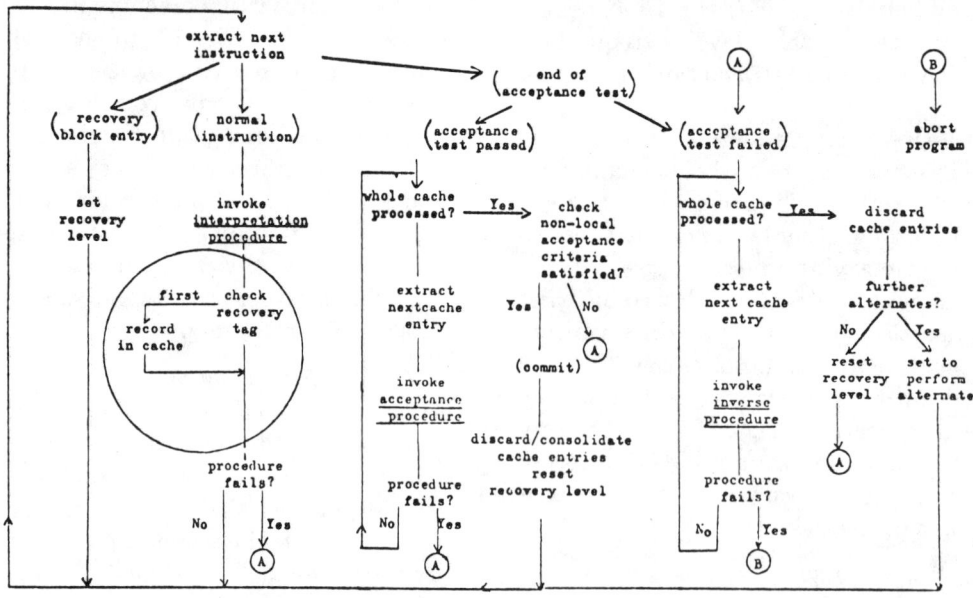

Fig. 13. Fault-tolerant interpreter.

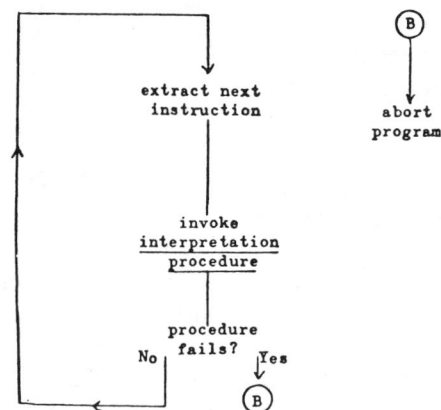

Fig. 14. Conventional interpreter.

region will be discarded in its entirety after it has been used for backing up a process. Similarly, if the recovery block or conversation is completed successfully, some entries will be discarded, but those that relate to variables which are nonlocal to the enclosing environment will be consolidated with the existing "program" in the underlying region of the cache.

This then is a very brief account, ignoring various simple but important "mere optimizations," of the main characteristics of a failure-tolerant virtual machine interface of the complete interpreter kind. Being so closely related to the basic recursive cache mechanism, it will perhaps be most readily appreciated by people who are already familiar with the published description [5] of the detailed functioning of one recursive cache mechanism.

VI. CONCLUSIONS

The techniques for structuring fault-tolerant systems which we have described have been designed especially for faults arising from design errors, such as are at present all too common in complex software systems. However we believe they are also of potential applicability to hardware and in particular allow the various operational faults that hardware can suffer from to be treated as simple special cases. In fact the techniques we have sketched for fault tolerance in multilevel systems would appear to provide an appropriate means of integrating provisions for hardware reconfiguration into the overall structure of the system. Indeed as a general approach to the structuring of a complex activity where the possibility of errors is to be considered, there seems to be no *a priori* reason why the structuring should not extend past the confines of the computer system. Thus, as others have previously remarked [2], the structuring could apply to the environment and perhaps even the activity of the people surrounding the computer system.

The effectiveness of this approach to fault-tolerant system design will depend critically on the acceptance tests and additional alternate blocks that are provided. An experimental prototype systems is currently being developed which should enable us to obtain experience in the use of this approach, to evaluate its merits, and to explore possible performance–reliability tradeoffs. In our opinion, one lesson is however already clear. If it is considered important that a complex system be provided with extensive error recovery facilities whose dependability can be the subject of plausible *a priori* arguments, then the system structure will have to conform to comparatively restrictive rules. Putting this another way, it will not be sufficient for designers to argue for the use of very sophisticated control structures and intercommunication facilities on the grounds of performance characteristics and personal freedom of design, unless they can clearly demonstrate that these do not unduly compromise the recoverability of the system.

ACKNOWLEDGMENT

The work reported in this paper is the result of the efforts of a sizeable number of people, all associated with the Science Research Council-sponsored project on system reliability at the University of Newcastle upon Tyne. Arising out of this work, patents have been applied for by the National Research Development Corporation. Those most directly responsible for the techniques of system structuring which form the central theme of this paper are J. J. Horning, R. Kerr, H. C. Lauer, P. M. Melliar-Smith, and the author. (Professor Horning, of the University of Toronto, Toronto, Ont., Canada, held a Senior Visiting Fellowship with the project during the Summer of 1973.)

The author has great pleasure in acknowledging his indebtedness to all his colleagues on the project, several of whom, and in particular P. M. Melliar-Smith, provided many useful acceptance tests and alternates for the author's activity in preparing this paper.

REFERENCES

[1] T. A. Anderson, "Provably safe programs," Comput. Lab., Univ. Newcastle upon Tyne, Newcastle upon Tyne, England, Tech. Rep., in preparation.
[2] C. T. Davies, "Recovery semantics for a DB/DC system," in *Proc. 1973 Ass. Comput. Mach. Nat. Conf.*, New York, N. Y., pp. 136–141.
[3] E. W. Dijkstra, "The structure of the "THE" multiprogramming system," *Commun. Ass. Comput. Mach.*, vol. 11, no. 5, pp. 341–346, 1968.
[4] C. Hewitt, "PLANNER: A language for proving theorems in robots," in *Proc. Int. Joint Conf. Artificial Intelligence*, Mitre Corp., Bedford, Mass., 1969, pp. 295–301.
[5] J. J. Horning, H. C. Lauer, P. M. Melliar-Smith, and B. Randell, "A program structure for error detection and recovery," in *Proc. Conf. Operating Systems: Theoretical and Practical Aspects*, IRIA, Apr. 23–25, 1974, pp. 177–193.
[6] H. C. Lauer, "Protection and hierarchical addressing structures," in *Proc. Int. Workshop Protection in Operating Systems*, IRIA, Rocquencourt, France, 1974, pp. 137–148.
[7] H. C. Lauer and D. Wyeth, "A recursive virtual machine architecture," Comput. Lab., Univ. Newcastle upon Tyne, Newcastle upon Tyne, England, Tech. Rep. 54, Sept. 1973.
[8] S. E. Madnick and J. W. Alsop, II, "A modular approach to file system design," in *1969 Spring Joint Comput. Conf., AFIPS Conf. Proc.*, vol. 34. Montvale, N. J.: AFIPS Press, 1969, pp. 1–13.
[9] D. L. Parnas, "Response to detected errors in well-structured programs," Dep. Comput. Sci., Carnegie-Mellon Univ., Pittsburgh, Pa., Tech. Rep., July 1972.
[10] W. H. Pierce, *Failure-Tolerant Computer Design*. New York: Academic, 1965.
[11] B. Randell, "Highly reliable computing systems," Comput. Lab., Univ. Newcastle upon Tyne, Newcastle upon Tyne, England, Tech. Rep. 20, July 1971.
[12] ——, "Research on computing system reliability at the University of Newcastle upon Tyne, 1972/73," Comput. Lab., Univ. Newcastle upon Tyne, Newcastle upon Tyne, England, Tech. Rep. 57, Jan. 1974.

Brian Randell was born in Cardiff, Wales, on April 26, 1936. He received the B.Sc. degree in mathematics from the University of London, London, England, in 1957.

From 1957 to 1964 he was employed with the English Electric Company Limited, where he worked on compilers for DEUCE and the KDF9, and was responsible for the Whetstone KDF9 compiler. From 1964 to 1969 he was employed with IBM working mainly at the IBM T. J. Watson Research Center, Yorktown Heights, N. Y. During that time he worked on the architecture of very high speed computers, multi-processing systems, and system design methodology. Since 1969 he has been Professor of Computing Science at the University of Newcastle upon Tyne, Newcastle upon Tyne, England. He is currently the principal investigator for the project on the design of highly reliable computing systems sponsored by the Science Research Council; co-author of the book *ALGOL 60 Implementation* (New York: Academic, 1964); and Editor of the book *The Origins of Digital Computers: Selected Papers* (New York: Springer-Verlag, 1973).

Mr. Randell is a member of the Association for Computing Machinery and a Fellow of the British Computer Society.

The *N*-Version Approach to Fault-Tolerant Software

ALGIRDAS AVIŽIENIS, FELLOW, IEEE

Abstract—Evolution of the *N*-version software approach to the tolerance of design faults is reviewed. Principal requirements for the implementation of *N*-version software are summarized and the DEDIX distributed supervisor and testbed for the execution of *N*-version software is described. Goals of current research are presented and some potential benefits of the *N*-version approach are identified.

Index Terms—Design diversity, fault tolerance, multiple computation, *N*-version programming, *N*-version software, software reliability, tolerance of design faults.

I. INTRODUCTION

THE transfer of the concepts of fault tolerance to computer software, that is discussed in this paper, began about 20 years after the first systematic discussion of fault-tolerant logic structures [49], [41], and the first introduction of some fault tolerance by duplication or triplication of hardware subsystems in first generation computers [43], [16], [18]. The 1950–1970 period was a time of evolution in both the theoretical development and the practical application of fault tolerance techniques in digital systems, well illustrated by the presentations at the first International Symposium on Fault-Tolerant Computing in March of 1971 [20]. In the subsequent decade, the field matured with the emergence of several successful system designs [6] followed by the appearance of the product line of Tandem computers [9].

All the efforts discussed above were aimed at the tolerance of physical faults, either of a permanent or transient nature. *Physical faults* are undesirable changes in the hardware components of the system, e.g., short circuits between two leads, open circuited transistor junctions, alpha particle impacts on dynamic MOSFET memory cells, etc. Such faults cause *errors* to appear in the information that is processed by the computing system. The errors most often appear as changes in the patterns of zeros and ones that represent the information. Other errors are time based: the information fails to arrive or arrives at the wrong time. Errors that are not detected and eliminated within the system are likely to lead to the *failure* of the computing system to deliver the expected service to other systems or to human users.

The function of fault tolerance is to preserve the delivery of expected services despite the presence of fault-caused errors within the system itself. Errors are detected and corrected, and permanent faults are located and removed while the system continues to deliver acceptable service. This goal is accomplished by the use of error detection algorithms, fault diagnosis, recovery algorithms, and spare resources. They are all integral parts of the fault-tolerant system, and may be implemented in hardware, firmware, or software.

In addition to physical faults, system failures are also caused by *design faults* and *interaction faults* [6]. These classes of faults originate due to the mistakes and oversights of humans that occur while they specify, design, operate, update, and maintain the hardware and software of computing systems. Fault avoidance and fault removal (after failure) have been generally employed to cope with design faults. Some research efforts to apply fault tolerance to software design faults have been active since the early 1970's; this paper reports the results and current work on the "*N*-version" approach that has been investigated by the Dependable Computing and Fault-Tolerant System research group at UCLA.

The *N*-version approach to fault-tolerant software depends on a generalization of the *multiple computation* method that has been successfully applied to the tolerance of physical faults. The method is reviewed and its application to the tolerance of software faults is discussed in the following section.

II. THE MULTIPLE COMPUTATION APPROACH AND ITS EXTENSION TO DESIGN DIVERSITY

Multiple computation is a fundamental method employed to attain fault tolerance. Multiple computations are implemented by N-fold ($N \geq 2$) replications in three domains: *time* (repetition), *space* (hardware), and *information* (software). In this section, a shorthand notation is employed to describe the various possible approaches to multiple computation. The nonfault-tolerant, or *simplex*, system is characterized by one execution (simplex time $1T$) of one program (simplex software $1S$) on one hardware channel (simplex hardware $1H$), and is described by the notation: $1T/1H/1S$.

One major distinction in fault-tolerant systems is between single-channel and multiple-channel architectures. The former provide only one physical (hardware) set of components needed for the computation. Error detection invokes recovery by a retry from a "rollback point" system state. This program rollback can succeed when the fault is transient, but will fail for permanent faults, leaving a safe shutdown of this $2T/1H/1S$ system as the only acceptable outcome. External repair service is then required to remove the fault and to return the system to an operational state. More than one retry is possible, and there can be multiple computations that use the same hardware and software, but replicate the execution N-fold in time: $NT/1H/1S$.

In the N-fold time cases (NT), the consecutive executions of a computation can employ new copies (identical replicas) of the program and associated data. A common practice in coping with system crashes is the loading from stable backup storage and running of a new copy of the program and data on the same hardware: $2T/1H/2S$. A more sophisticated fault tolerance approach that is, for example, used in Tandem computers [9], is the execution of another copy of the program that resides in a standby duplicate hardware channel: $2T/2H/2S$. It must be noted that the use of "new copies" of a program implies the existence of a *reference program* in stable storage from which the copies are made.

In a multiple-channel architecture that is limited to simplex time ($1T$), multiple computations take place as concurrent executions of N copies of the reference program on N hardware channels: $1T/NH/NS$. Examples of such systems are NASA's Space Shuttle with $N = 4$ [48], SRI's SIFT system with $N \geq 3$ [24], C. S. Draper Lab's Fault-Tolerant Multiprocessor with $N = 3$ [31], and AT&T Bell Laboratories' 1ESS central control with $N = 2$ [14]. It is evident that N-fold time may be introduced into multiple-channel architectures to produce additional variations of multiple computations. The general case is $NT/YH/ZS$, with Y channels and Z copies of the program, constrained by $NY \geq Z$.

The systems discussed above attain fault tolerance by the execution of multiple (N-fold, with $N \geq 2$) computations that have the same objective: to deliver a set of N results derived from a given set of initial conditions and inputs. The following two fundamental requirements apply to such multiple computations:

1) the *consistency* of initial conditions and inputs for all N computations must be assured; and

2) a reliable *decision algorithm* that determines a single *decision result* from the multiple results must be provided.

The decision algorithm may utilize only a subset of all N results for a decision; e.g., the first result that passes an acceptance test may be chosen. It is also possible that an acceptable decision result cannot be determined, and a higher level recovery procedure must be invoked. The decision algorithm is often implemented N times—once for each computation in which the decision result is used. In this case, only one computation is affected by the failure of any one implementation, such as a majority voter in triple-modular redundancy (TMR).

The usual partitioning of faults into "single fault" and "multiple fault" classes needs to be refined when we consider multiple computations. Faults that affect only one in a set of N computations are called *simplex* faults. A simplex fault does not affect other computations, although it may be either a single or a multiple fault within one channel. Simplex faults are very effectively tolerated by the multiple computation approach, as long as input consistency and a reliable decision algorithm are provided.

Faults that affect M out of the N separate computations are *M-plex* faults ($2 \leq M \leq N$); they affect M separate results from the set that is used to obtain the decision result. Typically, multiple occurrences of faults are divided into two classes: *independent* and *related*. We say that related *M-plex* faults are those for which a common cause that affects M computations exists or is hypothesized. Examples of common physical causes are: interchannel shorts or sneak paths, common power supply fluctuations, bursts of radiation, etc. The effects of related physical faults, i.e., the errors caused in the individual computations, are much more likely to be *distinct* than *identical* at the points at which the decision algorithm is applied.

Another class of related *M-plex* faults is quite different: they are *design faults* due to human mistakes committed during the design or the subsequent design modifications of a hardware or software element. All N computations that employ identical copies of that hardware or software element are affected by the design fault in the same manner when a given state of the element is reached, and the resulting errors are all identical at the decision algorithm, causing an erroneous decision result. Such total susceptibility to design faults is the most serious limitation of the multiple computation approach as it is currently applied in fault-tolerant system design.

A potentially effective method to avoid the identical errors that are caused by design faults in multiple computation systems is to use N independently designed software or/and hardware elements instead of identical copies that were generated from one design. This "design diversity" approach directly applies to the parallel (simplex time) systems $1T/NH/NS$, which can be altered to: 1) $1T/NH/NdS$, where NdS stands for *N-fold diverse software*, as used in N-version programming [5]; 2) $1T/NdH/NS$, where NdH stands for *N-fold diverse hardware*; and 3) $1T/NdH/NdS$. The N-fold time (NT) systems have been implemented as recovery blocks [47], with N sequentially applicable alternate programs that use the same hardware channel: $NT/1H/NdS$. An acceptance test is performed for fault detection, and the decision algorithm selects the first set of results that pass the test.

The use of N-version software introduces new "similarity" considerations for multiple results and for errors caused by M-plex faults. The results of individual versions often differ within a certain range when different algorithms are used in the diverse designs. Therefore, the decision algorithm may need to determine the decision result from a set of similar, but not identical, results. *Similar results* are defined to be two or more results (good or erroneous) that are within the range of variation that is allowed by the decision algorithm; consequently, a set of similar results is used to determine the decision result. When two or more similar results are erroneous, they are called *similar errors*. If the set of similar errors outnumbers the set of good (similar) results at a decision point, then the decision algorithm will arrrive at an erroneous decision result. For example, two similar errors will outweigh one good result in the three-version case, and a set of three similar errors will prevail over a set of two similar good results when $N = 5$. All possible errors caused by M-plex faults are now classified as either *distinct* or *similar*, and *identical* errors form a subset of *similar* errors.

When design faults occur in $M \geq 2$ diverse versions, the design faults may be either independent or related. An obvious criterion for discrimination is to designate those faults that cause similar errors at a decision point as related, and all others as independent. However, this naive criterion disregards the nature and origin of the design faults themselves. For example, it has been observed that two entirely different design faults have produced a pair of similar errors [7].

Our choice is to follow the preceding treatment of physical faults and to consider two (or $M > 2$) design faults as *potentially related* if they cause similar errors at a decision point. Potentially related faults are considered *related* if they are attributed to some common cause, such as a common link between the separate design efforts. Examples of a "common link" are: an ambiguous specification, a conversation between designers from two efforts, use of the same faulty compiler, or use of the same erroneous programmer's manual. If a common cause cannot be identified or hypothesized, the design faults are considered independent, although the errors they have caused are similar.

We anticipate situations in which two (or more) programmers will apparently quite accidentally make the same mistake. In that case, the preceding definition of related design faults allows the choice of either continuing the search for a nonapparent common cause, or considering the two faults to be independent and only coincidentally identical. This option appears to be a necessary condition at the present stage of our understanding of the causes of design faults.

III. Evolution of Fault Tolerance in Software

The evolution of fault tolerance in software has followed two distinct directions. The first direction consisted of the introduction of special fault detection and recovery features into single-version software. The second direction was the development of multiple-version diverse software for the purpose of attaining fault tolerance.

Considering single-version software, it is known that the first generation machine and assembly language programs already contained *ad hoc* provisions to detect abnormal behavior and to signal its presence to the operator. These fault detection provisions served to detect physical faults as well as software (design) faults introduced by programmers. A programmed time-out counter is a good example of such a fault detector. The sophistication of software fault detection increased with the evolution of operating systems, which took over the monitoring of the behavior of application programs. A large body of literature has evolved on the subjects of detection, confinement, and recovery from abnormal behavior of single-version software. Modularity, system closure, atomicity of actions, decision verification, and exception handling are among the key attributes of reliable single-version applications and system software. It is quite evident that these attributes remain desirable and advantageous in each version of the fault-tolerant multiversion software that will be discussed in the remainder of this paper.

Multiple-version software has remained of little interest to the mainstream researchers and developers of software for a relatively long time. Some suggestions of its potential usefulness had appeared in the early and mid-1970's [17], [21], [36], [19]. However, the first suggestion on record was made by Dr. Dionysius Lardner who, in 1834, wrote in "Babbage's calculating engine" as follows [42]:

"The most certain and effectual check upon errors which arise in the process of computation, is to cause the same computations to be made by separate and independent computers; and this check is rendered still more decisive if they make their computations by different methods."

The first long-term systematic investigation of multiple-version software for fault tolerance was initiated by Brian Randell at the University of Newcastle upon Tyne in the early 1970's [47], [1]. From this research evolved the *recovery block* (RB) technique, in which alternate software versions are organized in a manner similar to the dynamic redundancy (standby sparing) technique in hardware. Its objective is to perform run-time software (as well as hardware) fault detection by an acceptance test performed on the results delivered by the first version. If the acceptance test is not passed, recovery is implemented by state restoration followed by the execution of an alternate version on the same hardware ($NT/1H/NdS$). Recovery is considered complete when the acceptance test is passed. Several variations of the RB approach have been recently investigated [3], [11], [25], [30], [35], [50].

Another continuing investigation of multiversion software is the N-version programming (NVP) project started by the author at UCLA in 1975 [4]. N-fold computation ($1T/NH/NdS$, or $1T/NdH/NdS$) is carried out by using N independently designed software modules, or "versions," and their results are sent to a decision algorithm that determines a single decision result [5]. Other pioneering investigations of the multiversion software concept have been carried out at the KFK Karlsruhe, FRG [22], at the Halden Reactor Project, Norway [13], and at UC Berkeley and other organizations in the United States [46].

The fundamental difference between the RB and NVP approaches is the decision algorithm. In the RB approach, an acceptance test that is specific to the application program being implemented must be provided. In the NVP approach, the decision algorithm is a generic consensus algorithm that delivers an agreement/disagreement decision. Otherwise, both RB and NVP can be implemented for concurrent or sequential execution depending on the number of hardware channels available at once. Analytic models using queuing and Markov modeling techniques have been developed for the comparison of RB and NVP techniques with respect to time requirements and reliability improvement, allowing for the existence of similar errors in NVP and imperfect acceptance tests in RB [26], [37].

A number of variations and combinations of the RB and NVP approaches can be readily identified [2]. First, acceptance tests on individual versions can be employed to support the decision algorithms in NVP [33]. Second, fault detection and exception handling algorithms in individual hardware channels can help to distinguish physical faults from design faults. Third, the RB approach can concurrently use two (or more) hardware channels, either copied: $(N/2)$ $T/2H/NdS$, or diverse: $(N/2)$ $T/2dH/NdS$. A decision algorithm can support the acceptance tests, since two sets of results are made available in parallel, and real-time constraints can be met as long as one channel remains acceptable. The general diverse system is $NT/YdH/ZdS$ with $NY \geq Z$, that includes acceptance tests, exception handling, and the detection of physical faults in each channel to support the decision algorithm. Other diverse systems result when some features are deleted or diversity is reduced.

IV. N-Version Programming Experiments at UCLA

N-version programming is defined as the independent generation of $N \geq 2$ software modules, called "versions," from the same initial specification [5]. "Independent generation" means that programming efforts are carried out by individuals or groups that do not interact with respect to the programming process. Wherever possible, different algorithms, programming languages, environments, and tools are used in each separate effort. The goal of NVP is to minimize the probability of similar errors at decision points in an N-fold computation.

The purpose of the initial specification is to state the functional requirements completely and unambiguously, while leaving the widest possible choice of implementations to the N programming efforts. The specification also prescribes the special features that are needed to execute the set of N versions as an "N-version software unit" in a fault-tolerant manner. An initial specification defines: 1) the function to be implemented by the N-version software unit; 2) the cross-check points ("cc-points") at which the decision algorithm will be applied to the results of each version; 3) content and format of the cross-check vectors ("cc-vectors") to be generated at each cc-point; 4) the decision algorithm to be used at each cc-point; and 5) the response to the possible outcomes of decisions. The decision algorithm explicitly states the allowable range of variation in numerical results, if such a range exists, as well as any other acceptable differences in the version results such as extra spaces in text output or other "cosmetic" variations.

It is the fundamental conjecture of the NVP approach that the independence of programming efforts will assure a low probability that residual software design faults will lead to an erroneous decision by causing similar errors to occur at the same cc-point in two or more versions. Given a reasonable choice of cc-points and cc-vectors, the low probability of similar errors is expected to make N-version programming an effective method for achieving software fault tolerance. The effectiveness of the NVP approach depends on the validity of the conjecture, and an experimental investigation was deemed to be the essential next step. The initial NVP research effort at UCLA (1975–1978) addressed two questions: 1) which requirements (e.g., good specifications, choice of suitable types of problems, constraints on the nature of algorithms, timing constraints, decision algorithms, etc.) have to be met to make N-version programming feasible at all regardless of the cost; and 2) what methods should be used to compare the cost and the effectiveness of the NVP approach to the two alternatives: single-version programming and the recovery block approach.

The scarcity of previous results and an absence of formal theories on N-version programming led to the choice of an experimental approach: to choose some conveniently accessible programming problems, to assess the applicability of N-version programming, and then to proceed to generate a set of programs. Once generated, the programs were executed as N-version software units in a simulated multiple-hardware system, and the resulting observations were applied to refine the methodology and to build up the concepts of N-version programming. The first detailed review of the research approach and a discussion of two sets of experimental results, using 27 and 16 independently written programs, was published in 1978 [12].

The preceding exploratory research demonstrated the practicality of experimental investigation and confirmed the need for high quality software specifications. As a consequence, the first aim of the next phase of UCLA research (1979–1982) was the investigation of the relative applicability of various software specification techniques. Other aims were to investigate the types and causes of software design faults, to propose improvements to software specification techniques and their use, and to propose future experiments for the investigation of design fault tolerance in software and in hardware [33].

To examine the effect of specification techniques on multiversion software, an experiment was designed in which three different specifications were used. The first was written in the formal specification language OBJ [23]. The second specification language chosen was the nonformal PDL that was characteristic of current industry practice. English was employed as the third, or "control," specification language since English had been used in the previous studies [12]. Thirty programmers started the programming effort, and eighteen programs were delivered (seven from OBJ, five from PDL, and six from the English specification). The length of the programs varied from 217 to 689 PL/1 statements, averaging 392 statements per program.

The problem chosen for the experiment was an "airport

scheduler" program. This database problem concerns the operation of an airport in which flights are scheduled to depart for other airports and seats are reserved on those flights. The problem was originally an example of database system specification [15] and was later used to illustrate the use of OBJ [23]. Because the problem is transaction oriented, the natural choice of cross-check points was at the end of each transaction. With the OBJ specification as reference, a specification was written in PDL and another one in English. The OBJ specification was 13 pages long, the English specification took 10 pages, but PDL required 74 pages to contain the same specification [32]. The detailed description of the experiment has been reported in [32], and the main results have been presented in [33] and [7].

A major second generation experiment began in June of 1985. UCLA is cooperating with the University of Illinois, the University of Virginia, and North Carolina State University in a large-scale experiment sponsored by the NASA Langley Research Center. Twenty versions of a program to manage sensor redundancy in an aircraft and spacecraft navigation system are to be written by September of 1985. Hypotheses on similar errors have been formulated and will be validated, and the cost effectiveness and reliability increase of the N-version approach will be assessed. To establish a long-term research facility for these second generation experimental investigations, the DEsign DIversity eXperiment system (DEDIX), a distributed software supervisor and testbed system at the UCLA Center for Experimental Computer Science, has been designed and implemented [8]. A subsequent section of this paper describes the requirements, design, and implementation of DEDIX.

V. Principal Issues of N-Version Programming

The series of N-version programming experiments that were conducted at UCLA allowed us to identify several issues that require resolution in order to attain successful N-version fault tolerance in software. The key problems of implementing the multiversion software solution are discussed below.

Initial Specification

The most critical condition for the independence of design faults is the existence of a complete and accurate specification of the requirements that are to be met by the diverse designs. This is the "hard core" of this fault tolerance approach. Latent defects, such as inconsistencies, ambiguities, and omissions, in the specification are likely to bias otherwise entirely independent programming or logic design efforts toward related design faults. The most promising approach to the production of the initial specification is the use of formal, very-high-level specification languages [38], [44], [39]. When such specifications are executable, they can be automatically tested for latent defects and serve as prototypes of the programs suitable for assessing the overall design. With this approach, perfection is required only at the highest level of specification; the rest of the design and implementation process as well as its tools are not required to be perfect, but only as good as possible within existing resource constraints and time limits. The independent writing and subsequent comparison of two specifications, using two formal languages, is the next step that is expected to increase the dependability of specifications beyond the present limits. Our current investigation of specification methods is discussed in a subsequent section.

Independence of Design Efforts

The approach that is employed to attain independence of design faults in a set of N programs is maximal independence of design and implementation efforts. It calls for the use of diverse algorithms, programming languages, compilers, design tools, implementation techniques, test methods, etc. The second condition for independence is the employment of independent (noninteracting) programmers or designers, with diversity in their training and experience. Wide geographical dispersion and diverse ethnic backgrounds may also be desirable.

N-Version Execution Support

Implementation of N-version fault-tolerant software requires special support mechanisms that need to be specified, implemented, and protected against failures due to physical or design faults. These mechanisms fall into two categories: those *specific* for the application program being implemented, and those that are *generic* for the N-version approach. The *application-specific* class contains the specifications of: 1) the initial state of the program; 2) the inputs to be received; 3) the location of cross-check points (partitioning into modules); 4) the content and format of the cross-check vector at each cc-point (outputs are included here); 5) the algorithms for internal checking and exception handling within each version; and 6) the time constraints to be observed by each program module.

The *generic* class of support mechanisms forms the N-version execution support environment that includes: 1) the decision algorithm; 2) assurance of input consistency; 3) interversion communication; 4) version synchronization and enforcement of timing constraints; 5) local supervision for each version; 6) the global executive and decision function for the treatment of faulty versions; and 7) the user interface for observation, debugging, injection of stimuli, and data collection during N-version execution of application programs. The nature of the generic support mechanisms is illustrated in the discussion of the DEDIX N-version supervisor and testbed system that is described in the next section.

Protection of the Support Environment

The success of design fault tolerance by means of N-version software depends on uninterrupted and fault-free service by the N-version support environment. Protection against physical faults is provided by the physical distribution of N versions on separate machines and by the implementation of fault-tolerant communication linkages.

The SIFT system [24] and the DEDIX system [8] are suitable examples in which the global executive is also protected by N-fold replication. The remaining problem is the protection against design faults that may exist in the support environment itself. This may be accomplished by N-fold diverse implementation of the support environment. To explore the feasibility of this approach, the prototype DEDIX environment is currently undergoing formal specification. Subsequently, this specification will be used to generate diverse multiple versions of the DEDIX software to reside on separate physical nodes of the system. The practicality and efficiency of the approach remain to be determined.

Architectural Support

Current hardware architectures were not conceived with the goal of N-version execution; therefore, they lack supporting instructions and other features that would make N-version software execution efficient. For example, the special instructions "take majority vote" and "check input consistency" would be very useful. The practical applicability on N-version software in safety-critical real-time applications hinges on the evolution of custom-tailored instruction sets and supporting architectures.

Recovery of Failed Versions

A problem area that needs to be addressed is the recovery of a failed version at a cc-point in order to allow its continued participation in N-version execution. Since all versions are likely to contain design faults, it is critically important to recover versions as they fail rather than merely degrade to N-1 versions, then N-2 versions, and so on to shutdown. Recovery of a given version is difficult because the other (good) versions are not likely to have identical internal states; they may differ drastically in internal structure while satisfying the specification.

Modification of N-Version Software

It is evident that the modification of software that exists in multiple versions is more difficult. The specification is expected to be sufficiently modular so that a given modification will affect only a few modules. The extent to which each module is affected can then be used to determine whether the existing versions should be modified according to a specification of change, or the existing versions should be discarded and new versions generated from the appropriately modified specification. Experiments need to be conducted to gain insights into the criteria to be used for a choice.

Assessment of Effectiveness

The usefulness of the N-version approach depends on the validity of the conjecture that residual software faults in separate versions will cause very few, if any, similar errors at the same cc-points. Large-scale experiments need to be carried out in order to gain statistically valid evidence, and the "mail order software" approach offers significant promise. In an "international mail order" experiment, the members of fault tolerance research groups from several countries will use a formal specification to write software versions. It is expected that the software versions produced at widely separated locations, by programmers with different training and experience who use different programming languages, will contain substantial design diversity. In further experiments, it may be possible to utilize the rapidly growing population of free-lance programmers on a contractual basis to provide module versions at their own locations. This approach would avoid the need to concentrate programming specialists, have a low overhead cost, and readily allow for the withdrawal of individual programmers.

Cost Investigations

The generation of N versions of a given program instead of a single one shows an immediate increase in the cost of software prior to the verification and validation phase. The question is whether the subsequent cost will be reduced because of the ability to employ two (or more) versions to attain mutual validation under operational conditions. Cost advantages may accrue because of 1) the faster operational deployment of new software; and 2) replacement of costly verification and validation tools and operations by a generic N-version environment in which the versions validate each other.

VI. THE DEDIX SYSTEM: AN N-VERSION RESEARCH TOOL

In the course of previous experiments at UCLA, it became evident that the usual general-purpose computing services were poorly suited to support the systematic execution, instrumentation, and observation of N-version fault-tolerant software. In order to provide a long-term research facility for experimental investigations of design diversity as a means of achieving fault-tolerant systems, the UCLA Dependable Computing and Fault-Tolerant System research group has designed and implemented the prototype DEDIX (DEsign DIversity eXperiment) system [8], a distributed supervisor and testbed for multiple-version software, at the UCLA Center for Experimental Computer Science. DEDIX is supported by the Center's Olympus Net local network, which utilizes the UNIX-based LOCUS distributed operating system [45] to operate a set of 20 VAX 11/750 computers. The prototype DEDIX system is discussed in this section. DEDIX illustrates the solutions that were chosen for the N-version software implementation problems identified in the preceding section. The three following general requirements were established for DEDIX.

• *Transparency:* The application programmers are not required to take care of the multiplicity, and a version must be able to run in a system with any allowed value of N without modifications.

• *Distribution:* The versions should be able to run on separate physical sites of a network in order to take advantage of physical isolation between sites, to benefit from parallel execution, and to tolerate the crash of a site.

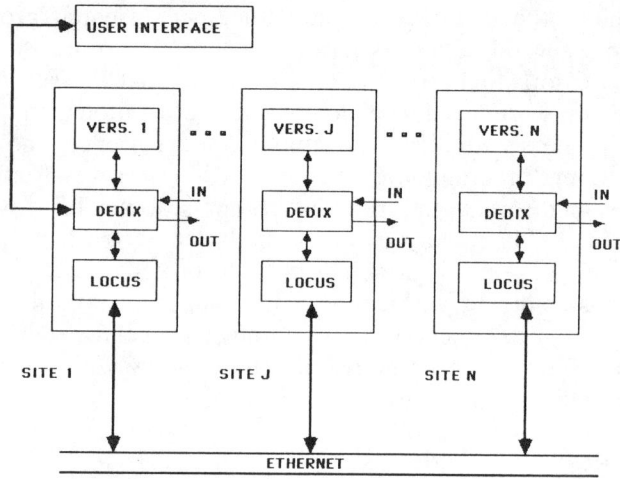

Fig. 1. DEDIX at *N* sites of Olympus Net.

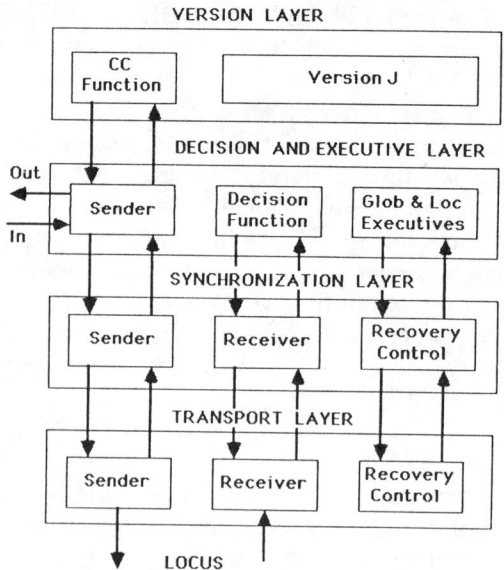

Fig. 2. Layers and entities at one site of DEDIX.

- *Environment:* DEDIX is designed to run on the distributed LOCUS environment at UCLA and must be portable to other UNIX environments. DEDIX must be able to run concurrently with all other normal activities of the local network.

The DEDIX structure can be considered as a network-based generalization of SIFT [24] that is able to tolerate both hardware and software faults. Both have similar partitioning, with a local executive and a decision algorithm at each site that processes broadcast results, and a copy of the global executive at each site that takes consistent reconfiguration decisions by majority vote. DEDIX is extended to allow some diversity in results and in version execution times. SIFT is a frame synchronous system that uses periodically synchronized clocks to predict when results should be available for a decision. This technique does not allow the diversity in execution times and unpredictable delays in communication that can be found in a distributed *N*-version environment. Instead, a synchronization protocol is used in DEDIX which does not make reference to global time within the system.

The purpose of DEDIX is to supervise and to observe the execution of *N* diverse versions of an application program functioning as a fault-tolerant *N*-version software unit. DEDIX also provides a transparent interface to the users, versions, and the input/output system so that they need not be aware of the existence of multiple versions and recovery algorithms. An abstract view of DEDIX in an *N*-site environment is given in Fig. 1. In summary, DEDIX provides the following services:

- it handles communications from the user and distributes them to all active versions;
- it handles requests from the versions to have their results (cc-vectors) processed, and returns decision results to the versions and to the user;
- it executes decision algorithms and determines decision results;
- it manages the input and output operations for the versions; and
- it makes reconfiguration and recovery decisions about the handling of faulty versions.

The DEDIX system can be located either in a single computer that executes all versions sequentially, or in a multicomputer system running one or more versions at each site. If DEDIX is supported by a single computer, it is vulnerable to hardware and software faults that affect the host computer, and the execution of *N*-version software units is relatively slow. In a computer network environment, the system is partitioned to protect it against most hardware faults. This has been done by providing each site with its own local DEDIX software, while an intersite communication facility is common to all computers. The DEDIX design is suitable for any specified number $N \geq 2$ of sites and versions, and currently accommodates the range $2 \leq N \leq 20$, with provision to reduce the number of sites and to adjust the decision algorithm upon the failure of a version or a site.

The prototpye DEDIX has been designed as a hierarchy of four layers to reduce complexity and to facilitate the inevitable modifications. Each site has an identical set of layers and entities as shown in Fig. 2. The purpose of each layer is to offer services to the higher layers, shielding them from details on how those services actually are implemented. The layers, discussed below, are the: *transport layer*, *synchronization layer*, *decision and executive layer*, and *version layer*.

The transport layer handles the communication of messages between the sites. It serves as the interface of DEDIX and the host LOCUS distributed operating system that manages intersite communication. The layer is intended to assure that messages are not lost, duplicated, damaged, or misaddressed, and it preserves the ordering of sent messages. The loss of communication with another site is reported to the layer above.

The synchronization layer at each site has a *sender* that broadcasts local results, and a *receiver* that collects messages with the results (cc-vectors) from other sites, using the services of the transport layer. The collected results are delivered to the decision function. The execution of versions at all sites needs to be event-synchronized to ensure that only results from corresponding cc-points are matched. A synchronization protocol has been designed to provide the service [27]. It ensures that the results that are supplied to the decision function are from the same cross-check (cc) point in each version. The versions are halted until all of them have reached the same cc-point, and they are not started again until the results are exchanged and a decision is made. To be able to detect versions that are "hung up" and to allow slow versions to catch up, a time-out technique is used by the protocol. Acknowledgments are employed to verify that each site has received enough results to make a decision.

The decision and executive (D&E) layer receives the cc-vectors from its local version directly and from all other versions via the synchronization layer, determines the decision result, establishes whether the local version is faulty or not, and makes recovery decisions. The D&E layer controls the input/output of the local version, and all exceptions that are not handled elsewhere are directed to this layer. This layer has four entities: a *sender*, a *decision function*, and two entities that control the recovery process—a *local executive* and a *global executive*. The *sender* receives the cc-vector result from the local version and returns the decision result to it after a decision has been taken. It also executes the disconnection of the local version, controls its input and output operations, and handles communications with both executives.

The decision function determines a single decision result from the N results of individual versions. DEDIX provides a generic decision algorithm which may be replaced by a user's algorithm provided that the interfaces are preserved. This allows application-specific decision algorithms to be incorporated in those cases where the standard mechanisms are inappropriate. The generic decision algorithm determines a decision by applying one of three agreement tests: 1) *bit by bit*— identical match only; 2) *cosmetic*—detecting character string differences caused by spacing, misspelling, or character substitution; and 3) *numeric*—integer and real number decisions. Numeric decisions use a median value such that, as long as the majority of versions are not faulty, the median of all responses is acceptably close to the desired value. Numeric values are allowed to differ within some "skew interval," thus allowing version results to be nonidentical but still useable in the numeric decision process.

The local executive takes action when the decision function indicates that the decision result is not unanimous, or when any other exception is signaled from the local version or another layer. The local executive will first try to recover locally before it either reports the problem to the global executive or, if it is considered as fatal to the site, closes down the site. Three classes of exceptions can occur. *Functional exceptions* are specified in the functional description of DEDIX and are independent of the implementation. Among them are deviations from a unanimous result, the case when a communication link is disconnected, and the case when a cc-vector is completely missing. For these exceptions, the local executive will attempt to keep the site active, possibly terminating the local version, while keeping the input/output operating. *Implementation exceptions* are dependent on the specific computer system, language, and implementation technique chosen. All UNIX signals, such as segmentation faults, process termination, invalid system call, etc. belong to this class. Other examples are all the exceptions defined in DEDIX, such as signaling when a function is called with an invalid parameter or when an inconsistent state exists. Most of those exceptions will force an orderly closedown of a site in order to be able to provide data for analysis. Finally, there are *exceptions generated by the local version*. The local version program may include provisions for exception handling and some of the exceptions may not be recoverable within the version. These exceptions are sent to the local executive which will terminate the local version while keeping the site alive.

The global executive collects error reports from the decision function and the local executive, exchanges error reports with every other active global executive, and decides on a new configuration based on all error reports. The global executive is invoked after a preset number of exchanges of results (i.e., number of decisions) has taken place. The number of exchanges is maintained as a consistent value at all sites. Thus, by referring to this number, it is possible to ensure that all correctly working sites will exchange error reports and decide on a reconfiguration at the same state of computation. This number is kept consistent by the synchronization protocol.

The version layer interfaces the Jth (local) version with the DEDIX system and alters the variables in the local cc-vector that disagree with the decision result produced by the decision function. The function doing the interfacing is called the cross-check, or CC, function since it is called at each cc-point. Pointers to the results to be corrected are sent as parameters to this function. The CC function transfers the version representation of results into the DEDIX cc-vector format, so that the internal representation of a cc-vector in DEDIX is hidden to the version program. The CC function also returns the decision result to the version.

The user interface of DEDIX allows users to debug the system as well as the versions, to monitor the operations of the system, to apply stimuli to the system, and to collect data during experiments. Several commands are provided. The *break* command enables the user to set breakpoints. At a breakpoint, DEDIX stops executing the versions and allows entering of commands. The *remove* command deletes breakpoints set by the break command. The *continue* command resumes execution of the versions at a breakpoint. The user may terminate execution using the *quit* command. The user can examine the current contents of the message passing through the transport layer by using the *display* command. Since every message is logged, the user may also specify conditions in the *display* command to examine any message logged previously. The user can also examine the internal system states by using the *show* command, e.g., to examine the breakpoints which have been set, the decision results, etc. The user can inject faults to the system by changing the system states, e.g., the cc-vector, by using the *modify* command. The user interface gathers data and collects statistics of the experiments. Every message passing the transport layer is logged into a file with a time stamp. This enables the user to do postexecution analysis or even replay the experiment. Statistics such as elapsed time, system time, number of cc-points executed, and their decision outcomes are also collected.

The prototype DEDIX system has been operational since early 1985. Several modifications have been introduced since then—most of them intended to improve the speed of the execution of N-version software. The first major test of DEDIX will be experimentation with the set of about 20 programs produced by the NASA-sponsored four-university project discussed in Section IV. At the same time, a formal specification effort for DEDIX is being initiated as described in the following section.

VII. Directions of Current Research

The N-version software research at UCLA has the following two major long-term objectives:

1) to develop the principles of implementation and experimental evaluation of fault-tolerant N-version software units; and

2) to devise and evaluate supervisory systems for the execution of N-version software in various environments.

The N-version implementation studies address the problems of: 1) methods of specification; 2) the verification of specifications; 3) the assurance of independence in designs; 4) partitioning and matching, i.e., good choices of cc-points and cc-vectors for a given problem; 5) the means to recover a failed version; 6) efficient methods of modification for N-version units; 7) evaluation of effectiveness and of cost; and 8) the design of experiments.

The research concerned with the supervisory systems deals with: 1) the functional structure of supervisors; 2) fault-tolerant supervisor implementation, including tolerance of design faults; 3) instrumentation to support N-version software experiments; 4) efficient implementation, including custom hardware architectures to support real-time execution; and 5) methods of supervisor evaluation.

Our past experience has pinpointed an effective specification as the keystone of success for N-version software implementation [7]. Significant progress has occurred in the development of formal specification languages since our previous experiments. Our current goal is to compare and assess the ease of use by application programmers of several formal program specification methods, including the OBJ specification language developed at UCLA [23] and used in our previous experiment; the Clear specification language developed at the University of Edinburgh and SRI International [10]; the Larch family of specification languages developed at M.I.T. and the Xerox Research Center [28]; the Ina Jo^{TM} specification language developed at SDC [34]; the Z specification language developed at Oxford University [29], and also Prolog and Concurrent Prolog as methods of formal specification.

The comparison focuses on several aspects of applicability: 1) the purpose and scope (problem domain); 2) completeness of development; 3) quality and extent of documentation; 4) existence of support environments; 5) executability and suitability for rapid prototyping; 6) provisions to express timing constraints and concurrency; 7) methods of specification for exception handling; 8) extensibility to specify the special attributes of fault-tolerant multiversion software. The goal is to choose two or more specification languages for an experiment in the design of fault-tolerant multiversion software. The experiment has two major elements: first, it is an attempt to attain concurrent verification of two specifications by symbolic execution with mutual interplay, that is, a "two-version" specification; and second, it provides an assessment of the ease of use of the specifications by application programmers in an N-version software experiment. It is conjectured that the application of two diverse formal specifications will help to eliminate residual specification faults and further increase the dependability of the specifications.

The next step in the development of DEDIX is the formal specification of parts of the current DEDIX prototype that are implemented in C, beginning with the synchronization layer, the decision function, and the local and global executives. The specification is intended to provide an executable version of the DEDIX supervisory operating system. This functional specification is expected to provide a starting point for a implementation for real-time systems. Furthermore, the specification can be independently reimplemented in C for the use of multiversion software techniques in the implementation of different sites of DEDIX. The goal is a DEDIX system that supports N-version application programs and which is itself diverse in its design at each site.

In the experimental evaluation of the N-version approach, the immediate goal is extensive experimentation with about 20 programs to be generated during the summer of 1985 by the four-university effort discussed in Section IV. For the next step, plans are being prepared for the "international mail order" experiment as discussed in Section V of this paper.

VIII. Conclusion: Some Potential Long-Range Advantages of Design Diversity

The most immediate and direct opportunity to apply N-version software is offered by multiple-channel systems that incorporate very complete tolerance of physical faults such as SIFT [24]. The hardware resources and some architectural features that can support N-version software are already present, and the implementation requires an extension of the existing physical fault tolerance mechanisms. Furthermore, hardware diversity can be introduced by choosing functionally compatible hardware building blocks from different suppliers for each channel.

A more speculative, and also more general, application of N-version software is its partial substitution for current software verification and validation (V&V) procedures. Instead of extensive preoperational V&V of a single program, two independent versions can be executed in an operational environment, completing V&V concurrently with productive operation. The increased cost of producing the software is compensated for by a reduction of the V&V time and an earlier deployment. Another advantage may be a decrease in the amount of human effort and complexity of software tools needed for the very thorough V&V effort. Design faults in the V&V software are also less critical. The user can take the less efficient ("backup") version off line when adequate reliability of operation is reached, and then bring it back for special operating conditions that require greater reliability assurance, especially after modifications or after maintenance. A potential system lifetime cost reduction exists because a duplex diverse system (possibly operating in the recovery block mode) can support continued operation after latent design faults are uncovered, providing very high availability. The cost of fault analysis and elimination also might be reduced due to the lesser urgency of the repair actions.

The possible use of a "mail-order" approach to the production of two or more versions of software modules suggests an intriguing long-range benefit of the N-version approach in software. Given a formal specification that includes a set of single-version acceptance tests, the versions of software can be written by programmers working at their own preferred times and locations, and using their own personal computing equipment. Two potential advantages are as follows.

- The overhead cost of programming that accrues in highly controlled professional programming environments could be drastically reduced through this approach that allows free play to individual initiative and utilizes low-cost home facilities.

- The potential of the rapidly growing number of freelance programmers to serve as "mail-order" programmers would be tapped through this approach. For various reasons, many individuals with programming talents cannot fill the role of a professional programmer as defined by today's rigorous approaches to quality control and the use of centralized sites during the programming process, but they may well succeed as independent programming contractors for N-version implementations.

Finally, an important reliability and availability advantage through design diversity may be expected for systems that use VLSI circuits. The growing complexity of VLSI circuits, with 500 000 gates/chip available today and 1 million gates/chip predicted for the near future, raises the probability of design faults since a complete verification of the design is very difficult to attain. Furthermore, the design automation and verification tools themselves are subject to undiscovered design faults. Even with multi-channel fault-tolerant system designs, a single design fault may require the replacement of all chips of that type since on-chip modifications are impractical. Such a replacement would be a costly and time-consuming process. On the other hand, use of N versions of VLSI circuits in a multiple-channel design does allow the continued use of chips with design faults, as long as their errors are not similar at the circuit boundaries where the decision algorithm is applied.

Design diversity may enable dependable operation throughout the lifetime of a multiple-channel system without a single chip having a perfect design, and without any single perfect program executing on those chips. The building of the first system of this kind will be a milestone in the evolution of fault-tolerant systems, and current results support the prediction that such systems should be in service by the year 2000.

ACKNOWLEDGMENT

Over the past several years, this research has been supported by the National Science Foundation under Grants MCS-72-03633, MCS-78-18918, and MCS 81-21696, by the Office of Naval Research under Contract N0014-79-C-0866, and by a research grant from the Battelle Memorial Institute. Current support is provided by a grant from the Advanced Computer Science Program of the Federal Aviation Administration. The major contributions to experimental research have been made by L. Chen and J. P. J. Kelly. The principal designers of the DEDIX system are P. Gunningberg, L. Strigini, P. Traverse, K.-S. Tso, and U. Voges. Thanks are due to T. Anderson and J.-C. Laprie for their thoughtful comments on this paper.

REFERENCES

[1] T. Anderson and P. A. Lee, *Fault Tolerance, Principles and Practice.* Englewood Cliffs, NJ: Prentice-Hall, 1981, pp. 249–291.
[2] T. Anderson, "Can design faults be tolerated?" *Fehlertolerierende Rechensysteme* in *Proc. 2nd GI/NTG/GMR Conf.* Bonn, West Germany, Sept. 1984, IFB vol. 84, Springer-Verlag, pp. 426–433.
[3] T. Anderson, D. N. Halliwell, P. A. Barrett, and M. R. Moulding, "An evaluation of software fault tolerance in a practical system," in *Dig. 15th Ann. Int. Symp. Fault-Tolerant Comput.*, Ann Arbor, MI, June 19–21, 1985, pp. 140–145.
[4] A. Avižienis, "Fault tolerance and fault intolerance: Complementary approaches to reliable computing," in *Proc. 1975 Int. Conf. Rel. Software*, Los Angeles, CA, Apr. 21–23, 1975, pp. 458–464.
[5] A. Avižienis and L. Chen, "On the implementation of N-version programming for software fault tolerance during execution," in *Proc. COMPSAC 77, 1st IEEE-CS Int. Comput. Software Appl. Conf.*, Chicago, IL, Nov. 8–11, 1977, pp. 149–155.
[6] A. Avižienis, "Fault tolerance: The survival attribute of digital systems," *Proc. IEEE*, vol. 66, pp. 1109–1125, Oct. 1978.
[7] A. Avižienis and J. Kelly, "Fault tolerance by design diversity: Concepts and experiments," *Computer*, vol. 17, no. 8, pp. 67–80, Aug. 1984.
[8] A. Avižienis, P. Gunningberg, J. P. J. Kelly, L. Strigini, P. J. Traverse, K. S. Tso, and U. Voges, "The UCLA DEDIX system: A distributed testbed for multiple-version software," in *Dig. 15th Annu. Int. Symp. Fault-Tolerant Comput.*, Ann Arbor, MI, June 19–21, 1985, pp. 126–134.
[9] J. F. Bartlett, "A 'NonStop' operating system," in *Proc. Hawaii Int. Conf. Syst. Sci.*, Honolulu, HI, Jan. 5–6, 1978, pp. 103–119; reprinted in D. P. Siewiorek and R. S. Swarz, *The Theory and Practice of Reliable System Design.* Bedford, MA: Digital Press, 1982, pp. 453–460.
[10] R. M. Burstall and J. A. Goguen, "An informal introduction to specifications using CLEAR," in *The Correctness Problem in Computer Science*, R. Boyer and H. Moore, Eds. New York: Academic, 1981, pp. 185–213.
[11] R. H. Campbell, K. H. Horton, and G. G. Belford, "Simulations of a fault-tolerant deadline mechanisms," in *Dig. 9th Annu. Int. Symp. Fault-Tolerant Comput.*, Madison, WI, June 1979, pp. 95–101.

[12] L. Chen and A. Avižienis, "N-version programming: A fault tolerance approach to reliability of software operation," in *Dig. 8th Annu. Int. Conf. Fault-Tolerant Comput.* (FTCS-8), Toulouse, France, June 21-23, 1978, pp. 3-9.

[13] G. Dahll and J. Lahti, "Investigation of methods for production and verification of highly reliable software," in *Proc. IFAC Workshop SAFECOMP 1979*, Stuttgart, Germany, May 16-18, 1979.

[14] R. W. Downing, J. S. Nowak, and L. S. Tuomenoksa, "No. 1 ESS maintenance plan," *Bell Syst. Tech. J.*, vol. 43, no. 5, pt. 1, pp. 1961-2019, Sept. 1964.

[15] H. Ehrig, H. Kreowski, and H. Weber, "Algebraic specification schemes for data base systems," in *Proc. 4th Int. Conf. Very Large Data Bases*, West Berlin, Germany, Sept. 13-15, 1978, pp. 427-440.

[16] "Information processing systems—Reliability and requirements," in *Proc. East. Joint Comput. Conf.*, Washington, DC, Dec. 8-10, 1953.

[17] W. R. Elmendorf, "Fault-tolerant programming," in *Proc. 1972 Int. Symp. Fault-Tolerant Comput.*, Newton, MA, June 19-21, 1972, pp. 79-83.

[18] R. R. Everett, C. A. Zraket, and H. D. Benington, "SAGE-a data-processing system for air defense," in *Proc. East. Joint Comput. Conf.*, Washington, DC, Dec. 1957, pp. 148-155.

[19] M. A. Fischler, O. Firshein, and D. L. Drew, "Distinct software: An approach to reliable computing," in *Proc. 2nd USA-Japan Comput. Conf.*, Tokyo, Japan, Aug. 26-28, 1975, pp. 573-579.

[20] G. C. Gilley, Ed., *Dig. 1971 Int. Symp. Fault-Tolerant Comput.*, Pasadena, CA, Mar. 1-3, 1971.

[21] E. Girard and J. C. Rault, "A programming technique for software reliability," in *Proc. 1973 IEEE Symp. Comput. Software Rel.*, New York, Apr. 30-May 2, 1973, pp. 44-50.

[22] L. Gmeiner and U. Voges, "Software diversity in reactor protection systems: An experiment," in *Proc. IFAC Workshop SAFECOMP 1979*, Stuttgart, Germany, May 16-18, 1979, pp. 75-79.

[23] J. A. Goguen and J. J. Tardo, "An introduction to OBJ: A language for writing and testing formal algebraic program specifications," in *Proc. Specific. Rel. Software*, Cambridge, MA, Apr. 3-5, 1979, pp. 170-189.

[24] J. Goldberg, "SIFT: A provable fault-tolerant computer for aircraft flight control," in *Inform. Processing 80 Proc. IFIP Congr.*, Tokyo, Japan, Oct. 6-9, 1980, pp. 151-156.

[25] S. T. Gregory and J. C. Knight, "A new linguistic approach to backward error recovery," in *Dig. 15th Annu. Int. Symp. Fault-Tolerant Comput.*, Ann Arbor, MI, June 19-21, 1985, pp. 404-409.

[26] A. Grnarov, J. Arlat, and A. Avižienis, "On the performance of software fault tolerance strategies," in *Dig. 10th Int. Symp. Fault-Tolerant Comput.*, FTCS-10, Kyoto, Japan, Oct. 1-3, 1980, pp. 251-253.

[27] P. Gunningberg and B. Pehrson, "Protocol and verification of a synchronization protocol for comparison of results," in *Dig. 15th Annu. Int. Symp. Fault-Tolerant Comput.*, Ann Arbor, MI, June 19-21, 1985, pp. 172-177.

[28] J. V. Guttag and J. J. Horning, "An introduction to the Larch shared language," in *Inform. Processing '83 Proc. IFIP Congr.*, Paris, France, Sept. 19-23, 1983, pp. 809-814.

[29] I. J. Hayes, "Applying formal specification to software development in industry," *IEEE Trans. Software Eng.*, vol. SE-11, pp. 169-178, Feb. 1985.

[30] H. Hecht, "Fault-tolerant software," *IEEE Trans. Rel.*, vol. R-28, pp. 227-232, Aug. 1979.

[31] A. L. Hopkins, Jr., T. B. Smith, III, and J. H. Lala, "FTMP—A highly reliable fault-tolerant multiprocessor for aircraft," in *Proc. IEEE*, vol. 66, pp. 1221-1239, Oct. 1978.

[32] J. P. J. Kelly, "Specification of fault-tolerant multi-version software: Experimental studies of a design diversity approach, Dep. Comput. Sci., Univ. California, Los Angeles, Tech. Rep. CSD-820927, Sept. 1982.

[33] J. P. J. Kelly and A. Avižienis, "A specification-oriented multi-version software experiment," in *Dig. 13th Annu. Int. Symp. Fault-Tolerant Comput.* (FTCS-13), Milano, Italy, June 28-30, 1983, pp. 120-126.

[34] R. A. Kemmerer, "Testing formal specifications to detect design errors," *IEEE Trans. Software Eng.*, vol. SE-11, pp. 32-43, Jan. 1985.

[35] K. H. Kim, "Distributed execution of recovery blocks: Approach to uniform treatment of hardware and software faults," in *Proc. IEEE 4th Int. Conf. Distributed Comput. Syst.*, San Francisco, CA, May 14-18, 1984, pp. 526-532.

[36] H. Kopetz, "Software redundancy in real time systems," in *Inform. Processing 74 Proc. IFIP Congr.*, Stockholm, Sweden, Aug. 5-10, 1974, pp. 182-186.

[37] J.-C. Laprie, "Dependability evaluation of software systems in operation," *IEEE Trans. Software Eng.*, vol. SE-10, pp. 701-714, Nov. 1984.

[38] B. H. Liskov and V. Berzins, "An appraisal of program specifications," in *Research Directions in Software Technology*, P. Wegner, Ed. Cambridge, MA: M.I.T. Press, 1979, pp. 170-189.

[39] P. M. Melliar-Smith, "System specifications," in *Computing Systems Reliability*, T. Anderson and B. Randell, Eds. New York: Cambridge University Press, 1979, pp. 19-65.

[40] B. Meyer, "A system description method," in *Int. Workshop Models and Languages for Software Specification and Design*, B. G. Babb, II, and A. Mili, Eds. Orlando, FL, Mar. 1984, pp. 42-46.

[41] E. F. Moore and C. E. Shannon, "Reliable circuits using less reliable relays," *J. Franklin Inst.*, vol. 262, no. 9 and 10, pp. 191-208 and 281-297, Sept.-Oct. 1956.

[42] P. Morrison and E. Morrison, Eds., *Charles Babbage and His Calculating Engines*. New York: Dover, 1961, p. 177.

[43] J. Oblonsky, "A self-correcting computer," in *Digital Information Processors*, W. Hoffman, Ed. New York: Interscience, 1962, pp. 533-542.

[44] D. L. Parnas, "The role of program specification," in *Research Directions in Software Technology*, P. Wegner, Ed. Cambridge, MA: M.I.T. Press, 1979, pp. 364-370.

[45] G. Popek et al., "LOCUS—A network transparent, high reliability distributed system," in *Proc. 8th Symp. Operating Syst. Principles*, Dec. 1981, pp. 169-177.

[46] C. V. Ramamoorthy et al., "Application of a methodology for the development and validation of reliable process control software," *IEEE Trans. Software Eng.*, vol. SE-7, pp. 537-555, Nov. 1981.

[47] B. Randell, "System structure for software fault tolerance," *IEEE Trans. Software Eng.*, vol. SE-1, pp. 220-232, June 1975.

[48] J. R. Sklaroff, "Redundancy management technique for space shuttle computers," *IBM J. Res. Develop.*, vol. 20, pp. 20-28, Jan. 1976.

[49] J. Von Neumann, "Probabilistic logics and the synthesis of reliable organisms from unreliable components," in *Automata Studies*, C. E. Shannon and J. McCarthy, Eds. Princeton, NJ: Princeton University Press, Ann. Math. Studies, 1956, no. 34, pp. 43-98.

[50] H. O. Welch, "Distributed recovery block performance in a real-time control loop," in *Proc. Real-Time Syst. Symp.*, Arlington, VA, 1983, pp. 268-276.

Algirdas Avižienis (S'55-M'56-F'73) was born in Kaunas, Lithuania, in 1932. He received the B.S., M.S., and Ph.D. degrees, all in electrical engineering, from the University of Illinois, Urbana-Champaign, in 1954, 1955, and 1960, respectively.

He has recently completed three years of service as Chairman of the Department of Computer Science, University of California, Los Angeles, where he has served on the faculty since 1962. He also directs the UCLA Dependable Computing and Fault-Tolerant System research group that he established in 1972. Current projects of the group include design diversity for the tolerance of design faults, faults tolerance in distributed systems, and fault-tolerant supercomputer architectures. From 1956 to 1960 he was associated with the Digital Computer Laboratory, University of Illinois, as a Research Assistant and Fellow participating in the design of the Illiac II computer. From 1960 to 1973 he directed research on fault-tolerant spacecraft computers at the Jet Propulsion Laboratory, California Institute of Technology, Pasadena. This effort resulted in the construction and evaluation of the experimental JPL STAR (self-testing-and-repairing) computer, for which he received a U.S. Patent in 1970. A paper that described the JPL STAR computer won the Best Paper selection of the IEEE TRANSACTIONS ON COMPUTERS in 1971.

Dr. Avižienis was elected Fellow of IEEE for his pioneering work in fault-tolerant computing. and also received the NASA Apollo Achievement Award, the Honor Roll of the IEEE Computer Group, the AIAA Information Systems Award, the NASA Exceptional Service Medal, and the IEEE Computer Society Technical Achievement Award. As a member of the IEEE Computer Society, he founded and was the first Chairman of the Technical Committee on Fault-Tolerant Computing (1969-1973) as well as the General Chairman of the First International Symposium on Fault-Tolerant Computing in 1971. He also served for four years as a member of the Computer Society Governing Board. Since 1980 he has been the first Chairman of Working Group 10.4 on "Reliable Computing and Fault Tolerance" of the International Federation for Information Processing.

Redundancy in Data Structures: Improving Software Fault Tolerance

DAVID J. TAYLOR, MEMBER, IEEE, DAVID E. MORGAN, MEMBER, IEEE, AND
JAMES P. BLACK, STUDENT MEMBER, IEEE

Abstract—The increasing cost of computer system failure has stimulated interest in improving software reliability. One way to do this is by adding redundant structural data to data structures. Such redundancy can be used to detect and correct (structural) errors in instances of a data structure. The intuitive approach of this paper, which makes heavy use of examples, is complemented by the more formal development of the companion paper, "Redundancy in Data Structures: Some Theoretical Results."

Index Terms—Binary trees, error correction, error detection, linear lists, redundancy, robust data structures, software fault tolerance, software reliability.

I. INTRODUCTION

THE INCREASE in complexity and size of modern software systems and the increase in society's dependence on computer systems has been accompanied by an increase in the costs associated with their failure. This has in turn created an interest in achieving reliable, fault tolerant systems. In this pair of papers, we discuss one particular approach to increasing fault tolerance: the detection and correction of errors in stored data structures. This paper presents a survey of related work, terminology, and an informal development of the approach, including some experimental results. The companion paper [24] complements this with a more rigorous treatment of the basic results, as well as extensions to them, and concludes with some remarks on the synthesis of robust data structures.

Avizienis [3] defines two complementary approaches to achieving software reliability: *fault intolerance* and *fault tolerance*. The former includes techniques applied during system development to ensure that the running system satisfies all reliability criteria *a priori*: examples are proofs of program correctness, structured design and programming methodology, and development aids for systematic testing and debugging. This approach cannot cope with residual design flaws, bugs, hardware malfunctions, or user errors, all of which suggest using the complementary approach of fault tolerance. This approach attempts to increase reliability by designing the system to continue to provide service in spite of the presence of faults.

Manuscript received September 21, 1979; revised April 10, 1980. This work was supported in part by the Natural Sciences and Engineering Research Council of Canada under Grants A3078 and A8116, and through a Postgraduate Scholarship.

The authors are with the Department of Computer Science and the Computer Communications Networks Group, University of Waterloo, Waterloo, Ont., Canada N2L 3G1.

The need for software to cope with its own errors, errors introduced by undetected hardware faults and mistakes by users seems to have been recognized first by designers of real-time control systems, notably telephone switching systems [4], [8]. More recently, designers of operating systems and database systems have also recognized that detection and correction of software-induced errors are important. (An example of this concern is shown in the design of IBM's OS/VS2-2 [22], [23], which contains error detection and recovery routines not included in previous IBM operating systems.)

Redundancy is the key to error detection, correction, and recovery [2], [3], [20]. Redundant data in the system are essential in order to detect and recover from many types of hardware or software malfunctions. Special software is required to maintain and make effective use of the redundant data; some redundant data may be essentially coded into this software. Other types of malfunctions can only be detected by observing the behavior of the system, and comparing this with known or expected behavior derived from analysis of a system model or experience using the system. There are, in fact, four forms of redundancy which can be used to enhance system fault tolerance: redundant hardware, redundant software, redundant data, and redundant information about the system's behavior. A compromise between the cost of failures and the cost of the facilities necessary to cope with them determines the amount and type of redundancy which should be used to improve reliability.

Recovery relies on the use of redundancy to reconstruct damaged data. The redundancy can be in the form of backup copies or can be achieved by using redundancy in the representation of the data. A systematic recovery technique is the use of "recovery blocks" and the associated "recovery cache" [21]. For each recovery block, a sequence of alternate sections of code is provided. Each alternate is tried in turn until the "acceptance test" associated with the recovery block is satisfied. After each unsuccessful alternate, the system state is reset from the recovery cache to its contents on entry to the block. Useful acceptance tests depend on the existence of appropriate redundancy.

Various ad hoc techniques have also been developed for using redundant representations of data for recovery. For example, Waldbaum [28] summarizes some techniques for use with a set of linked control blocks, and Lockemann and Knutsen [15] describe a particular technique for use in correcting disk allocation data after a system crash.

A general description of error redundancy in a database

environment is given by Fry and Sibley [9]. Many recovery techniques for database systems make use of backup copies of portions of the database. Some ways of making use of such backup copies in recovery are described in [6], [16].

Ideally, there should be systematic techniques for synthesizing the software components of a system to achieve specified levels of reliability and recoverability. There is also a need to analyze software systems to predict or measure their reliability. Attempts are being made to satisfy these needs: a good survey may be found in [2]. Unfortunately, there is little underlying theory to explain why one technique is better than another or to assist in the development of new techniques. Even when it is realized that redundancy is the key to performing error detection, diagnosis, and recovery, there is no systematic technique for adding redundancy to stored data, or for exploiting such redundancy.

The major goal of our research is to find where and how to apply redundancy to yield cost-effective fault tolerant systems. A little redundancy, thoughtfully deployed and exploited, can yield significant benefits for fault tolerance; however, excessive or inappropriately applied redundancy is pointless. These papers illustrate one way of measuring and comparing the effectiveness of alternative ways of structuring data, the goal being to find storage structures that are robust in the face of errors and failures. The work is in a sense parallel to (and complements) that of Gotlieb and Tompa [11] which provides a technique for selecting a storage structure from a set of alternatives based on efficiency considerations.

II. Terminology

In discussing fault tolerance, we will use some definitions suggested by Melliar-Smith and Randell [18]. A *failure* occurs when a system does not meet its specifications: it is an externally observable event. An *erroneous state* is a system state that can lead to a failure which we attribute to some aspect of that state. An *error* is that part of an erroneous state which can lead to a failure. A *fault* is a mechanical or algorithmic cause of an error. A *fault tolerant* system is one which attempts to prevent erroneous states from producing failures. This paper discusses the effect on fault tolerance of using redundancy in the representation of data structures.

The following definitions will be used in discussing data structures. A *data structure* is defined to be a logical organization of data. A *storage structure* is a representation of a data structure. The representation specifies whether nodes are to be adjacent or connected by pointers, what pointers are used, and so on. An *encoding* of a storage structure is its representation on a particular storage medium. The encoding specifies how pointers are represented (absolute, relative, etc.), what fields are packed into a single word, and so on. Thus, "binary tree" is a data structure; a representation in which there are pointers from each node to the left and right sons of the node is a storage structure for a binary tree; and if we also specify that pointers are stored as absolute addresses, that is an encoding of a binary tree. (This terminology is adapted from Tompa [27].)

We define a *data structure instance* to be a particular occurrence of a data structure. When the context makes the meaning clear, we will also use "data structure instance" to refer to the storage structure for the instance or its encoded form.

We define a *change* to be an elementary modification to the encoded form of a data structure instance. (The meaning of "elementary modification" can be specified to suit the environment; here it will mean the modification of a single word.) Since a change modifies a data structure instance at the encoding level, the effect of the change on the storage structure depends on the encoding used. There is a mapping which transforms a change into one or more "changes" in the storage structure. For simplicity, we will assume that each change corresponds to only one "change" in the storage structure unless the encoding is explicitly noted as packing two or more fields into one word. (Here, the only example of the latter case occurs in Section III-B.) We do not specify the types of faults which cause the changes, but the following are possibilities: hardware faults; "wild" stores by incorrect programs; incorrect update procedures; and incomplete execution of update procedures, possibly resulting from an unrelated event (e.g., an operating system crash). For this last possibility, the instance which has been partially updated is left some number of changes "away" from the initial configuration and from the final desired configuration.

To illustrate our definition of change, consider the following storage structure for a linear list. Suppose the list contains four items, each of the first three has a pointer to the next, and the last contains a null pointer:

$$A \to B \to C \to D \to NULL$$

If somewhere in storage there is a node which contains X and a null pointer, then a single change in the pointer of node C can produce

$$A \to B \to C \to X \to NULL$$

This single change effectively replaces D by X.

In this paper, only changes affecting structural information (such as pointers, counts, and identifier fields) will be considered. That is, we are concerned here with structural integrity rather than semantic integrity. *Semantic integrity* [12], [17], [19] concerns the meaning of the data being represented: does it correspond to a possible configuration of the real world entities being described? *Structural integrity* [10], [29] concerns the correctness of the representation of the data: whether pointers have values in the right range, whether internal structural redundancy is consistent, and so forth.

In order to discuss error detection and correction in instances of data structures, we must give our definition of a "correct" instance. For the purposes of this paper, we define an instance of a data structure to be "correct" if a "detection procedure" applied to the instance returns the value "correct."

Detection properties of a data structure encoding are stated in terms of changes. If a single change can transform a correct data structure instance into another correct instance, as in the linear list example above, the encoding has no detection capabilities. If at least two changes are required to transform any correct instance into another, then single change detection is possible. In general, if at least N changes are required to transform any correct instance into another, any set of one to N-1 changes can be detected.

If all sets of N or fewer changes can be detected, we say the encoding is *N-detectable* (i.e., its *detectability* is N). We say an encoding is *N-correctable* (i.e., its *correctability* is N) if there is a procedure which, for all sets of N or fewer changes, can take a correct instance modified by that number of changes and recreate the correct instance. Thus, we are interested in computing the minimum number of changes to produce, say, an undetectable error. (Note that N-detectability implies K-detectability for K < N, and similarly for correctability.) These definitions of detectability and correctability are related to Hamming's definitions for binary codes [13].

Although detectability and correctability are properties of the encoding of a data structure, it is often convenient to refer to them as properties of the storage structure. In general, the encoding itself will only be significant when it specifies that more than one field at the storage structure level is to be placed in a single word.

III. Robust Storage Structures

A robust storage structure is one containing redundant data which allow erroneous changes to be detected, and possibly corrected as well. Three commonly used forms of structural redundancy in data are a stored count of the number of nodes in a structure instance, identifier fields, and additional pointers [28].

A count of the number of nodes in an instance is often useful for purposes other than reliability. It is also one of the most commonly used techniques for improving the robustness of storage structures, since it is a simple technique to use and usually introduces little overhead.

An *identifier field* is a group of one or more words, usually at the beginning of a node, whose value is sufficient to determine the unique instance in the system to which the node belongs. As well, there may be different identifier field values associated with different types of nodes in an instance. Usually, given a particular pointer in a particular type of node, we know (by the rules governing the storage structure) that it must point to a node of a particular type. Thus, the path followed to a particular node is sufficient to determine its type and the value which should be stored in its identifier field. This situation, in which all identifier fields are redundant, is the only one which will be considered in these papers.

Algorithms which work with a storage structure usually require certain pointers between nodes in order to perform their functions. Additional pointers whose values could be deduced from other pointers may be added to the structure. These redundant pointers are a powerful tool in increasing storage structure robustness. In addition, they may sometimes make algorithms which work with the storage structure simpler or more efficient.

In this paper we consider storage structures which consist of a *header* and a (possibly empty) set of *nodes*. The header contains pointers to certain nodes of the instance or to parts of itself and may also contain one or more counts and identifier fields. Each node contains data items and structural information, which may be pointers and node type identifier fields. (If the header contains more than one part, we assume that all parts are accessible without following intra-header pointers. This is generally accomplished by storing the parts of the header as a contiguous vector.)

When identifier fields are used in an instance, we assume that they contain a value which appears in no other identifier fields in the system. This is an aspect of the "valid state hypothesis," which is a basic assumption used throughout these papers. The hypothesis is that the only pointers to nodes of an instance occur in the instance, and that the unique identifier value(s) for the instance appear only in its own identifier fields. Insofar as the theorems in the companion paper are concerned, we point out that it is possible to relax the valid state hypothesis, at the price of complication of their statement and proof [26].

We present below examples of several storage structures for linear lists and binary trees, and informally discuss their robustness. We also give some practical implementation considerations. Our purpose is to clarify the terms presented above, give an intuitive motivation for the theoretical results presented in the companion paper, and demonstrate that these techniques can be easily applied in practice.

A. Linear Lists

The easiest way of implementing a linear list is simply to store a pointer in each node to the next node of the list, placing a null pointer in the last node. Inserting nodes in, and deleting nodes from, instances of such a storage structure is quite simple and efficient, but the storage structure is not at all robust. Specifically, it is 0-detectable and 0-correctable: changing one pointer to null can reduce any list to the empty list. Such a storage structure contains no explicit redundancy and uses only one word of structural data in each node (the pointer field). Inserting a node in the list requires two changes, one in the inserted node and one in the preceding node.

A commonly used storage structure which is more robust adds an identifier field to each node, replaces the null pointer in the last node by a pointer to the header of the list, and stores a count of the number of nodes on the list. In this "single-linked" implementation, an additional word is added to each node of the list, and four changes are required to insert a node: two pointers, an identifier field, and the count. It also has the effect of making the storage structure 1-detectable, although it is still 0-correctable.

The 1-detectability is easily seen. A change to the count may be detected by comparing it against the number of nodes found by following pointers. An identifier change is trivial to detect. A pointer change may be detected either because the count does not agree, or because the changed pointer now points to a foreign node, which cannot have a valid identifier field under the valid state hypothesis. The reader can easily devise a pair of changes which produces a correct instance, thus proving that the storage structure is exactly 1-detectable. The 0-correctability is shown by the following example: modifying a pointer to shorten the apparent list makes it impossible to decide whether the count is wrong or whether some nodes have been deleted.

The most robust of commonly used list storage structures is the double-linked list. A double-linked list is a single-linked list with a pointer added to each node, pointing to the predecessor of the node on the list. This adds one more word of storage per node and increases the number of changes for inserting a node to six: two forward pointers, two backward pointers, an identifier field, and the count. This storage structure is 2-detectable and 1-correctable, essentially because it has two independent, disjoint sets of pointers, each of which may be used to reconstruct the entire list. (This result is proven in the companion paper.)

Finally, we may consider a novel storage structure, which is similar to the double-linked one, but in which the "backward" pointers point to the second preceding node rather than the immediately preceding node. The storage required per node is clearly the same as for a double-linked list, but one more change is required when inserting a node. (Three backward pointers must be changed, rather than two.) This storage structure, which is referred to as a "modified(2) double-linked list," is 3-detectable and 1-correctable. Fig. 1 shows a modified(2) double-linked list of five nodes. (The parameter 2 in the name is the distance spanned by the back pointer. A modified(3) double-linked list is 4-detectable, but still only 1-correctable. Increasing the parameter beyond 3 has no further effect on detectability or correctability.)

This last storage structure illustrates that the "standard" double-linked list implementation may not always be the best way of using two pointers per node in a linear list. If one is willing to pay a slight price in terms of update time, it is possible to achieve greater detectability using the modified(2) double-linked implementation.

We can summarize the robustness and the performance costs of these four storage structures in a "cost and effectiveness graph" (Fig. 2).

How could these detectability and correctability results be exploited in a real system? Could this be done at reasonable cost? Besides the obvious costs of increased storage and update time, what else is required to perform the error detection and correction?

In-line checks may be introduced into normal system code to perform error detection, and possibly correction, during regular operation. This introduces an unvarying amount of overhead. Alternatively, detection/correction programs (sometimes called "audit" programs [1]) may be run periodically, or when trouble is supected. The advantage is that their frequency may be varied according to criteria such as frequency of errors, system load, application criticality, etc. The classical example is automated telephone switching [1]. Some additional considerations may be found in [5], [28].

In order to indicate that the cost of detecting and correcting errors is not prohibitive, Fig. 3 shows a single error correction/double error detection procedure for standard double-linked lists. In the companion paper, we give a general correction theorem, and sketch a general correction procedure which has a polynomial, although rather excessive execution time. However, the procedure of Fig. 3 has O(n) execution time

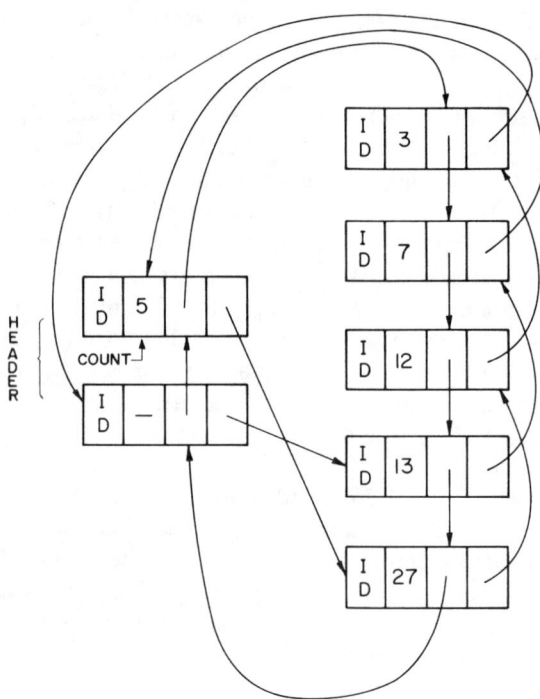

Fig. 1. Modified(2) double-linked list.

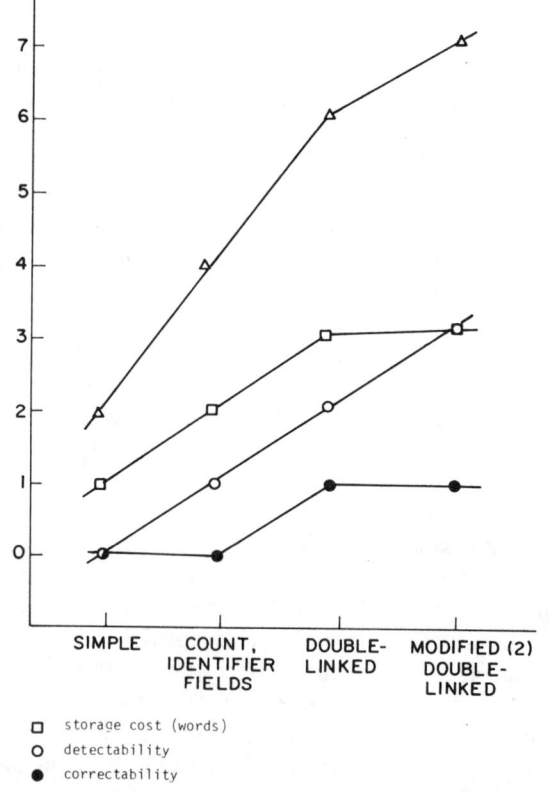

Fig. 2. Cost and effectiveness graph for linear list storage structures.

for an n-node list. The procedure scans the list in the forward direction until an identifier field error or forward/back pointer mismatch is detected. When this occurs, a reverse scan is initiated until a similar error is encountered, at which point repair is attempted. Fig. 4 gives an example, showing the applicable variables when L_REPAIR is called. The reader

```
procedure LIST-CORR (H, N)
begin
    pointer H, integer N, pointer P,
    pointer PREV-P, integer J;
    J ← 0;
    PREV-P ← H;
    P ← FORWARD(H);
    while (P ≠ H) do
    begin
        J ← J + 1;
        if (BACK(P) = PREV-P and ID(P) correct) then
        begin
            PREV-P ← P;
            P ← FORWARD(P);
        end
        else
        begin
            BACK-SCAN(H, P, PREV-P);
            return;
        end
    end
    if (BACK(H) ≠ PREV-P or ID(H) incorrect) then
    begin
        BACK-SCAN(H, P, PREV-P);
        return;
    end
    if (J ≠ N) then
        N ← J;
end

procedure BACK-SCAN (H, P, PREV-P)
begin
    pointer H, pointer P, pointer PREV-P
    pointer Q, pointer PREV-Q;
    PREV-Q ← H;
    Q ← BACK(H);
    repeat
    begin
        if (FORWARD(Q) = PREV-Q and ID(Q) correct) then
        begin
            PREV-Q ← Q;
            Q ← BACK(Q);
        end
        else
        begin
            L-REPAIR (P, PREV-P, Q, PREV-Q);
            return;
        end
    end
end

procedure L-REPAIR (P, PREV-P, Q, PREV-Q)
begin
    pointer P, pointer PREV-P, pointer Q, pointer PREV-Q;
    if (P = Q and ID(P) incorrect) then
        ID(P) ← correct i.d.
    else
        if (P = PREV-Q) then
            BACK(PREV-Q) ← PREV-P
        else
            if (PREV-P = Q) then
                FORWARD(PREV-P) ← PREV-Q
            else
                "multiple error";
end
```

Fig. 3. Linear list correction procedure.

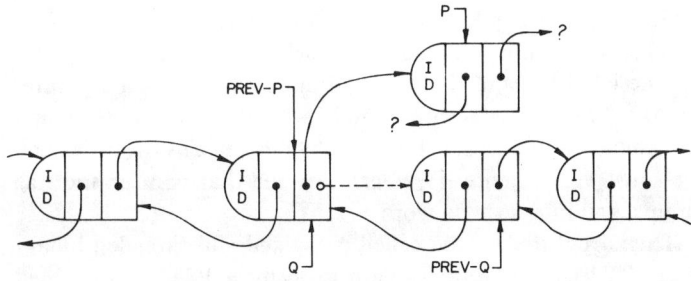

Fig. 4. Linear list correction. L–REPAIR will make the correction indicated by o– – →.

should be able to convince himself that the procedure corrects any single error to count, identifier, or pointer fields, and detects all double errors and some multiple errors. (This is proven in [25].) While LIST_CORR is shown in the form of an audit, it could easily be adapted to perform any "normal" processing required during list traversal, thus making it into an in-line check procedure.

B. Binary Trees

Binary trees are very commonly used data structures, but ad hoc detection and correction techniques for them are not as well developed as for linear lists. This section presents new techniques for achieving the same level of robustness in binary trees as is provided by the common techniques used for linear lists.

The usual storage structure for binary trees will be considered, namely, one in which each node of the tree contains two pointers, one to its left son and one to its right son. If either son does not exist, the corresponding pointer will have a null value. Procedures for traversing binary trees form the basis for detection and correction procedures. Generally, an in-order traversal will be used. In-order may be defined simply by: traverse the left subtree (in in-order), "visit" the root, traverse the right subtree (in in-order). This suggests an obvious recursive implementation; a simple nonrecursive implementation using a stack is also possible. For more details on tree traversal see [14, pp. 315–332].

Two obvious kinds of redundancy to add to a binary tree storage structure are identifier fields and a count of the number of nodes in the tree. As with linear lists, this yields 1-detectability and 0-correctability. Without this redundancy, the structure is 0-detectable and 0-correctable. Performing change detection is difficult because of problems associated with detecting the change of a pointer so that it points to a different subtree of the same size. It appears that all detection procedures which do not modify the tree structure instance require $O(n \log n)$ time and $O(n)$ working storage, for a tree of n nodes. (These are worst case results; better average case behavior could be obtained.)

A simple example will illustrate the source of the difficulty. Consider a three node tree: a root A and two sons of A, denoted B and C. Suppose the pointer from A to C is changed to point to B. The only difference from the original tree is that one node, B, now appears to be in two different locations in the tree. If modification is allowed we may set a flag in each node visited to detect duplication. However, if the tree may not be modified, we must compare each node against all other nodes in order to detect this type of change. The only effective way of detecting duplication is to store all node addresses in a structure which has $O(\log n)$ search and insertion times, thus producing the results cited above. An alternative is to rescan the previous part of the tree structure, thus eliminating the $O(n)$ storage space but increasing the execution time to $O(n^2)$. It is only necessary to test for duplication at leaf nodes; however, since in a balanced tree of n nodes there are approximately n/2 leaves, the above order notations are not changed.

Another kind of redundancy which is sometimes added to binary trees to improve efficiency is a "thread link" [14, pp. 319–320]. In the case of "right threading," which will be used here, each null right link is replaced by a pointer to the in-order successor of the node containing the thread link. A recursive characterization is that, for a node X, the final in-order node in X's left subtree contains a thread to X. A flag in each node is used to indicate whether the right pointer is a normal link or a thread. We assume that the encoding packs the right pointer and its associated flag into one word. As shown in [25, Section 5.4], this implementation is 1-detectable and a detection procedure exists which, for a tree of n nodes, requires $O(n)$ time and space proportional to the height of the tree ($O(\log n)$ for a balanced tree).

The threaded tree implementation is not 2-detectable, as illustrated in Fig. 5. The instance on the right differs in the count and one link from the instance on the left, and both are properly threaded binary trees.

We would like to obtain a 2-detectable, 1-correctable storage structure for a binary tree. As mentioned above for linear lists, the general correction theorem of the companion paper requires at least two edge-disjoint paths to each node of an instance, in order to prove that the structure is 1-correctable. Intuitively, this precludes disconnection of one or more nodes from the instance by a single change. This clearly implies that there be at least two pointers to each node, a condition which does not hold for threaded trees. We note that each node has exactly one nonthread link pointing to it and either zero or one thread links pointing to it. In fact, a node has a thread link pointing to it iff it has a nonnull left subtree. (If the left subtree is nonnull, the final in-order node in the subtree contains a thread to the node in question.) Thus, nodes with null left links have only one incoming edge, so an obvious

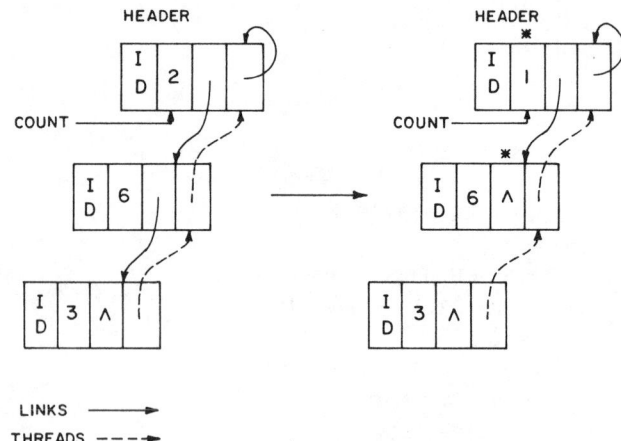

Fig. 5. An undetectable pair of changes to a threaded tree.

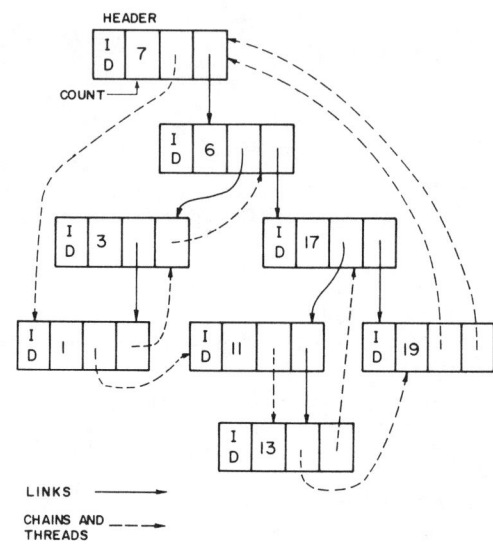

Fig. 6. A CT-tree of seven nodes and header.

possibility is to link these nodes together, using the left link field. A tag must be added to each node indicating the use of the left link, and the list head must now contain a pointer to the "first" node with a null left link. The nodes could be linked in any order, but for obvious reasons, in-order will be most convenient. (We again assume that pointer and flag are packed into a single word.)

This structure will be called a chained and threaded binary tree (CT-tree). The nodes with logically null left links, joined in in-order, will be called the chain, and the links joining them will be called chain links. Fig. 6 shows an example of a chained and threaded binary tree.

Fig. 7 is a detection procedure for chained and threaded binary trees. Its execution time is $O(n)$ for an n-node tree. The routine CHECK operates as follows. Given the header of a purported subtree T and a pointer CH to the first node which should be on T's chain, CHECK sets CH to the last in-order chain link in the subtree, and sets TH to the thread link of the final in-order node in the subtree. Calls to CHECK use the new values of CH and TH to verify that the tree is properly formed. CHECK also counts each node encountered

```
procedure CHECK_CT(T, N);
    pointer T;
    integer N;
    begin
    /* Given a purported tree root T, expected count N, and
    expected chain pointer CH, CHECK increments K by the
    number of nodes in the tree, and advances CH and TH to
    the outgoing chain and thread pointers. It makes
    recursive calls to itself to check each of its subtrees.
    */
    procedure CHECK (T, N, K, CH, TH);
        pointer T, CH, TH;
        integer N, K;
        begin
        K ← K + 1;
        if ID(T) incorrect then error_exit;
        if K > N then error_exit;
        if LTAG(T) = 'CHAIN' then
            /* Check expected chain pointer and update CH.*/
            if CH = T then CH ← LEFT(T)
            else error_exit
        else begin
            CHECK(LEFT(T), N, K, CH, TH);
            /*Verify proper threading of subtree.*/
            if TH ≠ T then error_exit;
            end;
        if RTAG(T) = 'THREAD' then
            /*Advance thread pointer.*/
            TH ← RIGHT(T)
        else CHECK(RIGHT(T), N, K, CH, TH);
        end CHECK;
    integer K;
    pointer CH, TH;
    /*Initialise call and verify subtree chain and thread.*/
    if T = null or ID(T) incorrect then error_exit;
    K ← 0;
    CH ← LEFT(T);
    CHECK(RIGHT(T), N, K, CH, TH);
    if N ≠ K or CH ≠ T or TH ≠ T then error_exit;
    end CHECK_CT;
```

Fig. 7. CT-tree detection procedure.

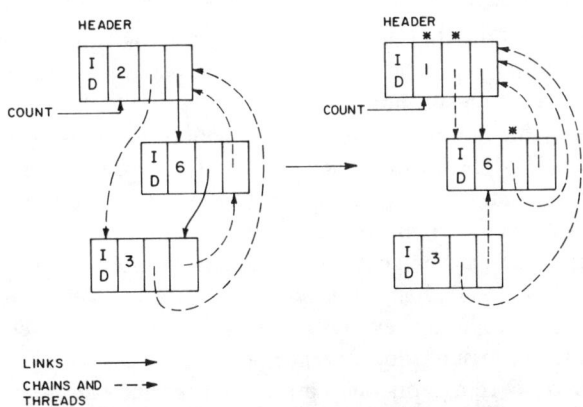

Fig. 8. Change in number of nodes in a CT-tree.

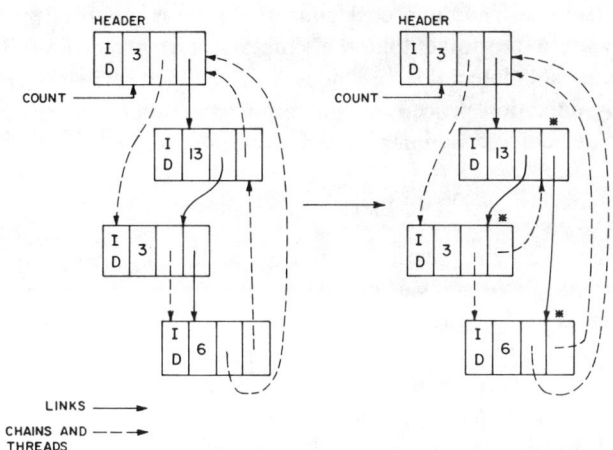

Fig. 9. Rearrangement of a CT-tree.

and terminates if this count exceeds N, the expected number of nodes in the tree. The enclosing routine CHECK-CT simply uses the header to initialize the call to CHECK, and to verify that the tree is properly chained and threaded to the header.

The detection procedure is presented to make formal our definition of a chained and threaded binary tree. However, exhibiting a detection procedure implies nothing about the robustness of this storage structure, which we claim is 2-detectable and 1-correctable. Given the 2-detectability, and the two edge-disjoint paths to every node (one using only chains and threads, the other using the normal tree pointers), the general correction theorem states that the structure is 1-correctable.

The following is an intuitive justification of the 2-detectability. Any set of changes which transforms one correct instance into another must either change the number of nodes in the instance, rearrange existing nodes, or replace one or more nodes in the instance with foreign nodes.

1) Change in Number: Deletion clearly requires fewer changes than insertion, as new identifier fields are required for new nodes under the valid state hypothesis. Any subtree may be deleted by changing the count, the incoming chain pointer, and either the left pointer to a chain or the right pointer to a thread, for a minimum of three changes. See Fig. 8.

2) Rearrangement: Clearly, both the normal tree structure and the chain/thread structure must be rearranged for the result to be a correct CT-tree. The case requiring the fewest changes occurs when a null and a nonnull subtree are exchanged, leaving the chain structure intact: the old thread becomes a right pointer, the incoming pointer to the subtree becomes a thread, and the outgoing thread of the subtree is updated, for a minimum of three changes. Updates which rearrange nonnull subtrees, which require changing the chain structure, or which rearrange interior nodes all require a larger number of changes. See Fig. 9.

3) Replacement: As the valid state hypothesis requires changing an identifier field for each replacement node, the minimum clearly occurs when a single foreign node replaces a single node of the instance. Besides the identifier field, we must change one incoming pointer, one incoming thread or chain, one outgoing chain or left pointer, and one outgoing thread or right pointer. This gives a minimum of five changes for replacing one or more nodes.

Thus, the minimum number of changes to transform one correct CT-tree into another is three for rearrangement and change in number, and five for replacement. Note that such changes do not necessarily leave the system in a valid state, as they may leave identifier fields and pointers in memory external to the changed instance. However, this is undetectable except by exhaustive memory search, which we exclude by assumption. Since at least three changes are required to transform one correct CT-tree into another, the detectability is exactly two.

The results obtained here for binary tree storage structures are summarized in a cost and effectiveness graph (Fig. 10). It should be noted that the simple storage structure with a count is 1-detectable but does not have a linear time, read-only detection procedure, whereas all the other detectabilities can be achieved by linear time procedures.

IV. Empirical Results

The preceding section assumed an "intelligent" source of changes, that is, we calculated the minimum number of changes to produce an uncorrectable or undetectable error. In this section we discuss some experiments which were performed to determine the effect of applying "random" changes to the encoding of a data structure instance.

Although the change sources are different, the analytical results do partially predict the results of the experiments. For example, if a storage structure is exactly 2-detectable, we know that any randomly selected change or pair of changes cannot produce an undetectable error, but that a set of three changes can. The experiments provide an indication of the probability that a set of three changes will produce an undetectable error.

It may be possible to calculate such probabilities directly from the specification of a storage structure, but at present only empirical results are available. (It should also be noted that the effect of applying random changes depends on various parameters which do not have to be considered when using an "intelligent adversary" model. How one selects "random changes" is clearly such a parameter. Less obviously, the size of the instance may also be a relevant parameter.)

A. Methodology

The basic experimental technique used was to introduce changes to encodings of data structure instances in a pseudorandom manner and observe the behavior of detection and correction routines applied to the changed instances.

The experiments work with data structures that appear to be on external storage. The most important reason for this is that external data structures constrain a program to perform all accesses through read and write routines, simplifying the experiments.

The data structures are actually kept in main storage, a large buffer being used to simulate a random-access file. A set of routines called the "IOSYS Pseudo File System," de-

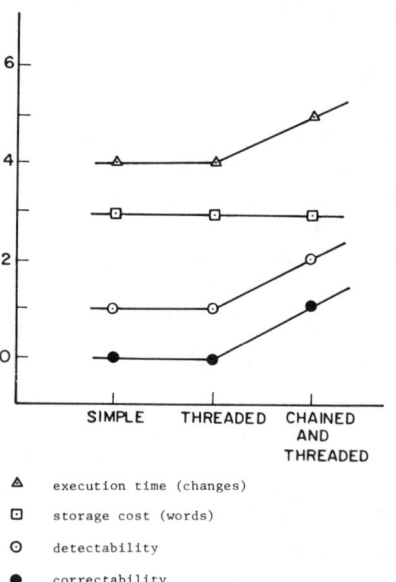

Fig. 10. Cost and effectiveness graph for binary tree storage structures.

veloped in order to perform the experiments, provides support for such simulated files, and provides various auxiliary services such as long-term storage of simulated files on real external storage. An important facility provided is the "mangler" which allows pseudorandom changes to be inserted in a simulated file.

There are many ways of introducing erroneous changes in a data structure instance (i.e., mangling it) in order to test its robustness. Alternative methods of mangling range from inserting random values into randomly selected locations to making subtle changes to carefully selected locations in the instance. If no use is made of knowledge of the storage structure, subtle combinations of changes that could be caused by software containing errors will occur with very small probability. If full knowledge of the data structure is used, it is likely that the mangler will only introduce those errors that the programmer thought of. A full discussion of manglers is beyond the scope of this paper.

The mangler used for these experiments is a compromise intended to minimize the disadvantages of either extreme. It is implemented as part of the write function of IOSYS. It pseudorandomly chooses whether or not to change the record being written, which word to change, and by what amount to change the word. Small increments or decrements are used for changes rather than arbitrary replacement of a word, since the chosen method tends to introduce more "subtle" changes.

For flexibility, the mangler is driven by a set of user-specified parameters which determine: the probability of mangling a record, the probability density of changes over the words of a record, and the maximum value to be used as an increment or decrement. There are presently two distributions available: uniform, and skewed towards the beginning of the record (where structural information is typically stored). The increment to be used is chosen uniformly from the integers in the range -max to max, excluding zero. All parameters can be specified individually for the separate simulated files.

B. Detectability Results

The purpose of the experiments was to estimate the probability of random changes producing undetectable errors in linear list storage structures. A routine "pretended" to delete records from a linear list by reading and writing those records which a delete routine would read and write. As records were written, words in the list nodes were "randomly" altered by adding or subtracting a small value. When a specified number of changes had been made, a detection procedure was executed to determine if the resulting instance could be detected as in error.

Three storage structures were tested in this experiment: the single-linked, double-linked, and modified(2) double-linked implementations described above. These have detectabilities of 1, 2, and 3, respectively, as described previously. For single-linked lists, 3000 sets each of one up to five changes were applied. For exactly two changes, five pairs of changes produced undetectable errors; no other number of changes produced undetectable errors. For both double-linked lists and modified(2) double-linked lists, 3000 sets of 1 to 12 changes were applied and no undetectable errors occurred.

Probably the most surprising aspect of these results is that single-linked lists seem more resistant to triples or quadruples of changes than to pairs of changes. It is hypothesized that this results from the tendency of sets of more than two changes to include destruction of an identifier field in addition to an otherwise undetectable set of changes.

C. Correctability Results

In order to study correctability, two additional concepts are needed. The first is called the *accessible set* of a data structure instance. It is the set of all nodes which can be accessed by following a sequence of pointers from the header of the structure. For a correct instance which does not contain pointers to other instances, the accessible set is simply the set of nodes which are (intuitively) "part of" the structure. We define the *correctability radius* to be one less than the minimum number of changes which can cause any node to become inaccessible.

No attempt was made to correct the instances found to be in error, but all the changed instances were checked to see if there was still a path to each node of the unchanged instance, which is a prerequisite for correction. We are particularly interested in determining how frequently disconnections occur once the correctability radius is exceeded. (In all the examples of Section III, the correctability radius is equal to the correctability.) Table I shows the probabilities of disconnecting an instance (destroying all paths to a node).

We can observe that for the first two storage structures there is a direct practical significance for the correctability radius (which is 0 for single-linked lists and 1 for double-linked lists). If the correctability radius is exceeded we immediately encounter a significant number of disconnections, precluding correction. The modified(2) double-linked implementation also experiences some disconnections as soon as the correctability radius is exceeded, but there are not nearly as many. Another much more robust storage struc-

TABLE I

Number of Changes	Single-linked	Double-linked	Modified(2) Double-linked
1	0.424 (0.406, 0.442)	0.00 (0.00, .001)	0.00 (0.00, .001)
2	0.675 (0.658, 0.692)	0.143 (0.131, 0.156)	0.008 (0.006, 0.012)
3	0.841 (0.828, 0.854)	0.332 (0.315, 0.349)	0.020 (0.015, 0.025)
4	0.942 (0.933, 0.950)	0.510 (0.492, 0.528)	0.044 (0.038, 0.052)
5	0.978 (0.972, 0.983)	0.655 (0.638, 0.672)	0.079 (0.070, 0.090)

The parenthesized figures are 95 percent confidence intervals.

ture, not described here, was also tested. It has a correctability radius of four, but in the experiment no disconnections were observed for sets of fewer than 14 changes, and even with as many as 20 changes applied, the number of disconnections was very small, not exceeding seven disconnections in 3000 trials in any of the test runs.

V. Conclusions

In this, the first of two companion papers, we have introduced the reader to concepts of robust data structures, and have given an informal analysis of the detectability and correctability of various implementations of linear lists and binary trees. Empirical results indicate that the effective detectability of a storage structure can be higher than the analytically determined worst case detectability.

We have seen that commonly used techniques, in the case of linear lists, can be quite effective. However, the modified(2) double-linked implementation suggests that the commonly used techniques may not necessarily be the best way of exploiting redundancy.

For binary trees, the authors are aware of no commonly used storage structures which are 1-correctable. The chained and threaded implementation described here is 1-correctable, uses no additional storage (assuming space is available for tag bits), and can still be updated in time proportional to the height of the tree.

There are three aspects of highly redundant structures which we have not discussed. One is simply that the increased complexity of the update routines may make programming errors more likely. The second is the propagation of erroneous changes by correct update routines. It appears that in many highly redundant structures the rate of error propagation is directly proportional to the detectability. The third aspect is that faulty update routines may make correlated erroneous changes to several fields. In particular, duplicated fields will often be changed to the same erroneous value. Therefore, redundant data in a structure should be as independent as possible from all other data in the structure. This consideration does not affect the theoretical results since they are only based on the number of changes; it could have a significant impact on the effective robustness of a storage structure, however.

We have attempted to give an informal description of our approach to improving data structure robustness, including definitions and examples. While the examples were concerned only with two simple data structures, we present more generally applicable formal results in the companion paper [24]. The companion paper also extends the basic framework to a restricted class of "compound" data structures, and discusses some of the design issues related to robust data structure synthesis.

References

[1] R. P. Almquist, J. R. Hagerman, R. J. Hass, R. W. Peterson, and S. L. Stevens, "Software protection in no. 1 ESS," in *Proc. Int. Switching Symp.*, 1972, pp. 565-569.

[2] T. Anderson and B. Randell, Eds., *Computing Systems Reliability*. Cambridge: Cambridge Univ. Press, 1979.

[3] A. Avizienis, "Fault-tolerance: The survival attribute of digital systems," *Proc. IEEE*, vol. 66, pp. 1109-1125, Oct. 1978.

[4] H. J. Beuscher, G. E. Gessler, D. W. Huffman, P. J. Kennedy, and E. Nussbaum, "Administration and maintenance plan," *Bell Syst. Tech. J.*, vol. 48, pp. 2765-2815, Oct. 1969.

[5] H. Y. Chang, "Hardware maintainability and software reliability of electronic switching systems," Infotech State of the Art Rep. 20: Comput. Syst. Reliability, pp. 455-479, 1974.

[6] P. A. Dearnley, "An investigation into database resilience," *Comput. J.*, vol. 19, pp. 117-121, May 1976.

[7] P. J. Denning, "Fault-tolerant operating systems," *Comput. Surveys*, vol. 8, pp. 359-389, Dec. 1976.

[8] R. W. Downing, J. S. Nowak, and L. S. Tuomenoksa, "No. 1 ESS maintenance plan," *Bell Syst. Tech. J.*, vol. 43, pp. 1961-2019, Sept. 1964.

[9] J. P. Fry, and E. H. Sibley, "Evolution of database management systems," *Comput. Surveys*, vol. 8, pp. 7-42, Mar. 1976.

[10] G. Giannotti, "Data base integrity," *Data Management*, vol. 12, pp. 22-25, May 1974.

[11] C. C. Gotlieb and F. W. Tompa, "Choosing a storage schema," *Acta Informatica*, vol. 3, pp. 297-319, 1974.

[12] M. M. Hammer and D. J. McLeod, "Semantic integrity in a relational data base system," in *Proc. Int. Conf. Very Large Data Bases*, Framingham, MA, Sept. 22-24, 1975, pp. 25-47.

[13] R. W. Hamming, "Error detecting and error correcting codes," *Bell Syst. Tech. J.*, vol. 26, pp. 147-160, Apr. 1950.

[14] D. E. Knuth, *The Art of Computer Programming*, vol. 1: Fundamental Algorithms, 2nd ed. Reading, MA: Addison-Wesley, 1973.

[15] P. C. Lockemann and W. D. Knutsen, "Recovery of disk contents after system failure," *Commun. Ass. Comput. Mach.*, vol. 11, p. 542, Aug. 1968.

[16] R. A. Lorie, "Physical integrity in a large segmented database," *ACM Trans. Database Syst.*, vol. 2, pp. 91-104, Mar. 1977.

[17] D. J. McLeod, "High level expression of semantic integrity specifications in a relational data base system," M.S. thesis, Dep. Elec. Eng. Comput. Sci., Massachusetts Inst. Technol., MIT/LCS/TR-165, June 1976.

[18] P. M. Melliar-Smith and B. Randell, "Software reliability: The role of programmed exception handling," in *Proc. ACM Conf. Language Design for Reliable Software*, Raleigh, NC, Mar. 28-30, 1977; also in *SIGPLAN Notices*, vol. 12, pp. 95-100, Mar. 1977.

[19] N. Minsky, "Files with semantics," in *Proc. ACM SIGMOD Int. Conf. Management of Data*, Washington, DC, June 2-4, 1976, pp. 65-73.

[20] B. Randell, "Operating systems: The problems of performance and reliability," in *Inform. Processing 71, Proc. IFIP Congr. 71*, Ljubljana, Yugoslavia, Aug. 23-28, 1971, pp. 281-290.

[21] —, "System structure for software fault tolerance," in *Proc. Int. Conf. Reliable Software*, Los Angeles, Apr. 21-23, 1975, pp. 437-449.

[22] A. L. Scherr, "The design of OS/VS2 Release 2," in *Proc. Nat. Comput. Conf.*, 1973, pp. 387-394.

[23] —, "Functional structure of IBM virtual storage operating systems, part II: OS/VS2-2 concepts and philosophies," *IBM Syst. J.*, vol. 12, pp. 382-400, 1973.

[24] D. J. Taylor, D. E. Morgan, and J. P. Black, "Redundancy in data structures: Some theoretical results," this issue, pp. 595-602.

[25] D. J. Taylor, "Robust data structure implementations for software reliability," Ph.D. dissertation, Dep. Comput. Sci., Univ. Waterloo, Ont., Canada, 1977.

[26] —, "Theoretical foundations for robust data structure implementations," Univ. Waterloo, Waterloo, Ont., Canada, Comput. Sci. Res. Rep. CS-78-52.

[27] F. W. Tompa, "Data structure design," in *Data Structures, Computer Graphics, and Pattern Recognition*, A. Klinger et al., Eds. New York: Academic, 1977, pp. 3-30.

[28] G. Waldbaum, "Audit programs—A proposal for improving system availability," IBM, Yorktown Heights, NY, Res. Rep. RC2811, Feb. 26, 1970.

[29] M. V. Wilkes, "On preserving the integrity of data bases," *Comput. J.*, vol. 15, pp. 191-194, Aug. 1972.

David J. Taylor (S'76-M'77) received the B.Sc. degree in mathematics from the University of Saskatchewan, Saskatoon, Sask., Canada, in 1972 and the M.Math and Ph.D. degrees in computer science from the University of Waterloo, Waterloo, Ont., Canada, in 1974 and 1977, respectively.

He is an Assistant Professor of computer science at the University of Waterloo. His field of research is the reliability of software systems and computer networks.

Dr. Taylor is a member of the IEEE Computer Society and the Association for Computing Machinery.

David E. Morgan (M'74) received the B.Sc. degree in mathematics from Rose Polytechnic Institute, Terre Haute, IN, the M.S. degree in mathematics from the University of Michigan, Ann Arbor, and the Ph.D. degree from the University of Waterloo, Waterloo, Ont., Canada.

He is an Associate Professor of Computer Science and Associate Director of the Computer Communications Networks Group at the University of Waterloo. He designed and developed a system for observing and controlling the behavior of computer networks and distributed systems. He has served as consultant to several U.S. and Canadian businesses and governmental organizations, and is Vice-President of Telecom Network Technology, Inc., a firm specializing in consulting services and technology transfer. While on sabbatical leave at Digital Equipment Corporation, he contributed to the design of tools for software engineering and systems for managing the behavior of a computer network. Earlier, as a member of technical staff at Bell Laboratories, he participated in the development of Bell's electronic switching systems and IBM's time-sharing system for the 360/67. He has authored several papers relating to the reliability, availability, maintainability, and performance of computer systems and networks.

Dr. Morgan is a member of the Association for Computing Machinery and a life member of Tau Beta Pi.

James P. Black (S'80) received the B.Sc. degree from the University of Calgary, Calgary, Alta., Canada, in 1975 and the Diplome d'Ingenieur from the Grenoble Polytechnic Institute, Grenoble, France, in 1977.

He is currently studying for the Ph.D. degree at the University of Waterloo, Waterloo, Ont., Canada. His fields of interest are software system reliability, queueing theory, and distributed computer systems.

Mr. Black is a member of the IEEE Computer Society and the Association for Computing Machinery.

DMERT: A Fault Tolerant Environment for Diverse Applications

D. J. Fitch

A. M. Guercio

K. W. Johnson

G. T. Surratt

AT&T Bell Laboratories
Naperville, Illinois 60566

ABSTRACT

Over the last few years there has been a marked increase in the demand for high availability computing. Traditional approaches to high availability were specialized single application systems. However, the entry of a wide range of users into fault tolerant computing requires a more flexible approach. The DMERT fault recovery meets these needs by providing centralized control and decision making while distributing responsibility for device dependent operations. The key elements of centralized control are progressive re-initialization, which ensures effective recovery, and configuration management, which provides a logical abstraction of the physical machine.

1. INTRODUCTION

The DMERT (Duplex Multi-Environment Real Time) operating [1], [2] provides an ultrahigh availability, real time environment. Although many earlier systems[3], [4], [5] provided similar environments, these systems supported either a single customer or a very narrow range of customers. Since the designers knew the hardware and software architecture of the end user's system, a centralized fault recovery strategy turned out to be very effective. However, DMERT supports Value Added Resellers (VARs) with diverse hardware and software architectures. Therefore, the centralized approach had to be augmented to provide greater flexibility without compromising the integrity of the system. DMERT's approach combines the following techniques to provide a system that, while complete in itself, allows both VARs and end users to tailor the system to their needs:

- centralized fault recovery control and decision making

- high level abstraction of the physical environment including
  - relationship between units
  - current status
  - fault characteristics (error thresholds)

- distributed responsibility for device dependent operations

- simple application interfaces

- manual overrides

These facilities allow DMERT to ensure the integrity of the system while providing the flexibility needed by its customers.

2. Fault Tolerant Environment

The DMERT fault recovery system shields both the application[1] and the remainder of the operating system from the details of the configuration of the physical machine by providing a virtual machine environment. Figure 1 depicts the virtual machine layers of the DMERT fault recovery system.

The innermost layer is the physical layer. DMERT runs on the AT&T 3B20D computer[6], whose hardware configuration is illustrated in Figure 2. The processors are duplicated with memory update and maintenance links connecting the two processors. Peripheral device controllers are dual-ported and duplicated. Peripheral devices are connected to one controller, that is, they are not dual-ported. Application hardware may be added at the processor level, at the device controller level and at the device level.

The second layer in the virtual machine environment provides centralized control. The primary elements of centralized control are <u>configuration management</u> and <u>progressive re-initialization</u>. Configuration management provides a logical abstraction of the configuration of the physical machine as well as a centralized decision making process for making unit removal or mate replacement decisions. Progressive re-initialization monitors the state of the machine to ensure that recovery actions succeed. If the actions are not successful, progressive re-initialization <u>escalates</u> the recovery action to a more drastic level.

The next layer is a well defined interface between the centralized control and each process in the system. The individual processes implement device dependent operations. Thus the responsibility for the actions is distributed to processes. Each process has a <u>fault</u> entry point which interfaces to configuration management and progressive re-initialization. The fault recovery system

---

1. We use the term <u>application</u> to refer to the process(es) provided by the customer or VAR.

recognizes a variety of error conditions, such as illegal instruction, privilege or protection violation, and reports these errors to both configuration management and the fault entry of the implicated process. The process can request process termination, a retry, or an initialization. While the individual process is responsible for correcting an error condition, progressive re-initialization software monitors for a recurrence of the problem. If the action taken by the process is ineffective, centralized control will escalate the recovery action.

A simple interface is provided between the processes and the centralized layer. There is a set of library functions for both configuration management and progressive re-initialization. There is also one specialized interface, the application interface process, as indicated in Figure 1. The application interface process differs from other processes in that it includes some portion of centralized control. This gives the application the capability to alter some of the progressive re-initialization parameters, thus giving it a degree of control over the progressive re-initialization strategy.

The simple interface to the fault recovery system extends to the operator interface. There is a menu type display for both initialization and configuration control. The operator represents the ultimate authority in the system and is given the capability to control the configuration and initialization level in addition to all the automatic actions.

The effect of this structure is that processes are supported by a fault-tolerant virtual machine. Certain capabilities are distributed to the various processes in the system while the centralized control provides a safety net backing up the processes' actions.

3. Progressive Re-initialization Strategy

DMERT's philosophy of fault tolerance is to match the level of recovery to the severity of the fault. Therefore, for a given hardware or software failure, a minimal, localized recovery procedure is attempted to minimize the effect on unrelated parts of the system. Localized recovery can be attempted because extensive fault detection mechanisms are provided which permit early error detection. If the effect of the failure is not local, but rather the failure has affected multiple processes or hardware units, then a system wide rollback procedure is attempted. Most work in progress will be continued or restarted automatically. If this type of recovery is not successful, then recovery actions will be automatically escalated to a system bootstrap. By monitoring recovery and by using a progressive re-initialization strategy, DMERT ensures that the failure will eventually be dealt with properly at the lowest possible recovery level and thereby avoid over-reacting to a failure and reducing processor availability unnecessarily.

3.1 Centralized Control

Although DMERT has responsibility for basic system recovery, the recovery system is flexible. If an application desires, it can tailor recovery actions to meet its needs. An application process can also provide its own recovery actions by using the fault entry interface to DMERT.

To provide this flexibility and still not jeopardize recovery, DMERT maintains control over system recovery by administering escalation level counters and automatically selecting different hardware configurations (processors and/or boot devices) to use on successive recovery attempts. When a system wide re-initialization occurs, processes are notified and an initialization interval is started. During this interval, an unsuccessful recovery attempt is automatically escalated to a higher level.

Different types of system monitoring are also provided. A sanity timer must be periodically reset; a timeout results in a switch to the mate processor. During a system re-initialization, basic system processes are expected to report to a central monitoring process. Failure of one of these processes to make this report results in an escalated system re-initialization. Additionally, there are many error sources, each with associated error thresholds. A recovery is initiated when an error rate becomes excessive.

3.2 Progressive Re-initialization

Because DMERT attempts to match recovery actions to the fault, a common error handler is called when an error occurs that does not cause an automatic switch to the mate processor. The error handler determines the type of error and the process that was executing when the error occurred or the device driver responsible for the unit that caused the error. The implicated process is then responsible for taking the appropriate recovery actions.

If the implicated process determines that localized recovery actions can not handle the condition, recovery is escalated to a system wide re-initialization. Each DMERT and application process is notified by its fault entry that a rollback type re-initialization is occurring and each process is expected to use its state information to clean up any transactions in progress. This level is the primary recovery mechanism in DMERT and does not require a system bootstrap. When possible, the initial recovery attempt uses the existing hardware configuration so that recovery occurs relatively quickly (a few hundred milliseconds). If the system fails to recover, a switch to the mate processor occurs automatically. If the memory in the mate processor is out-of-date, memory is copied by the switched-to processor before recovery proceeds. When memory must be copied, recovery time is longer and is a function of the amount of memory equipped. Because of the rollback strategy used and the automatic reconfiguration of processors that can occur, recovery at this level is usually successful.

When rollback is not successful, recovery actions are automatically escalated to a bootstrap from disk. Even when such a bootstrap occurs, several regions of memory and the Equipment Configuration Database (ECD) information are protected to maintain some continuity. Successively more severe levels of re-initialization involve re-initializing these protected regions and reloading the ECD. However, one protected memory region is preserved for the application and is initialized only by manual request or a power up bootstrap.

An application may determine that it needs to be re-initialized without causing a system wide re-initialization. To accomplish this, an "application only" re-initialization level is provided. Although no 3B20D computer hardware or DMERT software is re-initialized at this level, DMERT does administer the initialization interval so that actions used at successive recovery attempts are automatically escalated in severity. When "application only" recovery actions can not clear the problem, DMERT regains control to assure system recovery.

3.3 Manual Control

Although DMERT provides automatic recovery from faults, the system operator still retains control over the system. Recovery actions can be manually initiated using the system console. Any option manually selected takes precedence over automatically selected ones. The operator can force various combinations of processors and boot devices (disks) and can specify the recovery level to be attempted using the forced hardware configuration.

4. Configuration Management

DMERT provides a centralized configuration management capability consisting of an ECD and a Configuration Administrator (CONFIG) which utilizes the database to make configuration decisions. This capability is needed to assure high availability under hardware failure conditions. When a failure occurs, CONFIG quickly determines a viable alternate configuration of the hardware modules. DMERT's configuration management system was designed to provide a generalized solution to the configuration management problem because the 3B20D computer is an embedded processor in many of its applications. The consistent approach taken for all types of units permits application hardware to be easily included in the database and administered by CONFIG even though DMERT does not know the device's characteristics. Flexibility and expandability are key attributes of this solution.

4.1 Equipment Configuration Database

The ECD provides a hardware abstraction of the system. All information that recovery software needs to know about the hardware is contained in the ECD in concise standardized formats. This allows CONFIG to take a "total system" viewpoint because it can determine the state of all hardware units in the system without having to access any hardware or to have special cases for each type of unit.

The ECD has separate records for each hardware unit in the system. These records contain unit specific information such as state variables, equipage amounts, unit name, hardware type and version, channel address, interrupt numbers, software driver, and error counters and thresholds. Device drivers, performing part of their distributed fault recovery role, keep this data up-to-date as changes occur in their units. Thus the ECD always provides an accurate picture of the state of the system at any moment. The ECD also provides relational information about the physical interconnection of the hardware units and logical relationships between hardware units. This is depicted in Figure 3. The physical interconnection information denotes controlling and subordinate units and thus provides a system wide view of the physical layout of the units. The logical relationship information, which can be used to describe concepts of redundant units, backup units and spare units, enumerates the physical units which comprise the logical groupings.

As systems evolve over a period of time, records for additional hardware units and even new types of units can be easily added to the ECD. DMERT provides facilities and procedures for adding or removing hardware while the system is in service. Part of that procedure is the modification of the ECD to include or remove the records for the associated hardware units.

4.2 Configuration Administrator

CONFIG provides a consistent approach to handling hardware failures and system re-configurations. It is able to apply the same criteria to all types of units. This is made possible because of the ECD architecture, where standardized record formats are used for all hardware units. The procedures are device independent, relying only on information in the ECD. CONFIG does not control any hardware: it only makes the decision. Once the decision is made, the responsibility for performing the actual re-configuration is distributed to the appropriate device drivers.

CONFIG performs three functions associated with configuration control. These are the monitoring of error rates, the selection of an alternate configuration, and the notification of re-configuration. These functions will be discussed below. It should be noted that while CONFIG provides an automatic configuration control capability, the system configuration can be altered under extenuating circumstances by manual action or by specific software request.

As part of the generalized configuration management solution, DMERT permits the definition of error counters for each hardware module. Use of these error counters permits better characterization and resolution of failures and provides more flexibility in fault recovery actions. The error counters and associated thresholds are defined in ECD records for each unit. While the number of counters, the type of errors counted, and the error rate thresholds are all variable for each type of unit, the data format is common and CONFIG can administer all of the error counters with the data provided. Whenever a driver detects an error (failure), it notifies CONFIG, specifying the error number and the unit. As long as the error rate remains less than the threshold rate, the unit will remain in service. When the threshold rate is exceeded, CONFIG then proceeds to the selection of an alternate configuration.

When selecting an alternate configuration, CONFIG utilizes the physical interconnection and logical relationship information in the ECD. The physical interconnection information shows which subordinate units will have to be removed when the faulty unit is removed. The logical relationship information identifies possible replacement units. Basically, the unit removal criterion which CONFIG applies to all units is that a unit can be removed only if there is a replacement unit to take over its function, or the unit and its subordinates are designated in the ECD records as not being essential to the operation of the system.

CONFIG also utilizes the state information in the ECD unit records when selecting an alternate configuration. Those units which are not in service are disqualified from becoming replacement units. This assures that at least one of every "essential" unit will be in service in the new configuration. If CONFIG decides to remove a unit, it notifies the appropriate driver to carry out the removal. If the unit can not be removed because of a lack of replacement units, CONFIG notifies the driver that it must either quickly restore another unit or continue to use the faulty unit. At that point, recovery responsibility passes from CONFIG to the driver. If the driver continues to be unsuccessful with the faulty unit, it may escalate the recovery.

CONFIG provides a re-configuration notification function. This is triggered whenever a driver changes the state of a unit in the ECD. There are a number of DMERT processes which react to or record changes in configuration. The system status display on the operator's terminal, for example, must be updated whenever a re-configuration occurs. So, in an effort to keep them all up to date, CONFIG acts as the town crier by notifying all concerned processes of the state change for any unit.

Because CONFIG applies a consistent approach to unit removal and re-configuration for all types of units, it is easy to add new units to the system and have them included under CONFIG's administration. Error counters and thresholds provide a mechanism to accommodate the unique failure modes and recovery actions for different types of units and also provides flexibility for future fine tuning as experience is gained from field data.

5. Application Interfaces

Although the DMERT fault recovery subsystem is complete in itself, many of the applications built on it have special fault recovery needs. DMERT provides simple interfaces that allow its customers to tailor the system to meet these needs. Each of these interfaces has safeguards to ensure that DMERT's centralized control facilities are not compromised.

5.1 Progressive Initialization Parameters

The application can influence the progressive re-initialization strategy employed by DMERT by modifying the length of the initialization interval or by specifying the number of application supplied initialization levels for each DMERT level. DMERT also allows the application to call for a specific recovery level. To ensure that the progressive re-initialization strategy is not compromised, however, DMERT escalates requests for levels that have already been tried to the next appropriate level.

5.2 Application Specific Hardware

DMERT allows the application to represent its hardware in the ECD. The same completeness and consistency checks that are used for DMERT records are applied to these application records. After the records have been verified, DMERT will provide the same fault recovery capabilities for the application's hardware as it does for its own. In particular, it will notify the application when a unit has exceeded its error rate and what recovery action to take (e.g., initialize the unit or switch to its mate).

5.3 Application Interface Monitor

DMERT allows the application to provide an Application Interface Monitor (AIM). If provided, AIM will be notified of overload conditions, recovery actions and pending configuration changes. This allows DMERT to communicate effectively with a wide range of applications using a standardized interface.

6. Conclusion

DMERT's fault recovery system integrates two key concepts: centralized control and distributed responsibility. The implementation of these concepts in DMERT provides a flexible and general environment capable of achieving the same level of availability as conventional centralized approaches. There are currently in excess of 230 3B20D computers in operation since an initial deployment in September 1981. The applications using DMERT include: a digital telephone switching system[7], a database server[8], a backend file system[9], and an emulation of another machine[10]. The deployed machines are achieving an availability of 99.998%[11].

References

[1] M. E. Grzelakowski, J. H. Campbell, and M. R. Dubman, "DMERT Operating System," Bell System Technical Journal, Vol. 62, No. 1, Part 2, pp 303-323.

[2] N. A. Martellotto, "An Operating System for Reliable Real-Time Telecommunications Control," Fourth International Conference on Software Engineering for Telecommunication Switching Systems; University of Warwick, England; July 20-24, 1981.

[3] "No. 1 Electronic Switching System", Bell System Technical Journal, Vol. 43, September, 1964.

[4] "The 1A Processor," Bell System Technical Journal, Vol. 56, February 1977.

[5] "No. 2 ESS," Bell System Technical Journal, Vol. 48, October, 1969.

[6] W. N. Toy and L. E. Gallaher, "Overview and Architecture of the 3B20D Computer," Bell System Technical Journal, Vol. 62 No. 1, Part 2, pp 181-190.

[7] William Bridges Smith and F. T. Andrews, Jr., "No. 5 ESS - overview," Bell Telephone Laboratories, USA, International Switching Symposium, Montreal, Canada, September, 1981.

[8] "Network Services and the Network Control Point," National Electronics Conference, Technical Session 12, October, 1982.

[9] J. W. James and M. Marques, "The No. 4 ESS Attached Processor System" Second Annual Phoenix Conference, 1983 Conference Proceedings.

[10] J. R. Kane, M. W. Rolund and J. M. Scanlon, "The 3B Duplex Processor System and Its Application to TSPS; Part I, Description of the Process System," ISS '81 Proceedings.

[11] N. O. Whittington, L. C. Brown and N. X. DeLessio, "3BTM$_2$OD Computer System Field Experience," accepted for Proceedings of the International Switching Symposium, May 1984.

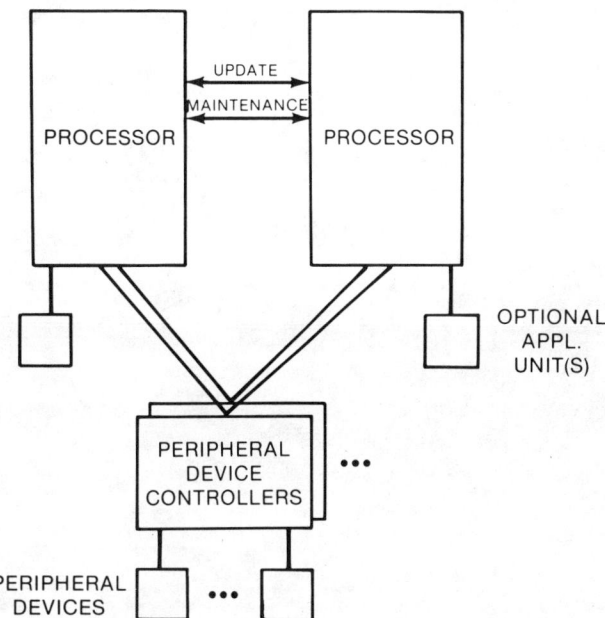

Configuration of the AT&T 3B20D Computer
FIGURE 2

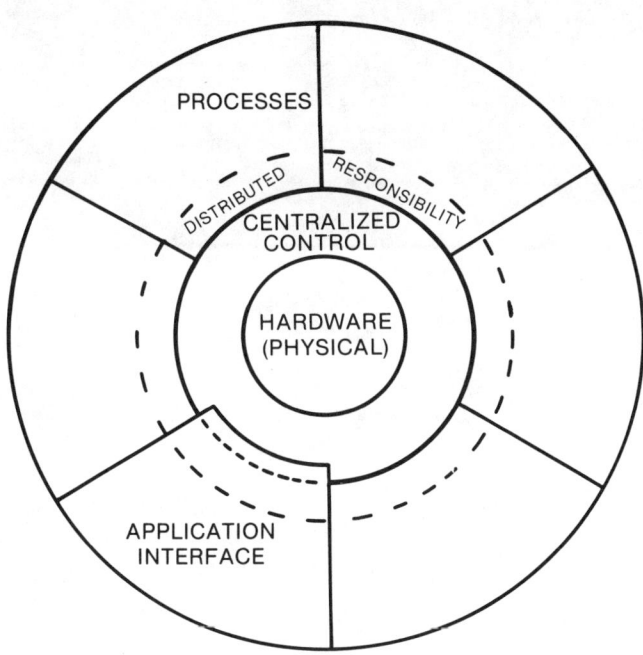

DMERT Fault Recovery Structure
FIGURE 1

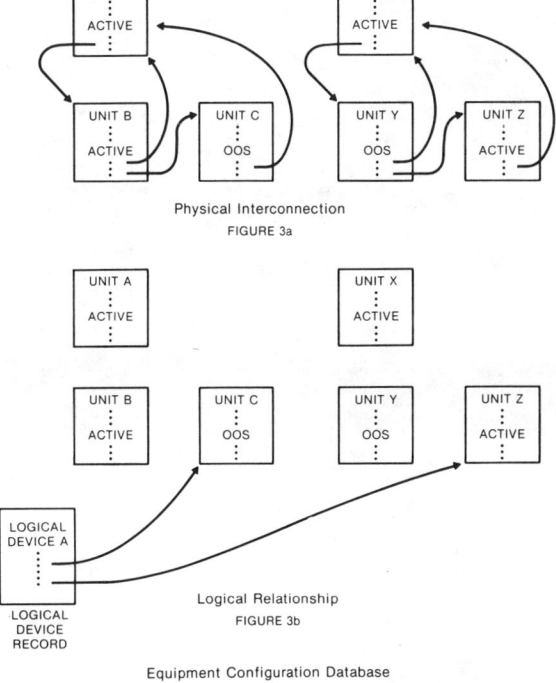

Physical Interconnection
FIGURE 3a

Logical Relationship
FIGURE 3b

Equipment Configuration Database
FIGURE 3

Chapter 6: Fault-Tolerant Memory Systems

Introduction

Computer memory systems have traditionally been one of the weakest reliability links in computer system designs. Whereas "soft" errors can often be tolerated by various combinational and sequential logic circuits, such errors can irreversibly destroy information vital to the operation of a system, and hence result in complete system failures. The overall consequences of memory errors differ for different applications. In the case of a real-time data acquisition and processing system, the temporary loss of some data might be equivalent to "noise" in a signal being acquired and manipulated, and hence can be tolerated as new data are acquired. In control applications, however, an erroneous memory bit could result in some irreversible action taking place in the system. In banking and other database applications, memory represents the most critical part of the system, and hence must be protected (both primary and secondary) at all costs. In military and aerospace systems, as in other control applications, single-bit errors could lead to complete system failure if they occur in vulnerable spots in the database or program store.

Fault-tolerant memory designs have traditionally been a part of most aerospace applications [DIC64,HOP78] and the Bell System Electronic Switching System (ESS) processors [DOW64], whereas most commercial systems, until recently, have been content with simple parity for error checking. The advent of VLSI circuit chips that implement various error-detection and error-correction schemes, however, plus the decreasing cost of memory chips, has made the use of redundancy for fault tolerance economically feasible, even for relatively low-cost systems. Meanwhile, ultrareliable designs continue to apply massive redundancy to achieve even higher degrees of fault tolerance.

This chapter will examine the various approaches to fault-tolerant memory system design at various levels. First, a brief summary of expected memory failures will be presented, considering both large memory systems and VLSI single-chip systems. Then various redundancy schemes designed to provide fault tolerance will be examined, with reliability models used to illustrate the performance of the various schemes. In addition to reliability, cost and performance (speed) overhead will be considered for the various schemes. Several case studies will be presented, considering both system and chip-level designs.

Memory Fault Models

Although semiconductor memory devices have proved to be a cost effective approach to memory system design, these devices tend to be more susceptible than other devices to various faults, both transient and permanent. Semiconductor memory failure modes have been examined in [SAR84,LAL85,SIE82], and can be summarized as being either in the individual memory cells or else in the common circuitry shared by the cells in the memory. A typical block diagram of a memory system is shown in Figure 6.1, consisting of common circuitry for address decoding, bus driving and control, and the memory array itself. In the case of the common circuitry, faults can either affect single bits read from or written to the array, as in the case of stuck-at failures of the pins of one of the common chips, or affect larger portions of a data word, as in the case of bus drivers failing or address decoders not selecting the memory at the proper time. These faults are summarized as follows:

Bus drivers/buffers: Failures include one bit or a group of bits stuck at logical one (s-a-1) or stuck at zero (s-a-0), a driver failing to turn on and thus leaving the bus in a "floating condition," and "bridging faults," i.e. adjacent bits of the driver affecting each other.

Address decoding: The primary failure mode is that of either selecting the memory when it is not being accessed or vice-versa. In the first case, data from the memory will be destroyed if inadvertently written to, or they will conflict with data from the proper unit if inadvertently selected during a read operation. In those cases where the memory fails to be selected when being requested, then write operations will not complete, plus memory read requests will result in a floating bus value being misinterpreted as data.

Control circuitry: A variety of improper operations can result from malfunctioning control circuitry, ranging from improper timing on read/write operations to spurious read/write cycles not corresponding to system requests. Of particular sensitivity is refresh control of dynamic RAM devices, which can result in lost data if not performed properly, and/or conflicts with read/write accesses to the memory array.

The memory array: While the individual bits of the memory array are susceptible to both hard and soft errors, the internal organization of the memory devices may be such as to exhibit other failure modes as well, where circuitry common to more than one bit within the device is affected. Such faults include entire rows or columns s-a-1/s-a-0, pattern-sensitive faults in which adjacent bits affect each other, and entire chip failures. The individual memory cells, depending on the technology used, can be affected by a

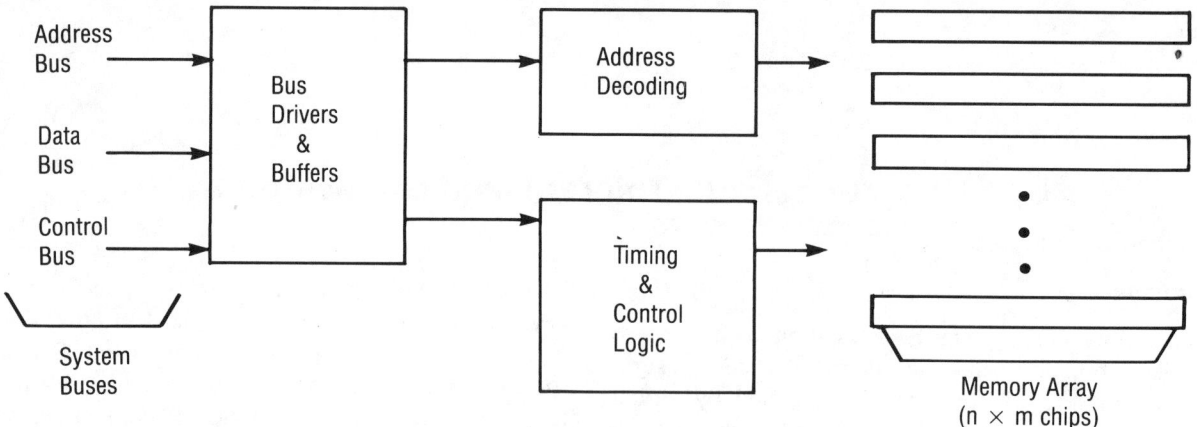

Figure 6.1. Typical Memory System Block Diagram

variety of "soft" (transient) errors caused by power fluctuations, borderline parameters, radiation effects, and so on. The affects of alpha particle radiation from the packaging material in dynamic and other volatile memories has received particular interest in the research community [MAY78].

While the above discussions have concentrated on logical (s-a-1,s-a-0) faults, bridging faults and other faults resulting in timing errors such as slow access times or write recovery times can be equally as damaging to the system.

Memory System Reliability Models

Reliability modelling of memory systems requires three separate activities. First, a reasonable model of each memory device and the various support circuits is needed. Second, a model of the simplex (non-redundant) memory system is needed to determine a "baseline" reliability that can be used to measure the reliability improvement gained through various fault-tolerant designs. In many cases, this baseline reliability in itself may be sufficiently high as to make the use of redundancy unnecessary in meeting the reliability goals of the system. In other situations, however, there may be requirements for some degree of fault tolerance coupled with the reliability goal. Finally, the effects of any redundancy techniques must be quantified to determine the reliability improvement gained through the use of those techniques, effects that can then be weighed against cost and performance tradeoffs to determine the desirability of using those techniques, given the system requirements.

The most commonly used method for determining the reliabilities of individual memory and support devices is to use the reliability handbook MIL-HDBK-217C [USD79], which provides information to model the reliabilities of most electrical devices. As an example, consider the expected reliability of a 64K x 1 dynamic RAM chip to be used in a memory subsystem. From the handbook, the following expression is used to compute the expected failure rate of the memory:

$$\lambda = \pi_L \pi_Q (C_1 \pi_T \pi_V \pi_{PT} + (C_2 + C_3) \pi_E) \qquad (6\text{-}1)$$

where:

π_L is a learning factor (10 for new devices, 1 otherwise).

π_Q is a quality factor, related to the screening of the part, ranging from 0.5 for the highest military grade to 35 for commercial.

π_T is a temperature acceleration factor, related to device technology, package, case temperature, and power dissipation.

π_V is a voltage stress factor, which is 1 for most devices and higher for CMOS parts with high power supply values.

π_{PT} is a PROM programming technique factor, dependant on the number of bits in the PROM (1 for non-PROMs).

π_E is an environmental factor, which takes into account shock, vibration, humidity, etc. (ranging from 1 for a benign ground environment to 10 for a missile launch).

C_1, C_2 are complexity factors, which are functions of the number of bits in the memory device.

C_3 is a package complexity factor, related to package type, and number of pins on the package.

For example, if a new 16-pin, non-hermetically sealed, commercially screened 64K × 1 NMOS dynamic RAM is to be used in a computer room application at a chip junction temperature of 25° C, then the chip reliability, from Equation (6-1) would be 24.2 failures/10^6 hours. If an established design, hermetically sealed, military screened version of the same chip were to be used instead, then failure rate would drop to 0.034 failures/10^6 hours. Formulas similar to Equation (6-1) exist in [USD79] for other semiconductor and other electrical devices as well, and would be used to estimate the reliabilities of various memory system support chips.

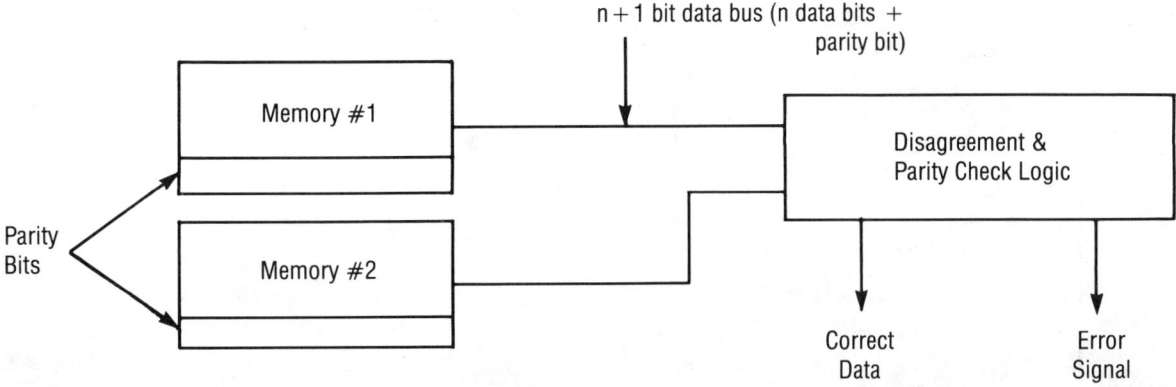

Figure 6.2. Duplex memory system with parity check. Disagreement check detects errors. Parity check indicates faulty member of disagreeing pair with output of other unit passed to system bus.

Once the reliabilities of the individual memory and support chips in the memory system are determined, then the overall non-redundant system reliability in a system consisting of n memory chips and m support chips can be given by:

$$R = \left(\prod_{i=1}^{m} R_i \right) \cdot Rb^n \quad (6\text{-}2)$$

where R_i is the reliability of the ith support component and Rb is the individual memory chip reliability. Note that Equation 6-2 represents the reliability of a series combination of devices, since all devices must work for proper system operation in the baseline memory.

Memory System Redundancy

Essentially, two general redundancy techniques have been employed for fault-tolerant memory system design, i.e. massive redundancy and information redundancy, in addition to a variety of combinations of the two. In using massive redundancy either the entire memory system is duplicated and a match circuit used to detect disagreement, as shown in Figure 6-2, or else the system is triplicated with a majority voter used to mask single errors in each bit, as shown in Figure 6.3. The latter approach has been used in the FTMP system [HOP78], where identical memories are grouped into triads, with all information passed between the memories and triads of processors over a triplicated bus. Voters at the inputs to each processor and memory mask any single error resulting from a failed memory or processor. In the case of duplex systems, simple comparison can identify an error in one copy of a memory, but it cannot identify the source of the error.

Consequently, errors cannot be corrected automatically. In the Saturn V launch vehicle computer system [DIC64], a duplex memory was augmented by adding a parity bit to each memory word in both copies of the memory. In this case, the match circuit detects the presence of an error condition, and the parity check circuit identifies the faulty module, so that the output of the remaining module can be automatically selected to provide continuous operation without the addition of extra processing cycles. The No. 1 ESS processor [DOW64] "call store" memory used a configuration similar to that used in the Saturn V system, except that there was no dynamic selection of the correct unit. Instead, an interrupt was generated on a mismatch and the faulty unit was identified by a diagnostic routine. This approach allowed the system to maintain logs of error trends, which was important because the system was designed for long-term operation, not the short mission time of the Saturn V system.

In comparing the relative reliabilities of the two schemes presented above, one must consider the fault coverage of the error-detection and error-correction techniques. In the duplex case, faults can exist in both memories and still be correctable so long as one of the two copies at each word position in the memory is error-free. If a fault does exist, then the match circuitry will detect the existence of any errors, with the parity check circuitry identifying the faulty unit, causing the error-free copy to be used and thus "correcting" the word. Being a simple parity check, of course, only an odd number of errors would be detectable in the faulty word. Given that each memory bit has a reliability of Rb, and assuming that multiple bit errors are unlikely to be compared to the probability of occurrence of single errors and that the check circuitry is error-free, then the reliability of the duplex-parity memory would be approximately

$$R = ((Rb^n + n*Rb^{(n-1)}*(1-Rb))*Rb^n)^K \quad (6\text{-}3)$$

where K is the number of words of memory and n is the word width. Note that the term inside the outer parentheses of Equation (6-3) represents the reliability of a single word of the memory, which is equal to the joint probability that one copy of the word contains no faults while the other contains no more than one error.

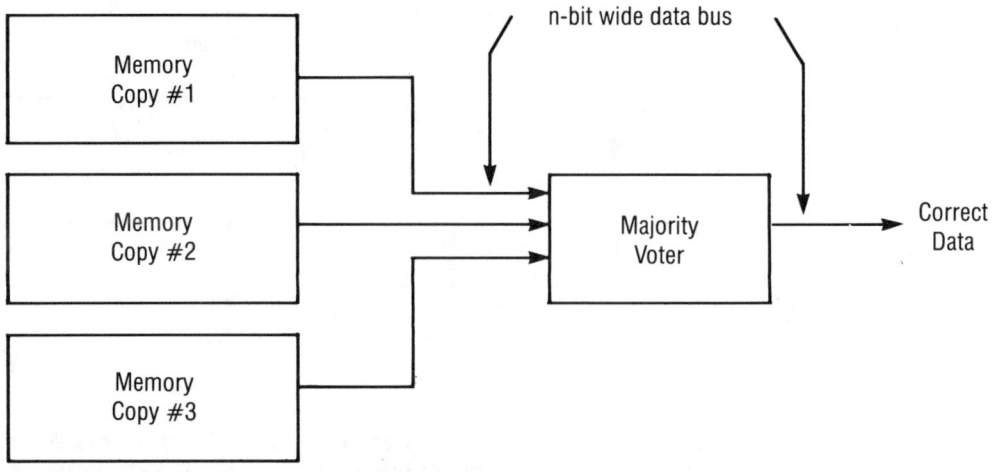

Figure 6.3. Triple-Modular Redundant (TMR) Memory Module. The majority voter corrects single errors at each bit position of each word of memory.

In the case of the TMR approach, fault coverage is improved in that the voter not only masks errors in each word of the memory, but also masks errors at each bit position within each word. Hence, there may exist errors in all three copies of one word of memory and yet the memory can still be corrected if the bit positions of the errors are different in each word. Hence, again assuming ideal error correcting circuitry, the reliability of this system is

$$R = ((Rb^3 + 3*Rb^2*(1-Rb))^n)^K \qquad (6\text{-}4)$$

where the term inside the outer parentheses represents the reliability of one word of the memory, which requires that at least two of the three bits at each of the n positions be correct in order to correct the entire word.

Figure 6.4 illustrates the relative difference in system reliability between the two redundancy approaches and also shows the reliability improvement over a simplex design, showing their respective reliabilities as functions of Rb. It can be seen that the TMR approach does indeed provide a reliability improvement over a duplex design through its increased fault coverage. However, the designer must determine whether or not this increase in reliability is worth the expense of the third copy of the memory plus the increase in the total bit failure rate.

In terms of overhead penalties, the relative performance degradation of parity check and match circuitry is comparable to that of majority voting, both essentially being exclusive-OR trees. Hence the two approaches exhibit similar characteristics. In both cases the performance penalty amounts to simply a few extra gate delay times added to the overall memory access time.

Information Redundancy in Memory Systems

Information redundancy consists of using redundant bits within a data word and a corresponding coding scheme that will allow erroneous code words to be detected and/or corrected. Coding techniques have been examined in considerable detail in the literature [SIE82,CHE84a,AIC84], and will not be covered in depth in this paper. Figures 6.5 and 6.6, however, summarize the basic concepts. Essentially, the redundant bits in the data word result in the overall space of N-tuples for the N-bit word being considerably larger than the actual code space of M-tuples, as shown in Figure 6.5. Code words are then selected so that the "Hamming distance," i.e. the number of bit positions in which the code words differ, is sufficiently large between any two code words to ensure that an n-bit error will result in a non-code word, allowing the error to be detected. For error correction, the resulting non-code word must be closer in Hamming distance to the original word than to any other code word.

This is illustrated in Figure 6.6a, which shows two code words separated by a Hamming distance of three. Any single fault in either word leaves the resulting word a distance of one from the original code word, and at least a distance of two from any other code word. Hence, the word can be correctly associated with the nearest code word, provided the number of errors does not exceed one. In the case shown in Figure 6.6a, if two errors occur in one of the code words, then the resultant could be a distance of one from the other code word and would be erroneously corrected to the closer word. One disadvantage of the above is that multiple errors will be misinterpreted and hence converted erroneously to other code words that will not be detected by the normal error detection mechanism. Increasing the minimum separation between the code words will allow multiple errors to be detected, the exact number depending on this minimum separation.

The most commonly used coding scheme is the simple parity code, in which one redundant bit is added to each data

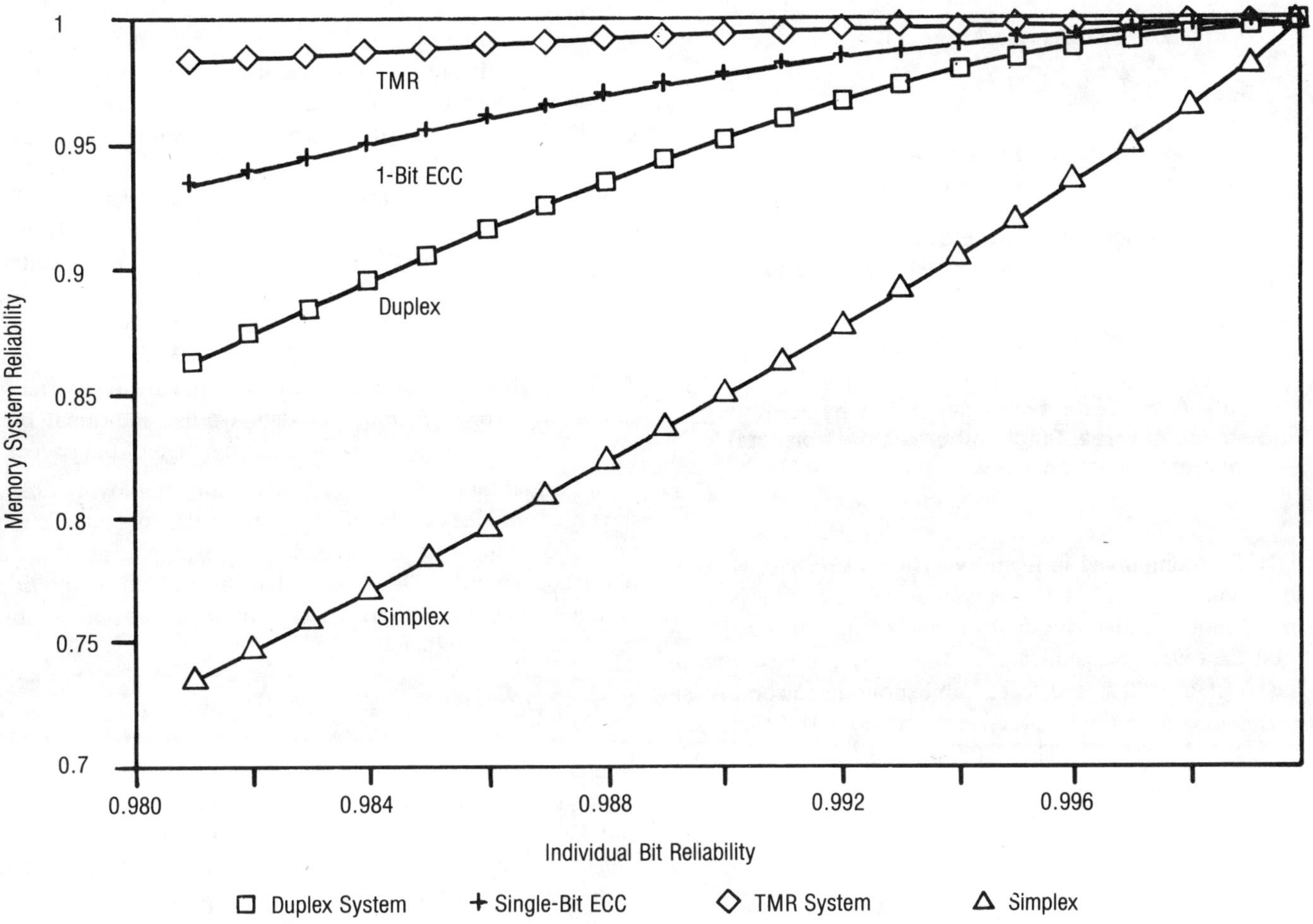

Figure 6.4. Comparison of fault-tolerant memory configurations.

word, dividing the overall binary space in half. In this case, each pair of code words has a minimum separation of two, as shown in Figure 6.6b. Any error (or odd number or errors) will result in a word halfway between two code words, and hence it is detectable although not correctable. Double errors (or any even number of errors) can turn one valid code word into another, and hence can go undetected. The primary advantages of parity codes are their low cost, requiring only one redundant bit, and a small exclusive-OR tree for generating and checking parity. However, if error correction is desired, one must have a minimum separation of three between any pair of code words, hence simple parity schemes are not sufficient and one must go to a more elaborate scheme. It should be noted that many systems group data bits into subsets, with a parity bit protecting each subset, thus allowing errors to be isolated to a "parity group" within the system. Such schemes tolerate a variety of errors in addition to simple single bit errors [SIE82].

Hamming codes and a variety of other coding schemes

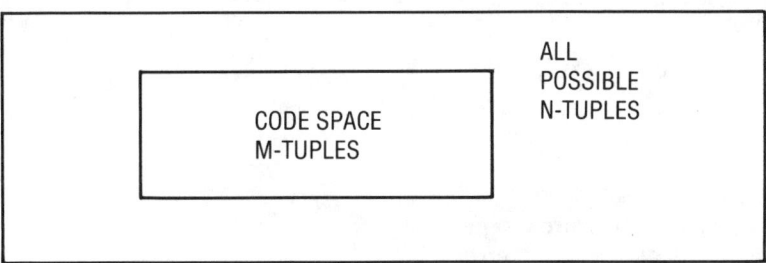

Figure 6.5. Encoding of M-bit data words into an N-bit code.

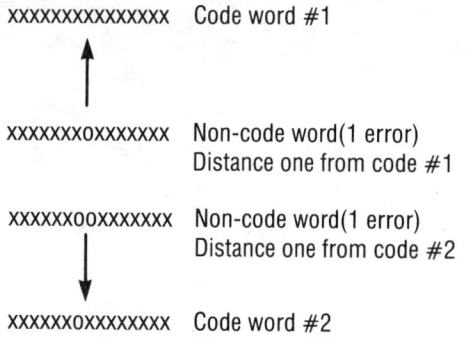

Figure 6.6a. Code words separated by Hamming distance of three. Single-bit errors are correctable to nearest code word.

have been employed in memory systems [SIE82,CHE84a] to provide error correction as well as detection. In the case of Hamming codes, $\log_2 b + 1$ check bits appended to a b-bit data word are sufficient to correct single-bit errors in the word, as well as to detect a number of other errors. As an example, consider the (7,4) code described in [LAL85], and shown in Figure 6.7. The notation (n,m) refers to a code word having n bits, of which m are data bits, and hence $n-m$ check bits. The check bits are computed from the following parity computation equations:

$$c1 = d1 \oplus d2 \oplus d4$$
$$c2 = d1 \oplus d3 \oplus d4 \quad (6\text{-}5)$$
$$c3 = d2 \oplus d3 \oplus d4$$

where $c1$ is the parity bit for the group containing $d1$, $d2$, and $d4$; $c2$ is the parity bit for the group containing $d1$, $d3$, and $d4$; and $c3$ is the parity bit for the group containing $d2$, $d3$, and $d4$. The parity bits are stored in memory with the data bits in the order shown in Figure 6.7. Upon reading the data, "syndrome" bits are computed as follows:

$$s1 = c1 \oplus d1 \oplus d2 \oplus d4$$
$$s2 = c2 \oplus d1 \oplus d3 \oplus d4 \quad (6\text{-}6)$$
$$s3 = c3 \oplus d2 \oplus d3 \oplus d4$$

```
xxxxxxxxxxxxxxxx    Code word #1
xxxxxxxxxoxxxxxxx   Non-code word (1 error)
xxxxxxxxxooxxxxxx   Code word #2
```

Figure 6.6b. Simple parity code with words separated by a Hamming distance of two. The error word can be detected but the source of the error cannot be uniquely determined to be code word #1 or #2.

A zero syndrome vector $(s3, s2, s1)$ computed from Equations (6-6) indicates the absence of errors, simply verifying the computations of Equations (6-5) used to generate the check bits originally. If the syndrome vector is non-zero, then its binary value points to the bit position in the data word $(c1,c2,d1,c3,d2,d3,d4)$ that is in error. For example, the data word 0010 would give $(c1,c2,c3) = 011$, and hence a code word 0101010. If bit $d3$ were to be changed to 0, giving 0101000, then the computed syndrome would be $(s3,s2,s1) = 110$. The binary value of the syndrome, 6, points to the sixth bit of the code word, $d3$, for correction. Although this particular code would erroneously "correct" double-bit errors to improper data words, additional bits could be added to increase the fault coverage of the code.

In evaluating the reliability of a memory employing ECC, the failure modes consist of any number of errors outside the correction capability of the code. For example, assume an N-bit code word with M redundant bits added to provide complete single-fault correction. In this case, given bit reliability Rb, we have

$$R = (Rb^{(N+M)} + (N+M)*Rb^{(N+M-1)}*(1-Rb))^K \quad (6\text{-}7)$$

where the term inside the outer parentheses represents the probability of either zero or one error within a given word, and K is the number of words in the memory. Figure 6.4 illustrates the reliability improvement of the ECC approach to that of the TMR and duplex systems presented above.

Recently, a number of IC manufacturers have developed chips which implement the error-detection and error-correction (EDC) features described above. A partial listing of these chips is given in Table 6.1. A typical block diagram of such a chip is shown in Figure 6.8. As data are written to

DATA WORD	(7,4) CODE WORD $(c1,c2,d1,c3,d2,d3,d4)$
0000	0000000
0001	1101001
0010	0101010
0011	1000011
0100	1001100
0101	0100101
0110	1100110
0111	0001111
1000	1110000
1001	0011001
1010	1011010
1011	0110011
1100	0111100
1101	1010101
1110	0010110
1111	1111111

Figure 6.7. Valid code words for a (7,4) Hamming code. All single-bit errors are correctable.

Table 6.1. Some Commercial EDC Devices.

Device	Basic Width /CBs	Expanded Width /CBs	Time to Compute CBs	Time to Detect Errors	Time to Correct Errors
AMD-2960	16/6	64/8	32ns	32ns	65ns
Intel-8206	16/6	80/9	42ns	52ns	67ns
National-DP8400	16/6	64/8	35ns	35ns	70ns
Signetics 74F630	16/6	——	20ns	25ns	25ns
Fairchild 74F632	32/7	——	38ns	30ns	30ns
Tex.Instr. 74ALS632A	32/7	——	35ns	26ns	58ns

Note: All include "byte" modification and use modified Hamming codes.

memory, they are directed to the data input latch of the EDC chip where they are used by the check-bit generation circuitry, with the resultant check bits written to memory with the data. Most of the commercial EDC chips utilize a modified Hamming code that will allow correction of all single errors and detection of all double and some other multiple errors. On READ operations, both the data and the check bits are loaded into input latches and the syndrome bits are computed. At this time, the syndrome is examined and appropriate error flags are raised, after which the syndrome is used to correct the data if a single-bit error is indicated. The corrected data are then passed to the system data bus. In the case of systems that write less than a full word of memory, most of the EDC chips will do a read-modify-write operation so that the new check bits will be computed for the entire word. The EDC chips listed in the table all have on-chip diagnostic modes, in addition to being able to be used without their error-correction features if more speed is required. In this case, the error signals would be used to generate processor interrupts that can then initiate error correction.

Recently, the use of EDC modules has begun to migrate onto the memory chips themselves in various forms [AIC84,KHA83,YAM84]. Because of yield considerations, most memory chips in recent years have included redundancy in the form of extra columns and/or rows of memory bits. In most of these devices, lasers or other means are used to deactivate faulty columns and replace them with spares as faults are detected during wafer probe and testing. The next logical step has been to use standard Hamming code techniques to eliminate the use of the manual reconfiguration of the memory chips. Faulty columns and/or rows of bits can

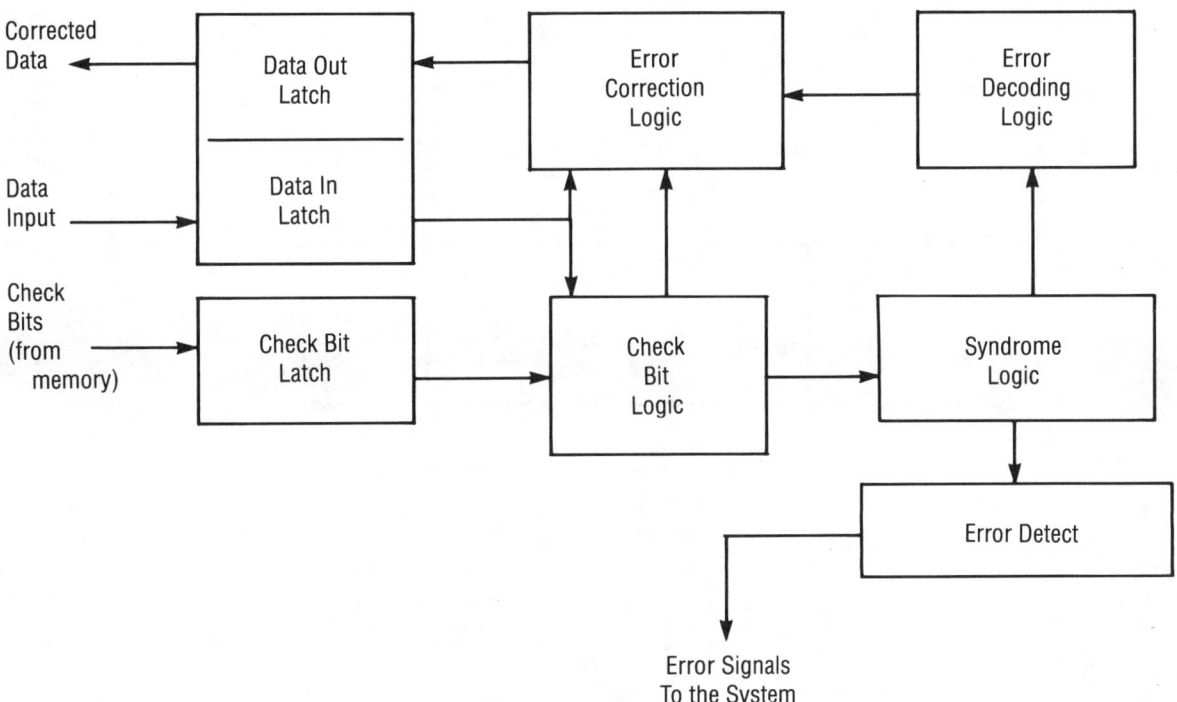

Figure 6.8. Typical Error-Correction- and Error-Detection-Unit (EDCU) Block Diagram.

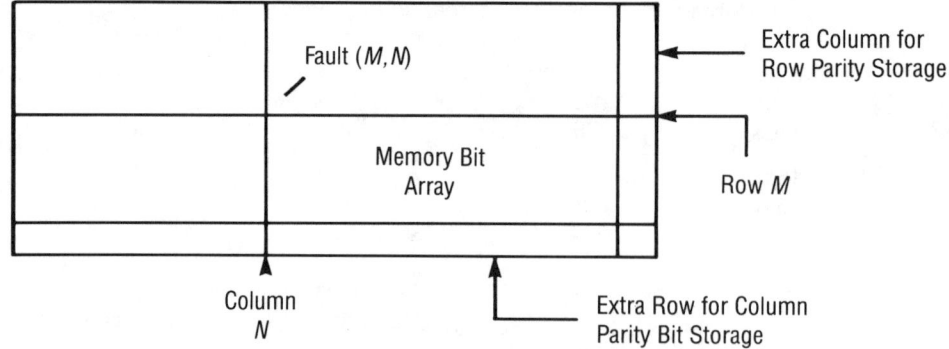

Figure 6.9. Product code organized memory. Row parity error in row *M* and column parity error in column *N* identify faulty bit at *(M,N)* in the memory array.

be simply corrected by the ECC mechanism, eliminating the need to replace them within the chip. In addition, the ECC mechanism can continuously mask "soft" errors in the chip, which cannot be done with the laser-manipulated on-chip redundancy. A typical example is a 256 × 4 ECL RAM chip described in [KHA83], in which each 4-bit "word" is stored with 3 check bits computed via a (7,4) Hamming code. This chip will continuously correct all single-bit errors in each word of the chip.

Another error-correction coding scheme that has been receiving increased attention for use in semiconductor memory applications is the use of two-dimensional parity in so-called product or block codes [TAN84, OSM82, EDW81]. As shown in Figure 6.9, a memory is organized into rectangular blocks, with a parity bit generated for each row and one for each column of each block. The presence of an error would be signaled when reading the row containing the error by the horizontal parity check on that row. Upon detecting the row parity error, a vertical parity check is performed on the columns of the block until the error is again detected. The intersection of the faulty row and column is the position of the erroneous bit, which can be toggled to correct it.

The block code approach is considerably less costly in terms of hardware than is the Hamming code approach described above, while providing reasonable error coverage. However, while the Hamming code can correct a single-bit error in each word of a memory array, the block codes cannot correct single-bit errors in two different words of the array if the errors are in the same column, because the vertical parity is unable to detect this double error condition, although the horizontal parity checks will still detect the errors in the two words. In terms of speed, the use of block coding requires a lengthy examination of column parities

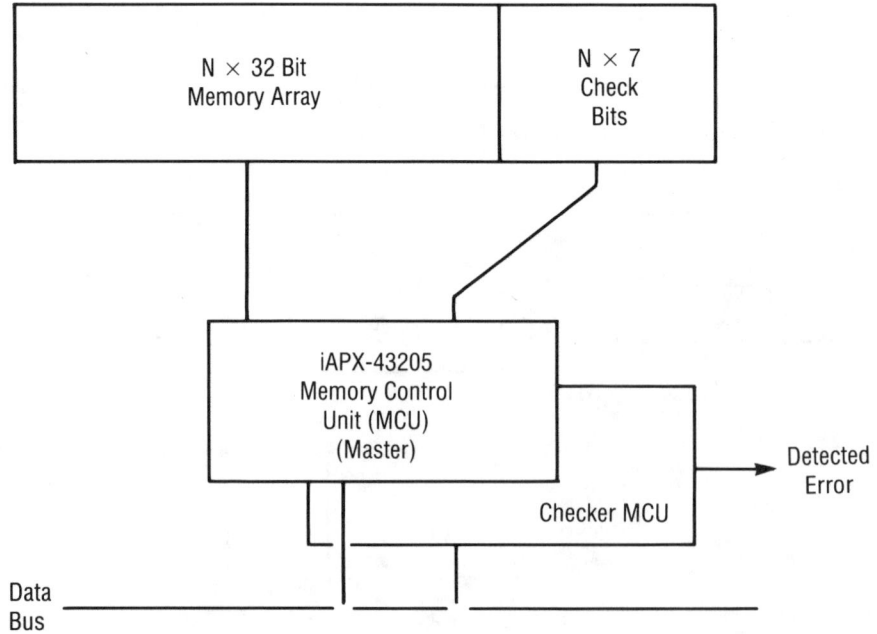

Figure 6.10. Intel iAPX-432 system memory using error coding in the memory array and duplex operation of the common circuitry, including the iAPX-43205 MCU.

following the detection of a row parity error, which represents a severe time penalty within that interval. If errors are infrequent, however, the overall time penalty might be considered negligible in many cases. As is the case with Hamming code techniques, the use of block codes has begun to move onto the memory chips themselves [TAN84,OSM82], with a substantial increase in performance over off-chip ECC mechanisms.

Other Memory Protection Techniques

The fault-tolerance techniques presented above are designed primarily to detect and correct errors within the memory array itself, although the duplex and TMR approaches can also be applied to the common circuitry in addition to the memory array. This approach was used by Intel in the design of the iAPX-432 memory subsystem support components [PET83]. As shown in Figure 6.10, the iAPX-43205 Memory Control Unit (MCU), is duplicated, with the copies operating in a standard duplex, matching mode, while a Hamming code is applied to the memory array. Consequently, all errors in one MCU are detected via the duplex match circuitry, while errors in the memory array are detected by the ECC. In addition, the duplex MCU will periodically test its bus drivers to detect any gross failure of those devices. All information entering and leaving the memory via the system bus is protected by a standard bit-per-byte interlaced parity.

The approach described above could conceivably be extended to provide even further memory protection by incorporating features similar to those used in memory management subsystems directly at the memory module. This would be especially useful in shared memory systems, where a faulty processor could damage information vital to other processors in the system. Memory management functions could verify the validity of each memory access and hence provide some protection against such malfunctions. Such a design is presented in [NEL85] which describes design of a fault-tolerant memory for the Auburn FTDCL multiprocessor system.

Summary

The incorporation of fault tolerance into memory system designs is perhaps the oldest and most widely used fault-tolerance technique. This is largely because of the maturity of coding theory, but it is also because of the relatively low cost of coding technique implementations as compared to other redundancy techniques, for a given level of reliability. These techniques have recently moved onto the VLSI memory devices themselves, both to ensure the reliability of the chip and to improve yield, since faulty rows and/or columns in a memory array can simply be left in place and then masked by the built-in redundancy. In the next few years, very few large systems will be without a memory incorporating ECC techniques, and in the not too distant future, these techniques will migrate into smaller systems as well.

C. L. Chen
M. Y. Hsiao

Error-Correcting Codes for Semiconductor Memory Applications: A State-of-the-Art Review

This paper presents a state-of-the-art review of error-correcting codes for computer semiconductor memory applications. The construction of four classes of error-correcting codes appropriate for semiconductor memory designs is described, and for each class of codes the number of check bits required for commonly used data lengths is provided. The implementation aspects of error correction and error detection are also discussed, and certain algorithms useful in extending the error-correcting capability for the correction of soft errors such as α-particle-induced errors are examined in some detail.

Introduction

In recent years *error-correcting codes* (ECCs) have been used increasingly to enhance the system reliability and the data integrity of computer semiconductor memory subsystems. As the trend in semiconductor memory design continues toward higher chip density and larger storage capacity, ECCs are becoming a more cost-effective means of maintaining a high level of system reliability [1–4].

A memory system can be made fault tolerant with the application of an error-correcting code; i.e., the mean time between "failures" of a properly designed memory system can be significantly increased with ECC. In this context, a system "fails" only when the errors exceed the error-correcting capability of the code. Also, in order to optimize data integrity, the ECC should have the capability of detecting the most likely of the errors that are uncorrectable.

Error-correcting codes used in early computer memory systems were of the class of *single-error-correcting* and *double-error-detecting* (SEC-DED) codes invented by R. W. Hamming [5]. A SEC-DED code is capable of correcting one error and detecting two errors in a codeword. The double-error-detecting capability serves to guard against data loss. In 1970, a new class of SEC-DED codes called *odd-weight-column* codes was published by Hsiao [6]. With the same coding efficiency, the odd-weight-column codes provide improvements over the Hamming codes in speed, cost and reliability of the decoding logic. As a result, odd-weight-column codes have been widely implemented by IBM and the computer industry worldwide [7–10]. Examples of systems which incorporate these codes are the IBM 158, 168, 303X, 308X, and 4300 series, Cray I, Tandem, etc. There are also various standard part numbers of these codes offered by many semiconductor manufacturers [11] (for example, the AM2960 and AMZ8160 of Advanced Micro Devices, the MC68540 of Motorola, the MB1412A of Fujitsu, and the SN54/74 LS630, LS631 of Texas Instruments).

The number of errors generated in the failure of a memory chip is largely dependent on the chip failure type. For example, a cell failure may cause one error, while a line failure or a total chip failure in general causes more than one error. For ECC applications, the memory array chips are usually organized so that the errors generated in a chip failure can be corrected by the ECC. In the case of SEC-DED codes, the one-bit-per-chip organization is the most effective design. In this organization, each bit of a codeword is stored in a different chip; thus, any type of failure in a chip can corrupt, at most, one bit of the codeword. As long as the errors do not line up in the same codeword, multiple errors in the memory are correctable.

Memory array modules are generally packaged on printed-circuit cards with current semiconductor memory technology, and usually a group of bits from the same card form a portion of an ECC codeword, as illustrated in **Figure 1**. With this

© **Copyright** 1984 by International Business Machines Corporation. Copying in printed form for private use is permitted without payment of royalty provided that (1) each reproduction is done without alteration and (2) the *Journal* reference and IBM copyright notice are included on the first page. The title and abstract, but no other portions, of this paper may be copied or distributed royalty free without further permission by computer-based and other information-service systems. Permission to *republish* any other portion of this paper must be obtained from the Editor.

multiple-bit-per-card type of organization, a failure at the card-support-circuit level would result in a byte error, where the size of the byte is the number of bits feeding from the card to a codeword. In this type of configuration, it is important for data integrity that the ECC be able to detect byte errors [12]. A SEC-DED code is in general not capable of detecting all single-byte errors. However, a class of SEC-DED codes capable of detecting all single-byte errors can be constructed [13, 14]. These are called *single-error-correcting double-error-detecting single-byte-error-detecting* (SEC-DED-SBD) codes.

There are certain design applications where the memory array cannot be organized in one-bit-per-chip fashion because of cost or other reasons such as system granularity or power restrictions. As chip density increases, it becomes more difficult to design a one-bit-per-chip memory system. For a multiple-bit-per-chip type of memory organization, a *single-byte-error-correcting double-byte-error-detecting* (SBC-DBD) code [15–20] would be more effective in error correction and error detection.

System reliability generally tends to decrease as the capacity of a memory system increases. To maintain the same high level of reliability, a *double-error-correcting triple-error-detecting* (DEC-TED) code may be used. However, this type of code requires a larger number of check bits than a SEC-DED code and more complex hardware to implement the functions of error correction and error detection [8, 15, 16].

An error-correcting code can be used to correct "soft" errors as well as hard errors. Soft errors are temporary errors such as α-particle-induced errors that disappear during the next memory write operation. With a maintenance strategy that allows the accumulation of hard errors, a high soft error rate would cause a high *uncorrectable error* (UE) rate. To reduce the UE rate that involves soft errors, a SEC-DED code can be modified to correct two hard errors or a combination of one hard and one soft error [21–25].

In this paper we review the current status of error-correcting codes for semiconductor memory applications and present the state of the art by describing the construction of four classes of error-correcting codes suitable for this type of design application. These four classes are SEC-DED codes, SEC-DED-SBD codes, SBC-DBD codes, and DEC-TED codes. For each class of code we provide the number of check bits required for commonly used data lengths, information that is particularly useful to designers for system planning. We also discuss the implementation aspects of error correction and error detection for these classes of error control codes. In addition, we describe a number of algorithms useful in extending the error-correcting capability of codes for the correction of soft errors such as α-particle-induced errors and other temporary errors.

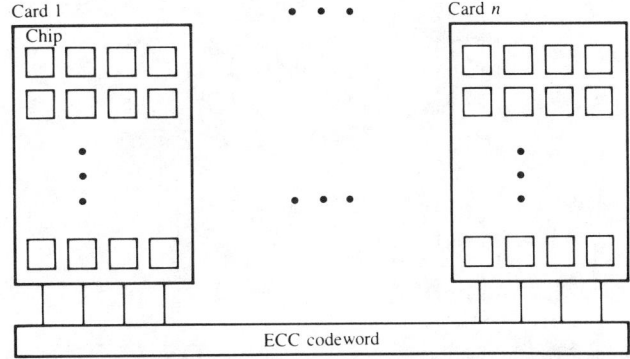

Figure 1 A 4-bit-per-card memory array.

Binary linear block codes

A binary (n,k) linear block code is a k-dimensional subspace of a binary n-dimensional vector space [8, 15, 16]. An n-bit codeword of the code contains k data bits and $r = n - k$ check bits. An $r \times n$ *parity check matrix* $\mathbf{H}$ is used to describe the code. Let $\mathbf{V} = (v_1, v_2, \cdots, v_n)$ be an n-bit vector. Then $\mathbf{V}$ is a codeword if and only if

$$\mathbf{H} \cdot \mathbf{V}' = \mathbf{0}, \tag{1}$$

where $\mathbf{V}'$ denotes the transpose of $\mathbf{V}$, and all additions are performed modulo 2.

The *encoding* process of a code consists of generating r check bits for a set of k data bits. To facilitate encoding, the $\mathbf{H}$ matrix is expressed as

$$\mathbf{H} = [\mathbf{P}, \mathbf{I}_r], \tag{2}$$

where $\mathbf{P}$ is an $r \times k$ binary matrix and $\mathbf{I}_r$ is the $r \times r$ identity matrix. Then the first k bits of a codeword can be designated as the data bits, and the last r bits can be designated as the check bits. Furthermore, the ith check bit can be explicitly calculated from the ith equation of the set of r equations in (1). A code specified by an $\mathbf{H}$ matrix of (2) is called a *systematic code*.

Any binary $r \times n$ matrix $\mathbf{H}$ of rank r can always be transformed into the systematic form of (2). Since the rank of $\mathbf{H}$ is r, there exists a set of r linearly independent columns. The columns of the matrix can be reordered so that the rightmost r columns are linearly independent. Applying elementary row operations [16] on the resultant matrix, a matrix of (2) is obtained. The systematic code obtained is equivalent to the code defined by the original $\mathbf{H}$ matrix. **Figure 2(a)** is an example of the parity check matrix of a (26,20) code in a nonsystematic form. Note that the last six columns of the matrix are linearly independent. The submatrix of the six columns can be inverted. The multiplication of the inverse of the submatrix and the transpose of the parity check matrix results in a matrix of systematic form shown in **Figure 2(b)**.

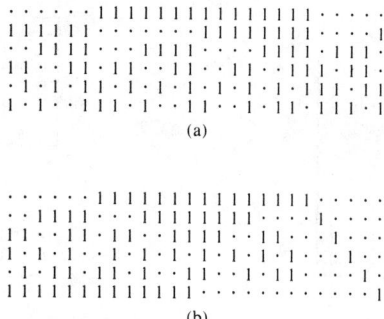

Figure 2 (26,20) code: (a) nonsystematic form; (b) systematic form.

Table 1 Average number of uncorrectable errors (UEs) with three memory systems employing different error control schemes: parity check, SEC-DED code, and DEC-TED code.

Time ($\times 10^3$ hrs.)	Parity check	SEC-DED	DEC-TED
0–10	49	3.2	0.56
0–20	81	5.2	0.96
0–30	111	6.9	1.3
0–50	168	9.3	2.0
0–80	253	13	2.9

Parity check: (9,8) code.
SEC-DED: (72,64) code.
DEC-TED: (80,64) code.

A word read from the memory may not be the same as the original codeword written in the same location. Let $U = (u_1, u_2, \cdots, u_n)$ be the word read from the memory. The difference between U and the original codeword V is defined as the *error vector* $E = (e_1, e_2, \cdots, e_n)$; i.e., $U = V + E$. The ith position of U is in error if and only if e_i is nonzero.

The *decoding process* consists of determining whether U contains errors and determining the error vector. To determine whether U is in error, an r-bit *syndrome* S is calculated as follows:

$$S = H \cdot U' = H \cdot (V' + E')$$
$$= H \cdot E'. \qquad (3)$$

If S is an all-zeros vector, the word U is assumed to be error-free. If S is a nonzero vector, it is used to determine the error vector.

The error-correcting capability of a code is closely related to the *minimum distance* of the code. The *weight* of a codeword is the number of nonzero components in the codeword. The *distance* between two codewords is the number of components in which the two codewords differ. The minimum distance d of the code is the minimum of the distances of all pairs of codewords. For a linear code, the minimum distance of the code is equal to the minimum of the weights of all nonzero codewords [8, 15, 16]. A code is capable of correcting t errors and detecting $t + 1$ errors if and only if $d > 2t + 1$.

In semiconductor memory applications, the encoding and the decoding of a code are implemented in a parallel manner. In encoding, the check bits are generated simultaneously by processing the data bits in parallel. In decoding, the syndrome is generated using the same hardware for the generation of the check bits. The error vector is then generated by decoding the syndrome bits in parallel. Finally, the errors are corrected by subtracting the error vector from the fetched word. The subtraction is accomplished by the bit-by-bit exclusive-or (XOR) of the components of the two vectors.

The reliability function of a memory system that employs an error-correcting code can be handled either analytically or through Monte Carlo methods [1–4, 26–28]. For a system with a simple architecture, an analytical approach may be possible. However, for a memory system consisting of hierarchical arrays, the memory reliability function is too intractable to handle analytically. Monte Carlo methods are considered a general approach to study the effectiveness of error-correcting codes and other fault-tolerant schemes [27, 28].

To demonstrate the reliability improvement obtainable with ECC, we consider three memory systems of four megabytes. The first system consists of eight memory cards and is designed with a parity check on each set of eight data bits. The second system consists of 18 memory cards and is designed with a (72,64) SEC-DED code. The last system consists of 20 memory cards and is designed with an (80,64) DEC-TED code. The memory chips for the systems are 16K-bit chips with 128 bit lines and 128 word lines in each chip. Each memory card contains an array of 32×9 chips for the first system, and an array of 32×4 chips for the other two systems. The failure rates of the chips and the card-support circuits are assumed to be the same as those described in [27]. When a UE occurs, the strategy is to replace the card that contains the UE and that has the largest number of defective cells.

The modeling tool of [27] is used to simulate the reliability of the three memory systems. The results of the simulation are shown in **Table 1**. The improvement factor of ECC over the parity check scheme on the number of UEs is over 15 for SEC-DED code and over 84 for DEC-TED code.

SEC-DED codes

The minimum distance of a single-error-correcting and double-error-detecting (SEC-DED) code is greater than or equal to four. Since an n-tuple of weight three or less is not a codeword, from Eq. (1) the sum of a set of three or fewer columns of the H matrix must be nonzero. In other words,

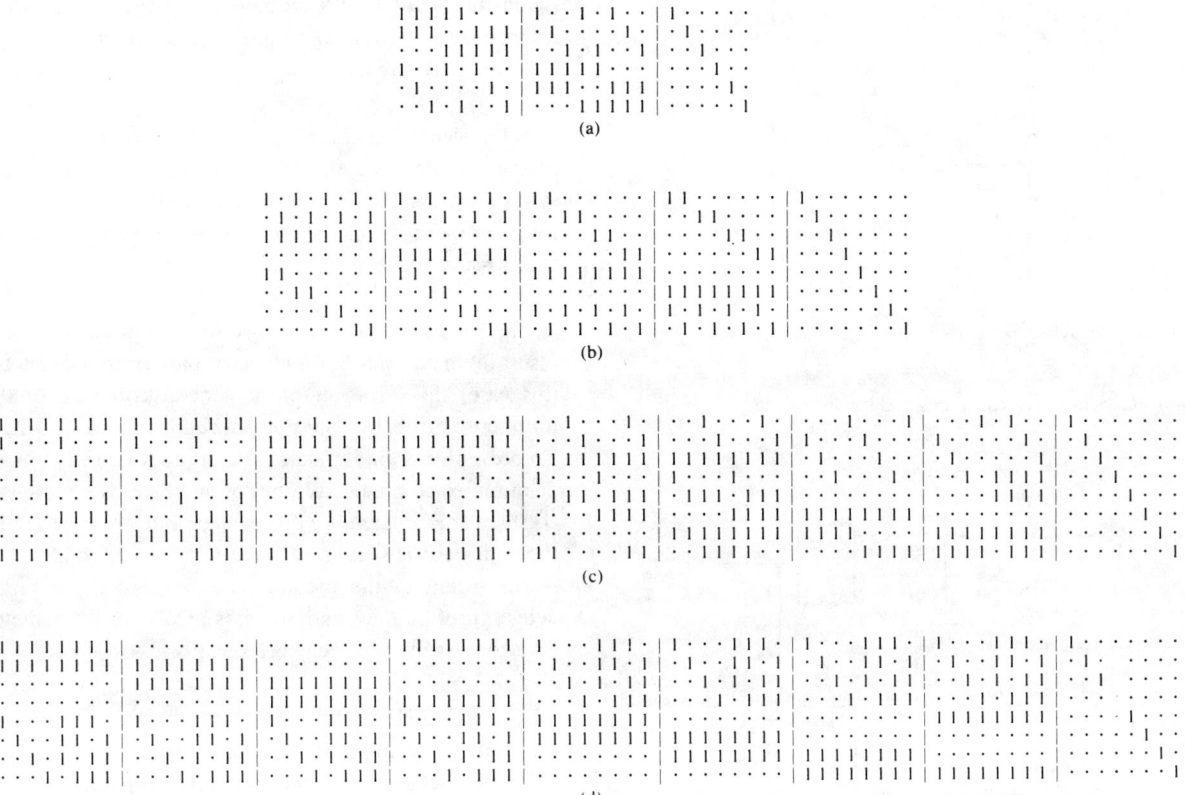

Figure 3 Parity check matrix of some SEC-DED codes: (a) (22,16) code (IBM System/3); (b) (40,32) code (IBM 8130); (c) (72,64) code (IBM 3033); (d) (72,64) code (IBM 3081).

any set of three columns of the **H** matrix are linearly independent. Thus, the **H** matrix of a SEC-DED code must satisfy the following conditions:

A1. The column vectors of the **H** matrix are nonzero and are distinct.

A2. The sum of two columns of the **H** matrix is nonzero and is not equal to a third column of the **H** matrix.

Note that the sum of two odd-weight r-tuples is an even-weight r-tuple. A SEC-DED code with r check bits can be constructed with its **H** matrix consisting of distinct nonzero r-tuples of odd weights. This is an odd-weight-column code of Hsiao [6].

The maximum code length of an odd-weight-column code with r check bits is 2^{r-1}, for there are 2^{r-1} possible distinct odd-weight r-tuples. This maximum code length is the same as that of a SEC-DED Hamming code. The maximum number of data bits k of a SEC-DED code must satisfy $k \leq 2^{r-1} - r$. **Table 2** lists the number of check bits required for a set of data bits. **Figure 3** shows examples of SEC-DED codes used in some IBM systems.

Most of the SEC-DED codes for semiconductor memory applications are *shortened codes* in that the code length is less

Table 2 Number of check bits required for SEC-DED codes.

Data bits	Check bits
8	5
16	6
32	7
64	8
128	9
256	10

than the maximum for a given number of check bits. There are various ways of shortening a maximum-length SEC-DED code. Usually a code designer constructs a shortened code to meet certain objectives for a particular application. These objectives may include the minimization of the number of circuits, the amount of logic delay, the number of part numbers, or the probability of miscorrecting triple errors [6].

In a write operation, check bits are generated simultaneously by processing the data bits in a parallel manner according to Eqs. (1) and (2). In a read operation, syndrome bits are generated simultaneously from the word read according to Eq. (3). Typically the same XOR tree is used to generate both the check bits and the syndrome bits (see **Figure 4**).

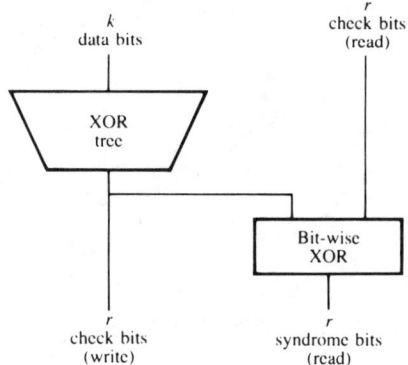

Figure 4 Generation of check bits and syndrome bits.

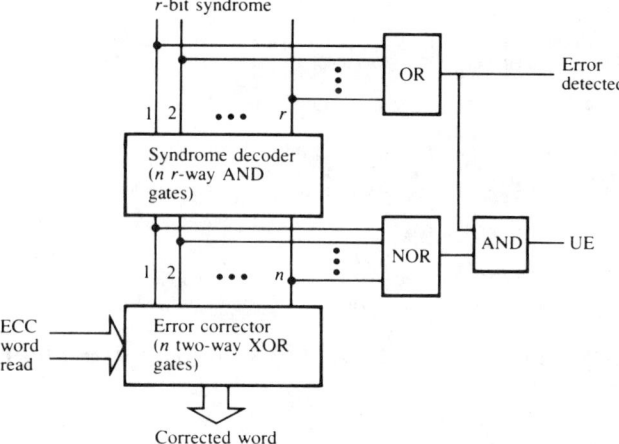

Figure 5 Error detection and correction block diagram.

An algorithm for correcting single errors and detecting multiple errors is described as follows:

1. Test whether **S** is **0**. If **S** is **0**, the word is assumed to be error-free.
2. If **S** $\neq$ **0**, try to find a perfect match between **S** and a column of the **H** matrix. The match can be implemented in n r-way AND gates.
3. If **S** is the same as the ith column of **H**, the ith bit of the word is in error.
4. If **S** is not equal to any column of **H**, the errors are detected as uncorrectable (UE).

This algorithm applied to a SEC-DED code corrects all single errors and detects all double errors. Multiple-bit errors may be detected or falsely corrected. The extent of multiple errors detected depends on the structure of the code.

As shown in **Figure 5**, hardware implementation of the error correction and detection mainly consists of an r-way OR gate for testing nonzero syndrome, n r-way AND gates for decoding syndromes, an n-way NOR gate for generating UE signal, and n two-way XOR gates for inverting the code bit in error. Additionally, an n-bit data register and control logic for timing are required.

A UE signal can also be generated based on the logical OR of the minterms of all UE syndromes. A subset of all UE syndromes is the set of even-weight syndromes caused by even numbers of errors. This subset of syndromes can be recognized by an r-way XOR gate.

The failure of a common logic support in the memory may result in an all-ones or an all-zeros pattern in a codeword. In this case, the error vector in general contains a multiple number of errors that are not detectable by a SEC-DED code. To prevent this kind of data loss, the code can be constructed or modified so that an all-ones or an all-zeros n-tuple is not a codeword. For example, if the check bits are inverted before the codeword is written into the memory, then all the codewords stored in the memory are nonzero. In general, the detection of all-ones and all-zeros errors can be achieved by inverting a subset of the check bits [9].

SEC-DED-SBD codes

In some applications it is required that the memory array chips be packaged in a b-bits-per-chip organization. A chip failure or a word-line failure in this case would result in a byte-oriented error that contains from 1 to b erroneous bits. Byte errors can also be caused by the failures of the supporting modules at the memory card level. The class of SEC-DED codes that are capable of detecting all single-byte errors (SEC-DED-SBD codes) may be used to maintain data integrity in these applications.

The **H** matrix of a SEC-DED-SBD code can be divided into N blocks of $r \times b$ submatrices, $\mathbf{B}_1, \mathbf{B}_2, \cdots, \mathbf{B}_n$, where $\mathbf{B}_i$ represents the parity checks for byte position i. From (3), the syndrome of a byte error at position i is a sum of the columns of $\mathbf{B}_i$ that correspond to the bit error positions within the byte. The syndromes of all possible byte errors at position i are the sum of all possible combinations of the columns of $\mathbf{B}_i$. Let $\langle \mathbf{B}_i \rangle$ denote the sums of all possible nonzero linear combinations of the columns of $\mathbf{B}_i$. Each member of $\langle \mathbf{B}_i \rangle$ should be nonzero and should not be equal to a column of $\mathbf{B}_j$, for $j \neq i$. Otherwise, the byte error at position i will be mistaken as no error or as a correctable single error at position j. Thus, the **H** matrix of a SEC-DED-SBD code must satisfy the conditions A1 and A2 given previously, as well as the following condition:

A3. Each vector of $\langle \mathbf{B}_i \rangle$ is nonzero and is not equal to a column vector of $\mathbf{B}_j$, for $j \neq i$.

For $b \leq 4$, most of the SEC-DED codes for practical applications can be *reconfigured* to detect single-byte errors. The reconfiguration involves the regrouping or rewiring of the

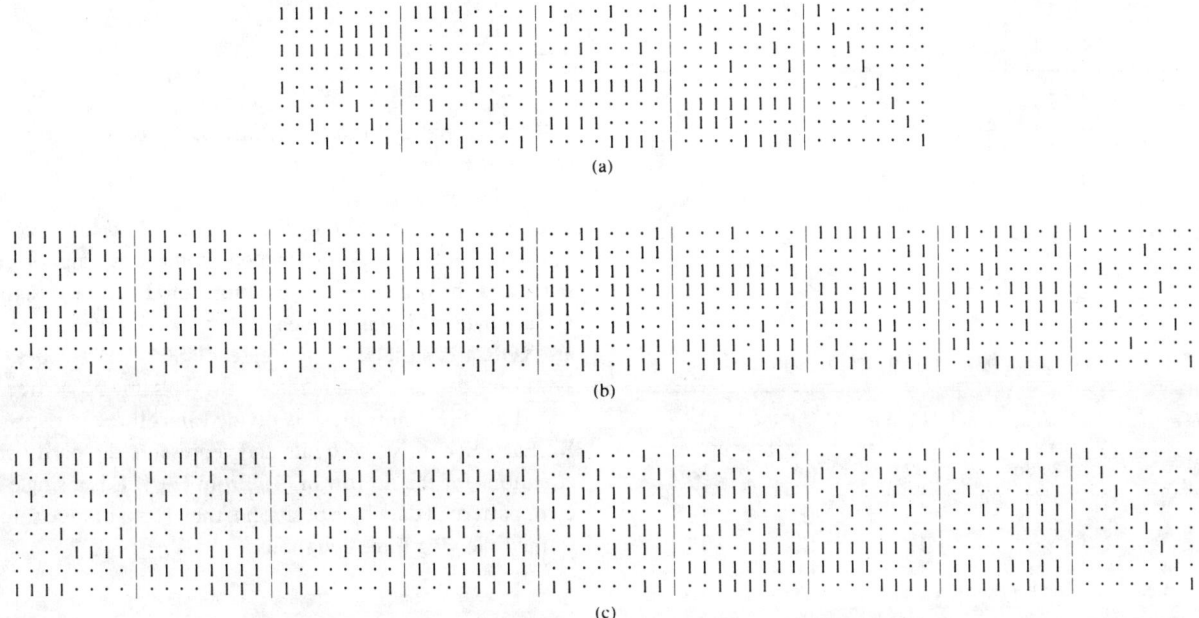

Figure 6 Examples of SEC-DED-SBD codes: (a) (40,32) code, $b = 4$; (b) (72,64) code, $b = 4$; (c) (72,64) code, $b = 3$ and $b = 4$.

bit positions of the original code. Since the same encoding and decoding hardware can be used, no additional hardware is required if a SEC-DED code can be reconfigured for single-byte error detection. **Figure 6** illustrates some examples of SEC-DED-SBD codes. The codes in Figs. 6(a) and (b) are obtained from those in Figs. 3(b) and (d) by reconfiguration, and the code in Fig. 6(c) is the same as that in Fig. 3(c). The (72,64) codes of Fig. 6 are those used in IBM systems 3081 and 3033.

Techniques for the construction of SEC-DED-SBD codes have been presented in [13, 14]. Let $N(r,b)$ be the code length in b-bit bytes. For $b = 3$, it is shown in [14] that optimal codes with $N(r,3) = \lfloor 2^{r-1}/3 \rfloor$, where $\lfloor x \rfloor$ denotes the integer part of x, can be constructed. For other values of b, the construction of the longest code for a given r is an open question. A list of the code lengths of some known SEC-DED-SBD codes is given in **Table 3**.

SBC-DBD codes

For a memory system packaged in a b-bits-per-chip organization, the reliability provided by a SEC-DED code may not be acceptable. To increase the reliability, a byte-oriented error-correcting code may be used [15–20, 29]. In this section, we discuss the construction and implementation of single-byte-error-correcting and double-byte-error-detecting (SBC-DBD) codes.

A codeword of a SBC-DBD code consists of N b-bit bytes. A binary b-tuple is considered an element of the finite field $GF(2^b)$ of 2^b elements [8, 15, 16]. For example, all binary 3-

Table 3 Code length in bytes for some SEC-DED-SBD codes.

r \ b	3	4	5	6	7	8	9
$b+1$	2	2	3	3	3	3	3
$b+2$	5	6	7	8	9	10	11
$b+3$	10	12	15	16	18	20	22
$b+4$	21	26	31	36	41	46	51
$b+5$	42	52	63	72	82	92	102
$b+6$	85	106	127	148	169	190	211

Table 4 All binary 3-tuples expressed as elements of $GF(8)$.

$0 = 0\ 0\ 0$
$x^0 = 1\ 0\ 0$
$x^1 = 0\ 1\ 0$
$x^2 = 0\ 0\ 1$
$x^3 = 1\ 1\ 0$
$x^4 = 0\ 1\ 1$
$x^5 = 1\ 1\ 1$
$x^6 = 1\ 0\ 1$

tuples can be assigned as the elements of $GF(8)$, as shown in **Table 4**. In the finite-field representation of b-tuples, the sum of two elements is the bit-by-bit XOR of the two associated b-tuples. The product of two elements X^i and X^j is X^k with $k = i + j \mod (2^b) - 1$. For example, $X^3 + X^6 = (1\ 1\ 0) + (1\ 0\ 1) = (0\ 1\ 1) = X^4$, and $X^3 \cdot X^6 = X^2$ from Table 4.

With the finite-field representation, an SBC-DBD code is a linear code over $GF(2^b)$ with a minimum distance $d \geq 4$. The

Figure 7 (10,7) SBC-DBD code with $b = 3$.

Table 5 Number of check bits required for SBC-DBD codes.

Bits per byte	Data bits per ECC word			
	16	32	64	128
2	8	10	10	12
3	9	12	12	12
4	12	12	14	16
$b > 5$	$3b$	$3b$	$3b$	$3b$

code can also be defined by the parity check matrix **H** of (1) and (2), with the components of the matrices and vectors considered elements of GF(2^b). Let $\mathbf{h}_i$, $1 \leq i \leq N$, be the column vectors of the **H** matrix. The SBC-DBD code must satisfy the following conditions:

B1. $h_i \neq X \cdot h_j$ for $i \neq j$, $X \in$ GF(2^b).
B2. $h_i + X_1 \cdot h_j \neq X_2 \cdot h_f$, for distinct i, j, f, and $X_1, X_2 \in$ GF(2^b).

Let r be the number of check bytes of an SBC-DBD code over GF(2^b). For $r = 3$, a code of length $N = 2 + 2^b$ bytes can be constructed by extending a Reed–Solomon code of length (2^b) – 1 [15–19]. The parity check matrix of the code can be expressed as

$$\mathbf{H} = \begin{bmatrix} \mathbf{I} & \mathbf{I} & \mathbf{I} & \cdots & \mathbf{I} & \mathbf{I} & \mathbf{O} & \mathbf{O} \\ \mathbf{I} & \mathbf{T} & \mathbf{T}^2 & \cdots & \mathbf{T}^{2^b-2} & \mathbf{O} & \mathbf{I} & \mathbf{O} \\ \mathbf{I} & \mathbf{T}^2 & \mathbf{T}^4 & \cdots & \mathbf{T}^{2(2^b-2)} & \mathbf{O} & \mathbf{O} & \mathbf{I} \end{bmatrix}, \quad (4)$$

where **I** is the $b \times b$ identity matrix, **O** is a $b \times b$ all-zero matrix, **T** is the $b \times b$ companion matrix of X, and X is a *primitive element* of GF(2^b) [15, 16]. If X is a root of the *primitive polynomial* $P(X) = a_0 + a_1X + a_2X^2 + \cdots + a_{b-1}x^{b-1}$, the companion matrix of X is

$$\mathbf{T} = \begin{bmatrix} 0 & 0 & \cdots & 0 & a_0 \\ 1 & 0 & \cdots & 0 & a_1 \\ 0 & 1 & \cdots & 0 & a_2 \\ \cdot & \cdot & & \cdot & \cdot \\ \cdot & \cdot & & \cdot & \cdot \\ 0 & 0 & \cdots & 1 & a_{b-1} \end{bmatrix}$$

For example, the companion matrix of X in Table 4 is

$$\mathbf{T} = \begin{bmatrix} 0 & 0 & 1 \\ 1 & 0 & 1 \\ 0 & 1 & 0 \end{bmatrix},$$

and the **H** matrix for a (10,7) SBC-DBD code with $b = 3$ is shown in **Figure 7**.

Using the **H** matrix of Eq. (4), the last three column positions of **H** can be designated as the positions of check bytes and the other column positions of **H** can be designated as data byte positions. The check bytes can be generated with an XOR tree just as in the case of SEC-DED codes. The syndrome can also be generated with the same XOR tree. For decoding, the syndrome **S** is divided into three parts, $\mathbf{S}_1$, $\mathbf{S}_2$, $\mathbf{S}_3$. Each $\mathbf{S}_i$ consists of b bits and represents the parity check equations for the ith row of (4). From (3), if **E** is a single-byte error pattern at data byte position i, then **E** is a unique solution to the following three equations:

$\mathbf{S}_1 = \mathbf{E}'$,

$\mathbf{S}_2 = \mathbf{T}^i \cdot \mathbf{E}'$,

$\mathbf{S}_3 = \mathbf{T}^{2i} \cdot \mathbf{E}'$.

On the other hand, if **E** is a byte error pattern at check byte position i, where $i = 1, 2$, or 3, then $\mathbf{E} = \mathbf{S}'_i$ and the other two subsyndromes are zeros. The following steps can be taken to find the correctable single-byte error patterns and to detect multiple uncorrectable byte errors.

1. If **S** is a zero vector, assume that there is no error. If **S** is nonzero, go to step 2.
2. If one of the subsyndromes $\mathbf{S}_i \neq \mathbf{0}$, and the other two subsyndromes are zero, $i = 1, 2, 3$, the check byte position i with error pattern S is assumed. Otherwise, go to step 3.
3. Assume that $\mathbf{E} = \mathbf{S}'_1$. Find i that satisfies $0 \leq i < N - 4$, $\mathbf{T}^i \cdot \mathbf{E}' = \mathbf{S}_2$, and $\mathbf{T}^{2i} \cdot \mathbf{E}' = \mathbf{S}_3$. If i has a solution, the byte error with pattern **E** at data byte position i is assumed. If i has no solution, then an uncorrectable error is detected.

A block diagram for the generation of the error pointers for the code of Fig. 7 is shown in **Figure 8**.

The extended Reed–Solomon codes defined in Eq. (4) are optimal in that no other SBC-DBD codes with three check bytes contain more data bytes. However, there exists only one code for a given byte size b. When b is small, the code may be too short for memory applications. For example, the code for $b = 2$ can only accommodate six data bits. This code certainly is not practical for most applications. In order to increase the code length for a given b, additional check bits are required.

Techniques for the construction of SBC-DBD codes for $r > 3$ can be found in [15, 16, 30, 31]. **Table 5** lists the minimum number of check bits required for some known SBC-DBD codes.

DEC-TED codes

A memory system with a large capacity or with high chip failure rates may use a double-error-correcting and triple-error-detecting (DEC-TED) code to meet its reliability requirements. A DEC-TED code is also attractive for a memory with a high soft error rate. Although there are schemes [21–25], to be discussed in a subsequent section, for a SEC-DED code to correct hard-hard and hard-soft types of double errors, these schemes cannot correct double soft errors and they require the interruption of a normal memory read operation. With a DEC-TED code, any combination of hard and soft double errors, including double soft errors, can be corrected automatically without system interruption.

A minimum distance of a DEC-TED code is at least equal to six. The parity check matrix **H** of a DEC-TED code must have the property that any linear combination of five or fewer columns of **H** is not an all-zeros vector.

A class of DEC-TED binary linear block codes can be constructed according to the theory of BCH codes [8, 15, 16, 32, 33]. Let X be a root of a primitive binary polynomial $P(X)$ of degree m. The powers of X can be considered elements of $GF(N)$, $N = 2^m$, and can be expressed as binary m-tuples. A binary code defined by (1) with the following parity check matrix is a DEC-TED code:

$$\mathbf{H} = \begin{bmatrix} 1 & 1 & 1 & \cdots & 1 \\ 1 & X & X^2 & \cdots & X^{N-2} \\ 1 & X^3 & X^6 & \cdots & X^{3(N-2)} \end{bmatrix}. \quad (5)$$

The powers of X in **H** are expressed in m-tuples. Since there are $2m + 1$ linearly independent row vectors in **H**, the number of check bits of the code is $2m + 1$. The code length is equal to $N - 1$. The code can be extended to length N by adding a column of 1 followed by $2m$ zeros. **Figure 9(a)** shows the parity check matrix of a (31,20) code constructed from Eq. (5).

A full-length BCH code can be shortened by deleting a number of columns from its **H** matrix. The shortened code has a minimum distance at least as large as the original code. The number of check bits of the shortened code may be less than the original code when proper bit positions are deleted [34–35]. In particular, let **Y** be a row vector in the space generated by the row vectors of **H**. Deleting the column positions of **H** where the corresponding positions of **Y** are ones, then the shortened **H** matrix has one fewer linearly independent row vector and the shortened code has one fewer check bit than the original code. **Table 6** presents a list of the number of check bits required for some DEC-TED BCH codes.

The **H** matrix defined by (5) can be transformed into the systematic form of (2) for the generation of check bits (see

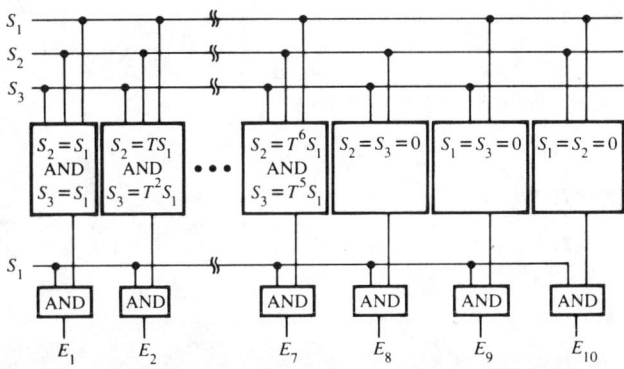

Figure 8 Generation of error vectors for a (10,7) SBC-DBD code with $b = 3$.

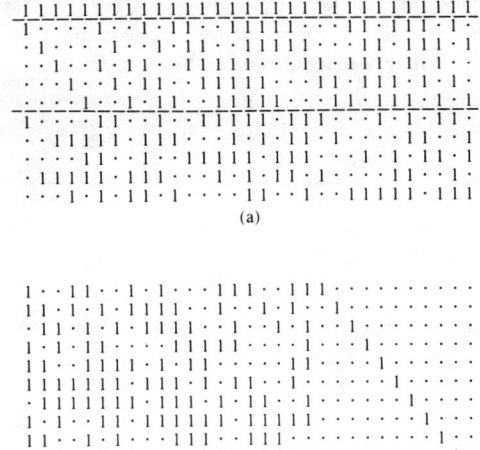

Figure 9 Parity check matrix of a (31,20) code: (a) nonsystematic form **H**; (b) systematic form **H1**.

Table 6 Number of check bits required for DEC-TED BCH codes.

Data bits	Check bits
8	9
16	11
32	13
64	15
2^m	$2m + 3$

Fig. 9 for example). Let **H1** be the parity check matrix in systematic form, and **T** be an $r \times r$ transformation matrix that satisfies

$$\mathbf{H} = \mathbf{T} \cdot \mathbf{H1}. \quad (6)$$

The generation of check bits from matrix **H1** can be imple-

Table 7 Example of locating erasures.

Direction of stuck faults	1 0 - - - - - 1
T_1 (WRITE)	1 1 0 0 1 1 0 0
T_1 (READ)	1 0 0 0 1 1 0 1
T_2 (WRITE)	0 0 1 1 0 0 1 1
T_2 (READ)	1 0 1 1 0 0 1 1
T_1 (READ) + T_2 (READ)	0 0 1 1 1 1 1 0
ERASURE ERROR	1 1 0 0 0 0 0 1

mented with an XOR tree. For decoding, it is convenient to define the syndrome **S** from (3) with the **H** matrix instead of the **H1** matrix. The syndrome can be generated using an XOR tree associated with the **H** matrix. Thus, two separate XOR trees are used to generate check bits and syndrome bits. The syndrome can also be generated by first generating **S1** from Eq. (3) with the **H1** matrix, then multiplying matrix **T** by **S1**. Using this approach, the same XOR tree can be used to generate check bits and **S1**. The validity of this procedure follows directly from Eq. (6).

The syndrome **S** can be divided into three parts, S_0, S_1, and S_2, where S_0 consists of one bit, and S_1 and S_2 consist of m bits. Let the bit positions of the code be assigned as the powers of X. Assume that E_1 and E_2 are the positions of two erroneous bits. Then $S_0 = 0$ and $S_1 = E_1 + E_2$, $S_2 = E_1^3 + E_2^3$. Since $S_1^3 + S_2 = E_1^2 E_2 + E_1 E_2^2 = E_1 E_2 S_1$, the error positions E_1 and E_2 are roots of the quadratic equation

$$S_1 y^2 + S_1^2 y + (S_1^3 + S_2) = 0. \tag{7}$$

On the other hand, if there is only one error, then $S_0 = 1$ and the error position is the root of the linear equation $y + S_1 = 0$.

The major part of the error correction is to find the error positions from the syndrome. Once the error positions are known, the errors are corrected by inverting the data bits at the error positions. The error positions are determined by solving Eq. (7). If $S_0 = 0$, and Eq. (7) has two solutions, then the solutions are the positions of two errors. If $S_0 = 1$, and Eq. (7) degenerates to a linear equation, then the solution is the position of a single error. Uncorrectable errors are detected if Eq. (7) has no solution when $S_0 = 0$, or Eq. (7) does not degenerate into a linear equation when $S_0 = 1$.

There are various schemes for solving Eq. (7) [36–38]. The equation can be solved algebraically using hardware that implements finite-field operations as in [36]. It can also be solved by substituting all possible solutions into the equation, as in [38]. Another approach is to store the error positions of correctable errors in a table. The syndrome is used as the address to the table of error positions [37].

Extended error correction

Errors in semiconductor memory can be broadly divided into hard errors and soft errors [24, 25]. Hard errors are caused by stuck faults or by permanent physical damage to the memory devices. Soft errors are temporary errors or α-particle-induced errors that will be erased during the next data storage operation. For this discussion, the errors that will stay in their locations during the next few write cycles are considered hard errors.

Error-correcting codes can be used to correct hard as well as soft errors. However, the maintenance strategy for a system may allow the hard errors to accumulate. The presence of errors in the memory increases the probability of uncorrectable errors (UE) due to the lineup of multiple errors in a codeword. The UE rate can be reduced by repair service scheduled periodically. It can also be reduced by extending the conventional error correction to some of the otherwise uncorrectable errors. The latter approach is especially attractive when the soft error rates are high, because it does not require the replacement of memory components. The extended error-correction schemes are discussed in this section.

The errors for which locations but not values are known are called *erasures* [15, 16]. Erasures are easier to correct than random errors. Let t and e be the number of random errors and erasures, respectively, that a code is capable of correcting; then the minimum distance d of the code must satisfy [15, 16],

$$2t + e < d. \tag{8}$$

For example, a SEC-DED code is capable of correcting one random error and one erasure.

In memory applications, the hard errors can be considered erasures if their locations can be identified. To locate the erasures of a particular word in the memory, we may apply some test patterns to the memory. Assume that any binary pattern can be written into the memory. An example is shown in **Table 7** for finding the locations of erasures with two test patterns, T_1 and T_2, of length 8, where T_2 is the complement of T_1. Before the test patterns are written into and read out of the memory, the word originally stored in the memory is read out and stored in a temporary storage. The erasure vector is obtained by the complement of T_1(READ) + T_2(READ). The locations of the erasures are indicated by the ones in the erasure vector. Since T_1 can be arbitrarily chosen, we may also use the word that originally stored in the memory as T_1. This approach for locating the erasures, known as the *double complement algorithm*, saves one write and one read operation. An example of the algorithm is shown in **Table 8**.

Some system designs permit only the codewords to be written into the memory [21, 22, 25]. If the complement of a codeword is not a codeword, then the approaches just described for the identification of erasures are not applicable. In this case, one solution is to design codes with some special properties [21, 22]. Another solution is to employ three test patterns in locating the erasures [25]. The test patterns are chosen in such a way that they contain at least one 1 and one 0 in every bit position. It can be shown that three test patterns are sufficient to satisfy this condition for any linear code.

Once the locations of the erasures are identified, algorithms can be designed to correct the hard and soft errors, provided that the number of errors satisfies Eq. (8). Assume that the double complement algorithm is applicable for locating the erasures. The following procedure can be used to correct up to two hard errors or a combination of one hard and one soft error for a SEC-DED code:

1. Read word T_1 from a memory location.
2. If a single error in T_1 is detected by the ECC logic, the error in the word is corrected, and the corrected codeword is sent out to its destination.
3. If uncorrectable errors in T_1 are detected by the ECC logic, the complement of T_1 is written into the same memory location. Then the word from the same memory location is read and complemented. Let the resultant word be T_3 (see Table 8).
4. If a single error in T_3 is detected by the ECC logic, the error is corrected. The corrected word is sent out to its destination and is also written into the same memory location.
5. If no error is detected by the ECC logic, T_3 is assumed error free. T_3 is sent out to its destination and is also written into the same memory location.
6. If uncorrectable errors are detected by the ECC logic, the original word is declared uncorrectable.

Note that double soft errors are not correctable by this procedure. All single errors are corrected at the normal speed. The correction of hard-hard and hard-soft types of double errors takes more time because additional write and read operations are involved. The procedure can be modified or refined to correct additional multiple hard errors [21, 24] at the expense of speed and cost. The procedure can also be extended to correct multiple errors beyond the random error-correcting capability of SBC-DBD codes and DEC-TED codes.

The procedure just described derives the information on erasures at the time when the double error occurs. A different method is to store the information on the erasure errors in a table [22]. This approach increases the speed of correcting double errors. However, the table has to be constantly updated to reflect the true status of the erasures in the memory.

There are other schemes for the correction of multiple erasures [39–41]. These schemes involve the design of codes

Table 8 Example of double complement algorithm.

Original word = T_1 (WRITE)	1 1 0 0 1 1 0 0
Hard and soft errors	H - - - - S -
T_1 (READ)	0 1 0 0 1 1 1 0
T_2 (WRITE) = $\overline{T_1 \text{ (READ)}}$	1 0 1 1 0 0 0 1
T_2 (READ)	0 0 1 1 0 0 0 1
T_1 (READ) + T_2 (READ)	0 1 1 1 1 1 1 1
Erasure error	1 0 0 0 0 0 0 0
$T_3 = \overline{T_2 \text{ (READ)}}$	1 1 0 0 1 1 1 0
Soft error = $T_3 + T_1$ (WRITE)	0 0 0 0 0 0 1 0

with additional check bits, which are used to mask the erasures in decoding. For example, a (76,64) code can be designed to correct double erasures and single random errors, and to detect double random errors [40].

Conclusions

Advances in semiconductor technology have brought about very high levels of integration, especially in the memory area where circuit densities are up to 256K bits per chip. In VLSI memory, higher density usually means a reduced signal-to-noise margin. It also increases the likelihood of soft errors due to radiation and other sources. Error-correcting codes have provided a very effective solution to these problems. They have become an essential part of modern memory design. In the future, the ECC could even be an integral part of the memory chips that manufacturers would offer.

In this paper, we have described the essentials of the principal error-correcting codes used in semiconductor memory design applications. The class of SEC-DED codes is currently most widely used throughout the industry. However, more powerful codes such as SBC-DBD and DEC-TED codes are quite likely to be used in future commercial systems.

Acknowledgment

Contributions made by D. C. Bossen are gratefully acknowledged.

References

1. L. Levine and W. Myers, "Semiconductor Memory Reliability with Error Detecting and Correcting Codes," *Computer* **9**, 43–50 (October 1976).
2. B. Richard, "Automatic Error Correction in Memory Systems," *Computer Design* **15**, 179–182 (May 1976).
3. P. K. Lala, "Error Correction in Semiconductor Memory Systems," *Electron. Eng.* **18**, 49–53 (January 1979).
4. A. V. Ferris-Prabhu, "Improving Memory Reliability through Error Correction," *Computer Design* **18**, 137–144 (July 1979).
5. R. W. Hamming, "Error Detecting and Error Correcting Codes," *Bell Syst. Tech. J.* **29**, 147–160 (April 1950).
6. M. Y. Hsiao, "A Class of Optimal Minimum Odd-Weight-Column SEC-DED Codes," *IBM J. Res. Develop.* **14**, 395–401 (July 1970).
7. M. Y. Hsiao, W. C. Carter, J. W. Thomas, and W. R. Stringfellow, "Reliability, Availability, and Serviceability of IBM Computer Systems: A Quarter Century of Progress," *IBM J. Res. Develop.* **25**, 453–465 (September 1981).

8. S. Lin and D. J. Costello, Jr., *Error Control Coding: Fundamentals and Applications*, Prentice-Hall, Inc., Englewood Cliffs, NJ, 1983.
9. G. R. Basham, "New Error-Correcting Technique for Solid-State Memories Saves Hardware," *Computer Design* **15**, 110–113 (October 1976).
10. D. Morris, "ECC Chip Reduces Error Rate in Dynamic RAMS," *Computer Design* **19**, 137–142 (October 1980).
11. D. P. Siewiorek and R. S. Swarz, *The Theory and Practice of Reliable System Design*, Digital Press, Digital Equipment Corporation, Bedford, MA, 1982.
12. D. C. Bossen, L. C. Chang, and C. L. Chen, "Measurement and Generation of Error Correcting Codes for Package Failures," *IEEE Trans. Computers* **C-27**, 201–204 (March 1978).
13. S. M. Reddy, "A Class of Linear Codes for Error Control in Byte-per-Package Organized Memory Systems," *IEEE Trans. Computers* **C-27**, 455–458 (May 1978).
14. C. L. Chen, "Error Correcting Codes with Byte Error Detection Capability," *IEEE Trans. Computers* **C-32**, 615–621 (July 1983).
15. E. R. Berlekamp, *Algebraic Coding Theory*, McGraw-Hill Book Co., Inc., New York, 1968.
16. W. W. Peterson and E. J. Weldon, Jr., *Error Correcting Codes*, 2nd ed., MIT Press, Cambridge, MA, 1972.
17. I. S. Reed and G. Solomon, "Polynomial Codes over Certain Finite Fields," *J. Soc. Ind. Appl. Math.* **8**, 300–304 (June 1960).
18. T. Kasami, S. Lin, and W. W. Peterson, "Some Results on Cyclic Codes Which are Invariant under the Affine Group and Their Applications," *Info. Control* **11**, 475–496 (November 1967).
19. J. K. Wolf, "Adding Two Information Symbols to Certain Nonbinary BCH Codes and Some Applications," *Bell Syst. Tech. J.* **48**, 2405–2424 (1969).
20. D. C. Bossen, "b-Adjacent Error Correction," *IBM J. Res. Develop.* **14**, 402–408 (July 1970).
21. W. C. Carter and C. E. McCarthy, "Implementation of an Experimental Fault-Tolerant Memory System," *IEEE Trans. Computers* **C-25**, 557–568 (June 1976).
22. C.-E. W. Sundberg, "Erasure and Error Decoding for Semiconductor Memories," *IEEE Trans. Computers* **C-27**, 696–705 (August 1978).
23. P. K. Lala, "An Adaptive Double Error Correction Scheme for Semiconductor Memory Systems," *Digital Processes* **4**, 237–243 (1978).
24. R. Nelson, "Effortless Error Management," *Computer Design* **21**, 163–168 (February 1982).
25. D. C. Bossen and M. Y. Hsiao, "A System Solution to the Memory Soft Error Problem," *IBM J. Res. Develop.* **24**, 390–397 (May 1980).
26. W. K. Mikhail, R. W. Bartoldus, and R. A. Rutledge, "The Reliability of Memory with Single-Error Correction," *IEEE Trans. Computers* **C-31**, 560–564 (June 1982).
27. C. L. Chen and R. A. Rutledge, "Fault-Tolerant Memory Simulator," *IBM J. Res. Develop.* **28**, 184–195 (1984, this issue).
28. M. R. Libson and H. E. Harvey, "A General-Purpose Memory Reliability Simulator," *IBM J. Res. Develop.* **28**, 196–205 (1984, this issue).
29. S. J. Hong and A. M. Patel, "A General Class of Maximal Codes for Computer Applications," *IEEE Trans. Computers* **C-21**, 1322–1331 (December 1972).
30. T. T. Dao, "Design and Implementation of a Non-Binary Code for Byte-Organized Memory with Binary and Quaternary Logics," *Proceedings of the 8th IEEE International Symposium on Multi-Valued Logic*, Rosemont, IL, May 1973, pp. 24–26.
31. S. Keneda and E. Fujiwara, "Single Byte Error Correcting Double Byte Error Detecting Codes for Memory Systems," *IEEE Trans. Computers* **C-31**, 596–602 (July 1982).
32. R. C. Bose and D. K. Ray-Chaudhuri, "On a Class of Error-Correcting Binary Group Codes," *Info. Control* **3**, 68–79 (March 1960).
33. A. Hocquenghem, "Codes Correcteurs d'Erreurs," *Chiffres* **2**, 147–156 (1959).
34. J. M. Goethals, "On the Golay Perfect Binary Code," *J. Comb. Theory* **11**, 178–186 (September 1971).
35. C. L. Chen, "On Shortened Finite Geometry Codes," *Info. Control* **20**, 216–221 (April 1972).
36. T. H. Howell, G. E. Gregg, and L. Rabins, "Table Lookup Direct Decoder for Double-Error Correcting BCH Codes Using a Pair of Syndromes," U.S. Patent No. 4,030,067, June 14, 1977.
37. J. T. Yamato and T. K. Tama, "Error Correcting and Controlling System," U.S. Patent No. 4,107,652, August 15, 1978.
38. P. Golan and J. Hlavicka, "New Method for Parallel Decoding of Double-Error Correcting Group Codes," *Proceedings of the 13th International Conference on Fault-Tolerant Computing*, Milan, Italy, June 1983, pp. 338–341.
39. B. S. Tsybakov, "Defects and Error Correction," *Problemy Peredachi Informatsii* **11**, 21–30 (1975).
40. A. V. Kuznetsov, T. Kasami, and S. Yamamura, "An Error Correcting Scheme for Defective Memory," *IEEE Trans. Info. Theory* **IT-24**, 712–718 (November 1978).
41. C. L. Chen, "Linear Codes for Masking Memory Defects," presented at the *IEEE International Symposium on Information Theory*, St. Jovite, Quebec, Canada, September 26–30, 1983.

Received June 30, 1983; revised September 26, 1983

C. L. (Jim) Chen *IBM Data Systems Division, P.O. Box 390, Poughkeepsie, New York 12602.* Dr. Chen is a senior engineer working on error-correcting codes and fault-tolerant memory systems. Before joining IBM in 1974, he held a postdoctoral position at the University of Hawaii and was a faculty member of the University of Illinois. He received his Ph.D. degree in electrical engineering from the University of Hawaii. Dr. Chen is a member of the Institute of Electrical and Electronics Engineers. He has received three IBM Invention Achievement Awards and one IBM Outstanding Innovation Award for his work on error-correcting codes.

M. Y. (Ben) Hsiao *IBM Data Systems Division, P.O. Box 390, Poughkeepsie, New York 12602.* Dr. Hsiao is a senior technical staff member and manager of the Laboratory Engineering Analysis Department. His current professional interests include research and development in computer reliability, availability, serviceability, error-correcting codes, error detection, failure-isolation techniques, and system engineering analysis. He joined IBM in Poughkeepsie in the Advanced Reliability Technology Department in 1960. From 1965 to 1967, he was on educational leave to the University of Florida, after which he returned to IBM as advisory engineer in the Reliability and Diagnostic Engineering Department. In 1969, he was promoted to senior engineer and manager of the Reliability Technology Department. He assumed his present position in 1979. Dr. Hsiao received his B.S. in electrical engineering in 1956 from Taiwan University, Taipei, his M.S. in mathematics in 1960 from the University of Illinois, and his Ph.D. in electrical engineering in 1967 from the University of Florida. He has seven IBM Invention Achievement Awards, two IBM Outstanding Innovation Awards, and a Corporate Award in the areas of error-correction codes, error detection, and failure-isolation techniques. He has authored and co-authored two books published in 1964 and 1968. Dr. Hsiao is a Fellow of the Institute of Electrical and Electronics Engineers and a member of the Fault Tolerant Computing Committee and IFIPS Committee on Reliable Computing and Fault Tolerance.

F. J. Aichelmann, Jr.

Fault-Tolerant Design Techniques for Semiconductor Memory Applications

Advances in semiconductor memory technology towards higher-density and higher-performance memory chips have created new reliability challenges for the memory system designer. An example would be the multiple-bit-per-chip organization with the chip outputs used in the same word. This design structure would be prone to uncorrectable errors with conventionally implemented single-error-correcting double-error-detecting codes. With these newer chips, memory system designers will have to give special attention not only to the types of failures but to ways of minimizing the system impact of reliability defects. In this paper, a number of design approaches are presented for minimizing the effects of chip failures through the use of organizational techniques and through enhancements to conventional error checking and correction facilities. The fault-tolerant design techniques described are compatible with most existing memory designs. An evaluative comparison of these techniques is included, and their application and utility are discussed.

Introduction

Computer memory chips containing 65 536 (64K) bits are now quite common, and chips of even greater bit densities are becoming available. In addition, each new computer system generation has seen a substantial increase in the number of memory chips used with a corresponding significant increase in memory capacity. However, larger-capacity memory systems utilizing higher-density memory chips are more susceptible to failures. This paper describes several of the most effective fault-tolerant design techniques useful in minimizing the consequences of these failures upon using systems. The primary objectives are to significantly reduce the sensitivity to defects (by minimizing the probability of their accumulation into failures, which can become uncorrectable errors), and to provide mechanisms for keeping the memory system operating once the failures exceed the capabilities of conventional *single-error-correcting double-error-detecting* (SEC-DED) *error checking and correction* (or *error-correcting code—ECC*) facilities [1].

The defect types that can occur for random-access memories of the dynamic MOSFET one-device-cell type [2, 3] can greatly influence the types of error control code selected as well as the amount of memory affected by these failures. The most common types of defect faults include the single-cell, word-line, bit-line, and chip-fail categories. In addition to these hard faults, this type of memory has been susceptible to soft failures caused by alpha-particle radiation [4], with a failure probability higher than the basic intrinsic chip failure rate. In order to minimize the consequences of these hard and soft error mechanisms, designers must take into account the interaction between the using system, the error checking and correction facilities used, and the chip configuration and associated memory organization. The incorporation of ECC logic for improving product reliability has been commonplace since the introduction of the IBM System/370 computers. Increased chip densities and multiple-bit-per-chip organizations have resulted in more complex designs, increasing the challenge to the designer [5]. Special attention has been placed on adapting serial coding techniques (e.g., Fire codes [6]) to random-access memories to help improve error control capabilities [7, 8].

The particular system maintenance strategy used can play an important role in fault tolerance because it can allow the physical replacement of failures to be deferred and to accumulate to a selected threshold. To minimize the system sensitivity to *uncorrectable errors* (UEs) when soft error rates are high, memory systems employ "scrubbing" [9, 10] of detected errors by correcting and rewriting into the same location. Scrubbing consists basically of the periodic reading and correction, if required, of the data stored at *all* memory addresses. (Additional details concerning the scrubbing operation are

© **Copyright** 1984 by International Business Machines Corporation. Copying in printed form for private use is permitted without payment of royalty provided that (1) each reproduction is done without alteration and (2) the *Journal* reference and IBM copyright notice are included on the first page. The title and abstract, but no other portions, of this paper may be copied or distributed royalty free without further permission by computer-based and other information-service systems. Permission to *republish* any other portion of this paper must be obtained from the Editor.

Copyright 1984 by International Business Machines Corporation; reprinted with permission.

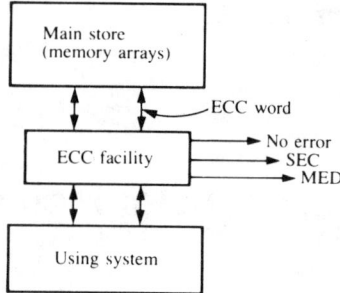

Figure 1 Simple memory system with error checking and correction facility.

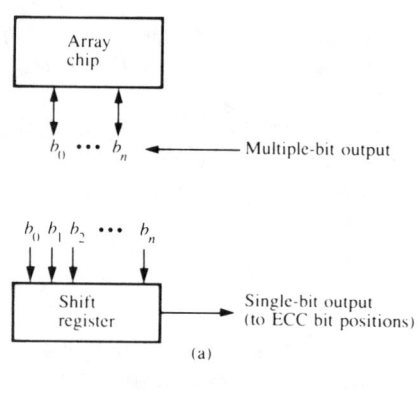

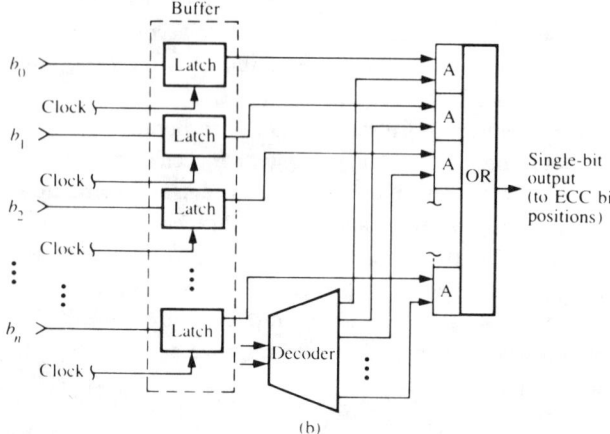

Figure 2 Bit scattering by simple redistribution or data steering: (a) through the use of shift registers; (b) through the use of gated latches.

between the memory arrays and the using-system interface. Such a configuration enables the correction and detection of simple errors (i.e., such as a single defect) and the reporting of status information (i.e., No Error, Single Error Correction—SEC, and Multiple Error Detection—MED). The effectiveness of the ECC facility will depend on the particular memory chip structure chosen as well as on the corresponding organization of how the data are assembled and sent to the using system.

This paper describes techniques designed to improve the effectiveness of conventional ECC by using data organizational schemes and by providing enhancements to existing ECC facilities to achieve improved fault tolerance. These techniques are compatible with most existing designs, do not require any using system intervention, and are self-contained within the memory system. The design techniques that we shall consider include

- bit scattering,
- sparing,
- complement/recomplement,
- consecutive correction, and
- prestorage protection.

The first two are organizational schemes and the latter three involve ECC facility enhancements. Techniques based on more complex multi-bit-correcting ECC code are not addressed since they typically impose increased system performance overhead.

The following sections of this paper describe the organizational techniques and the ECC enhancements. Presented first is the bit scattering technique, which includes data redistribution and address selection. That is followed by a description of how sparing can be used for arrays as well as for arrays and support logic. Subsequent sections deal with ECC enhancements based upon recovery by error erasure (complement/recomplement), knowledge of previous defect locations (consecutive correction), and the biasing of data words to conceal defects (prestorage protection). Additional sections deal with application and utility and include a summary and conclusion.

Bit scattering

Bit scattering is a design technique that minimizes the effect of chip defects by either distributing bits across different ECC words or by concentrating the failures within the smallest addressable section of memory. Bit scattering occurs in two forms: data steering (i.e., redistribution or fault alignment exclusion), and address selection.

Redistribution or *data steering* (also referred to as *fault alignment exclusion* [13]) is a buffering scheme used for multiple-bit-per-chip organizations by distributing the chip outputs across multiple ECC words [14]. **Figure 2** illustrates two

discussed subsequently in a later section.) Once a specified error-rate threshold has been exceeded, the using system can invoke reconfiguration and deallocation algorithms [9–12] to remove memory space from program use. It should be noted, however, that the deallocation of memory space can result in reducing memory capabilities on line, with corresponding potential for reducing overall system performance. The simplest type of fault-tolerant memory system is that shown in **Figure 1**, which incorporates a conventional ECC facility embodiments of this buffering: shift registers and gated latches. In both examples, a group of bits from a chip is buffered, with no more than a single bit position allocated to any ECC word. This results in minimizing the effects of multiple-bit chip-fail types of failures.

Address selection is a technique which is used to minimize the size of the failure (i.e., the number of pages affected) based upon word-line and bit-line failures. The address-selection technique is most effective for block-transfer-type memory applications. An example is a memory paging application which requires 32 iterative array selects from a 64K-bit memory array chip (see **Figure 3**). In this example, a page consists of $32 \times 4 = 128$ bits on a chip. Assume that the selected array is a $16K \times 4$-bit chip partitioned into two separate groups, each with its own support circuits. Each group consists of four identical sections, and each section is comprised of 64 word lines and 128 bit lines. Therefore, depending upon the method of data placement and subsequent retrieval for the 32 iterative selects, by word line or by bit line, the amount of defect contamination will be different. The reason for this is that each defect is not equally dependent upon type (i.e., bit-line or word-line) or the number of pages that reside in the defect region. Figure 3 illustrates the results of contiguous selection by word line, by bit line, and by intermixing between four and eight groups of bit lines and word lines to demonstrate the extent of memory space affected when the 32 iterative selects are completed for each page. As shown, by proper design choice it is possible to minimize the effects of defects due to word-line or bit-line failures. The particular choice depends upon application requirements.

Sparing

Sparing techniques are used to replace a defective component from an operating memory without requiring manual intervention [15]. The sparing concept can be used for arrays as well as for arrays plus supports. **Figure 4** depicts a selection partition suitable for simple spares. As shown, there is a group of memory arrays with a spare provided for appropriate activation. Any chip that fails in the memory array group can be substituted for (i.e., electronically replaced) by the spare chip. The substitution is accomplished by personalizing the selection logic via the data bus. When the high-order address bit selects the defective chip, the personalized selection logic performs the substitution.

The sparing concept can be extended to cover both arrays and support circuits by an appropriate memory organization. **Figure 5** shows a memory organization consisting of a group of 16 array cards or FRUs (*field-replaceable units*) each supplying an ECC word across a selection interval. Each FRU supplies an ECC word during a selection interval (i.e., a group of 16 ECC words are clocked and generated sequentially, one from each of the 16 array cards). For example, if Array Card

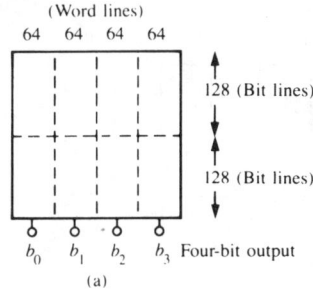

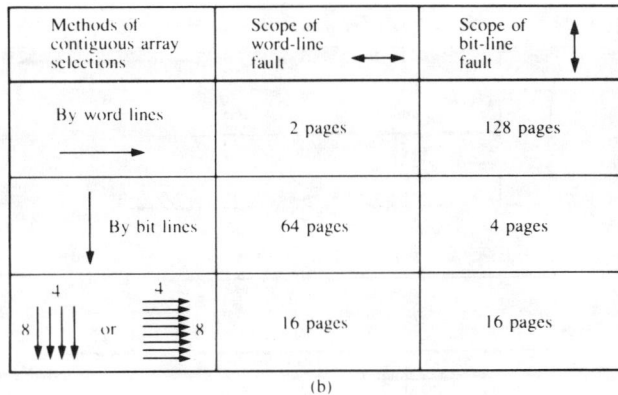

Figure 3 Bit scattering by address selection: (a) example memory structure; (b) fault consequences of contiguous array selection by word lines, by bit lines, or by intermixed groups of bit lines and word lines.

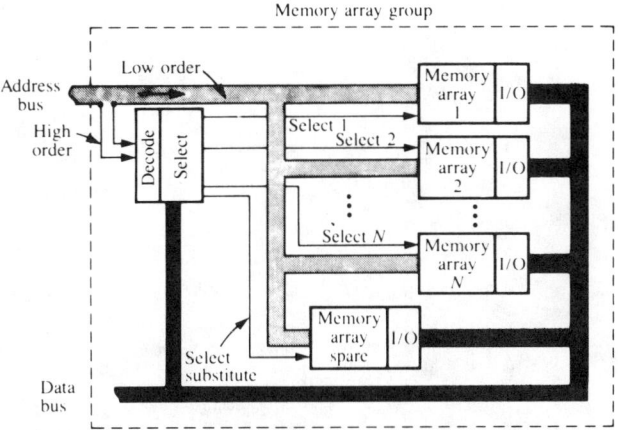

Figure 4 Example of selection partition suitable for simple (chip) paring.

3 (FRU 3) is defective, then when the defective card is to be clocked it is suppressed and an alternative or spare is substituted. As shown, by the addition of an alternate or spare FRU, sparing can be used to cover arrays as well as their support circuitry.

Note that, in order for the spare to be deployed, provision must be allowed for the shifting of data from the defective or failing unit into the spare unit. In addition, space must be

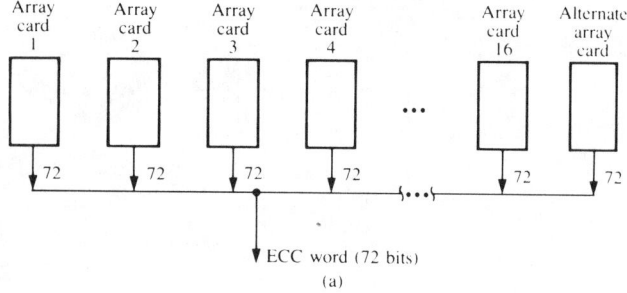

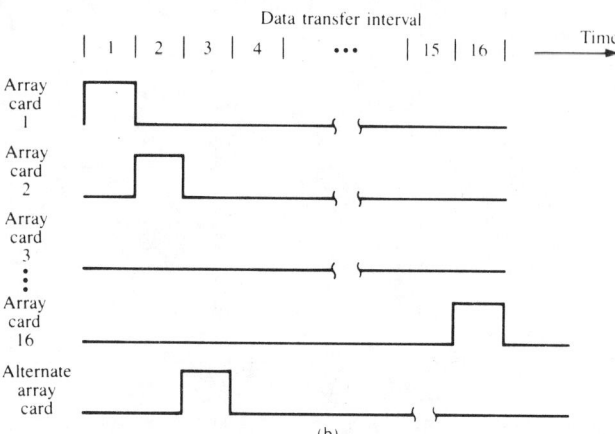

Figure 5 Example of sparing via alternative FRU: (a) memory organization; (b) ECC word generation sequence.

```
1 0 1 0 1 0 1 0 1      Correct data
    Z        α          Faults
1 0 0 0 0 0 1 0 1      Read from storage: UE
0 1 1 1 1 1 0 1 0      Complement, written
0 1 0 1 1 1 0 1 0      Read from storage
1 0 1 0 0̄ 0 1 0 1      Recomplement: CE
1 0 1 0 1 0 1 0 1      Correct data rewritten
1 0 0̄ 0 1 0 1 0 1      Read on refetch: CE
                (a)

1 0 1 0 1 0 1 0 1      Correct data
    Z    Z              Faults
1 0 0 0 0 0 1 0 1      Read from storage: UE
0 1 1 1 1 1 0 1 0      Complement, written
0 1 0 1 0 1 0 1 0      Read from storage
1 0 1 0 1 0 1 0 1      Recomplement: no errors
1 0 1 0 1 0 1 0 1      Correct data rewritten
1 0 0 0 0 0 1 0 1      Read on refetch: UE

1 0 1 0 1 0 1 0 1      Correct data
                (b)
```

Figure 6 Complement/recomplement error-erasure technique examples. Allows erasure of hard-stuck errors and identification/correction of intermittent (soft) errors. (a) Example 1: hard-plus-soft error; (b) Example 2: hard-plus-hard error. (Note: Z = hard error position; α = soft error position; UE = uncorrectable error indication from ECC logic, i.e., a MED signal; CE = correctable error; □ = correctable error position.)

available to accommodate the additional logic and spare arrays required and the system must be capable of tolerating a performance overhead.

Complement/recomplement

Complement/recomplement is a method of extending single-error-correction capabilities to correct for double errors by a read-invert-write-read-invert procedure [16]. This procedure allows the erasure of hard-stuck errors and provides an identification/correction capability for intermittent (soft) errors. **Figure 6** demonstrates this technique for two examples: a combination of hard and soft errors, and a combination of hard and hard errors. These samples each start with an *uncorrectable error* (UE) and finish with either a *correctable error* (CE) when soft defects align with hard defects, or *no error* when only hard defects exist.

A rewriting of the data after this procedure provides for a way of eliminating or "scrubbing" of soft errors [3, 10].

Consecutive correction

Consecutive correction is a design technique that increases the correction capabilities beyond conventional SEC-DED codes by modifying the structure of the ECC facility [17]. The principle of operation is based on the maintenance of a history of hard correctable errors, so that, when they accumulate into uncorrectable errors, the history information can be used to erase the original error and to correct the subsequent error. This operation is achieved by storing the syndromes of the initial single error into an array for subsequent use. When an uncorrectable error is detected in an ECC word, the prior correctable syndrome is used to erase the initial error and then the modified data are passed through the ECC facility for subsequent correction of the new error in the ECC word. **Figure 7** illustrates the structure of a typical conventional ECC facility for read operations. Syndrome bits (S_j) resulting from the comparison of the generated and received check bits are used by the error classifier to determine error conditions, while the error-bit locator decodes the syndrome to the defective location. **Figure 8** depicts the structure of a modified error-correction facility, which has added a correctable-bit-locator array, with its output coupled to the error-bit locator, and a feedback path from the data bit modifier for erasure of the original defect so that the new defect can be corrected. The control of the consecutive correction is controlled by the error classification, which uses the output (S'_j) of the correctable-bit locator when uncorrectable errors are detected (i.e., when there is an "even" output from the error classifier).

Prestorage protection

Prestorage protection is a design technique for extending the correction capabilities of conventional ECC facilities by biasing the data in an ECC word to conceal stuck bits. Making the stuck bit appear as a hidden fault enables the ECC to correct additional defects once they occur within the ECC word. The operation is accomplished by providing true and complement paths within the ECC facility based on the property that odd-weighted codes produce the same check bits for

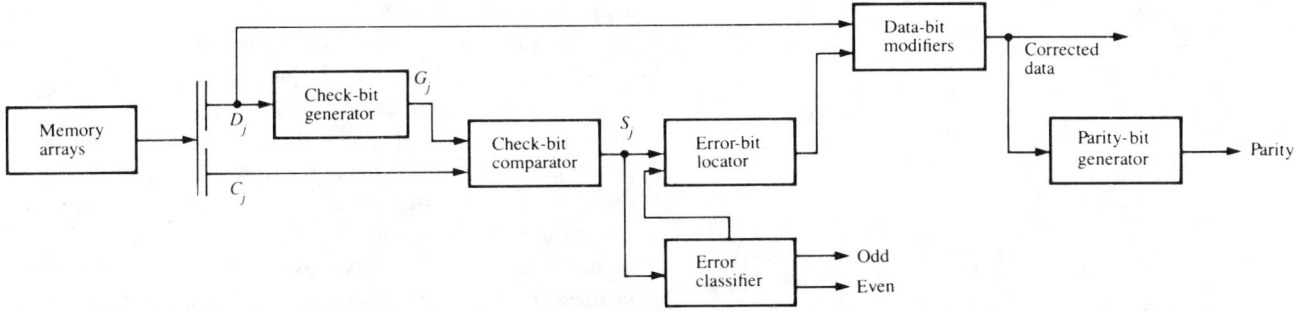

Figure 7 Structure of conventional ECC facility for memory read operations. (Note: D_j = data bits received from memory; C_j = check bits received from memory; G_j = new generated check bits; S_j = syndrome bits.)

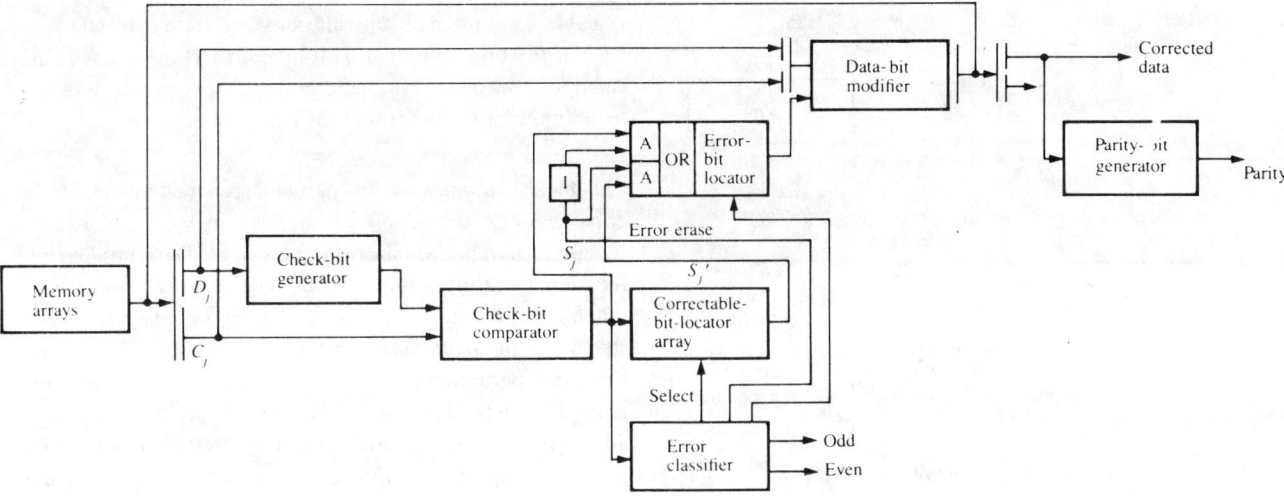

Figure 8 Structure of modified error-correction facility for consecutive correction technique.

either true or complement data bits. **Figure 9** depicts, in block diagram form, the modification to the ECC facility. The control or path selection is determined on the basis of the status bits generated from both paths. These status bits (MED, SEC, and No Error) determine which format the ECC word is in, true or complement.

The principle of operation is based upon biasing of the bits in an ECC word so that defects can be hidden (i.e., bit stuck at a value which is correct for the ECC word). As a result, depending upon the ECC word format, the code assignment (i.e., true or complement) can be selected to conceal hard errors. The following formats are available with an odd-weighted ECC code (i.e., check bits assigned as odd-weighted parity):

ECC word format	Resultant characteristics
True	D_j, C_j
Complement	$\overline{D_j}, \overline{C_j}$

This technique checks all memory stores for errors with a post-write procedure. If errors are found on a fetch of the

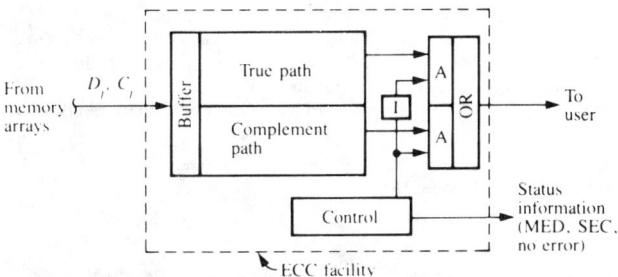

Figure 9 Modification of ECC facility for prestorage protection.

store, the data are stored in complemented form and left in that format if no errors are found. **Figure 10** illustrates this simplified post-write procedure. Subsequent memory fetches with this ECC facility require that the appropriate path, true or complement, be selected. This is accomplished via the six true and complement status bits that are tabulated in **Table 1(a)**. The MED/MED case denotes multiple errors and requires additional recovery via the complement/recomplement procedure, while the SEC/SEC case is unresolved due to code-

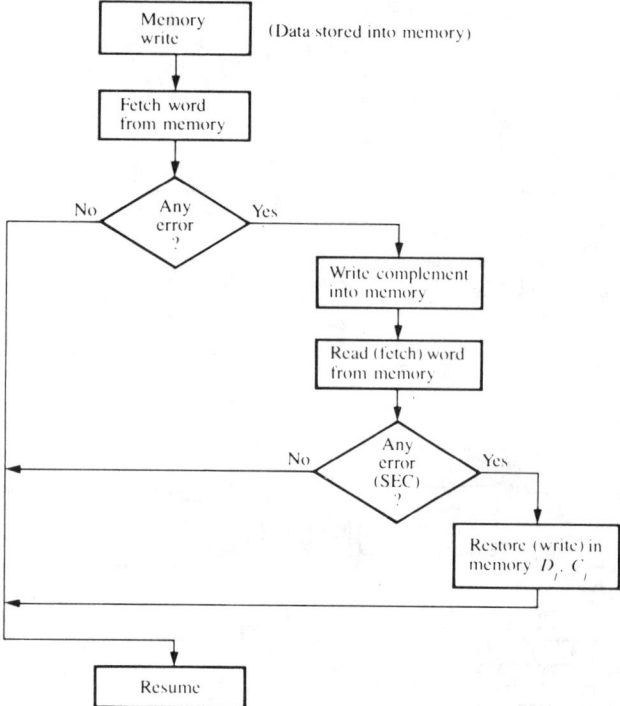

Figure 10 Post-write procedure for prestorage protection technique.

Table 1 Subsequent read recovery (following post-write procedure, for prestorage protection technique).

(a) Status conditions (from ECC, for control path selection)

True	Complement	Condition
No error	MED	No-error data in true form
MED	No error	No-error data in complement form
SEC	MED	Single-error data in true form
MED	SEC	Single-error data in complement form
MED	MED	Recovery via complement/recomplement
SEC	SEC	Possible check-bit-error data in complement form

(b) SEC/SEC determination:

Case	Test	Result
Case 1	Test with ones and zeros with bit comparison	No mismatch—soft-error data in true form
Case 2	Same test	Mismatch in data field—data in complement form
Case 3	Same test	Mismatch in check bits—hard-error data in true form

point limitations. The SEC/SEC determination can be resolved by a diagnostic test of ones and zeroes with bit comparison; this determination is described in **Table 1(b)**. An additional redundancy bit can be added to the scheme to reduce the read recovery operations.

Application and utility

The fault-tolerant design techniques just described satisfy a broad range of applications. The purpose of these schemes is to minimize the accumulation of errors from semiconductor memory defects so that the probability of exceeding the capabilities of the error-correction facility is minimized. The design techniques discussed all involve interaction between the actual memory circuits, the organization of the computer memory, the maintenance strategy, and the ECC facility. Two of these techniques are based on the chip structure and the memory organizational requirements of the using system, while the remaining three deal with enhancement of the ECC facility for specific situations.

Table 2 summarizes the failure-type coverage or effectiveness of the organizational fault-tolerant techniques. As indicated in the table, bit scattering and sparing are effective techniques for the control of the effects of hard errors.

Table 3 summarizes the particular characteristics of the enhanced-ECC-correction techniques, including a relative comparison in performance and hardware. The complement/recomplement procedure can be used not only as a recovery scheme but also to identify stuck bits by comparison (exclusive-or) of the *read data* with the *corrected data*. These locations can be used as the basis for forming a memory fault map. The method of consecutive correction does not require any multiple memory array cycles but rather uses multiple passes through the modified ECC structure. By proper design choice and implementation, this technique can provide a fast correction (i.e., at logic speeds) of double errors. The prestorage protection technique is most suitable for regions of memory that are designated as read mostly; otherwise performance can suffer. Those regions best suited are the areas of "core" or nucleus of operating systems, and source tables used in address translation applications. All of these techniques enhance the minimization of errors and deallocation.

Summary and conclusion

The progress of semiconductor memory technology has advanced in the industry from LSI to VLSI and will continue in the future. The accelerated progress in memory chip density coupled with larger-capacity memory applications will result in requirements for greater chip reliability and for greater system tolerance to errors. Fault-tolerant design techniques can be used to minimize the effects of failures in memory systems. As described, there are those techniques that are suitable for organization and address selection, and those that can be used to enhance the ECC capabilities of a given code. The appropriate application of these design techniques can reduce the number of uncorrectable errors and minimize the amount of replacement components necessary. These design approaches can be used either individually or collectively, and the suitability of each approach is dependent upon the specific application requirements. The using system can benefit not only from fewer errors but also from better performance whenever less memory will have to be deallocated.

References

1. C. L. Chen and M. Y. Hsiao, "Error-Correcting Codes for Semiconductor Memory Applications: A State-of-the-Art Review," *IBM J. Res. Develop.* **28**, 124–134 (1984, this issue).
2. C. H. Stapper, A. N. McLaren, and M. Dreckmann, "Yield Model for Productivity Optimization of VLSI Memory Chips with Redundancy and Partially Good Product," *IBM J. Res. Develop.* **24**, 398–409 (1980).
3. Ronald H. Sartore and David W. Gulley, "Fire Code Detects and Corrects Errors in Wide Word for Large RAMs," *Electronics* **55**, No. 11, 154–157 (June 2, 1982).
4. D. C. Bossen and M. Y. Hsiao, "A System Solution to the Memory Soft Error Problem," *IBM J. Res. Develop.* **24**, 390–397 (1980).
5. Harvey J. Hindin, "Error Detection and Correction Cleans Up Wide-Word Memory Act," *Electronics* **55**, No. 11, 153 (June 2, 1982).
6. P. Fire, "A Class of Multiple-Error Correcting Binary Codes for Non-Independent Errors," *Sylvania Report RSL-E-2*, Sylvania Reconnaissance Systems Laboratory, Mountain View, CA, 1959.
7. Mike Evans, "Nelson Matrix Can Pin Down 2 Errors per Word," *Electronics* **55**, No. 11, 158–162 (June 2, 1982).
8. Lionel White and Reddy Chitranjan, "Wide-Word 64K-Bit RAM Expands System Performance," *Electron. Design* **30**, No. 6, 231–238 (March 18, 1982).
9. Gary Ward, "Intelligent Memory Systems Can Operate Nonstop," *Electron. Design* **30**, No. 6, 243–250 (March 18, 1982).
10. F. J. Aichelmann, Jr., B. E. Bachman, and D. J. Perlman, "High Data Integrity Scheme for Memory Reliability," *IBM Tech. Disclosure Bull.* **22**, No. 11, 4933–4934 (1980).
11. F. J. Aichelmann, Jr., "Local Paging Memory Buffer for Minimizing Concurrence of Hard and Soft Data Errors," *IBM Tech. Disclosure Bull.* **22**, No. 11, 4931–4932 (1980).
12. John Reilly, Arthur Sutton, Robert Nasser, and Robert Griscom, "Processor Controller for the IBM 3081," *IBM J. Res. Develop.* **26**, 22–29 (1982).
13. D. C. Bossen, C. L. Chen, and M. Y. Hsiao, "Fault Alignment Exclusion for Memory Using Address Permutation," *IBM J. Res. Develop.* **28**, 170–176 (1984, this issue).
14. F. J. Aichelmann, Jr., "Memory Application of Multiple Bit Chips," *IBM Tech. Disclosure Bull.* **24**, No. 4, 2194–2196 (1981).
15. F. J. Aichelmann, Jr. and L. K. Lange, "Dynamic Allocation of Redundant Memory Components," *IBM Tech. Disclosure Bull.* **24**, No. 9, 4776–4778 (1982).
16. B. E. Bachman and S. M. Dobrzyuski, "Multiple Error Correction," *IBM Tech. Disclosure Bull.* **13**, No. 8, 2190 (1971).
17. F. J. Aichelmann, Jr., "Consecutive Error Correction," *IBM Tech. Disclosure Bull.* **24**, No. 11B, 6048–6049 (1982).

Received July 5, 1983; revised September 27, 1983

Frederick John Aichelmann, Jr. *IBM General Technology Division, East Fishkill facility, Hopewell Junction, New York 12533.* Mr. Aichelmann is a senior engineer in the Advanced Memory Development group at East Fishkill, working on advanced memory applications and fault-tolerant techniques. He joined IBM in memory development at Kingston, New York, in 1964. Since that time, he has participated in all aspects of memory development from ferrite products through semiconductor memories, including FET process, development, circuit design, and memory system development. Prior to joining IBM, Mr. Aichelmann was employed by RCA, working in satellite communications, magnetic recording, and video recording.

Table 2 Comparison of organizational fault-tolerant design techniques: Effectiveness as a function of failure (defect) type.

Technique	Deployment for effective failure-type coverage			
	Word-line failure	Bit-line failure	Chip failure	Support and array failure
Bit scattering				
Data redistribution	X	—	X	—
Address selection	X	X	—	—
Sparing				
Array	X[1]	X[1]	X	—
FRU	—	—	X	X

[1] Denotes second order, not primary, usage.

Table 3 Characteristics and comparison of enhanced-ECC-correction techniques.

Technique	Error-type coverage		General technique characterization
	Hard	Soft	1 Application deployment 2 Performance impact 3 Hardware implication
Complement/recomplement	X	X	1—Error-recovery and scrubbing of soft errors 2—Worst performance hit 3—Least hardware impact
Consecutive correction	X	X	1—Multi-bit correction, in lieu of spares, minimize deallocation 2—Least performance hit 3—Hardware intensive—worst hardware impact
Prestorage protection	X	X	1—Multi-bit correction, hard-error scrubbing where deallocation (core and nucleus) is not possible 2—Fast read, slow write 3—Increased hardware

In 1957, he received the B.S. in electrical engineering from the University of Virginia, with subsequent graduate study at the University of Pennsylvania. Mr. Aichelmann has received a Sixth-Level IBM Invention Achievement Award; he is a member of the Institute of Electrical and Electronics Engineers.

Fast RAM corrects errors on chip

Prototype random-access memory ups soft-error immunity with little penalty in access time but with increased yield

by Aurangzeb Khan, *Fairchild Camera & Instrument Corp., Mountain View, Calif.*

☐ Advances in fabrication technology that reduce device size foreshadow the freedom to extend functions in denser semiconductor memories. At the same time, eversmaller devices sap a memory's resistance to soft errors. That dilemma clearly points to its own resolution—a memory that integrates error-correction circuits on chip.

The usual response to soft errors—board-level error checking—falls far short for fast memories. Even the fastest of these solutions adds delays greater than the access times of high-speed emitter-coupled-logic random-access memories. With access times below 25 nanoseconds, such parts crop up in control stores, caches, and the like, where both data integrity and high speed are critical concerns. Although present parts have adequate immunity to soft errors, continued scaling down of device geometry and with it, cell standby current, bodes ill for bipolar RAMs, just as denser MOS chips have already run afoul of alpha particles.

A prototypical design for a high-speed error-correcting memory—a "resilient" ECL RAM—adds parity-generating and -checking circuits to a 256-by-7-bit array (Fig. 1) to increase soft-error immunity by several orders of magnitude. Three bits per word are used internally for error correction, and the RAM is pin-compatible with existing 256-by-4-bit parts for simplicity of application.

Fast logic circuits on chip substantially speed up error correction. Indeed, only a 5- or 6-ns penalty need be paid in access time for an optimal design. Finally, although the chip area of such a RAM will be some 75% larger than that of its conventional brethren, that cost can be partly offset: error-correcting circuitry turns flawed RAMs into functioning conventional ones.

To facilitate testing and evaluation of both the checking algorithm and the RAM, special operating modes are added. The data outputs can present either corrected data (the standard mode), uncorrected data, uncorrected parity bits, or corrected parity bits. The three latter modes can be accommodated in the standard pinout of a by-4-bit RAM by decoding nonstandard voltages (below the low logic level) applied to two of the data inputs.

System remedies

The transience and pervasiveness of soft errors make fault location and system diagnosis particularly troublesome. The traditional system approach has been to design a single-error–correction, double-error–detection (SEC-DED) scheme to evaluate encoded data on the system bus and call for an interruption and rereading of data found to be in error. SEC-DED hardware has not been universal, but rather custom-designed for each application. Until recently, composing such hardware has required 5 to 10 medium-scale integrated circuits and a concomitant increase in circuit-board space and power.

During the past two to three years, several semiconductor manufacturers have introduced large-scale ICs that add SEC-DED capabilities to a memory system. Typical of such products is the 74F418, a TTL chip from Fairchild. Housed in a 48-pin dual in-line package, the part operates on 39 input/output lines: 32 data bits and 7 check bits. Depending on the control inputs, the chip monitors bus data, generates check bits, and so on. Delay from data input to error correction is 55 ns; checking for multiple errors takes another 20 ns; and the corrected output follows 52 ns after that.

Parts such as the 74F418 are used primarily to ensure the integrity of data retrieved from main memory. Limitations to this technique include the requirement for substantial additional memory chips to hold the parity bits, as well as slower memory-access times. Because SEC-DED hardware works on the system's clock cycle, its operation is not and never can be transparent to the system. In other words, communication among the error-correcting

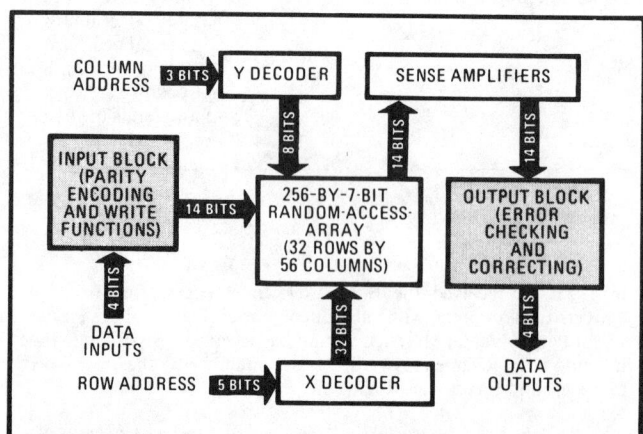

1. Resilient RAM. Logic circuits integrated with a 256-by-7-bit random-access memory encode parity bits before storing data and check and correct for errors during a read. On-chip error correction is a must for fast memories needing enhanced soft-error immunity.

Evaluating the RAM's resiliency

A by-7-bit emitter-coupled-logic random-access memory that uses 3 bits of each word for error correction has been designed as a pin-for-pin replacement of existing by-4-bit RAMs. The prototype design described in the accompanying article improves data integrity by a factor of 1,000 or more over a conventional RAM.

If the probability of any one bit suffering a soft error in a given time is P, the probability that a bit is good is $1-P$, and the chance that all bits of a 4-bit word are good is $(1-P)^4$. Without error correction, any error in the word causes a system error. Using conventional by-4-bit RAMS, such errors therefore occur with a probability of $1-(1-P)^4$ per word. Because P is so small, this expression is very nearly equal to $4P$.

For the 7-bit word of the error-correcting, or resilient, RAM, however, all single-bit errors are corrected and only multiple-bit failures cause a system error. The probability of any bit being bad and the other 6 good is $P(1-P)^6$, so the probability of any single-bit error in a word is $7P(1-P)^6$. System errors thus occur with a probability of $1-(1-P)^7-7P(1-P)^6$, or about $21P^2$ per word.

The ratio of probable system errors from the conventional RAM and the resilient RAM measures the improvement in data integrity: $4/21P$. In other words, the improvement is almost inversely proportional to the probability of an error because multiple-bit errors are about P times less likely to occur than single-bit errors.

Failure rates of 10^{-9} to 10^{-7} per hour have been estimated for RAMs. Thus, over the life of a system, P is likely to be 10^{-4} at the most. The resilient RAM therefore improves data integrity—extends the mean time between failures—by at least 1,000 times, and possibly much more.

---

chips and other system components is regulated by the system clock and necessarily slows memory operations. Thus, parts at present available to ensure data integrity are not useful in applications where performance is at a premium: control stores and cache memories.

For such applications, the system must be partitioned differently, transferring the error-correction functions to the chip level. Of course, communication between processing blocks on one chip is significantly faster than communication between chips. Also, for a given amount of power expended, speed improves far more for on-chip communications, and logic can be integrated with fast memory to provide automatic and continuous error correction. The additional processing is performed asynchronously at the optimal internal speed of the chip. Finally, this automatic and continuous error correction is transparent to the system designer. It follows that error correction is performed fastest and most simply on chip. The high-speed error-correcting RAM, or resilient RAM, is the direct consequence of this reasoning.

The resilient part can be made pin-compatible with existing simple memories. For systems with no SEC-DED circuitry, soft-error immunity can be obtained simply by replacing ordinary memory with resilient chips. Further, systems already employing error detection at the board level can readily implement two-stage checking.

The improvement in data integrity using resilient RAMs is roughly inversely proportional to the average probability of a random single-bit failure. In present RAMs, that number is already quite low. As a result, data integrity can be expected to improve 1,000 times or more (see "Evaluating the RAM's resiliency," above). What's more, the proposed RAM system can easily be designed to provide flags when a soft error is detected, thus helping in fault location and diagnosis. An on-chip counter could give a "replace chip" signal after some predetermined number of failures.

At the outset, the research leading to the resilient RAM addressed the problem of soft failures. However, it soon became apparent that circuitry developed for this function would not differentiate between soft and hard failures, but would be equally effective against the entire range of possible errors. The processing done in the resilient RAM constitutes dynamic redundancy, as opposed to the static redundancy more usually employed by manufacturers of dense MOS memories to catch hard errors only.

In dynamic redundancy, extra information regarding input data is developed in a systematic manner and stored together with the data. Upon a subsequent read request, the chip evaluates the stored information and data and automatically corrects any single-bit errors. In contrast, static redundancy calls for some number of replacement circuits to be fabricated with the host circuit. Defective circuits discovered during production testing are replaced with the redundant elements. If the number and kind of spare circuits match the number and kind of defects, such repairs succeed in increasing yield.

Although redundant elements increase chip area and thus decrease the pretesting yield, successful repairs increase the post-testing yield. Clearly, redundancy makes sense economically when the post-testing increase outweighs the pretesting decrease. Furthermore, when test costs are a large portion of the total chip cost, redundancy pays extra dividends, for the cost of the testing time is amortized over a larger number of good chips.

As opposed to static redundancy, dynamic redundancy provides fault tolerance when and where needed, on a continuous and automatic basis, and is self-diagnosing and self-reconfiguring (see "Dynamic redundancy for a megabit ROM," p. 128). Of course, a price is paid for such autonomous processing: the overhead for dynamic redundancy is generally much higher than that for a static implementation.

The dynamic redundancy of the resilient RAM presents a tradeoff between yield enhancement and soft-error immunity. That is, random hardware failures are effectively masked so that partially functioning arrays will appear good. If a soft error occurs in a word containing a hard error—a permanently bad bit—that soft error will not be corrected since the parity coding scheme can correct only one flaw. The RAM will still function; indeed, for the

Dynamic redundancy for a megabit ROM

Unlike static redundancy, where a limited set of devices can be hardwired into an integrated circuit once and for all, dynamic redundancy gives fault tolerance on a continuous and automatic basis. Such on-chip error checking and correction heals damaged memory bits whether those disturbances are permanent flaws or only transient upsets.

A design implementing the correction of soft, transient errors is detailed in the accompanying article. At the same time, dynamic redundancy for yield enhancement—correcting hard, permanent errors—is also proving valuable. At the International Solid State Circuits Conference in February, engineers from Japan's Hitachi Ltd. disclosed a megabit read-only memory that incorporates error-checking-and-correction circuitry and 192-K of overhead memory for parity storage.

Clearly, static redundancy for a ROM poses severe problems. Because the code is set during manufacture, redundant portions must be dedicated to particular rows or columns. For example, Oki Electric Co.'s megabit ROM, incorporating static redundancy, duplicates the entire array, for a 100% chip area penalty.

For dynamic redundancy, however, parity bits are readily calculated from the bit pattern and permanently stored along with the rest of the code. For the Hitachi chip, area is increased 20%. Measurements during pilot production confirm the prediction that the ROM's yield then increases about three times.

Although organized as 128-K by 8 bits, data is stored internally as 32-bit words to hold down the amount of overhead memory required for parity bits. Thus, 32 data and 6 parity bits are read out from the array on each access and sent to the ECC circuits. The two lowest-order address bits sent to a "nibble" decoder then select one 8-bit output word from the 32 error-corrected bits.

This scheme has the additional advantage that four adjacent bytes typically can be accessed in a total of 240 nanoseconds: 150 ns for the first one, and 30 ns each for the other three. The access time penalty of the ECC scheme is said to be less than 15%.

Fabricated in a 2-micrometer n-well complementary-MOS process, the ROM cell occupies 36 square micrometers for a chip size close to 80 square millimeters. Hitachi has recently announced plans and specifications for production versions.
—Roderic Beresford

---

prototype design presented, good chips could be obtained with up to one seventh of the memory matrix permanently bad, if the flaws occurred precisely one to a word. At the same time, however, a strategy for chip testing must provide a mechanism to distinguish between resilient RAMs and those with hard errors masked by the correction circuitry.

The most pervasive source of soft failures is alpha particles arising from trace contaminants in the packaging materials. Most soft errors therefore are random, occur infrequently relative to the system cycle time, and occur in a single bit. While disruption of active signals within the RAM is possible, no data on such events exists.

Also, soft errors can be caused by electrical noise: an "anemic" cell with a low voltage swing may be disturbed by the addressing of some other memory location. Guarding against such events is, however, primarily a circuit-design issue. Therefore, the resilient RAM's primary goal is the correction of random single-bit errors.

The resilient RAM has design constraints significantly different from those applicable to error correction at a system level or in other technologies. Those constraints follow not only from the nature of the soft-error problem but also from the requirement for high speed and the limitations on power dissipation.

The circuitry for error detection and correction should naturally be dense, fast, and simple to lay out. A viable ECL design must perform at the highest possible speed. Because additional delays due to coding data and checking for errors add directly to the write and access times for a RAM, they must be kept to a minimum. Furthermore, the high speed must be obtained within a maximum power constraint, typically around 1 watt or less for conventionally packaged ICs. That constraint mandates "focused" power—that is, channeling current to the critical transition paths of a circuit.

The Hamming scheme, besides being conceptually simple, meets the requirements for speed and density in coding and checking circuits. In particular, an implementation in the form of a programmable logic array is faster than the more usual cascaded exclusive-OR gates. PLAs also lay out simply and compactly. With them, the canonical form of the Hamming algorithm can be entered as microcode simply by defining appropriate transistor-emitter placements. A further benefit of PLAs is that the microcode can be altered by changing only one mask from among the entire set.

To derive the equations for the Hamming algorithm, the word size must be established. Even a moderately wide word will require a prohibitively large AND-OR

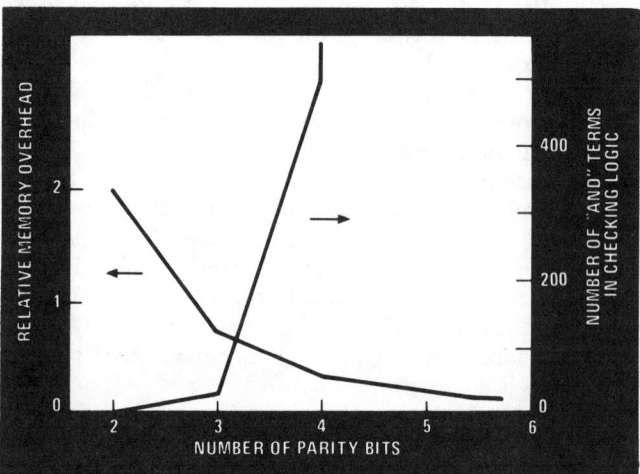

2. The tradeoff. The number of AND terms in the programmable logic array used for high-speed error checking prohibits wide data words. Thus overhead memory is 75%—3 parity bits for 4 data bits.

PARITY SCHEME FOR RESILIENT RAM								Encoding equations	Checking equations
		\multicolumn{7}{c	}{Data word}		
		P_0	P_1	D_0	P_2	D_1	D_2	D_3		
Check word	C_0	■		■		■		■	$P_0 = D_0 + D_1 + D_3$	$C_0 = P_0 + D_0 + D_1 + D_3$
	C_1		■	■			■	■	$P_1 = D_0 + D_2 + D_3$	$C_1 = P_1 + D_0 + D_2 + D_3$
	C_2				■	■	■	■	$P_2 = D_1 + D_2 + D_3$	$C_2 = P_2 + D_1 + D_2 + D_3$

array because the PLA implementation grows rapidly with the number of input variables.

Conventional implementations of the Hamming scheme employ a 16- or 32-bit word, reducing the memory overhead—the relative amount of additional storage required for the parity bits. Because a relatively long clock cycle is the usual time constraint, the logic functions are obtained with cascaded exclusive-OR gates, forgoing high-speed processing.

This approach runs precisely counter to the needs of the resilient RAM. Overhead memory is not prohibitive because, on chip, it adds minimal delay and uses area efficiently. Furthermore, a 16- or 32-bit word complicates the PLAs used for high-speed coding and checking.

As suggested in Fig. 2, the optimum number of parity bits is 3, allowing a word size of 4 bits. As mentioned, this overhead constitutes a substantial penalty in chip area, but it may be partly offset by resilient RAMs with stuck bits that function as well as conventional parts do. For P parity bits, the coding PLA requires P OR terms and AND terms numbering:

$$2^{(2^{(P-1)}-2)}P$$

The checking array needs P OR terms and twice as many AND terms as the coding array. With 3 parity bits, the coding and checking arrays have 12 and 24 AND terms, respectively.

The chosen scheme encodes even parity before storage and checks for odd parity upon retrieval of data. The table provides the relevant equations. As shown, the check word $C_2C_1C_0$ identifies the location of an erroneous bit in the 7-bit word $D_3D_2D_1P_2D_0P_1P_0$, where D indicates data bits and P parity bits.

Logic architecture

A prestorage block operates on input data prior to sending it to the memory array (Fig. 3). It provides the appropriate encoding bits and also allows deliberate insertion of an error into any bit of the word to be stored.

Each parity bit is generated in canonical form from four AND terms and one OR tie in the encoding PLA. The three encoding equations each take the form:

$$P = A + B + C = A\overline{BC} + ABC + \overline{A}B\overline{C} + \overline{AB}C$$

where A, B, and C represent appropriate data bits.

Using data set up on three probing pads, the error-insert address decoder provides a signal specifying in which of the seven locations an erroneous bit could be inserted. In a straightforward sequential design, the output of the 3-to-8 decoder that selects an error-insert location would control a 7-bit multiplexer in order to choose either true or complemented bits for transmission to the write circuitry.

The write circuitry would then use the read-write signal (R/W) derived from the chip-select ($\overline{CS}$) and write-enable ($\overline{WE}$) inputs to form the write 1 and write 0 signals:

$$W1 = \overline{R/W}\overline{M}$$
$$W0 = \overline{R/W}M$$

where M stands for the multiplexer output.

However, these operations can be performed twice as fast if done in parallel rather than sequentially. Multiplexing true and complemented data using the error-insert signal (EI) implements the function:

$$M = D\overline{EI} + \overline{D}EI$$

Thus, as illustrated in Fig. 3, write signals can be formed directly as:

$$W1 = \overline{R/W}\overline{M} = \overline{R/W(D+EI)}$$
$$W0 = \overline{R/W}M = \overline{R/W(\overline{D}+EI)}$$

with a single ECL stage delay, rather than the two-stage delays needed in a sequential implementation.

The read-write circuit's outputs are fed to the 256-by-7-bit array, which is organized as 32 rows and 56 columns in eight current-steering blocks. Thus, a 5-to-32 X

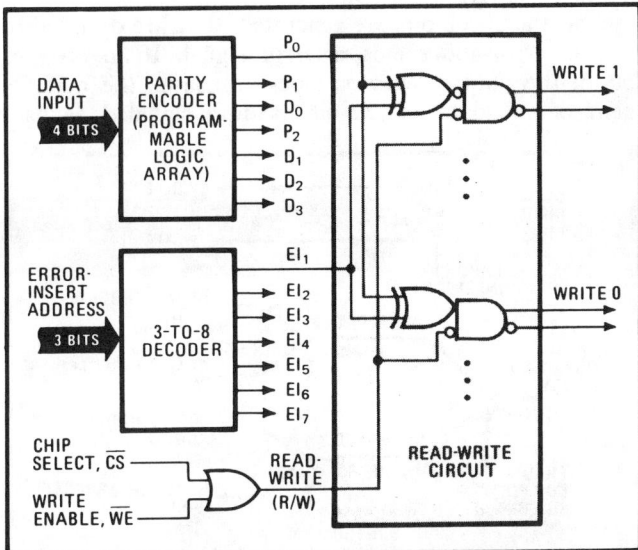

3. Fast coding. The input function block generates the 3 parity bits in a PLA and also allows a deliberate error insertion during wafer-level testing. The read-write circuit is a single ECL stage deep.

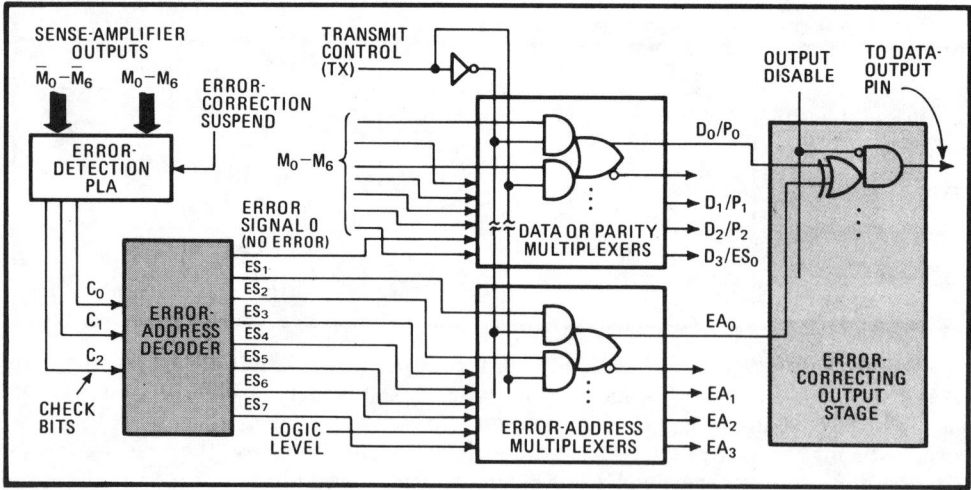

4. Checker. The output function block, driven by the sense amplifier, forms a check word ($C_2C_1C_0$), decodes it, and then sends either the data as it is retrieved or as its complement to the output. In order to assist in testing, the multiplexers permit parity bits to be observed at the outputs.

decoder and a 3-to-8 Y decoder accept the eight address-bit inputs and select one of 256 7-bit words for transmission to the sense amplifiers.

The 14 sense-amplifier outputs (true and complement data) drive an output function block (Fig. 4) when triggered by an external read request. This block also receives special nonstandard ECL signals from the first and second data-input pins: the error-correction–suspend and transmit-control signals, respectively.

The error-detection PLA generates a check word of 3 bits. If no single-bit error has occurred and the retrieved data is identical to the input data, then each check bit will be 0. However, if a single-bit error has occurred, the check bits, taken in correct order ($C_2C_1C_0$), signal the location of the erroneous bit. Also, if the error-correction–suspend signal is asserted, the check bits will remain 0 regardless of the data. This ECC-transparent mode allows uncorrected data to pass to the output, as is required in testing the RAM.

After the check bits are generated, they are decoded to give an error-address or no-error signal. If an error is found, the output function block transmits the complement of the data at the bit location signaled as bad.

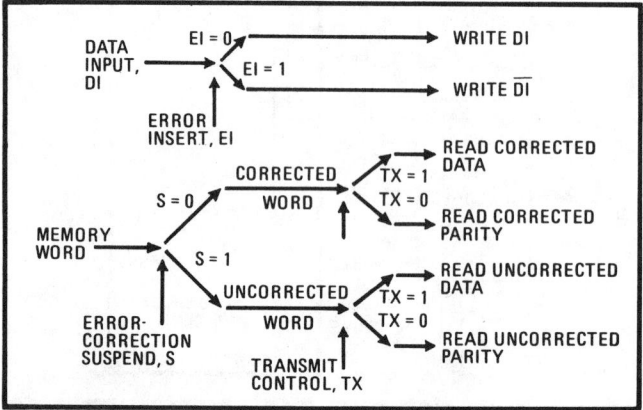

5. Testable. Special signals allow deliberate error insertion, disabling of the error-correction circuitry, and selection of parity bits for output. The RAM's extra circuitry is thus fully testable.

Otherwise, the data as retrieved from the array passes to the output. Furthermore, provisions are made to transmit parity bits instead of data bits to the output, opening the entire array to observation during testing.

To speed these operations, two decisions are made in parallel: whether to transmit data or parity bits to the output stage, and correspondingly, whether to transmit error-address signals for the data or parity bits. The output stage then sends either data as retrieved or its complement to the output pins.

The data/parity multiplexers implement the equation:

$$D/P = DTX + P\overline{TX}$$

where TX is the special transmit-control signal. Likewise, the error-address multiplexers use TX to select data-error (DE) or parity-error (PE) address signals:

$$EA = DETX + PE\overline{TX}$$

The data-output circuit then uses the foregoing results to pass either true or complemented data or parity bits to the pins:

$$DO = \overline{OD}(D/P\,\overline{EA} + \overline{D/P}\,EA)$$

The output disable signal, OD, is derived from $\overline{CS}$ and $\overline{WE}$. When transmitting parity bits, only three of the four bit locations are needed, so the fourth is used to carry the no-error signal.

Test strategies

Unlike the error-insert circuitry of the input function block, the special test features of the output block are made accessible to the user. The former is included to aid in evaluating the error-correction algorithm; the latter has several other purposes.

If the memory always corrects errors, single stuck bits will pass by the RAM tester unnoticed, because their erroneous data will be automatically corrected before presentation at the data ouputs. As noted, such chips improve yield by providing working conventional RAMs.

Obviously, however, it is vital to isolate fully functional chips, with their enhanced soft-error immunity, from those that become acceptable thanks to the on-chip processing. Through the multiplexing of data and parity bits and the ability to disable the error-detection PLA, the RAM array becomes fully testable—externally, electronically, and at will—without resort to internal probing. Figure 5 summarizes the test modes available.

Another approach to reducing soft-error susceptibility is through improvements in the fabrication process. Only by disabling the on-chip error detection can the relative effectiveness of such alternatives be estimated. □

Fault-Tolerant 256K Memory Designs

R. MICHAEL TANNER, MEMBER, IEEE

Abstract — A series of designs for a 256K memory are presented which integrate error-correcting coding into the memory organization. Starting from a simple single-error correcting product code, the successive designs explore trade-offs in coding efficiency, access delay, and complexity of communication and computation. In the most powerful design, all the 256K bits are organized so that they form a codeword in a double-error-correcting triple-error-detecting code derived from a projective plane. Because all of the bits are components of this single codeword, the coding efficiency is very high; the required parity check bits increase the storage by only 3 percent, approximately. Single error correction can take place at the time of a read with very little additional delay compared to that of a normal irredundant memory. Multiple error correction can be performed by the memory management system. A variety of failure modes, including failure of a whole column of one of the constituent 64 × 64 subarrays can be tolerated. Writing into the memory is somewhat slower than in a conventional memory, involving a read-write cycle.

Index Terms — Distributed, error-correction, fault-tolerant, memory, parallel, projective plane graph, redundancy, VLSI.

I. INTRODUCTION

THE increased vulnerability of high-density memory systems to both hard and soft errors had led to greater interest in the use of error-correcting codes to improve system reliability [10]. An approach now common in 16-bit word machines is to encode a word using a (22, 16, 4) single-error-correcting double-error-detecting modified Hamming code [8], [9]. Supporting modified Hamming code chips are commercially available (e.g., Texas Instruments SN54/74LS630). Elkind and Siewiorek [7] suggest the use of a block code in similar way. Bossen and Hsiao [3] discuss the use of a longer code of the same type in conjunction with a more powerful microcode and hardware correction algorithm.

Barton in his thesis [1] proposes the construction of a hierarchical memory based on multilayer error-correcting coding that can tolerate numerous faults. His design constitutes an architectural realization of the product codes of Elias [6], formed by iterating a Hamming code.

All of these approaches have a relatively high coding overhead inasmuch as a substantial fraction of the physical memory is devoted to the storage of redundant parity checks. This arises from the use of relatively short coding blocks chosen for the sake of keeping the encoding and decoding times short since these are a substantial part of the resulting memory access times.

The use of an error-correcting code for protecting a memory inevitably involves a tradeoff between coding efficiency on the one hand, and computation and communication costs on the other. As is well known in coding theory, to correct a fixed number of errors with very little coding overhead the block length of the code must be large, enabling dependencies to be distributed over many bits. Correspondingly, however, the computation of the correct value of any bit of the codeword must involve a large number of the bits of the codeword, implying in turn the need for communication lines to access the bits and delay in the computations that interrelate them.

In this paper we present a series of designs that achieve high coding efficiency by organizing the memory so that a large number if not all of the stored bits form a single codeword in a large block-length code. While the underlying principles can be applied at different levels of memory organization, depending on the interpretation of the basic memory unit, we will consider the design of a single chip 256K memory with one bit as the unit. In that context, our goal is to structure the code so that the communication lines required for error-correction are naturally available in customary VLSI circuit design.

Our first design is based on a simple product code [6], where many of the central issues can be seen clearly, unobscured by the subtlety of the code itself. In this design the efficiency is exceedingly high (only roughly $1/256$ of the memory is redundant parity checks) but communication requirements lead to excessive area penalties with current fabrication techniques. Then we present several variations on this basic code that illustrate tradeoffs the between coding efficiency, read delay, and complexity of communication and computation. All of these are single error-correcting, double error-detecting codes. The last is variant of the parity check product code design of Osman [11]. Finally, we consider a double error-correcting triple error-detecting graph code and algorithm suggested in [13] that achieves high coding efficiency at the expense of more complicated addressing.

II. A PRODUCT CODE DESIGN

A simple single error-correcting code can be formed from a parity check using the product code construction [6]. A set of information bits is used to form a $q \times l$ square array. A parity check bit is added to each row that is the parity sum of the information bits in that row. Then a parity check bit is added to each column that is the parity sum of the bits in that column (see Fig. 1). The array is then $(q + 1) \times (l + 1)$,

---

Manuscript received January 25, 1983. This work was supported in part by the Defense Research Projects Agency under Contract MDA 903-79-C-0680.

The author was with the Information Systems Laboratories, Stanford University, Stanford, CA 94305. He is now with the Department of Computer and Information Sciences, University of California, Santa Cruz, CA 95064.

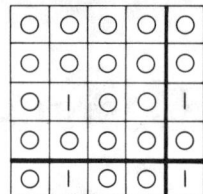

Fig. 1. Product code array.

with $(q + l + 1)$ parities added to the original information bits. The resulting code has minimum distance four since changing a single information bit requires changing three of the parity bits to maintain all the parity equations.

To correct a single error anywhere in the array, the parities of all of the rows are computed, as are the parities of all of the columns. A parity failure in exactly one row and exactly one column indicates an error in the bit in that row and column; more than one row parity failure or more than one column parity failure indicates the presence of multiple errors. Note that this permits any double error to be detected.

Now consider the bits in the array to be the bits stored in a RAM with the addresses in the array corresponding identically to the physical locations in the RAM. Let the information bits be $b(i,j), i = 0, \cdots, q - 1, j = 0, \cdots, l - 1$; the row parities are the bits $b(i, l), i = 0, \cdots, q$, and the column parities are the bits $b(q, j), j = 0, \cdots, l$. (Note that $b(q, l)$ is the parity sum of all of the information bits, whether computed as a sum of row parities or a sum of column parities.) Suppose that the values stored in the memory form a codeword in the product code in which at most a single error has occurred. To read bit $b(i,j)$ three values are needed

$$\sum_{t=0}^{q} b(t,j) + b(i,j) \tag{2.1}$$

$$\sum_{t=0}^{l} b(i,t) + b(i,j) \tag{2.2}$$

and $b(i,j)$ itself, where all sums are mod 2. The first is the sum of all bits in the column except the bit itself; the second is the sum of all bits in the row except the bit itself. By virtue of the parity check condition, if no errors have occurred all three values will be the same. The three sets of bits are disjoint, and a single error can effect at most one of the three. Consequently, if the value output from the memory is the majority vote of these three, it will be correct. However, a double error clearly will cause the emitted value to be in error. The presence of a double or multiple error would have to be detected by a systematic computation of the parity sets that looks for two or more row or two or more column parity violations.

In writing a bit into the memory, the object is to ensure that the memory is maintained as a codeword in the product code. The procedure is to update the codeword as a new value is entered. Initially, all bits in the memory are brought up as zero, obviously forming a codeword. To write $b(i,j)$, the currently stored value for it is read out using the single error correction procedure, along with the stored values for $b(i,l), b(q,j)$, and $b(q,l)$. If the new value of $b(i,j)$ agrees with the currently stored value, all four values are rewritten into the memory unchanged. If the new value differs from the stored value, all four values are complemented and then written back into the memory. It is easily verified that the new memory values form a codeword if the original values did, and that no errors are created by this procedure as long as the currently stored value for $b(i,j)$ is read out correctly.

Our first implementation of this code as a fault-tolerant memory is conceptually straightforward, although not necessarily practical. The code array described above is realized directly as a conventional RAM, with the addresses in the array corresponding identically to the physical locations in the RAM. One of the sums (2.1) or (2.2) will be easy to compute by taking advantage of the parallel read lines. For instance, if a row address enables an entire row, the parity sum of the row can be computed by placing a parity tree at the bottom of the array. The desired bit can be selected from the enabled row. If the RAM were symmetric with respect to rows and columns so that an entire column could be read out in parallel to a column parity tree, the bit and the outputs of the row tree and column tree could be fed to a gate to produce the corrected bit value. The obvious problem with this scheme, however, is the communication costs. Depending on the particular technology, providing parallel enable and outputs for both rows and columns could more than double the basic cell size.

To write a bit $b(i,j)$ into this memory, the bit as stored must be read using the correction circuit and $b(i,l), b(q,j)$, and $b(q,l)$ must be read out, complemented as necessary, and rewritten. For example, if the memory shown as an array in Fig. 1 is initially entirely zero, and $b(2,1)$ is to be written as one, the current value of $b(2,1)$, namely, zero, is determined by the correcting read. Since the value to be written differs from that stored, the stored values of $b(2, 1), b(2, 4), b(4, 1)$, and $b(4, 4)$ are all complemented and rewritten, leaving the memory values as shown in Fig. 1. Since $b(q, l)$ is examined when any bit is written, separate access to it should be provided. Parallel access to the other three bits is readily available with the symmetric RAM architecture described. The basic layout of this hypothetical memory is shown in Fig. 2.

For purposes of later comparison, note that the coding efficiency of this design is relatively high. For a 256K memory, only $2(512) + 1$ parity check bits are needed; approximately 1/257 of the memory is devoted to redundancy. Unfortunately, the area penalty for communication makes the coding efficiency irrelevant.

III. Graph Representation

The same code can be realized in different ways to achieve different tradeoffs. Before moving to the modifications, it will be useful to introduce the representation of this product code as a graph code [9], [12, pp. 136–138]. This abstract representation, which is discussed in detail in [13], enables the actual code structure to be seen clearly, independent of the particular architectural realization. It serves also to give a unifying perspective on both the product code and the more intricate projective plane code to be treated later.

In Fig. 3 the array product code is converted into a bipartite

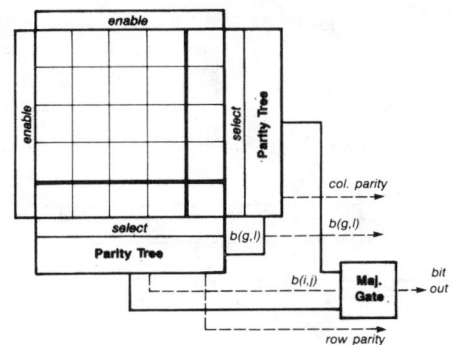

Fig. 2. Symmetric RAM.

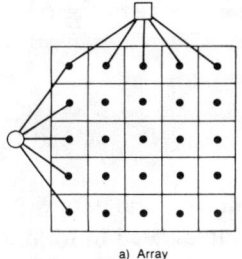
a) Array

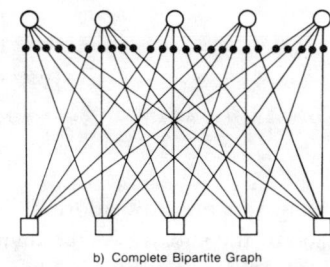
b) Complete Bipartite Graph

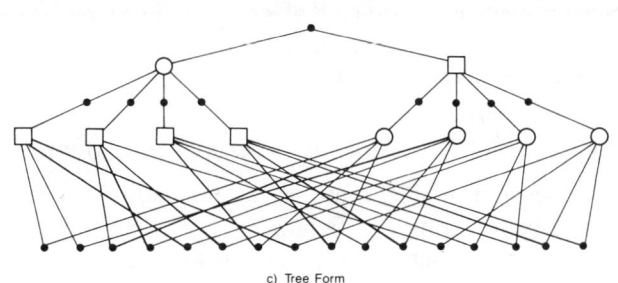
c) Tree Form

Fig. 3. Product code as graph code.

graph. A bit in the code is represented by a solid node, a parity check acting on a set of bits by a hollow node connected to the set of bits checked by the particular parity equation. In the product code, each bit is checked by a row parity check and a column parity check, and thus the bit nodes have degree two. The row parity nodes have degree l and the column nodes have degree q. The graph created by the array can be recognized as a bipartite graph built from a complete bipartite graph with the row and column nodes in two classes, as shown in Fig. 3(b). In Fig. 3(c) the graph is redrawn in tree form using an arbitrary bit as the root. The tree has the same form, no matter which bit is used as root. When the bit at the top of the tree is to be read, three values are required: the bit itself, the parity sum of its row, and the parity sum of its column. The access paths and addressing of the RAM architecture permit two actual parity trees to perform the computations for any desired bit.

Another way of thinking about the minimum distance of the code is in terms of the girth, or minimum cycle length, of the graph. To keep all the parity equations satisfied, a minimum weight word must form a cycle in the graph. The product code graph has girth 8, with a minimum cycle passing through $8/2 = 4$ bits. To change any single bit in the code while preserving all code equations requires that at least four bits must be changed. The suggested write procedure operates on a minimal set.

While the tree of Fig. 3(c) can represent the graph with an arbitrary bit at the root, additional insight into the code structure can be obtained by thinking of the bits at the bottom of the tree as the information bits and the root as the bit $b(q, l)$. If an information bit is changed, the bit on the path up the left-hand side of the tree from that bit to the root must be changed, the bit on the path up the right-hand side must be changed, and the root bit must be changed. It is clear, however, that the bits at the bottom of the tree can be assigned arbitrary values and all parity equations can be satisfied by proper choice of the bits at the next level and the root.

IV. LESS COMMUNICATION — MORE DELAY

A variant of the above design reduces the area penalty and maintains the coding efficiency by time multiplexing the output lines, thereby increasing the read delay. The new design comes from simply reinterpreting the product code graph as a RAM.

Taking $q = l$, the $(q + 1)^2$ bits are organized into a square $(q + 1) \times (q + 1)$ array as before, and the condition that the mod 2 sum of the bits in any row must be zero is imposed. Then, rather than requiring columns to sum to zero mod 2, we demand that the sum along any cyclic diagonal be zero

$$\sum_{k=0}^{q} b(i - k, k) = 0, \qquad \text{for all } i$$

where the sum is mod 2 and the index arithmetic is mod $(q + 1)$. The ith diagonal sum and the jth row share exactly one bit, and thus the code is isomorphic to the original code. Once again we can take the bits $b(i, j), i, j = 0, \cdots, q - 1$ to be the information bits. The bits $b(i, q), i = 0, \cdots, q - 1$ are determined by the row sums, and then the bits $b(q, j), j = 0, \cdots, q$ are determined by the diagonal sums. To write bit $b(i, j)$, bits $b(q, i)$, $b(i, q)$, and $b(q, i + j + 1)$ must be accessed.

To read a bit, the bit has to be accessed along with a corresponding row sum and a diagonal sum. As before, with a row enable and a parity tree at the bottom of the RAM, both the bit and the row sum can be obtained in one cycle. To obtain the diagonal sum, the RAM must be equipped with diagonal enable lines, and on a second cycle the diagonal address of the bit activates the appropriate diagonal. Diagonal address decoders actually must activate the two parts of the cyclically continued diagonal. This architecture is illustrated in Fig. 4. The same output lines then carry the values from the diagonal to the same parity tree. The resulting parity sum can then be combined with the bit value and row sum to produce the corrected value.

V. LOWER CODING EFFICIENCY — DECREASED DELAY

The need for multiplexing of the output lines arose because a large set of bits had to be accessed to read any one bit. The communication bottleneck can be alleviated by reducing the

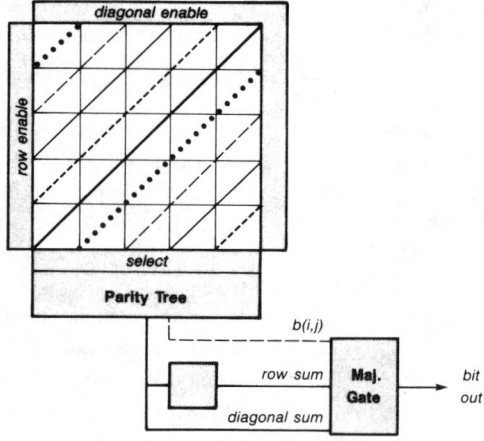

Fig. 4. Diagonal enable RAM.

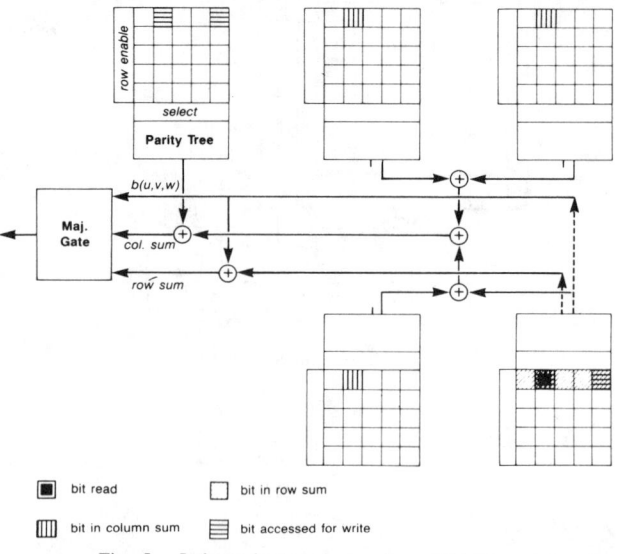

Fig. 5. Independent product code architecture.

coding efficiency. Clearly in the normal RAM architecture, all the bits in a given row are readily accessed. This suggests the use of an encoding in which all the bits required to decode a given bit are found in a single row [11]. While any error-correcting code could be used, the simplicity of the computations for both encoding and decoding the product code make it an attractive candidate. Consider, then, converting the $(q + 1) \times (q + 1)$ matrix into a single RAM row by concatenating the successive rows of the product code. The coding efficiency is greatest when q is large, and thus for the sake of coding efficiency, it would be preferable to have a highly rectangular $l \times (q^2 + 2q + 1)$ RAM. To preserve the aspect ratio of the RAM, we instead organize the bits into $q + 1$ subarrays each of dimension $l \times (q + 1)$. Let the bits be indexed by $b(u, v, w)$ where u gives the subarray, v gives the row in the subarray, and w gives the column in the subarray. The set of bits with a fixed v form a product code with u indexing the product code rows and w the product code columns. This organization is shown in Fig. 5 for $q = l = 4$.

To calculate the product code row sum for a particular bit $b(u, v, w)$, the row sum of the v row of the u subarray must be found. This can be achieved by having a parity tree associated with each subarray and the u address selects the appropriate parity tree output to be used. The product code column sum is the sum over u of the bits with the same v and w addresses. The addresses v and w are used to select a single bit from each of the subarrays; these are fed into a parity tree spanning the subarrays that produces the required sum.

For a fixed memory size, this organization into multiple, independent product code blocks decreases the coding efficiency. Using this approach to implement a 256K memory, we have $q = l = 64$ and $64(2(64) + 1)$ parities. The efficiency is that of the 64×64 product code, with roughly 1/33 of the memory devoted to parities. Nonetheless, the greatest area penalty is still not the storage for the parities; rather, is in providing the separate sense amplifiers for the separate subarrays and the parity trees. Note, however, that an entire column of one of the subarrays can fail without causing failure of the memory, assuming no other errors are present because any column contributes at most one bit to the output sum.

This form is the starting point for our final memory design.

Using separate row addressing and address computers with each of the subarrays, the memory is reintegrated to form a single codeword in a graph code derived from a projective geometry. The fraction of the memory devoted to parity check bits is virtually unchanged. Similar parity trees enable single error correction to take place at the time a bit is read. The code has minimum distance six, and is capable of performing double error correction.

VI. A Code Derived From a Projective Geometry

As discussed in [13], a projective geometry $PG(2, q)$ [4] can be used to construct a field plane hexagon code for any prime power q. By letting the points and lines represent parity checks and creating a bit node for every point–line pair, a bipartite graph is formed that has girth, or minimum cycle, of twelve. In such a graph, any bit node node can be used as the root of a "tree" analogous to that of Fig. 3(c) where no cycles are formed above depth 6. A graph of this type for $q = 2$ is shown in Fig. 6. Presently, we will construct the graph by starting from an actual tree and connecting the leaf edges at the bottom on one side of the tree to the leaf edges on the other side so as to guarantee that the graph thus formed has a minimum cycle of twelve.

Once the graph has been constructed, its implementation and use as a RAM are extensions of the techniques for the simple product code. Note, for example, that there are q^3 bit nodes at the bottom of the tree. These bottom nodes can be taken to be the actual data bits, with those higher in the tree being the parity checks.

Theorem 6.1: If the q^3 bits at the bottom of the tree are assigned arbitrary values, all of the parity equations can be satisfied by proper choice of the values of the remaining bits. The code is thus a $[(q + 1)(q^2 + q + 1), q^3, 6]$ code.

Proof: Consider the tree of Fig. 6. All of the parities at depth 5 can be satisfied by letting each bit at level 4 be the parity of all of the bits attached to the parity node below it. Similarly, the parities at depth three can be satisfied by proper choice of values for the bits at depth 2. Finally, both parities

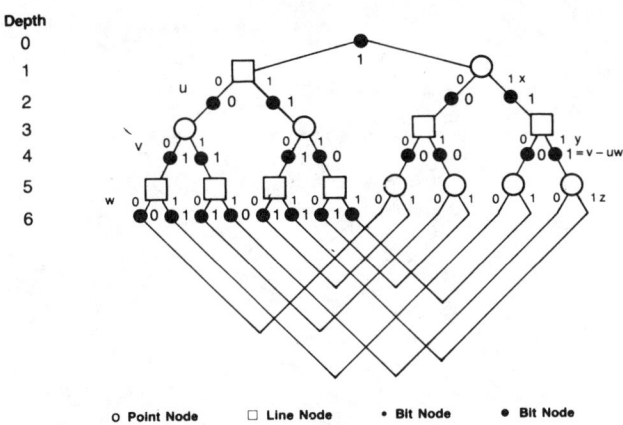

Fig. 6. An 8 bit ($q = 2$) memory in tree form.

at depth one are satisfied by letting the top bit be the parity of the left and right sets, which must be the same value, namely, the parity of all of the bits at the bottom of the tree.

The code is, in fact, a conventional circuit code [9], [12, pp. 136–138]. The tree forms a spanning tree, and thus is sufficient to establish the parity checks.

VII. Addressing

Each bit at the bottom of a closed tree such as Fig. 6 can be viewed as having two addresses, one defined by the path via the left half of the tree to the bit and another via the right. The graph is constructed by giving a mapping between the two address for any bit at the bottom. In defining the addressing system, we make use of arithmetic on a Galois field of q elements, GF(q). An introduction to the construction and use of finite fields adequate for our purposes is given in [12, Ch. 6].

The left-hand side of the tree provides a naturally $q$ary addressing of the bottom bits and the right-hand side provides a different $q$ary addressing. By employing a $(q + 1)$st symbol ϕ, we can give addresses to all of the bits in the tree in the form of 3-tuples on a $(q + 1)$ary alphabet. For addresses via the left half, the 3-tuples will be given in parentheses. For addresses via the right half, square brackets will be used. The bit at the top is $(\phi, \phi, \phi) = [\phi, \phi, \phi]$. The bits at depth 2 on the left are (u, ϕ, ϕ). Those at depth 4 are (u, v, ϕ) and the bottom bits as addressed via the left tree are (u, v, w). Similarly on the right, the bits are $[x, \phi, \phi]$ at depth 2, $[x, y, \phi]$ at depth 4, and $[x, y, z]$ at the bottom. The address components $u, v, w, x, y,$ and z can all be interpreted as elements of GF(q).

The linkage between the left and right halves of the tree formed by a data bit at the bottom can be represented by an address mapping $f:(u, v, w) \to [x, y, z]$ such that the address of a bit via the left half is (u, v, w) and its address via the right half is $[f(u, v, w)]$. In these terms, the code will have minimum distance six if the mapping f can be chosen so that no cycles of less than 12 exist in the graph.

Theorem 7.1: If the address mapping is given by $f(u, v, w) = [x, y, z] = [w, v - uw, u]$, with arithmetic on GF($q$), the graph has no cycles shorter than 12.

Proof: The mapping f is clearly a bijection. Also, it is easy to see that any cycle must have length 4, 8, or 12 because the graph is doubly bipartite; line nodes connect via bit nodes only to point nodes, not other line nodes, and vice versa. Obviously, no short cycle of 4 or 8 can pass through the root node, nor can one pass through a parity bit at depth 1. If there is a short cycle that passes through a parity node at depth 3 on the right-hand side, it must pass through a single parity at depth 5 on the left. However, any pair of bits with addresses (u_0, v_0, w_0) and (u_0, v_0, w_1), $w_0 \neq w_1$, have different x addresses on the right, and so such a cycle must pass through the parity node at depth one on the right. This implies that it has length 12 or greater. Similarly, no short cycle can pass through a single parity node at depth 5 on the right. The only remaining possibility is that there is a short cycle confined to nodes at depths five and six. If so, it must pass through four bits with left and right addresses of the form

$$(u_0, v_0, w_0) - [x_0, y_0, z_1]$$
$$(u_0, v_0, w_1) - [x_1, y_1, z_2]$$
$$(u_1, v_1, w_2) - [x_1, y_1, z_3]$$
$$(u_1, v_1, w_3) - [x_0, y_0, z_0].$$

By definition of f, this implies that $w_1 = w_2 = x_1$, $w_0 = w_3 = x_0$, $z_1 = z_2 = u_0$, and $z_0 = z_3 = u_1$. Then $y_1 = v_0 - u_0 w_1 = v_1 - u_1 w_1$ and $y_0 = v_0 - u_0 w_0 = v_1 - u_1 w_0$. Consequently,

$$v_0 - v_1 = w_1(u_0 - u_1)$$
$$= w_0(u_0 - u_1).$$

Since these are elements of a field and nonzero elements have multiplicative inverses, this implies that either $u_0 = u_1$ or $w_0 = w_1$, a contradiction. Therefore, no such cycle can exist and the graph has girth 12.

This mapping for $q = 2$ has been used in Fig. 6.

VIII. The Write Cycle and Correcting Read

As with the product code, writing into the memory consists of updating the stored values so that the memory always forms a codeword. If the memory is brought up with all bits set to 0, it clearly forms a correct codeword. To write a data bit, that bit as stored is read out of the memory along with the five other bits on the path from that bit to the top of the tree, including the bit at the top. If the value to be written is the same as the one read out, all six bits can be written back in unchanged. If the new value is different, all six values are complemented and then written back in. The memory addressing arrangement can permit all six of these bits to be accessed and written in parallel.

For this write procedure to function properly, the value read out must be correct. Otherwise, the complementing operation may itself create errors among the parity bits that can engender future read errors. Consequently, the value read out should be that provided by the error-correcting read procedure.

Reading with single error correction is, likewise, directly analogous to the procedure for the product code. Referring to Fig. 6, if no errors have occurred, the parity sum of the bits at depth 2 in the left half of the tree and the parity sum of bits at depth 2 in the right half both are the same as the value of the bit at the top of the tree. A majority vote of these three will give the correct value so long as at most a single error has occurred. The RAM organization contrives to make these three values available for any bit read.

The underlying code has minimum distance six and is thus capable of correcting double errors and detecting triple errors. The tree algorithm of [13] can be used for this purpose, and we will now show how it can be adapted to the memory context. To carry out the full double error correction procedure each time a bit is read would increase access delay and require substantial additional circuitry; a software implementation included in the system management program may be more appropriate. For example, this might be incorporated naturally into the refresh program for a dynamic memory.

The tree algorithm itself is not conceptually complicated. Given that the graph has girth twelve, any bit in the graph can be used as the root of a tree of the form given in Fig. 6. The bit at the top of the tree can be recaptured correctly despite the presence of two errors using a two stage procedure. In the first stage, all of the parities at depth 3 are computed. If any one of these indicates a parity failure, an "X," representing an uncertain state, is placed on the bit node adjacent to it on level 2. In the second stage, the parities at depth 1 take in values from the bits below and compute an estimated value for the bit at the top. If one or more of the values supplied by the bits below is an "X," the estimated value is also "X." If all the bits give values of 0 or 1, the estimated value is the value the top bit must have to make the parity correct. Three values, then, are available at the top node: an estimate from the left-hand side, an estimate from the right-hand side, and the stored value of the bit itself. To make a final decision on the top bit's value, an estimate of 0 or 1 is given a weight of 2. An estimate of "X" is given no weight. The value of 0 or 1 stored for the bit is given weight one. The value with the largest total weight is the answer. Thus conflicting 0 and 1 estimates will be decided by the stored value. One estimate of "X" and a conflict between the stored value and the other estimate goes in favor of the estimate. Two "X"'s and a stored value give the stored value, and so forth.

If no errors are present, the final decision will have the total weight of five for the correct value, and it is straightforward to check that a single error anywhere in the tree can cause a change in the final weight of at most two. Consequently, the final bit will be correct as long as two or fewer errors have occurred.

Before considering the details of carrying out this procedure, we turn to the description of the actual hardware, showing how the tree used to create the projective plane can be realized as a RAM architecture.

IX. Memory Organization

The starting point for the physical organization of the memory is the addressing given by the left-hand side of the tree. The data bits are stored in q subarrays, each with q rows and q columns. The subarrays are indexed by u, the rows by v, and the column within a subarray by w. The parity bits at depth 4 on the left-hand side can be stored as an extra column

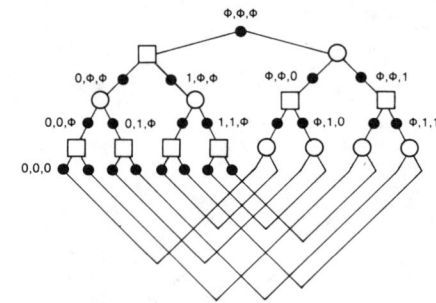

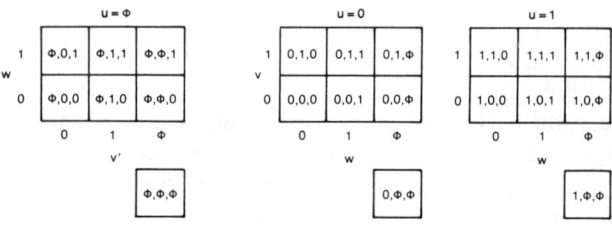

Fig. 7. Mapping the tree to an array.

in each u subarray. This is the form shown in Fig. 7, where the two main subarrays, $u = 0$ and $u = 1$, have an extra third column. The parity bits at depth two on the left are an additional bit associated with each u subarray, the (u, ϕ, ϕ) bit.

Now observe that when a bit with address (u_0, v_0, w_0), denoted by $b(u_0, v_0, w_0)$, is read, the correction procedure previously described requires the bit itself and two parity sums

$$b(u_0, v_0, \phi) + \sum_{w=0}^{q-1} b(u_0, v_0, w) + b(u_0, v_0, w_0) \quad (9.1)$$

and

$$b[x_0, y_0, \phi] + \sum_{z=0}^{q-1} b[x_0, y_0, z] + b[x_0, y_0, z_0] \quad (9.2)$$

where $f(u_0, v_0, w_0) = [x_0, y_0, z_0]$ and the sums are mod 2. The first sum is straightforward. It is the EXCLUSIVE-OR sum of the entire v_0 row of the u_0 subarray, including the extra (u_0, v_0, ϕ) bit, EXCLUSIVE-OR'd with the bit value itself. The bit value itself is added simply to cancel out its presence in the row sum. The second sum is less obvious, but note that

$$\sum_{z=0}^{q-1} b[x_0, y_0, z] = \sum_{u=0}^{q-1} b(u, v_0' + uw_0, w_0)$$

with $v_0' = (v_0 - u_0 w_0)$. The bit $b[x_0, y_0, \phi]$ can be viewed as a bit in another special subarray for the right-hand side of the tree with elements indexed by x_0 and y_0 or, equivalently, v_0' and w_0. This will be referred to as the (ϕ, v', w) subarray, shown as the $u = \phi$ array in Fig. 7. Similarly, the bits with addresses of the form $[x, \phi, \phi]$ can be stored in a (ϕ, ϕ, w) column appended to the $u = \phi$ subarray. The top (ϕ, ϕ, ϕ) bit is the extra bit for that subarray. The sum (9.2) is the EXCLUSIVE-OR sum of one bit from each main subarray, one bit from the (ϕ, v', w) subarray, and the bit itself. As before, the bit value itself is added back in to cause it to disappear from the final sum.

X. Parity and Address Computations

Both the computation of addresses on a Galois field and, to a lesser extent, the parallel parity computations are uncommon features in a memory design. We will now examine the actual circuitry required for these in closer detail.

In Fig. 8, a schematic diagram of the memory for $q = 4$ is given. When a bit is read, the input address is divided into three parts, u, v', and w. To facilitate address computation, the external address for a bit with internal address (u, v, w) is $(u, v' = v - uw, w)$. Of course, this makes no difference to the user. Each of the $q + 1$ different subarrays has a row-address computer that receives as inputs both v' and w and computes, using its own unique value of u, u_0, the row address for that subarray, $v' + u_0 w$. The multiplication is just multiplication by a constant on the field and is tantamount to a matrix multiplication over the base field [2]. For $q = 64$, the addition is simply a bit-wise EXCLUSIVE-OR of two six bit vectors. The entire computation for one subarray can be carried out with six multiple-input EXCLUSIVE-OR gates. Each of the main subarrays has a $(q + 1)$-input EXCLUSIVE-OR tree that computes the mod 2 sum of the bits in the row specified by the computed row address. The w address selects a bit from that row. The last bit in the row is the (u, v', ϕ) bit for that u_0.

The sum (9.1) is produced by letting the u address select a particular subarray. The w-selected bit of that subarray is the desired data bit and is placed on an output line. The output of the EXCLUSIVE-OR tree for that subarray is the first two terms of (9.1) and it is placed on a line leading to the "w sum out." The actual "w sum out," (9.1), is the EXCLUSIVE-OR of this with the selected bit.

The sum (9.2) is formed by another $(q + 1)$-input EXCLUSIVE-OR tree that combines the w-selected bits from each of the q subarrays and the bit from the w row and v' column of the (ϕ, v', w) additional subarray. The actual (u, v, w) bit is EXCLUSIVE-OR'd with this to give (9.2).

For the purposes of the WRITE operation, the previously mentioned six bits must be accessed. The first of these is the desired bit itself. The second is the bit in the extra column and same row of the u-selected subarray. The third is the extra bit for that subarray. The (ϕ, v', w) bit and the (ϕ, ϕ, w) bit are in the same row of the $u = \phi$ subarray. The sixth is the extra (ϕ, ϕ, ϕ) bit for that subarray, as shown in Fig. 7. The hardware can permit these to be written back in parallel since two bits from any subarray are always taken from the same row.

A quick glance at Fig. 5, the memory organization for the independent product codes, and Fig. 8, that for the projective plane code, reveals that they closely resemble each other. The key difference is that the single bits taken from each of the subarrays by the projective plane can all be in different rows. This creates an interdependence between the rows that is not present in the independent product code organization and enables the projective plane code to correct double errors. The price that must correspondingly be paid is that individual row addresses must be computed for each of the subarrays, and each subarray must have its own row address decoders.

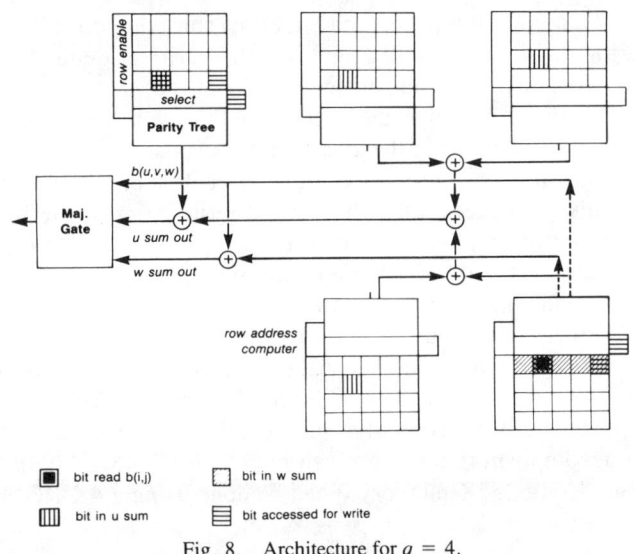

Fig. 8. Architecture for $q = 4$.

XI. Software Double Error Correction

Assuming randomly generated double errors are relatively rare, increasing access delay and circuit complexity to accommodate automatic double error correction by the hardware is not worthwhile. Rather, the memory management system should detect double errors by systematically surveying all of the parity check nodes in the graph as part of the refresh cycle. A multiple error is detected if there are more than two parity check failures or the two nodes with parity check failure do not check a common bit. Given that a double error has been detected, a conservative algorithm for eliminating it is to invoke the double error correcting tree algorithm described in Section VIII for all bits checked by a parity that is violated.

In order to carry out the tree algorithm for a particular bit, it is sufficient to have the three outputs generated automatically by the single error correction circuitry for all the bits at distance two from the bit in question. If the bit to be corrected is the top bit in a tree such as Fig. 6, the tree algorithm starts from estimates for the bits at depth 2 provided by the parities at depth 3. The estimate for a bit at depth 2 is, in fact, one of the three inputs to the majority logic gate when the bit at depth 2 is read. Consequently, if the three inputs to the majority logic gate are externally available, the software correction begins by reading the $2q$ bits at depth 2 to obtain the information on parity failures at depth 3. This information, combined with the three majority gate inputs from reading the top bit, is all that is needed for the tree algorithm.

To complete analysis, we must verify that the three inputs to the majority logic gate are available for all of the bits in the memory, including the parity bits. Equivalently, we need to show that a parity sum for each parity node in the graph can be computed. With an architecture such as that illustrated in Fig. 8, the parity of all rows of all subarrays must be even. These are computed by the hardware EXCLUSIVE-OR trees associated with each subarray. In terms of the tree of Fig. 6 with bit (ϕ, ϕ, ϕ) at the top, this includes all parity nodes at depth 5 on the left and depth 3 on the right. The EXCLUSIVE-OR tree that takes one bit from each subarray can compute all the parities at depth 5 on the right and the parity at depth 1 on the left. The remaining parities are the sums of the bits in the extra column as well as the isolated bit of each subarray. One method of computing these is to have a separate parity tree that operates on the extra column of each subarray. Alternatively, and preferably, the current parity sum of the bits in the extra column can easily be computed with a single EXCLUSIVE-OR and one additional bit of storage as the refresh cycle reads the successive rows.

Correction of double errors requires computation of the address function f; the need arises when the bits at distance two from a given bit must be found. The most difficult part of f is the multiplication of u and w over $GF(q)$. Two methods for accomplishing this are given in [2, pp. 47–48]. Alternatively, for a 256K memory it can be done using a 4K ROM.

XII. Other Failure Modes

The error correction capabilities of this memory design enable it to operate correctly despite the presence of circuit failures that effect more than an isolated bit. The memory can tolerate limited failures in the accessing lines and in the EXCLUSIVE-OR trees, and failure of an entire column of one of the subarrays. It is vulnerable inevitably to error in the final output stage, the three-input majority-logic circuit, and, to a lesser extent, to failure of the address computers and decoders.

The single error-correction procedure will handle all errors that affect only one of the inputs to the majority-logic circuit. If there are no errors in the bits, one of the EXCLUSIVE-OR trees can fail and only one of the three inputs will be wrong. Similarly, any single failure of one of the accessing lines leading to the final output circuit will not produce an output error. Note also that when any bit is read, at most one bit is taken from any given column in a given subarray. Thus, so long as there are no other bit errors involved, the memory can perform correctly despite such a column failure.

Address computer and decoder failures are clearly more damaging. A failure confined to one subarray can be tolerated if bits from that subarray are never actually used externally. If the subarray supplies only one bit for the global EXCLUSIVE-OR tree, obviously it cannot hurt the immediate output. Any attempt to read out a bit from that subarray, however, may cause it to furnish two incorrect values.

The circuit is also partially self-checking because one of the parity nodes in the graph is redundant. No matter what the pattern of bit errors, the number of parity checks that are not satisfied must be an even number. Each bit error causes two parity check violations, and the number of violations must always 0 mod 2. Therefore, if ever in refreshing the memory the management system finds an odd number of unsatisfied parity nodes, it indicates that there has been a failure in one of the circuits, not just a data error.

XIII. Conclusion

The memory design we have presented represents a conceptual departure from customary practice. By structuring the memory so that it forms a single codeword in an error-correcting code, we achieve the ability to correct all double errors, most triple errors, as well as a variety of other failures, while requiring only roughly 3 percent of the 256K memory to be devoted to redundant parity check bits.

Some additional delay occurs in when a bit is read out. The addresses must pass through one or two levels of EXCLUSIVE-OR's in the subarray address computers and the accessed bits are fed into a 65 input EXCLUSIVE-OR tree and then the three-input majority-logic circuit. When realized on a single chip, the increase in access time should still be less than that required to read information from a memory and pass it through error-correcting circuits on a separate chip. Writing a bit into the memory requires reading, modifying, and rewriting six bits, the minimum distance of the underlying error-correcting code. Both the area and time delay overhead should be comparable or slightly greater than that for the simple parity product codes of Section V and [11].

Although we have focused on a 256K chip and $q = 64$, the same design can be built for any prime power q, the powers of two being those of principle interest for computer systems. The interconnectivity of the memory is based on a projective plane graph. Additional error-correction power can be achieved by use of a graph such as a generalized quadrangle or other generalized n-gon [5], but the coding overhead will be higher and the addressing will be more complicated. Alternatively, following the principles of [13], a more powerful error-correcting code can be used in place of the simple parity, while preserving the same addressing and connectivity. It is questionable whether the additional computational delay and circuit complexity would be justified for normal applications. Similarly, as mentioned previously, the design may be used at a higher level with a larger basic unit such as a word, or memory chip with additional addressing, rather than a bit.

The architecture and algorithms we have proposed embody a number of tradeoffs. On the assumption that the actual random soft-error generation rate is typically very low, the parallelism in the error-correcting circuitry has been kept small, and internal correction only takes place at the time of a write or under control of the memory management system. If random error rate increases, the number of error-correction computations that take place in a given time interval must be increased correspondingly, either by more frequent visits by the management system or more internal parallel correction.

The enhanced reliability inherent in this design can be put to different purposes. On the one hand, chips that are fully tested and contain no flaws will have greater reliability in the field. On the other, chips with some manufacturing flaws can perform as though they were perfect irredundant memories. In this way the design strategy may effectively increase yields.

Acknowledgment

The author wishes to thank J. Greene for a presentation on fault-tolerant memories and R. Wellington-Oguri and A. El Gamal for helpful discussions on coding and memory design.

REFERENCES

[1] A. F. Barton, "A fault tolerant integrated circuit memory," Ph.D. dissertation, Dep. Comput. Sci., Calif. Inst. Tech., Apr. 1980.
[2] E. R. Berlekamp, *Algebraic Coding Theory*. New York: McGraw-Hill, 1968, pp. 44–51.
[3] D. C. Bossen and M. Y. Hsiao, "A system solution to the memory soft error problem," *IBM J. Res. Devel.*, vol. 24, no. 3, pp. 390–397, May 1980.
[4] P. J. Cameron and J. H. Van Lint, *Graph Theory, Coding Theory, and Block Designs*. Cambridge: Cambridge Univ. Press, 1975.
[5] P. Dembowski, *Finite Geometries*. New York: Springer-Verlag, 1968.
[6] P. Elias, "Error-free coding," *IRE Trans. Inform. Theory,* vol. PGIT-4, pp. 29–37, Sept. 1954.
[7] S. A. Elkind and D. P. Siewiorek, "Reliability and performance of error-correcting memory and register arrays," *IEEE Trans. Comput.*, vol. C-29, pp. 920–927, Oct. 1980.
[8] M. Y. Hsiao, "A class of optimal minimum odd-weight-column SEC-DED codes," *IBM J. Res. Devel.*, July 1970, pp. 395–401.
[9] D. A. Huffman, "Graph codes," unpublished, 1966.
[10] *Intel Corporation Memory Design Handbook,* pp. 4-13–4-33, Jan. 1981.
[11] F. I. Osman, "Error-correction technique for random-access memories," *IEEE J. Solid-State Circuits,* vol. SC-17, no. 5, pp. 877–881, Oct. 1982.
[12] W. W. Peterson and E. J. Weldon, *Error-Correcting Codes*. Cambridge, MA: MIT Press, 1972.
[13] R. M. Tanner, "A recursive approach to low-complexity codes," *IEEE Trans. Inform. Theory,* vol. IT-27, no. 4, pp. 533–547, Sept. 1981.

R. Michael Tanner (S'67–M'69) was born in Spanish Fork, UT, in 1946. He received the B.S. degree in 1966, the M.S. degree in 1967, and the Ph.D. degree in 1971 in electrical engineering, all from Stanford University, Stanford, CA.

From 1971 to 1972 he taught electrical engineering at Tennessee State University, Nashville, TN. Since 1972 he has been in the Department of Computer and Information Sciences, University of California, Santa Cruz, where he is currently an Associate Professor. His primary research interests are in error-correcting coding and complexity.

Error-Correction Technique for Random-Access Memories

FAZIL I. OSMAN, MEMBER, IEEE

Abstract—On-chip error correction for random-access memories is not very popular because of the high overhead necessary. This paper presents a technique that performs a single-bit correction and a double-bit detection on clocked memories where all column data is internally available, with an area penalty of less than 20 percent. The timing overhead for on-chip implementation is less than the time required to generate a parity bit. The detection and correction operation is transparent to the user and does not require different cycle times for the detection and for the correction.

I. INTRODUCTION

Error-correction coding has been applied to serial data links and storage as well as main memory systems [1]. Historically, more work has been done on serial error correction, producing some very fast and efficient codes. The Fire code is such an example. This trend has not, however, been present in computer main memory systems. Most memory systems are either 8 bits or 16 bits wide as in small systems and microprocessors or 32 bits or more in large systems such as mainframes and recently in VLSI processors. Single-bit error correction has such a high overhead for small systems that the small system users have limited themselves to single-bit error detection only using a parity bit. Large system users can usually afford the cost and area overhead for error-correction codes.

However, with technological improvements, cheaper and higher packing density main memory is becoming available to computer designers. The small system user is increasing the amount of main memory in his system and taking advantage of the low cost per bit to increase his system performance. Unfortunately, the larger amount of memory and higher sensitivity of the parts to α-particle errors means that the small system user as well as his larger system counterpart will need error correction. This paper presents an error-correction technique that is applicable to random-access memories (RAM's). Using this technique, single-bit error correction and double-bit error detection can be performed on a dynamic RAM with less than 20 percent area overhead. Moreover, by being implemented on the memory chip itself, it is transparent to the user. This means that the computer system designer can fit these parts into his system without having to interrupt his CPU for error-correction.

Section II will briefly describe error-correction techniques that have been used up to now in random-access memory systems. Section III will describe the proposed error-correction technique for RAM. Section IV will describe a hypothetical 8K $\times$ 8 DRAM to show the application of the technique to a DRAM and to calculate the area and timing overheads. Section V will give a brief resumé of some other possible applications of the technique. A summary of the paper is presented in Section VI.

II. PRESENTLY USED ERROR-CORRECTION TECHNIQUES FOR RAM

Small system users do not usually have error-correction capabilities, but usually rely on parity for the detection of a single-bit error. This has up to now been adequate. But, the small system designer is now using more main memory and the incidence of single-bit errors should increase.

Error-correction is possible for any width of data bus. The most commonly used code for single-bit error correction and double-bit detection is the Hamming code. Fig. 1 shows a graph of the memory overhead necessary for implementing the Hamming code. Using 25 percent as an arbitrary cutoff point for the cost effectiveness of error correction, it can be seen that it is not effective for data bus widths of less than 32 bits. Error correction using the Hamming code is used widely in large systems. Error-correction units such as Intel's 8206 [2] are available for this purpose. Memory overhead is not the only disadvantage of Hamming codes. Detection and correction take different amounts of time. For the small system user this causes a problem, as he has to halt his system during the correction and this might mean placing some sort of memory management unit between his processor and main memory.

One technique that offers a low memory overhead is the software/hardware technique proposed by Edwards [3]. The main memory is divided into blocks of a fixed size. To each byte, a parity bit is added as a horizontal parity. A vertical parity is generated and stored in the vertical parity memory as shown in Fig. 2. The vertical parity is the parity of the same bit position for all the bytes in the block. During normal operation, only the horizontal parity is checked. If a horizontal parity error is detected, the system goes into a software loop that generates the vertical parities for the block. The bit at the intersection of the horizontal and vertical parities is the failed bit. The main advantage of this technique is the low memory overhead, which can be as low as 1.2 extra bits depending upon the block size. The logic required is very simple as only parity generation is necessary. The main disadvantages are the completely different detection and correction times and the need for the system designer to understand and handle the correction technique. It is not a user-transparent technique.

Manuscript received March 1, 1982; revised June 23, 1982.
The author is with the Microcomponents Organization, Burroughs Corporation, San Diego, CA 92127.

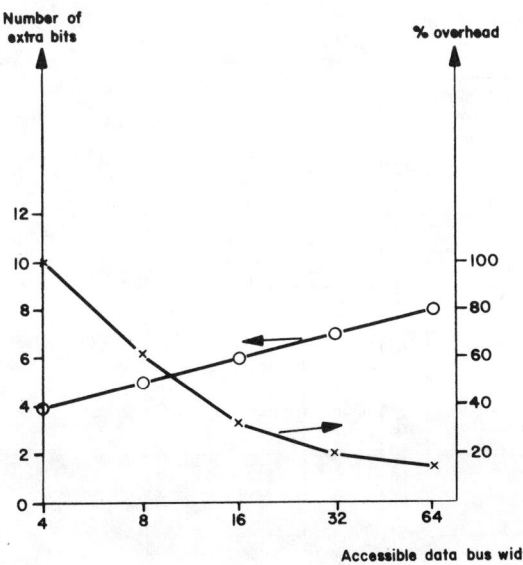

Fig. 1. Memory overhead for implementing a Hamming code.

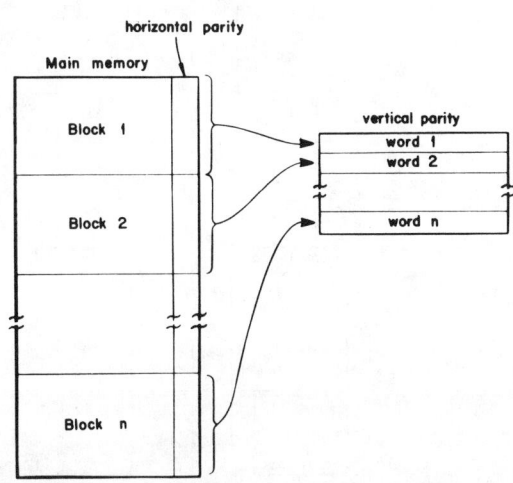

Fig. 2. In Edwards' method, a horizontal parity bit is added to each word and a vertical parity is generated for each block.

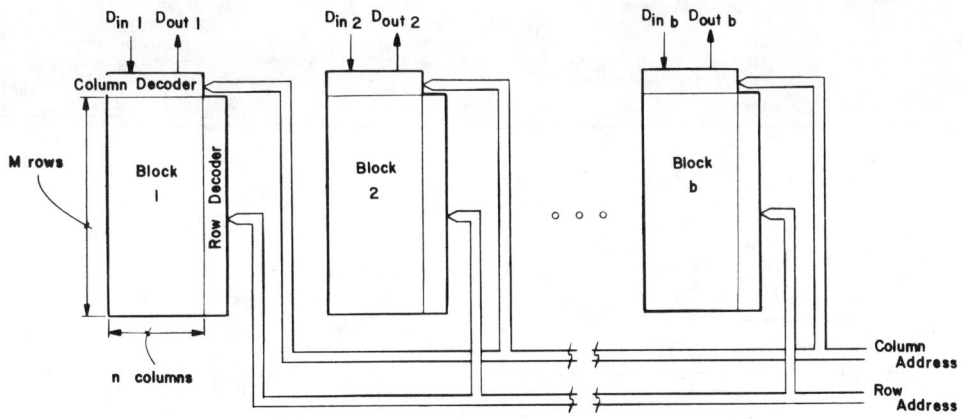

Fig. 3. Block diagram of a b bits wide memory array.

III. Description of the Proposed Technique

Similar to the Edwards technique, the proposed technique is based upon a block or product code. Although more sophisticated codes could be used for multiple-bit correction, the description here will be limited to a single-bit error correction and a double-bit error detection. It is orientated towards byte-wide memories.

Consider a memory array such as the one shown in Fig. 3. It consists of b blocks of memory where b is the memory width. Each block is implemented as an array of m rows and n columns, giving a total accessible memory capacity of $m \times n \times b$ bits ($m \times n$ words).

Single-bit error detection can be implemented on this memory array by having parity bits. Parity can be done in two ways as follows.

1) Row Parity: When accessing the memory, only 1 of m rows is accessed at a time. Data are available on the n columns in that row. Row parity can be implemented by adding an extra column $n+1$ to each block where the $n+1$th bit of each row will store the parity for that row, as shown in Fig. 4. The parity generation takes place in parallel with the column decode and does not significantly degrade the performance.

2) Block Parity: This is the usual technique of implementing parity for a byte-orientated memory. An extra block $b+1$ is added which stores the parity of the b bits for any particular row and column address combinations in the same address location on the $b+1$th block, as shown in Fig. 4.

These two parities can be used at the same time to implement a product code that allows a single-bit correction and double-bit detection. A single-bit error is defined as any one bit within the whole array failing, while a double-bit error is defined as any two bits within the whole array failing. As this technique generates parity bits for the row being accessed only, if two bits in different rows fail, they can both be corrected separately. A single-bit error is detected when block parity and row parity are flagged at the same time. Table I shows the different combinations of row and block parities and their interpretations for single-bit and double-bit errors. One advantage of this method is that detection of single-bit and double-bit errors only involves a parity generation and single-bit correction only requires a further inversion.

If this technique is to be considered for on-chip error correction and detection, both memory and logic overheads have to be considered. The memory overhead is dependent upon b,

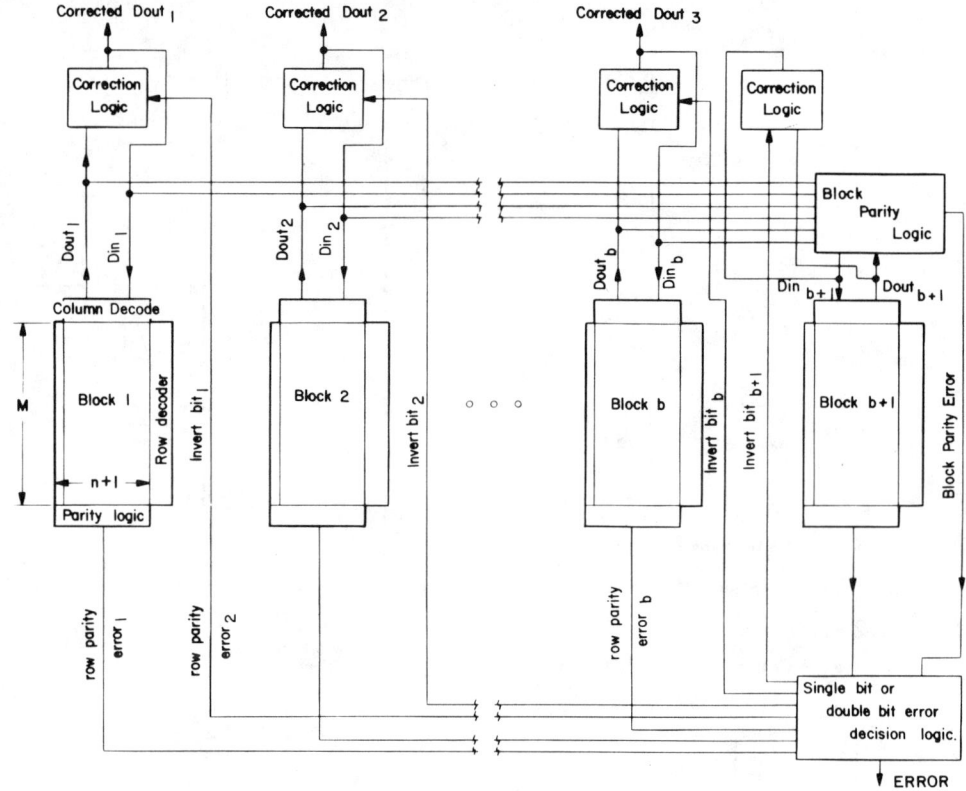

Fig. 4. Block diagram for single-bit correction and double-bit detection.

TABLE I
CONDITIONS FOR DIFFERENT TYPES OF ERRORS

ROW PARITIES	BLOCK PARITY	INTERPRETATION
$R_1 - R_{b+1} = 0$	0	No error.
$R_n = 1$ all other R's = 0	1	Single-bit error at $D_{out\ n}$. Inverted for correction.
$R_n = 1$ all other R's = 0	0	Single-bit error at block n. It is not the bit being accessed. Error will be corrected at access.
All R's = 0	1	Double-bit error in row.
$R_n = 1$, $R_m = 1$, all other R's = 0	0	Double-bit errors in block m & n.

Block parity key: 1=parity error is flagged. 0=no parity error. *Note*—Multiple-bit errors can also cause the conditions described in this table.

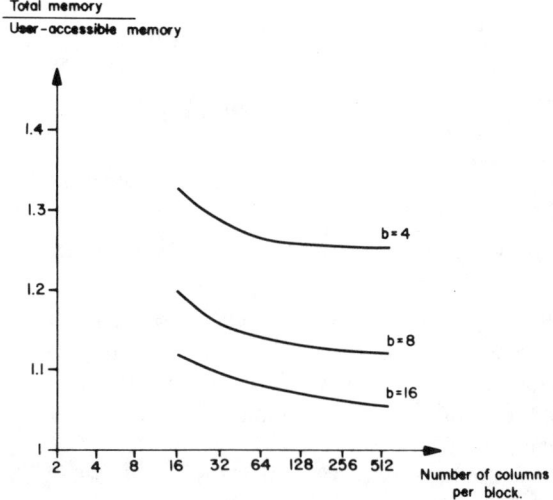

Fig. 5. Memory overhead for implementing row and block parities.

IV. TRADEOFFS FOR AN 8K × 8 SINGLE-BIT ERROR-CORRECTING DRAM

In order to prove the feasibility of this technique for present day technology, calculations have been done for an 8K × 8 DRAM. The most highly discussed source of single-bit and double-bit failures is α-particles. Single-bit errors are caused by hits on the memory cell or bit line and double-bit errors by hits between adjacent memory cells. It should be noted that double-bit errors in different rows can be corrected. The only type of double-bit error caused by a single α-particle is in the

the number of blocks in the user-accessible memory, and upon the number of columns n in each row of a block. Fig. 5 shows the variation of the memory overhead with these parameters. For the fastest possible error correction, the logic overhead in terms of Exclusive-OR gates is proportional to the number of columns n and the number of blocks b, as shown in Fig. 6.

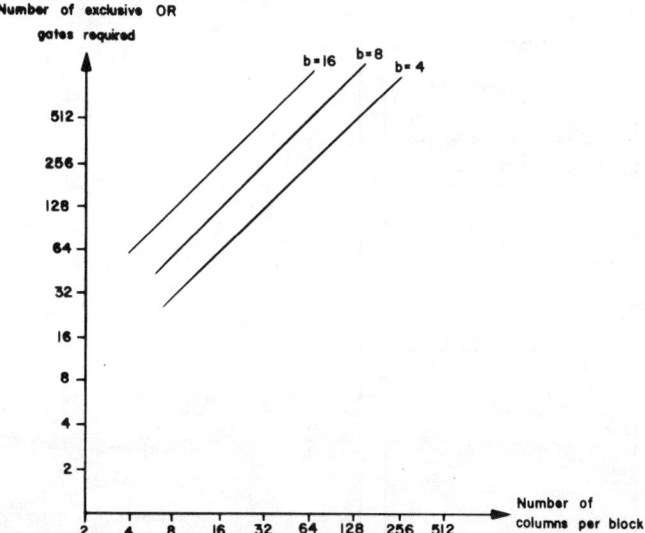

Fig. 6. Logic overhead for implementing row and block parities.

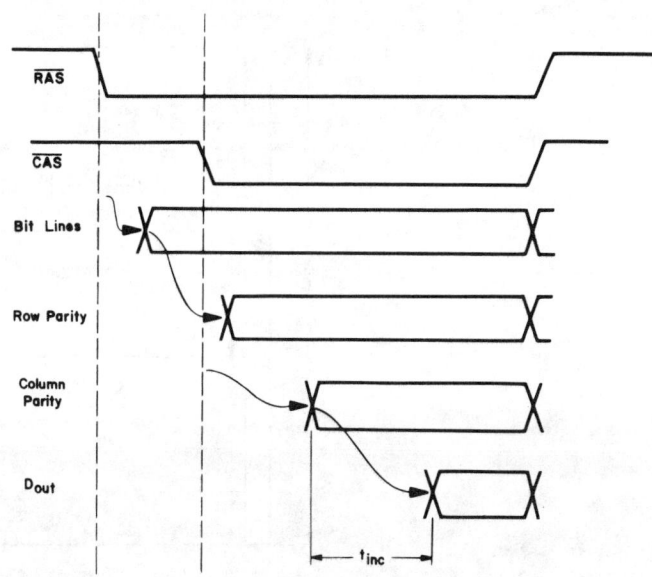

t_{inc} = increase in cycle time due to error-correction.

Fig. 7. Timing diagram for an error-correcting DRAM.

TABLE II
PIN-OUT FOR AN 8K × 8 ERROR-CORRECTING DRAM

Signal	Description
$\overline{RAS}$	Row address select
$\overline{CAS}$	Column address select
$\overline{WE}$	Write enable
VDD	Power supplies
VSS	
A0–A6	Address lines
IO1–8	D_{in} and D_{out} lines
$\overline{INIT}$	Memory initialization
ERROR	Double-bit error flag

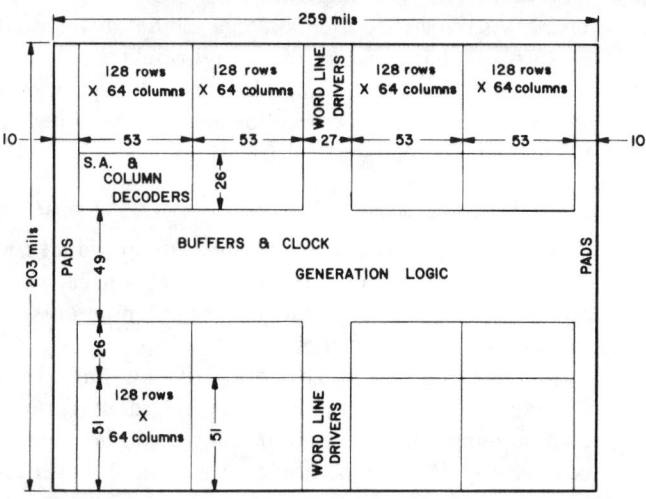

Fig. 8. Possible layout for an 8K × 8 DRAM. (*Note:* Figure not drawn to scale.)

two adjacent bits within the same row and block. Such an error can be corrected if each block of the memory is divided into odd and even rows. Instead of adding one extra column for the row parity, both an odd and an even column are added to store the parity of the odd and even columns, respectively.

The following are the main points that have been considered in the design of the memory chip.

1) Pin-Out: The smallest package that can be used is a 24 pin package. Table II shows the signals that will be used. $\overline{INIT}$ and ERROR are the only two signals that are necessary for the error-correction logic. The byte-wide data could be multiplexed for a 64K × 1 DRAM. This could not, however, be used in a 16 pin package because of the lack of pins for $\overline{INIT}$ and ERROR.

2) Timing Overhead: Row parity can be generated when the data is available on the bit lines and can be done in parallel with the column decoding. Block parity, on the other hand, can only be generated once the data has been selected. This means an increase in the cycle time. A timing diagram is shown in Fig. 7. The increase in the cycle time, however, should be less than the time taken to generate parity off-chip as timing skews are minimized on-chip.

3) Memory Initialization: Unlike main memory at present in small systems, the parity bits in the array have to be set. This can be done by using a combination of $\overline{RAS}$ and $\overline{INIT}$. This is similar in operation to a RAS-only refresh cycle. The two options there are to either set the memory data to an all-zero state or to set the parity bits and leave the main array to whatever state it is initialized. The advantage of the first option is that it would make an initialize cycle faster than the normal cycle. The latter option would allow for resetting the parity bits if a double-bit error is detected and is not considered critical. Correction of single-bit errors in parts of the array that are not being accessed can be done during a RAS-only refresh cycle. This would improve the reliability of the system.

4) Layout: In order to estimate the area increase for the error correction on-chip, data from a 3.5 μm lithography 64K DRAM was used. The cell size is 10.5 × 21 μm². Fig. 8 shows a possible layout for an 8K × 8 DRAM. The chip size is calculated as 203 × 259 mils². For the error-correction logic, the

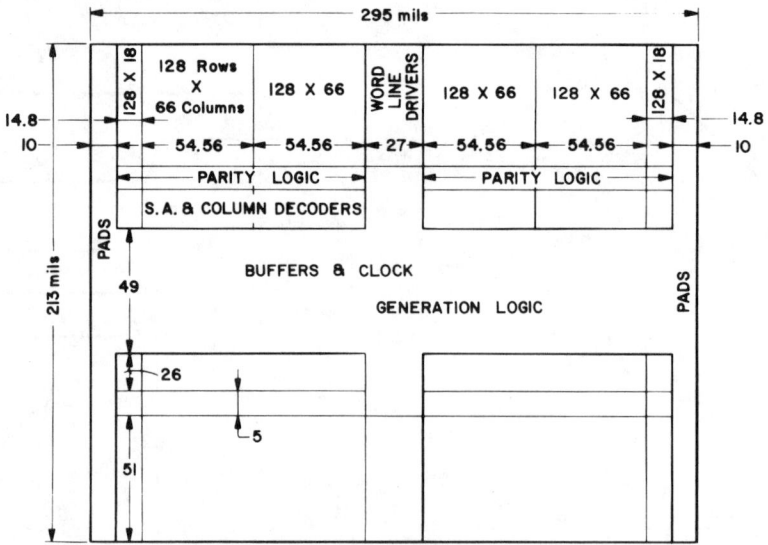

Fig. 9. Possible layout of an 8K × 8 DRAM with parity logic added.

area for each Exclusive-OR gate is estimated at 4.3 mils^2/gate. This gives the layout in Fig. 9 where the chip size is 213 × 295 mils^2, an area increase of 19.5 percent.

5) Testing: As the error-correction logic cannot differentiate between soft and hard errors, the array would have to be tested separately from the logic. This would require extra logic for disabling the error-correction logic. This overhead has not been included in the area calculations above.

V. Other Possible Applications of this Technique

What has been proposed is the application of a product code to RAM organization. Single-bit error correction capability has been shown. However, product codes have more possibilities than single-bit error correction.

1) Multiple-Bit Correction: The row parity bit could be replaced by multiple bits to allow for the generation of, for example, a Hamming code. The same thing could be done for the block parity. More work would have to be done to estimate the area penalty for such applications.

2) ROM Application: With decreasing linewidths, both RAM and ROM are getting denser. In order to increase yields, redundancy is being used in RAM. This technique cannot be applied to ROM because of the unique bit combination of each row and column. The only approach to redundancy in ROM has been 100 percent redundancy where each row is duplicated. A product code could be applied to ROM to correct single-bit failures if the extra time penalty is acceptable.

VI. Summary

A technique has been proposed to apply product codes to random-access memories. The main advantage of this technique is that the area overhead can be kept under 20 percent, as shown by calculations for an 8K × 8 DRAM. The timing penalty is similar to generating parity on the chip. All the logic can be made on-chip making the single-bit correction operation totally transparent to the user.

Acknowledgment

The author would like to thank T. Knudsen for all the time and effort he spent on the drawings and tables.

References

[1] W. W. Peterson and E. J. Weldon, Jr., *Error-Correcting Codes, 2nd Ed.* Cambridge, MA: M.I.T. Press, 1972.
[2] Intel Corporation data sheet, July 1981.
[3] L. Edwards, "Low cost alternative to Hamming codes corrects memory errors," *Comput. Des.*, pp. 132–148, July 1981.

Fazil I. Osman (M'74) was born in Mauritius in 1956. He obtained the B.Sc. degree with honors in electrical engineering and electronics from the University of Edinburgh, Edinburgh, Scotland, in 1978.

He worked at Burroughs Machines, Ltd., Cumbernauld, Scotland, from September 1978 to April 1981. The work he performed there included circuit design, memory system design for microprocessors, and wafer-scale integration. Since April 1981 he has been with the Microcomponents Organization, Burroughs Corporation, San Diego, CA, developing a CMOS process. He has had 2 patents filed while at Burroughs.

Chapter 7: VLSI Implementations of Redundancy Techniques

Overview

The previous chapter focused on the application of redundancy techniques to memory devices and memory systems. While state-of-the-art memory devices are VLSI, the regularity of memory architectures lends itself to redundancy implementations that may not be applicable to other types of devices or systems. Hence, this chapter covers the application of redundancy techniques to VLSI implementations other than memory.

Redundancy may be used in VLSI implementations to improve availability, reliability, detectability of errors, integrity, testability, or production yield. The use of redundancy for reconfigurable architectures has also been proposed. Redundancy may be applied on-chip, at the chip level, at the board level, at the subsystem level, or at the system level. In fact, combinations of the above may be justified in those cases in which redundancy is required at all levels. Definitive guidelines on the best level for application of techniques have not been developed.

Each goal given above is addressed in one or more of the reprints included in this chapter. The approaches range from system-level techniques to chip-level design considerations. A brief summary of the contribution of each reprint is given below with references to other pertinent articles. However, design for testability is considered beyond the scope of this book. Readers desiring a closer look at the testable design area are referred to the survey paper by Williams and Parker [WIL83], the reprint collection by Timoc [TIM85], or the tutorial by Reghbati [REG85].

Rennels et al. [REN78a], in the first paper reprinted in this chapter, propose a standard set of four VLSI components, or building blocks, to facilitate and systemitize the design of fault-tolerant computer systems. The building blocks (Core Building Block, Memory Interface Building Block, Bus Interface Building Block, and I/O Building Block) would provide fault-detection and recovery functions plus interface logic to permit straightforward design of a self-checking computer module (SCCM) using off-the-shelf processors and memory devices. SCCM's can then be employed in standalone or multiple computer configurations.

Each building block features the use of error-detection/correction codes, self-checking (morphic) logic, and/or duplication to provide internal fault detection. Additionally, the Core Building Block provides error detection for its associated SCCM and controls recovery or disabling of the module. A high level of coverage is thus provided which minimizes the hard-core requirements.

In theory, the building-block approach is significant since it permits design to occur at a system or subsystem level rather than at the logic level. Designers are thus spared the chore of designing circuitry to provide encoding and decoding, fault detection, and recovery. Also, a wide range of applications can be handled due to the flexibility of the approach. Other discussions of the building block approach are found in [REN78b] and [REN80].

In practice, the approach has to date had some notable commercial acceptance. Several semiconductor manufacturers, for example, offer products similar in function to the proposed Memory Interface Building Block. Such products include AMD 2960, Intel 8206, National DP 8400, Signetics/Fairchild 74F630, and TI 74LS630 series. The AMD 2960 is discussed in detail in Chapter 6. This application offers a big payoff in reliability gain for a memory using a relatively simple building block. Also, memory chip interfaces are reasonably standard. Products corresponding to other building blocks have not appeared because of standardization problems, complexity of the device, lower potential reliability gain, or lack of a market. The Intel 432 architecture also offers a modular approach to the design of fault-tolerant systems. However, Intel's approach differs significantly in detail to the Building Block approach as will be described in later paragraphs.

Sedmak and Liebergot [SED80], in the second paper reprinted in this chapter, have proposed a method for incorporating error detection inside VLSI functional chips. The approach evolved from a study to determine the most effective way to use VLSI in the design of a general-purpose computer while taking in to account cost, performance, and fault-tolerance issues.

Fault-tolerance goals were nearly 100% immediate fault detection, limited down-time instead of total fault masking, deferrable maintenance as opposed to automatic self-repair, complete recovery from transient or intermittent faults, and rapid and automatic fault isolation. Achieving the goals resulted in a 5.5% increase in chip count over a conventional VLSI-based design. However, a 55% increase in gate count was required in the CPU to provide fault detection and error handling.

Techniques employed to provide fault detection and error handling include internal duplicate complementary logic, a special purpose error-handling chip, error-detection and error-correction codes, duplication, self-checking checkers, and miscellaneous approaches for power and clock signals. Fault recovery is accomplished by masking errors in memory with SEC/DED codes and by operation retry for other non-memory faults.

Duplicate complementary logic is the most unique of the techniques employed and will be discussed in more detail below. The technique is implemented on-chip and consists of input code checkers, two blocks of functional logic, comparators, and error-multiplexing and encoding logic. One of the functional logic blocks realizes the "true" form of the chip output functions. The other block of functional logic realizes the "complement" form of the chip output functions. Outputs and selected intermediate signals of the two blocks are compared for error detection. Errors are reported to an error-handling chip via the on-chip error multiplexing and encoding logic. Input code errors are similarly reported.

Duplicate complementary logic offers several advantages over standard duplication. The common-mode problem is avoided since a chip-wide flaw or failure will not likely cause the two blocks to fail and to produce complementary outputs. Also, the approach minimizes the likelihood of bridging or shorting faults. Moreover, checking for errors on intermediate results will often result in earlier detection of a problem than will only checking for output errors. However, complementary logic does have several problems of its own, plus complementary circuits are not always easy to develop.

The last observation can be used as a justification for on-chip duplication rather than chip-level duplication. Clearly, chip-level duplication only permits output error detection which could increase error latency to an unacceptable level. However, while the above is true for error detection, error masking can perhaps be better realized with chip-level redundancy. Further study of the trade-offs between on-chip and chip-level redundancy is needed to more clearly understand the best applications of each.

The Intel i432 system architecture is described by Johnson [JOH84], in the next paper reprinted in this chapter, and also in [PET83]. Many interesting and useful architectural features are offered in the i432 including hardware support of objects and type managers. Such features allow efficient realization of information hiding and modular programming which in turn greatly simplifies the development and maintenance of complex software. The i432 also offers a range of features that permit the configuration of a wide spectrum of fault-tolerant systems. While the i432 was not successful in the market place, many of its features will likely appear in successful systems of the future.

The basic elements of an i432 system include the general data processor (GDP), I/O processor (IOP), bus interface unit (BIU), memory control unit (MCU), and system bus. Conceptually, the BIU and MCU components are reminders of the standard building blocks described by Rennels [REN78a]. A two-bit interlaced parity encoding is used on the system bus. Data stored in memory are encoded in a SEC/DED code using 7 check bits defined over the 16-bit data word and the corresponding physical address bits. This approach allows the detection of address errors in addition to providing the standard features of a SEC/DED code. The MCU also supports the use of a spare bit plane for configuring around hard failures in a single RAM component.

The i432 architecture supports up to 63 processor, I/O, and memory modules and up to 8 system buses. Multiple resources can be used to provide improved performance or to defer maintenance by offering the opportunity to reconfigure a system on restart around a failed component.

Systems of high integrity and high availability can be configured from i432 components by choosing to implement the confinement-area feature. Confinement areas limit damage from error propagation and localize recovery and repair. Error-detection mechanisms are placed at confinement-area boundaries to prevent inconsistent data from leaving one area and corrupting others. The primary error-detection technique employed for this purpose is functional redundancy checking (FRC). FRC is implemented at the chip level by duplication and on-chip by special error-detection logic. A pair of such chips is called a self-checking module.

Systems capable of continuous or non-stop operation may be configured by implementing module shadowing. A pair of self-checking modules operating in lockstep with complete and current backup of all data constitutes module shadowing. One module is active while the other is passive. The active/passive roles are switched after each bus request. Hence if a module fails, its shadow can take over the active role alone until repair is complete.

Tsao et al. [TSA82] describe, in the next paper reprinted in this chapter, an experimental microprocessor that incorporates fault-tolerance and testability features. The Fairchild F8 was chosen as the target architecture of the design primarily for its simplicity which was consistent with the experimental nature of the project. A primary goal was to investigate the applicability of various redundancy and testability techniques for on-chip realization of microprocessor designs.

Fault-tolerance features include error-detection and error-recovery capabilities. Single-bit odd parity is the only on-chip error-detection technique used for data-path logic. However, totally self-checking parity checkers are not used in order to conserve chip area. Whether or not to use totally self-checking checkers for such an application remains an open question. Perhaps they are justifiable since parity is the only on-chip technique employed in the data path. Detection of ALU errors is handled at the system level through a master/slave, duplicate-and-compare technique similar to that employed in the i432. As the technique is implemented, however, recovery is not possible from certain hard failures of the slave. Error detection in the control path is provided by self-checking PLA's.

Instruction retry is supported by the provision of shadow registers for the Accumulator and for the Scratch Pad Address Register. A register is also provided to save the most recently read value from the I/O bus. Testability has been improved through the implementation of a visibility bus that permits loading or reading of control path flip-flops while in a test mode.

Halbert and Bose [HAL84], in the paper reprinted in this chapter, describe an approach to the design of a VLSI self-checking microprocessor. The target architecture is that given by MIL-STD-1750A. General features of the design include on-chip error detection, an extensive use of PLA's in totally self-checking circuits, and a microprogram controller with high fault coverage. Goals for self-checking include fault-secureness for all modeled faults, self-testing for all modeled faults when built-in-test routines are run, and self-testing under normal use for as many faults as possible. Modeled faults include single stuck-at faults and transient faults in data storage cells. Redundancy methods used to achieve the goals include single-bit parity, k-variable two-rail logic, m-out-of-n codes, and duplication (possibly complementary).

Perhaps the most noteworthy contribution in [HAL84] is the method for realizing totally self-checking PLA's. Efficient PLA circuits including simple incrementers, a multifunction counter, small adders, and a microinstruction decoder have been designed using the method. A novel microstore addressing scheme employing m-out-of-n codes is also described.

Efficient realizations of totally self-checking PLA's is an important issue in the design of fault-tolerant VLSI devices. The reader wanting more information on the subject is referred to [WAN79] and [MAK82].

On-chip redundancy has been employed in the approaches described above for purposes of error detection, error correction, or testability improvement. Another approach to on chip redundancy has been presented by [LAL82]. On-chip redundancy has also been proposed for realizing restructurable systems (customization or fault tolerance) and for yield improvement in VLSI and WSI devices. Both of these applications are still in theoretical or early experimental stages of development. Much additional research is needed before any practical use of the ideas can be made. The final reprint [NEG86] in the chapter addresses these areas.

Many researchers [KOR81, SNY82, CHU83, PEL83, ROS83, KUN84, NEG86] have presented schemes for realizing restructurable architectures in VLSI or WSI devices. The paper by Negrini, Sami, and Stefaneli [NEG86] discusses the fault models expected in VLSI and WSI devices, which can be individual or clustered, and presents a number of reconfiguration algorithms. Two different types of algorithms are discussed to deal with both of the fault types, one making use of "structural redundancy," i.e. redundant rows and/or columns of cells to use in reassigning the functions of failed cells, and "temporal redundancy," in which an individual cell may perform multiple functions in several processing phases. The functions of the "normal" cell would be executed in one phase, and that of a failed cell in another, thus allowing continued operation without a great deal of redundancy in the cell array. Sample cell structures are also presented which support the various reconfiguration algorithms.

Another discussion of the design of reconfigurable arrays of processing cells is given by Koren [KOR81]. The approach uses an array of identical processing elements operating in a pipeline fashion. Processing elements can be interconnected to form a linear array, a rectangular array, or a binary tree. Each processing element consists of an application processor and a communication processor. The array can be configured during initialization to route around faulty elements for yield enhancement. Fault tolerance could similarly be provided by designing the processing elements as self-checking modules.

Mangir [MAN84a] discusses sources of failure and yield improvement for MOS VLSI. More specifically, the effects of scaling on MOS circuits are described along with resultant failure modes and the implications in terms of logical failures. Past approaches to yield-modeling are also reviewed. The primary contribution of the paper is the development of a model for yield improvement of VLSI circuits through the use of redundancy. The model indicates that on-chip redundancy can result in improved yield. However, the degree of improvement is influenced by several factors including defect density, interconnect area, randomness of intermodule interconnection pattern, module gate-to-pin ratio, testing coverage, and replacement coverage. Interested readers are also referred to [MAN82a, KOR84, MAN84b] for further discussions on the subject.

Finally, Lee and Shin [LEE84] propose to use VLSI real estate to implement hardware structures to support the software recovery block scheme developed by Randell [RAN75]. Recall that recovery blocks were discussed extensively in Chapter 5.

A STUDY OF STANDARD BUILDING BLOCKS FOR THE DESIGN OF FAULT-TOLERANT DISTRIBUTED COMPUTER SYSTEMS

David A. RENNELS
Jet Propulsion Laboratory
California Institute of Technology
Pasadena, CA 91103, USA

Algirdas AVIŽIENIS
Computer Science Department
University of California
Los Angeles, CA 90024, USA

Miloš ERCEGOVAC
Computer Science Department
University of California
Los Angeles, CA 90024, USA

Abstract

This paper presents the results of a study that has established a standard set of four semiconductor VLSI building-block circuits. These circuits can be assembled with off-the-shelf microprocessors and semiconductor memory modules into fault-tolerant distributed computer configurations. The resulting multi-computer architecture uses self-checking computer modules backed up by a limited number of spares. A redundant bus system is employed for communication between computer modules.

1. Introduction

Over the last decade a great deal of effort has been expended in the area of fault-tolerant computing [1], but the degree to which fault-tolerant computing has been utilized has been disappointing. Many early workers in the field expected to exert a strong influence on the next generation of computers, but this has not occurred. Manufacturers are going their own way, leaving the pursuit of fault-tolerance to a small number of government sponsors and academic investigators.

This paper summarizes an on-going study, being conducted at the Jet Propulsion Laboratory, which is directed at finding techniques to facilitate a wider use of fault-tolerant systems. The approach being taken is to define a small number of VLSI building block circuits which can be connected together with a variety of commercially available microprocessors and memories to implement a wide range of fault-tolerant computing systems.

The designs of the building blocks utilize already proven and accepted fault-tolerance techniques, e.g.: duplexing, error detecting and correcting codes, self-checking or morphic logic [2], etc. The primary goal is to attain a wide utilization of the building blocks in the near future. We depend on established results regarding the effectiveness of the fault-tolerance techniques [3], and therefore innovative modeling techniques are not developed in the present paper. The main criterion of choice for a particular technique is the generality and ease of utilization, rather than the highest reliability prediction with the least hardware investment. The second major goal is the manufacturing and extended testing of the building blocks in a prototype fault-tolerant distributed system. The term "Building Block" will be abbreviated to "BB" in the following discussion.

2. Applicability Conditions

The first problem in attaining wider use of fault-tolerance is to have devices in existence which allow its immediate utilization. The devices must allow implementation of different configurations of fault-tolerant computers, and they must also allow for the selective application of redundancy. A complex system contains system elements with a wide range of mission-criticality and with greatly differing failure rates. The system engineer often requires a high degree of redundancy protection for mission-critical computations, while computations for non-critical tasks may remain unprotected. This applies especially to multiple computer systems. For single computer applications, or for distributed systems, the manual (human) maintenance interval may vary from minutes to years, which implies an adjustable choice of spares. We have concluded that satisfying the following conditions will lead to a set of building block (BB) circuits that can be used in a variety of near-term applications.

(1) The number of distinct BB circuits must be small.
(2) They must interface directly with a variety of off-the-shelf microprocessor and memory circuits in order to achieve wide utilization.
(3) Currently existing busing and I/O standard should be followed as closely as possible. Advantages are compatibility, availability of existing interface circuits, and a backlog of experience on field performance.
(4) The resulting system architectures must display high coverage. Fault detection and recovery mechanisms must be nearly perfect for long-life systems whether or not human intervention for maintenance is available.
(5) For a majority of applications, periodic manual maintenance is possible; modules discarded by the system are replaced by spares while regular operation of the system continues. Design of the interface BBs should facilitate such repairs.
(6) The BBs must be manufactured and available for use by ongoing system development programs.
(7) The BB-based architectures should be sufficiently flexible to accomodate a wide range of application. They should provide the ability to handle an adjustable number of spare units as required by specific applications.
(8) Conceptual simplicity and ease of use are parameters which are sometimes overlooked, but they are important to promote widespread use of fault-tolerance. Fault-tolerant computing is conceived form the outside as an exotic and risky technology. Murky details within checking circuits and recovery algorithms add to this problem.

The first step in determining the functions of BB circuits is to examine the general types of fault-tolerant architectures for which the BB approach should be considered. Early fault-tolerant computers were partitioned into replaceable units below the level of a whole computer [4]. Due to the relatively high failure rates of SSI logic elements, the individual processors, memories, and I/O elements were diagnosed and replaced under control of a "hard core" module. Using microcomputer technology, a small computer is now of low enough cost and complexity that it can be replaced as a throw-away unit. This greatly simplifies system interfaces, removes maintenance connectors from the high-bandwidth internal buses, and simplifies hardcore elements by removing shared buses, synchronous clocks, and hardware recovery units. In view of this evolution of technology we have chosen a computer consisting of a processor, small memory, I/O, and intercommunication circuits as the basic replacement module in fault-tolerant BB architectures.

Our basic architectural unit is a Self-Checking Computer Module (SCCM), e.g., a small computer which is capable of detecting internal faults during normal operation. This module is constructed using off-the-shelf microprocessor and memory circuits connected with a set of VLSI building blocks. The SCCMs can be combined into a number of fault-tolerant configurations. The SCCM can be used (1) as a stand-alone configuration, (2) as a member of a voting or hybrid configuration, or (3) as a component of a distributed computing system. The self-checking attribute of the SCCM provides the requisite high coverage and allows a faulty SCCM to signal its failure to other SCCMs which can then implement fault recovery.

3. The Self-Checking Computer Module (SCCM)

A most important attribute of the set of BBs used to implement a SCCM is that they must allow any of a number of different processors to be used in the module. This requires finding a relatively standard set of interfaces which will match the BBs to most existing 16 bit microprocessors. The only standard interface which exists is the tri-state bus which conveys information between the processor and memory. The only standard interfacing technique is memory-mapped I/O. All I/O activations, intercommunications, reconfiguration and external diagnosis are commanded by reading from or writing into out-of-range addresses. The only requirements for interfacing the processor are compatibility with a 16-bit tri-state address and data busses, and common memory and DMA control signals. Figure 1 shows the SCCM, which contains four BB circuits: 1) an error detecting and correcting Memory Interface BB (MI-BB), 2) a programmable Bus Interface BB (BI-BB), 3) a Core-BB, and 4) a digital Input-Output BB (IO-BB). The BB circuits control and interface the various processor, intercommunication, memory, and I/O functions to the internal bus. Each BB is responsible for detecting faults in its associated circuitry and then signalling the fault condition to the Core-BB by means of a morphic internal fault indicator. The Core-BB receives the various fault indicators and also checks bus signals for proper coding. Upon detecting an error the Core-BB disables the bus control and I/O functions, isolating the SCCM from the rest of the system. The Core-BB can optionally (1) halt further processing until external intervention, or (2) attempt a rollback or restart of the processor, or (3) when fitted, initiate a memory reload from a local nonvolatile store and execute a program restart.

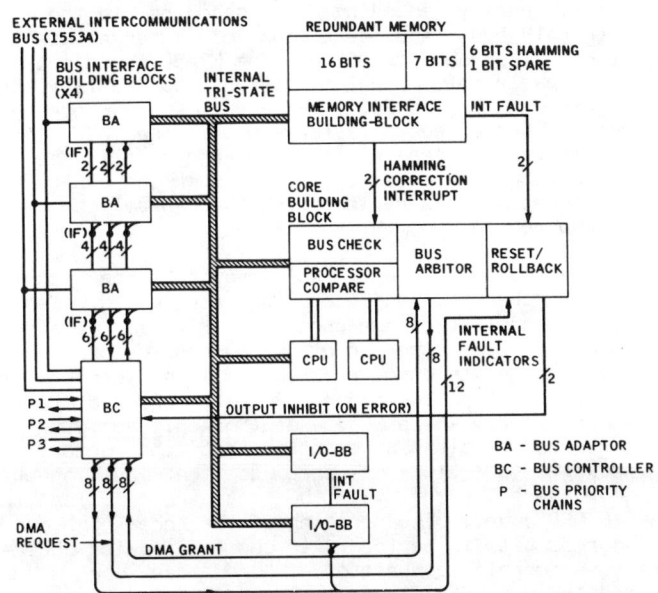

Figure 1: A Self-Checking Module (SCCM)

Repeated errors result in the disabling of the faulty SCCM by the Core-BB.

An important feature of this design is the reduction of hardcore elements by the use of morphic logic [2]. The SCCM is disabled by redundant power switches to its bus drivers and I/O drivers. They are controlled by a morphic "disable" signal from the Core-BB. Morphic logic is used throughout the Core-BB, its incoming error signals, and the checkers in the other BB circuits. Thus a faulty SCCM is designed to isolate itself from the rest of the system. Recovery is effected by another SCCM which is programmed to recognize the lack of activity from the faulty SCCM. The following is a brief description of the BB circuits used in the SCCM.

4. The Memory Interface BB (MI-BB)

The fault detecting and correcting MI-BB shown in Figure 2 interfaces a storage array (consisting of a redundant set of memory chips) to the SCCM internal bus. It provides Hamming correction to damaged

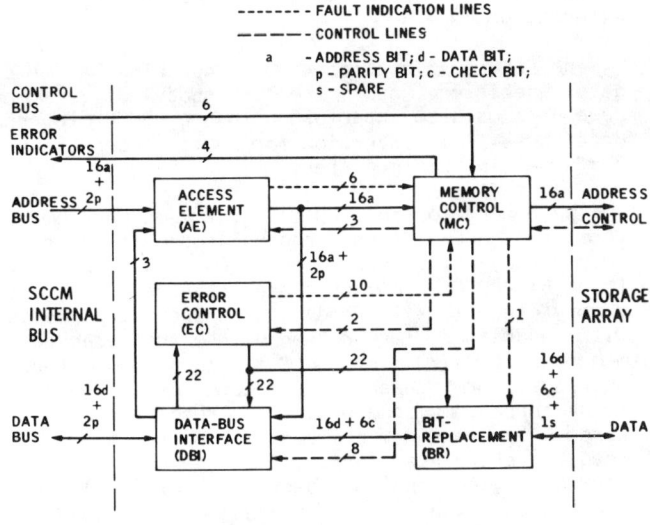

Figure 2: The Memory Interface Building Block (MI-BB)

memory data, replacement of a faulty bit with a spare, parity encoding and decoding to the SCCM internal bus, and detection of internal faults within its own circuitry. The MI-BB needs only to be capable of detecting errors to satisfy the requirement of a SCCM. However, memory represents most of the expected failures within the SCCM, and single-fault repair in this area will greatly improve SCCM reliability, even though the basic SCCM is treated as a replaceable (throw-away) item with backup spares.

The Access Element (AE) provides the address parity checking and decoding required to select a memory module (storage array plus MI-BB). It stores and validates the incoming address using a self-checking parity checker circuit. If no errors are detected, the low-order 13 bits are sent to the storage array where independent on-chip decoding is performed. (It is assumed that the memory is packaged one-bit per chip so that an on-chip addressing error will be detectable using the SEC/DED code.) The decoding of the three high order address bits is performed in duplex circuits checked by a morphic comparator. More than one memory module may be employed in the SCCM. The three high order address bits are used to select modules within the SCCM storage system. These bits are used as "soft names" and must be mapped into a physical module address. This mapping is carried out by a small associative memory, protected by duplication, which is loaded from the data bus in response to "Set Soft Name" commands.

The Error Control (EC) element is responsible for the generation of Hamming code check bits and syndromes, byte-parity generation and checking (for the SCCM internal bus), and error analysis. The circuits used in the EC are also self-testing. A single-bit error is corrected by decoding the syndrome generated from the word read from memory, in order to localize the faulty bit. The correction is performed by complementing the faulty bit. The correction mechanism can be disabled on system request to preserve the original data information for system diagnostics. An error analyzer within the EC collects various error indications such as single error, double error, and circuit error, which are recorded in an Error Status Word that can be transmitted over the external bus on system demand.

The Bit-Replacement (BR) element performs the reconfiguration of the storage array. It contains a multiplexor circuit which can replace any one bit plane in the memory with a single standby spare plane. The bit to be replaced is specified by an external command.

The Data Bus Interface (DBI) contains a memory data register and the tri-state drivers and receivers used to interface with the SCCM internal data bus. Bit inversion for Hamming correction is performed in this register.

The Memory Control (MC) element receives commands from the SCCM internal control bus which specifies "read" and "write" operations. For addresses less than 61,440 the commands are interpreted as normal memory operations. "Read" and "Write" instructions with addresses larger than 61,440 are reserved for memory-mapped I/O. A set of these out-of-range addresses are reserved for commands to the MI-BB. Among these commmands are: 1) read error status words, 2) read error position of faulty word, 3) read address of last error, 4) reset, 5) disable correction, 6) read redundant check bits, 7) replace a bit plane with a spare, and 8) set soft name.

From preliminary designs, the complexity of the MI-BB is estimated to be equivalent to 2000 gates. This implies a small failure rate with respect to the storage array. The MI-BB is readily implemented as a single LSI circuit.

5. The Bus Interface Building Block (BI-BB)

The BI-BB provides the mechanism by which information is transferred between SCCMs or between SCCMs and external I/O devices over the external bus system. The BI-BB can be microprogrammed to perform either the function of a Bus Adaptor or of a Bus Controller. The external bus system is being designed to utilize MIL STD 1553A communication formats and the Controller and Adaptor functions correspond to an "intelligent" version of the controller and terminal in that standard. Microprogrammed control is used in the BI-BB so that it can be reprogrammed to meet other communications formats.

The Bus Controller controls the movement of data over one of several external buses. Upon activation by its host SCCM, it reads a control table from the host SCCM's memory which specifies the source and destination of information required for the bus transfer along with the length of the transmission. The Controller then broadcasts the appropriate commands over the external bus system to "set-up" the transmitting and receiving Adaptors in other SCCMs. It monitors the subsequent transfer of information over the external bus, records status messages, and notifies the host SCCM upon completion of the transfer by means of an interrupt.

The Bus Adaptor serves as a passive interface to an external bus. After receiving a transmit command (over the external bus) by a Bus Controller, the Bus Adaptor locates the requested information in its host SCCM's memory. It extracts this information by cycle-stealing techniques and transmits it over the external bus. The Bus Adaptors designated (by the Bus Controller) as receivers extract this information from the bus and move it into specified areas in their host SCCM's memories. The SCCM can contain several Bus Adaptors to provide an interface to a number of redundant external buses. Communication with an SCCM can occur simultaneously over as many as three external buses without conflict (time delays) seen on any bus. A Bus Adaptor cannot initiate a bus transfer but only responds to the commands of a Bus Controller. Provision is made for sending discrete commands

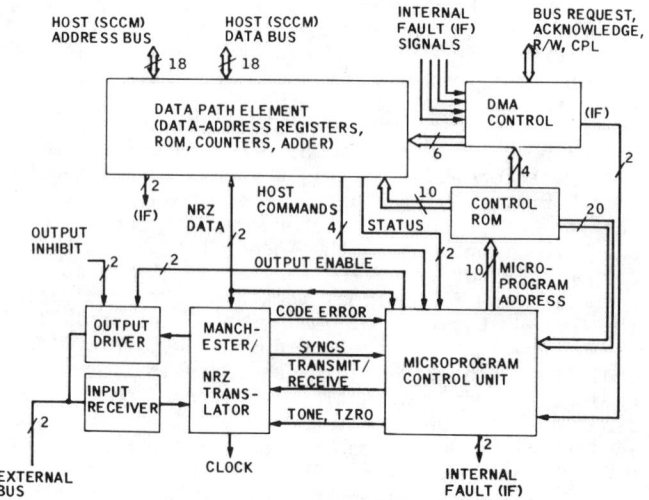

Figure 3: Bus Interface Building Block (BI-BB)

thorugh Bus Adaptors such as: power on, power off, halt, interrupt, reconfigure, etc.

The Bus Controller and Bus Adaptors are highly autonomous units which contain considerable internal microprogram sequencing to carry out their functions. A block diagram of the BI-BB is shown in Figure 3. It consists of five major elements, a Manchester/NRZ translator, a Microprogram Control Unit, a Control ROM, a Data Path Element, and a DMA Controller.

The Manchester/NRZ translator translates incoming Biphase Manchester into commands and data by supplying a bus-synchronized clock, command and data word-sync indicators, NRZ data, and parity and Manchester-error detection signals. It will also accept NRZ data, encode it, and output Manchester data for bus transmission, along with the associated commmand and data sync signals. This type of circuit is already available as a monolithic device.

The Microprogram Control Unit (MCU) is a microprogram sequencer. A microprogram location counter is started at one of several fixed addresses by command sync, data sync, or a host SCCM command (detection of an out-of-range address). The location counter proceeds through consecutive addresses or branches on the basis of incoming data, internal flags, or other internal circuit conditions. The microprogram sequencer is programmed to generate a unique set of address sequences for each type of incoming bus command, data sequence, or computer command. This output sequence is then mapped through a Control ROM to generate the detailed control signals required to drive the Data Path, MCU, and DMA Control elements. An additional function of the MCU is to collect morphic error indicators from the other BI-BB elements and also its own internal circuits. The error signals are reduced to a single internal fault output using a morphic reduction tree.

The Data Path element contains: 1) registers necessary to buffer addresses and data, 2) ROM to store memory protection bounds, data keys, and table addresses; and 3) an arithmetic-logic unit for addressing computations. The DMA Control element is responsible for obtaining control of the host SCCM's internal bus and transferring data between the BI-BB and host SCCM memory.

The fault detection techniques employed in the BI-BB are based on parity coding to protect memory information and duplication with morphic comparison for most of the logic circuitry. Preliminary designs indicate that this building block will have complexity equivalent to 7,000-10,000 gates.

6. The I/O Building Blocks (IO-BB)

Input-Output requirements of host systems in which the entire computer is embedded vary widely in voltage ranges, currents, and timing parameters. The approach best suited to building block development is to provide a standard set of functions which serve a majority of general applications. The user is required to supply any additional functions unique to his applications.

Candidate I/O functions are: 1) 16-bit parallel data in and out, 2) 16 bit serial data in and out, 3) a pulse sampling circuit, 4) a pulse counter, 5) a pulse generator, 6) an adjustable frequency generator, 7) an analog multiplexor with A/D converter, and 8) a high-rate DMA channel.

The circuitry for each I/O function is not complex and the implementation of fault detection is straightforward. Where bus information is preserved, parity checking is employed, other functions are protected by duplications with morphic comparison. The VLSI circuit density is sufficiently high that a number of I/O functions can be supplied on a single chip. The specific function which is required can be activated by connecting pins. This approach can reduce the inventory of I/O building blocks to two or three. One additional requirement is for redundant connection of I/O elements. To achieve redundancy in dedicated computer modules, two or more modules are cross-strapped; i.e., their inputs and outputs are hooked together. One computer is powered and the others are used as unpowered standby spares. When cross-strapped I/O is used, it is important that short-circuit protection be provided at all connections - otherwise a shorted I/O connection can inactivate all of the spares.

7. The Core Building Block (Core-BB)

The Core-BB is responsible for (1) detecting CPU (microprocessor) faults by synchronizing and comparing two duplex CPU's, (2) collecting fault indications from itself and other Building Blocks, and (3) disabling its host SCCM upon detection of a permanent fault. Three options are provided to attempt recovery from transient faults. These are: 1) Stop at first fault indication, wait for outside help; 2) rollback at first fault indication, stop if the fault recurs; 3) reload memory and restart, stop if fault recurs. In all cases Bus Controller and I/O outputs are inhibited as long as the SCCM is suspect; e.g., before a rollback or restart has been successfully completed.

Specific functions of the Core-BB are listed below: 1) compare two CPU's for disagreement; 2) parity encode CPU output for internal bus transmission; 3) check parity on the internal bus; 4) recognize Core-BB commands which can be sent from another SCCM through a Bus Adaptor as an out-of-range address (these are commands to halt and inhibit outputs, restart, and enable outputs of the receiving module); 5) allocate the internal tri-state bus amongst several DMA requests from the Bus Controllers, Adaptors, and I/O-BBs; 6) detect internal faults within the Core-BB; 7) collect internal fault indications from all others BBs within the SCCM; 8) disable SCCM output under fault conditions; 8) provide rollback/restart capability for transient fault recovery; 10) halt computation on recurring faults.

The Core-BB consists of three elements as shown in Figure 4. The Processor Check Element serves three functions: (1) to compare the outputs of two synchronous CPU's, (2) to encode and check internal bus parity, and (3) to recognize and decode commmands sent to the Core-BB through the internal bus. It contains self-checking parity checkers, a duplex command decoder, and morphic reduction trees.

The Bus Arbitration Element accepts morphic bus request signals from the various DMA controllers in other BB's. It obtains release of the internal bus by the CPU's, and grants access to requesting BB's on the basis of hardware priority. The Bus Available signal is sent as a morphic indicator to each requesting module. The Priority Resolver circuits are duplexed, one with true and the other with complement outputs and they are compared by a self-checking comparator.

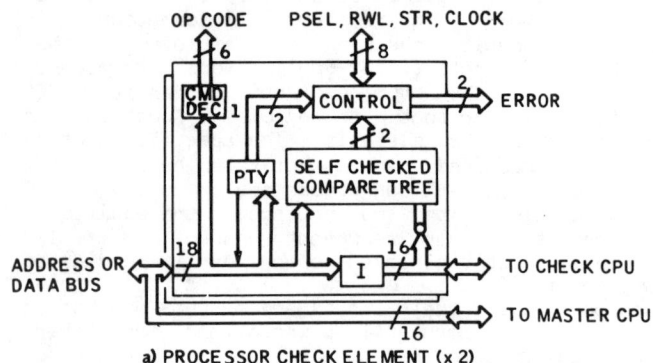

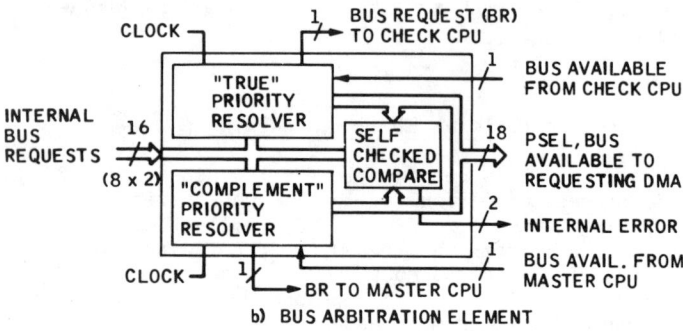

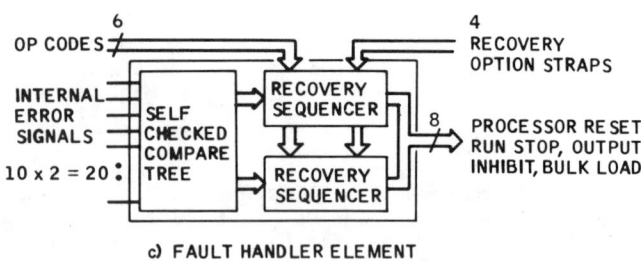

Figure 4: The Core Building Block

The Fault-Handler element accepts morphic fault indicators from the other BB's and from within the Core-BB. It reduces these to a single morphic master fault indicator which indicates a fault somewhere in the SCCM. This fault indicator triggers the removal of power from Bus Controllers output drivers, isolating the SCCM from the rest of the system. Duplex Recovery Sequencers are employed to implement optional transient recovery sequences. They are checked with a self-checking comparator.

8. Multiple Computer Configurations

With building block computer modules, such as the SCCM, which can detect their internal faults and disable themselves upon failure, it becomes possible to configure a set of these self-checking computers into a number of fault-tolerant configurations. Any set of SCCMs with redundancy can be viewed as a network in which intelligence exists at various places to detect and take over the function of a failed module. When several SCCMs are performing different tasks with a few back-up spares the configuration is a distributed system. When the machines and spares are dedicated to a single task, we have the simplified case of a single redundant computer. Thus, we will view all fault-tolerant configurations as networks of these self-checking machines.

A model architecture has been developed at the Jet Propulsion Laboratory for distributed processing. A breadboard has been constructed and used to implement the on-board processing functions of a planetary spacecraft [5]. The first breadboard has been built without fault-tolerant features, to evaluate the software and communications concepts which are employed. A second breadboard will utilize building-block SCCMs in a fault-tolerant configuration. This architecture, called the Unified Data System (UDS) is shown in Figure 5.

An advanced UDS architecture consists of a set of SCCMs connected by several external buses. The SCCMs, which utilize the same microprocessor and local software executive, fall into two types: (1) dedicated Terminal Modules, which are configured with I/O circuits to interface with peripheral subsystems (sensors, actuators, instruments, etc.) and with passive Bus Adaptors through which data can be entered or extracted from their local memories; and (2) non-dedicated High-Level Modules which are configured to coordinate the processing in various computers by control of an external (intercommunications) bus [6, 7]. A High-Level Module enters commands, data, and timing information into pre-arranged memory areas within the Terminal Modules. Each Terminal Module controls its local subsystem and delivers information to the UDS system by placing outgoing messages in predetermined locations of its memory, which are then extracted by a High-Level Module (via DMA) over the bus. The High-Level Modules are non-dedicated and contain little or no direct I/O functions.

9. Redundant Implementations

Since the Terminal Modules are connected directly to a specific peripheral subsystem, they must have dedicated spares which are also connected to the same subsystem. The amount of redundancy is determined by the criticality and failure rate of the associated subsystem. Since a Terminal Module cannot initiate a bus communication, it can only halt and signal an error. Recognition of a failed Terminal Module and commands for reconfiguration are the responsibility of a High-Level Module. High-Level Computer Modules are non-dedicated and can be backed up by a common pool of spares. In a distributed implementation, where several High-Level Modules perform different computations, we typically

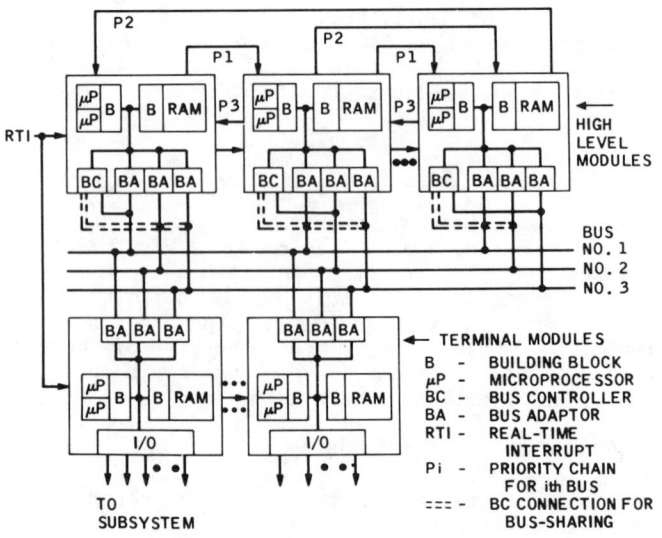

Figure 5: Distributed Building Block Computer Architecture

use a "hot" backup for critical functions, but not for functions which can allow the time to reload and restart a standby spare. (A "hot" backup is a spare SCCM which is programmed to take over a critical function and which maintains recent status information so that it can take over a failed function immediately). This property of not requiring "hot" backup modules for all computations reduces the sparing requirements.

Two fault-tolerant configurations are envisioned for the building-block SCCM systems: (1) distributed standby redundancy; and (2) a critical hybrid/voting configuration. In the standby-redundant configuration the High-Level Module containing the overall system control function is responsible for polling the various modules within the system to determine if a module has isolated itself due to a failure. This polling process can be carried out nearly automatically using the external bus system every few (10-100) milliseconds. (Bus system failures are determined by rerouting suspect messages through a different High-Level Module External Bus combination.) The High-Level Module is then responsible for directing the reload and/or reconfiguration function necessary to re-establish computation. Reconfiguration is accomplished through a Bus Adaptor by: (1) sending direct commands which set control levels in the module; (2) DMA inspection or loading of memory; or (3) effecting DMA read or write cycles to out-of-range addresses to directly command the Building Blocks. The controlling SCCM is backed up by a "hot" spare which interrogates its status and restart parameters on a periodic basis and which takes over upon failure of the master controller. In the critical hybrid/voting configuration two or more SCCMs are run concurrently with the same computations. If one fails, computation is continued by the other(s).

10. Conclusions

The current study has resulted in the definition and preliminary design of a small set of Building Block VLSI circuits which, if implemented, would allow the user to construct fault-tolerant systems out of existing microprocessors and memories in a straightfoward fashion. It has the significant advantage of allowing the use of proven processors and existing software. The next phase of this effort will be a detailed logic design of the four Building Block circuits and the implementation of a breadboard consisting of several SCCMs interconnected by the redundant external bus system. This step will be completed in 1979 and will provide the detailed experience necessary for a subsequent VLSI implementation of the Building Block circuits. When this step is accomplished, we expect that the systems engineer will have in hand the tools for the immediate and routine use of fault-tolerant computing.

11. Acknowledgment

This effort has been initiated by the Naval Ocean Systems Center, Code 923, San Diego, CA., and is being conducted at the Jet Propulsion Laboratory of the California Institute of Technology by agreement with the National Aeronautics and Space Administration. Part of the work was performed at the UCLA Computer Science Department under a subcontract from JPL. The work is sponsored by the Naval Electronic System Commmand, Washington, D.C., and directed by Mr. Nate Putler and Mr Larry Sumney of the Electronic Technology Division, ELEX 304. A special acknowledgement is due to Mr. Reeve Peterson and Dr. Ralph Martinez of the Naval Ocean Systems Center for their continued support and encouragement.

12. References

[1] A. Avizienis, "Fault-tolerant computing - progress, problems and prospects, " Proc. IFIP Congress 1977, Toronto, Canada, 405-420.

[2] W.C. Carter, et al., "Computer error control by testable morphic boolean functions - a way of removing hardcore," Digest 1972 Int. Symp. Fault-Tolerant Computing, June 1972, 154-159.

[3] D.A. Rennels, "Fault detection and recovery in a redundant computer using standby spares," Technical Report UCLA-ENG-7355, University of California, Los Angeles, June 1973.

[4] A. Avizienis, et al., "The STAR (Self-Testing-And-Repairing) computer: an investigation of the theory and practice of fault-tolerant computer design," IEEE Trans. Comput. vol. C-20, Nov. 1971, 1312-1321.

[5] D.A. Rennels, et al., "The Unified Data System: distributed processing network for control and data handling on a spacecraft," Proc. IEEE 1976 National Aerospace and Electronics Conf. (NAECON), May 1976, 283-289.

[6] B.M. Dobrotin and D.A. Rennels, "An application of microprocessors to a Mars roving vehicle," Proc. 1977 Joint Automatic Control Conf., June 22-24, 1977, 185-196.

[7] F. Lesh and P. Lecoq, "Software techniques for a distributed real-time processing system," Proc. IEEE 1976 National Aerospace and Electronics Conf. (NAECON), May 1976, 290-295.

AUTHORS

David A. Rennels was born in Terra Haute, Indiana. He received the B.S.E.E. ('64) from the Rose-Hulman Institute of Technology, the M.S.E.E. ('65) from Caltech and the Ph.D. ('73) in Computer Science from UCLA. He is currently a member of the Technical Staff at the Jet Propulsion Laboratory, working on fault-tolerant computing and distributed systems.

Algirdas Avižienis was born in Kaunas, Lithuania. He received the B.S. ('54), M.S. ('55) and Ph.D. ('60) degrees in Electrical Engineering from the University of Illinois. In 1960 he initiated research on fault-tolerant computing and later directed the JPL-STAR Computer project at JPL, where he is now an Academic MTS. Since 1962 he has been a faculty member at UCLA, where he is now a Professor in the Computer Science Department. He was the first chairman of the IEEE-CS TC on Fault-Tolerant Computing and the Chairman of FTCS-1 in 1971.

Miloš D. Ercegovac was born in Belgrade, Yugoslavia. He received his diploma ('65) in E.E. from the University of Belgrade and M.S. ('72) and Ph.D. ('75) degrees in Computer Science from the University of Illinois. He is currently an Assistant Professor in the Computer Science Department of UCLA. His research interests include computer architecture and fault-tolerant design, theory and practice of computer arithmetic, high speed systems and analysis of algorithms.

Fault Tolerance of a General Purpose Computer Implemented by Very Large Scale Integration

RICHARD M. SEDMAK and HARRIS L. LIEBERGOT

Reprinted from *IEEE Transactions on Computers*, Volume C-29, Number 6, June 1980, pages 492-400. Copyright © 1980 by The Institute of Electrical and Electronics Engineers, Inc.

Abstract—The construction of computer systems containing integrated circuit logic components with very large scale integration (VLSI), that is, many thousands of gates, is inevitable. Such levels of integration have already been achieved in memory components. There are significant problems in using some conventional fault-tolerant techniques in VLSI implementations for general purpose computers; consequently, modified approaches must be investigated.

This paper describes preliminary results of a research effort to design a general purpose computer with VLSI components which will achieve a level of fault detection, recovery, and failure isolation far exceeding non-VLSI implementations. The fundamental approach is to design and partition the logical elements in such a way that effective fault detection can be done by a novel method which places the detection responsibility inside the VLSI chip.

This approach results in an extremely high level of fault detection, and combined with certain other design techniques, also results in tolerance of most transient and many solid failures. Failure isolation is sufficiently exact that is unlikely that any diagnostic test or other maintenance action will be necessary to define the failing replaceable unit.

The rationale for the design tradeoffs which must be made in the development of a general purpose computer is also explored.

Index Terms—Availability, computer, fault detection, fault recovery, fault tolerance, maintainability, redundancy, reliability, self-checking, very large scale integration (VLSI).

I. INTRODUCTION

SEVERAL important past studies are pertinent to the background of this paper. Carter *et al.* [1] indicated in 1964 that intermittent failures contributed heavily to cases where systems were out of service for long periods of time, and that immediate detection of errors is of paramount importance in overcoming this problem. Carter and Schneider [2] discussed in 1968 the basic principles of self-checking circuits. In 1972, Mehta *et al.* [4] addressed the issue of internal redundancy but rejected it because the required redundancy was claimed to be excessive (more than double the simplex circuitry) and the technique was said to simplify only the diagnosis of internal faults. The authors suggested that an improved approach could be employed using an "Ambiguity Resolver" which, through an output testing circuit, simplifies the diagnosis of input faults. Arnold [5] in 1973 showed the importance of having fault detection and recovery for all of the elements of a machine in order to achieve high reliability.

Tanaka *et al.* [7] in 1977 described the use of duplication in some parts of a general purpose computer, the ACOS 800/900. Finally, an important paper by Carter *et al.* [8], at FTC7, concluded that complete checking of an LSI version of an IBM 360 would require (relative to the conventional 360 fault checking) only 6.5 percent more components, and that microinstruction and simple macroinstruction retry could be achieved with only one additional chip and no apparent speed degradation compared to the normal 360 performance.

II. BACKGROUND

The work whose results are described in this paper was an extension of a study aimed at designing an instruction processor and its associated input/output capability in such a way as to achieve lower cost and high reliability in the medium to large scale performance range. The vehicle technology for the original study was ECL LSI with scatterings of SSI and MSI. The subsequent study whose preliminary results are described in this paper concentrated on a VLSI (very large scale integration, more than 5000 gates/chip) implementation of the same design but with the major goal of improving cost and fault tolerance over the earlier version. An existing circuit technology and packaging were assumed but were coupled with future VLSI process parameters to allow the desired gate densities and propagation delays. A presupposition was that the high density was achievable and that yields and manufacturing costs were acceptable. The major question left to be addressed was how the thousands of gates in each chip could be most effectively employed in the design of a fault tolerant general purpose computer.

As is the case in most design efforts, three primary factors were considered and traded off against each other: cost, performance, and fault tolerance. In the past, systems engineers have realized that any attempt to improve significantly any one of those factors while holding another constant meant a significant degradation in the third factor. The advent of VLSI, however, seems to have affected that situation dramatically. Historically, a significant increase in the number of gates employed in a design translated directly into a rather significant rise in build cost. With VLSI, the economies are different: the rate of increase of cost as a function of added gates is greatly reduced. Thus, if a system designer wants to increase fault tolerance by adding circuitry while holding performance constant (or perhaps even increasing performance) the net

Manuscript received July 30, 1979; revised January 21, 1980.
The authors are with Sperry Univac, Blue Bell, PA 19424.

increase in manufacturing cost of the machine will be very small in comparison to costs for conventional designs of the past.

A. Fault-Tolerant Aspects

With respect to commercial general purpose computers, there are several parameters of the marketplace which affect the design of the fault-tolerant features, as follows:

1) Total fault masking via triple modular redundancy (TMR) is not needed if other techniques and procedures will limit down time to a small period relative to total production hours.

2) Maintenance calls to a customer site will be made for mechanical peripheral failures even if the central complex is failure-free. Thus, it is not absolutely necessary to provide a self-repairable central processor, although it is desirable to prevent emergency calls if the computer design can provide "deferrable" maintenance, particularly for the central complex.

3) Near 100 percent immediate fault detection is necessary; a fault must be detected in order to prevent generation of erroneous output, aid in error recovery, and provide failure isolation.

4) Complete recovery should be effected from transient or intermittent failures. This results partly from the extreme difficulty of locating such failures, and the fact that recovery can be accomplished primarily by temporal redundancy (retry) and so recovery is relatively economical.

5) The largest part of a service call is usually devoted to diagnosis. Therefore, low downtime is made possible by rapid fault isolation, hopefully without human intervention.

The fault-tolerant aspects of the proposed VLSI machine are designed to satisfy the preceding parameters.

III. General Structure of the Central Complex

The architecture of the processor described in this paper is based on a medium to large scale Sperry Univac 9000 Series CPU with virtual storage. A single macro-stream execution is carried out without the use of macro execution look ahead. Variable length instructions are permitted, as are byte-formatted and word-formatted data. The machine is microprogrammed with the bulk of the intelligence residing in microcode. Thus, very little random control logic is employed for acceleration of instruction execution. This last characteristic is primarily an outgrowth of the original version of the design rather than the VLSI implementation, where a bit of splurging in hardware to gain performance is economically justifiable.

Within the instruction processor, there is high utilization of resources such as shifters, buses, and register stacks. In addition, a large amount of time multiplexing is carried out during the four clock phases of the microcycle. Input/output is handled via a byte-oriented multichannel interface integrated into the processor. I/O activity is dealt with through interrupt driven microcode, although a significant amount of capability exists within the individual channels' logic.

Although an MOS circuit technology was assumed that lends itself to VLSI, other high-speed high-density technologies could also be used. It is because of the high gate densities that major improvements in fault tolerance can be made without commensurate additions to cost. A packaging approach was assumed that was compatible with VLSI circuit behavior and characterized by controlled interconnection parameters and multilayered printed circuit boards and backpanel.

By far the most important fault-tolerant feature in the computer design is fault detection. It is the cornerstone for the total fault-tolerant capability. It should be noted that the detection coverage includes not only IC chip failures, but also transient power fluctuations, clock failures, and mechanical interconnection failures such as backboard shorts, open foils, loose cables, etc. Thus, a fundamental design criterion for this machine is near 100 percent single fault detection, as detailed in the succeeding paragraphs.

IV. Detailed Fault-Tolerant Characteristics

Several important techniques have been employed in order to meet the preceding design objectives of fault detection, isolation, and recovery. These methods are listed below and will be discussed in order:

1) Internal redundancy using "complementary logic."
2) Error handling chip.
3) Error detection/correction codes and redundancy for checking interchip circuit networks.
4) Self-checking error checkers.
5) External to chip checking.

A. Generalized VLSI Chip

Fig. 1 shows the general structure of a typical VLSI chip in the proposed design. The bulk of the logic is contained in the area labeled Functional Logic and an area of approximately equal size labeled Duplicate Complementary Logic. The outputs of these blocks of logic as well as various intermediate results are fed to Comparators 1 to n. Output data and control information with code (ECC or parity) pass to the output pins.

The functional and duplicate circuits receive input data and control information from the input pins. This information is checked by Input Code Checkers 1 to m to verify that the input data are correct.

Power and ground inputs are redundant, and are fed separately to the functional and duplicate logic. The redundant power inputs are checked by a comparator. Clock inputs are fed to another checker, and also to logic blocks.

All checker outputs are in turn sent to the Error Multiplexing and Encoding Logic which feeds other output pins.

B. Fault Detection and Handling Techniques

1) Internal Redundancy Using "Complementary Logic"

An example of the kind of complementary duplication which is used in the VLSI chips is shown in Fig. 2. From the figure it is easy to see that for a given combinational logic element in the functional portion, the signals into and out of the gate will be of polarities opposite to those of the complementary portion. With sequential logic the same physical elements are

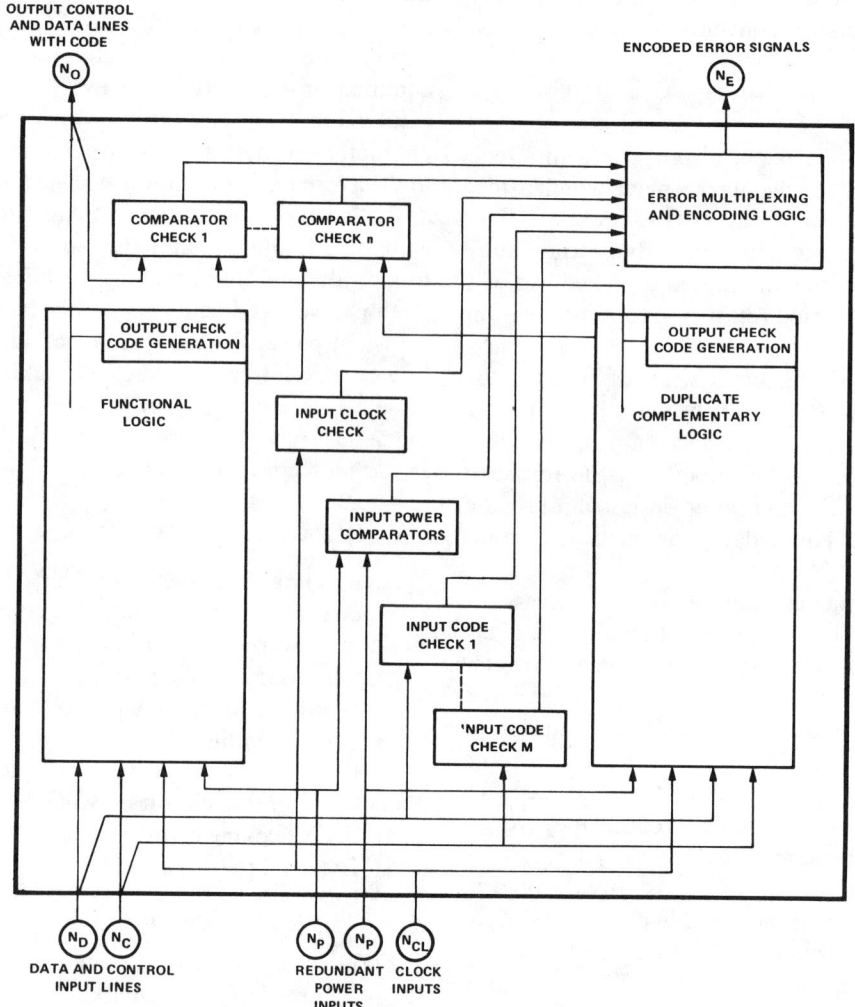

Fig. 1. Generalized VLSI chip.

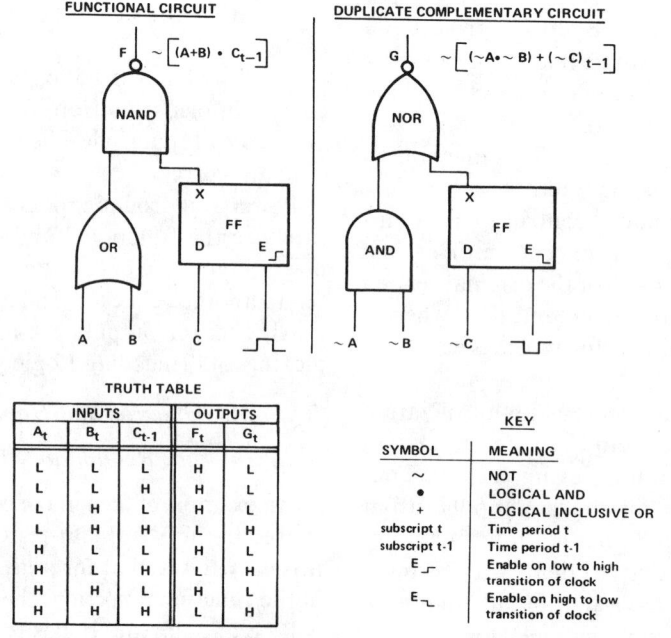

Fig. 2. Example of functional versus duplicate complementary circuits.

used; however, control signals and data stored in the functional logic have opposite polarities to those in the complementary logic. This technique serves two purposes: Firstly, it will eliminate a problem associated with applying the same mask or cell types twice internally—once for the functional logic and again for the redundant circuit. The problem is that failures (design, process, and wearout) undetected by the comparators could occur in noncomplementary duplication where a mask or cell fault might materialize in both the functional and duplicate circuits and thus create identical failure states. Secondly, the design with complementary duplication will be much less susceptible to bridging faults than noncomplementary duplication. This is due to the fact that there will be far fewer cases of long nets of metallization with the same Boolean function and the same polarity signal, which if bridged might result in an undetected error should a subsequent failure occur.

It has been discovered during the logic partitioning process that it is desirable to have, internal to each chip, one to four comparators, each associated with one of the four machine clock phases. Each comparator checks signals which are stable during the respective phases. This conclusion stems from the fact that, due to the high density of internal logic, it is often necessary to make comparisons of intermediate data or control results, rather than wait for the delayed chip outputs to become valid for comparison. For example, suppose in a given microinstruction, a register file embedded within a VLSI chip is written into but not subsequently read out until many microinstructions or even macroinstructions later. If a comparison is made only at the chip's final outputs, a failure to write the register properly would not be detected until much later, when the reading takes place; by that time a retry procedure might be impossible since needed retry data may have been discarded. If, however, a comparison of intermediate results is carried out, such as comparing the updated registers, the fault could be detected early enough to accomplish the retry. Using the same reasoning, it is evident that the practice of *externally* duplicating chips and comparing them is much less practical and useful with the advent of VLSI.

2) Error Handling Chip (EHC)

All error signals in the CPU are routed to VLSI chips known as the Error Handling Chips EHC's (for a given design, one may be sufficient if the number of error signals is low enough). Within this logic a portion of the merging, sorting, and isolation of faults takes place. As shown in Fig. 3, the EHC employs the various techniques depicted in Fig. 1, including internal duplication and fault detection. However, because of the critical nature of this logic, the EHC receives both the processor and console clocks (the console has a stand-alone, intelligent microprocessor), internally detects a failure in either one, and automatically switches to the operational clock inputs. Thus, a failure of the CPU clock will not prevent the correct status from being reported.

When more than one EHC is used, a tree structure is employed for the interconnection scheme. All the encoded error signals from the various VLSI chips come into the first level

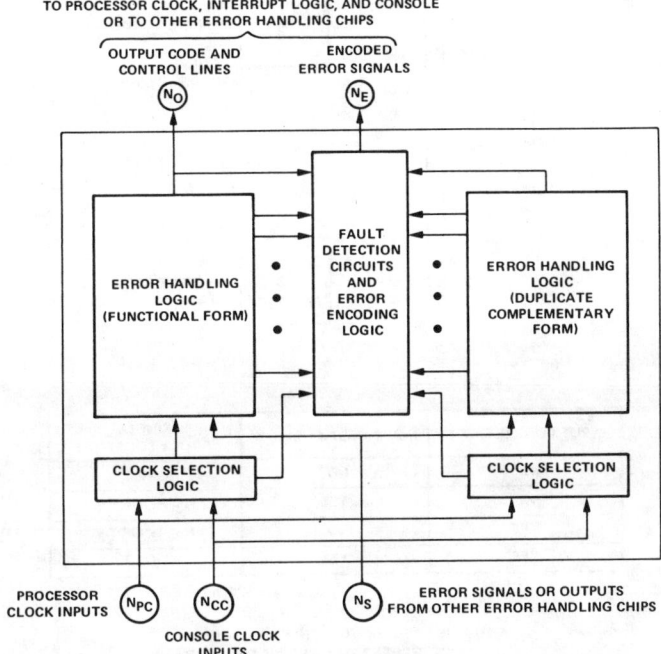

Fig. 3. Error Handling Chip.

of EHC's. At each level of the tree some preprocessing is carried out which results in a combining of the input error codes into a single code word of much fewer bits, through compaction of information (elimination of redundancies, removal of irrelevant data, etc.). After the various levels of preprocessing, the final outputs of the EHC tree are distributed to the microprogram control store addressing in order to carry out an error interrupt of the microcode. These outputs are also sent to the master clock generation for sequence controlling and to the stand-alone console for final fault processing and subsequent display of error status. By virtue of the internal checking schemes in the EHC, failures in these chips are also communicated to the console for display. There may be a need to provide fault injection capabilities for the EHC since it contains logic that reacts to error conditions and therefore does not change state frequently.

3) Error Detection/Correction Codes and Redundancy for Checking Interchip Nets

Referring again to Fig. 1, it has been indicated that error checking codes are carried on all compatible data or control lines between chips; in the case of singular or nonhomogeneous lines (such as a clear line), redundancy is employed. The primary code utilized is simple parity, or in cases where timing and pins permit, an ECC code.

An important characteristic of the approach considered in this study is that more than one fault detection circuit will exist in each VLSI chip and, in many cases, several chips will be in the same net, monitoring the same outputs. As a result of the vast amount of fault information available, a fine degree of isolation can be achieved during the preprocessing in the EHC's and final processing in the console logic. A simple case of isolating faults by monitoring of the outputs from several

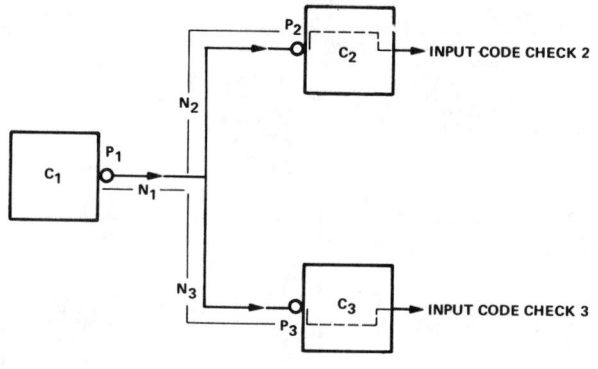

INPUT CODE CHECK 2?	INPUT CODE CHECK 3?	SINGLE FAULT LOCATION
NO	NO	NONE
NO	YES	N_3, P_3, OR C_3
YES	NO	N_2, P_2, OR C_2
YES	YES	N_1 OR P_1

NOTES
(1) "C" REFERS TO A CHIP
"N" REFERS TO A NET (SET OF SIGNALS)
"P" REFERS TO "PINS" (A SET OF PINS)
(2) ASSUMES NO INTERNAL CHIP FAILURE DETECTED IN C1.

Fig. 4. Single failure isolation in multiple branch net.

distinct error checking circuits is illustrated in Fig. 4. The diagram indicates that, depending on the combination of the two input code checks, the fault location can be isolated to one of the two net branches and its receiving chip, or to the portion of the net before the branch and its associated output pins.

4) Self-Checking Checkers

Each of the code checkers and comparators is implemented using a self-checking design approach. Therefore, each detection circuit is fault secure and self-testing for a single failure; special diagnostic procedures are not required to test it. Fig. 5 shows a sample circuit (described by Anderson [3]) that could be used in the construction of a self-checking comparator. This design represents only one approach; other circuits which are capable of distinguishing between single faults internal and external to the checker itself are presently being researched and could lead to even better isolation capabilities. The circuit in Fig. 5 when employed as a two bit comparator indicates a miscompare or checker failure when its outputs are the same and no failure when the outputs are different. A nice characteristic of this circuit is that its outputs will vary from (1, 0) to (0, 1) as the nonfaulty inputs vary, thus, expediting the detection of a fault in the checker. Since all of the nonchecker logic is redundant, and all checker logic is self-checking, the internal chip is completely checked for all single and many multiple faults.

As shown in Fig. 1, the various error checkers all feed into logic which multiplexes and encodes the signals for transmission to the EHC. This logic is also self-checking as are the encoded error signals. The purpose of the encoding approach is to reduce the number of output pins required for the error signals.

5) "External to Chip" Checking

In order to be complete in the fault detection design, the areas of power and clock generation and distribution must be handled and merit special mention. Since complete redundancy of power is not a design objective, there will be only one of each type power supply used. Appropriate sensors will detect supply failures at the output. From the output, power is supplied to each VLSI chip via multiple distinct backpanel buses, PC board connector pins, PC board buses, and VLSI chip pins. The signals at power pins from separate distribution runs are compared internally in the VLSI chip and a miscompare causes a unique error indication. This technique has the virtue of isolating a very troublesome failure (power distribution net) rather exactly.

The four phase clock system is distributed to almost all of the VLSI chips. Faults in the generation or distribution are detected by sending the master oscillator pulse train to each chip that receives the clocks and by implementing a local detection circuit on each of those chips. The following types of faults are detected through the circuit, which is driven by the crystal oscillator's buffered output:

a) Faulty oscillator.
b) Missing single or multiple phases.
c) Extreme out of tolerance phases(s).
d) Out of sequence phases(s).

By monitoring all VLSI chips for clock fault detections, the EHC will permit isolation of the failure to the clock generator, distribution net and pins, or to the receiving chip.

6) Checking Scheme Considerations

Various advantages and disadvantages can be identified for the internal checking scheme described in the preceding paragraphs. In its favor are the following points:

a) All single and many multiple transient or stuck-at faults detected.
b) Many bridging or shorting faults detected.
c) Many timing problems and race conditions can be found by virtue of the two different implementations internal to the chip.

On the other hand, several disadvantages can be cited:

a) More design time and effort are necessary for the two internal implementations even though the algorithms are the same. (However, effort is always needed to incorporate any fault tolerance in a design.)
b) The approach uses much of the gate density regardless of the partitioning of the logic. (However, because of pin limitations in VLSI, the number of usable internal gates will most likely be restricted.)
c) The internal duplication only simplifies the diagnosis of faults internal to a chip. (The problem has been dealt with through the incorporation of conventional checking techniques for detecting faults on interchip nets and pins. It should also be kept in mind that the redundancy scheme in itself greatly enhances failure isolation over other standard approaches.)
d) The complementary logic may be slightly slower than the functional logic due to the possible need for additional logic levels. The translation from functional to complementary logic

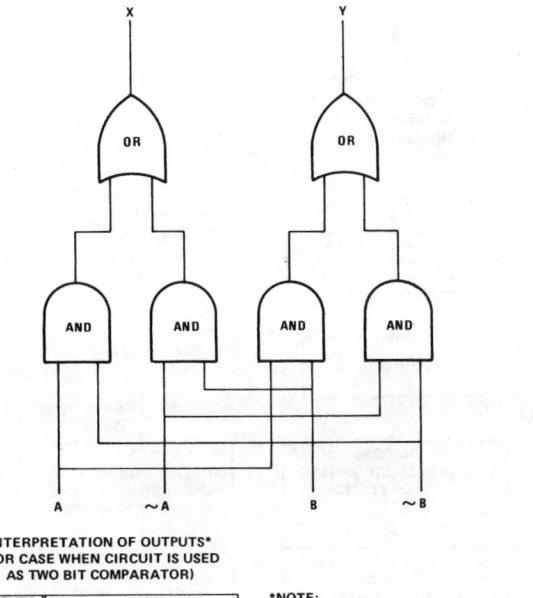

Fig. 5. Self-checking comparator: Possible basic building block circuit.

is not always on a one element to one element basis. (However, a balancing effect may occur since it sometimes requires fewer logic levels to implement the complementary version. In addition, even a net increase in the delay in the complementary version will not affect the overall machine performance and a delay can be tolerated by the detection logic.)

e) Although the pin limitation problem in VLSI has been identified, this fault tolerant approach seems to use more pins than conventional techniques. (However, for a small percentage increase of pins used for fault tolerance, error detection, recovery, and isolation characteristics have been dramatically improved over conventional techniques. In addition, a much higher utilization of the VLSI gate density is accomplished.)

C. Fault Recovery

The basic philosophy of fault recovery in this design is to mask solid failures only in the memories (main and control) via ECC, but attempt recovery from intermittent/transient failures anywhere else in the machine via an appropriate retry technique.

The ECC is a standard single error correcting/double error detecting implementation, and need not be further described. Single bit errors can be logged for failure isolation. However, it is valuable to indicate a certain philosophy here—that of putting as much control logic as possible in the control memory, rather than utilizing hardwired control logic. This is a fundamental design goal which results from the ease and economy of doing control logic fault recovery in memories via ECC.

Operation retry is the fundamental recovery technique for nonmemory faults. The three machine states of interest when a fault is detected are macroinstruction execution, I/O operations (since the channels are integrated with the CPU), and interrupt decode. In each case sufficient data will be stored to enable retry to take place from the appropriate restart point. A general flow of the actions of the machine when a fault is detected is shown in Fig. 6.

The particular VLSI chip or chips which detected the fault will send an error code to the Error Handling Chip. Several actions will then occur. The error code will be stored in a status register as a unique indicator of the fault. A signal is sent to the console to alert it that an error recovery sequence is being undertaken. (The console is a logically separate unit controlled by its own microprocessor and clock.) The console reads the error status register in the EHC and logs the data. The status that has been stored will point to the particular chip which failed, or may indicate that the failure was not in a chip. The CPU clock is stopped and a delay timer activated in order to allow any transient failures to pass.

After the delay has expired, the CPU clock is restarted and a retry microroutine is entered which attempts to retry the failing macroinstruction, interrupt, or channel function. This routine uses data which have been saved during the function execution in order to perform a valid retry operation. If the microroutine itself fails to operate correctly because the same or another error is detected, a second error code to the EHC will activate a solid failure procedure. In this case the CPU is stopped and a second signal is sent to the console microprocessor. Since the console microprocessor will have available some mass storage such as a floppy disk, it can take the error status and format a message to the console screen even with the CPU inactive. Due to the partitioning of the fault detection, the status will usually be sufficient to indicate the replaceable

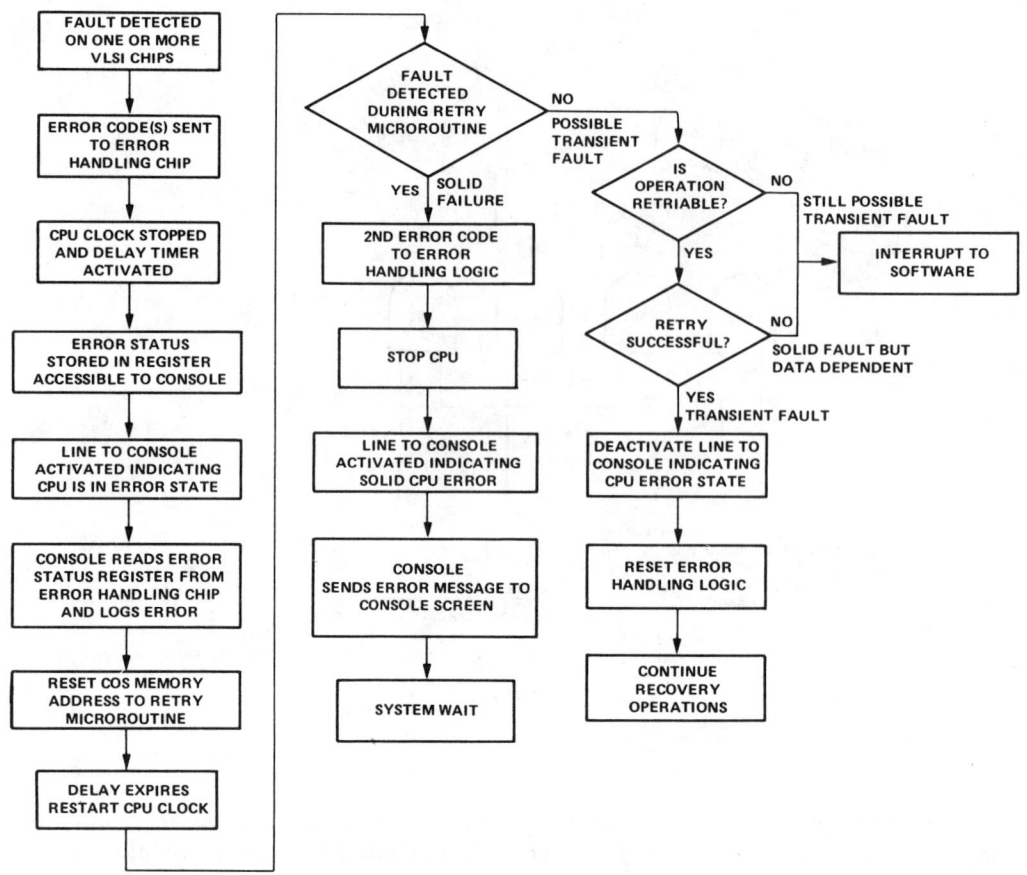

Fig. 6. Fault recovery procedure.

unit. So the message will appear resembling the following.

    CPU SOLID FAILURE
    CARD #28
    CHIP #A14

which indicates which VLSI chip on which printed circuit card has failed. Maintenance action is thus limited to chip replacement. A failure in the EHC itself will cause the same result via a separate set of lines to the console.

The rest of the retry routine is relatively conventional. If the retry is successful, the console microprocessor is notified accordingly. In this case, the console microprocessor will merely log the recoverable error status for future reference. If the retry is unsuccessful, an interrupt is taken to the software for appropriate action. In all cases the error status is recorded.

Thus, the design criteria in the fault recovery area are met: correction of single faults in the memory, retry of operations when faults occur in other areas, logging, and isolation of the faults.

A question which might arise involves the possibility of running simplex when a fault is detected in a VLSI chip. This would involve extra circuitry to allow the duplicated circuits to be run independently. Upon detection of a failure, test patterns would be run on each circuit to try to isolate the failure to one circuit or the other. Operations would then continue with the remaining circuit until the whole chip is replaced. This approach has not been actively considered because it violates one of the design criteria since there would be no fault detection in the chip running in simplex mode. The detailed failure isolation provided makes it unlikely that a machine would be out of service for an extended period, so the need for the simplex mode operation appears slight.

D. Failure Isolation

It may be of interest to note that the cost of maintenance of a system to the manufacturer may exceed the build cost over the system's lifetime. The main costs are due to diagnostics development and support, training, initial spare parts, customer engineering labor and replacement parts.

In a recent internal study of a system which does not have quite the detection/recovery/isolation capabilities described in this paper, the maintenance costs were estimated as follows:

Labor (Including Travel Time)	34 percent
Initial Spare Parts	26
Replacement Parts	21
Training	6
Diagnostic Development and Support	5
Other	8
Total	100 percent

It is expected that the design of this new machine will result in cost reductions in all of the above categories, in some cases by a significant amount.

The philosophy of having the logic partitioning and error detection immediately point to the replaceable unit means that for most failures diagnostics will be unnecessary. It was pointed out in the previous section that an unrecoverable error in the CPU will cause a message to be generated on the console screen which identifies the failing chip. Thus the diagnostic development effort is reduced, but not eliminated entirely, since verification of repair and general machine exercise programs will still be needed.

Certain failures such as backboard shorts, foil opens, power distribution and clock distribution failures may not point to the replaceable unit. In these cases, maintenance actions are suggested based on the ease of replacement. For example, if the input data or control signals to a VLSI chip are incorrect (see Fig. 4) then the failure could be at the chip pin input, the foil on the card containing the chip, in the backboard, the foil on the card from where the signals originated, or the output pin of the chip from where the signal originated. The console screen will indicate the appropriate procedure based on the error isolation provided—either chip or card replacement or a more extensive effort to examine the backboard and connectors. However, chip failures often constitute the majority of failures in a mature product.

It is quite obvious that the preceding types of failure indications lead to the ability to repair failures without the need for extensive training on diagnostic procedures, which forms the bulk of current training programs. The repair would usually be effected by a replacement of an IC chip, and possibly this chip would be socket mounted to ease the replacement process. So the cost of training customer engineers should be quite reduced.

In discussing initial spares and replacement parts, it is instructive to note that frequently the cost of multilayer printed circuit cards exceeds the cost of the chips which are contained on the card. In current systems where the replaceable unit is the card, the cost of initial spares is quite high, since a set of unique cards is required for each machine or for several machines depending on geographical proximity. Replacement costs are also high since the replaced board must be repaired and retested if possible, or scrapped otherwise. But in the proposed design, the replaceable unit is the chip (in most cases), and a set of chips can be placed in an appropriate geographical position (perhaps at each site). Of course, a set of boards may be required at some depot when the failure is a board failure rather than a chip failure. But this failure rate is much lower than the chip failure rate. Therefore, the cost of initial spares is markedly reduced, and replacement costs are less because there is much less board repair required.

Finally, it can be expected that labor costs will be reduced. Even if the failure rate of the machine were to be the same as current machines, the time to diagnose a problem will be cut dramatically on the average, and diagnosis is frequently up to 85 percent of the repair time. The reduction in diagnosis time will come about by the recovery from most intermittent errors without repair, by the logging of such recoveries indicating which chip is intermittent so that repair can take place when convenient, by reduction of diagnosis time per man, and by the near elimination of "difficult" problems which require excessive personnel and time.

E. Testing

The area of testing, particularly test set generation, has not been studied extensively for this project as yet. However, it is apparent that the necessity for testing is dramatically reduced with the proposed design. While testing general purpose computers at customer sites is currently used extensively for diagnostic purposes, the use of testing in the proposed design will be primarily for general system verification, usually at the beginning of the day or after a repair is made. As mentioned, diagnosis and isolation of the replaceable unit is intended to be automatic, in most cases. The penalty for a nonperfect test set will not be an undiscovered fault which might compromise data integrity, but rather detection of the fault at a less desirable time, i.e., during user operation, through dynamic checking hardware.

It is possible that development of a detailed test approach might affect the design somewhat, particularly if additional I/O pins on the VLSI chip are needed to access internal test points. However, note that with no additional points added, testing is still easier than in conventional highly microprogrammed CPU's, since with automatic fault detection the output of a test does not have to be compared with known correct data.

V. General

A. Effect of Design on Failure Rate

Since there is more circuitry and a few more chips in the proposed VLSI design than in an unchecked VLSI implementation, the absolute failure rate will be somewhat increased over an unchecked version. Limited experience on VLSI chip failure rates (and the fact that an unchecked design was never done in detail) makes it difficult to estimate precisely the difference in MTBF. Even so, the absolute failure rate is not necessarily the most important measure, since in current systems a single physical failure may cause multiple system failures. The physical failure may be intermittent or data dependent and the consequent difficulty of diagnosing the failure leads to the multiple system failures.

The proposed design offers two advantages which will tend to reduce the system failure rate. Firstly, the high degree of immediate fault detection and effective retry design means that few intermittent failures will cause a system failure since successful recovery is expected in most cases. Secondly, the detailed automatic error isolation will generally indicate the failing replaceable unit even on a transient failure; and thus, a replacement can be made easily after the first detected fault.

While VLSI chip failure information is scanty, it is likely that intermittent faults due to internal chip failure modes as well as design imperfections (noise, loading, race conditions) will be a fact of life. Therefore, it seems quite justified to add the additional detection/recovery/isolation circuitry which may lower the MTBF somewhat in order to raise the Mean Time Between System Failure significantly.

B. Cost Effectiveness

In considering the added cost of the approach discussed in this paper, it should be kept in mind that in designing with VLSI, the pin factor poses the greatest limitation. Internal duplication takes advantage of the often unusable logic space and at the same time requires very few signal pins for off-chip nets. In line with this reasoning, preliminary studies show that triple modular redundancy (TMR) could also be a practical technique to use in this technology. It is interesting to note that the pin limitation problem also necessitates the use of time multiplexing, busing, serializing, and encoding methods for interchip nets. Such tactics also facilitate the use of the various error checking code schemes discussed in this paper.

In comparison with MSI/LSI machines of this type, VLSI offers a reduction in the total number of logic boards and board types, lower cost, and at least similar performance. However, in contrast to a VLSI version using conventional fault detection techniques only (such as internal parity or other simple codes), the design described offers better isolation, detection of a larger set of faults, quicker detection and recovery, a drastic reduction in the need for diagnostics, and a much simpler maintenance procedure.

An examination of cost considerations reveals some surprising results. The logic overhead associated with fault tolerance consists of the duplicate complementary gates, comparators and other fault detection circuits, and Error Handling Chip logic. These circuits comprise approximately 55 percent of the total gates in the CPU. However, if one examines the incremental number of gates added to the design to proceed from a conventionally checked VLSI machine to the one presented here, the increase in VLSI *chip count* is only 5.5 percent. (A conventionally checked VLSI machine is assumed to be one having parity code on memories, complete checking for single faults in the data path, but no fault detection in the control logic.) Part of the reason for such a small percentage increase is the pin limitation effect discussed previously, whereby present VLSI chip design is bound more often by the number of pins than by the gate density. Thus the technique described here, which utilizes a large number of the unusable gates, does not require a large addition to the chip count over a conventionally checked VLSI computer. Note that the 5.5 percent chip count increase is based on the numbers of gates and pins assumed and the functions to be implemented for the proposed design. Other assumptions or functions might change this percentage, but the general conclusions on cost effectiveness should remain the same. It should also be noted that CPU's of the range described in this proposal at present typically form only 15 to 20 percent of the total system hardware cost, with peripherals forming the bulk of the rest of the cost.

VI. Conclusion

The advent of VLSI brings with it both unique problems and unique solutions in the design of the fault-tolerant capabilities of a general purpose computer. Conventional fault detection techniques which presume single bit failures may not be appropriate to some failure modes in chips of extremely high density. Even external duplication of chips results in a difficult recovery situation since a great deal of processing may have occurred between the time of physical failure and detection of the fault. However, the large number of gates available in VLSI combined with limited input/output pins permits the use of the general approach described in this paper and results in vastly superior fault-tolerant characteristics for a small cost increase.

The proposed design approach results in
1) Immediate detection of transient or stuck-at single faults.
2) Immediate detection of most multiple faults.
3) Immediate detection of most bridging faults.
4) Immediate detection of power and clock failures.
5) Opportunity to recover from most transient/intermittent failures.
6) Automatic isolation of the failing chip or interchip circuit network.
7) Small chip count increase (5.5 percent) over conventionally checked VLSI design.

References

[1] W. Carter et al., "Design of serviceability features for the IBM System/360," *IBM J.*, pp. 115-126, Apr. 1964.
[2] W. Carter and P. Schneider, "Design of dynamically checked computers," in *Proc. IFIP 68*, 1968, pp. 878-883.
[3] D. A. Anderson, "Design of self-checking digital networks using coding technique," Univ. of Illinois Coordinated Sci. Lab. Rep. R-527, Sept. 1971.
[4] M. A. Mehta et al., "Functions for improving diagnostic resolution in an LSI environment," in *Spring Joint Comput. Conf, AFIPS Conf. Rec.*, 1972.
[5] J. F. Arnold, "The concept of coverage and its effect on the reliability model of a repairable system," *IEEE Trans. Comput.*, vol. C-22, pp. 251-255, Mar. 1973.
[6] M. Breuer and A. Friedman, *Diagnosis and Reliable Design of Digital Systems*. Woodland Hills, CA: Computer Science Press, 1976.
[7] N. Tanaka et al., "Computer with designed-in duplication at device, module level," Tokyo Nikkei Electronics, Mar. 21, 1977.
[8] W. Carter et al., "Cost effectiveness of self-checking computer design," in *Proc. Int. Conf. FTC*, June 1977.

Richard M. Sedmak was born in Philadelphia, PA on March 17, 1949. He received the B.S. degree in electrical engineering in 1971 and the M.S. degree in business administration in 1973, both from Lehigh University, Bethlehem, PA.

Since joining the Sperry Univac, division of Sperry Corporation, Blue Bell, PA, in 1971, he has held various positions in system research and development organizations. Currently serving as Manager of Availability, Reliability, and Maintainability, he is engaged primarily in hardware and software reliability efforts.

Harris L. Liebergot was born in Philadelphia, PA on October 23, 1943. He received the B.S. degree in physics and the M.S. degree in electrical engineering from Drexel University, Philadelphia, PA, in 1966 and 1971, respectively. He is currently working towards the Ph.D. degree in information science at Drexel University.

In 1967 he joined the Sperry Univac, division of Sperry Corporation, Blue Bell, PA, as a Diagnostic Programmer. Since then he has held various positions in hardware and software design and communications systems reliability. He is currently Manager, System Availability in the Product Strategy and Requirements Department.

Want to select your level of fault tolerance? Intel's 432 offers three FT levels and the possibility of configuring a continuously operating system from mass-produced components.

The Intel 432: A VLSI Architecture for Fault-Tolerant Computer Systems

Dave Johnson, Intel Corporation

Reprinted from *Computer*, Volume 17, Number 8, August 1984, pages 40-48. Copyright © 1984 by The Institute of Electrical and Electronics Engineers, Inc.

In the past, fault-tolerant computer systems occupied a relatively narrow niche in the computer systems market. Most were—and are—designed to provide solutions for specific applications. As computers continue to take over more and more tasks critical to the successful operation of stores, hospitals, factories, and offices, the demand for fault tolerance and the scope of fault-tolerant systems has increased. Applications have expanded beyond the multimillion-dollar mainframe computer rooms and NASA satellites that brought the original demand for fault tolerance.

Current application needs for fault tolerance reflect five concerns:

(1) Reliability. Greater reliability is essential in even the most basic computer applications. As the cost of the system decreases, the cost of maintenance and downtime grow to dominate system life-cycle costs, dovetailing with the users' need for less expensive maintenance approaches. System manufacturers must offset the increasing cost of field service with systems that are more reliable and allow deferred repair.

(2) Integrity. The system must be able to detect failures, whether the applications are those of international corporations or small businesses with office automation file servers, but once a failure has occurred, the system must restore the data to a consistent state before allowing computation to proceed.

(3) Availability. As on-line access to information becomes more essential to an operation, long periods of downtime become less and less tolerable. The system must have the redundant resources to permit quick recovery. The allowable downtime varies, ranging from milliseconds for real-time control to five or 10 minutes for less critical office functions.

(4) Degradation. Some applications require the computer equipment to operate in isolated locations (drilling sites, relay stations, etc.). For these applications, the computer system must continue functioning for very long periods of time, even if operation of the system is degraded. Graceful degradation also permits a system manufacturer to defer repair of a system until a convenient time.

(5) Continuous operation. Because downtime can cause loss of business income—or even loss of life—continuous operation is required. Downtime must be held to an absolute minimum.

Matching the expanding demand for fault tolerance are the unfolding capabilities of VLSI. VLSI offers high functionality with low cost and high reliability per function. It can provide the added functionality and redundancy required in FT systems without adversely impacting system cost and reliability. Its technology can accommodate the growing demands for fault-tolerant systems.

Replication as a design strategy

Replication of standard building blocks to construct systems is a design strategy consistent with the needs of fault-tolerant systems and the constraints of VLSI technology. While traditionally a good engineering practice, until recently replication has been confined to relatively small subunits of a system. It simply was not cost-effective to construct a family of systems from a small set of building blocks based on a single technology.

Replication as a design strategy for all major units in a system requires that the design provide efficient load-sharing across resources and effective communication protocols between the multiple active agents in the system.

Keeping all of the processors active is fundamental to achieving the performance potential of the system. When replication is applied to all major units, load sharing becomes an issue for all resources. The design must ensure that all buses, memory modules, and I/O channels share the workload. Without effective sharing in these passive units of the system, bottlenecks and "hot spots" will develop, straining system capabilities.

A variety of communication protocol problems must be solved. Multiprocessor systems must share resources, buses, and memory structures and solve the race conditions that can arise from concurrent access and operation on data structures. These constraints exist at the lowest levels of hardware-bus protocols, as well as at the higher levels of communication between concurrent, cooperating processes in the software.

If the problems of load sharing and communication protocols can be solved, the potential of VLSI technology can be exploited and the increasing demand for fault-tolerant systems can be met. But development of VLSI components is a long and expensive task, and for design investment to bring dividends, the components must be mass-produced. A system-design approach based on replication—the multiplication of components to add capabilities—permits economical mass production of multipurpose components. Systems can then be assembled economically from mass-produced components to meet a wide range of special needs. The characteristics of a system based on VLSI replication also can satisfy the specifications of fault tolerance. Because the system is based on replicated units, it is possible to provide the redundant resources required for detection of and recovery from failures in the system. The cost of the fault-tolerant systems will be reduced because of the high-volume production of the components, even though the FT system itself may have relatively low volume.

Finally, replication makes it possible to construct a compatible family of systems covering a range of fault-tolerant levels. VLSI replication can provide software-transparent migration over a range of fault-tolerant options without penalties for unused fault-tolerant facilities in low-end systems. A design based on VLSI replication offers great potential for flexible, low-cost, fault-tolerant systems.

The Intel 432

One of the principle goals of the Intel 432 design effort was the construction of a robust computing environment. The 432 architecture was designed to take advantage of VLSI technology to reduce system costs in software, maintenance, and downtime.

The 432 VLSI components provide a flexible and robust environment with additional support logic for its fault-tolerant capabilities. The 432 provides comprehensive detection facilities for processor operations, as well as for buses and memories. Recovery is possible from both permanent and transient errors. Because detection and recovery are done totally in the VLSI components, there is no need for additional logic or diagnostic software.

Figure 1 shows the three dimensions of expansion that are made possible by replication of the 432 VLSI components. Replication allows increased processor performance and bus bandwidth, expands memory size and number of I/O channels, and increases fault-tolerant capabilities. Movement over this full range of options is transparent to the application software running on the machine. The user can configure the machine for a specific application. As the application requirements change, or as new requirements are added, the machine can be reconfigured to meet the needs of the newly defined environment.

The following sections describe how VLSI replication was used in the 432 to provide a flexible and general-purpose, fault-tolerant architecture. More detailed technical descriptions of the fault-tolerant mechanisms and timing can be found in the book by Siewiorek and Swarz,[1] in the Intel reference manual,[2] and in Johnson[3] and Peterson.[4] Siewiorek and Swarz provide historical perspective and a bibliography for most of the fundamental fault-tolerance techniques, including those used in the 432.

Entry-level 432 configuration

Figure 2 shows the basic 432 configuration. The system consists of three modules—processor, memory, and I/O channel—and a system bus. This configuration uses all five VLSI components in the 432 family: the generalized data processor, which consists of two VLSI components; the interface processor; bus interface unit; and memory control unit. The GDP and IP components were introduced early in 1980. The BIU and MCU were introduced early in 1983.

The 432 processors provide an object-based architecture that is the foundation for increased software productivity and reliability. The 432 hardware support of objects and type managers allows information-hiding and program-modularity to an extent impossible in more conventional architectures.[5-11] These functions greatly simplify the development and maintenance of complex software. The hardware run-time protection provides shared-object descriptions, but separate access descriptors. It is the key

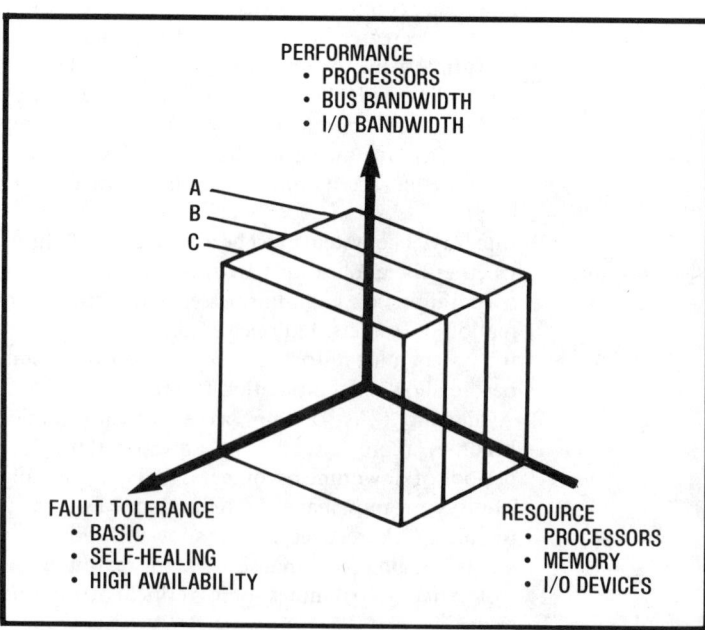

Figure 1. Flexible and modular expansion with (A) high-integrity fault tolerance; (B) high availability; and (C) continuous operation.

August 1984

to supporting multiple-language environments and the dynamic relationships that exist in an environment of cooperating, concurrent processes.

The BIU and MCU extend the logical robustness of the 432 processors into the system's physical implementation. The MCU provides all of the control and management functions required to operate a dynamic RAM memory array. Up to one megabyte of memory may be configured behind a single MCU. There are no point-to-point signals or daisy-chained signals. Arbitration, interprocessor communication, and memory accesses are all done over bused signal lines, making modular growth and on-line repair possible. Because signal definition is independent of the number of resources in the system, the presence or absence of any module cannot prevent communication between any other modules. There are no centralized bus masters or arbitration agents. All BIUs and MCUs on the system bus execute a cooperative arbitration algorithm that allows each component to track its own access on the bus.[2,4] The system bus defined by the BIU and MCU provides a uniform and regularly structured communications path that supports the modular expansion of both fault tolerance and standard system capabilities.

The system bus is a multiplex address and data bus consisting of 16 address and data lines supporting a 24-bit physical memory address space. Any individual bus transfer may contain from one to 16 bytes of data. To optimize the throughput of the bus, a bus transaction is split into separate request and reply packets. Requests and replies may be exchanged on the bus while a request is being serviced by the MCU. Each system bus provides 20 megabytes of instantaneous transfer bandwidth at 10 MHz, and as many as three requests may be outstanding at any given instant.

Even this basic 432 system has significant fault-tolerant facilities. Two bits of parity interlaced over alternate data and control lines detect errors on the system bus. The interlaced parity bits can detect all single failures, all double failures in adjacent signal lines, and a large number of other multiple-failure cases. Each memory array is protected by a seven-bit error correcting code that detects all single- and double-bit errors in the memory address or data and allows the correction of all single-bit data errors. Address errors are detected because the ECC check bits are computed from both the data to be stored and the address of the storage location. During normal operation, data is returned to the processor before the ECC check is complete. This early data return enhances performance by overlapping the bus operation and the ECC computation. If the MCU detects an error, it is reported in time to prevent the use of the flawed data.

After the system detects and reports an error, it will attempt to recover by retrying the outstanding access. During the clock cycle when the error is reported, all bus traffic is stopped and all outstanding bus requests are marked invalid. The system enters a waiting period that allows transient error conditions to subside. The length of this waiting period is set by software and may range from 16 microseconds to two seconds. After the waiting period, all pending accesses (including those outstanding at the time of the error) are retried by the BIUs. All writes are issued before reads to guarantee consistency of accesses partially completed before the wait.[2] The retry operation provides recovery in the case of transient bus and correctable memory errors.

The MCU also provides a mechanism that allows software to switch in a spare RAM bit should one of the RAM components in the memory array fail. The RAM array behind a MCU consists of 40 RAM chips: 32 data bits, seven ECC bits, and one spare bit. The spare bit can be switched in to replace any of the other 39 bit positions. The combination of a single bit-correcting ECC code and the spare RAM bit provides a very reliable, yet cost-effective memory array.

The facilities provided by the basic 432 configuration are designed to provide detection of and recovery from the most frequent causes of central system failures: soft errors in dynamic RAMs, hard failures in a single RAM component in a memory array, and transient errors on the system bus. No extra support logic is required.

Deferred maintenance

All basic units in the 432 configuration can be replicated to provide expansion of performance and system resources. A 432 system can be configured with up to a total of 63 processors, I/O, and memory modules. These modules can be interconnected with up to eight system buses, as shown in Figure 3. This expansion of system facilities has been achieved with the same five components used to construct the basic system, which illustrates that replication provides a broad range of performance and resource options. Hardware expansion is transparent to software, which does not need to know the number of resources available in the pool.

The 432 uses a cooperative, self-dispatching mechanism to distribute the workload between the available processors.[6,8-10,12] Whenever a processor is idle, the dispatching mechanism examines a dispatching queue for processes ready to run. If any are available, they are automatically picked up and execution is started.

The BIU and MCU provide interleaving mechanisms that distribute memory accesses across all of the available resources. The combination of memory and bus interleaving distributes memory addresses across eight memory modules on four system buses. Interleaving occurs on

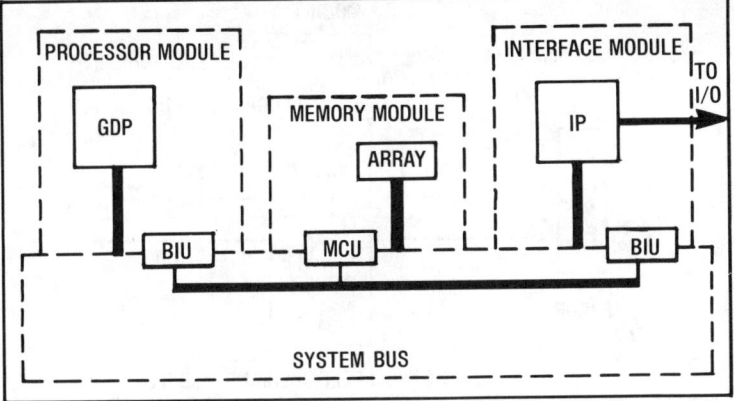

Figure 2. Basic 432 configuration.

16-byte boundaries. The 16-byte granularity is small enough to distribute the load effectively, but large enough to minimize the number of split accesses.

VLSI replication for system expansion allows multiple resources in the system. During normal operation, the multiple resources in the system are fully utilized to increase the performance and capabilities of the system. Bus signals for all communications eliminates the concern about serial paths chained through many modules in a system. Cooperative algorithms for processor dispatching and bus arbitration eliminate the need for critical "master" resources for system operation. The presence of these mechanisms in the 432 allows a level of flexibility and adaptability that has not been possible in the past. Figure 4 shows this level of system fault-tolerance expansion.

Because this expanded 432 system has more than one of every system resource, it can recover from permanent hardware failures without a service call. Retry and memory ECCs can be used to recover from transient failures. If the failure is not correctable, however, the system will crash. Then it can be restarted and reconfigured around the faulty resource. The multiple resources in the system allow restart from permanent hardware failures just as they do after a software crash. This *self-healing* system allows continued operation with maintenance deferred until it is convenient for the user and the service staff.

High integrity and high availability

Enhancing the detection facilities in the hardware increases both the availability and integrity of the system. The 432 central system is partitioned into a set of confinement areas, which form the basis for error detection and recovery. These mechanisms result from VLSI replication and have no impact on system performance.

Confinement areas limit damage from error propagation and localize recovery and repair. They are defined as units (module or system bus) of the system, which have a limited number of tightly controlled interfaces. Detection mechanisms are placed at every interface to prevent inconsistent data from leaving one confinement area and corrupting others.[12] The use of confinement areas significantly reduces the need for diagnostic probing as a method of fault isolation. Figure 4 shows the four types found in 432 systems.

The GDP confinement area includes the GDP, its associated BIUs, the processor bus, and module support logic. The only interfaces to a GDP confinement area are the memory buses. The BIUs check all of the information leaving the GDP module. Errors are detected by a duplicate GDP module that functions in a "checker" mode, performing functional redundancy checking (see Figure 5). Any disagreement is detected and signaled to the rest of the system.

GDPs are identified as "masters" or "checkers" at initialization. Both run in clock-cycle lockstep, but the master carries out the normal system operations while the checker duplicates the operation of the master. The checker's outputs are disabled, however, so it uses its comparison circuitry to detect any inconsistency between itself and the master.

Figure 6 shows the internal FRC logic in the VLSI components. No external logic is required. The FRC logic detects any operational error occurring in either the master or checker block of logic (GDP, BIUs, the local bus, and supporting logic). The master/checker pair is treated as a single, self-checking module, so when an FRC error is detected, no attempt is made to determine which unit is

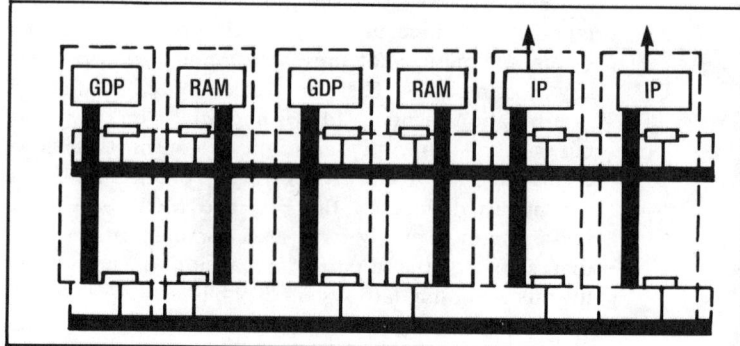

Figure 3. Expanded system configuration.

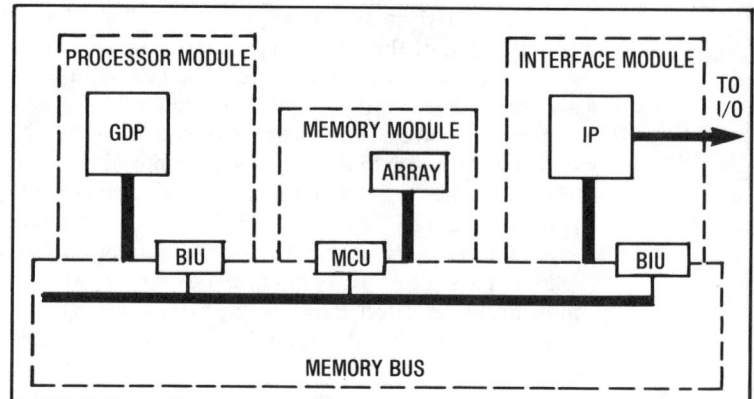

Figure 4. Intel 432 confinement areas.

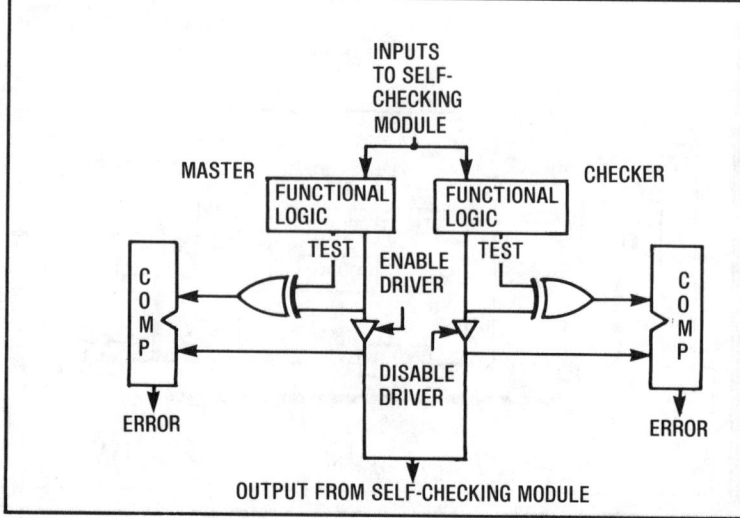

Figure 5. Functional redundancy checking in an Intel 432 system.

correct. A self-checking GDP module is shown in Figure 7. Periodic testing during normal operation uncovers latent failures in this critical block of comparison and fault-reporting logic of the checker.

The IP confinement area includes the IP, its associated BIUs, the processor bus, and support logic in the module. It interfaces to system memory buses and to an external I/O subsystem. IP interfaces to the memory buses are checked by the BIUs. The external I/O subsystem is checked by the IP component, which keeps errors off the peripheral subsystem bus. Here, however, application hardware or software must apply detection mechanisms to the peripheral subsystem. Error detection is performed by a duplicate checker as shown in Figure 8.

The memory confinement area includes the MCU, the RAM array, and the buses and support logic inside the module. A memory module has interfaces to two of the memory buses in the system. As in other modules, the MCU checks all information leaving the memory confinement area. Errors are detected by the ECC and FRC logic in the MCUs. The self-checking memory module has two MCUs and one memory array, as shown in Figure 9.

Each memory-bus confinement area includes a memory bus and the interface logic residing in the BIUs and MCUs attached to the memory bus. Each interfaces to all GDP and IP modules and to some of the memory modules. Every node (BIU or MCU) attached to such a bus checks the information it receives from the memory bus. Errors are detected by the two interlaced parity bits that cover the control and address/data lines, duplicated arbitration lines, and a protocol time-out; see Figure 10.

An example processor/memory operation clarifies the operation of the confinement areas. Assume a GDP makes a read request to a memory location; see Figure 11. That request is mapped through the BIU on the addressed memory bus. As the information flows onto the memory bus, it is checked by the BIU FRC detection mechanism. If no errors are detected, the information flows across the memory bus and into the addressed memory module. Before the information is accepted by the module, the MCU checks the parity bits for correctness. Any detected failure must have occurred in the memory-bus confinement area because the information was valid when it left the GDP confinement area. If the information is correct, the MCU performs the memory operation and returns data to the memory bus. As data flows onto the bus, it is again checked by the FRC and ECC detection mechanisms. Then, as the data flows into the GDP module from the memory bus, the parity bits are checked by the BIU.

The confinement area interfaces provide very tight error control and isolate the failure in one of the building blocks present in the system. The only remaining question concerns checking the detection mechanisms, virtually all of which are checked either as part of normal operation, or by special diagnostic commands to flush out latent faults.

During the clock cycle after detection of an error, an error message is broadcast to all the nodes in the system to identify the faulty confinement area, the type of error, and whether it is permanent or transient.[1,2,13] The error report informs the system that an error has occurred; this prevents other confinement areas from using the inconsistent data. It also provides the necessary information for system recovery.

The BIU and MCU use a simple mechanism for labeling an error as permanent or transient. The first time an error is reported, it is labeled as transient. If the same error is reported a second time (same error report twice in a row) within a software-specified time window ranging from 16 microseconds to two seconds, the error will be labeled permanent. If a permanent error occurs, the BIUs and MCUs deactivate the faulty unit and isolate it from the rest of the system. The components use the information in the error report as well as their own internal IDs to determine the

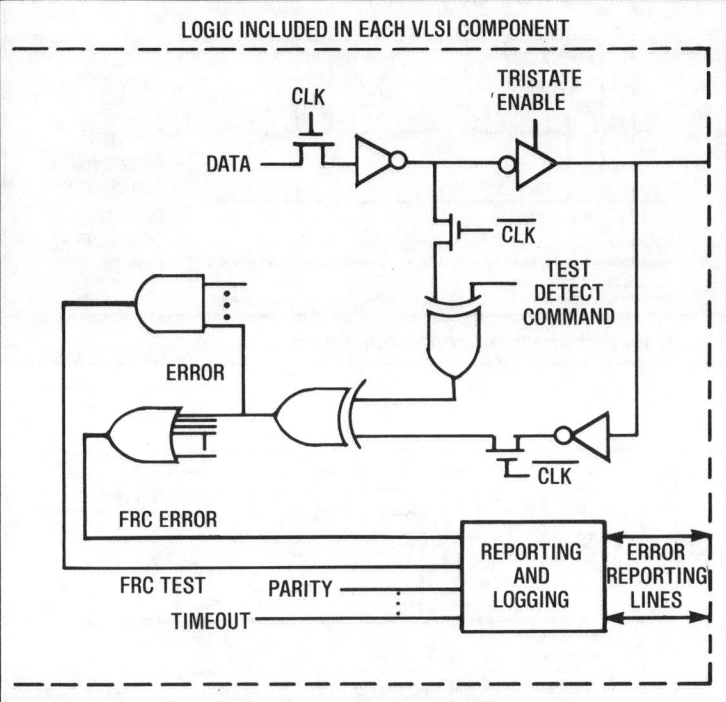

Figure 6. Internal functional redundancy checking circuitry.

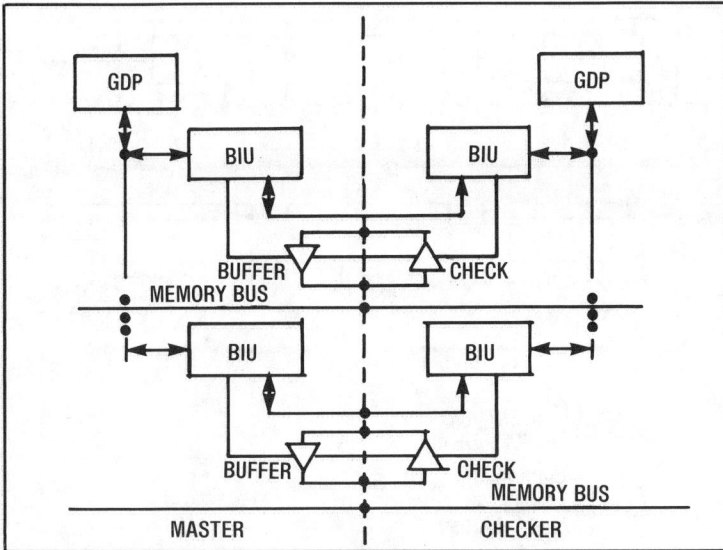

Figure 7. Generalized data processor module with functional redundancy checking.

correct actions in response to the error message. After recovery, the error message is recorded in a log register in every node in the system. This log is available to software for monitoring the health of the system.

The error messages are broadcast over a set of serial buses associated with each system and module data bus. Each system bus has a pair of lines that transmit the error message in parallel. Each module bus has a single line for error-message propagation. These error report lines are totally independent from the buses used during normal operation.

No single failure in the error reporting network can prevent the correct and timely reporting of an error in the system. A failure on one of these error-reporting buses is

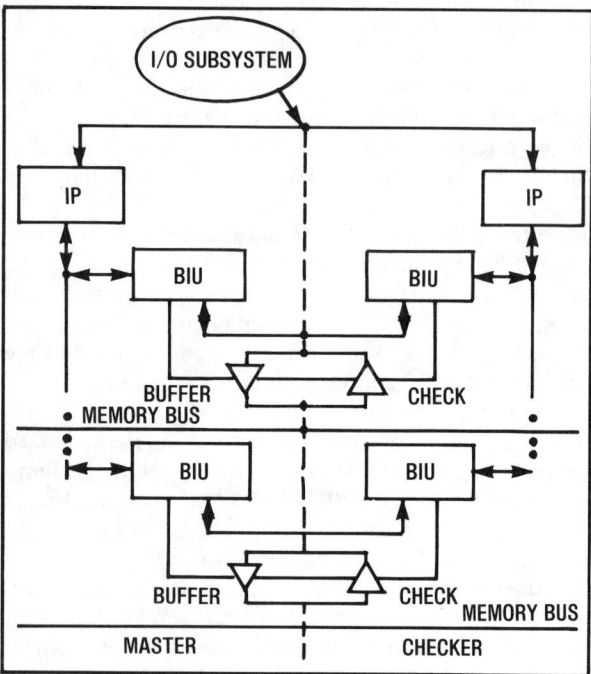

Figure 8. Error checking in an Interface Processor confinement area.

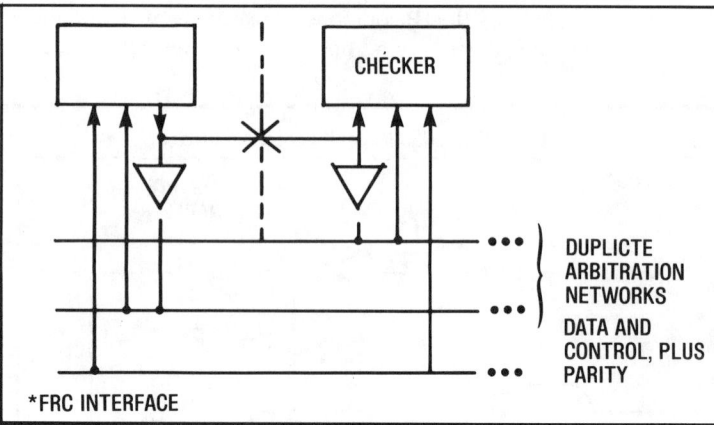

Figure 10. Self-checking on the memory bus.

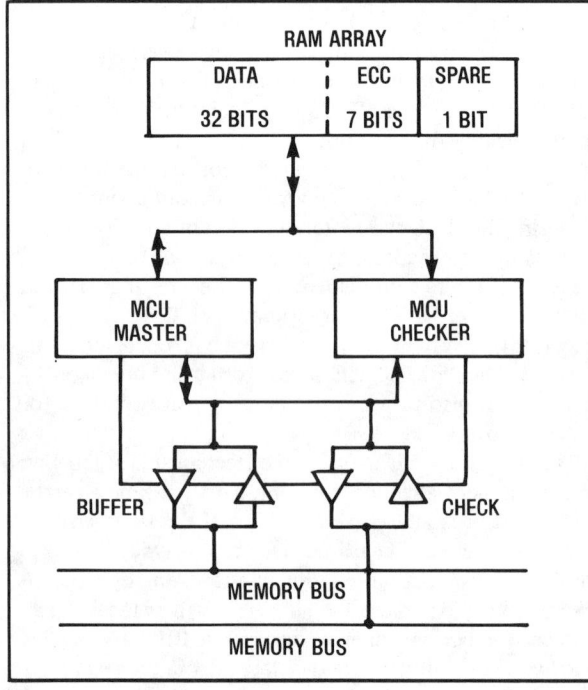

Figure 9. Self-checking in a memory confinement area.

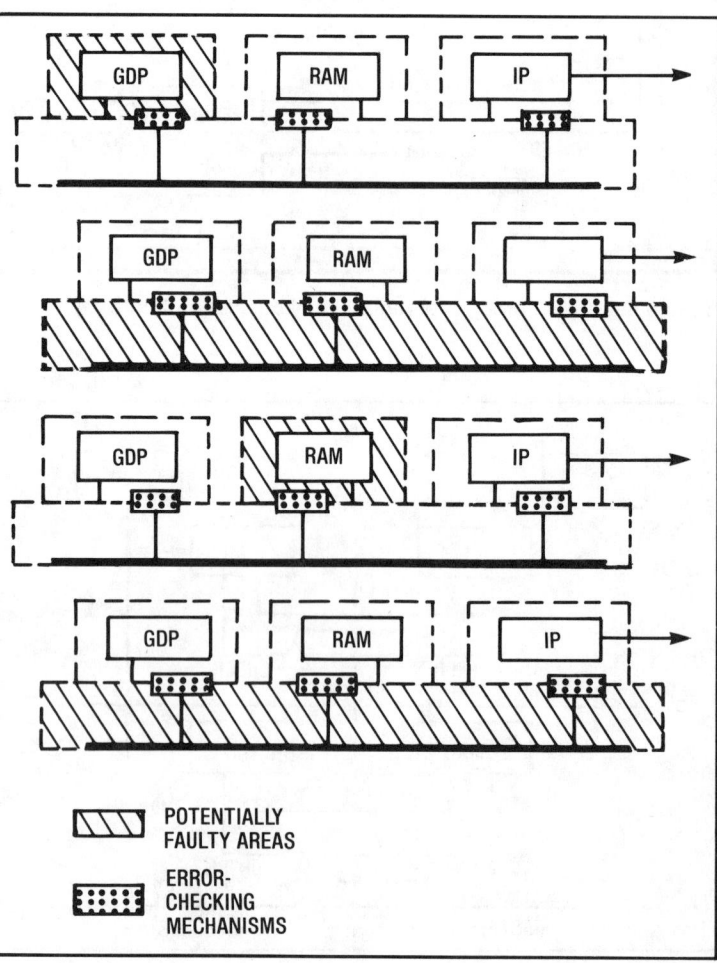

Figure 11. Confinement area operation.

August 1984

limited to one of the confinement areas, so it does not compromise system fault tolerance. Other error reporting buses (in the other confinement areas) take over the reporting responsibilities of a failed reporting bus.

Continuous operation

In deferred-maintenance and high-availability systems, the 432 uses VLSI replication to provide alternate resources for recovery. The 432 can also be configured to provide redundant resources for recovery to provide continuous operation. Alternate resources offer the same functions as primary resources but do not have the current-state information. Redundant resources provide a complete and current backup for the primary resource and allow a 432 system to recover from any detected failure without interruption to the executing software system.*

In 432 systems, software is responsible for policy decisions, while the hardware implements the chosen policy. The redundant configuration is established under software control. The recovery at the time of failure is handled completely in the BIU and MCU without software support or interruption.

By controlling configuration, management software can make decisions about optimal resource allocation as a function of current workload and resource availability. Depending on the situation, it could activate a spare module, degrade performance by removing a module from service, or degrade the fault-tolerant coverage by allowing a unit to continue operation without an active redundant module. This approach provides an architecture with the flexibility of a wide range of fault-tolerant options.

Redundant resources are provided in a 432 system by pairing every self-checking module in the system with a similar self-checking module. Pairs of self-checking modules operate in lockstep and provide a complete, current backup for all information in the module. This technique is known as "module shadowing" because the shadow is ready for immediate recovery should the primary module fail—or vice versa—or "quad-modular redundancy" because the 432 VLSI components are replicated four times (in the master and checker of each module pair).

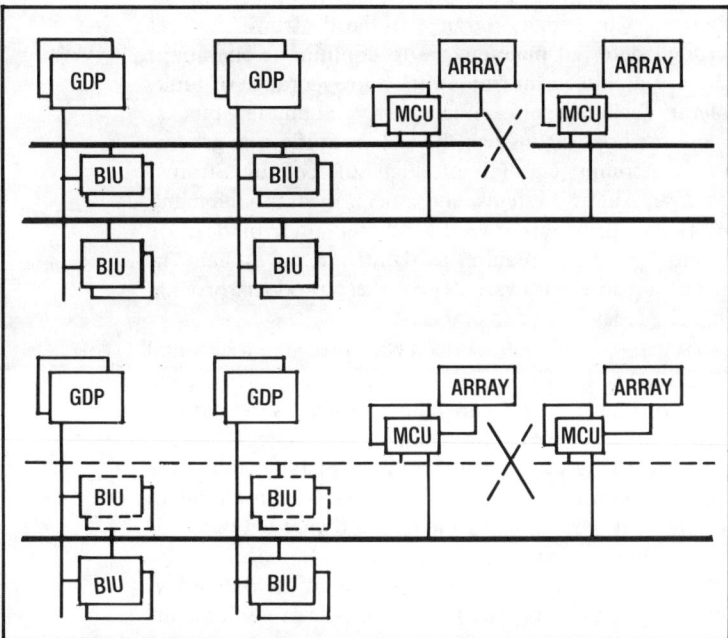

Figure 12. Bus reconfiguration.

This primary/shadow configuration allows recovery from any single failure in either module without any interruption to the logical software environment.

One module in the pair is the *active* module, while the other is *passive*. Initially, the primary module is the active module, taking responsibility for driving the memory bus for a request or reply. The passive module monitors the bus and arbitration lines in order to track the operation of the active module and maintain exactly the same state information as the active module. (Although data leaves only through the active module, it enters both modules).

The roles of active and passive module are switched after each bus request (reply for memory modules) issued by the module. This switching action exercises all the logic in the primary and shadow modules. Any latent failure in either module is detected immediately.

This primary/shadow configuration is established completely by software. There are no special signals connecting the two modules. Eliminating these connections is particularly important in applications involving long mission times where the allocation of spares is critical. The logic to perform this lockstep operation is contained in the BIU or MCU. Neither the processors nor the external logic is aware that the module is participating as one half of a primary/shadow pair.

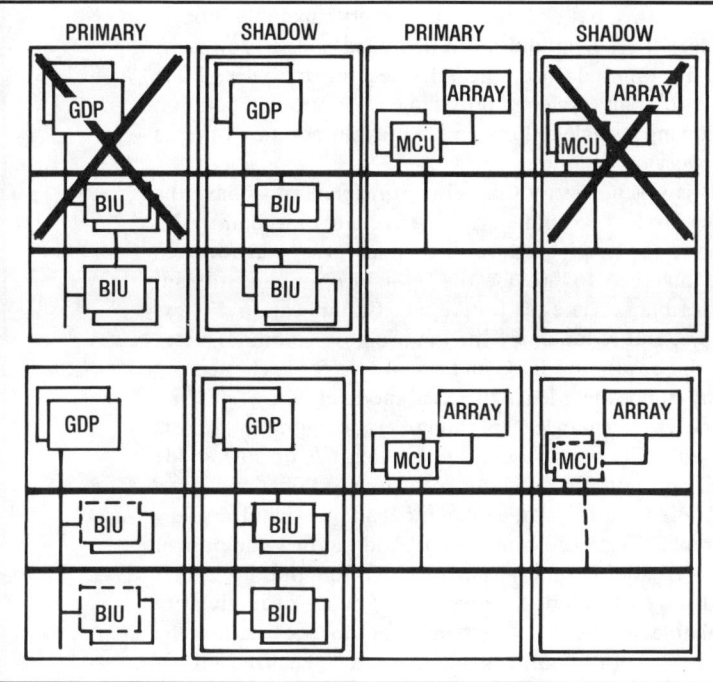

Figure 13. Module reconfiguration.

*Because of the recent release of the VLSI components, no MTBF or availability figures can be presented at this time.

It is important to understand that, whether active or passive, all detection mechanisms remain enabled and continuously check the operation of the module. The passive module checks itself, and so does not double-check the operation of the active module.

The 432 also provides redundancy for the bus-confinement areas, but because the buses do not hold state information, recovery requires only alternate—not redundant—buses. Each system bus may be paired with another system bus, and during normal operation, they run independently. Both contribute to the total bandwidth available in the system, but if one bus fails, the other bus is capable of handling the requests on the failed bus.

Bus traffic is rerouted by the BIUs and MCUs. The MCUs actually provide dual-ported access to the memory-array (only one port may be active). When a bus failure occurs, the MCUs on the failed bus will detach and activate their secondary memory port on the backup bus. The BIUs assist in this recovery operation by rerouting traffic from the faulty bus onto the backup bus. Then memory traffic originally interleaved across both buses is now routed onto the backup bus.

There is no centralized element that controls recovery in a 432 system. Each BIU and MCU executes an identical recovery algorithm in parallel. The components affected by the failure automatically take the appropriate recovery actions, while other components simply retry accesses that were outstanding at the time of the failure.

Reconfiguration and recovery are performed by the hardware without any software intervention. After recovery is complete, the hardware informs the system software of the error and subsequent recovery actions through an interrupt and through error logs. System software may now choose

- to maintain the full capabilities of the system and switch in a spare resource;
- to maintain fault tolerance and degrade preformance by switching out the unit that now lacks a shadow; or
- to maintain performance and run with an increased probability of failure by keeping the shadow unit in operation without bringing a spare on-line.

Figure 12 shows how a 432 system reconfigures around a bus failure. Normally, address interleaving directs traffic across both system buses. When a permanent error is detected in one bus, the BIUs connected to that bus become inactive and processor modules cease communication with the faulty bus. The MCUs attached to the faulty bus activate their backup bus port to isolate the memory array from the failed bus. The BIUs on the good bus activate their backup address recognition logic so that requests are routed onto the good bus. All accesses that were outstanding on the broken bus are then retried on the good bus.

Figure 13 shows the reconfiguration of a single logical GDP and single logical memory module after module failure. During normal operation, the modules operate as a primary/shadow pair, sharing all current state information. When a permanent error is reported in either the primary or shadow module, the remaining module takes over full responsibility for the continuing operation of the module. The BIUs or MCUs in the broken module shut down and isolate the failed module.

The 432 VLSI components provide a set of building blocks that allows the construction of a family of systems with a wide range of fault-tolerant capabilities. The fundamental 432 design strategy is VLSI replication, which permits an architecture with the flexibility to grow in performance, resources, and fault tolerance. In the area of fault tolerance, the emphasis is on providing an architecture that meets the growing demand for fault-tolerant systems. The demand is not focused solely on continuous operation, but spans a range of needs from low cost through deferred maintenance to continuous operation. The 432 architectural framework allows a range of fault-tolerant facilities from a small set of VLSI building blocks. These facilities distinguish the 432 from the new generation of commercial FT products offered by Stratus, Synapse, August Systems, and others. Even though many of these products are based on microprocessor technology, they require a significant investment in special-purpose hardware. Thus, these products provide only single-level fault tolerance.

VLSI replication allows the 432 to provide incremental functionality for incremental cost and eliminates the expense of unwanted FT capabilities. Then, as the requirements of an application change, the system can be modified to meet a new level of fault tolerance. Since the entire range of fault-tolerant facilities is transparent to software, it is possible to migrate software between 432 systems having different levels of fault tolerance.

For basic systems, a user may decide to use only a few detection mechanisms and provide recovery only for transient errors, but eliminate checkers for error detection and shadows for recovery. To reduce maintenance costs and increase system availability, a system may use all detection mechanisms, but without extra recovery capability. For instance, checker modules can be added and shadow pairs can be omitted from the self-checking modules. Fully fault-tolerant systems providing continuous operation following a single failure require only the addition of extra recovery capabilities.

It is not necessary that all confinement areas have the same level of redundancy. Since recovery mechanisms in each confinement area are independent, they can be mixed and matched to provide the optimal cost/fault-tolerant performance trade-off for the specific application. For example, full redundancy for the processor modules, retry for the buses, and ECC and a spare bit for each memory array can be included in different modules of a system that would offer a high level of fault tolerance without the costs of full duplication. Users can also upgrade or downgrade their configuration without software modifications.

These fault-tolerant capabilities can be expanded solely by replicating VLSI components, without new component types or additional external logic. The continuous operation stage of Figure 1 shows the full range of modularity available in the 432. Systems that do not require the highest level of fault tolerance are not penalized in any way—cost, size, or performance—for the unused fault-tolerant capabilities. *

Acknowledgments

Many people on the staff at Intel's Special Systems Operation contributed to the 432 fault-tolerant design effort. In particular, I would like to thank Tony Cornish, Dave Budde, Dave Carson, Craig Peterson, and Bill Corwin for their important contributions to the design work. Sudhir Bhagwan provided the management guidance required to complete the project, while Justin Rattner played a key role by establishing the overall 432 architecture and maintaining a stimulating and challenging engineering environment within SSO.

References

1. D. Siewiorek and R. Swarz, *The Theory and Practice of Reliable System Design,* Digital Press, Bedford, Mass., 1982.
2. *IAPX 432 Interconnect Architecture Reference Manual,* Intel Corp., Santa Clara, Calif., 1983.
3. D. Johnson et al., "Intel IAPX 432—VLSI Building Blocks for a Fault-Tolerant Computer," *AFIPS Conf. Proc.,* Vol. 52, 1983 NCC, AFIPS Press, Reston, Va., pp. 531-538.
4. C. Peterson et al., "Two Chips Endow 32-Bit Processor With Fault-Tolerant Architecture," *Electronics,* Vol. 55, No. 7, April 7, 1983, pp. 159-165.
5. E. Organick, *A Programmer's View of the Intel 432 System,* McGraw-Hill, New York, 1983.
6. *IAPX 432 GDP Architecture Reference Manual,* Intel Corp., Santa Clara, Calif., 1982.
7. S. Ziegler et al., "Ada for the Intel 432 Microcomputer," *Computer,* Vol. 14, No. 6, June 1981, pp. 47-56.
8. K. Kahn and F. Pollack, "An Extensible Operation System for the Intel 432," *Proc. Compcon Spring 81,* pp. 398-404.
9. G. Cox et al., "Interprocess Communication, and Processor Dispatching on the Intel 432," *ACM Trans. Computer Systems,* Vol. 1, No. 1, Feb. 1983, pp. 45-66.
10. K. Kahn et al., "IMAX: A Multiprocessor Operating System for an Object-Based Computer," *Proc. Eighth Symp. Operating System Principles,* Dec. 1981, pp. 127-136.
11. D. Kinder, "Transparent Multiprocessing Boosts Microcomputer Throughput," *Electronic Design News,* Vol. 30, No. 8, Apr. 15, 1982, pp. 159-170.
12. P. J. Denning, "Fault-Tolerant Operating Systems," *ACM Computing Surveys,* Vol. 8, No. 4, Dec. 1976, pp. 359-389.
13. D. Johnson, "Error Reporting in the Intel IAPX 432," *Proc. 14th Fault Tolerance Computing Seminar,* June 1984, pp. 24-28.

Dave Johnson works for Intel Corporation in Hillsboro, Oregon, where he was a principal designer of the 432 fault-tolerant system and is currently working on advanced systems technology. Before joining Intel in 1979, he worked for Burroughs in research and advanced development. He holds a BSEE from Washington University in St. Louis and an MS in computer science from the University of Utah. His address is M/S JF1-2-108, Intel Corporation, 2111 NE 25 Ave., Hillsboro, OR 97123.

The Design of C.fast:
A Single Chip Fault Tolerant Microprocessor

Michael M. Tsao, Andrew W. Wilson, Ralph C. McGarity
Chia-Jeng Tseng, and Daniel P. Siewiorek

Department of Electrical Engineering, and Computer Science Department,
Carnegie-Mellon University, Pittsburgh, Pennsylvania

ABSTRACT

During the spring of 1981, the authors were involved in a project to design a single chip fault tolerant microprocessor. The microprocessor chip has been fabricated by the Multi Project Chip (MPC) facilities, sponsored by the MOSIS group at USC-ISI. During the spring of 1982, eight prototypes were tested by the authors. This report presents a brief overview of the chip, examples of the reliability - testability techniques implemented, and some of the trade-off issues resolved during the design process. Three interesting techniques were implemented: a simple self checking scheme using parity code for PLA's, microinstruction retry of target machine instructions on detection of error in a duplicate, master- slave configuration, and a visibility register that uses the system I/O data bus as the visibility bus during test.

INTRODUCTION

The C.Fast[1] project attempted to accomplish four goals. The first goal was to provide the authors with experience in designing digital integrated circuits, especially microprocessors. This experience gave us a better basis from which to build a Design Automation (DA) system using a hierarchical structured design methodology. A second goal of the project was to explore ways to connect control signals to the data path part in a simple structured way with little random routing. A third goal was to try out some low cost reliability techniques at the integrated circuit (IC) chip design level. Three ideas implemented were parity checking on the the control PLA's and the concept of using the data path to act as a visibility bus for testing purposes. Shadow registers were used so that, on detection of errors, the target machine instruction can be retried. A final goal was to produce, as a by-product of the design effort, a set of register transfer (RT) level building blocks to be used by our DA programs.

The Fairchild F8 microprocessor [FAIR77] was chosen as the target machine for the following reasons. 1) It represents a "typical" microprocessor architecture of the mid-70's era. 2) The original F8, F3850, is an n-MOS chip, same as the MPC process. The minimum feature size used is similar to the current MPC process, where the minimum transistor gate area is 5 microns by 5 microns. 3) The complexity of the F8 is not very great, which made reimplementing the Instruction Set Processor (ISP) easier. 4) The original F8 is partitioned in such a way that we could implement the basic CPU chip in less than 24 pins, thus leaving some pins for our testability - reliability portion of the design. 5) As part of earlier research work, we have explored the question of implementing low cost fault tolerant features on an F8 system at the IC level.

CHIP OVERVIEW

The C.fast chip can be regarded as consisting of three interrelated sections: the control part, the data part and the reliability part (see Figure 1, and 2.) These sections were each under the control of a different designer, though naturally there was considerable consultation between them. A photomicrography of the prototype chip is shown in Figure 3. The major functional areas are identified on the floor plan, Figure 4.

---

[1] C.fast, in the PMS notation [SIEW81], stands for Computer: FAult-tolerant and Self Testing

The paper presented here is an excerpt of a project report "The MPC C.fast micro computer", available from the authors.

While working on this project, the authors were supported by the Defense Advanced Research Agency (DOD), ARPA Order No. 3579, monitored by the Air Force Avionics Laboratory under contract F33615-78-C-1551, and by National Science Foundation grant ENG-78-25399, and by the Carnegie-Mellon University Department of Electrical Engineering.

The views and conclusions contained in this document are those of the authors and should not be interpreted as representing the official policies, either expressed or implied, of the Defense Advanced Research Agency or the US Government, or other funding agencies.

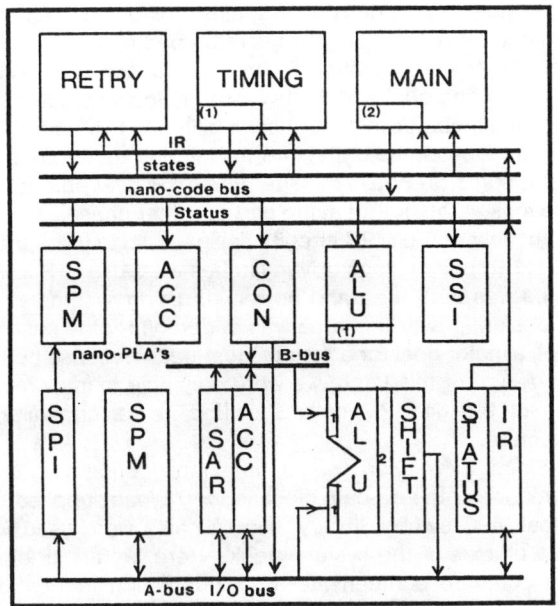

Figure 1: RT level block diagram of the C.fast microprocessor

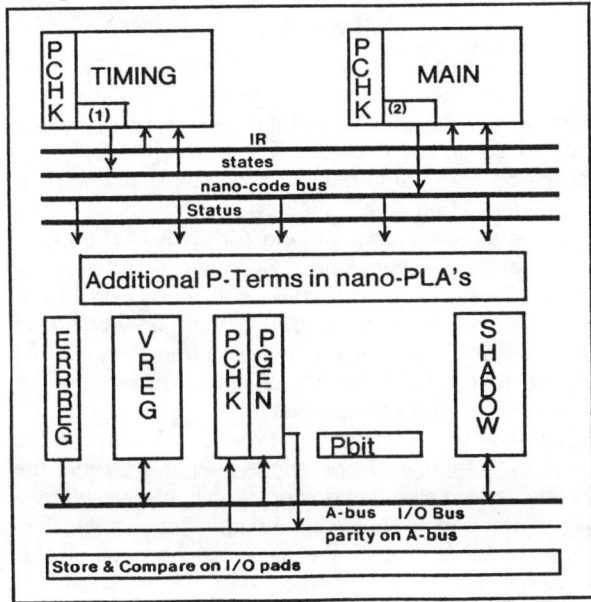

Figure 2: Block diagram of the testability-reliability portion of the C.fast

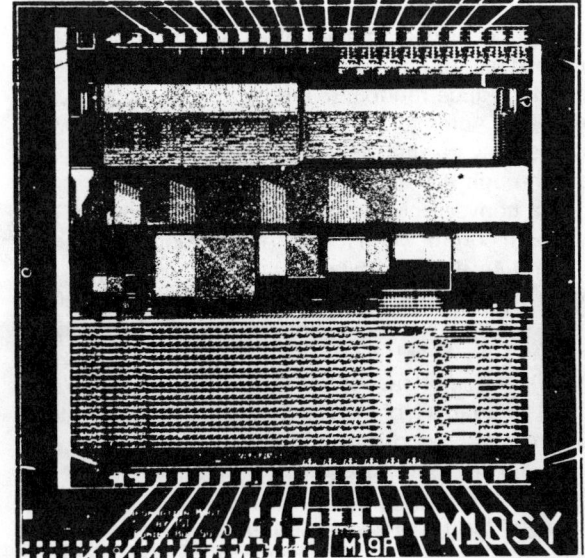

Figure 3: Photomicrography of the C.fast Prototype Chip

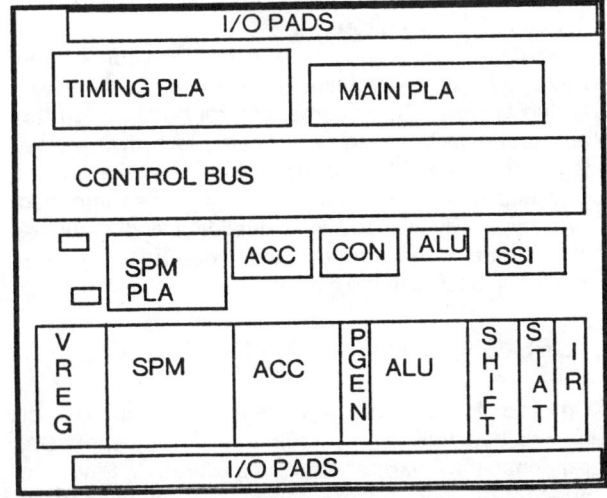

Figure 4: Major functional areas of the C.fast chip

The control is partitioned into two groups of PLA's. Three large PLA's control the instruction execution (TIMING PLA), provide correct sequencing for the external data bus (MAIN PLA), and attempt recovery after transient errors (RETRY PLA). These PLA's broadcast encoded commands on a control bus which traverses the chip in parallel with the data bus. Small decoder PLA's, (called Nano PLA's because of their resemblance to techniques used in nanocoding), produce the actual control signals for the data path elements using the broadcast microinstructions as inputs. This partitioning has produced a smaller and faster control section than would have been produced by a more conventional design methodology.

Information about the state of the data part is fed back to the control part through a status bus which is available to all PLA's. The extensive use of buses is intended to reduce random routing and is partly motivated by our Design Automation research. The use of a command bus allows easy testing since it can be made readable and writable through the visibility bus and the I/O bus. It also provides a convenient way for the Retry PLA to take over the data path control when it attempts instruction retry.

The data part is similar to the Cal Tech OM-2 data path chip [MEAD80]. Its similarities include a two phase clocking scheme, precharging of buses, use of a precharged Manchester carry chain in the Arithmetic Logic Unit (ALU), and interleaved data buses. It is different from the OM-2 in that all of the storage elements are static, although the latches driving the ALU are dynamic. Also several of the elements have been reworked so that there is a uniform control, power and ground scheme. One of the buses (called the B bus) is divided into several sections to increase parallelism. Other changes include passive pullups in some places, a different spatial ordering of ALU and Shifter, use of a more specialized shifter, and wider Vdd and ground wires. Embedded within the data path part are fault tolerant devices including a parity checker, parity generator, and shadow registers. Also added are a zero detector and a status register.

The chip is also serving as a test bed for several reliability and testability techniques. Testability is enhanced by allowing access to the internal control bus through the I/O bus via the visibility register. Fault tolerances against transient errors are derived from the pervasive parity checking and built-in retry algorithms. It is also intended that two chips will be used in a duplicate and compare system with one in the standby slave mode, ready to take over if an error occurs in the master.

DESIGN FOR FAULT TOLERANCE

In order to achieve a more reliable microprocessor system, we decided to use fault *tolerance* techniques, rather than fault *avoidance* techniques [ELKI81]. Since we had no control over the processing and manufacturing aspect of the project, we could not do anything about the fault avoidance area of reliability improvement. Furthermore, we wanted to explore the design space for low cost, (in terms of chip area), fault tolerance alternatives. For this chip, we employed a four-tier approach in improving the fault tolerant properties of this microprocessor. The goals were to improve the error detection and error recovery capability of the basic system.

Due to considerations of chip area, we did not duplicate everything, or implement complete self-checking, even in a duplex configuration. Therefore, it is impossible to recover from every possible permanent failure. However, by designing in the retry mechanism, and barring some special pathological common mode errors, a duplex configuration can recover from transient errors.

Conservative circuit level designs

A static latch design was used for all the flip-flop implementations, including the scratch pad memory (SPM) and all the temporary buffers. In this manner, one could hold off any one phase of the two-phase clock, thus trading off system speed for testing observability. In this particular implementation, some of the internal latches are latched on phase 1, some on phase 2. Therefore, it is desirable to be able to look at the output at the end on either phase.

In most of the MPC circuits designed up to the Spring of 1981, two phase clock driven latches were used. Such a design saves both area and power. In using a completely static design, power and area was traded off for the ease of control, a major goal for a testable test-bed. Because of the larger design of this latch, we were only able to implement 16 out of the 64 SPM cells specified in the original F8 architecture.

Since there were some questions concerning the performance of the on-chip clock input I/O pad supplied by the local MPC symbol library, two I/O pins were used for the two phases of the system clock. Here, we are trading off pin count to compensate for a fluctuating fabrication process.

Register Transfer (RT) level functional blocks

Data path part

Parity was used on all registers and the SPM's for error detection. All data transfers (one 8 bit byte at a time) between the processor chip and the memory system were assumed to be encoded by a single bit odd parity code. One of the on-chip parity checkers was used to check all off chip data transfers. All parity checkers were implemented as a sequence of nine XOR gates. Therefore, it is not a totally self checking (TSC) checker. It was felt that the additional chip area could not be justified in this particular case. However, since the same parity checkers were also used to check all on-chip data transfers, it could be debated that a TSC checker is a viable alternative for other systems of similar structures.

The issue of detecting ALU errors was handled at the system level. Since ALU operations seldom preserve the parity code used in all data transfers, again, it was felt that a parity predictor can not be justified here. The complexity of such a predictor is usually the same as the original ALU block [KHOD79]. Furthermore, since the original ALU design is usually at the "optimal" point in the design space, there is no easy way to generate a similarly optimal counterpart: the parity predictor. Therefore, it was decided that if one wants to check the ALU operations in a C.fast environment, one uses a second copy.

Shadow copy registers were inserted for the accumulator (ACC) and two other key registers, allowing for instruction retry. A more detailed discussion on these registers are presented in a later section.

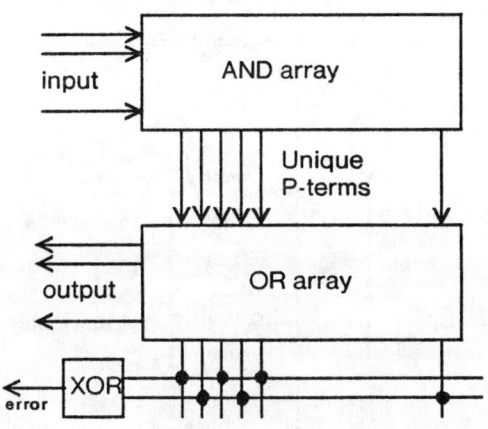

Figure 5: A Simple Self-Checking PLA

PLA's	Inputs	Outputs	P-Terms	Area Increases (%) over original	
TIMING	16	16	116	35	extra states
MAIN	14	11	114	9	extra nano codes
RETRY	12	22	61	...	F8 instruction retry
SPM	12	34	35	5	
ACC	8	17	23	91	shadow registers
CON	12	11	18	9	
ALU	9	13	12	0	
SSI	11	14	20	41	shadow status bits
VRE	4	7	8	...	visibility registers

Figure 6: Table of PLA area increases due to testability-reliability requirements

PLA implementation

Several alternative schemes for implementing a self checking PLA were investigated. A scheme similar to those proposed by Wang and Avizienis [WANG79] was chosen (see Figure 5.) The simplest one to implement involved restricting the product terms (P-terms) such that, for any input pattern, one and only one P-term is activated. It seems that this is a necessary condition on most of the TSC PLA algorithms. Since all the PLA's were designed using PLA generating programs, it was trivial to enforce the "uniqueness" condition. The "even" and "odd" P-terms were alternately placed next to each other, such that a shorted wire will activate terms from both classes. Additionally, two extra OR array output lines were inserted, one for the "even" P-terms, one for the "odd" P-terms. In this scenario, one checks for the unique activation of these two "parity" lines. There are several more complicated schemes that could have been employed, but all required designing a great deal of additional circuitry.

Microcode of Target Machine Instruction

In this design, the microcode is implemented in the control PLA's. On detection of an external bus transaction error (e.g. memory read), the entire system does a bus retry. (This may not always be possible for all microprocessor systems. It is dependent upon the types of support chips used in a micro computer system.) On detection of internal errors, such as those reported by the ALU input bus parity checker, the current target machine instruction is retried. This can be done only if there is sufficient redundant information. The goal was to make the fault tolerance aspect of the chip transparent to F8 software. Under this type of fault tolerant design, one can run an existing F8 program unmodified. Figure 6 lists the additional PLA area increases due to this aspect of the fault tolerant design.

The processor attempts to recover from errors through microcoded retry sequences. On detection of external bus transaction errors, (e.g. memory read), the entire system does a bus retry. While conceptually simple, the F8 implementation is complicated by the fact that critical address registers (including the program counter) are located off chip. For example, in order to reread an opcode byte, the program counter must be read into the processor a byte at a time, decremented, and written back to the memory control chip. The implementation of external retries with almost any other microprocessor would be considerably simpler.

On detection of internal errors, such as those reported by the ALU input bus parity checker, the current target machine instruction is re-executed. Two shadow registers are used to maintain the original state of the Accumulator and Scratch pad Address Register (ISAR), which are the only registers whose values may be modified (as opposed to overwritten). These Shadow registers are updated with the newly computed values during the instruction execution. The update operation overlaps the fetch phase of the next instruction, thus allowing full speed instruction execution. By using both principal internal data buses, simultaneous updates of both shadow registers are possible.

The third shadow register is used to save the most recently read value from the I/O bus. This register is not essential to the retry scheme, but avoids having to reread values from the external data bus, simplifying the retry process. Since the external Bus transaction itself will be repeated untill a good copy of the data has been received, the shadow register can be used to provide operands during retry of instructions which have suffered some other error while executing.

With these schemes all detectable transient data path errors can be recovered from. With some additional effort certain PLA parity errors could also have been addressed, however guarding against contamination of the shadow registers by the spurious microcode which might be generated would be difficult. Instead, system level duplicate-and-match strategies were invoked, as described elsewhere. The retry features provide software transparent fault tolerance for the F8, allowing existing F8 programs to execute without modification.

A Duplex, Master-Slave C.fast System

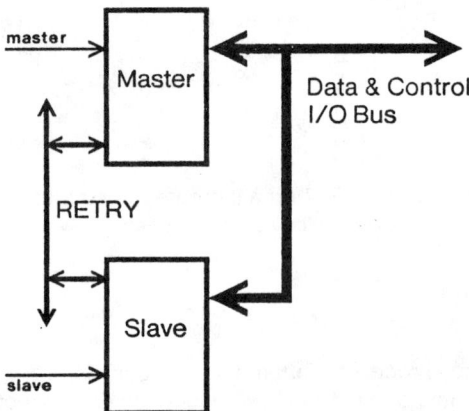

Figure 7: A Duplex, Master - Slave System

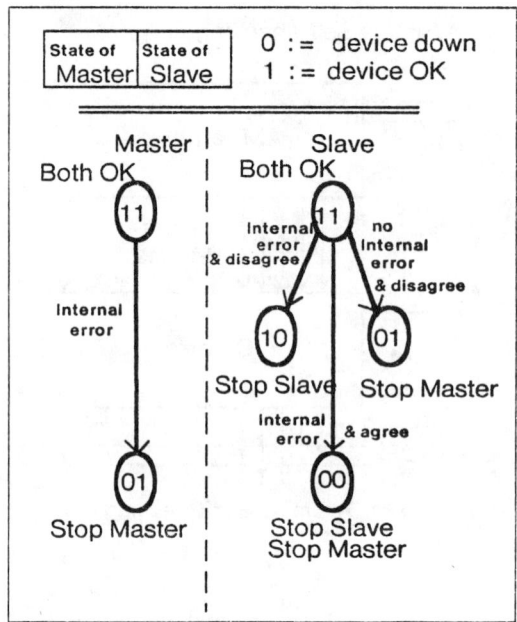

Figure 8: State diagram showing the states of a duplicate-match C.fast system After Retry

At the system level

Several possible scenarios were explored for this project. One alternative was a design similar to the Bell System local ESS processors [TOY78]. In such a design, in addition to some on board error detection mechanisms, one needs a central arbitrator. It was felt that a more "distributed" mechanism for fault isolation is more desirable. Another scheme considered was based on the SIFT-inspired algorithm [PEAS80]. In such a scenario, several cooperating processor exchanges messages until a consensus is reached. Based on the algorithm proposed by Pease, et. al., in the limiting case of having only two processors, one can detect errors but can not isolate the failing processor. Furthermore, for a two-copy systems, a more redundant communication path is required for the algorithm to work properly.

We chose to implement a master-slave, duplicate and compare system, Figure 7, similar to the Intel iAPX 432 system [JOHN82]. In this scenario, the slave microprocessor watches the output of the master in a lock step fashion. To implement this function, a set of latches and simple comparators were connected with all the tri-state I/O pads for the I/O bus data pins. On all clock cycles that invoke bus output, the slave microprocessor compares the output from the master with its own copy of the "proposed" output pattern. Since the comparator is situated right at the I/O pads, in a properly implemented system, there should not be any big speed penalty. At the same time, for additional error detection capabilities, the on board error detection mechanism is also in operation. In this manner, some of the ALU errors could also be detected. On disagreement, and also on detection of internal error, a system "retry" signal is activated. Both microprocessors perform one retry of the current target machine instruction. At the end of the retry cycle, the system can be in any one of the states shown in Figure 8.

In this proposed duplex and match system, the master has **NO** information about the state of the salve at the end of the retry cycles. The slave knows only what the master puts out on the I/O bus. One common alternative is for both copies to exchange some internal information. However, in our opinion, the additional cost (in chip area, complexity, design time, etc.) can not be justified in our particular situation. With the current scheme, total error detection and recovery is not guaranteed. However, the system can recover from certain types of error conditions, which will be discussed in the following section.

ERROR DETECTION CAPABILITIES

Since the proposed C.fast system does not really fit most of the traditional models of redundant systems, and it is very hard to put any meaningful reliability parameters on a prototype system, the following reliability analysis techniques are proposed, Figure 9 and Figure 10. Basically, the capability for error detection and error recovery of a properly implemented C.fast system is listed. For each type of failure, the proposed system can either detect the error, recover from the error, or miss it entirely. Therefore, this is not a totally fail-safe system. It is trading off the chip area against the capability for error detection and recovery. However, as designed, it does recover from transient errors through the retry mechanism.

Mechanism for Detecting Hard Failures

Chip Operations & Failure Locations	Single Copy	Duplex System
Data Transfer		
Single Point Failures	PARITY	PARITY *
Two Failures		
On Same Chip	MISSED	COMPARE **
Different Chip	N/A	PARITY
ALU Operations	MISSED	COMPARE **
Control PLA's		
Single Point Failures	SELF CHECKING	SELF CHECKING
Two Failures		
On Same Chip	MISSED	COMPARE **
Different Chip	N/A	SELF CHECKING

* Recovery is possible when the failed copy is disabled.

** Can recover IFF the slave failed.

Figure 9: Error Detection Capability Against Permanent Failures

Mechanism for Detecting Transient Errors

Chip Operations & Error Locations	Single Copy	Duplex System
Data Transfer		
Single Point Failures	PARITY *	PARITY *
Two Failures		
On Same Chip	MISSED	COMPARE *
Different Chip	N/A	PARITY *
ALU Operations	MISSED	COMPARE *
Control PLA's		
Single Point Failures	SELF CHECKING *	SELF CHECKING *
Two Failures		
On Same Chip	MISSED	COMPARE *
Different Chip	N/A	SELF CHECKING *

* Recovery is possible when RETRY is used.

Figure 10: Error Detection Capability Against Transient Errors

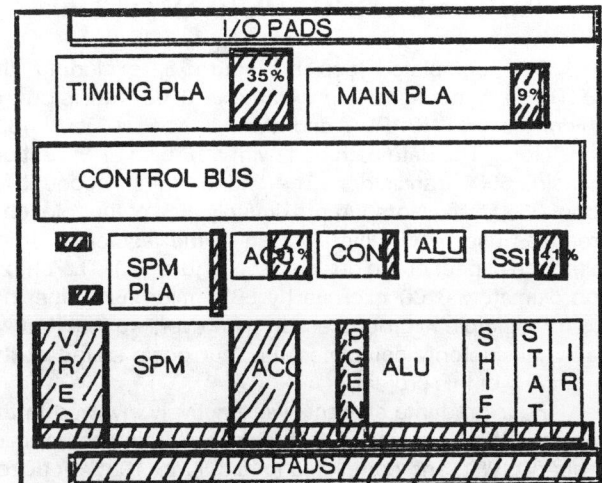

Figure 11: Chip Areas Used by Testability - Fault Tolerance Circuitries

DESIGN FOR TESTABILITY

A traditional microprocessor design can usually be grouped into the data path part and the control part. The data part is more observable from the off chip I/O pins. The control part is somewhat harder to control and even harder to observe. In most microprocessor designs, the only way to determine the proper operation of the control part is by observing the output of the data part. The goal for our testable microprocessor was to design a place where we can put a controllable and observable path (the visibility bus) between the control part and the data part, and route it to the off chip I/O pins.

In the C.fast microprocessor design, the main control PLA generates control information for the "control bus", not for the data part directly. This was done to optimize the area-speed trade-off. This control bus is converted into the "visibility" bus during the test mode. Extra circuitry was used for observing values of the control part, as well as jamming new values onto this visibility ("control") bus. Thus, the observability of the control part and the controllability of the data part was increased.

The controllability of the control part Finite State Machine (FSM) is increased by making it easier to write information into the FSM flip-flops (FF's). During test mode, these FF's can be loaded from the off chip data bus I/O pins via the visibility register and the visibility bus. The operation is very similar to all the scan-set ideas, such as the Level Sensitive Scan Design (LSSD) technique used on some IBM machines [EICH77]. On C.fast, the FF values can be loaded during the test mode write cycles. The microprocessor runs one or more executing cycles. The chip is set back to test mode, and the values stored by the visibility register are read off. One important difference is that the data reading and loading uses the 8-bit parallel I/O data bus pins. This design does not use shift-in and shift-out pins as in most scan set-like designs. Furthermore, the pins for controlling the test mode functions could be shared with the pins used for the fault tolerance operations. The extra pins do not visibly impact the total pin count.[2]

Additionally, portions of the FSM used for fault tolerance operations are highly observable during "normal" operations. The microprocessor can easily be fooled into an error recovery mode where the proper operation of the recovery FSM can be observed. The built-in error detectors also increase the testability of the chip.

There is a trade-off between this type of visibility register, using the microprocessor data bus for access, and the more traditional shift register type of testable designs. Obviously, the shift register approach is more general, able to be applied to all digital sequential circuits. However, the main argument in the C.fast case is to take advantage of a already highly structured design, such as used in many modern microprocessors. In such a situation, the visibility register may provide a better access method over the traditional shift register approach.

---

[2] We ran out of chip real estate in which to place the Retry PLA. However, all the associated control signals were placed. Using the visibility bus, the error recovery procedures can still be tested.

IMPLEMENTING THE PROTOTYPE

The completed design, Figure 3, excluding the RETRY PLA, contains approximately 13000 transistors, of which the TIMING PLA and the MAIN PLA uses 4300 transistors. The data path part, with a 16 byte SPM section, contains 5600 transistors. The "nano-PLA's" account for about 3000 transistors. Approximately 25% of the total chip area was use by circuits involved in the testability - fault tolerance aspect of the design, (see Figure 11.) The chip is approximately 6100 microns by 5800 microns, somewhat big for a simple microprocessor. However, we feel that we have satisfactorily completed the four goals stated at the beginning of this project.

Four graduate students were actively involved in the design. Work on the C.fast chip was initiated in mid-January, 1981, and completed in mid-June, 1981. A dozen or so CAD programs were used in designing the chip. To verify the correctness of the PLA microcode, the actual bit patterns for the PLA generator were used to drive a ISPS simulator of the micro machine. The completed design was submitted, and accepted by the MOSIS group at ISI at around October 1, 1981. It was returned to CMU by January 1, 1982. During the spring of 82, we interfaced the C.fast chip to an existing F8 prototyping board, and a DEC LSI-11 for testing. At of this writting, (April 10, 9182), we have discovered several design errors. But portions of the chip are operating as expected. More complete results of this testing phase will be reported during the conference presentation.

SUMMARY

It is in our opinion that we have satisfied the original four goals, set during the early days of January, 1981. In the fault tolerance, testability area, the main objective was to try out some design ideas: a simple self checking scheme using parity code for PLA's, microinstruction retry of target machine instructions on detection of an error in a duplicate, master- slave configuration, and a visibility register that uses the system I/O data bus as the visibility bus during testing. All together, not counting the unimplemented RETRY PLA, the extra circuitry increased the overall chip area by about 25% above the base design. In return for these increases, certain class of permanent failures can be detected in a properly implemented C.fast system. Furthermore, in a duplex configuration, the system can recover from all transient errors through the use of retry.

ACKNOWLEDGMENT

The authors would like to thank Bill Birmingham on the layout of the shifter section; Dr. Dennis Lunder, of Fairchild Microprocessor Product division, who donated a F387X PEP single board computer system, providing a test vehicle for our finished prototype; and John Chiesa for helping out with testing of the prototype. We would also like to thanks our colleagues at CMU's VLSI community. Without their many wonderful CAD programs, we could not have completed this design.

REFERENCES

[EICH77] E.B. Eichelberger, and T.W. Williams. "A Logic Design Structure for LSI Testing". *Proc. 14th Design Automation Conf."* June 77. pp 462-468.

[ELKI82] S.A. Elkind. "Reliability and Availability Techniques". in *"The Theory and Practice of Reliable System Design".* by D.P. Siewiorek, and R. Swarz. Digital Press. 1982.

[FAIR77] "F8 User's Guide." Fairchild. 1977.

[JOHN81] D.P. Siewiorek and D. Johnson. "A Design Methodology for High Reliability Systems: The Intel 432". in *"The Theory and Practice of Reliable System Design".* by D.P. Siewiorek, and R. Swarz. Digital Press. 1982.

[KHOD79] B. Khodadad - Mostashiry. *"Parity Prediction in combinational Circuits"* FTCS-9, pp 185-188.

[MEAD80] C. Mead, and L. Conway. *"Introduction to VLSI Systems".* Addison -Wesley. 1980.

[PEAS80] M. Pease, R. Shostak, and L. Lamport. "Reaching Agreement in the Presence of Faults." Journal of the Association for Computing Machinery. Vol. 27, No. 2, April 1980. pp 228-234.

[SIEW82] D.P. Siewiorek, C.G. Bell, and A. Newell. *"Computer Structures: Principles and Examples."* McGraw-Hill. 1982.

[TOY78] W.N. Toy. "fault-Tolerant Design of Local ESS Processors." Proceedings of the IEEE. Vol.66, No. 10, October 1978, pp. 1126-1145.

[WANG79] S.L. Wang and A. Avizienis. *"The Design of Totally Self Checking Circuits Using Programmable Logic Arrays"* FTCS-9, pp 173-180.

DESIGN APPROACH FOR A VLSI SELF-CHECKING
MIL-STD-1750A MICROPROCESSOR

M.P. Halbert and S.M. Bose

Cambridge Consultants Limited.
Science Park, Milton Road,
Cambridge, England. CB4 4DW.

ABSTRACT

A design approach is presented for a VLSI self-checking MIL-STD-1750A microprocessor. Concurrent hardware error detection techniques are employed to obtain 100% coverage of all modelled faults. A feature of the approach is the extensive use of programmable logic arrays (PLAs). A methodology is presented for interconnecting totally self-checking PLA building blocks to produce larger totally self-checking circuits. This is found to enable efficient implementation of many logic functions. To illustrate the practical application of the techniques, designs for two major microprocessor subsystems are discussed: the arithmetic units and the microprogram controller.

1. INTRODUCTION

The increasing dependence on computer systems in airborne applications has led to a growing demand for highly reliable but compact microprocessor systems. Triple or quadruple modular redundancy is widely employed to achieve reliability through fault-tolerance, but is frequently unacceptable on the grounds of power consumption and size. A more attractive option is the use of self-checking computer modules which require only duplication for single fault-tolerance.

Various attempts at implementing self-checking computers have been reported in the literature. One approach[4] involves duplication and comparison of standard microprocessors. Aiming at lower chip counts, others have tackled the design of VLSI microprocessors with fault detection mechanisms incorporated on-chip[3][5][7].

Falling into the latter category, this paper reports some early results from a study into the design of a VLSI microprocessor to implement the MIL-STD-1750A instruction set.

An important feature of our design approach is the extensive use of programmable logic arrays (PLAs) in totally-self-checking (TSC) circuit design. Building on the work of Wang and Avizienis[8], we have developed a design methodology for the interconnection of TSC PLAs to generate larger TSC circuits. The value of the techniques are demonstrated by their application to several important subsystems of the microprocessor, including various arithmetic units and the instruction decoder. Also reported is our approach to the microprogram controller which incorporates a number of novel techniques to achieve high fault coverage with low hardware overhead.

2. 1750A INSTRUCTION SET

MIL-STD-1750A defines the instruction set architecture for a 16-bit airborne computer[1]. The instruction set includes a wide range of arithmetic and logical instructions which operate on 16- or 32-bit integers and 32- or 48-bit floating point numbers. Ten addressing modes allow access to 64K words of logical memory, while a memory management option expands physical memory to 1M word. A comprehensive fault and interrupt handling structure enables an orderly response to a range of exception conditions, including memory faults, illegal instructions, illegal memory references and error detection by hardware built-in-test equipment (BITE).

Because MIL-STD-1750A does not define specific implementation details, it makes no comment on the implementation of BITE. The designer is therefore free to incorporate extensive error checking, and to utilize the interrupt structure for initiating retry, recovery or reconfiguration.

3. SIMPLEX DESIGN OF A 1750A PROCESSOR

We began by first developing a simplex hardware architecture capable of implementing the 1750A instruction set. A two-chip set is intended with the central processing unit (CPU) on one chip and memory management unit on the other. A block diagram of the CPU is shown in Fig. 1.

4. FAULT MODEL

The primary fault classes we have considered are single stuck gate terminals, and transient faults in data storage cells. Wherever possible we have also taken account of open circuit lines, short circuits between adjacent lines and multiple stuck-at faults. However, the probability of many of these faults is layout dependent, and at the design stage can only be modelled for regular structures such as memories and PLAs.

5. SELF-CHECKING DESIGN AIMS

The design aim is to produce a microprocessor which has the following properties.

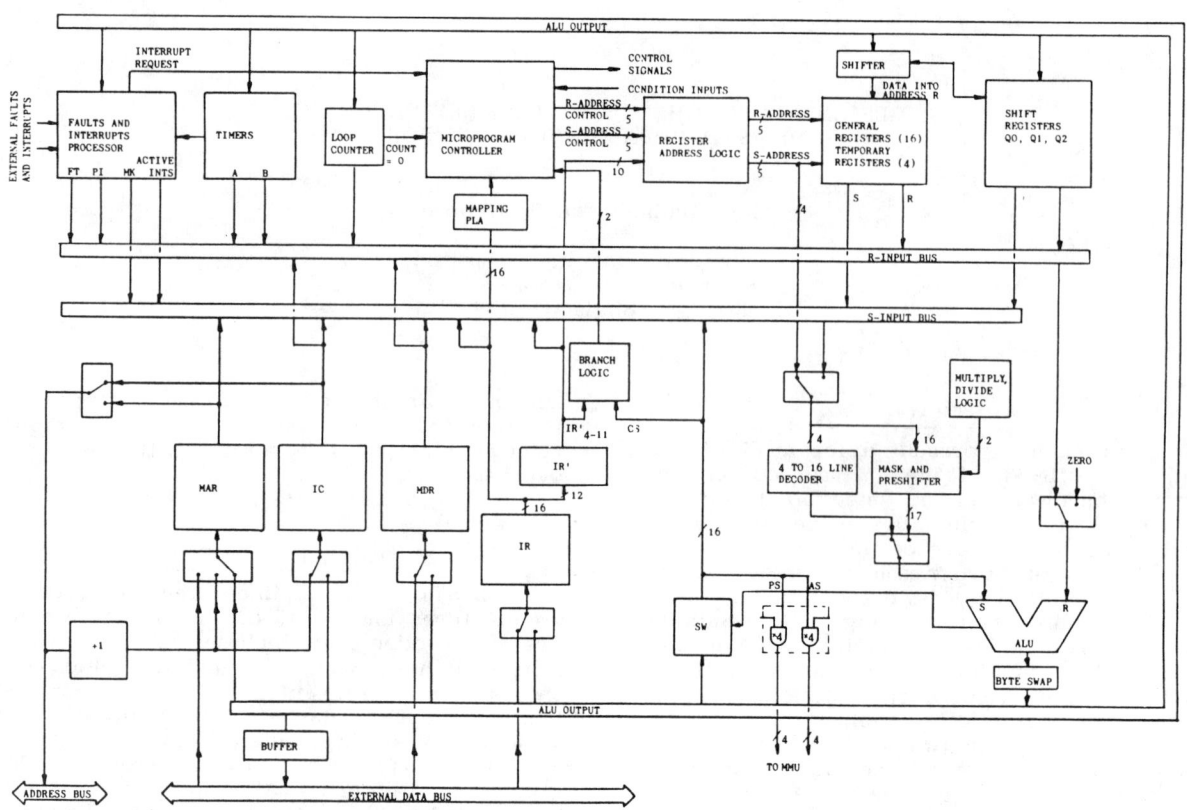

Fig. 1. Block diagram of the simplex MIL-STD 1750A microprocessor.

(1) Fault-secure for all modelled faults, ie. any fault which causes an error in the output must immediately be detected.

(2) Self-testing for all modelled faults when special built-in-test (BIT) routines are executed. These BIT routines are run from main memory and should be of practical size.

(3) Self-testing during normal use for as many faults as possible. Obviously 100% coverage cannot be guaranteed when running application programs, since certain exception conditions (e.g. illegal instructions) may never occur.

The motivation behind the above design aims is two-fold:

(1) The self-checking microprocessor forms the basis of a self-checking computer module; a fault-tolerant computer can be built by duplication of these modules.

(2) The processor's testability makes it possible to screen for latent faults before beginning a mission. Comprehensive testing at such times is important if high reliability is to be achieved through modular redundancy. As a bonus, the self-check capability can also assist with device screening during manufacture.

6. DESIGN METHODOLOGY

6.1 General

The requirement for 100% fault-secureness implies that concurrent error detection by on-chip hardware is essential. In general, we achieve this by:

- Information redundancy. Data words are encoded so that specified errors are detectable as code violations. Code checkers must also be TSC. We have found the most practical codes to be: single-bit parity; k-variable two-rail; m-out-of-n.

- Modular redundancy. In situations where the application of coding is impracticable, duplication is sometimes a more efficient approach. To avoid common mode failures or masking of shorted lines, it is often preferable if the duplicate module is implemented in complementary logic. A TSC comparator can be used to compare the outputs from the module pair.

Under fault-free conditions, each TSC code checker generates a two-rail complementary output; if the input is non-code, or if the checker is faulty, the two output lines assume the same logic value. The outputs of several checkers are condensed into one two-rail output by means of TSC k-variable two-rail checkers.

This leads ultimately to a single two-rail output to indicate the fault status of the entire processor to the outside world.

6.2 Background to the Use of PLAs

A key feature of our design approach is the extensive use of PLAs. PLAs have the advantages of regular structure and ease of layout, but are also attractive because of the ease with which bridging faults and contact faults can be modelled; as compared with random logic, this would appear to offer a more comprehensive representation of likely physical failures.

A method for designing TSC PLAs to implement general logic functions was described by Wang and Avizienis (W-A)[8]. They show that a PLA is TSC if it possesses the following four properties:

(1) The output belongs to a checkable code such that no output codeword covers any other.

(2) Each output pattern is expressed by its sum of products with minimum literals.

(3) The PLA is non-concurrent, i.e. for each input, one and only one product term is activated.

(4) Members of every pair of adjacent product terms belong to different output patterns, and members of every pair of adjacent output lines have different crosspoint device patterns.

A problem with this class of PLAs is that all possible binary patterns must be fed to the PLA to guarantee that it is completely tested. Consequently, checkable encoding of the input word is not possible, and protection against input errors is not provided. Unless this problem is solved, such PLAs cannot be used as a component in a totally self-checking system.

6.3 Interconnection of PLAs

We now describe an efficient method of interconnecting PLAs to form larger TSC networks. The essence of the method is:

- To eliminate the input inverters from each PLA, so that the AND-planes are effectively driven by two-rail codes.

- To choose two-rail output encoding for each PLA, so that the output of one PLA can directly drive the inputs of others.

Interconnected in this manner, a network of PLAs is automatically <u>fault-secure</u>. (The proof is based on the fact that a single fault can only cause uni-directional errors). To be <u>self-testing</u> however, the following conditions must be met.

(1) Each PLA in the network must be self-testing. This condition is satisfied by following the W-A design procedure.

(2) The entire network must be testable from the primary inputs, ie. a test set must exist which, when applied to the primary inputs, succeeds in applying a full test set to each PLA in the network. This condition cannot necessarily be met for any arbitrary partitioning of a circuit into individual PLAs. However, two expedients can be pursued to assist in meeting it: to maximise the range of codewords generated by each PLA, and to reduce the test set of each PLA. Both of these factors can be controlled to some extent by making different choices during the processes of 'don't care' assignment and literal minimisation. A logic simulator is a useful tool for verifying that chosen test sets do indeed achieve the desired fault coverage.

(3) Each PLA output must be code checked. This condition can be met either by dedicated code checkers, or in certain circumstances, by one or more of the PLAs to which the output is connected. The circumstances under which a TSC PLA can serve as a code checker for its inputs are covered by the theorem in the appendix. Briefly, a given two-rail input pair is code-checked if, for each product term, there is one AND-plane dot on either of the two input rows. The ability of PLAs to exhibit this code disjoint property saves considerably on dedicated checkers, and contributes greatly to the efficiency of the technique.

In general, the efficiency and testability of a network designed by this method is sensitive to the manner in which the network is partitioned into separate PLAs. If the number of inputs to each PLA is kept small, the total crosspoint device count will normally be low. The size of the test set too will be small. On the other hand, partitionings with larger PLAs sometimes have the advantage of lower propagation delays. One deciding factor between alternative partitionings is very often the number of dedicated checkers required. In this context, it is desirable if the design of individual TSC PLAs can be successfully completed without introducing extra output lines.

Although not all functions can be implemented efficiently by this method, many lead to elegant structures which are much more compact than equivalent implementations in duplicated random logic. Together with the other attractions of using PLAs in VLSI, the method has considerable potential for practical self-checking design.

7. ARITHMETIC UNITS

We have applied the above method to the design of several arithmetic units for the self-checking processor. These include:

- Simple incrementers for use in TSC, failsafe counters.

- A multi-function counter with facilities for increment, decrement, skip, hold and load.

- Small adders for use in the register addressing logic.

- Two designs for a full 16-bit eight-function arithmetic logic unit (ALU). One design is partitioned into two-bit slices with ripple carry between them, while another uses a simple form of lookahead carry.

Space precludes the description of the more complex circuits mentioned above. To provide an illustration of our method we describe below a simple four-bit adder with ripple carry.

7.1 4-bit adder with ripple carry

A simple design for a 4-bit adder is shown in Figure 2. The circuit comprises four single-bit adders, each with carry in and carry out. Each bit-slice is implemented in PLA and designed to be TSC according to the W-A method.

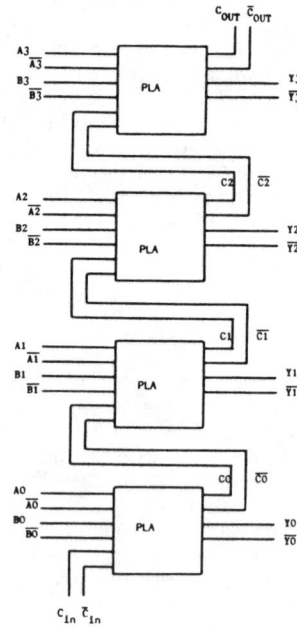

Fig. 2a.   The structure for a simple 4-bit adder.

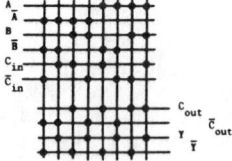

Fig. 2b.   The PLA used in the above adder.

The design procedure for each PLA is trivial in this case, since there is no scope for reduction of literals, and one product term is needed for each possible input pattern.

Key features of the adder circuit are:

- Two-rail codes are used on both the input and output of each PLA.

- According to the theorem in the appendix, each PLA serves as a two-rail code checker for its inputs. This makes the entire circuit code disjoint and also eliminates the need for a dedicated checker on the 'carry out' lines. The only checkers needed, therefore, are those on the primary outputs.

- The adders can be cascaded to any size, and can be used as building blocks in larger networks of PLAs.

- Although there are 512 possible codeword inputs, the complete adder can be tested with just 8 input patterns.

- The equivalent gate count of the adder is 48, considerably less than a duplicated random logic version of the same circuit.

- Faster adders can be achieved by implementing each two-bit adder with one PLA. The same kind of structure is obtained, but the carry propagates at twice the speed. Each PLA now requires 32 product terms.

8. MICROPROGRAM CONTROLLER

The microprogram controller demonstrates a wider range of the design techniques which we have employed in the self-checking microprocessor. The design, which is novel in several aspects, not only achieves 100% coverage of single faults, but does so efficiently. Depending on the final choice of encoding in the microinstruction, the device-count overhead introduced by the self-checking circuitry is between 15 and 30%. This compares extremely favourably with other approaches reported in the literature.

The requirements for the microprogram controller are as follows :

1. An instruction decoder which reads a 16-bit instruction word and generates two microprogram addresses: one for address mode calculation and the other for instruction execution. Since the instruction word is not fully coded, PLA provides a much more efficient implementation than ROM.

2. Conditional branch capability.

3. ROM microstore size of approximately 1K x 64 bits.

Figure 3 illustrates a TSC design for the controller. The reasons behind the major design decisions are described briefly in the following subsections.

8.1 Microstore addressing

An essential feature of the self-checking microprogram controller design is the technique for covering decoder faults in the microstore ROM. Methods in the literature include binary addressing with single-bit parity [6], full binary address recoding [3] and m-out-of-n code addressing [2]. The first two of these methods are not necessarily fault-secure for all address decoder faults, and in practice tend to rely on the coded microinstruction fields to detect errors. With m-out-of-n codes, it is possible to design an

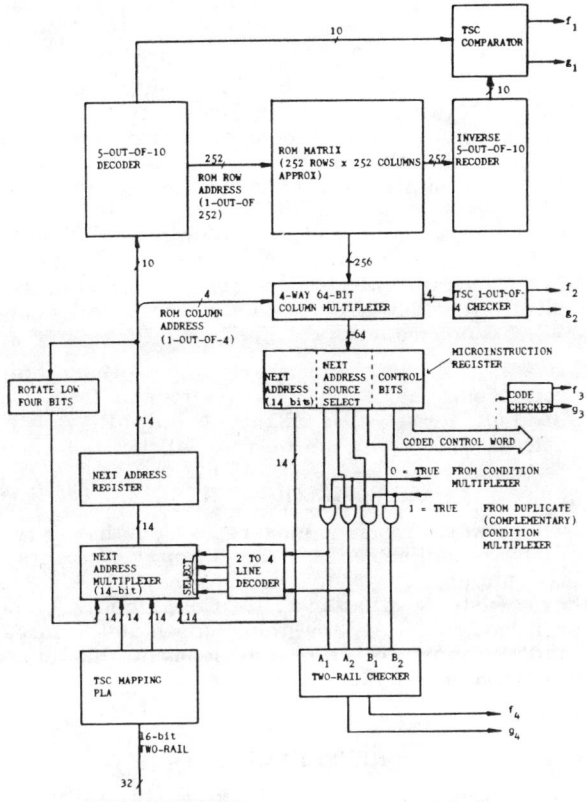

Fig. 3. The TSC microprogram controller.

address decoder and checker which can be proved TSC regardless of microinstruction contents.

In our design, a 5-out-of-10 code word is used to select 1-of-252 rows in the microstore ROM. These rows then drive an inverse 5-out-of-10 recoder. The output of this recoder is complementary to the original codeword and the two words can therefore be compared by a k-variable two-rail checker. This arrangement both checks the 5-out-of-10 code and is TSC for all decoder or recoder faults.

A method for sequence control, particularly conditional branching, is another important aspect. To overcome the problem that m-out-of-n codes possess no obvious sequence properties, we have adopted the following approach.

(a) The 1K x 64 ROM is implemented as a square matrix with 252 rows and 4 x 64 columns. The row address is in a 5-out-of-10 code and the column address is 1-out-of-4.

(b) A next address field in each microinstruction indicates the normal sequence of microinstructions.

(c) If a branch condition is true, the next instruction is taken from the same ROM row but the next column. Since this only involves rotation of the 1-out-of-4 column address, the address is trivial to generate. The advantage of this approach is that a second microinstruction field is not occupied by the alternative address.

(d) A next address multiplexer selects between the four alternative addresses, i.e. the normal next address, the conditional branch address, and the two mapping PLA outputs. Because the multiplexer and the next address register are handling m-out-of-n codewords they are fault-secure for all single faults, including those in the multiplexer address decoder.

8.2 Microinstruction Coding

Error detecting codes are required in the microinstructions to cover faults in microstore ROM bits and the column multiplexer. Since address decoder faults are already covered, a simple code which covers random bit errors is sufficient; more powerful codes to cover the multiple unidirectional errors caused by address decoder faults are unnecessary. Depending on the fault model adopted for ROM cells, any convenient choice of codes can be made for individual microinstruction fields. Single-bit parity, Hamming double error detecting or m-out of-n codes are all suitable.

8.3 PLA Instruction Decoder

Because of the requirement for a single large PLA as the instruction decoder, we were interested to discover whether the W-A procedure was able to yield a TSC design of practical proportions. The fact that it was able to do so with less than 20% increase in size indicates that this approach offers substantial savings over the opcode recode and compare approach suggested by Disparte .

The main steps involved in the design of the TSC mapping PLA are described below.

(1) TSC PLA outputs must be in a checkable code. Since the microstore addresses are m-out-of-n, this requirement is already met.

(2) Normally, the PLA must provide a full m-out-of-n code space to test its checker. In this case however, a dedicated checker is not required, since the m-out-of-n checker at the microstore ROM fulfils the function. Furthermore, a full m-out-of-n code space is not required, since the checker can be fully exercised by cycling of the microstore ROM.

(3) From a study of the 1750A opcode allocations, we identified the number of instruction types requiring distinct output patterns from the mapping PLA. Of these distinct patterns, 196 corresponded to legal instructions and the remainder to illegal opcodes.

(4) Minimisation of literals and elimination of concurrencies were simple for the legal instructions, since in general either 4 or 8 bits of the 16-bit instruction word were 'don't care'. Thus one product term was required for each legal instruction.

(5) Illegal opcodes were distributed fairly randomly about the 1750A opcode matrix, and it was not possible to minimise literals without introducing concurrencies. To overcome this problem, we divided the illegal opcodes into three groups and allocated different microprogram addresses for each. We were then able to minimise literals without introducing concurrencies. Sixteen product terms were needed to decode all illegal opcodes.

(6) The PLA input is two-rail encoded, thus providing protection against all unidirectional input errors.

The resulting PLA, which is TSC for all single and many multiple stuck-at faults, shorts and crosspoint defects, has 16 two-rail inputs, 212 product terms and 28 outputs. A complete test set comprises about 658 tests, of which some are illegal opcodes. Thus the PLA will not be completely tested in normal use, but can be checked by periodically running a small test routine.

9. CONCLUSION

Although further work is planned on detailed aspects of the design, the implementation of a self-checking 1750A microprocessor with 100% fault coverage is emerging as a practical proposition. Preliminary device counts suggest that the self-testing overheads will be in the range of 40 to 60%, depending on whether the main registers are protected with parity or two-rail codes.

An interesting outcome from our work to date is a methodology for interconnecting TSC PLAs which results in especially regular and efficient implementation of many logic functions. Considering the ease of PLA design and layout, together with the comprehensiveness of the fault model addressed, we believe that PLA implementations of this kind are suitable for wide application in future self-checking designs.

APPENDIX
Theorem

A non-concurrent PLA, in which each output pattern f_m is expressed by its sum of products with minimum literals and which has no two patterns f_m and f_n such that f_m covers f_n, serves as a two-rail code checker for the input rows x_i and $\bar{x}_i$ if

(a) for every product term, there is one dot in either row x_i or row $\bar{x}_i$, and

(b) any errors in the other input lines are in the same direction as errors in x_i and $\bar{x}_i$. Note that this condition is guaranteed when a single fault model is applied to a network of PLAs, since any errors will be unidirectional.

Proof

Consider the following input code violations in turn.

(1) If $x_i = \bar{x}_i = 0$, then condition (a) ensures that no product terms can be activated. The PLA output will have zeros in all bit positions and hence be non-code.

(2) If $x_i = \bar{x}_i = 1$, and the other input rows are correct two-rail codes, then two product terms will be activated, one corresponding to $x_i = 0$ and the other corresponding to $x_i = 1$. The output patterns belonging to these two terms must be different or else, when literals are minimised, we obtain one product term with no dots in rows x_i and $\bar{x}_i$. The PLA output will therefore represent two different codewords ORed together, and hence will be non-code.

(3) If $x_i = \bar{x}_i = 1$ and there exist other input rows such that $x_k = \bar{x}_k = 1$, then at least two product terms with different outputs will be activated. Again the output will be noncode.

ACKNOWLEDGEMENTS

This work was sponsored by the Royal Aircraft Establishment, Farnborough, Hants., U.K., under contract no. A81A/2111. The authors wish to thank L.R. Collingbourne and G.W. Wilcock of RAE for their continued interest in and support of the development of fault-tolerant airborne systems.

REFERENCES

1. Department of Defense, "Sixteen-bit Computer Instruction Set Architecture", MIL-STD-1750A (USAF), Notice 1, 21 May 1982.

2. DIAZ, M. and DE SOUZA, J.M., "Design of Self-Checking Microprogram Controls", Digest, 5th Intnl. Symp. on Fault-Tolerant Computing (FTCS-5), pp.137-142, Paris 1975.

3. DISPARTE, C.P., "A Self-Checking VLSI Microprocessor for Electronic Engine Control", Digest, 11th Intnl. Symp. on Fault-Tolerant Computing (FTCS-11), p. 253, June 1981.

4. RENNELS, D.A., "Architectures for Fault-Tolerant Space-craft Computers", Proc. IEEE, Vol. 66, Vol. 10, pp. 1255 - 1268, Oct. 1978.

5. SEDMAK, R.S. and LIEBERGOT, H.L., "Fault-Tolerance of a General Purpose Computer Implemented by Very Large Scale Integration", IEEE Trans. Computers, Vol C-29, No. 6, pp. 492 - 500, June 1980.

6. TOY, W.N., "Fault-Tolerant Design of Local ESS Processors", Proc. IEEE, Vol 66, No. 10, pp. 1126 - 1145, Oct. 1978.

7. TSAO, M.M., WILSON, A.M., McGARITY, R.C., TSENG, C.J., and SIEWIOREK D.P., "The design of C.fast: A Single Chip Fault-Tolerant Microprocessor", Digest, 12th Intnl. Symp. on Fault-Tolerant Computing (FTCS-12), pp. 63 - 69, June 1982.

8. WANG, S.L. and AVIZIENIS, A., "The Design of Totally Self-Checking Circuits using Programmable Logic Arrays", Digest, 9th Intnl. Symp. on Fault-Tolerant Computing (FTCS-9), pp. 173 - 180, June 1979.

Fault Tolerance Techniques for Array Structures Used in Supercomputing

Roberto Negrini, Mariagiovanna Sami, and Renato Stefanelli
Politecnico di Milano, Italy

We can change reconfiguration algorithms to suit varying requirements while keeping VLSI and WSI arrays and their hardware and software interfaces standard.

We can say that supercomputing systems appeared early in the history of data processing if we agree to define them as the fastest state-of-the-art machines that can be obtained at any given time.

Two philosophies of parallelism. Since advanced application areas have consistently demanded computing power and speed far greater than that obtainable from technology that incorporates conventional architectures, the only acceptable solution has always been to design nonconventional architectures that have a high degree of parallelism. Such an approach was already evident in the late fifties; later, the concept of parallelism was expanded and applied along two distinct philosophies.

In the first, *parallelism of operation* is introduced at the global-architecture level; that is, many processing units are used, and all are provided with program- and data-storage capabilities. The intrinsic parallelism of the given application algorithm is identified, and parallel tasks are executed by the different processing units. Communication overheads are a basic issue: The achieving of expected performance depends mainly on the distribution of tasks among processors and on interconnection topology. Thus, hardware and software aspects contribute equally to the effectiveness of a given solution.

The best-known example of this class is probably Illiac IV[1]; many examples that are more recent are available, although it appears that only a relatively small percentage of the architectures proposed has reached the implementation stage.[2,3,4]

In the second, *parallelism is localized* in a specific section of the computing system. Typically, this section is the arithmetic unit or, more in general, some coprocessor capable of executing a well-specified and restricted set of functions. In most instances, such functions are parallel mathematical operations like those used in signal processing (in particular, two-dimensional signal processing): Processing elements are similarly specialized and linked together to form arrays. The resultant "parallel machine" cannot perform as a stand-alone computer; it must be controlled by a more complex conventional system.

The two approaches are not mutually exclusive; on the contrary, both can be found in supercomputers dedicated to signal-processing applications. In such supercomputers, the special-purpose array machine is interfaced to the general-purpose host machine by means of highly standardized interfaces; one main result of such interfacing, discussed in recent literature,[5] concerns the possibility of mapping a number of relevant algorithms onto the same array structure (in the case of some classes of arrays). This mapping capability is of obvious importance, since it allows us to obtain the efficiency of special-purpose devices with standardized devices. To ensure its validity, reconfiguration for purposes of fault tolerance (and even functional reconfiguration[5]) must be completely transparent at the host-array interface as regards both hardware and software.

In this article, we deal with the second-named (standardized) class of parallel machines.

Fast, highly parallel, dedicated array units are well suited to VLSI or even WSI implementation because of the extreme regularity of their architecture and their interconnection locality. Given these attributes, it is reasonable, as H. T. Kung[6] suggests, to look for algorithms inherently suited to such arrays (signal-processing algorithms, for instance, fall within this class).

Among the most attractive examples of array units discussed in the literature are the CHiP structure[7] and, most notably, the class of systolic arrays.[6] On such architectures it is possible to activate a *wavefront computation mode*, in which computation propagates along one direction only for the various interconnection axes. (In this article, we restrict our consideration to architectures that permit wavefront computation.)

The systems we consider here are, then, regular interconnections of processing elements (*cells*), with information flowing in one direction only along all interconnection lines. We require that no memory devices be present in the array, with the possible exception of local "service" memories (for example, registers in serial arithmetic units). This limited use of memory elements is acceptable for attached processors that generally communicate by means of I/O lines with the main memories. (The presence of registers of course affects error latency, since we must recover correct information from all working registers.)

Whatever the particular algorithm—or class of algorithms—implemented by arrays of the types described above, fault tolerance is an important performance, particularly when VLSI or WSI devices are considered.

Dual purposes can be identified for fault-tolerance capacities. On the one hand, application areas are typically mission-critical ones (for example, space systems, military systems, and telecommunications), so that obtaining a longer lifetime for the array structure is a major requirement.

On the other hand (and in particular for wafer-scale integration devices), fault tolerance is the only solution capable of giving acceptable production yield because it permits preliminary self-testing and array reconfiguration that exploits cell and interconnection redundancy.

Fault-tolerance policies can be identified only if significant fault models are defined first. Since we are considering array-level policies here, we assume that error information about the individual cell is provided by self-testing techniques that associate binary error information with each cell. (The particular self-testing technique adopted depends, in general, on technology as well as on cell function.) Further identification of fault models follows different lines and depends on two main factors, namely

- Fault occurrence time (that is, the frequency of run-time faults and production-time faults), and
- The relative complexity of the single cell as against the complete device (for example, VLSI arrays of a—relatively limited—number of cells as compared with WSI arrays of a large number of cells).

The two factors are not independent; run-time faults are the most probable ones for VLSI devices, which can be assumed to be properly screened for production-time faults, while tolerance for production-time faults is necessary to ensure reasonable production yield for WSI devices. Reconfiguration algorithms are different for each type of integration; still, VLSI-type reconfiguration algorithms are capable of supporting some production-time faults if these are restricted to individual cells, while WSI-type algorithms are suited also for WSI run-time reconfiguration.

In the sequel, algorithms leading to fault tolerance through reconfiguration will be discussed for both fault models defined above. Some notable proposals introduced in recent literature will be considered; then, a unified approach to some classes of reconfiguration techniques will be presented.

These fault-tolerance techniques have been tested for array self-reconfiguration; they can, as well, be used for host-driven reconfiguration. The most interesting result of the unified approach that we propose in this article is that it permits the introduction of *standard* structures that support a variety of fault-tolerance algorithms. (These belong to either the structure-redundancy or time-redundancy approach.) Thus, changes in fault-tolerance requirements will be totally transparent at the hardware/software interface between systolic array and host processor.

An analysis of some existing approaches

Fault-tolerance achieved by introduction of spare elements and reconfiguration has long been used in multiple-processor systems.[8] Here, we review only some of the techniques that are relevant to the subject of our article.

Where discrete-processor architectures are concerned, the main goal, if N spare elements are present, is to achieve survival to up to N faults, in other words, to achieve 100 percent spares utilization. This is obvious, since in such cases the cost of processing elements is much higher than that of interconnections and of routing devices; another reason is that since in such architectures processing elements are usually proper CPUs, routing is program-controlled by the same working CPUs.

The case of VLSI arrays is different as regards both performances to be evaluated and reconfiguration management. While utilization of spares is, of course, still important, it is also fundamental to keep locality of interconnections as high as possible even after reconfiguration and to implement simple routing devices, both of which measures help to minimize (a) increase in silicon area and (b) time delays. This requirement of implementing simple routing devices is valid also for reconfiguration-controlling circuits whenever on-chip self-reconfiguration is adopted. It has been proved[9] that excessive increase of chip area due to introduction of fault-tolerance-related circuits has a negative effect on overall device reliability.

For these reasons, papers dealing with VLSI array reconfiguration strive to achieve a balance between reconfiguration effectiveness (that is, the probability of surviving up to x number of faults, given $N \geq x$ spares) and reconfiguration algorithm complexity. The relevance of this balance differs depending on the approach adopted for reconfiguration, namely

(a) Static reconfiguration, which is performed at production time,
(b) Dynamic reconfiguration, which is driven by a host at run-time, and
(c) Dynamic self-reconfiguration performed on-chip at run time.

A prerequisite for all three approaches is the availability of testing information about the individual cell.

In case (a), reconfiguration is uniquely determined at production time, and it is actuated, for the most part, by irreversible actions. Testing is performed externally, and no on-chip controlling circuitry is required. The complexity of the reconfiguration algorithm is not a critical issue, since it does not affect either circuit complexity or operation speed. (See Leighton and Leiserson [10] and Kung and Lam.[11])

Case (b) is justified when we consider that the array structures are driven by an external host that can perform reconfiguration-controlling actions on the basis of available error information. The problem of *error latency* (defined as the time that passes before the array is operating correctly again after occurrence of a fault) has to be taken into account, since reconfiguration is not undertaken at each array operation step. Locality of interconnection is an important consideration, but reconfiguration-controlling algorithms can be fairly complex since the host machine is usually a powerful one; thus, high probability of survival may be reached by means of complex algorithms. Some examples of case (b) are discussed by Batcher,[2] Snyder,[7] and Aubusson and Catt.[12]

Lastly, case (c). This type of reconfiguration, while obviously introducing additional costs as far as the array device itself is concerned (both for self-testing and for self-reconfiguration) helps to keep error latency low and does not add to host computation overhead. To reach a balance between probability of survival and the added silicon area required for reconfiguration, algorithms must be characterized by simplicity of implementation. Many proposals have been presented in the literature.[13-19]

Some techniques are suitable for both cases (b) and (c): Such techniques make use of interconnection networks and routing elements that are identical in both cases, while, obviously, they implement reconfiguration control in a different way. This suitability for both cases derives from the possibility of a formal, technology-independent definition for the reconfiguration techniques. We devote the next sections to their analysis.

Fault models and types of redundancy

The examples we treat in this article refer, typically, to two-dimensional systolic arrays; all the techniques described can easily be extended to different topologies.

We assume that self-testing information is associated with each cell, and that it is stored locally so as to keep track of error information. Under this setup, transient faults can be managed efficiently by resetting such information from time to time, since we make no assumption about how frequently the different faults occur.

We distinguish two different fault models:

• *Random fault distribution*. This model is well suited to VLSI devices and run-time fault occurrence: The devices it is applicable to consist of a (relatively) limited number of cells, and the number of spares also is rather limited, so high spares utilization must be reached.

• *Cluster fault distribution*. This model is well suited to production-time faults in wafer-scale devices, where fault causes can affect large areas of the wafer. (A comparable type of failure in a VLSI device would lead to discarding the device itself.) Since the relative complexity of cell as compared with wafer is lower than in the preceding model and the number of spares is high, spares utilization is not as important as in the other model. This second fault model also adapts to run-time random faults on the same device.

We also distinguish two redundancy types:

• *Structure redundancy*. This is the type of redundancy most usually considered in the literature; it involves introduction of spare cells (and of a corresponding interconnection structure). In array structures, spares are kept inactive as long as no fault is present, and begin operation only when it becomes necessary to substitute them for faulty cells. If the reconfiguration algorithm is sufficiently simple and fast, operation speed of the array does not change even after reconfiguration.

• *Time redundancy*. This approach has been used mainly for self-testing. The technique involves assigning to an array-processing step a number of operation phases. Working cells—by performing during repeated operation phases—perform the functions of faulty cells without the need of spare elements (complexity of the interconnection network and chip area increases). Processing speed decreases with respect to the nominal speed; thus, this approach can be considered effective only when the speed made possible by the array is greater than that required by the application, or when decreasing speed is an acceptable form of degradation. Since supercomputing involves high-speed computation requirements, we do not treat this type of approach in depth in this article.

Four different instances can thus be examined: One for each fault model and one for each type of redundancy. In the next sections, we present sample algorithms for the four instances.

A unified approach to reconfiguration involves two different problems.

The first problem is that of *routing data* through the reconfigurable array. This involves introduction of redundant links and of routing devices (such as multiplexers or switches) that permit us to create the correct paths by interconnecting suitable links. We preserve the locality of the interconnection network by abandoning the *direct substitution* philosophy adopted in discrete-elements architectures (by which a faulty cell is directly replaced by a spare) and by adopting the philosophy of global *deformations* of the whole array (these confine faulty cells and include suitable spares).

The routing structure depends on the different reconfiguration strategies adopted, *not* on the particular algorithm; that is, it depends on the number of deformations to be performed in the array to achieve reconfiguration. This keeps the routing structure valid for a number of alternative reconfiguration algorithms.

The second problem is that of *reconfiguration computation* as related to fault distribution and to either distribution-of-spares or time-redundancy strategy adopted. This involves definition and implementation of reconfiguration algorithms.

Our formal definition of algorithms (below) allows for two alternative implementation criteria, namely either by means of software on the host computer controlling the array, or by means of dedicated hardware, such as on-chip reconfiguration-controlling circuits. Both alternatives make use of the same routing structure defined in the first phase of operation, thus achieving further standardization of hardware interfaces.

A unified approach to reconfiguration: structure redundancy

We introduce here a class of reconfiguration algorithms that make use of simple patterns of spare elements. For rectangular arrays of $N*N$ "nominal" cells, spares are organized along the $(N+1)$th column and/or row.

As regards routing strategies: For a given fault distribution, reconfiguration is performed by a global procedure in which array functions are mapped onto the working cells by means of a global *renaming* process. If we define for each cell in the array

- *physical indices* (i,j) denoting position in the *physical* array consisting of all cells, and
- *logical indices* (i',j') that denote position in the *logical* array consisting of working cells only and implement all *functions* required by the array (Note: Conventionally, whenever a cell is not active, logical indices are set to 0),

then, reconfiguration can be seen as an algorithm of mapping logical onto physical indices. Whenever a given algorithm does not complete this mapping onto correctly working cells, a *fatal failure* condition is said to occur.

This approach allows us to define reconfiguration algorithms that preserve to a high degree the regularity and locality of interconnection networks. The effectiveness of the algorithms (which is, ultimately, the probability of survival they reach) is related to their complexity; still, all the algorithms are relatively simple, even the most effective ones. Requirements of locality and simplicity, on the other hand, mean that for some fault distributions, reconfiguration may be impossible even though there are still spare cells available.

A reconfiguration algorithm ultimately performs a deformation of the working array. It is possible to give a formal definition of all such algorithms;[20] here, we confine ourselves to an "intuitive" presentation of the approach and of a few main algorithms.

Consider the simplest case, in which we add to the array one (the rightmost) column of spares. If cell (i,j) is faulty, it is bypassed and logical indices (i',j') are associated with cell $(i, j+1)$; for all cells (i,k), $k>j$, logical indices are computed as $i'=i$, $k'=k-1$. Figure 1 shows the results of reconfiguration on a sample distribution of faults after running Algorithm 1 (see Table 1): Fatal failure is reached whenever there are two faulty cells in one row (the probability of survival is not very good, as shown by the statistical results in row 1, Table 1). Locality is high: Cell-to-cell paths never exceed length 2, if 1 is the distance between two physically adjacent cells.

Far better results can be achieved by adding both a column and a row of spares (the row at the bottom), thus adding $2N+1$ spares to an $N \times N$ array. A simple algorithm (described by Sami and Stefanelli[21] as "simple fault-stealing") acts as follows:

- The array is scanned from top to bottom, (that is, it is scanned for $1 \le i \le N$).

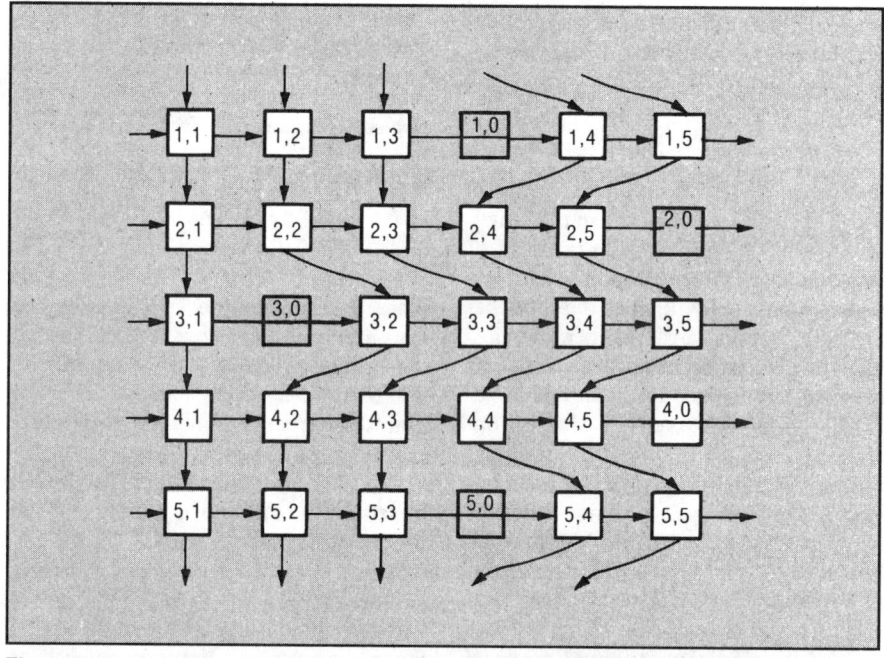

Figure 1. An example of reconfiguration achieved by Algorithm 1. (Shaded cells are faulty.)

Table 1.
Statistical results obtained from using four different algorithms to reconfigure a 20*20 array.

Algorithm	Array	No. of spares	No. of faults that can be overcome with probability		
			90%	75%	50%
1	20*20	20	2.6	4.2	5.8
2	20*20	41	12.1	15.5	19.1
3	20*20	41	23.1	25.0	28.0
4	20*20	41	31.5	34.4	36.8

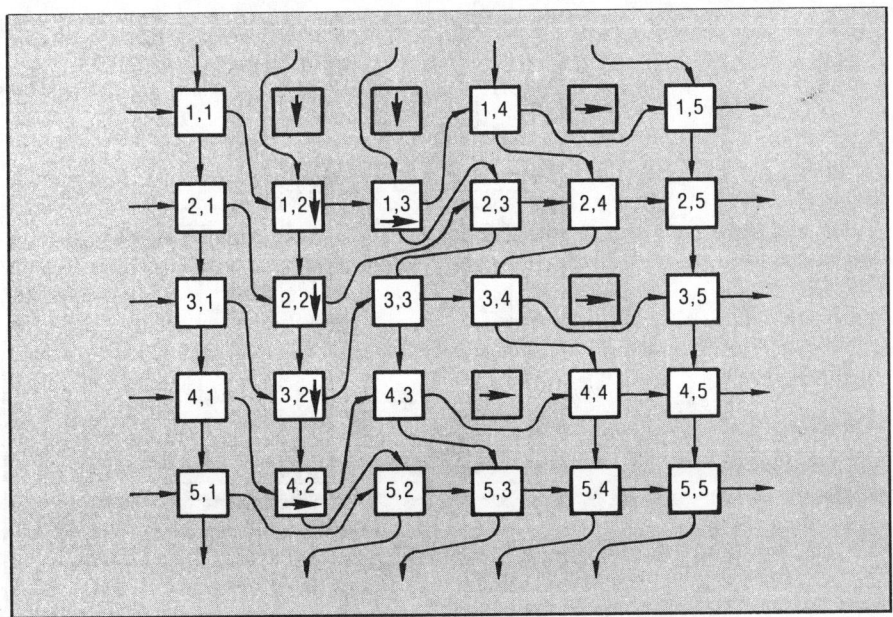

Figure 2. Reconfiguration achieved by Algorithm 2. (Shaded cells are faulty.)

- If in row i there is only one faulty or "stolen" cell, rightward reconfiguration is performed as described for Algorithm 1.

- Otherwise, the rightmost faulty or stolen cell invokes rightward reconfiguration, while all other faulty or stolen ones "steal" functions of cells in the corresponding positions of row $i+1$ (these last become "stolen cells"). Stealing by (i, j) implies associating logical indices (i', j') with the stolen cell, which then acts as if it were faulty by invoking reconfiguration in its turn.

- Fatal failure is reached whenever a stolen cell is faulty.

An example of reconfiguration performed by this second algorithm is given in Figure 2. As with Algorithm 1, locality is high (maximum path length is 3). Statistical results are given in row 2 of Table 1.

While still simple (circuits implementing it are suitable for on-chip self-reconfiguration), this algorithm's performance is limited by the dual conditions that rightward reconfiguration be reserved to the rightmost cell requiring it and that stealing be performed strictly along the columns. Loosening these limitations leads to better performances but also, obviously, to greater complexity. The first restriction is overcome by introducing *variable-choice stealing*, in which for each row, rightward reconfiguration is reserved to the faulty or stolen cell (if any) that could not invoke stealing along the column. Statistical results for this solution (Algorithm 3, Table 1) show a marked improvement over Algorithm 2. Finally, by combining this variable choice with a wider possibility for stealing (cell (i, j) may require stealing either from $(i+1, j)$ or, if this is faulty or stolen, from $(i+1, j+1)$) we reach a *complex stealing algorithm* (Algorithm 4, Table 1) characterized by very high probability of survival.

On the other hand, the complexity of this algorithm—and therefore of the circuits *computing* reconfiguration signals

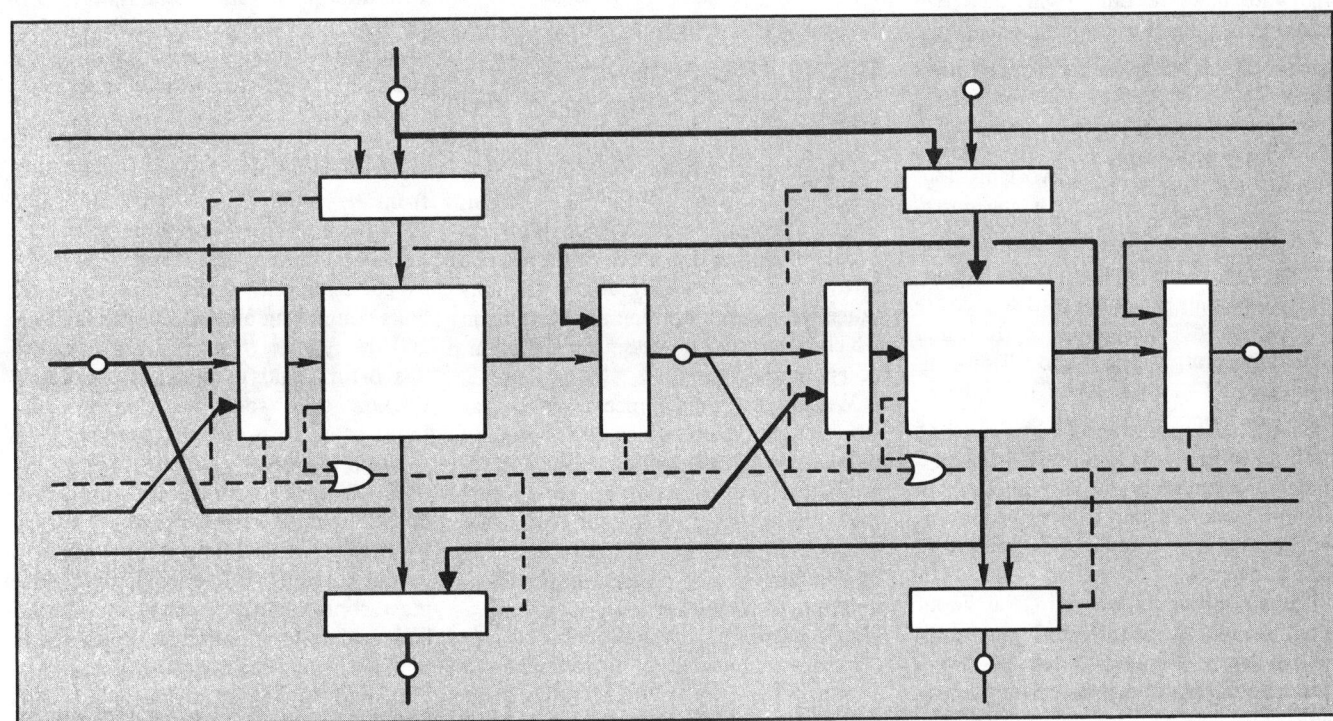

Figure 3. The interconnection structure and spare links corresponding to a single reconfiguration operator. (Thick lines denote active interconnections for a sample reconfiguration; broken lines represent reconfiguration-controlling signals.)

(*not* the circuits of the interconnection structure!)—makes it better suited to host-driven reconfiguration than to on-chip self-reconfiguration. It is not yet optimum, if an optimum algorithm is one that, when applied to a particular deformation and a given distribution of spares, leads to fatal failure only for such fault distributions as would not allow reconfiguration by any other algorithm applied to the same deformation. Host-driven reconfiguration makes even complex and time-consuming algorithms acceptable if they optimize spare utilization.

Consider now the basic interconnection structures supporting the various algorithms. For any algorithm involving deformation in *one* direction only, the general interconnection structure illustrated in Figure 3 can be used; it incorporates alternative links and one two-way multiplexer along each input and output point of each cell. (Thick lines denote active interconnections for a sample reconfiguration; broken lines represent signals controlling the multiplexers). This structure constitutes one layer of "reconfiguration shell" around the cell.

In the same way, any sequence of *two* deformations (for example, rightward and downward) that makes use of one spare row and one spare column will lead to two layers of shell and allow interconnections with a much larger set of cells; the elementary structure can be obtained by superimposing two shells like the one shown in Figure 3. (At the input and output points of a shell lies the working "logical" cell (i', j') created by the corresponding deformation, and on it, in turn, a second deformation may be applied).

Data-routing structures thus defined are "preliminary" ones; while correct and totally general, they are also silicon-consuming, and the number of multiplexers inserted along each path causes large delays.

Simpler interconnection structures can be devised by following, for the vertical and/or horizontal input to cell (i, j), all alternative paths coming from outputs of different cells, and substituting the "input shell" structure for (i, j) with one multiplexer that (1) has as many inputs as there are different paths and (2) is controlled by a function derived from the control signals to the 2-input multiplexers found on the various paths.

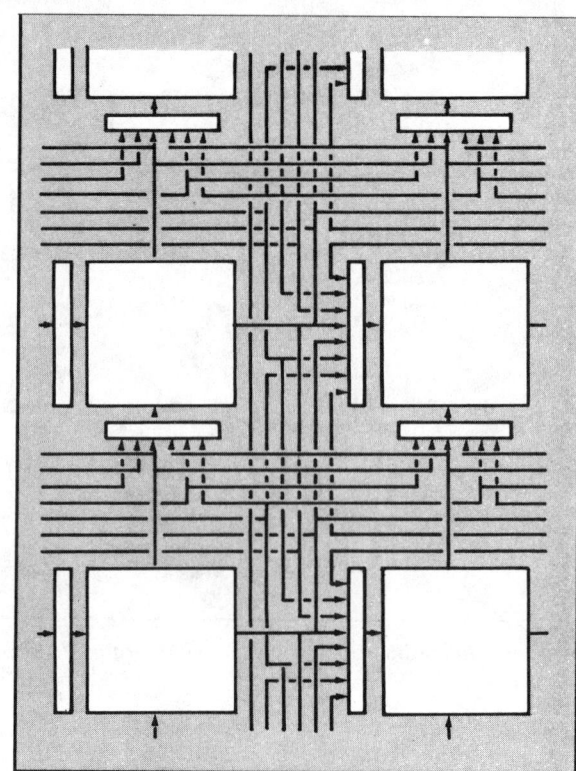

Figure 4. An interconnection structure for Algorithms 2 and 3. A single multiplexer is inserted between logically adjacent cells.

Thus, we finally achieve a simpler (if less regular) routing layout (see Figure 4). Some algorithms set limits to the possible values of reconfiguration signals of adjacent cells. This allows us to further simplify the corresponding interconnection structure.

Random distribution of faults: the time-redundancy approach

The algorithms discussed in the previous section (note that they set stringent limits to alternative path lengths) do not modify the operation speed of the systolic array. This is obviously of basic importance for supercomputing applications in which decreasing processing speed is unacceptable.

When speed requirements are not as stringent (or, when reducing the speed by one half is an acceptable measure of degradation necessitated by the presence of faults), if structure redundancy has to be overridden, an alternative is represented by *time redundancy*, a technique previously proposed for system-level self-testing.

In the time-redundancy mode of synchronous arrays, multiple operation phases are introduced for each processing step; any given working cell can be associated with different pairs of logical indices during the different operation phases. To this end, each cell is provided with suitable input and output latches: One for each phase. Assume, for example, two phases: A working cell (i, j) may be associated with logical indices (i', j') during the first phase and with (i'', j'') during the second phase. Operation is controlled by three staggered clocks associated, respectively, with first-phase and second-phase processing, and with input latch loading. (Again, a cell not working in a given phase is associated with logical indices set to 0.)

As a consequence of failure of cell (i, j), second-phase operation capacity and interconnection links would be "borrowed" from $(i-1, j)$. (Reconfiguration is, in such a case, performed only along the vertical axis.) To keep area redundancy as low as possible, only unit-length redundant links connecting any $(i, j-1)$ to $(i-1, j)$ and $(i-1, j)$ to $(i, j+1)$ are introduced; this, in turn, leads us to consider particular working cells, sometimes, as "pseudofaults" that is, as cells that are kept inactive *as if they were faulty*.

Satisfactory performances with a two-phase operation require a compromise between structure and time redundancy, so a row of spares is also added. This, for the most sophisticated algorithms, leads to high probability of survival. (For a 12 * 12 nominal array, we have 90 percent, 75 percent, and 50 percent probability of surviving, respectively, up to 20, 27.5 and 37.5 faults—a reasonable result if we consider that a two-phase operation adds, in

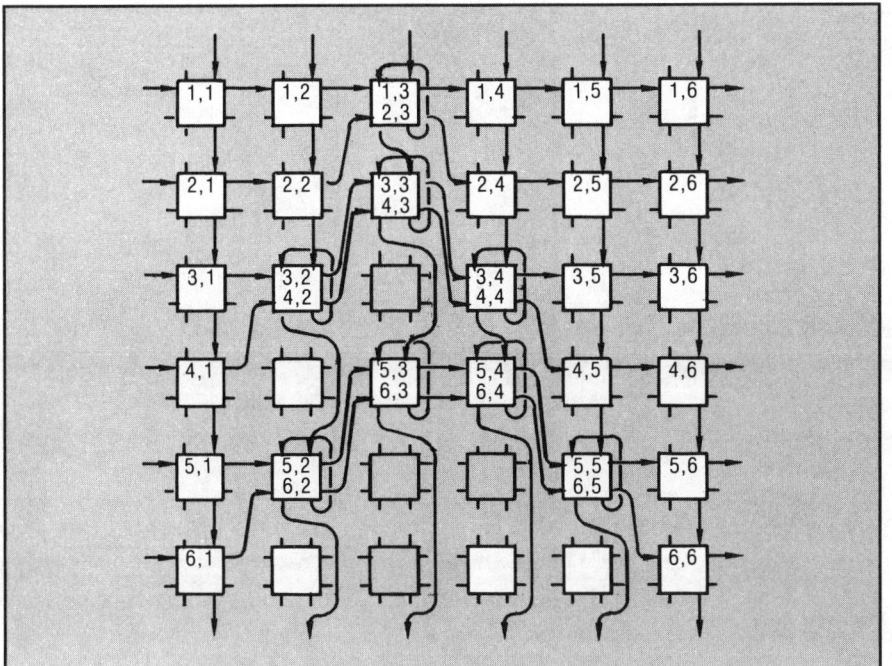

Figure 5. An example of reconfiguration achieved by the time-redundancy approach. The numbers shown inside cells are the logic indices of the working array. If a cell contains two pairs of indices, it works during both alternating phases and thus corresponds to two working logical cells. The upper pair of indices corresponds to the first working phase.

itself, N^2 "equivalent" spare cells to the basic single-phase array!)

Some alternative algorithms are discussed by Sami and Stefanelli[19]; as an example, consider Figure 5. Every cell appears to have two sets of possible connections with adjacent cells; actually, the upper horizontal and rightmost vertical links correspond to first-phase operation, the others to second-phase operation. (Pairs of logical indices associated with each cell for each operation phase are aligned with the links to which they correspond.) Pseudofaults are here clearly identified (by shaded boxes); maximum path length is never more than 2.

As in a previous example, the routing problem can be solved by building a standard shell structure around the basic cell to account for reconfiguration; the elementary shell is somewhat more complex than the one described in the section on the structural-redundancy approach, since two different data paths must be provided as inputs to the two latches along each axis. On the other hand, since reconfiguration is performed along one axis only, only one shell layer has to be introduced.

Cluster distribution of faults

A second important fault model is designed against the possibility that faults are "clustered" in relatively large silicon areas; such a model is typically required for wafer-scale integration arrays in which a large number of production defects have appeared. Thus, reconfiguration actions must isolate clusters of defects affecting not only processing cells but also data paths and even reconfiguration networks located inside faulty areas. Here also, as in the previous cases of VLSI-oriented solutions, the two different approaches of area and time redundancy can be introduced.

The area-redundancy approach. Large numbers of spares are required to recover from large numbers of faults: This is consistent with wafer-scale integration, which is well suited to implementation of large arrays of relatively simple processing cells. It is also consistent that some working elements work as "connecting elements" only.

In Negrini and Stefanelli,[18] a class of algorithms following these guidelines and differing in the number of spare data paths adopted has been introduced.

Figures 6(a) and (b) refer to one of these solutions and are based on a small set of alternative vertical and horizontal paths (respectively, 3 vertical and 5 horizontal). For any cell (i, j), only one vertical and one horizontal path are active; cells can be faulty, working, or acting just as connecting elements, as can be seen in the reconfiguration example in Figure 7.

Techniques for the VLSI fault model implicitly assume that areas between adjacent faulty cells are fault free, which would mean that reconfiguration signals can be created and propagated there. This assumption does not hold for the WSI fault models, which allow the presence of large faulty areas; therefore, different criteria for generation of reconfiguration signals must be introduced.

We adopt an approach, based on propagation of **request** and **acknowledge** reconfiguration signals throughout the whole array, that is capable of keeping active interconnection paths and active reconfiguration-controlling circuits from faulty areas.

The algorithm is composed of two successive phases:

(1) Propagation of vertical **request/acknowledge** signals from the bottom to the top of the array (creation of columns); and

(2) Subsequent propagation of horizontal **request/acknowledge** signals from left to right (creation of rows).

The basic principle can be seen in Figure 6(a), which describes reconfiguration of an array's column through utilization of spare paths. Cell (i, j) is requested so as to prolong a line as a consequence of some request signal **r** coming from a cell below, for example, cell $(i+1, j)$. It activates request **r1**: If cell $(i-1, j-1)$ is both working and not yet reserved, it generates acknowledge $\mathbf{a_1}$, which activates generation of acknowledge signal **a** in cell (i, j). Otherwise, cell (i, j) activates $\mathbf{r_2}$; again, if acknowledge $\mathbf{a_2}$ is not received, $\mathbf{r_3}$ is activated. If $\mathbf{a_3}$ also is not received, then acknowledge **a** is negated to cell $(i+1, j)$, which in turn will forward the request to cell $(i, j+1)$, and a similar process of request/acknowledge propagation will start again from this cell. Decreasing priorities

COMPUTER

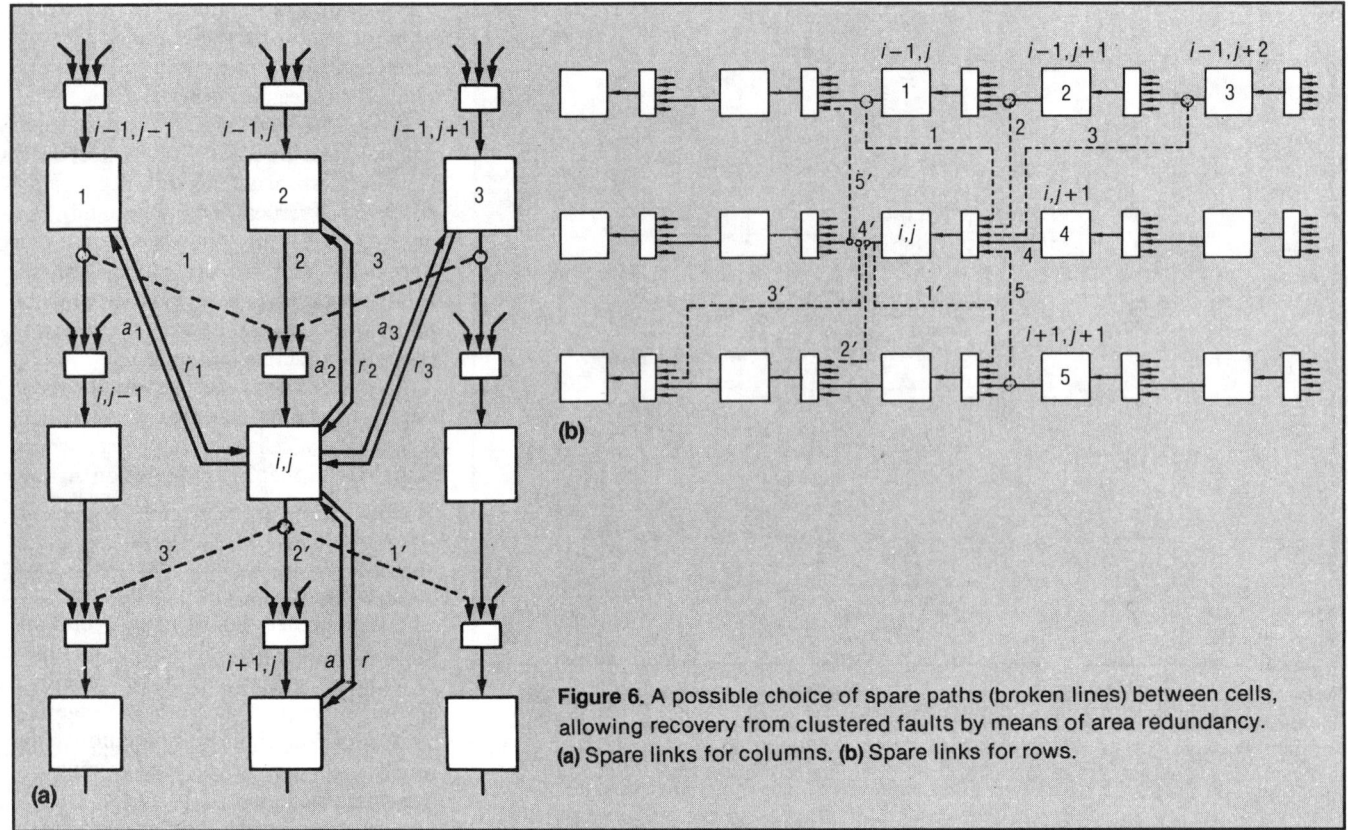

Figure 6. A possible choice of spare paths (broken lines) between cells, allowing recovery from clustered faults by means of area redundancy. (a) Spare links for columns. (b) Spare links for rows.

are associated with columns going from left to right: For example, if cell $(i-1, j)$ is requested at the same time by cells $(i, j-1)$ and (i, j), it acknowledges cell $(i, j-1)$ only. These priorities are the real core of the algorithm.

This procedure must be iterated by scanning the columns from left to right repeatedly until a stable configuration is achieved.

The same procedure can be applied to creation of rows. For example, in the case shown in Figure 6(b), where five pairs of horizontal paths are used, the algorithm would need five attempts to request the five horizontal neighbors in order. Values shown inside the cells represent both the order and priority of these requests.

During creation of rows it is also necessary to account for possible reconfiguration errors (a possible error instance is a row that does not cross all columns in proper order). Negrini and Stefanelli[18] prove that errors can be avoided by conditioning the horizontal control network through the **acknowledge** signals generated by the vertical control network.

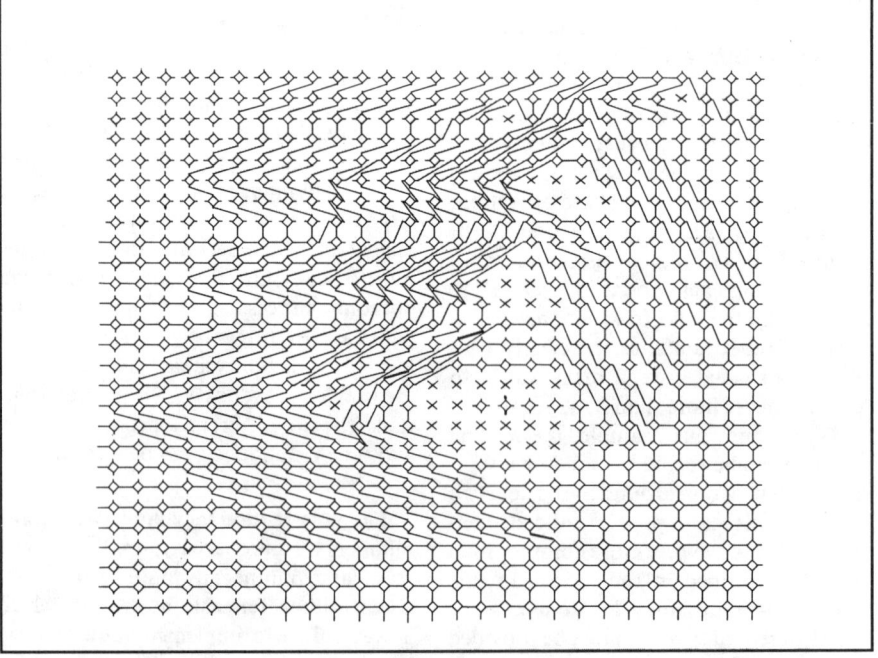

Figure 7. A complete reconfiguration achieved by means of the area-redundancy approach. Crossed cells (denoted "X") are faulty; completely interconnected cells form the working array; partially interconnected cells work as "links"; isolated cells are unused spares.

Figure 8. A complete example of reconfiguration achieved with the time-redundancy approach for clustered faults. The numbers shown inside cells are the logic indices of the working array, and cells working during both alternating phases contain the logic indices of both the corresponding logic cells.

Logic networks managing propagation of **request/acknowledge** signals are very simple.

Time-redundancy approach. For the time-redundancy approach, too, the WSI fault model implies that reconfiguration signals and data paths must completely avoid faulty areas.

As in the case of area redundancy, the problem is solved by adopting algorithms based on **request/acknowledge** signals exchanged among working cells. Reconfiguration is performed along both rows and columns (contrary to the VLSI case, where one deformation only is used).

Even if in pure time redundancy no spare processing elements are foreseen for use, algorithms similar to those suitable for the previous case of area redundancy can be identified.[22] It is necessary to describe a real processing cell as corresponding to two virtual ones, which in turn directly correspond to the two alternating operating phases.

Control networks and spare paths need not be duplicated in each cell; multiplexers governing the choice of spare paths change their active inputs alternatively, following the rhythm of the operating phases.

Among the algorithms that can be built in this way, the one adopted to solve instances like Figure 8 (the reconfiguration pattern was obtained by simulation) orders operations as follows:

(1) To prolong a row, a processing element (i, j) requests one of the six virtual cells of the three neighboring elements in the column at its right: $(i-1, j+1)$ $(i, j+1)$ $(i+1, j+1)$. The highest priority is given to the cell $(i-1, j+1)$ and the lowest to the cell $(i+1, j+1)$. Priorities tend to bend the rows, if possible, toward the upper edge of the array.

(2) To prolong a column, the processing element (i, j) requests one virtual cell from the following neighboring elements: $(i-1, j-1)$, $(i-1, j)$, $(i-1, j+1)$ and from (i, j) also, if there remains in it a free phase. Here, also, a fixed priority is given to the attempts: The highest to $(i-1, j-1)$ and the lowest to $(i-1, j+1)$. These priorities tend to favor bending of columns to the left.

Figure 8 shows also (inside the cells) the logical indices of the working $9*9$ array; the indices corresponding to the first alternating phase are written on top.

We have analyzed a set of methodologies aiming at fault tolerance through reconfiguration of VLSI and WSI arrays. All reconfiguration algorithms for these methodologies are associated with interconnection structures that, while easily far from optimal because they result in added silicon requirements and added delays, are characterized by extreme regularity and locality; moreover, further optimization is very simple. Thus, our unified approach can be seen as a preliminary design tool—one to be adopted during the first stages of design.

A most important aspect of the approach is that the same structure of interconnection links and interconnection-controlling circuits is kept valid for a number of reconfiguration algorithms of varying complexity and performance. While this is already interesting in the case of on-chip self-reconfiguration (since the most relevant part of the chip design is kept unchanged over a number of implementations) the interest obviously increases in the case of host-driven reconfiguration. In the latter case, reconfiguration algorithms can be changed dynamically to suit varying requirements while the array and its hardware and software interfaces are kept absolutely standard.

Our work up to now has been basically independent from functions performed by the single cell and, consequently, from the functional algorithm implemented by the whole array. Presently, we are considering the much more complex problem of extending this high standardization of array structure and interfaces supporting flexible reconfiguration techniques so as to take into account not only fault tolerance but also functional reconfiguration. This would be extremely useful in some real-time image-processing applications (for example, radar imaging); dynamic reconfiguration supported by standardized hardware should then lead to optimal global system performances. ☐

Acknowledgments

This work was supported in part by the European Economic Community as part of Project CVT.

References

1. W. J. Bouknight et al., "The Illiac IV System," *Proc. IEEE,* Vol. 60, No. 4, Apr. 1972, pp. 369-379.
2. K. E. Batcher, "Architecture of a Massively Parallel Processor," *Proc. Seventh Symp. Computer Architecture,* May 1980, pp. 168-173.
3. H. J. Siegel, "A Model of SIMD Machines and a Comparison of Various Interconnection Networks," *IEEE Trans. Computers,* Vol. C-28, No. 12, Dec. 1979, pp. 907-917.
4. S. P. Kartashev and S. I. Kartashev, "Problems of Designing Supersystems with Dynamic Architectures," *IEEE Trans. Computers,* Vol. C-29, No. 12, Dec. 1980, pp. 1114-1132.
5. K. S. Hedlund and L. Snyder, "Wafer-Scale Integration of Configurable Highly Parallel (CHiP) Processor," *Proc. Int'l Conf. Parallel Processing,* Aug. 1982, pp. 262-264.
6. H. T. Kung, "Why Systolic Architectures?" *Computer,* Vol. 15, No. 1, Jan. 1982, pp. 37-46.
7. L. Snyder, "Introduction to the Configurable, Highly Parallel Computer," *Computer,* Vol. 15, No. 1, Jan. 1982, pp. 47-56.
8. D. P. Siewiorek and R. S. Swarz, *The Theory and Practice of Reliable System Design,* Digital Press, Bedford, Mass., 1982.
9. R. M. Mangir and A. Avizienis, "Fault-Tolerant Design for VLSI: Effect of Interconnection Requirements on Yield Improvement of VLSI Design," *IEEE Trans. Computers,* Vol. C-31, No. 7, July 1982, pp. 609-615.
10. F. T. Leighton and C. E. Leiserson, "Wafer-Scale Integration of Systolic Arrays," *Second Symp. Foundations of Computer Science,* Oct. 1982, pp. 297-311.
11. H. T. Kung and M. S. Lam, "Fault-Tolerance and Two-Level Pipelining in VLSI Systolic Arrays," *Proc. MIT Conf. Advanced Research in VLSI,* Jan. 1984, pp. 74-83.
12. R. C. Aubusson and I. Catt, "Wafer-Scale Integration: A Fault-Tolerant Procedure," *IEEE J. Solid-State Circuits,* Vol. SC-13, No. 3, June 1978, pp. 339-344.
13. I. Koren, "A Reconfigurable and Fault-Tolerant VLSI Multiprocessor Array," *Proc. Eighth Symp. Computer Architecture,* 1981, pp. 425-442.
14. F. R. K. Chung, F. T. Leighton, and A. L. Rosenberg, "Diogenes: A Methodology for Designing Fault-Tolerant VLSI Processor Arrays," *Proc. 13th Int'l Symp. Fault-Tolerant Computing (FTCS-13),* June 1983, pp. 26-32.
15. M. G. Sami and R. Stefanelli, "Reconfigurable Architectures for VLSI Implementation," *Proc. Nat'l Computer Conf. (NCC-83),* May 1983, pp. 565-577.
16. J. Fried, "Wafer-Scale Integration of Pipelined Processors," *Proc. Int'l Conf. Computer Design (ICCD-84),* Oct. 1984, pp. 611-615.
17. D. S. Fussell and P. J. Varman, "Designing Systolic Algorithms for Fault Tolerance," *Proc. Int'l Conf. Computer Design (ICCD-84),* Oct. 1984, pp. 623-628.
18. R. Negrini and R. Stefanelli, "Algorithms for Self-Reconfiguration of Wafer-Scale Regular Arrays," *Proc. Int'l Conf. Circuits and Systems (ICCAS-85),* Oct. 1985, pp. 190-196.
19. M. G. Sami and R. Stefanelli, "Fault Tolerance of VLSI Processing Arrays: the Time-Redundancy Approach," *Proc. 1984 Real-Time Systems Symp.,* Dec. 1984, pp. 200-207.
20. R. Negrini, M. G. Sami, and R. Stefanelli, "Fault-Tolerance Approaches for VLSI/WSI Arrays," *Proc. Conf. Computers and Communication,* Mar. 1985, pp. 460-468.
21. M. G. Sami and R. Stefanelli, "Fault-Stealing: An Approach to Fault-Tolerance of VLSI Array Structures," *Proc. Int'l Conf. Circuits and Systems (ICCAS-85),* June 1985, pp. 205-210.
22. R. Negrini and R. Stefanelli, "Time Redundancy in WSI Array of Processing Elements," *Proc. Int'l Conf. Supercomputing Systems (SCS-85),* Dec. 1985, pp. 429-438.

Roberto Negrini received the Dr. Ing. degree in electrical engineering (summa cum laude) from the Politecnico di Milano, Italy, in 1974. He is currently an associate professor of computer science at the Dept. of Electronics at the Politecnico di Milano. His main area of interest is computer architecture—in particular, fault-tolerant multi-microprocessor systems, fault-tolerance in VLSI dedicated structures, and semicustom circuits.

Mariagiovanna Sami received her Dr. Ing. degree in electronics engineering from the Politecnico di Milano, Italy, in July 1966. She received her libera docenza in computers and switching theory in 1971. She is now a professor of computer science in the Dept. of Electronics at Politecnico di Milano.

Her research interests are in the area of distributed architectures, with particular reference to fault-tolerant architectures and computer reliability, and to design and testing of VLSI architectures. Her current research activities are mainly centered in the EEC-sponsored CVT project (Computer-aided design for VLSI in Telecommunications) and in the ESPRIT-sponsored project "ARTS-IP" (Architectures for Real-Time SAR Image Processing).

Renato Stefanelli received the Dr. Ing. degree in electrical engineering in 1956 at the Politecnico di Milano, Italy, and the libera docenza in computer engineering in 1964.

Stefanelli is a professor of computer architecture and of applied electronics at the Dept. of Electronics of the Politecnico di Milano. He is also director of the Computer Engineering Research Center of the Italian National Research Council (CNR) at the Politecnico di Milano.

His research interests focus on algorithms for pattern recognition, array processors for image analysis, fast arithmetic units, and fault tolerance in arithmetic units and in regular processing arrays.

Questions about this article can be addressed to Sami at the Politecnico di Milano, Dipartimento di Elettronica, Piazza Leonardo Da Vinci 32, 20133 Milano, Italia.

Bibliography

[ABR74]. J.A. Abraham and D.P. Siewiorek, "An Algorithm for the Accurate Reliability Evaluation of Triple Modular Redundancy Networks," *IEEE-TC*, Vol. C-23, No. 7, pp. 682-692, July 1974.

[ADA82]. G.B. Adams and H.J. Siegel, "A Multistage Network With an Additional Stage for Fault Tolerance," *Proc. 15th Hawaii Int'l. Conf. on System Sciences*, Jan. 1982.

[AIC84]. F.J. Aichelmann, Jr., "Fault-Tolerant Design Techniques for Semiconductor Memory Applications," *IBM JRD*, Vol. 28, No. 2, pp. 177-183, March 1984.

[AND76]. T. Anderson and R. Kerr, "Recovery Blocks in Action: A System Supporting High Reliability," *Proc. 2nd Int'l. Conf. on Software Engineering*, San Francisco, Calif., Oct. 1976, pp. 447-457.

[AND81]. T. Anderson and P.A. Lee, *Fault Tolerance Principles and Practices*, London: Prentice-Hall International, 1981.

[ARM61]. D.B. Armstrong, "A General Method of Applying Error Correction to Synchronous Digital Systems," *Bell System Technical Journal*, Vol. 40, No. 3, pp. 577-593, March 1961.

[AVI69]. A. Avizienis, "Digital Fault Diagnosis by Low-Cost Arithmetic Coding Techniques," *Proc. Purdue Centennial Year Symp. on Inf. Proc.*, Vol. I, pp. 81-91, Lafayette, Ind., April 1969.

[AVI71]. A. Avizienis, et al., "The STAR (Self-Testing and Repairing Computer: An Investigation of the Theory and Practice of Fault-Tolerant Computer Design," *IEEE-TC*, Vol. C-20, No. 11, pp. 1312-1321, Nov. 1971.

[AVI77]. A. Avizienis and L. Chen, "On the Implementation of N-Version Programming for Software Fault Tolerance During Program Execution," *Proc. of COMPSAC-77*, Chicago, Ill., Oct. 1977, pp. 149-155.

[AVI78]. A. Avizienis, "Fault-Tolerance: The Survival Attribute of Digital Systems," *Proc. of the IEEE*, Vol. 66, No. 10, pp. 1109-1125, Oct. 1978.

[AVI85]. A. Avizienis, et al., "The UCLA DEDIX System: A Distributed Testbed for Multiple-Version Software," *Proc. FTCS-15*, Ann Arbor, Mich., June 1985, pp. 126-134.

[AYA82]. J.-M. Ayache, et al., "REBUS, A Fault-Tolerant Distributed System for Industrial Real-Time Control," *IEEE-TC*, Vol. C-31, No. 7, pp. 637-647, July 1982.

[BAR78]. J.F. Bartlett, "A 'NonStop' Operating System," *Proc. Hawaii Int. Conf. of System Sciences*, Hoholulu, Haw., 1978, pp. 103-119.

[BEA78]. M.D. Beaudry, "Performance-Related Reliability Measures for Computing Systems," *IEEE-TC*, Vol. C-27, No. 6, pp. 540-547, June 1978.

[BOE75]. B.W. Boehm, R.K. McClean, and D.B. Urgrig, "Some Experience with Automated Aids to the Design of Large-Scale Reliable Software," *Proc. 1975 Int'l. Conf. on Reliable Software*, pp. 105-113.

[BOE76]. B.W. Boehm, "Software Engineering," *IEEE-TC*, Vol. C-25, No. 12, Dec. 1976, pp. 1226-1241.

[BOU69]. W.G. Bouricius, W.C. Carter and P.R. Schneider, "Reliability Modeling Techniques for Self-Repairing Computer Systems," *Proc. ACM Annual Conf.*, 1969, pp. 295-309.

[BOU71]. W.G. Bouricius, et al., "Reliability Modeling for Fault-Tolerant Computers," *IEEE-TC*, Vol. C-20, No. 11, pp. 1306-1311, Nov. 1971.

[BOW77]. P.W. Bowman, et al., "1A Processor-Maintenance Software," *Bell System Tech. J.*, Feb. 1977.

[BUR76]. D.D. Burchby, L.W. Kern, and W.A. Sturm, "Specification of the Fault-Tolerant Spaceborne Computer (FTSC)," *Proc. FTCS-6*, 1976, pp. 129-133.

[CAR72]. W.C. Carter, A.B. Wadia, and D.C. Jessep, Jr. "Computer Error Control by Testable Morphic Boolean Functions-A Way of Removing Hardcore," *Proc. FTCS-2*, Boston, Mass., pp. 154-159, 1972.

[CAR76]. W.C. Carter and C.E. McCarthy, "Implementation of an Experimental Fault-Tolerant Memory System," *IEEE-TC*, Vol. C-25, No. 6, June 1976, pp. 557-568.

[CAR83]. W.C. Carter, "Architectural Considerations for Detecting Run-Time Errors in Programs," *Proc. FTCS-13*, pp. 249-256, Milano, Italy, 1983.

[CHA72]. K.M. Chandy and C.V. Ramamoorthy, "Rollback and Recovery Strategies for Computer Programs," *IEEE-TC*, Vol. C-21, No. 6, pp. 546-556, June 1972.

[CHA75]. K.M. Chandy, "A Survey of Analytic Models of Rollback and Recovery Strategies," *Computer*, Vol. 8, No. 5, pp. 40-47, May 1975.

[CHE78]. L. Chen and A. Avizienis, "N-Version Programming: A Fault-Tolerance Approach to Reliability of Software Operation," *Proc. FTCS-8*, Toulouse, pp. 3-9, June 1978.

[CHE84a]. C.L. Chen and M.Y. Hsiao, "Error-Correcting Codes for Semiconductor Memory Applications: A State-of-the-Art Review," *IBM JRD*, Vol. 28, No. 2, pp. 124-134, March 1984.

[CHE84b]. C.L. Chen and R.A. Rutledge, "Fault-Tolerant Memory Simulator," *IBM JRD*, Vol. 28, No. 2, pp. 184-195, March 1984.

[CHE85]. M. Chester, "Fault-Tolerant Computers Mature," *Systems and Software*, pp. 117-129, March 1985.

[CHU83]. F.R.K Chung, F.T. Leighton, and A.L. Rosenberg, "Diogenes: A Methodology for Designing Fault-Tolerant VLSI Processor Arrays," *Proc. FTCS-13*, Milano, Italy, June 1983, pp. 26-31.

[CLA79]. J.B. Clary and R.A. Sacane, "Self-Testing Computers," *Computer*, Vol. 12, No. 10, pp. 49-59, Oct. 1979.

[CLA82]. E.M. Clarke and C.N. Nikolaou, "Distributed Reconfiguration Strategies for Fault-Tolerant Multiprocessor Systems," *IEEE-TC*, Vol. C-31, No. 8, pp. 771-784, Aug. 1982.

[COH83]. K.I. Cohen, "Multiprocessor Architecture Tunes In To Transaction Processing," *Electronics*, Jan. 27, 1983, pp. 94-97.

[COO76]. A.E. Cooper and W.T. Chow, "Development of On-Board Space Computer Systems," *IBM JRD*, Vol. 20, No. 1, pp. 5-19, Jan. 1976.

[COX78]. G.W. Cox and B.D. Carroll, "Reliability Analysis of Fault-Tolerant Memories," *IEEE-TR*, Vol. R-27, No. 1, pp. 49-54, April 1978.

[CRI81]. F. Christiam, "Exception Handling and Software-Fault Tolerance," *Proc. FTCS-11*, Kyoto, Japan, June 1981, pp. 97-103.

[DEA76]. D. DeAngelis and J. A. Lauro, "Software Recovery in the Fault-Tolerant Spaceborne Computer," *Proc. FTCS-6*, Pittsburgh, Penn., pp. 143-147, June 1976.

[DEN76]. P.J. Denning, "Fault Tolerant Operating Systems," *Computing Surveys*, Vol. 8, No. 4, Dec. 1976.

[DES78]. P.T. De Sousa and F.P. Mathur, "Sift-Out Modular Redundancy," *IEEE-TC*, Vol. C-27, No. 7, pp. 624-627, July 1978.

[DIC64]. M.M. Dickinson, et al., "Saturn V Launch Vehicle Digital Computer and Data Adapter," *Proc. FJCC-64*, pp. 501-516.

[DOB77]. B.M. Dobrotin and D.A. Rennels, "An Application of Microprocessors to a Mars Roving Vehicle," *Proc. 1977 Joint Automatic Control Conf.*, San Francisco, Calif., pp. 185-196, June 1977.

[DOW64]. R.W. Downing, J.S. Nowak, and L.S. Tuomenoksa, "No. 1 ESS Maintenance Plan," *Bell System Tech. J.*, Vol. 43, Sept. 1964, pp. 1961-2019.

[EDW81]. L. Edwards, "Low Cost Alternative to Hamming Code Corrects Memory Errors," *Computer Design*, pp. 132-148, July 1981.

[ELK80]. S.A. Elkind and D.P. Siewiorek, "Reliability and Performance of Error-Correcting Memory and Register Arrays," *IEEE-TC*, Vol. C-29, No. 10, pp. 920-927, Oct. 1980.

[ELE86]. Electronics Magazine Editorial Staff, "How Technology is Cutting Fault-Tolerance Costs," *Electronics*, Jan. 13, 1986, pp. 55-58.

[ELM72]. W.R. Elmendorff, "Fault-Tolerant Programming," *Proc. FTCS-2*, 1972, pp. 79-83.

[EMM84]. R. Emmerson and M.J. McGowan, "Fault Tolerance Achieved in VLSI," *IEEE Micro*, Vol. 4, No. 6, pp. 34-43, Dec. 1984.

[FAU82]. T.L. Faulkner, C.W. Bartlett, and M. Small, "Hardware Logic Design Faults-A Classification and Some Measurements," *Proc. FTCS-12*, Santa Monica, Calif., June 1982, pp. 377-380.

[FEN81]. T. Feng and C. Wu, "Fault-Diagnosis for a Class of Multistage Interconnection Networks," *IEEE-TC*, Vol. C-30, No. 10, Oct. 1981, pp. 743-758.

[FIT84]. D.J. Fitch, et al., "DMERT: A Fault Tolerant Environment for Diverse Applications," *Proc. FTCS-14*, June 1984, pp. 336-340.

[FRA84]. S.J. Frank, "Tightly Coupled Multiprocessor System Speeds Memory Access Times," *Electronics*, Jan. 12, 1984, pp. 164-169.

[FRE82]. R. Freiburghouse, "Making Processing Fail-Safe," *Mini-Micro Systems*, pp. 255-264, May 1982.

[GAN78]. T.F. Gannon and S.D. Shapiro, "An Optimal Approach to Fault Tolerant Software Systems Design," *IEEE-TSE*, Vol. SE-4, No. 3, pp. 390-409, Sept. 1978.

[GEI83]. R.M. Geist and K.S. Trivedi, "Ultrahigh Reliability Prediction for Fault-Tolerant Computer Systems," *IEEE-TC*, Vol. C-32, No. 12, pp. 1118-1127, Dec. 1983.

[GLA84]. S.D. Glazer, "Fault-Tolerant Mini Needs Enhanced Operating System," *Computer Design*, Aug. 1984, pp. 189-198.

[GOO80]. J.B. Goodenough and C.L. McGowan, "Software Quality Assurance: Testing and Validation," *Proc. of IEEE*, Vol. 68, No. 9, pp. 1093-1098, Sept. 1980.

[GRN80]. A. Grnarov, J. Arlay, and A. Avizienis, "On the Performance of Software Fault-Tolerance Strategies," *Proc. FTCS-10*, Kyoto, Japan, 1980, pp. 251-253.

[GRZ83]. M.E. Grzelakowski, J.H. Campbell, and M.R. Dubman, "DMERT Operating System," *Bell Sys. Tech. J.*, Vol. 62, No. 1, Part 2, Jan. 1983, pp. 303-322.

[HAL84]. M.P. Halbert and S.M. Bose, "Design Approach for a VLSI Self-Checking MIL-STD-1750A Microprocessor," *Proc. FTCS-14*, Kissimmee, Fla., pp. 254-259, June 1984.

[HAM50]. R.W. Hamming, "Error Detecting and Error Correcting Codes," *Bell System Tech. J.*, Vol. 29, No. 2, pp. 147-160, April 1950.

[HAN83]. R.C. Hansen, R.W. Peterson, and N.O. Whittington, "The 3B20 Processor & DMERT Operating System - Fault Detection and Recovery," *Bell System Tech. J.*, Vol. 62, No. 1, Part 2, pp. 349-366, Jan. 1983.

[HAY85]. J.P. Hayes, "Fault Modeling", *IEEE Design & Test,* April 1985, pp. 88-95.

[HEC76]. H. Hecht, "Fault-Tolerant Software for Real-Time Applications," *Computing Surveys,* Vol. 8, No. 4, Dec. 1976, pp. 391-407.

[HEC79]. H. Hecht, "Fault Tolerant Software," *IEEE-TR,* Vol. R-28, No. 3, pp. 227-232, Aug. 1979.

[HEC80a]. H. Hecht, "Current Issues in Fault Tolerant Software," *Proc. COMPSAC-80,* Chicago, IL, Oct. 1980, pp. 227-232.

[HEC80b]. H. Hecht, "Mini-Tutorial on Software Reliability," *Proc. COMPSAC-80,* Chicago, Ill., Oct. 1980, pp. 603-607.

[HEN83]. G. Hendrie, "A Hardware Solution to Part Failures Totally Insulates Programs," *Electronics,* Jan. 27, 1983, pp. 103-105.

[HOP71]. A.L. Hopkins, Jr., "A Fault-Tolerant Information Processing Concept For Space Vehicles," *IEEE-TC,* Vol. C-20, No. 11, Nov. 1971, pp. 1394-1403.

[HOP75]. A.L. Hopkins, Jr. and T.B. Smith, III, "The Architectural Elements of a Symmetric Fault-Tolerant Multiprocessor," *IEEE-TC,* Vo. C-24, No. 5, pp. 505-512, May 1975.

[HOP78]. A.L. Hopkins, Jr., et al., "FTMP—A Highly Reliable Fault-Tolerant Multiprocessor for Aircraft," *Proc. of IEEE,* Vol. 66, No. 10, pp. 1221-1239, Oct. 1978.

[HOR84]. R. Horst and S. Metz, "New System Manages Hundreds of Transactions Per Second," *Electronics,* April 19, 1984, pp. 147-151.

[HSI70]. M.Y. Hsiao, "A Class of Optimal Minimum Odd-Weight-Column SEC-DED Codes," *IBM JRD,* Vol. 14, No. 4, pp. 395-401, July 1970.

[INS83]. A.D. Inselberg, "Multiprocessor Architecture Ensures Fault-Tolerant Transaction Processing," *Mini-Micro Systems,* pp. 165-172, April 1983.

[JAC75]. L.A. Jack, et al, "Coverage Analysis of Self Test Techniques for Semiconductor Memories," Honeywell Corporation Tech. Rept. MR12399. Minneapolis, Minnesota, 1975.

[JEN63]. P.A. Jensen, "Quadded NOR Logic," *IEEE-TR,* Vol. R-12, No. 3, pp. 22-31, Sept. 1963.

[JOH84]. D. Johnson, "The Intel 432: A VLSI Architecture for Fault-Tolerant Computer Systems," *Computer,* Aug. 1984, pp. 40-48.

[KAT77]. J.A. Katzman, "System Architecture for Non-Stop Computing," *Proc. CompCon,* 1977, pp. 77-80.

[KAT78]. D. Katsuki, et al., "Pluribus—An Operational Fault-Tolerant Multiprocessor," *Proc. of IEEE,* Vol. 66, No. 10, pp. 1146-1159, Oct. 1978.

[KEI83]. P.A. Keiller, et al., "Comparison of Software Reliability Predictions," *Proc. FTCS-13,* Milano, Italy, June 1983, pp. 128-134.

[KEL83]. J.P. Kelly and A. Avizienis, "A Specification-Oriented Multi-Version Software Experiment," *Proc. FTCS-13,* Milano, Italy, pp. 120-126, June 1983.

[KHA83]. K.H. Khan, "Fast RAM Corrects Errors On Chip," *Electronics,* pp. 126-130, Sept. 8, 1983.

[KIM78]. K.H. Kim, "An Approach to Programmer-Transparent Coordination of Recovering Parallel Processes and Its Efficient Implementation Rules," *Proc. 1978 Int'l. Conf. on Parallel Processing,* Aug. 1978, pp. 58-68.

[KIM80]. K.H. Kim, "An Implementation of a Programmer-Transparent Scheme for Coordinating Concurrent Processes in Recovery," *Proc. COMPSAC-80,* 1980, pp. 615-621.

[KIM82]. K.H. Kim, "Approaches to Mechanization of the Conversation Scheme Based on Monitor," *IEEE-TSE,* Vol. SE-8, No. 3, pp. 189-197, May 1982.

[KIM84]. W. Kim, "Highly Available Systems for Database Applications," *ACM Computing Surveys,* Vol. 16, No. 1, March 1984, pp. 71-98.

[KIM85]. K.H. Kim, "Software Techniques for Fault Tolerance in BMD Computing Systems," Tech. Rept., Univ. of South Florida, May 14, 1985.

[KLA69]. T.F. Klaschka, "Reliability Improvement by Redundancy in Electronic Systems, II: An Efficient New Redundancy Scheme—Radial Logic," *Royal Aircraft Establishment,* Ministry of Technology 69045. Farnborough, U. K., 1969.

[KOH81]. W.H. Kohler, "A Survey of Techniques for Synchronization and Recovery in Decentralized Computer Systems," *Computing Surveys,* Vol. 13, No. 2, June 1981, pp. 149-183.

[KOP80]. H. Kopetz, "Software Design for Fault Tolerance," *Proc. COMPSAC-80,* Chicago, Ill., Oct. 1980, pp. 591-595.

[KOR81]. I. Koren, "A Reconfigurable and Fault-Tolerant VLSI Multiprocessor Array," *Proc. 8th Comp. Arch. Symp.,* Minneapolis, Minn., May 1981, pp. 425-442.

[KOR84]. I. Koren and M.A. Breuer, "On Area and Yield Considerations for Fault-Tolerant VLSI Processor Arrays," *IEEE-TC,* Vol. C-33, No. 1, pp. 21-27, Jan. 1984.

[KRA84]. G. Kravetz, "Fail-Safe Computers Increase Reliability, Lower Costs," *Mini-Micro Systems,* April 1984, pp. 121-130.

[KUN84]. H.T. Kung and M.S. Lam, "Fault-Tolerant VLSI Systolic Arrays and Two-Level Pipelining," *SPIE Proc. on Real-Time Signal Processing,* Vol. 431, 1983, pp. 143-158.

[LAL82]. P.K. Lala, "An Onchip Fault Tolerant Design Scheme," *Computer Design,* pp. 143-148, Aug. 1982.

[LAL85]. P.K. Lala, *Fault Tolerant and Fault Testable Hardware Design,* 1985, Prentice-Hall International, Englewood Cliffs, N.J.

[LEE79]. P.A. Lee, N. Ghani, and K. Heron, "A Recovery Cache for the PDP-11," *Proc. FTCS-9,* Madison, Wis., pp. 3-8, June 1979.

[LEE84]. Y. Lee and K.G. Shin, "Design and Evaluation of a Fault-Tolerant Multiprocessor Using Hardware Recovery Blocks," *IEEE-TC,* Vol. C-33, No. 2, pp. 113-124, Feb. 1984.

[LIB84]. M.R. Libson and H.E. Harvey, "A General-Purpose Memory Reliability Simulator," *IBM JRD,* Vol. 28, No. 2, pp. 196-205, March 1984.

[LIN70]. S. Lin, *An Introduction to Error-Correcting Codes.* Englewood Cliffs, N.J.: Prentice-Hall, Inc, 1970.

[LIN83]. S. Lin and D.J. Costello, Jr., *Error Control Coding: Fundamentals and Applications.* Englewood Cliffs, N.J.: Prentice-Hall, Inc, 1983.

[LIP77]. M. Lipow and T.A. Thayer, "Prediction of Software Failures," *Proc. 1977 Ann. Reliability and Maintainability Symp.,* Philadelphia, Penn., pp. 489-494, Jan. 1977.

[LON71]. R.L. London, "Software Reliability Through Proving Programs Correct," *Proc. FTCS-1,* Pasadena, Calif., March 1971, pp. 125-129.

[LOS76]. J. Losq, "A Highly Efficient Redundancy Scheme: Self-Purging Redundancy," *IEEE-TC,* Vol. C-25, No. 6, pp. 569-578, June 1976.

[MAK82]. G.P. Mak, J.A. Abraham, and E.S. Davidson, "The Design of PLAs with Concurrent Error Detection," *Proc. 1982 TESTCON,* pp. 303-310.

[MAN82a]. T.E. Mangir and A. Avizienis, "Fault-Tolerant Design for VLSI: Effect of Interconnection Requirements on Yield Improvement of VLSI Designs," *IEEE-TC,* Vol. C-31, No. 7, pp. 609-615, July 1982.

[MAN82b]. T. Mano, et al., "A Redundancy Circuit for a Fault-Tolerant 256K MOS RAM," *IEEE J. Solid State Circ.,* Vol. SC-17, No. 4, Aug. 1982, pp. 726-730.

[MAN84a]. T.E. Mangir, "Sources of Failure and Yield Improvement for VLSI and Restructurable Interconnects for RVLSI and WSI: Part I-Sources of Failures and Yield Improvement for VLSI," *Proc. IEEE,* Vol. 72, No. 6, pp. 690-708, June 1984.

[MAN84b]. T.E. Mangir, "Sources of Failure and Yield Improvement for VLSI and Restructurable Interconnects for RVLSI and WSI: Part II—Restructurable Interconnects for RVLSI and WSI," *Proc. IEEE,* Vol. 72, No. 12, pp. 1687-1694, Dec. 1984.

[MAR70]. B.D. Martin, "Data Subsystems for 12-Year Missions," *Astronautics and Aeronautics,* Sept. 1970, pp. 55-61.

[MAR85]. P.B. Mark, "The Sequoia Computer: A Fault-Tolerant Tightly-Coupled Multiprocessor Architecture," *Proc. 12th Computer Architecture Symp.,* 1985, pg. 232.

[MAT70]. F.P. Mathur and A. Avizienis, "Reliability Analysis and Architecture of a Hybrid-Redundant Digital System: Generalized Triple Modular Redundancy with Self-Repair," *Proc. AFIPS SJCC,* 1970, pp. 375-383.

[MAT71]. F.P. Mathur, "On Reliability Modeling and Analysis of Ultrareliable Fault-Tolerant Digital Systems," *IEEE-TC,* Vol. C-20, No. 11, pp. 1376-1382, Nov. 1971.

[MAT75a]. F.P. Mathur and P.T. deSousa, "Reliability Models of NMR Systems," *IEEE-TR,* Vol. R-24, No. 2, pp. 108-113, June 1975.

[MAT75b]. F.P. Mathur and P.T. deSousa, "Reliability Modeling and Analysis of General Modular Redundant Systems," *IEEE-TR,* Vol. R-24, No. 5, pp. 296-299, Dec. 1975.

[MAY78]. T.C. May and M.H. Woods, "A New Physical Mechanism for Soft Errors in Dynamic Memories," *16th Ann. Proc. Reliability Physics,* San Diego, Calif., pp. 33-40, April 1978.

[MCG84]. W.F. McGill and S.E. Smith, "Fault Tolerance in Continuous Process Control," *IEEE Micro,* Vol. 4, No. 6, pp. 22-33, Dec. 1984.

[MER76]. C. Meraud, et al., "Automatic Rollback Techniques for the COPRA Computer," *Proc. FTCS-6,* Pittsburgh, Penn., pp. 23-29, June 1976.

[MOR80]. D. Moriss, "ECC Chip Reduces Error Rate in Dynamic RAMs," *Computer Design,* pp. 137-142, Oct. 1980.

[NEG86]. R. Negri, M. Sami, and R. Stefanelli, "Fault Tolerance Techniques for Array Structures Used In Supercomputing," *Computer,* Vol. 19, No. 2, Feb. 1986, pp. 78-87.

[NEL75]. E.C. Nelson, "Software Reliability," *TRW Software Series TRW-SS-75-05,* Redondo Beach, Calif., Nov. 1975.

[NEL85]. V.P. Nelson, et al., "Fault Tolerance and Architectural Reliability in Distributed Data Processing Systems," Auburn Univ. Tech. Rept. AU-EE-85-0011-1, Sept. 1985.

[NES85]. E. Nestle and A. Inselberg, "The Synapse N+1 System: Architectural Characteristics and Performance Data of a Tightly-Coupled Multiprocessor System," *Proc. 12th Symp. on Computer Architecture,* 1985, pp. 233-239.

[NG80]. Y.W. Ng and A.A. Avizienis, "A Unified Reliability Model for Fault-Tolerant Computers," *IEEE-TC,* Vol. C-29, No. 11, pp. 1002-1011, Nov. 1980.

[OBR76]. F.J. O'Brian, "Rollback Point Insertion Strategies," *Proc. FTCS-6,* 1977, pp. 138-142.

[ORN76]. S.M. Ornstein, et al., "Pluribus-A Reliable Multiprocessor," *AFIPS Conf. Proc.,* Vol. 45, pp. 401-411, June 1976.

[OSM82]. F.I. Osman, "Error-Correction Technique for Random-Access Memories," *IEEE J. Solid-State Circ.,*

Vol. SC-17, No. 5, pp. 877-881, Oct. 1982.

[PEL83]. D.L. Peltzer, "Wafer-Scale Integration: The Limits of VLSI?," *VLSI Design*, pp. 43-47, Sept. 1983.

[PET72]. W.W. Peterson and E.J. Weldon, Jr., *Error-Correcting Codes*, 2nd Ed., Cambridge, Mass.: MIT Press, 1972.

[PET83]. C.B. Peterson, et al., "Two Chips Endow 32-Bit Processor with Fault Tolerant Architecture," *Electronics*, April 7, 1983, pp. 159-164.

[PET84]. H.N. Peterson, "Are Fault-Tolerant Industrial Control Systems Affordable?," *Texas Instruments Engineering Journal*, Vol. 1, No. 1, pp. 27-33, July-Aug. 1984.

[PIE65]. W. H. Pierce, *Fault Tolerant Design*, Orlando, Fla.: Academic Press, 1965.

[PRA80a]. D.K. Pradhan and J.J. Stiffler, "Error Correcting Codes and Self-Checking Circuits," *Computer*, Vol. 13, No. 3, pp. 27-37, March 1980.

[PRA80b]. D.K. Pradhan, "A New Class of Error-Correcting Codes for Fault-Tolerant Computer Applications," *IEEE-TC*, Vol. C-29, No. 6, pp. 471-481, June 1980.

[PRA81]. D.K. Pradhan and S.M. Reddy, "A Fault-Tolerant Communication Architecture for Distributed Systems," *Proc. FTCS-11*, pp. 214-220, Portland, Maine, June 1981.

[PRA86a]. D.K. Pradhan, (Ed.), *Fault-Tolerant Computing-Theory and Techniques*, Vol. I, Prentice-Hall, Englewood Cliffs, N.J., 1986.

[PRA86b]. D.K. Pradhan, (Ed.), *Fault-Tolerant Computing-Theory and Techniques*, Vol. II, Prentice-Hall, Englewood Cliffs, N.J., 1986.

[RAN75]. B. Randell, "System Structure for Software Fault Tolerance," *IEEE-TSE*, Vol. SE-1, No. 2, pp. 220-232, June 1975.

[RAO74]. T.R.N. Rao, *Error Coding for Arithmetic Processors*, Orlando, Fla.: Academic Press, 1974.

[REG85]. H.K. Reghbati, *Tutorial: VLSI Testing and Validation Techniques*. Washington, DC, IEEE Computer Society Press, 1985, IEEE Catalog No. EH0237-8.

[REN78a]. D.A. Rennels, et al., "A Study of Standard Building Blocks for the Design of Fault-Tolerant Distributed Computer Systems," *Proc. FTCS-8*, pp. 144-149, Toulouse, France, June 1978.

[REN78b]. D. A. Rennels, "Architectures for Fault-Tolerant Spacecraft Computers," *Proc. of IEEE*, Vol. 66, No. 10, pp. 1255-1268, Oct. 1978.

[REN80]. D.A. Rennels, "Distributed Fault-Tolerant Computer Systems," *Computer*, Vol. 13., No. 3, pp. 55-65, March 1980.

[REN84]. D.A. Rennels, "Fault-Tolerant Computing—Concepts and Examples," *IEEE-TC*, Vol. c-33, No. 12, pp. 1116-1129, Dec. 1984.

[ROH73]. J.A. Rohr, "STAREX Self Repair Routines: Software Recovery in The JPL STAR Computer," *Proc. FTCS-3*, Palo Alto, Calif., pp. 11-16, June 1973.

[ROS83]. A.L. Rosenberg, "The Diogenes Approach to Testable Fault-Tolerant Arrays of Processors," *IEEE-TC*, Vol. C-32, No. 10, pp. 902-910, Oct. 1983.

[SAR84]. D.B. Sarrazin and M. Malek, "Fault-Tolerant Semiconductor Memories," *Computer*, pp. 49-56, Aug. 1984.

[SCH78]. G.J. Schick and R.W. Wolverton, "An Analysis of Competing Software Reliability Models," *IEEE-TSE*, Vol. SE-4, No. 2, pp. 104-120, March 1978.

[SCH81]. F.B. Schneider and R.D. Schlichting, "Towards Fault Tolerant Process Control Software," *Proc. FTCS-11*, pp. 48-54, Portland, Maine, June 1981.

[SCO84]. R.K. Scott, et al. "Experimental Validation of Six Fault-Tolerant Software Reliability Models," *Proc. FTCS-14*, Kissimmee, Fla., pp. 102-107, June 1984.

[SED80]. R.M. Sedmak and H.L. Liebergot, "Fault Tolerance of a General Purpose Computer Implemented by Very Large Scale Integration," *IEEE-TC*, Vol. C-29, No. 6, pp. 492-500, June 1980.

[SER84]. O. Serlin, "Fault-Tolerant Systems in Commercial Applications," *Computer*, Aug. 1984, pp. 19-30.

[SHE80]. J.P. Shen and J.P. Hayes, "Fault Tolerance of a Class of Interconnection Networks," *Proc. 7th Ann. Symp. on Comp. Arch.*, May 1980, pp. 61-71.

[SHE82]. J.P. Shen and J.P. Hayes, "Synthesis of Fault-Tolerant Beta-Networks," *Proc. FTCS-12*, Santa Monica, Calif., June 1982, pp. 201-208.

[SHO68]. M.L. Shooman, *Probabilistic Reliability: An Engineering Approach*, Orlando, Fla.: McGraw-Hill Book Co., 1968.

[SHO77]. R.E. Shostak, et al., "Proving the Reliability of a Fault Tolerant Computer Design," *Proc. COMPCON*, Spring 1977, pp. 283-287.

[SHR85]. S.K. Shrivastava (ed.), *Reliable Computer Systems*, Berlin: Springer-Verlag, 1985.

[SIE77]. D. Siewiorek, M. Canepa, and S. Clark, "C.vmp: The Architecture and Implementation of a Fault Tolerant Multiprocessor," *Proc. FTCS-7*, Los Angeles, California, pp. 37-43, June 1977.

[SIE78a]. D.P. Siewiorek, et al., "A Case Study of C.mmp, Cm*, and C.vmp: Part I—Experiences with Fault Tolerances in Multiprocessor Systems," *Proc. of IEEE*, Vol. 66, No. 10, pp. 1178-1199, Oct. 1978.

[SIE78b]. D.P. Siewiorek, et al., "A Case Study of C.mmp, Cm*, and C.vmp: Part II—Predicting and Calibrating Reliability of Multiprocessor Systems," *Proc. of IEEE*, Vol. 66, No. 10, pp. 1200-1220, Oct. 1978.

[SIE82]. D.P. Siewiorek and R.S. Swarz, *The Theory*

and Practice of Reliable System Design, Bedford, Mass: Digital Press, 1982.

[SKL76]. J.R. Sklaroff, "Redundancy Management Technique for Space Shuttle Computers," *IBM JRD,* Vol. 20, No. 1, pp. 20-28, Jan. 1976.

[SMI83]. J.E. Smith and P. Lam, "A Theory of Totally Self-Checking System Design," *IEEE-TC,* Vol. C-32, No. 9, pp. 831-844, Sept. 1983.

[SNY82]. L. Snyder, "Introduction to the Configurable, Highly Parallel Computer," *Computer,* Vol. 15, No. 1, pp. 47-56, Jan. 1982.

[STA85]. J.A. Stankovic, *Reliable Distributed System Software.* Washington, D.C.: IEEE Computer Society Press; 1985.

[STI76]. J.J. Stiffler, "Architectural Design for Near-100% Fault Coverage," *Proc. FTCS-6,* 1976, pp. 134-137.

[STI78]. J.J. Stiffler, "Coding for Random Access Memories," *IEEE-TC,* Vol. C-27, No. 6, pp. 526-531, June 1978.

[TAN84]. R.M. Tanner, "Fault-Tolerant 256K Memory Designs," *IEEE-TC,* Vol. C-33, No. 4, April 1984, pp. 314-322.

[TAY80a]. D.J. Taylor, et al., "Redundancy in Data Structures: Improving Software Fault Tolerance," *IEEE-TSE,* Vol. SE-6, No. 6, pp. 585-594, Nov. 1980.

[TAY80b]. D.J. Taylor, D.E. Morgan, and J.P. Black, "Redundancy in Data Structures: Some THeoretical Results," *IEEE-TSE,* Vol. SE-6, No. 6, pp. 595-602, Nov. 1980.

[TAY82]. D.J. Taylor and J.P. Black, "Principles of Data Structure Error Corection," *IEEE-TC,* Vol. C-31, No. 7, pp. 602-608, July 1982.

[TIM83]. C. Timoc, et al., "Logical Models of Physical Failures," *Proc. International Test Conf.,* 1983, pp. 546-553.

[TIM85]. C. Timoc, *Selected Reprints on Logic Design for Testability.* Washington, D.C.: IEEE Computer Society Press, 1985.

[TOY78]. W.N. Toy, "Fault-Tolerant Design of Local ESS Processors," *Proc. of IEEE,* Vol. 66, No. 10, pp. 1126-1145, Oct. 1978.

[TRI82]. K.S. Trivedi, *Probability & Statistics with Reliability, Queuing, and Computer Science Applications,* Prentice-Hall, Inc., Englewood Cliffs, N.J., 1982.

[TRY62]. J.G. Tryon, "Quadded Logic." In Wilcox and Mann (eds.), *Redundancy Techniques for Computing Systems,* Washington, DC: Spartan Books, 1962, pp. 205-228.

[TSA82]. M.M. Tsao, et al., "The Design of C.fast: A Single Chip Fault Tolerant Microprocessor," *Proc. FTCS-12,* Santa Monica, Calif., June 1982, pp. 63-69.

[TUR76]. R. Turn, M.R. Davis, and R.N. Reinstedt, "A Management Approach to the Development of Computer-Based Systems," *Proc. 2nd Int'l. Conf. on Software Engineering,* IEEE, New York, Oct. 1976, pp. 305-311.

[USD79]. U.S. Department of Defense, *Military Standardization Handbook: Reliability Prediction of Electronic Equipment,* MIL-HDBK-217C, 1979.

[WAG73]. W.L. Wagoner, "The Final Report on a Software Reliability Study," Technology Division, The Aerospace Corp., El Segundo, Calif., Aug. 1973.

[WAK78]. J. Wakerly, *Error Detecting Codes, Self-Checking Circuits, and Applications,* New York: Elsevier North-Holland, Inc., 1978.

[WAN79]. S.L. Wang, and A. Avizienis, "The Design of Totally Self-Checking Circuits using Programmable Logic Arrays," *Proc. FTCS-9,* Madison, Wis., June 1979, pp. 173-180.

[WEN72]. J.H. Wensley, et al., "SIFT-Software Implemented Fault Tolerance," *Proc. AFIPS FJCC,* 1972, pp. 243-253.

[WEN76]. J.H. Wensley, et al., "The Design, Analysis, and Verification of the SIFT Fault-Tolerant System," *Proc. 2nd Int'l. Conf. on Software Engineering,* San Francisco, Calif., Oct. 1976, pp. 458-466.

[WEN78]. J.H. Wensley, et al., "SIFT: Design and Analysis of a Fault-Tolerant Computer for Aircraft Control," *Proc. of IEEE,* Vol. 66, No. 10, pp. 1240-1255, Oct. 1978.

[WEN81]. J.H. Wensley, "Fault-Tolerant Computers Ensure Reliable Industrial Controls," *Electronic Design,* June 25, 1981.

[WEN82]. J.H. Wensley and C.S. Harclerode, "Programmable Control of a Chemical Reactor Using a Fault Tolerant Computer," *IEEE-TIE,* Vol. IE-29, No. 4, pp. 258-264, Nov. 1982.

[WIL83]. T.W. Williams and K.P. Parker, "Design for Testability—A Survey," *Proc. of IEEE,* Vol. 71, No. 1, pp. 98-112, Jan. 1983.

[WIL84]. T.J. Williams, "The Development of Reliability in Industrial Control Systems," *IEEE Micro,* Vol. 4, No. 6, pp. 66-80, Dec. 1984.

[WUL75]. W.A. Wulf, "Reliable Hardware/Software Architecture," *IEEE-TSE,* Vol. SE-1, No. 2, pp. 233-240, June 1975.

[YAM84]. J. Yamada, et al., "A Submicron 1 Mbit Dynamic RAM with a 4-Bit-at-a-Time Built-In ECC Circuit," *IEEE J. Solid State Circ.,* Vol. SC-19, No. 5, Oct. 1984, pp. 627-632.

[ZOR85]. G. Zorpette, "Computers That Are 'Never' Down," *IEEE Spectrum,* April 1985, pp. 46-54.

Author Biographies

Victor P. Nelson is Associate Professor of Electrical Engineering at Auburn University. He has been involved in fault-tolerant computing since 1976 in research projects with the U.S. Air Force and the U.S. Army Ballistic Missile Defense Advanced Technology Center. In conjunction with the latter, he has directed the construction of the Fault Tolerance/Distributed Computing Laboratory at Auburn. Nelson has authored or co-authored numerous technical papers and reports in fault-tolerant computing as well as in other areas such as in microprocessor applications. He received the Ph.D. in electrical engineering from Ohio State University.

Dr. Nelson is a member of the Computer Society of the IEEE, IECI Society, ACM, Eta Kappa Nu, and Pi Mu Epsilon. He has served as vice-chair for fault tolerance of the Distributed Processing Technical Committee and as New Products Editor for *IEEE Micro*.

Bill D. Carroll is Professor and Chairman of the Computer Science Engineering Department of the University of Texas at Arlington (UTA). Previously he served on the Auburn University faculty for ten years and held a visiting appointment at the University of California, Berkeley. Dr. Carroll has also held engineering staff appointments at Texas Instruments and at General Dynamics. He received his Ph.D. degree in Electrical Engineering from the University of Texas, Austin in 1969.

His work in the field of fault-tolerant computing began in 1970. He has published numerous papers and technical reports on the subject. Dr. Carroll (with Dr. Victor P. Nelson) has developed and teaches a short course on fault-tolerant computing and also teaches a course on this subject at UTA. His current research interests are in reliability modeling and in architectures for fault-tolerant systems.

Dr. Carroll is also the co-author of a textbook on logic design and conducts research in computer-aided-engineering methodologies. He is an active volunteer with the IEEE Computer Society and the IEEE.